THE OXFORD HANDBOOK OF

POLITICAL

PSYCHOLOGY

SECOND EDITION

Edited by

LEONIE HUDDY, DAVID O. SEARS

and

JACK S. LEVY

OXFORD

UNIVERSITY PRESS

OXFORD
UNIVERSITY PRESS

Oxford University Press is a department of the University of Oxford.
It furthers the University's objective of excellence in research, scholarship,
and education by publishing worldwide.

Oxford   New York
Auckland   Cape Town   Dar es Salaam   Hong Kong   Karachi
Kuala Lumpur   Madrid   Melbourne   Mexico City   Nairobi
New Delhi   Shanghai   Taipei   Toronto

With offices in
Argentina   Austria   Brazil   Chile   Czech Republic   France   Greece
Guatemala   Hungary   Italy   Japan   Poland   Portugal   Singapore
South Korea   Switzerland   Thailand   Turkey   Ukraine   Vietnam

Oxford is a registered trademark of Oxford University Press
in the UK and certain other countries.

Published in the United States of America by
Oxford University Press
198 Madison Avenue, New York, NY 10016

Library of Congress Cataloging-in-Publication Data
The Oxford handbook of political psychology/[edited by] Leonie Huddy, David O. Sears,
and Jack S. Levy. — Second edition.
pages; cm
ISBN 978-0-19-976010-7 (pbk.: alk. paper)   1. Political psychology.   I. Huddy, Leonie.
JA74.5.O94 2013
320.01'9—dc23
2013003195

3 5 7 9 8 6 4
Printed in the United States of America
on acid-free paper

Contents

PART III MASS POLITICAL BEHAVIOR

PART IV INTERGROUP RELATIONS

About the Contributors

Ananthi Al Ramiah is Assistant Professor of Social Science (Psychology) at Yale-NUS College, Singapore. She works in the area of intergroup social psychology and has written articles on the role of intergroup contact and social identity in reducing prejudice, the antecedents of intergroup contact, and the impact of diversity on intergroup relations.

Daniel Bar-Tal is Branco Weiss Professor of Research in Child Development and Education at the School of Education, Tel Aviv University, Israel. He has published 20 books and over 200 articles and chapters in major social and political psychological journals, books, and encyclopedias. He served as President of the International Society of Political Psychology and received various awards for his work, including the Lasswell Award of the International Society of Political Psychology for "distinguished scientific contribution in the field of political psychology."

Michael Billig is Professor of Social Sciences at Loughborough University, UK. He has written books on a number of different subjects, including nationalism, psychoanalytic theory, rhetoric, ideology, and attitudes towards the British royal family. His latest book is *Learn to Write Badly: How to Succeed in the Social Sciences*" (published by Cambridge University Press, 2013).

Ted Brader is Professor of Political Science at the University of Michigan, USA, and Research Professor in the Center for Political Studies at the Institute for Social Research. He is the author of *Campaigning for Hearts and Minds* and currently serves as Associate Principal Investigator for the American National Election Studies and Associate Principal Investigator for Time-Sharing Experiments for the Social Sciences. His research focuses on the role of emotions in politics, political partisanship, media effects on public opinion, and other topics in political psychology. He serves on the Governing Council of the International Society of Political Psychology and has served on the editorial board for the journal *Political Psychology.*

Christia Brown is an Associate Professor of Psychology and Director of Children at Risk Research Cluster at University of Kentucky, USA. She has written numerous articles on children's gender and ethnic stereotypes, understanding of politics, and perceptions of discrimination. She had been awarded a major grant from the Foundation for Child Development for her research with Mexican immigrants in elementary schools.

Gian Vittorio Caprara is Professor of Psychology at the "Sapienza" University of Rome, Italy. His primary research interests focus on personality development and assessment, psychosocial adjustment, and personality and politics. He was President of the European Association of Personality Psychology from 1990 to 1992 and is a member of the Governing Council of the International Society of Political Psychology.

Dennis Chong is Professor and Chair of the Department of Political Science at the University of Southern California, USA. He studies American national politics and has published extensively on issues of decision-making, political psychology, social norms, rationality, tolerance, and collective action. He is the author of *Rational Lives: Norms and Values in Politics and Society*, a study of value formation and change, group identification, and conflict over social norms and values. He also wrote *Collective Action and the Civil Rights Movement*, a theoretical study of the dynamics of collective action as well as a substantial study of the American civil rights movement and the local and national politics that surrounded it. This book won the William H. Riker Prize, given by the Political Economy Section of the American Political Science Association. Professor Chong's current research on the influence of information and framing in competitive electoral contexts has received several national awards, including the APSA's Franklin L. Burdette / Pi Sigma Alpha Prize. An active member of the profession, Professor Chong has been elected to the Executive Council of the American Political Science Association, and he is coeditor of the book series Cambridge Studies in Public Opinion and Political Psychology, published by Cambridge University Press.

Susan Condor is Professor of Social Psychology in the School of Social Political and Geographical Sciences, at Loughborough University, UK. She has written numerous articles on vernacular political understanding. Her empirical work combines survey methodology with close textual analysis of the content and structure of political reasoning in formal political debate and unstructured everyday talk. She has held major research grants to study national framing in the British press, and identities, policy attitudes, and constructions of citizenship in the context of regional, English, UK, and European Union governance.

Stephen Benedict Dyson is Associate Professor of Political Science at the University of Connecticut, USA. He is the author of *The Blair Identity: Leadership and Foreign Policy* and numerous articles on political leaders, political psychology, and foreign policy. He serves on the editorial board of the journal *Foreign Policy Analysis*.

Stanley Feldman is Professor of Political Science at Stony Brook University, USA. He is the President of the International Society of Political Psychology from 2013 to 2014. He has published numerous papers on the structure and determinants of public opinion and ideology, values and politics, and the political effects of emotions.

Ronald J. Fisher is Professor of International Peace and Conflict Resolution in the School of International Service at American University, Washington, DC, USA. His primary interest is interactive conflict resolution, which involves informal third-party interventions in protracted and violent ethnopolitical conflict. His publications include a number of books at the interface of social psychology and conflict resolution as well as numerous articles in interdisciplinary journals including *Political Psychology*.

Carolyn L. Funk was an associate professor in the L. Douglas Wilder School of Government and Public Affairs at Virginia Commonwealth University, USA. She has written numerous articles using twin studies to examine the genetic and environmental influences on political behavior.

Eva G. T. Green is Senior Lecturer in Social Psychology at the University of Lausanne in Switzerland. Winner of several grants from the Swiss National Science Foundation, she has extensively published on prejudice and immigration attitudes, national identity, and social representations.

Eran Halperin is Senior Lecturer at the new school of psychology at the IDC, Herzliya, Israel. He got his PhD from the University of Haifa in 2007 (summa cum laude) and completed postdoctoral training (through a Fulbright Scholarship) at the Department of Psychology, Stanford University, in 2008. His work integrates psychological and political theories and methods in order to explain different aspects of intergroup (mostly intractable) conflicts. Dr. Halperin's main line of research focuses on the role of emotions and emotion regulation in determining public opinion about peace and equality, on the one hand, and war and discrimination, on the other. In addition, he is interested in the psychological roots of some of the most destructive political ramifications of intergroup conflicts (e.g., intolerance, exclusion, and intergroup violence). The unique case of Israeli society in general, and the Israeli-Palestinian conflict in particular, motivates his work and inspires his thinking. Hence, most of his studies are conducted within the context of this "natural laboratory."

Paul 't Hart is a Professor of Public Administration at the Utrecht School of Governance and Associate Dean at the Netherlands School of Government in The Hague, the Netherlands. His research interests include political and public sector leadership; elite behavior and group dynamics in government; policy evaluation and policy change; and the political psychology of crisis management. His recent books include *Dispersed Democratic Leadership*, *Framing the Global Meltdown*, *The Real World of EU Accountability*, *How Power Changes Hands*, *Prime-Ministerial Performance*, and the *Oxford Handbook of Political Leadership*. He is a coeditor of *Political Psychology* and recipient of the Erik Erikson Prize of the International Society for Political Psychology.

Matthew Hayes is an assistant professor at Indiana University, Bloomington, USA. Professor Hayes's research and teaching interests primarily focus on political behavior and racial and ethnic politics, with a particular interest in issues of representation and how institutions can shape individual political behavior. His current research investigates how citizens evaluate representation and whether substantive and descriptive representation can maximize satisfaction both for minorities and for whites. In addition to his primary research in race and representation, Professor Hayes has also conducted collaborative research with Professors Jeff Mondak and Damarys Canache examining the role of personality in shaping political attitudes and behaviors using survey data from across Latin and North America. Professor Hayes received his AB from the University of Chicago in 2006 and his PhD from the University of Illinois at Urbana-Champaign in 2013.

Richard K. Herrmann is Professor and Chair of the Department of Political Science at the Ohio State University, USA. He has published numerous pieces on the role perceptions play in international relations and for five years coedited the *International Studies Quarterly*. He has served on the policy planning staff at the US Department of State and from 2002 to 2011 was Director of the Mershon Center for International Security Studies.

Miles Hewstone is Professor of Social Psychology at the University of Oxford and Fellow of New College, UK. He has published widely in the field of social psychology, focusing on prejudice and stereotyping, intergroup contact, the reduction of intergroup conflict, sectarianism in Northern Ireland, and segregation and integration. He is a co-founding editor of the *European Review of Social Psychology*. He has presented his work to various public policy bodies and reviews and was recipient of the 2012 Kurt Lewin Award from the Society for the Psychological Study of Social Issues.

Robert Huckfeldt is Distinguished Professor of Political Science at the University of California, Davis, USA. He has written several books and a series of articles on the roles of social contexts and social networks for diffusion, persuasion, and conflict in politics.

Leonie Huddy is Professor of Political Science and Director of the Center for Survey Research at Stony Brook University, USA. She has written numerous articles and book chapters on political psychology, with a focus on the politics of intergroup relations. Huddy's research has been funded by the National Science Foundation. She is past editor of the journal *Political Psychology*, past president of the International Society for Political Psychology, and serves on the American National Election Studies (ANES) Board of Overseers and numerous editorial boards in political science.

Herbert C. Kelman is the Richard Clarke Cabot Professor of Social Ethics, Emeritus, at Harvard University, USA. A pioneer in the development of interactive problem solving, he has been engaged for some 40 years in efforts to resolve the Israeli-Palestinian conflict. His publications include *International Behavior: A Social-Psychological Analysis* (editor and coauthor, 1965) and *Crimes of Obedience: Toward a Social Psychology of Authority and Responsibility* (with V. Lee Hamilton, 1989). He is past president of the International Studies Association, the International Society of Political Psychology, and several other professional organizations.

Donald R. Kinder is the Philip E. Converse Collegiate Professor of Political Science at the University of Michigan, USA. A Fellow of the Center for Advanced Study in the Behavioral Sciences at Stanford, the Guggenheim Foundation, and the American

Academy of Arts and Sciences, Kinder is the author of *News That Matters* (1987), *Divided by Color* (1996), *Us against Them* (2009), and *The End of Race?* (2012), among other works.

Bert Klandermans is Professor in Applied Social Psychology at the VU University, Amsterdam, the Netherlands. He has published extensively on the social psychology of political protest and social movement participation. His *Social Psychology of Protest* appeared with Blackwell in 1997. He is the editor and coauthor (with Suzanne Staggenborg) of *Methods of Social Movement Research* (University of Minnesota Press, 2002) and (with Nonna Mayer) of *Extreme Right Activists in Europe* (Routledge, 2006). With Conny Roggeband he edited the *Handbook of Social Movements across Disciplines* (Springer, 2007). He is the editor of Social Movements, Protest, and Contention, the prestigious book series of the University of Minnesota Press and of *Sociopedia.isa*, a new online database of review articles published by Sage in collaboration with the International Sociological Association. He is coeditor of Blackwell/Wiley's *Encyclopedia of Social Movements*.

Robert Kurzban is Associate Professor in the Department of Psychology at the University of Pennsylvania, USA, and currently occupies the Rasmuson Chair of Economics at the University of Alaska, Anchorage, USA. His research primarily focuses on human social behavior from an evolutionary perspective. He serves as co-editor-in-chief of *Evolution and Human Behavior*, the flagship journal of the Human Behavior and Evolution Society.

Richard R. Lau is Professor of Political Science and Director of the Center for the Experimental Study of Politics and Psychology at Rutgers University, USA. His research focuses on information processing, political advertising, and voter decision-making. His research has been supported by the National Science Foundation, the National Institute of Health, the Carnegie Corporation, and the Ford Foundation. His most recent book (with David Redlawsk), *How Voters Decide* (Cambridge University Press, 2006), won the 2007 Alexander George Award from the International Society of Political Psychology for the best book in political psychology published in the previous calendar year.

Jack S. Levy is Board of Governors' Professor of Political Science at Rutgers University, USA. He is past president of the International Studies Association and of the Peace Science Society. Levy studies the causes of interstate war and foreign policy decision-making, including prospect theory, misperception and war, intelligence failure, learning from history, and time horizons. His most recent books include *Causes of War* (2010) and *The Arc of War: Origins, Escalation, and Transformation* (2011), each coauthored with William R. Thompson.

George E. Marcus is Professor of Political Science at Williams College, USA. He, with his colleagues, have written a number of books, among them, *Political Tolerance and American Democracy*, *With Malice toward Some: How People Make Civil Liberties Judgments*, and *Affective Intelligence and Political Judgment*. He is also the author of *The Sentimental Citizen* and *Political Psychology: Neuroscience, Genes, and Politics*. He has published in many political science journals and has received grants from the National Science Foundation, the National Endowment for the Humanities, the Sloan Foundation, the Ford Foundation, and the Carnegie Corporation, and held a residency at the Rockefeller Foundation Center in Bellagio, Italy.

Tali Mendelberg is Professor of Politics at Princeton University, USA. She is the author of *The Race Card: Campaign Strategy, Implicit Messages, and the Norm of Equality* (Princeton University Press, 2001), winner of the American Political Science Association's Woodrow Wilson Foundation Award for "the best book published in the United States during the prior year on government, politics or international affairs." She received the APSA Paul Lazarsfeld Award for the best paper in Political Communication, the APSA Best Paper Award in Political Psychology, the Carrie Chapman Catt Prize for Research on Women and Politics (honorable mention), and the Erik H. Erikson Early Career Award for Excellence and Creativity in the Field of Political Psychology. She has published articles in the *American Political Science Review, American Journal of Political Science, Journal of Politics, Public Opinion Quarterly, Perspectives on Politics, Political Behavior, Political Psychology,* and *Political Communication*. Her work has been supported by grants and fellowships from the National Science Foundation, the University of Pennsylvania, Harvard University, and the Center for Advanced Study in the Behavioral Sciences. She holds a PhD from the University of Michigan. Her areas of specialization are political communication; gender; race; public opinion; political psychology; and experimental methods.

Jeffery J. Mondak is the James M. Benson Chair in Public Issues and Civic Leadership in the Department of Political Science at the University of Illinois, USA. His research has appeared in numerous journals, including the *American Political Science Review,* the *American Journal of Political Science,* the *British Journal of Political Science,* and the *Journal of Politics*. His most recent book is *Personality and the Foundations of Political Behavior* (Cambridge University Press).

C. Daniel Myers is a Robert Wood Johnson Scholar of Health Policy at the University of Michigan, USA. In the fall of 2013, he will start as Assistant Professor of Political Science at the University of Minnesota, USA. His research focuses on the political psychology of democratic deliberation and other forms of political communication. His dissertation, "Information use in Small Group Deliberation," won the American Political Science Association's Experimental Research Section 2011 Best Dissertation Award.

Susan Allen Nan is Associate Professor of Conflict Analysis and Resolution and Director of the Center for Peacemaking Practice at the School for Conflict Analysis and Resolution at George Mason University, USA. Her main focus is on reflective practice and research that emerges from practice contexts. She has substantial expertise in intermediary roles and coordination among intermediaries, evaluation of conflict resolution initiatives, and theories of change and indicators of change in conflict resolution practice. She has engaged long term in conflict resolution in the Caucasus, as well as contributing to a variety of conflict resolution initiatives in the United States, eastern Europe, Eurasia, the Caribbean, South America, and Africa.

Yioryos Nardis is a PhD candidate in Communication Studies at the University of Michigan, USA. His research focuses on political communication from a comparative perspective. He is currently examining citizen apathy toward European Union integration and the role of the media in fostering engagement in EU politics.

Matthew T. Pietryka is a lecturer and postdoctoral fellow at the University of California, Davis, USA. He studies political communication and the role of social networks in political behavior.

Jerrold M. Post, M.D., is Professor of Psychiatry, Political Psychology, and International Affairs, and Director of the Political Psychology Program at George Washington University, USA. He was the founding director of the CIA's Center for the Analysis of Personality and Political Behavior, where he took the lead in preparing the Camp David profiles of Menachem Begin and Anwar Sadat. Dr. Post is author and/or editor of 11 books, including *The Psychological Assessment of Political Leaders*, and *Leaders and Their Followers in a Dangerous World*.

David P. Redlawsk is Professor of Political Science and Director of the Eagleton Center for Public Interest Polling at Rutgers University, USA. His most recent book with Caroline Tolbert and Todd Donovan is *Why Iowa? How Caucuses and Sequential Elections Improve the Presidential Nominating Process* (2011, University of Chicago Press). With Richard Lau he is the author of *How Voters Decide: Information Processing in Election Campaigns* (2006, Cambridge University Press) winner of the 2007 Alexander L. George Best Book Award from the International Society of Political Psychology. His research has been supported by multiple research grants from the National Science Foundation. He currently coedits the journal *Political Psychology*.

Jack Reilly is a PhD candidate in Political Science at the University of California, Davis, USA. He studies social networks and political discussion, with a focus on the political behavior and communication patterns of socially isolated individuals.

David O. Sears is Distinguished Professor of Psychology and Political Science at the University of California, Los Angeles, USA. He is a coauthor of *Obama's Race: The 2008 Election and the Dream of a Post-racial America* (2010) and *The Diversity Challenge* (2008). He received his PhD in Psychology from Yale University and is a former president of the International Society for Political Psychology and a former Dean of Social Sciences at UCLA.

Jim Sidanius is Professor in the departments of Psychology and African and African American Studies at Harvard University, USA. He received his PhD at the University of Stockholm, Sweden, and has taught at several universities in the United States and Europe, including Carnegie Mellon University, the University of Texas at Austin, New York University, Princeton University, the University of Stockholm, Sweden, and the University of California, Los Angeles. He has authored some 270 scientific papers. His primary research interests include the interface between political ideology and cognitive functioning, the political psychology of gender, institutional discrimination and the evolutionary psychology of intergroup conflict.

Christian Staerklé is Associate Professor of Social Psychology at the University of Lausanne in Switzerland. He has widely published on intergroup attitudes, cultural beliefs, and political legitimacy and has obtained many research grants from national and international research organizations. Staerklé is codirector of the social psychology graduate school of the universities of Geneva and Lausanne.

Janice Gross Stein is the Belzberg Professor of Conflict Management and the Director of the Munk School of Global Affairs at the University of Toronto, Canada. Her recent research focuses on the psychological dimensions of security and the changing meanings of humanitarianism.

Charles S. Taber is Professor of Political Science and Dean of the Graduate School at Stony Brook University, USA. He has written several books and many articles on political psychology and computational modeling in the social sciences. Winner of nine research grants from the National Science Foundation, Taber is a past editor of the journal *Political Psychology* and serves on numerous editorial boards in political science.

Cristian Tileagă is Lecturer in Social Psychology and member of the Discourse and Rhetoric Group at Loughborough University, UK. His research focuses on developing critical approaches for researching social and political life. He has written extensively on political discourse, the critical psychology of racism, collective memory, and social representations of national history. He is the author of *Political Psychology: Critical Perspectives* (forthcoming, Cambridge University Press) and *Discourse Analysis and Reconciliation with the Recent Past* (Romanian). He is coediting *Psychology and History: Interdisciplinary Explorations* (with Jovan Byford, Open University) and serves on editorial and advisory boards of international journals in Romania, Brazil, and Germany.

Tom R. Tyler is the Macklin Fleming Professor of Law and Professor of Psychology at Yale University, USA. His research explores the dynamics of authority in groups, organizations, and societies. In particular, he examines the role of judgments about the justice or injustice of group procedures in shaping legitimacy, compliance, and cooperation. He is the author of several books, including *The Social Psychology of Procedural Justice* (1988); *Social Justice in a Diverse Society* (1997); *Cooperation in Groups* (2000); *Trust in the Law* (2002); *Why People Obey the Law* (2006); and *Why People Cooperate* (2011).

Nicholas A. Valentino is Professor of Political Science and Research Professor in the Institute for Social Research at the University of Michigan, USA. He specializes in political psychological approaches to understanding public opinion formation, political socialization, information seeking, attitude change, and electoral behavior. His work employs experimental methods, online and laboratory surveys, and content analyses of political communication. His previous work has focused on the intersecting roles of racial attitudes and emotion in support for public policies related to race. He is currently exploring the causes of public opinion on issues related to globalization including immigration, terrorism, and job transfers in the United States and around the world.

Jojanneke van der Toorn is Assistant Professor in the Department of Psychology at Leiden University, the Netherlands. She holds MA degrees in Organizational Psychology and Cultural Anthropology from the Free University of Amsterdam and a PhD in Social Psychology from New York University. Her research focuses on processes of legitimation and the social psychological mechanisms implicated in social change and resistance to it. Her work has appeared in the *American Sociological Review*, the *Journal of Experimental Social Psychology*, *Political Psychology*, and *Social Justice Research*.

Jacquelien van Stekelenburg (PhD, VU University Amsterdam, 2006) is Associate Professor of Sociology at the VU University, Amsterdam, the Netherlands. She researches the social psychological dynamics of protest, with a special interest in identification, emotions, and ideologies as motivators for collective action.

Michele Vecchione is a researcher in psychology at the "Sapienza" University of Rome, Italy. His research interests focus on political psychology, multivariate statistics in the field of personality and social psychology, personality assessment, socially desirable responding and response biases, the role of individual differences in predicting individuals' preferences and performance, the issue of measurement invariance across cultural contexts and administration modes, and the longitudinal investigation of stability and change in personality.

David G. Winter is Professor of Psychology at the University of Michigan, USA. Within the field of personality and social psychology, his research focuses on power and power motivation, the motivational bases of leadership, and the psychological aspects of conflict escalation and war. He is the author of *Personality: Analysis and Interpretation of Lives*, as well as numerous articles in professional journals. He has been President and Councilor of the International Society of Political Psychology, and has received the society's Lasswell Award for scientific contributions.

Everett Young received his PhD in political science from Stony Brook University, USA, in 2009. He has taught courses in political psychology, American politics, and methodology at Florida State University and Washington University in St. Louis. He resides in Tallahassee, FL.

CHAPTER 1

....

INTRODUCTION

*theoretical foundations of
political psychology*

....

LEONIE HUDDY, DAVID O. SEARS,
AND JACK S. LEVY

POLITICAL psychology, at the most general level, is an application of what is known about human psychology to the study of politics. It draws upon theory and research on biopsychology, neuroscience, personality, psychopathology, evolutionary psychology, social psychology, developmental psychology, cognitive psychology, and intergroup relations. It addresses political elites—their personality, motives, beliefs, and leadership styles, and their judgments, decisions, and actions in domestic policy, foreign policy, international conflict, and conflict resolution. It also deals with the dynamics of mass political behavior: voting, collective action, the influence of political communications, political socialization and civic education, group-based political behavior, social justice, and the political incorporation of immigrants.

Since the publication of the first edition of the *Oxford Handbook of Political Psychology* in 2003, the field of political psychology has grown significantly. Research has been fueled by a mix of age-old questions and recent world events as social psychologists and political scientists have turned to psychology to understand the origins of political conservatism (Jost, Glaser, Kruglanski, & Sulloway, 2003), the historic election of an African American president in the United States (Tesler & Sears, 2010), spectacular acts of international terrorism such as the 2004 Madrid and the 2005 London train bombings and the September 11 attacks in the United States (Crenshaw, 2000; Lerner, Gonzalez, Small, & Fischhoff, 2003; Pyszczynski, Solomon, & Greenberg, 2003), anti-immigrant sentiment (Sniderman, Hagendoorn, & Prior, 2004; Sniderman & Hagendoorn, 2007), the failure of expert judgment (Tetlock, 2005), and the underpinnings of collective action (Simon & Klandermans, 2001).

Enlivened interest in the topics addressed by political psychologists goes hand in hand with a strong and increasingly global organization, the International Society of

Political Psychology (ISPP), and the growing circulation of *Political Psychology*, its well-respected journal. The journal has grown in stature in recent years. It ranked 12th in political science and 19th in social psychology in terms of its two-year impact factor in the 2011 Journal Citation Reports database, and was ranked even more highly in terms of its five-year impact (9th in political science and 14th in social psychology in 2011). There are also vibrant political psychology sections of major national and regional organizations such as the organized section of the American Political Science Association (APSA) and the European Consortium for Political Research (ECPR) Standing Group.

There is also an increased number of textbooks devoted to the field. Since the first version of this *Handbook* several good undergraduate texts devoted solely to political psychology have been published, including textbooks by Cottam, Dietz-Uhler, Mastors, and Preston (2010), Houghton (2009), Marcus (2012), a reader by Jost and Sidanius (2004), and a graduate-level text by McDermott (2004) on political psychology and international relations. Several major presses, including Cambridge, Oxford, and Routledge, now have book series in political psychology. There is also a steady stream of monographs published in the field each year, leading to the existence of three annual book prizes dedicated to political psychology: the Robert E. Lane book prize awarded by the Political Psychology Section of the American Political Science Association, and the Alexander George and David O. Sears prizes awarded by the International Society for Political Psychology.

The current edition of the *Handbook* takes stock of the past decade's developments in political psychology, building closely on the 2003 *Oxford Handbook of Political Psychology* (Sears, Huddy, & Jervis, 2003), and more loosely on two previous volumes: *Handbook of Political Psychology* (Knutson, 1973) and *Political Psychology* (Hermann, 1986). In this second edition of the *Oxford Handbook of Political Psychology* widely respected political scientists and psychologists summarize what psychology has contributed to our understanding of the political behavior of both political elites and ordinary citizens, and the insights into basic psychology obtained from research on political behavior. The chapters in the *Handbook* provide an overview of key terms, major theories, and cutting-edge research within both psychology and political science and will be an essential reference for scholars and students interested in the intersection of these two fields.

We designed the *Handbook* to provide a comprehensive and expertly distilled account of research in many subfields of political psychology for both the beginning graduate student and the more advanced scholar who may be new to a specific subfield or topic. But we should note that the original *Handbook* will remain a useful reference because it contains topics and discussions that are omitted from the current volume. Moreover, political psychology is a diverse and growing subfield and by necessity not all topics could be included in a single volume. We thought long and hard about a number of chapters that did not make it into this volume, including neuropolitics, the political psychology of terrorism, political impression formation, and the political psychology of obedience. These topics are touched on within different chapters but may constitute distinct chapters in a future edition of the *Handbook*.

In compiling this volume, we acknowledge the growing international flavor of contemporary political psychology, which explores topics as diverse as the dynamics of

American presidential elections, resistance to immigration in a globalized economy, and the role of emotion and threat in the decisions of political leaders. Where possible, authors of chapters in this volume have chosen examples of good political psychology research from around the globe, demonstrating the broad explanatory power of common psychological forces within different polities. Cognitive biases, authoritarianism, patriotism, ethnocentrism, and social conformity are not constrained by geographic boundaries but seem evident throughout the world, albeit in interaction with specific cultures and political systems.

1. WHAT IS POLITICAL PSYCHOLOGY?

At its core, political psychology concerns the behavior of individuals within a specific political system. Psychology alone cannot explain the Holocaust, intractable conflicts, war, or most other behavior of states or collective political actors in complex environments. Individuals do not act within a vacuum. Their behavior varies with, and responds to, differences in political institutions, political cultures, leadership styles, and social norms. As Levy notes in his chapter in this volume, psychology influences foreign policy behavior primarily through its interaction with specific aspects of the international system, national governments, and distinct societies. The same logic applies to a wide range of different phenomena. Consider research on authoritarianism. Do we look to the behavior of leaders or their followers to understand why citizens in the 1930s and 1940s followed fascist leaders who persecuted and killed millions of people? Were the atrocities committed in Nazi Germany and Stalinist Russia a function of political leadership, the support (acquiescence) of the public, or both? Some scholars attribute the Holocaust squarely to the psychology of authoritarian followers (Adorno, Frenkel-Brunswik, Levinson, & Sanford, 1950); others view it as a function of leadership and the pervasive human propensity to obey authority (Milgram, 1974); still others view it as the reaction of authoritarian individuals to social and political discord (Feldman & Stenner, 1997). In the end it is difficult to believe that someone with authoritarian tendencies will behave in exactly the same way under a fascist regime as in a liberal democracy.

A complex mix of individual psychology and political context also shapes public reactions to terrorism. Public support for anti-terrorism policies depends on how a threatened government reacts, the government's perceived competence and effectiveness in combatting terrorism, and a person's felt vulnerability to a future terrorist event. External forces such as the strength of government national security policy or terrorist determination and capabilities vary over time and across contexts, and they influence, in turn, whether a citizen feels anxious or angry in response to a terrorist event. Powerful terrorists and a weak government tend to generate anxiety among a threatened population, whereas a powerful government and weak terrorists will likely generate feelings of anger. Moreover, not everyone responds to threat in the same way, and individual psychological dispositions play an added role in determining whether someone reacts to terrorism with anger or anxiety. In general, a society dominated by feelings of anger may support aggressive antiterrorism action, whereas a population dominated by feelings of anxiety may oppose aggressive action that exacerbates the risk of terrorism (Huddy & Feldman, 2011; Lambert et al., 2010). Neither individual psychology nor political circumstances alone is likely to fully explain these reactions.

In a more general sense, questions about public reactions to terrorism or an authoritarian response to fascist rule are closely linked to one of the perennial questions raised by political psychology: how well are citizens equipped to handle their democratic responsibilities (Le Cheminant & Parrish, 2011)? Can they deliberate over the issues of the day fairly to arrive at a reasoned judgment, or conversely do they succumb to internecine enmities and fall victim to irrational intolerance? Many of the chapters in this *Handbook* grapple with such issues, underscoring the democratic capabilities of the citizenry while highlighting ways in which leaders and citizens fall short of the democratic ideal. The question of a citizenry's democratic competence is addressed very directly in the chapter by Myers and Mendelberg as they consider the psychology of political deliberation and the conditions under which it conforms to the democratic ideal of free, equal, and open dialogue. In reality, both citizens and leaders exhibit distorted reasoning and a slew of cognitive and emotional biases that are well cataloged in this volume. Partisan resistance to new information, ethnocentric reactions to immigrants, automatic and preconscious reactions to a political candidate's facial features, greater risk-taking in the face of losses than gains—the list goes on. Many of these same processes are at work among political leaders for whom partisan loyalties loom large, threat impairs their ability to deliberate rationally, and emotions such as humiliation and anger affect their political decisions. In that sense leaders are vulnerable to emotional and cognitive psychological biases similar to those observed within the electorate.

Yet democratic societies work, more or less, and political psychology has focused in recent years on individual differences among citizens to explain why a characterization of the public as biased, ethnocentric, fearful, or any other singular characterization is erroneous. Individual differences grounded in early socialization, genetic makeup, social context, and personality generate liberals and conservatives, Social Democrats and Christian Democrats, tolerant and intolerant individuals, more and less well informed citizens, and sectarian partisan elites. Politics emerges from such individual differences, leading to political disagreements that are visible and widely debated within well-functioning democratic societies. Even if citizens engage in biased reasoning, competing arguments are pervasive and difficult to avoid completely; the passionate are free to make their case, and the dispassionate can evaluate their efforts and arguments. The democratic process may be messy, unsatisfying, and frustrating, but it is inherently psychological. As scholars we need to know something about both a political system *and* human psychology to make sense of it. The interplay of psychology and politics, especially within democratic processes, is a central theme of this volume and lies at the core of many of its chapters.

2. Intellectual Underpinnings of Political Psychology

As we noted in the earlier edition of this *Handbook*, there is no one political psychology (Sears et al., 2003). Rather, researchers have employed a number of different psychological theories to study political behavior and attitudes. Some theories are more appropriate than others for analyzing certain political phenomena, as seen in many of the chapters in the *Handbook*. For example, in contemporary political psychology Freudian psychodynamics is commonly applied to questions concerning the psychology of political leaders, and discourse theory is applied specifically to the analysis of political rhetoric and communications. But some of the psychological approaches employed across these chapters are marshaled to understand diverse political phenomena. For example, the influence of cognitive and emotional processes on elite and citizen decision-making is discussed in a number of chapters. Basic aspects of the affective and cognitive system such as the link between anger and risk seeking or the limits of working memory and attention have broad ramifications for the study of political behavior across diverse political topics. To deepen insight into the intellectual underpinnings of political psychology, we lay out the major classes of psychological theories that have been applied to the study of political behavior (see also Cottam et al., 2010; Marcus, 2012; Sullivan, Rahn, & Rudolph, 2002). Each of the broad approaches we discuss contains several different theories and concepts yet are brought together by their focus on broadly similar psychological processes and mechanisms.

2.1. Rational Choice

Over the last five to six decades, rational choice theory has been a major influence on political science models of both elite and mass political behavior. This is understandable since democratic theory is predicated on the notion of a well-informed citizenry capable of handling and digesting information on issues of the day to arrive at well-informed decisions. As Chong explains in this *Handbook*, rational choice theory is built on a set of basic assumptions about human behavior that resemble the requirements for a well-functioning citizenry: first, individuals have consistent preferences over their goals, which are often defined as the pursuit of economic self-interest; second, individuals assign a value or utility to these goals; and third, probabilities are assigned to the different ways of achieving such goals. This culminates in Chong's definition of rational choice as "choosing the course of action that maximizes one's expected utility." If utilities, or goals, are equated with economic self-interest, as they often are, a rational choice model predicts that an individual will be motivated to act in ways that are most likely to pay the highest financial dividend. In politics, this translates into support of candidates and policies that are most likely to improve voters' economic bottom line and benefit them personally. Expectancy-value theory was formalized in psychology as an early version of the rational choice idea (Edwards, 1954; Fishbein & Ajzen, 1975).

As Chong notes in this *Handbook*, however, pure rationality is something of a fiction when applied to human behavior. Downs (1957) was the first to identify the paradox of voting, a major problem for rational choice theory, in which the costs of voting far exceed its expected benefit to one's self-interest, suggesting that it is irrational even though frequently practiced (see also Green & Shapiro, 1994). Since Downs, it has become increasingly clear that neither leaders nor citizens make entirely rational political decisions. Nonetheless, in many branches of political science, researchers are only slowly moving away from a rational model of human behavior. At the forefront of this effort lies pioneering research by social psychologists on systematic biases in human decision-making (Kahneman, 2011; Kahneman, Slovic, & Tversky, 1982).

In the *Handbook*, Stein provides a succinct account of a rationalist approach to threat in the field of international relations and highlights its inadequacy to fully explain elite behavior and decision-making. She documents a number of cognitive, motivational, and emotional biases that distort elite threat perceptions and reactions to threat. Herrmann attributes elites' images of other nations, in part, to similar cognitive and emotional biases; these images shape, in turn, elite responses to the actions and perceived intentions of other nations in which friend and foe are clearly distinguished. Levy develops this theme further and summarizes prospect theory (Kahneman & Tversky, 1979) as an alternative to rationalist expected utility as a theory of choice under conditions of risk. In something of an exception, however, Dyson and 't Hart caution against an excessive focus on cognitive and emotional biases among elite decision-makers and argue instead for a more pragmatic view of rationality, which they define as the best decision possible under current resource constraints.

At the level of mass politics, among the earliest challenges to rational choice were observations that major political attitudes were in place well before adults began contemplating the political arena, in studies of political socialization and voting behavior (see the chapter by Sears and Brown). Later challenges came from Kahneman and Tversky's findings on cognitive heuristics and biases, which blossomed into the subfield of behavioral decision theory and behavioral economics (Camerer, Loewenstein, & Rabin, 2004), fields that intersect quite closely with political psychology. Behavioral economics and other well-documented psychologically based deviations from rationality are discussed at some length in the chapter by Redlawsk and Lau on citizen political decision-making. Tyler and van der Toorn also note in their chapter that justice considerations often lead citizens to make political decisions that are at odds with their rational self-interest.

In conclusion, it is difficult to overstate the importance of rational choice theory as a foundational basis for democratic theory and a stimulus to political psychology research. Its emphasis on the structure of information, careful deliberation, and weighting of one's interests as essential to the formation of informed positions on political matters continues to serve as a baseline for much political psychology research. Rational choice theory may provoke political psychologists to document the ways in which human behavior fails to conform with its stringent expectations, but even in that role it is highly influential. Moreover, even to political psychologists the public's democratic shortcomings are cause for consternation no matter how well explained psychologically, suggesting some lingering desire for the normative standard of rational deliberation and well-informed political decisions.

2.2. Biopolitics

Over the last decade or so, social scientists have begun to view human behavior through the prism of biology with intriguing results: neuroscience sheds light on information processing and emotion, evolutionary psychology underscores the biologically adaptive role of various social behaviors, and behavioral genetics uncovers the heritability of many social and political behaviors (Hatemi & McDermott, 2011). Political psychology is also beginning to adopt this perspective, leading to a key focus on biological reasoning and evidence in several chapters in the volume, and a passing reference to biological evidence in many others.

At one level an explanation of human behavior grounded in evolutionary thinking seems entirely consistent with a focus on rationality since human behavior is functional within evolutionary theory, geared toward enhanced reproductive fitness via the process of natural selection. In the *Handbook*, Sidanius and Kurzban outline the basic principles of evolutionary psychology, examining the adaptive biological and reproductive benefits of many social and political behaviors, including cooperation and coordination. But whereas classic rational choice theory is focused on individual goal seeking and reward, evolutionary psychology grapples increasingly with the benefits of social and political behavior to the collective linked to the controversial theory of group selection (Wilson & Wilson, 2008). In that vein, Sidanius and Kurzban state succinctly and somewhat provocatively that "adaptations for political psychology are driven by the possibility of fitness gains through coordinated, cooperative activity with conspecifics." Such deviations from individual rationality are of central interest to political psychology.

Evolutionary psychology focuses on attributes of psychology common to all members of the species, but some questions tackled by biopolitics deal with marked individual variation in human behavior. Why are some people open to experience and others closed, or some conscientious and others not? In her chapter, Funk picks up where Sidanius and Kurzban leave off, providing an overview of major approaches to the study of genetic influences on political behavior that explain individual differences. She evaluates the degree to which different facets of political behavior can be traced back to genes and concludes that genes have extensive influence on political behavior, with heritability shaping a range of fundamental political orientations and behaviors, including political ideology, partisan identity, strength of partisanship, and political participation. This work raises many intriguing questions about the biological mechanisms through which genes influence political behavior, and Funk notes a number of studies in which political behavior is traced to specific genetic alleles that govern known biological processes.

Other chapter authors allude in passing to the growing field of biopolitics. Brader and Marcus discuss developments in the neural understanding of emotions, and Stein considers similar research in reference to the perception of threat among political elites. Huddy notes biological evidence in support of the primacy of in-group attachments, the speed with which in-group and out-group distinctions form in the brain, and the power of hormones such as oxytocin to generate positive in-group feelings. Kinder considers the possible genetic bases of racial prejudice. Dyson and 't Hart note research in which loss activates fear centers of the brain, helping to uncover the biological bases of loss aversion. Attention to the biological bases of political behavior will hopefully reinforce existing insights into political behavior, and help to identify basic biological pathways that may be central to an understanding of political psychology.

2.3. Personality and Psychodynamics

Many political psychologists have examined an individual's personality or characterological predispositions to explain the behavior of political leaders and the ideological choices of citizens. Personality is usually defined as a collection of relatively persistent individual differences that transcend specific situations and contribute to the observed stability of attitudes and behavior. In the last 10 years, political psychologists have shown renewed interest in stable personality traits and their effects on political attitudes and behavior based, in part, on growing consensus on the basic structure of personality traits.

Psychologists commonly identify five basic clusters of personality characteristics or traits—neuroticism, openness to experience, extraversion, conscientiousness, and agreeableness—commonly referred to as the five-factor or Big Five framework of personality. These dimensions are described in some detail and their links to political ideology examined in the *Handbook* by Caprara and Vecchione. The five-factor model has broad influence in political psychology and is touched on in *Handbook* chapters by Feldman, Funk, Taber and Young, Huckfeldt, and colleagues, and Winter. Caprara and Vecchione go beyond conventional accounts of personality within political psychology, however, to suggest that personality is broader than just traits and incorporates political values, such as egalitarianism and the need for security. These basic political values explain individual differences in political attitudes to an impressive degree, as discussed in the chapter on ideology by Feldman. Winter takes a similarly broad view of personality in his chapter on political elites, drawing on social context, personality traits, cognitions, and motives to analyze individual differences in elite behavior and decision-making.

Sigmund Freud had a great deal of influence on early political psychologists because his psychoanalysis of specific individuals lent itself well to the analysis of the personalities of specific political leaders. Harold Lasswell, in his *Psychopathology of Politics* (1930), was a pioneer in analyzing the personalities of political activists in terms of the unconscious conflicts that motivated their political activities. This approach led to numerous psychobiographies of famous leaders, such as the analysis of Woodrow Wilson by George & George (1956), or of Martin Luther by Erik Erikson (1958). Post employs an idiographic approach to perceptively analyze the personality of political leaders from a psychoanalytic perspective. This idiographic approach to personality and politics can be contrasted with the nomothetic approach discussed by Carprara and Vecchione, which statistically places large numbers of people at various positions on specific dimensions of personality.

Feldman adds an important caveat to the study of personality and politics, underscoring the critical interplay between personality traits and political systems. As he notes, political ideology is not simply a proxy for personality. Conservatives may be less open to experience than liberals, but how personality traits map onto political ideology within a given political system also depends on the structure of political parties, their number, strategically adopted issue positions, and additional religious-secular, racial, and other powerful cleavages within a society. In the end, personality is an important recent addition to the study of political psychology, but it cannot be considered in isolation from political context.

2.4. Cognitive and Affective Psychology

Cognitive psychology and neuroscience have had profound influence on political psychology through their discovery of key features of the cognitive system: limited attention and working memory, implicit attitudes that lie outside conscious awareness, the rapid formation of habitual mental associations, and the interplay of affect and cognition. In essence, the cognitive system is highly efficient, processing a great deal of information with relatively little mental exertion. Under appropriate conditions, individuals can override the human tendency toward fast and efficient decision-making (Kahneman, 2011). But political decision-making is often beset with biases that privilege habitual thought and consistency over the careful consideration of new information. This is not always bad. Indeed, in the realm of consumer and other choices such fast gut-level decisions are often superior to reasoned thought. But in the realm of politics, reliance on this form of reasoning privileges consistency through the process of motivated reasoning in which disagreeable or challenging information is quickly rejected. This can lead, in turn, to biased and suboptimal political decisions (Bartels, 1996).

In myriad ways, cognitive psychology has undermined the rational choice model of elite and public decision-making, and we briefly describe how awareness of each aspect of the cognitive system has shaped the study of political psychology over the last decade. Much of this research is dedicated toward understanding how well (or poorly) democratic citizens function and the degree to which they deviate from the normative ideal of rational decision-making.

2.4.1. *Cognitive Economy*

Clear limits on human information-processing capacity underlie the widespread use of cognitive heuristics or shortcuts, which can distort the decision-making of elites (Jervis, 1976; Larson, 1985) and members of the public. These limits often lead to what Simon (1957) refers to as "bounded rationality," discussed at some length in the *Handbook* chapter by Chong.

Levy discusses the impact of cognitive biases on foreign policy decision-making. He distinguishes between "cold," cognitive biases and "hot," affective biases. Cold biases are based on the application of straight cognitive heuristics such as anchoring, in which prior probability assessments exert a disproportionate weight and in which the updating of priors based on new information is slow and inefficient. Hot motivated biases, such as wishful thinking and cognitive consistency, help to preserve the integrity of one's belief system. Such biases in adulthood force an examination of the origins of attitudes and beliefs that require such vigorous defense, as developed in the chapter on childhood and adult development by Sears and Brown. Elite reliance on efficient cognitive biases is further developed in the chapter by Herrmann, in which he discusses the underpinnings of enemy images held by one nation's leaders of another.

Redlawsk and Lau turn to the use of cognitive heuristics among citizens and review work on behavioral decision theory, contrasting normative models with behavioral descriptions of how ordinary people make political decisions. Here too the cognitive limits on rationality lead to a variety of problem-solving strategies that involve cognitive shortcuts. The use of mental shortcuts is not necessarily pernicious, however. The chapters by Taber and Young and by Redlawsk and Lau suggest that the use of cognitive shortcuts for reasoned political deliberation may not be as bad for mass political decision-making as once feared (also see Lau & Redlawsk, 1997). Dyson and 't Hart make a similar point, underscoring the benefits of heuristic reasoning for elite decision-makers facing a crisis.

The need for cognitive efficiency and an awareness of the low priority of politics for many citizens leads to a particular focus within political psychology on information: citizens' depth of knowledge, how political information is acquired, and the sources to which citizens turn to acquire it. In the *Handbook*, Valentino & Nardis discusses Americans' relatively low levels of political knowledge. Huckfeldt, Mondak and colleagues explore in considerable detail the role of everyday conversation partners in conveying political information (and influence). They specifically discuss the role played by politically expert discussion partners and find that conversation with such knowledgeable individuals is reasonably common and influential, even if their arguments are not necessarily held in high regard. This provides an example of how citizens can reduce the effort involved in acquiring knowledge by obtaining political information from others within their immediate social circles.

2.4.2. *Implicit Attitudes and Automaticity*

Conscious cognitive activity is a limited commodity, and decisions are often made, and opinions influenced, by information outside conscious awareness. In reality, the brain is largely devoted to monitoring the body, and most of its activity lies outside consciousness, reserving conscious thought for important higher-level activities. Political psychologists might regard political decisions as a high-level activity warranting conscious deliberation, yet political attitudes can be influenced by information of which someone may be unaware. Taber and Young discuss this phenomenon most fully in their chapter, focusing on implicit attitudes that exist outside conscious awareness, and the automaticity of preconscious attitude activation. They characterize implicit attitudes as affective in nature, fast to take effect, and as interacting with explicit attitudes in various ways that deserve further research scrutiny. Several chapters discuss the widely used Implicit Association Test (IAT; Greenwald, McGhee, & Schwartz, 1998). Kinder extends this discussion to implicit racial attitudes, examining their nature and political effects. In their chapter, Al Ramiah and Hewstone note the influence of implicit attitudes on intergroup discrimination, including racially discriminatory behavior. Overall, the political influence of implicit attitudes and automaticity has been examined in a growing number of research studies concerned with racial attitudes, candidate choice, and the effects of political campaign ads.

Valentino and Nardis weave a discussion of preconscious attitudes into their chapter on political communication, in which they assesses the power of campaign ads, news media content, and other media coverage to sway the public. They regard preconscious attitudes as a source of consistency in political belief, concluding that "what we think of as political deliberation is mostly the post-hoc rationalization of pre-conscious evaluations." In other words, preconscious attitudes serve as attitudinal ballast that prevents someone from being readily persuaded by any one political message; in essence, contrary information is coded as disagreeable and rejected even before it is consciously considered. In that sense, preconscious attitude activation serves as a useful counterweight to persuasive political rhetoric.

The notion of automaticity shares an intellectual link with behaviorist theories that were much in vogue in the middle half of the 20th century. One version of behaviorist theories emphasizes the learning of long-lasting habits, which in turn guide later behavior. They were inspired by the classical conditioning studies of Pavlov, who showed that dogs could be conditioned to salivate at the sound of a bell if it were always followed by food; by the instrumental conditioning studies of Watson and Skinner, who showed that animals could develop complex habits if their behavior proved instrumental to the satisfaction of their basic needs such as hunger or thirst; and the imitative learning examined by Bandura, who showed that children would engage in imitative behavior without any involvement of need satisfaction. Such theories long dominated the analysis of mass political attitudes. The field of political socialization, as described in the chapter by Sears and Brown, developed from the assumption that children learned basic political attitudes (such as party identification and racial prejudice) from their families and friends, and that the residues of these early attitudes dominated their later political attitudes in adulthood, such as their presidential vote preferences, triggering a host of automatic associations not readily subject to conscious scrutiny.

2.4.3. *Spreading Activation and Habitual Association*

The process of automaticity is linked to the axiomatic notion, developed by Hebb (1949), that neurons that fire together, wire together. The simultaneous pairing of two objects in the environment leads to the firing of their relevant neurons. If this pairing persists, the brain associates the two objects habitually and recalls the second when primed with the first in a process of spreading activation. For example, if the word *liberal* is frequently associated in popular conversation with loose-living, pot-smoking, intellectual, or impractical dreamers, or the media depict African Americans in settings that emphasize their poverty, unemployment, and drug-related crimes, the terms will become connected mentally. This set of mental associations may lie at the heart of implicit racial, gender, and other group stereotypes discussed in the *Handbook* by Donald Kinder.

The existence of habitual associations in the brain results in consistent thought patterns that link, for example, abortion and liberal-conservative ideology, or positive feelings about capitalism and support for government fiscal austerity measures. In general, such associations anchor policy positions and contribute to attitude stability over time, especially among those who connect policies to stable political attitudes such as political ideology or other basic values. But habitual mental associations also vary among individuals; political sophisticates with strongly anchored political beliefs show stronger habitual mental associations than those with few or weakly held beliefs. The existence of consistent mental associations helps to explain why reframing a political issue—discussing a tax cut in terms of reduced government waste rather than growing inequality, for example—will be effective for citizens for whom the concept of a tax cut is not anchored by other stable political beliefs, but will be less successful among political sophisticates.

Understanding the factors or situations in which someone will scrutinize their habitual mental associations is of critical interest to political psychology and the study of a democratic citizenry more generally. In their *Handbook* chapter on political emotion, Brader and Marcus present evidence that habitual thought is less common when individuals feel anxious. Under those circumstances, citizens seek out new information, process it carefully, and are motivated to reach the "right" decision. The distinction between more and less effortful information processing is captured within dual-process models that posit both a superficial and more deliberate path to attitude change. The delineation of conditions under which citizens engage in careful political deliberation and are open to new information remains of key interest to political psychologists and will continue to stimulate research in both psychology and political science.

2.4.4. *Interplay of Affect and Cognition*

Contemporary political psychology draws heavily on affective processes. The previous volume of the *Handbook* was published at a time when individual information-processing and research on cognitive biases were popular topics within the study of political behavior. In the last decade, research on affect and emotion has increased exponentially in the social sciences, leading to a far more emotional and affect-laden view of political behavior that is manifestly apparent in the current volume. There was one chapter devoted to political emotions in the previous version of the *Handbook*, but few other chapters devoted much space to the topic. That has changed dramatically in the current volume, in which it is difficult to find a chapter that does not make at least passing reference to the role of political emotions in research on citizens or political elites.

In addition to Brader and Marcus's detailed discussion of political emotions, emotions surface in numerous ways in this edition of the *Handbook*. Stein discusses in considerable detail the influence of emotions on elites' perceptions of, and responses to, external threats. She builds on Brader and Marcus's discussion of the origins and cognitive consequences of different classes of emotions to explain the likely consequences of fear, humiliation, and anger for elite decision-making. Levy, Herrmann, and Dyson and 't Hart also touch on the role of emotion within elite decision-making. Positive and negative affect are integral components of implicit attitudes, as noted by Taber and Young, and in that sense emotion plays a very central role within modern attitude research in both psychology and political science. Al Ramiah and Hewstone consider evidence that members of minority groups react more strongly to negative implicit than explicit attitudes held by a majority group member, underscoring the power of implicit attitudes to shape interpersonal encounters. Kinder discusses the importance of affect to the study of racial prejudice. Huddy underscores the contribution of intergroup emotions to the development of group cohesion and political action. Bar-Tal and Halperan evaluate the importance of anger, hatred, fear, and humiliation to the development of intractable conflicts.

Brader and Marcus review research on political emotions in considerable detail. Their chapter underscores a fourth crucial aspect of the cognitive system, the intricate interplay between affect and cognition. Hot cognition underscores the degree to which motivational and affective states influence decision-making, and is discussed at some length by Taber and Young. Motivated reasoning serves as a pervasive example of hot cognition in which individuals are motivated to preserve their beliefs, oppose challenging or contradictory views, and dismiss the other side's arguments as far weaker than one's own. In essence, it produces rapid (and perhaps preconscious) dismissal of opposing views. The existence of motivated reasoning generates a paradox, however, when it comes to political sophisticates, who turn out to be most subject to automaticity and motivated reasoning. In Chong's words, "the beliefs of the best informed may reflect an ideologically distorted perspective rather than the objective state of the world," raising real questions about the rational basis of public opinion. If those with the information needed to make a fully informed decision are also the most biased in their reasoning, rational deliberation seems like an unattainable political ideal.

2.5. Intergroup Relations

In tandem with a growing interest in biology and emotions, contemporary political psychology is also increasingly focused on collective behavior and theories of intergroup relations as explanations for political behavior. The previous version of this *Handbook* contained four chapters linked to intergroup relations focusing on in-group identity, collective action, group prejudice, and intractable group conflict. In the current volume, the chapters explicitly devoted to intergroup relations have been expanded to additionally include conflict management, interpersonal social influence, small-group deliberation, immigration and multiculturalism, and discrimination. Moreover, the growing focus over the last 10 years on group-based political behavior is entwined with other changes that have occurred within the field of political psychology. Intergroup research is increasingly international in focus, drawing on common frameworks such as social identity theory to explain political behavior in numerous regions of the world. It also builds on an integrated model of affect and cognition, with affect playing an especially important role in motivating collective action and driving responses to societal and personal threat.

The field of intergroup relations does not embody a single theoretical approach; rather it draws on diverse psychological theories. But it is fair to say that many, if not most, analyses of collective behavior deviate from a rational choice account of human behavior. For instance, Sidanius and Kurzban note the power of collectives within human evolution and conclude that the need to cooperate is a basic and functional aspect of human society (even if not always completely rational for an individual). Early research on intergroup relations, conducted in the 1950s and 1960s, stressed the biased and emotional nature of out-group animosity, especially toward Jews and Negroes (Allport, 1954). Much attention was paid to the childhood socialization of prejudice and stereotyping, as indicated in the chapter by Sears and Brown. Research on the authoritarian personality, a highly influential study of prejudice, emphasized the importance of interrelated and emotionally motivated aspects of personality such as authoritarian submission and authoritarian aggression in the development of racial prejudice and anti-Semitism (Adorno et al., 1950).

More recent research on racial prejudice and intergroup relations has drawn on a mix of cognitive and affective factors to account for political group conflict, cohesion, and conformity. The limitations of the cognitive system, as discussed in numerous chapters of the *Handbook,* lead to the formation of simplistic group stereotypes that shape intergroup political behavior, as noted by Kinder, influence enemy images, as discussed by Herrmann, and affect the process of conflict resolution, as described by Fisher and colleagues. Group identities are linked to powerful emotions that generate anger and hatred and play a central role in accounts of international and domestic politics in

Handbook chapters by Stein, Huddy, Klandermans and van Stekelenburg, and Bar-Tal and Halperan.

Some accounts of intergroup behavior, such as realistic conflict theory, are consistent with rational choice and are often pitted against symbolic accounts of group political cohesion and conflict. Huddy highlights the distinction between social identity theory, which stresses social prestige and intergroup respect as motives for intergroup behavior (Tajfel, 1981; Tajfel & Turner, 1986), and realistic interest theories, which place emphasis on shared material interests and conflict over tangible resources (Blumer, 1958; Bobo & Tuan, 2006; Levine & Campbell, 1972; Sidanius & Pratto, 1999). A similar distinction between realistic and affective responses to members of an out-group surfaces in research on racial attitudes in Kinder's discussion of prejudice and Green and Staerklé's chapter on immigration and multiculturalism. On balance, there is greater support for symbolic than realistic sources of political group cohesion and conflict.

Threat plays a special role in the political life of a collective. It can galvanize and unify an in-group while leading to vilification of an out-group, and is thus particularly potent politically. Threat is widely discussed in *Handbook* chapters dealing with the political psychology of mass politics, including Huddy's chapter on in-group identities, Green and Staerklé's consideration of immigration and multiculturalism, Kinder's overview of racial prejudice, and Bar-Tal and Halperan's overview of intractable conflicts. The concept of threat has long dominated research on conflict within international relations, as noted at some length by Stein. Research on both mass and elite politics assesses the rationality of threat reactions and generally rejects that interpretation, at least in broad stroke. Highly distorted subjective judgments often influence elites' perception of threat, as noted in chapters by Levy, Stein, and Herrmann. Moreover, economic threats are typically less politically potent than cultural and other less tangible noneconomic threats in mass politics, as discussed in chapters by Huddy, Kinder, and Green and Staerklé.

Finally, humans' impressive capacity for cooperation, a topic discussed at length by Sidanius and Kurzban, leads us back to consider the political psychology of a collective. Tyler and van der Toorn consider the origins of societal justice in social and moral values that can govern cooperation and societal defection. They mention a provocative argument advanced by social psychologist Donald Campbell that values such as humanitarianism have arisen over time through social evolution as a way to curb more base instincts linked to self-interest. This raises an important consideration about the key role of social norms in political psychology. As social animals, humans are profoundly affected by social norms. Those norms are often learned early and well in the socialization process, as indicated by Sears and Brown. Such norms hold the potential for good as well as evil. Indeed some even argue that life in modern democratic societies is remarkably peaceable, that international violence is now at an all-time low, and that the horrors that were commonplace in the past, such as the widespread use of torture, are now widely condemned (Pinker, 2011). The globalization of economic life reflects international cooperation on a scale unimaginable in times past.

Have the scales tipped toward a more humane and cooperative world? Such a claim would undoubtedly be disputed by scholars of indigenous oppression, economic inequality, and other societal ills. Nonetheless, research on values and social justice opens political psychology to the positive forces of cooperation, tolerance, and respect on which modern democratic societies pivot. Adherence to a norm of cooperation may not be rational for an individual (if defined as the pursuit of self-interest) but can have clear advantages to human groups. The positive forces in human society are touched on only lightly in this *Handbook* but may come to play a larger role in future political psychology research (see Aspinwall & Satudinger, 2002; Monroe, 1996).

3. Organization of This Volume

We begin this volume with a section on broad psychological theories. This section includes basic psychological theories that concern personality, early childhood and adult development, rational choice, decision-making, the study of emotion, evolutionary psychology, genetics, and political rhetoric. Then we move to the substantive focus of different areas of political psychological research, which tend to cut across theoretical approaches. We start with elite behavior, first in the area of international relations and then in the area of domestic politics. The next section focuses on mass political behavior, including an analysis of political reasoning, political ideology, social justice, social influence, political communications, and political deliberation. The final section considers collective behavior, including identities, social movements, racial prejudice, migration and multiculturalism, discrimination, and intractable conflict.

We characterize political psychology as the application of psychology to politics, but we would like to see greater two-way communication between disciplines. Indeed, the study of political psychology provides potential insight into basic psychology, as is clear from the chapters in this volume. For example, Feldman discusses at some length the multidimensional nature of political ideology and conservatism that is at odds with their popular unidimensional conception in social psychology. Numerous chapters underscore the complexity of political sophistication, which cannot simply be equated with expertise and the efficient assimilation of new information but focuses instead on strong political biases, powerful partisan identities, and extensive motivated reasoning. While processes such as motivated reasoning are well known in psychology, they deserve even greater research attention within political psychology because of their political heft. Although many political psychologists, including authors in this volume, are drawn from the disciplines of psychology and political science, they also include historians, sociologists, anthropologists, psychiatrists, communications researchers, educators, and lawyers.

Before closing, we also want to refer the interested reader to several other recent volumes with different goals from our own but with somewhat similar titles. This *Handbook* is intended as a comprehensive statement of the current state of knowledge in political psychology. There are several other volumes in the *Oxford Handbooks* series that touch on similar aspects of political behavior but take a less explicitly psychological approach.

Handbooks edited by Russell Dalton and Hans-Dieter Klingemann (*The Oxford Handbook of Political Behavior*, 2007) and Robert Shapiro and Lawrence Jacobs (*The Oxford Handbook of American Public Opinion and the Media*, 2011) discuss topics such as political socialization, political communication, trust, and political emotions. The current volume goes more deeply into original psychological research, includes authors from both psychology and political science, and is unique in combining research on both elite and mass politics. The three handbooks provide excellent complementary reviews of political behavior research.

One other recent volume presents an interesting collection of individual research in political psychology. Borgida, Federico, and Sullivan edited *The Psychology of Democratic Citizenship* (2009), with chapters devoted to citizens' democratic capabilities. The volume includes scholars presenting their own research on political knowledge, persuasion, group identity, political tolerance, and the media. Topics and approaches overlap with those in the current *Handbook* but describe a single research enterprise rather than review a body of work, and are less singularly focused on psychological research and theory. Howard Lavine is the editor of the four-volume set *Political Psychology* (2010). The series includes reprints of classic articles in political psychology and is organized into four broad themes: theoretical approaches, public opinion, international relations, and intergroup relations. This series serves as an important reference work for students and scholars who wish to become acquainted with canonical writing and research studies in political psychology.

The current *Handbook* is a companion to these volumes in political psychology and political behavior that has a somewhat different purpose. This *Handbook* is the place to go to find out what is currently known about the many different fields in the umbrella topic of political psychology and learn more about psychology, political science, and their vibrant intersection.

REFERENCES

Adorno, T. W., Frenkel-Brunswik, E., Levinson, D. J., & Sanford, R. N. (1950). *The authoritarian personality*. New York: Harper & Row.

Allport, G. W. (1954). *The nature of prejudice*. Garden City, NY: Doubleday Anchor.

Aspinwall, L. G., & Staudinger, U. (Eds.). (2002). *A psychology of human strengths: Fundamental questions and future directions for a positive psychology*. Washington, DC: APA Books.

Bartels, L. M. (1996). Uninformed voters: Information effects in presidential elections. *American Journal of Political Science, 40*(1), 194–230.

Blumer, H. (1958). Race prejudice as a sense of group position. *The Pacific Sociological Review, 1*(1), 3–7.

Bobo, L. D., & Tuan, M. (2006). *Prejudice in politics: Group position, public opinion, and the Wisconsin treaty rights dispute*. Cambridge, MA: Harvard University Press.

Borgida, E., Federico, C. M., & Sullivan, J. (2009). *The political psychology of democratic citizenship*. New York: Oxford University Press.

Camerer, C. F., Loewenstein, G., & Rabin, M. (Eds.) (2004) *Advances in behavioral economics*. New York: Russell Sage.

Cottam, M. L., Dietz-Uhler, B., Mastors, E., & Preston, T. (2010). *Introduction to political psychology* (2nd ed.). New York: Psychology Press.

Crenshaw, M. (2000). The psychology of terrorism: An agenda for the 21st century. *Political Psychology, 21,* 405–420.

Dalton, R., & Klingemann, H. D. (2007). *The Oxford handbook of political behavior.* Oxford: Oxford University Press.

Downs, A. (1957). *An economic theory of democracy.* New York: Harper & Row.

Edwards, W. (1954). The theory of decision-making. *Psychological Bulletin, 51,* 380–417.

Erikson, E. H. (1958). *Young man Luther: A study in psychoanalysis and history.* New York: Norton.

Feldman, S., & Stenner, K. (1997). Perceived threat and authoritarianism. *Political Psychology, 18,* 741–770.

Fishbein, M., & Ajzen, I. (1975). *Belief, attitude, intention, and behavior: An introduction to theory and research.* Reading, MA: Addison-Wesley.

George, A. L., & George, J. L. (1956). *Woodrow Wilson and Colonel House: A personality study.* New York: Dover.

Green, D., & Shapiro, I. (1994). *Pathologies of rational choice theory: A critique of applications in political science.* New Haven, CT: Yale University Press.

Greenwald, A. G., McGhee, D. E., & Schwartz, J. L. K. (1998). Measuring individual differences in implicit cognition: The implicit association test. *Journal of Personality and Social Psychology, 74,* 1464–1480.

Hatemi, P. K., & McDermott, R. (2011). *Man is by nature a political animal: Evolution, biology, and politics.* Chicago: University of Chicago Press.

Hebb, D. O. (1949). *The organization of behavior.* New York: Wiley.

Hermann, M. G. (1986). *Political psychology.* San Francisco: Jossey-Bass.

Houghton, D. P. (2009). *Political psychology: Situations, individuals, and cases.* New York: Routledge.

Huddy, L., & Feldman, S. (2011). Americans respond politically to 9/11: Understanding the impact of the terrorist attacks and their aftermath. *American Psychologist, 66*(6), 455–467.

Jervis, R. (1976). *Perception and misperception in international politics.* Princeton, NJ: Princeton University Press.

Jost, J. T., Glaser, J., Kruglanski, A. W., & Sulloway, F. (2003). Political conservatism as motivated social cognition. *Psychologcial Bulletin, 129,* 339–375.

Jost, J. T., & Sidanius, J. (2004). *Political psychology.* New York: Psychology Press.

Kahneman, D. (2011). *Thinking, fast and slow.* New York: Farrar, Straus, and Giroux.

Kahneman, D., Slovic, P., & Tversky, A. (Eds.) (1982). *Judgment under uncertainty: Heuristics and biases.* New York: Cambridge University Press.

Kahneman, D., & Tversky, A. (1979). Prospect theory: An analysis of decision under risk. *Econometrica, 47,* 263–291.

Knutson, J. N. (Ed.). (1973). *Handbook of political psychology.* San Francisco: Jossey-Bass.

Lambert, A. J., Scherer, L. D., Schott, J. P., Olson, K. R., Andrews, R. K., & O'Brien, T. C. (2010). Rally effects, threat, and attitude change: An integrative approach to understanding the role of emotion. *Journal of Personality and Social Psychology, 98,* 886–903.

Lasswell, H. D. (1930). *Psychopathology and politics.* New York: Viking.

Larson, D. (1985). *Origins of containment.* Princeton, NJ: Princeton University Press.

Lau, R. R., & Redlawsk, D. P. (1997). Voting correctly. *American Political Science Review, 91,* 585–598.

Lavine, H. (2010). *Political psychology.* Thousand Oaks, CA: Sage.

Le Cheminant, W., & Parrish, J. M. (2011). *Manipulating democracy: Democratic theory, political psychology and mass media.* New York: Routledge.

Lerner, J. S., Gonzalez, R. M., Small, D. A., & Fischhoff, B. (2003). Effects of fear and anger on perceived risks of terrorism: A national field experiment. *Psychological Science, 14,* 144–150.

LeVine, R. A., & Campbell, D. T. (1972) *Ethnocentrism: Theories of conflict, ethnic attitudes, and group behavior.* New York: Wiley & Sons.

Marcus, G. E. (2012). *Political psychology: Neuroscience, genetics, and politics.* New York: Oxford University Press.

McDermott, R. (2004). *Political psychology in international relations.* Ann Arbor: University of Michigan Press.

Milgram, S. (1974). *Obedience to authority.* New York: Harper & Row.

Monroe, K. R. (1996). *The heart of altruism: Perceptions of a common humanity.* Princeton, NJ: Princeton University Press.

Pinker, S. (2011). *The better angels of our nature: Why violence has declined.* New York: Viking.

Pyszczynski, T., Solomon, S., & Greenberg, J. (2003). *In the wake of 9/11: The psychology of terror.* Washington, DC: American Psychological Association.

Sears, D. O., Huddy, L., & Jervis, R. (Eds.). (2003). *Oxford handbook of political psychology.* New York: Oxford University Press.

Shapiro, R., & Jacobs, L. (2011). *The Oxford Handbook of American Public Opinion and the Media.* New York: Oxford University Press.

Sidanius, J. & Pratto, F. (1999). *Social dominance: An intergroup theory of social hierarchy and oppression.* New York: Cambridge University Press.

Simon, B., & Klandermans, B. (2001). Politicized collective identity: A social psychological analysis. *American Psychologist, 56*(4), 319–331. doi:10.1037/0003-066X.56.4.319

Simon, H. A. (1957). *Models of man: Social and rational.* New York: Wiley.

Sniderman, P. M., Hagendoorn, L., & Prior, M. (2004). Predispositional factors and situational triggers: Exclusionary reactions to immigrant minorities. *American Political Science Review, 98*(1), 35–49.

Sniderman, P. M., & Hagendoorn, L. (2007). *When ways of life collide.* Princeton, NJ: Princeton University Press.

Sullivan, J. L., Rahn, W. M., & Rudolph, T. J. (2002). The contours of political psychology: Situating research on political information processing. In J. H. Kuklinski (Ed.), *Thinking about political psychology* (pp. 23–47) Cambridge, MA: Cambridge University Press.

Tajfel, H. (1981). *Human groups and social categories: Studies in social psychology.* Cambridge: Cambridge University Press.

Tajfel, H., & Turner, J. C. (1986). The social identity theory of intergroup behavior. In S. Worchel & W. G. Austin (eds.), *Psychology of intergroup relations* (2nd ed., pp. 7–24). Chicago: Nelson-Hall.

Tesler, M., & Sears, D. O. (2010). *Obama's race: The 2008 election and the dream of a post-racial America.* Chicago: University of Chicago Press.

Tetlock, P. (2005). *Expert judgment: How good is it? How can we know?* Princeton, NJ: Princeton University Press.

Wilson, D. S., & Wilson, E. O. (2008). Evolution "for the good of the group." *American Scientist, 96,* 380–389.

PART I

THEORETICAL APPROACHES

CHAPTER 2

···

PERSONALITY APPROACHES TO POLITICAL BEHAVIOR

···

GIAN VITTORIO CAPRARA AND MICHELE VECCHIONE

1. WHAT IS PERSONALITY?

1.1. Introduction

PERSONALITY is both a familiar and complex psychological concept, which refers to habitual and distinct patterns of physical and mental activity that distinguish one individual from another. Today personality is a popular explanatory concept in the domain of politics, due to the pervasive influence of the modern news media and their focus on the personality of political leaders. This has led political candidates to become more concerned with conveying favorable personal images and appealing narratives that are capable of attracting potential voters beyond the appeal of traditional political ideology. Voters' personality is no less important than leaders' personality within the analysis of contemporary political behavior. Voters' political preferences depend increasingly on their likes and dislikes of political candidates, and voter personality factors and related judgmental heuristics guide their political decisions to a greater degree than previously influential factors such as voter education, gender, and age.

In the present chapter we will address current views of personality to provide the conceptual frame within which to address the role of personality in contemporary politics. Then we will focus on the contribution of personality to an understanding of political behavior, highlighting how different components of personality, like traits, needs, values, self-beliefs, and social attitudes, shape citizens' ideological preferences and participation and leaders' perceived personality.

Personality can be viewed from two distinct perspectives that lead to a focus on different, although interdependent, courses of inquiry. One may view personality subjectively, from individuals' perspective, focusing on their private feelings, thoughts, and narratives about themselves and their life and thus on the enduring collection of personal qualities, attributes, and inclinations that convey a sense of personal identity. From this perspective, personality is a self-referential agentic system capable of self-regulation with a significant impact on the environment. Alternately, an objective view takes the perspective of an observer, from which personality may be viewed as the entire architecture of psychological characteristics that distinguish individuals one from another. From this perspective, personality is largely a social construction involving systems of beliefs about the qualities of individuals that dictate how individual differences in observed behaviors should be acknowledged and treated.

These two perspectives capture the way in which personality has been examined in the political domain. The first perspective has been adopted when the focus is on voters' and politicians' predispositions, beliefs, values, expectations, and behavior. The second perspective has been used to account for citizens' perceptions and impressions of political leaders' personal characteristics.

In this chapter, we address both of these views, first by reviewing major research contributions of the past, and second by pointing to current studies that attest to the effect of personality on political preferences and participation.

1.2. Personality as a Self-Regulatory System

Personality can be thought of as a dynamic system of psychological structures and processes that mediates the relationship between the individual and the environment and accounts for what a person is and may become. The overall organization of this complex system results from synergistic interactions among multiple subsystems (cognitive, affective, and behavioral), which convey, foster, and preserve a sense of personal identity (Caprara & Cervone, 2000).

Looking at the transactions of personality as a whole, we can either focus on its basic structure, or on the adaptive functions of its various components. As people exhibit consistent, stable patterns of experience and action that distinguish them one from another, some personality psychologists point to internal structures that set an individual's initial potential and dictate the kind of person one may become under given conditions. Other personality psychologists point, instead, to the processes through which people adapt to the environment, and they focus on the dynamic organization of components from which each individual's unity, coherence, and continuity derive.

Most personality psychologists would agree that personality science should address the entire psychological functioning of individuals and thus account for both the structure and dynamics of the system and how structures and processes act on one another (Caprara, 1996).

If we focus on psychological qualities that allow us to distinguish among people, personality can be viewed as consisting of traits or dispositions (e.g., extraversion), namely endogenous basic tendencies to exhibit consistent, stable patterns of experience and action across situations (McCrae & Costa, 2008). However, traits alone cannot account for the entire architecture of personality nor for its functioning: how predispositions generate stable patterns of behavior, how different behavioral tendencies operate in concert, and ultimately for the distinctive experience of each person. Personality should address the processes and mechanisms from which consistency, directionality and the sense of one's own individuality derive. This leads beyond the study of individual differences in traits to a comprehensive model of personality functioning that incorporates trait activation and orchestration under given physical and sociohistorical conditions.

In this regard, social learning theories have paved the way to a more comprehensive account of personality by pointing to the influence that social environment exerts in setting the conditions for the construction and functioning of personality. Such social cognitive approaches to personality have moved beyond a social learning model in pointing to the influence that individuals may exert on the environment as active agents that construe, select, and change the environments in which they live. From this social-cognitive perspective, needs, values and self-beliefs are just as important as traits in accounting for the internal organization of personality and individual differences that may significantly influence political behavior. Ultimately, conceptualizing personality as a self-regulatory system in the service of individual development and well-being has provided a common ground for reconciling different research traditions under broad assumptions, as we will discuss below.

It is a common assumption that genes and the brain form the remote basis of personality distinctive properties and characteristics by providing a vast amount of potential. Likewise it is a common assumption that people develop and function in ongoing processes of reciprocal interaction with their environment. Likely internal factors, in the form of cognitive, affective, and biological events, behavior, and the environment all operate as interacting determinants of what personality is at any moment within a network of reciprocal causation, and of what personality may become within the boundaries set by biological and social constraints. Finally, most would agree that unique capacities for self reflection, learning from one's own and from others' experience and forethought, accord people the power to regulate their behavior in accordance with their own aims and standards, to extend their control over the environment, and to contribute proactively to their own development. All this leads to a view of personality as a selective, generative and proactive system, not just reactive and adaptive. People do not consist of a set of tendencies that progress in a predetermined sequence toward inevitable end states. Although both cultural and biological factors contribute to the development of personality, people are not passive vessels who merely store genetic endowments and absorb environmental influences They, instead, are active agents who causally contribute to sign their course of life. In viewing personality as a complex system of psychological structures and processes through which people regulate their actions and experiences, one can identify three main sources of influence on personality development: nature, nurture, and the agentic person (see Funk, chapter 8, this volume; Sears and Brown, chapter 3, this volume).

Over the last several decades, personality psychologists have come to recognize that the development and functioning of personality cannot be properly understood without addressing its biological roots. Recent years in particular have witnessed enormous progress in our understanding of the genetic factors that function as distal determinants of personality, and of the brain systems that are more proximal determinants of personality functioning and development. At the same time similar progress has been made in understanding how social environments and interpersonal relations set the conditions for the expression of individuals' endowments and potentials.

In reality development involves continuous and reciprocal interactions between the person as a bio-psychological system and the social context in which they live. Genetic endowment equips people with a vast array of potential whose actualization is conditional on their experiences. Early contexts set the conditions for activation of processes and deployment of mechanisms that establish cognitive structures, emotional patterns, and habits that provide an individual with unity, continuity, coherence and agentic power.

Viewing personality as a dynamic and self-regulating system which develops and functions in an ongoing process of reciprocal interactions with the environment allows one to capture its multiform expressions and to appreciate the value of both behavioral stability and change. Stability is critical for preserving one's own identity, as well as for establishing and maintaining relations with others. Change on the other hand is no less critical over the entire life course to continuously respond to the environmental and to grant the full expression of one's own individuality. A person's actualization, in fact, depends upon their capacities to align their behavior to their values and to continuously adjust their strivings to the opportunities and constraints of their environment. Ultimately, both stability and change can be fully appreciated only by looking at the person as a whole in continuous transition toward new forms of organization across the life span.

Along this line of reasoning, caution is recommended when examining recent findings that point to the stability of political choices, and to the heritability of political attitudes and preferences (Alford, Funk, & Hibbing, 2005; Bouchard & Lohelin, 2001; Hatemi, Medland, Morley, Heath, & Martin, 2007; Hatemi et al., 2010). Genes likely set the potential for inclinations that under given conditions may turn into values, social attitudes, and political preferences (Smith, Oxley, Hibbing, Alford, & Hibbing, 2011). Although available findings are encouraging, we warn against premature conclusions about either the causes of political stability, or the pathways through which genes may affect political choices, both directly and indirectly via traits, values, and attitudes. One should also not underestimate variability in genetic expression that may stem from the impact of family environments and idiosyncratic experiences (see Funk, chapter 8, this volume).

1.3. Personality in Politics

Several basic and major features of personality are relevant in the political domain, including traits, needs and motives, self-beliefs, values, and social attitudes. Together they form layers of a hypothetical architecture of personality that operates at different levels and whose elements interact to various degrees. These features address different aspects of personality that shed light on its functioning.

Traits refer to the basic dispositions that predispose one to consistent patterns of thought, feeling, and action (McCrae & Costa, 2008). Needs concern people's conscious or unconscious wishes, desires, or goals (Winter, John, Stewart, Klohnen, & Duncan, 1998). Self-beliefs concern pervasive evaluations and expectations individuals hold about themselves and their life, including self-esteem and life confidence, one's ability to cope with challenging tasks and situations, such as self-efficacy. Values are cognitive representations of desirable, abstract, transsituational goals that serve as a guiding principle in everyday life. Social attitudes are dispositional evaluations, such as likes and dislikes of specific social objects, events, and behaviors that attest to an individual's social bonds and identity.

Traits are related to executive-behavioral functions and concern habitual behaviors, whereas needs, values, and self-beliefs are related to evaluative-motivational functions as they concern people's views of themselves and what they cherish in life. Within a comprehensive and thereby inclusive conception of personality, basic traits have been viewed as distal causes or potentials that precede and predispose one to adopt specific self-beliefs, values, and social attitudes that emerge under the influence of social experiences. Alternatively, basic needs have been viewed as antecedent to basic traits (Winter et al., 1998). Yet causal primacy cannot be easily assumed, since both traits and needs represent inherited features that are set early in life. We are thus inclined to view basic traits and needs as reflecting different, although linked, intrapersonal systems that operate in concert to account for an individual's course of action in manifold domains of functioning, including politics.

One may question whether needs, traits, self-beliefs, values, and social attitudes are sufficient to offer a comprehensive view of personality, and in particular whether intelligence, cognitive abilities, and cognitive styles should be included among the major features of personality. Likewise, most would agree that emotional intelligence, social intelligence, and wisdom should be included within a comprehensive view of personality features, because the notion of intelligence has been extended in the last several decades to include people's capacity to orchestrate their talents and take opportunities that will further their happiness and success. In this regard, we do not doubt that intelligence could enhance political knowledge, foster engagement, and promote leadership. Yet, to our knowledge, empirical support for this claim is less consistent than one would expect.

1.4. Differing Theoretical Approaches to the Study of Personality and Politics

Discussion regarding the influence of personal qualities in politics is long-standing if one includes the seminal intuitions of classic writers such as Machiavelli and Hobbes. In particular, concern for the role that temperament, character, and passion play in the fortune of leaders and in the behavior of followers precedes the inquiry of psychologists among prominent social scientists (Durkheim, 1933; Le Bon, 1895; Marx, 1844; Tarde, 1903; Weber, 1904). Earlier contributions of psychology go back to the early 1930s and developed over the next several decades in accordance with the approaches that dominated the field of personality at the time: first psychoanalysis, then social learning, and finally cognitive psychology.

Most of these earlier studies were conducted in North America, thus raising questions about the generality and applicability of their research findings to different cultures. Brilliant reviews focusing on the history of personality and politics research can be found in Knutson (1973), Sniderman (1975), Greenstein (1975), and Simonton (1990), and as a consequence we limit our discussion to the major contributions of this research over the last millennium. In the decades that precede and follow World War II, psychoanalysis seemed to provide a reasonable basis for selecting and organizing empirical findings relating personality types to political orientation (see also Post, chapter 15, this volume). For theorists who embraced psychoanalytic theory, political preferences and choices of leaders and followers were interpreted by making reference to unconscious drives and mechanisms. Classic examples based on this approach are the studies of Harold Lasswell (1930, 1948) on the motives behind political engagement (see Winter, chapter 14, this volume) and research under the lead of Theodor Adorno that focused on the authoritarian personality. The study by Adorno and colleagues (1950) was largely influenced by Freudian ideas about the role of drives and of defense mechanisms in the functioning of personality. The revisions of Marxian theory made within the Frankfurt school of social theory (Fromm, 1941; Horkheimer, 1936) about the role of family in the formation of individuals' character and in the reproduction of society, and a more or less explicit commitment to left ideals of the time, were also influential. Psychoanalytic concepts related to unconscious strivings, escape mechanisms, and psychodynamic conflicts were used by Adorno and colleagues (1950) to account for power motives, mass submission to authority, and uncritical adherence of people to totalitarian movements and regimes. Ultimately, nine tightly interrelated traits, including authoritarian aggression, authoritarian submission, conventionalism, anti-intraception, superstition and stereotypy, destructiveness and cynicism, projectivity, concerns over sexuality, and power and toughness, were regarded as distinctive of the authoritarian personality.

From a political standpoint, people with an authoritarian personality were described as those inclined to prejudice and an intolerance of diversity (authoritarian aggression), to follow strong leaders, to admire strength and toughness, to submit to symbols of power (authoritarian submission), and to prefer traditional and conventional values (conventionalism). The hierarchical structure of the patriarchal family, characterized by harsh, punitive parental discipline, was posited at the root of the deference toward authorities and thus at the core of a diffused mentality functional to the maintenance of past regimes whose totalitarian devolution lead to fascism and Nazism.

The authoritarian personality can be considered the first systematic study of the personality determinants of prejudice, and its impact spread much beyond psychology. A number of criticisms, however, followed earlier enthusiasm, leading to a progressive loss of confidence in the heuristic validity of the theory and its constructs (Brown, 1965; Sanford, 1973). Some criticisms were related to the unidimensionality of authoritarianism and to the psychometric properties of measures (Allport, 1954; Christie & Cook, 1958; Wilson, 1973). Others concerned the ideological biases of authors that led them to view authoritarianism as prototypical of right but not left ideologies (Eysenck, 1954; Rokeach, 1954). Eysenck (1954), in particular, noted considerable similarities between the personalities of National Socialists and Communists, despite their opposite positions on a traditional ideological continuum. He found that extremists on both the political Left (communists) and Right (fascists) were more tough-minded (e.g. highly authoritarian and aggressive) than moderates (conservatives and liberals).

In reality, authoritarian personality features were most common among those on the right of the political spectrum, although various psychological attributes of authoritarianism could also be found among supporters of left-wing ideologies. Rokeach (1956), for instance, found that extremists on the left and right shared a dogmatic personality and rigid thinking that led them to be more resistant than moderates to change and more receptive to closed-minded belief system. Thus other constructs, like dogmatism, intolerance of ambiguity, mental rigidity, closed-mindedness, and alienation, came to the fore as cognitive counterparts to authoritarianism (Budner, 1962; Rokeach, 1956; Seeman, 1959, 1966).

Among the few authors who have had direct access to the personality of political elites, Di Renzo (1963) found that members of the Italian neofascist Social Movement (MSI) scored higher in dogmatism than members of the Communist Party. Similar findings were found by Barker (1963) on a sample of US student activists. There are also sophisticated, in-depth case studies, employing psychobiography and historiographical analyses, that focus on the personalities of prominent politicians, using memoirs, archival documents, and available historical data. The studies by Erikson on Martin Luther (1958) and Mahatma Gandhi (1969), as those of George and George (1956) on Woodrow Wilson, represent classic examples of qualitative approaches to personality and political leadership that have captured the uniqueness of the single case and, at the same time, underscored the limitations in reliability and generalizability of such qualitative single-case studies. Earlier psychodynamic approaches were gradually replaced by new approaches focusing on a leader's worldview (Barber, 1965, 1972), interpersonal traits (Etheredge, 1978), motivations (Hermann, 1977; Winter, 1973; Winter & Stewart, 1977), cognitive styles (Suedfeld & Rank, 1976; Suedfeld & Tetlock, 1977), and leadership style (Simonton, 1986, 1988) (see Winter, chapter 14, this volume). Most leadership studies relied on indirect measures to assess personality, either adopting at-a-distance scoring systems or relying upon experts' evaluations.

Costantini and Craik (1980), however, achieved a direct description of members of California's presidential delegation slate across five US presidential campaigns, from 1968 to 1976. Self-reports on a standard personality inventory—the Adjective Check List (Gough & Heilbrun, 1965)—made possible comparisons between politicians and the general public and among politicians of opposite parties. Politicians reported a higher tendency than the general public to seek and maintain a role as leader in groups (*dominance*), to be assertive, outgoing, ambitious (*self-confidence*), and determined to do well (*achievement*). On the other hand, they showed a lower tendency than the general public to solicit sympathy, affection, or emotional support (*succorance*), to express feelings of inferiority through self-criticism, guilt, or social impotence (*abasement*), and to seek and sustain subordinate roles in relations with others (*deference*). Several differences were also discovered between politicians, reflecting their ideological positioning. Republican showed a higher tendency than Democrats to express optimism and positivity toward life, to be cheerful, interested in others, and ready to adapt (*personal adjustment*), to be tidy, neat, well organized (*order*), diligent, responsive to their obligations (*self-control*), and persistent in the activities undertaken (*endurance*). On the other hand, Democrats showed a higher tendency than Republican to act independently (*autonomy*), to avoid stability (*change*), to be flexible, spontaneous, and unconventional (*liability*), to maintain personal friendships (*affiliation*), to seek the attention of others (*exhibition*), and to solicit their sympathy or support (*succorance*). These findings were among the first to document systematic differences in personality between large groups of politicians from opposite sides of the political divide. However, only at the turn of the 1990s did the growing consensus on general systems to describe personality traits (Big Five) and values (Schwartz's model) give impulse to nomothetic studies and open new avenues to understand the links between personality and politics, and the psychological pathways by which personality influences political preferences and engagement.

2. PERSONALITY DETERMINANTS OF POLITICAL PREFERENCE

2.1. Basic Personality Traits and Their Political Effects

An impressive body of research has been accumulated in the last three decades positing five basic factors, the so-called Big Five (McCrae & Costa, 1996, 2008), at the roots of major individual differences in personality traits. The Big Five represent the meeting point of two traditions of research, based respectively on analysis the terms laypeople use to distinguish people one from another (i.e., the lexicographic tradition), and on analysis of questionnaire self-reports that assess major interindividual differences in personality (i.e., the factorial tradition). Findings from both research traditions identify five factors as the cornerstone of individual personality in virtually all cultures (McCrae & Allik, 2002). Despite some divergence among various authors regarding the name to be given to these various factors across cultural contexts (Digman, 1990; Goldberg, 1990; John, 1990), there is substantial agreement on the basic five traits: (1) extraversion (or energy), (2) agreeableness, (3) conscientiousness, (4) neuroticism (or emotional stability), and (5) openness to experience (or intellect). Extraversion refers to individuals' tendency to behave and react vigorously in different situations and is usually conveyed by adjectives such as dynamic, active, and sociable. Agreeableness refers to individuals' concern for altruism, generosity, and loyalty and is usually conveyed by adjectives such as kind, honest, and sincere. Conscientiousness refers to individuals' tendency to pursue order and meet one's own obligations and is usually conveyed by adjectives such as diligent, reliable, and precise. Emotional stability refers to the control of impulses and emotions and is usually conveyed by adjectives such as calm, patient, and relaxed. Finally, openness to experience refers to an interest in culture and curiosity about new experiences and is conveyed by adjectives such as innovative, imaginative, and creative.

Despite having been the target of various criticisms because they do not provide a fine-grained description of a single personality and account even less well for their functioning, at present the Big Five represent the most widely accepted model to address major individual differences in behavioral tendencies in manifold contexts, including politics (Mondak, 2010). Within this framework, numerous studies conducted in a variety of samples drawn from different countries focused on different political outcomes of these traits, including ideological left-right self-placement (Jost, 2006), voting choice (Caprara, Barbaranelli, & Zimbardo, 1999; Caprara, Schwartz, Capanna, Vecchione, & Barbaranelli, 2006; Schoen & Schumann, 2007), political candidate preference (Barbaranelli, Caprara, Vecchione, & Fraley, 2007), political party affiliation (Gerber, Huber, Doherty, & Dowling, 2012), and public policy preferences (Riemann, Grubich, Hempel, Mergl, & Richter, 1993; Schoen & Schumann, 2007).

Findings from the United States (Barbaranelli et al., 2007; Carney, Jost, Gosling, Niederhoffer, & Potter, 2008; Gerber, Huber, Doherty, Dowling, & Ha, 2010; Gosling, Rentfrow, & Swann, 2003; Jost, 2006; McCrae, 1996; Mondak & Halperin, 2008; Trapnell, 1994) and several European countries, such as Germany (Riemann et al., 1993; Schoen & Schumann, 2007), Italy (Caprara et al., 1999; 2006), Poland, and Belgium (Van Hiel, Kossowska, & Mervielde, 2000) have shown that individuals high in openness to experience tend to prefer parties and ideologies located in the left wing of traditional ideological cleavages. People high in conscientiousness instead tend to prefer right-wing and conservative ideologies, parties, and issues. Overall, the contribution of conscientiousness to political preference is smaller in magnitude than that of openness to experience. Thus, both in the United States and Europe, liberals and left-wing voters tend to present themselves as more open-minded, creative, and novelty seeking than conservatives and right-wing voters, who in turn tend to present themselves as more orderly, conventional, and organized than liberals and left-wing voters.

Findings regarding the political effects of energy/extraversion, agreeableness, and emotional stability are less robust and consistent across countries. In some studies, energy/extraversion was found to be associated with a preference for the rightist and conservative ideologies (Caprara et al., 1999; 2006; Gerber et al., 2010; Mondak & Halperin, 2008). Agreeableness was found to be related to a preference for liberal ideologies in some European countries, such as Italy and Germany, whereas results are mixed in the United States. Likely the relation of agreeableness with political orientation is complex and may vary through different cultural contexts and political systems, different facets of the trait (Jost, 2006), and different dimensions (social and economic) of political ideology (Gerber et al., 2010). Emotional stability predicted ideological self-placement in both Germany and the United States, although in the opposite direction. Whereas people high in emotional stability showed a preference for liberal parties in Germany (Schoen & Schumann, 2007), the inverse relationship was found in the United States, where people with high levels of emotional stability were more oriented toward conservative policies (Mondak & Halperin, 2008) and political parties (Gerber et al., 2010).

The average variance in ideological self-placement accounted for by the Big Five is roughly from 5% to 20%, whereas basic demographic variables such as gender, age, income, and educational level, typically used as predictors of political behavior by political scientists, do not account for more than 10%. A similar pattern is found in research on politicians: personality traits account for greater variance in their political behavior than do demographic characteristics.

In Italy, Caprara and colleagues conducted a first study on a sample of 103 male politicians equally distributed among members of the European Parliament, the Italian Parliament (Chamber and Senate), and three Italian provincial councils (Caprara, Barbaranelli, Consiglio, Picconi, & Zimbardo, 2003). A second study was conducted on a sample of 106 female members of the Italian Parliament, 70% of the entire population of female members (Caprara, Francescato, Mebane, Sorace, & Vecchione, 2010). In both studies politicians completed a standard questionnaire—the Big Five Questionnaire (BFQ, Caprara, Barbaranelli, Borgogni, & Perugini, 1993)—to assess their personality traits. Political orientation was operationalized as the affiliation with center-right or center-left coalitions. Results corroborated the pattern of differences found in the general population, with right-wing politicians scoring higher in energy/extraversion and conscientiousness than did left-wing politicians. No significant differences were found in agreeableness, openness to experience, and emotional stability. Findings from these studies also revealed that self-reported traits contribute to political affiliation of politicians far more than among voters (the percentage of variance accounted for was 36% among politicians and 5% among voters). This pattern of findings is consistent with early intuitions of Converse (1964), who found that a highly involved group of US politicians exhibited higher levels of intercorrelation among ideas and attitudes on various political issues than did the vast majority of Americans.

The political attitudes of politicians are likely to be highly constrained and tightly linked to ideological orientation, because of their high levels of education, political expertise, and sophistication, as suggested in Converse's (1964) seminal study. All these factors contribute to a politician's ideological coherence, and the congruence between their ideas and behavior. Thus, it is not surprising that the polarization in self-presentation between political elites of opposite ideological orientations is higher than among voters (Jost, 2006; Zaller, 1992).

Another interesting line of research has extended the analysis of the link between personality and political preference from individuals to communities, showing that geographical differences in voting patterns reflect differences in self-presentation among citizens living in different states (Rentfrow, Jost, Gosling, & Potter, 2009). Significant differences in openness to experience and conscientiousness have been found between red (Republican) and blue (Democratic) states, with higher levels of conscientiousness and lower levels of openness to experience observed in red than blue states.. Common living conditions and social influence may account for similarity in personality traits among inhabitants of the same region, at least in part. Further investigation is needed to establish whether certain states attract certain kind of personalities or whether living in certain states leads, through comparison, contagion, and social desirability, to conformity to styles of thinking, feeling, and behaving that ultimately affects citizens' self-presentation and vote choice.

While the above findings attest to stable and consistent patterns of relations between personality dispositions and ideological preferences, at least among citizens of Western established democracies, it is still possible that traits merely accompany political choice but do not causally influence them. In this regard other findings suggest that personality differences between liberals and conservatives begin in early childhood and affect political orientations throughout life (Block & Block, 2006), and that political ideologies may be shaped by genetic inheritance (Alford et al., 2005; Bouchard & Lohelin, 2001; Hatemi et al., 2007). Thus one might guess that the more preference and engagement rest upon genetic characteristics, the less they change over the course of life. Yet it is unlikely that heredity dictates preferences. Rather it is likely that genes set potentials that largely turn into habits and preferences through experiences that are socially situated. It has been argued (Franklin, 2004) that one's first encounter with voting has an effect over the entire course of life, with voters and abstainers repeating their original choices in future elections. After all, one may guess that early choices, whatever their distal determinants, tend to repeat over the course of life quasi-automatically as habits that attest to both the expressive and objective value of voting.

In reality, voting confronts citizen with a paradoxical dilemma: on the one hand voting has a highly symbolic value as an expression of citizens' right to voice their views; on the other hand it has very little practical value as single votes are somewhat irrelevant to the outcome of an election.

Ultimately the habit of voting or not voting is far from irrational, having both a symbolic function and negligible impact. Thus it would be unwarranted to conclude that stability arises to a greater degree from heredity than experience. In this regard the metaphor of elective affinities used by Jost, Federico, & Napier (2009) provides an elegant solution to the traditional dilemma about the primacy of person or situation, pointing to political choices as a result of the concerted action of individual proclivities and situational opportunities. Likely people whose genes and socialization experiences predispose them to certain political views vote in accordance with contingent political offers.

2.2. Needs

Needs and motives have been used interchangeably and often as synonymous to account for social behaviors; we define them as internal states or forces experienced as wishes and desires that lead to the achievement of specific goals. Among earlier taxonomies of needs, McClelland (1985) pointed to three basic motives, namely achievement, affiliation, and power, and attributed their relative dominance to early experiences and socialization processes. In this tradition Winter devised an at-a-distance scoring system that allowed researchers to assess these three motives in specific political leaders (Winter, 1987; 1998; 2002; 2003; 2005).

Later contributions, along the line of the "motivated social cognition" movement (Kruglanski, 1996), traced political reasoning and action to epistemic needs for knowledge and meaning (e.g., needs for order, structure, and closure), existential needs for safety and reassurance (e.g., needs to reduce and manage uncertainty and threat), and relational needs for affiliation and social identification (see Jost, Glaser, Kruglanski, & Sulloway, 2003a, for a review). Political conservatism in particular has been viewed as a belief system associated with the epistemic need for closure, serving an existential need for safety. It has been reasoned that people with high safety needs tend to be particularly sensitive to threats that may derive from change and uncertainty, and thus process information and organize knowledge in ways that tend to maximize stability, avoid change, and reduce uncertainty (Chirumbolo, 2002; Jost, Kruglanski, & Simon, 1999; Kemmelmeier, 1997; Kruglanski & Webster, 1996).

Yet it is unlikely that only people high in needs for safety and closure are attracted to conservative ideologies. In reality the influence that various needs exert on political decision and action rests upon individual predispositions as well as upon situations and events that in various ways challenge and make salient those needs. Thus even people low in safety needs may be sensitive to security appeals in times of uncertainty and danger, and even those with a moderate need for safety are attracted to conservative ideologies under conditions of great insecurity. In this regard empirical studies have shown that stimuli and situations of danger, threat, and loss can foster a preference for ideological conservatism: the more people are exposed to stimuli and events that elicit safety needs, the more conservative ideologies become appealing (Jost & Banaji, 1994; Jost, Banaji, & Nosek, 2004; Jost et al., 2007).

2.3. Basic Values and Core Political Values

Among personality features, basic values form a bridge between the functioning of individuals and of society. On the one hand, values attest to the pervasive influence that socialization practices and memberships in families, groups, class, and communities exert on individuals' development, identity and functioning (see Sears and Brown, chapter 3, this volume). On the other hand values underscore the crucial role individuals play in preserving and changing the guiding principles and the functioning of social systems (Caprara & Cervone, 2000; Hitlin, 2003). The importance of values for political behavior has been championed by the seminal contribution of Rokeach (1973, 1979) and later acknowledged by a number of scholars, who pointed to the central role of values in politics as major organizers of political judgments and preferences (Feldman,

2003; Feldman, chapter 19, this volume; Knutsen, 1995; Mitchell, Tetlock, Mellers, & Ordonez, 1993; Schwartz, 1994).

In the last decades the contribution of Schwartz and his colleagues led to a comprehensive theory on the nature, organization, and function of basic values (Schwartz, 1992; 2005; 2006; Schwartz & Bilsky, 1987), which paved the way for systematic research and comparisons among countries on the impact that values exert on both ideological self-placement (Piurko, Schwartz, & Davidov, 2011) and voting behavior (Barnea & Schwartz, 1998; Caprara et al., 2006). Schwartz's theory identifies 10 different motivational priorities common to people of many cultures and societies, which can be grouped into four higher-order dimensions: Openness to change values (self-direction, stimulation, hedonism) encourages independence of thought, feeling, and action, and receptiveness to change; conservation values (conformity, tradition, security) call for submissive self-restriction, preserving traditional practices, and protecting stability; self-transcendence values (universalism, benevolence) emphasize accepting others as equals and concern for their welfare; self-enhancement values (power, achievement) encourage pursuing one's own relative success and dominance over others.

Studies conducted in several countries showed that Schwartz's values discriminated significantly among voters of different political parties, and that the relevance of particular types of values to voting is a function of the ideological content of the political discourse (Barnea & Schwartz, 1998). In the 1988 Israeli elections, for instance, voters for liberal parties (e.g., MAPAM, Civil Rights Movement, Shinui, and Labor) attributed higher priority to self-direction (autonomy and self-actualization) and universalism (acceptance of others as equal). Voters for conservative parties (e.g., Moleet, Tehiya) gave higher priority to security values, which endorse protection of the social order and status quo (Barnea & Schwartz, 1998).

In the 2001 Italian elections, voters for the center-left attributed higher priority to the self-transcendence values of universalism and benevolence; voters for the center-right gave higher priority to the self-enhancement and conservation values of power, achievement, security, and conformity (Caprara et al., 2006). These results accord with the traditional view in Western democracies pointing to right and conservative ideologies as mostly concerned with individual success and social order, and to liberal ideologies as mostly concerned with equality and social justice.

Results from a sample of Italian politicians corroborated this pattern of relations (Caprara et al., 2010). Like traits, values have a stronger relation with political preference among political elites than among the general electorate. This further attests to the earlier reasoning of Converse (1964) about the constraints that lead sophisticated politicians to hold consistent attitudes. Findings demonstrate that basic values account for a greater portion of variance in voting than do traits (Caprara, Schwartz, Vecchione, & Barbaranelli, 2008), while demographic variables related to voters' social location, such as income and education, have no additional impact once values and traits have been taken into account. We view this finding in accordance with our idea of personality as a proactive self-regulating, agentic system operating in the pursuit of one's goals (Bandura, 1997, 2000; Caprara & Cervone, 2000). As people weigh alternative aspirations and goals in light of their personal priorities, values account for more variance than traits in predicting choices such as voting, the more their choices rest on conscious deliberation of alternative options (Caprara et al., 2006).

Longitudinal findings help to further clarify the pathways through which traits and values contribute to political preference. Traits measured during late adolescence, before the age of voting, contribute indirectly to later political orientation, through the effect of basic values (Caprara, Vecchione, & Schwartz, 2009). In particular, security and universalism values fully mediate the relations of openness to experience, agreeableness, and conscientiousness traits to voting choice and left-right ideology. These findings demonstrate the causal primacy of basic traits over basic values in the pathway to political orientation and choice, in accordance with the vast literature attesting to a significant genetic component of basic traits (Jang, McCrae, Angleitner, Riemann, & Livesley, 1998; Loehlin, McCrae, Costa, & John, 1998), and the importance of socialization experiences in channeling individual dispositions toward values.

Values operate as more proximal determinants of political choices than traits, orienting toward certain ideologies the more politics is instrumental to the pursuits of one's existential priorities. People who differ in their inherited trait dispositions may indeed be differently inclined to endorse basic values linked to liberal or conservative ideologies.

However, even basic values do not directly influence vote choice. Values that are mostly associated with the political domain may act as more proximal determinants of political choice than less overtly political values. Along this line of reasoning a number of authors (e.g., Converse, 1964; Feldman, 1988; Jacoby, 2006; McCann, 1997) have identified a set of core political values (also called "core political attitudes"), which refer to "overarching normative principles and belief assumptions about government, citizenship, and society" (McCann, 1997, p. 565), such as traditional morality (traditional religious and family values versus newer, permissive lifestyles), equality (egalitarian distribution of opportunities and resources), free enterprise (the noninterference of government in the economic system), civil liberties (freedom for everyone to act and think as they consider most appropriate), blind patriotism (unquestioning attachment to, and intolerance of criticism of, one's country), economic security (guarantee of job and income).

Differences in political attitudes have been extensively used to account for variations in policy preferences, voting behavior, and ideological identification. Pollock, Lilie, and Vittes (1993), for example, related core political attitudes to policy preferences regarding nuclear power. McCann (1997) demonstrated that voters for George Bush in the 1992 American elections scored higher on moral traditionalism and lower on egalitarianism than voters for Bill Clinton. Feldman (1988) showed that both equality and individualism correlate significantly with liberal-conservative ideological identification. Liberals attributed most importance to equality of opportunities, whereas conservatives valued most economic individualism.

Many studies have examined the political values of the general public, how they relate to one another, and which underlying set of principles accounts for their structure (Feldman, 1988; Judd, Krosnick, & Milburn, 1981; Zaller, 1992). It has been argued that basic values and core political values in concert may account for political choices much better than previous left and right, and liberal and conservative distinctions. Only recently, however, has the relation between basic values and core political values been addressed empirically. Schwartz, Caprara, and Vecchione (2010) have shown that core political values account for a substantial portion of variance (54%) in vote choice, largely mediating the contribution of basic values. Whereas basic values account for most of the organization of core political values, these in turn account for most of political preferences. The pursuit of basic values leads people to favor specific political attitudes and ideologies that can promote these basic values in particular political contexts. People who attribute high priority to security, for example, are likely to adopt nationalist political values in political contexts in which nationalism appears to promise greater security.

It is likely that core political values are the characteristic adaptations of basic values to specific political contexts. Yet one should not exclude significant variations across political contexts either in the relations among basic values and core political values or in the pathways conducive to political preference. It has been found, for instance, that basic values explain left-right political orientation more in European countries that share a long political tradition of liberal democracy (i.e. Germany, the Netherlands, and the United Kingdom) than in countries that have converted to democracy after a long totalitarian regime, like the post-Communist countries, where the left-right dimension has little coherent meaning (Piurko et al., 2011).

2.4. Social and Political Attitudes

Much research in recent years has focused on Right-Wing Authoritarianism (RWA, Altemeyer, 1996), and Social Dominance Orientation (SDO, Sidanius & Pratto, 1999) as major and proxy determinants of political orientation (Feldman, chapter 19, this volume; Sidanius & Kurzban, chapter 7, this volume). However, it is still a matter of contention as to whether individual differences in RWA and SDO should be traced to personality dispositions or to social attitudes.

The persistent and current interest of political psychologists in the authoritarian personality, despite criticisms of the approach, is due to the contributions of Altemeyer (1988, 1996, 1998), who abandoned earlier ideological and psychodynamic underpinnings of authoritarianism to develop the concept of RWA. According to Altemeyer RWA is a personality characteristic that includes three major features: authoritarian submission, authoritarian aggression, and conventionalism (1981, 1998). High-authoritarian individuals submit uncritically to authorities, carry aggressive feelings against people who deviate from the norms, and conform rigidly to conventional values.

Among social psychologists Pratto and colleagues originally conceived Social Dominance Orientation (SDO) as a "general attitudinal orientation toward intergroup relations, reflecting whether one generally prefers such relations to be equal versus hierarchical" and the "extent to which one desires that one's in-group dominate and be superior to out-groups" (Pratto, Sidanius, Stallworth, & Malle, 1994, p. 742).

Duckitt and Sibley (2010), finally, view RWA and SDO as two ideological attitude dimensions, which express distinct sets of motivational goals or values, namely "the respective competitive-driven motivation for group-based dominance and superiority (SDO), and threat-driven motivation for collective security and social cohesion (RWA)" (Duckitt, Wagner, du Plessis, & Birum, 2002) (p. 546). RWA entails "beliefs in coercive social control, in obedience and respect for existing authorities, and in conforming to traditional moral and religious norms and values" (Duckitt & Sibley, 2009, p. 100), and is mostly related to religiosity and valuing order, structure, conformity, and tradition, and the belief that the social world is dangerous and threatening. In contrast, SDO concerns "beliefs in social and economic inequality as opposed to equality, and the right of powerful groups to dominate weaker ones" (Duckitt & Sibley, 2009, p. 100), and is related to valuing power, achievement, and hedonism, and with the belief that the world is a ruthlessly, competitive jungle in which only the strong survive.

An extensive body of research from North America, New Zealand, and Europe, including ex-Communist countries, identifies both Right-Wing Authoritarianism and Social Dominance as robust predictors of a number of sociopolitical outcomes usually associated with right-wing ideologies, such as social and economic conservatism, generalized prejudice, intergroup hostility, nationalism, ethnocentrism, and antidemocratic sentiments (Altemeyer, 1998; Duckitt, 2006; Sidanius & Pratto, 1999; Pratto et al., 1994; Sibley, Robertson, & Wilson, 2006; Roccato & Ricolfi, 2005; Sidanius & Pratto, 1999).

Few investigations, however, have addressed the links between RWA and SDO and other personality features like basic traits and basic values to disentangle their relationships and to clarify the pathways through which they contribute to political preferences. Some authors have posited that conscientiousness and a lack of openness to experience are at the root of RWA. A lack of agreeableness and a lack of openness to experience have been posited, instead, as at the root of SDO (Akrami & Ekehammar, 2006; Ekehammar & Akrami, 2007; Sibley & Duckitt, 2008). Others have found that conservation values (security, conformity, and tradition) correlate with RWA, whereas self-enhancement values, above all power, correlate with SDO (Altemeyer, 1988).

Ultimately, Duckitt and Sibley (2010) have advocated a dual-process motivational (DPM) model in which individual factors and social experience in concert contribute to political preferences. In the posited model, personality traits influence ideological preference indirectly through the mediation of RWA and SDO (see also Duckitt, 2001; 2003). As argued by the authors, "RWA and SDO represent two basic dimensions of social or ideological attitudes, each expressing motivational goals or values made chronically salient for individuals by their social worldviews and their personalities" (Duckitt & Sibley, 2009, p. 298). High conscientiousness and low openness to experience may elicit the belief that the social world is an inherently dangerous and threatening place (as opposed to safe and secure), which predisposes individuals to become more authoritarian. Low agreeableness leads people to the belief that the world is competitive, which causes stronger endorsement of social dominance attitudes (Duckitt & Sibley, 2009). Social circumstances in their turn may further affect people's beliefs about the world, and thus their level of authoritarianism and social dominance, whose expression may vary to the degree to which social and economic contingencies lead people to perceive societal threat and danger (RWA), or intergroup inequality and competition (SDO) (Duckitt, 2006). Recent findings, for instance, indicate that the perception of threat from terrorism may activate more "authoritarian" views that result in support for restrictive government policies promoting order and safety (Hetherington & Suhay, 2011).

Despite diverse findings, research on SDO and RWA is largely consistent with the reasoning of Caprara, Schwartz, and colleagues about the influence of traits, values, and core political values on political attitudes (Caprara et al., 2006; Schwartz et al., 2010), as well as with the reasoning of Jost et al. (2009) about elective affinities between a person's proclivities and situational challenges and opportunities. People's predispositions and needs are turned into habits and values, depending on their early socialization and personal experiences. Likewise, situations provide the challenges and opportunities that allow values to turn into habits and action.

2.5. Cognitive Abilities and Styles

Cognitive abilities are generally referred to as an individual's propensity to comprehend complex ideas, adapt successfully to diverse environments, learn from experience, engage in reasoning, and use skills to solve a variety of problems. Although cognitive abilities are important features of a person's total functioning, little research has systematically addressed their influence on political preferences (see Van Hiel, Onraet, & De Pauw, 2010).

In a world in which most people achieve a relatively high level of education and in which success at school and at work largely depends on aspects of intelligence other than IQ, much of the impact of cognitive abilities and education on political preference is mediated by individual differences like traits and values, and their effects are likely to differ across social and political systems. In reality, cognitive styles, namely characteristic ways of conceptually organizing the environment, have long been associated with political preferences of both citizens and political elites (Tetlock, 1983, 1984, 1985; Tetlock & Suedfeld, 1988).

Earlier studies on authoritarianism (Adorno et al., 1950), intolerance of ambiguity (Frenkel-Brunswik, 1949), dogmatism (Rokeach, 1960), and uncertainty avoidance (Wilson, 1973) have demonstrated that political conservatives are less flexible than liberals in their way of thinking.

Integrative complexity has become a popular notion in recent research focused on the thinking and reasoning of voters and politicians (Suedfeld, Tetlock, & Streufert, 1992). Integrative complexity refers to the capacity of people to differentiate and integrate multiple points of view when addressing political matters. Whereas differentiation leads people to acknowledge and distinguish all the various aspects of an issue or a decision, integration leads people to make connections among various ideas and elements of judgment.

Earlier studies in Great Britain have shown that right-wing voters and political officials (members of the British House of Commons) report lower levels of integrative complexity than their left-wing counterparts (Sidanius, 1985, 1988; Tetlock, 1983, 1984). Content analysis of interviews with UK politicians and their policy statements have shown that liberal parliamentarians managed policy issues in more integratively complex ways than their conservative colleagues (Tetlock, 1983, 1984). Similar results were replicated in different political and cultural contexts, such as the Soviet Union (Tetlock, 1988), corroborating the so-called "rigidity of the Right" hypothesis, namely that conservative and right-wing ideological beliefs are associated with mental rigidity and low cognitive complexity.

Other studies, however, have found that extremists from both sides of the political spectrum show lower integrative complexity (e.g., Tetlock & Boettger, 1989) than their more moderate counterparts, in accordance with the ideological extremity hypothesis, namely that traces any extremism to low cognitive sophistication and high mental rigidity (see Jost, Glaser, Kruglanski, & Sulloway, 2003b; Greenberg & Jonas, 2003 for a review).

3. PERSONALITY DETERMINANTS OF POLITICAL PARTICIPATION

In many established democracies, the decline of voter turnout is viewed as a serious symptom of political disengagement (Dalton, 2004; Franklin, 2004). It is difficult to imagine a form of democracy that does not imply some form of active citizenry and responsible participation, and it is difficult to imagine a more reliable and succinct indicator of political engagement, although minimal, than voting. Even where democracy could fully rely on the effective functioning of institutions, lack of political participation would represent a *vulnus* for both individual and society (Allport, 1945; Lanning, 2008).

More than 40 years ago, Milbrath (1965) claimed there was a need to consider the role of personality in models of participation. Yet the lack of consensual theories and methods has represented a major limitation to the accumulation of knowledge in this case. Recent findings, however, attest that significant progress can be made in this domain. Traits, values, and perceived political self-efficacy beliefs, in particular, represent major features of personality that can contribute to understanding and promoting citizens' engagement in politics.

3.1. Traits, Values, and Political Participation

Studies conducted using the Big Five Model have found significant relations between basic traits, such as openness to experience and energy/extraversion, and various forms of political participation, like voting, contacting political representatives, campaigning for candidates, attending political meetings and rallies, attempting to persuade others on how to vote, contributing to organized political events, displaying yard signs and bumper stickers, donating money to political associations, movements or parties, distributing leaflets, and signing petitions (Anderson, 2009; Gerber et al., 2010; Mondak & Halperin, 2008; Mondak, Hibbing, Canache, Seligson, & Anderson, 2010; Steinbrecher & Schoen, 2010; Vecchione & Caprara, 2009). The effect of these traits is consistent across several countries from different continents (e.g., the United States, Germany, Italy, Venezuela, Uruguay), and persists even after other well-known determinants of civic engagement, like income and education, have been taken into account (Milbrath, 1965; Verba, Schlozman, & Brady, 1995). It is likely that both openness to experience and energy/extraversion account for individual differences in behavior, communication, and relational styles that are crucial for being successful in the political arena. Important ingredients of political activity such as keeping up to date with main political events, being receptive to a large variety of ideas and points of views, and interacting with a large diversity of people, may benefit from a genuine openness toward others and the world. In addition, several facets of energy/extraversion such as assertiveness, persuasiveness, and dominance, are crucial to participating and being successful in politics. Previous results suggest that extraversion is consistently related to leadership across study settings and leadership criteria (Judge, Bono, Ilies, & Gerhardt, 2002). Other findings have shown that politicians score higher than the general population on energy/extraversion (Best, 2011; Caprara et al., 2003).

These results are in accordance with those of Silvester and Dykes (2007), who focused on personal determinants of electoral success among a large sample of political candidates. Their study is unique in that it uses data from an assessment center set up by a major UK political party for selecting prospective parliamentary candidates. It has been found that both critical thinking and communication skills are significantly associated with candidates' political performance, as assessed through the percentage of votes achieved in the 2005 UK general election. As argued by Silvester (2008), "politicians must be able to shift through large amounts of information quickly, identify key arguments, balance conflicting demands and formulate responses" (p. 128). On the other hand, they must be able to communicate effectively across different audiences and communication media, as well as be able to persuade potential voters of their intentions (Silvester, 2008). It is likely that much of the capacity needed to analyze, organize, and integrate information and needed to convince and persuade people can be traced to basic traits like energy/extraversion and openness to experience, although not only these traits, and not directly.

Recent contributions have pointed to the role of personal values in affecting citizens' decision to vote. Although voting is the minimal expression of political participation, people have no reason to vote unless they perceive that voting serves to promote their personal priorities to a certain degree. Conversely, the more people perceive political programs as irrelevant to or incongruent with their values, interests, and priorities, the less voting is perceived as mandatory and the more people are inclined to abstain. Based on this reasoning, a recent study addressed the influence of personal values on electoral participation (Caprara, Vecchione, & Schwartz, 2012). In the Italian context, people who did vote assigned relatively high priority either to universalism values or to security values, namely the values appealed to by the two major political coalitions. Nonvoters, by contrast, attributed less importance than voters to values like universalism and security that were decisive in allocating left and right preferences, and assigned greater importance to values like stimulation and hedonism that have no impact on political preference. As neither coalition was associated with promoting the pursuit of excitement or pleasure, voting offered little payoff for reaching these goals that motivated nonvoters.

3.2. Perceived Political Efficacy

Political efficacy has been a popular and relevant concept in political science. First, Campbell, Gurin, & Miller (1954) conceptualized political efficacy as the "feeling that individual political action does have, or can have, an impact upon the political process, namely, that it is worthwhile to perform one's civic duties" (Campbell et al., 1954, p. 187). Although initially conceived as a unitary construct, it soon became clear that political efficacy included both judgments people make about their own capacities and their attitudes toward the political system. Then a number of authors suggested distinguishing between internal and external political efficacy, pointing respectively to two components of people's beliefs regarding their contribution to change in society (Converse, 1972; Craig, 1979; Gurin & Brim, 1984; Lane, 1959): people's beliefs regarding their ability to achieve desired results in the political domain and people's beliefs that the political system is amenable to change through individual and collective influence.

While a number of studies have shown that internal political efficacy plays an important role in promoting political participation and civic engagement (Abramson & Aldrich, 1982; Finkel, 1985; Madsen, 1987; Milbrath & Goel, 1977; Zimmerman, 1989), external political efficacy has been found to be associated with general trust in the functioning of the political system and institutions (Niemi, Craig, & Mattei, 1991).

A major limitation of the above findings is that most studies are not grounded in a comprehensive theory of personality functioning capable of accounting for why and how people's beliefs in their efficacy influence their political behavior. Social cognitive theory (Bandura, 1986; 1997) makes a useful contribution in this respect, placing political efficacy within a broad theory of human agency. The theory focuses on perceived political efficacy, which is defined as the judgments people make about their capacities to perform effectively in the political domain, and views this as a major determinant of political engagement. The theory states that (a) people are self-organizing, proactive, and self-regulating agents because of the self-reflective and forethoughtful properties of the human mind; (b) people's self-directive capacity operates through structures and mechanisms that grant control over the environment and set the course of people's own life; (c) people learn from their own and others' experience, infer their sense of efficacy from dealing successfully with challenging situations, engage in activities that give them satisfaction and self-worth, avoid behaviors that carry self-censure, and accord their behavior to the values they cherish while pursuing goals that they perceive as within their reach; (*d*) people make judgments about their capacities, namely self-efficacy beliefs, that are the most influential determinants of their efforts and accomplishments.

A broad literature documents the pervasive influence of perceived self-efficacy on cognition, motivation, learning, and performance, while diverse lines of research attest to the role that self-efficacy beliefs exert in sustaining intellectual development, social adjustment, and well-being while promoting academic achievement, work performance, and healthy habits. The judgments people make about their capacity to be effective in the realm of politics are critical to inclining them to devote the time and effort needed to stay informed and participate actively. Lacking a sense of personal efficacy may nurture both feelings of distance and alienation conducive to disenchantment and ultimately to withdrawal from politics.

A study by Caprara, Vecchione, Capanna, and Mebane (2009) illustrates the close link between political engagement and perceived efficacy. Italian politicians reported higher perceived political efficacy than political activists who, in turn, reported higher political self-efficacy than voters who were not political activists. This finding held regardless of the political orientation or ideology of the people involved. Other findings verify the mediational role that political self-efficacy beliefs play in linking openness to experience and energy/extraversion traits to political engagement (Vecchione & Caprara, 2009). Personality traits provide the potential for political activity, but they do not necessarily turn into political action. Likely values are crucial to channel traits, but values are not sufficient to grant that people will invest their talents and virtues in politics, unless properly equipped for the political arena. People can be extremely energetic and open-minded, but, whatever their value priorities, it is unlikely that they will get actively involved in politics unless they feel capable of doing what politics contingently requires.

4. NAVIGATING POLITICAL WATERS THROUGH PERSONALITY COMPASS

4.1. Dispositional and Likeability Heuristics: The Role of Traits in the Impressions and Evaluations Voters Draw from Politicians

Modern politics presents voters with an enormous amount of information from multiple sources. The media saturates the voting population with images designed to reflect, portray, invent, construe, and sometimes denigrate the personalities of political candidates. Given the enormous amount of information people have from multiple media sources about issues, candidates, parties, appeals, and negative campaigns, the task of making judgments about political personalities would seem to be a rather challenging one. Cognitive theorists argue that individuals navigate through the complexity of their political environments by using heuristics as efficient mental shortcuts for organizing information and simplifying political choices (Sniderman, Brody, & Tetlock, 1991). Likewise scholars of political reasoning have pointed to a variety of strategies that people use to make reasonable choices, given their bounded rationality (Delli Carpini, Huddy, & Shapiro, 1996; Popkin, 1991; Simon, 1985). One of these is a dispositional heuristic that anchors impressions and inferences about politicians' intentions to traits that are habitually used to describe oneself and others and that are most important within politics (Caprara & Zimbardo, 2004). Dispositional inferences about politicians may be spontaneously activated, as for any other person (Uleman, Newman, & Moskowitz, 1996), may summarize a variety of feelings and perceptions, and may carry specific attributions about politicians' motives and intentions. People are able to make judgments about a politician's competence after only a brief exposure to their visual image (Todorov, Mandisodza, Goren, & Hall, 2005). Dispositional constructs provide a parsimonious way to organize knowledge and to extend voters' control over politicians' future performance on the common assumption that personality dispositions are relatively stable.

A number of studies have shown that voters process information about candidates in a schematic fashion (Conover & Feldman, 1986); and that traits play an important role in organizing political knowledge preferences (Funk, 1999). Findings from several studies conducted in the United States and Italy have shown that voters' judgments of politicians can typically be traced back to two clusters of traits, which have been referred to as *integrity*, which represents a blend of agreeableness, conscientiousness, and emotional stability, and *leadership*, which represents a blend of energy/extraversion and openness to experience (Caprara, Barbaranelli, & Zimbardo, 1997; 2002). These dimensions largely overlap with the two personality features of politicians that have been frequently reported as being the most important among electorates in several democracies of the Western world (Popkin, 1991). Thus, when voters appraise the personalities of leading politicians, the typical five-factor structure collapses into two broader categories, that is, energy/extraversion and friendliness, which serve as the main anchors or *attractors* for evaluating politicians' personality and subsume the other dimensions of the Big Five. These are also the factors in which politicians report higher scores than nonpoliticians (Caprara et al., 2003).

The same simplified solution has been replicated in Italy for voter judgments of politicians with different degrees of political leadership, and with the major coalition leaders serving in different roles (Caprara, Barbaranelli, Fraley, & Vecchione, 2007). Replicating earlier findings from the United States (Miller, Wattenberg, & Malanchuk, 1986), this result suggests that judgmental categories used to evaluate politicians' personalities tend to remain remarkably stable over years, despite changes in their political responsibilities. The use of this kind of dispositional heuristic allows voters both to simplify the personal information that is made available about candidates and to anchor their judgments to personality traits that are most relevant for holding political offices.

As the media expose citizens to a huge amount of contrasting information, the simplified perceptions of the personalities of political leaders can be instrumental to a cognitively efficient strategy that leads voters to focus on what they care for and expect most from politicians at a given time in a given context. In doing so, they may sacrifice a more detailed, informative, fine-grained evaluation of the candidates' personalities. Yet a functional trade-off can take place between distinctiveness and comprehensiveness as latent factors become restricted in number but broadened in latitude.

Another form of judgmental heuristic at work in the political domain is a kind of likeability heuristic by which choices between people are weighted on the basis of the sympathy and positive affect they may elicit (Sniderman et al., 1991). The more a candidate is liked, the higher is his or her probability of attracting votes. A well-documented literature supports the hypothesis that individuals are most attracted by people who are similar to themselves (Byrne, 1971; Fiske, 2004; Klohnen & Luo, 2003). This attraction may serve a series of needs, such as personal coherence, belonging, and control over the environment. Both familiarity and a kind of egocentric favoritism may contribute to liking those who are perceived as similar to oneself (Byrne, Bond, & Diamond, 1968; Zajonc, 1980). People may like others who share the same preferences, proclivities, and aversions in order to be consistent and maintain a balanced state of feelings and cognitions (Heider, 1958), or because these shared attributes reaffirm and validate one's own (Fiske, 2004).

The similarity-attraction relationship has gradually gained support in different domains of political preferences. Physical similarity, for instance, proved influential in increasing candidate support in an experiment in which the degree of candidate-voter facial similarity was manipulated. People showed higher preference for facially similar candidates, even though participants were not aware of the similarity manipulation (Bailenson, Iyengar, Yee, & Collins, 2008).

Other studies have pointed to the role that personality traits may exert in anchoring and fostering similarity judgments. Findings drawn from the 2004 presidential election in the United States and from the 2006 Italian national elections have shown that voters generally perceive politicians for whom they vote as being most similar to themselves with respect to a variety of personality characteristics, while those they do not vote for are judged to be most different (Caprara, Vecchione, Barbaranelli, & Fraley, 2007). As traits allow voters to organize their impressions of politicians in a coherent fashion and to link politicians' perceived personalities to their own personalities, it is likely that traits are among the major elements through which the similarity-attraction principle operates in politics.

Whatever the source of similarity, whether physical or moral, whether real or just attributed, one cannot doubt the function that it exerts in building and keeping consensus. As people tend to like people whom they perceive as similar to themselves, voters will like and therefore vote for candidates they consider most similar. Thus, similarity promotes likeability, which in turn affects political judgments and choices. The more voters acknowledge in their leaders the same personal qualities that they use to characterize themselves, the easier it will be for voters to infer that their leader will act on their behalf and in accordance with a shared worldview.

4.2. A Congruency Model of Political Preference and Participation

Congruency between emotions, cognitions, and actions corresponds to a kind of necessity that marks our lives. Individuals feel uneasy when behavior does not fall in line with feelings and reasoning, and when emotions, thoughts, and actions are not in accordance with one another. In reality, it is a property of our self-system and a necessity of our social life to preserve a certain level of congruency between what we declare and what we do and between how we feel and how we present ourselves. Patterns of congruity between thoughts, emotions, and actions are at the core of our identity; they get associated with the experience of unity and continuity, allow us to make sense of others' behaviors, feelings, and thoughts on the assumption that what accounts for oneself also accounts for others, and, finally, contribute to the stability of the relationship among people, by conferring a sense of stability, predictability, and controllability to their exchanges.

Several findings support the view that a powerful congruency principle is functioning at different stages of political transactions, with personality evaluations playing a crucial role in making sense of both voters' preferences and politicians' appeals (Caprara & Zimbardo, 2004).

The congruency principle accounts for how the distinctive personality characteristics reported by leaders and followers can be traced back to common ideals that supply the emotional glue that bonds them together. The same principle operates in allowing voters to equate congruency in their habits, values, and preferences as diagnostic of a politician's ideological orientations. Next, it operates in how voters appraise politicians' personality, selecting those attributes that they believe to be most relevant to the political office and that they personally value most. Finally, it operates in how voters perceive politicians as similar to themselves, either because politicians and voters of the same coalition share similar values and habits, or because politicians tend to convey images that highlight traits that are most congruent with the political views they advocate. While the image that people have and cultivate of themselves serves as a compass to navigate the world of politics, congruency attests to the commonality of feelings, thoughts, habits, and ideals among partisans, while accentuating the distinctiveness among opponents.

Just as there is a match between what people report about themselves in the sphere of habits, needs, values, and political orientations, there is a similar match between the self-reported personality of voters and the perceived personality of preferred politicians. The same congruency principle may contribute to individuals' political engagement. The more voters' preferences meet political offerings that are congruent with the values that most account for their personal and social identity, the more they feel committed to vote and draw a sense of self-actualization from voting. The more voters acknowledge in other voters the same personal qualities that they use to characterize themselves, and the more they expect others will behave like them, the more they derive a sense of inclusion and collective efficacy. The more voters acknowledge in their leaders the same personal characteristics that they use to characterize themselves, the more they will draw a sense of control over their actions, and the easier it will be for them to make sense of their leader's choices. The more citizens feel close to their representatives, the more they have reason to believe that their own opinions count, and the more reason they have to pay the cost of political engagement.

As congruency is crucial in matching individuals' preferences and political offerings, personal and collective efficacy beliefs are crucial in sustaining political participation. Ultimately, congruency and efficacy go hand in hand in sustaining political participation: the more politics is perceived within the reach of their understanding and pursuits, the more people will have reason to invest in politics. Conversely, incongruency between leaders' behaviors, political programs, and citizen's priorities may fuel feelings of distance, alienation, and powerlessness conducive to various forms of democratic disenfranchisement, no matter whether due to self- or social exclusion. This may be the case when voters face a world of politics whose functioning is incomprehensible or beyond their control, when issues seem irrelevant, or when political programs are disjoined from people's priorities and values. Common sense dictates that people's engagement does not matter when leaders operate like members of a caste apart from other citizens.

5. Conclusions

The findings reported above demonstrate the contribution of personality science to an understanding of the psychological processes and structures that account for one's ideological orientation and level of political participation. They also highlight the contribution of personality science to an understanding of the personal determinants that are at the core of democratic consensus and a well-functioning democracy.

Democracy may be defined as the form of government that aims for the realization of self-determination and ultimately for the actualization of the potentials of self-reflective agents (Dahl, 2007; Post, 2006). In reality, the traditional ethos of democracy requires members to see themselves and treat each other as socially equal in their capacities to express their opinions and preferences in the pursuit of conditions that may maximize public welfare. Equality and freedom are ideals crucial to democracy, and granting citizens the best conditions to express their talents and potentials is crucial for the realization of those ideals.

People, in fact, are not just beings endowed with talents that predispose them to react in particular ways when confronted with particular stimuli or tasks, but beings endowed with a vast array of unexpressed capacities that are realized within appropriate environments. Potentials draw attention to the fact that personal qualities develop and express themselves through dynamic interactions between people and their sociocultural environment, assigning them a proactive role in selecting and changing the situations they encounter, and ultimately setting the course of their life. In this regard, understanding the development and functioning of personality is no less important than knowledge regarding the functioning of social institutions and government. Likewise, addressing the personality features that account for political behavior is no less important that addressing the processes and mechanisms that account for its development and change. This leads to research that extends beyond a study of needs and abilities to capture self-regulatory mechanisms that are at the core of human agency.

Ultimately we believe that the growth of personality and the growth of democracy are conditional and reciprocal. The growth of democracy should grant the conditions for the full expression of citizens' potentials and thus for the most knowledgeable political participation, while citizens' major engagement in politics should contribute to the democratization of the entire political process. To this aim further research is needed to identify the experiences and pathways conducive to the endorsement of worldviews and lifestyles that are most congenial to democracy and the policies that may promote and sustain those experiences.

Our reasoning draws upon knowledge and ideals of Western democracies, and one should be aware that the same reasoning may not apply to the same degree and in the same fashion to other social and cultural contexts where notions like human agency, personal and social identity, ideology, and political rights are expressed in different ways. In reality, one may doubt that the same principles apply in societies where women have no voice, dissenters are prosecuted, and power does not belong to the people.

References

Abramson, P. R., & Aldrich, J. H. (1982). The decline of electoral participation in America. *American Political Science Review, 76*, 502–521.

Adorno, T., Frenkel-Brunswik, E., Levinson, D., & Sanford, R. (1950). *The authoritarian personality*. New York: Harper.

Akrami, N., & Ekehammar, B. (2006). Right-wing authoritarianism and social dominance orientation: Their roots in Big Five personality factors and facets. *Journal of Individual Differences, 27*, 117–126. doi:10.1027/1614-0001.27.3.117

Alford, J. R., Funk, C. L., & Hibbing, J. R. (2005). Are political orientations genetically transmitted? *American Political Science Review, 99*, 153–167. doi:10.1017/S0003055405051579

Allport, G. W. (1945). The psychology of participation. *Psychological Review, 52*, 117–132.

Allport, G. W. (1954). *The Nature of Prejudice*. Cambridge, MA: Addison-Wesley.

Altemeyer, R. A. (1981). *Right-wing authoritarianism*. Manitoba: University of Manitoba Press.

Altemeyer, R. A. (1988). *Enemies of freedom: Understanding right-wing authoritarianism*. San Francisco: Jossey-Bass.

Altemeyer, R. A. (1996). *The authoritarian specter*. Cambridge, MA: Harvard University Press.

Altemeyer, R. A. (1998). The other "authoritarian personality." In M. P. Zanna (ed.), *Advances in experimental social psychology* (vol. 30, pp. 47–91). New York: Academic Press.

Anderson, M. R. (2009). Beyond membership: A sense of community and political behavior. *Political Behavior, 31*, 603–627. doi:10.1007/s11109-009-9089-x

Bailenson, J. N., Iyengar, S., Yee, N., & Collins, N. A. (2008). Facial similarity between voters and candidates causes influence. *Public Opinion Quarterly, 72,* 935–961. doi:10.1093/poq/nfn064

Bandura, A. (1986). *Social foundations of thought and action: A social cognitive theory.* Englewood Cliffs, NJ: Prentice Hall.

Bandura, A. (1997). *Self-efficacy: The exercise of control.* New York: Freeman.

Bandura, A. (2000). Exercise of human agency through collective efficacy. *Current Directions in Psychological Science, 9,* 75–78. doi:10.1111/1467-8721.00064

Barbaranelli, C., Caprara, G. V., Vecchione, M., & Fraley, R. C. (2007). Voters' personality traits in presidential elections. *Personality and Individual Differences, 42,* 1199–1208. doi:10.1016/j.paid.2006.09.029

Barber, J. D. (1965). *The lawmakers: Recruitment and adaptation to legislative life.* New Haven, CT: Yale University Press.

Barber, J. D. (1972). *The presidential character: Predicting performance in the White House.* Englewood Cliffs, NJ: Prentice-Hall.

Barker, E. N. (1963). Authoritarianism of the political right, center, and left. *Journal of Social Issues, 19,* 63–74. doi:10.1111/j.1540-4560.1963.tb00439.x

Barnea, M. F., & Schwartz, S. H. (1998). Values and voting. *Political Psychology, 19,* 17–40. doi:10.1111/0162-895X.00090

Best, H. (2011). Does personality matter in politics? Personality factors as determinants of parliamentary recruitment and policy preferences. *Comparative Sociology, 10,* 928–948.

Block, J., & Block, J. H. (2006). Nursery school personality and political orientation two decades later. *Journal of Research in Personality, 40,* 734–749. doi:10.1016/j.jrp.2005.09.005

Bouchard, T. J., Jr., & Lohelin, J. C. (2001). Genes, personality, and evolution. *Behavior Genetics, 31,* 23–73.

Brown, R. (1965). The authoritarian personality and the organization of attitudes. In R. Brown (ed.), *Social Psychology* (pp. 477–546). New York: Free Press.

Budner, S. (1962). Intolerance of ambiguity as a personality variable. *Journal of Personality, 30,* 29–59. doi:10.1037/0033-2909.129.3.339

Byrne, D. (1971). *The attraction paradigm.* New York: Academic Press.

Byrne, D., Bond, M. H., & Diamond, M. J. (1968). Responses to political candidates as a function of attitude similarity-dissimilarity. *Human Relations, 22,* 251–262. doi:10.1177/001872676902200305

Campbell, A., Gurin, G., & Miller, W. (1954). *The voter decides.* Evanston, IL: Row Peterson.

Caprara, G. V. (1996). Structures and processes in personality psychology. *European Psychologist, 1,* 14–26. doi:10.1027/1016-9040.1.1.14

Caprara, G. V., Barbaranelli, C., Borgogni, L., & Perugini, M. (1993). The Big Five Questionnaire: A new questionnaire to assess the five factor model. *Personality and Individual Differences, 15,* 281–288.

Caprara, G. V., Barbaranelli, C., Consiglio, C., Picconi, L., & Zimbardo, P. G. (2003). Personalities of politicians and voters: Unique and synergistic relationships. *Journal of Personality and Social Psychology, 84,* 849–856. doi:10.1037/0022-3514.84.4.849

Caprara, G. V., Barbaranelli, C., Fraley, R. C., & Vecchione, M. (2007). The simplicity of politicians' personalities across political context: An anomalous replication. *International Journal of Psychology, 42,* 393–405. doi:10.1080/00207590600991104

Caprara, G. V., Barbaranelli, C., & Zimbardo, P. (1997). Politicians' uniquely simple personalities. *Nature, 385,* 493. doi:10.1038/385493a0

Caprara, G. V., Barbaranelli, C., & Zimbardo, P. (1999). Personality profiles and political parties. *Political Psychology, 20,* 175–197. doi:10.1111/0162-895X.00141

Caprara, G. V., Barbaranelli, C., & Zimbardo, P. (2002). When parsimony subdues distinctiveness: Simplified public perception of politicians' personality. *Political Psychology*, 23, 77–96. doi:10.1111/0162-895X.00271

Caprara, G. V., & Cervone, D. (2000). *Personality: Determinants, dynamics and potentials.* Cambridge: Cambridge University Press.

Caprara, G. V., Francescato, D., Mebane, M., Sorace, R., & Vecchione, M. (2010). Personality foundations of ideological divide: A comparison of women members of parliament and women voters in Italy. *Political Psychology*, 31, 739–762. doi:10.1111/j.1467-9221.2010.00780.x

Caprara, G. V., Schwartz, S. H, Capanna, C., Vecchione, M., & Barbaranelli, C. (2006). Personality and politics: Values, traits, and political choice. *Political Psychology*, 27, 1–28. doi:10.1111/j.1467-9221.2006.00447.x

Caprara, G. V., Schwartz, S. H., Vecchione, M., & Barbaranelli, C. (2008). The personalization of politics: Lessons from the Italian case. *European Psychologist*, 3, 157–172. doi:10.1027/1016-9040.13.3.157

Caprara, G. V., Vecchione, M., Barbaranelli, C., & Fraley, R. C. (2007). When likeness goes with liking: The case of political preference. *Political Psychology*, 28, 609–632. doi:10.1111/j.1467-9221.2007.00592.x

Caprara, G. V., Vecchione, M., Capanna, C., & Mebane, M. (2009). Perceived political self-efficacy: Theory, assessment, and applications. *European Journal of Social Psychology*, 39, 1002–1020. doi:10.1002/ejsp.604

Caprara, G. V., Vecchione, M., & Schwartz, S. H. (2009). Mediational role of values in linking personality traits to political orientation. *Asian Journal of Social Psychology*, 12, 82–94. doi:10.1111/j.1467-839X.2009.01274.x

Caprara, G. V., Vecchione, M., Schwartz, S. H. (2012). Why people do not vote: The role of personal values. *European Psychologist*, 17, 266–278. doi:10.1027/1016-9040/a000099

Caprara, G. V., & Zimbardo, P. (2004). Personalizing politics: A congruency model of political preference. *American Psychologist*, 59, 581–594. doi:10.1037/0003-066X.59.7.581

Carney, D. R., Jost, J. T., Gosling, S. D., Niederhoffer, K., & Potter, J. (2008). The secret lives of liberals and conservatives: Personality profiles, interaction styles, and the things they leave behind. *Political Psychology*, 29, 807–840. doi:10.1111/j.1467-9221.2008.00668.x

Chirumbolo, A. (2002). The relationship between need for cognitive closure and political orientation: The mediating role of authoritarianism. *Personality and Individual Differences*, 32, 603–610. doi:10.1016/S0191-8869(01)00062-9

Conover, P. J., & Feldman, S. (1986). The role of inference in the perception of political candidates. In R. R. Lau & D. O. Sears (eds.), *Political cognition* (pp. 127–155). Hillsdale, NJ: Erlbaum.

Converse, P. E. (1964). The nature of belief systems in mass publics. In D. E. Apter (ed.), *Ideology and discontent* (pp. 206–261). New York: Free Press.

Converse, P. E. (1972). Change in the American electorate. In A. Campbell & P. E. Converse (eds.), *The human meaning of social change* (pp. 263–337). New York: Russell Sage Foundation.

Costantini, E., & Craik, K. H. (1980). Personality and politicians: California party leaders, 1960–1976. *Journal of Personality and Social Psychology*, 38, 641–661. doi:10.1037/0022-3514.38.4.641

Craig, S.C.(1979). Efficacy, trust, and political behavior: An attempt to resolve a lingering conceptual dilemma. *American Politics Quarterly*, 7, 225–239. doi:10.1177/1532673X7900700207

Christie, R., & Cook, P. (1958). A guide to published literature relating to the authoritarian personality through 1956. *Journal of Psychology*, 45, 171–199.

Dahl, R. (2007). *Sull'uguaglianza politica* [About political equality]. Rome: Laterza.

Dalton, R. (2004). *Democratic challenges, democratic choices: The erosion of political support in advanced industrial democracies.* Oxford: Oxford University Press.

Delli Carpini, M. X., Huddy, L., & Shapiro, R. (1996). *Research in micropolitics: Rethinking rationality.* Greenwich, CT: JAI Press.

Di Renzo, G. (1963). *Personalità e potere politico* [Personality and political leadership]. Bologna: il Mulino.

Digman, J. M. (1990). Personality structure: Emergence of the five-factor model. *Annual Review of Psychology, 41*, 417–440. doi:10.1146/annurev.ps.41.020190.002221

Duckitt, J. (2001). A cognitive-motivational theory of ideology and prejudice. In M. P. Zanna (ed.), *Advances in Experimental Social Psychology* (vol. 33, pp. 41–113). San Diego, CA: Academic Press.

Duckitt, J. (2003). Prejudice and intergroup hostility. In D. Sears, L. Huddy, & R. Jervis (eds.), *Oxford handbook of political psychology* (pp. 559–600). New York: Oxford University Press.

Duckitt, J. (2006). Differential effects of right wing authoritarianism and social dominance orientation on outgroup attitudes and their mediation by threat from and competitiveness to outgroups. *Personality and Social Psychology Bulletin, 32*, 1–13. doi:10.1177/0146167205284282

Duckitt, J., & Sibley, C. G. (2009). A dual process model of ideological attitudes and system justification. In J. T. Jost, A. C. Kay, & H. Thorisdottir (eds.), *Social and psychological bases of ideology and system justification* (pp. 292–313). New York: Oxford University Press.

Duckitt, J., & Sibley, C. G. (2010). Personality, ideology, prejudice, and politics: A dual process motivational model. *Journal of Personality, 78*, 1861–1894. doi:10.1111/j.1467-6494.2010.00672.x

Duckitt, J., Wagner, C., du Plessis, I., & Birum, I. (2002). The psychological bases of ideology and prejudice: Testing a dual process model. *Journal of Personality and Social Psychology, 82*, 75–93. doi:10.1037/0022-3514.83

Durkheim, E. (1933). *The division of labor in society.* New York: Free Press.

Ekehammar, B., & Akrami, N. (2007). Personality and prejudice: From Big-Five personality factors to facets. *Journal of Personality, 75*, 899–926. doi:10.1111/j.1467-6494.2007.00460.x

Erikson, E. H. (1958). *Young man Luther.* New York: Norton.

Erikson, E. H. (1969). *Gandhi's truth.* New York: Norton.

Etheredge, L. S. (1978). Personality effects on American foreign policy, 1898–1968: A test of interpersonal generalization theory. *American Political Science Review, 72*, 434–451.

Eysenck, H. J. (1954). *The psychology of politics.* New York: Routledge, Chapman & Hall.

Feldman, S. (1988). Structure and consistency in public opinion: The role of core beliefs and values. *American Journal of Political Science, 32*, 416–440.

Feldman, S. (2003). Values, ideology, and structure of political attitudes. In D. O. Sears, L. Huddy, & R. Jervis (ed.), *Oxford handbook of political psychology* (pp. 477–508). New York: Oxford University Press.

Finkel, S. E. (1985). Reciprocal effects of participation and political efficacy: A panel analysis. *American Journal of Political Science, 29*, 891–913. doi:10.2307/2111186

Fiske, S. T. (2004). *Social beings: A core motives approach to social psychology.* Hoboken, NJ: John Wiley.

Franklin, M. (2004). *Voter turnout and the dynamics of electoral competition in established democracies since 1945.* Cambridge: Cambridge University Press.

Frenkel-Brunswik, E. (1949). Intolerance of ambiguity as an emotional and perceptual variable. *Journal of Personality, 18*, 108–143. doi:10.1111/j.1467-6494.1949.tb01236.x

Fromm, E. (1941). *Escape from freedom.* New York: Rinehart.

Funk, C. L. (1999). Bringing the candidate into models of candidate evaluation. *Journal of Politics, 61,* 700–720. doi:10.2307/2647824

George, A. L., & George, J. L. (1956). *Woodrow Wilson and Colonel House: A personality study.* New York: Day.

Gerber, A. S, Huber, G. A., Doherty, D., & Dowling, C. M. (2012). Personality and the strength and direction of partisan identification. *Political Behavior, 34,* 653–688. doi:10.1007/s11109-011-9178-5

Gerber, A. S, Huber, G. A., Doherty, D., Dowling, C. M., & Ha, S. (2010). Personality and political attitudes: Relationships across issue domains and political contexts. *American Political Science Review, 104,* 111–133. doi:10.1017/S0003055410000031

Goldberg, L. R. (1990). An alternative "description of personality": The Big-Five factor structure. *Journal of Personality and Social Psychology, 59,* 1216–1229. doi:10.1037/0022-3514.59.6.1216

Gough, H. G., & Heilbrun, A. B. (1965). *The Adjective Check List manual.* Palo Alto, CA: Consulting Psychologists Press.

Gurin, P., & Brim, O. G. (1984). Change in self in adulthood: The example of sense of control. In P. B. Baltes & O. G. Brim (eds.), *Lifespan development and behavior* (vol. 6, pp. 281–334). New York: Academic Press.

Heider, F. (1958). *The psychology of interpersonal relation.* New York: John Wiley & Sons.

Hetherington, M., & Suhay, E. (2011). Authoritarianism, threat, and Americans' support for the war on terror. *American Journal of Political Science, 55,* 546–560. doi:10.1111/j.1540-5907.2011.00514.x

Horkheimer, M. (1936). Studien über Autorität und Familie. *Schriften des Instituts für Sozialforschung, 5,* 947.

Gosling, S. D., Rentfrow, P. J., & Swann, W. B., Jr. (2003). A very brief measure of the Big Five personality domains. *Journal of Research in Personality, 37,* 504–528. doi:10.1016/S0092-6566(03)00046-1

Greenberg, J. & Jonas, E. (2003). Psychological motives and political orientation—the left, the right, and the rigid: Comment on Jost et al. (2003). *Psychological Bulletin, 129,* 376–382. doi:10.1037/0033-2909.129.3.376

Greenstein, F. I. (1975). Personality and politics. In F. I. Greenstein & N. W. Polsby (eds.), *The handbook of political science* (vol. 2, pp. 1–92). Reading, MA: Addison-Wesley.

Hatemi, P. K., Hibbing, J. R., Medland, S. E., Keller, M. C., Alford, J. R., Smith, K. B., Martin, N. G., & Eaves, L. J. (2010). Not by twins alone: Using extended family design to investigate genetic influence on political beliefs. *American Journal of Political Science, 54,* 798–814. doi:10.1111/j.1540-5907.2010.00461.x

Hatemi, P. K., Medland, S. E., Morley, K. I., Heath, A. & Martin, N. C. (2007). The genetics of voting: An Australian twin study. *Behaviorial Genetics, 37,* 435–448. doi:10.1007/s10519-006-9138-8

Hermann, M. G. (Ed.). (1977). *A psychological examination of political leaders.* New York: Free Press.

Hitlin, S. (2003) Values as the core of personal identity: Drawing links between two theories of the self. *Social Psychology Quarterly, 66,* 118–137. doi:10.2307/1519843

Jacoby, W. G. (2006). Value choices and American public opinion. *American Journal of Political Science, 50,* 706–723. doi:10.1111/j.1540-5907.2006.00211.x

Jang, K. L., McCrae, R. R., Angleitner, A., Riemann, R., & Livesley, W. J. (1998). Heritability of facet-level traits in a cross-cultural twin sample: Support for a hierarchical model of personality. *Journal of Personality and Social Psychology, 74,* 1556–1565. doi:10.1037/0022-3514.74.6.1556

John, O. P. (1990). The "Big Five" factor taxonomy: Dimensions of personality in the natural language and in questionnaires. In L. A. Pervin (ed.), *Handbook of personality: Theory and research* (pp. 66–100). New York: Guilford Press.

Jost, J. T. (2006). The end of the end of ideology. *American Psychologist, 61,* 651–670. doi:10.1037/0003-066X.61.7.651

Jost, J. T., & Banaji, M. R. (1994). The role of stereotyping in system-justification and the production of false consciousness. *British Journal of Social Psychology, 33,* 1–27. doi:10.1111/j.2044-8309.1994.tb01008.x

Jost, J. T., Banaji, M. R., & Nosek, B. A. (2004). A decade of system justification theory: Accumulated evidence of conscious and unconscious bolstering of the status quo. *Political Psychology, 25,* 881–919. doi:10.1111/j.1467-9221.2004.00402.x

Jost, J. T., Federico, C. M., & Napier, J. L. (2009). Political ideology: Its structure, functions, and elective affinities. *Annual Review of Psychology, 60,* 307–337. doi:10.1146/annurev.psych.60.110707.163600

Jost, J. T., Glaser, J., Kruglanski, A. W., & Sulloway, F. J. (2003a). Political conservatism as motivated social cognition. *Psychological Bulletin, 129,* 339–375. doi:10.1037/0033-2909.129.3.339

Jost, J. T., Glaser, J., Kruglanski, A. W., & Sulloway, F. (2003b). Exceptions that prove the rule: Using a theory of motivated social cognition to account for ideological incongruities and political anomalies. *Psychological Bulletin, 129,* 383–393. doi:10.1037/0033-2909.129.3.383

Jost, J. T., Kruglanski, A. W., & Simon, L. (1999). Effects of epistemic motivation on conservatism, intolerance, and other system justifying attitudes. In L. Thompson, D. M. Messick, & J. M. Levine (eds.), *Shared cognition in organizations: The management of knowledge* (pp. 91–116). Mahwah, NJ: Erlbaum.

Jost, J. T., Napier, J. L., Thorisdottir, H., Gosling, S. D., Palfai, T. P., & Ostafin, B. (2007). Are needs to manage uncertainty and threat associated with political conservatism or ideological extremity? *Personality and Social Psychology Bulletin, 33,* 989–1007. doi:10.1177/0146167207301028

Judd, C. M., Krosnick, J. A., & Milburn, M. A. (1981). Political involvement and attitude structure in the general public. *American Sociological Review, 46,* 660–669.

Judge, T. A., Bono, J. E., Ilies, R., & Gerhardt, M. (2002). Personality and leadership: A qualitative and quantitative review. *Journal of Applied Psychology, 87,* 765–780.

Kemmelmeier, M. (1997). Need for closure and political orientation among German university students. *Journal of Social Psychology, 137,* 787–789. doi:10.1080/00224549709595501

Klohnen, E. C., & Luo, S. (2003). Interpersonal attraction and personality: What is attractive: Self similarity, ideal similarity, complementarity, or attachment security? *Journal of Personality and Social Psychology, 85,* 706–722.

Knutsen, O. (1995). Value orientations, political conflicts and left-right identification: A comparative study. *European Journal of Political Research, 28,* 63–93. doi:10.1111/j.1475-6765.1995.tb00487.x

Knutson, J. (1973). *Handbook of political psychology.* San Francisco: Jossey-Bass.

Kruglanski, A. W. (1996). Motivated social cognition: Principles of the interface. In E. T. Higgins & A. W. Kruglanski (eds.), *Social psychology: Handbook of basic principles* (pp. 493–520). New York: Guilford Press.

Kruglanski, A. W., & Webster, D. M. (1996). Motivated closing of the mind: "Seizing" and "freezing." *Psychological Review, 103,* 263–283.

Lane, R. E. (1959). *Political life.* New York: Free Press.

Lanning, K. (2008). Democracy, voting, and disenfranchisement in the United States: A social psychological perspective. *Journal of Social Issues, 64*, 431–446. doi:10.1002/9781444307337.ch1

Lasswell, H. D. (1930). *Psychopathology and politics.* New York: Viking.

Lasswell, H. D. (1948). *Power and personality.* New York: Norton.

Le Bon, G. (1895). *The crowd: A study of the popular mind.* London: Transaction Publishers.

Loehlin, J. C., McCrae, R. R., Costa, P. T., & John, O. P. (1998). Heritabilities of common and measure-specific components of the Big Five personality factors. *Journal of Research in Personality, 32*, 431–453. doi:10.1006/jrpe.1998.2225

Madsen, D. (1987). Political self-efficacy tested. *American Political Science Review, 81*, 571–582.

Marx, K. (1844). Economic and philosophical manuscripts. In *Early Writings* (R. Livingstone & G. Benton, trans.). New York: Vintage, 1975.

McCann, J. A. (1997). Electoral choices and core value change: The 1992 presidential campaign. *American Journal of Political Science, 41*, 564–583.

McClelland, D. C. (1985). *Human motivation.* Glenview, IL: Scott, Foresman.

McCrae, R. R. (1996). Social consequences of experiential openness. *Psychological Bulletin, 120*, 323–337. doi:10.1037/0033-2909.120.3.323

McCrae, R. R., & Allik, J. (2002). *The five-factor model of personality across cultures.* New York: Kluwer Academic/Plenum Publishers.

McCrae, R. R., & Costa, P. T., Jr. (1996). Toward a new generation of personality theories: Theoretical contexts for the five-factor model. In J. S. Wiggins (ed.), *The five-factor model of personality: Theoretical perspectives* (pp. 51–87). New York: Guilford.

McCrae, R. R., & Costa, P. T. (2008). The five-factor theory of personality. In O. P. John, R. W. Robins, & L. A. Pervin (eds.), *Handbook of personality: Theory and research* (3rd ed., pp. 159–181). New York: Guilford Press.

Milbrath, L. W. (1965). *Political participation: How and why do people get involved in politics?* Chicago: Rand McNally.

Milbrath, L. W., & Goel, M. L. (1977). *Political participation* (2nd ed.). Chicago: Rand McNally.

Miller, A. H., Wattenberg, M. P., & Malanchuk, O. (1986). Schematic assessments of presidential candidates. *American Political Science Review, 80*, 521–540.

Mitchell, P. G., Tetlock, P. E., Mellers, B. A., & Ordonez, L. (1993). Judgments of social justice: Compromise between equality and efficiency. *Journal of Personality and Social Psychology, 65*, 629–639. doi:10.1037//0022-3514.65.4.629

Mondak, J. J. (2010). *Personality and the foundations of political behavior.* Cambridge: Cambridge University Press.

Mondak, J. J., & Halperin, K. D. (2008). A framework for the study of personality and political behaviour. *British Journal of Political Science, 38*, 335–362. doi:10.1017/S0007123408000173

Mondak, J. J., Hibbing, M. V., Canache, D., Seligson, M. A., & Anderson, M. R. (2010). Personality and civic engagement: An integrative framework for the study of trait effects on political behavior. *American Political Science Review, 104*, 85–110. doi:10.1017/S0003055409990359

Niemi, R. G., Craig, S. C., & Mattei, F. (1991). Measuring internal political efficacy in the 1988 national election study. *American Political Science Review, 85*, 1407–1413.

Piurko, Y., Schwartz, S. H., & Davidov, E. (2011). Basic personal values and the meaning of left-right political orientations in 20 countries. *Political Psychology, 32*, 537–561.

Pollock, P. H., Lilie, S. A., & Vittes, M. E. (1993). Hard issues, core values and vertical constraint: The case of nuclear power. *British Journal of Political Science 23* (1): 29–50.

Popkin, S. (1991). *The reasoning voter.* Chicago: University of Chicago Press.

Post, R. (2006). Democracy and equality. *Annals of the American Academy of Political and Social Science, 603,* 24–36. doi:10.1177/0002716205282954

Pratto, F., Sidanius, J., Stallworth, L. M., & Malle, B. F. (1994). Social dominance orientation: A personal variable predicting social and political attitudes. *Journal of Personality and Social Psychology, 67,* 741–763. doi:10.1037/0022-3514.67.4.741

Rentfrow, P. J., Jost, J. T., Gosling, S. D., & Potter, J. (2009). Statewide differences in personality predict voting patterns in U.S. presidential elections, 1996–2004. In J. T. Jost, A. C. Kay, & H. Thorisdottir (eds.), *Social and psychological bases of ideology and system justification* (pp. 314–347). New York: Oxford University Press.

Riemann, R., Grubich, C., Hempel, S., Mergl, S., & Richter, M. (1993). Personality and attitudes towards current political topics. *Personality and Individual Differences, 15,* 313–321. doi:10.1016/0191-8869(93)90222-O

Roccato, M., & Ricolfi, L. (2005). On the correlation between right-wing authoritarianism and social dominance orientation. *Basic & Applied Social Psychology, 27,* 187–200. doi:10.1207/s15324834basp2703

Rokeach, M. (1954). The nature and meaning of dogmatism. *Psychological Review, 61,* 194–204.

Rokeach, M. (1956). Political and religious dogmatism: An alternative to the authoritarian personality. *Psychological Monographs, 70* (18, Whole No. 425), 43.

Rokeach, M. (1960). *The open and closed mind.* New York: Basic Books.

Rokeach, M. (1973). *The nature of human values.* New York: Free Press.

Rokeach, M. (1979). *Understanding human values: Individual and social.* New York: Free Press.

Sanford, N. (1973). Authoritarian personality in contemporary perspective. In J. N. Knutson, (ed.), *Handbook of political psychology* (pp. 139–170). San Francisco: Jossey Bass.

Schoen, H., & Schumann, S. (2007) Personality traits, partisan attitudes, and voting behavior: Evidence from Germany. *Political Psychology, 28,* 471–498. doi:10.1111/j.1467-9221.2007.00582.x

Schwartz, S. H. (1992). Universals in the content and structure of values: Theoretical advances and empirical tests in 20 countries. In M. Zanna (ed.), *Advances in experimental social psychology* (vol. 25, pp. 1–65). New York: Academic Press. doi:10.1016/S0065-2601(08)60281-6

Schwartz, S. H. (1994). Are there universal aspects in the structure and contents of human values? *Journal of Social Issues, 50,* 19–45. doi:10.1111/j.1540-4560.1994.tb01196.x

Schwartz, S. H. (2005). Basic human values: Their content and structure across cultures. In A. Tamayo & J. Porto (eds.), *Valores e trabalho* [Values and work]. Brasília: Editora Vozes.

Schwartz, S. H. (2006). Les valeurs de base de la personne: Théorie, mesures et applications [Basic human values: Theory, measurement, and applications]. *Revue française de sociologie, 42,* 249–288.

Schwartz, S. H. & Bilsky, W. (1987). Toward a universal psychological structure of human values. *Journal of Personality and Social Psychology, 53,* 550–562. doi:10.1037/0022-3514.53.3.550

Schwartz, S. H., Caprara, G. V., & Vecchione, M. (2010). Basic personal values, core political values and voting: A longitudinal analysis. *Political Psychology, 31,* 421–452. doi:10.1111/j.1467-9221.2010.00764.x

Seeman, M. (1959). On the meaning of alienation. *American Sociological Review, 24,* 783–791.

Seeman, M. (1966). Alienation, membership, and political knowledge: A comparative study. *Public Opinion Quarterly, 30,* 353–367. doi:10.1086/267429

Sibley, C. G., & Duckitt, J. (2008). Personality and prejudice: A meta-analysis and theoretical review. *Personality and Social Psychology Review, 12,* 248–279. doi:10.1177/1088868308319226

Sibley, C. G., Robertson, A., & Wilson, M. (2006). Social dominance orientation and right wing authoritarianism: Additive and interactive effects. *Political Psychology*, 27, 755–768. doi:10.1111/j.1467-9221.2006.00531.x

Sidanius, J. (1985). Cognitive functioning and sociopolitical ideology revisited. *Political Psychology*, 6, 637–661.

Sidanius, J. (1988). Political sophistication and political deviance: A structural equation examination of context theory. *Journal of Personality and Social Psychology*, 55, 37–51. doi:10.1037/0022-3514.55.1.37

Sidanius, J., & Pratto, F. (1999). *Social dominance: An intergroup theory of social hierarchy and oppression.* New York: Cambridge University Press.

Silvester, J. (2008). The good, the bad, and the ugly: Politics and politicians at work. In G. P. Hodgkinson & J. K. Ford (eds.), *International review of industrial and organizational psychology* (vol. 23, pp. 107–148). Chichester: John Wiley and Sons. doi:10.1002/9780470773277.ch4

Silvester, J., & Dykes, C. (2007). Selecting political candidates: A longitudinal study of assessment centre performance and political success in the 2005 UK general election. *Journal of Occupational and Organizational Psychology*, 81, 11–26. doi:10.1348/096317906X156287

Simon, H. A. (1985). Human nature in politics: The dialogue of psychology with political science. *American Political Science Review*, 79, 293–304.

Simonton, D. K. (1986). Presidential personality: Biographical use of the Gough Adjective Check List. *Journal of Personality & Social Psychology*, 51, 149–160. doi:10.1037/0022-3514.51.1.149

Simonton, D. K. (1988). Presidential style: Personality, biography, and performance. *Journal of Personality and Social Psychology*, 55, 928–936. doi:10.1037/0022-3514.55.6.928

Simonton, D. K. (1990). Personality and politics. In L. Pervin (ed.), *Handbook of personality* (pp. 670–692). New York: Guilford Press.

Smith, K. B., Oxley, D. R., Hibbing, M. B., Alford, J. R., & Hibbing, J. R. (2011). Linking genetics and political attitudes: Reconceptualizing political ideology. *Political Psychology*, 32, 369–397. doi:10.1111/j.1467-9221.2010.00821.x

Sniderman, P. M. (1975). *Personality and democratic politics.* Berkeley: University of California Press.

Sniderman, P. M., Brody, R. A., & Tetlock, P. E. (1991), *Reasoning and choice: Explorations in political psychology.* Cambridge: Cambridge University Press.

Steinbrecher, M., & Schoen, H. (2010). Personality and turnout in Germany: Evidence from the 2009 federal election. Typescript, University of Mannheim.

Suedfeld, P., & Rank, A. D. (1976). Revolutionary leaders: Long-term success as a function of changes in conceptual complexity. *Journal of Personality and Social Psychology*, 34, 169–178. doi:10.1037/0022-3514.34.2.169

Suedfeld, P., & Tetlock, P. E. (1977). Integrative complexity of communications in international crises. *Journal of Conflict Resolution*, 21, 169–184. doi:10.1177/002200277702100108

Suedfeld, P., Tetlock, P. E., & Streufert, S. (1992). Conceptual/integrative complexity. In C. P. Smith (ed.), *Motivation and personality: Handbook of thematic content analyses* (pp. 393–400). New York: Cambridge University Press.

Tarde, G. (1903). *The Laws of imitation.* New York: Henry Holt.

Tetlock, P. E. (1983). Cognitive style and political ideology. *Journal of Personality and Social Psychology*, 45, 118–126. doi:10.1037/0022-3514.45.1.118

Tetlock, P. E. (1984). Cognitive style and political belief systems in the British House of Commons. *Journal of Personality and Social Psychology*, 46, 365–375. doi:10.1037/0022-3514.46.2.365

Tetlock, P. E. (1985). Integrative complexity of American and Soviet foreign policy rhetoric: A time-series analysis. *Journal of Personality and Social Psychology*, 49, 1565–1585. doi:10.1037/0022-3514.49.6.1565

Tetlock, P. E. (1988). Monitoring the integrative complexity of American and Soviet policy rhetoric: What can be learned? *Journal of Social Issues*, 44, 101–313. doi:10.1111/j.1540-4560.1988.tb02065.x

Tetlock, P. E., & Boettger, R. (1989). Accountability: A social magnifier of the dilution effect. *Journal of Personality and Social Psychology*, 57, 388–398. doi:10.1037/0022-3514.57.3.388

Tetlock, P. E., & Suedfeld, P. (1988). Integrative complexity coding of verbal behavior. In C. Antaki (ed.), *Analyzing lay explanation: A casebook of methods* (pp. 72–87). Beverly Hills, CA: Sage.

Todorov, A., Mandisodza, A. N., Goren, A., & Hall, C. C. (2005). Inferences of competence from faces predict election outcomes. *Science*, 308, 1623–1626. doi:10.1126/science.1110589

Trapnell, P. D. (1994). Openness versus intellect: A lexical left turn. *European Journal of Personality*, 8, 273–290. doi:10.1002/per.2410080405

Uleman, J. S., Newman, L. S., & Moskowitz, G. B. (1996). People as flexible interpreters: Evidence and issues from spontaneous trait inference. In M. P. Zanna (ed.), *Advances in experimental social psychology* (vol. 29, pp. 211–279). San Diego, CA: Academic Press. doi:10.1016/S0065-2601(08)60239-7

Van Hiel, A., Kossowska, M., & Mervielde, I. (2000). The relationship between openness to experience and political ideology. *Personality and Individual Differences*, 28, 741–751. doi:10.1016/S0191-8869(99)00135-X

Van Hiel, A., Onraet, E., & De Pauw, S. (2010). The relationship between social-cultural attitudes and behavioral measures of cognitive style: A meta-analytic integration of studies. *Journal of Personality*, 78, 1765–1800. doi:10.1111/j.1467-6494.2010.00669.x

Vecchione, M., & Caprara, G. V. (2009). Personality determinants of political participation: The contribution of traits and self-efficacy beliefs. *Personality and Individual Differences*, 46, 487–492. doi:10.1016/j.paid.2008.11.021

Verba, S., Schlozman, K. L., & Brady, H. (1995). *Voice and equality: Civic voluntarism in American politics*. Cambridge, MA: Harvard University Press.

Weber, M. (1904). *Die protestantische Ethik und der Geist des Kapitalismus*. Tübingen: J.C.B. Mohr (Paul Siebeck).

Wilson, G. D. (Ed.). (1973). *The psychology of conservatism*. London: Academic Press.

Winter, D. G. (1973). *The power motive*. New York: Free Press.

Winter, D. G. (1987). Leader appeal, leader performance, and the motive profiles of leaders and followers: A study of American presidents and elections. *Journal of Personality and Social Psychology*, 52, 196–202.

Winter, D. G. (1998). Toward a science of personality psychology: David McClelland's development of empirically derived TAT measures. *History of Psychology*, 1, 130–153. doi:10.1037/1093-4510.1.2.130

Winter, D. G. (2002). Motivation and political leadership. In L. Valenty & O. Feldman (eds.), *Political leadership for the new century: Personality and behavior among American leaders* (pp. 25–47). Westport, CT: Praeger.

Winter, D. G. (2003). Measuring the motives of political actors at a distance. In J. M. Post (ed.), *The psychological assessment of political leaders: With profiles of Saddam Hussein and Bill Clinton* (pp. 153–177). Ann Arbor: University of Michigan Press.

Winter, D. G. (2005). Things I've learned about personality from studying political leaders at a distance. *Journal of Personality*, 73, 557–584. doi:10.1111/j.1467-6494.2005.00321.x

Winter, D. G., John, O. P., Stewart, A. J., Klohnen, E. C., & Duncan, L. E. (1998). Traits and motives: Toward and integration of two traditions in personality research. *Psychological Review, 105,* 230–250. doi:10.1037/0033-295X.105.2.230

Winter, D. G., & Stewart, A. J. (1977). Content analysis as a technique for assessing political leaders. In M. G. Hermann (ed.), *The psychological examination of political leaders* (pp. 27–61). New York: Free Press.

Zaller, J. R. (1992). *The nature and origins of mass opinion.* New York: Cambridge University Press.

Zajonc, R. B. (1980). Feeling and thinking: Preferences need no inferences. *American Psychologist, 35,* 151–175. doi:10.1037/0003-066X.35.2.151

Zimmerman, M. A. (1989). The relationship between political efficacy and citizen participation: Construct validation studies. *Journal of Personality Assessment, 53,* 554–566. doi:10.1207/s15327752jpa5303_12

CHAPTER 3

....

CHILDHOOD AND ADULT
POLITICAL DEVELOPMENT

....

DAVID O. SEARS AND CHRISTIA BROWN

IF the study of history considers human affairs through the lens of time as an independent variable, the study of human psychological development views individuals in terms of their life histories, employing the tool of time within the human life span. Accordingly, this chapter examines the life histories of political orientations as they evolve from early childhood through old age (for an earlier version, see Sears & Levy, 2003).

The life history perspective has a unique niche in political psychology in a variety of respects. It addresses the constant tension between continuity and change as played out throughout an individual's life span. Such an historical emphasis contrasts with more ahistorical approaches such as the rational choice theories drawn from the field of economics, or the behavioral decision theories drawn from psychology, or cognitive psychology more generally. Moreover, it helps us to understand the origins of orientations that are politically consequential among adults, whether concerning politics specifically (see Taber and Young, chapter 17, this volume; Feldman, chapter 19, this volume) or intergroup relations (see Huddy, chapter 23; Kinder, chapter 25; and Hewstone and Al-Ramiah, chapter 27, all in this volume). At a more practical, or ultimately perhaps impractical, level, the utopian spirit ranges far and wide among humans, including such disparate types as liberal social scientists, Jesus Christ, Adolf Hitler, and Vladimir Lenin, and sometimes centers on the hope that human progress might be aided by early intervention.

Time appears as an independent variable most often in three ways. One concerns the persisting effects of *early experiences*. Early studies of political socialization documented the appearance in childhood and adolescence of racial prejudice, national and other identities, party identification and ideology, and support for political leaders, regimes, and systems (see Renshon, 1977; Sears, 1975). Such youthful attitudes were generally assumed to be meaningful and to have lasting influence throughout the life span.

A second focus is upon "*the times*." Individuals' life histories are inextricably connected to what happens in the broader environment. Sometimes "the times" show dramatic changes, such as during the French Revolution, the emancipation of African American slaves, World War II, China's Cultural Revolution, or the abrupt collapse of the Soviet Union. More often change is significant but gradual, as in the slow changes since the New Deal in the American party system. Or sometimes change is so glacial it appears nonexistent, as in the American polity's commitment to freedom of speech and worship.

A third general approach looks for politically distinctive features of different *life stages*. Young children may have difficulty cognitively linking various aspects of their experience, delaying their appreciation of abstract concepts such as Congress or the Supreme Court. Adolescents may be especially vulnerable to "storm and stress" and drawn to unconventional behavior and to political rebellion, such as in the old French adage, "He who is not a revolutionary at 20 has no heart; he who is a revolutionary at 40 has no head." Young adults may be especially concerned about their own independent identity and be somewhat unmoored in society, and so more open to influence. Mature adults, embedded in work, home, and family, may show a stronger sense of self-interest. The elderly may flag in mental and physical energy, with consequences for the consistency and stability of their attitudes and for their level of political participation.

Previous review essays in handbooks of political psychology have been titled "political socialization" and have focused largely on the childhood acquisition of specifically political orientations (Merelman, 1986; Niemi, 1973). The application of preadult developmental approaches to political psychology has undergone considerable cycling in popularity. A generation ago, Greenstein (1970, p. 969) felt that "political socialization is a growth stock," and Sears (1975, p. 94) noted that "research output has increased at a geometric rate." A reaction then set in, characterizing political socialization as in a "bear market" (Cook, 1985) and challenging two often overly enthusiastic assumptions: of a "primacy principle," the staying power of early-acquired predispositions, and a "structuring principle," that early-acquired predispositions had special political power in adulthood (e.g., Searing, Schwartz, & Lind, 1973; Searing, Wright, & Rabinowitz, 1976). Some called for recognition of more openness to change through the life course; for example, that "change during adulthood is normal" (Sapiro, 1994, p. 204), and others that "learning and development are [not] completed by adulthood; rather they [constitute] a lifelong process" (Sigel, 1989, p. viii). Some trends in political science more generally also contributed to de-emphasis on preadult experience, especially economic theories focusing on the rational choices made by adults. Then, in some eyes, political socialization research experienced a "rebirth" (Niemi & Hepburn, 1995).

In contrast to that early focus on preadults, we broaden our scope to the full life span. We begin with a discussion of the preadult acquisition of basic political predispositions, with particular focus on the paradigmatic case of party identification in America, as well as on ethnic and racial prejudices and identities. We then consider the later life history of such predispositions, with particular attention to their persistence, and to the related "impressionable years" model postulating particular susceptibility to change in late adolescence and early adulthood, with applications to political generations. We conclude with some attention to the competing role of contextual changes in adulthood.

1. Childhood and Adolescence

1.1. Party Identification

The paradigmatic case of the development of political attitudes among preadults has been Americans' party identifications. In large part that is because party identification is by far the strongest and most consistent predictor of voting preferences in the world's oldest democracy. The early conventional wisdom was that "a man is born into his political party just as he is born into probable future membership in the church of his parents" (Hyman, 1959, p. 74).

The more complex theory then developed in *The American Voter* (Campbell, Converse, Miller, & Stokes, 1960) is perhaps the most influential in the study of American political behavior, based on a sequence of two questions asked of each survey respondent (see Huddy, chapter 23, this volume, for the exact wording). It described party identification as an attitudinal predisposition typically acquired in preadult life, often from the parental family; as highly stable over the life span; as the most powerful single factor in determining candidate evaluations and voting choices in partisan elections, and often issue preferences as well; as usually acquired and maintained without an elaborate accompanying ideological understanding about the positions of the two parties; with the *strength* of party identification (or its "crystallization") being thought to increase through the life cycle as the individual accumulated experience with the partisan electoral system, at least in periods of a stable party system (Campbell et al., 1960).

This early theory relied on less direct empirical assessment of these propositions than has later research. It relied on adults' recall of their earlier lives to establish early acquisition, familial influence, and stability over the life span; on cross-sectional correlations to establish its influence over candidate and issue preferences; on the paucity of adults' ideological thinking to establish that early acquisition of partisanship was not usually informed by larger ideological understandings; and only later on empirical tests of the strengthening of party identification with age (Converse, 1969; 1976).

Later research tested for the crystallization of preadults' party identifications directly (Sears & Valentino, 1997), using the criteria originally suggested by Converse (1964) for detecting belief systems (constraint across related attitudes, stability over time, and power over attitude formation toward new attitude objects), and found that adolescents' party identifications had crystallized almost to adult levels by the end of a presidential campaign. A similar study found that the party identifications of a large sample of entering college students had already crystallized approximately to adult levels, and that the adult demographic and value correlates of partisanship were largely in place already (Sears, Haley, & Henry, 2008).

The original hypothesis of preadult *family transmission* was later directly tested by Jennings and Niemi (1974; 1981), in their classic "Michigan socialization study," interviewing a national sample of high school seniors and their parents in 1965, with both samples again in 1973 and 1982, and with the student cohort along with children of the former students in 1997. They found substantial, though not perfect, parental transmission of party identification to their adolescent children, and lesser transmission of other political attitudes (Jennings, Stoker, & Bowers, 2009; also see Kroh & Selb, 2009, for evidence of successful parental transmission in the German multiparty system). Parent-child similarity of partisanship declined through the offsprings' early adulthoods (though not thereafter), as their own issue preferences had increasing influence (Beck & Jennings, 1991; Niemi & Jennings, 1991).

But plainly families vary considerably in their ability to pass their partisanship on to their offspring. The most politicized parents, and those with the most stable attitudes themselves, are consistently the most successful (Beck & Jennings, 1991; Jennings et al., 2009). Similarly, parental political interest produces greater influence, at least while the offspring continue to live with their parents (Fitzgerald, 2011). Wolak (2009) found greater crystallization of preadults' partisanship among adolescents who converse more politically with their parents. In the words of the authors of *The American Voter Revisited*, a recent reassessment of *The American Voter*, adolescents from politically uninvolved homes find themselves "largely adrift in partisan terms" (Lewis-Beck, Norpoth, Jacoby, & Weisberg, 2008, p. 141).

Politicized parents seem to be particularly successful because they most accurately communicate their political positions to their children (Niemi, 1974; Tedin, 1980). Variations in the quality of parent-child relationships, such as rebellions against parents, seem generally not to be central in success of transmission (Jennings & Niemi, 1974). Accuracy of perception of parental positions also helps to explain differences in transmission across attitude domains: parental attitudes are communicated more clearly in some (e.g., candidate choices in hotly contested elections) than others (e.g., political efficacy). Nevertheless, working in favor of parental transmission of partisanship is that it usually displays one of the strongest correlations of any attribute between spouses, suggesting that it plays a relatively important role in mate choice (Alford, Hatemi, Hibbing, Martin, & Eaves, 2011).

But the child's own political interest plays a role, suggesting that preadults are sometimes not mere passive recipients of political socialization but active participants (see similar findings from England and Germany; Zuckerman, Dasovic, & Fitzgerald, 2007). Interestingly, Fitzgerald and Curtis (2012), analyzing panel surveys in several countries, found that parental discord over politics tends to produce higher levels of political engagement over time in their offspring. And offspring sometimes influence parental attitudes, especially in domains in which they introduce more "modern" attitudes to their families (Sapiro, 2003; also see Fitzgerald, 2011 regarding nontraditional "rising parties" in Switzerland; or Zuckerman et al., 2007, in England and Germany).

The centrality of family transmission was originally proposed in an era of more frequent intact two-parent families than is the case now, with higher rates of divorce and never-married mothers, and in an era seemingly marked by more ritualized parent-child contact than today. Even so, the extension of the Michigan socialization study to the children of the original students shows quite convincingly that parent-child transmission in those families shows very much the same pattern as it did in the original families (Jennings et al., 2009). Indeed in some attitude domains it is even higher, such as in political ideology and racial attitudes. Nevertheless, parental absence, especially divorce (more than death, oddly) weakens preadults' political involvement (Sances, 2013).

"The times" are also implicated in the preadult acquisition of party identification. The original theory implied that it was transmitted in piecemeal fashion in the course of daily life. But if the key to successful political socialization is clear communication of stable parental attitudes, vivid *political events* might be important catalysts because their heavy information flows could provide occasions for such communication. Indeed Sears and Valentino (1997) found that the crystallization of adolescents' partisanship increased dramatically, almost to parental levels, through the course of a presidential campaign. No such increase occurred in adults' partisanship, which was already at high levels; nor toward attitudes objects peripheral to the campaign; nor during the less information-intense postcampaign year. Crystallization increased most among adolescents most engaged in interpersonal political communication (Valentino & Sears, 1998). Indeed longer-term interest in politics may be sparked if preadults enter the age of political awareness at times of heightened activity in the political arena (Wolak and McDevitt, (2011; also see Fitzgerald, 2011). Another study showed that highly visible female candidates produced more political involvement among adolescent girls due to greater political discussion within the family (Campbell & Wolbrecht, 2006). Other political events, such as 9/11, have also been shown to contribute to adolescents' political socialization (Gimpel, Lay, & Schuknecht, 2003).

1.2. Role of Government

At one time, childhood political socialization was thought to be a key element in installing a sense of government legitimacy and diffuse system support in mass publics. One vehicle for accomplishing that goal was to develop children's admiration for the most visible and personal symbol of government, the chief of state (Easton & Dennis, 1969). This line of research has been less active in recent years, perhaps due to questions about the durability of those early attitudes, and with recognition that children's supposed idealization of the American president was partly a function of the popularity of the incumbents when that early research was done (for a review, see Sears, 1975).

In the United States, most children learn about their presidents in the early school years (Easton & Dennis, 1969; Hess & Torney, 1967; Picard, 2005). At this age, children have a basic sense of the president being the leader of government. Their understanding of the methods, purposes, and effects of government increases across elementary school (Abraham, 1983). Across countries, children around age 8–10 tend to be quite positive about their government and its symbols (Sears, 1975).

Indeed some research indicates that children and early adolescents believe the government should play a larger role than do adults (Lopez & Kirby, 2005). For example, Brown, Mistry, and Bigler (2007) found that American children between the ages of 6 and 14 believed that the government should have played an important role in aiding the victims of Hurricane Katrina by providing houses, jobs for families, and money. A majority of ninth-graders in a national sample reported that the government should be responsible for providing free basic education and healthcare for everyone, and a sufficient standard of living for the elderly (Baldi, Ferie, Skidmore, Greenberg, & Hahn, 2001).

However, adolescents are less generally positive toward their government and its symbols than are younger children. They also begin to mirror adults' sometimes negative attitudes, such as in the case of the disgraced President Nixon. Affect toward less controversial symbols of the nation generally remains positive, however, such as toward the American flag and British monarchy (see Sears, 1975).

1.3. Civic Engagement

The early adolescent years mark the formation of attitudes toward civic engagement (Metz & Youniss, 2005). This is important because civic engagement in youth may be an important predictor of voting in adulthood (Youniss, McLellan, & Yates, 1997). At least having civic knowledge in high school is associated with whether youth think they will vote in the future (Krampen, 2000)

One challenge is defining civic engagement in a population too young to vote. Descriptions of civic engagement used in large international studies include social responsibility, loyalty, patriotism, a sense of political efficacy, trust in the government, participation in political discussions, knowledge of democracy, and having a concern for the welfare of others beyond oneself (Sherrod, Flanagan, & Youniss, 2002). Torney-Purta, Lehmann, Oswald, and Schultz (2001) go further and argue that developing citizenship should also include awareness of human rights, including respect for the political rights of women and ethnic minorities.

Not surprisingly, civic engagement increases across adolescence, in some respects attaining adult levels and in others falling short. For example, Moore, Lare, and Wagner (1985) found that most adolescents (90%) believe adults should vote and obey the law, though only half believed adults should be affiliated with a political party. About half of American adolescents in another study gave a correct definition of "democracy," divided among mentions of the freedoms and rights of the individual, majority rule, and the promise of civic equality (Flanagan, Gallay, Gill, Gallay, & Nti, 2005). Correct responses increased with age. Youth whose parents were more educated, and who engaged in family discussions of current events, were more likely to give a correct definition of democracy, paralleling the evidence on family political socialization cited earlier. Cognitive development may be involved as well: 14-year-olds have greater ability to view multiple sides of social problems and consider others' opinions than do 10-year-olds (Gallatin & Adelson, 1971).

Many point to the youthful socialization process as an important means of increasing civic engagement. Adolescents' subjective civic engagement, such as feeling politically competent and influential in shaping others' political views, is associated with greater participation in political activities in everyday life, such as having political discussions and watching political news reports (Krampen, 2000). Youth with civically engaged parents are more likely to be civically engaged (Flanagan, Bowes, Jonsson, Csapo, & Sheblanova, 1998). Civic education in youth settings (e.g., Torney-Purta et al., 2001) may also be important spheres in which youth can increase their civic knowledge, feel a sense of social responsibility, and increase their political self-efficacy.

1.4. Race and Ethnicity

In a diverse society, ethnicity and race are important social categories, influencing individuals' social attitudes and identities, among other things. Although there are important distinctions between race and ethnicity, children rarely make the distinction, so racial and ethnic attitudes and identities develop similarly and have similar implications. We will discuss the findings of race and ethnicity together.

1.4.1. Prejudice and Stereotyping

Most early research on the development of racial prejudice examined American and Canadian children (see Aboud, 1988 for a thorough review). More recent work with international samples has shown very similar findings. It indicates that children endorse racial stereotypes and show racial biases very early, before age 3, even before they can correctly identify their own race or ethnicity. In one American study, when children age 2½ were asked to choose photographs of unfamiliar peers they would like to play with, a majority of white and black children picked a same-race face (Katz & Kofkin, 1997).

By age 3, however, a majority of American white and black children alike began to choose a white peer (Katz & Kofkin, 1997). For white children, a bias favoring whites continues to increase until approximately age 7 or 8. Among black children, however, this white preference typically continues until about age 6, after which point they begin to show an own-race preference when picking a potential playmate. Kelly and Duckitt (1995) found a similar white preference among black South African children up to age 10. Originally it was argued that this early white preference shown by young black children was due to poor self-esteem (Clark & Clark, 1939). Contemporary researchers argue instead that it reflects children's recognition that being white is desirable because it is associated with higher social status (e.g., Aboud, 1988). In any case, by around age 10, white, black, Asian, and Latino children's attitudes have become more similar, with most children showing a slight preference for their own racial group (Aboud, 1988; Brown, Alabi, Huynh, & Masten, 2011; Katz & Kofkin, 1997).

Even when children show preferences for members of their own racial group, however, they do not necessarily express dislike or derogation toward members of other racial or ethnic groups. In one study, American children attributed positive traits and qualities to their own racial group and were neutral toward other racial groups (Cameron, Alvarez, Ruble, & Fuligni, 2001). However white children were more likely to endorse racial stereotypes than were children from other racial backgrounds (e.g., Aboud & Skerry, 1984). And in social contexts with more explicitly negative intergroup relations, such as Israel, children have been shown to endorse negative attitudes about the out-group (Bar-Tal, 1996; Brenick et al., 2010).

Although children show prejudices and stereotypes very early, their understanding of them develops more slowly, perhaps dependent on their cognitive development. In interviews with Mexican American and black children, Quintana (2007) found that children's understanding of ethnic prejudice is related to their more general perspective-taking abilities. For example, young children (ages 3–6) attributed prejudice to physical and observable preferences, such as, "They don't like their color." This parallels young children's general tendency to attend to observable, rather than abstract, characteristics of the environment. Even slightly older children (ages 6–8) attributed prejudice to literal, nonsocial reasons, such as "They may not like Mexico."

A big leap forward in the understanding of race, prejudice, and stereotypes occurs around ages 8 to 10. Children at this age now generally accept the view common among American adults that race is stable and inherited (Alejandro-Wright, 1985). They also often recognize the social components of prejudice, even suggesting that others might be prejudiced because of what they are taught at home (Quintana, 2007). Further, across this developmental period, children's knowledge of group differences in stereotyping increases steadily (e.g., "White people think black people are not smart"; McKown & Weinstein, 2003, p. 5). Children also become increasingly aware through the elementary school years of the implications of these stereotypes for group status. For example many black children rate occupations as lower status (i.e., earn less money, require less education) if performed by blacks rather than whites (Bigler, Averhart, & Liben, 2003).

Although culturally often confounded with race and ethnicity, social class is a more complex and abstract construct (i.e., with somewhat less visible and concrete markers compared to skin color). Children's understanding of social class, therefore, develops more slowly than their understanding of race, developing first in elementary school. Yet the two domains show striking parallels, at least in research on American children. Qualitative research with children living below the poverty line has shown that poor children often assume society views the poor as "troublemakers," "dirty," "stupid," and "disgusting" (Weinger, 1998, p. 108). They believe that the poor are not welcome in wealthier neighborhoods, that the poor are social outcasts, and that more affluent children are happier and more worry-free. Other research (Emler & Dickinson, 1985) has shown that middle-class children perceive greater income discrepancies than do working-class children between manual (e.g., road sweeper) and nonmanual labor jobs (e.g., teachers). Regardless of their own social class, however, children typically perceive income discrepancies on the basis of occupation to be justified (Emler & Dickinson, 1985).

Poor children's perceptions of negative stereotypes directed toward the poor parallel perceived racial stereotypes. For example, adolescents aged 11–16 consider poor people to be less intelligent and less able to make friends than wealthy people (Skafte, 1989). With age, stereotypes about the poor become more differentiated. For example, fourth-graders considered wealthy individuals to be better at sports, academics, and music relative to poor individuals. Sixth- and eighth-graders considered poor people advantaged in sports and disadvantaged in academics compared to wealthy people, while music tended to be a stereotype-neutral domain (Woods, Kurtz-Costes, & Rowley, 2005). American adolescents' explanations for, and evaluations of, poverty and economic inequality mirror those about racial differences, more often attributing poverty to such personal characteristics as work ethic and effort than to structural factors such as job availability, government supports, and discrimination (Leahy, 1990). Black or biracial children are more likely than white children to mention unemployment or lack of employment opportunities as the cause of poverty (Chafel & Neitzel, 2005).

Despite the continuing general preference for own-race members, racial stereotypes typically start to decline at around age 10, as demonstrated with a variety of methods (Aboud, 1988; Aboud & Skerry, 1984; Brown & Johnson, 1971; Katz, Sohn, & Zalk, 1975; Williams, Best, & Boswell, 1975) and in a variety of nations (Monteiro, de França, & Rodrigues, 2009; Augoustinos & Rosewarne, 2001; Boulton & Smith, 1996).

Why do children show an increase and then a decline around age 10 in own-race biases? A cognitive developmental theory of prejudice argues that young children are necessarily biased at a young age because of their cognitive limitations, but as they become more cognitively sophisticated, their racial attitudes become more tolerant (Aboud, 1988; Bigler & Liben, 1993). For example, children gradually develop multiple classification skills, such as the ability to recognize that people can simultaneously belong to two different categories. As a result they may begin to understand that children from different ethnic groups can look different from them externally but be similar to them internally, such as in interests and tastes (Aboud, 1988). Indeed, children who were taught to classify stimuli along multiple dimensions within an experimental paradigm showed lower levels of stereotyping after the acquisition of this cognitive skill (Bigler & Liben, 1993).

A different explanation for this age-related shift is that children become more familiar with social norms about the expression of racial biases. If so, explicit racial attitudes might show more reduced bias with age than would implicit attitudes (e.g., more quickly associating positive qualities with white faces than with black faces, and vice versa for negative qualities). Some preliminary research indicates that white children at age 6 have equivalent explicit and implicit racial biases, but by age 10 show reduced explicit racial bias along with continued implicit associations favoring whites over blacks (Baron & Banaji, 2006).

Although this shift with age could be due to children's growing awareness of social norms, it could also be due to their growing cognitive complexity such that they can hold both unbiased conscious and biased subconscious attitudes simultaneously. These two arguments are often pitted against one another, but they are not necessarily mutually exclusive.

In any case, by adolescence, youths typically understand prejudice at a broader, societal level and can compare their attitudes about their group to how their group is portrayed in the media (e.g., "If one [Mexican] did something, it's like all the Mexicans in the world did everything bad"). In addition, adolescents begin to be aware of structural forms of racism and cultural differences in the endorsement of stereotypes (Brown & Bigler, 2005).

Similarly, adolescents begin to develop attitudes about specific social policies that mirror those of adults. Substantial racial differences in attitudes about race-conscious social policies, such as affirmative action, emerge in late (e.g., 16- to 17-year-olds), rather than early (14- to 15-year-olds), adolescents (Hughes & Bigler, 2011). In addition, support for affirmative action became more closely linked to knowledge about historical racism among black youth. Similarly, white youth were less likely to support affirmative action if they held implicit antiblack biases. Support for school desegregation became more closely related with age to awareness of racial disparities and attributions of disparities to racism for both racial groups.

1.4.2. Racial and Ethnic Identity

Not only do children show preferences for some racial and ethnic groups and develop an awareness of prejudice, they must also place themselves *within* a racial or ethnic group and come to terms with their own group membership. Research has shown that children can label their own and others' race correctly by age 6 (Aboud, 1988; Katz & Kofkin, 1997). Racial and ethnic minority children are more likely to mention their ethnicity than are white children, however, and consider it more central to their sense of self (Ruble et al., 2004).

This early-acquisition point should be qualified, however. Although elementary school-age children are capable of identifying themselves by race, they may not consider race to be a salient aspect of their identity. Indeed, few young children mention race or ethnicity when describing themselves. Moreover, this early racial and ethnic identification is not necessarily terribly stable. One of the most important factors affecting ethnic identification seems to be context, particularly the school context. In one study, 85% of the youth who identified themselves as black /African American at sixth grade did so again when asked in eighth grade, but only if they attended a black majority school (the other students changed their identification to multiethnic). If they attended a Latino majority school, only 65% of such early black identifiers did so again later (one-third identifying as multiethnic and the others as Latino; Nishina, Bellmore, Witkow, & Nylund-Gibson, 2010).

Middle to late childhood (toward the end of elementary school) appears to be an important developmental period in which ethnic minority individuals think about and explore their ethnic identity (e.g., Marks, Szalacha, Lamarre, Boyd, & García Coll, 2007). Following this period of searching, adolescents achieve and make a commitment to an ethnic identity (Phinney, 1990), so well-developed ethnic identities only emerge in adolescence. In the United States, ethnic identities develop earlier among Latinos, Asians, and blacks than among whites (Brown et al., 2011). Studies consistently show ethnic group differences, such that the ethnic identity of European American adolescents is typically less salient, less developed, and less positive than that of ethnic minorities (i.e., African American, Latino, Native American, and Asian American; e.g., Roberts, Phinney, Masse, & Chenet, 1999; Sears, Fu, Henry, & Bui, 2003). Some research suggests that this ethnic difference is not apparent from the beginning, but only becomes evident among children in early adolescence (DuBois, Burk-Braxton, Swenson, Tevendale, & Hardesty, 2002).

Regardless of the exact age of development, the attainment of a well-developed ethnic identity is thought to be an important developmental milestone for racial or ethnic minority adolescents (Phinney, 1990; Quintana, 2007). It is a primary aspect of adolescents' developing self-concept and directly impacts a wide range of factors central to adolescents' daily lives (see Brown & Chu, 2012; Chao & Otsuki-Clutter, 2011). By college age, minorities' ethnic identification has become quite stable (Sears et al., 2003). It has been shown to be a complex and multidimensional component of the self-concept (see Ashmore, Deaux, & McLaughlin-Volpe, 2004 for a review; also Sellers, Rowley, Chavous, Shelton, & Smith, 1997).

1.4.3. Perceptions of Discrimination

Research psychologists have started to focus increasingly on racism from the targets' perspective, specifically on perceived racial or ethnic discrimination. Among very young children, exclusion of others based on social group membership appears to be the most recognizable form of discrimination (e.g., Killen & Stangor, 2001). During the elementary school years, children develop a more detailed and nuanced awareness of discrimination. In one study, most Dutch children (92%) were familiar with the meaning of discrimination by the age of 10, with name-calling being the most frequently cited example, followed by an unequal sharing of goods and social exclusion (Verkuyten, Kinket, & Van Der Wielen, 1997). Children avoided classifying negative behavior as discriminatory, however, if they considered either the target to be responsible for the negative behavior, or the perpetrator to have acted unintentionally. By age 10, the majority of children (90%) inferred that it was individuals' stereotypic beliefs that led them to engage in discrimination (McKown & Weinstein, 2003).

Peer discrimination seems to be the most common type perceived by children and adolescents (Brown et al., 2011; Fisher, Wallace, & Fenton, 2000). For example, one study found that the majority of black 10- to 12-year-olds reported having experienced at least one instance of racial discrimination from a peer, with verbal insults and racial slurs reported as the most common (Simons et al., 2002). Fisher et al. (2000) report similar findings with their sample of black, Latino, South Asian, East Asian, and white adolescents. Many children also reported being excluded from activities because of their race, and a small number of children reported being threatened with physical harm (Simons et al., 2002).

Children and adolescents also perceive discrimination within institutions and in public settings (Brown et al., 2011). More than half of one sample of black and Latino adolescents perceived themselves to have been hassled by store clerks and to have received poor service at restaurants because of their race (Fisher et al., 2000). Many children and adolescents also reported being suspected of wrongdoing (Simons et al., 2002) and more than a quarter reported being hassled by the police (Fisher et al., 2000). Children and adolescents also perceive discrimination by teachers in educational settings (Brown et al., 2011; Rosenbloom & Way, 2004). Half of one sample of black and Latino adolescents reported that they had been graded unfairly because of their race, and approximately a quarter felt they had been discouraged from joining advanced-level classes and disciplined wrongly by teachers because of their race (Fisher et al., 2000). Another study found adolescents perceiving discrimination by teachers to occur at least a couple of times a year (Wong, Eccles, & Sameroff, 2003).

Although perceptions of peer-based discrimination remain stable across adolescence, perceptions of adult-based discrimination (which can include educational and institutional discrimination) seems to increase with age (Greene, Way, & Pahl, 2006; Fisher et al., 2000). For example, eighth-grade black students, but not fourth- or sixth-grade students, blamed the government's response to Hurricane Katrina on race and class discrimination (Brown et al., 2007). Not surprisingly, youth of color and those with a strong ethnic identity perceive more discrimination than white youth and/or those with a less important ethnic identity (e.g., Fisher et al., 2000; Romero & Roberts, 1998).

Despite having a generally positive and optimistic view of the government, as indicated earlier, children do perceive inequalities in the presidency. In 2005, well before the formal candidacy of Barack Obama, Bigler, Arthur, Hughes, and Patterson (2008) found that most 5- to 10-year olds were aware of the lack of gender and racial diversity among past presidents. Older and black children were especially attentive to the lack of racial diversity. The most common explanation the children gave for this lack of diversity was that the dominant group (e.g., men or whites) wouldn't vote for anyone else, with only one-quarter of children attributing it to a lack of leadership abilities among women and minorities. A majority of girls and black and Latino children felt that boys and whites were happy that no woman, black, or Latino had ever been president.

1.4.4. Conclusions

In general, children hold biases about social groups from an early age. With age and cognitive development, these biases lessen, albeit never disappear entirely. Children continue to hold biases and make internal attributions, however, about socioeconomic status. With increasingly complex cognitive abilities, children begin to understand how biases, such as discrimination, can contribute to social inequalities in contexts such as presidential elections. As children enter adolescence, they can better understand the role of institutions (because of more advanced perspective-taking abilities). Thus, adolescents have distinct attitudes about government and their role in the political process. Some groups of adolescents (e.g., African Americans) are particularly supportive of the government playing a role in addressing social inequalities, and these early differences seem to foreshadow party identification differences in adulthood.

2. ADULT LIFE HISTORY

The American Voter's (Campbell et al., 1960) theory of party identification described earlier, with its focus on early learning, persistence, and later influence on voting behavior, provided a clear paradigm of lasting importance. Is it a useful model for thinking about political life histories more generally? Building on the various ways of thinking about time that we started with, four alternative models of the full political life cycle have been contrasted: (1) *persistence*: the residues of preadult learning persist through life; its variant, (2) *impressionable years*: orientations are particularly susceptible to influence in late adolescence and early adulthood, but tend to stabilize thereafter; its major alternative, (3) *lifelong openness*: individuals remain open to influence throughout later life, including by "the times"; and (4) *life cycle*: people show life stage-specific propensities (Alwin, Cohen, & Newcomb, 1991; Jennings & Niemi, 1981; Sears, 1975; Sears, 1983).

2.1. Persistence

2.1.1. Stability within Individuals

What is the plasticity of important political and social attitudes through the life span? From a political perspective, if the most important attitudes are essentially static after early life, public opinion would always be frozen in anachronisms. Modernizing change would occur primarily by replacement of older individuals by younger ones with fresher attitudes, rather than by conversion of adults based on the intrinsic merits of new views.

The most straightforward method for assessing persistence measures a given orientation in the same set of respondents at multiple points in time, in "longitudinal" or "panel" studies. The most representative samples come from several four-year panel studies conducted by the American National Election Studies (ANES). Party identification was the most stable attitude measured in those studies and indeed was almost perfectly stable with some correction for measurement unreliability (Converse & Markus, 1979). Similar conclusions have emerged from other such studies in the United States, Canada, Britain, and Germany (Green, Palmquist, & Schickler, 2002).

Three other studies yield evidence of stability across much longer periods of adulthood, though in less representative samples. The long-term Michigan socialization study of the student and parent cohorts described earlier found that party identification was highly stable through the mature adult years (Stoker & Jennings, 2008). The appraisal of its findings by Lewis-Beck et al. (2008, p. 143) was that in the parent cohort, "the degree of persistence over a nearly 20-year span is impressive, while in the student cohort, spending its youth in a particularly turbulent time in American politics and society," party identification "proves less stable" (p. 143) between the first two interviews, but highly stable through mature adulthood.

The classic "Bennington study" tracked a cohort of women who had attended Bennington College during the 1930s for nearly half a century afterwards (Alwin et al., 1991). Their partisanship showed extremely high stability from college graduation through adulthood: "The stability coefficient linking a latent attitude variable over roughly 50 years of the life-span is in the .70 to .80 range" (Alwin, 1993, p. 68; also see Alwin et al., 1991). The long-term Terman Study of Gifted Children tested the partisanship of a considerably larger and more heterogeneous sample, selected from high-IQ children in California public elementary schools after World War I, from 1940 to 1977 (approximately ages 30 to 67). Their party identifications were quite stable through the period, with a coefficient of .65 corrected for measurement error (Sears & Funk, 1999). The overall conclusion drawn from these panel studies is that party identification is "firm but not immoveable" (Lewis-Beck et al., 2008, p. 142).

The party identification of Americans, then, has become the paradigmatic case for attitudinal persistence. One caveat should be mentioned, however. The customary indicator of stability, a high test-retest correlation, can be somewhat misleading if the marginal frequencies have changed; individual attitudes may have changed even though relative rank orders may not have. The conclusion that party identification is highly stable required both high stability coefficients and a period in which basic party divisions remained more or less constant (Converse, 1976).

Some other attitudes show considerable stability over time. The conventional wisdom is that racial attitudes and basic ideological position are also among the most stable of Americans' political attitudes, though less than party identification (Converse & Markus, 1979; Stoker & Jennings, 2008; Sears, 1983; Alwin et al., 1991). For example, only 13% changed from "liberal" to "conservative," or vice versa, from about age 30 to retirement age in the Terman gifted children study (Sears & Funk, 1999). Moral attitudes, such as those toward abortion and marijuana, have also been found to be highly stable in some of these studies (Converse & Markus, 1979; Stoker & Jennings, 2008).

Political engagement is another product of preadult socialization that seems to be quite stable across the life cycle. Prior (2010) analyzed numerous panel surveys in four different countries and found adolescents' self-reported political interest highly stable well into adulthood. Men tend to be more psychologically involved in politics in adulthood than women are, and Wolak and McDevitt (2011) found that that gap exists already in adolescence. They also found that the occurrence of a political campaign season bolsters adolescents' political engagement, but does not eliminate the gender gap.

One potential general challenge to the persistence model is the pervasive correlation of higher education with political orientations. If those correlations are the products of higher education influencing the residues of preadult socialization, the impressionable years model might offer a better explanation for them. For example, political engagement is generally greater among the better educated. The association is typically strong, and the conventional inference is causal, that a college education contributes to various skills and interests that promote political sophistication, participation, and so on. Alternatively, selection effects may explain the association: perhaps the college-bound are more politically engaged even before attending a single class (Highton, 2009; Kam

& Palmer, 2008). As might be expected, unraveling the causal flows among such closely related variables both inspires debate and has led to the use of increasingly sophisticated methodologies (see Henderson & Chatfield, 2011; Kam & Palmer, 2011).

On the other hand, attitudes in many other policy domains intensely debated by political elites seem to show much less stability over time in the mass public (Converse, 1964; Converse & Markus, 1979). Rather than one model of the political life cycle fitting all, the trajectories of both individuals and aggregates are likely to vary across orientations. Why do some preadult orientations persist for so long when others are more open to change? The evidence on family transmission is a suggestive parallel. Persistence may stem from a high-volume and/or one-sided flow of communication in the individual's microenvironment. The opportunity to practice the orientation in conversation and behavior may also facilitate it. The meaning of the political object may need to be constant as well. For example, Americans' party identifications and racial attitudes are cases of relatively high levels of information flow, and so presumably are sources of conversation and opportunities for behavioral practice, conditions favorable to persistence (Valentino & Sears, 1998). But many policy issues scarcely come to public attention at all and so may involve considerably lower levels of such favorable conditions (Sears, 1983). And the cognitive meaning of the two parties, in terms of their positions on racial and other issues, changed dramatically in the 1960s, with the result that massive changes have occurred in white southerners' party identifications (Green et al., 2002; Osborne, Sears, & Valentino, 2011).

Persistence also should be greater for orientations toward attitude objects salient in early life than for those that only become salient later in life, even if in the same general domain. Here election campaigns as occasions for the socialization of partisanship may serve as a model, as indicated earlier. White adults' migration between the racially conservative South and the more racially liberal North is another example. Region of origin dominated whites' adult attitudes about older issues such as racial intermarriage, while region of adult residence had a stronger effect on issues that became prominent in later years, such as busing for school integration or affirmative action (Glaser & Gilens, 1997).

Many policy attitudes, however, do not show high levels of stability over time (Converse, 1964; Converse & Markus, 1979). Converse (1964; 2000) speculated that many were "non-attitudes," that many people simply had no fixed attitude toward issues they were only vaguely familiar with. Alternatively, Achen (1975) suggested that much observed attitude instability may simply be due to measurement error, perhaps due to ambiguous survey items. Yet a third possibility is that it reflects respondent ambivalence about the issue. If different and conflicting considerations come to mind in two different interviews, unstable summary responses may result (Zaller & Feldman, (1992). These issues remain somewhat unresolved (Converse, 2000; Kinder, 2006).

2.1.2. *Aggregate Stability*

Longitudinal studies are expensive and difficult to execute. The long-term studies often examine just one period and/or birth cohort, limiting their ability to distinguish persistence from cohort or period-specific effects. *Cohort analysis* can assess aggregate-level persistence using cross-sectional surveys conducted at different times with different samples. Indirect evidence of individual-level persistence is provided if each birth cohort maintains the same distribution of opinion as it ages, and individual-level change can be inferred if cohorts change over time. For example, the greatly increased support for general principles of racial equality among white Americans in the half-century after World War II (Schuman, Steeh, Bobo, & Krysan, 1997) is likely to be due primarily to a mixture of cohort replacement (more prejudiced older cohorts were gradually replaced by less prejudiced younger ones) and some liberalizing individual attitude changes within cohorts (period effects; Danigelis & Cutler, 1991; Firebaugh & Davis, 1988). These liberalizing trends within cohorts began to slow by the 1980s, especially on newer racial issues (Steeh & Schuman, 1991; Wilson, 1996; for similar analyses on broader ranges of attitudes, see Davis, 1992; Danigelis, Hardy, & Cutler, 2007).

Natural experiments also can provide indirect evidence about individual-level persistence by testing the resistance to change of presumably early-acquired attitudes when people are placed in altered attitudinal environments. For example, migration between congressional districts dominated by opposite parties influences adults' voting preferences and party identification (Brown, 1988). Some direct personal experiences in adulthood might also be expected to produce change. One common expectation is that the emergence of economic interests in adulthood will influence individuals' political attitudes. However, extensive research has found surprisingly limited evidence that self-interest has much effect on adults' political attitudes, as if earlier-acquired sociopolitical attitudes resisted such influences in adulthood (Citrin & Green, 1990; Sears & Funk, 1991; but see Chong, 2000).

Most of the literature has interpreted persistence, when it occurs, as a product of the psychological strength of the orientation. An alternative is that hereditary transmission dominates potential environmental influences (see Funk, chapter 8, this volume). Any impact of the direct indicators of family political socialization described earlier, such as clear parental attitudes and strong family communication, is inconsistent with the hereditary account. A nuanced version of the hereditary hypothesis has been offered by Hatemi et al. (2009), however. They too found convincing evidence of the family's role into early adulthood. But from age 21 on, cross-twin correlations begin to be larger for monozygotic (identical) twins than for dizygotic (fraternal) twins, a key finding for the hereditary view. Perhaps family influences get replaced by inherent hereditary tendencies when the individual leaves the parental nest. This is an area of research that will no doubt grow in the future.

2.2. The Impressionable Years

The "impressionable years" hypothesis (Sears, 1975) is a variant of the persistence hypothesis, suggesting a "critical period" in early adulthood when political orientations are especially open to influence. Mannheim (1952) speculated that the period might be approximately from ages 17 to 25. Three psychological propositions are involved. One is that core orientations are still incompletely crystallized as the individual enters that period, contrary to the persistence model, and gains may be seen through early adulthood. Second, that process should be complete as the individual enters mature adulthood, so crystallization should show only modest gains thereafter. And third, people may experience political life as a "fresh encounter" during that critical period, one that can seldom be duplicated later (Mannheim, 1952). In Erikson's (1968) terms, young adults are becoming more aware of the social and political world around them just when they are seeking a sense of self and identity. As a result, they may be especially open to influence at that stage.

On the first point, even attitudes that may be relatively highly crystallized by late adolescence may still show increased crystallization in early adulthood. Party identification followed that pattern in the Michigan socialization study, both showing greater stability than almost all other attitudes when the student sample left adolescence, and impressive gains through early adulthood (Jennings & Niemi, 1981). More recent studies show similar gains in early adulthood in racial attitudes, religiosity, and social dominance orientation (Henry & Sears, 2009; Sears & Henry, 2008; Ho et al., 2012).

Second, core orientations should be more stable over time once the individual is past the impressionable years. Data from two four-year NES panel studies show that all older cohorts had substantially more stable party identifications than did the youngest cohort (Alwin et al., 1991; Sears, 1983). The youngest cohort in the earlier study also showed greatly increased stability when re-sampled in the later study, when it was 16 years older, suggesting that the increased stability with age was an aging rather than a period effect (Alwin, 1993). The Michigan socialization study cited earlier also showed that high school seniors had substantially lower levels of attitude stability across early adulthood than did their parents in later adulthood. After the students reached their thirties, though, their attitudes had become as stable as their parents' attitudes (Lewis-Beck et al., 2008; Stoker & Jennings, 2008).

On the other hand, orientations that are subjected to strong information flows and regularly practiced might simply become stronger with age with no sharp discontinuity in early adulthood (Converse, 1969; Sears, 1983). Indeed cohort analyses in the United States show that each cohort expresses stronger party identifications as it ages, at least during what Converse (1976) described as the "steady state era" of roughly constant partisan divisions prior to the 1970s (Lewis-Beck et al., 2008; Miller & Shanks, 1996). Such aging effects have been obtained in the UK as well (Cassel, 1999).

If indeed attitudes that are well practiced become stronger with age, one might expect that the elderly would show the least change of all. Surprisingly enough, there is some evidence that the relationship of age to attitude stability follows an inverted-U pattern. Racial prejudice among whites in the 1972–1976 ANES panel study was least stable over time for the youngest (under 30) and oldest (over 60) age groups (Sears, 1981). Moreover, in a period of liberalizing racial attitudes, the oldest cohort actually liberalized the most. These findings held up with education controlled, and measurement reliability showed no slippage in the oldest cohort. Similar decreases in the stability of party identification occurred in two ANES panel studies, even with corrections for measurement unreliability (Alwin et al., 1991; Alwin, 1993). Why these attitudes might become more unstable in old age is unclear. However many of the ways in which people are socially embedded often do change in old age, in terms of work, residence, family, and other social networks, which may destabilize political attitudes.

The third implication is that core attitudes ought to become more resistant to influence as the individual ages. Three surveys analyzed by Visser and Krosnick (1998) yielded such effects. Another found that changes in one's youthful social environment, as indexed by demographic location, had considerably greater influence on levels of racial tolerance than changes later in life (Miller & Sears, 1986; also see Glaser & Gilens, 1997). In another study, migration between congressional districts dominated by opposite parties influenced adults' voting preferences and party identification, with greater change among those migrating earlier in life (Brown, 1988). However, another extensive cohort analysis of tolerance-related attitudes found as much intracohort change over time among older (60-plus) as among younger (under 40) adults (Danigelis et al., 2007).

An excellent case study of the impressionable years hypothesis examined the long-term effects on draft-eligible young men of being subjected to the draft lottery during the Vietnam War (Erikson & Stoker, 2011). A process for randomly assigning young men to draft-eligible status was instituted in 1969 to replace the system of college deferments that had been criticized as class-biased. Low lottery numbers, based on the individual's date of birth, made men more vulnerable to the draft. The Michigan socialization panel study was used because its youth cohort was exactly of the age to be included in the lottery. Those who had had the college deferments that were expiring were vulnerable; the noncollege members of the youth cohort were not, having already passed through exposure to the draft. Erikson and Stoker found that having low lottery numbers in the college group was much more strongly associated with opposition to the war than was the case among those whose military status had already been resolved one way or another. Moreover, the anticipation of vulnerability to the draft led to more antiwar attitudes than did actual past military service.

The impressionable years hypothesis is a good fit for what happened thereafter. In the 1973 interviews, lottery number trumped prelottery party identification as a predictor of preferences for the antiwar presidential candidate, George McGovern, reflecting the continuing influence of a significant event occurring in that earlier critical period. And in 1997, when the original student sample was middle-aged, lottery number still strongly predicted their attitudes toward the Vietnam War. Moreover, postlottery party identification dominated prelottery party identification in predicting key political attitudes among the lottery-vulnerable, but not among their counterparts who had been spared. The attitude changes that had occurred in the impressionable years were highly persistent, as was their continuing influence.

2.3. Political Generations

The impressionable years hypothesis focuses on the particular susceptibility to influence of individuals' attitudes in late adolescence and early adulthood. But if "the times"

(AKA the *zeitgeist*) embody compelling new ideas, sometimes people in that life stage can be influenced in common, producing generational differences. Mannheim (1952) suggested, more narrowly, that "generational units," or subsets of those in that impressionable stage (which, as indicated above, he arbitrarily defined as ages 17 to 25), may share powerful experiences that will mark them as distinctive for life. Either way, producing such generational effects requires both that individuals have a particular psychological openness at that life stage and that a cohort be exposed to unique and evocative political experiences in common.

Several such generational effects have received intensive empirical study. One is the "New Deal generation" in the United States. Youthful new voters who first entered the electorate during the 1930s remained substantially more Democratic into the 1950s, both in voting behavior and in party identification, than were earlier cohorts at similar ages (Campbell et al., 1960; Centers, 1950; Elder, 1974). The young protestors in the United States and Europe in the 1960s became another quite self-conscious generational unit. Most evidence indicates that their left-liberal distinctiveness persisted for many years thereafter, especially among those who actively engaged in protest. For example, the students in the Michigan socialization study who said they had been active as protestors in 1973 continued to be considerably more liberal than were college-educated nonprotestors, even as late as 1997 (Jennings, 1987; also see Fendrich & Lovoy, 1988; Marwell, Aiken, & Demerath, 1987; McAdam, 1989). Interestingly enough, their offspring were more liberal than the offspring of nonprotestors (Jennings, 2002). Even "engaged observers"—those who were attentive to the movements but not very active in them—showed lasting political effects years later (Stewart, Settles, & Winter, 1998).

Partisanship in the generation that immediately followed is another case in point. A number of issues divided both parties internally in the mid-1960s to mid-1970s, such as civil rights, conflict over the Vietnam War, and the Watergate scandal. Disenchantment with the parties ensued among many of their normal supporters, reducing the strength of partisanship in the generation then entering the electorate. Debates continue today over whether partisan strength among incoming youthful cohorts subsequently turned back up (Miller & Shanks, 1996), or whether that era foreshadowed a more lasting dealignment (Dalton, 2013; Hajnal & Lee, 2011; Wattenberg, 1998). Much turns on the seemingly arcane, but politically crucial, treatment of "leaning independents," those who declare they are "independent" rather than aligned with either party, but who also say they lean toward one party; specifically whether they are really "closet partisans" or more closely resemble dealigned independents. A related debate is whether the American public is now more politically polarized than ever (Abramowitz, 2010; Hetherington & Weiler, 2009) or remains mainly ideologically moderate but has simply "sorted" itself into more ideologically homogeneous parties (Fiorina, Abrams, & Pope, 2011; Levendusky, 2009).

Finally, a potentially rich line of investigation concerns persisting possible generational effects of political or social traumas, though much of this work has been left to nonquantitative historians. Loewenberg (1971), for example, suggests that the unusually powerful support for the Nazi regime among Germans born from 1900 to 1915 can be ascribed in part to the many traumas they had experienced in early life, including malnutrition and starvation, disease, parental neglect and permanent father absence, and hyperinflation. Direct exposure to political violence has been shown to increase the likelihood of psychopathology in studies from Israel and South Africa (Slone, Adiri, & Arian, 1998; Slone, Kaminer, & Durrheim, 2000). Even exposure to distal violence, such as the assassination of a popular leader, can have profound emotional effects in the short run (Raviv, Sadeh, Raviv, Silberstein, & Diver, 2000; Wolfenstein & Kliman, 1965), and perhaps long-term political effects as well (Sears, 2002).

However occasional generational effects more usually appear in the midst of a cloud of generational similarities. For example, Harding and Jencks (2003) found that pre-marital sex has become more morally acceptable in America since the early 1960s. They also found that younger cohorts have been more liberal throughout. But that may not be a generational effect. They found that the sharpest liberalizing changes occurred in *all* cohorts during a narrow window of time from 1969 to 1973. Current age differences, with older adults more conservative than the young, may therefore reflect aging rather than generational effects (also see Danigelis et al., 2007). Osborne et al. (2011) found both generational and within-cohort changes as southern whites moved from the Democratic to the Republican Party following racial liberalization of the national Democratic Party. Tessler, Konold, and Reif (2004) did find a lasting generational distinctiveness in attitudes toward the Boumedienne regime among Algerians who came of age in the 1960s and 1970s, but less clear differences in other orientations and/or other cohorts. And finally, Davis (2004) cautions against expecting both broad and sharp generational differences in social and political attitudes in the aftermath of the 1960s (also see Danigelis et al., 2007).

Another set of generational effects is reflected in *collective memory*, defined as "memories of a shared past that are retained by members of a group, large or small, that experienced it," especially "shared memories of societal-level events" (Schuman & Scott, 1989, pp. 361–362; also see Halbwachs [1950] 1980). Howard Schuman (e.g., Schuman & Corning, 2012) has extensively tested whether "national or world changes" occurring in one's impressionable years are especially likely to be recalled later as "especially important." The age cohort most likely to select World War II had been 20, on average, in 1943; the Vietnam War was selected by those averaging age 20 in 1968. Elderly Germans and Japanese in 1991 were especially likely to mention World War II (Schuman, Akiyama, & Knauper, 1998). Ascribing great importance to the assassination of JFK peaked among those who had been in childhood and adolescence in 1963. Even simple pieces of information, such as FDR's party, or the New Deal program called the WPA, have shown marked generational differences years later.

Collective memories, of course, can be the stuff of intense political debate. The period after 1880 is sometimes known as the "Second Civil War," as former Confederates and Unionists struggled to control the dominant narrative history of the original Civil War, including the role of slavery in causing the conflict, whether Grant or Lee was the superior general, which army was the more courageous, and whether the outcome was due to superior soldiering or to mere material wealth (Fahs & Waugh, 2004; Waugh, 2009).

Respondents were asked in 1990 whether the best analogy for the conflict in the Persian Gulf created by the Iraq leader Saddam Hussein's invasion of Kuwait was the incumbent President G. H. W. Bush's "Hitler" metaphor of a voracious dictator, or the opposition Democrats' "Vietnam" metaphor of a Third World quagmire. Those over 40 strongly preferred the Hitler analogy, whereas those under 40 were split evenly between the two analogies (Schuman & Rieger, 1992). Tellingly, once the American coalition went to war against Iraq, the Hitler metaphor became the overwhelming favorite, and generational differences disappeared. The collective memories held by ordinary people may sometimes not correspond to those of the political classes, as seen in Palestinians' beliefs about the 1948 Palestinian exodus from what is now Israel (Nets-Zehngut, 2011). The political classes emphasized Israeli-Palestinian conflict, and Israeli efforts to expel Palestinians from what became Israeli territory, a theme less common in ordinary Palestinians' collective memories.

Robert Jervis (1976) has applied this notion of collective memory to the question of how foreign policy decision-makers "learn from history." Political leaders who have dramatic and important firsthand experiences in politics when they are in the "impressionable years" may later apply those "lessons" to issues they must deal with as public officials. For example, Harry Truman, confronting the North Korean invasion of South Korea in 1950, and Lyndon Johnson, facing the Vietnam War, both recalled that the buildup to World War II had taught them the danger of not facing up to aggressors at an early stage. Colin Powell and other military leaders who had been young officers in the 1960s later applied the lesson of Vietnam to, among other things, the Persian Gulf War: don't go to war half-heartedly, they said; either stay out or go in with overwhelming force. The danger of those early-learned "lessons," as with any persisting generational effects, is of course that they are long out of date by the time the young person becomes a mature adult, as in the cliché that the military is always "fighting the last war."

2.4. Life Cycle Effects

These questions about the persistence of early learning, as opposed to the continuing openness to new experience, by no means exhaust the possible contributions of a life-span development approach to political psychology. Correlations of age with political orientations can logically reflect cohort, period, or life cycle effects. While these cannot be rigorously distinguished in cohort analyses (Mason, Mason, Winsborough, & Poole, 1973), given only two pieces of information (age and time of measurement), sometimes other information can help.

One common life cycle hypothesis is that people become more conservative with age. However, cohort analyses show that is not necessarily true either for partisanship or racial conservatism. In the 1950s, age was positively correlated with Republicanism, when the elderly came from pre–New Deal cohorts, a period of Republican dominance. In a later era, when the elderly were predominantly from the

"New Deal generation," they tilted toward the Democrats (Crittenden, 1962). And young voters moved sharply toward the Republicans during the Reagan era (Lewis-Beck et al., 2008; Miller & Shanks, 1996). These reflect generational rather than life cycle effects on partisanship. Danigelis et al.'s (2007) extensive cohort analyses comparing older and younger cohorts' trajectories found quite a mixture of intracohort changes, most in the direction of greater tolerance with age; but older cohorts never overshot younger ones.

Age also correlated positively with support for Jim Crow racism among whites in the decades after World War II (Schuman et al., 1997). However, as noted earlier, cohort analyses have shown waning support for it within cohorts of white Americans as they aged during that period, reflecting period and cohort, not life cycle, effects on racial conservatism (Sears, 1981; Firebaugh & Davis, 1988; Danigelis & Cutler, 1991). Indeed, life cycle effects on attitudes have generally been difficult to pin down (Alwin, 1993; Danigelis et al., 2007).

Young Americans usually show relatively low levels of political engagement, for example, in political information, newspaper reading, political interest, and voting turnout. Part of this is a life cycle effect, as young people generally have been less politically engaged than mature adults through most periods. But today it is partly a generational effect as well, surprisingly so since educational level is almost always correlated with more political engagement, and recent generations have received much more formal education (e.g., Delli Carpini, 2000). Putnam (2000) famously found declines in voter turnout, communal and organizational participation, and trust in people among more recent generations, arguing that they reflect a generational decline in "social capital." He suggests that the rise of television has disrupted such communal activities, though evidence for its role is necessarily somewhat indirect. Others implicate declines in newspaper reading and/or reduced perceived duty to vote in reduced voter turnout among the young (Dalton, 2008; Wattenberg, 2008). Still others conclude that the generational decline in turnout has generally largely resisted efforts at explanation (e.g., Highton & Wolfinger, 2001; Miller & Shanks, 1996).

Finally, the chronically low voting turnout of young people may indeed be a life cycle effect, but may perhaps reflect sociological as well as psychological processes. A psychological interpretation would be that consistent turnout develops through greater experience with the political system. A sociological alternative is that young people are distracted from civic duties by the press of various transitions into adult roles, such as leaving home, leaving school, entering the workforce, getting married, owning a home, and, often, moving geographically. If so, turnout might increase with age merely because people ultimately mature past such obstacles. Comparing these two views, Highton and Wolfinger (2001) found that successfully transitioning into such adult roles had quite mixed effects on turnout, whereas aging all by itself greatly increased it: having accomplished all six such adult tasks increased voting turnout by only 6%, a small fraction of the 37% turnout gap between the young and those over age 60. The authors prefer the more psychological explanation that "pure learning" may be responsible (p. 208).

3. Contextual Changes

3.1. Lifelong Openness

The challenges to the persistence and impressionable years models driven by researchers arguing for more lifelong openness have often provided valuable evidence, even if perhaps sometimes interpreted overly enthusiastically. An influential line of work argues that adults' partisanship is in fact responsive to "the times." The theory of "retrospective voting" suggests that party identification is constantly being modified by new information about the parties' performances (Fiorina, 1981). The notion of "macropartisanship" (Erikson, MacKuen, & Stimson, 2002) describes fluctuations over time in the aggregate distribution of party identification, sometimes over just a few days. Other research shows the influence of changes in candidate images, issues, or events (Niemi & Jennings, 1991; Dalton, 2013).

Beyond that, we simply wish to put up some cautionary flags. An impressive series of studies collected by Sigel (1989) examines the political effects of discontinuities within adulthood, such as entering the workplace, serving in the military, immigrating to a new country, participating in social movements, entering college, getting married, or becoming a parent. Each of these cases, as she notes, incorporates three elements that potentially can affect political attitudes: the crystallization of an individual's own unique identity, assumption of new roles, and coping with the novel and unanticipated demands of adulthood. However, all these specific discontinuities also occur most often in late adolescence and early adulthood, again suggesting such findings may better fit the impressionable years model. And even the mostly youthful but clearly evocative personal experience of military service in Vietnam was found by the Michigan socialization study to have only "modest" lasting political effects (Jennings & Markus, 1977).

Another caution involves the findings cited earlier that mature adults change their attitudes when they encounter major discontinuities in their attitudinal environments. But relatively few people are exposed to such discontinuities after early adulthood. For example, migration from an area dominated by one political party to an area dominated by its opponents does affect partisanship, but is almost three times as likely among young adults as among their elders (Brown, 1988). Migration between North and South affected white adults' racial attitudes, but only about 10% of them had engaged in such migration in both directions combined (Glaser & Gilens, 1997). The microenvironments represented by individuals' social networks also tend to be politically supportive, and indeed disagreements are underrecognized (see Huckfeldt, Mondak, Hayes, Pietryka, and Reilly, chapter 21, this volume). Normally environmental continuity is quite great, and when it breaks down, change may occur, but both environmental change, and any subsequent attitudinal change, are more common in the "impressionable years."

Nevertheless the broader political context can set conditions that facilitate such individual-level processes producing change in adults. For example, the polarization of party elites on racial issues led to a substantial shift of southern whites to Republicans beginning in the 1960s, though the exact mixture of cohort replacement and individual-level change is not clear cut (Osborne et al., 2011; Green et al., 2002; Miller & Shanks, 1996). The shift away from Jim Crow racism in the white public after the civil rights era (Schuman et al., 1997) was presumably facilitated by elite rejection of the southern segregation system, apparently resulting in a mixture of between- and within-cohort changes (Firebaugh & Davis, 1988).

Similarly, the life-cycle-based strengthening of party identification with age should partly be dependent on the stability of the party system itself. As noted earlier, in the United States, intraparty disputes in the period around the early 1970s resulted in reduced strength of partisanship in most cohorts as they aged, contrary to its usual trajectory. More generally, Converse (1969) found that age was associated with stronger party identifications in the mature democratic systems of the United States and UK, but considerably less so in the interrupted democratic systems in Germany and Italy and in the immature electoral system of Mexico. Even Russia, in the aftermath of the demise of the USSR, has yielded some evidence of nascent partisanship that is stable across elections and with meaningful underlying attitudinal cleavages (Brader & Tucker, 2001; Miller & Klobucar, 2000). In general the persistence model seems to work best for parties that are large and/or old, consistent with the notion that people are most likely to acquire and hold strong attitudes about visible and stable attitude objects (Converse & Pierce, 1992; Sears, 1983).

3.2. Immigration

As with many areas of political psychology, the available evidence about childhood and adult development rests heavily on the American political experience. It is not obviously the most typical case, given, among other things, its highly stable party system, even compared to other developed democracies. As noted above, examining people only in a stable political context risks overestimating the psychological basis for continuities within individual life histories. As one check, we can look at immigrants, who have experienced a variety of changes in their lives, including the political system they live in.

We start with the trajectory of national and ethnic identities after childhood. The persistence hypothesis would suggest that identification with the original nationality group might follow the dominant pattern of the European immigrants of a century ago, being stable within immigrants' life spans, and even passed on to their children, generating a strong ethnic group consciousness in politics (Alba, 1990; Alba & Nee, 2003; Wolfinger, 1965). On the other hand, contemporary youthful immigrants might later in life replace their original national identity (e.g., "Mexican") with an American ethnic identity (e.g., "Latino"), a process consistent with the impressionable years model. Perhaps in later generations the American ethnic identity might become secondary to identification with the destination nation (e.g., "American"), following acculturation through inter-marriage, residential and occupational integration, and/or socioeconomic mobility.

Another possibility, consistent with the "lifelong openness" view, is that such changes in identity might all occur within a single generation regardless of the immigrants' ages. A mixed alternative would be a more "segmented assimilation," in which some immigrants follow the trajectory of assimilation to American identities, while others remain poor and with low levels of education, their efforts rebuffed by discrimination, rejecting core American values, instead developing a strongly alienated ethnic identity (Portes & Rumbaut, 2001).

Several recent studies test these alternatives. Some surveys of Latino adults asked, "How do you primarily think of yourself: just as an American, both as an American and (ethnicity), or only as an (ethnicity)?" Latinos tended to pass through three distinct stages as a function of immigration status. Noncitizen immigrants tended to identify themselves primarily as ethnics, and to feel a strong sense of ethnic identity. Naturalized immigrants overwhelmingly said "both," and also had a fairly strong sense of ethnic identity. Nonimmigrant Latinos were less likely to categorize themselves primarily as ethnic, their ethnic identification was weaker, and they had stronger patriotism about America (Citrin & Sears, 2012). Quite similar differences emerged from a large study of Asian Americans (Wong, Ramakrishnan, Lee, & Junn, 2011). Non-citizens were more likely to identity with their national ethnic group (e.g., "Chinese") than were naturalized citizens or the US-born, and less likely to use a hyphenated identity ("Chinese American") or pan-ethnic identity ("Asian American"). Similar differences were found in a large study of Asian and Latino undergraduates at UCLA (Sears et al., 2003). These findings yield evidence of the persistence of early identities, and for a gradual assimilation process among immigrant families.

Immigrants to America also provide a test of the boundaries of *The American Voter's* theory of party identification. If preadult crystallization depends in part on political discussions with parents, presumably children in immigrant families should not usually acquire strong partisanship. They should not be likely to be exposed to much family transmission, since their noncitizen parents do not vote in the United States and so are likely to have weak partisan preferences. Indeed the study of incoming freshmen just cited (Sears, Haley, & Henry, 2008) found that immigrant Asian and Latino students had the least crystallized partisanship, the US-born from both groups were intermediate, and white students (almost all native-born) had the most.

Hajnal and Lee (2011) go further to distinguish a two-stage sequence of immigrants' acquisition of party identification. In the first stage, many immigrants do not respond at all to questions about party identification, as if the concept had little meaning for them. Instead of giving the conventional responses "Democrat," "Republican," or "Independent," they often responded "none," "neither," "other," or "don't know," and so forth, and so were classified as "non-identifiers." Surveys done in 2006 and 2008 found that over a third of the heavily immigrant groups, Latinos and Asian Americans, were non-identifiers, while only 7 percent of blacks and whites were. Only those who pass this first stage ever become classified as identifying with one of the two parties or as an Independent. Treating immigrants' party identifications in terms of this two-stage sequence reinforces the centrality of parental socialization to the acquisition of partisanship. For example, Asian Americans with parents who were non-identifiers were far more likely to be non-identifiers themselves than those with partisan parents. Those with a Democratic father were 66% Democratic and 10% non-identifiers. Only 37% of the offspring of non-identifier fathers became Democrats, while 34% became non-identifiers themselves (Wong, et al. 2011).

More broadly, immigrants to the United States appear gradually to assimilate to the partisan norms of the dominant society. For example, a straight-line assimilation theory about immigrant groups goes far to explain the gradual disappearance of non-identifiers with greater time in the host country, and in later generations, a process Hajnal and Lee (2011) call "incorporation" into the politics of the society. Recent immigrants are more likely to be non-identifiers than the foreign-born who have been in the country for longer, or than those born in the United States. For example, among Latinos, 56% of the foreign-born were non-identifiers, but only 25% of the immigrants who had been in the country for at least 27 years were, and among the US-born, only 26% were (Hajnal & Lee, 2011). Among Asian Americans, 59% of those who had immigrated within the previous four years were non-identifiers, against only 29% of those arriving at least 25 years earlier, and 24% of the US-born (Wong et al., 2011). Beyond that, other indicators of incorporation contribute to the acquisition of partisanship; e.g., being better-informed, and/or having a definite political ideology.

Socioeconomic attainment plays a greater role in the second stage, party choice, than it does in leaving the first, "nonidentifier," stage. Working-class contemporary Latino immigrants gradually come to identify with the Democratic Party, just as had those arriving a century earlier from Europe (Cain, Kiewiet, & Uhlaner, 1991; de la Garza, DeSipio, Garcia, Garcia, & Falcon, 1992). So higher income is associated, as might be expected, with being more likely to identify as a Republican (Hajnal & Lee, 2011).

But immigrants may also import old loyalties and antagonisms from their native countries, as the persistence model would suggest. For example, a majority of the immigrants from Cuba, Vietnam, Korea, and Taiwan, heavily composed of political refugees from Communism during the vigorously anti-Communist Reagan era, became Republicans, especially those fleeing at the height of Communist power. In a survey of Asian Americans, Vietnamese were more likely to identify as Republicans, whereas Japanese and Asian Indians were more likely to identify as Democrats (Wong, et al., 2011). Democrats command large majorities among those from Mexico or Puerto Rico, who tend to immigrate more often for economic reasons (Hajnal & Lee, 2011). There is also some evidence that involvement in a previous political system tends to foster immigrants' politicization. Black (1987) found that participation and partisanship in the Canadian political system were higher among the immigrants who had been the most interested in politics and politically active in their home countries.

Immigrants also provide an interesting test case of the hypothesis that partisanship strengthens with political experience, for which age is usually taken as a proxy. Immigrants enter at a variety of different ages, so age does not bear a uniform relationship to the amount of political experience they have had with the political system of the receiving nation. Rather, the strength of their partisanship should be a function of time since immigration. Indeed the longer immigrants have lived in the United States, and the more generations their families have been in the United States, the more likely they are to develop a party identification and identify as a strong partisan (Hajnal & Lee, 2011; Wong et al., 2011). Their age does not matter much. Of course time in the new nation is not the only important variable. Naturalized citizens are more likely to acquire a partisan preference, and citizenship explains some of the effects of time, as if time doesn't "count" for as much until citizenship occurs, consistent with the presumed role of practice in the development of a partisan preference (Hajnal & Lee, 2011; Wong et al., 2011).

4. Conclusions

In our view, continuing research on the questions that first animated the field of political socialization, and extended it to the broader life cycle, has yielded somewhat surprising levels of support for its initial suppositions. The importance of the early learning of partisanship, prejudice, and racial and ethnic identity now seems evident. Even proponents of a revisionist view suggest that the findings all "point to much continuity in political-response patterns over the course of an individual's life," notwithstanding the new tasks and roles they later encounter, as well as "considerable change in sociopolitical attitudes and behaviors" in response to new contingencies (Sigel, 1989, p. 458); in addition, "the weight of these studies suggests that we should not usually expect dramatic evidence of change during adulthood" (Sapiro, 1994, p. 204). Much recent research nicely documents the conditions under which adult change is most likely to occur. There may have been something of an overcorrection against the most enthusiastic early claims, with the center of gravity of the field perhaps swinging a bit too far away from recognition of the substantial early learning and persistence manifested by some predispositions.

In recent years new foci of attention have arisen, such as the importance of cognitive (in additional to social) factors in the development of racial and ethnic attitudes and the increasing political importance of ethnic and national identity, that require developmental analyses, even if not to the exclusion of alternative approaches. Moreover, long-term persistence now is seen as not merely a function of pure psychology but also of a supportive social and political milieu.

We close with ruminations about two limitations of the literature as we have presented it. It has been to an excessive degree generated within North America. This reflects both where the main body of such research has been done and, even more, the limits of the authors' own knowledge. It narrows us particularly in assessing how changing political contexts influence the individual. For example, we present no solid estimate of the extent to which the great experiments at society-molding "took" in the Soviet Union, Nazi Germany, Mao's China, or Khomeini's Iran. Second, we have reviewed a good bit of work on how specifically political events have influenced political development. But these are presumably a subset of the ways in which individuals interact with the events of the larger world. Psychologists have not generally been sufficiently attentive to those interactions (though see Stewart & Healy, 1989).

Finally, we should be cautious about normative implications of the research described here. On the matters taken up in this chapter, there is typically no one ideal outcome that all will agree to. The nature of politics—indeed, its primary raison d'être—is to adjudicate disputes over competing interests and preferences, not to ratify consensus over political ends. Even ethnocentrism and prejudice are often seen as justified by those who hold them, as harshly as they are condemned by their victims and their sympathizers. Stereotypes have their beneficial uses as simplifiers and organizers, as much as they harm their victims and limit the social skills and circles of their holders. The merits of assimilation and separation of conflicting groups can be and are legitimately debated. And, as often was said in the months after the terrorist attacks on the World Trade Center, one man's "terrorist" is another man's "freedom fighter." If political psychology can teach us anything, it is that we must all constantly struggle to balance the natural tendency to glorify the familiar and those most like us with the need to sympathetically take the perspective of others. Social scientists may engage that struggle in more intellectual terms than the ordinary person, but a struggle it remains.

REFERENCES

Aboud, F. E. (1988). *Children and prejudice.* New York: Blackwell.

Aboud, F. E., & Skerry, S. A. (1984). The development of ethnic attitudes: A critical review. *Journal of Cross-Cultural Psychology, 15,* 3–34.

Abraham, K. G. (1983). Political thinking in the elementary years: An empirical study. *Elementary School Journal, 84,* 221–231.

Abramowitz, A. (2010). *The disappearing center: Engaged citizens, polarization, and American democracy.* New Haven, CT: Yale University Press.

Achen, C. H. (1975). Mass political attitudes and the survey response. *American Political Science Review, 69,* 1218–1231.

Alba, R. D. (1990). *Ethnic identity: The transformation of white America.* New Haven, CT: Yale University Press.

Alba, R. D., & Nee, V. (2003). *Remaking the American mainstream: Assimilation and contemporary immigration.* Cambridge, MA: Harvard University Press.

Alejandro-Wright, M. N. (1985). The child's conception of racial classification: A socio-cognitive model. In M. B. Spencer, G. K. Brookins, & W. R. Allen (eds.), *Beginnings: Social and affective development of black children* (pp. 185–200). Hillsdale, NJ: Erlbaum.

Alford, J. R., Hatemi, P. K., Hibbing, J. R., Martin, N. G., & Eaves, L. J. (2011). The politics of mate choice. *Journal of Politics, 73,* 362–379.

Alwin, D. F. (1993). Socio-political attitude development in adulthood: The role of generational and life-cycle factors. In D. Krebs & P. Schmidt (eds.), *New directions in attitude measurement* (pp. 61–93). Berlin: de Gruyter.

Alwin, D. F., Cohen, R. L., & Newcomb, T. M. (1991). *Aging, personality and social change: Attitude persistence and change over the life-span.* Madison: University of Wisconsin Press.

Ashmore, R. D., Deaux, K., & McLaughlin-Volpe, T. (2004). An organizing framework for collective identity: Articulation and significance of multidimensionality. *Psychological Bulletin, 130,* 80–114.

Augoustinos, M., & Rosewarne, D. (2001). Stereotype knowledge and prejudice in children. *British Journal of Developmental Psychology, 19,* 143–156.

Baldi, S., Ferie, M., Skidmore, D., Greenberg, E., & Hahn, C. (2001). *What democracy means to ninth-graders: U.S. results from the international IEA civic education study (NCES 2001-096).* U.S. Department of Education, National Center for Educational Statistics. Washington, DC: U.S. Government Printing Office.

Baron, A., & Banaji, M. (2006). The development of implicit attitudes: Evidence of race evaluations from ages 6, 10, and adulthood. *Psychological Science, 17,* 53–58.

Bar-Tal, D. (1996). Development of social categories and stereotypes in early childhood: The case of "the Arab" concept formation, stereotype and attitudes by Jewish children in Israel. *International Journal of Intercultural Relations, 20,* 341–370.

Beck, P. A., & Jennings, M. K. (1991). Family traditions, political periods, and the development of partisan orientation. *Journal of Politics, 53,* 742–763.

Bigler, R. S., Arthur, A. E., Hughes, J. M., & Patterson, M. M. (2008). The politics of race and gender: Children's perceptions of discrimination and the U.S. presidency. *Analyses of Social Issues and Public Policy, 8,* 83–112.

Bigler, R. S., Averhart, C. J., & Liben, L. S. (2003). Race and the workforce: Occupational status, aspirations, and stereotyping among African American children. *Developmental Psychology, 39,* 572–580.

Bigler, R. S., & Liben, L. S. (1993). A cognitive-developmental approach to racial stereotyping and reconstructive memory in Euro-American children. *Child Development, 64,* 1507–1518.

Black, J. H. (1987). The practice of politics in two settings: Political transferability among recent immigrants to Canada. *Canadian Journal of Political Science, 20,* 731–753.

Boulton, M. J., & Smith, P. K. (1996). Liking and peer perceptions among Asian and White British children. *Journal of Social and Personal Relationships, 13,* 163–177.

Brader, T., & Tucker, J. A. (2001). The emergence of mass partisanship in Russia, 1993–1996. *American Journal of Political Science, 45,* 69–83.

Brenick, A., Killen, M., Lee-Kim, J., Fox, N., Leavitt, L., Raviv, A., Masalha, S., Murra, F.& Al-Smadi, Y. (2010). Social understanding in young Israeli-Jewish, Israeli-Palestinian, Palestinian, and Jordanian children: Moral judgments and stereotypes. *Early Education and Development, 21,* 886–911.

Brown, C., Alabi, B. O., Huynh, V. W., & Masten, C. L. (2011). Ethnicity and gender in late childhood and early adolescence: Group identity and awareness of bias. *Developmental Psychology, 47,* 463–471.

Brown, C. S., & Bigler, R. S. (2005). Children's perceptions of discrimination: A developmental model. *Child Development, 76,* 533–553.

Brown, C. S., & Chu, H. (2012). Discrimination, ethnic identity, and academic outcomes of Mexican immigrant children: The importance of school context. *Child Development, 83,* 1477–1485.

Brown, C. S., Mistry, R. S., & Bigler, R. S. (2007). Hurricane Katrina: Children's perceptions of race, class, and government involvement amid a national crisis. *Analyses of Social Issues and Public Policy, 7,* 191–208.10.

Brown, G., & Johnson, S. P. (1971). The attribution of behavioural connotations to shaded and white figures by Caucasian children. *British Journal of Social & Clinical Psychology, 10,* 306–312.

Brown, T. A. (1988). *Migration and politics: The impact of population mobility on American voting behavior.* Chapel Hill: University of North Carolina Press.

Cain, B. E., Kiewiet, D. R., & Uhlaner, C. J. (1991). The acquisition of partisanship by Latinos and Asian Americans. *American Journal of Political Science, 35,* 390–422.

Cameron, J. A., Alvarez, J. M., Ruble, D. N., & Fuligni, A. J. (2001). Children's lay theories about ingroups and outgroups: Reconceptualizing research on prejudice. *Personality and Social Psychology Review, 5,* 118–128.

Campbell, A., Converse, P. E., Miller, W. E., & Stokes, D. E. (1960). *The American voter.* New York: Wiley.

Campbell, D. E., & Wolbrecht, C. (2006). See Jane run: Women politicians as role models for adolescents. *Journal of Politics, 68,* 233–247.

Cassel, C. A. (1999). Testing the Converse party support model in Britain. *Comparative Political Studies, 32,* 626–644.

Centers, R. (1950). Children of the New Deal: Social stratification and adolescent attitudes. *International Journal of Opinion and Attitude Research, 4,* 315–335.

Chafel, J., & Neitzel, C. (2005). Young children's ideas about the nature, causes, justification, and alleviation of poverty. *Early Childhood Research Quarterly, 20,* 433–450.

Chao, R. K., & Otsuki-Clutter, M. (2011). Racial and ethnic differences: Sociocultural and contextual explanations. *Journal of Research on Adolescence, 21,* 47–60.

Chong, D. (2000). *Rational lives.* Chicago: University of Chicago Press.

Citrin, J., & Green, D. P. (1990). The self-interest motive in American public opinion. In S. Long (ed.), *Research in micropolitics* (vol. 3, pp. 1–28). Greenwich, CT: JAI Press.

Citrin, J., & Sears, D. O. (2012). The politics of multiculturalism and the crisis of American identity. Manuscript.

Clark, K. B., & Clark, M. K. (1939). Segregation as a factor in the racial identification of Negro pre-school children: A preliminary report. *Journal of Experimental Psychology, 8,* 161–163.

Converse, P. E. (1964). The nature of belief systems in mass publics. In D. E. Apter (ed.), *Ideology and discontent* (pp. 206–261). New York: Free Press of Glencoe.

Converse, P. E. (1969). Of time and partisan stability. *Comparative Political Studies, 2,* 139–171.

Converse, P. E. (1976). *The dynamics of party support: Cohort-analyzing party identification.* Beverly Hills, CA: Sage.

Converse, P. E. (2000). Assessing the capacity of mass electorates. *Annual Review of Political Science, 3,* 331–353.

Converse, P. E., & Markus, G. B. (1979). Plus ça change...: The new CPS election study panel. *American Political Science Review, 73,* 32–49.

Converse, P. E., & Pierce, R. (1992). Partisanship and the party system. *Political Behavior, 14,* 239–259.

Cook, T. E. (1985). The bear market in political socialization and the costs of misunderstood psychological theories. *American Political Science Review, 79,* 1079–1093.

Crittenden, J. (1962). Aging and party affiliation. *Public Opinion Quarterly, 26,* 648–657.

Dalton, R. J. (2008). *The good citizen: How a younger generation is reshaping American politics.* Thousand Oaks, CA: CQ Press.

Dalton, R. J. (2013). *The apartisan American: Dealignment and changing electoral politics.* Thousand Oaks, CA: CQ Press.

Danigelis, N. L., & Cutler, S. J. (1991). An inter-cohort comparison of changes in racial attitudes. *Research on Aging, 13,* 383–404.

Danigelis, N. L., Hardy, M., & Cutler, S. J. (2007). Population aging, intracohort aging, and sociopolitical attitudes. *American Sociological Review, 72*, 812–830.

Davis, J. A. (1992). Changeable weather in a cooling climate atop the liberal plateau: Conversion and replacement in forty-two general social survey items, 1972–1989. *Public Opinion Quarterly, 56*, 261–306.

Davis, J. A. (2004). Did growing up in the 1960s leave a permanent mark on attitudes and values? *Public Opinion Quarterly, 68*, 161–183.

de la Garza, R. O., DeSipio, L., Garcia, F. C., Garcia, J., & Falcon, A. (1992). *Latino voices: Mexican, Puerto Rican, & Cuban perspectives on American politics.* Boulder, CO: Westview Press.

Delli Carpini, M. X. (2000). Gen.com: Youth, civic engagement, and the new information environment. *Political Communication, 17*, 341–349.

DuBois, D. L., Burk-Braxton, C., Swenson, L. P., Tevendale, H. D., & Hardesty, J. L. (2002). Race and gender influences on adjustment in early adolescence. *Child Development, 73*, 1573–1592.

Easton, D., & Dennis, J. (1969). *Children in the political system: Origins of political legitimacy.* New York: McGraw-Hill.

Elder, G. H., Jr. (1974). *Children of the great depression.* Chicago: University of Chicago Press.

Emler, N., & Dickinson, J. (1985). Children's representation of economic inequalities: The effects of social class. *British Journal of Developmental Psychology, 3*, 191–198.

Erikson, E. H. (1968). *Identity, youth, and crisis.* New York: Norton.

Erikson, R. S., MacKuen, M. B., & Stimson, J. A. (2002). *The macro polity.* New York: Cambridge University Press.

Erikson, R. S., & Stoker, L. (2011). Caught in the draft: The effects of Vietnam draft lottery status on political attitudes. *American Political Science Review, 105*, 221–236.

Fahs, A., & Waugh, J. (eds.). (2004). *The memory of the Civil War in American culture.* Chapel Hill: University of North Carolina Press.

Fendrich, J. M., & Lovoy, K. L. (1988). Back to the future: Adult political behavior of former student activists. *American Sociological Review, 53*, 780–784.

Fiorina, M. P. (1981). *Retrospective voting in American national elections.* New Haven, CT: Yale University Press.

Fiorina, M. P., with Abrams, S. J., & Pope, J. C. (2011). *Culture war? The myth of a polarized America* (3rd ed.). Boston, MA: Longman.

Firebaugh, G., & Davis, K. E. (1988). Trends in antiblack prejudice, 1972–1984: Region and cohort effects. *American Journal of Sociology, 94*, 251–272.

Fisher, C. B., Wallace, S. A., & Fenton, R. E. (2000). Discrimination distress during adolescence. *Journal of Youth and Adolescence, 29*, 679–695.

Fitzgerald, J. (2011). Family dynamics and Swiss parties on the rise: Exploring party support in a changing electoral context. *Journal of Politics, 73*, 783–796.

Fitzgerald, J., & Curtis, K. A. (2012). Partisan discord in the family and political engagement: A comparative behavioral analysis. *Journal of Politics, 74*, 129–141.

Flanagan, C. A., Bowes, J. M., Jonsson, B., Csapo, B., & Sheblanova, E. (1998). Ties that bind: Correlates of adolscents' civic commitments in seven countries. *Journal of Social Issues, 54*, 457–475.

Flanagan, C. A., Gallay, L. S., Gill, S., Gallay, E., & Nti, N. (2005). What does democracy mean? Correlates of adolescents' views. *Journal of Adolescent Research, 20*, 193–218.

Gallatin, J., & Adelson, J. (1971). Legal guarantees of individual freedom: A cross-national study of the development of political thought. *Journal of Social Issues, 27*, 93–108.

Gimpel, J. G., Lay, J. C., & Schuknecht, J. E. (2003). *Cultivating democracy: Civic environments and political socialization in America.* Washington, DC: Brookings Institution Press.

Glaser, J. M., & Gilens, M. (1997). Interregional migration and political resocialization: A study of racial attitudes under pressure. *Public Opinion Quarterly, 61,* 72–86.

Green, D., Palmquist, B., & Schickler, E. (2002). *Partisan hearts and minds: Political parties and the social identities of voters.* New Haven, CT: Yale University Press.

Greene, M. L., Way, N., & Pahl, K. (2006). Trajectories of perceived adult and peer discrimination among Black, Latino, and Asian American adolescents: Patterns and psychological correlates. *Developmental Psychology, 42*(2), 218–238.

Greenstein, F. I. (1970). A note on the ambiguity of "political socialization": Definitions, criticisms, and strategies of inquiry. *Journal of Politics, 32,* 969–978.

Hajnal, Z. L., & Lee, T. (2011). *Why Americans don't join the party: Race, immigration, and the failure (of political parties) to engage the electorate.* Princeton, NJ: Princeton University Press.

Halbwachs, M. ([1950] 1980). *The collective memory.* New York: Harper.

Harding, D. J., & Jencks, C. (2003). Changing attitudes toward premarital sex: Cohort, period, and aging effects. *Public Opinion Quarterly, 67,* 211–226.

Hatemi, P. K., Funk, C. L., Medlund, S., Maes, H. M., Silberg, J. L., Martin, N. G., & Eaves, L. J. (2009). Genetic and environmental transmission of political attitudes over the life cycle. *Journal of Politics, 71,* 1141–1156.

Henderson, J., & Chatfield, S. (2011). Who matches? Propensity scores and bias in the causal effects of education on participation. *Journal of Politics, 73,* 646–658.

Henry, P. J., & Sears, D. O. (2009). The crystallization of racial prejudice across the lifespan. *Political Psychology, 30,* 569–590.

Hess, R. D., & Torney, J. V. (1967). *The development of political attitudes in children.* Chicago: Aldine.

Hetherington, M. J., & Weiler, J. D. (2009). *Authoritarianism and polarization in American politics.* New York: Cambridge University Press.

Highton, B. (2009). Revisiting the relationship between educational attainment and political sophistication. *Journal of Politics, 71,* 1564–1576.

Highton, B., & Wolfinger, R. E. (2001). The first seven years of the political life cycle. *American Journal of Political Science, 45,* 202–209.

Ho, A. K., Sidanius, J., Pratto, F., Levin, S., Thomsen, L., Kteily, N., & Sheehy-Skeffington, J. (2012). Social dominance orientation: Revisiting the structure and function of a variable predicting social and political attitudes. *Personality and Social Psychology Bulletin, 38*(5), 583–606.

Hughes, J., & Bigler, R. S. (2011). Predictors of African American and European American adolescents' endorsement of race-conscious social policies. *Developmental Psychology, 47,* 479–492.

Hyman, H. H. (1959). *Political socialization.* Glencoe, IL: Free Press.

Jennings, M. K. (1987). Residues of a movement: The aging of the American protest generation. *American Political Science Review, 81,* 367–382.

Jennings, M. K. (2002). Generation units and the student protest movement in the United States: An intra- and intergenerational analysis. *Political Psychology, 23,* 303–324.

Jennings, M. K., & Markus, G. B. (1977). The effect of military service on political attitudes: A panel study. *American Political Science Review, 71,* 131–147.

Jennings, M. K., & Niemi, R. G. (1974). *The political character of adolescence.* Princeton, NJ: Princeton University Press.

Jennings, M. K., & Niemi, R. G. (1981). *Generations and politics.* Princeton, NJ: Princeton University Press.

Jennings, M. K., Stoker, L., & Bowers, J. (2009). Politics across generations: Family transmission reexamined. *Journal of Politics, 71,* 782–799.

Jervis, R. (1976). *Perception and misperception in international politics.* Princeton, NJ: Princeton University Press.

Kam, C. D., & Palmer, C. L. (2008). Reconsidering the effects of education on political participation. *Journal of Politics, 70,* 612–631.

Kam, C. D., & Palmer, C. L. (2011). Rejoinder: Reinvestigating the causal relationship between higher education and political participation. *Journal of Politics, 73,* 659–663.

Katz, P., & Kofkin, J. (1997). Race, gender and young children. In S. Luthar, J. Burack, D. Cicchetti, & J. Weisz (eds.), *Developmental psychopathology: Perspectives on adjustment, risk, and disorder* (pp. 51–74). New York: Cambridge University Press.

Katz, P. A., Sohn, M., & Zalk, S. R. (1975). Perceptual concomitants of racial attitudes in urban grade-school children. *Developmental Psychology, 11,* 135–144.

Kelly, M., & Duckitt, J. (1995). Racial preference and self-esteem in black South African children. *South African Journal of Psychology, 25,* 217–223.

Killen, M., & Stangor, C. (2001). Children's social reasoning about inclusion and exclusion in gender and race peer group contexts. *Child Development, 72,* 174–186.

Kinder, D. R. (2006). Belief systems today. *Critical Review: Special Issue on Democratic Competence, 18,* 197–216.

Krampen, G. (2000). Transition of adolescent political action orientations to voting behavior in early adulthood in view of a social-cognitive action theory model of personality. *Political Psychology, 21,* 277–297.

Kroh, M., & Selb, P. (2009). Inheritance and the dynamics of party identification. *Political Behavior, 31,* 559–574.

Leahy, R. L. (1990). The development of concepts of economic and social inequality. *New Directions for Child Development, 46,* 107–120.

Levendusky, M. (2009). *The partisan sort: How liberals became Democrats and conservatives became Republicans.* Chicago: University of Chicago Press.

Lewis-Beck, M., Norpoth, H., Jacoby, W. G., & Weisberg, H. F. (2008). *"The American Voter" revisited.* Ann Arbor: University of Michigan Press.

Loewenberg, P. (1971). The psychohistorical origins of the Nazi youth cohort. *American Historical Review, 76,* 1457–1502.

Lopez, M. H., & Kirby, E. (2005). Electoral engagement among minority youth. The Center for Information & Research on Civic Learning & Engagement (CIRCLE). Retrieved on September 28, 2006, from http://www.civicyouth.org/PopUps/FactSheets/FS_04_Minority_vote.pdf

Mannheim, K. (1952). The problem of generations. In P. Kecskemeti (ed.), *Essays on the sociology of knowledge.* (pp. 276–322). London: Routledge & Keagan Paul.

Marks, A. K., Szalacha, L. A., Lamarre, M., Boyd, M. J., & García Coll, C. (2007). Emerging ethnic identity and interethnic group social preferences in middle childhood: Findings from the Children of Immigrants Development in Context (CIDC) study. *International Journal of Behavioral Development, 31,* 501–513.

Marwell, G., Aiken, M. T., & Demerath, N. J., III. (1987). The persistence of political attitudes among 1960s civil rights activists. *Public Opinion Quarterly, 51,* 359–375.

Mason, K. O., Mason, W. M., Winsborough, H. H., & Poole, W. K. (1973). Some methodological issues in cohort analysis of archival data. *American Sociological Review, 38,* 242–258.

McAdam, D. (1989). The biographical consequence of activism. *American Sociological Review, 54,* 744–760.

McKown, C., & Weinstein, R. S. (2003). The development and consequences of stereotype consciousness in middle childhood. *Child Development, 74,* 498–515.

Merelman, R. M. (1986). Revitalizing political socialization. In M. G. Hermann (ed.), *Political psychology* (pp. 279–319). San Francisco, CA: Jossey-Bass.

Metz, E. C., & Youniss J. (2005). Longitudinal gains in civic development through school-based required service. *Political Psychology, 26,* 413–437.

Miller, A. H., & Klobucar, T. F. (2000). The development of party identification in post-Soviet societies. *American Journal of Political Science, 44,* 667–685.

Miller, S., & Sears, D. O. (1986). Stability and change in social tolerance: A test of the persistence hypothesis. *American Journal of Political Science, 30,* 214–236.

Miller, W. E., & Shanks, J. M. (1996). *The new American voter.* Cambridge, MA: Harvard University Press.

Monteiro, M., de França, D., & Rodrigues, R. (2009). The development of intergroup bias in childhood: How social norms can shape children's racial behaviors. *International Journal of Psychology, 44,* 29–39.

Moore, S. W., Lare, J., & Wagner, K. A. (1985). *The child's political world: A longitudinal perspective.* Westport, CT: Praeger.

Nets-Zehngut, R. (2011). Palestinian autobiographical memory regarding the 1948 Palestinian exodus. *Political Psychology, 32,* 271–295.

Niemi, R. G. (1973). Political socialization. In J. N. Knutson (ed.), *Handbook of political psychology.* San Francisco, CA: Jossey-Bass, 117–138.

Niemi, R. G. (1974). *How family members perceive each other.* New Haven, CT: Yale University Press.

Niemi, R. G., & Hepburn, M. A. (1995). The rebirth of political socialization. *Perspectives on Political Science, 24,* 7–16.

Niemi, R. G., & Jennings, M. K. (1991). Issues and inheritance in the formation of party identification. *American Journal of Political Science, 35,* 970–988.

Nishina, A., Bellmore, A., Witkow, M. R., & Nylund-Gibson, K. (2010). Longitudinal consistency of adolescent ethnic identification across varying school ethnic contexts. *Developmental Psychology, 46,* 1389–1401.

Osborne, D., Sears, D. O., & Valentino, N. A. (2011). The end of the solidly Democratic South: The impressionable-years hypothesis. *Political Psychology, 32,* 81–108.

Phinney, J. S. (1990). Ethnic identity in adolescents and adults: Review of research. *Psychological Bulletin, 108,* 499–514.

Picard, C. J. (2005). Comprehensive curriculum: Kindergarten social studies. Louisiana Department of Education.

Portes, A., & Rumbaut, R. G. (2001). *Legacies: The story of the immigrant second generation.* Berkeley: University of California Press.

Prior, M. (2010). You've either got it or you don't? The stability of political interest over the life cycle. *Journal of Politics, 72,* 747–766.

Putnam, R. D. (2000). *Bowling alone: The collapse and revival of American community.* New York: Simon & Schuster.

Quintana, S. M. (2007). Racial and ethnic identity: Developmental perspectives and research. *Journal of Counseling Psychology, 54,* 259–270.

Raviv, A., Sadeh, A., Raviv, A., Silberstein, O., & Diver, O. (2000). Young Israelis' reactions to national trauma: The Rabin assassination and terror attacks. *Political Psychology, 21,* 299–322.

Renshon, S. (ed.). (1977). *Handbook of political socialization: Theory and research.* New York: Free Press.

Roberts, R., Phinney, J., Masse, L., & Chenet, R. (1999). The structure of ethnic identity of young adolescents from diverse ethnocultural groups. *Journal of Early Adolescence, 19,* 301–322.

Romero, A. J., & Roberts, R. E. (1998). Perception of discrimination and ethnocultural variables in a diverse group of adolescents. *Journal of Adolescence, 21,* 641–656.

Rosenbloom, S. R., & Way, N. (2004). Experiences of discrimination among African American, Asian American, and Latino adolescents in an urban high school. *Youth and Society, 35,* 420–451.

Ruble, D. N., Alvarez, J., Bachman, M., Cameron, J., Fuligni, A., Coll, C. G., & Rhee, E. (2004). The development of a sense of "we": The emergence and implications of children's collective identity. In M. Bennett & F. Sani (eds.), *The development of the social self* (pp. 29–76). New York: Psychology Press.

Sances, M. W. (2011). Disenfranchisement through divorce? Estimating the effect of parental absence on voter turnout. *Political Behavior, 35,* 199–213.

Sapiro, V. (1994). Political socialization during adulthood: Clarifying the political time of our lives. *Research in Micropolitics, 4,* 197–223.

Sapiro, V. (2003). Theorizing gender in political psychology research. In D. O. Sears, L. Huddy, & R. Jervis (eds.), *The Oxford handbook of political psychology* (pp. 601–635). New York: Oxford University Press.

Schuman, H., Akiyama, H., & Knauper, B. (1998). Collective memories of Germans and Japanese about the past half-century. *Memory, 6,* 427–454.

Schuman, H., & Corning, A. (2012). Generational memory and the critical period: Evidence for national and world events. *Public Opinion Quarterly, 76,* 1–31.

Schuman, H., & Rieger, C. (1992). Historical analogies, generational effects, and attitudes toward war. *American Sociological Review, 57,* 315–326.

Schuman, H., & Scott, J. (1989). Generations and collective memories. *American Sociological Review, 54,* 359–381.

Schuman, H., Steeh, C., Bobo, L., & Krysan, M. (1997). *Racial attitudes in America: Trends and interpretations* (rev. ed.). Cambridge, MA: Harvard University Press.

Searing, D. D., Schwartz, J. J., & Lind, A. E. (1973). The structuring principle: Political socialization and belief systems. *American Political Science Review, 67,* 415–432.

Searing, D. D., Wright, G., & Rabinowitz, G. (1976). The primacy principle: Attitude change and political socialization. *British Journal of Political Science, 6,* 83–113.

Sears, D. O. (1975). *Political socialization.* In F. I. Greenstein & N. W. Polsby (eds.), *Handbook of political science* (vol. 2, pp. 93–153). Reading, MA: Addison-Wesley.

Sears, D. O. (1981). Life stage effects upon attitude change, especially among the elderly. In S. B. Kiesler, J. N. Morgan, & V. K. Oppenheimer (eds.), *Aging: Social change* (pp. 183–204). New York: Academic Press.

Sears, D. O. (1983). The persistence of early political predispositions: The roles of attitude object and life stage. In L. Wheeler & P. Shaver (eds.), *Review of personality and social psychology* (vol. 4, pp. 79–116). Beverly Hills, CA: Sage.

Sears, D. O. (2002). Long-term psychological consequences of political events. In K. R. Monroe (ed.), *Political psychology* (pp. 249–269). Mahwah, NJ: Lawrence Erlbaum Associates.

Sears, D. O., Fu, M., Henry, P. J., & Bui, K. (2003). The origins and persistence of ethnic identity among the "new immigrant" groups. *Social Psychology Quarterly, 66,* 419–437.

Sears, D. O., & Funk, C. L. (1991). The role of self-interest in social and political attitudes. In M. Zanna (ed.), *Advances in experimental social psychology* (vol. 24, pp. 1–91). Orlando, FL: Academic Press.

Sears, D. O., & Funk, C. L. (1999). Evidence of the long-term persistence of adults' political predispositions. *Journal of Politics, 61*, 1–28.

Sears, D. O., Haley, H., & Henry, P. J. (2008). Cultural diversity and sociopolitical attitudes at college entry. In J. Sidanius, C. van Laar, S. Levin, & D. O. Sears, *The diversity challenge: Social identity and intergroup relations on the college campus* (pp. 65–99). New York: Russell Sage Foundation.

Sears, D. O., & Henry, P. J. (2008). The overall effects of college on students' sociopolitical attitudes. In J. Sidanius, C. van Laar, S. Levin, & D. O. Sears, *The diversity challenge: Social identity and intergroup relations on the college campus* (pp. 100–135). New York: Russell Sage Foundation.

Sears, D. O., & Levy, S. (2003). Childhood and adult political development. In D. O. Sears, L. Huddy, & R. Jervis (eds.), *The Oxford handbook of political psychology* (pp. 60–109). New York: Oxford University Press.

Sears, D. O., & Valentino, N. A. (1997). Politics matters: Political events as catalysts for preadult socialization. *American Political Science Review, 91*, 45–65.

Sellers, R. M., Rowley, S. A. J., Chavous, T. M., Shelton, J. N., & Smith, M. A. (1997). Multidimensional inventory of black identity: A preliminary investigation of reliability and construct validity. *Journal of Personality and Social Psychology, 73*, 805–815.

Sherrod, L. R., Flanagan, C., & Youniss, J. (2002). Dimensions of citizenship and opportunities for youth development: The what, why, when, where, and who of citizenship development. *Applied Developmental Science, 6*, 264–272.

Sigel, R. S. (Ed.). (1989). *Political learning in adulthood*. Chicago: University of Chicago Press.

Simons, R. L., Murry, V., McLoyd, V., Lin, K., Cutrona, C., & Conger, R. D. (2002). Discrimination, crime, ethnic identity, and parenting as correlates of depressive symptoms among African American children: A multilevel analysis. *Development and Psychopathology, 14*, 371–393.

Skafte, D. (1989). The effect of perceived wealth and poverty on adolescents' character judgments. *Journal of Social Psychology, 129*, 93–99.

Slone, M., Adiri, M., & Arian, A. (1998). Adverse political events and psychological adjustments: A cross-cultural study of Israeli and Palestinian children. *American Academy of Child & Adolescent Psychiatry, 3*, 1058–1069.

Slone, M., Kaminer, D., & Durrheim, K. (2000). The contribution of political life events to psychological distress among South African adolescents. *Political Psychology, 21*, 465–487.

Steeh, C., & Schuman, H. (1991). Changes in racial attitudes among young white adults, 1984–1990. *American Journal of Sociology, 96*, 340–367.

Stewart, A. J., & Healy, J. M. (1989). Linking individual development and social changes. *American Psychologist, 44*, 30–42.

Stewart, A. J., Settles, I. H., & Winter, N. J. G. (1998). Women and the social movements of the 1960's: Activists, engaged observers, and nonparticipants. *Political Psychology, 19*, 63–94.

Stoker, L., & Jennings, M. K. (2008). Of time and the development of partisan polarization. *American Journal of Political Science, 52*, 619–635.

Tedin, K. L. (1980). Assessing peer and parent influence on adolescent political attitudes. *American Journal of Political Science, 24*, 136–154.

Tessler, M., Konold, C., & Reif, M. (2004). Political generations in developing countries: Evidence and insights from Africa. *Public Opinion Quarterly, 68*, 184–216.

Torney-Purta, J., Lehmann, R., Oswald, H., & Schultz, W. (2001). *Citizenship and education in 28 countries: Civic knowledge and engagement at age fourteen*. Amsterdam: International Association for the Evaluation of Educational Achievement.

Valentino, N. A., & Sears, D. O. (1998). Event-driven political communication and the preadult socialization of partisanship. *Political Behavior, 20*, 127–154.

Verkuyten, M., Kinket, B., & Van Der Wielen, C. (1997). Preadolescents' understanding of ethnic discrimination. *Journal of Genetic Psychology, 158*, 97–112.

Visser, P. S., Krosnick, J. A. (1998). Development of attitude strength over the life cycle: Surge and decline. *Journal of Personality and Social Psychology, 75*, 1389–1391.

Wattenberg, M. P. (1998). *The decline of American political parties, 1952–1996*. Cambridge, MA: Harvard University Press.

Wattenberg, M. P. (2008). *Is voting for young people?* Boston, MA: Pearson Longman.

Waugh, J. (2009). *U.S. Grant: American hero, American myth*. Chapel Hill: University of North Carolina Press.

Weinger, S. (1998). Poor children "know their place": Perceptions of poetry, class and public messages. *Journal of Sociology & Social Welfare, 25*, 100–118.

Williams, J. E., Best, D. L., & Boswell, D. A. (1975). The measurement of children's racial attitudes in the early school years. *Child Development, 46*, 494–500.

Wilson, T. C. (1996). Cohort and prejudice: Whites' attitudes toward blacks, Hispanics, Jews, and Asians. *Public Opinion Quarterly, 60*, 253–274.

Wolfenstein, M., & Kliman, G. (Eds.). (1965). *Children and the death of a president*. Garden City, NY: Doubleday.

Wolfinger, R. E. (1965). The development and persistence of ethnic voting. *American Political Science Review, 59*, 896–908.

Wolak, J. (2009). Explaining change in party identification in adolescence. *Electoral Studies, 28*, 573–583.

Wolak, J., & McDevitt, M. (2011). The roots of the gender gap in political knowledge in adolescence. *Political Behavior, 33*, 505–533.

Wong, C. A., Eccles, J. S., & Sameroff, A. (2003). The influence of ethnic discrimination and ethnic identification on African American adolescents' school and socioemotional adjustment. *Journal of Personality, 71*, 1197–1232.

Wong, J. S. (2000). The effects of age and political exposure on the development of party identification among Asian American and Latino immigrants in the United States. *Political Behavior, 22*, 341–371.

Wong, J., Ramakrishnan, S. K., Lee, T., & Junn, J. (2011). *Asian American political participation: Emerging constituents and their political identities* New York: Russell Sage Foundation.

Woods, T. A., Kurtz-Costes, B., & Rowley, S. J. (2005). The development of stereotypes about the rich and poor: Age, race, and family income differences in beliefs. *Journal of Youth and Adolescence, 34*, 437–445.

Youniss, J., McLellan, J. A., & Yates, M. (1997). What we know about engendering civic identity. *American Behavioral Scientist, 40*, 620–631.

Zaller, J., & Feldman, S. (1992). A simple theory of the survey response: Answering questions versus revealing preferences. *American Journal of Political Science, 36*, 579–616.

Zuckerman, A., Dasovic, J., & Fitzgerald, J. (2007). *Partisan families: The social logic of bounded partisanship in Germany and Britain*. Cambridge: Cambridge University Press.

CHAPTER 4

··

DEGREES OF RATIONALITY
IN POLITICS

··

DENNIS CHONG

RATIONAL choice theory is both a normative standard and empirical model of behavior. As a theory of behavior, it predicts (or prescribes) how an individual will (or should) choose from alternative courses of action given his objectives and beliefs about the instrumental relationship between those alternatives and his goals. The economic version of the theory is often referred to as omniscient rationality because it assumes perfect, unbounded, or substantive rationality (Becker, 1976; Elster, 1989; Rubinstein, 1998; Simon, 1995). A perfectly rational individual has a complete and coherent set of preferences, gathers an appropriate amount of information depending on the significance of the choice, forms beliefs about the alternatives that reflect the relevant information or evidence needed to make the decision, and chooses the action that is optimally related to his beliefs and goals.

The extent to which ordinary citizens behave rationally in politics is an empirical question considered in this chapter. Do people choose actions that are optimally related to their beliefs and goals? Are their preferences coherent, and do their beliefs correspond to the evidence they have gathered? Do individuals seek the proper amount of evidence, given their goals and beliefs?

As we shall see, in studying the political psychology and behavior of citizens, every facet of the rational choice model appears to be violated to some degree. People prefer policies and engage in behavior such as voting that do not further their self-interest. Their preferences are often unstable, inconsistent, and affected by how alternatives are framed. They do not always respond to new information by updating their beliefs and modifying their preferences in accord with their goals. They do not gather enough information to make the optimal choice.

Such departures from rational choice, however, raise a paradox. The paradox is that it is irrational for the average citizen to invest much time and effort becoming informed and making political decisions (Downs, 1957; Hardin, 2006). The economics of information constrain rational choice, because all political preferences and decisions may be compromised by the initial choice of citizens to economize on their effort. Given that substantive rationality depends critically on the optimal use of information to achieve one's goals, can citizens who rationally pay slight attention to politics still make rational political decisions? We would expect the quality of decisions to *vary* depending on the circumstances of the decision and the decision-maker.

In evaluating the rationality of preferences and behavior, much depends on our standards of rationality. In the omniscient or perfectly rational model, if we know people's goals and objective circumstances, we can predict their choices because we assume they have the capacity and knowledge to make the proper inferences. People who do not always uphold the standards of economic rationality are often better described as being boundedly rational (Conlisk, 1996; Rubinstein, 1998; Simon, 1985, 1995). In contrast to perfect economic rationality, bounded rationality assumes that people are instrumental in their actions, but will devote only so much time and resources to achieving their goals. Try as they might to make good decisions, they can make mistakes gathering and assessing evidence and reasoning from means to ends (Hirschman, 1982; Riker, 1995).

The decision-making procedures of boundedly rational individuals will vary according to the demands of the problem and the abilities of the decision-maker. To explain and predict people's behavior, we have to study their subjective motivations and goals, the information they possess, and their inferences about the consequences of alternative courses of action. All such deliberative procedures may be construed as being boundedly rational even if they vary in the degree to which they produce substantively rational outcomes (Simon, 1985, 294). If people are not universally rational, perhaps they are more likely to be rational when making decisions in some contexts (e.g., when decisions involve greater stakes or when they are more determined to make the right choice). And if their choices are not objectively rational, perhaps they are rational within the bounds of their limited knowledge, capacity, and motivation.

In this chapter, I explore both the economic and the psychological rationality of political choice. I begin by outlining the assumptions of rational choice theory and discussing variations on those assumptions to accommodate a more realistic individual psychology. I then evaluate the political attitudes and behavior of citizens in different contexts of decision-making. I focus specifically on the degree to which people make optimal (i.e., self-interested) policy choices; whether low or limited information rationality is substantively rational (and whether individuals who gather more information do better); whether beliefs are updated and information is processed rationally; and whether preferences are consistent across alternative framings of issues.

In discussing the empirical results in these areas of research, we shall see that the major deduction of rational choice theory that citizens do not have an incentive to devote much attention to politics casts a shadow on all of the topics we examine. When individuals are not motivated, they have less knowledge of the implications of policies, rely more heavily on partisan and ideological cues and other shortcuts to make choices, are less affected by substantive arguments, and more likely to engage in motivated reasoning. A more psychologically realistic model of political decision-making, however, can explain when decisions will deviate to a greater or lesser degree from optimal rational choice. Because decision-making exacts costs and can be improved through practice, incentives, and learning, bounded rationality, with its imperfections, should be regarded as an extension of economic reasoning rather than its contradiction (Conlisk, 1996).

Finally, I will discuss how normative standards of decision-making vary and are applied inconsistently across these topics of research. In particular, responsiveness to information is valued in some contexts, but stability of preferences (or resistance to information) is considered desirable in other instances. I will close with other examples of inconsistency in the normative evaluation of decision-making including the treatment of party cues and motivated reasoning.

1. Assumptions of Rational Choice Theory

Rational choice theory[1] assumes that individuals have preferences that reflect their desires and goals. The goals that people aspire to can be left open-ended in the model, although many rational choice analyses assume further that individuals are self-interested and more likely to give priority to goals (both economic and social) that bring benefits to themselves rather than to others (e.g., Chong, 2000; Harsanyi, 1969).

However people define their goals is secondary to having a consistent set of preferences for these goals. An individual's preferences among a set of alternatives can be ordered if preferences are complete (a is preferred to b, or b is preferred to a, or one is indifferent between a and b) and internally consistent or "transitive" (if a is preferred to b, and b is preferred to c, then a is preferred to c). An individual is rational if these preferences are coherent and if choices are logically derived from them (i.e., a rational individual chooses the most preferred outcome).

Intransitive preferences can arise if people switch dimensions when evaluating different pairs of outcomes (Shepsle & Bonchek, 1996). This can occur, for example, when different pairs of candidates evoke different dimensions of evaluation (domestic vs. foreign policy or character traits) so that candidate x trumps candidate y on foreign policy, candidate y trumps candidate z on domestic policy, and candidate z trumps candidate x on character issues. As I will discuss later, these are framing issues that presumably can be moderated if all of the evaluative criteria are made explicit in the context of choice.

What is the rule or principle that leads to the preference ordering? Because people have multiple goals (e.g., money, profits, power, social status, etc.) and costs accompany the actions taken to obtain these goals, there are invariably trade-offs among the available alternatives. Intuitively, people are able to choose between such alternatives, so they must possess a method for comparing them. The concept of utility allows us to make comparisons among different kinds of costs and benefits by reducing them to a common underlying scale. A utility function translates the goods that people seek into a value.

People select the best available means to satisfy their preferences given their beliefs about what different actions will produce. Because the relationship between alternative means and ends is often uncertain, it is instrumentally rational to act in accord with one's beliefs about the likelihood that different courses of action will achieve one's goals. Outcomes are therefore assigned a utility value, and beliefs about the likelihood that an action will lead to the preferred outcome are assigned a probability. If choices lead to outcomes with certainty, then the rational choice is a simple matter of selecting the alternative at the top of the preference ordering. When there is uncertainty about the consequence of actions, the expected utility of an action combines the respective utilities of the possible outcomes of an action with their corresponding probabilities.

A rational choice therefore entails choosing the course of action that maximizes one's expected utility.

1.1. Economic and Psychological Rationality

Economic rationality and bounded rationality make different assumptions about the information level and cognitive ability of individuals (Hogarth & Reder, 1987; Kahneman, 2003; Simon, 1995). Bounded rationality assumes there is individual and contextual variation in decision-making processes and outcomes (Conlisk, 1996; Gigerenzer & Goldstein, 1996; Lupia & McCubbins, 1998; Popkin, 1991; Simon, 1985, 1995). Decision-making procedures will vary by the importance of the issue and the motivations, abilities, and predispositions of the individuals forming judgments.

People, therefore, are not naturally or intuitively capable of making optimal choices in the more realistic psychology of bounded rationality. Rather, they sometimes choose poorly when compromising between effort and optimization. Hirschman (1982) suggests that "mistake making is one of the most characteristic of human actions, so that a good portion of the social world becomes unintelligible once we assume it away" (p. 81). Likewise, Riker (1995) notes: "There are degrees of difficulty in choosing instruments. Hence the model does not require instrumental accuracy, although it does require that...people do try to choose instruments that they believe, sometimes mistakenly, will achieve their goals" (p. 25).

Psychological and experimental research has produced a catalog of studies demonstrating the irrationality of individuals within particular contexts (Rabin, 1998). Clearly people are fallible in how they make decisions, often make mistakes, do not always seek to maximize utility, or fail to do so because of cognitive limitations. People often lack rational consistency in their preferences (Tversky & Thaler, 1990). They use evidence incorrectly or prejudicially and often draw overly confident conclusions from insufficient data (Gilovitch, 1991).

Whether these are conclusive demonstrations of widespread irrationality or only limited exceptions to rationality is debated. Among the major objections to the external validity of survey and experimental demonstrations of irrational behavior are that participants are not provided sufficient incentives to perform well on pencil-and-paper exercises, they are given novel problems without an opportunity to learn from their errors of reasoning, and there is usually no debate and discussion in the experiments to guide how individuals evaluate their alternatives (Camerer & Hogarth, 1999; Chase, Hertwig, & Gigerenzer, 1998; Gigerenzer, 1991; Riker, 1995, Wittman, 1995). Inconsistencies of choice and miscalculations are presumed more likely when there is little at stake and the alternatives are unfamiliar to the chooser. As Elster (1990) notes: "The central issue is whether people deal irrationally with important problems" (p. 40).

Of course, the necessity of incentives, education, and debate to induce rational choice acknowledges individual and situational influences on the substantive rationality of decisions. Decision-making can be aligned on a continuum that ranges from intuitive to effortful processing or "System 1" (intuition) versus "System 2" (reasoning) decision processes (Kahneman, 2003). Intuition is fast, automatic, affective, and effortless judgment, while reasoning is slow, objective, rule-based, and effortful. Similarly, dual-process cognitive models differentiate between "central" (or systematic) and "peripheral" processing of information depending on the effort expended by the decision-maker (e.g., Fazio & Olson, 2003; Petty & Cacioppo, 1986; Petty & Wegener, 1999). There is a trade-off between effort and accuracy. The idea of "satisficing" is that people establish an outcome that is adequate for their purposes and terminate their search when they find something that achieves that standard (Simon, 1957). People have to decide on both the quality of the outcome they seek and the amount of effort they are willing to invest to achieve that outcome. Simon (1990) therefore calls reason "a gun for hire" because deliberate, rational decision-making will be employed only under certain conditions.

Indeed, experimental research identifies where monetary incentives will sometimes improve performance (but sometimes make no difference). Incentives make the greatest difference when they motivate increased effort and if effort is relevant to improved performance. Effort works in combination with existing cognitive capital. When there is insufficient capital (skills, heuristics, experience, and know-how), increased effort can be futile. Conversely, if there is sufficient capital for the task, then adding incentives may not have a marginal effect on performance (Camerer & Hogarth, 1999). Monetary incentives therefore appear to have a qualified effect on rational choice. Larger incentives may induce more effort, but unless there is accompanying expertise, the additional effort may be fruitless. Witness the consequential errors people make in their financial investments (Benartzi & Thaler, 1995; Kahneman, 2003).

A separate issue is the extent to which incentives, education, and debate are relevant to mass political decision-making. For example, it is not clear how frequently we can depend on errors of perception and framing being corrected. "The fact that behavior may be changed after the subjects have been informed of their 'mistakes' is of interest, but so is behavior absent the revelation of mistakes because, in real life, explicit 'mistake-identifiers' rarely exist" (Rubinstein, 1998, p. 22). The impact of incentives also needs to be evaluated in light of the small expected value of most decisions (such as voting) that citizens make in politics. Much political analysis therefore concerns the quality of reasoning and choice when people are not well informed and highly motivated.

In the following sections, we will observe that people often fall short of the standards of rational choice not only because they are paying limited attention to politics, but also because of natural biases in how people process information. There is also evidence harmonious with a boundedly rational framework that consistency of preferences and the quality of judgment and choice varies systematically with changing motivations and incentives.

2. Do People Maximize Self-Interest?

A direct test of rational choice theory is whether people are maximizing utility when they take positions on public policies. Self-interested optimizers ought to prefer policies that yield the greatest benefits for themselves.

In public opinion surveys, however, the influence of self-interest on policy preferences has often proved to be weaker than general orientations such as political ideology, party identification, and political values. Compared to self-interest, people's values and their sociotropic evaluations are better predictors of their candidate preferences and their views in a variety of domains, including government spending, law and order, race and gender issues, social welfare policy, and foreign affairs (Citrin & Green, 1990; Sears & Funk, 1991). Likewise, in elections, voters are more apt to evaluate how the national economy, rather than their own personal economic status, will be affected by different candidates' policies (Kinder & Kiewiet, 1981).

The minor influence of self-interest on political choice is puzzling in light of the centrality of economic performance and standard-of-living issues in electoral campaigns. Politicians spend much of their efforts trying to convince voters that life will be materially better under their policies. Yet the respondents in mass opinion surveys seem to care less about their own personal stakes in policies than about whether those policies promote the national welfare or serve longstanding values.

I will explore reasons for the weak correlation between self-interest and political preferences, identify conditions that appear to strengthen the influence of self-interest, and discuss the theoretical implications of these results for our understanding of rationality. Part of the explanation for these results lies in the conceptualization and measurement of interests, and part lies in the cognitive and political constraints on the pursuit of self-interest through public policy.

2.1. Defining and Measuring Self-Interest

In testing the influence of self-interest, conceptual problems disentangling the sources of one's interests have been circumvented to some extent by defining self-interest as the tangible, relatively immediate, personal or family benefits of a policy. By definition, this narrow conceptualization of self-interest excludes the possibility that self-interest may be pursued through expressive or other-regarding actions or through long-term calculations. A narrow conception of self-interest also reduces the correlation between indicators of self-interest and measures of values such as ideology, partisanship, and egalitarianism, so that the relative influences of interests and values on policy preferences can be more clearly assessed. Broader conceptions of interests may yield somewhat different interpretations of the findings, but existing studies tend to concentrate on the conditions under which narrowly defined self-interests will influence policy positions.

Survey analyses of self-interest have generally sidestepped people's reasons for their policy preferences. Researchers typically make inferences about respondents' self-interest by making their own analysis of the consequences of the policy for different social groups in society and testing whether groups with a greater interest are more likely to support the policy. They assume, for example, that the unemployed will be more likely than the employed to want the government to guarantee employment, or that those without health insurance will have more to gain from supporting a national healthcare plan than those who are insured.

However, there is usually no independent confirmation that the respondents share similar beliefs about the impact of the policy. When people express preferences that contradict their interests, it is possible they knowingly choose an alternative that is not in their objective self-interest. Alternatively, their preferences may be consistent with their own analysis of their interests given their (possibly mistaken) beliefs about the policy. Again, the economics of information provides little incentive for citizens to acquire much policy knowledge even if some public policies (e.g., Social Security and healthcare reform) can have an immediate impact on citizens, and in these instances we would expect people to be motivated to learn more about the policy (Campbell, 2002). Thus a possible explanation for why self-interest exhibits only modest influence in shaping opinions is that people are frequently unaware of the implications of the policies for themselves and their families. The little information they have will often be partisan and ideological information that provides tidy though not necessarily accurate information about the costs and benefits of policies. When direct benefits are not self-evident, and the consequences of the policy are difficult to analyze, an ideological interpretation may be warranted as the best substitute.

2.2. When Costs and Benefits Are Magnified

We still might expect ideology and partisanship to be overridden when there is a clear understanding (even if sometimes simplistic) of what side of the policy benefits one the most. Indeed, studies that report more substantial self-interest effects have typically focused on policies that offer unambiguous benefits or impose tangible costs (Citrin & Green, 1990; Sears & Funk, 1991). Sears and Citrin (1985) found a strong relationship between owning one's home and voting for Proposition 13, a measure that slashed property tax rates in California. Green and Gerken (1989) and

Dixon, Lowery, Levy, and Ferraro (1991) found that smokers were significantly more opposed to smoking restrictions and cigarette taxes than were nonsmokers. Crow and Bailey (1995) found that regular drinkers were less likely than nondrinkers to support enhanced efforts to control drunk driving and underage drinking. Wolpert and Gimpel (1998) found that gun owners were consistently less likely than those who do not own guns to support proposals to ban handguns or to impose a waiting period for purchasing a gun.

The common element in all of these studies is that the policy being considered was clearly going to help or hurt some elements of the population more than others. For example, homeowners knew that Proposition 13 provided them with a large, immediate, and enduring financial benefit, whereas the hypothetical loss of government services carried relatively little weight (Sears & Citrin, 1985). Similarly, those who own a gun or intend to buy one can see that a waiting period will restrict their freedom. Therefore, instrumental reasoning and self-interested decision-making (i.e., rational choice) are more likely to be manifest when people can see that a policy will have a significant impact on their lives. On this point, analysts in both the social psychological and rational choice traditions are in agreement (Aldrich, 1993; Chong, 2000; Citrin & Green, 1990; Elster, 1990; Taylor, 1989).

2.3. Priming Self-Interest

In addition to the variation in issue content, individual differences in awareness and attentiveness can affect the connection between self-interest and policy choices. Both one's level of stored information and the content of cueing communications modify the priority given to self-interest in decision-making. People who are generally informed about politics or who constitute the attentive public on a particular issue are more likely to know how alternative policy proposals would affect them (Converse, 1964; Zaller, 1992). For those who are less cognitively skilled or engaged, the cues available to them at the moment of choice should be more influential in determining whether they will be motivated by self-interest (Sears & Lau, 1983; Taylor, Peplau, & Sears, 1994).

Critical to the role of self-interest in political reasoning, then, is whether the material benefits of a policy are visible, or cognitively accessible, to the decision-maker (Young, Thomsen, Borgida, Sullivan, & Aldrich, 1991). Pursuing this line of thinking, Sears and Lau (1983) showed that the relationship between self-interest and vote choice became stronger when respondents were asked about their personal economic situation *before* they were asked their candidate preference. Moreover, when their self-interest is primed, respondents are more likely to agree with egoistic justifications for a policy and less likely to accept reasons founded on broader, symbolic attitudes (Young et al., 1991; Taber & Young, chapter 17, this volume).

Chong, Citrin, and Conley (2001) further illustrate the conditional effects of self-interest in their survey experimental analysis of three policy issues—Social Security, the home mortgage interest tax deduction, and health benefits for domestic partners. They show that people in the key beneficiary categories (i.e., the elderly, homeowners, and unmarried individuals) recognize their own self-interest and act upon it without prompting when the policy has obvious implications for them; however the influence of self-interest is magnified significantly when people are primed to think about the personal costs and benefits of the policy. In contrast, people with a smaller stake in an issue are less likely to choose on the basis of self-interest and more likely to be influenced by their values and symbolic predispositions, especially when exposed to information that cues such concerns.

2.4. Uninformed Self-Interest

Even such affirmations of self-interested motivation are arguably crude approximations of carefully calculated rational choices. Bartels (2008) demonstrates that popular support for the tax cuts in 2001 and 2003 under President George W. Bush essentially boiled down to the perception among individuals that they personally were paying too much income tax. Other considerations about the growth of inequality in society, the negative social impact of inequality, and the unequal distribution of benefits of the Bush tax cuts in favor of the rich made little difference. While this suggests that voters cared only about the implications of the cuts for themselves, Bartels says average citizens (in contrast to the wealthy) were myopically self-interested in their support of the tax cuts because they failed to consider the ramifications of reduced taxes for cuts in government programs and increases in state and local taxes that would likely negate any tax savings at the federal level. Along the same line we could say that California voters were equally unenlightened when they supported Proposition 13 in California, the quintessential example in the literature of when self-interest supposedly dominated choices. Here is where the voter as consumer is an apt analogy, as consumers are often similarly myopic; for example, they buy low-price energy inefficient appliances even though in the long run these will cost more to operate than the more expensive but more efficient models (Conlisk, 1996, p. 672).

Such an interpretation, of course, holds the citizen against an objective criterion of self-interest and discounts their beliefs about the impact of tax cuts on the economy. Surveys have found that a majority of Americans believe that tax cuts help the economy, while only a fraction will say that tax cuts hurt the economy (AEI, 2011). Another revealing survey finding that might help to explain why lower- and middle-income individuals are reluctant to support tax increases on the wealthy is that they believe that politicians who target the wealthy for higher taxes will eventually also increase taxes on the middle class (AEI, 2011).

Survey analysis on the effect of different framings of tax cuts shows that support for tax cuts declines when people are given a choice between lowering taxes or maintaining spending on domestic programs such as education (Hacker & Pierson, 2005). These findings *might* be interpreted as support for the idea that information about trade-offs makes people more rational by causing them to take account of the benefits that are lost with tax cuts. The competitive frame provides respondents with information about both costs and benefits, and their preferences change as a consequence. But in this competitive context, either preference on the issue could conceivably be consistent with self-interest—supporters might be myopic in wanting something now, and opponents might be enlightened enough to resist the immediate temptation of a tax cut in favor of social programs that benefit them. (However, it also *may* be more plausible to say that people are giving greater weight to social values that support education and other social programs than to say they are becoming more self-interested. It is not clear they feel they are getting a better material return from these programs than they are from the tax cut; perhaps they simply feel that education is something they should support.)

2.5. When Self-Interest Matters

In keeping with a contextual approach to decision-making, the question to explore is not whether but *when* self-interest matters. (Redlawsk and Lau make a similar argument at the end of chapter 5 in this volume). Self-interest is more likely to matter when people actually have a stake in a policy and can see that they have a stake. Whether they can recognize those stakes depends on the transparency of the policy, the clarity with which the policy is presented to them, and their capacity to understand the implications of the policy. When their objective interests are debatable, when the implications of a policy are hard to discern or are obscured by political persuasion, or when they are not directly affected by the policy, people will rely more heavily on general political orientations (such as ideology and partisanship) that offer guidance in the absence of other criteria. Future research on rational choice should include a wider range of issues that differ systematically according to the size and clarity of their benefits and costs. A second task is to improve the measurement of both self-interest and values by developing more reliable measures of beneficiary classes and the specific values that are relevant to the policies.

3. LOW-INFORMATION RATIONALITY?

In politics, citizens will seek economical strategies to reason through their choices and hope to make adequate decisions even if they are generally not well informed. An obvious question is the quality of their political choices, which is analogous to the issue raised by economists of whether boundedly rational economic behavior leads to the same market outcomes as optimal behavior (e.g., Akerlof & Yellen, 1985). To what extent does economizing on deliberation produce outcomes that deviate from substantive or unbounded rationality?

The consequences of being uninformed may not be as severe as once thought. Although citizens devote little time to politics, they may learn just enough to make reasonable choices by capitalizing on politically relevant information available as a by-product of everyday routines (Downs, 1957; Fiorina, 1981; Popkin 1991; Lupia and

McCubbins, 1998). Voters may be unfamiliar with substantive issues, but they nevertheless can evaluate candidates using more easily acquired data, such as recent economic trends, the partisanship and personal characteristics of candidates, the candidates' ideologies, and the identities of opinion leaders and interest groups that endorse the candidates (Brady & Sniderman, 1985; Fiorina, 1981; Key, 1966; Lau & Redlawsk, 1997; 2001; Popkin, 1994; Sniderman, Brody, & Tetlock, 1991). In so doing, voters can draw conclusions without making a detailed study of the issues.

3.1. Measuring Performance

If we are using a normative standard of rationality, the right preference toward policies and candidates would be the position taken by a person who possessed all relevant information about the alternatives, analyzed and weighed that evidence properly, and chose the alternative that maximized his or her expected utility. Perfectly informed individuals in the electorate are an ideal type, like the omniscient rational actor. Researchers could analyze the issues and candidates and substitute their well-informed definition of the optimal choice for different types of voters, which is essentially the strategy taken in the studies testing for self-interested policy preferences. The analyst infers that a policy benefits some groups more than others and tests whether individuals in those groups actually provide greater support for the policy.

A more neutral method to define optimal choice focuses on the preferences of individuals who are significantly better informed than others because of their social position, educational level, or interest in following public affairs. If better-informed individuals have gathered sufficient information to understand the consequences of the policy, they should be more likely to identify the side of the policy that furthers their interests. Therefore we might take the preferences of the most-informed members of the public and compare them against the preferences of less-informed individuals, controlling for their demographic characteristics. Differences in preference by information level would suggest that information changes beliefs about the implications of the alternatives and improves the fit between preferences and goals.

A related approach to gauging the efficacy of low-information choice is to provide individuals with additional information about the alternatives and to measure the extent to which the new information changes their preferences. This can be done experimentally by randomly assigning individuals to a treatment group in which they receive relevant information about a policy; these individuals are then compared to a control group that was not provided this information. A before-after design can also be used to measure the preferences of a panel of individuals before and after they are informed about the alternatives.

Finally, an approach used specifically to test the value of possessing easily acquired but potentially useful heuristic information is to compare the preferences of individuals who possess the heuristic information against the preferences of those who are more fully informed about the alternatives.

3.2. The Impact of Information on Preferences

Virtually all of the studies reviewed here have found that possessing greater information tends to change preferences, which indicates that less-informed citizens are not making optimal choices. (See the discussion by Huckfeldt, Mondak, Hayes, Pietryka, and Reilly, chapter 21, this volume.) Delli Carpini and Keeter (1996) found that group differences between men and women, blacks and whites, and younger and older individuals sharpened among the best-informed members of the groups compared to the groups taken as wholes.

Bartels (1996) examined the effects of general knowledge on presidential vote choices. The average (absolute) deviation between actual and fully informed voter preferences in the six elections from 1972 to 1992 was approximately 10%, with effects being greater in some demographic categories than others. Bartels calculates that if voters chose randomly, the average deviation from fully informed voters would be on the order of 20%; therefore, the limited information possessed by the electorate as a whole shaves the magnitude of error in judgments by about 50%.

Althaus (1998) estimates that fully informed collective public opinion is more supportive of government services and higher taxes, but also (paradoxically?) more opposed to expanding government power; in the realm of social policy, fully informed opinion was generally more liberal except on the issue of affirmative action.

Gilens (2001) uses a standard for informed opinion that is based on specific policy knowledge rather than general political knowledge. He shows that specific information alters preferences over and above general knowledge: support for new prison construction is lowered when respondents are told that crime rates are declining, and support for foreign aid increases when respondents are informed that foreign aid is a trivial portion of federal spending. As in studies that simulate the preferences of a fully informed public, these findings suggest that lacking specific information leads to choices that are suboptimal in the sense of not aligning with the preferences one would hold if better informed. Furthermore, the addition of policy specific information seems to have its greatest impact on those who already possess high levels of general knowledge, because they are better equipped to process the new information and to update their preferences.

There is no handy criterion to assess whether citizens are doing adequately if suboptimally with the trade-off they are making between gathering more information and the quality of their decisions. Bartels asks (1996, p. 221): "Does the attractiveness of democracy as a political system depend in any fundamental way upon the degree of correspondence between the opinions the public actually expresses about a given candidate or policy and the opinions it would express if it was 'fully informed'? ... If deviations between actual and "fully informed" preferences of the magnitude reported here will not shake anyone's confidence in democracy, would deviations twice as large do so? Ten times as large?"

In their study of voter choice, Lau and Redlawsk (1997; 2006; Redlawsk & Lau, chapter 5, this volume) take the more sanguine position that most voters choose the candidate who is consistent with their stated beliefs and interests. By their definition, the correct vote is the vote that one would make with complete information about the candidates. Using two alternative measures of correct voting, they conclude from experimental and survey data that between two-thirds and three-quarters of the electorate is voting correctly. Whether an error rate of one-quarter to one-third of the electorate is excessive in a democratic system is an open question.

Even if additional information does change beliefs and choices, it is a separate question whether the cost of obtaining that information is worth the benefits associated with the new preferences. People may be more likely to "get it right," but the consequences of making good political choices for one's life may be minor.

3.3. Knowing Just Enough versus Knowing a Lot

Demonstrating that general and specific knowledge leads to different (more optimal) policy or candidate preferences suggests that heuristics are not fully compensatory for those with low information levels. This may be an overstatement because some people may acquire the relevant cues in policy campaigns when the issue is salient, and the key test is whether there are some heuristics that substitute adequately for more detailed knowledge. In Lupia's (1994) study of several California initiatives on auto insurance rates, voters' knowledge of the details of the initiatives made little difference in their voting behavior beyond their knowledge of the auto insurance industry's position on each initiative. Voters who knew only the insurance industry's stance voted similarly to those who knew additional factual details of the initiatives.

There is of course an inherent ambiguity in using the well informed as a standard for evaluating whether people are expressing optimal preferences. If information does not change preferences, then it does not produce any new knowledge (as defined by Lupia & McCubbins (1998), knowledge helps to predict the consequences of a policy relative to one's goals). Therefore, the marginal value of the information is zero, and people should not pay anything to obtain it. By definition, if the information has value, it should affect preferences. We cannot always tell, simply by comparing the preferences of informed and uninformed people, whether the information has marginal value. If there is no difference between these groups, the information may not have been valuable *or* the well informed may have failed to make rational use of the information. Thus, in Lupia's study, highly informed voters may have derived no additional value from the details of the initiative measures, or they may have ignored such information and focused primarily on the alignment of the lobbying groups and consumer interest groups on each measure. We cannot escape this ambiguity unless we have a separate standard for the relevance of the information to the decision.

The upshot of these studies is mixed. There is a price paid for cutting corners in gathering information. Nonetheless the drop-off in performance may be tolerable depending on one's standards for decision-making. The deviations in preferences produced by more information are consistent and statistically significant, but there is also evidence indicating that voters tend to choose the right candidate given their priorities and criteria.

As will be apparent in the following discussion of motivated reasoning, the best informed may be an imperfect standard of good decision-making because they are also the most partisan and ideological members of the electorate. Ideology and party identification can motivate biased interpretations of evidence, especially when that evidence has partisan implications. Therefore, the beliefs of the best informed may reflect an ideologically distorted perspective rather than the objective state of the world. Those who are less ideological may have more accurate beliefs about aspects of the world that are subject to ideological or partisan conflict. The stronger tendency of more informed individuals to engage in motivated reasoning raises question about using this group as the standard for optimal preferences.

4. ARE BELIEFS FORMED AND UPDATED RATIONALLY?

In the normative model of rational decision-making, individuals gather information and weigh its applicability to the choice they have to make. If the evidence is relevant to the choice at hand, they will modify their beliefs to take account of the new information. If these new beliefs change their evaluation of the relationship between the alternatives and their goals, they will change their preference among the alternatives.

The studies I discuss in this section show that reasoning on the basis of limited information and low motivation to engage in deliberate processing of information can give rise, ironically, to motivated reasoning. Although motivated reasoning is often warranted by the circumstances of the decision-maker and can even be logically coherent, it reduces the value of information in politics relative to simpler and sometimes more superficial cues.

4.1. Biased Information Processing

One of the biases of human decision-making is that people will shape their beliefs of the world to make them consistent with their preferences rather than form their preferences based on an objective assessment of the state of the world (Kunda, 1990). In politics, where disputes over the interpretation and significance of information are common, people often interpret the same facts or events from a biased partisan or ideological perspective.

A fundamental tenet of rationality is that one's desires should not guide one's beliefs, as in motivated reasoning or cognitive dissonance reduction (Elster, 1990). The classic demonstration of motivated reasoning is Lord, Ross, and Lepper's (1979) study of attitudes toward the death penalty. After reading strong and weak arguments on both sides of the issue, supporters and opponents of the death penalty became more polarized and sure of their positions. Each side accepted the arguments consistent with their original position and argued against inconsistent claims, resulting in stronger attitudes following the debate than before.

Motivated reasoning is appropriate within limits, as "it is also inappropriate and misguided to go through life weighing all facts equally and reconsidering one's beliefs anew each time an antagonistic fact is encountered. If a belief has received a lifetime of support, it is justified to be skeptical of an observation or report that calls the belief into question, but to readily accept evidence that supports its validity" (Gilovitch, 1991, pp. 50–51; see also Hardin, 2009, p. 8). Ideological and religious belief systems may receive greater reinforcement and social support from those we know and respect than objective beliefs about the world. Therefore, we should anticipate that partisanship and ideology might have a greater influence on how people interpret the political world than objective facts. The crux of the issue is how responsive individuals are to new information. If they are responsive, are they using evidence properly? To what extent do existing (prior) evaluations persist in the face of contrary evidence?

Studies pointing to the rationality of voters have offered evidence of their responsiveness to changing information. Page and Shapiro (1992) argue that public opinion, as a collective entity, is generally stable when conditions are constant and dynamic in response to new events and information "that rational citizens would take into account" (p. 56). Similarly, Stimson's (2004) theory of the public mood describes a responsive electorate (led by *some* attentive citizens) that moderates and influences the ideological thrust of public policy. The theory of retrospective voting (Downs, 1957; Fiorina, 1981; Key, 1966; Popkin, 1994) maintains that voters are capable of evaluating and responding to the recent performance of the incumbent administration even if they are not well informed on the policy platforms of the parties. In general this research credits the public with being able to discern the direction of public policy, evaluate the competence of the party in power, and respond to political events in a reasonably accurate manner.

Responsiveness to events alone provides evidence that people have reasons for their actions (a minimum standard of rationality) but does not mean that voters are giving proper weight to information in their opinions and preferences. For example, Achen and Bartels (2009) took a closer examination of what voters appear to be keying on when they make retrospective assessments of the administration's performance. They found that voters react to many irrelevant events, have a short memory and time frame—focusing on recent performance and ignoring earlier events—and base their decisions on outcomes beyond the control of the administration.

4.2. Partisan Biases in Information Processing

Both memory-based and online models of public opinion assume motivated reasoning, especially among partisans who are most knowledgeable about politics. An axiom of the

RAS (Receive-Accept-Sample) model of public opinion (Zaller, 1992) is that individuals accept or reject information they receive depending on its relationship to their partisan and ideological predispositions. The more highly informed individuals will be the most biased because they will be more likely to recognize the partisan cues in information. Lodge and Taber's (2000; 2013) online model assumes that all decisions are motivated, but sometimes they are motivated to achieve accuracy and other times they are motivated to achieve a desired conclusion (which they call, appropriately, a "partisan mode"). Their John Q. Public (JQP) model (Kim, Taber, & Lodge, 2010) emphasizes the persistence of attitudes and partisan polarization of preferences in the course of a campaign.

Gerber and Green (1998; see also Green, Palmquist, & Schickler, 2002) are in the minority when they argue that there is no partisan resistance to information. According to them, the evaluations of people with different party identifications move along parallel paths in response to new information, which is consistent with unbiased information processing. Bartels (2002) argues on the contrary that such parallel shifts in opinion confirm partisan biases. In his interpretation of unbiased processing, as evidence is accumulated, partisans should converge in their evaluations and eventually reach a consensus if they agree on the meaning of the evidence. The rate of convergence depends on the weight of the evidence (cf. Bullock, 2009). An analysis of 92 topics of opinion change between 1990 and 1992 using the NES panel survey showed that partisan bias was significant in 83 instances. What is more, partisan biases extend to objective facts. For example, Democrats and Republicans polarize in their beliefs about whether income differences have increased or decreased in the past 20 years. Thus, not only do opinions vary by ideology and party, but so do perceptions of the state of the world (Bartels, 2008).

If individuals are motivated by a combination of accuracy and consistency, then partisan biases expressed in response to factual questions may reflect the dominance of the consistency goal. Survey respondents may simply have greater accessibility to partisan perceptions than to facts even when they know the facts, and surveys may not provide respondents with sufficient incentive to retrieve the correct answer from their memories (Prior, 2007). Alternatively, people may not have the specific knowledge they are being tested on, so they use their political values as a heuristic to fill in details they do not know. This is a shortcut that sometimes works, as in the case of the likeability heuristic (Brady & Sniderman, 1985) that allows people to infer the policy positions of social groups.

The impact of substantive information is weakened when people are inclined to impute facts using their partisan values, or if their interpretation of the information is shaped by their prior attitudes and beliefs. Cohen's (2003) ingenious experiment on the relative influence of partisan cues and policy features shows how party cues affect the subjective meaning and interpretation of seemingly objective information. The experiment presented participants with two contrasting versions—generous or stringent—of a social welfare policy. Judging each policy on its merits, respondents preferred the version that was consistent with their ideological values. But when the policies were attributed to either the Democratic or Republican Party, liberal respondents favored the Democratic-labeled policy whether it was generous or stringent, and conservatives favored the Republican-labeled policy irrespective of details. Furthermore, greater cognitive effort did not change partisan biases in evaluating the policies.

Therefore, people's prior opinions about the group interests championed by the two parties were so strong that they had difficulty believing the Republican Party would ever be more sympathetic toward the poor. Any policy that appeared more generous than a rival Democratic policy was assumed to have some hidden features that undermined its ostensible benefits.

Within the confines of the experiment, this type of motivated reasoning appears irrational, but in the real political world, such assumptions about the relative sympathies of the two parties toward social welfare policy are warranted, and relying on party cues might be a more reliable decision rule than an independent analysis of the features of the policies. There is valid reason, rooted in long-term party reputations, to doubt that a Republican program would be more sympathetic to the poor; it may appear so in the capsule summary, but in the respondent's mind, there must be strings attached to undermine the attractiveness of the program. What would happen if the experimenter added the proviso: these are *identical* programs and will be implemented *identically*, except for variations in spending levels and duration? In this case, we might expect respondents to pay more attention to comparing absolute spending levels and time frames for the programs.

The Iraq war represents the most vivid recent example of motivated reasoning among Democratic and Republican identifiers (Gaines, Kuklinski, Quirk, Peyton, & Verkuilen, 2007; Jacobson, 2006; Prasad et al., 2009).Reactions to new information about the absence of weapons of mass destruction (WMDs) in Iraq varied significantly between Democrats and Republicans. Democrats updated their beliefs and increasingly withdrew support for the war when its justification was undermined; Republicans were much slower to revise their beliefs, and those who did supplied new reasons to justify the war, such as the need to overthrow a brutal dictator or to prevent Iraq from being a haven for Al-Qaeda (Jacobson, 2006).

4.3. The Relevance of Facts

A manipulation that strengthens the impact of a "fact" is to make people commit to its relevance. Kuklinski and colleagues (1997) designed a survey experiment that divided participants into two groups. Individuals in Group 1 gave their estimated and preferred levels of welfare spending and their attitude toward welfare spending; in Group 2, individuals gave the same estimates, but before they were asked their attitude toward welfare sending, they were given the true level of welfare spending (which was typically higher than either their estimated or preferred levels). "Group 2 respondents expressed more support for welfare spending than those in Group 1. In this extreme condition, in other words, factual information made a difference" (Kuklinski & Quirk, 2000, p. 173).

Kuklinski and Quirk describe the condition as "extreme" to mean the extraordinary effort that must be made to get people to update their beliefs and attitudes. The implication is that rational individuals should be more easily persuaded by good evidence. An alternative interpretation is that the participants had an attitude toward welfare programs that was not based on knowledge of the actual level of government spending, but simply on their belief that an excessive amount was being spent.

Specific quantitative facts, within bounds, are probably irrelevant for most policy preferences. People do not form their attitudes toward criminal justice based on the number of prisons in the United States. Nor does their attitude toward immigration rest on the annual number of immigrants who enter the country. Instead, people have a more ordinal (and numerically elastic) belief that, for example, there are "too many" people locked in prison or the pace of immigration is "too fast." Such qualitative judgments can accommodate virtually any actual statistics. Learning the exact numbers will not change those impressions; instead the meaning of the numbers (too high or too low) will be shaped by one's attitudes, not vice versa.

Gaines et al. (2007) substantiate this point in a panel study of attitudes toward the Iraq war. They show that new information about growing American casualties and failure to find WMDs in Iraq tends to be discounted as being irrelevant when it runs against strong partisan predispositions. In general, new facts do not change opinions as much as the perceived implications of those facts, which are themselves subject to partisan biases.

People are often uncertain about facts and how facts apply to the policy they are evaluating. Information competes with simpler cues that people receive about a policy. These cues also tell them which policy is best for them and which facts are relevant. Source cues especially can deflect attention from the substantive content of messages as well as shape interpretation of the information, so that the persuasiveness of the message depends on one's attitude toward the source. People not only have to be given incentives to study the information, but the information has to be presented in a way that increases its salience and credibility. A problem with low information rationality is that relevant substantive information is less likely to be given its due when individuals prefer taking a shortcut to making a careful evaluation of evidence.

People's certainty about the source's credibility can cause them to change their beliefs about both facts and applicability, especially if their prior beliefs about these facts and their applicability are weak. If an original position in favor of a policy is supported by a credible source and a set of beliefs about the facts, but these beliefs about the facts change because of new information, the new facts may be judged irrelevant (especially if the source remains steadfast but instead changes its rationale for the policy). The source prevails in this conflict because its policy position presumably incorporates all of the information in the situation that has a bearing on the decision. When source cues are so strong, information takes a back seat. Furthermore, following a source cue is not necessarily based on peripheral processing of information. Individuals may scrutinize the credibility of the source carefully. Therefore, party identification is a simple cue to follow, but it can reflect either central or peripheral processing.

The signal from a cue can also lead to an inference about what the facts must be using the following reasoning: the source has all the facts and supports the policy; any fact or consequence of the policy that is relevant to the source's position must be true or the source would not have endorsed the policy. If a person believes strongly that a fact is relevant but is uncertain if the fact is true, the signal from the source cue will strengthen belief that the fact is true (Lauderdale, 2010).

These dynamics of opinion indicate that Bayesian, unbiased, and rational have been incorrectly equated. There are cases of information processing that are consistent with Bayesian reasoning but that seem plainly unreasonable and ideologically dogmatic. "Opinion change in accordance with Bayes' rule may often be biased, and in extreme cases it may approach delusion, as long as it does not manifest internal contradictions" (Bartels, 2002, p. 126). Accordingly, Achen and Bartels (2009) show that it is possible to construct a Bayesian model in which partisan biases reflect cognitive inferences as opposed to wishful thinking; motivated reasoning is consistent with Bayesian updating when party identification is strong and the voter learns little information about the issue except that it has partisan relevance.

4.4. Overcoming Bias

Models of information processing hypothesize that people can correct their misperceptions when they have an incentive to make superior decisions. The relative emphasis on directional and accuracy goals will vary with the context of the decision. Individuals need not be consistent decision-makers across contexts because decisions differ in their complexity and individuals have varying motivations and opportunities to process information carefully (Lodge & Taber, 2000).

Studies show that increasing the incentive for accuracy (e.g., by telling people their decisions would have to be justified, would be made public, would have an effect on their own or other people's lives) without changing the attractiveness of particular outcomes, leads to more careful processing of information and reduces cognitive biases (e.g., stereotyping, group bias, primacy effects, anchoring effects in probability judgments, fundamental attribution errors) (Freund, Kruglanski, & Ajzen, 1985; Kruglanski & Freund, 1983; Petty & Cacioppo, 1986; Tetlock, 1983; 1985). (Note that in these decision and judgment tasks the participants did not have motivation to prefer one outcome to another, but they were motivated to care about arriving at an accurate judgment.) Fishkin and colleagues (Fishkin, Luskin, & Jowell, 2002; Fishkin, 2006) show that in carefully regulated deliberative contexts that emphasize rational evaluation of evidence, citizens develop coherent preferences across issues, become more informed about issues, and change their policy preferences following discussion with policy experts and fellow citizens.

But in order for accuracy incentives to reduce cognitive biases, individuals have to possess and employ reasoning strategies that improve choice (Camerer & Hogarth, 1999). Some kinds of problems may not benefit from greater effort if the effort promotes resorting to reasoning processes that are faulty, or if the problem is too difficult to solve so that effort is irrelevant or even counterproductive. A common circumstance in politics is that information is disputed among experts, and many people do not have the knowledge or ability to sort through competing claims even if they were motivated to do so.

In nonpolitical experiments there is typically a consensus on the quality of arguments among participants. Participants are not predisposed by their partisanship or ideologies to favor or oppose these arguments, so they are able to interpret the arguments more objectively than, for example, the arguments used in Cohen's (2003) "party over policy" paper. In Cohen's study, there was considerable cognitive elaboration occurring among participants, but it was aimed toward increasing consistency with prior attitudes toward the parties. In addition, in the political world, objectivity in assessing arguments may be compromised by strong prior attitudes toward the subject.

Although Achen and Bartels (2009) found a preponderance of motivated reasoning in their analysis of National Election Survey data, they did confirm that information effects are larger when individuals have personal concerns for the issue and receive considerable information about it. Their prime example is how women's attitudes toward abortion rights changed as Democratic and Republican Party positions evolved in the 1970s and 1980s. Women cared more than men about this issue, and informed women were more likely than informed men to change parties during the 1980s as the abortion issue and contrasting party positions became salient.

In their studies of vote choice, Lau, Anderson, & Redlawsk (2008; also Redlawsk & Lau, chapter 5, this volume) hypothesize that correct voting is related to increased motivation to make a good decision (operationalized as caring who wins); expertise (political knowledge and education); the availability of an effective heuristic; more informative campaigns (reflected in increased campaign spending); and simplicity and clarity of choice (i.e., ideologically distinct candidates, and fewer candidates should make correct voting easier to accomplish). Likewise, Hillygus and Shields (2009) found that voters respond to campaign information about the issue positions of candidates if the issue is sufficiently important to them. The alternative perspective (e.g., Lenz, 2009) is that voters are modifying their views over the course of the campaign to match those of the candidate they prefer. This alternative explanation seems unlikely among the persuadable partisans identified by Hillygus and Shields because their issue preferences were measured early in the campaign and the issues examined were deemed important by the voters, making it more likely that they had strong opinions on these issues that would not easily be changed.

In general, exposure to strong contrary arguments and their repetition should reduce biased processing because it is more difficult to discount strong arguments (Petty & Cacioppo, 1986, p. 164). There is evidence that motivated reasoning among voters can be gradually overcome with an accumulation of evidence, as voters do not indefinitely reject contrary evidence once they have formed a preference (Redlawsk, Civettini, & Emmerson, 2010).

In sum, we assume that rational citizens will incorporate information that is relevant to the decision. Accuracy is pursued if the decision is salient and the consequences are important; for example, more information is sought and evidence is reviewed more evenhandedly. But in politics this process can be muddled by the quality of information and debate over the facts and the applicability of those facts to the decision. Most of our information is obtained by trusting sources, not by independently verifying the truth of a claim. Virtually all public policy claims are disputed in varying degrees (see Chong & Druckman's (2010a) analysis of the large number of opposing frames used in political debates), making it difficult for citizens to identify what is true or relevant. In the following section, I will discuss how the prevalence of framing effects means that citizens rarely have a clear understanding of what facts and consequences are relevant to the policy. Ironically, motivated reasoning from partisan preferences to beliefs about policies is one of the ways that individuals resist framing effects.

5. Framing of Political Preferences

Rationality presumes that individuals have coherent preferences that are invariant to how the alternatives are described. The research on framing offers pervasive evidence that alternative (and sometimes logically equivalent) descriptions of the same policy can produce significantly different responses. In perhaps the most famous example, devised by Tversky and Kahneman (1981), individuals reversed their preferences in selecting between risky choices by preferring the risk-averse option when it was framed in terms of gains, but the risk-seeking alternative when the same outcomes were framed as losses. (See Jack Levy's discussion in chapter 10 of this volume of framing and preference reversals in international relations.)

In politics, changes in the labeling of alternatives can have marked effects on public opinion. Familiar examples include substituting "the poor" for "those on welfare," or referring to groups that oppose the right to an abortion as "anti-abortion" rather than "pro-life" (Bartels, 2003). Similarly, public preferences can be markedly affected by selectively highlighting certain positive or negative characteristics or consequences of the policy. A frequently cited example involves a political extremist group that is planning a public rally (Chong & Druckman, 2007, Nelson, Clawson, & Oxley, 1997; Sniderman & Theriault, 2004). If respondents are reminded by the survey question that free speech rights are at stake, they are inclined to support the group's right to stage the rally. But if they are reminded instead that the rally might spark violence, they switch their position and prefer to stop the rally from taking place.

Framing effects undermine the assumption of consistent preferences that underlies rational choice theory. In all of these instances, preferences should be invariant to changes in the framing of the alternatives. If framing effects are sufficiently common, they reduce the validity of public preferences expressed in surveys and elections, and challenge the notion of popular sovereignty in democratic theory.

5.1. The Psychology of Framing

To understand how framing occurs, consider the structure of an attitude. A person's attitude toward an object is the product of his beliefs about it. Framing presumes a mixture of positive and negative beliefs and therefore some degree of ambivalence. For example, a person may believe that an extremist group is entitled to free speech but may also believe that a rally would pose a danger to public safety. Whichever belief has greater weight will determine his or her attitude on the issue. Framing influences people's attitudes by affecting the relative weights they give to competing considerations. Equivalence frames are logically equivalent but convey different connotations or meaning, and issue frames emphasizing alternative considerations of the policy are not equivalent, but they represent the same basic options with alternative descriptions of their features (Jou, Shanteau, & Harris, 1996). Both equivalence and emphasis frames steer respondents to a particular interpretation or connotation of the problem.

People vary in the strength and reliability of their attitudes. Some people have strong attitudes that are based on a clear subset of beliefs. Others have beliefs that incline them in different directions, but do not have a settled understanding of the relevance of alternative considerations or aspects of the problem. Framing effects are more likely when people do not have a strong attitude or preference based on a well-defined set of considerations. Instead they passively accept the narrow conceptualization of the issue or problem provided to them (Kahneman, 2003, p. 1459) and are unable or unmotivated to generate additional features of the problem.

Stability of preferences depends on individuals being able to retrieve and evaluate the same set of relevant considerations independent of the framing of the question. This is likely to be difficult for all but well-informed and motivated respondents. For example, lawyers and judges display stable preferences on civil liberties issues when they consistently apply general legal principles to a variety of controversies involving the First Amendment rights of unpopular groups (Chong, 1996). More commonly, however, ordinary citizens are highly susceptible to framing because they have neither formal training nor strong beliefs on most issues.

5.2. Qualification of Framing Effects

A number of scholars (e.g., Wittman, 1995; Riker, 1995) have argued that experimental demonstrations of framing lack external validity because they exclude features of the political world (incentives, debate, learning) that would mitigate the effects generated in the laboratory. The magnitude of framing effects also can be moderated by the wording of problems, changing numerical details, strong attitudes, greater cognitive ability, increased contemplation, and the need to provide a rationale for one's preferences (Druckman, 2001; Kuhberger, 1998; Miller and Fagley, 1991).

Druckman (2004) provides persuasive evidence of contextual and individual variation in the size of framing effects on equivalence-framing problems. Expertise reduces framing effects, and counterframing and heterogeneous discussion also temper framing effects by increasing the accessibility of alternative interpretations of the problem so that one is not swayed disproportionately by a one-sided frame. Sniderman and Theriault (2004) also show that simultaneous competition between frames increases the likelihood that people will choose policy alternatives that are consistent with their values. Chong and Druckman (2007; 2010b) demonstrated experimentally that competing frames offset framing effects when the opposing frames are of comparable strength. However, they also found that the canceling effects of simultaneous competition between frames do not extend to dynamic competition between the same frames received over time. When competing frames are received sequentially over time, as in a political campaign, most individuals become newly susceptible to the last frame they receive because early framing effects tend to decay. An important qualification on this result is that people who engage in effortful processing of initial messages develop surprisingly stable—and rigid—opinions that are resistant to framing compared to those who rely on memory-based processing.

5.3. Information or Framing Effects?

A charitable interpretation of many examples of framing effects is that people are being guided by the connotations of frames rather than being misled or deceived. Alternative frames change the problem for the respondent by providing new information and highlighting what is relevant. For example, respondents are reasonable to believe the hate group rally poses a threat to public safety if the survey item explicitly mentions "the possibility of violence," but not otherwise. This interpretation of framing fits well with Simon's (1985) description of the problem solver as one "who is provided in advance with a knowledge of neither alternatives nor consequences—and who may even discover what his or her goals are in the course of the problem-solving process" (p. 295).

Framing and information effects have a different normative status in the study of public opinion even though they describe similar processes. Framing effects are said to undermine the validity of public opinion, while information effects demonstrate the public is responsive to substantive policy details. A possible distinction is that information introduces new considerations that change people's beliefs and preferences. In contrast, framing might operate by increasing the accessibility and applicability of existing beliefs rather than generating new ideas. Many examples of framing, however, probably result from a combination of learning and framing in which new arguments and beliefs are introduced and made applicable through repetition (Chong & Druckman, 2010b).

A telling example of the parallels between research on information and framing is Gilens's (2001) study, cited above, of the effect of specific policy information on attitudes toward new prison construction and foreign aid. Gilens found that information about declining crime rates reduced support for new prison construction. But this information could have been framed differently, and there is likely an alternative representation that would induce a different effect on policy preferences. Imagine how preferences would be affected if we used the following frame to connect the ideas that prison sentences have increased and crime rates have declined: "Given that crime rates have declined as incarceration rates have increased, do you support construction of new prisons?" This alternative "information" or frame would probably lead people to be more supportive of building additional prisons. Similarly, instead of pointing out that foreign aid amounts to less than 1% of federal spending (which increased support for foreign aid in Gilens's study), what would happen if this percentage instead were framed as an absolute dollar amount? Respondents who were told that about $50 billion of the current budget was devoted to foreign aid may be more likely to feel this was too much spending. These examples are meant to illustrate that information effects can be as problematic as framing effects in raising concerns about the reliability of public preferences.

5.4. Motivated Reasoning as a Source of Consistency

It is also instructive to juxtapose motivated reasoning and framing. The problem of motivated reasoning can be summarized as too little responsiveness to information that is relevant to the decision. Conversely, the problem of framing is too much responsiveness to the description of alternatives. The paradox is that in the framing research, resistance to framing usually is viewed positively (i.e., reflecting well on respondents), while in the motivated reasoning research, individuals who do not respond to information generally are evaluated negatively.

The inconsistent treatment of partisan motivations in these two areas of research highlights the need for a consistent criterion. Linking options to partisan endorsements is an especially effective way to reduce framing effects (Druckman, 2001, p. 248). Party endorsements provide supplemental cues to respondents about how to choose consistently between alternative framings of the same policy. As Druckman (2001, p. 237) writes: "many people have well developed preferences towards parties or other elites.... Thus, they are able to make consistent choices and are less susceptible to framing effects—they simply opt for the alternative endorsed by their party." Partisanship can diminish the effects of framing, of course, but this may be due mainly to motivated reasoning. Consistency potentially comes at a cost (cf. Cohen's findings on party versus policy) if it reflects only peripheral attention to party cues rather than analysis of information. Therefore the source of stability must be considered when evaluating the quality of decisions made. If people are able to choose consistently with the assistance of a party cue, they may also be misled by party cues to adopt positions they would not support on the strength of arguments. Weak arguments could just as easily be bolstered by strong peripheral cues as are stronger arguments.

Framing is inherently a reflection of ambivalence (Chong & Druckman, 2010; Popkin, 1991; Zaller, 1992). Ambivalence can be resolved (and stability achieved) in different ways, including reliance on ideological values or partisan cues, online processing, motivated reasoning, or rational deliberation. But we should not assume that anything that reduces framing effects is a positive outcome. It is a separate research question to analyze whether individuals are making good procedural decisions according to rational criteria.

Stability allows for consistency of preferences, which is a minimal qualification for rationality. Whether those preferences reflect reliable information and efficient matching of means to ends should also be considered when evaluating the rationality of preferences. In the preceding section, I discussed how strong arguments can prevail over weak arguments if people engage in deliberate processing of information, but it is not necessarily the case that either strong arguments or frames are more compelling on substantive grounds. Their appeal may simply be their ease of comprehension, emotional resonance, or association with an attractive source. There has been little systematic analysis of the qualities of frames that make them effective (Petty & Cacioppo, 1986).

I would argue, on normative grounds, that ambivalence is best resolved through reconciliation of competing ideas—aggregation and evaluation of relevant information to make choices that are instrumentally related to one's goals. In experiments on framing, however, only a small subset of people aggregate and balance information received over time (Chong & Druckman, 2007; 2010). More often, individuals are vulnerable to the vagaries of the timing and framing of communications because they do not engage in effortful processing of information.

In closing, it is useful to recall that the earliest framing effects in surveys were unintended. Survey researchers discovered that different phrasings of the question produced significant differences in the marginal distribution of opinion and sometimes in the correlations between opinions (Schuman & Presser, 1981). At the time, these framing effects were blamed on researchers more than on respondents. For example, the practice of using two-sided questions and bipolar scales is a response to the biases created by one-sided representations of issues such as acquiescence. When the NES changed the wording of issue questions to include opposing liberal and conservative positions, the ideological consistency of people's attitudes increased significantly (Nie, Verba, & Petrocik, 1976; Sullivan, Piereson, & Marcus, 1978). Attitudes can also be more reliably measured using batteries of items rather than single questions. These lessons are disconnected from recent discussions of framing, where competition substitutes for balanced items or attitude scales that present respondents with multiple considerations. In general, the same factors, including improvements in measurement, that increase the reliability of attitude reports should also reduce the prevalence of framing effects.

6. Conclusion

In everyday life, people assume that others are rational in the sense of having reasons for their actions that often derive from self-interest. This is an unstated assumption that guides human interaction. It is not always true, but it is sufficiently valid that people are able to explain and anticipate the behavior of others. Rationality therefore is the baseline against which behavior is measured.

Research in political psychology and behavior is similarly framed by assumptions of rationality. Rationality is the standard against which we evaluate individual decision-making. We assess the quality of public opinion and public choice by comparing it against a normative standard of how people ought to evaluate information, policies, and candidates. It is desirable that people not only have coherent beliefs and preferences, but that they hold reasonably accurate perceptions of the world, are open to new information, and are able to correctly connect means to their goals in light of these (reasonable) beliefs. Elster (1990) refers to rational choice as a normative theory first and an explanatory theory only when it assumes that people will abide by the normative standard of rationality.

Decision-making is assumed to be constrained by the economics of information: knowledge has value but is costly to obtain. Sometimes the costs are too high and cannot be justified given the expected benefit of obtaining the knowledge, such as the cost of gathering detailed information about candidates for election. Much knowledge is therefore discovered as a byproduct of other activities. People acquire it freely as part of their routine daily activities—for example, listening to the news while driving to work—and by relying on sources that share their interests and subsidize costs by analyzing and distilling information for them. If it is rational to limit one's attention to politics, it is also rational to restrict one's participation to relatively costless activities such as voting.

The rational choice explanation for voting, of course, is seen as the problem that falsified the theory (Green & Shapiro, 1994). The average individual derives negligible instrumental benefits from voting because any material policy differences between the parties are discounted by the almost-zero probability that one's vote will affect the outcome of the election (Downs, 1957). The logical deduction from this assumption is that if voters are concerned only about policy benefits, no one would ever bother to vote because the cost exceeds the benefit.

For some reason, this deduction has been regarded as significantly more problematic than the corollary deduction that voters also will have little or no incentive to gather information. Whereas no analysis of political attitudes and behavior questions the economics of information, the calculus of voting is dismissed as false. It *is* false in the sense that some people do indeed vote in large-scale elections, but some people also possess political knowledge, and it is not clear whether even the modest amounts of information held by the public is too much for a rational actor concerned only with the instrumental value of knowledge. The kinds of noninstrumental explanations (e.g., politics as recreational or expressive behavior) given for highly knowledgeable citizens have not undercut the economic theory of information in the same way that noninstrumental motives for voting have been seen as fatal to the theory of participation.

The most important lesson from the logic of voting is that citizens will place a low value on voting and even successful efforts to lower the costs of voting will have only marginal effects. As Schattschneider (1960) noted a half century ago: "The fact that something like forty million adult Americans are so unresponsive to the regime that they do not trouble to vote is the single most truly remarkable fact about it" (p. 99). What is more, "With some important exceptions, the most striking fact about the phenomenon is that it seems to be voluntary" (p. 98). The only countries that experience extremely high levels of turnout are those that impose penalties for not voting, which confirms that the value of voting is perceptibly small among many voters.

While the benefits of voting are small, so are the costs. The low cost of voting explains why small manipulations of subjective perceptions, social pressures, and the salience of civic norms can push people into the voting booth. A simple knock on the door from a campaign worker reminding one of Election Day can make a significant difference in the decisions of many (Gerber & Green, 2000). Politicians have a much greater stake in the outcome of the election, and they will create incentives and reduce costs to encourage higher turnout rates. Field experimental work by Gerber, Green, and colleagues has established the impact of social pressure on voter turnout, and more fundamentally the social esteem that is attributed to a person who votes (Gerber, Green, & Larimer, 2008). These studies indicate that nonpolicy social motivations for voting can be both instrumental and self-interested.

If there is general acceptance that rational choice theory is the best explanation for the limited engagement of citizens, there is much less agreement about the rationality of decisions that citizens make when they pay so little attention to politics. I have interspersed my review with comments about the inconsistent application of normative standards in the study of political attitudes. Let me close by briefly bringing together these observations:

We encountered several instances in which the same findings were interpreted and evaluated differently depending on whether the focus of research was on framing, information processing, updating of beliefs, cues and heuristics, or the stability and consistency of preferences. What is virtuous and desirable in one context is a troubling feature of decision-making in another context. For example, consider the following competing claims:

- People exhibit weak attitudes and inconsistent preferences when they are moved by alternative framings of policy alternatives. Alternatively, people respond to information rationally by updating their beliefs and adjusting their political preferences. Is opinion change in response to information different from a framing effect? Some demonstrations of information effects look suspiciously like a framing effect, although information effects are judged positively, but framing effects are judged negatively because they suggest that people have incoherent preferences. In all likelihood, the psychological processes underlying attitude change in response to frames and information are the same. If we believe it is desirable for people to be affected by information, we should consider whether there are parallel conditions in which people ought to be influenced by framing.
- Party cues are helpful heuristics because they override framing effects and create consistent preferences on issues. Alternatively, partisan values motivate biased information processing that reduces the influence of relevant arguments. Depending on the context, relying on party cues to make decisions can be interpreted as either undermining or facilitating rational choice. For example, people exhibit more rationally consistent preferences across alternative frames

when they rely on party or other endorsement cues to guide their choices. But in the study of motivated reasoning, partisans maintain stable opinions only because they irrationally ignore or discount contrary evidence and fail to update their beliefs.

- The most highly informed individuals are most likely to know their interests and use information optimally in connecting means to ends. Alternatively, the most highly informed are most likely to engage in motivated reasoning and to have distorted beliefs about the state of the world. Because motivated people also tend to be motivated reasoners, research on the effects of information should not simply assume that those who have more knowledge are more enlightened about political issues. The reasoning of highly informed individuals can fall considerably short of the standards of unbiased information processing. Knowledge can facilitate motivated reasoning because knowledgeable individuals have readily available reasons for accepting supportive evidence and rejecting contrary evidence. Therefore the most informed individuals may not hold optimal preferences if those preferences stem from false beliefs.
- Information changes policy preferences. Alternatively, more information does not change preferences because people have access to reliable heuristics. Generally, I think we prefer to see that substantive information makes a difference in how people decide. Yet there are two competing normative interpretations of these alternative conclusions: We are reassured when information matters because it proves that paying attention to politics can make a difference, even if many citizens know relatively little. However, if information makes no difference, this may also be a reassuring result if it indicates that people are able to make the equivalent of informed decisions with low effort and information.

All political decisions have to be explained and evaluated within the context in which they are made, as the procedures used to make decisions should be judged differently when the consequences are either large or small. A recurring theme here is there are no easy solutions to the low incentives to participate in mass electoral politics. Low motivation encourages limited information acquisition, peripheral processing of evidence, uncertain and unstable preferences, and motivated reasoning. Politics encourages the use of heuristics because the nature of interests are disputed and hard to discern, and the credibility of factual claims often cannot be judged independently of the partisan and ideological cues attached to them. Although there is evidence consistent with bounded rationality that increased incentives and motivation can moderate biases and errors in decision-making, an inherent and inescapable feature of mass democratic politics that limits individual participation is the diluted value of a single opinion or vote.

NOTES

1. See Elster (1986); Kreps (1990); Little (1991); Rubinstein (1998); Shepsle & Bonchek (1996); also Redlawsk & Lau, chapter 5, this volume.

REFERENCES

Achen, C., & Bartels, L. M. (2009). Musical chairs. Manuscript.

Akerlof, G. A., & Yellen, J. L. (1985). Can small deviations from rationality make significant differences to economic equilibria? *American Economic Review, 75*(4), 708–720.

Aldrich, J. H. (1993). Rational choice and turnout. *American Journal of Political Science, 37*(1), 246–278.

Althaus, S. L. (1998). Information effects in collective preferences. *American Political Science Review, 92*(2), 545–558.

Bartels, L. M. (1996). Uninformed voters: Information effects in presidential elections. *American Journal of Political Science, 40*(1), 194–230.

Bartels, L. M. (2002). Beyond the running tally: Partisan bias in political perceptions. *Political Behavior, 24*(2), 117–150.

Bartels, L. M. (2003). Democracy with attitudes. In M. B. MacKuen & G. Rabinowitz (eds.), *Electoral democracy* (pp. 48–82). Ann Arbor: University of Michigan Press.

Bartels, L. M. (2008). *Unequal democracy: The political economy of the new Gilded Age.* New York: Russell Sage Foundation.

Becker, G. S. (1976). *The economic approach to human behavior.* Chicago: University of Chicago Press.

Benartzi, S., & Thaler, R. (1995). Myopic loss aversion and the equity premium puzzle. *Quarterly Journal of Economics, 110*(1), 73–92.

Bowman, K. & Rugg, A. (2011, April 11). Public opinion on taxes: 1937 to today. Retrieved from http://www.aei.org/files/2011/04/11/AEIPublicOpinionTaxes2011.pdf.

Brady, H., & Sniderman, P. M. (1985). Attitude attribution: A group basis for political reasoning. *American Political Science Review, 79*(4), 1061–1078.

Bullock, J. (2009). Partisan bias and the Bayesian ideal in the study of public opinion. *Journal of Politics, 71*(3), 1109–1124.

Camerer, C. F., & Hogarth, R. M. (1999). The effects of financial incentives in experiments: A review and capital-labor-production framework. *Journal of Risk and Uncertainty, 19*(1–3), 7–42.

Campbell, A. (2002). Self-interest, Social Security, and the distinctive participation patterns of senior citizens. *American Political Science Review, 96*, 565–574.

Chase, V. M., Hertwig, R., & Gigerenzer, G. (1998). Visions of rationality. *Trends in Cognitive Science, 2*(6), 206–214.

Chong, D. (1996). Creating common frames of reference on political issues. In D. C. Mutz, P. M. Sniderman, & R. A. Brody (eds.), *Political persuasion and attitude change* (pp. 195–224). Ann Arbor: University of Michigan Press.

Chong, D. (2000). *Rational lives: Norms and values in politics and society.* Chicago: University of Chicago Press.

Chong, D., Citrin, J., & Conley, P. (2001). When self interest matters. *Political Psychology, 22*(3), 541–570.

Chong, D., & Druckman, J. N. (2007). Framing public opinion in competitive democracies. *American Political Science Review, 101*(4), 637–655.

Chong, D., & Druckman, J. N. (2010a). Identifying frames in political news. In Erik P. Bucy and R. Lance Holbert (eds.), *Sourcebook for political communication research: Methods, measures, and analytical techniques.* New York: Routledge.

Chong, D., & Druckman, J. N. (2010b). Dynamic public opinion: Communication effects over time. *American Political Science Review, 104*(4), 663–680.

Citrin, J., & Green, D. P. (1990). The self-interest motive in American public opinion. *Research in Micropolitics, 3*(1), 1–28.

Cohen, G. L. (2003). Party over policy: The dominating impact of group influence on political beliefs. *Journal of Personality and Social Psychology, 85*(5), 808–822.

Conlisk, J. (1996). Why bounded rationality? *Journal of Economic Literature, 34*(2), 669–700.

Converse, P. (1964). The nature of belief systems in mass publics. In D. E. Apter (ed.), *Ideology and discontent* (pp. 206–261). New York: Free Press.

Crowe, J. W., & Bailey, W. J. (1995). Self-interest and attitudes about legislation controlling alcohol. *Psychological Reports, 76*, 995–1003.

Delli Carpini, M. X., & Keeter, S. (1996). *What Americans know about politics and why it matters.* New Haven, CT: Yale University Press.

Dixon, R. D., Lowery, R. C., Levy, D. E., & Ferraro, K. F. (1991). Self-interest and public opinion toward smoking policies: A replication and extension. *Public Opinion Quarterly, 55*(2), 241–254.

Downs, A. (1957). *An economic theory of democracy.* New York: Harper & Row.

Druckman, J. N. (2001). The implications of framing effects for citizen competence. *Political Behavior, 23*(3), 225–256.

Druckman, J. N. (2004). Political preference formation: Competition, deliberation, and the (ir) relevance of framing effects. *American Political Science Review, 98*(4), 671–686.

Elster, J. (Ed.). (1986). *Rational choice.* New York: New York University Press.

Elster, J. (1989). *The cement of society.* New York: Cambridge University Press.

Elster, J. (1990). When rationality fails. In K. S. Cook & M. Levi (eds.), *The limits of rationality* (pp. 19–51). Chicago: University of Chicago Press.

Fazio, R. H., & Olson, M. A. (2003). Attitudes: Foundations, functions, and consequences. In M. A. Hogg & J. Cooper (eds.), *The handbook of social psychology* (pp. 139–160). London: Sage.

Fiorina, M. P. (1981). *Retrospective voting in American national elections.* New Haven, CT: Yale University Press.

Fishkin, J. (2006). Beyond polling alone: The quest for an informed public. *Critical Review, 18*(1 & 3), 157–165.

Fishkin, J. S., Luskin, R. C., & Jowell, R. (2002). Deliberative polling in Britain. *British Journal of Political Science, 32*(3), 455–487.

Freund, T., Kruglanski, A. W., & Shpitzajzen, A. (1985). The freezing and unfreezing of impressional primacy: Effects of the need for structure and the fear of invalidity. *Personality and Social Psychology Bulletin, 11*(4), 479–487.

Gaines, B. J., Kuklinski, J. H., Quirk, P. J., Peyton, B., & Verkuilen, J. (2007). Same facts, different interpretations: Partisan motivation and opinion on Iraq. *Journal of Politics, 69*(4), 957–974.

Gerber, A. S., & Green, D. P. (1998). Rational learning and partisan attitudes. *American Journal of Political Science, 42*(3), 794–818.

Gerber, A. S., & Green, D. P. (2000). The effects of canvassing, telephone calls, and direct mail on voter turnout: A field experiment. *American Political Science Review, 94*(3), 653–663.

Gerber, A. S., Green, D. P., & Larimer, C. W. (2008). Social pressure and voter turnout: Evidence from a large-scale field experiment. *American Political Science Review, 102*(1), 33–48.

Gigerenzer, G. (1991) How to make cognitive illusions disappear: Beyond "heuristics and biases." *European Review of Social Psychology, 2*, 83–115.

Gigerenzer, G., & Goldstein, D. G. (1996). Reasoning the fast and frugal way: Models of bounded rationality. *Psychology Review, 103*(4), 650–669.

Gilens, M. (2001). Political ignorance and collective policy preferences. *American Political Science Review, 95*(2), 379–396.

Gilovitch, T. (1991). *How we know what isn't so: The fallibility of human reason in everyday life.* New York: Free Press.

Green, D. P., & Gerken, A. E. (1989). Self-interest and public opinion toward smoking restrictions and cigarette taxes. *Public Opinion Quarterly, 53*(1), 1–16.

Green, D. P., Palmquist, B., & Schickler, E. (2002). *Partisan hearts and minds: Political parties and the social identities of voters.* New Haven, CT: Yale University Press.

Green, D., & Shapiro, I. (1994). *Pathologies of rational choice theory: A critique of applications in political science.* New Haven, CT: Yale University Press.

Hacker, J. S., & Pierson, P. (2005). Abandoning the middle: The Bush tax cuts and the limits of Democratic control. *Perspectives on Politics, 3*(1), 33–53.

Hardin, R. (2006). Ignorant democracy. *Critical Review, 18* (1), 179–195.

Hardin, R. (2009). *How do you know?* Princeton, NJ: Princeton University Press.

Harsanyi, J. C. (1969). Rational-choice models of political behavior vs. functionalist and conformist theories. *World Politics, 21*(4), 513–538.

Hillygus, D. S., & Shields, T. G. (2009). *The persuadable voter: Wedge issues in presidential campaigns.* Princeton, NJ: Princeton University Press.

Hirschman, A. O. (1982). *Shifting Involvements: Private interest and public action.* Princeton, NJ: Princeton University Press.

Hogarth, R. M., & Reder, M. W. (1987). *Rational choice: The contrast between economics and psychology.* Chicago: University of Chicago Press.

Jacobson, G. C. (2006). *A divider not a uniter: George W. Bush and the American people.* New York: Longman.

Jou, J., Shanteau, J., & Harris, R. J. (1996). An information processing view of framing effects. *Memory & Cognition, 24*(1), 1–15.

Kahneman, D. (2003). Maps of bounded rationality: Psychology for behavioral economics. *American Economic Review, 93*(4), 1449–1475.

Key, V. O., Jr. (1966). *The responsible electorate.* Cambridge, MA: Belknap Press.

Kim, S., Taber, C. S., & Lodge, M. (2010). A computational model of the citizen as motivated reasoner: Modeling the dynamics of the 2000 presidential election. *Political Behavior, 32*(1), 1–28.

Kinder, D. R., & Kiewiet, D. R. (1981). Sociotropic politics: The American case. *British Journal of Political Science, 11*(2), 129–161.

Kreps, D. M. (1990). *A course in microeconomic theory.* Princeton, NJ: Princeton University Press.

Kruglanski, A. W., & Freund, T. (1983). The freezing and unfreezing of lay-inferences: Effects on impressional primacy, ethnic stereotyping, and numerical anchoring. *Journal of Experimental Social Psychology, 19*(5), 448–468.

Kuhberger, A. (1998). The influence of framing on risky decisions: A meta-analysis. *Organizational Behavior and Human Decision Processes, 75*(1), 23–55.

Kuklinski, J. H., & Quirk, P. J. (2000). Reconsidering the rational public: Cognition, heuristics, and mass opinion. In A. Lupia, M. D. McCubbins, & S. L. Popkin (eds.), *Elements of reason: Understanding and expanding the limits of political rationality* (pp. 153–182). New York: Cambridge University Press.

Kunda, Z. (1990). The case for motivated political reasoning. *Psychological Bulletin, 108*(3), 480–498.

Lau, R. R., Anderson, D. J., & Redlawsk, P. (2008). An exploration of correct voting in recent U.S. presidential elections. *American Journal of Political Science, 52*(2), 395–411.

Lau, R. R., & Redlawsk, D. P. (1997). Voting correctly. *American Political Science Review, 91*(3), 585–598.

Lau, R. R., & Redlawsk, D. P. (2006). *How voters decide: Information processing in an election campaign.* New York: Cambridge University Press.

Lau, R. R., & Redlawsk, D. P. (2001). Advantages and disadvantages of cognitive heuristics in political decision making. *American Journal of Political Science, 45*(4), 951–971.

Lauderdale, B. E. (2010). Why are political facts so unpersuasive? Manuscript.

Lenz, G. S. (2009). Learning and opinion change, not priming: Reconsidering the priming hypothesis. *American Journal of Political Science, 52*(4), 827–837.

Little, D. (1991). *Varieties of social explanation.* Boulder, CO: Westview Press.

Lodge, M., & Taber, C. S. (2000). Three steps toward a theory of motivated political reasoning. In A. Lupia, M. McCubbins, & S. Popkin (eds.), *Elements of reason: Cognition, choice, and the bounds of rationality* (pp. 182–213). New York: Cambridge University Press.

Lodge, M., & Taber, C. S. (2013). *The rationalizing voter.* New York: Cambridge University Press.

Lord, C. G., Ross, L., & Lepper, M. (1979). Biased assimilation and attitude polarization: The effects of prior theories on subsequently considered evidence. *Journal of Personality and Social Psychology, 37*(11), 2098–2109.

Lupia, A. (1994). Shortcuts versus encyclopedias: Information and voting behavior in California insurance reform elections, *American Political Science Review, 88*(1), 63–76.

Lupia, A., & McCubbins, M. D. (1998). *The democratic dilemma: Can citizens learn what they need to know?* New York: Cambridge University Press.

Miller, P. M., & Fagley, N. S. (1991). The effects of framing, problem variations, and providing rationale on choice. *Personality and Social Psychology Bulletin, 17*(5), 517–522.

Nelson, T. E., Clawson, R. A., & Oxley, Z. M. (1997). Media framing of a civil liberties conflict and its effect on tolerance. *American Political Science Review, 91*(3), 567–583.

Nie, N. H., Verba, S., & Petrocik, J. R. (1976). *The changing American voter.* Cambridge, MA: Harvard University Press.

Page, B. I., & Shapiro, R. Y. (1992). *The rational public: Fifty years of trends in Americans' policy preferences.* Chicago: University of Chicago Press.

Petty, R. E., & Cacioppo, J. T. (1986). The elaboration likelihood model of persuasion. In L. Berkowtiz (ed.), *Advances in experimental social psychology* (pp. 123–205). New York: Academic Press.

Petty, R. E., & Wegener, D. T. (1999). The elaboration likelihood model: Current status and controversies. In S. Chaiken & Y. Trope (eds.), *Dual-process theories in social psychology* (pp. 41–72). New York: Guilford Press.

Popkin, S. L. (1994). *The reasoning voter: Communication and persuasion in presidential campaigns* (2nd ed.). Chicago: University of Chicago Press.

Prasad, M., Perrin, A. J., Bezila, K., Hoffman, S. G., Kindleberger, K., Manturuk, K., & Powers, A. S. (2009), There must be a reason: Osama, Saddam, and inferred justification. *Sociological Inquiry, 79*(2), 142–162.

Prior, M. (2007, April). Is partisan bias in perceptions of objective conditions real? The effect of an accuracy incentive on the stated beliefs of partisans. Paper presented at the 65th Annual Meeting of the Midwest Political Science Association, Chicago, IL.

Rabin, M. (1998). Psychology and economics. *Journal of Economic Literature, 36*(1), 11–46.

Redlawsk, D. P., Civettini, A. J. W., & Emmerson, K. M. (2010). The affective tipping point: Do motivated reasoners ever "get it"? *Political Psychology, 31*(4), 563–593.

Riker, W. H. (1995). The political psychology of rational choice theory. *Political Psychology, 16*(1), 23–44.

Rubinstein, A. (1998). *Modeling bounded rationality.* Cambridge, MA: MIT Press.

Schattschneider, E. E. (1960). *The semisovereign people: A realist's view of democracy in America.* New York: Holt, Rinehart, and Winston.

Schuman, H., & Presser, S. (1981). *Questions and answers in attitude surveys: Experiments in question form, wording, and context.* New York: Academic Press.

Sears, D. O., & Citrin, J. (1985). *Tax revolt: Something for nothing in California* (enlarged ed.). Cambridge, MA: Harvard University Press.

Sears, D. O., & Funk, C. L. (1991). The role of self-interest in social and political attitudes. *Advances in Experimental Social Psychology, 24*(1), 1–91.

Sears, D. O., & Lau, R. (1983). Inducing apparently self-interested political preferences. *American Journal of Political Science, 27*(2), 223–252.

Shepsle, K. A, & Bonchek, M. S. (1996). *Analyzing politics: rationality, behavior, and institutions.* New York: Norton.

Simon, H. A. (1957). *Models of man: Social and rational.* New York: Wiley.

Simon, H. A. (1985). Human nature in politics: The dialogue of psychology with political science. *American Political Science Review, 79*(2), 293–304.

Simon, H. A. (1990). Alternative visions of rationality. In P. K. Moser (ed.), *Rationality in action: Contemporary approaches* (pp. 189–204). New York: Cambridge University Press.

Simon, H. A. (1995). Rationality in political behavior. *Political Psychology, 16*(1), 45–61.

Sniderman, P. M., Brody, R. A., & Tetlock, P. E. (1991). *Reasoning and choice: Explorations in political psychology.* New York: Cambridge University Press.

Sniderman, P. M., & Theriault, S. M. (2004). The structure of political argument and the logic of issue framing. In W. E. Saris & P. M. Sniderman (eds.), *Studies in public opinion: Attitudes, nonattitudes, measurement error, and change* (pp. 133–165). Princeton, NJ: Princeton University Press.

Stimson, J. (2004). *Tides of consent.* New York: Cambridge University Press.

Sullivan, J. L., Piereson, J. E., & Marcus, G. E. (1978). Ideological constraint in the mass public: A methodological critique and some new findings. *American Journal of Political Science, 22*(2), 233–249.

Taylor, M. (1989). Structure, culture and action in the explanation of social change. *Politics and Society, 17*(2), 115–162.

Taylor, S. E., Peplau, L. A., & Sears, D. O. (1994). *Social psychology* (8th ed.). Englewood Cliffs, NJ: Prentice-Hall.

Tetlock, P. E. (1983). Accountability and the perseverance of first impressions. *Social Psychology Quarterly, 46*(4), 285–292.

Tetlock, P. E. (1985). Accountability: A social check on the fundamental attribution error. *Social Psychology Quarterly, 48*(3), 227–236.

Tversky, A., & Kahneman, D. (1981). The framing of decisions and the psychology of choice. *Science, 211* (4481), 453–458.

Tversky, A., & Thaler, R. H. (1990). Anomalies: Preference reversals. *Journal of Economic Perspectives, 4*(2), 201–211.

Wittman, D. (1995). *The myth of democratic failure: Why political institutions are* Chicago: University of Chicago Press.

Wolpert, R. M., & Gimpel, J. G. (1998). Self-interest, symbolic politics, and public attitu toward gun control. *Political Behavior, 20*(3), 241–262.

Young, J., Thomsen, C., Borgida, E., Sullivan, J. L., & Aldrich, J. H. (1991). When self-interest makes a difference: The role of construct accessibility in political reasoning. *Journal of Experimental Social Psychology, 27*(3), 271–296.

Zaller, J. R. (1992). *The nature and origins of mass opinion.* New York: Cambridge University Press.

CHAPTER 5

....

BEHAVIORAL
DECISION-MAKING

....

DAVID P. REDLAWSK AND RICHARD R. LAU

1. INTRODUCTION

....

JUDGMENT and choice are at the core of all politics. Given Easton's (1953) definition of politics as the "authoritative allocation of values," then the *study* of politics must certainly involve, as a central organizing theme, how those authoritative allocation decisions are made. Broadly speaking, political decision-making falls into two domains. One concerns how *individual* political actors, whether politicians or ordinary citizens, make political decisions. For the most part this first perspective views decision-making as a question of individual psychology: individual preferences, information search, evaluation, and choice. A second domain considers how the *institutions* of politics—the legislative, executive, judicial, and bureaucratic branches of government, as well as organizations that interact with them—make decisions. All institutions are made up of individuals, of course, but all institutions also have their own particular ways—laws, traditions, "standard operating procedures"—for gathering information, aggregating preferences, and taking actions. In many instances, institutional norms and procedures can override individual decision-making processes. March (1994) tries to capture this difference in perspectives by asking whether decision-makers are generally seen as autonomous actors or as being primarily guided by the "systematic properties of an interacting ecology" (p. ix).

Without meaning to minimize the importance of institutional factors in political decisions, we focus on how individual actors make political decisions. Individual decision-making has been a primary concern of psychologists and behavioral economists. In contrast, most economists, sociologists, and organizational theorists study larger aggregates like institutions and firms. The literatures are largely distinct; both are voluminous. For good overviews of research aimed more at the institutional level, the reader is referred to the many works of March (e.g., 1988; 1994; March & Olson, 1989; March & Simon, 1958) and the earliest research of Simon (1947). Allison and Zelikow (1999) do an excellent job of contrasting the two perspectives in the context of the Cuban Missile Crisis (see also Dyson and 't Hart, chapter 13, this volume).

Our goal is to provide a general framework for studying individual decision-making that applies to both everyday citizens and to political elites. Political elites and common citizens differ not only in the amount of expertise they typically bring to the decision-making task, however, but also in the *type* of decisions they are asked to make. Even so, the examples and extensions of the basic decision-making framework here will concentrate the decision-making of everyday citizens, and in particular on voter decision-making. One very important topic of elite decision-making, foreign policy, is the specific focus of the chapter by Levy in this volume (chapter 10). We develop our framework within the broader program of behavioral decision theory (Edwards, 1961; Einhorn & Hogarth, 1981; Hastie & Dawes, 2001) contrasting this psychological approach with rational choice theory (RCT), which, while generally ignoring much of what we know about limitations of human cognition, purports to provide "as-if" models of individual decision-making. Dennis Chong says more about RCT in his chapter in this volume (chapter 4), where he compares it directly to psychological approaches to political behavior.

Political scientists rarely differentiate between "judgment" and "decision-making." The two have often been linked (e.g., Slovic & Lichtenstein, 1971; Billings & Scherer, 1988; Gilovich & Griffin, 2010), and normatively they are equivalent in the sense that normally a decision-maker *should* choose an alternative if and only if it is preferred more than any other. But as Johnson and Russo (1984) argue, "*choosing* one alternative from a set can invoke difference psychological processes than *judging* alternatives which are presumably evaluated one at a time" (p. 549) (emphasis in original). Judgment involves the evaluation of a single entity along some dimension: how heavy or light, or bright or dark, an object is (psychophysical judgment); how attractive/funny/likable/smart some person is (person judgment); how likely some event is to occur (probabilistic judgment). Judgment thus involves mapping some ambiguous stimuli onto a perceptual system. The tendency to make judgments is particularly true of entities—that is, people—in the social world. The chapter by Valentino and Nardis in this volume (chapter 18) reviews this literature as it applies to perceptions of political actors.

A decision, in contrast, involves a *choice* between two or more alternatives: *whether* to take drugs, *whom* to marry, *when* to retire, *which* candidate to support in the election. Each alternative is associated with a set of beliefs about the outcomes that are believed to be associated with each alternative, and every outcome must be associated with a value or preference, although these beliefs and values may well be idiosyncratic to every decision-maker. But making a choice implies more *commitment* to the chosen alternative than making a judgment suggests about the judged entity, and may well also involve searching for reasons to *justify* the choice (Slovic, Fischoff, & Lichtenstein, 1982). People make judgments all the time without necessarily "putting those judgments into action."

Decisions are often treated as if they are nothing more than choosing the most highly evaluated alternative. This is a mistake, for at least two reasons. First, people (and institutions) make all sorts of decisions without first globally evaluating the alternatives. "Spur of the moment" decisions are of this type, as are habitual or "standing" decisions (Quadrel, Fischhoff, & Davis, 1993), but the problem is much broader than this. If you knew you were going to die tomorrow, you might think carefully about what your last meal should be and where to eat it. But most of the time the decision to eat Chinese or Italian or Mexican food is not made because of any judgment about the quality or tastiness or healthiness of these different cuisines, nor because of any judgment about the quality of the service or the skill of the chef in any of the nearby restaurants, but rather because you "feel" like having Chinese tonight. Such decisions may also be generated from gut responses—that is, emotional drives rather than our active thinking.

We suspect, however, that the vote decision in particular—or any choice between different *people*—is rarely made without first forming some global evaluation of the different candidates for the position, no matter how little information goes into the evaluation. So candidate evaluation is intimately involved in the vote choice. But a second reason that it is wrong to equate judgment and decision-making is that global evaluations, even when they are made, do not necessarily dictate choice. People may vote "strategically"—that is, choose a less preferred alternative because their most preferred candidate has no chance of winning (Cox, 1997). People may vote for a candidate they do not particularly like for some reason largely external to the decision itself (acting "against my better judgment"), for example to please a parent or girlfriend. Or they may simply find it a challenge to "vote correctly" (Lau & Redlawsk, 1997). Elsewhere (Lau & Redlawsk, 2006, chap. 8) we develop this argument in more detail. For now, we will leave the literature on person (candidate) impression to the chapter by Valentino and Nardis in this volume (chapter 18) and focus here on processes that generally lead to decisions, though necessarily we cannot completely ignore judgment in doing so.

The rest of this chapter proceeds by laying out more fully a general framework for what constitutes a "decision," a discussion that begins with the classic economic *rational choice* approach to decision-making associated with von Neumann and Morgenstern (1947). This approach has been regularly used as a normative standard against which particular decisions can be judged. No one who has actually observed decision-making believes that RCT provides an accurate *description* of how decision-makers actually behave, however, and we will spend more time discussing an approach that takes accurate description as its primary goal: *behavioral decision theory* (BDT). BDT takes as its starting point a very different (and more limited) view of human cognitive abilities than RCT. Ironically, this more limited starting point provides many more dimensions along which to study decision-making. Consequently we will spend some time discussing *process tracing* methods for studying decision-making. Finally we examine how the psychological models from BDT have been applied to voter decision-making.

2. Rational Choice, or Economic, Theories of Decision-Making

In its most general form, a decision involves multiple alternatives, beliefs about outcomes, and values associated with those outcomes. Economists have generally been concerned with how consumers and firms make decisions. Their earliest theories were normative in orientation, describing how decision-makers *should* behave. At the same time the research seemed also to suggest people *could* behave in the "rational" ways described by the theories. If people failed to meet normative standards, it was due to errors—biases—that could, given sufficient information and ample learning opportunities, be overcome with appropriate effort. This standard RCT approach views humans (*homo economicus*) as "omniscient calculators" (Lupia, McCubbins, & Popkin, 2000) or demons (Gigerenzer & Todd, 1999) who can readily perform the cognitive manipulations required to reach a decision given adequate motivation. Other social sciences, including social psychology (see Gilovich & Griffin, 2010) and political science (Downs, 1957) adopted these theories to describe their own types of decision-making.

Our intent is not to survey the literature in RCT—see Chong's chapter (chapter 4) in this volume for a more complete version. But it is important to understand what motivated the development of BDT as a reaction to the excesses in attempting to make RCT fit what people actually do. The term "rational" has become loaded, and has many different meanings (March, 1978; Rubenstein, 1998). But for the most part our interest is in *procedural rationality*; has a rational process been followed during information search, evaluations, and choice? A "rational choice" is one, then, based on relatively fixed preferences and following a *logic of consequence*, by which current actions are dictated by anticipation of the value associated with future outcomes (March, 1994). Rational decision-makers are motivated to maximize their "interests," although the theory is silent about what those interests ought to be. This restriction on the meaning of rationality also draws attention to the fact that RCT does not guarantee that the value-maximizing outcome *will* be obtained, only that it is the most likely outcome.

When RCT considers risk, it has an "expected value" framework. Decision-makers should gather sufficient information about every plausible course of action. Every consequence or outcome associated with each alternative is assumed to have a certain fixed value for the decision-maker. The value of the outcomes associated with each alternative, weighted by their expected probability of occurring, are combined in a simple additive fashion to determine the overall value associated with each alternative. After going through this process of information gathering and alternative evaluating, decision-makers choose among alternatives by some value-maximizing process (e.g., choose the alternative with the greatest expected value; choose the alternative that minimizes the worst thing that would be associated with every alternative—i.e., minimizes maximum regret).[1]

The most general expectancy-value theory is *subjective expected utility* (SEU) theory (von Neumann & Morgenstern, 1947; see also Raiffa, 1968; Hastie & Dawes, 2001). The concept of "utility" is a clever solution to a very tricky analytic problem. If all outcomes were easily evaluated in terms of money—say a proposed tax cut that is designed to spur the economy—it would be a relatively simple matter to compare the desirability of any two outcomes to each other. But they cannot. Some outcomes have primarily expressive costs and benefits—a peaceful world, greater social equality—that cannot easily be translated into monetary values. This makes the prospect of comparing two such outcomes to each other quite daunting. The problem is one of *incommensurability*—the inability to directly compare the various outcomes. And the clever solution of subjective expected utility theory is to use the hypothetical concept of subjective "utility" into which all costs and benefits can be translated. With this assumption, all values (i.e., utilities) become commensurable, and an expected value analysis can proceed.

But would anyone actually do this? Rationally, a decision-maker must seek out all relevant information (with "relevance" usually defined subjectively as anything the decision-maker cares about). Even assuming he has a "utility register" in his brain that can easily assign utilities to different outcomes, once there are more than a few outcomes to keep in mind, each weighed by some subjective probability of occurring, keeping track of the calculations becomes quite challenging.

Many RCT models, most notably Downs (1957), consider the cost of gathering information as a means of limiting the burdens on the decision-maker. Such models can be viewed as "optimization under constraints." New information should be gathered until the marginal costs of additional information exceed the marginal returns from that information. Although considering information costs seems at first glance a plausible way of limiting cognitive effort, in fact any stopping rule actually takes more cognitive effort to employ (Gigerenzer & Todd, 1999; Vriend, 1996). In practical terms, information search—data gathering—is probably the most effortful and influential aspect of decision-making, yet it is outside the realm of most RCT models.

There are two issues here, one concerning ability, the second concerning motivation. Is it *possible* for the unaided decision-maker to craft anything but the simplest decisions in the manner directed by the rational choice approach? Given the number of computations involved, and the limitations of working memory (see below), the answer must be no. Give that same person a pencil and paper, however, and the answer is probably yes—for the most part the computational demands are within reason, and the memory problem can be overcome by simply making lists of pluses and minuses associated with any alternative.

But *would* many decision-makers go to all this effort to make a decision? Here the issue of motivation arises, and it is a serious challenge to RCT. Citizens *could*, probably, follow most of the dictates of subjective expected utility theory for arriving at a good decision about which candidate to support in an election—but why would they bother? It is a lot of work to learn everything there is to know about the competing candidates. According to the theory, it is only rational for someone to expend all of this effort if the expected value of making the correct vote choice is greater than the cost of all of this information gathering and computation. A serious conundrum in RCT is the problem of *stopping* information search. How can anyone know if the cost of the next piece of information exceeds its value? As best as we can tell, RCT is silent on this question, but it is a point made explicit by Gigerenzer and colleagues (1999), as we describe below.

It is important to realize that we are not just trading off the greater expected utility of, say, Roger Republican winning rather than Debra Democrat, against the information gathering and computation costs that it takes to figure out which candidate to support. That utility could be substantial. But it must be weighed against the probability that one vote will determine the outcome of the election—and that probability is, for all practical purposes, nil. In other words, even if the difference in utilities associated with either candidate's victory is quite large, *everyone is still going to receive that utility irrespective of how they vote.* This is another example of the collective-action problem. Figuring out which candidate to vote for—indeed, going to the polls at all—is, according to RCT, an irrational activity. This argument can be pushed further, but the only way "rationality" can be saved is by adopting the economist's notion of "revealed preferences": because people *do* vote, we know the utility of voting must be greater than the costs. Thus notions like fulfilling one's "civic duty" are given great utility (Riker & Ordeshook, 1968). Unfortunately, this "solution" quickly makes the entire approach tautological.[2]

That so many people nonetheless *do* bother to vote suggests either that many people are irrational or that RCT is somehow flawed. The flaw, we think, is not in assuming that people want to be rational, but in *pretending that people actually make decisions* this way. March (1994) captures this perfectly when he asks if "decision-makers pursue a logic of consequence, making choices among alternatives by evaluating their consequences in terms of prior preferences" (p. viii). A "logic of consequence" simply does not describe how people make the vast majority of the decisions they make in all aspects of their lives, including (but certainly not restricted to) politics.

The subjective expected utility approach should not be applied as a behavioral description of how people (or organizations) actually make decisions. But this limitation does not eliminate the most attractive aspects of the perspective; its strong normative component and great "theoretical utility" in allowing researchers to make predictions of many types of behavior, particularly in the aggregate when individual stochastic deviations from rationality cancel out. If a decision-maker were to follow the dictates of RCT, she would be assured that she would likely make what is, for her, the "best" decision. Given certain reasonable (but not indisputable) assumptions, such as maximizing the interests of the most people, the rationality of individual decision-making can also be "aggregated up" to make normative judgments about institutional arrangements for decision-making (see Jones, 1994).

3. BEHAVIORAL DECISION THEORY

In contrast to the normative focus of RCT, BDT takes as its primary goal describing, and thus understanding, how people actually make decisions. Every study of decision-making in the real world has shown that rarely are all alternatives known, all outcomes considered, or all values evoked simultaneously. People generally settle for alternatives that are "good enough" rather than value maximizing. Named by Edwards (1961), BDT begins with the view of humans as *limited information processors*, with neither the motivation nor the ability to make the sort of "consequential" calculations described by rational choice (Anderson, 1983; Gilovich & Griffin, 2010; Hastie & Dawes, 2001; Simon, 1979; 1990; 1995). The term "cognitive miser" was once popular to represent this view (Taylor, 1981), but that term is misleading in that it suggests a conscious hoarding of cognitive resources, which is simply inaccurate. "Bounded rationality," coined by Simon (1947, 1957) is a better term to characterize human cognition.

3.1. Cognitive Limits on Rationality

But what, exactly, are the bounds on information processing? Bounded rationality is thoroughly described in Chong's chapter in this volume (chapter 4), but let us highlight where some of the limits on omniscience occur and are very clear. We can categorize them as limitations on processing and limitations on retrieval. Processing limitations begin with our sense organs. Except perhaps for mothers, human beings do not have eyes in the back of their heads nor ears that can hear distant conversations. Even limiting consideration to sights that are somehow before our eyes and sounds that are nearby, there is usually more in our visual and auditory fields than can be processed because all incoming stimuli must pass through "short-term" or "working" memory, which has a very limited capacity (of approximately 7, ± 2, bits of information; Miller, 1956). This attention bottleneck is in practice the most important "bound" on classic rationality. As a consequence, attention and factors that influence it are crucially important to information processing. The limits on working memory also dictate that most information processing will occur *serially*, one goal at a time.

Now, *if* an incoming stimulus is processed by working memory—and again, that is a big if—it can be more or less permanently stored in long-term memory. Long-term memory is usually envisioned as an associative network of nodes and the connections between them that for all practical purposes has an unlimited capacity. *Retrieval* from long-term memory, on the other hand, is far from perfect, and is a function of how the initial stimulus was processed (that is, what was associated with it), preexisting memory structures (schemas) related to it, the frequency and recency of exposure to the same stimulus (which influences the strength of the connections between nodes), and so on (Anderson, 1983; Simon, 1957, 1979). Limits on memory retrieval mean that one of the fundamental assumptions of rational decision-making, that people *have* preexisting preferences for outcomes, and that they are relatively *fixed* and *immediately available*, is frequently not going to be the case (Zaller & Feldman, 1992). Together, these cognitive limitations make the omniscient calculator of *homo economicus* an unapproachable ideal.

3.2. So, How Do People Cope?

We assert that people *want* to make good decisions—they just generally cannot do so in the ideal manner described by RCT. So human beings have developed mechanisms, or rules, to deal with information overload. These mechanisms are typically employed automatically without conscious forethought. Most are quite general and have ramifications for many aspects of human life. For example, *categorization* or grouping seems to be a basic property of human perception, such that when a new stimulus is perceived, the first thing people try to do is categorize the stimulus as another instance of some familiar group (Rosch, 1978). Category-based (or schema-based) processing is cognitively efficient because once a stimulus is perceived as another instance of some preexisting category, the details of the new stimulus can be largely ignored and "default values" associated with the category can be assumed to hold. Conover and Feldman (1989) and Lodge (Hamill, Lodge, & Blake, 1985; Lodge & Hamill, 1986) provide many political examples of such processing.

Decision-makers seem to simplify their task in at least three fundamental ways: decomposition, editing, and heuristic use.

- *Decomposition* means breaking a decision down into component parts, each of which is presumably easier to evaluate than the entire decision. Problem decomposition is closely related to the specialization and division of labor that is essential in any successful organization.
- *Editing* refers to eliminating (i.e., ignoring) relevant aspects of a decision. Voters might simplify their task by restricting attention to familiar candidates, effectively removing one or more alternatives from the choice set. "Single issue voters" limit the number of "outcomes" associated with each candidate to a manageable number, thus also largely avoiding the need to resolve goal conflicts. A decision-maker could simply count the number of pluses and minuses associated with each alternative rather than trying to weight them by importance or devise an evaluative scale with more than two levels. All of these editing procedures would greatly simplify any decision.
- *Heuristics* are problem-solving strategies (often employed automatically or unconsciously) that serve to "keep the information processing demands of the task within bounds" (Abelson & Levi, 1985, p. 255). They are cognitive shortcuts, rules of thumb for making certain judgments or inferences that are useful in decision-making. Their key attribute is that heuristics reduce the need for the complete search for alternatives and their consequences dictated by RCT.

These three very general simplification mechanisms are applied to many different types of decisions by all types of people. We can adopt an evolutionary perspective and conclude that they must, in general, "work," in the sense of producing choices that are, if not optimal, at least "good enough" most of the time to encourage their reproduction—and rarely bad enough to lead to extinction (Simon, 1957; also see Gigerenzer & Todd, 1999 for development of this argument).

Nonetheless, it is important to recognize that all three of these mechanisms can at times lead to poor decisions. Decomposition, for example, can lead to very embarrassing results when the components of a decision are treated as independent when in fact they are not. A candidate who stresses one set of policies in personal appearances and another set of policies in political advertisements at best puts forth a very diffuse and unfocused message and at worst can be caught espousing contradictory policies. Editing can lead to poor decisions when the ignored aspects of the decision would result, cumulatively, in a new preference order across alternatives if those ignored aspects had been considered. And heuristics can lead to systematic biases when the reason the heuristic is generally effective (e.g., more frequent occurrences really *are* easier to recall; numerical anchors provided by the decision context usually *are* reasonable) is not true in some particular instance (see Lau & Redlawsk, 2001a).

While editing in particular would seem to align nicely with processes described by political scientists such as single-issue voting, there has been little research into the first two mechanisms, while a large literature has developed about heuristics and their role in decision-making. This literature takes two directions. In one, exemplified by the heuristics and biases program of Kahneman & Tversky (1973; 1984; Tversky & Kahneman, 1973; 1974; 1981; 1986; 1992), heuristics lead to bias—failures of rational decision-making. The use of heuristics is not so much adaptive as something to be minimized, in order to make better decisions.

Gilovich and Griffin (2010) see Tversky and Kahneman's research as arising out of a "guiding evolutionary principle . . . that existing processes in perceptional analysis were co-opted as tools for higher level cognitive processing" (p. 545). Heuristics that might have been adaptive in pretechnological environments can lead to bias in the complex environment of modern society. Tversky and Kahneman (1974) identify three common cognitive heuristics employed in lieu of detailed information gathering and analysis. While allowing decision-makers to simplify complex judgments by focusing on a small subset of all possible information, they come with the likely cost of failing to maximize utility. These heuristics include *availability*—judging frequency, probability, and causality by how accessible or available concrete examples are in memory, or how easy it is to generate a plausible scenario; *representativeness*—assigning specific instances to specific categories (stereotypes, schemata) according to how well the specific instance fits the essential properties of one category rather than another; and *anchoring and adjustment*—forming a tentative response first and then adjusting by reviewing relevant data. These processes are ubiquitous; the problem is how to make good decisions in spite of them. The overarching conclusion of this program of research is that in the end decision-makers do cope with their cognitive limits by using heuristics, but using these heuristics results—most often—in a lower-quality decision than if a fully rational process had been used.

The heuristics and biases program examines the limits of rational decision-making while arguing that utility maximizing is the normative standard against which decisions should be tested. But earlier work by Simon (1957) rejects this normative criterion for a standard of bounded rationality through satisficing. Decision-makers can cope with their cognitive limits and make "rational" decisions if we loosen the definition to be "good enough" rather than maximizing. Satisficing assumes that decision-makers set aspiration levels for every attribute of judgment about which they care, and consider alternatives one at a time in random order, continuing to search until an alternative is discovered that meets or exceeds the aspiration level for every criterion. Search then stops and this alternative is chosen. If no such alternative is found, aspiration levels are lowered and the process repeated until an alternative that "satisfies" all criteria is found. Satisficing involves relatively simple cognitive processes. An alternative is sought that is satisfactory on every criterion of judgment, *without* comparing the alternatives to each other. Indeed, some alternatives may be totally ignored, and there is no guarantee that anything approaching the "best" alternative will be selected. Obviously the *order* in which alternatives are considered can completely determine which alternative is selected.

Satisficing provides a framework for the second perspective on the role of heuristics, the "adaptive toolbox" of Gigerenzer and his colleagues (1999; 2008). Their "fast and frugal" heuristics build on Simon's insight that decision-making operates within the interaction between an organism's cognitive limits and the environment in which it exists. They posit an "ecological rationality" where fast and frugal heuristics are an even more efficient and effective decision-making approach than satisficing. A satisficer, in effect, edits the decision environment, deciding to choose the alternative that is good enough. As long as good enough is good enough to survive, there is no reason to maximize. But this process still takes more cognitive effort than any of a number of fast and frugal heuristics that can be consciously adapted as needed based on the context of the decision to be made.

Thus Gigerenzer and his colleagues take a different approach to the study of heuristics, viewing them as adaptive mechanisms—rules of thumb—that can be fruitfully used in the modern world. There are a number of these "simple heuristics" of which satisficing is but one, though it is the most complicated one. Much easier is applying an ignorance-based heuristic like recognition, which draws from our innate ability to recognize a cue from experience and to apply it quickly and effectively. Additional heuristics in the adaptive toolbox include a series of "one-reason" heuristics, such as "Take the Best," which posits simply using the most accessible or apparently relevant information to make a quick decision. Take the Best includes rules for information search, stopping search, and making a choice, and thus is also more comprehensive than standard RCT models, which have a hard time explaining how and when information search stops. An application of Take the Best by Graefe and Armstrong (2010) found that identifying what voters consider the "most important problem" in polls, and assuming they use that one issue to determine their preferred candidate—that is, they "take the best" candidate on this one issue—results in a model that predicts election outcomes as well as econometric models.

While there are other fast and frugal heuristics, the point here is that decision-makers can rely on multiple heuristics adaptable to particular decision environments. With ecological rationality, a decision's "rationality" is based not on cost-benefit analysis and complicated information search, but on how well the decision fits with the environmental structure in which it is made.

We can make sense of many of the diverse findings of BDT by suggesting that decision-makers are generally guided by two competing goals: (1) *the desire to make a good decision*; and (2) *the desire to reach a decision with the minimal cognitive effort* (see, for example, Lau & Redlawsk, 2006; Payne, Bettman, & Johnson, 1993). This leads to another important distinction between RCT and BDT. RCT focuses attention on the *structure* or *elements* of a decision—the multiple alternatives and the value of the different outcomes that are associated, with some probability, with each alternative. BDT, in contrast, is much more likely to be concerned with the dynamic *processes* of *how decisions are made*, focusing on information search and strategies for making choices. The underlying assumption of much of this research is that the best way to study decision-making is to observe it while the decision is being made (Abelson & Levi, 1985).

4. UNDERSTANDING DECISION STRATEGIES

Behavioral decision researchers have developed several *process tracing* methodologies for studying decisions "while they happen," including verbal protocols (Ericsson & Simon, 1984) where decision makers talk out loud as they make their choices. But by far the most popular methodology is the *information board* (Carroll & Johnson, 1990). If studying verbal protocols resembles eavesdropping on a decision as it is being made, information boards are more like voyeurism. Information boards generally present subjects with some sort of matrix where the alternatives under consideration are placed in columns and the different attributes of choice (that is, the outcomes associated with every alternative) are the rows. The actual information is hidden from view, and decision-makers must *actively* decide to learn any specific bit of information by choosing a particular cell of the matrix. Every action the decision-maker takes is recorded, so that at the end there is a complete record of what the decision-maker accessed, how long every bit of information was considered, and the order in which it was examined.

Process tracing lets the researcher see the decision strategies that people use. A decision strategy is a set of mental and physical operations employed in reaching a decision. It includes identifying alternatives, searching for information about the possible outcomes associated with each alternative, making probabilistic judgments about the likelihood of those different outcomes, searching through memory to determine how much each of those outcomes is valued and how important it is in this particular context, and so on. A decision strategy also includes a method for choosing among the alternatives. Elsewhere (Lau & Redlawsk, 2006) we have described decision strategies in detail; here we will just quickly summarize. BDT researchers have identified a number of different decision strategies that differ in terms of how cognitively difficult they are to use, how much of the available information they consider, and their likelihood of reaching a "best" decision. We will refer to strategies that employ all available information as decision *rules* and those that ignore some information as decision *heuristics*.

4.1. Categorizing Decision Strategies

Decision strategies are typically categorized in the literature by the extent to which they confront or avoid conflict (Billings & Marcus, 1983; Ford et al., 1989). When one alternative is preferred on one dimension of judgment but a different alternative is preferred on another dimension, the potential for value conflict or trade-offs exists.[3] *Compensatory* strategies are cognitively complex information integration rules where decision-makers are assumed to assign a value to every attribute associated with each alternative. Some of those values can be positive and others negative, but when they are combined into an overall evaluation or decision, a positive value on one dimension can *compensate for* or trade off against a negative value on another dimension. Different compensatory strategies vary on the extent to which information is weighted and whether outcome importance or probability is considered, but they are all based on full information, that is, the decision-maker includes all relevant attributes and outcomes for all relevant alternatives.

Noncompensatory strategies rely on incomplete information search to avoid conflicts. Negative values on one attribute or possible outcome cannot trade off against positive values on another attribute or outcome; instead, alternatives are eliminated once negative information is encountered, or some attributes are simply ignored. Incommensurability is not a problem. A great deal of research has shown that most decision-makers, most of the time, try to avoid value trade-offs (Hogarth, 1987). But this avoidance has a cost: potentially fewer value-maximizing decisions. Some noncompensatory strategies rely on considering only a limited subset of attributes for all alternatives, while others focus on a subset of alternatives. If decision-makers use compensatory strategies, process tracing will show reasonably equal information search across alternatives and attributes. But if the cognitively limited decision-maker uses heuristics and other simplifying strategies, this will appear as imbalanced search, with some alternative and attributes receiving more attention than others, suggesting a noncompensatory strategy is in use.

Where some compensatory strategies—particularly the expected utility (EU) rule—map onto RCT in its full-blown mode, others are more akin to boundedly rational search. While all compensatory strategies require full information search, some simplifying heuristics may still be used, including assuming weights/probabilities are 1.0 for each attribute (EqW; Hastie & Dawes, 2001; Einhorn & Hogarth, 1975), limiting the evaluation to the frequency of good and bad features (FreqGB; Alba & Marmorstein, 1987), or comparing alternatives one attribute at a time, calculating the differences between each and summarizing (AddDif rule). In a simplified version of AddDif, the majority of confirming dimensions heuristic (MCD), alternatives are compared pairwise on every dimension, but only to judge which is preferred, and then to keep the winning (or confirming) alternative to compare to another until all alternatives have been considered.

Described earlier, Simon's satisficing heuristic was the first and most famous non-compensatory strategy identified (SAT; Simon, 1957). Satisficers are looking to meet an aspiration level and take the first alternative they run across that meets that level. The lexicographic heuristic (LEX) considers the value of every alternative on the most important attribute of judgment and selects the alternative with the highest value (Tversky, 1969). If two or more alternatives are tied, those alternatives are compared on the second most important attribute, and so on, until only one remains. A third non-compensatory strategy is the elimination-by-aspects heuristic (EBA; Tversky, 1972), which combines satisficing and lexicographic strategies and is generally simpler than both of them. As with LEX, decision-makers rank the attributes of judgment in terms of importance, and consider the most important first. As with SAT, decision-makers have an aspiration level for every attribute. Alternatives are eliminated if they do not meet or exceed the aspiration level of each attribute; attributes are examined in decreasing order of importance until only one alternative remains. Like SAT and LEX, EBA avoids conflicts by eliminating alternatives before conflicts occur. (For an application of one form of EBA heuristic to decision-making in foreign policy, see Jack Levy's discussion of "poliheurisitc theory" in chapter 10 in this volume.)

The preceding descriptions of different decision strategies are idealized accounts, of course, and would rarely be observed in such pure states. One may well ask, then, how do we tell which strategy a decision-maker is using? A very important finding of BDT research is that *different patterns of information acquisition clearly reflect distinguishable choice strategies.* Thus a key to understanding any decision is observing how people acquire information, because this in turn sheds light on the decision rules or heuristics that people follow in making their choice.

4.2. Measures of Information Search

Information boards provide a large amount of detailed information about the process of decision-making, particularly information search. Since decision-makers are cognitively limited and will almost certainly make any complex decision without full information, the order of information acquisition can be crucially important. It should be obvious that *how much* information is obtained can influence choice. Somewhat less obviously, even controlling on amount of information, *how* information comes to a decision-maker can also influence choice. As summarized in table 5.1, each of the decision strategies specifies a particular depth and order of information search.

Consider first the *depth* of information search. Rationally, all relevant information about every alternative should be obtained. With information boards it is easy to calculate the proportion of all alternatives, all attributes, and all possible information about every alternative that is considered, and so on—all reasonable measures of the depth of

Table 5.1 Characteristics of Different Decision Strategies

Decision rule	Type	Depth of search	Variance of search	Sequence of search	Cognitive effort
Weighted Additive Rule (WAdd) or Expected Utility Rule (EU)	Compensatory	Very Deep	Equal	Alternative-Based	Very High
Equal Weights Heuristic (EqW)	Compensatory	Deep	Equal	Alternative-Based	Moderately High
Frequency of Good and Bad Features Heuristic (FreqGB)	Compensatory	Deep	Equal	Alternative-Based	Moderate
Additive Difference Rule (AddDif)	Compensatory	Very Deep	Equal	Attribute-Based	Very High
Majority Confirming Dimensions Heuristic (MCD)	Compensatory	Deep	Equal	Attribute-Based	Moderately High
Satisficing Heuristic (SAT)	Noncompensatory	Depends: Shallow to Deep	Generally Unequal	Alternative-Based	Moderately Low
Lexicographic Heuristic (LEX)	Noncompensatory	Generally Shallow	Generally Unequal	Attribute-Based	Moderately Low
Elimination-by-Aspects Heuristic (EBA)	Noncompensatory	Generally Shallow	Generally Unequal	Attribute-Based	Low

information search. Compensatory decision strategies assume that all relevant information about every alternative will be considered, and thus search will be relatively deep. Each of the noncompensatory strategies allows for much shallower search, although the choice set and aspiration levels could be such that all information ends up being considered before a satisfactory alternative is found, or all but one alternative eliminated.

We can also consider the *sequence* of information acquisition. Irrespective of how much information is gathered, the search sequence can be relatively ordered, or largely haphazard. Using an information board sequence can be studied formally with a "transition analysis" (Jacoby, Chestnut, Weigl, & Fischer, 1976). *Ordered search* is of two types, as follows.

- With *alternative-based* search (more formally, intra-alternative, interattribute), sometimes also called *holistic* search, decision-makers consider the different alternatives sequentially. A voter following this search strategy would learn about the issue stands, political experience, personal values, and whatever else he considered important about one candidate in an election, before trying to learn the same information about a second candidate, and so on, until all of the competing candidates are explored. WAdd, EU, EqW, FreqGB, and SAT all assume alternative-based searching.

- With *attribute-based* search (intra-attribute, interalternative), sometimes also called *dimensional* search, a decision-maker chooses one attribute for consideration and compares the values of all competing candidates on that issue, before turning to another attribute and comparing all of the competing alternatives on it. AddDif, MCD, LEX, and EBA all assume attribute-based searching.

Haphazard search, then, is everything else—interattribute, interalternative transitions.[4]

Most research using information boards focuses on the relative proportion of alternative-based to attribute-based search, with the latter usually considered cognitively easier (Russo & Dosher, 1983; Rahn, 1993). But either type of ordered search must be much simpler, cognitively, than haphazard search. When information acquisition is completely under the decision-maker's control, as it is with information boards, the great majority of all transitions are ordered (Jacoby, Jaccard, Kuss, Troutman, & Mazursky, 1987), reflecting the decision-maker's overriding goal of minimizing cognitive effort. Ordered information can be processed and stored more efficiently, aiding decision-making. When information acquisition is not entirely controllable, however—as with, we would argue—an election, the sequence in which information becomes available, the structure of information in the environment, and the decision-maker's ability to at least partially restructure that sequence in some coherent manner can have important effects on decision-making, even changing preferences among alternatives (Tversky & Sattath, 1979).

A third measure is the *variance* of information search across alternatives. Compensatory strategies all assume that the same information should be considered for every alternative, while noncompensatory strategies allow for unequal search across alternatives. Thus the within-subject variance in the amount of information considered about each alternative is another way to distinguish between choice strategies. Compensatory strategies dictate equal variance, while noncompensatory strategies allow for unequal search. Variance measures are particularly useful in distinguishing between decision strategies when task constraints (e.g., time) make it impossible for all information to be considered.

Comparable alternatives are those about which the same attribute information is known, as is always possible with a standard information board. *Noncomparable alternatives*, on the other hand, are those with at least some attributes that are unique to each alternative (Johnson, 1986). Alternatives can be *inherently* noncomparable—guns versus butter, say—or de facto noncomparable because information about some alternatives exists but is unknown to the decision-maker. Rationally, information that is available about some but not all alternatives should be ignored in making a choice—but we suspect it rarely is. Instead, people use what information they have and whenever possible make category-based inferences about the missing information. More generally, however, the possibility (probability, in most instances) of incomplete search of available information means that virtually any decision may involve noncomparable alternatives.

5. Determinants of Choice Strategies: Deciding *How* to Decide

Having described a number of different decision strategies, and means of determining when a particular strategy is being employed, it is worth asking whether these strategies are available to and used by almost everyone, or if instead different people tend to *specialize* in the use of one or another strategy, employing it across different types of decisions. Asked differently, are there some people who tend to be very rational and methodical in their decision-making, while others typically employ more intuitive and heuristic-based decision strategies? The broad answer is that there is little evidence for systematic individual differences in use of these different strategies. Instead, *almost all people seem to have available a wide variety of different decision strategies that they can and do employ in making decisions.* Choice of decision strategy seems to be highly contingent on the nature of the decision task (Payne et al., 1993, Lau & Redlawsk, 2006). Hence BDT research, rather than searching for individual differences in decision-making, has instead focused on contextual factors that make it more likely that one or another strategy will be employed.[5]

One very important set of factors involves the complexity or size of the decision task. *Task complexity* is usually defined in terms of the number of alternatives under consideration and the number of different attributes across which they vary; the more complex the task, the more reliance on simplifying decision heuristics. This is true for both variation in the number of alternatives (Lau & Redlawsk, 2001b) and the number of attributes under consideration (Keller & Staelin, 1987), although the former seems to have much more consistent effects than the latter. Generally speaking, decision-makers rely on noncompensatory decision strategies when there are more than two alternatives, but they may use compensatory strategies if there are only two alternatives Tversky, 1972).

There are additional factors that can affect the difficulty of the choice facing decision-makers, holding task size constant. One is *time pressure*, which may shift a decision-maker's goals from accuracy to efficiency. Thus decision-makers faced with time pressure—say the deadline of Election Day—may accelerate processing (that is, work faster); reduce the amount of information considered, focusing on the most important factors; or change decision strategies, shifting from a compensatory to a noncompensatory strategy (Holsti, 1989; Payne, Bettman, & Johnson, 1988; see also Dyson and 't Hart, chapter 13, this volume). Another factor that affects task complexity is the similarity of the alternatives to each other. When alternatives are very *dis*similar, it is relatively easy to distinguish between them and choose the best one. A noncompensatory choice strategy might very well lead to a different choice than a compensatory strategy, however. When alternatives are relatively similar to each other, it is much more difficult to find the best alternative (Lau & Redlawsk, 2001a). Depth of search should increase (Bockenholt, Albert, Aschenbrenner, & Schmalhofer, 1991), and decision-makers may be more likely to employ a compensatory decision strategy. Decision-makers may also infer that when a decision is difficult, the alternatives must be relatively equally attractive, while in an easy decision they must be far apart (Liberman & Forster, 2006). Of course, it usually doesn't matter very much if one picks the second- or third-best alternative if they are all very similar to each other.

The more *important* the decision is to the decision-maker, the more she will be motivated by decision accuracy rather than decision ease, and the greater will be the effort expended in making the decision (Payne et al., 1993). Thus information search should be deeper, and compensatory decision strategies will be more likely to be employed (Lindberg, Garling, & Montgomery, 1989). This reasoning assumes that deeper information search leads to better decisions, a conclusion that is easy to reach granted omniscient rationality and demonic abilities, but may not actually hold for limited information processors. Indeed, we (Lau & Redlawsk, 2006) as well as Gigerenzer & Goldstein (1999; Czerlinski, Gigerenzer, & Goldstein, 1999) have demonstrated at least some instances when additional information actually results in lower-quality judgments.

Variations in *how information is displayed* or becomes available are also known to affect decision-making. Information rarely becomes available in an orderly, controllable manner, especially in the context of political decisions. If information is obtained about alternatives sequentially, the decision-maker has little choice but to engage in alternative-based decision strategies, while simultaneous acquisition of information about multiple alternatives makes attribute-based search possible (Tversky, 1969). More subtle variations of information display can also make alternative-based or attribute-based processing more likely (e.g., Herstein, 1981) and even determine whether particular information is utilized at all (Russo, 1977). During an election campaign, watching a rally, speech, or party convention for a single candidate provides primarily alternative-based information; a political debate, on the other hand, provides largely attribute-based information (Rahn, Aldrich, & Borgida, 1994). The *completeness* of the information—that is, whether the same information is available about every alternative—determines whether inferences about the missing data are necessary (Ford & Smith, 1987) but can also influence whether information "outside of the box" is even considered in making the decision.

6. Studying the Vote Decision: Dynamic Process Tracing

When political scientists attempt to understand individual vote decisions, they typically turn to the sample survey as their methodology of choice (e.g., Campbell, Converse, Miller, & Stokes, 1960; Fiorina, 1981; Lazarsfeld, Berelson, & Gaudet, 1944; Miller & Shanks, 1996; Nie, Verba, & Petrocik, 1976). Surveys do an excellent job of recording what decision was made (e.g., Are you going to vote in the upcoming election? Which candidate do you support?), but they are a poor vehicle for studying *how* that decision was reached. Surveys usually ask about opinions or decisions that were reached some time in the past, and thus the information provided is based on respondents' memories. Moreover, the reasons people provide for why they might vote for or against a candidate are often *justifications* of a decision already reached rather than a veridical representation of the information that went into that decision (Lau, 1982; Rahn, Krosnick, & Breuning, 1994; Civettini & Redlawsk, 2009). And it may be that voters keep an "online tally" or summary evaluation of familiar candidates in their heads, which they update whenever new information is encountered, but often forget the details of that new information (Lodge, McGraw, & Stroh, 1989; Lodge, Steenbergen, & Brau, 1995; but see Redlawsk, 2001; Lau & Redlawsk, 2006 for the role memory plays in choice). Memory, then, usually provides a poor trace of how a decision was reached.

More recently, political scientists have turned to experiments—laboratory, field, and survey based—to better address the causal questions raised in voter decision-making. Our particular approach has been to use process-tracing experiments. Studies of voting using the standard information board we described above have provided some insights (Herstein, 1981; Riggle & Johnson, 1996; Huang, 2000; Huang & Price, 2001). Yet this standard information board provides a poor analog to a political campaign since the decision-maker can access any information any time he wants. Campaigns, though, have a dynamic quality about them such that information easily available today might be harder to find tomorrow. All information on a standard board is equally easy to access, while in a political campaign certain types of information (e.g., hoopla and horse race) are typically easier to find than others (e.g., detailed issue stands). Decision-makers must actively choose to learn about the alternatives with a standard information board, but much information during political campaigns (e.g., political commercials) comes without any active effort by the decision-maker to learn that information. And, most important, decision-making with an information board is far too "manageable," too controllable, too easy; while during a typical high-level political campaign (e.g., presidential elections and many statewide races), voters can be overwhelmed by far more information than they can possibly process. This latter point may be even truer in the age of the Internet and information overload. In many ways the static information board represents an ideal world for decision-making that can be contrasted to an actual political campaign.

The trade-offs between internal and external validity with any methodology are well known. We have sought a middle ground for studying the vote decision, trying to devise a more ecologically valid research technique that would approximates the realities of modern political campaigns while still providing the experimental control and detailed evidence on information search that is available from a traditional information board (Lau, 1995; Lau & Redlawsk, 2006). To accomplish these goals we have designed a *dynamic process-tracing environment* (DPTE), retaining the most essential features of the standard information board while creating a better analog of an actual political campaign.[6] DPTE has the information boxes scroll down a computer screen rather than sitting in a fixed location (see Redlawsk, 2004; Lau & Redlawsk,

2006; Redlawsk & Lau, 2009 for details). If a standard information board is artificial because it is static and too "manageable," DPTE potentially overwhelms participants (voters) with information. If the static board is unrealistic by making all information available all the time, we mimic the ongoing flow of information during a campaign with the scrolling, where information available today might be much harder to find tomorrow. If the standard information board is artificial because all types of information are equally available, DPTE realistically models the relative ease or difficulty of learning different types of information during a campaign. And if a standard information board only allows for information actively accessed by the decision-makers, we provide voters with a good deal of relevant information "free of charge" in the form of campaign advertisements that occasionally take over the computer screen without any active decision on the voter's part to learn that information. Our research program aims to discover which of the various findings of the BDT literature apply to voting during political campaigns.

We have used DPTE to examine cognitive heuristics and other aspects of "low information rationality" that are common explanations for how people make pretty good decisions without a lot of cognitive effort, and without gathering an inordinate amount of information (Lau & Redlawsk, 2001a; 2006). We have also been explicit in recognizing that a vote *decision*, made in the context of an election campaign where voters know they must ultimately make a choice, is in important ways different from the process of making a judgment or forming an evaluation (such as of an incumbent president's job performance), even though it is common to treat the two as essentially identical.

We disagree. If voters are motivated by the desire to make good decisions and the desire to make easy decisions, storing in memory nothing more about the candidates than summary evaluations is certainly an *easy* way to make a decision, but it is not a particularly *good* way, especially if those evaluations are formed on the basis of two independent sets of criteria. A good decision, as most people intuitively realize, should be based on *comparing* alternatives on a *common* set of criteria, and to do that—except in fairly artificial or contrived situations—requires memory of the particulars upon which an evaluation is based. We have very clear evidence that memory matters to decision quality (Redlawsk, 2001; Lau & Redlawsk, 2006).

Recently we have used DPTE to look more closely at affective processes such motivated reasoning (Kunda, 1987; 1990). In our earlier studies we found evidence that voters were more positive in their evaluations of liked candidates for whom they learned negative information, than those for whom all they learned was positive (Redlawsk, 2002). More recently we have identified ways that memory is enhanced or conditioned by affect (Redlawsk, Lau, & Civettini, 2006; Civettini & Redlawsk, 2009) and at how long polarization might go on before voters begin to re-evaluate and more accurately update their priors (Redlawsk, Civettini, & Emmerson, 2010). Other work using DPTE has examined cognitive processing and aging (Lau & Redlawsk, 2008) and the role gender of candidates and voters plays in information processing (Ditonto & Andersen, 2011; Ditonto, Stalsburg, & Andersen, 2010; Redlawsk & Lau, 2008). The methodology is extremely flexible, allowing us to examine many different questions, the common thread of which is the examination of evaluation and choice as information flows over time.

7. VOTER DECISION-MAKING AND BEHAVIORAL DECISION THEORY

So what do we know about voters, given the basic precepts of behavioral decision theory? We turn now to an overview of recent voter decision-making research that implicitly or explicitly takes a perspective supported by BDT. Again this literature is huge, and we are not going to pretend to cover it all here. Instead we will focus on a few key strands. First, the psychological work in heuristics discussed earlier led to questions about how and when voters use heuristics and the extent to which these heuristics help or hurt. Second, we examine a developing literature that asks to what extent people (voters) are accurate in updating their evaluations. The question is whether voters operate "rationally" as Bayesian updaters, or whether instead they are motivated reasoners (Kunda, 1987; 1990) who maintain existing evaluations rather than challenge them with new information. Third, we examine the question of whether voters do a better (or worse) job by using heuristics, motivated reasoning, or by adopting more or less rational strategies using a standard we call a "correct vote" (Lau & Redlawsk, 1997).

7.1. Heuristics and Voter Decision-Making

Political scientists have looked to rehabilitate voter decision-making ever since *The American Voter* (Campbell et al., 1960) taught us that the capacity of American voters appears to fall well below the standards thought necessary for voters to hold their representatives accountable. We learned that voters have no sense of ideology and no real interest or knowledge of issues, and seem to vote guided mainly by the "nature of the times." A decades-long debate ensued over voters' ability to make good decisions. In many ways the debate became tedious, with the accepted wisdom that most voters were either through lack of ability or lack of motivation, just not doing a very good job.

Samuel Popkin, in his book *The Reasoning Voter* (1991), took issue with this accepted wisdom, arguing voters could make perfectly fine decisions using "gut rationality" or "limited information rationality." Voters can use the limited information they receive through daily life as a kind of heuristic to make sense of politics. Sniderman, Brody, and Tetlock (1991) extended this positive view of heuristic-based voting by arguing citizens could reason through political issues by simplifying the tasks and relying on the interaction of cognition and affect. That is, voters typically can identify what they like and don't like. They may in fact be able to identify groups as well and use the affect they have toward them to help make sense of the political world. The argument is much more nuanced than this, of course, but the point is that a "likeability heuristic" can be applied so that knowing what group one likes and knowing what political actor the group likes (endorsements) can allow the voter to transfer that affect to the political actor. But while heuristics may thus facilitate decision quality, they also require a modicum of information—if one does not know that the ACLU stands for something, then knowing the ACLU endorses a candidate or an issue is not very useful. Sniderman et al. were careful to note that heterogeneity in political sophistication leads to different expectations on the effectiveness of heuristic and nonheuristic processing.

Pushing back on this effort to rehabilitate at least some American voters, Bartels (1996) argued that it is naive at best to think that heuristics can replace actual information. Setting a standard based on the most sophisticated voters in the American National Election Studies, Bartels then asked whether less sophisticated voters—whom he *presumed* were using heuristics—actually voted as if they were sophisticated. The answer of course was no. Bartels ran a series of simulations that showed that some demographic groups would have voted differently in the aggregate if all voters made the same choices as the most knowledgeable. His conclusion was that heuristics simply could not be working since aggregate vote totals would have changed, even though no actual election outcome would have flipped.

But Bartels could not tell if voters were using heuristics, who was using them, and what heuristics were in use. The limitations of survey data mean that he could only assume that sophisticates did not need to use heuristics and nonsophisticates did use them, and used them badly. In order to do more than assume, we must observe the voter decision-making process as it happens, which can best be done in an experimental environment. Using DPTE, we followed voters in the lab, examining their heuristic use. The results (Lau & Redlawsk, 2001a; 2006) suggest that while heuristics are used by everyone—both sophisticated and nonsophisticated—their effectiveness in improving voter decision quality varies. In particular, some heuristics help *sophisticated* voters when the political environment is predictable, but lead to lower-quality decisions when the political environment is not aligned as they expect. And our findings suggest nonsophisticates gain little from the heuristics we tested. Kuklinski, Quirk, Jerit, and Rich (2001) make a similar point, finding that the nature of the information environment can either improve or detract from political decision-making. Some skepticism over the value of heuristics to "solve" the problem of uninformed voters is clearly warranted.

Yet a number of studies have shown that heuristics appear, if not to make nonsophisticates who use them act as political sophisticates, at least to help them make some decisions that are better than they might otherwise make. Boudreau (2009) reports experiments where an endorsement cue leads to better decisions by unsophisticated experimental participants, closing their gap with sophisticates. Levendusky (2010) found that as elite cues become clearer—because of political polarization of elites—the mass public is better able to adopt more consistent attitudes. Hobolt (2007) shows that voters in European Union referendums rely on an endorsement heuristic and that this aids some voters—those sophisticated enough to know party positions in the first place. Likewise Arceneaux and Kolodny (2009) examine endorsements, finding that in a field experiment endorsements provided some voters with a useful heuristic that allowed them to compensate for a lack of awareness. Interestingly, this worked only if the endorsement included contextual information about who the endorser was. These latter two studies comport with Sniderman et al.'s (1991) likeability heuristic.

7.2. Online Processing and Motivated Reasoning

Acting much like heuristics, *online processing* (Lodge et al., 1989; Redlawsk, 2001) builds on the well-established tendency of humans to make relatively effortless evaluations of other people rapidly, with no need to recall from memory what went into those evaluations (Hastie & Park, 1986). Evaluation takes place as information is encountered, and an online tally (Lodge et al., 1989), summarizing the affective value of that information, is updated, after which the actual information itself can be discarded. Contrasted with *memory-based processing*, online processing is quick and easy, in the sense that when a decision must be made, a voter need only query the online tallies for the candidates and choose the more highly evaluated one. Memory-based decisions require the extra effort of querying memories for the candidates, and then forming an evaluation and making a choice (Kelly & Mirer, 1974). Thus Lodge et al. (1995) argue that since voters are essentially making an impression-based decision, online processing is the default.

Yet as we noted above, our own work using dynamic process tracing (Redlawsk, 2001; Redlawsk, 2004; Lau & Redlawsk, 2006) finds a significant role for memory in voter decision-making, given the asymmetric information flows of the typical political campaign. Some of the variance in findings can be attributed to methods. Lodge uses information sheets showing research participants all the attributes of a single political figure in an easy-to-use format, minimizing the need to engage memory. On the other hand, DPTE presents asymmetric information mimicking a campaign, and the research participant must make a *choice*. This makes memory recall necessary to make the comparisons between candidates that facilitate high-quality decision-making.

More important to the question of rational decision-making is evidence that online processing is part of a broader evaluative process that may operate against "accurate" updating in the face of new, contradictory information. *Motivated reasoners* (Kunda, 1987; 1990; Redlawsk, 2002; Lodge & Taber, 2005; Taber & Young, chapter 17, this volume) strive to maintain their existing evaluations, discounting, counterarguing, and otherwise dismissing information running counter to their preferences. It is not hard to see how such processes would fly in the face of rational evaluations, where new negative information must lower an evaluation as readily as new positive information must increase it. For voters with existing evaluations and preferences, it appears quite difficult to move them in the correct direction (Redlawsk et al., 2010; Redlawsk, 2002; Redlawsk, 2006; Taber & Lodge, 2006). This effect appears attenuated when people are held accountable for their decisions (Redlawsk, 2001; Scholten, van Knippenberg, Nijstad, De Dreu, 2007); accuracy goals inhibit online processing.

But partisan motivations are at the core of much of politics. If such motivations are in opposition to accuracy goals, then motivated reasoners are unlikely to meet even low standards for rational decision-making. Gaines and colleagues (2007) show how interpretations of the same information create divergent beliefs on the Iraq war, which lead to divergent opinions, with better-informed citizens most likely to show this effect. Lebo and Cassino (2007) identify how partisan motivated reasoning has implications for presidential approval ratings. And Kopko, Bryner, Budziak, Devine, and Nawara (2011) even find motivated reason effects in ballot counting, especially when rules governing assessing voter intent are ambiguous.

Recently, we have suggested that while motivated reasoning effects are consistent and perhaps even inevitable, all hope for accurate voter decision-making is not lost (Redlawsk et al., 2010). At some point the amount of information encountered that is in opposition to the existing evaluation may overwhelm motivated processes. At this tipping point, voters seem to recognize that the world is not what they thought it was, and they update with greater accuracy. It appears that as the amount of incongruency grows, anxiety grows about the lack of agreement between the existing evaluation and the mounting new evidence. This may then act to motivate a different process—what Marcus, Neuman, and MacKuen (2000) call "affective intelligence," switching processing from the maintenance of existing evaluation to an effort to more systematically process new information.

7.3. Decision Quality

Elections have typically been studied by historians, journalists, and political scientists, all of whom are chiefly concerned with which candidate or which party won the most votes. Yet there is another way to look at the vote decision that is more compatible with a BDT perspective: Did the voter choose *correctly*—that is, did the voter select the candidate who, in some normative sense, from the voter's own perspective was the best one? By "best" we mean voting in accord with "fully informed preferences" (Dahl, 1989)— what the voter *would have* decided had she had full information about all of the candidates available to her. This has been a primary focus of our research (Lau, Anderson & Redlawsk, 2008; Lau, Patel, Fahmy, & Kaufman, 2013; Lau & Redlawsk, 1997; 2001a; 2001b; 2006; 2008; Patel, 2010; Redlawsk, 2002; 2004).

Various individual difference factors, including knowledge, interest, and motivation, have all been linked to correct voting (Lau, Anderson, & Redlawsk, 2008; Lau & Redlawsk, 2006). But we have also looked at many of the decision strategies described earlier. Probably our most important finding is that voters' decision strategies influence the *quality* of the choices they make—a finding with implications extending well beyond political campaigns. What we found is that voters often make *better* decisions with *less* information, a finding clearly at odds with rational decision-making models (Lau & Redlawsk, 2006).

Given a standard for voter decision quality, we need to ask under what institutional conditions voters do a better or worse job. We have begun to do this in the American presidential election context (Lau et al., 2008), where we found that a major third-party candidate on the ballot increases the difficulty of the choice and commensurately lowers the probability of a correct choice. Similarly a crowded ballot—defined as the presence of initiative and referenda on the ballot—decreases the attention voters can devote to the presidential election and decreases the level of correct voting. On the other hand, the more intense (competitive) a campaign—and thus the more relevant information available to voters—the more likely a correct vote.

It seems likely that other institutional arrangements would play an important role in correct voting, and warrant exploration of correct voting in a comparative context (Lau et al., 2011). Preliminary results across 69 elections and 33 democracies suggest that information availability (political rights), the ideological distinctiveness of the candidates, and clear lines of responsibility (parliamentary systems with single-party governments, and presidential systems with unified government) are all associated with higher levels of correct voting, while incentives for personal (as opposed to party) votes, which increase learning requirements for each election, and (as in the United States) the number of parties on the ballot, are associated with lower levels of correct voting (see also Hines, 2008).

Environmental contexts might impact correct voting, in particular the social networks in which voters are embedded. Richey (2008) examines the political discussion environment, finding that as voters interact with more knowledgeable discussants, correct voting is increased. But McClurg, Sokhey, and Seib, (2009) using their own dynamic process-tracing approach, found that disagreements within a social network may drive down the level of correct voting. Socially mediated information can cause voters to pay attention, but Ahn, Huckfeldt, and Ryan (2010) found that "when the subject's prior beliefs conflict with the informant's message, the subjects are generally well advised to rely on their own priors. This is especially true among the well-informed" (Ahn, et al., p. 780). Ryan (2010) further shows that while expertise available within social networks can improve voter decision-making, an individual's own knowledge plays an important role. Much more remains to be done to understand the contexts under which decision quality—a correct vote—is more or less likely.

8. A Quick Word on Behavioral Decision Theory and Emotion

Emotion is tricky, and until quite recently political scientists have paid it scant attention. But emotions, we are learning, are critical to decision-making. People without the capacity for emotion are generally without the capacity for making decisions, even if otherwise psychologically undamaged (Damasio, 1999). Kahneman writes that even "[u]tility cannot be divorced from emotion" (2003, p. 706). While this topic is covered in great detail by Brader and Marcus in this volume (chapter 6), a few points might be useful here. One is that evidence is strong that one's mood can act as a cue during information processing, which can be incorporated into perceptions of the information environment, in a process called affect-as-information (see Wyer, Clore, & Isbell, 1999 for a review). Second, mood may activate positive or negative information and lead to changes in its accessibility (Clore & Huntsinger, 2007).

Third, emotional states may trigger processing styles, so that people in positive states process information differently than those feeling negative. Positive feelings tend to result in less effortful processing, while negative feelings lead to more careful systematic consideration of new information (Park & Banaji, 2000). Drawing on this dual-process idea, Marcus et al. (2000; Marcus & MacKuen, 1993) have posited affective intelligence theory, where anxiety arising from an unexpected stimulus activates a surveillance system that attempts to make sense of the incoming stimulus, interrupting the dispositional system that otherwise would result in less effortful processing. The result, they suggest, is that anxious voters may be better voters (Redlawsk et al., 2010). Yet we doubt that anxiety would improve decision-making in all circumstances. Clinically high levels of anxiety, for example, can be seriously deleterious to effective cognitive processing (Clark & Beck, 2010), but even much lower levels of anxiety are often associated with learning deficits (Eysenck, Derakshan, Santos, & Calvo, 2007; MacIntyre & Gardner, 1994). And while low to moderate levels of anxiety have been shown to disrupt reliance on automatic heuristic-based processing and to increase interest in contemporary information (MacKuen, Wolak, Keele, & Marcus, 2010), too much information search may lower decision quality (Lau & Redlawsk, 2006).

Marcus, MacKuen, Wolak, and Keele (2006) make the important point that emotions must be thought of as more than a simple positive-negative valence. Instead, discrete emotions—such as anxiety, enthusiasm, and anger—are key to understanding affect. Gilovich and Griffin (2010) provide a nice summary of the research in psychology on these points, while Isbell, Otatti, and Burns (2006) review the implications of this research for political decision-making.

This new turn toward emotions brings us to the very old idea of "gut" feelings that a choice is right or wrong. Damasio's (1999) work provides important context, describing how as decisions are made, our mind and body interact; we may well "feel" a choice before we can think about it. In political science, Popkin (1991) developed this argument quite a while ago. People may operate on a very simple heuristic—what feels right. After all, decision-making is in the end about how we will feel in some future—more or less happy, more or less sad—if we make a particular choice.

Perhaps our increasing understanding of emotion can bridge between RCT and psychological theories, an argument developed by Bueno de Mesquita and McDermott (2004). Kim (Kim, Taber, & Lodge, 2010) models this process by linking cognitive and affective processing in an agent-based computational model that does a much better job than a Bayesian updating model in predicting individual change in evaluations as information is encountered and processed. This model works well because it combines both affective and cognitive processing, where each interacts with the other. In many respects work like this defines the newest frontier in our quest to understand how decisions are made in the real world of the decision-maker rather than in the idealized world of rational choice.

9. CONCLUSION

We began by considering the classic, rational choice perspective on decision-making, but suggested that a behaviorally oriented theory based on a view of humans as limited information processors was a more useful and accurate perspective if the goal is to understand how decisions are actually made. We have tried to shape our review of the BDT literature so as to highlight issues that should be of use to political psychologists. The focus on description in the BDT literature can leave the casual reader of that literature with a view more of the trees than of the forest. Our goal was to provide a map of the forest rather than describe all the trees, because the latter obscures the fact that while the *process* of making a decision is much more varied than the single ideal procedure suggested by RCT, it is still far from random (Jacoby et al., 1987). The *regularities* in human behavior are what social scientists must study, and there are more than enough in the decision-making field to go around.

Can RCT and BDT approaches ever be reconciled? It is fairly easy to integrate the notion of bounded rationality into a rational choice perspective. Information costs have long been recognized as an integral part of the approach (e.g., Downs, 1957; Fiorina, 1981). Bounded rationality provides a more complete understanding, not only in terms of the costs of *gathering* the information but also in terms of the costs of *utilizing* it once it has been gathered. Some versions of RCT view decision-makers as "intendedly rational," doing the best they can under the circumstances and with acknowledged cognitive limitations (Jones, 1994; Lupia et al., 2000). But this reconciliation misses the boat. Sometimes people *are* intendedly rational; but much more often they make decisions automatically or semiautomatically with no conscious consideration of how or why they are choosing as they are. The view of decision-makers as "omniscient calculators," even as an ideal, should probably be dropped: it can be misleading when people confuse "ought" with "is" and as a consequence set unrealistically high standards (Lau & Redlawsk, 1997). But the normative concerns of RCT are important, and the guidelines of procedural rationality are worthwhile standards for making good decisions. Rather than intendedly rational behavior, however, we would characterize most decision-making—and certainly most political decision-making—as *semiautomatic rule following*, with any conscious deliberation focused on determining which heuristic is appropriate rather than on value maximization.

We echo Kahneman (1994) in arguing that instead of asking *whether* decisions are rational or not, or revising our definition of "rationality" so that it can include more actual choice behavior, a better question for future decision research to address is *under what conditions* decision-makers are at least "reasonably" rational in their decision processes (see also Chong, chapter 4, this volume); and when they are not, *what cognitive shortcuts or heuristics they employ* in lieu of thorough information search and value-maximizing choice strategies. People can, and often do, follow a logic of consequence, if not omnisciently, at least reasonably, given their cognitive limitations. And people can, and often do, make many decisions automatically, by unconsciously following well-learned rules for making decisions. The question for political psychologists is not whether people are always or ever procedurally rational in their decision processes, but what they do when they are not, and what effect it has on the quality of the decision that is reached.

As political scientists, we also are interested in the implications of information processing and decision-making for institutional design. Of course there is the possibility of assessing different institutions and systems for the degree that they do or do not improve decision-making by both political elites and the mass public. Our own idea of "voting correctly" is one possible way for doing this. But a recent paper by a computer scientist suggests another possible implication: that knowing how voters process information might allow us to design systems that "support information gathering, organizing, and sharing, deliberation, decision making, and voting" (Robertson, 2005). As the world moves online, decision tasks like voting become both simultaneously more information rich, and yet potentially more difficult. BDT can help us understand both the strengths and weaknesses of how people make decisions, perhaps leading to system designs that play to the strengths and minimize the weaknesses. Robertson's goal strikes us as a challenging one, but one that is worth pursuing.

ACKNOWLEDGEMENT

We thank Zaid Abuhouran of Rutgers University for his diligent research assistance.

NOTES

1. When people refer to a "best" solution, they usually mean the value-maximizing alternative. Rational choice assumes decision-makers follow formal mathematical principles in making their probability judgments and value assessments, including regularity, independence from irrelevant alternatives, transitivity, procedure invariance, dominance, and all the dictates of Bayes's theorem. These principles are quite logical and intuitive and are widely accepted by decision-makers when they are explained. Hastie and Dawes (2001) summarize these principles, writing that a decision can be considered "rational" if it (1) is based on the status quo of current assets such that losses or forgone gains are equivalent; (2) is based on all possible/plausible outcomes associated with the choice; and (3) where

risk is involved, does not violate any of the basic rules of probability. As it turns out, this is a higher bar than it seems.

2. See Green and Shapiro (1994) for an elaborate presentation of this argument, Simon (1985; 1995) for its essence, and Aldrich (1993) or Friedman (1995) for various responses from the rational choice perspective.

3. If one alternative is preferred to all others on every dimension of judgment, it "dominates" the other alternatives (Hastie & Dawes, 2001), and there should be no conflict in making a decision.

4. One other type of transition is possible: intra-attribute, intra-alternative, that is, reaccessing the same item of information. This type of transition can usually be considered a random error.

5. The one exception to this statement is *expertise*, which has been a major focus of attention in the field; see, for example, Fiske, Lau, and Smith (1990) and Lau and Erber (1985).

6. The most recent version of the DPTE system is available to any researcher wishing to develop process-tracing experiments, at http://www.processtracing.org.

References

Abelson, R. P., & Levi, A. (1985). Decision making and decision theory. In G. Lindzey & E. Aronson (eds.), *Handbook of social psychology* (3rd ed., vol. 1, pp. 231–209). New York: Random House.

Ahn, T. K., Huckfeldt, R., & Ryan, J. B. (2010). Communication, influence, and informational asymmetries among voters. *Political Psychology 31*, 763–787.

Alba, J. W., & Marmorstein, H. (1987). The effects of frequency knowledge on consumer decision making. *Journal of Consumer Research 14*, 14–26.

Aldrich, J. H. (1993). Rational choice and turnout. *American Journal of Political Science, 37*, 246–276.

Allison, G. T., & Zelikow, P. D. (1999). *Essence of decision: Explaining the Cuban Missile Crisis* (2nd ed.). New York: Longman.

Anderson, J. R. (1983). *The architecture of cognition*. Cambridge, MA: Harvard University Press.

Arceneaux, K., & Kolodny, R. (2009). Educating the least informed: Group endorsements in a grassroots campaign. *American Journal of Political Science, 53*, 775–770.

Bartels, L. M. (1996). Uninformed votes: Information effects in presidential elections. *American Journal of Political Science, 40*, 194–231.

Billings, R. S., & Marcus, S. A. (1983). Measures of compensatory and noncompensatory models of decision behavior: Process tracing versus policy capturing. *Organizational Behavior and Human Performance, 31*, 331–352.

Billings, R. S., & Scherer, L. L. (1988). The effects of response mode and importance on decision-making strategies: Judgment versus choice. *Organizational Behavior & Human Decision Processes, 41*, 1–19.

Bockenholt, U., Albert, D., Aschenbrenner, M., & Schmalhofer, F. (1991). The effects of attractiveness, dominance and attribute differences on information acquisition in multiattribute binary choice. *Organizational Behavior and Human Decision Processes, 49*, 258–281.

Boudreau, C. (2009). Closing the gap: When do cues eliminate differences between sophisticated and unsophisticated citizens? *Journal of Politics, 71*, 964–976.

Bueno de Mesquita, B., & McDermott, R. (2004). Crossing no mans land: Cooperation from the trenches. *Political Psychology, 25,* 271–287.

Campbell, A., Converse, P. E., Miller, W. E., & Stokes, D. E. (1960). *The American voter.* Chicago: University of Chicago Press.

Carroll, J. S., & Johnson, E. J. (1990). *Decision research: A field guide.* Beverly Hills, CA: Sage.

Civettini, A. J. W., & Redlawsk, D. P. (2009). Voters, emotions, and memory. *Political Psychology, 30,* 125–151.

Clark, D. A., & Beck, A. T. (2010). *Cognitive therapy of anxiety disorders: Science and practice.* New York: Guilford Press.

Clore, G. L., & Huntsinger, J. R. (2007). How emotions inform judgment and regulate thought. *Trends in Cognitive Science, 2,* 393–399.

Conover, P. J., & Feldman, S. (1989). Candidate perception in an ambiguous world: Campaigns, cues, and inference processes. *American Journal of Political Science, 33,* 912–940.

Cox, G. W. (1997). *Making votes count: Strategic coordination in the world's electoral systems.* Cambridge: Cambridge University Press.

Czerlinski, J., Gigerenzer, G., & Goldstein, D. G. (1999). How good are simple heuristics? In G. Gigerenzer, P. M. Todd, & the ABC Research Group (eds.), *Simple heuristics that make us smart* (pp. 97–118). New York: Oxford University Press.

Dahl, R. A. (1989). *Democracy and its critics.* New Haven, CT: Yale University Press.

Damasio, A. R. (1999). *The feeling of what happens: Body, emotion and the making of consciousness.* London: Heinemann.

Ditonto, T., & Andersen, D. J. (2011). Two's a crowd: Women candidates in concurrent elections. Paper presented at the Annual Meeting of the Midwest Political Science Association, Chicago, IL.

Ditonto, T., Stalsburg, B., & Andersen, D. J. (2010). Intersectional stereotypes: How gender, race and partisan stereotypes interact in evaluations of political candidates. Paper presented at the Annual Meeting of the American Political Science Association, Washington, DC.

Downs, A. (1957). *An economic theory of democracy.* New York: Harper and Row.

Easton, D. (1953). *The political system: An inquiry into the state of political science.* New York: Knopf.

Edwards, W. (1961). Behavioral decision theory. *Annual Review of Psychology, 12,* 473–498.

Einhorn, H. J., & Hogarth, R. M. (1975). Unit weighting schemes for decision making. *Organizational Behavior and Human Performance, 13,* 171–192.

Einhorn, H. J., & Hogarth, R. M. (1981). Behavioral decision theory: Processes of judgment and choice. *Annual Review of Psychology, 32,* 53–88.

Ericsson, K. A., & Simon, H. A. (1984). *Protocol analysis: Verbal reports as data.* Cambridge, MA: MIT Press.

Eysenck, M. W., Derakshan, N., Santos, R., & Calvo, M. G. (2007). Anxiety and cognitive performance: Attentional control theory. *Emotion, 7,* 336–353.

Fiorina, M. P. (1981). *Retrospective voting in American national elections.* New Haven, CT: Yale University Press.

Fiske, S. T., Lau, R. R., & Smith, R. A. (1990). On the variety and utility of political knowledge structures. *Social Cognition, 8,* 31–48.

Ford, J. K., Schmitt, N., Schechtman, S. L., Hults, B. M., & Doherty, M. L. (1989). Process tracing methods: Contributions, problems, and neglected research questions. *Organizational Behavior and Human Decision Processes, 43,* 75–117.

Ford, J. K., & Smith, R A. (1987). Inferential beliefs in consumer evaluations: An assessment of alternative processing strategies. *Journal of Consumer Research, 14,* 363–371.

Friedman, D. (1995). Monty Hall's three doors: Construction and deconstruction of a choice anomaly. *The American Economic Review, 88*, 933–946.

Gaines, B. J., Kuklinski, J. H., Quirk, P. J., Peyton, B., & Verkuilen, J. (2007). Same facts, different interpretations: Partisan motivation and opinion on Iraq. *Journal of Politics, 69*, 957–974.

Gigerenzer, G. (2008). Why heuristics work. *Perspectives on Psychological Science, 3*, 20–29.

Gigerenzer, G., & Goldstein, D. G. (1999). Betting on one good reason: The take the best heuristic. In G. Gigerenzer, P. M. Todd, & the ABC Research Group (eds.), *Simple heuristics that make us smart* (pp. 75–95). New York: Oxford University Press.

Gigerenzer, G., & Todd, P. M. (1999). Fast and frugal heuristics: The adaptive toolbox. In G. Gigerenzer, P. M. Todd, & the ABC Research Group (eds.), *Simple heuristics that make us smart* (pp. 75–95). New York: Oxford University Press.

Gilovich, T. D., & Griffin, D. W. (2010). Judgment and decision making. In S. T. Fiske, D. T. Gilbert, & G. Lindzey (eds.), *Handbook of social psychology* (5th ed., vol. 2, pp. 542–588). Hoboken: John Wiley and Sons.

Graefe, A., & Armstrong., J. S. (2010). Predicting elections from the most important issue: A test of the take-the-best heuristic. *Journal of Behavioral Decision Making, 25*, 41–48.

Green, D. P., & Shapiro, I. (1994). *Pathologies of rational choice theory: A critique of applications in political science.* New Haven, CT: Yale University Press.

Hamill, R., Lodge, M., & Blake, F. (1985). The breadth, depth, and utility of class, partisan, and ideological schemata. *American Journal of Political Science, 29*, 850–870.

Hastie, R., & Dawes, R. M. (2001). *Rational choice in an uncertain world* (2nd ed.). New York: Harcourt Brace Jovanovich.

Hastie, R., & Park, B. (1986). The relationship between memory and judgment depends on whether the task is memory-based or on-line. *Psychological Review 93*, 258–268.

Herstein, J. A. (1981). Keeping the voter's limits in mind: A cognitive process analysis of decision making in voting. *Journal of Personality and Social Psychology, 40*, 843–861.

Hines, E. (2008). Voting correctly in Europe. PhD dissertation, University of Iowa.

Hobolt, S. B. (2007). Taking cues on Europe? Voter competence and party endorsements in referendums on European integration. *European Journal of Political Research, 46*, 151–182.

Hogarth, R. M. (1987). *Judgment and choice* (2nd ed.). New York: Wiley.

Holsti, O. R. (1989). Crisis decision making. In P. E. Tetlock, J. L. Husbands, R. Jervis, P. C. Stern, & C. Tilly (eds.), *Behavior, society, and nuclear war* (vol. 1, pp. 8–84). New York: Oxford University Press.

Huang, L. (2000). Examining candidate information search processes: The impact of processing goals and sophistication. *Journal of Communication, 50*, 93–114.

Huang, L., & Price, V. (2001). Motivation, goals, information search, and memory about political candidates. *Political Psychology, 22*, 665–692.

Isbell, L. M., Otatti, V. C., & Burns, K. C. (2006). Affect and politics: Effects on judgment, processing, and information seeking. In D. Redlawsk (ed.), *Feeling politics: Emotion in political information processing* (pp. 57–86). New York: Palgrave Macmillan.

Jacoby, J., Chestnut, R. W., Weigl, K. C., & Fischer, W. (1976). Pre-purchasing information acquisition: Description of a process methodology, research paradigm, and pilot investigation. *Advances in Consumer Research, 5*, 546–554.

Jacoby, J., Jaccard, J., Kuss, A., Troutman, T., & Mazursky, D. (1987). New directions in behavioral process research: Implications for social psychology. *Journal of Experimental Social Psychology, 23*, 146–175.

James, W. (1884). What is an emotion? *Mind, 9*, 188–205.

Johnson, M. D. (1986). Modeling choice strategies for noncomparable alternatives. *Marketing Sciences, 5*, 37–54.

Johnson, E. J., & Russo, J. E. (1984). Product familiarity and learning new information. *Journal of Consumer Research, 11*, 542–550.

Jones, B. D. (1994). *Reconceiving decision-making in democratic politics: Attention, choice, and public policy.* Chicago: University of Chicago Press.

Kahneman, D. (1994). New challenges to the rationality assumption. *Journal of Institutional and Theoretical Economics, 150*, 18–36.

Kahneman, D. (2000). Experienced utility and objective happiness: A moment-based approach. In D. Kahneman & A. Tversky (eds.), *Choices, values, and frames* (pp. 201–208). New York: Cambridge University Press.

Kahneman, D. (2003). A perspective on judgment and choice: Mapping out bounded rationality. *American Psychologist, 58*, 697–720.

Kahneman, D., & Tversky, A. (1972). Subjective probability: A judgment of representativeness. *Cognitive Psychology, 3*, 430–454.

Kahneman, D., & Tversky, A. (1973). On the psychology of prediction. *Psychological Review, 80*, 237–251.

Kahneman, D., & Tversky, A. (1979). Prospect theory: An analysis of decision under risk. *Econometrica, 47*, 263–291.

Kahneman, D., & Tversky, A. (1982). The psychology of preferences. *Scientific American, 246*, 160–173.

Kahneman, D., & Tversky, A. (1984). Choices, values, and frames. *American Psychologist, 39*, 341–350.

Keller, K. L., & Staelin, R. (1987). Effects of quality and quantity of information on decision effectiveness. *Journal of Consumer Research, 14*, 200–213.

Kelly, Jr., S., & Mirer, T. W. (1974). The simple act of voting. *The American Political Science Review, 68*, 572–591.

Kim, S., Taber, C. S., & Lodge, M. (2010). A computational model of the citizen as motivated reasoner: Modeling the dynamics of the 2000 presidential election. *Political Behavior, 32*, 1–28.

Kopko, K. C., Bryner, S. M., Budziak, J., Devine, C. J., & Nawara, S. P. (2011). In the eye of the beholder? Motivated reasoning in disputed elections. *Political Behavior, 33*, 271–290.

Kuklinski, J. H., Quirk, P. J., Jerit, J., & Rich, R. R. (2001). The political environment and citizen decision making: Information, motivation, and policy tradeoffs. *American Journal of Political Science, 45*, 410–424.

Kunda, Z. (1987). Motivation and inference: Self-serving generation and evaluation of evidence. *Journal of Personality and Social Psychology, 53*, 636–647.

Kunda, Z. (1990). The case for motivated political reasoning. *Psychological Bulletin, 108*, 480–498.

Lau, R. R. (1982). Negativity in political perception. *Political Behavior, 4*, 353–378.

Lau, R. R. (1995). Information search during an election campaign: Introducing a process tracing methodology to political science. In M. Lodge & K. McGraw (eds.), *Political judgment: Structure and process* (pp. 179–205). Ann Arbor: University of Michigan Press.

Lau, R. R., Anderson, D., & Redlawsk, D. P. (2008). An exploration of correct voting in recent U.S. presidential elections. *American Journal of Political Science 52*, 395–411.

Lau, R. R., & Erber, R. (1985). An information processing perspective on political sophistication. In S. Kraus & R. Perloff (eds.), *Mass media and political thought* (pp. 17–39). Beverly Hills, CA: Sage.

Lau, R. R., Patel, P., Fahmy, D. F., & Kaufman, R. R. (2013). Correct voting across 33 democracies. *British Journal of Political Science.* DOI: http://dx.doi.org/10.1017/S0007123412000610, Published online: 06 March 2013.

Lau, R. R., & Redlawsk, D. P. (1997). Voting correctly. *American Political Science Review, 91,* 585–599.

Lau, R. R., & Redlawsk, D. P. (2001a). Advantages and disadvantages of cognitive heuristics in political decision making. *American Journal of Political Science, 45,* 951–971.

Lau, R. R., & Redlawsk, D. P. (2001b). An experimental study of information search, memory, and decision making during a political campaign. In J. H. Kuklinski (ed.), *Citizens and politics: Perspectives from political psychology* (pp. 136–159). Cambridge: Cambridge University Press.

Lau, R. R., & Redlawsk, D. P. (2006). *How voters decide: Information processing during an election campaign.* New York: Cambridge University Press.

Lau, R. R., & Redlawsk, D. P. (2008). Older and wiser? The effects of age on political cognition. *Journal of Politics, 70,* 168–185.

Lau, R. R., & Sears, D. O. (1986). Social cognition and political cognition. In R. R. Lau & D. O. Sears (eds.), *Political cognition: The 19th annual Carnegie symposium on cognition* (pp. 347–366). Hillsdale, NJ: Erlbaum.

Lazarsfeld, P. F., Berelson, B. R., & Gaudet, H. (1944). *The people's choice.* New York: Columbia University Press.

Lebo, M. J., & Cassino, D. (2007). The aggregated consequences of motivated reasoning and the dynamics of partisan presidential approval. *Political Psychology, 28,* 719–746.

Levendusky, M. S. (2010). Clearer cues, more consistent voters: A benefit of elite polarization. *Political Behavior, 32,* 111–131.

Levy, J. (1997). Prospect theory, rational choice, and international relations. *International Studies Quarterly, 41,* 87–112.

Liberman, N., & Forster, J. (2006). Inferences from decision difficulty. *Journal of Experimental Social Psychology, 42,* 290–301.

Lindberg, E., Garling, T., & Montgomery, H. (1989). Differential predictability of preferences and choices. *Journal of Behavioral Decision Making, 2,* 205–219.

Lodge, M., & Hamill, R. (1986). A partisan schema for political information processing. *American Political Science Review, 80,* 505–519.

Lodge, M., McGraw, K. M., & Stroh, P. (1989). An impression-driven model of candidate evaluation. *American Political Science Review, 83,* 399–420.

Lodge, M., Steenbergen, M. R., & Brau, S. (1995). The responsive voter: Campaign information and the dynamics of candidate evaluation. *American Political Science Review, 89,* 309–326.

Lodge, M., & Taber, C. S. (2005). The automaticity of affect for political leaders, groups, and issues: An experimental test of the hot cognition hypothesis. *Political Psychology, 26,* 455–482.

Lupia, A., McCubbins, M. D., & Popkin, S. L. (2000). Beyond rationality: Reason and the study of politics. In A. Lupia, M. D. McCubbins, & S. L. Popkin (eds.), *Elements of reason: Cognition, choice, and the bounds of rationality* (pp. 1–20). New York: Cambridge University Press.

MacIntyre, P. D., & Gardner, R. C. (1994). The effects of induced anxiety on three stages of cognitive processing in computerized vocabulary learning. *Studies in Second Language Acquisition, 16,* 1–17.

MacKuen, M., Wolak, J., Keele, L., & Marcus, G. E. (2010). Civic engagements: Resolute partisanship or reflective deliberation. *American Journal of Political Science, 54,* 440–458.

March, J. G. (1978). Bounded rationality, ambiguity, and the engineering of choice. *Bell Journal of Economics, 9,* 578–608.

March, J. G. (1988). *Decisions and organizations.* Oxford: Blackwell.

March, J. G. (1994). *A primer on decision making.* New York: Free Press.

March, J. G., & Olson, J. P. (1989). *Rediscovering institutions: The organizational basis of politics.* New York: Free Press.

March, J. G., & Simon, H. A. (1958). *Organizations.* New York: Wiley.

Marcus, G. E., & MacKuen, M. B. (1993). Anxiety, enthusiasm, and the vote: The emotional underpinnings of learning and involvement during presidential campaigns. *American Political Science Review, 87,* 672–685.

Marcus, G. E., MacKuen, M. B., Wolak, J., & Keele, L. (2006). The measure and mismeasure of emotion. In D. P. Redlawsk (ed.), *Feeling politics: Emotion in political information processing* (pp. 31–46). New York: Palgrave MacMillan.

Marcus, G. E., Neuman, W. R., & MacKuen, M. B. (2000). *Affective intelligence and political judgment.* Chicago: University of Chicago Press.

McClurg, S., Sokhey, A., & Seib, D. (2009). Social networks and correct voting: A dynamic, processing approach. Paper presented at the Annual Meeting of the Southern Political Science Association, New Orleans, LA.

Miller, G. A. (1956). The magical number seven, plus or minus two: Some limits on our capacity for processing information. *Psychological Review, 63,* 81–97.

Miller, W. E., & Shanks, J. M. (1996). *The new American voter.* Cambridge, MA: Harvard University Press.

Nie, N. H., Verba, S., & Petrocik, J. R. (1976). *The changing American voter.* Cambridge, MA: Harvard University Press.

Park, J., & Banaji, M. R. (2000). Mood and heuristics: The influence of happy and sad states on sensitivity and bias in stereotyping. *Journal of Personality and Social Psychology, 67,* 1005–1023.

Patel, P. (2010). The effect of institutions on correct voting. PhD dissertation, Rutgers University.

Payne, J. W., Bettman, J. R., & Johnson, E. J. (1988). Adaptive strategy selection in decision making. *Journal of Experimental Psychology: Learning, Memory, and Cognition, 14,* 534–552.

Payne, J. W., Bettman, J. R., & Johnson, E. J. (1993). *The adaptive decision maker.* New York: Cambridge University Press.

Popkin, S. L. (1991). *Reasoning and choice: Communication and persuasion in political campaigns.* Chicago: University of Chicago Press.

Quadrel, M. J., Fischhoff, B., & Davis, W. (1993). Adolescent (in)vulnerability. *American Psychologist, 48,* 102–116.

Rahn, W. M. (1993). The role of partisan stereotypes in information processing about political candidates. *American Journal of Political Science, 37,* 472–496.

Rahn, W. M., Aldrich, J. H., & Borgida, E. (1994). Individual and contextual variations in political candidate appraisal. *American Political Science Review, 88,* 193–199.

Rahn, W. M., Krosnick, J. A., & Breuning, M. (1994). Rationalization and derivation processes in survey studies of political candidate evaluation. *American Journal of Political Science, 38,* 582–600.

Raiffa, H. (1968). *Decision analysis: Introductory lectures on choices under uncertainty*. Reading, MA: Addison-Wesley.

Redlawsk, D. P. (2001). You must remember this: A test of the on-line model of voting. *Journal of Politics, 63*, 29–58.

Redlawsk, D. P. (2002). Hot cognition or cool consideration? Testing the effects of motivated reasoning on political decision making. *Journal of Politics, 64*, 1021–1044.

Redlawsk, D. P. (2004). What voters do: Information search during election campaigns. *Political Psychology, 25*, 595–610.

Redlawsk, D. P. (2006). Motivated reasoning, affect, and the role of memory in voter decision-making. In D. P. Redlawsk (ed.), *Feeling politics: Emotion in political information processing* (pp. 87–108). New York: Palgrave Macmillan.

Redlawsk, D. P., Civettini, A. J. W., & Emmerson, K. M. (2010). The affective tipping point: Do motivated reasoners ever "get it"? *Political Psychology, 31*, 563–593.

Redlawsk, D. P., & Lau, R. R. (2008). Gender and Candidate Information Processing. 2008. Paper presented at the Annual Meeting of the International Society of Political Psychology, Paris, France.

Redlawsk, D. P., & Lau, R. R. (2009). Understanding individual decision making using process tracing. Paper presented at the General Conference of the European Consortium for Political Research, Potsdam, Germany.

Redlawsk, D. P., Lau, R. R., & Civettini, A. (2006). Affective intelligence and voter information. In W. R. Neuman, G. Marcus, M. B. MacKuen, & A. Crigler (eds.), *The affect effect: Dynamics of emotion in political thinking and behavior* (pp. 152–179). Chicago: University of Chicago Press.

Richey, S. (2008). The social basis of voting correctly. *Political Communication, 25*, 366–376.

Riggle, E. D. B., & Johnson, M. M. S. (1996). Age differences in political decision making: Strategies for evaluating political candidates. *Political Behavior, 18*, 99–118.

Riker, W. H., & Ordeshook, P. C. (1968). A theory of the calculus of voting. *American Political Science Review, 62*, 25–42.

Robertson, S. (2005). Voter-centered design: Toward a voter decision support system. *ACM Transactions on Computer-Human Interaction, 12*, 263–292.

Rosch, E. (1978). Principles of categorization. In E. Rosch & B. B. Lloyd (eds.), *Cognition and categorization* (pp. 28–50). Hillsdale, NJ: Erlbaum.

Rubenstein, A. H. (1998). *Modeling bounded rationality*. Cambridge, MA: MIT Press.

Russo, J. E. (1977). The value of unit price information. *Journal of Marketing Research, 14*, 193–201.

Russo, J. E., & Dosher, B. A. (1983). Strategies for multiattribute binary choice. *Journal of Experimental Psychology: Learning, Memory and Cognition, 17*, 676–696.

Ryan, J. B. (2010). The effects of network expertise and biases on vote choice. *Political Communication, 27*, 44–58.

Scholten, L., van Knippenberg, D., Nijstad, B. A., & De Dreu, C. K. W. (2007). Motivated information processing and group decision-making: Effects of process accountability on information processing and decision quality. *Journal of Experimental Social Psychology, 43*, 539–552.

Simon, H. A. (1947). *Administrative behavior*. New York: Macmillan.

Simon, H. A. (1957). *Models of man: Social and rational*. New York: Wiley.

Simon, H. A. (1979). Information processing models of cognition. *Annual Review of Psychology, 30*, 363–396.

Simon, H. A. (1985). Human nature in politics: The dialogue of psychology with political science. *American Political Science Review, 79*, 293–304.

Simon, H. A. (1990). A mechanism for social selection and successful altruism. *Science, 250*, 1665–1668.

Simon, H. A. (1995). Rationality in political behavior. *Political Psychology, 16*, 45–61.

Slovic, P., Fischoff, B., & Lichtenstein, S. (1982). Response mode, framing, and information processing effects in risk assessment. In R. Hogarth (ed.), *New directions for methodology of social and behavioral science: The framing of questions and the consistency of response* (pp. 21–36). San Francisco: Jossey-Bass.

Slovic, P., & Lichtenstein, S. (1971). Comparison of Bayesian and regression approaches to the study of information processing in judgment. *Organizational Behavior and Human Performance, 6*, 649–744.

Sniderman, P. M., Brody, R. A., & Tetlock, P. E. (1991). *Reasoning and choice: Explorations in political psychology*. New York: Cambridge University Press.

Taber, C. S., & Lodge, M. (2006). Motivated skepticism in political information processing. *American Journal of Political Science, 50*, 755–769.

Taylor, S. E. (1981). The interface of cognitive and social psychology. In J. Harvey (ed.), *Cognition, social behavior, and the environment* (pp. 189–211). Hillsdale, NJ: Erlbaum.

Tversky, A. (1969). Intransitivity of preferences. *Psychological Review, 76*, 31–48.

Tversky, A. (1972). Elimination by aspects: A theory of choice. *Psychological Review, 79*, 281–299.

Tversky, A., & Kahneman, D. (1973). Availability: A heuristic for judging frequency and probability. *Cognitive Psychology, 5*, 207–232.

Tversky, A., & Kahneman, D. (1974). Judgment under uncertainty: Heuristics and biases. *Science, 185*, 1124–1131.

Tversky, A., & Kahneman, D. (1981). The framing of decisions and the psychology of choice. *Science, 211*, 453–463.

Tversky, A., & Kahneman, D. (1986). Rational choice and the framing of decisions. *Journal of Business, 59*, S251–S278.

Tversky, A., & Kahneman, D. (1992). Advances in prospect theory: Cumulative representation of uncertainty. *Journal of Risk and Uncertainty, 5*, 297–323.

Tversky, A., & Sattath, S. (1979). Preference trees. *Psychological Review, 86*, 542–573.

von Neumann, J., & Morgenstern, O. (1947). *Theory of games and economic behavior*. Princeton, NJ: Princeton University Press.

Vriend, N. J. (1996). Rational behavior and economic theory. *Journal of Economic Behavior & Organization, 29*, 263–285.

Wyer, R. S., Clore, G. L., & Isbell, L. M. (1999). Affect and information processing. In M. P. Zanna (ed.), *Advances in Experimental Social Psychology* (vol. 31, pp. 1–77). San Diego, CA: Academic Press.

Zaller, J., & Feldman, S. (1992). A simple theory of the survey response: Answering questions versus revealing preferences. *American Journal of Political Science, 36*, 579–166.

CHAPTER 6

....

EMOTION AND POLITICAL PSYCHOLOGY

....

TED BRADER AND GEORGE E. MARCUS

1. INTRODUCTION

....

IT is timely, given the explosion of interest in emotion over the past 20-plus years, to briefly reflect on the history of research on political emotion. In the 1980s an earlier handbook, Margaret Hermann's *Political Psychology* (1986), did not have a chapter on emotion, nor did Greenstein and Lerner's still earlier *A Source Book for the Study of Personality and Politics* (1971). That emotion was largely ignored in the 1970s and 1980s should be, on reflection, a bit of surprise. For from the very outset of Western thought, reason and emotion were understood as the two fundamental qualities of human nature (Aristotle, 1954; Aristotle, 1983; Plato, 1974). Indeed it was the purpose of that inquiry to learn how to reconcile the presumed agonistic relationship between these two core faculties (Nussbaum, 1986).[1]

The period of inattention to emotion reflected, we believe, two presumptions. First, that emotion was mysterious or elusive and, hence, not amenable to scientific inquiry. And, second, that emotion would prove to be a declining force as the growth of and reliance on scientific knowledge, joined with expansive public education, would enable reason to take up the central role in politics (Marcus, 2002).[2] Beginning in the 1980s emotion began its move to center stage in both psychology and political science. Since then, the number of published articles with the words "affect" or "emotion" in the title has grown exponentially (Brader, Marcus, & Miller, 2011). Reflecting the growth of research, two recent textbooks on political psychology have chapters devoted to emotion and politics (Cottam, 2004; Houghton, 2009).

We first offer an overview and critical reflections on the dominant theoretical approaches to emotion and politics. Second, we consider the antecedents and functions that have been posited to distinguish a number of common emotional states. Third, we examine the rapidly accumulating evidence that emotions shape attention, decision-making, attitudes, and action in the realm of politics. Finally, we conclude with some reflections on important and promising paths forward in the study of emotion and political psychology.

2. MAJOR THEORETICAL PERSPECTIVES

Two broad approaches are evident in the long history of interest in emotion. We can term them the "outside in" and "inside out" approach. The "outside in" approach began with the earliest efforts of humans to understand ourselves. It has been with us ever since. The "inside out" approach is far more recent, enabled by advances in technology.

Scholars adopting an "outside in" approach infer the constitution and causes of emotions from verbal reports of experiences and observations of behavior (Darwin, 1998; Ekman & Rosenberg, 2005; Frijda, 1986; Izard, 1991; Lazarus, 1991; Plutchik, 1980; Schwarz & Clore, 2003; Tomkins, 2008; Zajonc, 1980). Much as has been the case with many other longstanding psychological concepts—intelligence, motive, memory, and attitudes, "outside in" scholars infer from a reasoned examination of human behavior that the brain is engaged with emotion.[3] From what scholars see "outside," they infer what's going on "inside." They observe manifestations of emotion in facial expression, in gesture, tone, or as reported verbally by subjects. They must deduce its latent qualities from what they, and we, can observe, though that does not preclude speculation, as for example Descartes "locating" the source of emotion in the pineal gland (Descartes, 1989). Practitioners of the "outside in" approach do not directly study the brain's role in generating emotions and therefore, setting aside occasional speculations, tend not to offer precise accounts of how emotion is produced by the brain.

The "inside out" approach—facilitated by technological advances that permit better observation and measurement of brain activities—involves direct investigation of neural processes that engage affect (Adolphs, Tranel, Damasio, & Damasio, 1995; Damasio, 1994; Gray, 1987; LeDoux, 1995; Panksepp, 1998; Rolls, 2005). This focus on neural processes generated new insights. First, for most neuroscientists, the subjective experience of affect is of only peripheral interest. As Cacioppo and colleagues (Cacioppo, Berntson, Norris, & Gollan, 2011, p. 34) note:

> There is an understandable appeal to settling for feelings as the appropriate data to model in the area of affect. It is these feelings that some theorists seek to describe, understand, and explain. The structure and processes underlying mental contents are not readily apparent, however, and most cognitive processes occur unconsciously with only selected outcomes reaching awareness.

Neuroscientists instead shifted attention to the role of neural processes that subserve emotion. This in turn led to finding that these same processes also subserve various adaptive processes, such as attention and decision-making. Second, neuroscientists argue that affect is inherently appraisal and that a separate and subsequent stage of "cognitive" interpretation is not an essential ingredient to making affect meaningful (Cacioppo & Decety, 2009; Marcus, 2012). We return to this point below, as the concepts *affect, cognition,* and *appraisal,* as scientific terms, have become increasingly problematic.

2.1. Primary Theoretical Approaches

There are three primary theoretical approaches to emotion in broad use today, though there are many specific variants within each. Evolving initially from the "outside in" tradition, there are approach-avoidance theories and appraisal theories. Theories of affect as neural process exemplify the "inside out" perspective. We review each in turn.

2.1.1. Approach-Avoidance Theories

Here affect functions to solve the problem of approach and avoidance. Affect is often understood as a simple valence assessment of circumstances (or stimuli) as either punishing or rewarding. Affect is thus critical to identifying stimuli as either rewarding, hence justifying approach, or punishing, thus warranting avoidance. This notion undergirds modern attitude theories, where liking-disliking constitutes the critical affective dimension of attitudes (Eagley & Chaiken, 1993; Fishbein & Ajzen, 1975). It also underlies Damasio's (Damasio, 1994) conception of "somatic markers" as automatic preconscious signals that facilitate decision-making by sorting good from bad in our environment on the basis of past associations. Similarly, political psychologists adopting a "hot cognition" approach in the study of motivated reasoning see affect as the decisive initial assessment of reward and punishment (Lodge & Taber, 2013).

On one hand, scholars have long found this a convenient and useful way to simplify affective experience: Does she like or dislike that policy? Are voters in a good or bad mood? Is his partisan identity based more on attraction to one party or repulsion from the other? Much research on both explicit and implicit attitudes (toward racial groups, political parties, political candidates, etc.) continues to focus on a simple positive-negative dimension of affect (see Taber & Young, chapter 17, this volume). On the other hand, after some 30 years of analysis in innumerable studies, it is clear that affective subjective experience is not well described by only a single valence dimension (Larsen & McGraw, 2011; Marcus, 2003). Scholars from diverse approaches have found it increasingly useful to make finer differentiations among emotions. Once reliance on a single approach-avoidance conception of emotion, and measures that reproduce that conception (e.g., feeling thermometers), is relaxed so as to accommodate what is now known about the complex and multifaceted character of (preconscious and postawareness) appraisals—see figure 6.2 and attendant discussion below—a richer array of insights is likely to follow.

2.1.2. Appraisal Theories

Appraisal theories are among the leading contemporary approaches to make finer distinctions among emotions. As the name implies, their focus is the appraisals, conceived as cognitive interpretations of the significance of a situation for one's goals, that trigger emotions (Smith & Ellsworth, 1985). Both conscious and preconscious appraisals are possible (Lazarus, 1991; Scherer, Schorr, & Johnstone, 2001). Specific theories seek to offer a unique one-to-one mapping between appraisal pattern and emotion, in order to explain why we observe variation in emotional experiences across individuals and situations. To empirically test these relationships, some studies ask subjects to describe situations in which they felt particular emotions (Roseman, Antoniou, & Jose, 1996; Smith & Ellsworth, 1985), while others experimentally manipulate the attributes of scenarios (along posited appraisal dimensions) to test whether those situations generate the predicted emotions (Roseman, 1991).

Each theory conceives of a slightly different inventory of appraisals and emotions. Smith and Ellsworth (Smith & Ellsworth, 1985), for example, map six appraisal dimensions (of eight initially considered) on fifteen emotions. The dimensions include pleasantness, certainty, attention, anticipated effort, responsibility, and situational control. The nature of their contributions differed. Pleasantness explained a great deal of variance in emotional experiences, while situational control explained only a small portion; but the latter was particularly essential to discriminating among negative emotions like sadness, anger, fear, and disgust. Other theories conceptualize and label the appraisals differently, though there is clearly overlap. Having focused on five appraisals in earlier work (Roseman, 1991), Roseman et al. (1996) found that seven appraisals work best to predict 17 emotions: unexpectedness, situational state (present/absent), motivational state (reward/punish), probability (certain/uncertain), control potential, problem source, and causal agency (circumstances, others, or self).

In a final example, Lazarus (1991) identifies a "core relational theme" for each emotion, or what that emotion signals about the ongoing relationship between a person and her environment. Six appraisals—three primary, three secondary—evaluate the meaning of a situation and trigger the appropriate emotion. Primary appraisals, which concern "the stakes," include goal relevance, goal congruency, and type of ego-involvement. Secondary appraisals, which concern how the situation will be resolved, include blame/credit, coping potential, and future expectations. A situation must be perceived as "goal relevant" for any emotion to be triggered.

Several studies draw on appraisal theories to isolate the causes and explain the emergence of distinct emotions with political consequences (Brader, Groenendyk, & Valentino, 2010; Huddy, Feldman, & Cassese, 2007; Just, Crigler, & Belt, 2007; Steenbergen & Ellis, 2006; Valentino, Brader, Groenendyk, Gregorowicz, & Hutchings, 2011). However, to date, most of this research tends not to advance an entire appraisal account, but rather adopts isolated propositions related to a subset of specific emotions and appraisals as needed for the study in question (but cf. Roseman, Abelson, & Ewing, 1986).

2.1.3. Neural Process Theories

Beginning in the 1980s neuroscientists advanced accounts of the neural processes that generated affective response (Adolphs & Spezio, 2006; Adolphs, Tranel, & Damasio, 1998; Bechara, Damasio, Tranel, & Damasio, 1997; Gray, 1987; Gray, 1990; LeDoux, 1993; LeDoux, 2000; Rolls, 1999). Although researchers have identified multiple neural systems that generate distinct emotions (Panksepp, 1998), early work placed a heavy emphasis on two dimensions of affective appraisal, one most often labeled "positive" (a dimension that arrayed affect from moribund to enthusiastic), the second labeled "negative" (a dimension that ranged from calm to anxious and fearful). Each of these invoked neural processes that in turn influenced downstream cognitive and behavioral processes. By the late 1990s and early 2000s, researchers from multiple perspectives found it increasingly useful to take notice of a third dimension, anger (Huddy et al., 2007; Lerner & Keltner, 2001; Marcus, Neuman, & MacKuen, 2000; Panksepp, 1998).[4] This dimension is held to produce affects that range from calm to heightened aversion (e.g., rage, bitterness, anger, contempt, disgust, and so on).

The most prevalent theoretical formulation in political psychology, the theory of affective intelligence, evolved similarly from an initial focus on two dimensions, an anxiety dimension and an enthusiasm dimension (Marcus & MacKuen, 1993; Marcus, 1988) to adopting the current three-dimensional view (MacKuen, Wolak, Keele, & Marcus, 2010; Marcus et al., 2000; Marcus, 2002). The virtue of this formulation is that it makes an explicit case for the adequacy of the now widely adopted three-dimensional structural account of affective appraisals. Enthusiasm generates hypotheses about when people become engaged in politics in various ways and their reliance on extant identifications and convictions (Brader, 2006; Marcus et al., 2000). Anxiety generates hypotheses about attention, learning, and reliance on contemporary considerations (Brader, 2006; MacKuen, Marcus, Neuman, & Keele, 2007; Marcus & MacKuen, 1993). Aversion/anger generates hypotheses about the role of normative violations, and defensive and aggressive actions to protect extant identifications and convictions (Huddy et al., 2007; MacKuen et al., 2010).

2.2. Critical Considerations

Before turning to research on causes and consequences of emotion, we need to review a few of the concepts that scholars have used to describe emotion. Theoretical perspectives have appeared at different times, applying somewhat different presumptions, often unstated, about terms that, while appearing to be scientific, are just as often vernacular in meaning. This raises the risk of overly plastic meanings inasmuch as lay ideas are often plural in their meanings. Three frequently used terms recur in various accounts of emotion. Moreover, these conceptual terms are central to describing the phenomenon and imputing the mechanisms that control and give rise to the appearance of this or that emotion. The core terms requiring some excavation are *discrete*, *appraisal*, and *cognition*, with the latter two terms often paired, as in "cognitive appraisal." These terms have come to be used in various ways that often lead to confusion.

2.2.1. *What Does It Mean to Say an Emotion Is Discrete or Dimensional?*

There are two meanings of the term "discrete" apparent in the literature, one more casual and one more conceptually dense. The first is an assertion that different emotions need to be kept clearly discriminated. As a vernacular term, used in that fashion, the claim that an emotion is discrete is an appropriate way to make an introductory claim. But even in that usage the term is merely preliminary unless then linked to a recognized taxonomy of emotion states so that the affective state in question is explicitly related to the other specified affect states. This has been done in the case of "basic emotions." Various scholars have enumerated what they take to be the core fundamental affects. Though not all agree on the final array, they typically identify something like 8 to 12 "basic emotions" (Frijda, Kuipers, & Schure, 1989; Ortony, Clore, & Collins, 1989; Roseman, 1984). This second use of the term advances a richer imputation, one that holds that each discrete emotion is a bounded domain that has some homogenous quality both as to its antecedents and its consequences. This second meaning and usage is best grasped by comparison to another frequently used approach to depicting emotion, that of treating affective states as aligned along one or more dimensions.

Consider anxiety from a dimensional point of view. Anxiety, conceived as an affective dimension, is typically regarded as an appraisal of uncertainty. In this dimensional view, affective states of anxiety depict different degrees of uncertainty, hence uniting semantic terms such as *tranquil, calm, uneasy, jittery, nervous,* and *fearful* as "marking" different degrees of anxiety, arrayed from less to more. From a discrete perspective, while *jittery* and *fearful* might be seen as describing different intensities of anxiety, the emotions of *tranquility* and *calmness* would more likely be regarded as a different, discrete affective state, one to be contrasted to *anxiety.*

Figure 6.1 provides a further example of the sorts of differences that can distinguish discrete and dimensional approaches. The figure displays four common feeling words— *lethargic, withdrawn, congenial,* and, *enthusiastic.* Part A shows how these four affective states could be construed when applying a discrete approach. In this case, for illustrative purposes, we "organize" the four emotional states, in the way a cognitive appraisal theorist might, that is, according to the evaluations presumed to give rise to these four

A. Hypothetical Example of Discrete Organization of Selected Emotions

	Regarding	
Valence	Self-regarding	Other-regarding
Positive (approach)	*Enthusiastic*	*Congenial*
Negative (avoidance)	*Lethargic*	*Withdrawn*

B. Hypothetical Example of Dimensional Organization of Selected Emotions

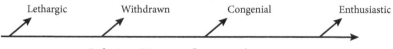

Enthusiasm Dimension (less to more)

FIGURE 6.1 Sample Taxonomies: Discrete and Dimensional Typologies of Emotion

discrete states. Part B shows how applying a dimensional approach might array them along a single dimension.

If we asked subjects to rate how well each of these affect words describe diverse scenarios, we would likely find that each of these terms is thought to be most applicable to quite different circumstances. Having found that people systematically differentiated these four terms, a scholar could conclude that these are distinct emotions produced by applying a self-regarding versus other-regarding consideration, thereby differentiating *enthusiastic* and *lethargic* from *withdrawn* and *congenial*. And that scholar might also conclude that subjects differentiated appetitive (i.e., positive) outcomes from aversive (i.e., negative) outcomes, thus differentiating *enthusiastic* and *congenial* from *withdrawal* and *lethargic*. These two general abstract considerations when jointly applied generate the four distinct affect states as depicted in Part A of figure 6.1. Thus, data and conception converge.

However, if we asked how *enthusiastic, lethargic, withdrawn,* or *congenial* they felt in different settings, we might well find that the reported levels each rise and fall in a correlated fashion. Indeed, they might be so highly correlated that they converge to a single dimension. Here again, conception and measurement converge.

In Part A, each of the four affect terms is located in its own cell, emphasizing its unique features, presumably produced by the joint application of two abstract considerations. In Part B of figure 6.1, we see these same affect terms "marking" different levels of a positive affective state, ranging from very low to very high, generated by a single appraisal, that of the likelihood of securing a positive outcome (either in the past, present, or future).

Testing the validity of these two perspectives turns on resolving three issues. First, they clearly differ as to number of antecedent factors that generate the affects (i.e., two or one). Second, they presumably differ in "downstream" consequences (though not all theories produce explicit theoretical claims thereon). Third, is there neurological evidence on the mechanisms by which these (and other) affects are generated? As we shall suggest below, however, these two accounts need not be treated as mutually exclusive.

2.2.2. *What Does It Mean to Say That Appraisals Are Central to Emotion?*

Affective reactions are expressed in facial display, posture, gesture, vocal timbre, and so forth. Emotions, it is now generally agreed, are generated by neural processes in the brain. The neural processes engaged with emotion are very fast, cycling on the order of five times faster than conscious awareness and producing their appraisals prior to conscious awareness (Rolls, 1999; Rolls, 2005). This requires fundamental rethinking about the relationship between affect and cognition. Affective preconscious appraisals execute faster than and arise before consciousness. But the traditional definition of cognition, a word derived from Latin, to cogitate, to think, has long been perceived as taking place only "inside" the mind where cogitating takes place.

Consciousness—the subjective arena wherein feeling and thinking seem to play out—offers the false sensation of instantaneous and comprehensive access to external affairs. In fact, consciousness is not instantaneous. During the time that it takes the brain to construct consciousness, our brains are active in understanding our circumstances through very fast appraisals of the somatosensory and sensory streams along with integrating those appraisals with our goals so as to enact habituated actions (Marcus, 2012). We subjectively experience events around us as if the events and their mental representation in conscious awareness are concurrent. But this apparent concurrence is itself a fabrication by preconscious neural processes (Libet, 2004; Libet, Gleason, Wright, & Pearl, 1983; Libet, Wright, Feinstein, & Pearl, 1979). Given that subjective experience seems to give instant and veridical access to the world, it is not surprising that initial research suggesting that humans react to external events before they are conscious of those events (Zajonc, 1980) was met with considerable skepticism and resistance (Kunst-Wilson & Zajonc, 1980; Lazarus, 1982; Lazarus, 1984; Tsal, 1985).[5] Hence, the more potent differentiation between consciousness and affect is not spatial but temporal. And it is well established that people act on these preconscious appraisals (Bechara et al., 1997; Todorov & Ballew, 2007).

Early cognitive theories of affect arose before this new understanding and thus often presumed that thinking of some sort was necessary to interpret affective reactions so as to make them coherent and subjectively meaningful. As a result, researchers risked conflating self-reported interpretations of when and why subjects felt a particular emotion with the temporally prior and "hidden" processes by which affective responses are generated. Put differently, some cognitive appraisal accounts seemed to confuse structural accounts, which posit implicit "rules" by which situational antecedents elicit distinct emotions, with the actual process giving rise to emotions (Clore & Ortony, 2008).

In contrast, like other neural process accounts, the most prevalent approach in political science—the theory of affective intelligence (Marcus et al., 2000; Marcus, 2002)—holds, in its current form, that there are three preconscious appraisals that generate the array of emotions that people experience at the outset of exposure to some stimulus (whether new or old, contemporaneously present, recalled from prior exposure, or part of some imagined future). Of the three, two are ubiquitous, levels of *enthusiasm* ranging from lethargic to enthusiastic, and levels of *anxiety* ranging from calm to anxious. The third, which they label *aversion*, is a situational appraisal manifest only when confronting familiar punishing circumstances.[6]

Preconscious appraisals and postawareness appraisals can both influence subjective affective states. However, disentangling the contributions of pre- and postawareness processes requires some rethinking about the terms cognition and appraisal. Most researchers, regardless of approach, now use *appraisal* to refer to the brain's assessment of some internal or external situation. There remains considerable disagreement over whether to call all appraisals *cognitive* or even what doing so implies (Scherer et al., 2001). The everyday meaning of the word cognition has long been equated with conscious thought or, at least, higher cortical mental functions. In the wake of long-running and attention-getting debate over the "primacy" of affect and cognition (Lazarus, 1982; Lazarus, 1984; Zajonc, 1980), many psychologists and neuroscientists have adopted an expanded definition of cognition as applying to any sort of information processing in the brain. From this perspective, cognitive appraisals can be understood to encompass anything from preconscious perceptions that arise directly from somatosensory and sensory inputs to extended conscious rumination about the meaning of events.

We argue that this "resolution" does more to obscure than to clarify. A multitude of brain processes, including many long associated with "cognition," occur at a preconscious level. Calling nearly everything the brain does "cognition" seems less than helpful to understanding how a host of distinct and interdependent processes function to regulate behavior.

The field, therefore, would benefit from shifting away from this terminology (and the seemingly intractable debate it invites) to specify more concretely the process by which the brain translates sensory and somatosensory inputs into differentiated emotional reactions, as well as how those emotions translate in turn into behavioral responses. In our view, scholars should focus directly on the temporal dimension, endeavoring to understand how preconscious and postawareness processes each contribute to emotional episodes. Subjective feeling states result from a sequential series of appraisals that have both "upstream" (preconscious) and "downstream" (conscious) aspects.

Such a temporal focus may productively turn attention to understanding better which appraisals, and thus which emotional states (or levels of emotional differentiation), can and do arise at a preconscious stage and which arise only, or mainly, with conscious reflection. For example, it is now widely accepted among both cognitive appraisal theorists and neuroscientists that basic preconscious appraisals of situations as something like desirable/undesirable (i.e., good/bad) set in motion positive/negative affective responses automatically—that is, outside subjective control and often outside of awareness (Clore & Ortony, 2008; Keltner & Lerner, 2010; LeDoux, 1996). In contrast, some evaluations suggested by cognitive appraisal theories may not be apt for preconscious affective appraisals, which are very fast, concerned with deft execution of action plans (including speech), and rely on the tight integration of current expectations with somatosensory input and fast sensory appraisals. Thus, an important and open question for future research is which appraisal dimensions require conscious awareness and which can occur at a pre-conscious stage. Appraisals of novelty/familiarity? Degree of situational control? Self/other causal responsibility? Certain/uncertain outcomes? Scholars have even dubbed certain affects as "self-conscious emotions" (see below), implying a more elaborate process of comparing the performance of the self with social expectations and norms. But does the social comparison underlying such emotions imply conscious awareness? The answer remains unclear.

From this broader understanding, both neural process theories, such as the theory of affective intelligence, and cognitive appraisal theories posit appraisal as an essential

t_0 arrival of sensory and somatosensory signals in the brain
t_1 conscious awareness
t_2 elaboration or consolidation of affective experience
t_3 further downstream changes

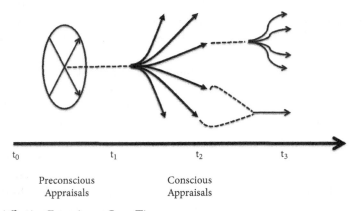

t_0 $\qquad$ t_1 $\qquad$ t_2 $\qquad$ t_3

Preconscious   Conscious
Appraisals   Appraisals

FIGURE 6.2 Affective Experience Over Time

function of conscious and affective processes. This would suggest that earlier efforts to integrate discrete and dimensional accounts in a "hierarchical" structure (Tellegen, Watson, & Clark, 1999a; 1999b) might be more usefully reconceived not in spatial terms, higher or lower, but rather in temporally arrayed "layers," with earlier states swiftly being elaborated by downstream appraisals. This suggestion, as shown in figure 6.2, allows for multiple appraisals, some very early with others falling along later in the time course of affective experience.

For example, as illustrated in the figure, initial preconscious appraisals may trigger emotions along a couple of fundamental dimensions, such as anxiety-calm and enthusiasm-lethargy. Subsequent appraisals may shape affective responses into a broader array of specific emotional states, such as anger, fear, sadness, disgust, shame, and joy. Finally, as conscious awareness and interpretation of emotions unfolds further, and emotions become infused with greater cognitive input, individuals may experience still more subtle variations in affect—for example, as angry-like reactions differentiate into anger, frustration, contempt, and resentment (Clore, Ortony, Dienes, & Fujita, 1993)—or the blending of affects into a unique emotional state—such as sadness and joy melding into a feeling of nostalgia as one reflects on happier past times (Holak & Havlena, 1998). In this way, the elaboration shown in figure 6.2 suggests one way to account for the richness of affective experience while also relying on the more parsimonious account of the early stages of preconscious appraisal. Though it should be added that for at least some circumstances, notably those when people confront very familiar stimuli (e.g., people, slogans, groups, circumstances, etc.) rather than an unfolding richness we might find, in some circumstances, the affective space collapsing even to a single valence dimension (Marcus et al., 2000).

3. ANTECEDENTS AND FUNCTIONS OF EMOTIONS

This section is divided into brief discussions of emotions or "families of emotions." Our goal is to provide readers with a sense of the most relevant distinctions among emotions, as suggested by the research literature to date, including their antecedents and functions. These categories do not reflect any particular theory, but instead identify for readers distinctions that have proven useful for social and political psychologists across a variety of studies and perspectives. Indeed, as noted earlier, one theory might argue for tying multiple categories to a single affective dimension, while another theory might insist on splitting a single category apart into even finer distinctions. This is also not an exhaustive list. Some emotions—surprise, jealousy, regret, sympathy, to name a few— have received little or no attention from political psychologists to date.[7]

3.1. Enthusiasm, Hope, Pride, and Joy

This set of emotions illustrates well the tension between vernacular labels that attempt to assign meaning to our experiences and scientific categories that mark distinct psychological processes. They are central examples of what are often called positive or "feel-good" emotions, and they are indeed associated with pleasurable feelings and an approach orientation. There are some ready differences in the way people use these terms in everyday life. Joy and happiness often refer most directly to feelings of pleasure and may describe even more broadly a positive mood or general satisfaction with life (Fredrickson, 2003). Enthusiasm suggests a more specific state of excitement and expectation for what's happening and what's ahead. Hope implies a prospective orientation, yearning for better things. Pride, in contrast, is a more retrospective feeling of pleasure and confidence due to one's success.

Thus, one might be tempted to treat these as distinct categories and yet, for all the differentiation in meaning attached to the labels, it has been difficult to differentiate these emotions observationally (based on self-reports and the like) and especially by their consequences.[8] They appear very similar in terms of neural, physiological, expressive, cognitive, and behavioral responses. Several scholars have argued that these feelings emerge from one emotional system—variously given labels such as the behavioral approach system (Gray, 1987), the seeking system (Panksepp, 1998), or the disposition system (Marcus et al., 2000)—that functions to regulate and adapt behavior toward the pursuit of rewards. People experience the emotional state associated with feelings of enthusiasm, joy, and so on, when the system receives positive feedback about that pursuit, namely when rewards appear within reach, are getting closer, or have been attained. This emotion generates the physical and mental resources for maintaining and focusing interest and engagement with the pursuit of those rewards in question, motivating the expenditure of further effort to reach the goal. In the service of such goal-seeking, this system also facilitates the learning of routines (habits of mind and body) and regulates their execution.

Political psychologists have shown that enthusiasm—typically measured as a scale that combines self-reported feelings from this set of emotions (e.g., "hopeful," "proud," "enthusiastic," "happy")—increases interest in political processes, motivates political action, and strengthens reliance on prior convictions in making political choices (Brader, 2006; Marcus et al., 2000; Valentino et al., 2011). What triggers enthusiasm in the political domain? In general, political psychologists have devoted less effort to uncovering the antecedents of politically consequential emotions than the effects. But experimental research has highlighted a few sources of political enthusiasm. These can be substantive in origin, such as reassuring news stories about the enactment of desired policies (MacKuen et al., 2010), the positive economic impact of social trends (Brader, Valentino, & Suhay, 2008), or the lead one's party has in the polls (Valentino, Hutchings, Banks, & Davis, 2008). Enthusiasm can also be triggered in somewhat more superficial (yet equally consequential) ways, such as by the smile of a charismatic politician (Sullivan & Masters, 1988b) or the use of uplifting music and feel-good imagery in campaign advertising (Brader, 2006).[9]

There is much more to learn about this set of emotions. Despite the difficulties mentioned earlier, there has been some effort to differentiate further among so-called "positive" emotions. For example, some associate pride with an expressive impulse (Lazarus, 1991) and argue, therefore, it may particularly motivate people to put their views and accomplishments on display through public discussion or the wearing and posting of political messages (Corrigan & Brader, 2011). Research on "self-conscious emotions" also differentiates pride by highlighting its relationship to feelings of shame and guilt (see below). Scholars also have suggested other potential consequences of enthusiasm, joy, or other "positive" emotions that remain relatively little explored in the political realm. Evidence in social psychology suggests these emotions can stimulate creative, playful thinking that leads to new solutions (Fredrickson, 2003) and assist recovery from stressful states, from "laughing off" a scare to coping with aversive events such as disaster or terrorist attacks. Similarly, the past decade has seen increased interest in investigating the impact of political humor, but we are not aware of any such studies to date that treat audience reactions to successful attempts at political humor explicitly as an emotion (i.e., *amusement*) and pursue its effects accordingly.

3.2. Sadness and Disappointment

If the preceding set of emotions is associated with the successful pursuit and acquisition of rewards, sadness and disappointment are clearly related to the reverse: failure and loss. Not surprisingly, therefore, dimensional accounts such as the theory of affective intelligence posit these emotions as products of negative feedback from the same emotional system that generates enthusiasm. Vernacular usage can imply subtle distinctions in meaning for how feelings are labeled in this category: one is sad, not disappointed, at the loss of a loved one. But this may simply reflect differences in intensity; a person who failed to achieve a goal she had been pursuing might describe herself as disappointed, sad, or depressed, as the importance of the goal and the magnitude of the failure increase. Is there an emotional difference between the loss of something valued and the failure to obtain rewards? Evidence on the behavioral consequences does yet not fully support such a distinction. Sadness and disappointment motivate withdrawal and more effortful processing of information, encouraging individuals to accept the loss, reflect on their situation, and change goals and plans accordingly (Bonanno, Goorin, & Coifman, 2008).

Although these emotions are ubiquitous and explicitly part of prominent theories, their political antecedents and implications are little studied. So much of politics seems to be about stirring up passions, the heavy emphasis on high-arousal emotions such as enthusiasm, fear, and anger, is perhaps understandable. However, sadness and disappointment are hardly irrelevant to the political domain. How does sadness affect the behavior of citizens experiencing a sense of collective and, at times, personal loss following events such as deadly terrorist attacks, a devastating natural disaster, or the death of a beloved leader? Or what about the consequences of disappointment felt at the failure of one's "side" in an election, a war, or international competition? By and large, the answers await further study.

3.3. Fear and Anxiety

Fear is the most studied emotion, not only within political psychology (e.g., see Stein, chapter 12, this volume), but also in the social sciences writ large. The terms fear and anxiety (along with numerous other cognates: alarm, worry, terror, etc.) typically refer to the same emotion in everyday discourse, conveying at most differing intensities of feeling. Although scholars broadly agree that these are at least very closely related "defensive" emotions, some draw distinctions between the terms. For example, clinical psychologists distinguish between generalized anxiety disorders and specific fears (phobias) that afflict individuals (Öhman & Mineka, 2001; Öhman & Soares, 1993; Öhman, Dimberg, & Esteves, 1989). Other researchers have pointed to neurological and behavioral differences between an emotional state (fear) associated with clear threats and more purely avoidance reactions, on one hand, and one (anxiety) associated with ambiguous threats and a mix of approach reactions and risk aversion, on the other (Gray & McNaughton, 2000; Perkins, Inchley-Mort, Pickering, Corr, & Burgess, 2012). Nonetheless, to date, most political psychologists use these labels interchangeably. On a practical level, research subjects in surveys and experiments seem to use the terms to report the same latent emotional experience, and such self-reports remain the principal method of measuring emotions. It remains to be seen whether political psychologists can isolate more subtle differences in these emotional responses and trace them in turn to meaningfully distinct political consequences.

The disproportionate scholarly attention focused on fear clearly reflects the centrality and importance of its function in human life. Fear is a product of an emotional system—sometimes named the behavioral inhibition system (Gray, 1987), the surveillance system (Marcus et al., 2000), or simply the fear system (Panksepp, 1998)—that monitors the environment for potential threats and adapts behavior accordingly. It may be activated as an innate response to certain classes of events that portend danger (e.g., unexpected loud noises, large objects quickly approaching) or as a learned response to just about anything that has become associated with danger (LeDoux, 1996). Novelty, or uncertainty, can trigger anxiety, since what is unknown may also be dangerous. Fear interrupts ongoing behavior, while redirecting attention and other cognitive activity toward dealing with the threat. Specifically, it prompts individuals to seek out information related to the threat and to reconsider courses of action to deal with the danger in light of present circumstances. It motivates people to remove the danger, if that is readily doable, or, if not, to remove themselves from the danger. Thus, fear motivates (and prepares the body for) risk-aversive behavior, including actions aimed at prevention and protection, conciliatory acts, hiding, and flight. The impact of fear on memory is more complex, with evidence that it can both enhance the encoding and recall of memories and yet also interfere with encoding and recall.

What arouses fear among citizens? As with enthusiasm, political psychologists have demonstrated that it can be triggered by both substantive and superficial stimuli. Subliminal images of snakes and skulls (Way & Masters, 1996a; Way & Masters, 1996b) and the discordant music and violent images that serve as a backdrop to campaign advertising (Brader, 2006) generate anxiety that spills over to affect the way voters process political information and make decisions. Of course, fear is often activated directly by threats conveyed by the very events, people, and policies at the heart of political life, including, for example, the worried or uncertain expressions of political leaders (Sullivan & Masters, 1988b), campaign news suggesting a preferred candidate is losing (Valentino et al., 2008) or does not have the policy positions or character one hoped (Redlawsk, Civettini, & Emmerson, 2010), stereotypic portrayals of threatening out-groups (Brader et al., 2008), news of deadly viral outbreaks (Brader et al., 2010), or images of terrorist attacks (Gadarian, 2010; Lerner, Gonzalez, Small, & Fischhoff, 2003; Merolla & Zechmeister, 2009).

3.4. Calmness and Serenity

If feelings of fear arise from threatening conditions, then serenity or calmness is the state that prevails only when threats are absent. Perhaps for this reason, dimensional accounts of emotion, which place fear and calmness as poles on a single axis, give greater recognition to this emotional state. The theory of affective intelligence, for example, posits that calmness is generated when the surveillance system indicates everything is safe and expected (Marcus et al., 2000). In contrast, discrete emotion accounts rarely include this emotion in their lists. We are aware of no research on the political antecedents and implications of serenity. This is understandable, given that the emotional state implies that "not much is happening," but it nonetheless seems to hold potential significance for politics that has gone unexplored. For example, leaders may wish to restore calm to a public upset about the threat of war, disease, terrorism, or other crisis. Whereas numerous studies in political psychology have investigated how to make citizens more anxious, none yet have investigated how to make them more calm.

3.5. Anger

The status of anger has posed particular difficulties for dimensional models of emotion. Although people clearly *experience* anger as distinct from fear, self-reported feelings of anger often accompany those of fear. and the structural analyses have typically placed anger and fear in very close proximity (Tellegen et al., 1999a; 1999b). This makes considerable sense in light of the fact that many of the same situations that produce fear also produce anger (Berkowitz & Harmon-Jones, 2004; Berkowitz, 1988). Nevertheless, anger appears to be an "approach" emotion (Carver, 2004) and, as such, its consequences often seem to have more in common with enthusiasm than fear. In light of this, Carver recasts the dimension underlying the behavioral approach system such that sadness anchors the low end when rewards vanish or are recognized as unobtainable, but anger and frustration emerge along the middle of the dimension when rewards are seen as slipping away but still within reach. Another dimensional account, affective intelligence theory, has also evolved to argue that aversion—defined as a cluster of feelings that includes anger, disgust, contempt, and hatred—is activated by the same system that produces enthusiasm (i.e., the disposition system), specifically when *familiar* disliked or threatening stimuli present themselves (MacKuen et al., 2010).

Whatever the challenges to defining its "place" in the structure of emotions, anger clearly has distinct effects. Indeed, one of the most important contributions of political psychology's growing attention to emotions in recent years has been to explain why threatening or aversive circumstances in politics often produce such divergent reactions. Social scientists have long recognized that "threat" has a strong influence on individuals but previously did not differentiate or reconcile its myriad effects. In contrast to those who are anxious, angry citizens cling tightly to their prior convictions and are less receptive to new considerations or opposing points of view. Anger is a particularly powerful mobilizing force that motivates people to take and support risky, confrontational, and punitive actions.

What triggers anger? Anger emerges in situations when people are threatened or find obstacles blocking their path to reward (see also Huddy, chapter 23, this volume). The primary function of the set of effects just described is to marshal the cognitive and physical resources necessary to overcome such obstacles or threats. But we have already noted that anger and fear frequently co-occur. Moreover, fear is also a response to threats, and sadness is also a response when rewards are not obtained. So what *distinctively* triggers anger? Beyond the presence of threats and obstacles, four antecedents receive considerable discussion in the literature: (1) an external cause, especially the intentional actions of some "freely acting" agent who can be blamed (Lazarus, 1991; Smith & Ellsworth, 1985); (2) coping potential, or the perception that one has some control over the situation (Carver, 2004; Frijda, 1986; Lazarus, 1991); (3) perception that the situation is unfair, illegitimate, or undeserved (Averill, 1983; Roseman, 1991); and (4) the familiarity of a threat (Marcus, 2002). Some have argued that many or all of these factors may constitute sufficient rather than necessary conditions for the arousal of anger; no one is essential, but each strengthens the likelihood and experience of an anger response (Berkowitz & Harmon-Jones, 2004).

By conducting further research to isolate the causes of anger as distinct from other "negative" emotions, political psychologists can shed light on the origins of public outrage and contribute to a greater understanding of anger among psychologists generally (Krosnick & McGraw, 2002). Steenbergen and Ellis (2006), for example, draw on survey data to suggest that anger toward presidential candidates may be rooted in assessments of unfair or morally wrong actions. Other studies have found that intentionality of the wrongdoer increases anger in criminal justice opinions (Petersen, 2010) and, in experimental research, that situational blame and control trigger anger distinctly from fear in response to threatening news (Brader et al., 2010).

3.6. Disgust

Much as it requires some effort to disentangle anger from fear, even more effort is required to pull apart disgust and anger (Hutcherson & Gross, 2011). The co-occurrence of self-reported disgust and anger to any specific elicitor is high; numerous studies use "disgusted" as an indicator term in constructing scales for anger (Conover & Feldman, 1986; MacKuen et al., 2010; Valentino et al., 2011). The theory of affective intelligence explicitly conceptualizes disgust as a marker for an emotional state called "aversion," which is also indicated by feelings of anger, contempt, and hatred (MacKuen et al., 2010). Despite this close entanglement with anger, however, disgust reactions also clearly arise from a distinctive and very old neural and physiological process that has evolved to avoid and expel contamination (Rozin, Haidt, & McCauley, 2008). When people smell decomposing bodies or urine-saturated alleyways, when they see cockroaches crawling across food or maggot-infested wounds, they automatically wrinkle their nose, curl their upper lip, and even feel nauseous. Disgust motivates individuals to stay away from noxious or impure stimuli and, if necessary, to purge and cleanse themselves of the possible contaminants. Scholars have recently begun to examine more fully the social and political implications of disgust, building on the recognition that disgust reactions in human societies seem to have been extended beyond the realm of physical impurity to the realm of moral impurity (Schnall, Haidt, Clore, & Jordan, 2008).

3.7. Shame, Embarrassment, Guilt, and Pride

The last set of emotions more fully represents a family or class of emotions. Although there has been difficulty and disagreement in distinguishing among some of these feeling terms, no scholars propose that they all constitute a single emotional state or dimension. Many scholars instead consider it useful to categorize these affective states together under the label "self-conscious emotions" (Tracy, Robins, & Tangney, 2007). They are triggered by preconscious or conscious appraisals evaluating the self, specifically comparing how well or poorly oneself has performed with respect to a socially prescribed standard or norm (Lewis, Haviland-Jones, & Barrett, 2008). Both the experience and the anticipation of experiencing these emotions can influence behavior, typically motivating people toward greater adherence with social standards.

Ordinary people (and some researchers) use shame and guilt interchangeably, but mounting research suggests two clearly distinct emotional processes are at work (Tangney, Stuewig, & Mashek, 2007): the first, labeled shame, is triggered when negative self-evaluation is leveled at the whole self ("I am a bad person"), while the second, guilt, is triggered when negative self-evaluation is focused on a specific behavior ("I did a bad thing"). The divergent consequences are stark. Shame, by far the more painful experience, causes feelings of powerlessness and worthlessness; motivates a desire to hide, deny, or escape the situation; inhibits empathy; provokes externalization of blame and destructive anger; and is associated with a host of psychological disorders (depression, post-traumatic stress disorder, suicidal thoughts, etc.). In contrast, guilt elicits feelings of remorse and regret over actions; causes heavier focus on the consequences of behavior for others; and motivates reparative actions such as confession, apologies, efforts to make amends, and desire to improve future behavior. Embarrassment manifests as a relatively mild feeling (Lewis et al., 2008), triggered by norm violations, social awkwardness, and feeling exposed (i.e., conspicuous); it motivates conciliatory behavior, attempts to win the approval of others in the group, and conformity with social norms (Tangney et al., 2007). Finally, pride is triggered by a positive self-evaluation for meeting standards or other socially valued outcomes and encourages further conformity with standards.

Although these emotions may seem more the province of interpersonal relations than politics, they bear ample relevance for politics. Self-conscious emotions likely facilitate the informal policing and maintenance of group norms (e.g., reciprocity, civility, acquiescence) that enable cooperation and reinforce power structures in communities, formal organizations, social movements, or any peer network. For example, the experience of embarrassment or pride at finding oneself out of or in line, respectively, with the political values of one's group elicits greater adherence and application of those values (Suhay, 2008). Politicians and activists try at times to explicitly "shame" (usually meaning guilt or embarrassment, by the definitions above, and so illustrative of the confusion over terms) citizens or leaders into "doing what is right." During the civil rights movement, Martin Luther King Jr. used these emotional tactics when he pointed to the hypocritical gap between American principles and the realities of racial inequality, and again when he told white audiences that the "tragedy" of their times lay not in the violent actions of bad people, but rather in the "appalling silence and indifference of the good people." Without directly measuring emotions, recent studies highlight the way get-out-the-vote efforts can motivate greater adherence to civic duty and thereby boost turnout—ostensibly by evoking self-conscious emotions through the actual or threatened publication of names and voting records to neighbors or members of the community (Gerber, Green, & Larimer, 2010; Panagopoulos, 2010). As a final example, citizens may experience collective guilt for the harmful actions of group members (past or present), which in turn may motivate support for reparative policies and political action on behalf of such goals (Leach, Iyer, & Pederson, 2006; Pagano & Huo, 2007).

4. POLITICAL CONSEQUENCES OF EMOTIONS

Research on the political consequences of emotions to date has spanned several important substantive domains of politics, including voter decision-making in election campaigns; reactions to war, terrorism, disaster; the effects of mass-mediated messages; the formation of policy preferences; and the evolution of political activism and social movements. We offer a brief and necessarily selective overview of a fast-growing body of evidence demonstrating that emotions shape political outcomes in a multitude of ways. We organize this discussion according to types of effects, ranging from how emotions affect preferences over individual and collective political actions, thus shaping both public opinion and political participation, to how they influence the very processes of attention, information processing, and decision-making. In the concluding section of the chapter, we also highlight some new or neglected areas ripe for further consideration by political psychologists.

4.1. Motivation for Personal and Political Action

In adapting behavior to meet situational needs, emotions prepare the body for and provide an impulse toward certain courses of action, sometimes called *action tendencies* (Frijda, 1986). As a result, they can shape both the private and public actions of citizens. High-arousal emotions, such as fear, enthusiasm, and anger, provide the motivation for citizens to become engaged with and participate in politics generally (Marcus et al., 2000). Of these, the impact of fear seems most variable and the impact of anger seems most reliably potent, but both appear to depend on the resources or efficacy of the individual (Brader, 2006; Rudolph, Gangl, & Stevens, 2000; Valentino et al., 2011; Valentino, Banks, Hutchings, & Davis, 2009; see also Valentino & Nardis, chapter 18, this volume). Political psychologists should also take note of recent work in political sociology that documents the critical role of emotions in motivating and sustaining collective action in protests, social movements, and other forms of political activism (Goodwin, Jasper, & Polletta, 2001; Gould, 2009; Jasper, 1998; 2011; see also Klandermans & Stekelenburg, chapter 24, this volume).

The action tendencies ascribed to fear, anger, enthusiasm, sadness, and other emotions are quite distinct, of course, though such implications remain relatively underexplored in the field. Fear and anger, for example, have divergent effects not only on the assessment of risks, but also actual risk-taking behavior. In the shadow of terrorist attacks, fearful citizens perceive greater risks and are more likely to engage in precautionary actions like screening mail and restricting travel, while angry citizens perceive less risk and engage in more risk-acceptant behaviors (Lerner et al., 2003). Similarly, facing a potentially deadly viral outbreak, angry citizens were more likely to write officials demanding investigation and prosecution of those who caused the outbreak, while fearful citizens were more likely to engage in preventative or protective behaviors, such as wearing a mask, increased hand washing, and reading up on the disease (Brader et al., 2010). We should expect similar emotion-specific patterns for explicitly political actions where this is a fit between action tendency and type of behavior; for example, pride ought to promote expressive displays of group loyalty, while anger ought to motivate participation in confrontational protests or other forms of political aggression.

4.2. From Action Tendencies to Political Attitudes

Much of politics involves collective and representational action, with governments, political parties, or other groups acting ostensibly on behalf of others. In many or even most cases, citizens do not act directly to pursue their goals for society, but instead express support for particular policies or outcomes and choose leaders who will pursue them. Thus, action tendencies should manifest as much in preferences for public action (i.e., public opinion) as in individual participatory acts.

Indeed, scholars have found that emotions inform preferences and policy-related attitudes across several policy domains. For example, anger and anxiety have been the focal emotions for studies of public reactions to terrorism, with anxiety leading to more risk-averse or isolationist policy preferences and anger leading to more support for more confrontational policies (Fischhoff, Gonzalez, Lerner, & Small, 2005; Huddy, Feldman, Taber, & Lahav, 2005; Lambert et al., 2010; Lerner et al., 2003; Skitka, Bauman, Aramovich, & Morgan, 2006; Small, Lerner, & Fischhoff, 2006). Across a range of behaviors, anger seems to promote a more confident, aggressive response during crises, while fear causes individuals to pull back or proceed with caution (see also Druckman & McDermott, 2008). Similarly, anxiety and anger seem to make individuals more and less receptive, respectively, to compromise (MacKuen et al., 2010).

We also see emotions affecting opinions and decisions in the domain of morality. While many have held that such decisions ought to rely on explicit principles, the sentimental approach has long held that normative actions are embedded in early habits of right action sustained by emotional foundations (Frazer, 2010; Hume, 1975; 1984; Smith, 1959). A modern-day sentimentalist is Jonathan Haidt (2001). In his moral foundations theory (Haidt & Joseph, 2007; Haidt, 2008), Haidt grounds moral judgment in emotions. He argues that five foundations—harm/care, fairness/reciprocity, in-group/loyalty, authority/respect, purity/sanctity—elicit the key emotions of disgust and empathy that motivate action intended to sustain the moral codes in question.

This formulation has stimulated and exemplified work on so-called moral emotions (Tangney et al., 2007). That body of work includes studies examining the role of shame, embarrassment, and pride in promoting adherence to group values in democratic life (Suhay, 2008), the role of empathy and guilt in promoting support for humanitarian and reparative actions during war (Pagano & Huo, 2007), and the role of anger and guilt in punishing norm violations (Nelissen & Zeelenberg, 2009). A cluster of recent studies considers the role of disgust in moral judgments and behavior. Studies focusing on both traits (i.e., general sensitivity to disgust reactions) and situational reactions find that disgust causes individuals to make harsher moral judgments (Eskine, Kacinik, & Prinz, 2011; Helzer & Pizarro, 2011; Pizarro, Inbar, & Helion, 2011; Wheatley & Haidt, 2005). Research in the United States also suggests that disgust reactions push people toward identifying as politically conservative (Inbar, Pizarro, Iyer, & Haidt, 2012; Inbar, Pizarro, Knobe, & Bloom, 2009). Finally, disgust is associated with morally conservative policy positions, especially on issues linked to perceived impurity, such as abortion and homosexuality (Inbar & Gilovich, 2011; Inbar et al., 2009).

4.3. Information Processing and Decision-Making

It has now become conventional wisdom that humans have two modes of decision-making, the so-called dual-process model. For a review see Evans (2008). The essential claim is that there is a fast system that relies primarily on processes not present in consciousness, and there is a slow system that makes use of deliberative, introspective, and thoughtful processes resident in consciousness. Emotion is increasingly understood to play a principal role in shaping which route, or path, is active and in serving to sustain each. This is important in part because if citizens, and leaders, have two modes of judgment, each activated in different circumstances, then understanding the strengths and liabilities of each shapes what we can expect of citizens and their leaders under circumstances when judgment processes differ. This has normative as well as empirical implications (Marcus, 2013). Such process-focused research examines how affective appraisals shape attention and judgment, by shifting from swift reliance on extant convictions and habits to deliberative processes.

Several studies explore the impact of emotions on attention and learning. Many find that fear causes citizens to desire and seek out more political information (Brader et al., 2008; Huddy et al., 2007; Marcus et al., 2000; Valentino et al., 2008). This search for information tends to be selectively focused on what may be useful for the situation at hand (Brader, 2006; Valentino et al., 2009), but also broader and more balanced, as it is less shaped by partisan or other confirmatory biases (MacKuen et al., 2010; Valentino et al., 2009). In many cases, though perhaps not all (Feldman & Huddy, n.d.), this seeking increases relevant factual knowledge (Marcus et al., 2000; Valentino et al., 2008; Valentino et al., 2009). The effects of anger diverge sharply from this pattern. For example, anger appears to reduce the amount of time actually spent visiting political websites, shrink the number of web pages visited, and narrow searches to opinion-confirming sources, produce less thoughtful opinions, and inhibit accurate recall of information (Geva & Skorick, 2006; MacKuen et al., 2007; Redlawsk, Civettini, & Lau, 2007; Valentino et al., 2008; Valentino et al., 2009). In sum, these findings confirm that there exist two different decisions-making modes, one triggered by anger, focusing on defense of extant convictions and hence disinterested in disconfirming evidence or new information triggered, and a second, more deliberative and open mode that is triggered by anxiety.

Much of the research on decision-making and affect has been shaped by the theory of affective intelligence (Marcus et al., 2000). That account holds that anxiety increases attention to contemporary information relevant to the decision choice, while both anger and enthusiasm lead to automatic reliance on relevant convictions. Numerous studies indeed find that political judgments of anxious citizens are more responsive to available information (e.g., media messages, campaign content) and less closely tied to predispositions (e.g., party identification or ideology) or prior attitudes, while anger and enthusiasm push decision-making in the opposite direction (Brader et al., 2008; Brader, 2006; Druckman & McDermott, 2008; MacKuen et al., 2007; Marcus, Sullivan, Theiss-Morse, & Stevens, 2005; Merolla & Zechmeister, 2009; Parker & Isbell, 2010; Redlawsk et al., 2010).[10] Banks and Valentino (2012) have applied the same interest in anger and anxiety to racial attitudes and find that anxiety undermines reliance on convictions, while anger strengthens it. Finally, Small and Lerner (2008) look at how a different emotion, incidental sadness, affected welfare policy judgments. Similar to what others have found for anxiety, sadness stimulated deeper processing of information and more attention to situational attributions, leading individuals to support more generous assistance.

5. Going Forward

Emotions have become a vibrant research topic within political psychology. As a result, we have a learned a great deal about the impact of emotions on opinion formation and political behavior, especially in electoral settings and under the threat of war or terrorism. Most attention has fallen on enthusiasm, fear, and anger, with only incipient consideration of other emotions to date. We are confident that research in the years ahead will deepen and broaden our understanding of these emotions and their implications for politics. It will also be important for political psychologists to devote greater study to the antecedents of political emotions, about which we know far less, and to illuminate the full range of relevant emotions or emotional dimensions. For all its recent vigor, this field of inquiry remains relatively young. There are many productive paths forward as the field expands. We conclude this chapter by highlighting a number of theoretical, methodological, and substantive issues that merit attention from political psychologists over the next decade.

5.1. Theoretical Testing and Integration

Research in this field has been predominantly theory-driven, in the sense of proceeding from theoretical propositions about the function and operation of emotions in the human brain. Most studies, however, have been content to take up isolated propositions without situating their tests in a fuller theory of political emotions. Work on the theory of affective intelligence (Marcus et al., 2000) is the major exception. Nonetheless, studies have drawn—some loosely, some directly—on a number of related theoretical perspectives from social psychology and neuroscience, including cognitive appraisal theories (Scherer et al., 2001), appraisal tendency theory (Lerner & Keltner, 2000), the affect-as-information model (Schwarz & Clore, 2003), terror management theory (Landau et al., 2004), the hot cognition hypothesis (Lodge & Taber, 2005; Lodge & Taber, 2013), and intergroup emotions theory (Mackie & Smith, 2004). To the extent such perspectives are useful for understanding emotions in the domain of politics, political psychologists should extend or adapt them as necessary to articulate full theoretical accounts of political emotions. Moreover, with few exceptions, researchers have focused largely on testing propositions in accordance with a single perspective rather than testing competing theoretical explanations. The theoretical development of this field requires explicit consideration of how well empirical tests accord with not just one, but multiple theories.

At the same time, there is considerable potential for theoretical integration as well as differentiation. For example, one need not see approaches like affective intelligence and cognitive appraisal theories as inherently or completely incompatible, given that they tend to emphasize different aspects of emotional response (e.g., preconscious versus postconscious appraisals). Indeed, by taking greater note of the temporal resolution, it is not hard to envision affective responses in the brain as multilayered. On one level, the brain may automatically encode and respond to sensory data with positive and negative affects as a useful mechanism for sorting objects and experiences according to their implications for the self, consistent with the hot cognition and somatic marker hypotheses (Damasio, 1994; Lodge & Taber, 2005). On another level, preconscious appraisals may further differentiate emotional responses through the activation of a limited set of modular or dimensional systems that adapt behavior to meet the needs of the situation, consistent with affective intelligence theory (Marcus et al., 2000), affective neuroscience approaches (Panksepp, 1998), and functional evolutionary accounts (Tooby & Cosmides, 2008). On yet a third level, postconscious appraisals may enable highly differentiated self-understandings of emotional responses that shape subsequent efforts to manage both the experience and expression of those emotions, consistent with cognitive appraisal theories (Lazarus, 1991; Scherer et al., 2001; Tracy et al.,

2007). Tellegen, Watson, and Clark (Tellegen et al., 1999a; 1999b), for example, find support for a three-level hierarchical structure of affective experience, moving from global bipolar affect to discrete emotions, based on self-report data. Efforts at theoretical integration and consideration of the multilayered nature of affective experience can improve our understanding of each constituent emotional process as well as focus our attention on which processes are most relevant for illuminating particular political experiences.

5.2. Measurement

Issues of measurement pose some familiar and some unique challenges to the study of emotions that have received relatively light consideration and treatment within political psychology. Psychologists have used a variety of tools to try to measure emotional reactions, including most notably verbal self-reports, psychophysiological measures, and human coding of facial or other body movements (Larsen & Fredrickson, 1999). Self-reports are by far the most common form of measurement in social and political psychology owing to ease of use and low cost. But reliance on verbal reports is tricky for at least three reasons. First, people have tenuous access to their emotional states—indeed, emotions frequently occur outside of conscious awareness. Second, as with any self-reported behavior, subjects can censor or edit their answers to meet perceived social expectations. Third, as discussed earlier, the vagaries of everyday language do not align perfectly with scientific conceptions. A person might equally well use the terms "disgusted" or "angry" to describe his reaction at another individual's transgression, and yet also use "disgusted" to describe his feelings at seeing insects in his food, when "angry" would not be a suitable descriptor. Similarly, in the English vernacular, people might say they are "anxious" either when they are worried (i.e., fearful) or when they are eagerly anticipating (i.e., enthusiastic about) what is to come.

   In light of these problems, it is tempting to turn to biological aspects of emotional response that do not require conscious awareness, cannot be easily controlled, and are not filtered through linguistic conventions. Paul Ekman and his students, for example, have developed and refined a detailed system for coding facial expressions that has been subject to extensive cross-cultural validation and application in numerous domains (Ekman & Rosenberg, 2005). Others have deployed a variety of tools to monitor directly such bodily reactions as heart rate, skin conductance, muscle tension, electrical activity, and blood flow. These techniques come with their own serious handicaps, however. Both facial coding and psychophysiological monitoring are laborious and require direct observation of subjects, often under highly controlled conditions. Some of the methods—electroencephalogram (EEG), facial electromyography (EMG), and functional magnetic resonance imaging (fMRI)—are particularly apt to feel invasive and artificial. Moreover, while emotions are clearly tied to patterns of visceral and brain activity, decades of research have failed to yield evidence of a clear one-to-one correspondence between specific emotional states and autonomic, visceral, and brain indicators (Larsen, Bernston, Poehlmann, Ito, & Cacioppo, 2008).

In view of the particular strengths and weaknesses of each measurement approach, specific studies and especially extended research programs tend to benefit from triangulating through the use of multiple methods (Larsen & Fredrickson, 1999). Nonetheless, given the predominance of self-reports and their necessity for survey studies, greater attention is warranted to best practices in obtaining reliable and valid emotional self-reports. Two useful guidelines that emerge relatively clearly from earlier work (Marcus, MacKuen, Wolak, & Keele, 2006) include (1) asking about the intensity (how much?) of emotions toward some target yields results comparable to asking about the frequency (how often?) of such emotions (both are superior to offering binary response options or a checklist); and (2) as with any latent construct, multiple-item scales yield stronger measures; specifically it is typically critical to include two cognate terms and preferably three or more for each emotion (dimension) the researchers seeks to tap, especially if the goal is to differentiate among highly correlated positive or negative affects (e.g., fear vs. anger vs. sadness).

Recent research in progress parallels other work in survey methodology by assessing the costs and benefits of question-and-response formats in self-administered questionnaires, relevant both for laboratory studies and for the increasingly prevalent use of Internet surveys. For example, the use of a sliding scale generates more reliable and valid measures in many situations (Marcus, Neuman, & MacKuen, 2009). Consistent with other work on survey methods, the use of a grid format to administer a battery of emotion items notably reduces completion time over asking items separately on sequential computer screens. However, subjects seem to report stronger positive emotions and weaker negative emotions when presented with a grid relative to answering the items sequentially (Brader, Valentino, & Karl, 2012).[11]

One question that arises often concerns the level of specificity required vis-à-vis the target of emotion. For example, if one wishes to examine the impact of anxiety on voting decisions, what is the appropriate target for the emotional self-report question? Should we expect only anxiety about the candidates or the choice between them to be relevant? How about more diffuse but obviously politically relevant anxiety about the current conditions or future direction of the country? How about anxiety over frequently relevant issues, such as anxiety about economic conditions, security in an age of terrorism, or cultural change at the hands of large-scale immigration? Finally, is it possible that anxiety over seemingly unrelated matters—stresses about an impending deadline at work, nervousness over an upcoming romantic date, the presence of a snake in the room—could affect voting decisions as well? Research to date suggests that integral and incidental affects produce similar behavioral consequences (Adolphs, 2009; Brader, 2005; Isbell & Ottati, 2002; Small et al., 2006; Way & Masters, 1996b). That said, studies in political psychology largely have failed to compare directly whether target specificity moderates the impact of emotional responses.

5.3. Promising Avenues for Future Research

In addition to the preceding theoretical and methodological issues, many substantive topics are ripe for further consideration. One is the link between *emotions* and *personality.* In recent years, political psychology has seen renewed interest in personality, especially from a trait theory perspective (see Caprara and Vecchione, chapter 2, this volume). Psychologists have long posited the existence of trait analogs to specific emotional states, for example, "trait anxiety," "trait anger," and "disgust sensitivity" (Haidt, McCauley, & Rozin, 1994; Spielberger & Sydeman, 1994; Watson & Clark, 1991). These traits may be conceptualized as an individual's propensity to experience certain emotions more (or less) often and more (or less) intensely, perhaps due to a greater (or lower) sensitivity to the associated environmental triggers or the tendency to generate relevant appraisals. Thus, a person who quickly becomes enraged at the slightest provocation is likely to score high in trait anger. Researchers often treat emotional traits and states as interchangeable predictors when pursuing the implications of particular emotions (Inbar & Gilovich, 2011; Inbar et al., 2009; Lerner & Keltner, 2000).

Emotions have also been tied to more general personality constructs. For example, two scales promulgated as part of a more comprehensive five-factor model of personality (the "Big Five") are closely associated with emotions. Specifically, the trait of extraversion is linked to the experience of positive emotions, and the trait of neuroticism is linked to the experience of negative emotions (McCrae & Costa, 2003). Another general construct is empathy, which is regarded as a disposition that has both cognitive and affective elements (Davis, 1994; Morrell, 2010). Empathy concerns an individual's ability or tendency to understand and react emotionally to other people's experiences. It inhibits aggression and antisocial behaviors that are harmful to others (Tangney et al., 2007).

The antecedents of political emotions are a neglected topic in research generally, but what research has been done is predominantly focused on situational rather than predispositional triggers. Only a handful of studies have considered how personality traits influence the experience and expression of political emotions (Bizer et al., 2004; Marcus, Sullivan, Theiss-Morse, & Wood, 1995; Wolak & Marcus, 2007). Further research in this vein can shed light, for example, on who is apt to be most responsive to specific types of emotional appeals—persuaded to reconsider one's views when faced with a fear-inducing threat, mobilized to political violence when angered by injustice, motivated to vote by a guilt-inflected reminder of civic duty, or moved to volunteer out of sympathy when officials plea for help in the wake of disaster. Some researchers also have suggested links between emotional traits and the development of liberal-conservative political orientations (Inbar, Pizarro, & Bloom, 2008; Jost, Glaser, Kruglanski, & Sulloway, 2003).

A second broad domain for future research is the role of emotions in group processes, both *intragroup* and *intergroup relations.* What role do emotions play in tying citizens together and directing the activities within small advocacy groups, election campaign teams, large political organizations, or social movements? How do emotions shape the relationship between leaders and followers? Such questions about intragroup dynamics are hardly new (Finifter, 1974; Verba, 1961), but they have slipped out of focus in contemporary political psychology (Mendelberg, 2005). In the 1980s and early 1990s, researchers at Dartmouth College laid down a sizable foundation of work on how emotional expressions and nonverbal behavior shape the relationships between leaders and followers in mass societies (Masters & Sullivan, 1989a; 1989b; McHugo, Lanzetta,

Sullivan, Masters, & Englis, 1985; Sullivan & Masters, 1988a; 1988b; Warnecke, Masters, & Kempter, 1992; Way & Masters, 1996a; 1996b). However, studies of the topic have become less frequent (Bucy & Bradley, 2004; Bucy & Grabe, 2008; Bucy & Newhagen, 1999; Glaser & Salovey, 1998; Stewart, Waller, & Schubert, 2009; Stroud, Glaser, & Salovey, 2005) and have focused almost exclusively on political candidates, especially US presidential candidates. Political psychologists have yet to delve far into studying how emotions shape the bonds among group members or between leaders and followers in small-scale political organizations, protest movements, or in authoritarian societies.

One place to start, for example, is for political psychologists to engage with recent work in political sociology, which has begun to explore the ways in which emotions shape the development, maintenance, and activities of advocacy groups and social movements (Barbalet, 2001; Goodwin et al., 2001; Gould, 2009; Jasper, 2011; see also Klandermans & Stekelenburg, chapter 24, this volume). Given strong interest in political discussion and deliberation (see Myers & Mendelberg, chapter 22, this volume), another fruitful avenue for future research is to examine the implications of emotions for communication and decision-making in deliberative settings (Hickerson & Gastil, 2008; MacKuen et al., 2010). Yet a third possibility is for political psychologists to take seriously the affective nature of social and political group identities. Emotions may be useful indicators of the strength of in-group identification (Greene & Elder, 2001), but specific emotions experienced as a group member have more nuanced implications for whether and what sorts of actions she is willing to undertake (see Huddy, chapter 23, this volume).

In contrast, research on intergroup processes—prejudice, conflict, cooperation— has flourished in contemporary political psychology (e.g., see chapters in this volume by Kinder, chapter 25; Green and Staerklé, chapter 26; Hewstone and Al-Ramiah, chapter 27; and Bar-Tal and Halperin, chapter 28). Negative affect, ranging from mild dislike to intense hatred, has long been a defining element of prejudice toward out-groups. But, when probed, people express a much more complex array of negative emotions toward out-groups—anger, fear, pity, disgust, guilt—and, in some cases, even positive emotions—sympathy, gratitude, and admiration. Although simple, summary measures of prejudice or "group affect" are useful as ubiquitous, powerful predictors of behavior, political psychologists should move away from heavy reliance on prejudice to take greater account of specific out-group emotions, which will lead to much finer-grained insights about the causes and consequences of both intergroup conflict and cooperation.

Two very similar, relatively new theories in social psychology—Intergroup Emotions Theory (Mackie & Smith, 2004; Mackie, Devos, & Smith, 2000) and a Sociofunctional Threat-Based Approach to Intergroup Affect (Cottrell & Neuberg, 2005)—provide promising foundations for pursuing this work. Each posits that distinct appraisals or threat perceptions of out-groups evoke specific emotions toward those groups, leading to distinctive "profiles" or patterns of emotions—anger, fear, disgust, pity, envy—that members of one group feel toward each out-group in their environment (Dasgupta, DeSteno, Williams, & Hunsinger, 2009; Iyer & Leach, 2008). Given what has been learned about the function and consequences of specific emotions, these theories point the way to distinct predictions for political attitudes and behavior depending on the outgroup implicated. Very little work to date has tested such political implications (Cottrell, Richards, & Nichols, 2010; Dumont, Yzerbyt, Wigboldus, & Gordijn, 2003), and thus political psychologists could contribute greatly to the development of these perspectives and enrich their own understanding of intergroup relations in doing so (see both Huddy, chapter 23, and Stein, chapter 12, this volume).

A third direction for future research is the study of *individual and institutional efforts to control emotions*. While there is considerable psychological research on individuals' efforts to regulate their own emotions, research on efforts to influence the emotions of others for political purposes is relatively rare. Studies of the antecedents of political emotions lag behind studies of effects and have focused predominantly on the individual appraisals, situational outcomes, and events depicted in news stories. In contrast, few studies examine explicit efforts to influence emotions, especially those with a recurring or institutionalized basis.

One limited exception is research on the use of emotional appeals in electoral or issue advocacy messages to sway audiences (Brader, 2006; Huddy & Gunnthorsdottir, 2000; Roseman et al., 1986; Weber, Searles, & Ridout, 2011). Even this small body of work focuses more on the effectiveness of specific emotional triggers than on the strategy and tactics adopted by candidates, political parties, and interest groups. There are many questions we could ask about such emotional strategies in political communication (Brader & Corrigan, 2005; Ridout & Searles, 2011; Weber et al., 2011): Which emotion or mix of emotions do these political actors try to evoke in their audiences? Does the desire to elicit specific emotions affect decisions about who is targeted and when? To what extent do political actors condition their emotional strategies on the emotional strategies of their rivals?

Political efforts at manipulating emotions, of course, extend well beyond campaign and issue ads. Numerous other recurring events in and out of election campaigns are occasions for eliciting public emotions: party conventions, campaign rallies, national parades, state funerals, and high-profile political speeches (e.g., the State of the Union speech, with its perennial presidential invocation of national achievements and future goals delivered to a regular refrain of congressional applause and cheers). From time to time, political leaders launch "campaigns" to persuade the public toward some course of action (e.g., extending rights to protect previously marginalized groups, passing legislation to reform healthcare access, preparing the country for war). In studying how and why politicians try to elicit emotions in these persuasive campaigns, it is equally important to consider the limits on their capacity to generate the desired emotions (cf. Lupia & Menning, 2009).

Not all efforts at emotional control aim at arousing emotions; some seek to inhibit or quell emotions. Take, for example, certain courtroom rituals in the United States. Officers of the court convey and expect a serious, civil demeanor. A bailiff or other officer instructs those present to rise and to be silent. A judge may insist on keeping "order in the court" in the face of emotional outbursts and limit the introduction of evidence when she deems its emotional impact to outweigh its probative value. Such rituals can serve other important purposes as well, but they are designed in part to inhibit the role of emotions in judicial proceedings.[12] Political psychologists need to study efforts to inhibit or lessen emotional arousal, a topic they have to date largely ignored, for such efforts play a role in both ritual and extraordinary aspects of political life. Leaders, for example, often try to calm their citizens during crises or when they worry that fear will turn into panic or anger into violence—speaking to the country in the wake of military attacks, civil unrest, terrorism, natural or civil disaster, political shootings, or economic collapse ("The only thing we have to fear is fear itself"). One challenge faced by governments in the United States and elsewhere following terrorist attacks has been how to balance the need to encourage the public to stay alert for threats while also reassuring them that they are safe. Autocratic leaders try to manage emotions at least as much as their democratic counterparts. Just as leaders in China, Iran, or elsewhere may foment public anger at foreign powers, for example, they may also try to restrain such emotions in service of their domestic and foreign policy goals (e.g., Stockman, 2013). How effective are such attempts to keep public emotions "under control" or to assuage fear, anger, or other already-aroused emotions? Does the level of difficulty and the effectiveness of particular approaches vary across emotions?

Finally, a fourth frontier ripe for further study is the *resonance of emotional appeals with past experience and present context*. Most research on the impact of emotionally evocative messages focuses tightly on differences across appeals and individuals, with little consideration of how the emotional appeal resonates with the audience. In some cases, success in eliciting emotions may depend on how appropriately the appeal fits with "tenor of the times" or the current "public mood." Is it possible to stoke economic anxieties in a time of prosperity, or generate partisan enthusiasm after a string of political losses? In other cases, a topic—crime, perhaps—may be perpetually more susceptible to fear appeals. The impact may also depend on resonance with an individual's prior experiences. Is it easier to arouse anger (moral outrage) among those who have experienced injustice themselves or witnessed it firsthand? Researchers should also be mindful of the temporal dimension: how long does emotional resonance last, how quickly does it decay?

These suggestions—personality, group dynamics, external control, resonance—are hardly exhaustive of promising directions for future work. Replication and extension of existing lines of research on antecedents and effects of emotions will also be important; so too are the issues of theoretical development and methodological refinement mentioned earlier. In a relatively short time, research on emotions has gone from a topic that received little explicit consideration in studies of politics to a central theme in political psychology. We have tried to highlight in this chapter how much we have learned from this explosion of interest already, as well as to suggest several next steps for the advancement of the field. We suspect that the relevant chapter in the third edition of the *Political Psychology* handbook, 10 or more years from now, will provide even greater cause for celebration at the progress in our understanding of the political psychology of emotions.

NOTES

1. The longevity of that conception is remarkable. As we write this chapter, the investment company Raymond James has as its principal advertising theme: "When investing, we remove the vagaries of emotion. Because they are vagaries." Their advertising text continues: "Just to make one thing perfectly clear, we are not some unfeeling financial automatons. Emotions are a wonderful thing. It's just that emotions can trump logic and play havoc with investing." The remainder of the ad text continues in that same vein: turbulent, irrational emotions that, while making us human, compete with cold implacable but efficacious reason.

2. For more on conceptions of emotion and its relationship to reason, see (Frazer, 2010; Krause, 2008).

3. As with "intelligence" and "attitudes," as research has continued, these homogenous concepts soon confronted disconfirming results. Rather than splitting these concepts into separate scientific categories, in the main, accommodation was achieved by adding subcategories to account for otherwise discrepant results. Hence we have now multiple forms of intelligence rather than one, and we now have "implicit" and "explicit" attitudes. In each instance the option of concluding that these concepts are flawed was rejected. Thus implicit and explicit attitudes continue to be categorized as attitudes even though they have quite different properties (e.g., the former most likely are located in procedural memory and are nonverbal; while the latter are located in semantic memory and are verbal in character).

4. Though here, as elsewhere, Roger Masters and his colleagues were examining this affect well before others turned to it (Masters & Sullivan, 1989a; 1989b; 1993; McHugo, Lanzetta, Sullivan, Masters, & Englis, 1985; Sullivan & Masters, 1988a; 1988b), as were Conover and Feldman (1986).

5. That it takes, using Libet's estimate, 500 milliseconds for conscious representations to arise and that affective appraisals arise in less than 100 milliseconds both before and "outside" of consciousness is now widely accepted and often demonstrated, as for example in Todorov's work (Todorov & Ballew, 2007; Willis & Todorov, 2006).

6. We will not be surprised to find that these three dimensions are insufficient. Work, largely done with animals, argues for a distinction between fear and anxiety largely having to do with the role of memory in enabling conditioning for one, fear, but not for the other, anxiety (Davis & Shi, 1999; Davis, 1992a; 1992b; Davis, Walker, Miles, & Grillon, 2010).

7. For example, empathy has long been of interest, and it has been proposed as a vital and distinct facet of affect shaping particular "we" versus "they" interactions (Brothers, 1989; Chlopan, McCain, Carbonell, & Hagen, 1985; Morrell, 2010).

8. In his cognitive appraisal account, Lazarus (1994) in fact differentiates them into at least three categories: joy/enthusiasm, pride, and hope. But this is consistent with our argument in that Lazarus's distinctions are based on the relational (self-environment) meaning of the emotions, not on evidence of their empirical consequences.

9. Although, in many cases, it may seem obvious what makes people feel happy or enthusiastic, it is not always so. For example, Hutchings, Valentino, Philpot, and White (2006) experimentally manipulated news stories to emphasize either similarity or difference in the racial policy stances of George W. Bush and Al Gore in the 2000 election. Blacks responded with significantly higher enthusiasm for Gore in the "difference condition," even though what differed was not a more positive take on Gore's position,

but instead the implication that Bush was more hostile to black interests (than in the similarity article).

10. There are those who dissent on the persuasiveness of these studies (Ladd & Lenz, 2008; 2011), though see (Brader, 2011; Marcus, MacKuen, & Neuman, 2011).

11. It remains unclear from the extant studies which set of responses—grid or sequential— yields more valid measures.

12. At the same time, of course, some aspects of court proceedings are clearly intended to arouse emotions. For example, in criminal trials, prosecutors may use horrific photos of the crime scene to elicit disgust and harsher judgments, or some jurisdictions may allow emotional testimony from family and friends at sentencing hearings.

REFERENCES

Adolphs, R. (2009). The social brain: Neural basis of social knowledge. *Annual Review of Psychology, 60,* 693–716.

Adolphs, R., & Spezio, M. (2006). Role of the amygdala in processing visual social stimuli. *Progress in Brain Research, 156* (Chapter 20), 363–378.

Adolphs, R., Tranel, D., & Damasio, A. R. (1998). The human amygdala in social judgment. *Nature, 393,* 470–474.

Adolphs, R., Tranel, D., Damasio, H., & Damasio, A. R. (1995). Fear and the human amygdala. *Journal of Neuroscience, 15*(9), 5879–5891.

Aristotle. (1954). *Rhetoric* (W. R. Roberts, trans.). New York: Modern Library.

Aristotle. (1983). *The politics* (rev. ed., T. A. Sinclair, trans.). New York: Penguin.

Averill, J. R. (1983). Studies on anger and aggression: Implications for theories of emotion. *American Psychologist, 38*(11), 1145.

Banks, A. J., & Valentino, N. (2012). Emotional substrates of white racial attitudes. *American Journal of Political Science, 56*(2), 286–297.

Barbalet, J. M. (2001). *Emotion, social theory, and social structure: A macrosociological approach.* New York: Cambridge University Press.

Bechara, A., Damasio, H., Tranel, D., & Damasio, A. R. (1997). Deciding advantageously before knowing the advantageous strategy. *Science, 175* (February 28), 1293–1295.

Berkowitz, L. (1988). Towards a general theory of anger and emotional aggression: Implications of the cognitive-neoassociationalistic perspective for the analysis of anger and other emotions. In R. S. Wyer Jr. & T. K. Srull (eds.), *Advances in social cognition.* Hillsdale, NJ: Erlbaum.

Berkowitz, L., & Harmon-Jones, E. (2004). Toward an understanding of the determinants of anger. *Emotion, 4*(2), 107.

Bizer, G. Y., Krosnick, J. A., Holbrook, A. L., Wheeler, S. C., Rucker, D. D., & Petty, R. E. (2004). The impact of personality on cognitive, behavioral, and affective political processes: The effects of need to evaluate. *Journal of Personality, 20*(5), 995–1028.

Bonanno, G. A., Goorin, L., & Coifman, K. G. (2008). Sadness and grief. In M. Lewis, J. M. Haviland-Jones, & L. F. Barrett (eds.), *Handbook of Emotion* (3rd ed., pp. 797–810). New York: Guilford Press.

Brader, T. (2005). Striking a responsive chord: How political ads motivate and persuade voters by appealing to emotions. *American Journal of Political Science, 49*(2), 388–405.

Brader, T. (2006). *Campaigning for hearts and minds: How emotional appeals in political ads work.* Chicago: University of Chicago Press.

Brader, T. (2011). The political relevance of emotions: "Reassessing" revisited. *Political Psychology*, 32(2), 337–346.

Brader, T., & Corrigan, B. (2005). Emotional cues and campaign dynamics in political advertising. Proceedings from Annual Meeting of the American Political Science Association, Washington DC.

Brader, T., Groenendyk, E. W., & Valentino, N. (2010). Fight or flight? When political threats arouse public anger and fear. Proceedings from Annual Meeting of the Midwest Political Science Association, Chicago.

Brader, T., Marcus, G. E., & Miller, K. L. (2011). Emotion and public opinion. In R. Y. Shapiro & L. R. Jacobs (eds.), *Oxford Handbook of American Public Opinion and the Media* (pp. 384–401). Oxford: Oxford University Press.

Brader, T., Valentino, N., & Karl, K. L. (2012). The measurement of political emotion: How I feel depends on how you ask. Proceedings from Annual Meeting of the American Political Science Association, New Orleans.

Brader, T., Valentino, N. A., & Suhay, E. (2008). What triggers public opposition to immigration? Anxiety, group cues, and immigration threat. *American Journal of Political Science*, 52(4), 959–978.

Brothers, L. (1989). A biological perspective on empathy. *American Journal of Psychiatry*, 146(1), 10–19.

Bucy, E. P., & Bradley, S. D. (2004). Presidential expressions and viewer emotion: Counterempathic responses to televised leader displays. *Social Science Information*, 43(1), 59–94.

Bucy, E. P., & Grabe, M. E. (2008). "Happy warriors" revisited: Hedonic and agonic display repertoires of presidential candidates on the evening news. *Politics and the Life Science*, 27(1), 78–98.

Bucy, E. P., & Newhagen, J. E. (1999). The emotional appropriateness heuristic: Processing televised presidential reactions to the news. *Journal of Communication*, 49(4), 59–79.

Cacioppo, J. T., Berntson, G. G., Norris, C. J., & Gollan, J. K. (2011). The evaluative space model. In P. A. M. Van Lange, A. W. Kruglanski, & E. T. Higgins (eds.), *Handbook of Theories of Social Psychology* (pp. 42–64). Thousand Oaks, CA: Sage.

Cacioppo, J. T., & Decety, J. (2009). What are the brain mechanisms on which psychological processes are based? *Perspectives on Psychological Science*, 4(1), 10–18.

Carver, C. S. (2004). Negative affects deriving from the behavioral approach system. *Emotion*, 4(1), 3–22.

Chlopan, B. E., McCain, M. L., Carbonell, J. L., & Hagen, R. L. (1985). Empathy: A review of available measures. *Journal of Personality and Social Psychology*, 48, 635–653.

Clore, G. L., & Ortony, A. (2008). Appraisal theories: How cognition shapes affect into emotion. In M. Lewis, J. Haviland-Jones, & L. F. Barrett (eds.), *Handbook of emotion* (3rd ed., pp. 628–642). New York: Guilford Press.

Clore, G. L., Ortony, A., Dienes, B., & Fujita, F. (1993). Where does anger dwell? In R. S. Wyer & T. S. Srull (eds.), *Perspectives on anger and emotion* (pp. 57–87). Hillsdale, NJ: Lawrence Erlbaum.

Conover, P., & Feldman, S. (1986). Emotional reactions to the economy: I'm mad as hell and I'm not going to take it any more. *American Journal of Political Science*, 30, 30–78.

Corrigan, B., & Brader, T. (2011). Campaign advertising: Reassessing the impact of campaign ads on political behavior. In S. K. Medvic (ed.), *New directions in campaigns and elections* (pp. 79–97). New York: Routledge.

Cottam, M. L. (2004). *Introduction to political psychology.* Mahwah, NJ: Lawrence Erlbaum.

Cottrell, C. A., & Neuberg, S. L. (2005). Different emotional reactions to different groups: A sociofunctional threat-based approach to "prejudice." *Journal of Personality and Social Psychology, 88*(5), 770–789.

Cottrell, C. A., Richards, D. A. R., & Nichols, A. L. (2010). Predicting policy attitudes from general prejudice versus specific intergroup emotions. *Journal of Experimental and Social Psychology, 46*(2), 247–254.

Damasio, A. R. (1994). *Descartes' error: Emotion, reason and the human brain.* New York: G. P. Putnam's Sons.

Darwin, C. (1998). *The expression of the emotions in man and animals* (3rd ed.). New York: Oxford University Press.

Dasgupta, N., DeSteno, D., Williams, L. A., & Hunsinger, M. (2009). Fanning the flames of prejudice: The influence of specific incidental emotions on implicit prejudice. *Emotion, 9*(4), 585–591.

Davis, M. H. (1992a). The role of the amygdala in conditioned fear. In J. P. Aggleton (ed.), *The amygdala: Neurobiological aspects of emotion, memory, and mental dysfunction* (pp. 255–305). New York: Wiley-Liss.

Davis, M. H. (1992b). The role of the amygdala in fear and anxiety. In *Annual Review of Neuroscience* (Vol. 821, pp. 353–375).

Davis, M. H. (1994). *Empathy: A social psychological approach.* Madison, WI: Brown & Benchmark.

Davis, M. H., & Shi, C. (1999). The extended amygdala: Are the central nucleus of the amygdala and the bed nucleus of the stria terminalis differentially involved in fear versus anxiety? *Annals of the New York Academy of Sciences, 877,* 281–291.

Davis, M. H., Walker, D. L., Miles, L., & Grillon, C. (2010). Phasic vs sustained fear in rats and humans: Role of the extended amygdala in fear vs anxiety. *Neuropsychopharmacology, 35*(1), 105–135.

Descartes, R. (1989). *The passions of the soul* (S. H. Voss, trans.). Indianapolis, IN: Hackett.

Druckman, J. N., & McDermott, R. (2008). Emotion and the framing of risky choice. *Political Behavior, 30*(3), 297–321.

Dumont, M., Yzerbyt, V., Wigboldus, D., & Gordijn, E. H. (2003). Social categorization and fear reactions to the September 11th terrorist attacks. *Personality and Social Psychology Bulletin, 29*(12), 1509–1520.

Eagley, A. H., & Chaiken, S. (1993). *The psychology of attitudes.* Forth Worth, TX: Harcourt Brace Jovanovich.

Ekman, P., & Rosenberg, E. L. (2005). *What the face reveals: Basic and applied studies of spontaneous expression using the facial action coding system (FACS)* (2nd ed.). New York: Oxford University Press.

Eskine, K. J., Kacinik, N. A., & Prinz, J. J. (2011). A bad taste in the mouth: Gustatory disgust influences moral judgment. *Psychological Science, 22*(3), 295–299.

Evans, J. S. B. T. (2008). Dual-processing accounts of reasoning, judgment, and social cognition. *Annual Review of Psychology, 59,* 255–278.

Feldman, S., & Huddy, L. (N.d.). The paradoxical effects of anxiety on political learning. Manuscript.

Finifter, A. (1974). The friendship group as a protective environment for political deviants. *American Political Science Review, 68*(2), 607–625.

Fischhoff, B., Gonzalez, R. M., Lerner, J. S., & Small, D. A. (2005). Evolving judgments of terror risks: Foresight, hindsight, and emotion. *Journal of Experimental Psychology: Applied, 11,* 124–139.

Fishbein, M., & Ajzen, I. (1975). *Belief, attitude, intention and behavior: An introduction to theory and research.* Reading. MA: Addison-Wesley.

Frazer, M. (2010). *The enlightenment of sympathy.* New York: Cambridge University Press.

Fredrickson, B. L. (2003). The value of positive emotions. *American Scientist, 91,* 330–335.

Frijda, N. H. (1986). *The emotions.* Cambridge: Cambridge University Press.

Frijda, N. H., Kuipers, P., & Schure, E. T. (1989). Relations among emotion, appraisal, and emotional action readiness. *Journal of Personality and Social Psychology, 57*(2), 212–228.

Gadarian, S. K. (2010). The politics of threat: How terrorism news shapes foreign policy attitudes. *Journal of Politics, 72*(2), 469–483.

Gerber, A. S., Green, D. P., & Larimer, H. W. (2010). An experiment testing the relative effectiveness of encouraging voter participation by inducing feelings of pride or shame. *Political Behavior, 32*(3), 409–422.

Geva, N., & Skorick, J. M. (2006). The emotional calculus of foreign policy decisions: Getting emotions out of the closet. In D. Redlawsk (ed.), *Feeling politics: Emotion in political information processing* (pp. 209–226). New York: Palgrave Macmillan.

Glaser, J., & Salovey, P. (1998). Affect in electoral politics. *Personality and Social Psychology Review, 2*(3), 156–172.

Goodwin, J., Jasper, J. M., & Polletta, F. (2001). *Passionate politics: Emotions and social movements.* Chicago: University of Chicago Press.

Gould, D. B. (2009). *Moving politics: Emotion and ACT UP's fight against AIDS.* Chicago: University of Chicago Press.

Gray, J. A. (1987). *The psychology of fear and stress* (2nd ed.). Cambridge: Cambridge University Press.

Gray, J. A. (1990). Brain systems that mediate both emotion and cognition. *Cognition and Emotion, 4*(3), 269–288.

Gray, J. A., & McNaughton, N. (2000). *The neuropsychology of anxiety: An enquiry into the functions of the septo-hippocampal system* (2nd ed.). New York: Oxford University Press.

Greene, S., & Elder, L. (2001). Gender and the psychology of partisanship. *Women and Politics, 22,* 63–84.

Greenstein, F. I., & Lerner, M. (1971). *A source book for the study of personality and politics.* Chicago: Markham.

Haidt, J. (2001). The emotional dog and its rational tail: A social intuitionist approach to moral judgment. *Psychological Review, 108*(4), 814–834.

Haidt, J. (2008). Mortality. *Perspectives on Psychological Science, 3*(1), 65–72.

Haidt, J., & Joseph, C. M. (2007). The moral mind: How five sets of innate intuitions guide the development of many culture-specific virtues, and perhaps even modules. In P. Carruthers, S. Laurence, & S. Stich (eds.), *The innate mind* (pp. 367–392). Oxford: Oxford University Press.

Haidt, J., McCauley, C., & Rozin, P. (1994). Individual differences in sensitivity to disgust: A scale sampling seven domains of disgust elicitors. *Personality and Individual Differences, 16*(5), 701–713.

Helzer, E. G., & Pizarro, D. A. (2011). Dirty liberals! Reminders of physical cleanliness influence moral and political attitudes. *Psychological Science, 22*(4), 517–522.

Hermann, M. G. (1986). *Political psychology.* San Francisco: Jossey-Bass.

Hickerson, A., & Gastil, J. (2008). Assessing the difference critique of deliberation: Gender, emotion, and the jury experience. *Communication Theory, 18*(2), 281–303.

Holak, S. L., & Havlena, William J. (1998). Feelings, fantasies, and memories: An examination of the emotional components of nostalgia. *Journal of Business Research, 42*(3), 217–226.

Houghton, D. P. (2009). *Political psychology: Situations, individuals, and cases.* New York: Routledge.

Huddy, L., Feldman, S., & Cassese, E. (2007). On the distinct political effects of anxiety and anger. In W. R. Neuman, G. E. Marcus, M. Mackuen, & A. N. Crigler (eds.), *The affect effect: Dynamics of emotion in political thinking and behavior* (pp. 202–230). Chicago: University of Chicago Press.

Huddy, L., Feldman, S., Taber, C., & Lahav, G. (2005). Threat, anxiety, and support of antiterrorism policies. *American Journal of Political Science*, 49(3), 610–625.

Huddy, L., & Gunnthorsdottir, A. H. (2000). The persuasive effects of emotive visual imagery: Superficial manipulation or the product of passionate reason? *Political Psychology*, 21(4), 745–778.

Hume, D. (1975). *Enquiries concerning human understanding and concerning the principles of morals* (3rd ed.). Oxford: Clarendon Press.

Hume, D. (1984). *A treatise of human nature.* London: Penguin.

Hutcherson, C., & Gross, J. J. (2011). The moral emotions: A social-functionalist account of anger, disgust, and contempt. *Journal of Personality and Social Psychology*, 100(4), 719–737.

Hutchings, V. L., Valentino, N., Philpot, T., & White, I. K. (2006). Racial cues in campaign news: The effects of candidate strategies on group activation and political attentiveness among African Americans. In D. Redlawsk (ed.), *Feeling politics* (pp. 165–186). New York: Palgrave Macmillan.

Inbar, Y., & Gilovich, T. (2011). Angry (or disgusted), but adjusting? The effect of specific emotions on adjustment from self-generated anchors. *Social Psychology and Personality Science*, 2(6), 563–569.

Inbar, Y., Pizarro, D. A., & Bloom, P. (2008). Conservatives are more easily disgusted than liberals. *Cognition and Emotion*, 23(4), 714–725.

Inbar, Y., Pizarro, D. A., Iyer, R., & Haidt, J. (2012). Disgust sensitivity, political conservatism, and voting. *Social Psychology and Personality Science*, 3(5), 537–544.

Inbar, Y., Pizarro, D. A., Knobe, J., & Bloom, P. (2009). Disgust sensitivity predicts intuitive disapproval of gays. *Emotion*, 9(3), 453–439.

Isbell, L. M., & Ottati, V. C. (2002). The emotional voter. In V. C. Ottati, R. S. Tindale, J. Edwards, F. B. Bryant, L. Heath, L., Y. Suarez-Balcazar, & E. J. Posavac (eds.)., *The social psychology of politics* (pp. 55–74). New York: Kluwer Academic/Plenum.

Iyer, A., & Leach, C. W. (2008). Emotion in inter-group relations. *European Review of Social Psychology*, 19(1), 86–125.

Izard, C. E. (1991). *The psychology of emotions.* New York: Plenum.

Jasper, J. M. (1998). The emotions of protest: Affective and reactive emotions in and around social movements. *Sociological Forum*, 13(3), 397–424.

Jasper, J. M. (2011). Emotions and social movements: Twenty years of theory and research. *Annual Review of Sociology*, 37, 285–303.

Jost, J. T., Glaser, J., Kruglanski, A. W., & Sulloway, F. J. (2003). Political conservatism as motivated social cognition. *Psychological Bulletin*, 129(3), 339–375.

Just, M. R., Crigler, A. N., & Belt, T. L. (2007). Don't give up hope: Emotions, candidate appraisals, and votes. In W. R. Neuman, G. E. Marcus, A. N. Crigler, & M. B. MacKuen (eds.), *The affect effect: Dynamics of emotion in political thinking and behavior* (pp. 231–259). Chicago: University of Chicago Press.

Keltner, D., & Lerner, J. S. (2010). Emotion. In S. Fiske, D. Gilbert, & G. Lindzey (eds.), *Handbook of social psychology* (pp. 317–352). New York: Wiley.

Krause, S. R. (2008). *Civil passions: Moral sentiment and democratic deliberation.* Princeton, NJ: Princeton University Press.

Krosnick, J. A., & McGraw, K. M. (2002). Psychological political science versus political psychology true to its name: A plea for balance. In K. R. Monroe (ed.), *Political psychology* (pp. 79–94). Hillsdale, NJ: Lawrence Erlbaum.

Kunst-Wilson, W. R., & Zajonc, R. B. (1980). Affect discrimination of stimuli cannot be recognized. *Science, 207,* 557–558.

Ladd, J. M., & Lenz, G. S. (2008). Reassessing the role of anxiety in vote choice. *Political Psychology, 29*(2), 275–296.

Ladd, J. M., & Lenz, G. S. (2011). Does anxiety improve voters' decision making? *Political Psychology, 32*(2), 347–361.

Lambert, A. J., Scherer, L. D., Schott, J. P., Olson, K. R., Andrews, R. K., O'Brien, T. C., et al. (2010). Rally effects, threat, and attitude change: An integrative approach to understanding the role of emotion. *Journal of Personality and Social Psychology, 98*(6), 886–903.

Landau, M. J., Solomon, S., Greenberg, J., Cohen, F., Pyszczynski, T., Arndt, J., et al. (2004). Deliver us from evil: The effects of mortality salience and reminders of 9/11 on support for President George W. Bush. *Personality and Social Psychology Bulletin, 30*(9), 1136–1150.

Larsen, J. T., Bernston, G. G., Poehlmann, K. M., Ito, T. A., & Cacioppo, J. T. (2008). The psychophysiology of emotion. In M. Lewis, J. M. Haviland-Jones, & L. F. Barrett (eds.), *Handbook of Emotions* (3rd ed., pp. 180–195). New York: Guilford Press.

Larsen, J. T., & McGraw, A. P. (2011). Further evidence for mixed emotions. *Journal of Personality and Social Psychology, 100*(6), 1095–1110.

Larsen, R. J., & Fredrickson, B. L. (1999). Measurement issues in emotion research. In D. Kahneman, E. Diener, & N. Schwarz (eds.), *Well-being: The foundations of hedonic Psychology* (pp. 40–60). New York: Russell Sage.

Lazarus, R. S. (1982). Thoughts on the relations of emotion and cognition. *American Psychologist, 37,* 1019–1024.

Lazarus, R. S. (1984). On the primacy of cognition. *American Psychologist, 39,* 124–129.

Lazarus, R. S. (1991). *Emotion and adaptation.* New York: Oxford University Press.

Lazarus, R. S., & Lazarus, B. N. (1994). *Passion and reason: Making sense of our emotions.* New York: Oxford University Press.

Leach, C. W., Iyer, A., & Pederson, A. (2006). Anger and guilt about ingroup advantage explain the willingness for political action. *Personality and Social Psychology Bulletin, 32*(9), 1232–1245.

LeDoux, J. E. (1993). Emotional memory systems in the brain. *Behavioural Brain Research, 58,* 68–79.

LeDoux, J. E. (1995). Emotion: Clues from the brain. *Annual Review of Psychology, 46,* 209–235.

LeDoux, J. E. (1996). *The emotional brain: The mysterious underpinnings of emotional life.* New York: Simon & Schuster.

LeDoux, J. E. (2000). Emotion circuits in the brain. In W. M. Cowan, E. M. Shooter, C. F. Stevens, & R. F. Thompson (eds.), *Annual Reviews Neuroscience* (vol. 23, pp. 155–184). Palo Alto, CA: Annual Reviews.

Lerner, J. S., Gonzalez, R. M., Small, D. A., & Fischhoff, B. (2003). Effects of fear and anger on perceived risks of terrorism: A national field experiment. *Psychological Science, 14*(2), 144–150.

Lerner, J. S., & Keltner, D. (2000). Beyond valence: Toward a model of emotion-specific influences on judgement and choice. *Cognition and Emotion, 14*(4), 473–493.

Lerner, J. S., & Keltner, D. (2001). Fear, anger, and risk. *Journal of Personality and Social Psychology*, *81*(1), 146–159.

Lewis, M., Haviland-Jones, J. M., & Barrett, L. F. (2008). *Handbook of emotions* (3rd ed.). New York: Guilford Press.

Libet, B. (2004). *Mind time: The temporal factor in consciousness*. Cambridge, MA: Harvard University Press.

Libet, B., Gleason, C. A., Wright, E. W., & Pearl, D. K. (1983). Time of conscious intention to act in relation to onset of cerebral activity (readiness-potential). *Brain*, *106*, 623–642.

Libet, B., Wright, E. W. Jr., Feinstein, B., & Pearl, D. K. (1979). Subjective referral of the timing for a conscious sensory experience. *Brain*, *102*, 1597–1600.

Lodge, M. G., & Taber, C. S. (2005). The automaticity of affect for political leaders, groups, and issues. *Political Psychology*, *36*(3), 455–482.

Lodge, M. G., & Taber, C. S. (2013). *The rationalizing voter*. New York: Cambridge University Press.

Lupia, A., & Menning, J. O. (2009). When can politicians scare citizens into supporting bad policies? *American Journal of Political Science*, *53*(1), 90–106.

Mackie, D. M., Devos, T., & Smith, E. R. (2000). Intergroup emotions: Explaining offensive action tendencies in an intergroup context. *Journal of Personality and Social Psychology*, *79*(4), 602–616.

Mackie, D. M., & Smith, E. R. (2004). *From prejudice to intergroup emotions: Differentiated reactions to social groups*. New York: Psychology Press.

MacKuen, M. B., Marcus, G. E., Neuman, W. R., & Keele, L. (2007). The third way: The theory of affective intelligence and American democracy. In A. Crigler, G. E. Marcus, M. MacKuen, & W. R. Neuman (eds.), *The affect effect: The dynamics of emotion in political thinking and behavior* (pp. 124–151). Chicago: University of Chicago Press.

MacKuen, M. B., Wolak, J., Keele, L., & Marcus, G. E. (2010). Civic engagements: Resolute partisanship or reflective deliberation. *American Journal of Political Science*, *54*(2), 440–458.

Marcus, G. E. (1988). The structure of emotional response: 1984 presidential candidates. *American Political Science Review*, *82*(3), 735–761.

Marcus, G. E. (2002). *The sentimental citizen: Emotion in democratic politics*. University Park: Pennsylvania State University Press.

Marcus, G. E. (2003). The psychology of emotion and politics. In D. O. Sears, L. Huddy, & R. Jervis (eds.), *Oxford handbook of political psychology* (pp. 182–221). Oxford: Oxford University Press.

Marcus, G. E. (2012). *Political psychology: Neuroscience, genetics and politics*. New York: Oxford University Press.

Marcus, G. E. (2013). Reason, passion, and democratic politics: Old conceptions—new understandings—new possibilities. In J. E. Fleming (ed.), *Nomos LIII: Passions and emotions*. New York: New York University Press.

Marcus, G. E., & MacKuen, M. (1993). Anxiety, enthusiasm and the vote: The emotional underpinnings of learning and involvement during presidential campaigns. *American Political Science Review*, *87*(3), 688–701.

Marcus, G. E., MacKuen, M. B., & Neuman, W. R. (2011). Parsimony and complexity: Developing and testing theories of affective intelligence. *Political Psychology*, *32*(2), 323–336.

Marcus, G. E., MacKuen, M. B., Wolak, J., & Keele, L. (2006). The measure and mismeasure of emotion. In D. Redlawsk (ed.), *Feeling politics: Emotion in political information processing* (pp. 31–45). New York: Palgrave Macmillan.

Marcus, G. E., Neuman, W. R., & MacKuen, M. B. (2000). *Affective intelligence and political judgment*. Chicago: University of Chicago Press.

Marcus, G. E., Neuman, W. R., & MacKuen, M. B. (2009). Measuring subjective emotional response: New evidence on an alternative method. Proceedings from Annual Scientific Meeting of the International Society of Political Psychology, Dublin.

Marcus, G. E., Sullivan, J. L., Theiss-Morse, E., & Stevens, D. (2005). The emotional foundation of political cognition: The impact of extrinsic anxiety on the formation of political tolerance judgments. *Political Psychology, 26*(6), 949–963.

Marcus, G. E., Sullivan, J. L., Theiss-Morse, E., & Wood, S. L. (1995). *With malice toward some: How people make civil liberties judgments*. New York: Cambridge University Press.

Masters, R. D., & Sullivan, D. (1993). Nonverbal behavior and leadership: Emotion and cognition in political attitudes. In S. Iyengar & W. McGuire (eds.), *Explorations in political psychology* (pp. 150–182). Durham, NC: Duke University Press.

Masters, R. D., & Sullivan, D. G. (1989a). Facial displays and political leadership in France. *Behavioral Processes, 19*(1), 1–30.

Masters, R. D., & Sullivan, D. G. (1989b). Nonverbal displays and political leadership in France and the United States. *Political Behavior, 11*(2), 123–156.

McCrae, R. R., & Costa, P. T. (2003). *Personality in adulthood: A five-factor theory perspective* (2nd ed.). New York: Guilford Press.

McHugo, G. J., Lanzetta, J. T., Sullivan, D. G., Masters, R. D., & Englis, B. (1985). Emotional reactions to expressive displays of a political leader. *Journal of Personality and Social Psychology, 49*, 1512–1529.

Mendelberg, T. (2005). Bringing the group back into political psychology: Erik H. Erikson Early Career Award Address. *Political Psychology, 26*(4), 637–650.

Merolla, J. L., & Zechmeister, E. J. (2009). *Democracy at risk: How terrorist threats affect the public*. Chicago: University of Chicago Press.

Morrell, M. E. (2010). *Empathy and democracy: Feeling, thinking, and deliberation*. University Park: Pennsylvania State University Press.

Nelissen, R. M. A., & Zeelenberg, M. (2009). Moral emotions as determinants of third-party punishment: Anger, guilt, and the functions of altruistic sanctions. *Judgment and Decision Making, 4*(7), 543–553.

Nussbaum, M. C. (1986). *The fragility of goodness: Luck and ethics in Greek tragedy and philosophy*. New York: Cambridge University Press.

Öhman, A., Dimberg, U., & Esteves, F. (1989). Preattentive activation of aversive emotions. In T. Archer & L. G. Nilsson (eds.), *Aversion, avoidance, and anxiety: Perspectives on aversively motivated behavior* (pp. 169–193). Hillsdale, NJ: Lawrence Erlbaum.

Öhman, A., & Mineka, S. (2001). Fears, phobias, and preparedness: Towards an evolved module of fear and fear learning. *Psychological Review, 108*(3), 483–522.

Öhman, A., & Soares, J. J. F. (1993). On the automatic nature of phobic fear: Conditioned electrodermal responses to masked fear-relevant stimuli. *Journal of Abnormal Psychology, 102*(1), 121–132.

Ortony, A., Clore, G. L., & Collins, A. (1989). *The cognitive structure of emotions*. New York: Cambridge University Press.

Pagano, S. J., & Huo, Y. J. (2007). The role of moral emotions in predicting support for political actions in post-war Iraq. *Political Psychology, 28*(2), 227–255.

Panagopoulos, C. (2010). Affect, social pressure, and prosocial motivation: Field experimental evidence of the mobilizing effects of pride, shame, and publicizing voter behavior. *Political Behavior, 32*(3), 369–386.

Panksepp, J. (1998). *Affective neuroscience: The foundations of human and animal emotions*. New York: Oxford University Press.

Parker, M. T., & Isbell, L. M. (2010). How I vote depends on how I feel: The differential impact of anger and fear on political information processing. *Psychological Science, 21*(4), 548–550.

Perkins, A. M., Inchley-Mort, S. L., Pickering, A. D., Corr, P. J., & Burgess, A. P. (2012). A facial expression for anxiety. *Journal of Personality and Social Psychology, 102*(5), 910–924.

Petersen, M. B. (2010). Distinct emotions, distinct domains: Anger, anxiety and perceptions of intentionality. *Journal of Politics, 72*(2), 357–365.

Pizarro, D. A., Inbar, Y., & Helion, C. (2011). On disgust and moral judgment. *Emotion Review, 3*(3), 267–268.

Plato. (1974). *The Republic* (2nd ed., D. Lee, trans.). New York: Penguin.

Plutchik, R. (1980). *Emotion: A psychoevolutionary synthesis.* New York: Harper & Row.

Redlawsk, D. P., Civettini, A. J., & Emmerson, K. M. (2010). The affective tipping point: Do motivated reasoners ever "get it"? *Political Psychology, 31*(4), 563–593.

Redlawsk, D. P., Civettini, A. J., & Lau, R. R. (2007). Affective intelligence and voting: Information processing and learning in a campaign. In W. R. Neuman, G. E. Marcus, A. Crigler, & M. MacKuen (eds.), *The affect effect: Dynamics of emotion in political thinking and behavior* (pp. 152–179). Chicago: University of Chicago Press.

Ridout, T. N., & Searles, K. (2011). It's my campaign and I'll cry if I want to: How and when campaigns use emotional appeals. *Political Psychology, 32*(3), 439–458.

Rolls, E. T. (1999). *The brain and emotion.* New York: Oxford University Press.

Rolls, E. T. (2005). *Emotion explained.* New York: Oxford University Press.

Roseman, I. J. (1984). Cognitive determinants of emotions: A structural theory. In P. Shaver (ed.), *Review of personality and social psychology* (vol. 5, pp. 11–36). Beverly Hills, CA: Sage.

Roseman, I. J. (1991). Appraisal determinants of discrete emotions. *Cognition and Emotion, 5*(3), 161–200.

Roseman, I. J., Abelson, R. P., & Ewing, M. F. (1986). Emotions and political cognition: Emotional appeals in political communication. In R. Lau & D. O. Sears (eds.), *Political cognition* (pp. 279–294). Hillsdale, NJ: Lawrence Erlbaum.

Roseman, I. J., Antoniou, A. A., & Jose, P. E. (1996). Appraisal determinants of emotions: Constructing a more accurate and comprehensive theory. *Cognition and Emotion, 10*, 241–277.

Rozin, P., Haidt, J., & McCauley, C. C. (2008). Disgust. In M. Lewis, J. M. Haviland-Jones, & L. F. Barrett (eds.), *Handbook of emotions* (3rd ed., pp. 757–776). New York: Guildford Press.

Rudolph, T. J., Gangl, A., & Stevens, D. (2000). The effects of efficacy and emotions in campaign involvement. *Journal of Politics, 62*(4), 1189–1197.

Scherer, K. R., Schorr, A., & Johnstone, T. (2001). *Appraisal processes in emotion: Theory, methods, research.* New York: Oxford University Press.

Schnall, S., Haidt, J., Clore, G. L., & Jordan, A. H. (2008). Disgust as embodied moral judgment. *Personality and Social Psychology Bulletin, 34*(8), 1096–1109.

Schwarz, N., & Clore, G. L. (2003). Mood as information: 20 years later. *Psychological Inquiry, 14*(3&4), 296–303.

Skitka, L. J., Bauman, C. W., Aramovich, N. P., & Morgan, G. S. (2006). Confrontational and preventative policy responses to terrorism: Anger wants a fight and fear wants "them" to go away. *Basic and Applied Social Psychology, 28*(4), 375–384.

Small, D. A., & Lerner, J. S. (2008). Emotional policy: Personal sadness and anger shape judgments about a welfare case. *Political Psychology, 29*(2), 149–168.

Small, D. A., Lerner, J. S., & Fischhoff, B. (2006). Emotion priming and attributions for terrorism: Americans' reactions in a national field experiment. *Political Psychology, 27*(2), 289–298.

Smith, A. (1959). *The theory of moral sentiments*. Indianapolis, IN: Liberty Fund.

Smith, C. A., & Ellsworth, P. C. (1985). Patterns of cognitive appraisal in emotion. *Journal of Personality and Social Psychology, 48*(4), 813–838.

Spielberger, C. D., & Sydeman, S. J. (1994). State-trait anxiety inventory and state-trait anger expression inventory. In M. E. Maurish (ed.), *The use of psychological testing for treatment planning and outcome assessment* (pp. 292–321). Hillsdale, NJ: Lawrence Erlbaum.

Steenbergen, M. R., & Ellis, C. (2006). Fear and loathing in American elections: Context, traits, and negative candidate affect. In D. Redlawsk (ed.), *Feeling politics: Emotion in political information processing* (pp. 109–134). New York: Palgrave Macmillan.

Stewart, P. A., Waller, B. M., & Schubert, J. N. (2009). Presidential speechmaking style: Emotional response to micro-expressions of facial affect. *Motivation and Emotion, 33*(2), 125–135.

Stockman, D. (2013). *Media commercialization and authoritarian rule in China*. New York: Cambridge University Press.

Stroud, L. R., Glaser, J., & Salovey, P. (2005). The effects of partisanship and candidate emotionality on voter preference. *Imagination, Cognition, and Personality, 25*(1), 25–44.

Suhay, E. (2008). Group influence and American ideals: How social identity and emotion shape our political values and attitudes. PhD dissertation, University of Michigan.

Sullivan, D. G., & Masters, R. D. (1988a). Emotions and trait attributions in the evaluation of political leaders: Experimental evidence. Paper presented at the Annual Meeting of the American Political Science Association.

Sullivan, D., & Masters, R. (1988b). Happy warriors: Leaders' facial displays, viewers emotions, and political support. *American Journal of Political Science, 32*(2), 345–368.

Tangney, J. P., Stuewig, J., & Mashek, D. J. (2007). Moral emotions and moral behavior. *Annual Review of Psychology, 58*, 345–372.

Tellegen, A., Watson, D., & Clark, L. A. (1999a). Further support for a hierarchical model of affect. *Psychological Science, 10*(4), 307–309.

Tellegen, A., Watson, D., & Clark, L. A. (1999b). On the dimensional and hierarchical structure of affect. *Psychological Science, 10*(4), 297–303.

Todorov, A., & Ballew II, C. C. (2007). Predicting political elections from rapid and unreflective face judgments. *PNAS, 104*(46), 17948–17953.

Tomkins, S. S. (2008). *Affect imagery consciousness: The complete edition*. New York: Springer.

Tooby, J., & Cosmides, L. (2008). The evolutionary psychology of the emotions and their relationship. In M. Lewis, J. M. Haviland-Jones, & L. F. Barrett (eds.), *Handbook of emotion* (3rd ed., pp. 114–137). New York: Guilford Press.

Tracy, J. L., Robins, R. W., & Tangney, J. P. (2007). *The self-conscious emotions: Theory and research*. New York: Guilford Press.

Tsal, Y. (1985). On the relationship between cognitive and affective processes: A critique of Zajonc and Markus. *Journal of Consumer Research, 12*, 358–362.

Valentino, N. A., Banks, A. J., Hutchings, V. L., & Davis, A. K. (2009). Selective exposure in the Internet age: The interaction between anxiety and information utility. *Political Psychology, 30*(4), 591–613.

Valentino, N. A., Brader, T., Groenendyk, E. W., Gregorowicz, K., & Hutchings, V. L. (2011). Election night's alright for fighting: The role of emotions in political participation. *Journal of Politics, 73*(1), 156–170.

Valentino, N. A., Hutchings, V. L., Banks, A. J., & Davis, A. K. (2008). Is a worried citizen a good citizen? Emotions, political information seeking, and learning via the Internet. *Political Psychology, 29*(2), 247–273.

Verba, S. (1961). *Small groups and political behavior: A study of leadership.* Princeton, NJ: Princeton University Press.

Warnecke, A. M., Masters, R. D., & Kempter, G. (1992). The roots of nationalism: Nonverbal behavior and xenophobia. *Ethology and Sociobiology, 13,* 267–282.

Watson, D., & Clark, L. A. (1991). Self- versus peer ratings of specific emotional traits: Evidence of convergent and discriminant validity. *Journal of Personality and Social Psychology, 60*(6), 927–940.

Way, B., & Masters, R. (1996a). Emotion and cognition in political-information processing. *Journal of Communications, 46*(3), 48–65.

Way, B. M., & Masters, R. D. (1996b). Political attitudes: Interactions of cognition and affect. *Motivation and Cognition, 20,* 205–236.

Weber, C., Searles, K., & Ridout, T. N. (2011). More than a feeling: The strategic use and consequence of emotion in campaign advertisements. Proceedings from the Annual Meeting of the Midwest Political Science Association, Chicago, IL.

Wheatley, T., & Haidt, J. (2005). Hypnotic disgust makes moral judgments more severe. *Psychological Science, 16,* 780–784.

Willis, J., & Todorov, A. (2006). First impressions: Making up your mind after a 100-Ms exposure to a face. *Psychological Science, 17*(7), 592–598.

Wolak, J., & Marcus, G. E. (2007). Personality and emotional response: Strategic and tactical responses to changing political circumstances. *Annals of the American Academy of Political and Social Sciences, 614*(1), 172–195.

Zajonc, R. B. (1980). Feeling and thinking: Preferences need no inferences. *American Psychologist, 35*(2), 151–175.

....

CHAPTER 7

TOWARD AN EVOLUTIONARILY INFORMED POLITICAL PSYCHOLOGY

....

JIM SIDANIUS AND ROBERT KURZBAN

He who would fully treat of man must know at least something of biology, of the science that treats of living, breathing things, and especially of that science of evolution which is inseparably connected with the great name of Darwin.

Theodore Roosevelt, 1910

ROOSEVELT's admonition notwithstanding, researchers working in the social sciences have historically kept themselves isolated from biology. This is changing, and biological ideas have been used productively in anthropology (Brown, 1991; Symons, 1979; Wrangham & Peterson, 1996), sociology (Dietz, Burns, & Buttel, 1990), psychology (Cosmides, Tooby, & Barkow, 1992), and economics (Bowles & Gintis, 1998; Hoffman, McCabe, & Smith, 1998; Hodgson, 2004). In this chapter we will argue that ideas drawn from evolutionary biology can similarly be used to deepen our insight into issues in political psychology and, indeed, that understanding evolution by natural selection is critical for an understanding of human behavior in general.

In the first section of this chapter, we review the basic principles of evolution by natural selection and discuss how these principles apply to understanding human psychology. The second section discusses a small number of applications of evolutionary approaches to important issues in political psychology. In particular, we look at the evolution of cooperation, ethnocentrism, sex differences in political behavior, the pervasiveness of intergroup bias and conflict, why discrimination is often directed more extremely toward males rather than females of subordinate groups, and the intersection between arbitrary-set and gender discrimination. Throughout, it will be our position that theory in the social sciences should be consistent with and informed by what is known in the biological sciences in a way that mirrors the multileveled conceptual integration in the natural sciences (Barkow, Cosmides, & Tooby, 1992).

Biological approaches to understanding human behavior are still looked upon with skepticism in many circles. In part, this skepticism arises because early attempts to integrate biological principles into the social sciences were often deeply flawed (see Kitcher, 1985) and sometimes used as a political tool to justify inhumane and oppressive social policy. A second reason for this widespread skepticism is that those outside the field hold incorrect beliefs about the assumptions and theoretical commitments undergirding evolutionary psychology (Kurzban & Haselton, 2006).

Because we cannot change the past to redress the first problem, an additional goal we pursue here is to mitigate the effects of the second. In particular, we emphasize that, contrary to popular misconceptions, *the evolutionary approach is not an endorsement of the "nature" side of the nature/nurture debate*; rather, it rejects this dichotomy as fundamentally ill-conceived. Evolutionary psychology changes the axis of debate to one in which what is at stake is the nature of the cognitive adaptations that characterize the human mind.

1. Basic Principles of Evolution by Natural and Sexual Selection

Understanding the evolutionary psychological approach requires a basic understanding of evolutionary theory and, more specifically, theories of the evolution of cooperation. Because many of these ideas are discussed at length elsewhere (Dawkins, 1976; Dugatkin, 1997; Sober & Wilson, 1998; Williams, 1966), we present only a brief sketch here.

We begin at the beginning. At some point in deep time, the first replicators emerged: entities that made copies of themselves. Some of these copies were not exact, and those new entities that made copies faster than others became more numerous. Over time, replicators (later, genes) that led to improved reproductive outcomes were retained. With some relatively unimportant exceptions, the genes in organisms today are those that were successfully passed down the generations because they produced design features that led to their own propagation (Darwin, 1859).

Genes influence their rate of replication through their effects on the organism's phenotype, its physical structure and behavior. Changes in genes that increase the rate of their own replication, mediated by the design changes they produce in the organism, spread in a population. For this reason, the eloquent biologist Richard Dawkins (1976) referred to genes as "selfish": the only thing that genes "care" about, that is, that influences whether or not they will persist, is the rate at which they replicate relative to other genes.

More specifically, genes that cause the phenotype to be altered in such a way that the organism is better able to solve a specific *adaptive problem*, a task that influences its rate of reproduction, such as finding food, attracting mates, avoiding predators, and so forth, are subject to selection. In short, *natural selection results in the gradual accumulation of design features that improve the functional fit between an organism and its environment.* Because no force other than natural selection is known by which complex functional organization can emerge from chance processes, *any complex functional features of organisms' phenotypes can be attributed to the process of natural selection* (Williams, 1966). These features are called *adaptations*.

Natural selection, unlike the individual organism, "sees" the results of strategies embodied by different genotypes and "chooses" the one that fares better than the others in terms of replication, or fitness. The evolutionary process is thus rational in the sense that it obeys the game-theoretical calculus, with strategies persisting solely on the basis of the number of offspring that they leave. The strategies that are selected, in contrast, will not necessarily appear rational at all (Cosmides & Tooby, 1994; Kurzban, 2003). Strategies, to persist, must simply be the optimal decision rule available among the existing possibilities. While the process of evolution is algorithmic, the adaptations, the cognitive information-processing circuits that this process builds, are necessarily heuristic, shaped by their performance in the environmental circumstances of the organism (Symons, 1992).

1.1. Sexual Selection and Parental Investment Theory

Darwin (1871) argued that an important factor determining the number of offspring an individual left was its ability to obtain matings. This idea explained why certain traits are unique to one sex: intrasexual competition for mates could drive adaptations in one sex but not the other. Similarly, preferences on the part of one sex for particular traits in the other could select for traits designed for being maximally attractive as a mate. Darwin referred to this process as "sexual selection."

This is a specific case of a more general rule about adaptations in species with two sexes. In many domains, the adaptive problems faced by members of both sexes are identical (e.g., finding food, avoiding predators), leading to selection for the same adaptations in both sexes. However, in cases in which adaptive problems differ, selection favors adaptations specific to each sex's adaptive problem. For example, in species in which one sex is differentially responsible for hunting, we might expect that individuals of that sex will be better adapted for this particular task.

An important further development of sexual selection theory was Trivers's (1972) theory of parental investment. Trivers began with the idea that species differ in the extent to which they invest in their offspring and expend resources nurturing them to sexual maturity. Further, in many species, the costs of nurturing young are not evenly divided between the sexes. In species in which one sex invests in offspring more than the other, the investing sex becomes a valuable resource for the less-investing sex. That is, organism A becomes valuable to organism B insofar as organism A expends time and energy contributing to the success of organism B's offspring. Further, the greater the asymmetry in investment between the sexes, the more intense competition for sexual access to the higher-investing sex is likely to be. Usually, in sexually reproducing species, the male (defined as the sex with the smaller gamete) invests less time and effort than the female, though this is not true for all species (see also Bateman, 1948).

A consequence of differential parental investment is that the sex that invests less will tend to have greater variance in reproductive success. If one sex invests minimally in offspring, this sex can, if able to obtain a large number of matings, produce a large number of offspring. In contrast, for the greater-investing sex, because resources are always limited, the maximum reproductive output will tend not to be constrained by matings, but rather by factors such as resource acquisition. Thus, the lesser-investing sex should be expected to have adaptations designed to obtain many matings, while the greater-investing sex should be expected to have adaptations designed to secure resources.

Sex differences in reproductive strategies have important behavioral consequences for sex differences in humans (Symons, 1979; see below). It is worth noting that unlike the case of gender, sex in biology, is a clear-cut, discrete variable. Many species have two morphs, a male and a female, and these morphs are reliably reproduced from generation to generation. Adaptations unique to each morph can evolve because of this consistency.

1.2. The Evolution of Altruism and Cooperation

This "selfish" view of the gene does not entail the idea that altruism and cooperation, issues central to many questions in political psychology, will never be observed. There are a number of ways, either by design or by accident, that organisms benefit one another. For example, a buzzard might fly toward a carcass for the straightforward reason that it is looking for a meal. The fact that other scavengers can follow the first one and so similarly feed themselves does not mean that the genes that produce the buzzard's behaviors persisted *because* they helped other organisms—this is merely a byproduct. However, some features of organisms are indeed designed to deliver benefits to others at a cost to themselves (where costs and benefits should always be understood to be denominated in the currency of reproductive fitness).

Kin selection. Hamilton (1964) pointed out that a gene could increase in frequency both by replicating itself and by replicating identical copies of itself. Further, he noted that identical copies of genes were differentially likely to be found in organisms related by descent. Hamilton's ideas suggested calculating a gene's fitness (rather than an individual's) by including relatives' reproduction in addition to the individual's own, and are therefore also known as "inclusive fitness theory." The crucial insight of the theory was that selection could favor genes that generated altruistic behavior toward relatives.

There are important restrictions on the operation of this process, including (1) the probability that an identical copy of the gene in question is found in the recipient of the altruistic act, and (2) the relationship between the size of the costs incurred and the benefits delivered. Consider a gene that coded for the delivery of miniscule benefits to a distantly related other at a large cost to the self. This gene would compare unfavorably to alternative designs that were more discriminating in altruistic practices (i.e., delivered large benefits to more closely related others at small cost to self), and would soon vanish from the gene pool.

More precisely, Hamilton quantified the restrictions on the evolution of kin altruism with his inequality, known as Hamilton's rule,

$$C < rB,$$

where C and B are the magnitudes of the costs incurred and benefits delivered and r is the coefficient of relatedness, the probability that an exact copy of the gene is present in the target of altruism by virtue of descent. Thus, as genealogical distance increases, the ratio of the benefit to the cost must correspondingly increase for selection to favor the altruistic gene.

It is important to bear in mind that this analysis only makes sense at the level of the gene. From the standpoint of one gene, it makes no difference which other genes reside in the target organism, or how many genes the target organism shares with the organism in which the altruistic gene is found. "Genetic similarity," therefore, in the sense of proportion of shared genome, is not a useful concept in understanding kin selection (Tooby & Cosmides, 1989).

1.2.1. Reciprocal Altruism

A second theory explaining the evolution of cooperation, reciprocal altruism theory, used the Prisoner's Dilemma (PD) as a model (Axelrod & Hamilton, 1981). In the PD, two organisms engage in an interaction such that each has two options, a cooperative one (C), and a noncooperative one (D, for "defect"). If both cooperate, both are better off than if both defect. However, the payoffs are structured such that regardless of what the other organism does, each organism is itself better off if it defects (see figure 7.1).

Trivers (1971) argued that this structure characterized many potential interactions among organisms of the same species and was a useful model for understanding how cooperation could emerge. In particular, he showed that if organisms interacted repeatedly, cooperative strategies could be selected for if organisms conditioned their moves

	C	D
C	5, 5	0, 8
D	8, 0	3, 3

FIGURE 7.1 Payoff structure for the Prisoner's Dilemma. Each player can choose to cooperate (C) or defect (D). Payoffs to the players are listed row, column.

on their partner's previous moves. Thus, if one organism had a strategy such that it cooperated if and only if its partner cooperated on previous moves, and the benefits to cooperation were sufficiently large, a strategy that conditionally cooperated could do better than one that always defected (see also Axelrod & Hamilton, 1981). On the other hand, the bulk of research over the last 30 years seems to indicate that the reciprocal altruism and related phenomena appear to exist in no more than a modest number of species (Hammerstein, 2003).

1.2.2 Multilevel (Group) Selection

In the 1950s and 1960s evolutionary biologists often explained apparent acts of altruism, such as a meerkat giving a warning signal at the approach of a predator, as done for the good of the group rather than for the benefit of the animal uttering the warning. In what became known as "group selection" theory, it was suggested that some members of a population would sacrifice their own reproductive success for the benefit of the group (Wynne-Edwards, 1962; Emerson, 1960). The difficulty with this view is that individuals in a group that carry mutations causing them to benefit themselves at the expense of the group out-reproduce more cooperative group members, leading ultimately to the replacement of cooperative types with selfish types (Maynard Smith, 1964; Williams, 1966).

However, the group selection model, once seemingly condemned to theoretical oblivion, has subsequently been revived and shown to be viable (Hamilton, 1975; Wilson, 1975; Sober and Wilson, 1998). The argument is as follows. Consider a "group" to be any set of individuals that have a fitness impact on one another. Assume that groups consist of two types of individuals, "altruistic" and "selfish" types. In all groups, altruists are at a disadvantage (being altruistic) and leave fewer descendents than selfish types. However, critically, groups that have more altruistic types leave more descendents, in aggregate, than groups with fewer altruistic types. Now, even though altruists are at a disadvantage within all groups, if the reproductive advantage that accrues to individuals in groups that consist of a larger fraction of altruistic types is sufficiently great, the frequency of altruistic types in the whole population (i.e., across both groups combined) can increase from one generation to the next (see Wilson and Sober, 1998, pp. 23–26, for a clear mathematical demonstration of this counterintuitive result). The extent to which having altruistic types in a group increases reproductive success for members of that particular group compared with the fitness advantage selfish types have over altruists within individual groups determines whether or not genes for altruistic trait will increase in frequency in the whole population.

This version of group selection, also called multilevel selection, should not be understood as an alternative to the genic view of evolution by natural selection. Rather, these models are simply another way to do the "bookkeeping," keeping track of genes' success by looking at their relative replication rates within and between groups (Reeve, 2000). No matter how the score is kept, the critical factor is the proportion of genes of one type relative to genes of the alternative type in the total population in successive generations. The effects that a gene has on its own replication rate determine whether or not it will spread in a population. Multilevel selection illustrates that considering genes' effects at different levels of analysis can clarify the level at which adaptations evolve. However, it is to be noted that recent work has shown that multilevel selection and kin selection to be essentially equivalent (see Lehmann, Keller, West, & Roze, 2007).

1.3. Evolutionary Psychology

Having outlined the major features of the theory of evolution by natural and sexual selection, we now discuss how these general ideas inform our understanding of human psychology. The evolutionary view helps to guide hypotheses about the mind in a number of ways. First, the focus on adaptive problems helps carve nature at its joints—it tells us the kinds of tasks our minds might be designed to perform. Second, it constrains the potential hypothesis space to explore: the only design features the mind is likely to have are those that would have served functions associated with the lifestyle of our hunter-gatherer ancestors (see below). Similarly, the models of cooperation discussed above generate game-theoretical constraints on the nature of cooperative psychology—we should be skeptical of models of psychology that appear to be un-evolvable. Finally, the evolutionary view makes clear that organisms are composed of numerous, functionally specialized integrated components. We should expect the same to be true of the human mind. This insight leads to a core component of the evolutionary approach: domain specificity.

1.3.1. Domain Specificity

Adaptive problems that organisms face, such as finding food, avoiding predation, attracting a mate, and so on, depend on their lifestyles. Further, these challenges cannot all be solved with the same structures, or mechanisms. This is why organisms have different parts, each one designed for a particular function. The variety of human organs reflects this principle: lungs are for the exchange of gasses, hearts are for pumping blood, and so forth.

Problems associated with information processing, the function of the brain, are no different. The brain, and the nervous system more generally, is designed to take in information from the world, process it, and generate adaptive behavior. However, because different adaptive problems require different kinds of information-processing systems to solve them, the brain consists of specialized machinery to solve these problems. This is obvious in the context of neural circuits associated with the senses, such as vision and hearing, but should be expected to be true of circuits designed to solve other kinds of problems—recognizing faces, selecting food, finding mates, maintaining friendships, and so forth (Tooby & Cosmides, 1992).

This conclusion represents a central conceptual element of the evolutionary psychological approach. The principle of domain specificity suggests that we should expect brains to consist of a large number of functionally specialized circuits designed by natural selection to solve the adaptive problems faced by our ancestors. This contrasts with other views prevalent in the social sciences that construe the brain as a very general learning machine (see Tooby & Cosmides, 1992; Plotkin, 1997 for a discussion).

1.3.2. *Learning and Culture*

A second critical element of the evolutionary approach is the rejection of the nature/nurture distinction. For any trait of any organism, it must be true that changes to its genes or its developmental environment could alter the trait—the construction of the phenotype is inherently an interaction. So, as Tooby and Cosmides (1992) put it, "*everything,* from the most delicate nuance of Richard Strauss's last performance of Beethoven's Fifth Symphony to the presence of calcium salts in his bones at birth, is totally and to exactly the same extent genetically and environmentally codetermined" (pp. 83–84, italics original).

Thus, *it is senseless to counter a claim that a given behavior is the product of an interaction between the environment and genes with the claim that the behavior is "cultural" or "learned."* [1] *Every* behavior "is" *both* "environmental" and "biological" in the sense that every behavior has both environmental and genetic causes—labeling behaviors as either carries no meaning. What is at stake is the nature of human developmental programs and the information acquisition mechanisms they build: the cognitive systems that construct knowledge from interaction with the environment. The reproductive outcomes produced by different developmental programs over evolutionary time led to the retention of the programs that regulated development, including learning in its many forms, in adaptive ways (Tooby & Cosmides, 1992).

1.3.3. *Minds Are Adapted to Ancestral Environments*

The specialized neural circuits that humans possess should be expected to be well designed to solve the adaptive problems faced by our hunter-gatherer ancestors (Tooby & Cosmides, 1990). Natural selection is a gradual process, requiring a large number of generations for the accumulation of complex design. Further, natural selection can only act relative to stable features of organisms' environment. That is, for evolution to result in a trait that guides adaptive behavior in response to particular environmental conditions, these conditions must be present with sufficient frequency over a sufficiently long period for the slow accretion of incrementally more adaptive design modifications.

For this reason, we should expect human minds to be well designed to solve the adaptive problems our ancestors faced during the course of human evolution. Because anthropological evidence suggests that our ancestors lived in small hunter-gatherer bands, human cognitive adaptations are likely to be designed to solve adaptive problems associated with this lifestyle. In contrast, because agriculture and high population densities are recent phenomena (evolutionarily speaking), we should not expect human cognitive adaptations to be designed specifically to solve the unique problems associated with these elements of modern life (Tooby & Cosmides, 1990). On the other hand, recent empirical work has shown that coevolutionary feedback between culture and genetics has contributed to accelerated kinetic changes in humans over the last 10,000 years (see Cochran, & Harpending, 2009).

1.3.4. Merits of Adaptationism

Adaptationism, the idea that organisms are designed by natural selection to solve adaptive problems faced during their evolutionary history, has been applied to every species that biologists study. Indeed, most biologists would not consider an analysis of any species possible without reference to evolutionary theory. This is simply because an organism's selective history has shaped and sculpted the species-typical design embodied by the organism.

Humans, as biological entities, are no different. All of their design features, including their cognitive mechanisms of learning, reasoning, emotion, planning, and so on, are products of the process of evolution by natural selection. A great deal is now known about the way that the process of natural selection operates, and about humans' ancestral past, allowing biologically informed researchers to apply this knowledge to generate new and useful predictions about a multitude of domains of human psychology (see Tooby and Cosmides, 2005). Trying to understand humans and their interactions with other humans without the benefits of adaptationist thinking is an unnecessary handicap.

Below, we attempt to show some of the ways in which the evolutionary view can be profitably deployed in understanding human social life, and used to make new and novel predictions that can be subjected to additional testing. It is important to note in this regard that hypotheses about human psychology and behavior derived from an evolutionary viewpoint are no less falsifiable than hypotheses derived from any perspective (see Ketelaar and Ellis, 2000, for a discussion.)

1.4. The Relevance of Evolutionary Perspectives to Political Psychology

In the remainder of this chapter we will suggest that an evolutionary perspective helps us to understand certain political phenomena with a depth, breadth, and novelty that has not been possible in the past. It is worth beginning with a question that seems so obvious it does not get asked. Why do humans have politics at all? This question becomes more compelling when it is pointed out that politics, in a recognizable form, does not seem to characterize behavior in most other species. Politics, being fundamentally about social relationships, is important in social species. Orangutans, largely solitary creatures, seem to have little political sophistication. Bee social life, on the other hand, is so complex that their behavior evokes political metaphors ("queens" and "citizens"; Dugatkin, 1999).

In applying the insights of an evolutionary perspective to the domain of political psychology, we would like to suggest that *adaptations for political psychology are driven by the possibility of fitness gains through coordinated, cooperative activity with conspecifics.*

1.4.1. Why Humans Have Politics

What was it about human evolutionary history that led to features that characterize human political psychology: within- and between-group hierarchy, xenophobia, coalitional psychology, and so on? Harcourt (1992), in his discussion of nonhuman primate coalitions, suggests there are ecological preconditions for coalitions, namely stability in group membership, variation in members' abilities, and a "rich, divisible resource, compactly distributed." He also suggests there are information-processing requirements—choosing partners and manipulating alliances is a complex endeavor.

In terms of ecological conditions, it is likely human bands were at least relatively stable over our evolutionary history and, importantly, hunted large game (Lee & DeVore, 1968). Successful big-game hunting hints at the presence of mechanisms that allow complex, interindividual coordination allowing the production of a "rich, divisible" resource that makes gains in trade possible—hunters who are successful on a given day have meat to spare, while those who are not are hungry. If this situation is possibly reversed in the future, there is the potential for consumption smoothing, trading meat for a reciprocal obligation.

Indeed, there is evidence that humans have adaptations designed for social exchange, and, more specifically, detecting and punishing violators of social exchanges (Cosmides & Tooby, 1992). These adaptations might not have evolved specifically for the political arena, but, once in place, might have been critical to the evolution of adaptations more specific to political domains. In addition, the evolution of punishment psychology, though still incompletely understood, has been shown to be potentially important for the generation of group-based cooperation (Boyd & Richerson, 1992).

Taken together, the ability to coordinate and the ability to punish cheaters might have laid the groundwork for adaptations designed to form factions within groups. To the extent that factions could appropriate resources, those best able to form and maintain dominant factions would have been at a profound reproductive advantage. In a species in which multiple factions are forming, it is not hard to imagine increasingly sophisticated mechanisms for detecting alliances (Kurzban, Tooby, & Cosmides, 2001) and manipulating the alignments of those in one's social world (Byrne & Whiten, 1988).

Humans are known to be polygynous, to at least some extent (e.g., Low, 1988). So there might have been large potential fitness gains if males in groups could exploit the reproductive females of other groups. The ability to coordinate activities, coupled with adaptations to punish defectors against the group, could have led to cognitive adaptations designed to exploit other groups' resources, especially reproductive females (Kurzban & Leary, 2001; Tooby & Cosmides, 1989).

Finally, the presence of adaptations designed for within-group power, as well as adaptations designed for between-group conflict and exploitation, sets up an intriguing dynamic. While an individual's interests might lie in exploiting as many other members of one's own group as possible to maximize appropriation of the group's resources, divided and conflict-ridden groups might have been at a severe disadvantage if between-group conflict were relatively common. This creates a tension between within-group and between-group success that mirrors the tension described above.

This tension might help explain what appears to be "leadership" and "followership" psychology, the desire for power (see van Vugt & Kurzban, 2007) and people's preferences for strong leaders, even if leadership comes at the price of sacrificing rights or freedoms (Boehm, 1999; Fromm, 1941). In a world with between-group conflict in which victors obtain sizable fitness gains, selection might favor mechanisms designed to support a leader, increasing the chance of victory, even though one's share of the gains might be less than proportionate. If between-group pressures were sufficiently strong, individuals who created within-group tension by contesting power might have been at a selective disadvantage. Once cognitive mechanisms were in place for coalitions to work effectively, selection might have favored mechanisms that motivated the individual to seek subordinate positions in existing coalitions rather than superordinate positions in weaker groups.

Thus, we argue that *human political psychology is that bundle of adaptations designed for seeking within-group power and influence, combined with the adaptations designed for between-group conflict and exploitation.* The complexities of human political behavior are an outcome of this dynamic.

2. Four Specific Applications of Political Psychology

While some effort has recently been made to apply an evolutionary approach to the study of world politics, including interstate cooperation and conflict, and the dynamics of international political economy (e.g., Thayer, 2004; Thompson, 2001), thus far the most widespread uses of the adaptationist approach to politically relevant behaviors are to be found within four other domains. These include (*a*) the dynamics of ethnocentrism, intergroup conflict, and intragroup cooperation, (*b*) sex differences in political behavior, (*c*) the emergence of group-based social hierarchy, and (*d*) the gendered nature of intergroup discrimination. In the remainder of this chapter we will explore adaptationist perspectives on each of these four domains in turn.

2.1. Ethnocentrism and Intragroup Cooperation

Ethnocentrism, or the preference for and belief in the superiority of one's own ethnic group, was known to be a widespread feature of human sociality even before William Graham Sumner coined the term in 1906. Since Sumner's time, continued ethnographic and experimental research has further confirmed the essentially ubiquitous preference for "Us" vs. "Them" (e.g., Eibl-Eibesfeldt, 1979). The well-known "minimal groups experiments" conducted by Tajfel and his colleagues (1978; see also Huddy, chapter 23, this volume) have demonstrated the ease with which in-group favoritism is elicited. Not only has the tendency towards in-group favoritism been found to hold across different ethnicities, nations, and cultures, but there has not been a single culture in which these results have failed to replicate (for a review, see Mullen, Brown, &

Smith, 1992). Furthermore, recent evidence indicates that automatic in-group bias is not only to be found among *Homo sapiens*, but among other primate species as well. For example, Mahajan and colleagues (2011) examined intergroup bias among rhesus macaques (*Macaca mulatta*). In a suite of experiments, Mahajan and colleagues found that macaques were able to distinguish in-group from out-group faces and showed greater vigilance toward out-group members, and even displayed greater vigilance toward objects associated with out-group members. Most interestingly, however, Mahajan and colleagues developed a Looking Time Implicit Association Test (based upon the well-known Implicit Association Test (IAT); see Greenwald & Banaji, 1995). Using this approach, the researchers discovered that, just as with humans, the macaques automatically evaluated the out-group members negatively and the in-group members positively.

Numerous theorists have spent the last 40 years trying to make sense of these basic findings, the dominant interpretation being that in-group bias is an effort to enhance one's positive social distinctiveness and/or reduce subjective uncertainty (see Huddy, chapter 23, this volume; see also Grieve & Hogg, 1999; Turner, 1999). However, these proximal explanations seem unlikely from a functional or adaptationist perspective (see Leary & Downs, 1995), and we suggest that a richer understanding of ethnocentrism can be found by considering its ultimate (evolutionary) roots.

Early attempts at developing an evolutionary theory of ethnocentrism used Hamilton's (1964) kin-selection theory of inclusive fitness, generalizing from dyadic interactions to group-level interactions. These models began with the idea that human evolution occurred in the context of small groups of genetically related individuals (e.g., brothers, sisters, nephews, cousins, etc.). Within such groups, the average degree of interindividual relatedness groups was assumed to be higher than the average degree of interindividual relatedness between groups. Thus, ethnocentrism was regarded as a form of extended kin selection and nepotism (see van den Berghe, 1981; Jones, 2000).

This model, however, can be criticized on at least two grounds. First, these arguments require very specific population structures in order to work. For example, if within-group mating was low while migration rates between groups were sufficiently large, kin selection forces would be insufficient to select for group-level altruistic behavior (Boyd & Richerson, 1985). Jones (2000) reported average coefficients of relatedness within groups for a number of modern tribal societies in the .05 to .1 range. Jones suggests that for kin selection to operate, this range would require "substantial" benefits to be conferred on fellow group members over time scales of tens of thousands of years.

An additional problem is that these kin selection processes are strongest in the context of one's closest relatives, which necessarily also means the smallest number of other individuals. The problem of getting cooperation to remain stable in larger kin networks, therefore, is that the relatively stronger forces of the smaller component kin groups are very likely to destabilize the larger level of organization (Richerson & Boyd, 1998). A related problem is that because of the nature of inheritance, kin selection forces fall off exponentially with the distance between relations. The coefficient of relatedness for first cousins, for example, is .125, meaning that kin selection will only operate when the benefits conferred are eight times as great as the costs to the altruistic individual (see Hamilton's rule, above).

An alternative to kin selection is the possibility that human cooperation in groups can be explained by a process of cultural group selection (Boyd & Richerson, 1985). Assume that different groups have adopted different social norms to govern their behavior, and these norms are followed by everyone in the group. Some groups will, by chance, have norms that are beneficial to the group as a whole, and some will have norms that are group-wise detrimental. Over time, the norms of the groups that are group-wise beneficial will tend to spread because of the greater relative success enjoyed by groups with cooperative norms. This structure can be understood as a cultural selection process that favored groups that were cooperative in interactions within groups and competitive in interactions between groups.

This argument turns critically on groups consisting of individuals who share the same values and norms. As with the genetic version, cultural group selection models require that cooperative individuals be grouped differentially with other cooperative individuals. To the extent that migration (of norms rather than genes) between groups or other processes mix selfish and cooperative individuals together, the group selection process is inhibited. Conversely, to the extent that groups are homogenous with respect to these norms, the cultural group selection process is facilitated.

Boyd and Richerson (1985) argued that a distinctive feature of humans is that they tend to adopt the ideas and practices that are common within their group. This conformist tendency they believe is an adaptation designed to acquire ideas or information that others in the population have found to be good ones. Gil-White (2001a) extended this idea, arguing that the conformist tendency in the context of interpersonal interactions was driven by the fact that coordinating one's actions to achieve mutually beneficial outcomes is easier when individuals share the same norms. In the modern cultural environment, for example, each individual is best off stopping on red and going on green. Deviating from local customs can have seriously detrimental effects. The process of conformism facilitates cultural group selection by homogenizing groups with respect to norms, avoiding the barrier to group selection posed by migration.

The advantages of sharing norms and acquiring the cultural practices of those around you might also explain why people everywhere use markers of group identity, cultural "badges" such as social customs, traditions, scarification, styles of dress, haircuts, language, and dialect (see Alexander, 1979; Dawkins, 1976; Eibl-Eibesfeldt, 1998; Reynolds, Falger, & Vine, 1987; Symons, 1979; van den Berghe, 1978; 1981). Boyd and Richerson (1987), for example, have suggested that ethnic markings might have emerged to allow individuals to identify precisely which other people individuals ought to be imitating.

Whatever the reason for the practice, cultural marking might provide another explanation for human large-scale cooperation. Some have argued that adaptations originally designed to confer benefits on genetic kin were co-opted to include individuals who share these cultural badges. Altruism, nepotism, and cooperation, originally bestowed upon close relatives, were extended to members of "fictive kinship" groups. For example, Wiessner (1998, p. 134) suggested that the evolution of socially defined kinship was "a critical adaptation of *Homo sapiens*. It permitted the construction of broad social security networks for risk reduction by granting access to human and natural resources lying outside the group. Losses due to fluctuations in natural resources, inability to find mates, conflict, and so on, could then be absorbed by a broader population." Thus, because of the human ability for symbol construction and abstraction, what began as a form of narrow in-group cooperation and ethnocentrism based upon the degree of genetic relatedness (kin selection) was transformed into the potential for in-group cooperation and ethnocentrism on a much broader scale and encompassing an almost infinitely large number of socially defined "kin" (see also Efferson, Lalive, & Fehr, 2008).

The strength of the relationship between ethnocentrism and socially constructed kinship is illustrated by the fact that political appeals to ethnocentric, patriotic, and xenophobic identity are very often framed by the use of familial and kinship terms (e.g., motherland, fatherland, "brothers in arms") and by the invocation of "myths of blood" and common descent (e.g., "the founding fathers"; see, e.g., Johnson, 1986; Johnson, Ratwik, & Sawyer, 1987).

Although the definitional characteristics and boundaries of in-groups and out-groups show remarkable plasticity over different social and political contexts, certain types of in-group/out-group boundaries seem to recur. Some work in developmental psychology and cognitive anthropology suggests that humans possess specialized mechanisms designed to parse the social world into particular kinds of human groups (Gil-White, 2001b). These systems seem to be sensitive to visual cues (Hirschfeld, 1996), and track those cues that correlate with coalitional alliance structures. The sensitivity to visual information might explain in part why "race" is one persistent group boundary. However, racial cues appear to be no different from other kinds of visual markings. Consistent with an earlier conception of "race" as an "arbitrary set" (i.e., Sidanius, 1993), Kurzban et al. (2001) provide evidence supporting the view that, rather than racial categorization being an automatically recruited natural category, "racial" classification might be an eradicable construct that persists only so long as it is actively maintained through being linked to parallel systems of social alliance.

The idea that "racial" categories are not as fundamental to social cognition and social choice as previously thought (e.g., Brewer, 1988) is also attested to by more recent evidence showing that the biased social choices of five-year-old children appear to be primarily based on accent rather than visual cues of "race" (Kinzler, Shutts, DeJesus, & Spelke, 2009). Once again, the bulk of this evidence suggests that both children and adults evaluate and prefer others on the basis of perceived coalitional groups that were relevant during human prehistory, and not on the basis of relatively recently invented social categories such as "race" (see also Kinzler & Spelke, 2011).

In sum, while an evolutionary perspective might lead us to expect ethnocentrism to be the default condition among human populations, it is also clear that the precise form, intensity, and lethality of this ethnocentric response depends upon a host of ecological, situational, and contextual factors. Thus, everything else being equal, the intensity of ethnocentrism might be related to factors such as economic uncertainty and scarcity, population density, idiosyncratic psychological proclivities of particular political elites, and the nature of political ideologies.

There are two primary lessons to be taken from the evolutionary approach to ethnocentrism and its associated phenomenon of in-group cooperation. The first is that any discussion of cooperation within or ethnocentrism between groups must begin with biologically sound assumptions about what could, in principle, have evolved. Models of the evolution of in-group cooperation must always show what prevents less cooperative strategies from invading populations of cooperative individuals. Second, the evolutionary view binds the issues of cooperation and competition. Models of the evolution of cooperation at the group level are always implicitly and often explicitly also models of in-group favoritism and ethnocentric competition. Evolutionarily speaking, the world of genetic fitness is zero sum. There are no genetic winners without genetic losers.

2.2. Sex Differences in Political Behavior

An evolutionary understanding of sex differences with respect to political attitudes and behaviors begins with an appreciation of the slightly different reproductive constraints and opportunities faced by males and females over the course of human evolutionary history. We suggest that the evolution of subtle differences in the cognitive adaptations employed by males and females have had profound implications for sex differences in political attitudes, political behavior, and social structure in general.

The reasoning behind these expectations is generated by the implications of Darwin's sexual selection theory and Trivers's (1972) parental investment theory, discussed above. Trivers argued that in sexually reproducing organisms, reproductive effort will be some combination of two basic activities: (*a*) mating effort—the time and effort devoted to finding and attracting mates, and (*b*) parental effort—the time and effort devoted to the care of offspring. Any sex difference in the potential variance in the rate of reproduction can create a sex difference in the relative effort devoted to one reproductive strategy versus the other. Because there is no monotonic relationship between the number of mates human females have sexual access to and their reproductive success, they will maximize fitness by devoting relatively more effort to parental rather than mating activities. In contrast, because human males are potentially able to produce a large number of offspring, their fitness will be maximized by devoting relatively more effort to mating rather than parenting activities (see Clutton-Brock, 1991). Thus, over evolutionary time, for males there will be a strong positive relationship between the number of mates they have sexual access to and their reproductive success.

These differential reproductive constraints confronting the two sexes have additional important consequences. Females, for example, should be expected to be substantially choosier in their selection of mates. Among social primates (e.g., baboons, chimpanzees, and humans) as well as several other species, females are attracted to males with demonstrably good health and vigor, high social status, control over valued economic resources, and an apparent willingness to deploy these resources on behalf of her and her offspring (Buss, 1989; Pawlowski & Dunbar, 1999). In general, males will be sub-stantially less choosy in their mate choice, exploiting mating opportunities because additional copulations, even with low-quality mates, can be a benefit for males, while constituting a substantial cost for females.

Because of their substantially higher levels of investment in offspring, human females are a limited reproductive resource for males, leading to higher levels of intrasexual competition among males. This expresses itself not only in direct competition over sex-ual access to females, but also in relatively high levels of male versus male competition for social status, power, and economic resources. For males, relatively high resources often led to high levels of reproductive success, typically because successful males have had sexual access to multiple and more fertile mates (e.g. Hopcraft, 2006; von Reuden, Gurven, & Kaplan, 2011). For example, powerful male rulers of the world's first major empires (e.g., the Aztec, Inca, and Chinese empires) had exclusive access to harems including as many as 10,000 wives (Betzig, 1993). In contrast, while females also need resources in order to raise healthy children and will engage in competition to get these resources, it will not benefit them to incur very large risks in order to accumulate *very* large amounts of resources because they will generally be unable to convert these sur-plus resources into reproductive success. In fact, not only will the marginal reproductive utility of additional resources generally be lower for females than for males, but intense striving after these additional resources might even lower their reproductive success (Hawkes, O'Connell, & Rogers, 1997; Packer, Collins, Sindimwo, & Goodall, 1995).

The different selection pressures acting on males and females over deep time are likely to have produced cognitive adaptations with somewhat different design features. Mate preference is one area in which these differences are clear: men and women put differ-ent weight on the traits that are most important in their long-term mates (although both sexes also place weight on similar qualities such as kindness and intelligence; Buss, 1989). The political implications of these male/female differences in reproductive strate-gies are then fairly straightforward. If it is true that, over evolutionary time, the fitness returns of obtaining control over other people and their resources were greater for males than for females, it is reasonable to expect that selection would have led to greater tastes for acquiring and exerting political power and dominance in males than in females.

A good deal of empirical evidence is consistent with these expectations. For example, patriarchy, or the disproportionate exercise of political and military power by males, appears to be a human universal (e.g., Goldberg, 1993; Rosaldo, 1974; Sanday, 1974, Harris, 1993). As of this writing, approximately 70% of human societies have only male political leaders, while in the remaining societies, the more powerful the political posi-tion is, the more likely it is to be occupied by a male (Whyte, 1978, 1979). Although there are a number of *matrilineal* societies (i.e., societies in which ancestral descent is traced through the female line) and societies in which individual rulers have been women (e.g., Queen Elizabeth I of England, Angela Merkel of Germany), there have been no recorded societies in human history in which women have held a disproportionate amount of elite political power.[2] While it is clear that the *degree* of patriarchy shows meaning-ful and sometimes dramatic variation across cultures (e.g., contemporary Sweden vs.

Afghanistan), social contexts, and time periods, the presence of patriarchy itself appears to be aHuman universal. Furthermore, patriarchy is not only characteristic of human societies, but with a few exceptions is also characteristic of most other species of social mammals.[3]

There are also consistent male/female differences in power-relevant sociopolitical attitudes. While men and women do share overlapping distributions in sociopolitical attitudes (as in just about every other characteristics such as psychical size and strength), mean differences between the sexes show males to be consistently more militaristic, ethnocentric, xenophobic, ethnically discriminatory, antiegalitarian, punitive, and positively disposed to the predatory exploitation of out-groups than are women (e.g., Ekehammar, 1985; Ekehammar & Sidanius, 1982; Furnham, 1985; Marjoribanks, 1981; Pratto, Stallworth, & Sidanius, 1997; Shapiro & Mahajan, 1986; Sidanius and Ekehammar, 1980; 1983; Smith, 1984; Togeby, 1994).

Given the nature of the politically relevant attitudinal differences between men and women, some theorists have described the sociopolitical attitudes of men as being more "hierarchy-enhancing," while those of women as being more "hierarchy-attenuating" (see Sidanius & Pratto, 1999).[4] While there is good reason to expect relatively stable male/female differences with respect to this continuum, these differences do not *necessarily* have to express themselves as differences in partisanship or political party preference. Rather, male/female differences in basic sociopolitical orientation should only be expected to manifest themselves as differences in partisanship to the extent to which political parties take differing, visible, and stable positions along this "hierarchy-enhancing versus hierarchy-attenuating" continuum.

Therefore, given our evolutionary assumptions discussed above, there is reason to believe that, everything else being equal, males should have a greater generalized predisposition to compete against, extract resources from, and subordinate the generalized "other" than females. The desire to establish and maintain systems of socioeconomic exploitation of and dominance over other groups has been captured by the construct of *social dominance orientation* (SDO; Pratto, Sidanius, Stallworth, & Malle, 1994; Sidanius & Pratto, 1999; see also Altemeyer, 1998; Whitley, 1999). SDO is conceptually and empirically distinct from more familiar constructs such as individual dominance, racism, authoritarianism, and political conservatism, yet shows strong and consistent relationships with a number of politically relevant attitudes and behaviors such as generalized ethnic prejudice, sexism, militarism, patriotism, nationalism, political conservatism, just-world beliefs, racial and social welfare policy attitudes, criminal justice and immigration attitudes, partisanship, and voting behavior.[5]

Based on these ideas, we expect men to have significantly higher average levels of SDO women. That this is, in fact, the case is one of the most well-documented findings within the social dominance literature and has been demonstrated across a broad range of cultures and social situations (see especially Sidanius & Pratto, 1999; see also Heaven & Bucci, 2001; Sidanius, Levin, Liu, & Pratto, 2000; Sidanius, Pratto, & Bobo, 1994; Sidanius, Pratto, & Brief, 1995). In the most recent and comprehensive study of this relationship to date, Lee, Pratto, and Johnson (2011) performed a meta-analysis of the relationship between sex and SDO using 118 independent reports of 206 independent samples, and employing 52,826 participants across 22 countries. The results showed an average effect size for the sex difference on SDO that was substantially larger than the average effect size for differences between high- and low-powered social groups more broadly defined.[6]

This sex difference in SDO implies that one of the fundamental reasons for the broadly observed "gender gap" in sociopolitical attitudes[7] has to do with male/female differences in the willingness to exercise dominance over others. To test this idea, Sidanius and Pratto (1999) examined the relationships between sex and a wide range of political attitudes (e.g., racism) and political policy preferences (e.g., aid to the poor) using several independent samples and across Israel, Sweden, and the United States. Consistent with expectations, social dominance orientation was found to mediate the relationship between gender and these attitudes in 98% of the cases and account for more than 50% of the covariation between sex, on the one hand, and political attitudes and policy preferences on the other.[8]

2.3. The Emergence of Group-Based Social Hierarchy

Recall we have argued that males can improve their reproductive success by acquiring additional mates, whereas females generally cannot. One of the primary means by which males can acquire reproductively desirable females is by the accumulation of power, status, and dominance—goals leading to relatively intense intrasexual competition among males. As part of this enterprise, human males form *expropriative coalitions* (e.g., gangs, raiding parties, armies), engaging in intergroup warfare and extracting social and economic resources from other groups of males (Tiger, 2007). Consistent with the observation of greater levels of attitudinal militarism among males, discussed above, Tooby and Cosmides (1989) argue that the differential reproductive benefits to males and females of coordinated conflict has led to a domain-specific cognitive adaptation in human males for "coalitional psychology" (see also Bugental & Beaulieu, 2009; Kurzban & Leary, 2001), designed in part to motivate competitive intergroup behavior.

This reasoning is consistent with the observation that warfare has been, and remains, an essentially an all-male activity. For example, in Murdock and White's (1969) ethnographic study of 224 known human societies around the world, the waging of war was found to be an *exclusively* male activity. While women have certainly participated in warfare and have been known to defend themselves, their homes, and their children, there is not a single recorded event in human history of women organizing and constituting armies for the purposes of conquest or intergroup predation (e.g., Keegan, 1993).

Because males have a greater tendency to strive toward political power, status, the accumulation of social resources, and the formation of predatory coalitions against other groups, we should not only expect to observe patriarchy and male-driven intergroup conflict, but within complex and large human social systems, we should also observe hierarchically structured sets of relations between "groups" or coalitions of males. Male coalitions with more efficient and powerful political, organizational, and/or military capabilities are able to extract economic and social resources from less powerful male coalitions. Because of the great human flexibility in constructing these in-group/out-group or coalitional boundaries, these hierarchically structured social groups can manifest themselves in any number of different ways, including conceptualization in terms of castes, estates, clans, lineages, nationalities, tribes, ethnic groups, "races," sports teams and social classes. Because of this definitional plasticity, social dominance theorists refer to such groups as *arbitrary sets*, and the hierarchical arrangement of these groups as *arbitrary-set hierarchy* (Sidanius & Pratto, 1999). Thus, as both Chagnon (1979) and Betzig (1993) suggest, the net result of this more expropriative and power-oriented male reproductive strategy is not only the patriarchic control of women, but also the development and maintenance of systematic economic and military inequality between arbitrary sets in general.

Many social scientists have tended to assume that patriarchy/sexism and racism are almost functionally and psychologically equivalent (e.g., Fernandez, Castro, & Torrejon, 2001; Marti, Bobier, & Baron, 2000). They are both regarded as forms of prejudice against stigmatized out-groups and thus are both assumed to be subject to the same psychological principles and constraints. In contrast, Sidanius and Pratto (1999) argue that while patriarchy and arbitrary-set hierarchy share some of the same causative roots (i.e., the relative male predisposition toward social predation), and the two forms of social hierarchy tend to be correlated across societies (see Sidanius & Pratto, 1999), these two systems of social organization are, nonetheless, qualitatively different. Of the several distinctions that can be drawn between patriarchic and arbitrary-set forms of social organization (see Sidanius & Veniegas, 2000), three are critically important for our argument here.

First, unlike different "races," members of the two sexes are objects of the other sex's desire. Each sex has a stake in the continued existence of the other. This is not necessarily true of arbitrary sets (e.g., Afro- and Euro-Americans), between whom it is not uncommon to witness genocidal or near genocidal violence (e.g., the complete extinction of the Tasmanian Aboriginals at the hands of the Australians in 1876; see Thayer, 2004). While violence against women by men is, of course not unknown, sexual genocide would represent the destruction of a scarce resource desired by men.

Second, there has been a tendency to regard sexism and patriarchy as essentially misogynist projects and driven by male hatred of and contempt for women (e.g., Dworkin, 1974; Mies, Bennholdt-Thomsen, & von Werlhof, 1988). In contrast, the evolutionary perspective suggests that patriarchy should be primarily seen as a project of *control* rather than a project of *aggression* (i.e., aggression defined as a desire to harm). Because males were critically dependent upon females for reproductive success, they should be inclined toward the restriction and control of female sexuality and of the resources on which females depend. Among other things, this implies that patriarchy is substantially more *paternalistic* than *misogynist* in nature.[9] Thus, rather than being a group against whom males must compete for precious reproductive resources, females have historically *been* the precious reproductive resource over which males competed with each other. While it is certainly true that females compete against one another for desired mates, they will generally not compete against one another for simultaneous sexual access to multiple mates, nor does this competition reach the ferocity of organized violence and warfare.

Third, by definition, patriarchy is an intersexual phenomenon and subject to all of the constraints described above. In contrast, because most arbitrary sets are patriarchically structured groups (e.g., tribes, clans, nations, estates, social classes), arbitrary-set confrontations are also essentially male-on-male phenomena and conceived of in male-gendered terms. For example, Eagly and Kite (1987) found that stereotypes of national groups were more strongly correlated with people's stereotypes of men than with their stereotypes of women. Similarly, Zarate & Smith (1990) found that men are more readily perceived in terms of their race than are women.

2.4. The Gendered Nature of Intergroup Conflict

These distinctions between patriarchy and arbitrary-set hierarchy lead us to counterintuitive expectations regarding the basic nature of intergroup discrimination. Because patriarchy is a project of *inter*sexual social control, while arbitrary-set confrontation is essentially a project of *intra*sexual competition, the primary targets of arbitrary-set aggressive discrimination are therefore more likely to be out-group males than out-group females. Thus, while females (regardless of arbitrary-set group membership) will be the targets of patriarchic control, one should expect that males will be the primary targets of aggressive arbitrary-set discrimination. Social dominance theorists have referred to this as the *out-group male target hypothesis* (OMTH).[10]

There is a good deal of archival evidence supporting the out-group male target hypothesis in that arbitrary-set discrimination against out-group males tends to be significantly more common and severe than arbitrary-set discrimination against out-group females. Evidence of this effect can be found across many different content domains, including the criminal justice system, the labor market, the housing sector, and the retail market (see Sidanius & Pratto, 1999; Sidanius & Veniegas, 2000). As one example, McDonald, Navarrete, and Sidanius (2011) found that black males were imprisoned at a rate six times greater than that of white males. In contrast, the racial disparity between black and white females was substantially less extreme, with black females being imprisoned at a rate only three times greater than white females. Although the overall level of ethnic disparity was not as severe with respect to the white/Latino contrast, the same relative severity against the Latino males was found here as well.

Archival evidence of the out-group male target hypothesis can also be found in the relatively egalitarian country of Sweden. For example Arai and Thoursie (2009) found that Asian, African, and Slavic immigrants to Sweden could significantly increase their labor market earnings by switching their names from foreign-sounding to Swedish-sounding names. Even more interesting, the positive earnings effect of a name change was moderated by the gender of the immigrant. Immigrant women benefited significantly more by switching to Swedish-sounding names than did immigrant men (see also le Grand & Szulkin, 2002).

Field experimental evidence consistent with the out-group male target hypothesis is also to be found in a two-stage employment audit study by Arai, Bursell, and Nekby (2008). In the first stage of their experiment, 283 equivalent curriculum vitae (CV) pairs were sent to prospective Swedish employers. The only difference between the CVs was that one name within each pair was Swedish, while the other name in that pair was Arabic. The results showed a relatively large and significant callback gap such that the CVs from Swedish-sounding applicants were much more likely to get a follow-up call than CVs from Arabic-sounding applicants, regardless of applicant sex. Most relevant for our discussion here, however, is what happened in the second stage of their experiment. In this phase, 292 CV pairs were sent to employers, but the applications with Arabic names were enhanced by having approximately two more years of work-relevant job experience. Under these conditions, the callback gap between Swedish and enhanced Arabic applications among females was eliminated. Most noteworthy for us here, however, and in stark contrast to the results for women, the callback gap between Swedish and enhanced CVs for Arab males not only failed to decrease, but *actually increased*. In other words and in stark contrast to the results for females, the greater the Arab males' relative job qualifications, the greater the degree of job discrimination against them.

There is also good experimental evidence from the laboratory supporting OMTH. Öhman and Mineka (2001) reasoned that because of our deep history of exposure to dangerous and nondangerous animals (e.g., snakes,and spiders vs. rabbits and butterflies respectively), conditioned fear responses toward danger-relevant animals should be more difficult to extinguish than conditioned fear responses toward danger-irrelevant animals.[11] In a very influential extension of this conditioned fear paradigm, Olsson, Ebert, Banaji and Phelps (2005) reasoned that since out-groups have represented danger-relevant social objects over the course of human evolutionary history, conditioned fear toward out-group members should extinguish substantially more slowly than should conditioned fear towards in-group members. Using photos of in-group and out-group males, their experimental results were consistent with expectations. For both black and white subjects, once one was conditioned to fear specific members of the racial out-group, this fear did not readily extinguish when the pictures of the out-group members were no longer associated with the unconditioned stimulus (i.e., electric shock and white noise). In contrast, conditioned fear to specific members of the in-group did readily extinguish when unconditioned stimuli were removed.

Using OMTH as a theoretical framework, Navarrete et al. (2009) extended this conditioned fear paradigm one step further. Olsson et al (2005) used only pictures of in-group and out-group *male* targets. Navarrete and his colleagues reasoned that because it was out-group males rather than out-group females who represented the greatest physical threat over evolutionary time, fear-extinction bias should only be found when using male targets but not female targets. This is exactly what their experimental results showed.

Further experimental evidence consistent with the expectations of OMTH was recently generated in simulated shoot / don't shoot scenarios conducted by Plant, Goplen, and Kunstman (2011). In the shoot / don't shoot experimental design, test subjects are very briefly shown images of in-group and out-group targets, some of whom are armed (e.g., carrying a gun or a knife in their hands), and some of whom are unarmed (e.g., carrying a cell phone or comb in their hands). The subjects' task is to decide whether to shoot the very briefly displayed target image or not. Plant and colleagues found that respondents were much more likely to be threatened by, and thus mistakenly to shoot, unarmed black male targets than other any other race-by-sex combination. Most tellingly, respondents were no more likely to mistakenly shoot black female targets than to shoot either white male or white female targets.

In addition, and in line with the consistent findings of higher SDO and xenophobia levels among men than among women (discussed earlier), there is now good experimental evidence that males are also more likely to discriminate in favor of the in-group than are females (e.g., Yamagishi & Mifune, 2009), especially when the targets are out-group males (e.g., Carlsson & Rooth, 2007; Fershtman & Gneezy, 2001; Navarrete, McDonald, Molina, & Sidanius, 2010).

Finally, recent empirical evidence indicates that males and females discriminate against out-group males for somewhat different reasons. While male discrimination against out-group males appears to be primarily motivated by a combination of aggression and social dominance orientation, female discrimination against out-group males appears to be primarily motivated by fear, especially fear of sexual coercion and molestation (see McDonald, Asher, Kerr & Navarette, 2011; Navarrete et al., 2010). For example, using reasoning inspired by an evolutionary perspective, Navarrete et al. (2009) found that women's menstrual cycle and conception risk were strongly influential on their degree of out-group bias. The greater their risk of impregnation, the greater the fear of out-group males ($r = .40$). Furthermore, this relationship was moderated by women's sense of vulnerability to sexual coercion; the more sexually vulnerable women felt, the stronger was the relationship between conception risk and racial bias against out-group males. In a follow-up study, McDonald, Asher, et al. (2011) did a conceptual replication of the Navarrete et al. (2009) findings by showing that conception risk was significantly related to intergroup bias only among those women who perceived the out-group males as physically formidable. Most importantly perhaps, these relationships held even when the in-group and out-group classifications consisted of essentially fictitious, or minimal, groups as well as real racial groups (i.e., blacks and whites).

The combination of the ideas that males are the primary targets of intergroup discrimination, and that intergroup discrimination and xenophobia are driven by different motives among males and females, has recently been labeled as the *theory of Gendered Prejudice* (McDonald, Navarrete, & Sidanius, 2011). Ultimately what the theory of Gendered Prejudice implies is that one cannot fully understand the sociopsychology of intergroup conflict and discrimination without incorporating an understanding of the political psychology of sex. While the predictions made above fall rather easily out the assumptions of evolutionary psychology, these predictions are not as easily derivable using the standard social science model.

3. Summary and Conclusions

This chapter has been devoted to discussing how an evolutionary perspective can inform and deepen our understanding of human political behavior. In doing this, we have tried to make three major points. First, we have presented the basic principles of modern evolutionary thinking and tried to correct the ways in which modern evolutionary thinking has been misinterpreted and misunderstood. Among the most deeply rooted misapprehensions is the idea that evolutionary thinking is necessarily an exercise in genetic determinism. While some 19th-century Darwinian approaches to human behavior were indeed deeply infected with a simplistic and highly deterministic view of human action (e.g., Galton, 1892; Spencer, 1862), contemporary evolutionary psychology emphasizes the deep and complex interaction between evolved cognitive mechanisms and environmental contexts, rejecting the social Darwinism of the past and the "nature versus nurture" dichotomy of the present as fundamentally ill-conceived.

Second, we suggested that some of the most straightforward applications of evolutionary theory to an understanding of political behavior can be found in the domains of ethnocentrism and intergroup conflict, the political psychology of sex, and the resilience of patriarchic and arbitrary-set social hierarchies. Thus for example, while there has been a distinct tendency to regard both sexism and racism as very similar, if not identical psychosocial phenomena, an evolutionary approach allows us to understand both why and how these two forms of social oppression should differ one from the other. While the domains of ethnocentrism, group conflict, intragroup cooperation, the political psychology of sex, and social hierarchy are the most obvious areas in which one might fruitfully apply an evolutionary approach to political behavior, these are certainly not the only domains possible. We look forward to additional applications of these ideas in the future (e.g., international relations).

Third and finally, it bears emphasizing that the evolutionary view does not replace psychological, sociological, or historical approaches, nor does it deny the existence of learning or socialization. Rather, the evolutionary perspective suggests that proposed learning mechanisms ought to be consistent with what is known about natural selection and cognition. Information that is "cultural," in the sense of information that is localized in a spatially and temporally contiguous set of human minds, is nonetheless acquired by evolved learning systems (see e.g., Boyer, 1994; Boyd & Richerson, 1985). In short, rather than regard socialization and evolutionary explanations as mutually hostile and competing cosmologies, we are suggesting the necessity of integrating the two sets of explanations into an internally consistent and congruent paradigm. Thus, we could regard socialization processes as the more proximal, yet nonetheless evolved sources of human action. We suggest that major and continued progress in our understanding of human political behavior will be greatly facilitated by the achievement of vertical integration across the social sciences, including an appreciation of the evolved character of the human mind (Cosmides et al., 1992). We will not be able to successfully confront the challenges to our continued existence (e.g., war), or the affronts to democratic values (e.g., racism, sexism, plutocracy, kleptocracy) until we achieve a much better understanding of the complex and multileveled manner in which the psychological mechanisms that underlie human political behavior have been shaped by evolutionary processes.

NOTES

1. "Culture" and "learning" are also not *alternative* explanations for claims that a given behavior, such as voting, is caused by the operation of an evolved psychological mechanism. To object to such a claim requires either (1) an alternative to evolution as an explanation for organized functional complexity (of which none are currently on offer), or (2) dualism (i.e., that mechanisms are not required for generating behavior). Of course, all events are multiply caused. The claim here is a weak one: that evolution must be one of the many causal agents in functionally organized biological systems.

2. Goldberg's (1993, pp. 231–247) careful ethnographic analysis has debunked the alleged exceptions to this rule (e.g., the Iroquois, the Hopi, the Jivaro).

3. For a description of patriarchy among other, nonhuman primate species, see de Waal, 1993, and Eibl-Eibesfeldt, 1989. Among the few exceptions to patriarchic rule among primates are bonobos, rhesus macaques and Muriqui monkeys (see Castillo, 1997).

4. By the term "hierarchy-enhancing," social dominance theorists mean the generalized desire to establish a hierarchical system of power relations between dominant and subordinate groups.

5. See, e.g., Altemeyer, 1998; Bates & Heaven, 2001; Danso & Esses, 2001; Heaven, 1999; Heaven & Bucci, 2001; Heaven, Greene, Stones, & Caputi, 2000; Jackson & Esses, 2000; Jost & Thompson, 2000; Martinez, Paterna, Rosa, & Angosto, 2000; Kteily, Sidanius, & Levin, 2011; Roccato et al., 2000; Pratto et al., 1994; Schwarzwald & Tur-Kaspa, 1997; Sidanius & Pratto, 1999; Strunk & Chang, 1999; Walter, Thorpe, & Kingery, 2001; Whitley, 1999; Whitley & Aesgisdottir, 2000.

6. While Lee et al. (2011) found a cross-nationally consistent tendency for men to have significantly higher SDO scores than women, this finding was moderated by the degree of collectivism and national GDP. Despite this moderation, the weak version of the invariance hypothesis was still found to hold, in that women were never found to have significantly higher SDO than men.

7. See e.g., Fite, Genest, & Wilcox, 1990; Norrander, 1999; Studlar, McAllister, & Hayes, 1998; Trevor, 1999; Wirls, 1986.

8. For a fascinating discussion of genetics and socio-olitical attitudes, see chapter 8 by Funk in this volume.

9. See Jackman (1994) for an empirical demonstration of this distinction. See also Glick and Fiske's (1996) distinction between hostile and benevolent sexism.

10. Previously known as the *subordinate male target hypothesis* (see Sidanius & Pratto, 1999).

11. In classical conditioning, a conditioned (CR) response is a response to a previously neutral stimulus, which has been paired with a noxious stimulus. For example, if one becomes frightened by the sight of a blue flower (conditioned stimulus) that has been consistently paired with receiving an electric shock (unconditioned stimulus).

REFERENCES

Alexander, R. D. (1979). *Darwinism and human affairs*. Seattle: University of Washington Press.

Altemeyer, B. (1998). The other "authoritarian personality." In M. P. Zanna (ed.), *Advances in experimental social psychology* (pp. 47–92).San Diego, CA: Academic Press.

Arai, M., Bursell, M., & Nekby, L. (2008). Between meritocracy and ethnic discrimination: The gender difference. IZA Discussion Paper Series No. 3467.

Arai, M., & Thoursie, P. S. (2009). Renouncing personal names: An empirical examination of surname change and earnings. *Journal of Labor Economics, 27*(1), 127–147.

Axelrod, R., & Hamilton, W. D. (1981). The evolution of cooperation. *Science, 211*(4489), 1390–1396.

Barkow, J. H., Cosmides, L., & Tooby, J. (1992). *The adapted mind: Evolutionary psychology and the generation of culture*. New York: Oxford University Press.

Bates, C., & Heaven, P. C. L. (2001). Attitudes to women in society: The role of social dominance orientation and social values. *Journal of Community & Applied Social Psychology, 11*(1), 43–49.

Bateman, A. J. (1948). Intrasexual selection in Drosophila. *Heredity, 2,* 349–368.

Betzig, L. (1993). Sex, succession, and stratification in the first six civilizations: How powerful men reproduced, passed power on to their sons, and used power to defend their wealth, women, and children. In L. Ellis (ed.), *Social stratification and socioeconomic inequality,* vol. 1: *A comparative biosocial analysis* (pp. 37–74). New York: Praeger.

Boehm, C. (1999). *Hierarchy in the forest: The evolution of egalitarian behavior*. Cambridge, MA: Harvard University Press.

Bowles, S., & Gintis, H. (1998). The moral economy of communities: Structured populations and the evolution of pro-social norms. *Evolution and Human Behavior, 19*(1), 3–25.

Boyd, R., & Richerson, P. J. (1985). *Culture and the evolutionary process*. Chicago: University of Chicago Press.

Boyd, R., & Richerson, P. J. (1987). The evolution of ethnic markers. *Cultural Anthropology, 2*(1), 65–79.

Boyd, R., & Richerson, P. J. (1992). Punishment allows the evolution of cooperation (or anything else) in sizable groups. *Ethology & Sociobiology, 13*(3), 171–195.

Boyer, P. (1994). Cognitive constraints on cultural representations: Natural ontologies and religious ideas. In L. A. Hirschfeld & S. A. Gelman (eds.), *Mapping the mind: Domain specificity in cognition and culture* (pp. 391–409).New York: Cambridge University Press.

Brewer, M. B. (1988). A dual process model of impression formation. In T. K. Srull & R. S. Wyer Jr (eds.), *Advances in Social Cognition* (vol. 1, pp. 1–36). Hillsdale, NJ: Lawrence Erlbaum.

Brown, D. E. (1991). *Human universals*. Philadelphia, PA: Temple University Press.

Bugental, D. B., & Beaulieu, D. A. (2009). Sex differences in response to coalitional threat. *Evolution and Human Behavior, 30*(4), 238–243.

Buss, D. M. (1989). Sex differences in human mate preferences: Evolutionary hypotheses tested in 37 cultures. *Behavioral & Brain Sciences, 12*(1), 1–49.

Byrne, R. W., & Whiten, A. (1988). *Machiavellian intelligence: Social expertise and the evolution of intellect in monkeys, apes, and humans.* New York: Oxford University Press; Oxford: Clarendon Press.

Carlsson, M., & Rooth, D.-O. (2007). Evidence of ethnic discrimination in the Swedish labor market using experimental data. *Labour Economics, 14*(4), 716–729.

Chagnon, N. A. (1979). Is reproductive success equal in egalitarian societies? In N. A. Chagnon & W. Irons (eds.), *Evolutionary biology and human social behavior: An anthropological perspective* (pp. 374–402). North Scituate, RI: Duxbury Press.

Clutton-Brock, T. H., & Scott, D. (1991). *The evolution of parental care.* Princeton, NJ: Princeton University Press.

Cochran, G., & Harpending, H. (2009). *The 10,000 year explosion: How civilization accelerated human evolution.* New York: Basic Books.

Cosmides, L., & Tooby, J. (1994). Better than rational: Evolutionary psychology and the invisible hand. *American Economic Review, 84*(2), 327–332.

Cosmides, L., & Tooby, J. (1992). Cognitive adaptations for social exchange. In J. H. Barkow, L. Cosmides, & J. Tooby (eds.), *The adapted mind: Evolutionary psychology and the generation of culture* (pp. 163–228). New York: Oxford University Press.

Cosmides, L., Tooby, J., & Barkow, J. H. (1992). Introduction: Evolutionary psychology and conceptual integration. In J. H. Barkow, L. Cosmides, & J. Tooby (eds.), *The adapted mind: Evolutionary psychology and the generation of culture* (pp. 3–15). New York: Oxford University Press.

Danso, H. A., & Esses, V. M. (2001). Black experimenters and the intellectual test performance of white participants: The tables are turned. *Journal of Experimental Social Psychology, 37*(2), 158–165.

Darwin, C. (1871). *The descent of man, and selection in relation to sex*: London: John Murray.

Darwin, C. (1859). *On the origin of species by means of natural selection: or The preservation of favoured races in the struggle for life.* London: John Murray.

Dawkins, R. (1976). *The selfish gene.* New York: Oxford University Press.

de Waal, F. B. M. (1993). Sex differences in chimpanzee (and human) behavior: A matter of social values? In M. Hechter, L. Nadel, & R. E. Michod (eds.), *The origin of values* (pp. 285–303). Hawthorne, NY: Aldine de Gruyter.

Dietz, T., Burns, T. R., & Buttel, F. H. (1990). Evolutionary theory in sociology: An examination of current thinking. *Sociological Forum, 5*(2), 155–171.

Dugatkin, L. A. (1999). *Cheating monkeys and citizen bees: The nature of cooperation in animals and humans.* New York: Free Press.

Dugatkin, L. A. (1997). *Cooperation among animals: An evolutionary perspective.* New York: Oxford University Press.

Dworkin, A. (1974). *Woman hating*: New York: Dutton.

Eagly, A. H., & Kite, M. E. (1987). Are stereotypes of nationalities applied to both women and men? *Journal of Personality and Social Psychology, 53*(3), 451–462.Efferson, C., Lalive, R., & Fehr, E. (2008). The coevolution of cultural groups and ingroup favoritism. *Science, 321*(5897), 1844–1849.

Eibl-Eibesfeldt, I. (1979). *The biology of peace and war: Men, animals, and aggression*: New York: Viking Press.

Eibl-Eibesfeldt, I. (1989). *Human ethology*: New York: Aldine de Gryuter.

Eibl-Eibesfeldt, I., & Salter, F. K. (1998). *Ethnic conflict and indoctrination: Altruism and identity in evolutionary perspective*: New York: Berghahn Books.

Ekehammar, B. (1985). Sex differences in socio-political attitudes revisited. *Educational Studies, 11*(1), 3–9.

Ekehammar, B., & Sidanius, J. (1982). Sex differences in sociopolitical attitudes: A replication and extension. *British Journal of Social Psychology, 21*(3), 249–257.

Emerson, A. E. (1960). The evolution of adaptation in population systems. In S. Tax and C. Callender (eds.), *Evolution after Darwin: The University of Chicago centennial* (vol. 3, pp. 307–348). Chicago: Chicago University Press.

Fernandez, M. L., Castro, Y. R., & Torrejon, M. J. S. (2001). Sexism and racism in a Spanish sample of secondary school students. *Social Indicators Research 54*(3), 309–328.

Fershtman, C., & Gneezy, U. (2001). Discrimination in a segmented society: An experimental approach. *Quarterly Journal of Economics, 116*(1), 351–377.

Fite, D., Genest, M., & Wilcox, C. (1990). Gender differences in foreign policy attitudes: A longitudinal analysis. *American Politics Quarterly, 18*(4), 492–513.

Fromm, E. (1941). *Escape from freedom*: New York: Henry Holt.

Furnham, A. (1985). Adolescents' sociopolitical attitudes: A study of sex and national differences. *Political Psychology, 6*(4), 621–636.

Galton, F. (1892). *Hereditary genius: An inquiry into its laws and consequences*. London: Watts.

Gil-White, F. J. (2001a). Are ethnic groups biological "species" to the human brain? *Current Anthropology, 42*(4), 515–554.

Gil-White, F. J. (2001b). Sorting is not categorization: A critique of the claim that Brazilians have fuzzy racial categories. *Journal of Cognition & Culture, 1*(3), 219–249.

Glick, P., & Fiske, S. T. (1996). The ambivalent sexism inventory: differentiating hostile and benevolent sexism. *Journal of Personality and Social Psychology, 70*, 491–512.

Goldberg, S. (1993). *Why men rule: A theory of male dominance*. Chicago: Open Court.

Greenwald, A. G., & Banaji, M. R. (1995). Implicit social cognition: Attitudes, self-esteem, and stereotypes. *Psychological Review, 102*(1), 4–27.

Grieve, P. G., & Hogg, M. A. (1999). Subjective uncertainty and intergroup discrimination in the minimal group situation. *Personality & Social Psychology Bulletin, 25*(8), 926–940.

Hammerstein, P. (2003). Why is reciprocity so rare in social animals? A protestant appeal. In P. Hammerstein (ed.), *Genetic and cultural evolution of cooperation: Dahlem workshop report* (pp. 83–93). Cambridge, MA: MIT Press.

Hamilton, W. D. (1964). The genetical evolution of social behavior. *Journal of Theoretical Biology, 7*(1964), 1–52.

Hamilton, W. D. (1975). Innate social aptitudes of man: An approach from evolutionary genetics. In R. Fox (ed.), *Biosocial anthropology* (pp. 133–156). New York: Wiley.

Harcourt, A. H. (1992). Coalitions and alliances: Are primates more complex than non-primates? In A. H. Harcourt & F.s B. M. de Waal (eds.), *Coalitions and alliances in humans and other animals* (pp. 445–471). Oxford: Oxford University Press.

Harris, M. (1993). The evolution of gender hierarchies: A trial formulation. In B. D. Miller (ed.), *Sex and gender hierarchies* (pp. 57–79). Cambridge: Cambridge University Press.

Hawkes, K., O'Connell, J. F., & Rogers, L. (1997). The behavioral ecology of modern hunter-gatherers, and human evolution. *Trends in Ecology & Evolution, 12*(1), 29–32.

Heaven, P. C. L. (1999). Attitudes toward women's rights: Relationships with social dominance orientation and political group identities. *Sex Roles, 41*(7–8), 605–614.

Heaven, P. C. L., & Bucci, S. (2001). Right-wing authoritarianism, social dominance orientation and personality: An analysis using the IPIP measure. *European Journal of Personality*, 15(1), 49–56.

Heaven, P. C. L., Greene, R. L., Stones, C. R., & Caputi, P. (2000). Levels of social dominance orientation in three societies. *Journal of Social Psychology*, 140(4), 530–532.

Hirschfeld, L. A. (1996). *Race in the making: Cognition, culture, and the child's construction of human kinds*. Cambridge, MA: MIT Press.

Hodgson, G. M. (2004). *Evolution of institutional economics: Agency, structure and Darwinism in American institutionalism*. London: Routledge.

Hoffman, E., McCabe, K. A., & Smith, V. L. (1998). Behavioral foundations of reciprocity: Experimental economics and evolutionary psychology. *Economic Inquiry* 36(3), 335.

Hopcraft, R. L. (2006). Sex, status and reproductive success in the United States. *Evolution and Human Behavior*, 27, 104–120.

Jackman, M. R. (1994). *The velvet glove: Paternalism and conflict in gender, class, and race relations*. Berkeley: University of California Press.

Jones, D. (2000). Group nepotism and Human kinship. *Current Anthropology*, 41, 779–809.

Johnson, G. R. (1986). Kin selection, socialization, and patriotism: An integrating theory. *Politics and the Life Sciences*, 4(2), 127–154.

Johnson, G. R., Ratwik, S. H., & Sawyer, T. J. (1987). The evocative significance of kin terms in patriotic speech. In V. Reynolds, V. S. E. Falger, & I. Vine (eds.), *The sociobiology of ethnocentrism: Evolutionary dimensions of xenophobia, discrimination, racism, and nationalism*, Beckenham, Kent: Croom Helm.

Keegan, J. (1993). *The history of warfare*. New York: Knopf.

Ketelaar, T., & Ellis, B. J. (2000). Are evolutionary explanations unfalsifiable? Evolutionary psychology and the Lakatosian philosophy of science. *Psychological Inquiry*, 11(1), 1–21.

Kinzler, K. D., Shutts, K., DeJesus, J., & Spelke, E. S. (2009). Accent trumps race in guiding children's social preferences. *Social Cognition*, 27(4), 623–634.

Kinzler, K. D., & Spelke, E. S. (2011). Do infants show social preferences for people differing in race? *Cognition*, 119(1), 1–9.

Kitcher, P. (1985). *Vaulting ambition: Sociology and the quest for human nature*. Cambridge, MA: MIT Press.

Kurzban, R. (2003). Biological foundations of reciprocity. In E. Ostrom & J. Walker (eds.), *Trust, reciprocity, and gains from association: Interdisciplinary lessons from experimental research* (pp. 105–127). New York: Russell Sage Foundation.

Kurzban, R., & Haselton, M. G. (2006). Making hay out of straw? Real and imagined controversies in evolutionary psychology. In J. H. Barkow (ed.), *Missing the revolution: Darwinism for social scientists* (pp. 149–161). Oxford: Oxford University Press.

Kurzban, R., & Leary, M. R. (2001). Evolutionary origins of stigmatization: The functions of social exclusion. *Psychological Bulletin*, 127(2), 187.

Kurzban, R., Tooby, J., & Cosmides, L. (2001). Can race be erased? Coalitional computation and social categorization. *Proceedings of the National Academy of Sciences of the United States of America*, 98(26), 15387–15392.

Leary, M. R., & Downs, D. L. (1995). Interpersonal functions of the self-esteem motive: The self-esteem system as sociometer. In M. H. Kernis (ed.), *Efficacy, agency, and self-esteem* (pp. 123–144). New York: Plenum Press.

Lee, I-C., Pratto, F., & Johnson, B. T. (2011). Intergroup consensus/disagreement in support of group-based hierarchy: An examination of socio-structural and psycho-cultural factors. *Psychological Bulletin*, 137(6), 1029–1064.

Lee, R. B., & DeVore, I. (Eds.). (1968). *Man the hunter.* Chicago: Aldine.

le Grand, C., & Szulkin, R. (2002). Permanent disadvantage or gradual integration: Explaining the immigrant-native earnings gap in Sweden. *Labour, 16*(1), 37–64.

Lehmann, L., Keller, L., West, S., & Roze, D. (2007). Group selection and kin selection: Two concepts but one process. *Proceedings of the National Academy of Sciences of the United States of America, 104*(16), 6736–6739.

Low, B. S. (1988). Pathogen stress and polygyny in humans. In L. Betzig, M. B. Mulder, & P. Turke, (eds.), *Human reproductive behavior: A Darwinian perspective* (pp. 115–127). Cambridge: Cambridge University Press.

Mahajan, N., Martinez, M. A., Gutierrez, N. L., Diesendruck, G., Banaji, M. R.,& Santos, L. R. (2011). The evolution of intergroup bias: Perceptions and attitudes in rhesus macaques. *Journal of Personality & Social Psychology, 100*(3), 387–405.

Marjoribanks, K. (1981). Sex-related differences in socio-political attitudes: A replication. *Educational Studies, 7*(1), 1–6.

Marti, M. W., Bobier, D. M., & Baron, R. S. (2000). Right before our eyes: The failure to recognize non-prototypical forms of prejudice. *Group Processes & Intergroup Relations, 3*(4), 403–418.

Martinez, C., Paterna, C., Rosa, A. I., & Angosto, J. (2000). El principio de jererguia social como explicacion: Del prejuicio y el rechazo a la accion positiva [The principle of social hierarchy as explanation: From prejudice and rejection to positive action]. *Psicologia Politica, 21,* 55–71.

Mayell, H. (2003). Genghis Khan a prolific lover, DNA data implies. *National Geographic News, February 14.* http://news.nationalgeographic.com/news/2003/02/0214_030214_genghis.html

McDonald, M. M., Asher, B. D., Kerr, N. L., & Navarette, C. D. (2011). Fertility and intergroup bias in racial and minimal-group contexts: Evidence for shared architecture. *Psychological Science, 22*(7), 860–865.

McDonald, M. M., Navarette, C. D., & Sidanius, J. (2011). Developing a theory of gendered prejudice: An evolutionary and social dominance perspective. In R. M. Kramer, G. J. Leonardelli, & R. W. Livingston (eds.), *Social cognition, social identity, and intergroup relations: A festschrift in honor of Marilynn B. Brewer* (pp. 189–220). New York: Psychology Press.

Mies, M., Bennholdt-Thomsen, V., & von Werlhof, C. (1988). *Women: The last colony.* London: Zed Books.

Mullen, B., Brown, R., & Smith, C. (1992). Ingroup bias as a function of salience, relevance, and status: An integration. *European Journal of Social Psychology, 22*(2), 103–122.

Murdock, G. P., & White, D. R. (1969). Standard cross-cultural sample. *Ethnology, 8*(4), 329–369.

Navarrete, C. D., McDonald, M. M., Molina, L. E., & Sidanius, J. (2010). Prejudice at the nexus of race and gender: An outgroup male target hypothesis. *Journal of Personality & Social Psychology, 98*(6), 933–945.

Navarrete, C. D., Olsson, A., Ho, A. K., Mendes, W. B., Thomsen, L., & Sidanius, J. (2009). Fear extinction to an out-group face: The role of target gender. *Psychological Science, 20*(2), 155–158.

Norrander, B. (1999). The evolution of the gender gap. *Public Opinion Quarterly, 63*(4), 566–576.

Öhman, A., & Mineka, S. (2001). Fears, phobias, and preparedness: Toward an evolved module of fear and fear learning. *Psychological Review, 108*(3), 483–522.

Olsson, A., Ebert, J. P., Banaji, M. R., & Phelps, E. A. (2005). The role of social groups in the persistence of learned fear. *Science, 309,* 785–787.

Packer, C. D., Collins, A., Sindimwo, A., & Goodall, J. (1995). Reproductive constraints on aggressive competition in female baboons. *Nature, 373*(6509),60–63.

Pawlowski, B., & Dunbar, R. I. M. (1999). Impact of market value on human mate choice decisions. *Proceedings of the Royal Society: Biological Sciences, 266*(1416), 281–285.

Plant, E. A., Goplen, J., & Kunstman, J. W. (2011). Selective responses to threat: The roles of race and gender in decisions to shoot. *Personality and Social Psychology Bulletin, 37*(9), 1274–1281.

Plotkin, H. C. (1997). *Evolution in mind: An introduction to evolutionary psychology.* Cambridge, MA.: Harvard University Press.

Pratto, F., Sidanius, J., Stallworth, L. M., & Malle, B. F. (1994). Social dominance orientation: A personality variable predicting social and political attitudes. *Journal of Personality & Social Psychology, 67*(4), 741–763.

Pratto, F., Stallworth, L. M., & Sidanius, J. (1997). The gender gap: Differences in political attitudes and social dominance orientation. *British Journal of Social Psychology, 36*(1), 49–68.

Reeve, H. K. (2000). Book review of *Unto others: The evolution and psychology of unselfish behavior,* by E. Sober & D. S. Wilson. *Evolution and Human Behavior, 21*(2000), 65–72.

Reynolds, V., Falger, V. S. E., & Vine, I. (1987). *The sociobiology of ethnocentrism: Evolutionary dimensions of xenophobia, discrimination, racism, and nationalism.* Beckenham, Kent: Croom Helm.

Richerson, P. J., & Boyd, R. (1998). The Evolution of human ultra-sociality. In I. Eibl-Eibisfeldt & F. Salter (eds.), *Ideology, warfare, and indoctrinability* (pp. 71–95). New York: Berghan Books.

Rosaldo, M. Z. (1974). Woman, culture, and society: A theoretical overview. In M. Z. Rosaldo & L. Lamphere (eds.), *Women, culture and society* (pp. 17–42). Stanford, CA: Stanford University Press.

Sanday, P. R. (1974). Female status in the public domain. In M. Z. Rosaldo & L. Lamphere (eds.), *Women, culture and society* (pp. 189–206). Stanford, CA: Stanford University Press.

Shapiro, R. Y., & Mahajan, H. (1986). Gender differences in policy preferences: A summary of trends from the 1960s to the 1980s. *Public Opinion Quarterly, 50*(1), 42–61.

Sidanius, J., & Ekehammar, B. (1980). Sex-related differences in socio-political ideology. *Scandinavian Journal of Psychology, 21*(1), 17–26.

Sidanius, J., & Ekehammar, B. (1983). Sex, Political party preference and higher-order dimensions of socio-political ideology. *Journal of Psychology, 115*(2), 233.

Sidanius, J., Levin, S., Liu, J., & Pratto, F. (2000). Social dominance orientation, anti-egalitarianism and the political psychology of gender: An extension and cross-cultural replication. *European Journal of Social Psychology, 30*(1), 41–67.

Sidanius, J. (1993). The psychology of group conflict and the dynamics of oppression: a social dominance perspective. In S. Iyengar & W. McGuire (eds.), *Explorations in political psychology* (pp. 183–219). Durham, NC: Duke University Press.

Sidanius, J., & Pratto, F. (1999). *Social dominance: An intergroup theory of social hierarchy and oppression.* New York: Cambridge University Press.

Sidanius, J., Pratto, F., & Brief, D. (1995). Group dominance and the political psychology of gender: A cross-cultural comparison. *Political Psychology, 16,* 381–396.

Sidanius, J., Pratto, F., & Bobo, L. (1994). Social dominance orientation and the Political psychology of gender. A case of invariance? *Journal of Personality & Social Psychology, 67*(6), 998–1011.

Sidanius, J., & Veniegas, R. C. (2000). Gender and race discrimination: The interactive nature of disadvantage. In S. Oskamp (ed.), *Reducing prejudice and discrimination the claremont symposium on applied social psychology* (pp 47–69). Mahwah, New Jersey: Lawrence Erlbaum Associates.

Smith, J. M. (1964). Group selection and kin selection. *Nature, 201*(4924), 1145–1147.

Smith, T. W. (1984). The polls: Gender and attitudes toward violence. *Public Opinion Quarterly, 48*(1B), 384–396.

Sober, E., & Wilson, D. S. (1998). *Unto others: The evolution and psychology of unselfish behavior.* Cambridge, MA: Harvard University Press.

Spencer, H. (1862). *First principles.* London: Williams and Norgate.

Studlar, D. T., McAllister, I., & Hayes, B. C. (1998). Explaining the gender gap in voting: A cross-national analysis. *Social Science Quarterly, 79*(4), 779.

Sumner, W. G. (1906). *Folkways: A study of the sociological importance of usages, manners, customs, mores, and morals*: Boston: Ginn.

Symons, D. (1979). *Evolution of human sexuality.* New York: Oxford University Press.

Symons, D. (1992). On the use and misuse of Darwinism in the study of human behavior. In J. H. Barkow, L. Cosmides, & J. Tooby (eds.), *The adapted mind: Evolutionary psychology and the generation of culture* (pp. 137–159). New York: Oxford University Press.

Tajfel, H. (1978). *Differentiation between social groups: Studies in the social psychology of intergroup relations.* Oxford: Academic Press.

Thayer, B. A. (2004). *Darwin and international relations: On the evolutionary origins of war and ethnic conflict.* Lexington: University Press of Kentucky.

Thompson, W. R. (2001). *Evolutionary interpretations of world politics.* New York: Routledge.

Tiger, L. (2007). *Men in groups.* New Brunswick, NJ: Transaction.

Togeby, L. (1994). The Gender Gap in Foreign Policy Attitudes. *Journal of Peace Research, 31*(4), 375–392.

Tooby, J., & Cosmides, L. (1989). Kin selection, genic selection, and information-dependent strategies. *Behavioral and Brain Sciences, 12*(3), 542–544.

Tooby, J., & Cosmides, L. (1990). The past explains the present: Emotional adaptations and the structure of ancestral environments. *Ethology and Sociobiology, 11*(4), 375–424.

Tooby, J., & Cosmides, L. (1992). The psychological foundations of culture. In J. H. Barkow, L. Cosmides & J. Tooby (eds.), *The adapted mind: Evolutionary psychology and the generation of culture* (pp. 19–136). New York: Oxford University Press.

Tooby, J., & Cosmides, L. (2005). Conceptual foundations of evolutionary psychology. In D. M. Buss (ed),. *The handbook of evolutionary psychology* (pp. 1–67). Hoboken, NJ: John Wiley & Sons.

Trevor, M. C. (1999). Political socialization, party identification, and the gender gap. *Public Opinion Quarterly, 63*(1), 62–89.

Trivers, R. L. (1971). The evolution of reciprocal altruism. *Quarterly Review of Biology, 46*(1), 35.

Trivers, R. L. (1972). Parental investment and sexual selection. In L. D. Houck & L. C. Drickamer (eds.), *Foundations of animal behavior: Classic papers with commentaries* (pp. 136–179). Chicago: University of Chicago Press.

Turner, J. C. (1999). Some current issues in research on social identity and self-categorization theories. In N. Ellemers, R. Spears, & B. Doosje (eds.), *Social identity: Context, commitment, content* (pp. 6–34). Malden, MA, Blackwell.

Van Vugt, M., & Kurzban, R. (2007). Evolutionary or origins of leadership and followership: managing the social mind. In. J. P. Forgas, M. G. Haselton, & von Hippel, W. (eds.), *The 9th Sydney Symposium of Social Psychology: The evolution of the social mind* (pp. 229–244). New York: Psychology Press.

Van Den Berghe, P. L. (1978). Race and ethnicity: A sociobiological perspective. *Ethnic and Racial Studies, 1*, 401–411.

Van Den Berghe, P. L. (1981). *The ethnic phenomenon*: New York: Elsevier.

Von Reuden, C., Gurven, M., & Kaplan, H. (2011). Why do men seek status? Fitness payoffs to dominance and prestige. *Proceedings of the Royal Society, 278*, 2223–2232.

Walter, M. I., Thorpe, G. L., & Kingery, L. R. (2001). The common beliefs survey-III, the situational self-statement, and affective state inventory and their relationship to authoritarianism and social dominance orientation. *Journal of Rational-Emotive & Cognitive-Behavior Therapy, 19*(2), 105–118.

Whitley, B. E. (1999). Right-wing authoritarianism, social dominance orientation, and prejudice. *Journal of Personality and Social Psychology, 77*(1), 126–134.

Whitley, B. E., Jr., & Ægisdóttir, S. (2000). The gender belief system, authoritarianism, social dominance orientation, and heterosexuals' attitudes toward lesbians and gay men. *Sex Roles, 42*(11–12), 947–967.

Whyte, M. K. (1978). Cross-cultural codes dealing with the relative status of women. *Ethnology, 17*(2), 211–237.

Whyte, M. K. (1979). *The status of women in preindustrial societies*. Princeton, NJ: Princeton University Press.

Wiessner, P. (1998). Indoctrinability and the evolution of socially defined kinship. In I. Eibl-Eibesfeldt (ed.), *Ethnic Strife and indoctrination: Altruism and identity in evolutionary perspective* (pp. 133–150). New York: Berghahn Books.

Williams, G. C. (1966). *Adaptation and natural selection: A critique of some current evolutionary thought*: Princeton, NJ: Princeton University Press.

Wilson, D. S. (1975). A theory of group selection. *Proceedings of the National Academy of Sciences of the United States of America, 72*(1), 143.

Wilson, E. O. (1975). *Sociobiology: The new synthesis*. Cambridge, MA: Belknap Press of Harvard University Press.

Wirls, D. (1986). Reinterpreting the gender gap. *Public Opinion Quarterly, 50*(3), 316–330.

Wrangham, R. W., & Peterson, D. (1996). *Demonic males: Apes and the origins of human violence* (D. Peterson, ed.). Boston: Houghton Mifflin.

Wynne-Edwards, V. C. (1962). *Animal dispersion in relation to social behaviour*. New York: Hafner.

Yamagishi, T., & Mifune, N. (2009). Social exchange and solidarity: In-group love or out-group hate? *Evolution and Human Behavior, 30*(4), 229–237.

Zarate, M. A., & Smith, E. R. (1990). Person categorization and stereotyping. *Social Cognition, 8*(2), 161–185.

CHAPTER 8

GENETIC FOUNDATIONS OF POLITICAL BEHAVIOR

CAROLYN L. FUNK

WE are entering a new era for political behavior research—one in which we begin to fully integrate biological, behavioral, and environmental factors into our theoretical models and understanding of political behavior. I focus in this chapter on the role of genetic influences in social and political attitudes and behaviors and how these are changing our understanding of how citizens think about and participate in democratic society.

This is an exciting time for research in this area and a particularly ripe moment for political psychologists to influence development of the field. While earlier models of political behavior focused mostly on the social environment, newer research has led to a renewed interest in the role of individual characteristics such as personality (see Caprara and Vecchione, chapter 2, this volume) and a new focus on the role of genetic influences on at least some political behaviors. Further, our understanding of environmental influences is being re-evaluated in light of evidence showing that the roles of what geneticists call the "shared environment," encompassing family socialization and more, is smaller than previously understood. Thus, we are faced with an array of new empirical evidence that strongly highlights our need for better theoretical models of political behavior and greater attention to the mechanisms linking genetic and environmental factors—whether from the home environment, personal experiences, or the wide array of other social forces in our lives.

There are a number of reasons why it is important to better understand the antecedents of political behavior. Findings from this line of research indicate that much past research has omitted key processes for understanding political behavior writ large, which may lead to reconceptualizations of key constructs from political cleavages, and to theories of political learning and remedies for political problems in society. And understanding the degree of heritability linked to the constructs of interest in political behavior research can have important consequences. For example, Tesser (1993) showed that attitudes higher in heritability are manifested more quickly and are more resistant to change (also see Olson, Vernon, Harris, Lang, 2001). Situational factors (or experimental manipulations or other environmental treatments) can have a weaker effect on phenotypes with greater heritability; thus the conclusions drawn from studies of these situational factors can be misleading if they are based on a single phenotype or ignore the possibility that response heritability moderates the treatment effect.

The research linking genetic influences with political behavior is still in its infancy, and new findings are being produced at a rapid pace. In this chapter, I review what we know about the biological bases of political behavior, including political ideology, partisanship, interest and knowledge about politics, and political participation. For each, I highlight what is known, what is largely speculative, and what needs to be addressed in future research. Future research will need to focus on identifying the mechanisms through which genetic and environmental factors interact. To do so, the field also needs more theoretical development to help identify the most fruitful avenues for study.

1. GATHERING EVIDENCE ABOUT GENETIC INFLUENCES

The research tools for testing the influence of genetic and environmental influences on social behavior require an array of methods outside the typical social scientist's toolkit. These include twin studies, adoption studies, extended family studies, genetic allele association studies and genome-wide linkage studies. These techniques require a much broader range of training than is commonly offered in the social sciences. And this line of research is reshaping the meaning of multidisciplinary research to include a much broader array of disciplines and expertise.

This section gives a brief primer on the behavioral genetic techniques used to study political behavior. Political behaviors such as ideology, political knowledge, interest, and participation are but a small piece of the kinds of behaviors that can be examined using these techniques. The field of behavioral genetics encompasses all sorts of behaviors, including cognitive abilities and disabilities, psychiatric disorders such as schizophrenia, and psychopathologies such as anxiety disorders, autism, and attention-deficit disorders. The behavioral genetics textbook by Plomin, DeFries, McClearn, and McGuffin (2008) provides an accessible and comprehensive overview of the field, and a wide array of other works cover these techniques in greater depth (see, e.g., Eaves, Eysenck, & Martin, 1989; Medland & Hatemi, 2009). Genes are the basic unit of hereditary analysis whether that analysis concerns plants, humans, or other animals. Alleles are specific forms of genes; for some genes, people vary in the specific alleles in their genetic makeup. The combination of an individual's genetic alleles is called its genotype. The phenotype refers to the specific traits and behaviors exhibited by an individual. The key question of behavioral genetics research is whether (and how much) differences in genotypes account for the observed differences across individuals, or in the parlance of behavioral geneticists, in phenotypic differences.

1.1. Establishing a Genetic Influence on a Phenotype

1.1.1. Twin and Adoption Studies

Twin studies are a mainstay of genetic research. The twin study design is used as a first step to establish whether or not there is a substantial genetic component for a given phenotype (i.e., any observable characteristic or "trait"). Twin studies estimate the amount of variance in a phenotype that can be attributed to either genetic or environmental sources. The environment is used in the broadest sense, to encompass all variation attributable to the social environment, namely anything that cannot be attributed to genetics.

The partitioning of variance into genetic and environmental components is possible because monozygotic twins (MZ) are genetically identical (sharing 100% of their genes), whereas dizygotic twins (DZ) (and other siblings) share on average 50% of their segregating genes (because these siblings arise from two different ova fertilized by different sperm). For any trait that is partly heritable, the tendency for MZ twins to share that characteristic should be stronger than the tendency for DZ twins to share that characteristic. If a characteristic comes solely from the environment, there should be no difference between the degree of similarity between MZ twin pairs and DZ twin pairs on that characteristic. Thus, the combination of MZ and DZ twin pairs, raised by the same parents in the same home environment, provides a natural experiment that can separate the effects of familial background and socialization from genetic effects.

Typically, the analysis partitions the variance into one of three sources: additive genetic (A), common or shared environment (C), and unique or unshared environment (E). The A factor reflects the combination of all additive genetic influences and thus reflects the influence of the shared genes between twin pairs. The nature of the genetic influence is assumed to be additive, meaning that the effects of the alleles at a genetic locus and across loci "add up" to influence behavior.[1] C reflects all environmental factors that make family members similar; this is typically thought of as the extent to which family and parental socialization makes members of the same family more similar than would be predicted solely from their genetic relationships. E reflects the unique or unshared environmental influences that make members of the same family different; it reflects the unique reactions or experiences of an individual to the environment.

There are several ways to generate the estimates of ACE including correlation-based techniques, known as the Falconer method, regression-based techniques (DeFries-Fulker models), and maximum likelihood structural equation techniques (for more details see Medland & Hatemi, 2009). A key benefit of the Falconer method stems from the relative simplicity of the calculation and the relative ease of interpretation. The estimate of the heritability between twin pairs using the Falconer method is the difference between the polychoric correlations for MZ pairs and DZ pairs on a given phenotype multiplied by 2 (i.e., $2 \times (MZ - DZ)$). Shared environment variance is estimated by $(2 \times DZ) - MZ$ and the unshared environment variance is calculated as $1 - MZ$. Thus, Falconer estimates can provide a useful first cut at the variance components analysis.

These analyses are typically confirmed with the more precise estimates of maximum likelihood structural equation estimates.

Variants of the twin design include twins reared apart in different households and extended family designs that make use of both twin similarity and similarity with parents and nontwin siblings. Adoption studies follow a logic similar to that of twin studies in making use of the known genetic similarity between biological relatives and adopted relatives to partition the variance into additive genetic and environmental components. A number of other variants on the naturally occurring twin design experiment are used to understand selected traits (see Segal, 2010).

The twin design is widely used in the behavioral genetics, psychology, and medical literatures. The design requires a special sample, making it time-consuming and costly to identify twins for potential study and then to collect data from them on the desired attributes. There are a handful of twin registries in the United States and in other countries (e.g., Australia, Sweden, Denmark) that are used to facilitate the process. Each of these samples is essentially a convenience sample of twins; as such, variance estimates from twin studies are considered specific to a given twin population. It is helpful when the results from twin studies can be replicated across multiple samples. The method is an important first step in identifying phenotypes with substantial genetic variance; such evidence supports the need for follow-up research.

1.1.2. *The Equal Environments Assumption*

The most common critique of twin studies stems from concerns about the equal environments assumption (EEA), which assumes common environmental influences on the phenotype being studied are the same for MZ and DZ twins. If MZ twins not only share more of their genetic code but also more of their environmental experiences for reasons that extend beyond their genetic similarity, relative to DZ twins, then variance attributed to genetics may actually be the result of environmental forces. The concern is that heritability estimates will be inflated while the effect of shared environment will be underestimated if this assumption is violated. Concerns about the EEA must be evaluated in the context of the specific phenotype under study. MZ twins may well have more similar environments than DZ twins in ways that are unrelated to the phenotype or trait of interest in a particular study. Past research has shown that MZ twins are more likely than DZ twins to be dressed alike and share the same bedroom and friends, for example (Kendler, Heath, Martin, & Eaves, 1987, Loehlin & Nichols, 1976). But a serious violation of the EEA would entail those more similar environmental influences accounting for greater co-twin similarity on the specific trait of interest, such as political ideology, knowledge, interest, or participation in politics. Thus, the EEA may be problematic for some traits but not others.

There have been a number of approaches to addressing the EEA. Studies with twins reared apart provide one powerful approach to controlling for possible violations of the EEA. Twins who think of themselves as "identical" or "fraternal" are sometimes mistaken about whether, in fact, they were born from a single fertilized egg that split in two (monozygotic twins) or from two separately fertilized eggs (dizygotic twins). Thus, another approach to testing the EEA analyzes (mis)perceptions of zygosity to determine whether actual or perceived zygosity explains concordance of behavior between twin pairs.

Other approaches involve controls for environmental factors that are plausibly related to the phenotype; studies using this approach have found little evidence that the EEA critique jeopardizes inferences that genetics influence political behavior to date. For example, a study of voter turnout by Fowler, Baker, and Dawes (2008) tested for a number of other factors reflecting more similar environments such as party membership, education levels, personality measures, and some other indicators of socioeconomic status such as housing values but found no evidence that similarity between twin pairs on the likelihood of showing up to vote were explained by similarity of environments in these other ways. Smith Alford, Hatemi, Eaves, Funk, and Hibbing (2012) controlled for both similarity in childhood environment (based on a four-item scale of sharing a bedroom, sharing friends, dressing alike, and being in the same school classrooms) and degree of mutual influence between adult twin pairs (measured by frequency of contact) when estimating the degree of genetic and environmental influence on political ideology. The degree of co-twin similarity in political ideology was not explained solely by these indicators of similarity of environment. Formal tests of both concepts (childhood similarity and mutual influence) as moderators of ACE indicated that estimates of A from studies without such controls are fairly robust. One study has also controlled for the extent of contact between twins when estimating heritability in an extended family design that includes parents and other, nontwin siblings (see Hatemi et al., 2010); incorporating similarity of environment in the SEM models had little substantive impact on estimates of ACE.

A study by Hatemi, Funk, et al. (2009) using a longitudinal design also found little basis for the idea that the EEA accounts for significant effects in the genetic and environmental transmission of political ideology. This analysis found no difference between the degree of MZ and DZ twin pair similarity in political ideology during the adolescent years, when environments should plausibly be most similar. Evidence of genetic influences did not emerge until the young adult years and was linked with leaving the parental home.

It is also possible to derive heritability estimates from other kinds of samples, making reliance on a twin design and concerns about the EEA moot. For example, Visscher and colleagues (2006) derived heritability estimates for height similar to those produced by twin analyses based on genotyping a large sample of nontwin siblings. Data from large samples with the kinds of measures needed to apply these techniques to other phenotypes is not yet available. As more large data sets become available with genetic markers and measures for a wider range of phenotypes, however, reliance on the classic twin design, and therefore concerns about the EEA, may fade.

1.1.3. Assortative Mating

Assortative mating is another assumption of the twin design; in this case the assumption suggests a potential bias in the opposite direction, toward overestimating environmental influences. Assortative mating refers to a tendency to choose mates, such as spouses, that are more similar to the self on the phenotype of interest than would be expected by chance. If mating is not random with regard to the trait of interest—be that height or intelligence or political attitudes and ideology—then variance components estimates will be biased toward underestimating additive genetic influences because the assumption that genetic traits in DZ twin pairs will correlate at .50, on average, is built on the assumption that biological parents will have a zero correlation, on average, for the same traits and these traits are not genetically influenced. If tall men mate with tall women, their offspring will, on average, be taller than the offspring of shorter men who mate with shorter women. In this way, assortative mating tends to increase the genetic variability of a given trait in the population. Assortative mating does not affect the correlations between MZ twins because they are genetically identical. It raises the correlations between DZ twin pairs, however, because of the greater genetic similarity passed on through their parents. Thus, the difference between co-twin correlations for MZ versus DZ twins will be smaller and variance partioning models will underestimate the effect of additive genetics and overestimate the effect of the shared environment. As with the EEA, concerns about assortative mating must be assessed in the context of a specific phenotype of interest. Assortative mating tends to be quite low for personality characteristics and many physical traits; it is substantial for education levels and general levels of cognitive ability, for example. Assortative mating is likely to be a significant concern for political phenotypes. Spousal pairs appear to select mates, in part, for similarity of social and political attitudes; thus, it is important to include the effect of assortative mating in variance partitioning models of ACE (Hatemi et al., 2010; also see Alford, Funk, & Hibbing, 2005; Eaves et al., 1999). Doing so entails including data from parents in addition to twin pairs on the phenotype (or trait) of interest for the study.

1.1.4. *Measurement Error*

Variance estimates of genetic and environmental influences also include some degree of measurement error, of course. In practice, measurement error is inseparable from the residual effect of the unshared environment in many twin study analyses. A few studies have included repeated measures of key concepts that allow model estimates to account for measurement error. In one study on political ideology, Hatemi et al. (2010) showed that controlling for measurement error decreases the estimated variance from the unique environment, as expected, making the relative share of explained variance from additive genetics larger.

1.1.5. *Multivariate Genetic Analysis*

Recent research on political behavior is moving beyond estimates of a single phenotype and looking to the relationships between genetic and environmental factors across a set of related political phenotypes. This approach uses multivariate genetic analysis to estimate the extent to which genetic and environmental factors that affect one trait also affect another trait or set of other traits. One example of this approach has led to the concept of "generalist genes" that affect an array of different learning disabilities (Plomin

& Kovas, 2005). Multivariate genetic analyses sometimes suggest that the same genetic influences affect a range of related phenotypes (as for the class of phenotypes related to cognitive ability) or that the heritability of one variable mediates some or all of the heritability of another variable due to its genetic overlap. Univariate analyses of social and political values show that each of several values have significant genetic and unique environmental influences. A multivariate genetic analysis of these values addresses whether the same genetic and environmental influences underlie each value. In one such test, Funk and colleagues (2012) found that measures of ideology, egalitarianism, right-wing authoritarianism, and an index of social values share common genetic and environmental influences, although they also have unique influences. Thus, the measures cannot be conceptualized as reflecting the same underlying phenotype, but about half of the variance of each measure can be attributed to factors common across the set of values, especially shared genetic influence.

1.2.   Connecting Specific Genes with Phenotypes

Molecular genetic research attempts to identify the specific genes responsible for the heritability of a given phenotype. Genome-wide linkage and association studies take an inductive approach to linking specific genes with phenotypes. The analysis identifies one or more regions of the genome where shared ancestry between relatives correlates with the relative's similarity on a particular phenotype of interest. Such studies are data-driven analyses with large samples designed to generate more specific hypotheses about the linkage between specific genes, or more likely regions of the genome, and phenotypes. Research to date suggests that the heritability of complex traits is often due to small effects on many, not one, gene. With many thousands of genetic markers, this approach helps identify more fruitful areas for further testing. One such study conducted on a large sample of twins from Australia by Hatemi et al. (2011) on political ideology identified four potential linkage regions within which follow-up research can test for genetic loci. Candidate gene studies test whether a particular genetic marker is associated with a specific phenotype. Studies are limited by the genetic markers available in a data set typically developed for applications rather far afield from political behavior research purposes (see Fowler & Dawes, 2008; Fowler, Settle, & Christakis, 2011). And, given the size and complexity of the human genome, it is neither practical nor sound to test an association between genes and phenotypes without a strong theoretical or empirical rationale.

1.3.   Connections with Other Biological Processes

While beyond the scope of this chapter, neuroscientific and psychophysiological techniques for the study of political behavior are also burgeoning across a number of social scientific disciplines. This line of research is important for helping connect the dots between genetics and complex social and political behaviors because most believe that the paths from genes to social and political phenotypes operate through the physiological variations in brain structure and function. Recent research is looking more closely at the biological markers that distinguish self-identified liberals from conservatives. For example, brain responses to situational cues can differ for liberals and conservatives. Amodio and colleagues (2007) tested for an association between self-identity as a liberal or conservative and a neurocognitive index of conflict monitoring, where a mismatch between one's habitual response tendency and the responses required by the current situation results in increased activity in the brain's anterior cingulated cortex region. Liberals were significantly more likely than conservatives to exhibit conflict-related neural activity when response inhibition was required; conservatives were more likely to show a greater persistence in a habitual response pattern, despite situational cues that this response pattern should change. Their findings are consistent with the idea that liberals, relative to conservatives, exhibit a greater openness to new experiences and higher tolerance for ambiguity and complexity.

Other work finds that differences between political sophisticates and novices arise from use of different neural substrates. In a study with college students, those more knowledgeable about politics (and active in either the Young Democrat or Young Republican club) showed increases in their blood oxygen level-dependent functional magnetic resonance imaging above a resting baseline in the premedial parietal cortex region of the brain when answering questions about national politics. By contrast, novices (those with little knowledge about national politics) show a pattern of decreased activation in the same regions. This pattern is consistent with a long line of research in neuroscience showing diminished brain activity when people are engaged in a variety of technical cognitive tasks and suggests that political novices respond to questions about politics as a form of technical cognition (Fowler & Schreiber, 2009; Schreiber, 2007).

Other biomarkers have also been found to distinguish self-identified conservatives from liberals. Oxley and colleagues (2008) found that conservatives are more likely than liberals to exhibit startle reflexes when presented with visual and auditory fear stimuli. And recent research suggests that liberals and conservatives differ in their reaction to and ability to detect odors associated with androstenone (Alford et al., 2011). Thus, involuntary physiological reactions have also been shown to correlate with political ideology. Most researchers in this area expect an indirect link between specific genes and political behavior through biological processes and systems (e.g., Jost, 2009; Smith, Oxley, Hibbing, Alford, & Hibbing, 2011). These lines of research may be useful in identifying the pathway from genes to specific biological processes to political behaviors.

Genetic research related to political phenomena is still in the beginning stages. New developments are occurring at a rapid pace as researchers begin to gather richer data sets from which to test the role of genetics in political behavior and adopt more sophisticated models for estimating the effects of genetic and environmental factors. These more complex statistical models are likely to dominate future research as the field begins to think seriously about how to integrate genetic influences into models of political behavior, but as with other social research, insight from these approaches will also hinge on strong theoretical models that address the mechanisms linking genetic and environmental factors.

2. The Genetic Origins of Political Behavior

Below, I review what we know about the genetic bases of political behavior, including political ideology, partisanship, interest and knowledge about politics, and political participation. Research in this area is starting to accumulate at a rapid pace, but much remains to be done; this includes building-block thinking to catalog and conceptualize which constructs are genetically transmitted to a substantial degree and which are transmitted almost exclusively by environmental factors. This effort requires deeper theoretical understanding about the concepts under study, an area where political psychology is well poised to contribute.

2.1. Political Ideology and Other Value Orientations

Research, to date, shows a substantial genetic component in the transmission of value orientations, particularly, liberal or conservative ideology. A number of twin studies have used the Wilson-Patterson Index of issue positions on a large number of social and political topics to gauge an overall direction of liberal or conservative beliefs. This approach measures ideology in terms of consistency in the direction of issue positions along a liberal-conservative continuum (see Wilson & Patterson, 1968); the scales used in past twin studies have included about 25 to 50 items in order to capture a wide range of issues. All such studies using this index have shown a substantial genetic influence on ideology (roughly 40% to 60% of the variance, with a smaller effect of the shared environment and substantial unique environmental effects); evidence comes from samples of twins from Australia (Martin et al., 1986), twins reared apart (Bouchard et al., 2003), a large-scale sample of twins in the United States conducted in the 1980s (Alford et al., 2005; Eaves et al., 1999), and a more recent survey of US twins (Funk et al., 2012). These findings were replicated with modeling techniques for family-wide correlations (for twin pairs, parents, and nontwin siblings), which accounted for assortative mating and measurement error (Hatemi et al., 2010).

The Wilson-Patterson Index of ideology is not the only way to conceive of and operationalize ideology, of course. Much research in political behavior has relied on a measure of ideology based on self-identification along a liberal or conservative continuum. Such a classification could well be based on a self-assessment of the degree of consistency in one's issue positions—in effect, having the respondent do the work of the Wilson-Patterson Index in one fell swoop—but it could also involve other judgments including group identity with a camp of "liberals" or "conservatives," for example. It is important, then, to test the influence of genetic and environmental influences for other indicators of ideology. Funk and colleagues (2012) tested both the Wilson-Patterson Index of ideology and a self-identification of ideology along a seven-point scale; they found the same pattern of substantial genetic and unique environmental effects and a minimal shared environment effect for both indicators of ideology.

Some scholars also argue that political ideology cannot be properly assessed as a unidimensional construct (see Feldman, chapter 19, this volume). Since the Wilson-Patterson Index involves positions across a wide range of issues of the day, it is also possible to treat subsets of issues as separate factors. Funk and colleagues (2009) conducted an ACE analysis for four subfactors of the Wilson-Patterson Index (representing religion, militarism, rule-breaking, and small government). They found the same general pattern of results, substantial genetic and unique environmental influences, for each of the four subfactors, with roughly 40% of the variance attributed to genetic influence on each subscale.

Genetic factors underlying political ideology are not expressed until young adulthood. Hatemi, Funk, et al. (2009) analyzed a longitudinal sample of US twins in childhood and adolescence along with a cross-sectional sample of adult twins, ages 18 to 60 years and older. They found no evidence of genetic influences on the Wilson-Patterson Index of liberal-conservative ideological orientations until early adulthood. Between the ages of 9 and 17, individual differences in ideological orientations were accounted for by a mix of shared and unique environmental influences; the role of shared environment influences accumulated strongly throughout adolescence. The expression of genetic influences is not shown until early adulthood and intriguingly is associated with leaving the parental home. Twins in the age 21 to 25 birth cohort exhibit genetic influences on political ideology, but this expression is almost solely limited to those who no longer live in the parental home. (Twins of the same age cohort living with their parents exhibit the same pattern seen with younger adolescents of shared and environmental influences.) The sizable genetic influence first expressed in early adulthood remained stable across adults of all ages. These results fit nicely with models of political socialization that emphasize a shift at young adulthood during an "impressionable years" period (Sears, 1983). And they highlight the complex interactions between genes and environmental influences. Shared environmental influences on political ideology, including those from the immediate family, are substantial and increase strongly from early to late adolescence, while genetic influences are substantial but only expressed starting in early adulthood, when a presumably powerful social environment changes.

Interestingly, evidence of genetic influences appears to be weaker when it comes to the strength of ideology, as opposed to the direction of beliefs. Settle, Dawes, and Fowler (2009) report a small effect of additive genetics in explaining individual differences in the extremity of self-identified ideology; they found ideological extremity to be largely explained by unique environmental factors for this small sample of adults twins in the United States who attended a twin "festival." (Extremity of ideology is based on four-point measure created by "folding" ideological self-placement at the midpoint, thus ranging from moderate to either very liberal or very conservative.) Funk Smith, Alford, and Hibbing (2010) also found a weaker, though still significant, genetic influence on extremity of self-identified ideology, relative to the pattern found for direction of ideological positions on the Wilson-Patterson Index. Their study also used a folded measure of self-identification of ideology among a sample of about 1,200 adult twins in the United States.

2.1.1. *Mechanisms Connecting Genes and Ideology*

A handful of studies have begun to identify specific genes or gene-environment interactions influencing political ideology. Hatemi et al. (2011) conducted the first genomewide linkage analysis of liberal-conservative ideological orientations, a method that can help identify likely regions of the genome for further research. They found four specific chromosomal regions that appear to be strongly linked to political orientations in a large sample of Australian twins and their family members. The data suggest a need for more research about the role of glutamate, specifically the NMDA glutamate receptor, in political ideology. Glutamate is a neurotransmitter known to be important for learning and memory. NMDA is linked to cognitive performance, including information processing, organization, capacity for abstract thought, and could be related to cognitive flexibility or openness to new ideas, which Jost, Glaser, Kruglanski, and Sulloway (2003) hypothesized is linked to political ideology.

A few studies have tested whether specific genes are associated with political phenotypes. Settle, Dawes, Christakis, and Fowler (2010) conducted genetic allele association tests on a representative sample of adolescents and young adults in the United States. They focused on the 7R variant of the dopamine receptor D4 gene, a gene associated with risk-taking and novelty-seeking. Importantly, they also test whether the social context interacts with this dopamine receptor gene to influence political ideology. They find that teenagers who report larger social networks *and* have the DRD4 7R variant are more likely to self-identify as liberals (about six years later) than do those without this gene or with smaller social networks during their teenage years. A related study suggests that social networks are correlated with particular genotypes (Fowler et al., 2011). Social friendship groups show clustering on the dopamine receptor D2 (DRD2) genotype, while a negative correlation was found between social networks and the CYP2A6 genotype (another gene that has been associated with openness). Thus, resemblance among friends on phenotypes such as political ideology may stem from a complex mix of factors, including an active choice of friends with genotypic similarities or differences. The pattern suggests an interaction between genes and the environment whereby an individual's genetic makeup creates a propensity to seek out environmental circumstances that are compatible with his or her genetic makeup.

2.1.2. *Other Values: Authoritarianism, Social Orientations, Egalitarianism*

Ideology is often treated as an underlying value orientation or core predisposition that, in turn, serves as an antecedent for attitudes and beliefs on political issues. Scholars diverge over how best to conceptualize values and which deep-seated core beliefs are important for structuring issue attitudes (for a review see Feldman, chapter 19, this volume). Other scholars eschew an emphasis on values as core predispositions and focus, instead, on personality traits as important precursors to political attitudes. The line between values and personality traits is sometimes blurry, as with concepts such as right-wing authoritarianism (Altemeyer, 1996) and social dominance orientation (Sidanius & Pratto, 1999; Pratto, Sidanius, Stallworth, & Mall, 1994). Regardless of the conceptual label used, most seem to agree that predispositions based on constructs that reach beyond a narrow political domain structure political orientations and political attitudes. It is important to test for the influence of genetic and environmental influences across a wide range of related constructs, beyond the Wilson-Patterson Index of ideology. There have been limited measures to do so until quite recently.

McCourt, Bouchard, Lykken, Tellegan, and Keyes (1999) found a substantial role for genetics in an analysis of twins reared apart on Altemeyer's right-wing authoritarianism scale. Their findings were consistent with an adoption study by Scarr and Weinberg (1981) using the F-scale. And a recent US twin study replicated these findings using a variant of the authoritarianism scale (Funk et al., 2012).

Smith et al. (2011) hypothesized that individual dispositions toward social rules, order, and behavioral conduct are the psychological foundation for political ideology. They developed a measure to capture these deep-seated social orientations called the Society Works Best Index. In a first test of this measure, results support the idea that there is a sizable genetic component of social orientations (Funk et al., 2012). The same study also found a sizable genetic influence on a multi-item index of egalitarianism— a concept thought to reflect deep-seated orientations about the procedures by which goods are distributed in society or the outcomes of that process (see Feldman, 1988; Feldman & Steenbergen, 2001). Across the five measures of value orientations in the Funk et al. study, the results supported a sizable influence of both genetic and unique environmental influences, with a smaller effect from the shared environment.

Kandler, Bleidorn, and Riemann (2011), using a sample of twins and their family members in Germany, analyzed genetic and environmental influences on value orientations of support for social equality versus inequality, and support for system change versus stability. This extended twin family design allowed controls for assortative mating, which as mentioned earlier tends to be weak for personality traits but more sizable for political orientations. Kandler et al. found sizable genetic influences, particularly in orientations toward system change.

One common framework for thinking about personality uses the Big Five (or five-factor model) of personality traits (McCrae & Costa, 2003). The dimensions of the Big Five are openness to experience, conscientiousness, extraversion, agreeableness, and emotional stability. A number of studies have investigated the influence of the Big Five on political ideology; these findings suggest that openness to experience predicts a liberal ideology, while conscientiousness predicts a conservative ideology (see Caprara and Vecchione, chapter 2, this volume; Carney, Jost, Gosling, & Potter, 2008; Gerber, Huber, Doherty, Dowling, & Ha, 2010; Mondak, 2010). A number of behavioral genetic studies have included measures of the Big Five over the years, and these consistently find that personality traits are strongly heritable (explaining about 40% to 60% of the variance) (see, e.g., Bouchard & Loehlin, 2001; Jang, McCrae, Angleitner, Riemann, & Livesley, 1998; Kandler et al., 2010; Loehlin, 1992; Loehlin, McCrae, Costa, & John, 1998). Other research using adult twin data collected in Germany over three time points spanning 13 years allows attention to more complex models of interaction between genes and environmental forces in personality traits over the life span (Bleidorn et al., 2010; Kandler et al., 2010). They found stability of personality traits to be largely explained by genetic influences, possibly through experiences resulting from genotype-environment correlations where individuals select social environments that are correlated with their personality traits, which in turn lead to experiences that affect personality. Thus, their findings suggest a complex interplay between genes and environmental factors on personality over the life course.

2.2. Party Affiliation and Strength of Partisanship

A handful of studies have tested the heritability of partisan affiliations, with the pattern of findings dependent on the specific construct examined. Analysis of the Virginia 30K twins in the United States from the 1980s finds a relatively low heritability coefficient for identification with a political party[2] and a much larger role for shared environmental factors (Alford et al., 2005; Hatemi, Alford, Hibbing, Martin, & Eaves, 2009). A study of Australian twins by Hatemi, Medland, Morley, Heath, and Martin (2007) also found a small additive genetic effect for partisanship and a larger effect for shared environmental factors in an analysis of whether respondents "think of themselves" as belonging to the Labor Party or to one of the more conservative parties in Australia (i.e., the Conservative, Liberal, or National party).[3] More recent twin samples in the United States suggest a more substantial role for genetic influence, however. Funk et al. (2010) found that both genetic and unique environmental factors explain the lion's share of variance in party identification, with a minimal role of the shared environment. Using a small sample of twins attending a twin festival in the United States, Settle et al. (2009) found genetic, shared environment and unique environmental effects to explain roughly equal portions of the variance in party identification. Thus, the role of genetic and environmental factors in explaining the direction of partisan affiliation in the United States remains under some debate, and very little research has explored these patterns in other party systems.

A study by Dawes and Fowler (2009) suggests that the likelihood of forming a political attachment is influenced by genetic factors, regardless of the pattern of effects in the direction of partisanship. They used genetic allele association tests on a representative sample of adolescents and young adults in the United States and found an association between the DRD2 dopamine receptor gene and the likelihood of identifying with either political party (regardless of direction). The dopamine neurotransmitter system is associated with a number of different regulatory functions (including control of movement, cognition, mood, and reward-driven learning); the D2 receptor has been associated with differences in cognitive functioning and the formation of social attachments. Those with two A2 alleles of the DRD2 were more likely to identify with a party than those with either one or no A2 alleles, a pattern that holds for both Democrats and Republicans. These results raise new questions about the correlation between parent and child party affiliation. While the tendency for offspring to attach to the same political party as their parents has often been interpreted in terms of parental transmission of party attachment that is reinforced over time, it is also possible that the tendency to affiliate or attach to a political party stems from inheritance of a specific gene form of the DRD2.

Studies looking at the strength of partisanship find a sizable role of genetic and unique environmental factors. Using a "folded" measure of partisanship, Settle et al. (2009) found a sizable role for genetic and unique environmental factors in explaining the strength of partisanship.[4] Similarly, Hatemi, Alford, et al. (2009) found the probability of holding a strong party affiliation (as opposed to no tie or to a weak party tie) was explained by a combination of genetic and unique environmental factors with little influence of the shared environment.[5]

One way to conceive of partisanship is through the lens of group affiliation. Alford et al. (2005) reported a sizable heritable component of affect toward the Republican and Democratic parties in the United States. About 30% of the variance in relative liking for Republicans and Democrats was explained by genetic factors, with the lion's share of the remaining variance explained by unique environmental factors. Thus, whether the construct concerns the direction of party affiliation or the likelihood of identifying with a party, or the strength of that identity or favoritism for one's own party (and hostility to another party), each may show a different pattern of genetic and environmental effects and potentially different underlying mechanisms linking genes to partisanship.

A number of studies have tested the genetic and environmental transmission of religious affiliation and religiosity (for a review see Funk, 2011). More broadly, a couple of recent studies have begun to test the genetic underpinnings of in-group favoritism and out-group hostility. Lewis and Bates (2010) tested the genetic and environmental factors underlying in-group favoritism for religious, ethnic, and racial groups. Univariate analyses suggest a substantial role of genetic and unique environmental factors with a small shared environmental effect. Multivariate analyses support a mixed model with both common factors under a central affiliation mechanism and influences that are unique to each type of group affiliation. Other research suggests that the underlying processes may vary when it comes to out-group hostility. Univariate analyses based on a sample of white US twins by Civettini and Miller (2011) found that out-group attitudes toward African Americans, Hispanics, and Asian Americans are explained by genetic and unique environmental factors, with little role for the shared environment. Affect toward the in-group (whites), by contrast, was explained largely by unique environmental factors, with a small effect from shared environmental factors, and essentially no role for genetic factors. Thus, the role of genetic influences appears to be quite different for in-group as compared with out-group attitudes. This distinction is in line with other studies on in-group and out-group processes (see Huddy, chapter 23, this volume). This line of research may lend insight into political and other group identities as well.

2.3. Political Knowledge, Interest in Politics, and Efficacy

A handful of studies are turning to other political concepts, including political knowledge, sophistication or expertise, interest in politics, and beliefs about internal efficacy. In a first test of these concepts, Funk et al. (2010) found a substantial role for genetics in a five-item index of general knowledge about politics. About half of the variance in a sample of US twins was explained by additive genetics, with the remainder explained by the unique environment (and essentially no role for shared environmental factors). These findings are consistent with an independent analysis using the same data by Arceneaux, Johnson, and Maes (2011); bivariate analyses also suggest that the same genetic factors influence or predispose individuals toward both political knowledge and educational attainment.

A similar, though somewhat weaker, pattern emerges for self-reported interest in politics and beliefs about political efficacy. Univariate analyses of interest in politics find about 40% of the variance explained by additive genetic factors, with the remainder attributed to the unique environment and essentially no role for shared environmental influences (Funk et al., 2010; Arceneaux et al., 2011). Klemmensen and colleagues (2011) also find a sizable role for genetic factors, using slightly different measures of political interest, in a sample of Danish twins. Their analyses also suggest an AE pattern whereby the variance is split between genetic and unique environmental factors and the shared environment explains essentially none of the variance. Bivariate analyses between political interest and political efficacy suggest a common latent genetic factor.

2.4. Voter Turnout and Political Participation

Genetic research is also aimed at understanding the potential role of genetic and environmental forces on citizen participation. Research, to date, finds a substantial role for genetics in voter turnout and other forms of citizen participation; current thinking hypothesizes an indirect linkage between genes and participation, but many questions remain about the nature of those mediators and the mechanisms at work.

Fowler et al. (2008) showed that habitual voter turnout is associated with genetic factors. In their analysis of twins from Los Angeles, they found roughly half (53%) of the variance in turnout across eight local county, primary, and statewide elections can be attributed to additive genetic factors; about 35% is attributed to shared environment, and a small portion (12%) is attributed to unique environment. One of the key strengths of their study stems from the use of validated turnout data for registered voters, rather than self-reports of voting.

They replicated this result for self-reported turnout in a single election and for an index of participation with a representative sample of young adults in the United States. For both behaviors, they found a strong role for genetic factors. Fully 72% of the variance in turnout was attributed to additive genetic factors, and 60% of the variance in political participation was attributed to genetics. They found a smaller role for shared relative to unique environmental influences.

One interpretation of these findings centers on an indirect role of genetics through an association with broader prosocial tendencies. Rather than expecting to identify a "gene for voting," Fowler, Dawes, and colleagues speculate that the set of genes whose expression, in combination with environmental factors, regulate political participation are likely related to social behaviors more generally. Two studies seek to identify the specific mechanism involved.

Dawes and Fowler (2009) tested whether the dopamine D2 receptor gene (DRD2) mediates the relationship between identification with a political party (regardless of direction) and voter turnout. They estimate the direct and indirect effects of DRD2 on voter turnout among this sample of young adults in the United States using a bootstrapping technique. Their results suggest an indirect effect of DRD2 on voting through its effect on the likelihood of identifying with a political party; there was no direct effect between this gene and the likelihood of voter turnout.

Another genetic association study by Fowler and Dawes (2008) looked at the relationship between the MAOA and 5HTT genes, both associated with the metabolism of serotonin in the brain. The serotonin neurotransmitter system is associated with a large number of social behaviors (including the regulation of mood, appetite, memory, and learning); in other studies, 5HTT and MAOA have been associated with antisocial behavior in response to social stressors. Fowler and Dawes hypothesize that the social stress of a preferred candidate potentially losing an election will decrease the odds that individuals with a genetic makeup that makes them particularly sensitive to social conflict will vote. (Conversely, those having either the long version of the 5HTT gene or high version of the MAOA polymorphism are hypothesized as more likely to turn out.) The analysis of this representative sample of young adults in the United States found a small direct effect of the MAOA on self-reported turnout in the most recent presidential election and a larger indirect effect between the 5HTT and turnout through an association with religious involvement. The probability of voting was greater only among those with a particular allele form of the 5HTT (the long form) who also attended religious services more frequently. Interestingly, the interaction effect seemed to account for the direct relationship found between church attendance and turnout. Their findings suggest a heretofore unexplored mechanism linking religious observance with voter behavior. The authors speculate that religious observance and political activity share a willingness and interest in affiliating or attaching with a social group, which may account for the interactive effect.

Others have focused on the possibility of an indirect relationship between genetic factors and political participation through personality tendencies. A number of studies have found a strong association between personality and political participation. Denny and Doyle (2008) report that personality characteristics of being aggressive, hard-working, and even-tempered are related to voter turnout in Britain, even after controlling for a host of other factors. Mondak and Halperin (2008) tested the relationship between the Big Five personality factors and a large set of political attitudes and behaviors in the United States. In addition to associations between personality attributes (especially openness to experience and conscientiousness) and partisanship, ideological orientations and political attitudes, they found traits of openness and extroversion related to the frequency of engaging in political discussions and the likelihood of holding opinions on a range of political topics. Elsewhere, Mondak, and colleagues (2011) found openness to experience and extroversion related to political participation in Uruguay and Venezuela; conscientiousness predicted participation in political protests.

A role for genetics in personality is well established in the behavioral genetics literature (Bouchard & McGue, 2003; Bouchard & Loehlin, 2001; Eaves et al., 1989; Loehlin, 1992; Pedersen, Plomin, McClearn, & Friberg, 1988; Tellegen et al., 1988). Past studies have estimated that about 40% to 60% of the variance for key personality attributes such as the Big Five is due to additive genetic factors; notably, there is little evidence of assortative mating effects in personality. Given the known role of genetics in personality, research on the correlation between personality and participation speaks to a potential mediating role for personality attributes in connecting genes with participation and engagement in democratic politics. New research is now turning to this question. Findings from one such study conducted with a sample of twins and their family members in Germany suggest that some of the similarity between parents and their offspring in political attitudes can be accounted for by shared genetic variance in personality traits. This study is consistent with multivariate genetic analyses on US twins, showing that the Big Five personality traits are largely distinct from value orientations such as political ideology (Funk et al., 2009). Further research looking at the potential mediating role of personality in political attitudes and behavior using twin data collected in the United States and Australia is likely to be available soon.

Other behaviors relevant to citizen participation in democracy. A growing body of research is aimed at testing the degree of genetic transmission and neurological correlates of other behaviors relevant to participation, including helping behavior, altruism, cooperation, trust, and risk-taking. The findings are varied. Rushton Fulker, Neale, Nias, Eysenck (1986) report a sizable role of genetics in explaining self-reported helping behaviors. Other studies (Koenig, McGue, Krueger, & Bouchard, 2007; Rushton, 2004) report a smaller genetic effect on self-reported helping behaviors in a sample of male twins; the genetic effects were shared with those explaining religiousness.

Recent research using public choice games has tested the role of genetic and environmental factors in behavior using samples of twins from both Sweden and the United States. Cesarini et al. (2008) found a modest role of genetic influences on behavioral indicators of trust in a public choice game. The same authors also found a modest role of genetic influences in giving and risk-taking behavior in the context of public choice games (Cesarini, Dawes, Johannesson, Lichtenstein, & Wallace, 2009). A larger role for genetic factors explained individual differences in rejecting offers in an ultimatum game; there was little evidence of shared environmental influences in explaining ulti-matum game behavior (Wallace, Cesarini, Lichtenstein, & Johannesson, 2007). This line of research is just starting to be developed, with more research using twins in economic games along with hypothetical versions of such games in the United States and Australia likely to be in the research literature soon.

3. CONNECTING GENETIC AND ENVIRONMENTAL INFLUENCES

The idea that genetic factors could (and do) account for some of the individual differ-ences in intelligence or cognitive abilities, psychiatric diseases such as schizophrenia, and personality is widely accepted (e.g., Bouchard & McGue, 2003; Eaves et al., 1989). The same idea when applied to social and political attitudes has long been considered counterintuitive. Fully accepting the empirical evidence that these kinds of political phenotypes are, in part, stemming from genetic factors will require an adjustment to our assumptions and models about the development of political behavior. But few expect these influences to operate as either/or phenomena. The key intellectual questions focus on a gene-environment interaction.

And we cannot simply stop at the idea that a complex interaction of genes and the environment underlies political behavior (see Maccoby, 2000); we need to be much more specific about the nature of the interaction, the environments, and the genes in order to gain any leverage in understanding. There are a number of ways in which genes and the environment are thought to interact. Three primary models of a gene-environment (GE) correlation are an active, passive, and a reactive or evocative GE cor-relation (see Bouchard, 1997; Loehlin, 2010; Plomin et al., 2008; Plomin, DeFries, & Loehlin, 1977).

An active GE correlation includes what Bouchard called experience-producing drives (1997), whereby those with a genetic predisposition or motivation tend to seek out and experience particular behaviors and environments that, in turn, influence phenotypic expression. One example consists of a genetic predisposition for sensation-seeking whereby high sensation-seeking individuals are more likely to engage in different activi-ties than lower sensation-seeking people; their peer groups are also likely to differ on these dimensions, as will their reactions to their experiences and environments. Along these lines, Eaves et al. (1999) suggest that small initial genetic differences may encour-age people to seek out particular kinds of experiences; these, in turn, are "augmented over time by the incorporation into the phenotype of environmental information, corre-lated with the genotype, in a continual process of sifting and evaluation" (p. 79); also see Scarr & McCartney, 1983). A similar idea extends to political environments. Individuals select social environments (such as friend groups and spouses) that are correlated with their political orientations, and these selection processes in turn lead to experiences that influence political attitudes and orientations. Thus, the underlying process connecting genetic factors to differences in adult attitudes may operate through iterative behavioral preferences that indirectly reflect their genes.

A passive model of GE argues that parents simultaneously influence the genetic and environmental experiences of their children by providing their children with genes conducive to particular phenotypes and also with environments that may foster the expression of genetic tendencies. The study by Dawes and Fowler (2009) evokes this kind of model as one possible interpretation of their findings. An offspring's tendency to affiliate with a political party may stem from an inherited gene form that predisposes the individual to affiliate with groups and a family or other social environment that encourages group affiliation in the political domain.

An evocative interaction stems from the tendency for others to respond differently to individuals depending on their characteristics such as physical attributes, personality tendencies, or abilities and deficits in abilities. Thus, genetic predispositions tend to evoke reactions and environmental experiences that foster gene expression.

Beyond these three types of GE correlations, there is also a host of ways to think about "the environment," ranging form prenatal environments, to parent and sibling environments, to peers and other environments outside the family. Thus, identifying the mechanisms underlying GE correlation is highly complex, requiring a strong theoretical rationale to help identify the most fruitful avenues for research.

The genetic underpinnings of political behavior are an exciting frontier for political behavior research. Empirical findings are now amassing at a rapid pace as new data sources become available and increasingly sophisticated modeling techniques are being applied to the study of political behavior. The growth of research in this area highlights the critical and ongoing need for better theoretical models and conceptual clarity about the findings to date and the likely mechanisms that link genes and behavior. This is a need that political psychology is particularly well suited to address with its strong grounding in psychological theory-building and its tradition of multidisciplinary research.

Research on the heritability of ideology and other values, partisanship, political interest and knowledge about politics, and participation makes it clear the role of genetics in political behavior varies depending on the construct. For example, the degree to which genetic factors influence attitude positions ranges along a continuum. These differences are consequential; attitudes higher in heritability tend to be expressed more quickly, are more resistant to social conformity pressures, and are more influential in social reactions. A number of studies have shown a sizable role for genetic (and unique environmental) factors in ideological orientations along a liberal-conservative continuum. The relative contribution of genetic factors is much more varied when looking across constructs such as party affiliation. And it even varies when considering the direction of beliefs as opposed to the intensity or strength of beliefs. These findings challenge researchers to think more clearly about the differences among these constructs and to ground further explorations in theoretical expectations about which constructs are likely to be strongly and weakly transmitted through genetic factors.

Several researchers have speculated about an indirect relationship between genes and attitude positions through value orientations, partisan and other group identifications, intelligence, personality temperaments, or specific biochemical differences in behavioral reactions. Much work remains to thoroughly test these potential mediating factors.

Genetic association studies that can link specific genes to specific opinions and behaviors are promising, especially where other known correlates of the genetic allele can help point the way to specifying the mechanisms at work. Some researchers have begun down this path, but much more work of this sort is needed. Similarly, neuroscientific methods for studying social behavior are allowing new linkages to be drawn between genes and neurological processes with the expression, formation, and modification of attitudes. The challenge ahead is twofold: first, to select areas of study that are theoretically grounded and thus hold the most promise, and, second, to fully integrate the findings across these different techniques into our theoretical models and understanding of political behavior.

NOTES

1. It is also possible for the effects of alleles to vary depending on the presence of other alleles. These interactive effects are called nonadditive genetic influences. Nonadditive genetic effects might be present if there is evidence of a genetic effect that does not tend to run in families, such as that observed when DZ twin pairs are not similar on a characteristic while MZ pairs are highly similar. Models partioning the variance of genetic and environmental influences can include either additive genetic influences or nonadditive genetic effects.
2. Party identification is based on a five-point measure with those not able or not willing to make a choice on the scale omitted from the analysis.
3. The authors treat this measure as reflecting vote choice.
4. Partisan identification is based on a seven-point scale that ranges from strong Democrat to strong Republican. Strength of partisanship is based on four-point scale that "folds" identification at the midpoint, with independents at one end of the scale and strong partisans at the other end.
5. The party identification question asked on the Virginia 30K twin survey is different from that on other surveys. The question stem asks for party affiliation; the response options combine a party label with a frequency of support for the party. Nonpartisans are classified as those selecting the midpoint on the scale. Those answering "some other party" and "prefer not to answer" or not answering are omitted from analyses.

REFERENCES

Alford, J. R., Funk, C. L., & Hibbing, J. R. (2005). Are political orientations genetically transmitted? *American Political Science Review, 99*, 153–168.

Alford, J. R., Smith, K. B., Balzer, A. J., Gruszczynski, M. W., Jacobs, C. M., & Hibbing, J. R. (2011). Political orientations may be related to detection of the odor of Androstenone. Paper presented at the Annual Meetings of the Midwest Political Science Association, Chicago, IL. March 31–April 3.

Altemeyer, B. (1996). *The authoritarian specter*. Cambridge, MA: Harvard University Press.

Amodio, D. M., Jost, J. T., Masters, S. L., & Lee, C. M. (2007). Neurocognitive correlates of liberalism and conservatism. *Nature Neuroscience, 10*, 1246–1247.

Arceneaux, K., Johnson, M., & Maes, H. H. (2011). The genetic basis of political sophistication. Paper presented at the Annual Meetings of the Midwest Political Science Association, Chicago, IL, March 31–April 3.

Bleidorn, W., Kandler, C., Hulsheger, U. R., Riemann, R., Angleitner, A., & Spinath, F. M. (2010). Nature and nuture of the interplay between personality traits and major life goals. *Journal of Personality and Social Psychology, 99*, 366–379.

Bouchard, T. J. (1997). Experience producing drive theory: How genes drive experience and shape personality. *Acta Paediatrica Supplement, 422*, 60–64.

Bouchard, T. J., Jr., & Loehlin, J. C. (2001). Genes, evolution, and personality. *Behavior Genetics, 31*, 243–273.

Bouchard, T. J., Jr., & McGue, M. (2003). Genetic and environmental influences on human psychological differences. *Journal of Neurobiology, 54*, 4–45.

Bouchard, T. J., Jr., Segal, N. L., Tellegen, A., McGue, M., Keyes, M., & Krueger, R. (2003). Evidence for the construct validity and heritability of the Wilson-Patterson conservatism scale: A reared-apart twins study of social attitudes. *Personality and Individual Differences, 34*, 959–969.

Carney, D. R., Jost, J. T., Gosling, S. L., & Potter, J. (2008). The secret lives of liberals and conservatives: Personality profiles, interaction styles, and the things they leave behind. *Political Psychology, 29*, 807–840.

Cesarini, D., Dawes, C. T., Fowler, J. H., Johannesson, M., Lichtenstein, P., & Wallace, B. (2008). Heritability of cooperative behavior in the trust game. *Proceedings of the National Academy of Sciences, 105*, 3721–3726.

Cesarini, D., Dawes, C. T., Johannesson, M., Lichtenstein, P., & Wallace, B. (2009). Genetic variation in preferences for giving and risk taking. *Quarterly Journal of Economics, 124*, 809–824.

Civettini, A. J. W., & Miller, B. (2011). Genetic and environmental influences on in-group and out-group attitudes. Paper presented at the Annual Meetings of the Midwestern Political Science Association, Chicago, IL, March 31–April 3.

Dawes, C. T., & Fowler, J. H. (2009). Partisanship, voting, and the dopamine D2 receptor gene. *Journal of Politics, 71*, 1157–1171.

Denny, K., & Doyle, O. (2008). Political interest, cognitive ability and personality: determinants of voter turnout in Britain. *British Journal of Political Science, 38*, 291–310.

Eaves, L. J., Eysenck, H. J., & Martin, N. G. (1989). *Genes, culture and personality: An empirical approach*. London: Academic Press.

Eaves, L. J., Heath, A. C., Martin, N. G., Maes, H. H., Neale, M. C., Kendler, K. S., Kirk, K. M., & Corey, L. (1999). Comparing the biological and cultural inheritance of personality and social attitudes in the Virginia 30,000 study of twins and their relatives. *Twin Research, 2* (June), 62–80.

Feldman, S. (1988). Structure and consistency in public opinion: The role of core beliefs and values. *American Journal of Political Science, 31*, 416–440.

Feldman, S., & Steenbergen, M. (2001). The humanitarian foundation of public support for social welfare. *American Journal of Political Science, 45*, 658–677.

Fowler, J. H., Baker, L. A., & Dawes, C. T. (2008). The genetic basis of political participation. *American Political Science Review, 102* (2), 233–248.

Fowler, J. H., & Dawes, C. T. (2008). Two genes predict voter turnout. *Journal of Politics, 70* (3), 579–594.

Fowler, J. H., & Schreiber, D. (2009). Biology, politics, and the emerging science of human nature. *Science, 322,* 912–914.

Fowler, J. H., Settle, J. E., & Christakis, N. A. (2011). Correlated genotypes in friendship networks. *PNAS, 108*(5), 1993–1997.

Funk, C. (2011). Connecting the social and biological bases of public opinion. In R. Y. Shapiro and L. R. Jacobs (eds.), *The Oxford Handbook of American Public Opinion and Media* (pp. 416–435). Oxford University Press.

Funk, C. L., Smith, K. B., Alford, J. R., & Hibbing, J. R. (2010). Toward a modern view of political man: Genetic and environmental transmission of political orientations from attitude intensity to political participation. Paper presented at the Annual Meetings of the American Political Science Association, Washington, DC, September 2–5.

Funk, C. L., Smith, K., Alford, J. R., Hibbing, M., Hatemi, P. K., Krueger, R. F., Eaves, L. J., & Hibbing, J. R. (2009). Genetic and environmental transmission of value orientations: A new twin study of political attitudes. Paper presented at the Annual Meetings of the American Political Science Association, Toronto, Canada, September 3–6.

Funk, C. L., Smith, K. B., Alford, J. R., Hibbing, M. V., Eaton, N. R., Krueger, R. F., Eaves, L. J., & Hibbing, J. R. (2012). Genetic and environmental transmission of political orientations. *Political Psychology.* doi: 10.1111/j.1467-9221.2012.00915.x

Gerber, A. S., Huber, G. A., Doherty, D., Dowling, C. M., & Ha, S. E. (2010). Personality and political attitudes: Relationships across issue domains and political contexts. *American Political Science Review, 104,* 111–133.

Hatemi, P. K., Alford, J. R., Hibbing, J. R., Martin, N. G., & Eaves, L. J. (2009). Is there a party in your genes? *Political Research Quarterly, 62,* 584–600.

Hatemi, P. K., Funk, C. L., Medland, S., Maes, H. M., Silberg, J. L., Martin, N. G., & Eaves, L. J. (2009). Genetic and environmental transmission of political attitudes over a life time. *Journal of Politics, 71,* 1141–1156.

Hatemi, P. K., Gillespie, N. A., Eaves, L. J., Maher, B. S., Webb, B. T., Heath, A. C., Medland, S. E., Smyth, D. C., Beeby, H. N., Gordon, S. D., Montgomery, G. W., Zhu, G., Byrne, E. M., & Martin, N. G. (2011). A genome-wide marker analysis of liberal and conservative political attitudes. *Journal of Politics, 73,* 271–285.

Hatemi, P. K., Hibbing, J. R., Medland, S. E., Keller, M. C., Alford, J. R., Smith, K. B., Martin, N. G., & Eaves, L. J. (2010). Not by twins alone: Using the extended family design to investigate genetic influence on political beliefs. *American Journal of Political Science, 54,* 798–814.

Hatemi, P. K., Medland, S. E., Morley, K. I., Heath, A. C., & Martin, N. G. (2007). The genetics of voting: An Australian twin wtudy. *Behavior Genetics, 37*(3), 435–448.

Jang, K. L., McCrae, R. R., Angleitner, A., Riemann, R., & Livesley, W. J. (1998). Heritability of facet-level traits in a cross-cultural twin sample: Support for a hierarchical model of personality. *Journal of Personality and Social Psychology, 74,* 1556–1565.

Jost, J. T. (2009). "Elective affinities": On the psychological bases of left-right differences. *Psychological Inquiry, 20,* 129–141.

Jost, J. T., Glaser, J., Kruglanski, A. W., & Sulloway, F. J. (2003). Political conservatism as motivated social cognition. *Psychological Bulletin, 129,* 339–375.

Kandler, C., Bleidorn, W., & Riemann, R. (2011). Left or right? Sources of political orientation: The roles of genetic factors, cultural transmission, assortative mating, and personality. *Journal of Personality and Social Psychology.* doi:10.1037/a0025560

Kandler, C., Bleidorn, W., Riemann, R., Spinath, F. M., Thiel, W., & Angleitner, A. (2010). Sources of cumulative continuity in personality: A longitudinal multiple-rater twin study. *Journal of Personality and Social Psychology, 98*, 995–1008.

Kendler, K. S., Heath, A. C., Martin, N. G., & Eaves, L. J. (1987). Symptoms of anxiety and symptoms of depression: Same genes, different environments? *Archives of General Psychiatry, 44*, 451–457.

Klemmensen, R. K., Hatemi, P. K., Hobolt, S. B., Dinesen, P. T., Skytthe, A., & Norgaard, A. S. (2011). Heritability in political interest and efficacy across cultures: Denmark and the United States. Annual Meetings of the Midwest Political Science Association, Chicago, IL. March 31–April 3, 2011.

Koenig, L. B., McGue, M., Krueger, R. F., & Bouchard, T. J., Jr. (2007). Religiousness, antisocial behavior, and altruism: Genetic and environmental mediation. *Journal of Personality, 75*(2), 265–290.

Lewis, G. J., & Bates, T. C. (2010). Genetic evidence for multiple biological mechanisms underlying in-group favoritism. *Psychological Science, 21*(11), 1623–1628.

Loehlin, J. C. (1992). *Genes and environment in personality development.* Newbury Park, CA: Sage.

Loehlin, J. C. (2010). Environment and the behavior genetics of personality: Let me count the ways. *Personality and Individual Differences, 49*, 302–305.

Loehlin, J. C., McCrae, R. R., Costa, P. T., Jr., & John, O. P. (1998). Heritabilities of common and measures-specific components of the Big Five personality factors. *Journal of Research in Personality, 32*, 431–453.

Loehlin, J. C., & Nichols, R. C. (1976). *Heredity, environment, and personality.* Austin: University of Texas Press.

Maccoby, E. E. (2000). Parenting and its effects on children: On reading and misreading behavior genetics. *Annual Review of Psychology, 51*, 1–27.

Martin, N. G., Eaves, L. J., Heath, A. C., Jardine, R., Feingold, L. M., & Eysenck, H. J. (1986). Transmission of social attitudes. *Proceedings of the National Academy of Sciences, 15*, 4364–4368.

McCourt, K., Bouchard, T. J., Jr., Lykken, D. T., Tellegan, A., & Keyes, M. (1999). Authoritarianism revisited: Genetic and environmental influence examined in twins reared apart and together. *Personality and Individual Differences, 27*, 985–1014.

McCrae, R. R., & Costa, P. T., Jr. (2003). *Personality in adulthood: A five-factor theory perspective* (2nd ed.). New York: Guilford Press.

Medland, S., & Hatemi, P. (2009). Political science, biometric theory, and twin studies: A methodological introduction. *Political Analysis, 17*, 191–214.

Mondak, J. J. (2010). *Personality and the foundations of political behavior.* New York: Cambridge University Press.

Mondak, J. J., Canache, D., Seligson, M. A., & Hibbing, M. V. (2011). The participatory personality: Evidence from Latin America. *British Journal of Political Science, 41*, 211–221.

Mondak, J. J., & Halperin, K. D. (2008). A framework for the study of personality and political behavior. *British Journal of Political Science, 38*, 335–362.

Olson, J. M., Vernon, P. A., Harris, J. A., & Lang, K. L. (2001). The heritability of attitudes: A study of twins. *Journal of Personality and Social Psychology, 80*, 845–860.

Oxley, D. R., Smith, K. B., Alford, J. R., Hibbing, M. V., Miller, J. L., Scalora, M., Hatemi, P. K., & Hibbing, J. R. (2008). Political attitudes vary with physiological traits. *Science, 321*, 1167–1170.

Pedersen, N. L., Plomin, R., McClearn, G. E., & Friberg, L. (1988). Neuroticism and extraversion, and related traits in adult twins reared apart and reared together. *Journal of Personality and Social Psychology, 55*, 950–957.

Plomin, R., DeFries, J. C., & Loehlin, J. C. (1977). Genotype-environment interaction and correlation in the analysis of human behaviour. *Psychological Bulletin, 84*, 309–322.

Plomin, R., DeFries, J. C., McClearn, G. E., & McGuffin, P. (2008). *Behavioral genetics* (5th ed.). New York: Worth.

Plomin, R., & Kovas, Y. (2005). Generalist genes and learning disabilities. *Psychological Bulletin, 131*(4), 592–617.

Pratto, F., Sidanius, J., Stallworth, L. M., & Malle, B. F. (1994). Social dominance orientation: A personality variable relevant to social roles and intergroup relations. *Journal of Personality and Social Psychology, 67*, 741–763.

Rushton, J. P. (2004). Genetic and environmental contributions to pro-social attitudes: A twin study of social responsibility. *Proceedings of the Royal Society, 271*, 2583–2585.

Rushton, J. P., Fulker, D. W., Neale, M. C., Nias, D. K. B., & Eysenck, H. J. (1986). Altruism and aggression: The heritability of individual differences. *Journal of Personality and Social Psychology, 50*(6), 1192–1198.

Scarr, S., & McCartney, K. (1983). How people make their own environments: A theory of genotype → environment effects. *Child Development, 54*, 424–435.

Scarr, S., & Weinberg, R. A. (1981). The transmission of authoritarianism in families: Genetic resemblance in social-political attitudes?. In S. Scarr (ed.), *Race, social class, and individual differences in IQ* (pp. 399–427). Hillsdale, NJ: Erlbaum.

Schreiber, D. (2007). Political cognition as social cognition: Are we all political sophisticates? In W. R. Neuman, G. E. Marcus, M. MacKuen, & A. Crigler (eds.), *The affect effect: Dynamics of emotion in political thinking and behavior* (pp. 48–70). Chicago: University of Chicago.

Sears, D. O. (1983). The persistence of early political predispositions. In L. Wheeler & P. Shaver (eds.), *Review of personality and social psychology* (pp. 79–115). Beverly Hills, CA: Sage.

Segal, N. L. (2010). Twins: The finest natural experiment. *Personality and Individual Differences, 49*, 317–323.

Settle, J. E., Dawes, C. T., Christakis, N. A, & Fowler, J. H. (2010). Friendships moderate an association between a dopamine gene variant and political ideology. *Journal of Politics, 72*(4), 1189–1198.

Settle, J. E., Dawes, C. T., & Fowler, J. H. (2009). The heritability of partisan attachment. *Political Research Quarterly, 62*, 601–613.

Sidanius, J., & Pratto, F. (1999). *Social dominance: An intergroup theory of social hierarchy and oppression.* New York: Cambridge University Press.

Smith, K. B., Alford, J. R., Hatemi, P. K., Eaves, L. J., Funk, C. L., & Hibbing, J. R. (2012). Biology, ideology and epistemology: How do we know political attitudes are inherited?. *American Journal of Political Science, 56*, 17–33.

Smith, K. B., Oxley, D. R., Hibbing, M. V., Alford, J. R., & Hibbing, J. R. (2011). Linking genetics and political attitudes: Reconceptualizing political ideology. *Political Psychology, 32*(3): 369–397.

Tellegen, A., Lykken, D. T., Bouchard, T. J., Jr., Wilcox, K. J., Segal, N. L., & Rich, S. (1988). Personality similarity in twins reared apart and together. *Journal of Personality and Social Psychology, 54*, 1031–1039.

Tesser, A. (1993). The importance of heritability in psychological research: The case of attitudes. *Psychological Review, 100*, 129–142.

Visscher, P. M., Medland, S. E., Ferreira, M. A. R., Morley, K. I., Zhu, G., Cornes, B. K., Montgomery, G. W., & Martin, N. G. (2006). Assumption-free estimation of heritability from genome-wide identity-by-descent sharing between full siblings. *PLoSGenetics*, 2(3), 316–324.

Wallace, B., Cesarini, D., Lichtenstein, P., & Johannesson, M. (2007). Heritability of ultimatum game responder behavior. *Proceedings of the National Academy of Sciences*, 104(40), 15631–15634.

Wilson, G. D., & Patterson, J. R. (1968). A new measure of social conservatism. *British Journal of Social and Clinical Psychology*, 7, 264–269.

CHAPTER 9

··

POLITICAL RHETORIC

··

SUSAN CONDOR, CRISTIAN TILEAGĂ, AND
MICHAEL BILLIG

1. INTRODUCTION

··

THE topic of political rhetoric concerns the strategies used to construct persuasive arguments in formal public debates and in everyday political disputes. The study of political rhetoric therefore touches upon the fundamental activities of democratic politics.
As Kane and Patapan (2010, p. 372) observe, "because public discussion and debate are
essential in a democracy, and because leaders are obliged to rule the sovereign people
by means of constant persuasion, rhetoric is absolutely central." Going further, Dryzek
(2010) notes that rhetoric is also central to grass-roots political action: "Rhetoric facilitates the making and hearing of representation claims spanning subjects and audiences...democracy requires a deliberative system with multiple components whose
linkage often needs rhetoric" (pp. 319–339).[1]

Since the previous edition of the *Handbook* in 2003, academic writing on political
rhetoric has greatly increased in volume and diversified in perspective. This work now
spans a range of disciplines, including linguistics, political theory, international relations, communication studies, and psychology. At the time of writing, there existed no
integrative accounts of this body of literature. The task of summarizing the field is complicated by the fact that dialogue between academics working in different disciplinary
contexts is often limited. In addition, the topic of political rhetoric is not always clearly
demarcated from cognate constructs, including political narrative (Hammack & Pilecki,
2012), framing (Chong, chapter 4, this volume), communication (Valentino & Nardis,
chapter 18, this volume), conversation (cf. Remer, 1999), discourse (e.g., Fairclough &
Fairclough, 2012), or deliberation (see Myers & Mendelberg, chapter 22, this volume).

Despite the diversity of approaches adopted and the overlap with other topics
addressed in political psychology, it is nevertheless possible to identify some distinctive

aspects to theory and research on political rhetoric. First, contemporary scholars of political rhetoric tend to draw inspiration directly from classical writings on the subject. In the case of rhetorical psychology, this has involved the use of classical scholarship as a source of insights about human mentality as well as about the structure and function of persuasive argument. Second, authors who write on the subject of political rhetoric often adopt a critical perspective in relation to their academic discipline of origin. In political science, the study of rhetoric may be presented as an alternative to established perspectives on political beliefs and decision-making. In social and political psychology, interest in rhetoric arose as part of the "turn to language," a movement that involved a rejection of cognitivism, and a commitment to approaching talk and text as strategic communicative action rather than as expressions of inner psychological processes, states, or traits (e.g. Burman & Parker, 1993; Edwards, 1997; Harré & Gillett, 1994; Potter, 2000; Potter & Wetherell, 1987; Shotter, 1993).

Although the subject of rhetoric clearly pertains to spoken and written language, empirical research has generally proceeded independently of methodological advances in the analysis of communication. However, some linguists have recently begun to advocate closer dialogue between students of rhetoric and researchers concerned with the fine details of discourse and stylistics (Foxlee, 2012), and scholars in communication studies have begun to consider the application of field methods to the in situ study of the rhetoric of protest movements (Middleton, Senda-Cook, & Endres, 2011). Similarly, unlike many other perspectives that originated from the "turn to language," rhetorical psychologists have not traditionally promoted any specific methodological technique. On the contrary: Billig (1988a) originally advocated traditional scholarship as an alternative to methodology for the interpretation of ideological themes in political rhetoric. More recently, psychological researchers have studied examples of political rhetoric using a variety of research techniques, including discourse analytic approaches to assist the identification of interpretative repertoires, and conversation analysis for the fine-grained analysis of the details of political speeches and arguments. Researchers with an explicitly political agenda may also adopt critical discourse analytic methods.

2. CHANGES AND CONTINUITIES IN SCHOLARSHIP ON POLITICAL RHETORIC

2.1. What Is "Rhetoric"?

In his monograph *The Rhetoric of Rhetoric*, Booth (2004, p. xiii) noted a "threatening morass of rival definitions." On the one hand, the term *rhetoric* can pertain to vacuous, insincere speech or political "spin" (Partington, 2003), as reflected in English expressions such as "mere rhetoric," "empty rhetoric," or "rhetorical question." Bishop Whatley introduced his textbook *Elements of Rhetoric* with the comment that the title was "apt to suggest to many minds an associated idea of empty declamation, or of dishonest artifice" (1828, p. xxxi). Were Bishop Whatley writing today, this cautionary note to his readership might still be warranted. Contemporary writers are still inclined to cast political rhetoric as the antithesis of action (e.g. Browne & Dickson, 2010; McCrisken, 2011) or reality (e.g. Easterly & Williamson, 2011; Hehir, 2011). On the other hand, the term *rhetoric* may also be used in a more positive sense: to refer to the practical art of effective communication. In *Institutio Oratoria*, the Roman rhetorician Quintilian defined rhetoric as the science of "speaking well." An alternative, related use of the term pertains to the study of the art of effective communication. This is illustrated by Aristotle's (1909, p. 5) well-known assertion that the function of rhetoric is "not to persuade, but to discover the available means of persuasion in each case." It is this, more neutral, conception of rhetoric that currently predominates.

Classical accounts of rhetoric focused on formal, public speech (the term *rhetoric* derives from the Greek, ῥήτωρ, meaning *orator*). However, contemporary authors have extended the scope of rhetorical scholarship to include informal talk (e.g., Billig, 1991), texts (e.g., Spurr, 1993), photography and visual images (Hill & Helmers, 2004), maps (Wallach, 2011), cartoons (Morris, 1993), film (Morreale, 1991), digital communication (Zappen, 2005), architecture (Robin, 1992), graphic art (Scott, 2010), and even food (Frye & Bruner, 2012).

Classical work on rhetoric was not confined to the political sphere. Aristotle described *political* (deliberative) oratory as argument that is concerned with weighing up alternative future courses of action relating to finances, war and peace, national defense, trade, and legislation. He distinguished this kind of talk from *judicial* (or forensic) oratory, practiced in the law courts, which focuses on questions of accusation, justice, and truth concerning past events, and from *epideictic* (ceremonial) oratory, concerned with the attribution of praise or censure in the present.[2] Contemporary scholars have further extended the sphere of application of rhetorical studies, often believing like Booth (2004 p. xi) that "[r]hetoric is employed at every moment when one human being intends to produce, through the use of signs or symbols, some effect on another." However, as Gill and Whedbee (1997) noted, it is still commonly supposed that "the essential activities of rhetoric are located on a political stage" (p. 157).

2.2. Changing Contexts of Political Rhetoric

Current studies of rhetoric continue to draw inspiration from classical works, such as Cicero's *De Oratore*, Qunitilian's *Institutio Oratoria*, and Aristotle's *Rhetoric*. At the same time, it is recognized that the contexts in which, and media through which, political rhetoric now operates are in many respects very different from the situation facing the classical Greek or Roman orator (see also Valentino & Nardis, chapter 18, this volume).

In the classical period, political oratory required a loud voice and formal gestures, as orators spoke in person to mass audiences. In the modern world, political oratory is typically mediated to distal audiences by textual or electronic means of communication often blurring the distinction between politics and entertainment (van Zoonen, 2005). This has impacted upon political rhetoric in a number of ways. For example, political leaders now often adopt an informal, conversational style as evidenced in particular in the genre of the televised political interview. The distinction between public and private aspects of political discourse is collapsing (Thompson, 2011), resulting in a rise of self-expressive politics and the personalization of formal political rhetoric. In addition, whereas classical work on political rhetoric focused on oratory, more recent work has come to focus on what Barthes (1977) called the "rhetoric of the image," which was not envisaged by the purely verbal logic of traditional rhetoric (Roque, 2008).[3]

The fact that political rhetoric is now often conveyed through television, newsprint, or e-communication has resulted in a diversification of potential audiences. Perelman and Olbrechts-Tyteca (1969) distinguish between the *particular audience* (the people being specifically addressed in a particular communication) and the *universal audience*, comprising all those who might in principle hear or dis/agree with the message. In either case, the audiences may be *composite* in character, composed of subgroups with multiple, often competing, views and interests. Van Eemeren (2010) distinguishes between two types of composite audience: *mixed* audiences, comprising individuals and subgroups with different starting points in relation to a communicator's topic or message, and *multiple* audiences, comprising individuals and groups with different (possibly incompatible) commitments in relation to the issue under discussion. The increased use of mediated communication increases the potential diversity of the audiences that a political communicator is expected to address in a single speech or text. In addition, the situation may be further complicated by the fact that the audiences being addressed in a particular communication need not always correspond with the constituencies that a speaker is claiming to represent, or toward whom she or he may be held politically accountable.[4]

The increasing importance of the mass and electronic media has also resulted in the effective rhetorical context of formal political communications becoming extended both temporally and spatially. The British MP Harold Wilson once famously remarked that "a week is a long time in politics." However, the fact that records of political debates, speeches, and other forms of communication are increasingly easy to retrieve through electronic search-engines means that political rhetoric can now have an infinite half-life, with the consequence that words uttered or written at one point in time may be retrieved and used in a different context (e.g. Antaki & Leudar, 1991).

Since the previous edition of the *Handbook* in 2003, academic authors have been paying increasing attention to the impact of new media technologies on political rhetoric. Bennett and Iyengar (2008) suggest that the potential impact of new technologies might eventually render previous academic perspectives on media effects obsolete. In particular, they draw attention to the ways in which new technologies afford increasing selective exposure to political information, the fragmentation of audiences, and the decline of inadvertent citizen exposure to political information through the media. Some authors have emphasized the democratizing potential of new technologies, which afford cosmopolitan communication between citizens (Mihelj, van Zoonen, & Vis, 2011) and which are capable of bridging different social networks (Hampton, 2011). New technologies may facilitate direct communication between citizens and decision-makers, citizens' active production of political messages, and collective political protest. Facebook and Twitter certainly facilitated the informal political communication of protesters in the Arab revolution, *indignados* in Madrid, and the Occupy movement.

However, some authors have been more skeptical about the actual effects of the digital revolution on political rhetoric and engagement. For example, Jouët, Vedel, and Comby (2011) observed that French citizens still obtain political information primarily from the mass media, and Jansen and Koop (2005) reported that Internet discussion boards during British Columbia's election were dominated by a relatively small number of users. Deacon and Wring (2011) suggested that the promise of the Internet as a campaign tool in the British general election of 2010 turned out to have been overrated. Similarly, in their analyses of videos and comments posted to YouTube in response to the Dutch anti-Islam video *Fitna*, van Zoonen and colleagues argue that YouTube enabled the airing of a wide variety of views, but at the same time actually stifled dialogue between those supporting or opposing the stance of the video (van Zoonen et al., 2010; 2011).

2.3. Recent Trends in Research on Political Rhetoric

Early contributions to rhetorical psychology often drew attention to the rhetorical aspects of everyday political attitudes. Subsequent research in this vein has considered the argumentative strategies employed by members of the general public to justify political participation and nonparticipation (Condor & Gibson, 2007), and to present views concerning immigration, racism, multiculturalism, and citizenship in such a manner that conforms to norms of public reason (Figgou & Condor, 2007; Gibson & Hamilton, 2011).

More commonly, research on political rhetoric focuses on real-world contexts of political engagement. This has included work on the rhetorical strategies adopted by social movements (Chavez, 2011; Endres & Senda-Cook, 2011), protest groups (Griggs & Howarth, 2004; Sowards & Renegar, 2006), and E-activist groups (Eaton, 2010; Sommerfeldt, 2011). However, most empirical studies of political rhetoric continue to focus on formal political communication, including parliamentary debates (e.g., Every & Augoustinos, 2007; Vanderbeck & Johnson, 2011), political campaigns and marketing (e.g., Fridkin & Kenney, 2011; Jerit, 2004; Payne, 2010), and high-profile speeches, texts, or films and historical documents (e.g. Terrill, 2009; 2011; Tileagă, 2009; 2012). Popular awareness of Barack Obama's rhetorical skill has led to a recent revival of academic interest in the oratory styles of particular political leaders (e.g., Coe & Reitzes, 2010; Isaksen, 2011; Grube, 2010; Toye, 2011; Utley & Heyse, 2009).

The substantive topics investigated in studies of political rhetoric tend to reflect political concerns of the day. Current research continues to focus on issues related to political rhetoric in debates concerning national identity (Condor, 2011; Finell &

Liebkind, 2010); immigration and citizenship (e.g., Boromisza-Habashi, 2011; Every & Augoustinos, 2007); foreign policy (Kratochvil, Cibulková, & Beneš, 2006), and the legitimation of war (Bostdorff, 2011; Oddo, 2011). Recently, researchers have turned their attention to rhetoric concerning climate change (Kurtz, Augoustinos, & Crabb, 2010), terrorism (De Castella & McGarty, 2011), and the "war on terror" (Esch, 2010; Kassimeris & Jackson, 2011; Kaufer & Al-Malki, 2009).

Empirical analyses of political rhetoric often focus on specific argumentative devices, tropes, or commonplaces. In this respect, researchers are inclined to foreground the micro-features of communication that are often overlooked in research that treats political discourse as a reflection of cognitive activity rather than as a form of communicative action. For example, analyses of conceptual or integrative complexity in political talk and text typically treat clichés ("cryptic or glib remarks"), idioms, satire, and sarcasm as unscoreable (Baker-Brown et al., 1992). In contrast, in rhetorical analyses, figures of speech are typically treated as important argumentative devices. Contemporary research has focused on questions related to the strategic use of metaphors (Ferrari, 2007), proverbs (Orwenjo, 2009), slogans (Kephart & Rafferty, 2009), humor (Dmitriev, 2008; Timmerman, Gussman, & King, 2012), politeness (Fracchiolla, 2011; Shibamoto-Smith, 2011), and appeals to common-sense values such as "change" (Roan & White, 2010), "choice" (Gaard, 2010), and "community" (Buckler, 2007) in political talk and texts. Over the past few years, scholars have demonstrated an increased concern over the use of religious language and idioms in formal political rhetoric (e.g., Kaylor, 2011; Marietta, 2012; Stecker, 2011; Terrill, 2007).

In view of the range of work that now exists on the subject, it is not possible to provide a comprehensive account of academic perspectives on political rhetoric in a single chapter. In the following pages we will focus specifically on the ways in which recent studies of political rhetoric relate to two key topics of interest to political psychologists: argument, and identity.

3. POLITICAL RHETORIC AND ARGUMENTATION

The term "argument" may be applied to a range of phenomena, including disputes between individuals or groups, and to coherent sets of statements justifying a single premise ("line of argument"). In its most inclusive sense, all verbal behavior might potentially qualify for the label of "argument." For example, Potter (1997) suggests that descriptive discourse necessarily has offensive (critical) aspects insofar as it explicitly or implicitly seeks to undermine rival versions of events, and defensive (justificatory) aspects insofar as speakers attempt to shore up their accounts from attack by rivals.[5]

Authors who focus on the argumentative aspects of political rhetoric often position themselves in direct opposition to other existing academic accounts of political opinions, belief, and action. In *Arguing and Thinking*, Billig (1987) presented rhetorical psychology as an alternative to standard social scientific approaches to reasoning, attitudes, and ideology. Hopkins and Kahani-Hopkins (2004; 2006; 2009) set their rhetorical approach to social and self-categorization processes as an alternative to reified social psychological perspectives on context, identity, and leadership. Finlayson (2006; 2007; Finlayson & Martin, 2008) offer rhetorical political analysis (RPA) as an alternative to established political science perspectives on ideas and beliefs. In all of these cases, the authors suggest that a focus on rhetorical argument might counter a tendency on the part of social scientists to prioritize consensus over contestation. In fact, theorists who foreground the argumentative character of political rhetoric often treat the very idea of political "consensus" itself as a strategic rhetorical construction (e.g. Beasley, 2001; Edelman, 1977; Weltman & Billig, 2001), and analyze the ways in which speakers may work up images of unanimity in an effort to represent a particular state of affairs as indisputable (e.g., Potter & Edwards, 1990).

In this section of the chapter we will focus on three areas of work of particular relevance to political psychology: the rhetorical psychology perspective on the argumentative nature of thinking and attitudes; the ideological dilemmas perspective on the argumentative aspects of ideology, and the rhetorical political analysis perspective on the argumentative aspects of policy decision-making.

3.1. Rhetorical Psychology

3.1.1. *Arguing and Thinking*

Rhetorical psychologists adopt the view that the same principles underlie both public oratory and private deliberation. The idea that human thought evidences similarities with public arguments draws on a long tradition of scholarship. For example, Francis Bacon suggested that "the solitary thinker uses rhetoric to excite his own appetite and will in a sort of intrapersonal negotiation—that is...to 'talk oneself into something'" (Conley, 1990, p. 164). Billig similarly suggests that the principle difference between deliberative oratory and the internal deliberations of thinking "is that in the latter one person has to provide both sets of arguments, as the self splits into two sides, which debate, and negate, each other" (Billig, 1991, p. 48).[6] More recently, Billig (2008) has pointed out that in the eighteenth century, the Third Earl of Shaftesbury also viewed thinking as being argumentative and has argued that many of the ideas of current approaches to critical psychology can be traced back to Shaftesbury's largely forgotten work.

Billig contrasts this perspective on thinking as argument with cognitive psychology models that characterize human reasoning, problem-solving, and decision-making as a matter of information processing or rule following. Drawing from the sophist Protagoras's famous maxim, "In every question, there are two sides to the argument, exactly opposite to each other," Billig contends that just as public argument is two-sided, so too is the solitary psychological process of thinking. Because both sides to an argument can produce reasonable justifications, and both can counter the criticisms of each other, the process of thinking is not necessarily motivated by a drive toward consistency. On the contrary, in the course of deliberation people often find themselves moved by the spirit of contradiction. Rhetorical psychology hence substitutes the conventional psychological image of the human thinker as a rule-following bureaucrat with the image of the human thinker as a deliberator "shuttling between contrary opinions" (Billig, 1996, p. 186).

Psychologists have long considered the process of categorization to be "the foundation of thought" (Bruner, Goodnow, & Austin, 1956), and it has often been held that categorization involves an economy of mental or discursive effort. For example, Morley (1886) described labels as "devices for saving talkative persons the trouble of thinking" (p. 142). More recently, Rosch (1978) famously described the function of category systems as "to provide maximum information with the least cognitive effort" (p. 28). In contrast, Billig suggests that these accounts of categorization presented a distinctly one-sided image of the capacities of human beings as reasoning subjects. To accept the argumentative, two-sided nature of thinking is to appreciate the capacity of people to employ categories, but also to engage in the opposite cognitive and rhetorical operation of particularization.

Insofar as categories are understood as rhetorical phenomena, the process of categorization need not be understood to save people the trouble of thinking. On the contrary, when used in the course of communication, categories typically constitute objects of deliberation and the topics of argument. Any act of generalization can always be potentially negated by a particularization, treating a particular object or event as a "special case." In the course of conversation, generalizations are typically qualified, as a speaker employs a category while also acknowledging the existence of exceptions. Moreover, people can debate the merits of classifying people or events in one way rather than another, the defining attributes of a category, the inferences that may be drawn from knowledge of category membership, and the appropriate use of labels.

These considerations have particular relevance to political psychology insofar as many of the basic categories of contemporary political discourse are essentially contested (Gallie, 1956), that is, they are the subject of continual disputes that cannot be settled by "appeal to empirical evidence, linguistic usage, or the canons of logic alone" (Gray, 1978, p. 344), such as "power," "democracy," "representation," and "liberty." Conventionally, social and political psychologists have been inclined to treat political constructs as variables that can be relatively easily operationalized and measured. For example, researchers investigate the "effects of power" on political cognition or action, the situations under which intergroup behavior is "determined by fairness motives," the extent to which individuals or groups differ in their understanding of "equality," and so forth. In contrast, researchers adopting a rhetorical perspective are more disposed to study the ways in which actors pursue political projects through flexible and strategic appeals to particular understandings of power, fairness, and equality. For example, Summers (2007) analyzed debates in Western Australian parliamentary speeches supporting or opposing the Lesbian and Gay Law Reform Act, and observed how *both* sides of the debate used appeals to equality, human rights, democracy, and the interests of children, which the speakers treated as rhetorical bottom-lines. Similarly, research has noted how arguments designed to support, and to oppose, various forms of ethnic discrimination may both appeal to shared liberal values of equality, fairness, and individualism (e.g., Augoustinos, Tuffin, & Every, 2005).

Nick Hopkins, Steve Reicher, and Vered Kahani-Hopkins adopted a rhetorical approach to social categorization in a program of research investigating the strategies used by politicians and political activists for the purposes of political mobilization (e.g., Hopkins and Kahani-Hopkins, 2004; Hopkins & Reicher, 1997; Hopkins, Reicher, & Kahani-Hopkins, 2003; Kahani-Hopkins & Hopkins, 2002; Reicher & Hopkins, 1996; 2001). These authors based their work on self-categorization theory (Turner, Hogg, Oakes, Reicher, & Wetherell, 1987) but argued that a reliance on laboratory experimentation could lead social psychologists to overlook the extent to which social categories may represent the object of, rather than merely a prior condition for, political contestation. As Hopkins and Kahani-Hopkins (2004) put it:

> Whilst experimental research has many strengths, there is a danger that an exclusive reliance on laboratory-based paradigms restricts the development of theory. Most obviously, as such paradigms are weak in exploring processes of argument there is a danger that theories of categorization underplay the importance of rhetoric and dispute. (p. 42).

As an example of work combining self-categorization theoretic perspectives with a rhetorical approach to categorization we may consider Hopkins and Kahani-Hopkins's (2004) analysis of the rival social category constructions mobilized in texts by groups of Muslim activists in Britain. On the one hand, the Muslim Parliament of Great Britain represented Islam and the West as entirely incompatible categories, such that any accommodation to Western societies or values would necessarily compromise Muslim identity. This category scheme did not simply sharply differentiate Muslim from non-Muslim Britons, but it also facilitated identification between British Muslims and the global Muslim umma. Advocates of this position adopted the view that categories of ethnicity and nationality were incompatible with Muslim identity and, further, that these constructs were themselves part of an ideological strategy promulgated by Western governments aiming to undermine Muslims' political consciousness.

In contrast, members of the UK Imams and Mosques Council argued that British Muslims were an integral part of British society. Rather than viewing the West as embodying the antithesis of Islamic values, these activists pointed to the existence of shared values. Proponents of this position not only challenged the idea that participation in a Western community subverted Muslim identity, but also argued that identification with non-Muslims was in fact an integral aspect of Muslim identity. In this case, the Islamic umma was construed as a heterogeneous group that instantiated the very values of tolerance and diversity necessary to function actively and effectively in a modern multicultural society.

Hopkins and Kahani-Hopkins's analysis highlighted a series of issues that are often overlooked in experimental studies of self-categorization processes. First, they did not consider category homogeneity, distinctiveness, or entitativity simply as the cognitive antecedents to, or consequences of, social categorization. Rather, these phenomena were viewed as the subject and outcome of active debate. Second, by treating social categorization as a rhetorical phenomenon, Hopkins and Kahani-Hopkins were able appreciate how the meanings of Islam and "the West" were established in an extended line of argument in which the speaker also constructed a version of group interests, social contexts, and the legitimacy of particular future courses of action. Finally, by approaching these competing category schemes as aspects of strategic rhetoric, the authors were able to appreciate their dialogic qualities. The two representational schemata that Hopkins and Kahani-Hopkins identified in British Muslim activists' rhetoric were not simply two mirror-image versions of the categories of Muslim and the West. Rather, each version was produced in such a way as to address, and to attempt to undermine, the other.

3.1.2. *Attitudes as Advocacy*

Although rhetorical psychologists draw attention to the flexible, and often contradictory, ways in which people can describe and evaluate political actors and events, they do not overlook the extent to which individuals and groups may display consistency in political opinions (cf. Caprara and Vecchione, chapter 2, this volume). For example, Hopkins and Kahani-Hopkins (2004) did not find members of the Muslim Parliament of Great Britain switching back and forth between arguing that Western policies of cultural accommodation threatened the integrity of Muslim identity, and arguing in support of the UK government's Community Cohesion program. On the contrary, the various British Muslim political activists maintained a relatively clear and consistent line of argument. Billig suggests that when social actors adopt and defend a particular point of view, their behavior might be likened to that of a public advocate "who has decided upon a single stance and is orating upon the virtues of the chosen position" (1996, p. 186).

Rhetorical psychology does not treat an individual's assertion of attitudes and opinions as a straightforward report of their subjective appraisals.[7] Rather, the act of claiming an attitude or offering an opinion involves an intervention into a public controversy.[8] This means that not all beliefs qualify as attitudes (Billig, 1988b). Within a given social context there will be certain matters that are treated as noncontroversial, commonsensical. It is only on potentially disputable matters that an individual can be said to hold opinions or express attitudes.

Insofar as attitudes constitute stances in a public debate, any line of argument (*logos*) only makes sense in relation to alternative arguments (*anti-logoi*). Sometimes a speaker may explicitly set out the *anti-logoi* to his or her own position. In other situations, a speaker may leave the *anti-logos* implicit. However, merely to declare oneself to favor capital punishment is, by implication, to take a stance against the abolition of the death penalty; to declare oneself pro-life is to oppose pro-choice arguments; to proclaim one's support for gun control is implicitly to take issue with the arguments of the firearms lobby; to argue in favor of multicultural policies of social integration is to take a position against the view that Muslim identity is fundamentally incompatible with Western values.

In ordinary social life, advocacy does not simply involve adopting a position for or against some state of affairs, as is normally required of research respondents when faced with an attitude scale or opinion survey. When expressed in the course of everyday conversation, attitude avowals are typically accompanied by reasons, whether these are direct justifications for the views proposed or criticisms of competing positions. The internal consistency of these lines of argument may represent an important consideration, but not because human beings have an inner drive or need for cognitive consistency. Rather, the internal coherence of attitude avowals, and the reliability with which an individual adopts a particular stance over a period of time, may be rhetorically motivated insofar as charges of inconsistency may weaken the force of an argument. It follows that individuals need not always attend to the logical consistency of their accounts. Indeed, discourse analysts have often pointed to variation in positions that a speaker may endorse in the flow of mundane talk. However, insofar as a speaker is publicly adopting a particular stance on a controversial issue, the need to maintain (or at least be seen to maintain) a consistent argument may become a relevant concern.

An interactional requirement for consistency need not, however, lead to rhetorical inflexibility. When presenting their attitude on a particular issue, people do not merely have a set of relevant considerations that they present identically on each occasion the topic arises. Instead, they tailor their argument to the rhetorical context in which they are talking.[9] Even individuals with strong, crystallized political views show a good deal of flexibility in their talk. For example, in a study of the way that families in England talked about the British royal family, Billig (1991; 1992) notes one case in which everyone agreed that the father had strong views against the monarchy. He constantly argued with his wife and children on the topic. However, in his arguments the father did not merely repeat the same statements, but flexibly managed his arguments to counter those of the other members of his family. Moreover, he alternated between radical and conservative rhetoric, as he counterposed his *logoi* to the *anti-logoi* of his family, presenting himself at one moment as a radical opposing the Establishment, and at other times as the defender of British values.

Billig (1989) distinguishes two ways in which individuals may be understood to hold a view in relation to a public controversy. *Intersubjective* perspectives presume the existence of a singular, ultimately discernable, empirical reality. In this case, disagreement may be attributed to initial error on the part of at least one of the parties concerned. In contrast, *multisubjective* perspectives treat dispute as the result of plural, and potentially irreconcilable, values or points of view. Like anything else, the intersubjective or multisubjective character of a dispute may, itself, constitute an object of contestation. Moreover, individuals need not always adopt a consistent position on whether a particular clash of political views should be regarded as a disagreement over matters of (singular) fact or of (multiple) competing values. For example, Condor (2011) reported how the same UK politicians could treat an attitude in favor of multiculturalism as a matter of multisubjectivity when discussing the EU (displaying respect for the rights of other

EU states to adopt assimilationist policies of social integration) while treating this as a matter of intersubjectivity in a UK context, in which case all alternative perspectives were presented as irrational and misguided.

3.2. Ideological Commonplaces and Ideological Dilemmas

Billig (1987) notes how classical rhetoricians advised speakers to advance their cases by using commonplaces (*topoi*): references to facts or moral values that will be shared by audiences. Formal political rhetoric often involves the use of commonplaces that appeal to the common sense of audiences. McGee (1980) coined the term *ideograph* to describe this phenomenon:

> An ideograph is an ordinary-language term found in political discourse. It is a high order abstraction representing commitment to a particular but equivocal and ill-defined normative goal. It warrants the use of power, excuses behavior and belief which might otherwise be perceived as eccentric or antisocial, and guides behavior and belief into channels easily recognized by a community as acceptable and laudable. (p. 15)

We noted in section 2 that a good deal of current empirical research involves identifying the use of *virtue words* (McGee, 1980, p. 6) such as "community," "change," or "choice" and mapping their rhetorical functions in specific arguments.

McGee suggests that ideographs may provide a basis for shared understanding between speakers and grounds for coordinated action, "when a claim is warranted by such terms as 'law,' 'liberty,' 'tyranny,' or 'trial by jury,'...it is presumed that human beings will react predictably" (McGee, 1980, p. 6). However, the fact that the key terms of political debate are essentially contestable means that although speakers often *treat* appeals to values such as fairness, the national interest, or human rights as if they were noncontentious, there is no guarantee that their audience will necessarily accept their argument. In practice, it is always possible for these appeals to be opened up for critical consideration or for exceptions to be made for particular cases.

Many social scientific accounts of ideology treat social actors as the passive recipients of inherited belief systems. From this kind of perspective, ideology is viewed as a conservative force, preventing challenges to the political status quo (Jost, Federico, & Napier, 2009) and imposing an overarching consistency to thoughts, beliefs, and values (cf. Nelson, 1977). Billig suggests that an understanding of ideology as systems of social and psychological "constraint" could be corrected by attending to the presence of contrary themes within ideological systems. Social scientists often draw attention to the contradictory nature of social maxims (many hands make light work *but* too many cooks spoil the broth). Conventionally, such contradictions have been viewed as evidence of the irrationality of common sense (cf. Billig, 1994; Shapin, 2001). In contrast, Billig argues that the contrary aspects of cultural common sense in fact represent the preconditions for two-sided argument, and consequently for rhetorical deliberation within and between members of a particular society. From this perspective, the ordinary person "is not a blind dupe, whose mind has been filled by outside forces and who reacts unthinkingly. The subject of ideology is a rhetorical being who thinks and argues with ideology" (Billig, 1991a, p. 2).

Billig's (1987) ideas concerning the productive potential of opposing topoi were developed in the text *Ideological Dilemmas* (Billig et al., 1988), which presented a series of case studies illustrating how contradictions within liberal ideology (between competing values of equality versus respect for authority, of fairness as equity or equality, of individualism versus the common good) played out in everyday debates concerning gender, education, prejudice, health, and expertise. The ambivalent quality of these arguments was not seen to reflect a lack of engagement or sophistication on the part of the speakers. On the contrary, it was precisely the availability of opposing themes that enabled ordinary people to find the familiar puzzling and therefore worthy of deliberation.

Although Billig and his colleagues assumed a liberal democratic political culture as part of the background against which everyday talk took place, they did not explicitly consider how dilemmatic themes operate in deliberation over political issues. However, subsequent research has applied the ideological dilemmas approach to everyday political reasoning on issues such as unemployment (Gibson, 2011), gender inequality (Benschop, Halsema, & Schreurs, 2001; Stokoe, 2000), and nationality and citizenship (e.g., Bozatzis, 2009; Condor, 2000; 2006; Condor & Gibson, 2007; Sapountzis, 2008).

Billig and his colleagues note that communicators do not always attend to dilemmatic aspects of discourse overtly. On occasions, "Discourse which seems to be arguing for one point may contain implicit meanings which could be made explicit to argue for the counter-point" (p. 23). An example of implicit ideological dilemmas is provided by Condor's (2011) analysis of political speeches in favor of "British multiculturalism." Condor observes that the speakers often referred explicitly to their *anti-logoi*: arguments in favor of ethnic or cultural nationalism, exemplified by Victorian imperialist discourses. However, analysis of the texts of these speeches showed that the arguments put forward by advocates of British multiculturalism rested upon the claim that the contemporary UK represented a "special case." Consequently, far from opposing the general ideology of ethnic nationalism, the speakers were in fact presupposing a normal social order of national ethnic homogeneity. Moreover, the specific topoi that the speakers invoked in the course of justifying British multiculturalism in fact closely echoed the ideograms employed by previous generations of politicians in epideictic rhetoric celebrating the aesthetic, moral, economic, and political value of British Imperialism.

3.3. Rhetorical Political Analysis

Although the rhetorical turn in the social sciences often involved a specific focus on political oratory and argument, until recently this work has been relatively neglected by political theorists (Garsten, 2011) and political scientists (Finlayson, 2004; 2006;

2007). Arguing that approaches based on rational choice theory embrace "too narrow a concept of reasoning" (2007, p. 545), Finlayson's alternative, which he terms rhetorical political analysis (RPA), recast political decision-making as a collective, argumentative activity.

Finlayson notes that democratic politics is premised on the assumption of the "irreducible and contested plurality of public life" (2007, p. 552) and that political ideas and beliefs "are always turned into arguments, into elements of contestable propositions...which, if they are to survive, must win adherents in a contest of persuasive presentation" (p. 559). Politics is hence not characterized by beliefs or decisions per se, but by "the presence of beliefs in contradiction with each other" (p. 552). Finlayson argues that political rhetoric deals both with areas of empirical uncertainty (in Billig's terms, *intersubjective* disagreement) and also disputes that result from the fact that citizens approach the same issue from different perspectives (Billig's *multisubjective* disagreement).

Like Billig, Finlayson suggests that political categories typically constitute the object of contestation. Taking the example of poverty (cf. Edelman, 1977), he observes that political deliberation does not only concern "the best policy instrument for alleviating poverty but how poverty should be defined (and thus what would actually constitute its alleviation), whether or not poverty is a problem, and if it is, then the kind of problem it might be (a moral, economic, social or security problem)" (2007, p. 550).

Finlayson argues that political reasoning is necessarily dialogic, insofar as any political theorist needs to justify his or her beliefs to others who may well adopt very different points of view. Moreover, he suggested that political ideas and beliefs are not simply expressed in the course of debate, but rather that political concepts, values, and intentions are in fact formulated through an ongoing process of argument. Similarly, although policymaking involves the formation of political consensus, this process need not involve the discovery of common interests or views, but rather the construction of agreement through the process of argument.

At present, little research has been conducted within the RPA perspective (although see Finlayson & Martin's [2008] analysis of Tony Blair's last speech to the UK Labour Party Conference in 2006). However, Finlayson (2006; 2007) provides a general outline of the ways in which future empirical work might develop.[10] First, RPA would approach any particular political debate in relation to its original rhetorical context, and also with a view to the ways in which the mediated character of contemporary politics can serve to render rhetorical situations fluid and ambiguous. Second, analysis should consider how the topic (the point of the controversy or bone of contention) is itself argumentatively established. Specifically, this would involve (1) *factual conjecture*: if/that a state of affairs exists (e.g., has Iraq attempted to purchase yellowcake uranium from Niger?); (2) *definition*: naming the issue, (e.g., "the Iraq war," "war in Iraq," "Operation Iraqi Freedom," "preventive war," "occupation of Iraq," "illegal invasion"); (3) *assessment* of the nature of the act or policy (e.g., is Western military intervention in Iraq a defense of national interests, a response to human rights violations, "the central front in the War on Terror," or a "fatal mistake"?); (4) *the boundaries of legitimate argument*: the rules concerning who, when, and where an issue may be discussed.

Third, RPA would analyze the substantive content of any particular political argument. This would include attention to (1) the ways in which the policy under dispute is framed in relation to the axes of the universal and the particular; (2) the formulation of specific states of affairs through metaphor, and narrative sequencing, and the use of rhetorical commonplaces; (3) modes of persuasive appeal: whether the speaker is appealing to ethos, pathos, or logos; (4) genre: how speakers cast their talk as deliberative, forensic, or epideictic; (5) how particular policy recommendations are rhetorically linked to general ideological or party political commitments.

In many respects, Finlayson's RPA is similar to Billig's approach to rhetorical psychology. However, there are three important differences between the perspectives. First, RPA focuses on formal political decision-making, emphasizing public clashes of views between individuals or groups, each adopting one-sided (largely institutionalized) standpoints. In contrast, rhetorical psychology often focuses on private deliberation on the part of individuals. This is reflected in the different ways in which the two perspectives consider the "ideological" aspects of political argument (rhetorical psychology emphasizing conflicts within wide-scale ideological systems, RPA stressing the consolidation of distinct political belief systems).

Second, RPA focuses on political decision-making, the resolution of dispute, and the ways in which political actors may construct robust arguments that can subsequently form the basis for collaborative action. In contrast, rhetorical psychology tends to stress the open-ended quality of argumentation. Billig draws on Shaftesbury's idealized view of a society in which there is a wonderful mix of "contrarieties," filled with debate, difference, and mockery: "In this image of utopia, the lion does not lie down in silence with the lamb, but the Epicurean and stoic meet again and again to argue, to seek truth and to laugh" (Billig, 2008, p. 134).

Third, RPA does not consider issues relating to the construction of self or social identity, matters that Finlayson devolved to discursive psychology (e.g., 2006, p. 539). As we shall see in the next section, rhetorical psychology, in common with many other perspectives on political language and communication, regards identity concerns as centrally and necessarily implicated in all political rhetoric.

4. POLITICAL RHETORIC AND IDENTITY

As we noted in section 2, Aristotle argued that audiences could be swayed not only by the style and content of an argument, but also the character projected by the speaker (*ethos*). Classical theorists identified three categories of ethos: *phronesis* (involving wisdom and practical skills), *arete* (morality and virtue), and *eunoia* (goodwill towards the audience).

In contemporary studies of political rhetoric, questions relating to ethos are often framed as a matter of the "identity" of the communicator. The term identity is ambiguous, and academic discussions of political rhetoric have approached the issue of communicator identity in various ways. Some theorists have simply refused the identity construct, insofar as it might be understood to imply a singular or fixed sense of self (see Charland, 1987). More commonly, researchers have focused communicator identity as a rhetorical production. In *A Rhetoric of Motives* Burke (1969) suggested that identification lies at the heart of all persuasive rhetoric for "you persuade a man [*sic*] only insofar as you can talk his language by speech, gesture, tonality, order image, attitude, idea, identifying your ways with his" (p. 55). Burke called this projected commonality between speaker and audience *consubstantiality*. In this section, we will limit ourselves to discussing some of the strategies that contemporary political communicators may use to achieve consubstantiality when faced with composite audiences of the type outlined in section 2. First, we consider how speakers may present their own rhetorical projects as exercises in political consensus. Second, we consider cases in which politicians appeal explicitly to broadly defined in-groups. Third, we examine the ways in which political commentators address aspirational categories, representing consubstantiality as a future project rather than a current condition. Finally, we discuss how speakers may implicitly display allegiance with mixed and multiple audiences, focusing in particular on the use of first-person pronouns.

4.1. Taking and Avoiding Sides

One way in which a political communicator may deal with the problem of audience diversity is simply to side with one group against another. An example of the way in which a speaker may orient herself toward the establishment of consubstantiality with a distal community of representation rather than their immediate audience is provided by Rapley's (1998) analysis of the maiden speech of Pauline Hanson, the independent Australian MP elected on an anti-immigration stance. Hanson did not claim commonality with the fellow members of parliament that she was ostensibly addressing. Instead, she stressed her commonality with the broader public. Hanson claimed to speak "just as an ordinary Australian" and not as "a polished politician," asserting that "my view on issues is based on commonsense, and my experience as a mother of four children, as a sole parent, and as a business-woman running a fish and chip shop" (Rapley, 1998, p. 331).

Rhetorical strategies are often polyvalent, serving a number of communicative functions simultaneously. In this case, through the act of siding with the "ordinary people" in opposition to the "the elite," Hanson was also rhetorically enacting her commitment to populist political ideology. However, in democratic political contexts, communicators who identify with more mainstream political parties are often confronted with a rhetorical dilemma. As Ilie (2003) observes, formal political debate often involves competing normative injunctions:

> Parliamentary debates presuppose, on the one hand, a spirit of adversariality, which
> is manifested in position claiming and opponent-challenging acts, and, on the other

hand, a spirit of cooperativeness, which is manifest in joint decision-making and cross-party problem-solving processes in order to reach commonly acceptable goals regarding future policies and suitable lines of action at a national level. (p. 73)

More generally, although democratic political discourse operates within what Atkins (2010) terms *the context of hegemonic competition*, at the same time, politicians who adopt an overtly adversarial stance may be criticized for their adherence to a particular ideology (Kurtz et al., 2010), charged with prioritizing partisan party interests over common national interests (Dickerson, 1998), or accused of negative political campaigning (cf. Fridkin & Kenney, 2011). Moreover, when individuals or groups are attempting to mobilize support in a majority-rule political system, it is often in their interests to appeal to as many sectors of their universal audience as possible.

One strategy that a politician may employ to avoid being seen to side with a particular section of the audience or community of representation involves presenting an argument in such a way as to appear to incorporate a range of divergent points of view. Fløttum (2010) reported a strategy that she termed the *polemical not*, in which a speaker suggests that his or her rhetorical project goes beyond current divisive arguments. As an example, Fløttum quoted from an address by Tony Blair to the European Union in 2005:

> The issue is **not** between a "free market" Europe and a social Europe, between those who want to retreat to a common market and those who believe in Europe as a political project.

Here we can see Blair advocating an understanding of the "issue" that will move beyond the petty squabbles between those holding incompatible views on the European Union. Significantly, Blair's account of his own position was evasive (cf. Bull, 2008). At no stage did he explicitly state what the "issue" actually was.

A related technique that politicians commonly use in formal public addresses is to present adversarial politics, itself, as their own personal anti-logos. In the United States, this kind of rhetorical strategy may be given a particular inflection when it is used in conjunction with an appeal to what Beasley (2001) termed the "shared beliefs hypothesis," according to which American national identity is essentially grounded in an adherence to a shared set of political principles. As an example, we may consider Barack Obama's famous "Yes We Can" speech presented after his success in the Democratic presidential primary in South Carolina in 2008.

> We're up against decades of bitter partisanship that cause politicians to demonize their opponents instead of coming together to make college affordable or energy cleaner. It's the kind of partisanship where you're not even allowed to say that a Republican had an idea, even if it's one you never agreed with....
>
> So understand this, South Carolina. The choice in this election is not between regions or religions or genders. It's not about rich vs. poor, young vs. old. And it is not about black vs. white. This election is about the past vs. the future. It's about whether

we settle for the same divisions and distractions and drama that passes for politics today or whether we reach for a politics of common sense and innovation, a politics of shared sacrifice and shared prosperity.

Once again, we can see the use of the *polemical not*, this time applied to a gamut of forms of "divisive" identity politics and "bitter" partisan political positions. By opposing opposition, and demonizing demonization, Obama presented himself and his policies as opposing nobody.

4.2. Explicit Appeals to Common In-group Membership

When faced with the need to appeal to mixed or multiple audiences, political communicators often attempt to regroup a composite audience into a single rhetorical entity (Perelman & Olbrechts-Tyteca, 1968). We have already seen how self-categorization theorists have drawn attention to the ways in which grass-roots political activists attempt to mobilize support by formulating common category memberships. Extending this to the sphere of formal political action, Reicher and Hopkins (2001) argue that political leaders act rhetorically as *entrepreneurs of identity*. According to this perspective, effective political leadership requires (1) regrouping diverse communities into a single overarching identity category; (2) framing the (aspiring) leader's own political project as the instantiation of the norms and values of that identity category, and (3) the (aspiring) leader's self presentation as a prototypical in-group member.

Reicher and Hopkins (2001) illustrate this process in a program of research conducted in Scotland, in which they show how electoral candidates attempted to maximize their appeal by framing both themselves and their audience in national terms. However, candidates defined this superordinate national identity in such a way as to present their own party's political program as expressing the qualities and values that they attributed to the Scottish people in general. Members of the left-wing Labour Party characterized Scots as inherently egalitarian, welfarist, and opposed to privilege. In contrast, Conservative Party candidates characterized Scots as hard-working and entrepreneurial. In all cases, the candidates presented themselves as prototypical members of the national community, not simply endorsing but also instantiating the virtues ascribed to their imagined community of representation.

As we noted earlier, rhetorical strategies are often polyvalent. A clear example of the ways in which the act of appealing explicitly to a common rhetorical in-group may also entail framing a political issue in a particular way and establishing the legitimacy of a particular course of action (cf. Finlayson, 2006) is provided in Tileagă's (2008) analysis of the former president Ion Iliescu's addresses in the Romanian Parliament during official commemorations of the Romanian revolution of 1989. These official commemorations took place in the context of a series of ongoing political controversies, including competing accounts of over the "events" of the revolution (the thousands of innocent deaths), and debates concerning Iliescu's own role in the overthrow of Ceauşescu and his own sudden rise to power. In addition, commentators were questioning the absence of specific policies designed to confront the legacy of the communist past, for example, the failure to establish laws limiting the political influence of former members of the Communist Party or collaborators of the secret services.

Tileagă notes how, against this background, Iliescu used the occasions of the official commemorations to establish a particular identity in relation to the Romanian people, which also served to promote his own preferred version of the revolution. In the opening section of his speeches, Iliescu used both formal forms of address ("Ladies and gentlemen, senators and deputies," "Distinguished members of the legislative bodies") and informal forms of address ("Dear friends from the days and nights of the December revolution," "Dear revolutionary friends"). The formal forms of address indexed Iliescu's institutional identity and representative capacity. Through the informal forms of address, Iliescu positioned himself within the imagined community of "revolutionaries" (a post-1989 descriptor conferred on anyone who was seen as having actively taken part in the revolution). In so doing, Iliescu presented himself as the possessor of firsthand, insider knowledge of the revolutionary events This identity claim thus established Iliescu's category entitlement to pass judgment on the events in question, which he used to warrant his preferred version of the events as "pure" revolution, and in so doing countered alternative versions of the Romanian revolution as a coup d'etat involving the Securitate (the secret police), or a foreign plot to force Ceauşescu from office.

4.3. Constructing Aspirational Identities

It is not always possible or expedient for a communicator to address a composite audience as a single group. One alternative involves a strategy that Frank (2011) termed *constitutive futurity*. This refers to a form of representation in which the object of political address (e.g., the "nation") is projected into an undetermined future. In this way, a speaker is not confined to constructing a common rhetorical in-group located in the narrative here-and-now, but can speak to, and on behalf of, "a people that is not ... yet" (p. 182).

Rogers (2012) suggests that the use of aspirational (rather than descriptive) appeals to common identity may have particular purchase when a speaker is acting as advocate for a group that is currently positioned outside, or on the margins of, a particular political community, as exemplified in Martin Luther King's (1963) "I Have a Dream" speech. Rogers focuses in particular on the strategies that W. E. B. Du Bois[11] employed in his collection of polemical essays, *The Souls of Black Folk* (1903). Rogers argues that Du Bois was faced with a specific rhetorical problem when addressing white audiences summed up by the question, "How will you move the people so that they will embrace an expanded view of themselves?" (p. 194). He suggests that Du Bois managed this by constructing an in-group that shared a common *political horizon* rather than a common identity in the historical present (cf. Dunmire, 2005).

Du Bois started out by extorting his (white) readership to sensitivity concerning the experiential aspects of social and political exclusion. Having established the audience's normative commitment to his rhetorical project through appeals to empathy, Du Bois went on to evoke in the reader a sense of shame for complicity in the suffering of black folks ("Let the ears of a guilty people tingle with truth"). Throughout, Du Bois adopted a complex authorial footing that invoked a distinction between (white) readers, the author, and black folk, but at the same time presented them all as participating in a common ideological project "in the arrival of a truth hitherto unavailable" (p. 196). This shared horizon involved for the white audiences the prospect of a new, extended sense of selfhood based on a sense of common emotional dispositions.[12]

4.4. Implicit Displays of Rhetorical Alignment

Although studies of the microfeatures of political rhetoric often focus on the ways in which political communicators overtly proclaim their membership of a particular category, researchers have also drawn attention to the ways in which social identities may be flagged implicitly, though dress, body posture, style of speech, and use of pronouns. The political alignments that people project through nonverbal media of communication do not always square with the ways in which they describe themselves. Condor and Abell (2006) consequently argue for the need to distinguish between explicit identity *avowals* (verbal acts of self-description) and implicit identity *displays* (the public performance of an identity).

An interesting example of the use of clothing to implicitly display multiple political allegiances is provided by Ahmed's (1997) analysis of Mohammed Ali Jinnah, the "Great Leader" of Pakistan (see also Reicher & Hopkins, 2001, p. 171). Ahmed described how Jinnah (a liberal, Anglicized individual who did not speak Urdu) used clothing to signal his identification with Muslims throughout the Indian subcontinent by adopting the coat (*sherwani*) worn in Aligarh, the cap (*karakuli*) worn by Muslims in North India, and the trousers (*shalwar*) worn in the areas that were to become West Pakistan.

Perhaps the most obvious way in which a speaker may implicitly display alignment with others is through the use of first-person plural pro-terms: "we," "us," or the possessive "our." Moss (1985, p. 86) suggests that the repeated use of "we" in political rhetoric serves to coalesce speaker and audience "so that the immediate impression is one of unity and common purpose." In addition, we may note that a particular advantage of pronouns lies in their capacity to signal a supposed unity and common purpose implicitly.

Some research has mapped the ways in which historical transformations in political alignment have been signaled through a communicator's use of the first-person plural. For example, Ventsel (2007) analyzes speeches made by the new political elite after the Soviet occupation of Estonia in 1940. He notes that immediately after the occupation, "we" was used simply to refer to the local communists who had carried out the coup, but it soon came to be used in a more inclusive sense, to construct a unified subject including both communist leaders and the people. However, within a year, a new addressee-exclusive "we" emerged, one that indexed the new leaders' alignment with the Party as opposed to the People.

Other research has compared the ways in which different politicians use personal pronouns to implicitly align themselves with particular groups. For example, Proctor and Su (2011) analyze the ways in which the various candidates used pronouns in interviews and debates in the run-up to the 2008 US presidential election. They noted that, in interview settings, Sarah Palin generally used "we" and "our" to signal solidarity with Americans and Alaskans, but rarely to signal solidarity with her running partner, presidential candidate John McCain. In contrast, Hillary Clinton generally used "we" to identify with the US government and the Democrats, but more rarely to indicate national identification. Barack Obama was most likely to use the first-person plural to refer to his campaign crew and to Americans.

4.5. Who Are "We"? Flexibility and Vagueness in the Use of First-Person Pronouns

Although there are some circumstances in which it may be expedient for a speaker to index his or alignment with a particular section of the audience, as we have already noted, politicians are often concerned to maintain alignment with diverse groups. Some analyses of political rhetoric have emphasized how communicators adopt a *segmental technique*, addressing different sections of their composite audience sequentially. In this context, first-person plural pronouns may represent a useful resource insofar as the use of "we" and "us" can enable a speaker to align him- or herself sequentially with different (possibly conflicting) subgroups without obviously appearing to shift narrative footing. For example, Wilson (1990) and Maitland and Wilson (1987) analyze speeches presented by Margaret Thatcher while she was prime minister of the United Kingdom. Within the same speech, and even within the same sentence, she could use "we" to align herself with the Conservative Party, the Government, the British citizenry, or all right-thinking people.

Myers (1999) observed that one problem with the segmental technique is that it does not enable speakers to ingratiate themselves "simultaneously to the diverse components of a composite audience" (p. 56). Studies of political rhetoric have noted how communicators often employ strategic ambiguity, formulating arguments in a manner that is sufficiently vague as to admit a variety of possible interpretations. Vague formulations can serve a dual rhetorical function for a political communicator. First, they may be acceptable to (or at least difficult to challenge by) various sections of a heterogeneous audience. Second, while appearing decisive, they do not in fact commit the speaker to any particular course of action, therefore allowing for future flexibility in political rhetoric and policy decisions whilst maintaining an apparent stance of ideological commitment and consistency of purpose. Fortunately for political communicators, the precise referent of first-person plural pronouns can be so vague as to elude even professional linguists (Borthen, 2010).

Duncan (2011) reports a particular variety of strategic ambiguity that he terms *polemical ambiguity*. This involves a speaker using strong dualistic formulations, but expressing them through forms of wording that are so vague that the precise nature of the argument is unclear to potential allies in the audience, while potentially alienated groups perceive a clear message with which they can identify. As an example, Duncan took the case of President George W. Bush's speech to a joint session of the US Congress on September 20, 2001, in which he was addressing the composite audience of the members of Congress and also the universal audiences of the American people, and by implication, "the leadership and citizenry of all other nations in the world, as well as terrorist groups … [in short] the entire planet" (p. 457). Duncan noted Bush's heavy use of "globe-sweeping antithes[es]" (p. 458): right versus wrong, good versus evil, us versus them (see also Coe, Domke, Graham, John, & Pickard, 2004; Lazar & Lazar, 2004). This polemical style was, Duncan observed, accompanied by the consistent use of vague and ambiguous referents, as illustrated by the text's well-known climax:

> And **we** will pursue nations that provide aid or safe haven to terrorism. Every nation in every region now has a decision to make: Either **you** are with **us** or **you** are with the terrorists. From this day forward, any nation that continues to harbor or support terrorism will be regarded by the United States as a hostile regime.

The meaning of phrases such as "aid or safe haven to terrorism," or "harbor or support terrorism" is unclear, and Bush's argument would be hard to refute on either epistemological or moral grounds. Of particular relevance to our current concerns is the ambiguity of Bush's use of pronouns: *we, us,* and *you.* In all cases, these pronouns clearly do not include "the terrorists" (whoever they may be). However, in context, *you* could refer to "any nation, nations, or peoples, whether currently an ally, enemy, or neutral" (Duncan, 2011, p. 458). *We* and *us* could mean "the United States, all Americans, Republicans, supporters of the Bush administration, North Atlantic Treaty Organization (NATO) members, the Western world, peace-loving peoples, or just the winners" (p. 458).

4.6. Using Pronouns to Display Complex Political Allegiances

In English, as in many other European languages, the first-person plural can be used in an inclusive or an exclusive sense. Terms such as "we" and "us" can, on occasions, exclude either the speaker or the audience. For example, a *speaker-exclusive* "we" (De Cock, 2011) can be used to signal allegiance rather than literal identification, as exemplified by Churchill's famous speech, made after the evacuation of Dunkirk in 1940: "**We** shall fight on the beaches, **we** shall fight on the landing grounds." As Wilson, (1990) observed, Churchill was not suggesting that he personally would be participating in the armed combat. The speaker-exclusive "we" may also be used to display goodwill toward, or shared common ground in relation to, those very communities of opinion with whom a speaker is currently disagreeing. The following example has been taken from W. E. B. Du Bois's 1928 speech, *The Negro Citizen.*[13]

> So, too, in the matter of housing, recreation and crime **we** seem here to assume that a knowledge of the facts of discrimination and of the needs of the colored public are sufficient, with faith, hope and charity, to bring ultimate betterment.

Du Bois was arguing that mere knowledge of the disadvantages faced by African Americans would not be sufficient to ensure progressive social change. Consequently, he was not using *we* to signal his acceptance of a common point of view. Rather, his use of *we* in this context is indexing his empathy with, and goodwill toward, the audience.In other situations, political commentators may include themselves in the pronoun "we" but exclude their audience. The use of an *addressee-exclusive* "we" is perhaps most obvious in cases where politicians use first-person plural pronouns to refer specifically to their political party or to the government. The following example was taken from a speech by Vernon Coaker MP, delivered to the Centenary Conference of the Irish Labour Party in 2012[14]:

> **We** in the Labour Party will speak up for the peace and progress—as the party who in government helped with others to bring about the Good Friday Agreement and all that flowed from it—and **we** will stand up for fairness in tough times.

Even in cases such as this, the precise referent of the pronoun may remain underdetermined. Coaker, a member of the British Labour Party, regularly slipped between using "we in the Labour Party" as (nationally) audience-exclusive and as (politically) audience-inclusive.[15]

Addressee-exclusive we's can also be used to soften disagreement. Fløttum (2010) quoted the following extract from an address made by Tony Blair to the European Parliament in 2005:

> **We** talk of crisis. Let **us** first talk of achievement.

Blair was presenting the discourse of "crisis" as his antilogos. Consequently, in this utterance, *we* actually means "they" or "you," and *us* means "me." One might reasonably suppose that Blair's objective in referring to his political adversaries as "we" was to display a general sense of empathy and goodwill. However, we cannot tell whether audiences did, in fact, interpret his words in this way. Depending on context, speaker-exclusive "we's" can be interpreted as markers of empathy, or as coercive or condescending.

The referents of first-person plural pronouns are not confined to the narrative present. As a consequence, a communicator can use terms such as "we" or "our" to display consubstantiality with historically expanded social categories, and to construct aspirational in-groups (Condor, 2006). This is illustrated in the following extract from a speech presented by George W. Bush to the Pentagon in 2003:

> **We cannot** know the duration of this war, yet **we know** its outcome: **We will** prevail...the Iraqi people will be free, and **our world** will be more secure and peaceful.

Bush's first two uses of **we** are within present-tense clauses and conjure up the image of shared experience between people existing in the narrative here-and-now. However, his third and fourth use of the firstperson plural (*we* will…, *our* world will…) projects his rhetorical in-group into an indeterminate future, possibly beyond the lifetimes of the people included in his first two synchronic we's.

4.7. Using First-Person Plural Pronouns to Convey Ideological Messages

We have already noted how a speaker may use explicit identity appeals not simply as a generic means by which to enlist an audience, but also to establish a commitment to a particular ideological project. When speakers enlist audiences using first-person plural pronouns, ideological messages may be imported into their arguments more subtly.

Linguists have noted how the referent of first-person plural pronouns may "wander" (Petersoo, 2007) within speeches or texts and even within single sentences or phrases. The slippery nature of terms such as "we" and "us" means that they can be used to link a potentially contentious political concept to a relatively benign one. For example, in political discourse, authors may start out by using "we" as a reference to themselves and their immediate audience, but then slip to using "we" to refer to the government, and to using "our" to refer to the economy or the armed services (e.g., "the strength of our economy"). In this way, a speaker may subtly elide the interests of the audience with those and with the government, the military, or corporate business (Fairclough, 2000).

This capacity for construct elision through referent slippage takes its most extreme form in what Billig (1995) terms the *syntax of hegemony*, in which the vagueness of first-person plural pronouns establishes a functional equivalence between a particular group and universal humanity. As Billig (1995, p. 90) observes, by mobilizing a nonspecific "we," political orators can present the interests of their party, government, nation as coinciding with those of the entire world, "so long as 'we' do not specify what 'we' mean by 'we,' but instead allow the first person plural to suggest a harmony of interests and identities."

This kind of rhetorical formulation has been most extensively studied in New World Order rhetoric on "the war on terror" (e.g., Coe et al., 2004; Leudar, Marsland, & Nekvapil, 2004; Lazar & Lazar, 2004). As we saw from the quotation from George W. Bush's 2001 speech cited above, in US foreign policy statements, "we" can both be used to signify the United States and also to refer to a US-led system of collective security. An example of the use of the syntax of hegemony can be seen in the quotation from George W. Bush's 2003 speech cited above:

> **We** cannot know the duration of this war, yet **we** know its outcome: **We** will prevail…the Iraqi people will be free, and **our world** will be more secure and peaceful.

From the context, "we" could refer equally to the United States or to the coalition. However, "our world" could be interpreted as a universal referent, suggesting that the US national or international military alliance is defending universal interests and universal values of freedom, security, and peace.

As we noted earlier, the allegiances that a communicator displays through the use of pronouns need not always square with the identities to which they explicitly lay claim. Condor (2006) coined the term *forked tongue strategy* to refer to a situation in which a speaker explicitly claims one identity and ideological commitment in principle, while displaying a different set of allegiances and ideological commitments through deictic reference. As an example, let us consider the following stretch of talk taken from the opening statement by the chair of a meeting of the Scottish National Party, reported in Reicher and Hopkins, (2001, p. 165).

> Fellow Scots! It gives me great pleasure to welcome you all here tonight. And when I say "fellow Scots" I include all those categories excluded by Nicholas Fairbairn. And I also include all **our** English friends who live among **us**, and who have chosen to throw in their lot with **us**, more than a few.

Reicher and Hopkins's original analysis focused on the explicit message conveyed in this stretch of talk. They noted how the speaker was invoking an inclusive in-group, thus potentially maximizing his potential constituency of representation. In his metadiscursive move ("And when I say 'fellow Scots'"), the speaker argued that this category construction reflects his party's ideological commitment to a civic understanding of Scottish identity, one that was not shared by the Conservative Party (whose more exclusive definition of the category of Scots had been exemplified in a speech made four days earlier by the MP Nicholas Fairbairn). For present purposes, however, the significant aspect of this stretch of talk lies in the way in which, in the very course of proclaiming his inclusive understanding of Scottish identity, the speaker uses pronouns to implicitly exclude people born in England ("*our* English friends") from the Scottish national "us."

5. CONCLUDING REMARKS

The study of rhetoric is necessarily a reflexive enterprise. Anyone who writes on the subject of rhetoric is also using rhetoric. Throughout this chapter, we have noted some of the difficulties involved in summarizing the topic of political rhetoric for a mixed and multiple audience of political psychologists. In the first place, it is not easy to place the subject into a tidy academic pigeonhole. Work on political rhetoric is not the province of any particular discipline, and there is no single essential feature that can be used to distinguish theory and research on political rhetoric from work on political argument, debate, communication, or discourse. In part, our aim in this chapter has been to provide a coherent overview of theoretical and empirical work that was originally conceived and written within a variety of academic traditions.

Any discussion of rhetoric in general, and political rhetoric in particular, cannot easily be delimited historically. In this chapter we have emphasized recently published work in order to update the information conveyed in the previous edition of the *Handbook*. However, because contemporary scholars continue to use classical terminology and to draw upon the writings of Aristotle, Plato, and Cicero, we cannot simply confine past writing on rhetoric to academic history. More generally, it is difficult for an author to structure an overview of work on political rhetoric in the standard narrative form conventionally used for reviewing a body of psychological research. Many contemporary authors would resist the idea that their work is "progressing" beyond the classical tradition. Moreover, much of the recent work on political rhetoric tends to take the form of individual piecemeal studies, rather than systematic, incremental, research programs.

On the one hand, the disconnected character of much current research on political rhetoric might reasonably be regarded as a problem. Certainly, the lack of cross-referencing between articles on similar issues (especially common when this work has been conducted by academics with different disciplinary affiliations) is regrettable, not least because individual authors often coin neologisms, leading to a confusing diversity of terminology to refer to what are, essentially, similar considerations. On the other hand, it is important to recognize that many of the apparent problems that confront anyone attempting to review work on political rhetoric are also reflections of the very nature of the subject matter. Rhetoric is essentially and inevitably complex, reflexive, argumentative, fluid, and contextual. Consequently, political psychologists who have been trained in the technē of operationalization and experimental control may find the study of rhetoric something of an intellectual culture shock.

In the worlds of political rhetoric, constructs cannot be marshaled into dependent, independent, moderating, and mediating variables. Analyses of specific examples of political rhetoric do not treat context as a predesignated setting in which, or to which, individuals respond. Rather, the "rhetorical situation" is itself understood to be constituted through the process of argument. Analysis of the fine detail of political rhetoric reveals social categories and stereotypes to be the objects of continual contestation, and draws our attention to the ways in which political actors may attend to multiple facets of their identity simultaneously.

Consideration of the ways in which people structure and respond to political arguments shows that their actions are not solely determined by particular norms rendered salient by a specific social context, nor are they motivated simply by a need to reduce subjective uncertainty. On the contrary, political communications are typically formulated with a view to dilemmatic epistemological and moral concerns, and to competing prescriptive norms for action. Kane and Patapan (2010) describe political rhetoric as the "artless art," in recognition of the fact that political leaders need to use rhetoric without appearing to do so. Effective political communicators also need to deal with a range of additional competing demands, such as demonstrating consistency in defense of a particular ideological project while avoiding charges of partiality; or mobilizing identity categories while at the same time maintaining the appearance of rational disinterest (Potter & Edwards, 1990).

Billig ([1987] 1996) borrows the 16th-century rhetorician Ralph Lever's term "witcraft" to describe the skilful and creative ways in which professional politicians and ordinary social actors formulate arguments in the context of debate. By paying attention to the fine details of political argumentation, we can appreciate how speakers can mobilize similar considerations to support quite different rhetorical ends, and how the same rhetorical project may be supported by an infinite number of possible lines of argument. In short, political communicators use language and other symbolic resources flexibly, creatively, and ironically to construct new patterns of argument, and to undermine the newly constructed claims of their opponents. Consequently, any quest for general laws, which neatly map particular rhetorical forms onto specific functions, will necessarily be doomed to failure.

For researchers accustomed to parsing human behavior into factors and levels, into stable entities or quantifiable dimensions, the study of political rhetoric confronts us with the apparent chaos of an underdetermined and monstrous realm where utterances are polyvalent, actions evasive, and values dilemmatic, and where factual assertions and appeals to consensual common sense may be successful insofar as they are, in practice, radically ambiguous. For the scholar of rhetoric, on the other hand, these complexities are regarded as evidence of witcraft, of the inventiveness, playfulness, and deadly seriousness of human social and political life.

ACKNOWLEDGMENTS

The authors wish to thank Nick Hopkins, Alan Finlayson and Neil Foxlee for their help in preparing this essay, and Leonie Huddy for invaluable editorial advice.

NOTES

1. Contemporary commentators often suggest that rhetorical scholarship may itself promote a democratic message insofar as it holds out the "promise of reason" against the "brute force" of violence, or authoritarian coercion (Gage, 2011). Theorists who adopt a rhetorical perspective often challenge deficit models of mass publics (Troup, 2009) insofar as they recognize, and celebrate, ordinary citizens' capacity to engage in open-ended reasoning and rational debate about public affairs.

2. Garver (2009) has questioned whether actual instances of rhetorical argument easily fit into this classificatory scheme.

3. Notwithstanding an in-principle recognition of the importance of the visual aspects of political rhetoric, most empirical research continues to focus on the spoken and written word, seldom even considering the ways in which information and evaluation may be

conveyed through intonation, facial expressions, or hand movements (cf. Mendoza-Denton & Jannedy, 2011; Streeck, 2008).

4. Political "representation" may itself be understood in various ways (Pitkin, 1967; Saward, 2010). In democratic regimes, an elected representative may be positioned as *delegates*, acting as spokesperson for their constituents, or as *trustees*, charged with using their expert skills to serve the best interests of those they represent, even if their arguments do not necessarily reflect the immediate will of the people themselves. Spokespeople for nongovernmental organizations may claim to represent the interests of a particular constituency without the members ever being consulted. Finally, an individual or group can adopt the stance of defending the interests or rights of animals or "the planet," a practice that might be understood as a form of *stewardship*.

5. This inclusive notion of rhetoric is not universally accepted. For example, Bitzer (1968) restricted his construct of the *rhetorical situation* to settings in there is an exigency that is capable of being modified though discourse, and where there is an audience that is potentially capable of being influenced by the discourse and acting as mediators of change.

6. Billig (1996; Shotter & Billig, 1998) noted parallels between rhetorical psychology and Wittgenstein's (1953) understanding of language as the vehicle of thought (remark 329), and Bakhtin's (1981) perspective on thought as inner speech.

7. For a similar perspective on attitudes as evaluative discourse, see Potter (1998).

8. In this respect, rhetorical psychology focuses on what social psychologists have traditionally termed verbal or public (as opposed to private and implicit) attitudes.

9. At the time that Billig was developing rhetorical psychology, social psychologists typically endorsed what subsequent commentators called a *file draw model* of attitudes, according to which individuals hold opinions on all manner of issues that they simply retrieve from memory for the purposes of responding to survey questions. More recent perspectives on attitudes as online constructions (e.g. Schwarz, 2007) differ from Billig's approach insofar as they regard attitudes primarily as mental phenomena, but share his concern for the ways in which attitude statements are formulated in local interaction.

10. Although Finlayson distinguished RPA from linguistic and critical discourse analytic approaches, in practice his account of the ways in which RPA might inform empirical research has much in common with these perspectives. In addition, Finlayson's focus on the use of rhetoric in political decision-making has clear parallels with Fairclough and Fairclough's (e.g. 2012) critical discourse analytic approach to *practical reasoning*.

11. Du Bois had received training in classical rhetoric at Harvard (Rampersad, 1976).

12. This observation has parallels with recent social psychological work that has considered the role of intergroup emotions such as empathy (Dovidio et al., 2010) shame and guilt (Lickel, Steele, & Schmader, 2011) in promoting support for minorities on the part of majorities.

13. National Interracial Conference, December 1928, Washington, DC.

14. April 17, 2012, speech reported at http://www.publicservice.co.uk/feature_story. asp?id=19629.

15. In addition, when a politician uses a political-party or government "we," it is not always clear whether the speaker is necessarily signaling his or her own personal commitment to the content of a message. Bull and Fetzer (Bull & Fetzer 2006; Fetzer & Bull, 2008) have noted how politicians may on occasions use a collective (normally party) "we" to avoid being held personally accountable for a potentially contentious view or course of action.

REFERENCES

Ahmed, A. (1997). *Jinnah, Pakistan and Islamic identity*. London: Routledge.

Antaki, C., & Leudar, I. (1991). Recruiting the record: Using opponents' exact words in parliamentary argumentation. *Text, 21*, 467–488.

Aristotle. (1909). *Rhetorica*. Cambridge: Cambridge University Press.

Atkins, J. (2010). Moral arguments and the justification of policy. *British Journal of Politics and International Relations, 12*, 408–424.

Augoustinos, M., Tuffin, K., & Every, D. (2005). New racism, meritocracy and individualism. *Discourse & Society, 16*, 315–340.

Baker-Brown, G., Ballard, E., Bluck, S., deVries, B., Suedfeld, P., & Tetlock, P. (1992). *Scoring manual for integrative and conceptual complexity*. University of British Columbia.

Bakhtin, M. (1981). *The dialogic imagination* (M. Holquist, ed., C. Emerson & M. Holquist, trans.). Austin: University of Texas Press.

Barthes, R. (1977). Rhetoric of the image. In *Image, music, text* (S. Heath, ed. and trans.) (pp. 32–51). New York: Hill and Wang.

Beasley, V. (2001). The rhetoric of ideological consensus in the United States. *Communication Monographs, 68*, 169–183.

Bennett, W. L., & Iyengar, S. (2008). A new era of minimal effects? *Journal of Communication, 58*, 707–731.

Benschop, Y., Halsema, L., & Schreurs, P. (2001). The division of labour and inequalities between the sexes: An ideological dilemma. *Gender, Work and Organization, 8*, 1–18.

Billig, M. (1985). Prejudice, categorization and particularization—from a perceptual to a rhetorical approach. *European Journal of Social Psychology, 15*, 79–103.

Billig, M. ([1987] 1996). *Arguing and thinking: A rhetorical approach to social psychology*. Cambridge: Cambridge University Press.

Billig, M. (1988a). Methodology and scholarship in understanding ideological explanation. In C. Antaki (ed.), *Analysing everyday explanation* (pp. 199–214). London: Sage.

Billig, M. (1988b). Rhetorical and historical aspects of attitudes: The case of the British monarchy. *Philosophical Psychology, 1*, 83–103.

Billig, M. (1989). The argumentative nature of holding strong views—a case-study. *European Journal of Social Psychology, 19*, 203–223.

Billig, M. (1991). *Ideology and opinions*. London: Sage.

Billig, M. (1992). *Talking of the royal family*. London: Routledge.

Billig, M. (1994). Rhetorical and ideological dimensions of common sense. In J. Siegfried (ed.), *The status of common sense in psychology* (pp. 121–145). Westport, CT: Ablex.

Billig, M. (1995). *Banal nationalism*. London: Sage.

Billig, M. (2001). Humour and hatred: The racist jokes of the Ku Klux Klan. *Discourse and Society, 12*, 267–289.

Billig, M. (2008). *The hidden roots of critical psychology*. London: Sage.

Billig, M., Condor, S., Edwards, D., Gane, M., Middleton, D., & Radley, A. R. (1988). *Ideological dilemmas: A social psychology of everyday thinking*. London: Sage.

Bitzer, L. (1968). The rhetorical situation. *Philosophy and Rhetoric, 1*, 1–14.

Booth, W. (2004). *The rhetoric of rhetoric*. Oxford: Blackwell.

Boromisza-Habashi, D. (2011). Dismantling the antiracist "hate speech" agenda in Hungary: An ethno-rhetorical analysis. *Text & Talk, 31*, 1–19.

Borthen, K. (2010). On how we interpret plural pronouns. *Journal of Pragmatics, 42*, 1799–1815.

Bostdorff, D. (2011). Epideictic rhetoric in the services of war. *Communication Monographs, 78,* 296–323.

Bozatzis, N. (2009). Occidentalism and accountability: Constructing culture and cultural difference in majority Greek talk about the minority in Western Thrace. *Discourse & Society, 20,* 431–453.

Browne, J., & Dickson, E. (2010). "We don't talk to terrorists": On the rhetoric and practice of secret negotiations. *Journal of Conflict Resolution, 54,* 379–407.

Bruner, J., Goodnow, J., & Austin, G. (1956). *A study of thinking.* New York: Wiley.

Buckler, S. (2007). Theory, ideology, rhetoric. *British Journal of Politics and International Relations, 9,* 36–54.

Bull, P. (2008). "Slipperiness, evasion and ambiguity": Equivocation and facework in non-committal political discourse. *Journal of Language and Social Psychology, 27,* 324–332.

Bull, P., & Fetzer, A. (2006). Who are we and who are you? The strategic use of forms of address in political interviews. *Text & Talk, 26,* 3–37.

Burke, K. (1969). *A rhetoric of motives.* Berkeley: University of California Press.

Burman, E., & Parker, I. (1993). *Discourse analytic research.* London: Routledge.

Charland, M. (1987). Constitutive rhetoric: The case of the Peuple Quebecois. *Quarterly Journal of Speech, 73,* 133–150.

Chavez, K. (2011). Counter-public enclaves and understanding the function of rhetoric in social movement coalition-building. *Communication Quarterly, 59,* 1–18.

Coe, K., Domke, D., Graham, E. S., John, S. L., & Pickard, V. W. (2004). No shades of gray: The binary discourse of George W. Bush and an echoing press. *Journal of Communication, 54,* 234–252.

Coe, K., & Reitzes, M. (2010). Obama on the stump: Features and determinants of a rhetorical approach. *Presidential Studies Quarterly, 40,* 391–413.

Condor, S. (2000). Pride and prejudice: Identity management in English people's talk about 'this country'. *Discourse and Society, 11,* 163–193.

Condor, S. (2006). Temporality and collectivity: Images of time and history in English national representation. *British Journal of Social Psychology, 45,* 657–682.

Condor, S. (2011). Rebranding Britain? Ideological dilemmas in political appeals to "British multiculturalism." In M. Barrett, C. Flood, & J. Eade (eds.), *Nationalism, ethnicity, citizenship: Multidisciplinary perspectives* (pp. 101–134). Cambridge Scholars.

Condor, S., & Abell, J. (2006). Vernacular accounts of national identity in post-devolution Scotland and England. In J. Wilson & K. Stapleton (eds.), *Devolution and identity* (pp. 51–76). Aldershot: Ashgate.

Condor, S., & Gibson, S. (2007). "Everybody's entitled to their own opinion": Ideological dilemmas of liberal individualism and active citizenship. *Journal of Community and Applied Social Psychology, 6,* 178–199.

Conley, T. (1990). *Rhetoric in the European tradition.* Chicago: University of Chicago Press.

Deacon, D., & Wring, D. (2011). Reporting the 2010 general election: Old media, new media – old politics, new politics. In D. Wring & R. Mortimore (Eds.), *Political communication in Britain: the leader debates, the campaign and the media in the 2010 general election* (pp. 281–303). Palgrave: Macmillan.

De Castella, K., & McGarty, C. (2011). Two leaders, two wars. *Analysis of Social Issues & Public Policy, 11,* 180–200.

De Cock, B. (2011). Why we can be you. *Journal of Pragmatics, 43,* 2762–2775.

Dickerson, P. (1998). I did it for the nation: Repertoires of intent in televised political discourse. *British Journal of Social Psychology, 37,* 477–494.

Dmitriev, A. (2008). Humor and politics. *Russian Social Science Review, 49,* 53–89.

Dovidio, J. F., Johnson, J. D., Gaertner, S. L., Pearson, A. R., Saguy, T., & Ashburn- Nardo, L. (2010). Empathy and intergroup relations. In M. Mikulincer & P. R. Shaver (eds.), *Prosocial motives, emotions, and behavior* (pp. 393–408). Washington, DC: American Psychological Association.

Dryzek, J. S. (2010). Rhetoric in democracy. *Political Theory, 38,* 319–339.

Du Bois, W. E. B. (1903). *The souls of black folk.* New York: Bantam.

Duncan, M. (2011). Polemical ambiguity and the composite audience. *Rhetoric Society Quarterly, 41,* 455–471.

Dunmire, P. (2005). Preempting the future: Rhetoric and ideology of the future on political discourse. *Discourse & Society, 16,* 481–513.

Easterly, W., & Williamson, C. (2011). Rhetoric versus reality: The best and worst of aid agency practices. *World Development, 39,* 1930–1949.

Eaton, M. (2010). Manufacturing community in an online activist organization: The rhetoric of MoveOn.org's e-mails. *Information, Communication & Society, 13,* 174–192.

Edelman, M. (1977). *Political language: Words that succeed and policies that fail.* New York: Academic Press.

Edwards, D. (1997). *Discourse and cognition.* London: Sage.

Endres, D., & Senda-Cook, S. (2011). Location matters: The rhetoric of place in protest. *Quarterly Journal of Speech, 97,* 257–282.

Esch, J. (2010). Legitimizing the "war on terror." *Political Psychology, 31,* 357–391.

Every, D., & Augoustinos, M. (2007). Constructions of racism in the Australian parliamentary debates on asylum seekers. *Discourse & Society 18,* 411–436.

Fairclough, I., & Fairclough, N. (2012). *Political discourse analysis.* London: Routledge.

Fairclough, N. (2000). *New labour, new language?* London: Routledge.

Ferrari, F. (2007). Metaphor at work in the analysis of political discourse. *Discourse & Society, 18,* 603–625.

Fetzer, A., & Bull, P. (2008). "Well I answer it by simply inviting you to look at the evidence": The strategic use of pronouns in political interviews. *Journal of Language and Politics, 7,* 271–289.

Figgou, L., & Condor, S. (2007). Categorising category labels in interview accounts about the "Muslim minority" in Greece. *Journal of Ethnic and Migration Studies, 33,* 439–459.

Finlayson, A. (2004). Political science, political ideas and rhetoric. *Economy and Society, 33,* 528–549.

Finlayson, A. (2006). For the sake of argument: Re-imagining political communication. *Soundings, 44,* 34–43.

Finlayson. A. (2007). From beliefs to arguments: Interpretative methodology and rhetorical political analysis. *British Journal of Politics and International Relations, 9,* 545–563.

Finlayson, A., & Martin, J. (2008). "It ain't what you say . . .": British political studies and the analysis of speech and rhetoric, *British Politics, 3,* 445–464.

Finell, E., & Liebkind, K. (2010). National symbols and distinctiveness. *British Journal of Social Psychology, 49,* 321–341.

Fløttum, K. (2010). EU discourse: Polyphony and unclearness. *Journal of Pragmatics, 42,* 990–999.

Fracchiolla, B. (2011). Politeness as a strategy of attack in gendered political debate. *Journal of Pragmatics, 43,* 2480–2488.

Frank, D. (2011). Obama's rhetorical signature. *Rhetoric and Public Affairs, 14,* 605–630.

Fridkin, K., & Kenney, P. (2011). Variability in citizens' reactions to different types of negative campaigns. *American Journal of Political Science, 55,* 307–325.

Frye, J., & Bruner, M. (Eds.). (2012). *The rhetoric of food: Discourse, materiality, and power.* London: Routledge.

Foxlee, N. (2012). An introduction to rhetoric and rhetorical criticism. Presentation to the Language, Ideology and Power Research Group (LIP), LAEL, Lancaster University, April 30.

Gaard, G. (2010). Reproductive technology of reproductive justice? An ecofeminist, environmental justice perspective on the rhetoric of choice. *Ethics and the Environment, 15,* 103–130.

Gage, J. (Ed.). (2011). *The promise of reason: Studies in the new rhetoric.* Carbondale: Southern Illinois University Press.

Gallie, W. B. (1956), Essentially contested concepts. *Proceedings of the Aristotelian Society, 56,* 167–198.

Garsten, B. (2011). The rhetoric revival in political theory. *Annual Review of Political Science, 14,* 159–180.

Garver, E. (2009). Aristotle on the kinds of rhetoric. *Rhetorica, 27,* 1–18.

Gibson, S. (2011). Dilemmas of citizenship: young people's conceptions of un/employment rights and responsibilities. *British Journal of Social Psychology, 50,* 450–468.

Gill, A., & Whedbee, K. (1997). Rhetoric. In T. A. van Dijk (Ed), *Discourse as structure and process* (pp. 157–184). London, Sage.

Gray, J. (1978). On liberty, liberalism and essential contestability. *British Journal of Political Science, 8,* 385–402.

Griggs, S., & Howarth, D. (2004). A transformative political campaign? The new rhetoric of protest against airport expansion in the UK. *Political Ideologies, 9,* 181–201.

Grube, D. (2010). The rhetorical framing of policy intervention. *Australian Journal of Political Science, 45,* 559–578.

Hamilton, L., & Gibson, S. (2011). The rhetorical construction of polity membership. *Journal of Community and Applied Social Psychology, 21,* 228–242.

Hammack, P., & Pilecki, A. (2012). Narrative as a root metaphor for political psychology. *Political Psychology, 33,* 75–103.

Hampton, K. (2011). Comparing bonding and bridging ties for democratic engagement: Everyday use of communication technologies within social networks for civic and civil behaviors. *Information, Communication & Society, 14,* 510–528.

Harré, R., & Gillett, G. (1994). *The discursive mind.* London: Sage.

Hehir, A. (2011). *The responsibility to protect: Rhetoric, reality and the future of humanitarian intervention.* Hampshire: Palgrave Macmillan.

Hill, C., & Helmers, M. (2004). *Defining visual rhetorics.* Mahwah, NJ: Lawrence Erlbaum.

Hopkins, N., & Kahani-Hopkins, V. (2004). The antecedents of identification: A rhetorical analysis of British Muslim activists' constructions of community and identity. *British Journal of Social Psychology, 43,* 41–57.

Hopkins, N., & Kahani-Hopkins, V. (2006). Minority group members' theories of intergroup contact. *British Journal of Social Psychology, 45,* 245–264.

Hopkins, N., & Kahani-Hopkins, V. (2009). Reconceptualising "extremism" and "moderation": From categories of analysis to categories of practice in the construction of collective identity. *British Journal of Social Psychology, 48,* 99–113.

Hopkins, N., & Reicher, S. (1997). Social movement rhetoric and the social psychology of collective action. *Human Relations, 50,* 261–286.

Hopkins, N., Reicher, S., & Kahani-Hopkins, V. (2003). Citizenship, participation and identity construction: Political mobilization amongst British Muslims. *Psychologica Belgica, 43,* 33–54.

Ilie, C. (2003). Discourse and metadiscourse in parliamentary debates. *Journal of Language and Politics, 2*, 71–92.

Isaksen, J. (2011). Obama's rhetorical shift. *Communication Studies, 62*, 456–471.

Jansen, H., & Koop, R. (2005). Pundits, ideologues, and the ranters: The British Columbia election online. *Canadian Journal of Communication, 30*, 613–632.

Jerit, J. (2004). Survival of the fittest: Rhetoric during the course of an election campaign. *Political Psychology, 25*, 563–575.

Jost, J. T., Federico, C. M., & Napier, J. L. (2009). Political ideology: Its structure, functions and elective affinities. *Annual Review of Psychology, 60*, 307–337.

Jouët, J., Vedel, T., & Comby, J.-B. (2011). Political information and interpersonal conversations in a multimedia environment. *European Journal of Communication, 26*, 361–375.

Kane, J., & Patapan, H. (2010). The artless art: Leadership and the limits of democratic rhetoric. *Australian Journal of Political Science, 45*, 371–389.

Kahani-Hopkins, V., & Hopkins, N. (2002). 'Representing' British Muslims: The strategic dimension of identity construction. *Ethnic and Racial Studies, 25*, 288–309.

Kassimeris, G., & Jackson, L. (2011). The West, the rest and the "war on terror." *Contemporary Politics, 17*, 19–33.

Kaufer, D., & Al-Malki, A. (2009). The war on terror through Arab-American eyes: the Arab-American press as a rhetorical counter-public. *Rhetoric Review, 28*, 47–65.

Kaylor, B. (2011). *Presidential campaign rhetoric in an age of confessional politics.* Lanham, MD: Lexington Books.

Kephart, J., & Rafferty, S. (2009). "Yes we can": Rhizomic rhetorical agency in hyper-modern campaign ecologies. *Argumentation & Advocacy, 46*, 6–20.

Kratochvil, P., Cibulková, P., & Beneš, V. (2006). Foreign policy, rhetorical action and the idea of otherness. *Communist and Post-Communist Studies, 39*, 491–511.

Kurtz, T., Augoustinos, M., & Crabb, S. (2010). Contesting the "national interest" and maintaining "our lifestyle": A discursive analysis of political rhetoric around climate change. *British Journal of Social Psychology, 49*, 601–625.

Lazar, A., & Lazar, M. (2004). The discourse of the New World Order. *Discourse & Society, 15*, 223–242.

Leudar, I., Marsland, V., & Nekvapil, J. (2004). On membership categorization: "Us," "them" and "doing violence" in political discourse. *Discourse and Society, 15*, 243–266, H.

Lickel, B., Steele, R., & Schmader, T. (2011). Group-based shame and guilt. *Social and Personality Psychology Compass, 5*, 15163.

Maitland, K., & Wilson, J. (1987). Pronominal selection and ideological conflict. *Journal of Pragmatics, 11*, 495–512.

Marietta, M. (2012). *The politics of sacred rhetoric.* Waco, TX: Baylor University Press.

Mendoza-Denton, N., & Jannedy, S. (2011). Semiotic layering through gesture and intonation: A case study of complementary and supplementary multimodality in a political speech. *Journal of English Linguistics, 39*, 265–299.

McCrisken, T. (2011). Ten years on: Obama's war on terrorism in rhetoric and practice. *International Affairs, 87*, 781–801.

McGee, M. C. (1980). The "ideograph": A link between rhetoric and ideology. *Quarterly Journal of Speech, 66*, 1–16.

Middleton, M., Senda-Cook, S., & Endres, D. (2011). Articulating rhetorical field methods. *Western Journal of Communication, 75*, 386–406.

Morris, R. (1993). Visual rhetoric in political cartoons. *Metaphor & Symbolic Activity, 8*, 195–211.

Moss, P. (1985). The rhetoric of defence in the United States: language myth and ideology. In P. Chilton (Ed.), Language and the nuclear arms debate (pp 45–62). London: Pinter.

Mihelj, S., van Zoonen, L., & Vis, F. (2011). Cosmopolitan communication online. *British Journal of Sociology*, 62, 613–632.

Morley, J. (1886). *Critical miscellanies* (vol. 1). London: Macmillan.

Morreale, J. (1991). The political campaign film: Epideitic rhetoric in a documentary frame. In F. Biocca (ed.), *Television and political advertising* (pp. 187–201). Hillsdale, NJ: Lawrence Erlbaum.

Myers, F. (1999). Political argumentation and the composite audience: A case study. *Quarterly Journal of Speech*, 85, 55–71.

Nelson, J. S. (1977). The ideological connection. *Theory and Society*, 4, 421–448.

Oddo, J. (2011). War legitimation discourse: Representing 'Us' and 'Them' in four U.S. Presidential Addresses. *Discourse & Society*, 22, 287–314.

Orwenjo, D. (2009). Political grandstanding and the use of proverbs in African political discourse. *Discourse and Society*, 20, 123–146.

Partington, A. (2003). *The linguistics of political argument*. London: Routledge.

Payne, J. (2010). Narrating the change: Presidential campaigning rhetoric 2008. *American Behavioral Scientist*, 54, 335–336.

Perelman, C., & Olbrechts-Tyteca, L. (1969). *The new rhetoric* (J. Wilkson & P. Weaver, trans.). Notre Dame: University of Notre Dame Press.

Petersoo, P. (2007). What does "we" mean? *Journal of Language and Politics*, 6, 419–436.

Pitkin, H. (1967). *The concept of representation*. Berkeley: University of California Press.

Potter, J. (1997). *Representing reality*. London: Sage.

Potter, J. (1998). Discursive social psychology: From attitudes to evaluative practices. *European Review of Social Psychology*, 9, 233–266.

Potter, J. (2000). Post-cognitive psychology. *Theory & Psychology 10*, 31–37.

Potter, J., & Edwards, D. (1990). Nigel Lawson's tent: Discourse analysis, attribution theory and the social psychology of fact. *European Journal of Social Psychology*, 20, 405–424.

Potter, J., & Wetherell, M. (1987). *Discourse and social psychology*. London: Sage.

Proctor, K., & Su, L. (2011). The first person plural in political discourse. *Journal of Pragmatics*, 43, 3251–3266.

Rampersad, A. (1976). *The art and imagination of WEB Du Bois*. New York: Schocken Books.

Rapley, M. (1998). "Just an ordinary Australian": Self-categorization and the discursive construction of facticity in "new racist" political rhetoric. *British Journal of Social Psychology*, 37, 325–344.

Reicher, S., & Hopkins, N. (1996). Self-category constructions in political rhetoric: An analysis of Thatcher's and Kinnock's speeches concerning the British miners' strike (1984–5). *European Journal of Social Psychology*, 26, 353–371.

Reicher, S., & Hopkins, N. (2001). *Self and nation*. London: Sage.

Remer, G. (1999). Political oratory and conversation. *Political Theory*, 27, 39–65.

Roan, A., & White, C. (2010) A rhetoric of change. *Australian Journal of Political Science*, 45, 337–352.

Robin, R. (1992). *Enclaves of America: Rhetoric of American political architecture abroad*. Princeton, NJ: Princeton University Press.

Rogers, M. (2012). The people, rhetoric and affect. *American Political Science Review*, 106, 188–203.

Roque, G. (2008). Political rhetoric in visual images. In E. Weigand (ed.), *Dialogue and rhetoric* (pp. 185–193). Amsterdam: John Benjamins.

Rosch, E. (1978). Principles of categorization. In E. Rosch & B. B. Lloyd (eds.), *Cognition and categorization* (pp. 27–48). Hillsdale, NJ: Erlbaum.

Sapountzis, A. (2008). Towards a critical social psychological account of national sentiments. *Social and Personality Psychology Compass, 2*, 34–50.

Saward, M. (2010). *The representative claim*. Oxford: Oxford University Press.

Schwarz, N. (2007). Attitude construction: valuation in context. *Social Cognition, 5*, 638–656.

Scott, D. (2010). *Poetics of the poster: The rhetoric of image/text*. Liverpool: Liverpool University Press.

Shapin, S. (2001). Proverbial economies. *Social Studies of Science, 31*, 731–769.

Shibamoto-Smith, J. (2011). Honorifics, "politeness" and power in Japanese political debate. *Journal of Pragmatics, 43*, 3707–3791.

Shotter, J. (1993). *Conversational realities: Constructing life through language*. London: Sage.

Shotter, J., & Billig, M. (1998). A Bakhtinian psychology: From out of the heads of individuals into the dialogues between them. In M. Gardiner & M. M. Bell (eds.), *Bakhtin and the human sciences* (pp. 13–29). London: Sage.

Sommerfeldt, E. (2011). Activist e-mail action alerts and identification. *Public Relations Review, 37*, 87–89.

Sowards, S., & Renegar, V. (2006). Reconceptualizing rhetorical activism in contemporary feminist contexts. *Howard Journal of Communications, 17*, 57–74.

Spurr, D. (1993). *The rhetoric of empire*. Durham, NC: Duke University Press.

Stecker, F. (2011). *The podium, the pulpit and the Republicans*. Santa Barbara, CA: Praeger.

Streeck, J. (2008). Gesture in political communication. *Research on Language and Social Interaction 41*, 154–186.

Stokoe, E. (2000). Toward a conversation analytic approach to gender and discourse. *Feminism and Psychology, 10*, 552–563.

Summers, M. (2007). Rhetorically self-sufficient arguments in Western Australian parliamentary debates on Lesbian and Gay Law Reform. *British Journal of Social Psychology 46*, 839–858.

Terrill, R. (2007). Rhetoric, religion and the civil rights movement 1954–1965. *Rhetoric & Public Affairs, 10*, 744–746.

Terrill, R. (2009). Unity and duality in Barack Obama's "A More Perfect Union." *Quarterly Journal of Speech, 95*, 363–386.

Terrill, R. (2011). An uneasy peace: Barack Obama's Nobel Peace Prize lecture. *Rhetoric and Public Affairs, 14*, 761–779.

Thompson, J. B. (2011). Shifting boundaries of public and private life. *Theory, Culture & Society, 28*, 49–70.

Tileagă, C. (2008). What is a "revolution"? National commemoration, collective memory and managing authenticity in the representation of a political event. *Discourse & Society, 19*, 359–382.

Tileagă, C. (2009). The social organization of representations of history. *British Journal of Social Psychology, 48*, 337–355.

Tileagă, C. (2012). Communism and the meaning of social memory. *Integrative Psychological & Behavioral Science, 46*, 475–492.

Timmerman, D., Gussman, G., & King, D. (2012). Humor, race and rhetoric. *Rhetoric Review, 31*, 169–187.

Toye, R. (2011). The rhetorical premiership: A new perspective on prime ministerial power since 1945. *Parliamentary History, 30*, 175–192.

Turner, J. C., Hogg, M. A., Oakes, P. J., Reicher, S. D., & Wetherell, M. S. (1987). *Rediscovering the social group: A self-categorization theory*. Oxford: Blackwell.

Utley, E., & Heyse, A. (2009). Barack Obama's (im)perfect union. *Western Journal of Black Studies, 33*, 153–163.

Van Eemeren, F. H. (2010). *Strategic manouvering in argumentative discourse*. Amsterdam: John Benjamins.

Van Zoonen, L. (2005). *Entertaining the citizen: When politics and popular culture converge*. Oxford: Rowman & Littlefield.

Van Zoonen, E., Vis, F., Mihelj, S. (2010) Emerging citizenship on YouTube: activism, satire and online debates around the anti-Islam video Fitna. *Critical Discourse Studies, 7*, 249–261.

Van Zoonen, L., Vis, F., & Mihelj, S. (2011). YouTube interactions between agonism, antagonism and dialogue: Video responses to the anti-Islam film Fitna. *New Media & Society, 16*, 1–18.

Vanderbeck, R., & Johnson, P. (2011). If a charge was brought against a saintly religious leader whose intention was to save souls. . .: an analysis of UK Parliamentary debates over incitement to hatred on the grounds of sexual orientation. *Parliamentary Affairs, 64*, 652–673.

Ventsel, A. (2007). the construction of the 'we'-category. *Sign Systems Studies, 35*, 249–266.

Wallach, Y. (2011). Trapped in mirror-images: The rhetoric of maps in Israel/Palestine. *Political Geography, 30*, 358–369.

Weltman, D., & Billig, M. (2001). The political psychology of contemporary anti-politics. *Political Psychology, 22*, 367–382.

Whatley, R. (1828). *Elements of rhetoric*. London: John Murray.

Wilson, J. (1990). *Politically speaking*. Oxford: Blackwell.

Zappen, J. (2005). Digital rhetoric: Toward an integrated theory. *Technical Communication Quarterly, 14*, 319–325.

CHAPTER 10

......

PSYCHOLOGY AND FOREIGN POLICY DECISION-MAKING

......

JACK S. LEVY

POLITICAL psychology occupies an uncertain space in the study of international relations and foreign policy. Longstanding but gradually receding conceptions of the international relations field as a series of paradigmatic clashes among realist, liberal, Marxist, and constructivist approaches, or even between rationalism and constructivism, leave little if any room for the beliefs, personalities, emotions, perceptions, and decision-making processes of individual political leaders.[1] Many of the leading research programs in the international relations field today—including realist balance-of-power and power transition theories, the bargaining model of war, democratic peace and capitalist peace theories, and a variety of institutionalist theories—give little or no causal weight to the role of individual political leaders. Debates in international political economy generally focus on system, state, and society-centered approaches while neglecting the individual level altogether (Ikenberry, Lake, & Mastanduno, 1988). Constructivist approaches, which should in principle be open to the inclusion of psychological variables, have until recently given little attention to individual agency (Shannon and Kowert, 2012).[2]

At the same time, however, explanations of many consequential historical events give considerable causal weight to the role of individual political leaders. Few would think of explaining World War II or the Holocaust without Hitler, Soviet policy in the 1930s and 1940s without Stalin, Chinese foreign policy without Mao, or contemporary Russian policy without Putin.[3] The decisive role of individual leaders is not limited to autocratic states. Many explanations of the United States' invasion of Iraq in 2003 emphasize the critical role of George W. Bush. These and countless other examples have led some IR scholars to acknowledge that "who leads matters" (Hermann, Preston, Korany, & Shaw, 2001) and to emphasize the important role of psychological variables in foreign policy decision-making and international interactions.

These different perspectives reflect a tension between the goals of constructing parsimonious and generalizable theoretical explanations of international behavior and of providing nuanced and descriptively accurate explanations of individual historical episodes. Many would agree that the inclusion of psychological variables seriously complicates the first task but is necessary for the second task. It is not coincidental that the majority of applications of psychological models to foreign policy and international relations have involved case studies of a small number of historical cases.

Psychology can affect foreign policy in a number of ways and at a number of different stages in the policymaking process. My primary focus is on the impact of psychology on judgment and decision-making on foreign policy issues by political leaders. I say relatively little about the important topics of heuristics and biases, emotions, personality, images of the adversary, threat perception, crisis decision-making, or psychobiography, which are discussed by Sears and Brown, chapter 3; Chong, chapter 4; Condor, Tileagă, and Billig, chapter 9; Stein, chapter 12; Dyson and 't Hart, chapter 13; Winter, chapter 14; Post, chapter 15; and Fisher, Kelman, and Nan, chapter 16, in this volume; or about the psychological aspects of societal-level variables influencing foreign policy—political culture, public opinion, nationalism, and other forms of mass attitudes and behavior—which are covered in chapters on socialization, group identity, public opinion, intractable conflict, and conflict management.

I begin this chapter with some general conceptual issues confronting the application of psychological variables to foreign policy and international relations. I then undertake a brief survey of the evolution of applications of psychology to the study of foreign policy. I argue that the turning point in the systematic development of a cognitive paradigm of foreign policy analysis came with Jervis's (1976) seminal study of perceptions and misperceptions in international politics. After noting important subsequent developments, including the incorporation of motivation and affect, I turn to a more detailed discussion of particular research traditions. I examine longstanding research programs on historical learning and on prospect theory. I then consider more recent developments, including the Rubicon model of war, poliheuristic theory, and research on time horizons. I conclude with a brief discussion of some other areas of foreign policy analysis that would benefit from greater attention to political psychology.[4]

1. CONCEPTUAL ISSUES

My brief introductory remarks alluded to the influential "levels of analysis" framework, which is most often used as a typology of causal variables for explaining foreign policy behavior. Most treatments include the individual as well as societal, governmental, and nation-state levels of analysis.[5] Although Waltz (1959) conceived of the individual image in terms of a universal human nature, and although most evolutionary approaches fit this framework (Thayer, 2004; Sidanius & Kurzban, chapter 7, this volume), most subsequent treatments of the individual level focus on factors varying across individuals. These include belief system, personality, emotional makeup, political socialization, learning from history, information processing, leadership style, attitude toward risk, time horizons, gender, and other factors. The working assumption is that individual leaders have a causal impact on outcomes. The counterfactual implication is that if a different individual with different characteristics had occupied a key leadership position, the outcome might very well have been different.[6]

One source of confusion in the literature derives from the fact that the levels-of-analysis framework can be applied to both independent and dependent variables—to the former as a system for the classification of causal variables, and to the latter as an identification of the units whose behavior or patterns is to be explained—individual, organization, state, dyad, system. The problem is compounding by scholars' failure to highlight how they are using the concept.

The fact that independent variables at one level can influence dependent variables at various levels highlights some analytic limitations in psychological explanations for foreign policy behavior and international outcomes. First, individual-level psychological variables cannot by themselves provide a logically complete explanation of foreign policy, which is a state-level dependent variable. Psychological variables must be integrated into a broader theory of foreign policy that incorporates state-level causal variables and that explains how the preferences, beliefs, and judgments of the leading decision-maker (along with those of other key actors) get aggregated into a foreign policy decision for the state.[7] Psychology cannot be divorced from politics in explanations for foreign policy.

Similarly, because war and other forms of strategic interaction are the product of the joint actions of two or more states at the dyadic or systemic levels, individual-level psychological variables (or societal and governmental-level variables) cannot by themselves provide a logically complete explanation for war or for other international patterns. Such explanations must be subsumed within a theory of bargaining or strategic interaction that includes dyadic or system-level causal variables.

This logic served as the basis for Kelman's (1965, pp. 5–7) critique of some of the early work by psychologists and psychiatrists on war and peace. Kelman argued that this work was "removed from the interaction between nations" and that

> it makes little sense to speak of *a* psychological theory of war or of international relations. There cannot be a psychological theory that is complete and self-contained.... There can only be a general theory of international relations in which psychological factors play a part, once the points in the process at which they are applicable have been properly identified. Within such a framework, however, psychological—and, particularly, social-psychological—analyses can potentially make a considerable contribution.

These conceptual problems inherent in assessing the relationship between psychology and foreign policy are compounded by methodological problems. The psychological theories from which foreign policy analysts draw are based on carefully controlled experimental studies with extensive replication. Although there are ongoing debates about the internal validity of many of these studies, which lead to continuing refinements and increasingly robust results, problems of internal validity pale in comparison to problems of external validity that plague any effort to generalize to the complex world of foreign policy decision-making (Holsti, 1976; Herrmann, 1988; McDermott, 2004, chap. 2).

One problem is that individuals selected into political leadership roles differ from the college students that typically serve as subjects in many experiments. In the absence of explicit controls there is a possibility that selection-based differences, not hypothesized causal variables, account for observed causal effects in the laboratory (Sears, 1986). Foreign policy-making also differs from the laboratory in terms of the stakes involved. The higher stakes facing political leaders as compared to experimental subjects create higher levels of stress—and the suboptimal performance that generally follows from it (Holsti and George, 1975)—that are difficult or impossible to duplicate in the laboratory.[8] Moreover, real-world decisions generally involve a series of judgments and decisions over time, which are difficult to replicate in more restricted laboratory experiments.

Another limitation on the generalizability of typical experiments in social psychology to foreign policy behavior is that most of these experiments ignore the political and strategic context of decisions. This includes the organizational and institutional contexts within which decisions are made, the accountability of decision-makers to domestic constituencies, and the international context, which includes conflicts of interests between states, bargaining to resolve those conflicts, and multiple diplomatic audiences. The neglect of the strategic context of foreign policy decisions often leads to an overestimation of the impact of actors' flawed judgments and choices and underestimation of the role of genuine conflicts of interests and domestic constraints (Jervis, 1976, pp. 3–4).

International relations scholars have attempted to get around the limitations of experiments through the use of historical case studies. They often have difficulty, however, in finding comparable cases for the purposes of controlled comparison and ruling out alternative interpretations. In addition, the universe of cases for many of the things we want to explain—major wars or revolutions, for example—is relatively small and context dependent. As Tetlock (1998, p. 870) notes, "The tape of history runs only once."

2. The Evolution of the Study of Psychology and Foreign Policy

It would be useful to put applications of psychology to foreign policy into the broader context of the study of foreign policy, which has evolved in significant ways over the last half-century.[9] Prior to the 1960s, foreign policy analysis (now the common name for the subfield) was more descriptive and prescriptive than theoretical. It typically involved single case studies that were bounded in space and time and that did little to facilitate broader theoretical generalizations. The most widely used text in the field for many years (Macridis, 1958) organized the subject around countries, not around analytic themes.

Foreign policy analysis was also more outcome oriented than process oriented. Scholars were more interested in describing the foreign policies of states, and providing general interpretations based on different conceptions of policy goals and strategies for advancing those goals, than in looking inside the "black box" of decision-making and analyzing the processes through which foreign policy is actually made. There was no well-developed paradigm of foreign policy analysis.

Many scholars implicitly adopted a rationalist framework in which states have certain "national interests" that political leaders attempt to maximize through a careful weighing of costs and benefits. This framework was not fully systematized, however, until Allison (1971) constructed a rational unitary actor model of foreign policy. Allison's "Model I" emphasized the specification of state goals, the identification of alternative strategies for achieving those goals, the assessment of the consequences of each strategy, and the selection of the strategy that maximized state goals. This model left no role for political leaders' distinctive beliefs, experiences, personalities, or emotional states.

It was social psychologists and personality theorists, rather than political scientists, who demonstrated the greatest initial interest in the psychological dimensions of international relations.[10] This went back to the 1930s and 1940s, a context defined by the experiences of the two world wars. Not surprisingly, the focus was on the psychology of war and war prevention. The growing interest in the study of attitudes (Thurstone & Chave, 1929) led to the examination of attitudes toward war, nationalism, and aggression (Droba, 1931; Stagner, 1942; May, 1943).

Following Freud's emphasis on aggressive instincts as the root cause of war (Einstein & Freud, 1932), there was considerable interest in applying psychoanalytic perspectives to the study of war (Durbin & Bowlby, 1939). Much of the focus was on "human nature" as an intractable cause of war. The concept of human nature raised some difficult conceptual and causal questions, however, and within a decade psychologists began emphasizing the cultural sources of war and the changes in attitudes and institutions that might alleviate war (Allport, 1945). Later, scholars began arguing that the proper question was not aggression per se but the political and international contexts under which war as politically organized violence was most likely to occur, the processes that contributed to war, and the place of psychology in these broader contexts (Kelman, 1965). As a consequence, analyses of the role of human nature, and much other early work by psychologists and psychiatrists as well, had little impact on the study of war and peace in political science.[11]

Psychoanalytic studies that implied variation across individuals, however, continued to have some influence. This often took the form of psychobiography or psychohistory, which attempted to explain political behavior in terms of early childhood experiences or development crises later in adulthood.[12] One of the first such studies was Walter Langer's ([1943] 1972) psychobiography of Hitler (see Post, chapter 15, this volume). The most influential study was George and George's (1956) analysis of Woodrow Wilson, which provided a psychodynamic explanation of Wilson's life and political career, including his decisive role in the US debate about the League of Nations. The Georges argued that Wilson's low self-esteem and repressed anger toward his demanding father led Wilson to a compensatory drive for power and refusal to compromise.[13] Psychoanalytic perspectives also influenced some of the early "operational code" analyses of political belief systems (Leites, 1951).

Interest in psychobiographical approaches began to wane by the 1970s, however, with a shift in orientation toward more parsimonious and empirically testable theories and with the development of alternative psychological frameworks. Despite the decline of psychobiography, scholars continued to show an interest in more general (and more easily testable) models of personality and foreign policy (Greenstein, 1975; Etheridge, 1978; Hermann, 1980; Winter, 1992; this volume, chap. 14; George and George, 1998; Post, 2003).

Meanwhile, by the 1950s and 1960s social psychologists had begun to move away from a reductionist perspective that traced causality in international affairs exclusively to individual needs, motivations, and tendencies, and toward a view that recognized the political and international context of foreign policy behavior. In doing so, they started having more of an impact on the study of foreign policy in political science. The influence of social psychologists' studies of foreign policy attitudes and their social, demographic, and personality correlates is evident in Almond's (1950) classic study of changing "moods" in American foreign policy. Scholars analyzed the psychology of nationalism and of national ideologies more generally and conducted cross-national studies of images and stereotypes of other nations (Campbell & LeVine, 1961). Most of this work focused on the mass level, however, and still gave relatively little attention to the mechanisms through which shifting public moods were translated into state foreign policy actions.[14] It was not until the late 1960s that social psychologists began focusing on elite perceptions and choice in foreign policy (DeRivera, 1968; White, 1968).

By this time, the first really systematic analysis of foreign policy in the international relations field had emerged, the "decision-making approach" of Snyder, Bruck, & Sapin ([1954] 1962). Reflecting the growing dissatisfaction with the rational, unitary, apolitical, and outcome-oriented focus of many existing studies of foreign polity, Snyder and his colleagues argued that understanding state behavior required focusing on political elites—and especially their conceptions of the national interest and "definition of the situation," the domestic political contexts in which they operated, and the nature of information and communication. Although this "first-wave" decision-making approach (Art, 1973) allowed a substantial role for individual psychology, there was little explicit theorizing about the influence of psychological variables in the foreign policy process. Scholars incorporated political leaders' worldviews but generally treated them as exogenous and made little attempt to explain the social, intellectual, and psychological processes that generated them. Psychological variables were given even less attention in the "second wave" of decision-making studies. These studies emerged with Allison's (1971) elaboration of a organizational process model based on standard operating procedures, and a governmental politics model based on bargaining between the heads of different agencies with different policy preferences and different degrees of power and influence.

Growing dissatisfaction with the neglect of psychological variables in the leading paradigms of foreign policy analysis led to a number of studies in which political psychology was central. One was Wohlstetter's (1962) analysis of information process-ing in the American intelligence failure at Pearl Harbor. Overturning the conventional wisdom that the primary source of intelligence failure was the lack of adequate informa-tion, Wohlstetter argued that the real problem in 1941 was not the lack of information but the excess of information and the inability to distinguish informative signals from background noise. She also emphasized the compartmentalization of information in different bureaucratic agencies. Wohlstetter gave relatively little attention, however, to the particular cognitive mechanisms contributing to the inability to distinguish signals from noise.

Whereas Wohlstetter (1962) focused on information processing, George (1969) focused on the content of individual belief systems in his study of the "operational codes" of political leaders. Influenced by the cognitive revolution in social psychol-ogy, and shifting away from the psychobiographical approach that he had done much to advance, George reformulated Leites's (1951) earlier work on the operational code of the Politburo. He eliminated the psychoanalytic component, focused on the cognitive dimensions, and generally tried to shift the focus toward a more social scientific orienta-tion. He urged analysts to focus on those beliefs that "can be inferred or postulated by the investigator on the basis of the kinds of data, observational opportunities, and meth-ods generally available to political scientists" (p. 195).

George argued that an individual's beliefs are interdependent, consistent, hierar-chically organized around a small set of "master beliefs," and resistant to change. The anchors of belief systems include philosophical beliefs about the nature of politics and conflict and instrumental beliefs about the efficacy of alternative strategies for advanc-ing one's interests.[15] Images of the enemy are a particularly important component of operational code belief systems.[16]

This new formulation was the basis for studies of the operational codes of a num-ber of political leaders, including John Foster Dulles (Holsti, 1970) and Henry Kissinger (Walker, 1977). Others developed new typologies for operational codes (Holsti, 1977), further grounded the concept in terms of the emerging literature on cognitive schemas and scripts (George, 1969), and, in some cases, began to reincorporate personality ele-ments into the operational code (Walker, 1995). Some question, however, whether the increasing complexity of the operational code concept has significantly enhanced its explanatory power (Walker, 2003). Other scholars adopted other frameworks for the study of leaders' belief systems, including cognitive mapping (Axelrod, 1976).

By the late 1960s, in response to Soviet-American crises over Berlin and especially over Cuba, scholars began examining crisis decision-making. They gave particular attention to the impact of stress induced by the high stakes, short decision time, and surprise associated with acute international crises (Hermann, 1972; Holsti & George, 1975). One influential research program was the Stanford project on International Conflict and Integration. This "1914 project" was novel both in its application of medi-ated stimulus-response models to international politics, and in its use of formal content analyses of diplomatic documents to examine decision-makers' perceptions and the discrepancy between perceptions and reality (Holsti, 1972; North, 1967). Other scholars provided more detailed historical case studies of crisis decision-making (Brecher & Geist, 1980; Stein & Tanter, 1980).

The 1914 studies demonstrated that political leaders misperceived the capabilities and intentions of their adversaries in systematic ways. They did little, however, to specify the causal mechanisms that drove misperceptions or to assess the causal impact of misperceptions on foreign policy choices and international outcomes. These were among the many contributions of Jervis's (1976) classic study *Perception and Misperception in International Politics*. Jervis provided a comprehensive survey of theory and experimental evidence from many diverse areas of cognitive and social psychology bearing on questions of perception and misperception in international relations, illustrated by a wide range of historical examples.

Jervis also provided a framework for thinking about the role of psychological variables in a way that avoided the "overpsychologizing" of earlier social-psychological approaches. Jervis identified alternative systemic and domestic explanations for the observed behavior and discussed the types of evidence and research designs that would be appropriate to empirically differentiate among these competing explanations. This attention to alternative explanations, threats to valid inference, and to research designs for dealing with these inferential problems was an important methodological contribution to the application of psychological models to foreign polity behavior, complementing Jervis's many theoretical contributions.

Jervis' (1976) study symbolized the coming of age of a systematic "cognitive paradigm" of foreign policy analysis, and it contributed significantly to the growing interest in psychological approaches to international relations.[17] The basic premises of the cognitive approach are that the world is extraordinarily complex, incoherent, and changing. People are limited, however, in their mental capacities to process information and fully satisfy standards of ideal rationality in their attempts to maximize their interests. They adopt a number of cognitive shortcuts or heuristics (Kahneman, Slovic, & Tversky, 1982; Kahneman, 2011) that help to impose some degree of simplicity and orderliness on a complex and uncertain world in order to make that world more comprehensible. These heuristics may serve people very well in a wide variety of situations, but they are also the source of significant errors and biases. These are cognitive or "unmotivated" biases, and they occur independently of emotions or interests. People may try to act rationally, but they do so within their simplified mental representations of reality, and their behavior is best described as "bounded rationality" (Simon, 1957; March, 1978; Jones, 1999; Redlawsk & Lau, chapter 5, this volume; Chong, chapter 4, this volume).

A central proposition of the cognitive paradigm is that an individual's cognitive predispositions or mindsets play a disproportionate role in shaping his or her perceptions. This leads to a general tendency to selective attention to information, to premature cognitive closure, for people to see what they expect to see based on prior beliefs and worldviews, and consequently to the perseverance of beliefs. In other words, perception is more theory-driven than data driven (Jervis, 1976).[18]

Jervis (1976) wrote at the peak of the "cognitive revolution" in social psychology.[19] His discussion of the role of emotion or motivation in perception was limited to one chapter on the influence of people's desires and fears on judgment and decision-making. These factors, in contrast to those associated with a purely cognitive view, lead to "motivated biases," or motivated reasoning (Kunda, 1990; see, in this volume, Sears & Brown, chapter 3; Condor, Tileagă, & Billig, chapter 9; Taber & Young, chapter 17). Motivated biases are driven by people's emotional needs, by their need to maintain self-esteem, and by their interests—diplomatic, political, organizational, or personal. The result is "wishful thinking": people what they *want* to see rather than what they *expect* to see. Motivated reasoning serves to rationalize policies that support one's interests and emotional needs.

Motivated biases are most likely to manifest themselves in decisions involving high stakes and consequential actions that might affect important values or trade-offs among important values. The resulting stress from threats to basic values often leads decision-makers to deny those threats or the need to make trade-offs between values (Holsti & George, 1975). Although judgments of the probability and utility of outcomes should be made independently in any rational calculus, in fact the desirability of an outcome often influences the perceived likelihood that it will occur. Many argue, for example, that the George W. Bush administration's strong preferences for war against Iraq in 2003, in conjunction with the belief that the existence of an Iraqi nuclear weapons program constituted the best way to mobilize domestic support for war, led through motivated biases to exaggerated perceptions that Iraq had nuclear weapons (Duelfer and Dyson, 2011).

Attention to the role of affect and motivation in judgment and decision-making began to grow after the publication of *Decision Making* by social psychologists Janis and Mann (1977).[20] International relations scholars soon began to incorporate these factors into their theories, but only gradually (Cottam, 1977; Lebow, 1981; Jervis, 1985; Stein, 1985). Cognitive and motivated biases generate some of the same pathologies of judgment and decision, and it is often difficult to empirically differentiate between the two. The belief that a cognitive model was more parsimonious and more easily testable led most international relations scholars to continue to give priority to cognitive over motivational explanations.[21]

This began to change by the end of the 1990s, following a shift toward a greater emphasis on emotions in social psychology and in the study of American politics (see, in this volume, Chong, chapter 4; Condor, Tileagă, & Billig, chapter 9; Taber & Young, chapter 17). Accompanying this change in emphasis was a conceptual transformation from the view that emotions are a source of deviation from rationality to a view in which emotions were necessary for rationality (Damasio, 1994). This argument was reinforced by the development of neuroscience and the ability to distinguish centers of cognition and emotion in the human brain (Marcus, 2012). In international relations, Mercer (2005) rejected the common view that psychology can only explain deviations from rationality and argued that psychology should be used to explain accurate judgments as well as erroneous ones. He also argued that many beliefs—including trust and credibility—are based on emotion as much by cognition.

There has been a lot of work in the last decade on the impact of emotion on foreign policy decision-making (Crawford, 2000; Rosen, 2005, chap. 2; McDermott, 2004, chap. 6). More recently, McDermott (2008) looked at the impact of illness, including its emotional consequences, on presidential decision-making. Lebow (2010) and Lindemann (2010) each emphasize the political psychology of recognition, the drive for self-esteem, and the impact of past humiliations in the processes leading to war. Many other research programs incorporate motivational mechanisms. Most variants of the diversionary theory of war (Levy, 1989) emphasize political leaders' use of military force externally to invoke the symbols of the nation, engage mass emotions, and generate a rally round the flag effect to bolster their political support. Many civil war theorists emphasize the impact of symbolic politics and emotions at the mass level in the outbreak and evolution of civil wars (S. Kaufman, 2006).

Many of the applications of social psychology to international relations in the last three decades have followed Jervis (1976) and focused on the psychology of threat perception, with particular attention to the role of cognitive and motivated biases. The literature on threat perception, which I surveyed in my chapter in the first edition of the *Handbook*, is covered in detail by Stein (chapter 12, this volume). Consequently, I will direct my efforts elsewhere in the remainder of this chapter. I focus on a number of specific research areas: learning, including both the updating of beliefs and learning from historical analogies; the application of the Rubicon model of action phases to overconfidence in judgments about war; prospect theory; polihheuristic theory; and time horizons, including applications of discounting models and of construal-level theory.[22]

3. SOME SPECIFIC RESEARCH PROGRAMS

3.1. Learning and Foreign Policy

There are at least two different ways in which scholars have applied social psychology to questions of learning in foreign policy judgment and decision-making. One involves the general question of how beliefs change in response to new information.[23] The other involves the use of historical analogies.

Most conceptions of rational learning are based on Bayesian updating, which involves the revision or updating of prior probability assessments (priors) in response to observed events according to Bayes's rule.[24] Rational learning is efficient, in that the successive updating of prior beliefs generates revised estimates that quickly converge to the "true" value, regardless of the accuracy of one's priors. Experimental and field research has demonstrated, however, that people systematically deviate from the normative Bayesian standard by giving disproportionately more weight to prior beliefs and less to new information. As a result, updating is often slow and inefficient. This pattern is explained by the cognitive bias literature in terms of the perseverance of beliefs due to selective attention, cognitive dissonance, and other biases. It is explained by the literature on decisional heuristics by the "anchoring and adjustment" heuristic. Prior beliefs serve as a cognitive anchor that impedes appropriate and efficient updating based on new information. This robust pattern is demonstrated in many carefully controlled experimental studies on anchoring and adjustment (Kahneman et al., 1982; Kahneman, 2011).

Anchoring has important implications for threat perception. Once beliefs that the adversary is either hostile or benign are formed, they are resistant to change.[25] An illustrative example of the resistance to the updating of beliefs in response to new information is the Israeli intelligence failure in 1973. The leading interpretation of that failure emphasizes that Israeli political and military leaders and the intelligence community shared the belief that (1) Egypt would not go to war unless it was able to mount air strikes deep into Israel in order to neutralize Israel's air force, and that (2) Syria would not go to war without Egypt. The first condition of this "conception" was not satisfied, so evidence of large Syrian and Egyptian deployments near Israeli borders was interpreted not as preparations for an attack but instead as routine Egyptian military exercises and Syrian defensive moves. Israel's Agranat Commission (1974) attributed the intelligence failure to the "persistent adherence to 'the conception' " (Shlaim, 1976; Stein, 1985).[26]

This is not to say that beliefs never change. Beliefs can change if information deviating from prior beliefs is strong and salient, if it arrives all at once, if there are relatively objective indicators to provide a baseline for the evaluation of the accuracy of beliefs, if decision-makers operate in "multiple advocacy" decision-making units, and if they are self-critical in their styles of thinking (George, 1980; Jervis, 2010; Tetlock, 1998, p. 880). Moreover, when belief change occurs, is generally follows the cognitive-consistency principle of least resistance. When people are faced with repeated inconsistencies between their belief systems and the world they observe, they first change tactical beliefs about the best means to particular ends. They change their strategic assumptions and orientation only after the failure of tactical solutions, and they reconsider their basic goals or objectives only after repeated strategic failures. Change in fundamental beliefs is often so psychologically difficult that it is likely to occur only in conjunction with a major change in personnel or regime (Tetlock, 1991, pp. 27–31).

Another line of research on learning focuses on the question of how political leaders learn from history. In the absence of well-defined theories to guide decision-makers in making inferences about likely outcomes, they often turn for guidance to "lessons of the past" from historical analogies. It is often said, for example, that generals are always fighting the last war, and that political leaders are always trying to avoid the mistakes of the past. One of the most influential analogies for the last half-century of international relations is the "Munich analogy," associated with the "lesson" that appeasement never works. The Munich analogy had a profound effect on American decision-making in the Korean War, the Vietnam War, and the 1990–1991 Persian Gulf War (May, 1973; Khong, 1992). Similarly, the "Vietnam analogy," which many interpret to suggest that any US intervention involves a strong risk of ending up in a quagmire, itself had a significant impact on American foreign policy for decades.

The phenomenon of learning from history has attracted considerable attention among international relations theorists (Jervis, 1976; Vertzberger, 1990; Khong, 1992; Levy, 1994; Stein, 1994). The learning process is often explained in terms of analogical reasoning, which is often linked to the "availability" heuristic, in which judgments of probability are shaped by events that are familiar, salient, and that come easily to mind (Tversky & Kahneman, 1974; also Sears & Brown, chapter 3, this volume; Condor, Tileagă, & Billig, chapter 9, this volume). The problem is that these events do not constitute a representative sample for the purpose of drawing inferences, and consequently judgments based on availability are often quite misleading.

The number of historical analogies from which individuals might learn is enormous, but there is a tendency to learn from events that have a major impact, affect the individual or his society directly, occur recently in time, and that are observed firsthand and at a formative period in a person's life. People tend to ignore the role of contextual factors and draw universal lessons rather than conditional lessons. As Jervis (1976, p. 228) argued, "People pay more attention to *what* has happened than to *why* it has happened. Thus learning is superficial, overgeneralized.... Lessons learned will be applied to a wide variety of situations without a careful effort to determine whether the cases are similar on crucial dimensions."

The lessons an individual learns from a historical analogy can also be significantly shaped by the extent to which she or he thinks counterfactually about the analogy, and these counterfactual assumptions may themselves be shaped by preexisting theoretical assumptions (Tetlock, 2005). The "Munich analogy" is based in part on the counterfactual assumption that standing up to Hitler at Munich would have prevented war. Most historians regard that proposition as highly unlikely (Steiner, 2011), and the fact that appeasement failed against Hitler does not mean that appeasement will never work against any opponent under any circumstances.

Hypotheses on learning provide potentially powerful explanations of political leaders' beliefs and judgments, but demonstrating that leaders actually learn from history (accurately or otherwise) and that lessons learned have a causal impact on behavior is often a daunting task. It is also possible that the causal arrow is reversed: instead of learning from history, political leaders may use history to gain political support for their preexisting policy preferences, reversing the causal arrows. There are two possible mechanisms here. In the strategic use of history, leaders deliberately select certain historical analogies and interpret them in a way to influence others to support the leader's preferred policy. Alternatively, motivated biases may subconsciously lead an individual to search for historical analogies that reinforce his or her preexisting policy preferences. It is not a surprise, from this perspective, that opposite sides of a policy debate emphasize different historical analogies or interpret the same analogy in different ways, as illustrated by how the Vietnam analogy was used in subsequent political debates in the United States. Researchers need to construct research designs that facilitate the ability to distinguish between genuine learning and both the strategic use of history and the role of motivated biases (Jervis, 1976; Khong, 1992; Levy, 1994).

3.2. The Rubicon Model of War

Many of the biases discussed in the last section contribute to overconfidence in probability judgments. In fact, many scholars have pointed to the overconfidence of political and military leaders on the eve of war, leading them to inflated expectations not only of victory but of a relatively quick victory with tolerable costs (White, 1968; Jervis, 1976; Levy, 1983; Johnson, 2004). Much has been written, for example, about the "short-war illusion" prior to World War I and US overconfidence in Vietnam, Iraq, and other wars. Yet we also know that fear, insecurity, and anxiety are a persistent feature of international politics and that leaders often exaggerate the capabilities and hostile intentions of their adversaries, frequently resulting in arms races and dangerous conflict spirals. This pattern of fear and insecurity, on the one hand, and military overconfidence, on the other, presents a puzzle, especially if we have reason to believe that information about relative capabilities is relatively constant. Johnson and Tierney (2011) have attempted to resolve this puzzle through an argument based on Heckhausen and Gollwitzer's (1987) "Rubicon model of action phases."

The theory of action phases, which has been influential in psychology (Gollwitzer, 2011) and which has important implications for conceptions of rationality and for decision-making in a wide variety of contexts, is that processes of judgment and decision-making vary over time. In the predecision phase, people tend to adopt a "deliberative" mindset, where alternative options and their possible consequences are carefully compared. In the postdecisional or implementation phase of decision-making people shift from making a decision to thinking about how to implement it. In this latter phase they are more vulnerable to psychological biases, including diminished receptivity to incoming information, and increased vulnerability to selective attention, tunnel vision, cognitive dissonance, self-serving illusions, and illusion of control. Consequently, people are generally prone to overconfidence and to engage in increasingly risky and aggressive actions.[27] With respect to war, when leaders come to believe that war is imminent (and thus cross a psychological Rubicon), they switch from a "deliberative" mindset to an "implemental" one, and from a more neutral analytic perspective to an overconfident one (Johnson and Tierney, 2011).

The Rubicon model is a potentially important contribution to our understanding of decision-making in international relations and elsewhere. It provides an overarching framework for integrating a diverse set of psychological biases, and its central proposition that processes of judgment and decision may vary over different stages in the decision-making process or in different contexts is quite plausible.[28] The Rubicon model appears to resolve the puzzling combination of insecurity and overconfidence in the processes leading to war, and it provides a useful contrast to rationalist bargaining models that assume that decisions on all aspects of policy are driven by the same rational processes.

In answering some questions, however, the Rubicon model raises others. Whereas the Rubicon model posits that overconfidence is reinforced by an illusion of control in the final phase of decision-making and implementation, earlier research points to common feelings of the loss of control over events (Langer, 1975). A number of IR scholars have emphasized that a sense of the loss of control as war approaches is common and consequential because it can lead decision-makers to abandon attempts to manage the crisis to avoid war and instead to prepare for war, which generates a momentum of its own (Lebow, 1987, chap. 3; Jervis, 1989, 153–164). We need to know which pattern is more likely, for what kinds of individuals in which contexts, for decision-making in general and for war in particular. There is also a need for more empirical work to ascertain the extent to which political and military leaders become more overconfident as war approaches. Leaders sometimes grow more pessimistic as the reality of war approaches, but calculate that inaction would only lead to a worsening of their position and poorer odds in the future.

3.3. Prospect Theory

For many years scholars explained individual choice behavior by the normative expected-utility model (Redlawsk and Lau, chapter 5, this volume; Chong, chapter 4, this volume), and they assumed that nonrational behavior was too unpredictable to model. The development of prospect theory (Kahneman and Tversky, 1979) posed a powerful challenge to expected-utility theory by providing a systematic and tractable explanation for a variety of seemingly nonrational behaviors.[29] Prospect theory is now the leading alternative to expected utility as a theory of choice under conditions of risk. It is influential in many social science disciplines, and it has played an important role in the development of behavioral economics. In political science, prospect theory has been particularly influential in international relations, in part because the choices of individual leaders have a greater impact than in domestic policy. Here I summarize the theory and briefly mention some of its implications for foreign policy and international relations.[30]

Whereas expected-utility theory defines value in terms of net assets, prospect theory posits that people are more sensitive to changes in assets than to net asset levels. People "frame" choice problems around a reference point ("reference dependence"), give more weight to losses from that reference point than to comparable gains ("loss aversion"), and make risk-averse choices when possible outcomes are positive and risk-acceptant choices where possible outcomes are negative (the "domain of losses").[31] Their strong aversion to losses, particularly to "dead" losses that are perceived as certain (as opposed to those that are perceived as probabilistic), lead them to take significant risks in the hope of avoiding a certain loss, even though the result may be an even greater loss and even though the expected value of the gamble may be considerably lower than the value of the certain loss. In addition, people value things in their possession more than comparable things not in their possession (the "endowment effect"). Consequently, actual losses hurt more than do forgone gains.[32]

Because value is defined in terms of gains and losses relative to a reference point, how people identify their reference points is critical. A change in reference point can lead to a change in preference ("preference reversal") even if the values and probabilities associated with possible outcomes remain unchanged. People facing decisions over medical treatments, for example, respond differently to the likelihood of a 90% survival rate than to a 10% mortality rate, although the two are mathematically equivalent.

Almost all applications of framing to political science focus on the effects of farming on choice rather than on the sources of framing, and thus give little attention to the question of why people select one reference point rather than another. One thing we do know, however, is that although people often frame choice problems around the status quo, they are sometimes influenced by expectation levels, aspiration levels, and social comparisons to select a different reference point. There is substantial evidence, for example, that people "renormalize" their reference points after making gains much faster than they do after incurring losses. This helps to explain why people go to such lengths to recover "sunk costs," contrary to the prescription of microeconomic theory to think on the margin and ignore sunk costs.[33] Renormalizing after making gains, and treating subsequent retreats from those gains as losses, helps to explain why, in the words of Daryl Hannah's character in the 1987 movie *Wall Street*, "When you've had money and lost it, it's much worse than never having had it at all."

Applications of these basic principles to foreign policy and international relations have led to a variety of interesting and intuitively plausible propositions.[34] (1) Because decision-makers usually take the status quo as their reference point, and because the costs of moving away from the status quo are treated as losses and overweighted relative to the benefits (gains) of doing so, states have a greater-than-expected tendency to remain at the status quo (the "status quo bias").[35] This helps to explain policy continuity.[36] (2) State leaders take more risks to maintain their international positions, territory, and reputations against potential losses than they do to enhance their positions. As Dennis Ross (1984, 247) argued, Soviet leaders were willing to engage in the "use of decisive and perhaps risky action far more readily for *defending* as opposed to *extending* Soviet gains." (3) domestic publics punish political leaders for incurring losses more than they reward them for making gains (Nincic, 1997).

(4) Leaders of declining states tend to frame reference points around their current position, define inaction and continued decline as a loss, and take excessively risky[37] actions in attempt to avoid losses and restore current position. This reinforces incentives for declining states to adopt preventive war strategies (Levy, 2008a), as illustrated by Japan's decision to attack an increasingly powerful United States at Pearl Harbor in 1941 (Taliaferro, 2004). (5) The fact that people are slow to accept losses and take risks to eliminate losses makes sunk costs important and contributes to entrapment in escalating conflicts (Brockner & Rubin, 1985), as illustrated by the United States in Vietnam and in Iraq and the Soviet Union in Afghanistan (Taliaferro, 2004).

With respect to strategic interaction between states, (6) if one state makes gains at another's expense, the winner generally renormalizes its reference point and takes excessive risks to defend the new status quo against subsequent losses. The loser does not adjust to the new status quo but instead takes excessive risks to recover its losses and return to its reference point. As a result, both sides engage in riskier behavior than a standard expected value calculus predicts. (7) Deterring an adversary from making gains is easier than deterring it from recovering losses or compelling it to accept losses.[38] (8) Reaching a negotiated settlement is more difficult than expected-utility theory predicts because people overweight what they concede in bargaining relative to what they get in return. This "concession aversion" is comparable to the status quo bias in individual decision-making. (9) It is easier for states to cooperate in the distribution of gains than in the distribution of losses, because political leaders will take more risks and bargain harder to minimize their share of the costs than to maximize their share of the gains. This explains why distributive issues are easier to resolve than redistributive issues.

Many of these hypotheses resonate well with common understandings of international politics, but validating them empirically raises difficult conceptual and methodological problems (Levy, 1997; O'Neill, 2001). Although hypotheses on reference dependence, loss aversion, and preference reversals have been systematically validated in laboratory experiments involving individual behavior in simple choice problems, generalizing them to the world of international relations raises a host of new issues. The key variables of interest in international relations—relative power, reputation, and the external security of states and the internal security of political elites, among others—are extraordinarily difficult to measure on an interval scale. This makes it difficult to demonstrate convincingly that choice is determined by framing, loss aversion, and risk orientation instead of by the maximization of expected value, as the conventional wisdom suggests.

Proponents of prospect theory also face the important task of developing hypotheses on how actors identify their reference points. Prospect theory remains a reference-dependent theory without a theory of the reference point (Levy, 1997).[39] Although standard process tracing through case studies can be useful (Davis, 2000; McDermott, 1998; Taliaferro, 2004), scholars should also explore the potential utility of more formal content analysis (Levi & Whyte, 1997) or other methodologies. It is also important to think about alternative sources of risk orientation (Sitkin & Pablo, 1992), including individual personality and experience (Kowert & Hermann, 1997), culture and ideology, gender, and leadership selection in different regimes.

Whereas prospect theory is a theory of individual choice under conditions of risk, international relations involve decisions by collective decision-making bodies who must act strategically in anticipation of the strategic behavior of adversaries and allies and also the reactions of domestic audiences. In addition, the world of international relations involves choices under conditions of uncertainty (where probabilities, and even the set of feasible outcomes, are unknown), rather than risk (where the probabilities of all possible outcomes are known). Former US Secretary of Defense Donald Rumsfeld is often ridiculed for his statement that "There are known knowns...known unknowns...[and] unknown unknowns," but Rumsfeld succinctly captured some important analytic distinctions.[40]

3.4. Poliheuristic Theory

Expected-utility theory and prospect theory are each compensatory theories of decision. Positive outcomes along one dimension can compensate for negative outcomes along another dimension. If decision-makers value one dimension so highly that they refuse to consider any strategy that falls below an acceptable level on that dimension, regardless of the benefits along another dimension, they have "lexicographic" preferences and follow a noncompensatory decision rule (see Redlawsk & Lau, chapter 5, this volume).[41] Mintz (1993; 2004) incorporated this decision rule into his "poliheuristic theory" of decision, which now constitutes a lively research program in international relations.[42] The decision problem is usually framed as one in which one state actor faces a threat from another and has several policy alternatives or strategies from which to chose, including doing nothing, breaking diplomatic relations, imposing economic sanctions, or a range of military actions. Each of these alternatives has consequences along several value dimensions—military, economic, domestic political, reputational, and so on.

Poliheuristic theory posits a two-stage decision-making process. In the first stage actors eliminate all strategies that are expected to lead to unacceptable outcomes on a particular dimension.[43] In the second stage they select the strategy with the highest expected utility. Mintz and his colleagues initially left it open as to which was the noncompensatory dimension. Subsequent experimental and case study research soon revealed that it was domestic dimension that is generally given primacy in a wide range of international contexts. This is intuitively quite plausible: political leaders often reject any strategy that might jeopardize their domestic positions.

To explore and test poliheuristic theory, Mintz and his colleagues have used both historical case studies and a computerized "decision-board." The latter is an important methodological innovation in foreign policy analysis because it facilitates the tracing of information search and decision-making processes under different conditions (Mintz et al., 1997).[44] Decision boards can be used, for example, to see whether individuals organize their information search by examining one strategy at a time and determining its consequences for different values before moving on to the next strategy, or whether they focus on different interests or values (such as domestic politics) and look at how each strategy might affect that dimension.

Poliheuristic theory provides an important alternative to compensatory models of decision-making and to utility-based models. The two-stage character of the model, which incorporates a noncompensatory decision rule in the first stage and a compensatory expected-utility decision rule in the second stage, is intriguing. It captures a basic intuition about the unwillingness of political leaders to do anything that might significantly threaten their domestic political positions. One question it raises, however, is whether all foreign policy decisions are truly noncompensatory—whether, for example, particularly acute external threats to national security interests might induce some leaders in some kinds of regimes to incur "unacceptable" domestic political costs to safeguard state interests.

3.5. Time Horizons

Scholars and other observers have long recognized that the time horizons of political leaders influence their foreign policy decisions. Just like individuals in their personal lives, political leaders must make choices involving trade-offs between current benefits and future costs (or current sacrifices for future benefits), both for the country and for their own political fortunes. How they make those trade-offs is profoundly affected by their time horizons. It is often said, for example, that political decision-makers have short time horizons, and that those time horizons are shortened further by acute international and domestic crises (Holsti, 1989). Decisions about whether to initiate a preventive war against a rising adversary are significantly influenced by the trade-offs one is willing to make between the risks of war now and the risks of war under increasingly unfavorable circumstances later (Levy, 2008a).

Yet the concept of time horizons remains remarkably undertheorized. Time horizons are rarely incorporated into most models of foreign policy or strategic interaction. One important exception is Axelrod's (1984) influential model of cooperation in iterated Prisoner's Dilemma games. In contrast to the single-play game Prisoner's Dilemma game, in which rational players should not cooperate, cooperation in the iterated game is rational if the "shadow of the future" (discount factor) is sufficiently high. Axelrod follows the standard practice in economics of using an exponential discounting model based on the assumption that the discount rate is constant from one period to the next.[45] Recent econometric models in political science have begin to incorporate exponential discounting.

A growing body of experimental and field research in behavioral economics and social psychology on discounting behavior, however, has found that individual discounting behavior differs from the assumptions of the standard exponential discount function (Loewenstein, Read, & Baumeister, 2003). More specifically, discount rates for most people tend to decline over time rather than remain constant. What this means is that people discount the immediate future more, but the distant future less, than the exponential discounting model suggests. That is, a descriptively accurate discount function is steeper for the near future and flatter for the more distant future.

One consequence of declining discount rates is that what is expected to happen tomorrow matters less than standard discount models predict (for a given discount rate). Another consequence is dynamic inconsistency and preference reversals. An actor may prefer to receive x now to receiving y tomorrow, but prefer y in t periods from now to x the period before. I may prefer to get up early and work on this paper, and set my alarm early to facilitate that, but when the alarm goes off prefer to sleep a while longer.

Actual discounting behavior can be better captured by a hyperbolic function than by an exponential function. In contrast to the constant-rate exponential discounting function, which is mathematically tractable (converging, and avoiding troubling preference reversals), the more descriptively accurate hyperbolic discounting model is not tractable: in addition to its dynamic inconsistency, it does not converge. Consequently, it does not permit analytic solutions to many economic models. This helps to explain the persistence of the exponential discounting model despite its descriptive inaccuracy.

This problem has led some to propose a "quasi-hyperbolic discount function" (Laibson, 1997), which incorporates a steep drop in the first period but constant-rate discounting after that. This function provides a closer fit to the data than does the exponential function, and it converges and permits analytic solutions. Streich and Levy

(2007) demonstrate that if actors behave as quasi-hyperbolic discounters rather than as exponential discounters, cooperation in iterated Prisoner's Dilemma games is more difficult than Axelrod's (1984) model implies.

Research has uncovered additional patterns that run contrary to the assumptions of the standard exponential discounting model (Loewenstein et al., 2003; Streich & Levy, 2007). Discount rates are lower for large payoffs than they are for small payoffs, which means that people give proportionately greater weight (in terms of discounted present value) to large future payoffs than to smaller future payoffs. There are also framing effects related to reference points. People tend to discount future gains more than they do future losses, and thus give more weight to future losses than to comparable future gains. This is another demonstration of the disproportionate and enduring psychological effects of losses relative to gains. This pattern reinforces the concession aversion and the impediments to negotiated solutions because it leads people to overweight the future costs from current concessions relative to their future benefits. Still another pattern, which runs contrary to the standard economic assumption that people prefer positive payoffs sooner rather than later, is that people often prefer improving sequences.[46] Theories of negotiation, bargaining, and conflict resolution would do well to incorporate some of these patterns.

Time horizons involve more than just the shape of an actor's discount function. Studies of discounting, whether economic or behavioral, implicitly assume that although people apply different weights to outcomes in the near future and more distant future, they basically reason in the same way about those outcomes. This assumption is questioned by an important line of research in social psychology, *temporal construal theory*, or construal-level theory (Liberman & Trope, 1998; Trope & Liberman, 2000). The theory, which is backed by substantial experimental evidence, posits that people think about near-term outcomes or strategies in relatively low-level and concrete terms embedded in a particular context, but that they think about more distant outcomes and strategies in more abstract and decontextualized terms.

This is consequential. More abstract and less context-specific representations generally lead to more optimistic expectations because they exclude "the devil in the details." Lower-level representations of the immediate future include more details and lead to more pessimistic assessments. Those details also facilitate assessments of the consequences of various actions and hence the feasibility of achieving short-term goals. The absence of these concrete details in distant outcomes make such assessments more difficult. Consequently, whereas outcomes in the immediate future are evaluated in terms of their feasibility, more distant outcomes tend to be evaluated in terms of their desirability. This implies that calculations about the immediate future are more likely to be based on expected-utility (or prospect-theoretic) calculations than are calculations about the distant future.[47]

The implications of construal-level theory for foreign policy and international relations are quite profound but neglected until recently. Rapport (2012/13) uses the theory to explain the widely recognized tendency for states to underestimate the long-term costs of military interventions and to fail to engage in extensive planning for the ending phases of a war, including occupation. Scholars have spent a fair amount of effort try-ing to explain the systematic underestimation of long-term costs and the absence of planning—by the United States in Iraq, the Soviet Union in Afghanistan, and numer-ous other cases. Rapport proposes a novel psychological explanation based on construal level theory.

Rapport shows that the absence of planning cannot be traced to high discounting of the future, because political leaders and military planners vary in their time horizons. They just think differently about the immediate and distant futures. Rapport demon-strates that those actors with long time horizons think about the future in abstract terms and tend to emphasize the desirability of future goals while neglecting their feasibility and the details of implementation, just as construal-level theory predicts. Those who place less weight on the future tend to focus on operational details and the feasibility of various strategies.

Krebs and Rapport (2012) apply temporal construal theory to several central ques-tions in the international relations field—international cooperation, preventive war, and coercion. They argue that temporal construal makes international cooperation some-what less difficult than standard cooperation theories suggest. Actors are more focused on the desirability of distant outcomes than on their feasibility, which generates greater optimism about the future, less concern about the future enforcement of current bar-gains, and a greater willingness to reach a negotiated settlement.

4. Conclusions

By any measure, the study of psychology and international relations has progressed enormously over the last half-century. Five or six decades ago much of the research on the psychology of foreign policy and war was conducted by psychologists who gave lit-tle attention to the political and strategic contexts in which foreign policy decisions are made. International relations theorists were beginning to develop political decision-making frameworks that incorporated a potentially important role for psychological variables, but they did not construct specific testable hypothesis or explore their under-lying psychological mechanisms. By the mid-1970s, however, IR scholars had started to develop a more systematic cognitive research program that built on new develop-ments in social psychology and that recognized the importance of the political context of individual decision-making. Within a few years, scholars gradually began incorpo-rating motivational and affective dimensions of judgment and decision-making.

One can now identify a variety of research programs on the political psychology of foreign policy and international relations. They build on different psychological the-ories, apply their models to a wide variety of substantive contexts, and make varying degrees of effort to integrate individual decision-making into more general frameworks of foreign policy and strategic interaction. They use different methodologies, including individual and comparative case studies, quantitative content analyses and surveys, aggregate data analysis, and, increasingly, experiments.

Each of these methods has its own advantages and limitations. Experiments are most effective in imposing scientific controls, but the problems of generalizing to the high-stakes and high-stress world of elite decision-making in international relations are formidable. Historical case studies are immersed in that world, but they face the problem of ruling out alternative explanations. Historical case studies are also more susceptible to the influence of the analyst's own theoretical biases on his or her interpretation; analysts are as susceptible as actors to the tendency to see what they expect to see or want to see. Threats to internal validity can be minimized by clearly specifying alternative interpretations and by applying the same standards of evaluation to alternative interpretations as to one's own (George & Bennett, 2005). The problem of generalizing from a handful of detailed case studies remains, but that problem can be reduced by identifying a carefully matched set of cases, by constructing "hard" tests, and by employing multimethod research designs.[48]

There are a number of different directions for future research that have the potential to make significant contributions to our understanding of foreign policy and international relations. My selection of specific research programs to survey in some detail in this chapter suggests some that I think are important but underdeveloped. A leader's willingness to take risks has undeniable importance in decisions for war, but IR scholars have given relatively little attention to this critical variable. Formal decision and game-theoretic models recognize that risk propensities are important but treat them exogenously and often assume either risk neutrality or risk aversion. Prospect theory provides a plausible account of the conditions under which risk acceptance is likely to emerge, but it ignores the possibility that risk attitudes might vary across individuals, cultures, or ideologies, or that political recruitment mechanisms in certain kinds of states might favor individuals with a particular kind of risk orientation.[49]

In addition, whereas prospect theory, like expected-utility theory, assumes that probabilities are known, decision-makers make choices in a world in which probabilities are unknown, which introduces an additional level of complication. This leads George and Smoke (1974, p. 528) to distinguish between calculable and incalculable risks and to argue that deterrence is probably more effective against an actor who perceives incalculable risks than high but calculable risks. This hypothesis draws support from evidence in experimental economics suggesting that people have an aversion to incalculable risks (Camerer, 1995, pp. 644–646).[50] People are more risk averse in response to "unknown unknowns" than they are to "known unknowns." We need more exploration of how different kinds of decision-makers respond to uncertainty and ambiguity as well as to risk under different conditions. We also need more work on the evaluation of potential events with extremely low probabilities (Taleb, 2007).

One particularly important area for future research on threat perception lies at the intersection of political psychology and game theory. Most discussions of threat perception focus primarily how one state perceives adversary intentions or capabilities or both while ignoring how the adversary attempts to influence the way it is perceived by others by strategically manipulating the images it projects. The game-theoretic literature on "signaling" (Banks, 1991; Wagner, 1989; Schultz, 1998) incorporates the behavior of both sender and receiver, but it assumes that signals are perceived and interpreted as intended by the sender. It ignores the psychology of threat perception and the substantial evidence that the way signals are perceived and interpreted is significantly shaped and distorted by the receiver's prior belief system, emotional needs, political interests, and organizational culture, often leading to significant distortions in the way she interprets those signals.

This is an important omission for policy as well as for theory. The manipulation of images will be most effective if the sender understands the psychology of threat perception and shapes his projection of images to exploit the proclivities of the receiver. At the same time, threat assessment will be more accurate if it incorporates the adversary's incentives to influence the way others perceive them. An integrated theory of signaling and threat perception that includes the manipulation of images, the psychology of threat perception, and the strategic interaction between them is a potentially fruitful area for future research (Jervis, 2002), one that would be advanced by attention to experimental research in behavioral game theory (Camerer, 2003).

There are other bodies of literature in international relations that could be enriched by incorporating political psychology. Liberal international theories give considerable attention to the importance of ideas and their impact on outcomes (Goldstein & Keohane, 1993), but they generally treat ideas exogenously and give little attention to the sources of ideas and how they might change. It is difficult to assess the causal impact of ideas, however, without understanding their origins. If ideas change in response to changing international structures, those ideas do not have an autonomous causal impact on policy outcomes. Hypotheses on the causal influence of ideas would be more convincing if they were linked theoretically to a model of how ideas originate and change, which should be informed by the political psychology of belief updating.

Similarly, constructivist theories of international politics could also benefit from greater attention to the literature on political psychology (Shannon & Kowert, 2012). The emphasis on the *social* construction of meanings, identities, and worldviews gives priority to the social and cultural sources of identity formation while minimizing the role of psychology. Among other things, it downplays the individual psychological needs that are satisfied by those identities and that systematically shape the social construction of identities (Kowert & Legro, 1996; Goldgeier, 1997). The incorporation of psychological variables and their interaction effects into social and cultural explanations of identity would create a better balance between social structures and individual agency in constructivist research.

Still another area in which greater attention to political psychology could enhance our understanding of foreign policy and international relations is foreign economic policy and international political economy. This field has been dominated by structural approaches that basically ignore individual-level sources of behavior and indeed the decision-making process itself. As I noted earlier, levels-of-analysis frameworks in international political economy omit the individual level. Yet it is hard to look at governmental and nongovernmental responses to the financial crises of 2008–2009 and the European debt crisis a couple years later without concluding that individual belief systems, judgments, and decision-making played a key role in shaping those responses, and that other individuals in the same positions might have made different decisions with different consequences. We need more research on how decision-making on economic issues is shaped by actors' beliefs about the international political economy, the economic lessons they draw from history,[51] their priorities among different economic values and perceptions of threats to those values, their time horizons and the kinds of trade-offs they are willing to make between current and future costs and benefits, and consequently in their economic policy preferences.

This leaves a broad agenda for future research on the political psychology of foreign policy and international relations. We need to pay particular attention to the interaction effects between psychological variables and the political and strategic context of decision-making. Although some applications of psychology attempt to contrast analytically distinct psychological models of foreign policy with alternative realist or domestic political models, this is probably not the most useful way to proceed. Psychological models alone do not provide complete explanations for international relations because they fail to explain how international and domestic conditions shape preferences and beliefs, or how the policy process aggregates individual preferences and beliefs into policy outputs for the state. The psychology of judgment and decision-making in foreign policy interacts with the political context, which varies in complex and contingent ways. Psychology plays an important role in foreign policy decision-making, but analyzing the psychological sources of foreign policy is too important to leave to the psychologists.[52]

Notes

1. Realists focus on states or groups trying to maximize power and security in an anarchic system lacking an authoritative decision mechanism. Liberals emphasize the role of domestic interests, institutions, information, and values, along with patterns of economic relationships, in shaping state goals and interactions. Constructivists emphasize the importance of identities, ideas, norms, and meanings, and how they are socially constructed, reproduced, and changed though repeated interactions. There are numerous variations within each approach. For competing theoretical perspectives, see Carlsnaes, Risse, & Simmons (2013).

2. Constructivism's neglect of individual psychology is reflected in standard typologies of systemic, norm-centric, rule-based, and societal forms of constructivism (Hopf, 2002). Alexander Wendt (1999), the most influential constructivist in international relations, explicitly adopts a state-as-unitary-actor framework that neglects domestic and individual-level influences.

3. A stronger statement of this argument is the "great man theory": history is shaped primarily by heroic individuals through their, wisdom, power, charisma, and skill (Carlyle [1840] 1888; Hook [1945] 1992).

4. For a more complete survey of the wide range of applications of social psychology to foreign policy and international relations, see Tetlock (1998) and McDermott (2004). On judgment and decision-making see Gilovich and Griffen (2010).

5. Waltz (1959) distinguished among individual, nation-state, and system-level "images" of war; Singer (1961) coined the phrase "levels of analysis"; Rosenau (1966) disaggregated the nation-state level into distinct societal and governmental components; and Jervis (1976) constructed a separate decision-making level. Other disciplines employ similar distinctions. Attribution theory's distinction between situational and dispositional sources of behavior (Nisbett & Ross, 1980) is comparable to system and unit-level variables, the latter referring to the aggregation of factors internal to the nation-state (Waltz, 1979).

6. Criteria for assessing such counterfactual propositions are discussed in Levy (2008b).

7. In a highly centralized state the preferences and perceptions of the dominant decision-maker may determine state foreign policy, but in that case the centralized nature of the state itself is part of the explanation. The fact that non-psychological variables are a necessary part of the explanation does not preclude the possibility that psychological variables carry the greatest causal weight in explaining particular foreign policy behavior or international outcomes.

8. Higher stakes also give leaders greater incentives to expend the mental energy to make rational decisions and to learn from their mistakes. Behavioral economists have constructed experimental designs to compensate for this effect (Camerer, 1995).

9. For surveys see Hudson (2007) and Mintz & DeRouen (2010).

10. Lasswell (1930; 1935) was an important exception.

11. In his comprehensive and interdisciplinary *Study of War*, for example, Quincy Wright (1942) gave far less attention to the psychological dimensions of war than to anthropological, sociological, economic, or political perspectives.

12. For useful reviews see Tetlock, Crosby, and Crosby (1981), Loewenberg (1982), McDermott (2004, chap. 6), and Post (chapter 15, this volume).

13. The power motive was developed more systematically by Winter (1973).

14. For reviews of early social-psychological studies relating to foreign policy and international relations see Klineberg (1950; 1965), Kelman (1965), and DeRivera (1968).

15. On the various ways George incorporated political psychology into theories of foreign policy decision-making, deterrence and coercive diplomacy, and crisis management, see Renshon & Renshon (2008) and other articles in that special issue of *Political Psychology*.

16. Images of the enemy are also central in scholarship outside of the operational code research program (Finlay, Holsti, & Fagen, 1967; Holsti, 1967; White, 1968; Herrmann, chapter 11, this volume).

17. Steinbrunner's (1974) "cybernetic" and cognitive models of decision making were also important.

18. Although most scholars interpret these various manifestations of theory-driven observation as cognitive, they can also be motivated. The emotional discomfort of maintaining a belief system composed of inconsistent elements leads people to reduce or eliminate those inconsistencies (Festinger, 1957).

19. For a discussion of relevance of the cognitive revolution for political science see Larson (1985).

20. Earlier, Janis (1972) developed a model of "groupthink," a tendency toward concurrence-seeking and conformity within cohesive groups driven by social pressure and individual insecurities. See 't Hart (1990) and the discussion by Dyson and 't Hart (chapter 13, this volume).

21. For a good attempt to empirically differentiate between cognitive and motivated biases in threat perceptions in the period leading to World War I, see Kaufman (1994).

22. Readers interested in more extensive surveys of the literature on political psychology and international relations should consult Goldgeier (1997), Tetlock (1998), Mintz and Derouen (2010), and McDermott (2004).

23. It is useful to distinguish "diagnostic learning" about values of certain parameters, such as adversary hostility, from "causal learning" about the validity of causal propositions, such as the likelihood that military threats work to induce compliance (Levy, 1994).

24. For an accessible discussion of Bayesian updating see Anderson and Holt (1996).

25. See the discussion of enemy stereotypes in Herrmann's chapter in this volume (chapter 11).

26. For an alternative interpretation, which emphasizes not the shared beliefs of the Israeli establishment but instead the idiosyncratic beliefs, personality, leadership style, and (non) actions of the Israeli director of military intelligence, see Bar-Joseph and Levy (2009). For general theoretical studies of intelligence failure, see Kam (1989) and Jervis (2010).

27. Much earlier, Janis (1968) posited a similar model of decision stages and emphasized the dissonance-reducing functions of overconfidence.

28. This is also a central theme of dual-process theories (Chaiken & Trope, 1999; Kahneman, 2011), which have been influential in social psychology but which have yet to have much influence in international relations.

29. Wakker (2010, 2), conceiving of theory as formal theory, described prospect theory as "the first rational theory of irrational behavior."

30. For theoretical developments, experimental tests, and applications of prospect theory in many disciplines, see Kahneman and Tversky (2000).

31. For example, when given a choice between $40 for certain and a 50/50 chance of getting nothing or $100, most people prefer to lock in the certain gain of $40. When given a choice between a $40 loss and a 50/50 chance of no losses and a $100 loss, most people prefer the gamble in the hope of avoiding the certain loss. In each case, they choose the option with the lower expected value.

32. For example, people generally get more upset when they fail to sell a stock that then goes down, than when they fail to buy a stock that then goes up by the same amount.

33. This helps explain why a basketball player is most likely to commit a foul immediately after he or she loses the ball or makes another mistake.

34. For applications to international relations see Jervis (1992), McDermott (1998), Davis (2000), Taliaferro (2004), and the June 1992 and April and June 2004 special issues of *Political Psychology*. For applications to American politics and the law, see Levy (2003). I focus on prospect theory's treatment of value. For its treatment of probabilities see Kahneman & Tversky (1979; 2000).

35. "Greater than expected" is measured relative to the predictions of expected-utility theory for a risk neutral actor.

36. At the domestic level, citizens often prefer a barely acceptable status quo to risking change. One commentator on the Russian election of March 2012 argued that for economically struggling Russians, "any desire to live better is outweighed by a persistent fear of living worse" (Schwartz, 2012, A6).

37. Relative to the predictions of expected-utility theory for a risk-neutral actor.

38. This represents a modification of (and explanation for) Schelling's (1966) argument that deterrence is easier than compellence.

39. For research in psychology see Frisch (1993).

40. Department of Defense news briefing, February 12, 2002.

41. This is an extreme form of loss aversion.

42. For an extensive bibliography see http://portal.idc.ac.il/en/PADA/publications/Pages/Bibliography.aspx.

43. This is reminiscent of Tversky's (1972) "elimination by aspects" model (Redlawsk & Lau, chapter 5, this volume).

44. See also Redlawsk and Lau (chapter 5, this volume), who have successfully applied decision boards in the study of voting behavior.

45. The discount rate r is inversely related to the discount factor δ, so that $\delta = 1/(1 + r)$. The lower the discount rate, the less one discounts the future, the higher the discount factor, and the greater the "discounted present value" of future payoffs.

46. This might be the result of an "anticipation effect," in which the process of waiting and thinking about a positive future payoff creates a positive utility (Loewenstein, 1987). It might also result from reference dependence, in that declining benefits might be perceived as losses relative to the initial reference point.

47. A key question is how distant the distant future has to be before these patterns are evident (Rapport, 2012/13).

48. An ideal form of a hard test, if it can be found, is through a "least likely" case design, for which prior theoretical expectations lead one to believe that the case is unlikely to support one's preferred hypothesis (and, ideally, is likely to support the leading alternative). Allison (1971) examined the Cuban Missile Crisis because the severity of threats to the national interests made it a least likely case for his organizational process and governmental politics models and a most likely case for his rational unitary actor model. The support of a hypothesis by a least likely case provides confidence in the more general validity of a hypothesis. Least likely case logic is based on what I call the "Sinatra inference": if I can make it there, I can make it anywhere (Levy, 2008c, p. 12). The inverse logic applies to a "most likely" case.

49. Risk orientation also varies across gender, with men being more risk acceptant than women in most task domains (Harris, Jenkins, & Glaser, 2006). Men also tend to be more overconfident than women, though this is highly dependent on task domain (Lundeberg, Fox, & Punccohar, 1994; Barber & Odean, 2001).

50. What this means is that "subjects would rather bet on known probabilities p than on known probability distributions of probability (compound lotteries) with a mean of p" (Camerer, 1995, p. 646).

51. For a study of economic decision making in 2008–2013, for example, it would be useful to explore the impact of historical analogies drawn from the Great Depression and the recession of 1937.

52. Undoubtedly psychologists have a similar view about leaving the study of politics to political scientists.

References

Agranat Commission. (1974). *The Agranat report*. Tel Aviv: Am Oved. (Hebrew)

Allison, G. T. (1971). *Essence of decision: Explaining the Cuban Missile Crisis*. Boston: Little, Brown.

Allport, G. W. (1945). Human nature and the peace. *Psychological Bulletin, 42*, 376–378.

Almond, G. A. (1950). *The American people and foreign policy*. New York: Harcourt Brace.

Anderson, L. R., & Holt, C. A. (1996). Classroom games: Understanding Bayes' rule. *Journal of Economic Perspectives, 10*, 179–187.

Art, R. J. (1973). Bureaucratic politics and American foreign policy: A critique. *Policy Sciences*, 4, 467–490.

Axelrod, R. (1984). *The evolution of cooperation*. New York: Basic Books.

Axelrod, R. (Ed.). (1976). *The structure of decision: The cognitive maps of political elites*. Princeton, NJ: Princeton University Press.

Banks, J. S. (1991). *Signaling games in political science*. New York: Routledge.

Barber, B. M., & Odean, T. (2001). Boys will be boys: Gender, overconfidence, and common stock investment. *Quarterly Journal of Economics*, 116, 261–292.

Bar-Joseph, U., & Levy, J. S. (2009). Conscious action and intelligence failure. *Political Science Quarterly*, 124, 461–488.

Brecher, M., & Geist, B. (1980). *Decisions in crises: Israel, 1967 and 1973*. Berkeley: University of California Press.

Brockner, J., & Rubin, J. Z. (1985). *Entrapment in escalating conflicts: A social psychological analysis*. New York: Springer-Verlag.

Camerer, C. F. (1995). Individual decision-making. In J. H. Kagel & A. E. Roth (eds.), *The handbook of experimental economics* (pp. 587–703). Princeton, NJ: Princeton University Press.

Camerer, C. F. (2003). *Behavioral game theory: Experiments in strategic interaction*. New York: Russell Sage.

Campbell, D. T., & LeVine, R. A. (1961). A proposal for cooperative cross-cultural research on ethnocentrism. *Journal of Conflict Resolution*, 5, 82–108.

Carlsnaes, W., Risse, T., & Simmons, B. A. (2013). *Handbook of International Relations* (2nd ed.). London: Sage.

Carlyle, Thomas. ([1840] 1888). *On heroes, hero-worship and the heroic in history*. New York: Stokes & Brother.

Chaiken, S., & Trope, Y. (Eds.). (1999). *Dual-process theories in social psychology*. New York: Guilford Press.

Cottam, R. W. (1977). *Foreign policy motivation: A general theory and case study*. Pittsburgh, PA: University of Pittsburgh Press.

Crawford, N. C. (2000). The passion of world politics: Propositions on emotion and emotional relationships. *International Security*, 24, 116–156.

Damasio, A. (1994). *Descartes' error: Emotion, reason, and the human brain*. New York: Putnam.

Davis, J. W., Jr. (2000). *Threats and promises*. Baltimore, MD: Johns Hopkins University Press.

DeRivera, J. H. (1968). *Psychological dimension of foreign policy*. Columbus, OH: Merrill.

Droba, D. D. (1931). Effect of various factors on militarism-pacifism. *Journal of Abnormal and Social Psychology*, 26, 141–153.

Duelfer, C. A., & Dyson, S. B. (2011). Chronic misperception and international conflict: The U.S.-Iraq experience. *International Security*, 36, 73–100.

Durbin, E. F. M., & Bowlby, J. (1939). *Personal aggressiveness and war*. London: Kegan Paul.

Einstein, A., & Freud, S. (1932). *Why war?* Paris: International Institute of Intellectual Cooperation.

Etheridge, L. (1978). *A world of men: The private sources of American foreign policy*. Cambridge, MA: MIT Press.

Festinger, L. (1957). *A theory of cognitive dissonance*. Stanford, CA: Stanford University Press.

Finlay, D., Holsti, O. R., & Fagen, R. (1967). *Enemies in politics*. Chicago: Rand McNally.

Frisch, D. (1993). Reasons for framing effects. *Organization Behavior and Human Decision Processes*, 54, 399–429.

George, A. L. (1969). The "operational code": A neglected approach to the study of political leaders and decisionmaking. *International Studies Quarterly*, 13, 190–222.

George, A. L. (1980). *Presidential decisionmaking in foreign policy: The effective use of information and advice.* Boulder, CO: Westview.

George, A. L., & Bennett, A. (2005). *Case studies and theory development in the social sciences.* Cambridge, MA: MIT Press.

George, A. L., & George, J. L. (1956). *Woodrow Wilson and Colonel House: A personality study.* New York: John Day.

George, A. L., & George, J. L. (1998). *Presidential personality & performance.* Boulder, CO: Westview.

George, A. L., & Smoke, R. (1974). *Deterrence in American foreign policy.* New York: Columbia University Press.

Gilovich, T. G., & Griffen, D. W. (2010). Judgment and decision making. In S. T. Fiske, D. T. Gilbert, & G. Lindzey (eds.), *Handbook of social psychology* (5th ed., vol. 1, pp. 542–588). New York: Wiley.

Goldgeier, J. M. (1997). Psychology and security. *Security Studies, 6,* 137–166.

Goldstein, J., & Keohane, R. O. (1993). *Ideas and foreign policy.* Ithaca, NY: Cornell University Press.

Gollwitzer, P. M. (2011). Mindset theory of action phases. In P. A. M. Van Lange, A. W. Kruglanksi, & E. T. Higgins (eds.), *Handbook of theories of social psychology* (vol. 1, pp. 526–545). London: Sage.

Greenstein, F. I. (1975). *Personality and politics.* New York: Norton.

Harris, C. R., Jenkins, M., & Glaser, D. (2006). Gender differences in risk assessment: Why do women take fewer risks than men? *Judgment and Decision Making, 1,* 48–63.

Hart, P. 't (1990). *Groupthink in government: A study of small groups and polity failure.* Amsterdam: Swets and Zeitlinger.

Heckhausen, H., & Gollwitzer, P. M. (1987). Thought contents and cognitive functioning in motivational versus volitional states of mind. *Motivation and Emotion, 11,* 101–120.

Hermann, C. F. (Ed.). (1972). *International crises: Insights from behavioral research.* New York: Free Press.

Hermann, M. G. (1980). Explaining foreign policy behavior using the personal characteristics of political leaders. *International Studies Quarterly, 24,* 7–46.

Hermann, M. G., Preston, T., Korany, B., & Shaw, T. M. (2001). Who leads matters: The effects of powerful individuals. *International Studies Review, 3,* 83–132.

Herrmann, R. K. (1988). The empirical challenge of the cognitive revolution: A strategy for drawing inferences about perceptions. *International Studies Quarterly, 32,* 175–203.

Holsti, O. R. (1967). Cognitive dynamics and images of the enemy. *Journal of International Affairs, 21,* 16–29.

Holsti, O. R. (1970). The "operational code" approach to the study of political leaders: John Foster Dulles' philosophical and instrumental beliefs. *Canadian Journal of Political Science, 3,* 123–157.

Holsti, O. R. (1972). *Crisis, escalation, war.* Montreal: McGill-Queens University Press.

Holsti, O. R. (1976). Foreign policy formation viewed cognitively. In R. Axelrod (ed.), *The structure of decision: The cognitive maps of political elites* (pp. 18–54). Princeton, NJ: Princeton University Press.

Holsti, O. R. (1977). *The "operational code" as an approach to the analysis of belief systems.* Final Report to the National Science Foundation, Grant No. SOC 7515368. Duke University.

Holsti, O. R. (1989). Crisis decision making. In P. E. Tetlock, J. L. Husbands, R. Jervis, P. C. Stern, & C. Tilly (eds.), *Behavior, society, and nuclear war* (vol. 1, pp. 8–84). New York: Oxford University Press.

Holsti, O. R., & George, A. L. (1975). The effects of stress on the performance of foreign policy-makers. In C. P Cotter (ed.), *Political science annual* (pp. 255–319). Indianapolis: Bobbs-Merrill.

Hook, Sydney. ([1945] 1992). *The hero in history.* New Brunswick, NJ: Transaction.

Hopf, T. (2002). *Social construction of international politics: Identities and foreign policies, Moscow, 1955 & 1999.* Ithaca, NY: Cornell University Press.

Hudson, V. M. (2007). *Foreign policy analysis.* Lanham, MD: Rowman & Littlefield.

Ikenberry, G. J., Lake, D. A., & Mastanduno, M. (1988). Introduction: Approaches to explaining American foreign economic policy. *International Organization, 42,* 1–14.

Janis, I. L. (1968). Stages in the decision-making process. In R. P. Abelson, E. Aronson, W. J. McGuire, T. M. Newcomb, M. J. Rosenberg, & P. H. Tannenbaum (eds.), *Theories of cognitive consistency: A sourcebook* (pp. 577–588). Chicago: Rand McNally.

Janis, I. L. (1972). *Victims of groupthink: A psychological study of foreign-policy decisions and fiascos.* Boston: Houghton Mifflin.

Janis, I. L., & Mann, L. (1977). *Decision making: A psychological analysis of conflict, choice, and commitment.* New York: Free Press.

Jervis, R. (1976). *Perception and misperception in international politics.* Princeton, NJ: Princeton University Press.

Jervis, R. (1985). Perceiving and coping with threat. In R. Jervis, R. N. Lebow, & J. G. Stein, *Psychology and deterrence* (pp. 13–33). Baltimore, MD: Johns Hopkins University Press.

Jervis, R. (1989). *The meaning of the nuclear revolution.* Ithaca, NY: Cornell University Press.

Jervis, R. (1992). Political implications of loss aversion. *Political psychology, 13,* 87–204.

Jervis, R. (2002). Signaling and perception: Drawing inferences and projecting images. In K. R. Monroe (ed.), *Political psychology* (pp. 293–312). Mahwah, NJ: Erlbaum.

Jervis, R. (2010). *Why intelligence fails: Lessons from the Iranian revolution and the Iraq war.* Ithaca, NY: Cornell University Press.

Johnson, D. P. (2004). *Overconfidence and war: The havoc and glory of positive illusions.* Cambridge, MA: Harvard University Press.

Johnson, D. P., & Tierney, D. (2011). The Rubicon theory of war: How the path to conflict reaches the point of no return. *International Security, 36,* 7–40.

Jones, B. D. (1999). Bounded rationality. *Annual Review of Political Science, 2,* 297–321.

Kahneman, D. (2011). *Thinking, fast and slow.* New York: Farrar, Straus and Giroux.

Kahneman, D., Slovic, P., & Tversky, A. (Eds.). (1982). *Judgment under uncertainty: Heuristics and biases.* Cambridge: Cambridge University Press.

Kahneman, D., & Tversky, A. (1979). Prospect theory: An analysis of decision under risk. *Econometrica, 47,* 263–291.

Kahneman, D., and Tversky, A. (Eds.). (2000). *Choices, values, and frames.* New York: Cambridge University Press.

Kam, E. (1989). *Surprise attack.* Cambridge, MA: Harvard University Press.

Kaufman, C. D. (1994). Out of the lab and into the archives: A method for testing psychological explanations of political decision making. *International Studies Quarterly 38,* 557–586.

Kaufman, S. J. (2006). Symbolic politics or rational choice? Testing theories of extreme ethnic violence. *International Security, 30,* 45–86.

Kelman, H. C. (1965). Social-psychological approaches to the study of international relations: Definition of scope. In H. C. Kelman (ed.), *International behavior: A social psychological analysis* (pp. 3–39). New York: Holt, Rinehart and Winston.

Khong, Y. E. (1992). *Analogies at war.* Princeton, NJ: Princeton University Press.

Klineberg, O. (1950). *Tensions affecting international understanding.* New York: Social Science Research Council.

Klineberg, O. (1965). *The human dimension in international relations.* New York: Holt, Rinehart and Winston.

Kowert, P. A., & Hermann, M. G. (1997). Who takes risks: Daring and caution in foreign policy making. *Journal of Conflict Resolution, 41,* 611–637.

Kowert, P., & Legro, J. (1996). Norms, identity, and their limits: A theoretical reprise. In P. J. Katzenstein (ed.), *The culture of national security: Norms and identity in world politics* (pp. 451–497). New York: Columbia University Press.

Krebs, R. R., & Rapport, A. (2012). International relations and the psychology of time horizons. *International Studies Quarterly, 56,* 530–543.

Kunda, Z. (1990). The case for motivated political reasoning. *Psychological Bulletin, 108* (3), 480–498.

Laibson, D. (1997). Golden eggs and hyperbolic discounting. *Quarterly Journal of Economics, 112,* 443–477.

Langer, E. J. (1975). The illusion of control. *Journal of Personality and Social Psychology, 32,* 311–328.

Langer, W. C. ([1943] 1972). *The mind of Adolf Hitler: The secret wartime report.* New York: Basic Books.

Larson, D. W. (1985). *Origins of containment: A psychological explanation.* Princeton, NJ: Princeton University Press.

Lasswell, H. D. (1930). *Psychopathology and politics.* Chicago: University of Chicago Press.

Lasswell, H. D. (1935). *World politics and personal insecurity.* New York: McGraw-Hill.

Lebow, R. N. (1981). *Between peace and war.* Baltimore, MD: Johns Hopkins University Press.

Lebow, R. N. (1987). *Nuclear crisis management.* Ithaca, NY: Cornell University Press.

Lebow, R. N. (2010). *Why Nations Fight: Past and Future Motives for War.* New York: Cambridge University Press.

Leites, N. (1951). *The operational code of the Politburo.* New York: McGraw-Hill.

Levi, A. S., & Whyte, G. (1997). A cross-cultural exploration of the reference dependence of crucial group decisions under risk. *Journal of Conflict Resolution, 41,* 792–813.

Levy, J. S. (1983). Misperception and the causes of war, *World Politics, 36,* 76–99.

Levy, J. S. (1989). The diversionary theory of war: A critique. In M. I. Midlarsky (ed.), *Handbook of war studies* (pp. 259–288). London: Unwin-Hyman.

Levy, J. S. (1994). Learning and foreign policy: Sweeping a conceptual minefield. *International Organization, 48,* 279–312.

Levy, J. S. (1997). Prospect theory, rational choice, and international relations. *International Studies Quarterly, 41,* 87–112.

Levy, J. S. (2003). Applications of prospect theory to political science. *Synthese, 135,* 215–241.

Levy, J. S. (2008a). Preventive war and democratic politics. *International Studies Quarterly, 52,* 1–24.

Levy, J. S. (2008b). Counterfactuals and case studies. In J. M. Box-Steffensmeier, H. E. Brady, & D. Collier (eds.), *Oxford handbook of political methodology* (pp. 627–644). New York: Oxford University Press.

Levy, J. S. (2008c). Case studies: Types, designs, and logics of inference. *Conflict Management and Peace Science, 25,* 1–18.

Liberman, N., and Trope, Y. (1998). The role of feasibility and desirability considerations in near and distant future decisions: A test of temporal construal theory. *Journal of Personality and Social Psychology, 75,* 1: 5–18.

Lindemann, T. (2010). *Causes of war: The struggle for recognition.* Colchester, UK: ECPR Press.

Loewenberg, P. (1982). *Decoding the past: The psychohistorical approach*. Berkeley: University of California Press.

Loewenstein, G. (1987). Anticipation and the valuation of delayed consumption. *Economic Journal*, 97, 666–684.

Loewenstein, G., Read, D., and Baumeister, R. F. (2003). *Time and decision: Economic and psychological perspectives on intertemporal choice*. New York: Russell Sage.

Lundeberg, M. A., Fox, P. W. & Punccohar, J. (1994). Highly confident but wrong: Gender differences and similarities in confidence judgments. *Journal of Educational Psychology*, 86, 114–121.

Macridis, R. C. (1958). *Foreign policy in world politics*. Englewood Cliffs, NJ: Prentice-Hall.

McDermott, R. (1998). *Risk-taking in international polities: Prospect theory in American foreign policy*. Ann Arbor: University of Michigan Press.

McDermott, R. (2004). *Political psychology in international relations*. Ann Arbor: University of Michigan Press.

McDermott, R. (2008). *Presidential leadership, illness and decision making*. New York: Cambridge University Press.

March, J. G. (1978). Bounded rationality, ambiguity, and the engineering of choice. *Bell Journal of Economic Management Science*, 9, 587–608.

Marcus, G. E. (2012). *Political psychology: Neuroscience, genetics, and politics*. New York: Oxford University Press.

May, E. R. (1973). *Lessons of the past*. London: Oxford University Press.

May, M. A. (1943). *A social psychology of war and peace*. New Haven, CT: Yale University Press.

Mercer, J. (2005). Rationality and psychology in international politics. *International Organization*, 59, 77–106.

Mintz, A. (1993). The decision to attack Iraq: A noncompensatory theory of decision making. *Journal of Conflict Resolution*, 37, 595–618.

Mintz, A. (2004). How do leaders make decisions? A poliheuristic perspective. *Journal of Conflict Resolution*, 48, 3–13.

Mintz, A., and DeRouen, K., Jr. (2010). *Understanding foreign policy decision making*. New York: Cambridge University Press.

Mintz, A., Geva, N., Redd, S. B., & Carnes, A. (1997). The effect of dynamic and static choice sets on political decision making. An analysis using the decision board platform. *American Political Science Review*, 91, 553–566.

Nincic, M. (1997). Loss aversion and the domestic context of military intervention. *Political Research Quarterly*, 50, 97–120.

Nisbett, R., & Ross, L. (1980). *Human inference: Strategies and shortcomings of social judgment*. Englewood Cliffs, NJ: Prentice-Hall.

North, R. C. (1967). Perception and action in the 1914 crisis. *Journal of International Affairs*, 21, 103–122.

O'Neill, B. (2001). Risk aversion in international relations theory. *International Studies Quarterly*, 45, 617–640.

Post, J. M. (2003). *The psychological assessment of political leaders*. Ann Arbor: University of Michigan Press.

Rapport, A. (2012/13). The long and short of it: Cognitive constraints on leaders' assessments of 'postwar' Iraq. *International Security*, 37, 133–171.

Renshon, J., & Renshon, S. A. (2008). The theory and practice of foreign policy decision making. *Political Psychology*, 29, 509–536.

Rosen, S. P. (2005). *War and human nature*. Princeton, NJ: Princeton University Press.

Rosenau, J. N. (1966). Pre-theories and theories of foreign policy. In R. B. Farrell (ed.), *Approaches to comparative and international politics* (pp. 27–92). Evanston, IL: Northwestern University Press.

Ross, D. (1984). Risk aversion in Soviet decisionmaking. In Jiri Valenta and William Potter (eds.), *Soviet Decisionmaking for National Security* (pp. 237–251). London: Allen & Unwin.

Schelling, T. C. (1966). *Arms and influence*. New Haven, CT: Yale University Press.

Schultz, K. A. (1998). Domestic opposition and signaling in international crises. *American Political Science Review, 92,* 829–844.

Schwartz, M. (2012). For struggling Russians, fear of return to hardship of '90s fuels support for Putin. *New York Times*, March 4, p. A6.

Sears, D. (1986). College sophomores in the laboratory: Influences of a narrow data base on psychology's view of human nature. *Journal of Personality and Social Psychology, 51,* 515–530.

Shannon, V. P., & Kowert, P. A. (Eds.). (2012). *Psychology and constructivism in international relations: An ideational alliance*. Ann Arbor: University of Michigan Press.

Shlaim, A. (1976). Failures in national intelligence estimates: The case of the Yom Kippur War. *World Politics, 28,* 348–380.

Simon, H. A. (1957). *Models of man*. New York: Wiley.

Singer, J. D. (1961). The level-of-analysis problem in international relations. *World Politics, 14,* 77–92.

Sitkin, S. B., & Pablo, A. L. (1992). Reconceptualizing the determinants of risk behavior. *Academy of Management Review, 17,* 9–38.

Snyder, R. C., Bruck, H. W., & Sapin, B. (Eds.). ([1954] 1962). *Foreign Policy Decision-making*. New York: Free Press.

Stagner, R (1942). Some factors related to attitude toward war, 1938. *Journal of Social Psychology, 16,* 131–142.

Stein, J. G. (1985). Calculation, miscalculation, and conventional deterrence, II: The view from Jerusalem. In R. Jervis, R. N. Lebow, & J. G. Stein (eds.), *Psychology and deterrence* (pp. 60–88). Baltimore, MD: Johns Hopkins University Press.

Stein, J. G. (1994). Political learning by doing: Gorbachev as uncommitted thinker and motivated learner. *International Organization, 48,* 155–184.

Stein, J. G., & Tanter, R. (1980). *Rational decision-making: Israel's security choices, 1967*. Columbus: Ohio State University Press.

Steinbrunner, J. D. (1974). *The cybernetic theory of decision*. Princeton, NJ: Princeton University Press.

Steiner, Z. (2011). *The triumph of the dark: European international history, 1933–1939*. New York: Oxford University Press.

Streich, P., & Levy, J. S. (2007). Time horizons, discounting, and intertemporal choice. *Journal of Conflict Resolution, 51,* 199–226.

Taliaferro, J. W. (2004). *Balancing risks: Great power intervention in the periphery*. Ithaca, NY: Cornell University Press.

Taleb, N. N. (2007). *The black swan: The impact of the highly improbable*. New York: Random House.

Tetlock, P. E. (1991). Learning in U.S. and Soviet foreign policy. In G. W. Breslauer & P. E. Tetlock (eds.), *Learning in U.S. and Soviet foreign policy* (pp. 20–61). Boulder, CO: Westview.

Tetlock, P. E. (1998). Social psychology and world politics. In D. Gilbert, S. Fiske, & G. Lindzey (eds.), *Handbook of social psychology* (4th ed., pp. 868–912). New York: McGraw-Hill.

Tetlock, P. E. (2005). *Expert political judgment: How good is it? How can we know?* Princeton, NJ: Princeton University Press.

Tetlock, P. E., Crosby, F., & Crosby, T. L. (1981). Political psychobiography. *Micropolitics, 1*, 191–213.

Thayer, B. A. (2004). *Darwin and international relations: On the evolutionary origins of war and ethnic conflict*. Lexington: University Press of Kentucky.

Thurstone, L. L., & Chave, E. J. (1929). *The measurement of attitude*. Chicago: University of Chicago Press.

Trope, Y., & Liberman, N. (2000). Temporal construal and time-dependent changes in preference. *Journal of Personality and Social Psychology, 79*(6), 876–889.

Tversky, A. (1972). Elimination by aspects: A theory of choice. *Psychological Review, 79*(4), 281–299.

Tversky, A., & Kahneman, D. (1974). Judgment under uncertainty: Heuristics and biases. *Science, 185*, 1124–1131.

Vertzberger, Y. Y. I. (1990). *The world in their minds*. Stanford, CA: Stanford University Press.

Wagner, R. H. (1989). Uncertainty, rational learning, and bargaining in the Cuban missile crisis. In P. C. Ordeshook (ed.), *Models of strategic choice in politics* (pp. 177–205). Ann Arbor: University of Michigan Press.

Wakker, P. P. (2010). *Prospect theory: For risk and ambiguity*. New York: Cambridge University Press.

Walker, S. G. (1977). The interface between beliefs and behavior: Henry Kissinger's operational code and the Vietnam War. *Journal of Conflict Resolution, 11*, 129–168.

Walker, S. G. (1995). Psychodynamic processes and framing effects in foreign policy decision-making: Woodrow Wilson's operational code. *Political Psychology, 16*, 697–717.

Walker, S. G. (2003). A cautionary tale: Operational code analysis as a scientific research program. In C. Elman & M. F. Elman (eds.), *Progress in international relations theory* (pp. 245–276). Cambridge, MA: MIT Press.

Waltz, K. N. (1959). *Man, the state, and war*. New York: Columbia University Press.

Waltz, K. N. (1979). *Theory of international politics*. Reading, MA: Addison-Wesley.

Wendt, A. (1999). *Social theory of international politics*. New York: Cambridge University Press.

White, R. (1968). *Nobody wanted war*. New York: Doubleday.

Winter, D. G. (1973). *The power motive*. New York: Free Press.

Winter, D. G. (1992). Personality and foreign policy: Historical overview of research. In E. Singer & V. Hudson (eds.), *Political psychology and foreign policy* (pp. 79–101). Boulder, CO: Westview.

Wohlstetter, R. (1962). *Pearl Harbor. Warning and decision*. Stanford, CA: Stanford University Press.

Wright, Q. (1942). *A study of war*. Chicago: University of Chicago Press.

....

CHAPTER 11

PERCEPTIONS AND IMAGE
THEORY IN INTERNATIONAL
RELATIONS

....

RICHARD K. HERRMANN

1. INTRODUCTION

....

CRONBACH (1957) described social psychology as divided into two disciplines, one that explained an actor's behavior from the outside, relying on the notion of the environment (Skinner, 1960), and the other explaining behavior from the inside, relying on the concept of personality. In international relations theory a similar division was evident in the 1950s. One school sought to explain state behavior from the outside, looking primarily at the distribution of power in the system and the external constraints and incentives it represented for any particular state. Another school sought to explain state behavior by examining the various motives and perceptions that prevailed in each state (Sprout, 1965). Both schools of thought employed the basic methods of positivist research, defining concepts, laying out deductive models, and pursuing empirical tests (Riker, 1962). Where they differed was with regard to their assumptions about the nature of decision-making (Snyder, Bruck, & Sapin, 1962).

Do people respond to the external environment as if they were rationally maximizing the payoffs available given the objective situation? That was the question that lay at the center of the dispute between the two perspectives. The first school of thought argued that it made sense to assume actors did perceive the environment correctly and did decide rationally (see the discussions by Redlawsk & Lau, chapter 5, this volume; and by Chong, chapter 4, this volume). Scholars in this school assumed actors would make mistakes, but learn from them and over time act as if they were rational players responding to objective incentive structures. The second school doubted that people would perceive the situation in the same way, even over time, and would therefore be making decisions in quite different constructions of reality employing rather different logics (Brecher, 1972; 1973; Rummel, 1975). Whereas in the first perspective scholars expected people to formulate probabilistic expectations and learn efficiently from experiential feedback, in the second perspective scholars expected people to operate with too little appreciation for uncertainty and, consequently, to be overconfident and slow to learn that they were wrong (Steinbruner, 1974).

The stakes involved in the debate as it came into the international realm were high. Great powers arrayed large armies against one another and counted on nuclear deterrence to keep the peace. If environmental conditions mostly understood as the distribution of power determined strategic choice and people were processing calculations in a rational fashion, then signaling resolve and intention might be understood as fairly straightforward (Schelling, 1966). On the other hand, if people were seen as operating with very different constructions of reality and updating in biased and distinctly different ways, then the room for serious misunderstanding and failed communication was high (George & Smoke, 1974; Green, 1968). Whereas in the first model nuclear deterrence seemed especially robust and highly sophisticated logics of signaling appropriate (Achen & Snidal, 1989), in the later model it seemed dangerous, and models that assumed the signals sent were the messages received were seen as too optimistic (Jervis, 1989; Jervis, Lebow, & Stein, 1985). Those advocating more attention to the psychological processes were perhaps willing to agree that the rational models were appropriate ideals to strive for when teaching professionals how to approach the task of decision-making (Steinbruner, 1974). They thought, however, that they were poor descriptions of how people actually did make decisions (R. W. Cottam, 1977; Jervis, 1976).

To understand how decisions were made, those promoting the psychological approach argued that more attention needed to be paid to how people perceived the situations they faced and the instrumental assumptions they held about casual relationships (Axelrod, 1976; Bodenhausen, 1993). Simon (1985) argued that knowing these things would explain far more than knowing in the abstract that people weighed benefits against costs. Of course, inferring what someone else values and identifying how that person sees the world is an empirical challenge that is extremely difficult to overcome (Herrmann, 1988). There are not agreed-upon indicators of underlying values, motives, or perceptions, and the incentives to deceive people on these matters, especially in the geopolitical world, is well understood (Jervis, 1970).

It was the sense that studying how people constructed reality was crucially important yet very hard to do that led to the concentration on images and mindsets. It also gave rise to theories that connected these cognitive concepts to underlying processes and motivations. This chapter lays out briefly the case for studying perceptions and images and then in section 3 turns to the question of how to do it. In that section, various ways of thinking about mental models are introduced and the notion of concentrating on perceptions of basic strategic relationships explained. The impact these mental models have on the search for and processing of new information is discussed, as is their effect on behavioral inclinations. Section 4 turns to the question of where these mental models come from and why they form and operate as they do. Here attention is directed to both the need to manage large amounts of information and the desire to protect self-esteem as explanations for why mental representations form as they do and for how these cognitive images make decision-making easier. Special attention is paid to how people balance their sentimental feeling about other countries with their cognitive constructions of them. Section 5 closes the chapter by identifying some of the questions this tradition still faces and the direction it may take in the future.

2. WHY STUDY IMAGES? WHAT DO THEY DO?

As already indicated, the study of perception was driven by the failure of theories that relied on purely material factors to explain the outbreak of war and the conclusion of peace. Wars seemed to start because parties had different estimates of the balance of power between them and different perceptions of their intentions and the intentions of others (Kray et al., 2010; Lebow, 1981). Initiators lost, suggesting error in this regard was not all that infrequent and the ability to predict war from power estimates alone was not all that impressive. Neorealists shifted away from a theoretical dependence on power as an objective factor and toward the idea that perceptions of security that rested on estimates of relative power and assumptions about the intentions of other countries were most important (Walt, 1987; Waltz, 1979). There was a recognition that rather than viewpoints converging as might be expected if materialist factors reigned supreme, perceptions instead varied greatly across countries and within countries.

The differences in elite perceptions often runs parallel to vastly different understandings of what is happening and why among the general public. The differences in what is taken to be almost conventional wisdom in one country compared to the next can be stark. Take, for example, the recent war in Iraq. While the Pew Center for the Study of the People and the Press found that most people in France (82%) and Germany (69%) thought leaders in Washington lied on purpose and were not misinformed about weapons of mass destruction, fewer than a third (31%) of the Americans saw it this way (Center, 2004). Nearly two-thirds in France (61%) and Germany (65%) perceived the War on Terror as a pretext motivated by desire for domination, while two-thirds (67%) of Americans thought it was motivated by real fear and concern for security. Numerous studies of American opinion on the war found that perceptions within the United States also varied widely. The partisan gaps between Republican and Democrats on the causes of the war, whether weapons of mass destruction had been found, and whether the progress was being made were so large that they were often taken as evidence of sharp polarization (Baum & Groeling, 2010).

Of course during the Cold War the argument between hawks and doves on the basic offensive or defensive character of the Soviet Union drove much of the interest in studying different perceptions (Holsti & Rosenau, 1984). It also drew attention to the inherent uncertainty involved when making strategic judgments. The behavior of others could be explained as a product of both its motivation to achieve certain aims and its power to do so (Herrmann, 1985). Unfortunately, measuring either motives or power was not easy to do, and the task was made only more difficult because any inference about one was dependent on an assumption about the other. There were no agreed-upon indicators of various offensive and defensive motivations (Jervis, 1970). Nor were there any agreed-upon ways to decide how to weigh a country's capabilities against the difficulty of the tasks it was trying to accomplish, which was the most common way of thinking about power as a relative phenomenon (Morgenthau, 1973, pp. 154–156). Moreover, it was impossible to estimate how hard a country was trying to achieve something without making assumptions about the options it had available. Of course, determining the options it had available usually involved estimating its power, which was often inferred from its success and failure in previous contests but any inferences drawn from these outcomes rested on an assumption about how hard the country was trying. At this point, the logic became circular. The inherent complexities involved with these judgments became especially clear as people tried to explain the outcomes in asymmetric conflicts like the wars in Vietnam and Afghanistan (George & Simons, 1994). Making matters only worse was the multidimensional nature of power and no agreed-upon way to add across its various elements to arrive at a net assessment in a specific context (Baldwin, 2002).

On closer inspection, the key concepts in the dominant theories used to explain international relations were often not tied closely to operational measures and were so loosely translated into concrete settings that their content seemed to be determined post hoc by the outcome as much as by any empirical strategy that allowed them to be used ex ante. This meant that important judgments about foreign countries remained nonfalsifiable. There was no definitive way to show that a motivational attribution was wrong or that an estimate of power was misplaced. As Jervis (2010, p. 170) has pointed out, the consequence of this was that despite the volumes of argument about the nature of the Soviet Union, almost nobody changed his or her mind in light of someone else's argument. The situation today regarding different views of China's intentions or Iran's power looks quite similar. Because these basic perceptions of other countries are not anchored solidly in agreed-upon methods for empirical testing, they are likely to vary a great deal and yet be crucially important.

The pictures people have of other countries become central building blocks in their identification of the threats and opportunities their country faces. These images of others can become assumptions that are so taken for granted that they produce routinized habits that define basic parameters of what is seen as in a country's interest or contrary to it. In case after case, it is the failure to rethink and adjust preexisting beliefs to incoming information that is seen as at the root of intelligence failures (Jervis, 2010, [[/ 169–171). Mintz (2003) suggests that we ought to think of decision-making as a two-stage process in which in the first stage decision-makers narrow the menu for choice by the use of one or more heuristics. These first-stage cognitive shortcuts, Mintz (2004) contends, reject alternatives that are unacceptable to the policymaker on a critical dimension or dimensions. The substantive content of these dimensions can vary, but whatever they are they evoke psychological processes that reduce the choices under active consideration. Mintz argues that a more rational analytic assessment of competing options occurs only after this first cognitive stage has narrowed the options. (See Levy's summary of Mintz's [2004] "poliheuristic theory" in chapter 10 in this volume.)

Of course, basic cognitive understandings and processes may also determine the meaning that is attached to various actions and words. They do this by defining the context in which these moves are embedded. Given that many actions can have multiple purposes, and words can be used both to communicate and to deceive, these prior beliefs, consequently, can affect what the moves of others are thought to signal and thereby complicate communication. They can even lead people to interpret moves made by third parties as signals sent by the second party, when, in fact, they were moves entirely determined by the third party. This was common in the Cold War, when people frequently saw third parties as proxies and dominoes (Jervis & Snyder, 1991). Tetlock and Lebow (2001) found that these basic images shaped the lessons people drew from historical outcomes. They did this by affecting the counterfactual thought experiments people imagined as plausible. Johnson and Tierney (2006) argue that these sorts of images even determined the perception people formed of who won and lost and why.

As studies attached more and more importance to perceptions and images, increasing attention turned to how to determine what they were. This involved both developing the conceptual infrastructure needed to describe them in a parsimonious way and strategies for connecting these abstractions to operational indicators. The first task meant understanding the character of mental models and their operation. The second task meant identifying prototypic patterns to look for and creating theories that explained why they formed. I turn to the first task next and the second task in section 4.

3. Perceptions, Gestalts, and Mental Models

When thinking about another country or strategic situation a person might have many ideas in play. The person could be thinking about the geographic location of the other country, the way its people look and dress, its military history, and its economic strength. Or the observer may also be picturing its topography and leaders, along with its monuments and cultural practices, its religion, and even its food. Beyond these country-specific attributes, one may also be thinking about certain ways most countries in general behave. George (1993, pp. 117–125) called this latter sort of information *generic knowledge*. Because it was easy to see that the number of features a description might include was very large, scholars sought to organize the descriptive task in ways that would facilitate the comparison of beliefs and worldviews. This often began with a fairly inductive strategy but moved toward a more deductively organized search as the study of schemata and scripts became popular.

Giving people a long list of countries and asking them to sort them into groups was one way scholars used to explore the dimensions people brought to mind when they thought about countries (for a review of categorization strategies see M. Cottam, 1986). These studies reaffirmed the importance of geography and sometimes alliances but did not seem to reveal the sort of considerations that were central to people as they thought about how to behave toward a foreign country. For that, it was necessary to concentrate on beliefs thought to be more proximate to strategic decision-making. The operational code seeks to do this by concentrating on philosophical and instrumental beliefs (George, 1969; Leites, 1951; Schafer & Walker, 2006). A scholar can describe subjects' beliefs about the essential conflictive or harmonious nature of the political system, their optimism about the prospects for success, and their sense as to whether political developments are predictable or not and how much of that is under their control. On the instrumental side, these operational code descriptions include a summary of subjects' ideas on how to calculate risk, their understanding of timing, and their judgments about the utility of different ways of exercising influence (Walker, 1990). The theoretical reasoning behind the 10 questions comprising the code was not developed fully, and a second tradition developed that took a more inductive approach. Cognitive maps were designed to describe the affective, substantive, policy, and value concepts in a person's speech and to track the linkages the person drew between them (Axelrod, 1976). The maps allowed the scholar to graphically present the person's causal reasoning.

Sometimes these cognitive maps became enormously complicated as scholars tried to capture a person's reasoning. Computers could be used to keep track of the linkages, but how to use this description to make strategic decisions was not clear. It was difficult to see the forest for the trees and hard to determine what the overall behavioral inclination would be. Constructing the maps also required access to the casual reasoning people were employing. This was sometimes available long after the fact in archival records but difficult to obtain in more contemporary settings. As in most operational code analyses, here too the measurement strategy typically took the words people used at face value. The assumption was the words directly revealed the thinking behind them. This, however, was not always accepted as a reasonable assumption in the political setting. Predictive expectations were also hard to deduce from both operational codes and cognitive maps because the various beliefs were treated as independent of one another, allowing for nearly infinite combinations and logic chains.

Scholars from a gestalt tradition approached the task differently. They believed the elements in a mindset or perception of another were so unified as a whole that it did not make sense to describe the parts as if they were separate one from the other. Instead of describing each piece independently, this strategy described whole impressions. Looking at their different features and across common dimensions, a researcher could compare them, but they would, nevertheless, be treated as wholes in which the subparts did not simply add up but instead interacted to produce integrated results. Asch (1952), for example, found that as people formed impressions of others, some items, especially how warm or cold they thought the other person was, affected the meaning they attached to the remaining features that they attributed to the other person. A smart, talented, rich women who was cold left a quite different impression than one who was smart, talented, rich, and warm. Asch found that switching the smart, talented, rich, or female attributes made less difference in the overall impression than changing the cold to warm or vice versa. Consequently, in this approach, the pieces going into an impression were not seen as equal. Some were more important and seen to be at the center of the gestalt.

Boulding (1959), developing a theory of international relations built on this basic gestalt idea, argued that the perceived hostility or friendliness of another country was the primary component in a person's image of that country. In his theory of national images, Boulding argued that the perceived strength or weakness of the other country was a second key component of the image and that with these two components it was possible to predict what sorts of behavior toward the other country someone operating with that image would be inclined to prefer (Boulding, 1956). Deutsch and Merritt (1965) went on to define images as "combinatorial constructs" that represented the integration of these dimensions. Scott (1965) explained how the images provoked emotions that then fueled the behavioral inclinations. Richard Cottam (1977) continued in this tradition, arguing that along with the threat or opportunity that was perceived and the perception of relative power, judgments about the relative cultural status of other countries were also central to the national gestalt, shaping both emotional sentiments and behavioral preferences.

Susan Fiske's (Fiske, Cuddy, & Glick, 2006; Fiske, Cuddy, Glick, & Xu, 2002) subsequent work in social psychology has found repeatedly that when describing a person's beliefs about another person, it is the warmth and competence they attribute to the other person that is critical. Herrmann, Voss, Schooler, and Ciarrochi (1997), building on Cottam, has found that in the political realm perceived goal interdependence and perceived relative power play an analogous role. In other words, perceived threats and opportunities that reflect the evaluation of how the other country's goals fit with those of one's own country act like warm and cold attributes, while estimates of relative power resemble perceptions of competence. Both lines of research have found that concentrating on these two dimensions of a gestalt is a parsimonious way of describing perceptions of others. It leads to predictions about both the emotional sentiments and strategic behaviors these perceptions lead to. Herrmann has continued to include judgments about cultural status as a third dimension, arguing it affects the norms people expect to prevail in the relationship between the self and other in a way that goal interdependence and relative power alone do not.

From the outset, Boulding (1956) directed attention to relationships, not simply to images of the other. His notions of friendliness and power implied something about both the self and the other. K. J. Holsti (1970) identified 17 role conceptions in international relations that defined different configurations of self and other. He argued these were driven by perceptions of threat and relative capabilities, along with economic needs and ideological principles. Alan Fiske (1991) has proposed a general theory of relationships arguing that central to them is the expected norms of exchange. He argues there are four ideal-typical such norms. They are market pricing, equality matching, communal sharing, and authority ranking. His argument is that people's mental construction of a relationship includes the norms seen as appropriate for exchange. In other words, when they imagine self and other, they also imagine whether the relationship between them warrants accepting the lead of the other (authority ranking), taking care of the other (communal sharing), or simply trading goods of equal amount or comparable market value. Fiske finds that disagreement over what norms should prevail can be an important source of conflict in a relationship.

Herrmann and Fischerkeller (1995) argue that perceived cultural status plays an important role in shaping the expectations for which norms of exchange will be expected. They draw on Horowitz's (1985, pp. 147–149, 167–171) finding that one source of serious violence between ethnic groups is the inclination of one group to see itself as more advanced in cultural terms and the other as backward, and then from this assume that norms of authority ranking should prevail. This sort of thinking underpinned caste and racial systems in numerous societies and was typical in many relationships between European imperial nations and their African and Asian colonies. These perceptions of cultural status, Herrmann and Fischerkeller argue, affect expectations about what sorts of rules of war, if any, would be respected by the other country and what sorts of self-restraint, therefore, should be exercised. These cultural judgments would also affect the perception of trustworthiness and the perceived likelihood agreements would be honored.

While much of the early work on images in international relations concentrated on enemy images that were prominent during the Cold War (Finlay et al., 1967; Silverstein, 1989), Cottam (1977) concentrated on the images associated with empire. The enemy relationship, he argued, was characterized by a combination of perceptions of threat, of comparable capability, and of comparable cultural status. This gestalt, Cottam argued, produced antagonistic behavioral inclinations and stereotypic descriptions that justified the use of large-scale violence against the other country. Although this gestalt when prevailing on both sides of a relationship can produce mirror images that lead to spiral escalation (Broffenbrenner, 1961; Jervis, 1976), the parties operating with it are often wary of direct attacks on one another, fearing the costs of war. After all, they see the other country as possessing comparable capability. Cottam argued it made sense to examine other mental constructions of a relationship that would lead to a more aggressive attack. Herrmann (1985) built on this idea by developing a gestalt that featured perceived opportunity in combination with perceived inferior capability and comparable cultural status that he called the *degenerate*. This, he argued, was a better description of how Hitler perceived France.

Another gestalt that has received a good deal of attention features a self that perceives the other as representing a perceived opportunity, and as inferior in capability and lower in cultural status. Cottam argued this was a reasonable description of the perception imperial leaders had of their colonies. The gestalt leads to a behavioral inclination to intervene in the other country and to impose control over it. Cottam described how the gestalt also associated with a stereotype that justified this control by picturing the other country as in danger of being ruled by terrible leaders, populated with people not yet motivated by nationalism, and unable to overcome its problems without tutelage. He, like Herrmann (1988) and Martha Cottam (1994) after him, laid out the basic architecture of the stereotype. It has been described in great detail in numerous regional settings (Jahoda, 1999; Porch, 1986; Said, 1979). The cultural dimension has also figured prominently in the analysis of dehumanization and infra-humanization.

The demonization of the adversary is a common feature in intensely violent conflicts. The process can both make violence more likely by making the normative prohibitions against killing seem less relevant, and be caused by violent conflict as people wrestle with justifying their actions. More will be said about the causes of demonization shortly; here the key point is that when people dehumanize others, they are in effect diminishing the other's cultural status. Haslam (2006) points out this is done in two ways, both by denying that the other has the attributes intrinsic to human nature and by denying that the other has the attributes that are widely agreed to distinguish humans from other species. For instance, when moral sensibility, refinement, civility, and rationality are taken out of a picture, the other person starts to resemble an animal. Likewise, when interpersonal warmth, emotional responsiveness, cognitive openness, and a sense of individuality and agency are erased, the other person starts to resemble a machine. In both cases, by altering the human basis of the other, the image affects both the expectations about the norms the other is likely to respect and judgments about the sort of treatment the other deserves.

Whether we use a two or three-dimensional model, the basic gestalts can be used to define ideal-typical relationships. This has been done often in the case of enemy relationships and asymmetric imperial ones. As ideal-typical constructions, the extreme versions of these gestalts do not describe any particular person's worldview. Instead, they provide a set of referents against which to compare actual perceptions. Nothing in this approach suggests that everyone operates with extreme perceptions of threat or radically different perceptions of relative power and status. To the contrary, it uses the extreme version to describe the mental landscape the way geographers use the North and South Pole to describe various locations. This mapping allows the easy comparison of constructions on dimensions found to associate with behavioral inclinations. These inclinations affect both the words used to describe the other country and the deeds directed at it.

Ole Holsti (1967) explored perceived threat and the enemy image it gave rise to in great depth. He found that the underlying perceptions of threat and power led John Foster Dulles to describe the Soviet Union in terms closely resembling a stereotype. This enemy image, he argued, included cognitive parts that made it nearly invulnerable to disconfirmation. Aggressive behavior affirmed the picture of an evil and power-hungry other. At the same time, the other's more cooperative behavior was attributed to the other's weakness and inability to carry out aggression, or to the success of deterrence. If these explanations seemed too implausible to accept, then the cooperative behavior of the other could be dismissed as a tactical feint sure to be followed by a future aggressive move. Holsti pointed out that in this inherent bad-faith model, there was very little the other country could do to change the perception of its intentions short of complete surrender. In more contemporary bargaining theory, credible commitments are often defined as those that persuade the observer that the other will still find it in its interest to comply in the distant future (Lake, 2010–2011, p. 23). These outcomes are hard to imagine when the observer is convinced the other has evil intentions, operates in bad faith, and will never abandon those goals. (See Stein's discussion, in chapter 12 of this volume, of the impact of emotions on threat perception.)

Beyond this, the existing image operates as a cognitive schema that not only shapes the interpretation of new information but also affects the search for new information (Sherman, Judd, & Park, 1989). Like other schemata, these images are clusters of knowledge that hang together and thereby lead people to notice evidence that is consistent with it, ignore or misread information that is not, and confuse what parts of the image actually have empirical evidence supporting them and which parts do not (Abelson, Dasgupta, Park, & Banaji, 1998; Campbell, 1967; Fiske & Taylor, 1991). One thing schemata do is help people to fill in information that they are missing about the other. When people do this, they usually fill in information consistent with the schema. Schemata also make it easier for people to retrieve from memory pieces of information that fit with the stereotype. To see how powerful ally, enemy, and dependent images were as schemata for American decision-makers, Martha Cottam (1986) deployed a survey and examined inclinations toward schema-consistent pictures. Herrmann et al. (1997) ran experiments giving subjects only a few pieces of information about another country and then asking subjects what they thought about other aspects of the country that had not been described. The inclination to fill in schema-consistent attributes was evident in enemy, ally, degenerate, and colony images. Alexander, Brewer, and Herrmann (1999) replicated the endeavor, looking also to see if a barbarian stereotype had schemata-like properties.

From Boulding on, the studies relying on historical case studies described the association between ideal typical gestalts and strategic preferences. Holsti worked these out for the enemy configuration, explaining John Foster Dulles's commitment to containment and even rollback. Shimko (1991) updated that sort of analysis, using it to explain the policy preferences of leaders in the Reagan administration. Herrmann (1986) found that images of the Soviet Union associated with policy support at the public level. Hurwitz and Peffley (1990) went much further, building a general theory to explain how these images combined with core values to produce policy preferences. They found that these images determined the lessons people drew from the collapse of the Soviet Union (Peffley & Hurwitz, 1992) and the end of the Cold War. Tetlock (1999) found similar effects among an elite academic sample.

Martha Cottam (1994) also made a case for the causal significance of images. She argued that the material and structural conditions in Latin America could not explain the variation in US intervention. Washington intervened, for instance, in Guatemala in 1954 and Cuba in 1960 but not in Bolivia in 1952 even though the material conditions in all three cases were similar. By contrasting US policy toward Chile, where the US intervened, between 1970 and 1973 with its policy toward Peru, where it did not, between 1968 and 1971, she made a similar argument. That is, she contended that the political and structural geopolitical conditions were similar and would have predicted intervention in both cases, while the study of prevailing imagery would predict intervention only in the cases where it in fact happened. Cottam provided an interpretation of why stereotypic images formed in some cases and not in others. Her argument revolved around the influence of specific leaders and the process of domestic political contest. She emphasized that regardless of why certain views prevailed in Washington, the prevalence of these images was associated with specific behavior.

Herrmann and Fischerkeller (1995) developed strategic scripts that they argued were associated with five stereotypic images. They argued that although stereotypic images may not associate strongly with individual actions, they would associate with sets of actions. Using Robert Abelson's (1976) notion of a script to describe a set of interrelated actions, they constructed five strategic scripts that were constituted of multiple objectives and policy tracks. They linked theoretically the enemy image to a containment script, the ally image to an institutional cooperation script, the degenerate image to a revisionism script, the imperialist image to an independent fortress script, and the colony image to an intervention script. They explored the empirical strength of the association in a preliminary way by treating the Persian Gulf as a microcosm of international politics and examining the multiple relationships between the United States, the Soviet Union, Iran, and Iraq.

Using gestalts and schemata as organizing concepts helped to simplify the task of describing international worldviews and strategic assumptions. It provided a structure around which to compare these things and narrowed the focus to a few tractable dimensions. It also drew attention to the stickiness of gestalts and images once they formed and explained why they were sometimes nearly invulnerable to disconfirmation. These tools allowed scholars to meet some of the challenge inherent in shifting to a more phenomenological perspective. At the same time, they did not satisfy the desire to explain what was driving international politics. This is because it was still not clear where these cognitive beliefs came from. Although they could be used as independent variables measured empirically, there was a desire to treat them as dependent variables, explaining why they formed as they did. Of course, this was a difficult question in the midst of a cognitive revolution that was fueled by the realization that people read stimuli in different ways and develope worldviews and beliefs in a fashion not always predictable from material conditions alone. Nevertheless, the investigation has been active.

4. The Origins of Images

If as Cronbach suggested, psychology in the 1950s incorporated two disciplines, one focused on the person and the other on the situation, then the resolution of the personality-versus-situation divide in the 1970s was to incorporate into the conception of personality invariance the subject's cognitive construction of the situation (Cronbach, 1975). This interactionist perspective, as Mischel and Shoda (1998; 1999) called it, emphasized the cognitive aspects of the personality construct. It reflected the move toward cognitive explanations and away from depth psychology and psychoanalytic explanations that featured motivations and drives emanating from within the person. Kurt Lewin's field theory (M. Deutsch, 1968) had encouraged the move to temporally proximate causes, arguing that tying putative causes that may have occurred several decades earlier to contemporary behavior left too much room for interpretation among a veritable grab bag of possible causes that were evident in the stream of a life's history.

By the 1970s, the preference for explanations that featured contemporary cognitions over emotions and underlying motivations was clear. These types of explanations were seen as more parsimonious. Why attribute to underlying unobservable motives the patterns in thought and biases that could be explained by cognitive factors? That, anyway, was the thinking moving much of the cognitive revolution as it made its impact on the study of international relations. It led scholars to study the operation of schemata, the various heuristic rules people employed, and the ways they went about calculating risks and expected utilities (Jervis, 1976; Vertzberger, 1990). At the same time, even if not as prominent, interest in emotions and motivations persisted, as did theoretical efforts to connect them to the cognitive items. By now, the balance between interest in strictly cognitive and more motivationally inclined perspectives has evened out, and the two orientations have come to share an interest in how emotions might tie them together. Here I will start with cognitive explanations and then turn to motivational theories.

4.1. Cognitive Inclinations

Jervis (1976, pp. 58–84) compared the model of rational deterrence in which signaling is assumed to be efficient to the model of spiral escalation in which even a bit of worst-case analysis and risk aversion can fuel unnecessary escalation and in which substantial misperceptions are not unusual. In reviewing the sources of misperception, he concentrated on strategies for managing the flow of information. The notion that people were cognitive misers often overwhelmed by too much information and anxious to manage it in useful and convenient ways directed attention to the shortcuts they used to do this. One of the most common shortcuts is to operate with categories that countries can be placed in and then use the category's general attributes to describe the country rather than concentrate on its idiosyncratic detail. If simple categories like good and bad are used, then people will be inclined to see all goods things as going together and bad things likewise. This could mean that countries seen as friendly are also seen as honest and as having a good government, and unfriendly countries seen as just the opposite.

This focus on categories more easily explains why people use general schemata to describe specific cases than it explains why countries are put into a category in the first place. One cognitive explanation for that might feature common heuristics people are known to employ (Kahneman, Slovic, & Tversky, 1982). (For more detailed discussions of cognitive heuristics or shortcuts, see Redlawsk & Lau, chapter 5, this volume; and Taber & Young, chapter 17, this volume.) For example, they might use the category that is most available or easiest to bring to mind. Similarly, they could notice one feature of the other country that they thought was most representative of a category and then catalog the country in that category without properly assessing all the other attributes of the country to see if the fit was really the most likely one. Of course, to calculate the likelihood a country belongs in a certain category, we needs to know the frequency of that type of country in the international system. Jervis explained that base rates of this type are not easy to imagine in international relations (Jervis, 1986). It is not clear even on what dimensions the different types would be tracked and base rates established (Jervis, 2010, pp. 193–195). Instead of thinking about the problem in terms of base rates and probabilities, cognitive misers are more likely to overvalue highly vivid information that carries an emotional charge when making the classification.

Beside the inclination to simplify, the cognitive explanations draw attention to the asymmetry in information that people have about their own country and other countries. Jervis (1976, pp. 319–329) found, for example, that one of the most common patterns was for people to perceive the decision-making in the other country, or even set of countries, as centralized and rational, while recognizing that in their own country it involved multiple factions, competing interests, and sometimes numerous veto-players. This could reflect their much greater familiarity with the internal workings of their own country and the limited information they have about different leaders, interests groups, and social movements in the other country. Jervis's students did more with information asymmetries, explaining the persistence of images and, in turn, reputation in terms of a fundamental attribution bias.

Because people are often paying attention to their own country, they are likely to become aware that its behavior varies across situations. Because they attend to other countries less frequently, they may not be aware of the variation in its behavior and instead only know about its behavior in a single context. Social psychologists have argued for decades that this produces an attribution bias (Jones & Nisbett, 1971; Ross, 1977). With more knowledge about variation in hand, people when explaining their own behavior are more likely to see situational causes. When explaining the behavior of other people, they are more likely to attribute behavior to dispositional causes. This is because they are less familiar with the other's behavior across many different situations. Mercer (1996) figured this asymmetry would have important implications for debates about the importance of demonstrating resolve in order to establish and preserve reputation. He argued that it would make convincing enemies that you were tough easier and convincing allies that you were dependable harder.

Mercer argued leaders who see another country as an enemy typically attribute its behavior to disposition, seeing its activity as evidence of resolve and aggressive intent. Predisposed both to hang on to their initial image of the enemy country and to make dispositional attributions for others, leaders tend to be insensitive to case-specific information. This mean that although a leader may worry that an adversary will come to doubt the leader's resolve because of behavior in a single case, in fact, adversaries typically see leaders as resolved and do not question that dispositional attribution. This means that leaders have a much easier time preserving a reputation for toughness in enemy relationships than they fear. Press (2005) subsequently found that perceptions that an adversary has interests at stake do more to strengthen credibility than the adversary's past behavior in conflict situations.

Because allies operate in cognitive terms like part of the in-group or self, people are inclined to make situational attributions when explaining an ally's moves. This means that people attend to the variation in the ally's behavior across situations and are less certain about its disposition. Mercer reasoned that this would make it harder to reassure an ally that you were dependable. Consequently, the real challenge, given attribution bias, is preserving reputation in the eyes of allies, not in the eyes of enemies—just the opposite of what leaders typically think.

Hopf (1994) explored the impact Third World conflicts had on Soviet views of American resolve. If the attribution argument outlined above is correct, then US moves in Vietnam, Nicaragua, Angola, and the host of other places in the Cold War's periphery should have less impact on Soviet views of US resolve than American leaders feared. Instead of needing to show resolve in each case, the attribution theory outlined above would expect Soviet enemy images of the United States to sustain the perception of aggressive US intent and toughness. Moreover, Soviet conclusions about the credibility of Washington's general deterrence would not be much affected by these peripheral conflicts. Rather than drawing a generalization from them, the persisting image operating as a generalization in its own right would drive the interpretation of the specific case. Hopf found, parallel to Mercer, that reputation, in this case tied to deterrence, was easier to sustain than US leaders believed.

In later work, Hopf (2002), working at the sociological level, argued that the way other countries are understood reflected the way social relationships are understood domestically. In other words, people learn from their interpersonal experience what certain archetypes look like and how they relate to one another. These can come from daily life, popular discourse, the arts, perhaps fairly tales, and today the movies. The notion is that these roles and relationships are then the categories and scripts that people have available when trying to make sense of foreign countries. Larson (1985) made a parallel argument, albeit at the individual and psychological rather than sociological level, when explaining where the prevailing US perceptions of the Soviet Union came from at the outset of the Cold War. Building on Bem's (1972) self-perception theory, she explained how President Truman came to understand Stalin and Soviet politics through the experiences he had had competing in domestic American politics.

A final cognitive explanation for where perceptions of threat and enemy images come from concentrates on the information people derive from their perception of the ideology prevailing in a foreign country. For example, people in democracies might focus on that feature and categorize other democratic countries as allies, or at least in the likely-to-be-reasonable category. They might put nondemocracies in the enemy, or need-to-be-wary-of, category. It is common in explanations of why democracies do not go to war against one another to see these types of arguments (Russett, 1993). Haas (2005) studied the degree to which perceptions of threat emanate from perceptions of the prevailing ideology in another country and found this to be more important than estimates of power. In his study, however, the scope was limited to great powers, so the range on the power dimension was limited.

Of course what is hard to explain with a focus on matching ideologies are dramatic changes in alliance patterns when ideologies do not change. For example, the United States and China went from adversaries to partners in the matter of a decade without a change in ideology in either country. China's embrace of Pinochet's Chile in this time frame was perhaps even more revealing, although Moscow's alliance with Iraq while Saddam Hussein was publicly executing the leadership of the Iraqi community party raised similar questions. So did the US policy embracing Islamic militants in Afghanistan's mujahideen and then opposing them in the Taliban. Likewise, the threat Americans saw from Iran but not from Saudi Arabia suggested more was going on than simply reading domestic ideologies. Actually, the sometimes-dramatic swings in how countries are perceived and then described are not easy to explain with cognitive theories that typically feature continuity. Motivated theories, on the other hand, see these cognitive processes as affected by interest and expect change in them as interests fluctuate.

4.2. Underlying Motives

In 1690 John Locke concluded, "all men are liable to error; and most men are, in many points, by passion or interests, under temptation to it." Clearly, motivated reasoning is not a new idea. By this point, the social psychological evidence substantiating that identities and interests affect how people see the world is strong (S. T. Fiske, 2004; Jost, Glaser, Kruglanski, & Sulloway, 2003; Kunda, 1990; Morton, Haslam, Postmes, & Ryan, 2006; Taber & Lodge, 2006; Chong, chapter 4, this volume; Stein, chapter 12, this volume). If the cognitive approaches were more plentiful at the height of the cognitive revolution, this is much less true now. Of course, there were theories positing motivated reasoning in the international realm throughout. One of the more popular of these theories emphasized economic factors and professional role considerations, concluding that where you stand depends on where you sit (Allison, 1971). Fred Greenstein and Richard Immerman (1992) show in the context of John F. Kennedy's discussions with Dwight D. Eisenhower about Indochina how participants in a single meeting can hear and later recall very different things depending on the interests and expectations they bring into the meeting.

Lebow (1981) argued it was not simply economic self-interest that motivated but personal power too. He explained that when leaders worry about their domestic weakness, they might be motivated to construct of picture of the external world that overestimates their relative power and downplays the likely retaliatory moves of other countries. The "windows of opportunity" that appear open when this occurs, according to Lebow, can lead to wars the initiator is likely to lose. Snyder (1991) developed another explanation for why countries bite off more than they can chew that emphasized the need to maintain a winning domestic coalition. He argued that to sustain large coalitions comprised of diverse interests, it was necessary to logroll and give everybody part of what they wanted. The desire to serve everyone's interests led, he argued, to overextension, especially in authoritarian systems where the public space for counterarguments was constrained. This overextension was also hidden by a motivated desire to believe in the myths of empire. These myths often began as arguments made by elites to mobilize mass support by making imperial control appear possible and not excessively costly. For example, some of these myths described the adversary as a paper tiger that was likely to retreat in the face of strength; others described the colonies as receptive to the colonizer's influence. Over time, these images often created a blowback in which the elites not only were constrained by the public they had mobilized, but also came to believe in the myths they had created.

Solingen (1998) expanded on this basic idea and proposed a theory that featured two types of coalitions, one that derived its wealth and authority from the commercial market that was global, and the other that derived its wealth and authority by claiming it defended the nation and its culture from global influences. In this theory, the people in the first coalition are motivated to see others as less threatening and to see interdependent cooperation as both fruitful and safe, while those in the second coalition are motivated to see other countries as threatening and national security as more vulnerable. In this theory, cognitive worldviews are not formed exclusively from the internal process of logrolling and interests cumulating, but also from the interaction with regional neighbors. In other words, there is process that is both motivated and reactive to external feedback. It is easier to sustain either of the ideal-typical motivated worldviews and strategies when neighbors doing the same thing reinforce them.

In his classic formulation of realism, Morgenthau (1973, pp. 327–329) did not stress economic interest as much as he did nationalistic universalism. His notion was that identity with the nation in an era of mass politics had changed international relations in a fundamental way. It led people to confuse their national interests and particular values with normative codes that had universal validity. He assumed they wanted to pursue their material self-interest but were constrained by normative prohibitions that limited this pursuit. To free themselves from these normative limitations, Morgenthau argued, people were motivated to believe in self-serving pictures of both other countries and specific situations (p. 252). These would at first be the propaganda used to mobilize domestic support, but over time become the constructions leaders came to use in their own thinking. Morgenthau reasoned that the closer you came to power and the more you bore the responsibility for decisions, the more you would be motivated to believe in the self-serving images (pp. 88–91). After all, they would make it easier both to decide and to act by erasing, at least from conscious consideration, difficult moral trade-offs.

Cottam's (1977) theory provided a psychological underpinning consistent with Morgenthau's contention that moved the reasoning in a more substantively specific direction. Cottam built on Fritz Heider's (1958) balance theory. Heider argued that people were motivated to balance the sentiments they felt about another person with their cognitive picture of that person. According to Heider, people are inclined to construct a cognitive picture of someone they like emotionally that features attributes they also like and think are positive. They are uncomfortable, he reasoned, with including attributes in the picture that are vile and negative. For those they disliked or hated, the inclination is just the opposite. In that case, people prefer cognitive constructions that feature negative attributes and minimize positive ones. Cottam posited that in international relations, sentiment is determined by whether the other country is willing to cooperate with one's country on one's country's terms. It gets stronger as the interests at stake increase and the cooperation becomes more important. It also increases with the importance people put on their attachment to the nation (M. L. Cottam & R. W. Cottam, 2001, pp. 87–122).

If threat and opportunity are seen as analogous to sentiments, then the more intense those feelings become the more pressure there is to construct balanced cognitive pictures of those evoking these feelings. In other words, as the feeling that another country has goals that threaten one's own increases, so does the inclination to construct a cognitive picture of that other country that features negative items (Reeder, Pryor, Wohl, & Griswell, 2005). Demonizing it in this way makes it easier to act on the feeling of threat. It does that by relaxing normative prohibitions a person would otherwise feel should constrain his or her behavior. It creates a context in which lying, torture, and even killing can become seen as warranted. By adopting caricatures of the other people that portray them in animalistic or mechanistic terms, the balance process can strip away their humanity, leaving a cognitive stereotype that makes engaging in otherwise unacceptable behavior toward them easier by allowing people to engage in it while still retaining a positive image of themselves (Castano & Giner-Sorolla, 2006; Goff, Eberhardt, Williams, & Jackson, 2008; Leyens et al., 2000; Maoz & McCauley, 2008).

The enemy image can be understood as a product of these balance processes. Feeling great threat from another country that is powerful could motivate people to construct a picture of that country that justifies destroying it or at least its government. The full force of these feelings of fear may be unconscious, but they are thought to produce a conscious description of the other country that highlights its evil intentions, unlimited ambitions, and ruthless brutality. Stopping it becomes seen as not just morally permitted but morally required. Of course, for people to act, they need to believe action is not only appropriate but also likely to be effective. An enemy picture that features a dangerous foe could intimidate and paralyze. The balanced stereotype includes the description of the other as a paper tiger. This image can neutralize that fear. Paper tigers in Chinese parades, after all, are hollow. The notion is that this internal vulnerability will lead the enemy to retreat when it runs into foreign opposition. The stereotype also pictures the other country as monolithic and united, making it easier to imagine the whole population as blameworthy. This feature becomes more important psychologically when contemplating total war in an era of strategic bombing. It allows people to question whether there really are any "innocent" civilians.

Although perceptions of threat and the enemy image have received a lot of attention, it is necessary also to understand the effects of perceived opportunity. Without development along those lines too, we are left with conceptual tools that cannot distinguish between threat and opportunity. Both Morgenthau and Cottam recognized that states most often describe their own imperialism as stimulated by defensive concerns and by their desire to counter someone else's imperialism. Neither, however, thought this was the real story. They assumed that direct intervention to take control in a foreign country often derives from leaders' perception of opportunity to use the target country instrumentally in advancing their own country's interests. Of course, in an era in which sovereignty and self-determination are norms, the picture that balances the desire to seize the opportunity while still allowing intervention and taking control needs to relax this moral constraint. It needs to do this while, at the same time, protecting the self-image of the intervener as morally upstanding. The enemy image does not accomplish this, but the colony image does.

In the colony stereotype, the other country is described as facing a choice between moderate responsible leaders and radical xenophobic ones, with the former described as motivated by genuine concern for national development and the later described as motivated by self-serving desire for power and often extremist religious or ideological dogmas. Because the good, moderate, responsible leaders are either at risk of being overthrown or unable to unseat the bad, radical ones, intervention is necessary. Because the good, moderate, responsible leaders are pictured as not capable of developing the country without tutelage, and the rest of the population is described as too poor and backward to care much about nationalism and self-determination, the outside exercise of control is pictured as not only morally warranted but a noble mission. The stereotype transforms the desire to take advantage of the opportunity into a conscious picture that describes doing so as generous and self-sacrificial. It can lead the person operating with this stereotype to anticipate gratitude rather than resentment on the part of the colony population.

Fitzsimons and Shah (2008) find that people are inclined to evaluate more positively those who are instrumentally valuable to them. They find people are also inclined to draw closer to these people. At the same time, Gruenfeld, Inesi, Magee, and Galinsky (2008) find that when there is a large asymmetry in power, the more powerful are likely to engage in objectification. That means they are inclined toward a process of subjugation whereby people, like objects, are treated as a means to an end. The approach to them is driven by the target's usefulness, defined in terms of the perceiver's goals. This means giving priority to what is good for the perceiver even when it means ignoring or violating what is best for the target. Rather than resisting the desire to exploit others, the sentiment toward them is determined by their willingness to cooperate. Those who will cooperate are seen positively and those who will not are demonized. Gruenfeld's group explores this process in the realm of unequal power relationships and gender. In the political realm, it fits with the asymmetric relationship typically producing colony images. In that stereotype, those willing to cooperate are seen as caring about the development of their country, while those who will not cooperate are demonized and described as self-interested and so extreme as to be crazy. The more stereotypical the image becomes, the sharper this dichotomization is drawn.

This theory of motivated images predicts that imagery can change quite dramatically and quickly as a function of the other's willingness to cooperate. This is different than the prediction of image persistence that is common in the cognitive theories already discussed. When conscious imagery is motivated by the underlying assessment of the goal interdependence, those dehumanized in the enemy construction or the radical extremists in the colony construction can become human and moderate almost overnight. Intense enemy images can be forgotten quite quickly, as seen in the popular American views of Russia and Japan. In the colony stereotype, leaders featured as good guys or bad guys can also be flipped around quickly depending on their readiness to cooperate. In the case of the US occupation of Iraq, for example, the Sunni resistance was initially seen as radical extremists tied to al-Qaeda but in remarkably short order was reimagined as the Sons of Iraq and pictured as the moderate-responsible leaders of the Sunni Awakening. What changed, of course, was their willingness to cooperate with the occupation forces. Equally dramatic reconstructions are evident in numerous other cases; for example, the new pictures of Maoist China popular in the Washington that followed Beijing's readiness to cooperate against the Soviet Union in the 1970s, the shift in American perceptions of Ethiopia and Somalia in the 1980s, and the transformation of American pictures of the good Afghan mujahideen into the bad Afghan Taliban in the 1990s.

When conscious imagery is serving a functional purpose, it can not only change quickly as the functional purpose does, but can also include contradictions across cases. For instance, when describing a noncooperating others, the observer may use a feature to demonize them, perhaps claiming they are too religious or to ready to use violence, and when describing cooperating others use these same features in a fashion that puts a positive spin on them, for example, saying the other believes in God and is ready to defend moral convictions. Likewise, conscious constructions can object to one country as too radical because it allows religion and backward tradition to dominate politics and describe another as simply traditional and conservative. In this theory, the difference really driving the conscious picture is not so much along the dimensions being identified (e.g., religiosity) as connected to the other's willingness to cooperate. Prevailing American images of Iran and Saudi Arabia illustrate that pattern.

The balance theory that underpins this motivated theory of imagery distinguishes between the unconscious gestalts taken as a combination of judgments that operate as sentiments and the conscious images that are treated as mental representations. It assumes the unconscious judgments about threats and opportunities in combination with estimates of relative power and cultural status are doing the strategic work. Many times, they may reflect quite rational estimates of opportunity and threat and reasonable estimates of relative power, as suggested by the examples above. On the other hand, the underlying sentiments driving these core strategic judgments may not always be well founded. The key idea in this theory of motivated reasoning is that whatever the underlying sentiments are, they are producing a resultant conscious imagery that makes it easier to act on the strategic desires. These images may seem like little more than propaganda and be assumed to reflect only elite efforts to manipulate public opinion, but in this theory, they are more than that. They become psychological defenses that elites come to believe in as they act on their strategic desires.

If this is true, then the images evident in verbal descriptions reveal the underlying sentiments driving the process. In other words, the enemy imagery reveals underlying perceived threat and the colony image reveals underlying perceived opportunity. Instead of taking verbal rhetoric at face value, as in more cognitive approaches, in this approach the theory of imagery is used to interpret what the rhetoric means. Rather than looking for direct statements about threat and opportunity, in this approach, the focus is on the resemblance between the imagery used and the balanced stereotypes. There is a presumption that people disguise their sentiments, even from themselves, so they can act on them while bolstering their positive self-image.

There are other theories of motivated reasoning that, rather than focusing on strategic drivers that can often change, concentrate on aspects of a person's personality that are mostly constant. Lasswell (1930; 1948), for example, emphasized the psychodynamic need for power and the pathologies it produced. White (1965; 1968) concluded that stereotypes like the diabolical enemy and what he called "black-and-white" thinking followed from these needs for both power and prestige. Etheredge (1978) built further on Lasswell's work and described syndromes he attributed to emotion-based projective intuition. In his study of career US Foreign Service officers, Etheredge argued their views reflected a dramatized version of events derived from their need to see themselves as part of an epic, heroic story.

Robins and Post (1997) built a theory of paranoia that derives from a psychiatric perspective. They posit a need for enemies in the subconscious of some people, especially those who are narcissistic. On the basis of this assumption, they propose a multidimensional explanation that connects underlying psychological maladies to political mindsets. They analyze hate in this regard, concentrating on leaders including Pol Pot, Idi Amin, Joseph Stalin, and Adolf Hitler. They extend their analysis to religious extremists and terrorists as well. Like Lasswell, they view motives as residing in personality and more invariant over time than the sentiments assumed to be shaping balance theory. Heider did not describe the inclination to balance sentiments and conscious cognitive pictures as pathology but rather as a feature of the healthy person trying to maintain a positive self-image. The balance process makes it easier to act as you want and still feel good about yourself. Heider expected people to resist and reject, possibly angrily, efforts to undermine their balance process and suggested that stripping away their comfort providing conscious imagery could lead to serious mental distress.

Recently, Sullivan, Landau, and Rothschild (2010, p. 434) have argued that "people are motivated to perceive themselves as controlling their environment yet realize that their lives can be negatively affected by myriad diffuse and capricious hazards." Their contention is that people narrow their focus from the multiplicity of things that could hurt them to a focal person or group that can be effectively controlled, managed, or understood. In this way, they reduce the threat they feel to their own sense of control. It comes at the cost, however, of attributing exaggerated influence to enemies. In this way, enemyship serves a psychological function, compensating for perceptions of reduced control over the environment.

The balance process would lead to stereotypes only in the cases of intensely felt threats and opportunities. Some people may be inclined to feel these sentiments more often and more passionately than others. One factor that may explain individual differences in this regard is the importance they attach to the group that is the object of the threat or opportunity. Drawing on social identity theory (Brown, 2000), Cottam and Cottam (2001) expected people who attach to the nation more deeply to be more likely to feel threats and opportunities more intensely. If that is the case, they are be more likely to adopt images of others countries that resemble more closely the well-known stereotypes. Federico, Gloec, and Dial (2005), operating in a more cognitive vein, find that the need for closure that could produce results similar to those expected in the theory of images is moderated by identification with the national in-group.

Differences in the degree of attachment to the nation should not only affect enemy and colony images but ally images too. Ally images are presumed to facilitate cooperating with another country by easing concerns about the other country's possibly unsavory attributes. It erases them and portrays the other country in positive terms that emphasize its virtue. If that is correct, then nationalists should not simply dislike foreign countries more than less nationalistically inclined people, which might be the prediction of traditional theories of ethnocentrism. Instead, they should both hate enemies more and like allies more than those people who attach to the nation less strongly. This is what Herrmann, Isernia, and Segatti (2009) find in both the United States and Italy.

5. FUTURE DIRECTIONS

The role group attachments play in triggering emotions raises a broader question about emotions in intergroup relations. This has become the subject of substantial interest and is an obvious avenue for future research (Mackie, Devos, & Smith, 2000; Smith, Seger, & Mackie, 2007). Perceiving threat and opportunity may be analogous to what Heider called like and dislike, but explorations into emotions have found that this dichotomy may be too simple. Emotions can be thought of with more discriminating concepts like fear, anger, hope, and joy. When sentiment is divided this way, the emotions do not appear to have similar impact on cognition. For example, anger may reduce the search for information and reaffirm a commitment to preexisting images, while fear might motivate a search for more information and careful reassessment of extant beliefs. Emotions are covered in detail by Brader and Marcus (chapter 6, this volume), so I will not delve into this further here but simply point to emotions' role in shaping cognitive models and connecting underlying motivational sentiments to imagery as a place where future research looks promising.

A related question still needing more attention is how to change images. Of course, this is at the heart of many strategies for conflict resolution (Fisher, Kelman, & Nan, chapter 16, this volume), so again the comments here will be brief. There has been a great deal of work on changing enemy images through strategies of reassurance.

Broffenbrenner (1961) called attention to this decades ago as he tried to de-escalate spiral conflicts by cracking mirror images. Osgood (1962) proposed gradual reciprocal reduction in tension as one way to do this. Larson (1997) found that during the Cold War the great powers missed several promising opportunities for de-escalation because they were so distrustful. Her conclusion, consistent with Osgood, is that repeated moves might be needed to overcome the inherent bad faith in the enemy image. Much less attention has been paid to changing colony and imperial images, where the underlying sentiments are more asymmetrical both in terms of felt threats and opportunities and in terms of estimates of power.

Of course, the popularity of stereotypical images in intense threat or opportunity relationships gives rise to institutions and bureaucratic agencies that develop a vested interest in the perpetuation of the image. During the Cold War, the offices, groups, and companies that developed an interest in defense spending were important sources of information and brakes on rapid change in prevailing imagery. Today, the industry that has grown up around combating terrorism and containing the proliferation of weapons of mass destruction is a similar brake on change in prevailing American views of countries and movements in the Middle East. As we move to the political and sociological levels, it becomes clear that changing imagery is more than a psychological endeavor. It requires a change in the interests that benefit from and sustain the prevailing imagery. Even at the individual level, if imagery is motivated by underlying interests, changing images will require more than simply providing more information to overcome misperception. It will require addressing the interests and passions driving the construction.

Zartman (2000) argues that not all conflicts are rooted simply in misperception and a unwarranted fear. Some are rooted in genuine conflicts of interest and the conviction on both sides that they can win outright. Zartman doubts that until both sides have tried to achieve victory and failed or for other reasons have concluded that unilateral victory is impossible, negotiations are unlikely to produce resolution. For example, in the conflict between Arabs and Israel, he believes, feelings of threat and opportunity coupled with estimates of superior power, now or in the future, have repeatedly derailed talks. Until these images change, in his view, the conflict is not ripe for resolution. This is consistent with what the balance theory of imagery predicts as well. In that theory, negotiations and public diplomacy might try to chip away at the prevailing imagery but this is not likely to produce change. Rather, the expectation is that the protagonists will see these efforts at public diplomacy as part of the contest for popular support and little more than debating points. Unless moves are made that affect the underlying drivers, the prospect that images will change is seen as minimal.

The most common approach to conflict management is to separate the combatants and keep them from hurting one another by institutionalizing that separation. This can involve demilitarized zones and various confidence-building measures, and the imposition of peacekeeping forces. This strategy and its numerous tactical options have been successful in maintaining peace when implemented carefully. It may reduce perceptions of threat over time, but the reassurance need not have that effect. The reason for this is that the parties to the conflict may attribute the other's compliant and peaceful behavior to the imposition of the institutional constraints. They might not see any change in the character of the other. This is especially likely when the institutions enforcing the separation are strong. In other words, it is possible for confidence in an institution to grow independent of increasing confidence in the adversary. It is possible that over time the imagery of each other may grow even more stereotypical as the two parties are kept apart and come to see each other as enduring rivals with deeply conflictive goals. This becomes more likely as new generations grow up never having known the other country in any other way.

One way for dealing with the problem inherent in separation may be to promote identity with a common superordinate in-group (Dovidio & Gaertner, 2008). How this will affect imagery is another question that deserves more attention in the future. Like the previous question related to social and political groups, however, this one takes the focus to an aggregate level and beyond the individual. It embeds the construction of images in the broader social processes of communication, socialization, and political contest over which ideas and constructions will prevail. Bridging the individual and group levels will be critical in any strategy designed to change images and may be the domain where research in the future will be most fruitful.

The turn toward phenomenological approaches long ago was motivated partly by an interest in behavior, not just outcomes. The sense was that explaining foreign policy choices meant understanding the mindset and perceptions of the people making the decisions. Realists did not argue against this so much as contend instead that regardless of what people thought they might be capable of the outcome of their actions would be determined by material factors. Realists figured that people who misperceived reality would not survive for long in the international system. It made sense, therefore, realists argued, to concentrate theoretically on objective material factors. They believed that just as in the physical world, where it makes sense to emphasize the constraining effects of gravity regardless of whether people perceive it or understand it, it made sense in the political world to emphasize objective effects of power. Of course, advocates of phenomenological approaches agreed that understanding power was important, but they did not see the analogy the realists counted on as particularly apt. In the physical world, they argued, gravity is not the product of anyone's decision. In the political world, constraints often are.

Countries rarely employ all the capabilities that they have available. How far they go to protect their interests and what they decide their interests are are the product of a political process. The decisions in that process are often shaped in fundamental ways by both the perceptions people have of the situation they face and the understandings people have regarding what sort of actions produce what sorts of outcomes. In this way, their mindsets and mental images become important causal factors affecting not only their actions but, because those actions often determine the constraints others face, outcomes too. When beliefs and perceptions are seen as important explanatory variables, the importance of how best to conceptualize and measure them increases. This chapter has traced how that increased interest has played out in the study of international relations.

As the study of beliefs progressed, attention turned to identifying the most parsimonious ways to unpack the concept. The dimensionality and structure of impressions and perception generated a steady stream of research. So did the effort to identify stereotypical patterns in the substantive content of people's mental pictures of other people and relationships. The connection between these mental images and behavioral choices also commanded attention, especially the connection between stereotypical dehumanizing pictures and violence. Image theory sought to systematize these relationships and expand the focus beyond the sort of dehumanization common in enemy images. It included images common in colony and imperial relationships as well. In those cases, it was not always just violence that characterized the behavior but also domination and control.

Image theory also assumed that the images people operated with at the conscious level were often pictures that balanced the inclinations to act that came from both emotional sentiments and normative prescriptions. These balanced images often created a picture that relaxed the normative constraints and made acting on the sentiment easier. In this way, the images were motivated by the underlying inclinations. The interest in motivated reasoning has grown substantially over the past three decades. Likewise, there is serious interest now in the relationship between emotions and cognitive images and judgments. Those are questions that should be more amenable to study given the now quite large literature on the importance, structure, and origins of perceptions summarized in this chapter.

REFERENCES

Abelson, R. (1976). Script processing in attitude formation and decision making. In J. Carroll & J. Payne (eds.), *Cognition and social behavior* (pp. 33–45). Hillsdale, NJ: Lawrence Erlbaum Associates.

Abelson, R., Dasgupta, N., Park, J., & Banaji, M. (1998). Perceptions of collective other. *Personality and Social Psychology Review*, 2, 243–250.

Achen, C. H., & Snidal, D. (1989). Rational deterrence theory and comparative case studies. *World Politics*, 41(2), 143–169.

Alexander, M. M., Brewer, M. R., & Herrmann, R. (1999). Images and affect: A functional analysis of out-group stereotypes. *Journal of Personality and Social Psychology*, 77 (July), 78–93.

Allison, G. T. (1971). *Essence of decision: Explaining the Cuban Missile Crisis*. Boston: Little, Brown.

Asch, S. (1952). *Social psychology*. Englewood Cliffs, NJ: Prentice-Hall.

Axelrod, R. (1976). *The structure of decision: The cognitive maps of political elites*. Princeton, NJ: Princeton University Press.

Baldwin, D. A. (2002). Power and international relations. In W. Carlsnaes, T. Risse, & B. A. Simmons (eds.), *Handbook of international relations* (pp. 177–191). London: Sage.

Baum, M. A., & Groeling, T. (2010). Reality asserts itself: Public opinion on Iraq and the elasticity of reality. *International Organization*, 64(3), 733–764.

Bem, D. J. (1972). Self-perception theory. In L. Berkowitz (ed.), *Advances in experimental social psychology* (vol. 6, pp. 1–61). New York: Academic Press.

Bodenhausen, G. V. (1993). Emotions, arousal, and stereotypic judgments: A heuristic model of affect and stereotyping. In D. M. Mackie & D. L. Hamilton (eds.), *Affect, cognition, and stereotyping: Interactive processes in group perception* (pp. 13–37). San Diego, CA: Academic Press.

Boulding, K. (1956). *The image.* Ann Arbor: University of Michigan Press.

Boulding, K. (1959). National images and international systems. *Journal of Conflict Resolution, 3,* 120–131.

Brecher, M. (1972). *The foreign policy system of Israel: Setting, image, process.* New Haven, CT: Yale University Press.

Brecher, M. (1973). Images, process and feedback in foreign policy: Israel's decision on German reparations. *American Political Science Review, 67,* 73–102.

Broffenbrenner, U. (1961). The mirror image in Soviet-American relations: A social psychologist's report. *Journal of Social Issues, 17,* 45–56.

Brown, R. (2000). Social identity theory: Past achievements, current problems and future challenges. *European Journal of Social Psychology, 30*(6), 745–778.

Campbell, D. T. (1967). Stereotypes and the perception of out-group differences. *American Psychologist, 22,* 812–829.

Castano, E., & Giner-Sorolla, R. (2006). Not quite human: Infrahumanization in response to collective responsibility for intergroup killing. *Journal of Personality and Social Psychology, 90*(5), 804–818.

Center, P. R. (2004). *A year after Iraq: Mistrust of Americans in Europe ever higher, Muslim anger persists.* The Pew Research Center for the People and the Press.

Cottam, M. L. (1986). *Foreign policy decision making: The influence of cognition.* Boulder, CO: Westview.

Cottam, M. L. (1994). *Images and intervention: U.S. policies in Latin America.* Pittsburgh: University of Pittsburgh Press.

Cottam, M. L., & Cottam, R. W. (2001). *Nationalism and politics: The political behavior of nation states.* Boulder, CO: Lynne Rienner.

Cottam, R. W. (1977). *Foreign policy motivation: A general theory and a case study.* Pittsburgh: University of Pittsburgh Press.

Cronbach, L. J. (1957). The two disciplines of scientific psychology. *American Psychologist, 12* (November), 671–684.

Cronbach, L. J. (1975). Beyond the two disciplines of scientific psychology. *American Psychologist, 30* (February), 116–127.

Deutsch, K., & Merritt, R. (1965). Effects of events on national and international images. In H. C. Kelman (ed.), *International behavior: A social-psychological analysis* (pp. 130–187). New York: Holt, Rinehart and Winston.

Deutsch, M. (1968). Field theory in social psychology. In G. Lindzey & E. Aronson (eds.), *The handbook of social psychology* (2nd ed., pp. 412–487). Reading, MA: Addison-Wesley.

Dovidio, J. F., Gaertner, S. L. & Saguy, T. (2008). Commonality and the complexity of "we": Social attitudes and social change. *Personality and Social Psychology Review, 13*(3), 3–20.

Etheredge, L. (1978). *A world of men: The private sources of American foreign policy.* Cambridge, MA: MIT Press.

Federico, C. M., Gloec, A., & Dial, J. L. (2005). The relationship between the need for closure and support for military action against Iraq: Moderating effects of national attachment. *Personality and Social Psychology Bulletin 1*(5), 621–632.

Finlay, D., Holsti, O., & Fagen, R. (1967). *Enemies in politics*. Chicago: Rand McNally.

Fiske, A. P. (1991). *Structures of social life: The four elementary forms of human relations*. New York: Free Press.

Fiske, S. T. (2004). Intent and ordinary bias: Unintended thought and social motivation create casual prejudice. *Social Justice Research, 17*(2), 117–127.

Fiske, S. T., Cuddy, A. J. C., & Glick, P. (2006). Universal dimensions of social cognition: Warmth and competence. *Trends in Cognitive Science, 11*(2), 77–83.

Fiske, S. T., Cuddy, A. J. C., Glick, P., & Xu, J. (2002). A-model of (often mixed) stereotype content: Competence and warmth respectively follow from perceived status and competition. *Journal of Personality and Social Psychology, 82*(6), 878–902.

Fiske, S. T., & Taylor, S. E. (1991). *Social cognition*. New York: Random House.

Fitzsimons, G. M., & Shah, J. Y. (2008). How goal instrumentality shapes relationship evaluations. *Journal of Personality and Social Psychology, 95*(2), 319–337.

George, A. L. (1969). The "operational code": A neglected approach to the study of political leaders and decision-making. *International Studies Quarterly, 13*(2), 190–222.

George, A. L. (1993). *Bridging the gap: Theory and practice in foreign policy*. Washington DC: United States Institute of Peace Press.

George, A. L., & Smoke, R. (1974). *Deterrence in American foreign policy: Theory and practice*. New York: Columbia University Press.

George, A. L., & Simons, W. E. (Eds.). (1994). *The limits of coercive diplomacy* (2nd ed.). Boulder, CO: Westview.

Goff, P. A., Eberhardt, J. L., Williams, M. J., & Jackson, M. C. (2008). Not yet human: Implicit knowledge, historical dehumanization, and contemporary consequences. *Journal of Personality and Social Psychology, 94*(2), 292–306.

Green, P. (1968). *Deadly logic: The theory of nuclear deterrence*. New York: Shocken Books.

Greenstein, F. & Immerman, R. (1992). What did Eisenhower tell Kennedy about Indochina? The politics of misperception. *Journal of American History, 79*(2), 568–597.

Gruenfeld, D. H., Inesi, M. E., Magee, J. C., & Galinsky, A. D. (2008). Power and the objectification of social targets. *Journal of Personality and Social Psychology, 95*(1), 111–127.

Haas, M. L. (2005). *The ideological origins of great power politics, 1789–1989*. Ithaca, NY: Cornell University Press.

Haslam, N. (2006). Dehumanization: An integrative review. *Personality and Social Psychology Review, 10*(3), 252–264.

Heider, F. (1958). *The psychology of interpersonal relations*. New York: John Wiley.

Herrmann, R K.. (1985). *Perceptions and behavior in Soviet foreign policy*. Pittsburgh: University of Pittsburgh Press.

Herrmann, R. K. (1986). The power of perceptions in foreign-policy decision making: Do views of the Soviet Union determine the policy choices of American leaders? *American Journal of Political Science, 30*(4), 841–875.

Herrmann, R K. (1988). The empirical challenge of the cognitive revolution: A strategy for drawing inferences about perceptions. *International Studies Quarterly, 32*(2), 175–120

Herrmann, R. K., & Fischerkeller, M. P. (1995). Beyond the enemy image and spiral model: Cognitive-strategic research after the Cold War. *International Organization, 49*(3), 415–450.

Herrmann, R. K., Isernia, P., & Segatti, P. (2009). Attachment to the nation and international relations: Dimensions of identity and their relationship to war and peace. *Political Psychology, 30*(5), 721–754.

Herrmann, R. K., Voss, J., Schooler, T., & Ciarrochi, J. (1997). Images in international relations: An experimental test of cognitive schemata Policy. Pittsburgh: University of Pittsburgh Press.

Holsti, K. J. (1970). National role conceptions in the study of foreign policy. *International Studies Quarterly, 14*, 233–309.

Holsti, O. R. (1967). Cognitive dynamics and images of the enemy. In O. H. D. Finlay, & R, Fagen (eds.), *Enemies in politics* (pp. 25–96). Chicago: Rand McNally.

Holsti, O. R., & Rosenau, J. N. (1984). *American leadership in world affairs: Vietnam and the breakdown of consensus*. Boston: Allen Unwin.

Hopf, T. (1994). *Peripheral visions: Deterrence theory and American foreign policy in the Third World, 1965–1990*. Ann Arbor: University of Michigan Press.

Hopf, T. (2002). *Social construction of international politics: Identities and foreign policies, Moscow, 1955 and 1999*. Ithaca, NY: Cornell University Press.

Horowitz, D. L. (1985). *Ethnic groups in conflict*. Berkeley: University of California Press.

Hurwitz, J., & Peffley, M. (1990). Public images of the Soviet Union: The impact on foreign policy attitudes. *Journal of Politics, 52*(1), 3–8.

Jahoda, G. (1999). *Images of savages: Ancient roots of modern prejudice in Western culture*. London: Routledge.

Jervis, R. (1970). *The logic of images in international relations*. Princeton, NJ: Princeton University Press.

Jervis, R. (1976). *Perception and misperception in international politics*. Princeton, NJ: Princeton University Press.

Jervis, R. (1986). Representativeness in foreign policy judgments. *Political Psychology, 7*(3), 483–505.

Jervis, R. (1989). *The meaning of the nuclear revolution: Statecraft and the prospect of Armageddon*. Ithaca, NY: Cornell University Press.

Jervis, R. (1989). Rational deterrence: Theory and evidence. *World Politics, 41*(2), 183–207.

Jervis, R. (2010). *Why intelligence fails: Lessons from the Iranian Revolution and the Iraq war*. Ithaca, NJ: Cornell University Press.

Jervis, R., Lebow, R. N., & Stein, J. G. (1985). *Psychology and deterrence*. Baltimore, MD: Johns Hopkins University Press.

Jervis, R., & Snyder, J. (Eds.). (1991). *Dominoes and bandwagons: Strategic beliefs and great power competition in the Eurasian Rimland*. New York: Oxford University Press.

Johnson, D. D. P., & Tierney, D. (2006). *Failing to win: Perceptions of victory and defeat in international politics*. Cambridge, MA: Harvard University Press.

Jones, E. E., & Nisbett, R. E. (1971). The actor and the observer: Divergent perceptions of the causes of behavior. In E. E. Jones, D. E. Kanouse, H. H. Kelley, R. E. Nisbett, S. Valins, & B. Weiner (eds.), *Attribution: Perceiving the causes of behavior* (pp. 79–94). Morristown, NJ: General Learning Press.

Jost, J., Glaser, J., Kruglanski, A., & Sulloway, F. J. (2003). Political conservatism as motivated social cognition. *Psychological Bulletin, 129*(3), 339–375.

Kahneman, D., Slovic, P., & Tversky, A. (Eds.). (1982). *Judgment under uncertainty: Heuristics and biases*. Cambridge: Cambridge University Press.

Kray, L. J., George, L. G., Liljenquist, K. A., Galinsky, A. D., Tetlock, P. E., & Roese, N. J. (2010). From what might have been to what must have been. *Journal of Personality and Social Psychology, 98*(1), 106–118. doi:10.1037/a0017905

Kunda, Z. (1990). The case for motivated reasoning. *Psychology Bulletin, 108*(3), 480–498.

Lake, D. A. (2010–2011). Two cheers for bargaining theory: Assessing rationalist explanations of the Iraq war. *International Security, 35*(3), 7–52.

Larson, D. W. (1985). *Origins of containment*. Princeton, NJ: Princeton University Press.

Larson, D. W. (1997). *Anatomy of mistrust: U.S.-Soviet relations during the Cold War*. Ithaca, NJ: Cornell University Press.

Lasswell, H. (1930). *Psychopathology and politics*. Chicago: University of Chicago Press.

Lasswell, H. (1948). *Power and personality*. New York: Norton.

Lebow, R. N. (1981). *Between peace and war: The nature of international crisis*. Baltimore, MD: Johns Hopkins University Press.

Lebow, R. N., & Stein, J. G. (1989). Rational deterrence theory: I think, therefore I deter. *World Politics, 41*(2), 208–224.

Leites, N. (1951). *The operational code of the Politburo*. New York: McGraw-Hill.

Leyens, J. P., Paladino, P. M., Rodriguez, R. T., Vaes, J., Demoulin, S., Rodriguez, A. P., & Gaunt, R. (2000). The emotional side of prejudice: The role of secondary emotions. *Personality and Social Psychology Review, 4*, 186–197.

Mackie, D. M., Devos, T., & Smith, E. R. (2000). Intergroup emotions: Explaining offensive action tendencies in an intergroup context. *Journal of Personality and Social Psychology, 79*(4), 602–616.

Maoz, I., & McCauley, C. (2008). Threat, dehumanization, and support for retaliatory aggressive policies in asymmetric conflict. *Journal of Conflict Resolution, 52*(1), 93–116.

Mercer, J. (1996). *Reputation and international politics*. Ithaca, NY: Cornell University Press.

Mintz, A. (2004). Foreign policy decision making in familiar and unfamiliar settings. *Journal of Conflict Resolution, 48*(1), 91–104.

Mintz, A. (Ed.). (2003). *Integrating cognitive and rational theories of foreign policy decision making*. New York: Palgrave Macmillan.

Mischel, W., & Shoda, Y. (1998). Reconciling processing dynamics and personality dispositions. *Annual Review of Psychology, 49*, 229–258.

Mischel, W., & Shoda, Y. (1999). Integrating dispositions and processing dynamics within a unified theory of personality: The cognitive-affective personality system. In L. A. Pevin & O. P. John (eds.), *Handbook of personality* (2nd ed., pp. 197–218). New York: Guilford Press.

Morgenthau, H. J. (1973). *Politics among nations: The struggle for power and peace* (5th ed.). New York: Alfred A. Knopf.

Morton, T. A., Haslam, S. A., Postmes, T., & Ryan, M. K. (2006). We value what values us: The appeal of identity-affirming science. *Political Psychology, 27*(6), 823–838.

Osgood, C. (1962). *An alternative to war or surrender*. Urbana: University of Illinois Press.

Peffley, M., & Hurwitz, J. (1992). International events and foreign policy beliefs: Public response to changing Soviet-U.S. relations. *American Journal of Political Science, 36*(2), 431–461.

Porch, D. (1986). *The conquest of Morocco*. New York: International Publishing Corporation.

Press, D. G. (2005). *Calculating credibility: How leaders assess military threats*. Ithaca, NY: Cornell University Press.

Reeder, G. D., Pryor, J. B., Wohl, M. J. A., & Griswell, M. L. (2005). On attributing negative motives to others who disagree with our opinions. *Personality and Social Psychology Bulletin, 31*(11), 1498–1510.

Riker, W. (1962). *The theory of political coalitions*. New Haven, CT: Yale University Press.

Robins, R. S., & Post, J. (1997). *Political paranoia: The psychopolitics of hatred*. New Haven, CT: Yale University Press.

Ross, L. (1977). The intuitive psychologist and his shortcomings: Distortions in the attribution process. In L. Berkowitz (ed.), *Advances in experimental social psychology* (vol. 10, pp. 173–220). New York: Academic Press.

Rummel, R. J. (1975). *Understanding conflict and war: The dynamic psychological field.* New York: John Wiley & Sons.

Russett, B. (1993). *Grasping the democratic peace: Principles for a post–Cold War world.* Princeton, NJ: Princeton University Press.

Said, E. W. (1979). *Orientalism.* New York: Vintage.

Schafer, M., & Walker, S. (Eds.). (2006). *Beliefs and leadership in world politics: Methods and applications of operational code analysis.* New York: Palgrave Macmillan.

Schelling, T. C. (1966). *Arms and influence.* New Haven, CT: Yale University Press.

Scott, W. (1965). Psychological and social correlates of international images. In H. Kelman (ed.), *International behavior: A social-psychological analysis* (pp. 70–103). New York: Holt, Rinehart, and Winston.

Sherman, S., Judd, C., & Park, B. (1989). Social cognition. *Annual Review of Psychology, 40,* 281–326.

Shimko, K. L. (1991). *Images and arms control: Perceptions of the Soviet Union in the Reagan administration.* Ann Arbor, MI: The University of Michigan Press.

Silverstein, B. (1989). Enemy images: The psychology of U.S. attitudes and cognitions regarding the Soviet Union. *American Psychologist, 44*(6), 903–913.

Simon, H. (1985). Human nature in politics: The dialogue of psychology with political science. *American Political Science Review, 79*(2), 292–304.

Skinner, B. F. (1960). *Behavior theory and conditioning.* New Haven, CT: Yale University Press.

Smith, E. R., Seger, C. R., & Mackie, D. M. (2007). Can emotions be truly group level? Evidence regarding four conceptual criteria. *Journal of Personality and Social Psychology, 93*(3), 431–446.

Snyder, J. (1991). *Myths of E: Domestic politics and international ambition.* Ithaca, NY: Cornell University Press.

Snyder, R., Bruck, H., & Sapin, B. (1962). *Foreign policy decision-making: An approach to the study of international politics.* New York: Free Press.

Solingen, E. (1998). *Regional orders at century's dawn: Global and domestic influences on grand strategy.* Princeton, NJ: Princeton University Press.

Sprout, H., & Sprout, M. (1965). *The ecological perspective on human affairs with special reference to international relations.* Princeton, NJ: Princeton University Press.

Steinbruner, J. D. (1974). *The cybernetic theory of decision: New dimensions of political analysis.* Princeton, NJ: Princeton University Press.

Sullivan, D., Landau, M. J., & Rothschild, Z. K. (2010). An existential function of enemyship. *Journal of Personality and Social Psychology, 98*(3), 434–449. doi:10.1037/a0017457

Taber, C. S., & Lodge, M. (2006). Motivated skepticism in the evaluation of political beliefs. *American Journal of Political Science, 50*(3), 755–769.

Tetlock, P. E. (1999). Theory-driven reasoning about plausible pasts and probable futures in world politics: Are we prisoners of our preconceptions? *American Journal of Political Science, 43*(2), 335–366.

Tetlock, P. E., & Lebow, R. N. (2001). Poking counterfactual holes in covering laws: Cognitive styles and historical reasoning. *American Political Science Review, 95*(4), 829–843.

Vertzberger, Y. Y. I. (1990). *The world in their minds: Information processing, cognition, and perception in foreign policy decisionmaking.* Stanford, CA: Stanford University Press.

Walker, S. G. (1990). The evolution of the operational code analysis. *Political Psychology, 11*(2), 403–418.

Walt, S. M. (1987). *The origins of alliances.* Ithaca, NY: Cornell University Press.

Waltz, K. (1979). *Theory of international politics*. Reading, MA: Addison-Wesley.

White, R. K. (1965). Images in the context of international conflict: Soviet perceptions of the U.S. and the U.S.S.R. In H. C. Kelman (ed.), *International behavior: A social-psychological analysis* (pp. 236–276). New York: Holt, Rinehart, & Winston.

White, R. K. (1968). *Nobody wanted war: Misperception in Vietnam and other wars*. Garden City, NY: Doubleday.

Zartman, I. W. (2000). Ripeness: The hurting stalemate and beyond. In P. C. Stern & D. Druckman (eds.), *International conflict resolution after the Cold War* (pp. 225–250). Washington, DC: National Academy Press.

CHAPTER 12

....

THREAT PERCEPTION IN INTERNATIONAL RELATIONS

....

JANICE GROSS STEIN

SCHOLARS in international relations have long given threat perception a central role in theories of war, deterrence and compellence, alliances, and conflict resolution. Thucydides wrote the foundational text on threat assessment and the need to balance against or ally with a threatening power. Yet at the core of theories of balance of power, of alliances, and of war was a largely unexamined concept of threat perception. Threat was conveniently equated to power, largely to military power, and scholars moved easily from "objective" measures of power to threat assessment, assuming equivalence between the two. Only in the last several decades have scholars begun to look seriously at intention as a source of threat that is independent of military capabilities and build models that focus explicitly on intention in their explanations of the causes of war (Walt, 1985). This strand of scholarship produced what is generally considered "rationalist" models of deterrence and of war where signaling and credibility are the core analytic puzzles (Schelling, 1960; 1966; Fearon, 1995).

At almost the same time, scholars in international relations schooled in political psychology, led by Robert Jervis, began to explore threat "perception" and "misperception," paying careful attention to the variance between what leaders perceive as threatening and what the evidence of intentions and military capabilities suggest (Jervis, 1976; Stein, 1982). In the first section of this chapter, I begin by looking at five nonpsychological explanations of threat perception that scholars in international relations have identified. I then examine the contribution of political psychologists as they brought fundamentally different theoretical perspectives to the analysis of threat perception.

Before turning to the examination of theories of threat perception, I briefly define the two key terms, threat and perception. Threats can be verbal and physical. Verbal threats are conditional statements designed to signal the capacity and intention to inflict harm if desired results are not forthcoming. Verbal threats usually take the form of if-then statements: if you do not do as I ask, I will inflict the following harm on you. Deterrent threats require the target to refrain from committing acts that the threatener does not like, and compellent threats require the target to engage in actions that they do not wish to do. Leaders do not always threaten verbally; they can also use nonverbal signals to communicate the seriousness of their intent to punish undesirable behavior. They may withdraw their ambassadors, put their forces on alert, or move forces to contested borders. Finally, in international politics, the accumulation of economic and military power may be perceived as threatening by others, even if that is not its principal purpose.

Threats do not unambiguously speak for themselves. Understanding the meaning of threats is mediated by the perception of the target. Perception is the process of apprehending by means of the senses and recognizing and interpreting what is processed. Psychologists think of perception as a single unified awareness derived from sensory processes while a stimulus is present. Perception is the basis for understanding, learning, and knowing and the motivation for action. Especially important in processes of individual perception are emotional states, information processing, and patterns of inference and attribution. At the collective level, processes of perception are more difficult to identify. Understandings are shared and communicated, as are emotions, to create a collective mood. In this sense, threats are socially constructed within and among private and public conversations of experts, political leaders, and publics (Meyer, 2009).

1. Nonpsychological Explanations of Threat Perception

Central to many rationalist accounts of threat perception is the argument that leaders perceive threat and go to war because they do not have complete information. Privately held information creates uncertainty, and in this context, states at times have an incentive to misrepresent information about their capabilities and their intentions (Fearon, 1995; Powell, 2006). This deliberate misrepresentation and the consequent difficulty in establishing the credibility of signals is an important part of the story of crisis escalation, deterrence failure, and war. If both parties accurately and completely represented their privately held information, rationalists expect, states could determine the outcome of a hypothetical confrontation and the "loser" would forgo engagement. This logic sees war as a result of inaccurate threat perception that flows from deliberate misrepresentation or signals that are not credible.

The emphasis of these rationalist accounts is largely on the dilemmas that the "sender" of the signals confronts in formulating credible commitments rather than on the perceptual dynamics of the perceiver. Implicit in these accounts, nevertheless, is the argument that if the sender's commitments are not credible to the receiver, the receiver may not perceive their meaning and consequently choose an inappropriate course of action. The silent, largely unexamined variable in rationalist accounts is the dynamics of threat perception by those who are the target of the signal. As Robert Jervis (2002) argues, the logic of signaling implies a logic of perception; signals that are sent acquire meaning when they are perceived.

When is this kind of misrepresentation and deceptive signaling most likely to occur? When, in other words, is the credibility of threats, a concern primarily of the sender rather than the perceiver, especially difficult to establish? Changes in the distribution of capabilities have long been identified as one condition that complicates credibility. The arguments of "offensive realists" are at first glance not directly relevant because they bypass signaling and the credibility of commitment and, reasoning directly from a shifting balance of power, suggest that rising powers will challenge as soon as they are able to do so (Mearsheimer, 2003; Elman, 2004,). Some strategic commentary today, for example, casts China as a rising power that will threaten the interests of the United States as the power balance shifts. Some draw a straightforward equivalence between rising power and the likelihood of aggressive behavior as the balance shifts and assess a rising trajectory of power as inherently threatening (Friedberg, 2000; 2005; Goldstein, 2005; 2007). Others expect military conflict even while China remains relatively weak (Christensen, 2001; 2006).

These arguments nevertheless indirectly open space for the analysis of signaling and credibility, attempts to prevent challenge and war. In a context where challenge is more likely, threat-based strategies of deterrence, compellence, and containment become important. Here rationalist arguments about signaling and the credibility of commitments become important. Credible commitments are important because they are markers of the future, a signpost that leaders can use to assess intentions and threat not only in the present but in the future (Mercer, 1996; Press, 2005).

Rationalists argue that leaders have strong incentives to bluff or deceive, to exaggerate their capabilities to conceal their weakness, especially when they fear attack. Evidence now suggests that Saddam Hussein, his eye on his historic enemy—Iran—deliberately did not reveal that he had ended his nuclear, chemical, and biological weapons programs. He could not credibly commit to the United States that he had ended his programs to develop weapons of mass destruction without undermining his deterrent capability with Iran. That inability to make a credible commitment pushed up the perception of threat among those in the Bush White House who were already inclined to see Saddam as a threat to US interests (Lake, 2011). Generically, the difficulty of making credible commitments complicates signaling for the sender, but it simultaneously complicates threat perception for the receiver.

Signaling and threat perception also become more difficult when intentions are difficult to read because of the workings of the security dilemma (Jervis, 1978; Glaser, 1977; 1992; 2010; Kydd, 1997a; 1997b; 2005; Booth and Wheeler, 2008; Tang, 2009; Fearon, 2011). A security dilemma arises between two states that are both "security seekers." When one takes defensive action to protect itself, but that defensive action can also be read as offensive, the other misperceives intention and misreads the type of state the other is. This process begins a mutual misperception of each other's defensive intentions as threatening that can culminate in a spiral into war. When sovereignty is contested, for example, the consolidation and defense of the territorial status quo can be viewed as aggressive, especially when it entrenches a disadvantage for one side. As a result, both sides may see their own actions as defensive and the other's as threatening, resulting in spirals of hostility as each seeks to bolster its control of contested territory. The culprit is not directly in the way leaders process information, but in the inherent ambiguity of the information they get and the poor diagnostics available to distinguish defensive from offensive intent. The security dilemma, which is most acute when offense is indistinguishable from defense, complicates signaling and threat perception and makes escalation likely because of the difficulty of reading intentions and the tendency to prepare for the worst case (Glaser & Kaufman, 1988; Jervis, 1978).

Closely related are "status dilemmas," which can explain competitive behavior among security seekers. Here states value status as well as security. A status dilemma occurs when two states would be satisfied with their status if they had perfect information about each other's beliefs. Without this kind of information, one set of leaders may perceive that its status is being challenged even when it is not. These leaders then take action to reassert their status, action that the other perceives as threatening. And so the spiral begins (Lebow, 2010; Wohlforth, 2009).

A third set of variables that can shape threat perception are the structural attributes of the political system. Organizational and bureaucratic politics can produce pathologies where leaders structure problems in ways that increase their importance and push hard for solutions that advance their institutional interests. These institutional interests can generate and benefit from either a heightened or reduced level of threat assessment. Those who seek to draw resources, for example, from those agencies that are responsible for preventing threat and managing the response tend to push for lower threat assessments. Contrary to conventional wisdom, these kinds of politics operate even during crises, despite leaders' attempts to extract national perspectives and limit parochial and institutional threat perceptions (Allison & Zelikow, 1999). A related but distinct argument focuses on organizational failure, on the inability of large and complex organizations to get information up the chain of command to leaders in a timely way. Investigations of the failure of US intelligence to read accurately the threat posed by Osama bin Laden and al-Qaeda highlighted the difficulty in sharing information across agencies and the challenge of capturing the attention of senior leaders in a noisy and crowded environment. Here leaders underestimated the threat not because parochial institutions succeeded in biasing the flow of information but because information simply did not flow in a timely and coordinated way.

A fourth set of variables in the explanation of threat perception is sociocultural. Domestic society and its accompanying identities influence how a state's decision-makers perceive threat (Hopf, 2002; Herrmann, chapter 11, this volume). Identity conditions threat assessments so strongly that the material balance of power becomes less important (Rousseau, 2006). A related argument suggests that political cultures that promote militarism and hypernationalism tend to be distrustful of outsiders, prone to defensiveness and worst-case thinking, and invested in the heightened perception of threat from external enemies. Kim Jong-il, when he was leader of North Korea, justified the sacrifices the impoverished population had to make by constant references to the existential threat posed by the United States and South Korea. For much of the Cold War, leaders in the Soviet Union and the United States made constant references to the threat posed by the other.

These heightened threat perceptions can be explained in several different ways. It is possible that North Korea's leaders accurately perceived the threat from the United States, but deliberately exaggerated and manipulated the threat to mobilize domestic forces and constrain opposition. Here they would have been instrumentally rational, using a heightened level of threat perception to achieve domestic goals. There is no direct evidence available about the dynamics of the threat perceptions of Kim Jong-il, but scholarly analysis of the US perception of the Soviet threat during the Cold War provides little support for an argument of instrumental rationality. Rather, the threat was exaggerated because of emotional beliefs, incomplete information, institutional dynamics, and cultural practices. Threat becomes culturally routine, embedded in political institutions, and acquires an almost taken-for-granted quality. Under these conditions, collective threat perceptions become highly resistant to change. In both these cases, scholars move back and forth between the individual and the collective level, a challenge that I deal with explicitly when I examine psychological explanations of threat perception.

Finally, scholars have identified the breaking of norms as a critical signal that elevates threat perception. The principal factor that elevated Roosevelt's assessment of the threat posed by Nazi Germany was Hitler's violation of the norm of political accommodation in the Munich crisis. What mattered were not the growing military capabilities of Germany, but rather Roosevelt's perception of German intentions that were shaped by the violation of a well-accepted procedural norm (Farnham, 2003).

These five sets of variables—changing balances of power and the attendant difficulty the sender faces in making commitments credible to the perceiver, security and status dilemmas that make intentions difficult to read and threats difficult to assess, institutional interests, political culture, and the violation of norms—complicate threat perception. The first of these variables—changing balances of power—is systemic and can create incentives for senders to withhold private information and thereby complicate the perception of threat by those who receive the signals. The second derives from ambiguity in the environment—in the case of the security dilemma, an environment in which offense and defense are difficult to distinguish, and in the case of status dilemmas, an environment where the determinants of status are ambiguous—which makes threat perception immensely more difficult. The next two are domestic and shape the environment in which threat assessment takes place. These arguments edge close to psychological arguments insofar as they assume implicitly, in interest-based arguments, that in an uncertain environment, people are motivated to construct threat assessments one way rather than another. The last is grounded in normative theory and the expectations that are derived from adherence to norms. None of these explanations, however, explicitly builds in psychological explanations that help to explain what appear to be anomalous patterns of threat perception at the individual level, nor do they deal with the difficult problem of how psychological moods that shape threat perception become collective and shared.

2. Psychological Explanations of Threat Perception

A recent study of the Iraq war in 2003 concludes that rationalist explanations of war are incomplete and need to be complemented by psychological explanations of threat perception and decision-making. Lake (2011, p. 9) sets the rationalist model of privately held information and deliberately deceptive signals against a psychological model of cognitive biases that impaired threat perception and decision-making. Although the key players were intentionalist, or minimally rational, he argues, "the key information failures were rooted in cognitive biases in decision making, not intentional misrepresentations by the opponent. Both the United States and Iraq engaged in self-delusions, biased decision making, and failures to update prior beliefs that are inconsistent with the assumption that actors will seek out and use all available information."

This is a strong indictment of purely rational models of incomplete information and signaling as a sufficient explanation, an indictment that is rooted in evidence of exaggerated threat perceptions by the Bush administration and Saddam's underestimation of the threat posed by the Bush administration to the survival of his regime. Nevertheless judgments of the accuracy and the adequacy of threat perception are both conceptually and empirically difficult to make, in part because the term is used to describe both an outcome and a process (Jervis, 1976).

When misperception describes an outcome, it is the difference between perceptions ex ante and the reality ex post. It is only possible, however, to make these judgments of accuracy or inaccuracy ex post; ex ante judgments are always uncertain. When misperception is used as process, it generally refers to the deviation from some standard model of rational information processing. Again what the standard is and how elastic the boundaries are, is open to question: what, for example, constitutes a rational or optimal search for information? How much information is enough? When does additional search provide diminishing marginal returns? These are extraordinarily difficult questions to answer empirically, and scholars themselves are vulnerable to the "hindsight bias" when answering the question after the fact; they know where the needle is in the haystack (Fischoff, 1975).

Arguments of "misperception" and "miscalculation" are built on the assumption that accurate perception and calculation are possible, that there is some standard, some boundary, which separates inaccuracy from accuracy. Yet this boundary is extraordinarily difficult to establish, even after the fact. Historians writing years later with full access to documentary evidence argue about intentions. There are multiple, at times overlapping explanations of why leaders would deliberately distort the signals they send about their capabilities and their intentions.

As we have seen, leaders may send distorted signals because they are attempting to cover weakness. A second, quite different, explanation emphasizes interests and the constraints imposed by multiple constituencies in "two-level" games (Evans, Jacobsen, & Putnam, 1993). Leaders may be speaking to multiple constituencies simultaneously and therefore have an incentive to distort either their intentions or their capabilities or both. Saddam Hussein did so when, constrained by his ongoing concern about Iran, he refused to acknowledge publicly that he had ended his unconventional weapons program. He therefore faced enormous difficulty in making his commitments credible to the United States. These difficulties have led scholars to set aside the question of accuracy, to abandon the systematic study of misperception, and to focus rather on patterns of perception under different circumstances (Jervis, 1976; Levy, 2003, p. 262). Are certain kinds of actors, situations, or crises associated with particular patterns of threat perception?

A second challenge is that most scholars have identified patterns of perception that deviate from rationality in the context of crises and war. They have not paid commensurate attention to identifying patterns of perception when threat assessment is stable and routine, or when threat assessment does not culminate in violence. It is likely that leaders systematically make cognitive "errors" in their information processing, and therefore these "errors" are not a significant contributor to crisis escalation or the outbreak of war. It is more than two decades since Jervis called for the systematic study of perceptions across a range of outcomes, but little research of that kind exists (Jervis, 1988, p. 680).

In this chapter, I look at the perceptions of intentions and of capabilities as the core elements of threat assessment. It is these two elements—capabilities and intentions—that have long been at the center of threat assessment and the modeling of rational deterrence and other threat-based strategies. Neither category is unproblematic. Intentions assume purposeful behavior, but psychological research has demonstrated that people are not always aware of their preferences and that their preferences may not be stable over time (Kahneman & Tversky, 1979). Capabilities are often difficult to assess. There are obvious and easily counted assets in assessing military capabilities, for example, but less tangible factors such as morale, motivation, loyalty, and leadership are more difficult to assess. Psychological studies of cognitive biases are helpful in explaining patterns of threat perception and in assessing the distance between these patterns of threat perception and the heuristic provided by rational models of information processing.

3. COGNITIVE BIASES AND HEURISTICS

Forty years ago, psychologists started a "cognitive revolution" as they rejected simple behaviorist models and looked again at the way people made inferences and judgments. They brought the "mind" back into psychology. Although this was not at all its purpose, the cognitive revolution is now widely understood largely as a commentary on the limits to rationality; some psychologists explicitly developed models that demonstrated the "deviations" from rationality. At the time, rationality was formulated in a very precise way as the capacity to maximize subjective expected utility; a microeconomic model became the foundation of rationality. To put the argument differently, the capacity for human reason was translated as rationality defined in microeconomic terms. (On rationality see Redlawsk & Lau, chapter 5, this volume; Chong, chapter 4, this volume.) "Misperception" and "miscalculation" were consequently defined against this narrow template of rationality.

How is this "cognitive revolution" relevant to the study of international politics? Political psychologists drew on the cognitive revolution to inform their study of inference, judgment, and decision-making by political leaders engaged in interactive bargaining with others even as they negotiated domestically with important constituencies. Situated at the apex of these complex strategic and multilayered games, political leaders, like everyone else, are limited in their capacity to process information. Their rationality is bounded (Simon, 1957; March, 1978; Jones, 1999). Because their rationality is bounded, people use a number of cognitive shortcuts and heuristics to simplify complexity and manage uncertainty, handle information, make inferences, and generate threat perceptions. Analysis of these cognitive shortcuts explains the threat perceptions that individual leaders make.

Research has now cumulated to show that people rarely conform to the expectations of the abstract rational model (Kahneman, Slovic, Tversky, 1982; Kahneman, 2011; Hogarth & Goldstein, 1996; Dawes, 1998; Hastie & Dawes, 2001; Gilovich, Griffin, & Kahneman, 2002). Cognitive psychology has demonstrated important differences between the expectations of rational decision models and the processes of attribution and estimation that people frequently use. It explains these differences by the need for simple rules of information processing and judgment that are necessary to make sense of environments that are both uncertain and complex. People have a preference for simplicity, they are averse to ambiguity and dissonance, and they misunderstand fundamentally the essence of probability (Dawes, 1998; Tetlock, 2005). We are not intuitively good at estimating probabilities. Together, these attributes compromise the capacity for rational inference.

3.1. Simplicity

Political leaders trying to assess a threat need to make a very complex world somewhat simpler. To do so, they unconsciously strip the nuance, the context, the subtleties out of the problems they face in order to build simple frames. Stripping out the context when assessing threat can lead to very oversimplified judgments. President George H. W. Bush famously said when Iraq invaded Kuwait in 1990 that Saddam Hussein was "another Hitler." Whatever Saddam was, it is difficult to argue that he was comparable to Hitler either in his intentions or his capabilities: the scope of his ambition or the numbers that he had killed did not compare to Hitler, nor did his relative military capabilities. That kind of simplified reasoning by analogy to develop a threat assessment is not uncommon.

3.2. Consistency

Cognitive psychologists have produced robust evidence that people strongly prefer consistency, that they are made uncomfortable by dissonant information, and that they consequently deny or discount inconsistent information to preserve their beliefs. They have a strong tendency to see what they expect to see based on their existing beliefs. This drive for consistency impairs processes of estimation and assessment. Exposure to contradictory information frequently results in the strengthening of beliefs (Anderson, Lepper, & Ross, 1980; Anderson, 1983; Hirt & Sherman, 1985).

The lengths policymakers will go to defend forecasts gone wrong are quite remarkable (Tetlock, 1998). Threat assessment is fundamentally a forecasting activity; it generates an estimate of what is likely to happen in the future. The contemporary debate about the trajectory of China, for example, is a debate about whether China is likely to threaten the status quo in the future as it grows relatively stronger. Much of the work of cognitive psychology has been done in the laboratory with students, and experts have questioned how well the results travel into international politics. That question has been largely put to rest by a remarkable study of the forecasts made by foreign policy experts in different cultures (Tetlock, 2005).

Experts on foreign policy generally continued to defend the forecasts they had made, even after what they expected did not happen. Tetlock (2005, p. 129) identifies seven categories of belief system defenses: challenging whether the local conditions required by the forecast were satisfied; invoking the unexpected occurrence of a shock; invoking a close-call counterfactual—"I almost got it right"; using an "off-on-timing" argument—"I'm ahead of my time; history will prove me right"; declaring that international politics is hopelessly indeterminate and consequently unpredictable; defiantly asserting that they made the "right mistake" and would do it again; and insisting that unlikely things sometimes happen.

The same kind of self-serving bias in information processing that cognitive psychologists have documented in the laboratory has also been confirmed among political experts. Tetlock also finds a relationship between the size of the mistakes and the activation of defenses. The more confident experts were in their original forecast or threat assessment, the more threatened they were when they were faced with disconfirming evidence, and the more motivated they were to use one or more of the seven defenses to preserve their beliefs. "Defensive cognitions," Tetlock (2005, p. 137) argues, "are activated when forecasters most need them." When political experts most needed to revise their judgments, they were least open to revision. If these patterns of thinking are characteristic among experts in international politics, they are as likely, if not more so, to be present among political leaders estimating threat. Deeply rooted cognitive processes systematically work against rational expectations of appropriate diagnostic updating.

When beliefs and arguments do change, they generally change in lumpy, bumpy ways that reflect somewhat arbitrary patterns in the information and basic processes of attribution.

There is some evidence, however, that is more encouraging. It comes from the close analysis of differences among foreign policy experts in their willingness to entertain the possibility that they were wrong. Not all experts were resistant to change all the time. Drawing on a well-known distinction made by Isaiah Berlin, Tetlock classified foreign policy experts as "foxes" or "hedgehogs." Hedgehogs know "one big thing" extremely well and extend what they know into other domains of foreign policy analysis. Foxes, on the other hand, know many small things, are generally skeptical of grand overarching schemes, stitch together assessments with different threads of knowledge, and are skeptical of prediction in world politics (Kruglanski & Webster, 1996, pp. 263–268; Berlin, 1997; Tetlock, 2005, pp. 73–75).

The evidence shows that the foxes do much better at short-term forecasting within their broad domain of expertise than do hedgehogs. The worst performers are hedgehogs who make long-term predictions, usually with considerable confidence. Hedgehogs are generally people with strong needs for structure and closure, who are most likely to discount and dismiss inconsistent evidence when it contradicts their preconceptions. The more knowledge hedgehogs have, the better equipped they are to defend against inconsistency. Foxes are skeptical of deductive approaches, more likely to qualify analogies by looking for disconfirming information, more open to competing arguments, more prone to synthesize arguments, more detached, and, not surprisingly, more likely to admit they were in error in their threat assessment. The hallmark of the foxes is their more balanced assessments and style of thinking about the world. Foxes have "a style of thought that elevates no thought above criticism" (Tetlock, 2005, pp. 88, 118). Rational models do not capture these differences in cognitive styles, the variation across political leaders who may be more like hedgehogs or foxes and consequently generate different kinds of threat assessments.

Related evidence suggests the concerning proposition that policymakers are predisposed to believe advisers who are hawks rather than doves. Scholars constructed a comprehensive list of psychological biases identified in the last 40 years of research and, in a remarkable result, found that all the biases predisposed leaders to believe the hawks. Basic psychological impulses incline national leaders to exaggerate the evil intentions of adversaries. Exaggerated threat perception is not random, but both systematic and deeply embedded in psychological processes (Kahneman & Renshon, 2007, p. 36). These processes take leaders far beyond prudential reasoning and reasoned assessment of threat.

3.3. Poor Estimators

People are not intuitive probability thinkers. They depart systematically from what rational models of information processing and objective probability calculations would dictate in the estimates they make. "Human performance suffers," argues Tetlock, "because we are, deep down, deterministic thinkers with an aversion to probabilistic strategies that accept the inevitability of error" (2005, p. 40). Foreign policy experts are no exception. Where we can compare their estimates to those that would be generated by objective calculations of probability, experts do surprisingly poorly. Highly educated specialists in foreign affairs approached only 20% of the ideal across all exercises (Tetlock, 2005, p. 77). They do so because they think causally rather than pay attention to the frequencies with which events occur. Experts tend to overestimate the likelihood of threat, for example, because they can easily imagine the causal pathways to war, a highly salient occurrence that they have likely studied (Tversky & Kahneman, 1983; Koehler, 1996). They pay less attention to the threats that did not lead to war and to the frequency of threats over an extended period of time

To make matters more difficult, likely states of the world are very difficult to estimate. In world politics, there are no repeated trials with large numbers. Leaders responsible for estimating threat do not live in a world of risk, where the probability distributions are known and the task is to estimate the likelihoods. Analysts, even the best informed, cannot know the probability, for example, of another attack by militants against civilian infrastructure in the United States or the United Kingdom. There have been too few such attacks to generate any reasonable estimate of likelihood. Those seeking to anticipate threat work in a structurally uncertain environment, where they generally have no access to probability distributions. This world of structural uncertainty is one that is particularly uncomfortable psychologically, and it is under these conditions that leaders, just like experts, are likely to seek the certainty, the false certainty, of order and control.

Cognitive psychology has identified a number of heuristics and biases that people use in environments of risk and uncertainty that can impair processes of judgment (Tversky & Kahneman, 1973; Nisbett & Ross, 1980; Kahneman et al., 1982; Fiske & Taylor, 1984; Jervis, 1986; von Winterfeldt & Edwards, 1986). Heuristics are convenient shortcuts or rules of thumb for processing information. Three of the best documented heuristics are *availability, representativeness,* and *anchoring.* The availability heuristic refers to people's tendency to interpret ambiguous information in terms of what is most easily available in their cognitive repertoire (Tversky & Kahneman, 1973; Ross & Sicoly, 1979; Taylor, 1982). The heuristic of representativeness refers to people's proclivity to exaggerate similarities between one event and a prior class of events, typically leading to significant errors in probability judgments or estimates of frequency (Kahneman & Tversky, 1972; 1973; Tversky & Kahneman, 1982). The heuristic of anchoring refers to an estimation of magnitude or degree by comparing it with an "available" initial value (often an inaccurate one) as a reference point and making a comparison (Fiske & Taylor, 1984, pp. 250–256, 268–275). In a world of uncertainty, leaders search for the relevant reference classes to anchor their judgments (Tversky & Kahneman, 1974). Initial judgments or prior beliefs serve as a conceptual anchor on the processing of new information and the revision of estimates.

Bayesian models of rational processing assume the updating of prior beliefs in response to new information, but evidence from cognitive psychology suggests that these processes are more conservative than rational models suggest, weighed down by prior beliefs and initial estimates. The implications for threat perception are considerable; once an estimate of threat is generated, it anchors subsequent rates of revision so that revision is slower and less responsive to diagnostic information. Threat perceptions consequently become embedded and resistant to change.

So do beliefs that an adversary will not attack. These conservative processes of information processing are present in almost all intelligence failures. Josef Stalin ignored evidence that was inconsistent with his belief that Adolf Hitler would not turn away from the western front and attack the Soviet Union. In 1973, Israel's decision-makers, although deeply aware of Egypt's determination to regain the Sinai, were nevertheless convinced that President Sadat would not attack until the Egyptian Air Force could attack deep behind Israel's lines. They systematically discounted evidence that was inconsistent with this core belief until they received information of an impending attack directly from one of their own agents who had penetrated the highest levels of decision-making in Cairo (Stein, 1985). Similarly, in the United States, although very senior officials warned of the intention of al-Qaeda to strike the United States, officials failed to update their estimates as they receive disconnected pieces of information before September 11. Preexisting beliefs anchored their judgments.

Yet conservatism does not hold unconditionally. The centrality of beliefs and the pattern of attribution have both been identified as predictors of the likelihood of revision and, by extension, of changes in estimates and judgment. Change is also a function of the rate at which discrepant information occurs, and how diagnostic the information is. Contradictory evidence dispersed across many instances should have a greater impact on estimates than a few isolated examples (Crocker et al., 1983). As people consider information inconsistent with previous knowledge, they incorporate into their estimates the conditions under which the belief does not hold, permitting gradual change and adjustment (Higgins & Bargh, 1987, p. 386). When people are faced with repeated inconsistencies, they change their least-central beliefs first (Tetlock, 1998). Important beliefs are challenged only when there is no other way to account for contradictory data that people consider diagnostic. Greater change will occur when information arrives in large batches, rather than bit by bit. President George H. W. Bush did not change his estimate of the threat posed by the Soviet Union even though the new Soviet leader, Mikhail Gorbachev, made a series of unilateral gestures to the United States. Only when information about large changes arrived in a rush did he finally change his threat perception. Even the strongest beliefs cannot withstand the challenge of strongly incongruent information over time (Markus & Zajonc, 1985).

Significant change in estimates of threat also occurs when subjects are exposed to incongruent information and are persuaded that the behavior is not arbitrary, but reflects the nature of the target. During the Balkan Wars in the 1990s, Croatian and Muslim leaders did not change their perception of the threat from Serbia because they attributed the change in Serbian policy to their military setback in Krajina. Change occurs when inconsistent information is attributed to dispositional rather than situational factors.

Cognitive processes of attribution also shape threat perception. One of the most pervasive biases is the fundamental attribution error, where people exaggerate the importance of dispositional over situational factors in explaining the behavior of others. They tend to place heavier emphasis on personality attributes than on the constraints that the other faces (Nisbett & Ross, 1980). Closely related is the actor-observer bias, in which people tend to overemphasize the role of a situation in their behaviors and underemphasize the role of their own personalities.

These biases can work together to increase threat perception. First, people tend to consider their own behavior differently than the behavior of others. They use a double standard. When the government of North Korea makes a threatening statement in the talks about its nuclear program, leaders in Washington see that threat as a function of the kind of regime that Pyongyang is, but explain their response as evidence of the situation they confront. The double standard in reasoning is clear and can lead to significant and reciprocal overestimation of threat in strategic interactions that take place against a background of enmity. The fundamental attribution error and the actor-observer bias, working together, can explain reciprocal patterns of escalating threat perception and the dynamics of the spiral model that occur when the security dilemma is acute. The two can reinforce each other to enable exaggerated threat perception, reciprocal escalatory steps, and a spiral of hostility. They can also explain the embedding of conflict over time so that it becomes protracted and resistant to resolution.

4. Loss Aversion, Framing, and Risk Propensity

Foreign policy decision-makers, like people generally, are not neutral about risk. Risk-propensity affects both perception of risk and response to risk. Prospect theory is among the most influential theories of risk propensity, and while it is a primarily a theory of decision, of response to risk, it also speaks to the perception of risk. Prospect theorists posit that people are more sensitive to relative changes in assets than to net asset levels, that they frame choice around a reference point, and that they give more weight to losses from that reference point than to comparable gains in constructing their assessments of risk (Kahneman & Tversky, 1979; 2000; Tversky & Kahneman, 1992; Levy, chapter 10, this volume). People also systematically overvalue certain losses relative to probable larger losses.

The impact of loss aversion on threat perception is considerable (Jervis, 1992; Stein & Pauly, 1992; Farnham, 1994; Levy, 1997; McDermott, 1998; Davis, 2000). Leaders are likely to be more sensitive to threats to what they already have, because they tend to value what they have—the "endowment effect"—more than comparable assets that they do not have (Kahneman, Knetsch, & Thaler, 1990, p. 1342; Jervis, 1992).

Prospect theory has considerable implications for rational theories of deterrence. Theories of deterrence are premised on rational choice, the expectation that the deterrer threatens harmful consequences that will exceed the benefits of what a would-be challenger wants to do. Challengers calculate their subjective expected utility, understand that the likely costs would exceed the benefits, and refrain from action. That is exactly how Israel's decision-makers thought of Egyptian calculation from 1970 to 1973. But President Sadat behaved not as rational deterrence theory but rather as prospect theory suggests. Leaders tend to be risk averse in the domain of gain and risk acceptant in the domain of loss, when they perceive a heightened threat, or when they face the likelihood of loss of something that matters to them. Sadat never normalized for the loss of the Sinai in 1967 and therefore chose as his reference point not the status quo but Egyptian possession of the Sinai. He was consequently in the domain of loss and prepared to be extraordinarily risk-acceptant in his choices. He designed his strategy around Israel's deterrence—its superiority in the air and on the ground—and his generals planned a limited strike across the Suez Canal under the protection of a missile shield (George & Smoke, 1974; Stein, 1985). Israel's decision-makers systematically underestimated the threat from Egypt because they missed the impact of loss aversion on Sadat's calculation of risk and subsequent decision.

Prospect theory, although primarily a theory of decision, is nevertheless a very useful screen for the "defender" to assess the likelihood of threat from a would-be "challenger." It would have been a far more useful theoretical screen for Israel's leaders to assess the likely threat from Egypt before the Sinai was returned than a lens of rational choice configured as subjective utility maximization. Prospect theory suggests that leaders need to be especially vigilant in their threat assessment when their adversary is in the domain of loss (Levy, 2003, p. 271). Under these circumstances, leaders run a risk of underestimating rather than overestimating threat.

The need for simplicity and consistency, the impediments to probabilistic thinking, the predisposition to loss aversion, and framing effects are often treated as deviations from rational models of deterrence. Rational choice remains the default, and these "deviations" are treated as limiting conditions. Yet the robustness of psychological models is now supported by a generation of research that establishes these patterns as the norm rather than the exception. New research in neuroscience has added to the complexity by bringing emotion back into reason.

5. Emotion and Threat Perception

Cognitive psychologists and prospect theorists, despite their evidence-based critique of models of (microeconomic) rationality, have moved only one degree away from the fundamental assumption of utility-maximizing rationality. They continue to set rationality as the default and then explore the consequences of systematic "errors" and "deviations," of "constrained" or bounded" rationality. These "deviations" from rationality only make sense against a background of a narrowly conceived microeconomic concept of rationality as an accounting of probability and value.

Two decades of research in neuroscience have reshaped our understanding of the relationship between emotion, perception and cognition (Brader & Marcus, chapter 6, this volume). Two results stand out. First, information processing seems not to be the result only of a deliberative thought process, but largely of preconscious neurological processes. The brain can absorb about 11 million pieces of information a second but can only process 40 consciously. The unconscious brain manages the rest. Second, emotion is primary and plays a dominant role in perception and thought. Research on emotion is having a significant impact on the analysis of a wide range of global issues: theories of deterrence (Mercer, 2005; 2010), reputation and signaling (Mercer, 1996; 2010), nuclear proliferation (Hymans, 2006), the war on terror (Bennett, 2002; Saurette, 2006; Blieker & Hutchison, 2008; Crawford, 2009), and revenge, anger, and humiliation as responses to threat and motives for war (Gries, 2004; Saurette, 2006; Löwenheim & Heimann, 2008; Lebow, 2010).

What is emotion? There is widespread theoretical dispute about the conceptualization of emotion. Political psychologists are sensitive to the complex siting of emotion at the interface of structure and action, material and psychological processes, and neurological and sociopolitical processes: "Emotion is a large set of differentiated, biologically-based complex[es] that are constituted, at the very least, by mutually transformative interactions among biological systems (e.g., cognition, physiology, psychology) and physical and sociocultural ones" (McDermott, 2004, p. 692).[1]

5.1. Emotion and Rationality

In seminal research, Damasio (1994) demonstrated that patients who sustained injuries to those parts of the brain that are central to the processing of emotion were incapable of making rational decisions. Elliott, his patient, suffered a brain injury in that part of the brain that controls emotions, but he was then, to his doctor's astonishment, unable to distinguish among important and unimportant cues and make rational decisions. Damasio's work ignited a research program on the relationship between cognition and emotion, a program that confirms that behavior is strongly influenced by finely tuned affective systems (LeDoux, 1996; Panksepp, 1998; Rolls, 1999). "When these systems are damaged or perturbed by brain injury, stress, imbalance in neurotransmitters, or the 'heat of the moment,' the logical-deliberative system—even if completely intact, cannot regulate behavior appropriately" (Camerer, Loewenstein, & Prelec, 2005, p. 11). Neuropsychologists, who begin by emphasizing the materiality of emotions, reject a separation between cognition and emotion as untenable. The one is embedded within the other. And by extension, rationality and emotion are interdependent, not opposite to one another. Rationality, in short, presupposes and indeed requires emotion.

There is growing consensus that emotion is "first"; because it is automatic and fast, and operating below the threshold of conscious awareness, it plays a dominant role in shaping perception and behavior (LeDoux, 1996; Winkielman & Berridge, 2004). We generally feel before we think, and, what is even more surprising, often we act before we think. There is widespread consensus that the brain implements "automatic processes" that are faster than conscious deliberations with little or no awareness or feeling of effort (Bargh, Chaiken, Raymond, & Hymes, 1996; Bargh & Chartrand, 1999). Not surprisingly, the conscious brain then interprets behavior that emerges from automatic, affective processes as the outcome of perception and deliberation.

How do neuroscientists analyze the relationship between emotion and cognition? "Dual-process" theories in psychology provide an account of how a phenomenon can occur as a result of two different processes, one implicit and the second explicit (Barrett, Tugade, & Engle, 2004; Kahneman, 2003; 2011; Sloman, 1996; Sun, 2002). Implicit systems are automatic, fast, evolved early, use parallel processing, have high capacity, are not reflexive, and are effortless, while explicit systems are conscious, controlled, relatively slow, evolve late, use sequential processing, are limited by attentional and working memory resources, and are effortful (MacDonald, 2008).

Building on the work of dual-process theorists, some psychologists and neuroscientists conceive of two separate operating systems in the brain: emotion and reason (LeDoux, 2000; Sloman, 1996). "Emotions influence our decisions," argues Jonathan Cohen. "They do so in just about every walk of our lives, whether we are aware or unaware of it, and whether we acknowledge it or not" (2005, p. 1). The brain, Cohen explains, has different kinds of mechanisms; one, which includes emotional responses, can respond automatically, quickly, and definitively but is relatively inflexible. Cognition is less rapid and has limited capacity but is more flexible. There is a trade-off between the speed and specialization of emotions and the generality of reflection. In the circumstances of modern life, these systems may prescribe different perceptions and responses.

Kahneman calls the first, emotion-based system of processing "intuitive" and "associative" and the second system "reasoned" and "rule-governed" (Kahneman, 2011). The first system is preconscious, automatic, fast, effortless, associative, unreflective, usually with strong emotional bonds, and slow to change. The second system is conscious, slow, effortful, reflective, rule-governed, and flexible. The vast majority of processing occurs through the first system, which draws heavily on emotions and, in a competition between the two, always trumps the rule-governed, reasoned system. It is extraordinarily difficult, Kahneman concludes, for the second system to educate the first.

5.2. Emotion and Perception

There is ongoing debate about the impact of emotion on information processing and perception. One approach treats emotion as information. Emotions carry information to people about their unconscious processes, which then become conscious thoughts and feelings and affect their perceptions and beliefs (Clore, 1992; Clore & Gasper, 2000; Clore, Schwarz, & Conway, 1994; Schwarz, 1990; Schwarz & Clore, 1983; Mercer, 2010). In this sense, emotions do not follow cognitive appraisal but create appraisals through the information they provide (Lerner & Keltner, 2001; Lerner, Small, & Loewenstein, 2004).

Evolutionary approaches see emotions as adaptive programs of action that have evolved over time to ensure survival and then reproduction (Frijda, 1988; Berkowitz, 1999). They understand emotions as superordinate programs that gather information from the environment and organize the raw data of experience prior to the conscious processes of thought. Emotions serve as switches, turning on and off depending on the environmental demands of the moment (Tooby & Cosmides, 2003, p. 116). These rapid and efficient judgments about the significance of social threat are important for the survival of the species. People are programmed to detect threatening faces, faces with angry expressions (Green & Philips, 2004).

Evolutionary inheritance does not always serve contemporary leaders well in their complex and uncertain environments. In an emotionally charged environment, threat detection based on the erroneous identification of objects is especially likely. It is individuals' emotional states that constitute a primary influence in automatic threat detection and the bias is in favor of overdetection rather than underestimation (Baumann & DeSteno, 2010). Knowledge of situational and dispositional constraints on the ability of emotion to bias threat detection would be valuable so that leaders could become more aware of the potential influence of their emotions on their perceptions of threat.

Political and social psychologists see evolutionary arguments as necessary but not complete. What, they ask, governs these switches, beyond the imperative of physical survival? It is social context that makes emotions meaningful (Saurette, 2006, pp. 507–508). It is only with a shared sense of what constitutes appropriate social behavior that a person, a people, or a government feels humiliated or threatened. When the flag of one nation is burned by another, the humiliation and anger that follows flow from a shared understanding that the burning of a flag is a deliberately insulting and threatening act. Physiological processes are layered by social knowledge that shapes the appropriateness of anger and fear and perceived threat. It is in this sense that emotions need to be conceived not only as an individual experience but also as a social process (Ross, 2006).

The analysis of emotions outside the laboratory presents theoretical and methodological challenges. Theoretically, there is no fundamental agreement on what constitutes the basic emotions, and the core emotions are not easily disentangled. At the individual level, emotions do not leave visible traces unless the observer is in direct contact with the participant, and participants are not always aware and self-conscious about their emotional response. These challenges are not unique, however, to the analysis of emotions, but are present in the analysis of perception and cognition as well. Scholars need to examine carefully the complex interconnections among emotion, perception, and cognition as they construct new, more complex models of the ways people feel and think.

5.3. Fear and Threat Perception

Among the emotions generally considered to be basic, the impact of fear is the most widely studied. Fear has been central to the study of foreign policy and international politics. From Thucydides, the great student of the Peloponnesian War, to Hobbes, who wrote about the state of anarchy that induced fear, to Morgenthau, the 20th-century classical realist who started his analysis of international politics with a Hobbesian analysis of international anarchy that generated fear and an unending search for power, realists have premised their analyses of international politics on the ubiquity of fear. In these realist and rationalist accounts, however, fear remains an assumption, unexplored, rather than a dynamic process that is experienced.

Neuropsychologists and behavioral economists treat fear very differently. Fear is conditioned in part by our evolutionary makeup and is frequently evoked by crude or subliminal cues. Fear typically peaks just before a threat is experienced and is highly dependent on mental imagery and vividness. It is, of course, highly adaptive; fear heightens attention and vigilance and prepares people to respond to what they perceive as imminent danger. Neuroscientists have now demonstrated that fear conditioning, however, may be permanent, or at least is far longer lasting than other kinds of learning. "To the extent that these differences exist between the calculus of objective risk and the determinants of fear, and to the extent that fear does play an important part in risk-related behaviors," argue Loewenstein and his colleagues, "behavior in the face of risk is unlikely to be well-described by traditional consequentialist models" (Loewenstein, Rick, & Cohen, 2008, p. 280). Fear, in other words, lasts longer than the threat and can become a learned response that is embedded over time.

It is not surprising then, that more than a decade after 9/11, leaders and publics in the United States still identify the threat of a terrorist attack as one of their primary concerns. Threat perception remains high and shapes foreign and domestic policy even though no major attack has succeeded in the years that followed. That several attacks have been aborted is undoubtedly a part of the continuing public and political focus on terrorism. But fear conditioning is also part of the explanation. Through repeated practice and institutionalization, a self-sustaining climate of fear was created in the United States by the Bush administration (Crawford, 2009; Meyer & Miskimmon, 2009). Once a threat is perceived and institutionalized, it becomes self-perpetuating, and it consequently becomes far more difficult to wind down the well-established embedded threat perceptions that drive conflict.

5.4. Humiliation and the Escalation of Threat

The well-known "ultimatum game" highlights the cognitive and emotional elements at play in decision making. The game comes out of economics but has direct relevance to threat perception as well. In the game, a powerful country offers a less powerful state only a small part (10%) of an available asset. If the less powerful leader accepts this "unfair" offer, she walks away with her small share, but if she rejects the offer, both parties get nothing because the asset remains contested. Rational models would dictate that she accept whatever she is offered, because "something is always better than nothing" in a one-play game. But participants in multiple experiments in North America do not play that way; they overwhelmingly reject offers that are much below 50%. An emotional response likely precedes conscious calculation and the decision to reject the offer. Research in anthropology demonstrates that this norm of fairness varies across cultures; culture deeply shapes cognition and emotion (Henrich, 2000).

That emotional response likely explains in part why leaders reject offers on global issues that they consider unfair or humiliating (Fattah & Fierke, 2009). One party—a state—has access to a given resource—wealth, vast natural resources, highly sophisticated military technology, the headwaters of a river—and can propose how the resource should be split. If the other party accepts the proposal, then the resource is divided as they have agreed. If the split is rejected, neither receives anything and the game is over. Conflict likely follows. As we have seen, the second party should accept anything that it is offered, because anything is clearly better than nothing. And again, the first party, knowing that for the other anything is better than nothing, should rationally offer as little as possible. Yet parties reject offers that they consider humiliating.

Perhaps those who rejected the offer were worried about their bargaining reputation and their capacity to make credible threats for the next round, as rational deterrence theory says they should. But when reputational effects were removed from consideration—when resolve and concerns about "costly signals" were taken off the table because they were told that they would play the game only once—they responded the same way. When asked why they rejected an offer that would give them something rather than nothing, they responded that the offer was humiliating and unfair. They quickly and intuitively rejected an offer that gave them something, but humiliated them in the process. Their rejection was driven by a strong, negative emotional response embedded in cultural norms of fairness and justice.

Threats that targets perceive as humiliating are likely to evoke anger and provoke the risk-acceptant response that a threat-based strategy is designed to avoid. The attacks on the World Trade Center and the Pentagon were deliberately designed to humiliate the United States, by attacking its visible symbols of power, by piercing its sense of invulnerability, by violating its sense of self-respect and honor. President Bush, humiliated and angered, lashed back, first against those who gave al-Qaeda shelter but then inexplicably against Saddam Hussein in Iraq, in a campaign described as "shock and awe" to give forcible description to American power (Saurette, 2006).

5.5. Emotion and the Credibility of Deterrent Threats

Cognitive models have long informed the study of deterrence (Jervis, Lebow, & Stein, 1985; Lebow & Stein, 1994), but building emotions into the explanation is shedding new light on old problems. The credibility of threats, an essential component in theories of deterrence, compellence, and bargaining, is not only a property of the sender, as some formal models of signaling suggest, but also a function of the beliefs of the receiver (Mercer, 2010). And these beliefs are not only cognitive but emotional as well. The emotional cues that signals evoke—fear, anger—matter insofar as these emotions then prompt beliefs and action in turn. Research demonstrates that fear prompts uncertainty and risk-averse action, while anger prompts certainty and risk acceptance. Threats that evoke fear, unless they evoke loss avoidance, are likely to prompt hesitancy and a risk-averse response; indeed, that is the purpose of most deterrent threats. Frightening threats are less likely to be successful, however, when they are designed to compel adversarial leaders to act.

Research also demonstrates that credibility, a fundamental component to theories of action in international politics, is emotional as well as cognitive. Credibility is not simply a function of either the cost of the signal or past behavior. It is an emotional belief that is held by its intended receiver; the belief that another's commitment is credible depends on the selection and interpretation of evidence and on the assessment of risk, both of which rely on emotion (Mercer, 2010). Russia's credibility is not only a function of what its leaders say and do, or have said and done, but what Georgia's leaders think Moscow will say and do, and what they think about that government is partly a function of what they feel.

Psychological explanations call into question reputational models based only on past behavior of states or on the costliness of signals, the traditional determinants of resolve. Leaders in deterrent relationships worry about their credibility, about the other's perception of their determination to fulfill their threats should compliance not be forthcoming. Under these conditions, an infinite regress of emotional expectations about resolve is likely (Mercer, 2010). Because Israel's leaders believe that what Hamas's leaders think of them matters, their emotional beliefs about what Hamas's leaders think about Israel matter. Israel's leaders beliefs may be—and have been in the past—significantly at variance from what Hamas's leaders actually believe about Israel's resolve. Israel's leaders nevertheless became locked into a conversation with themselves about their fragile or deteriorating reputation for resolve and have gone to war to preserve their reputation, even though they do not and cannot control how Hamas's leaders perceive Israel's threat to go to war should Hamas launch rockets across the border.

Building emotion in as a driver of threat perception changes the analysis of reputation based solely on past behavior or costly signals. Past behavior rarely speaks for itself but is felt and understood in multiple ways by others. What the deterrer feels and thinks of as a "costly" signal may not necessarily be felt as costly by a would-be challenger. Cost, as we know from our own experience, is subjective.

Emotion is an assimilation mechanism that influences the selection and interpretation of evidence in threat perception. (See the discussions of motivated reasoning by Chong, chapter 4, this volume, and by Taber & Young, chapter 17, this volume.) In 2009, Israeli and American leaders had access to almost all the same data and evidence on Iran's nuclear program; there is extensive intelligence sharing among the two countries. Yet American officials estimated a much longer time horizon—five years—for the development of a nuclear weapon by Iran than did Israel's officials, who estimated a year or two. The difference in threat perception is not explainable by the evidence but by the higher emotional loading of the likelihood of an Iranian bomb for Israel's leaders that shaped threat perception.

Building emotions—fear, anger, and humiliation—into the analysis illuminates the complexity of designing threat based strategies that are subtle and calibrated to likely emotional responses. Threat-based strategies that rely exclusively on rational calculation by an adversary and ignore the interaction among cognitive heuristics and emotional states, as well as the political and institutional context, are likely to misfire badly (Stein, 1988).

5.6. Fear, Threat, and Risk-Taking

It is not only the powerful, long-term consequences of fear that matter to foreign policy decision-making and international politics. Emotions also help to explain patterns of risk-taking in foreign policy. Prospect theory, formulated originally as a correction to rationalist accounts of decision-making, nevertheless implies more than the argument that the propensity to take risk is a function of situation and thinking. It is also about feelings. People *feel* more pain from losses than they *feel* pleasure from equivalent gains. It is this asymmetry in feeling that underlies decision-makers' efforts to avoid loss. Fear is such a powerful emotional experience in part because the *pain* of loss is commensurately greater than the *pleasure* of equivalent gain. It is this kind of dynamic, for example, that has led decision-makers who feel threatened to use their weapons early—sometimes starting a war—rather than risk the loss of these weapons later on. This is the most dangerous dynamic of escalation that scholars have identified, a dynamic that is very difficult to control until leaders feel reassured that their military capabilities will survive a debilitating first strike. This logic of fear of loss underlay the dangerous early decade of the Cold War, which then took decades of effort and billions of dollars of investment in hardening missile sites to wind down. This same incendiary dynamic of fear, threat perception, loss aversion, and risk acceptance underlies nightmare scenarios between South and North Korea and between Iran and its neighbors and makes the management of these relationships so dangerous and so delicate.

6. EMOTIONS AND COLLECTIVE APPRAISAL

In the last decade, scholars in international relations have paid attention to how emotions become collective, how they are shared, and whether we can speak of the "mood" of a nation (Ross, 2006; Saurette, 2006; Hall & Ross, 2011). At least two explanations of the creation of collective emotion are plausible.

Epidemiological and viral models are one obvious explanation of the diffusion of emotion from an individual to a larger group. Emotion is an individual property, but the individual is embedded in a social context, picks up cues from her environment, reacts emotionally to those cues, and diffuses emotion back to others. The spread of basic emotions from one individual to another is similar to other contagious processes where physical proximity matters (Hatfield, Cacioppo, & Rapson, 1994). One can "catch" an emotion very much as one can "catch" a cold (Hatfield et al., 1994; Neumann & Strack, 2000; Ilies, Wagner, & Morgeson, 2007). The direct "spread" of emotions explains diffusion within a small group but cannot provide an account of the collective emotions that are shared by large publics that are not physically proximate. Even if we allow for the impact of electronic and digital media, where messages laden with emotion can go "viral," a contagion model does not adequately explain why we are not continuously in a heightened state of arousal as we pick up the emotional cues of others.

An alternative approach suggests that emotions spread through processes of social appraisal. Emotions are spread "based on social appraisal [that] occurs because someone else's perceived affect carries information that alters our appraisal of the emotional meaning of what is happening" (Parkinson & Simons, 2009, p. 1071). Some emotions are likely to be contagious because they signal threats and opportunities in the social environment, while others require some shared social understanding or shared identity (Ross, 2006). Humiliation, for example, implies an understanding of the social norms that set social standards of appropriate behavior, for without that shared understanding, it is impossible to design strategies that humiliate.

A third approach speaks directly to shared social identity. Intergroup emotions theory (IET) holds that intergroup emotions are experienced by an individual when she identifies strongly with a group, making that group part of her psychological self. People have different levels of the self, both individual and collective (Smith, Seger, & Mackie, 2007). These group-level emotions are distinct from the emotions that occur primarily at the individual level; they depend on the person's degree of group identification, are socially shared within a group, and contribute to regulating both intra- and intergroup attitudes and behavior (Huddy, chapter 23, this volume). Experimental evidence suggests that group emotions may be important contributors to large-scale social change. All three of these mechanisms work through the individual's set of social relationships and connections to society, its norms, and its understandings. In this context, threats to the group are perceived as threats to the self and are internalized.

A second-order explanation puts the collective at the center and argues that collectivities experience emotions. This is a difficult argument, because it attributes to the collective what is an embodied individual experience: "states are not gigantic calculating machines," argues Hymans (2010, p. 462), "they are hierarchically organized groups of emotional people." It is difficult to conceive, some argue, that the fear after 9/11 that was widely shared in the United States was transmitted from individual to individual. Rather fear and the consequent perception of threat was a collective experience, evoked by trauma, enabled by political leaders, echoed over and over by the media, reinforced by practices designed to safeguard aircraft from hijacking and a system of public alerts, and institutionalized through the creation of new processes and practices. In this sense of shared institutions and practices, scholars claim, a collective climate of fear was created (Hall & Ross, 2011).

There is considerable evidence that manipulation of fear is common in post-traumatic societies that builds a shared identity based on a "safe inside" and a "threatening outside" (Hutchison & Bleiker, 2008). Communities that constitute themselves around an external threat are especially likely to legitimate policies of violence and revenge (Edkins, 2003). In the wake of a terrorist attack against civilians, some evidence suggests that threat perception and anxiety are distinct but related public reactions. Anxiety or fear increases risk aversion, potentially undercutting support for military action, while perceived threat increases the desire for retaliation and revenge. Some data suggest that the majority of Americans who perceived a high threat of future terror attacks against the United States but were not overly anxious about the consequences—I'm going to live my life; these attacks are random—supported the Bush administration's policies both at home and internationally (Huddy, Feldman, Taber, & Lahav, 2005). Similar evidence from the analysis of Israeli public opinion suggests that those who felt personally fearful were more supportive of compromise (Maoz & McCauley, 2009). Related research suggests that when the threatening idea of mortality is made salient, negative attitudes toward those who are perceived as threatening increase substantially (Greenberg, Simon, Pyszczynski, Soloman, & Chatel, 1992).

Collective emotions are central to workings of the international order. Fear is an emotional state, one indicator of pessimism about the future. Collective emotions are also cognitive, one person's sense of how pessimistic others are and their perceptions of how pessimistic still others are. An individual's mood is in part a function of the mood of others, and, in this sense, it is as reasonable to speak of a collective mood as it is to speak of shared norms.

Collective moods can set the context against which political leaders make their choices. Aware of the wave of public anger over the inaction of his government after North Korea shelled the island of Yeonpyeong in 2010, killing 4 civilians and wounding more than 40, President Lee Myung-bak of South Korea escalated his response through large military exercises, provoking threats of retaliation from North Korea in return. Here, the collective "mood," monitored in public opinion surveys and interviews and echoed and fueled in newspapers, was one of the factors that contributed indirectly to the highest level of tension on the Korean peninsula in 60 years.

7. CONCLUSION

There has been significant progress in the analysis of the close interconnections between cognition and emotion. Emotion and cognition are no longer conceived as alternative explanations, as they were as recently as a decade ago in the analysis of the political psychology of international relations, but rather as complementary. What people feel influences what they perceive and the way they think.

This understanding of the interconnectedness of emotion and perception opens an important research agenda for scholars of psychology and international politics. First, scholars will have to grapple systematically with the impact of fear, anger, and humiliation on threat perception at the individual level of leaders. Do different kinds of emotions produce differences in threat perceptions, which in turn produce different responses? Scholars have been calling for this kind of systematic and controlled inquiry. Empirical studies are urgently needed, but little progress has been made.

The lack of progress is attributable in part to the difficulty of systematically studying emotion outside the laboratory. New research findings are coming from work done with individuals subject to imaging technology under controlled laboratory conditions. How can these arguments be examined, exported, and refined in the political world? How can they inform the big research questions that have long preoccupied scholars of international relations? These are difficult but not impossible challenges, challenges that political psychologists have long grappled with. Thinking and feeling outside the laboratory cannot be directly observed, but scholars can draw on archives, documents, diaries, leaked cables, interviews, and polls to assess what leaders and publics feel, what they perceive, and what they think. Scholars working with this kind of evidence have long known that no one source is determining, that multiple streams of evidence increase confidence, and that the interpretative skills of the trained scholar will always matter. Experimental research and simulation may be valuable complements to the detailed search for emotional traces in documents and interviews. Although this may seem like a daunting task, it is not much easier, as I have argued, to find empirical traces of intentions.

Second, analysts have to grapple with threat perception not only at the individual level but also at the small group and the broader collective level. Rarely do individual leaders develop threat perceptions in isolation from their colleagues and the broader social and political surround. Yet theories of the impact of collective emotions on collective perceptions are not well developed.

Emotions are embodied experiences. We feel them physically, often before we are fully aware, but we feel them as individuals. How emotions move from the individual to the collective is still inadequately articulated. Constructivists offer one set of arguments, as do sociological institutionalists and political psychologists, but we will need more tightly reasoned and better supported explanations, supported by evidence, if we are to avoid the fallacy of attributing to the group the properties of the individual. Groups, after all, do not feel or think; individuals do. How emotions become social and how collectivities build shared threat perceptions are important theoretical and methodological challenges as this research agenda moves ahead.

Third, scholars in international relations ask: how important is the psychology of emotion and cognition in comparison to other explanations of threat perception? To ask this question is to ask a larger question: how important is agency in the explanation of these kinds of international outcomes? Once we move away from exclusively structural explanations and acknowledge a role for human agency, then any explanation of threat perception encompasses the analysis of feeling and information processing as essentials, as the core constitutive elements. The interesting question then becomes: what kinds of emotions have what kinds of impact on information processing and perception, under what kinds of political conditions? When, for example, does fear-driven threat perception lead to loss aversion and risky behavior, and when does it lead to retreat and risk-averse behavior? When does humiliation-driven threat perception provoke anger and revenge, and when does it lead to retreat and passivity? Answers to these kinds of questions are critical to theories of all threat-based strategies. Scholars need to specify how emotion would modify existing theories as well as the range and types of emotions that matter.

More challenging will be integrating psychological theories into broader theories of international relations. This chapter began with an analysis of the inability of models of strategic interaction and bargaining theories to explain why the threat perception of Saddam Hussein escalated so dramatically and why the confrontation led to war. Rationalist accounts of strategic interaction cannot explain why American leaders perceived Iraq as so much more threatening in 2003 than in 1998 (Lake, 2011, p. 28). These accounts privilege capabilities and intentions to explain changes in threat perception, but Iraq's capabilities did not grow significantly, and the same leader remained in power. Rationalist theories do not give much weight to the difference in the beliefs of the Clinton and Bush administrations, yet the difference in beliefs between the senior leaders in the two administrations mattered enormously in the way they perceived the threat emanating from Saddam. Misrepresentation by the other side was far less important than self-delusion. The United States systematically discounted its own costs of fighting, and Saddam ignored obvious signals of the Bush administration's resolve. What matters is that these biases were motivated: "Neither side wanted to know about itself or the other information that would have challenged its prior beliefs or slowed the march to war" (Lake, 2011, p. 45).

Lake's analysis of the patterns of threat perception and the road to war in 2003 leads him to call for a "behavioral theory of war," a suggestion very like the recommendation that psychological theories be integrated with models of strategic interaction (Jervis, 2002; Levy, 2003, pp. 272–273; Lake, 2011, pp. 45–47). Much of what is important in international relations—war and peace, deterrence and collaboration—is the result of strategic interaction. A focus on the emotional cognition of threat perception allows researchers to identify those psychological processes that are especially relevant to models of strategic interaction.

Underlying all these opportunities for fruitful research and the integration of psychology into theories of international politics is the necessity to leave behind, once and for all, an understanding of psychology as an explanation of deviation from rational choice. What we have learned in the last two decades is that without emotion, there is no rationality. It is this fundamental change in our understanding of the relationship between emotion and cognition, at both the individual and collective levels, that should inform the research agenda of the next decade.

NOTE

1. The concepts "emotion," "affect," "feelings," and "moods" are not identical, and their ontological and metaphysical foundations are disputed. The disputes arise partly because of the wide range of disciplines that are deeply interested in emotion. I use "emotion" as an

umbrella term to include the experience that is rooted in physiological changes in the body and the awareness of that experience. Emotion is embodied experience in the moment. I may experience fear, for example, as a pulsating heartbeat and sweating with no conscious awareness yet that I am frightened, much less what is frightening me. A feeling refers to the conscious awareness that I am afraid of something specific, while "mood" generally refers to a more diffuse and unfocused experience. Affect is defined more precisely as "positively or negatively valenced subjective reactions that a person experiences at a given moment in time" (Camerer et al., 2005, p. 39). It is the way people represent the value of things as good or bad and, so technically, is one dimension of emotion (McDermott, 2004).

REFERENCES

Allison, G., & Zelikow, P. (1999). *Essence of decision: Explaining the Cuban Missile Crisis* (2nd ed.). New York: Addison-Wesley.

Anderson, C., Lepper, M. R., & Ross, L. (1980). Perseverance of social theories: The role of explanation in the persistence of discredited information. *Journal of Personality and Social Psychology, 39*, 1037–1049.

Anderson, J. R. (1983). *The architecture of cognition*. Cambridge, MA: Harvard University Press.

Bargh, J. A., Chaiken, S., Raymond, P., & Hymes, C. (1996). The automatic evaluation effect: Unconditional automatic attitude activation with a pronunciation task. *Journal of Experimental Social Psychology, 32*, 104–128.

Bargh, J. A., & Chartrand, T. L. (1999). The unbearable automacity of being. *American Psychologist, 54*, 462–479.

Barrett, F. L., Tugade, M. M., & Engle, R. W. (2004). Individual differences in working memory capacity and dual-process theories of the mind. *Psychological Bulletin, 130*, 553–573.

Baumann, J., & DeSteno, D. (2010). Emotion guided threat detection: Expecting guns where there are none. *Journal of Personality and Social Psychology, 99*, 595–610.

Bennett, W. J. (2002). *Why we fight: Moral clarity and the war on terrorism*. New York: Doubleday.

Berkowitz, L. (1999). Anger. In T. Dalgleish & M. J. Power (eds.), *Handbook of cognition and emotion* (pp. 411–428). New York: Wiley.

Berlin, I. (Ed.). (1997). *The proper study of mankind*. New York: Farrar, Straus and Giroux.

Blieker, R., & Hutchinson, E. (2008). Fear no more: Emotions and world politics. *Review of International Studies, 34*, 115–135.

Booth, K., & Wheeler, N. J. (2008). *The security dilemma: Fear, cooperation and trust in world politics*. New York: Palgrave Macmillan.

Camerer, C., Loewenstein, G., & Prelec, D. (2005). Neuroeconomics: How neuroscience can inform economics. *Journal of Economic Literature, 43*, 9–64.

Christensen, T. J. (2001). Posing problems without catching up: China's rise and challenges for U.S. security policy. *International Security, 25*, 5–40.

Christensen, T. J. (2006). Fostering stability or creating a monster? The rise of China and U.S. policy toward East Asia. *International Security, 31*, 81–126.

Clore, G. L. (1992). Cognitive phenomenology: Feelings and the construction of judgment. In L. L. Martin & A. Tesser (eds.), *The construction of social judgments* (pp. 133–163). Hillsdale: Erlbaum.

Clore, G. L., & Gasper, K. (2000). Feeling is believing: Some affective influences on belief. In N. H. Frijda, A. S. R. Manstead, & S. Bem (eds.), *Emotions and beliefs: How feelings influence thoughts* (pp. 10–44). Cambridge: Cambridge University Press.

Clore, G. L., Schwarz, N., & Conway, M. (1994). Affective causes and consequences of social information processing. In R. S. Wyer & T. K. Srull (eds.), *Handbook of social cognition* (vol. 1, pp. 323–417). Hillsdale, NJ: Erlbaum.

Crawford, N. (2009). Human nature and world politics. *International Relations, 23,* 271–288.

Crocker, J., & Weber, R. (1983). Cognitive processes in the revision of stereotypic beliefs. *Journal of personality and social psychology, 45,* 961–977.

Damasio, A. (1994). *Descartes' error: Emotion, reason, and the human brain.* New York: Putnam.

Davis, J. W., Jr. (2000). *Threats and promises.* Baltimore, MD: John Hopkins University Press.

Dawes, R. (1998). Judgment and choice. In D. Gilbert, S. Fiske, & G. Lindzey (eds.), *Handbook of social psychology* (pp. 497–548). New York: McGraw Hill.

Edkins, J. (2003). *Trauma and the memory of politics.* Cambridge: Cambridge University Press.

Elman, C. (2004). Extending offensive realism: The Louisiana purchase and America's rise to regional hegemony. *American Political Science Review, 98,* 563–576.

Evans, P., Jacobsen, H., & Putnam, R. (Eds.). (1993). *Double-edged diplomacy: International bargaining and domestic politics.* Berkeley: University of California Press.

Farnham, B. (1994). *Taking risks/avoiding losses.* Ann Arbor: University of Michigan Press.

Farnham, B. (2003). The theory of democratic peace and threat perception. *International Studies Quarterly, 47,* 395–415.

Fattah, K., & Fierke, K. M. (2009). A clash of emotions: The politics of humiliation and political violence in the Middle East. *European Journal of International Relations, 15,* 67–93.

Fearon, J. D. (1995). Rationalist explanations for war. *International Organization, 49,* 379–414.

Fearon, J. D. (2011). Two states, two types, two actions. *Security Studies, 20,* 431–440.

Fischoff, B. (1975). Hindsight does not equal foresight: The effect of outcome knowledge on judgment under uncertainty. *Journal of Experimental Psychology: Human Perception and Performance, 1,* 288–299.

Fiske, S. T., & Taylor, S. E. (1984). *Social cognition.* Reading, MA: Addison Wesley.

Friedberg, A. L. (2000). The struggle for mastery in Asia. *Commentary, 110,* 17–26.

Friedberg, A. L. (2005). The future of U.S.-China relations: Is conflict inevitable? *International Security 30,* 7–45.

Frijda, N. H. (1988). The laws of emotion. *American Psychologist, 43,* 349–358.

George, A., & Smoke, R. (1974). *Deterrence in American foreign policy.* New York: Columbia University Press.

Gilovich, T., Griffin, D., & Kahneman, D. (Eds.). (2002). *Heuristics and biases: The psychology of intuitive judgment.* Cambridge: Cambridge University Press.

Glaser, C. L. (1977). The security dilemma revisited. *World Politics, 50,* 171–201.

Glaser, C. L. (1992). Political consequences of military strategy: Expanding and refining the spiral and deterrence models. *World Politics, 44,* 497–538.

Glaser, C. L. (2010). *Rational theory of international politics.* Princeton, NJ: Princeton University Press.

Glaser, C. L., & Kaufman, C. (1988). What is the offense-defense balance and can we measure it? *International Security, 22,* 44–82.

Goldstein, A. L. (2005). *Rising to the challenge: China's grand strategy and international security.* Stanford, CA: Stanford University Press.

Goldstein, A. L. (2007). Power transitions, institutions, and China's rise in East Asia: Theoretical expectations and evidence. *Journal of Strategic Studies, 30,* 639–682.

Green, M. J., & Philips, M. L. (2004). Review: Social threat perception and the evolution of paranoia. *Neuroscience and Biobehavioral Review, 28,* 333–342.

Greenberg, J., Simon, L., Pyszczynski, T., Soloman, S., & Chatel, D. (1992). Terror management and tolerance: Does mortality salience always intensify negative reactions of those who threaten one's world view? *Journal of Personality and Social Psychology, 73*, 5–18.

Gries, P. H. (2004). *China's new nationalism*. Berkeley: University of California Press.

Hall, T. & Ross, A. G. (2011). Mapping affect for IR. Manuscript.

Hastie, R., & Dawes, R. M. (2001). *Rational choice in an uncertain world: The psychology of judgment and decision making*. Thousand Oaks, CA: Sage.

Hatfield, E., Cacioppo, J. T., & Rapson, R. L. (1994). *Emotional contagion: Studies in emotion and social interaction*. New York: Cambridge University Press.

Henrich, J. (2000). Does culture matter in economic behavior? Ultimatum game bargaining among the Machiguenga of the Peruvian Amazon. *American Economic Review, 90*, 973–979.

Higgins, E. T., & Bargh, J. A. (1987). Social cognition and social perception. *Annual Review of Psychology, 38*, 369–425.

Hirt, E. R., & Sherman, S. J. (1985). The role of prior knowledge in explaining hypothetical events. *Journal of Experimental Social Psychology, 21*, 519–543.

Hogarth, R., & Goldstein, W. (Eds.). (1996). *Judgment and decision making: An interdisciplinary reader*. Cambridge: Cambridge University Press.

Hopf, T. (2002). *Social construction of international politics: Identities and foreign policies, Moscow, 1955 and 1999*. Ithaca, NY: Cornell University Press.

Huddy, L., Feldman, S., Taber, C., & Lahav, G. (2005). Threat, anxiety, and support of antiterrorism policies. *American Journal of Political Science, 49*, 593–608.

Hutchison, E., & Bleiker, R. (2008). Emotional reconciliation: Reconstituting identity and community after trauma. *European Journal of Social Theory, 11*, 385–403.

Hymans, J. E. C. (2006). *The psychology of nuclear proliferation: Identity, emotions, and foreign policy*. Cambridge: Cambridge University Press.

Hymans, J. E. C. (2010). The arrival of psychological constructivism. *International Theory, 2*(3), 461–467.

Ilies, R., Wagner, D. T., & Morgeson, F. P. (2007). Explaining affective linkages in teams: Individual differences in susceptibility to contagion and individualism-collectivism. *Journal of Applied Psychology, 92*, 1140–1148.

Jervis, R. (1976). *Perception and misperception in international politics*. Princeton, NJ: Princeton University Press.

Jervis, R. (1978). Cooperation under the security dilemma. *World Politics, 30*, 167–214.

Jervis, R. (1986). Representativeness in foreign policy judgments. *Political Psychology, 7*, 483–505.

Jervis, R. (1988). War and misperception. *Journal of Interdisciplinary History, 18*, 675–700.

Jervis, R. (1992). Political implications of loss aversion. *Political Psychology, 13*, 87–204.

Jervis, R. (2002). Signaling and perception: Drawing inferences and projecting images. In K. R. Monroe (ed.), *Political psychology* (pp. 293–312). Mahwah, NJ: Erlbaum.

Jervis, R., Lebow, R. N., & Stein, J. G. (1985). *Psychology and deterrence*. Baltimore, MD: Johns Hopkins University Press.

Jones, B. D. (1999). Bounded rationality. *Annual Review of Political Science, 2*, 297–321.

Kahneman, D. (2003). A perspective on judgment and choice. *American Psychologist, 58*, 697–720.

Kahneman, D. (2011). *Thinking, Fast and Slow*. New York: Farrar, Strauss and Giroux.

Kahneman, D., Knetsch, J. L., & Thaler, R. H. (1990). Experimental tests of the endowment effect and the Coase theorem. *Journal of Political Economy, 98*, 1325–1348.

Kahneman, D., & Renshon, J. (2007). Why hawks win. *Foreign Policy, 158*, 34–38.

Kahneman, D., Slovic, P., & Tversky, A. (Eds.). (1982). *Judgment under uncertainty: Heuristics and biases.* Cambridge: Cambridge University Press.

Kahneman, D., & Tversky, A. (1972). Subjective probability: A judgment of representativeness. *Cognitive Psychology, 3*, 430–454.

Kahneman, D., & Tverksy, A. (1973). On the psychology of prediction. *Psychological Review, 80*, 237–251.

Kahneman, D., & Tversky, A. (1979). Prospect theory: An analysis of decision under risk. *Econometrica, 47*, 263–291.

Kahneman, D., & Tversky, A. (Eds.). (2000). *Choices, values and frames.* Cambridge: Cambridge University Press and the Russell Sage Foundation.

Koehler, D. J. (1996). A strength model of probability judgments for tournaments. *Organizational Behavior and Human Decision Processes, 66*, 16–21.

Kruglanski, A. W., & Webster, D. M. (1996). Motivated closing of the mind: "Seizing" and "freezing." *Psychological Review, 103*, 263–283.

Kydd, A. (1997a). Game theory and the spiral model. *World Politics, 49*, 371–400.

Kydd, A. (1997b). Sheep in sheep's clothing: Why security seekers do not fight each other. *Security Studies, 7*, 114–155.

Kydd, A. (2005). *Trust and mistrust in international relations.* Princeton, NJ: Princeton University Press.

Lake, D. (2011). Two cheers for bargaining theory: Assessing rationalist explanations of the Iraq war. *International Security, 35*, 7–52.

Lebow, R. N. (2010). *Why nations fight: Past and future motives for war.* Cambridge: Cambridge University Press.

Lebow, R. N., & Stein, J. G. (1994). *We all lost the Cold War.* Princeton, NJ: Princeton University Press.

LeDoux, J. (1996). *The emotional brain: The mysterious underpinnings of emotional life.* New York: Simon and Schuster.

LeDoux, J. (2000). Emotional circuits in the brain. *Annual Review of Neuroscience, 23*, 155–184.

Lerner, J. S., & Keltner, D. (2001). Fear, anger, and risk. *Journal of Personality and Social Psychology, 81*, 146–159.

Lerner, J. S., Small, D. A., & Loewenstein, G. (2004). Heart strings and purse strings: Carryover effects on economic decisions. *Psychological Science, 15*, 337–341.

Levy, J. S. (1997). Prospect theory, rational choice, and international relations. *International Studies Quarterly, 41*, 87–112.

Levy, J. S. (2003). Political psychology and foreign policy. In D. O. Sears, L. Huddy, & R. Jervis (eds.), *Oxford handbook of political psychology* (pp. 253–284). New York: Oxford University Press.

Loewenstein, G. F., Rick, S., & Cohen, J. D. (2008). Neuroeconomics. *Annual Review of Psychology, 59*, 647–672.

Löwenheim, O., & Heimann, G. (2008). Revenge in international politics. *Security Studies, 17*, 685–724.

MacDonald, K. (2008). Effortful control, explicit processing, and the regulation of human evolved predispositions. *Psychological Review, 115*, 1012–1031.

Maoz, I., & McCauley, C. (2009). Threat perceptions and feelings as predictors of Jewish-Israeli support for compromise with Palestinians. *Journal of Peace Research, 46*, 525–539.

March, J. G. (1978). Bounded rationality, ambiguity, and the engineering of choice. *Bell Journal of Economic Management Science, 9,* 587–608.

Markus, H., & Zajonc, R. (1985). The cognitive perspective in social psychology. In G. Lindzey & E. Aronson (eds.), *Handbook of social psychology* (3rd ed., pp. 137–230). New York: Random House.

McDermott, R. (1998). *Risk taking in international relations.* Ann Arbor: University of Michigan Press.

McDermott, R. (2004). The feeling of rationality: The meaning of neuroscientific advances for political science. *Perspectives on Politics, 2,* 691–706.

Mearsheimer, J. (2003). *The tragedy of great power politics.* New York: Norton.

Mercer, J. (1996). *Reputation and international politics.* Ithaca, NY: Cornell University Press.

Mercer, J. (2005). Rationality and psychology in international politics. *International Organization, 59,* 77–106.

Mercer, J. (2010). Emotional beliefs. *International Organization, 64,* 1–31.

Meyer, C. O. (2009). International terrorism as a force of homogenization? A constructivist approach to understanding cross-national threat perceptions and response. *Cambridge Review of International Affairs, 22,* 647–666.

Meyer, C. O., & Miskimmon, A. (2009). Perceptions and response to threats: Introduction. *Cambridge Review of International Affairs, 22,* 625–628.

Neumann, R., & Strack, F. (2000). Mood contagion: The automatic transfer of mood between persons. *Journal of Personality and Social Psychology, 79,* 211–223.

Nisbett, R. E., & Ross, L. (1980). *Human inference: Strategies and shortcomings of social judgment.* Englewood Cliffs, NJ: Prentice-Hall.

Panksepp, J. (1998). *Affective neuroscience: The foundations of human and animal emotions.* New York: Oxford University Press.

Parkinson, B., & Simons, G. (2009). Affecting others: Social appraisal and emotion contagion in everyday decision making. *Personality and Social Psychology Bulletin, 35,* 1071–1084.

Powell, R. (2006). War as a commitment problem. *International Organization, 60,* 169–203.

Press, D. G. (2005). *Calculating credibility: How leaders assess military threats.* Ithaca, NY: Cornell University Press.

Rolls, E. T. (1999). *The brain and emotion.* New York: Oxford University Press.

Ross, A. G. (2006). Coming in from the cold: Constructivism and emotions. *European Journal of International Relations, 12,* 197–222.

Ross, M., & Sicoly, F. (1979). Egocentric biases in availability and attribution. *Journal of Personality and Social Psychology, 37,* 322–336.

Rousseau, D. L. (2006). *Identifying threats and threatening identities.* Stanford, CA: Stanford University Press.

Saurette, P. (2006). You dissin me? Humiliation and post-9/11 global politics. *Review of International Studies, 32,* 495–522.

Schelling, T. C. (1960). *The strategy of conflict.* Cambridge, MA: Harvard University Press.

Schelling, T. C. (1966). *Arms and influence.* New Haven, CT: Yale University Press.

Schwarz, N. (1990). Feelings as information: Informational and motivational functions of affective states. In E. T. Higgins & R. M. Sorrentino (eds.), *Handbook of motivation and cognition: Foundations of social behavior* (pp. 527–561). New York: Guilford Press.

Schwarz, N., & Clore, G. L. (1983). Mood, misattribution, and judgments of well-being: Informative and directive functions of affective states. *Journal of Personality and Social Psychology, 45,* 513–523.

Simon, H. A. (1957). *Models of man.* New York: Wiley.

Sloman, S. A. (1996). The empirical case for two systems of reasoning. *Psychological Bulletin, 119,* 3–22.

Smith, E. R., Seger, C. R., & Mackie, D. M. (2007). Can emotions be truly group level? Evidence regarding four conceptual criteria. *Journal of Personality and Social Psychology, 93,* 431–446.

Stein, A. A. (1982). When misperception matters. *World Politics, 34,* 505–526.

Stein, J. G. (1985). Calculation, miscalculation, and conventional deterrence, II: The view from Jerusalem. In R. Jervis, R. N. Lebow, & J. G. Stein (eds.), *Psychology and deterrence* (pp. 60–88). Baltimore, MD: John Hopkins University Press.

Stein, J. G. (1988). Building politics into psychology: The misperception of threat. *Political Psychology, 9,* 245–271.

Stein, J. G., & Pauly, L. (Eds.). (1992). *Choosing to cooperate: How states avoid loss.* Baltimore, MD: John Hopkins University Press.

Sun, R. (2002). *Duality of the mind.* Mahwah, NJ: Lawrence Erlbaum.

Tang, S. (2009). The security dilemma: A conceptual analysis. *Security Studies, 18,* 587–623.

Taylor, S. E. (1982). The availability bias in social perception and interaction. In D. Kahneman, P. Slovic, & A. Tversky (eds.), *Judgment under uncertainty: Heuristics and biases* (pp. 190–200). Cambridge: Cambridge University Press.

Tetlock, P. E. (1998). Social psychology and world politics. In D. Gilbert, S. Fiske, & G. Lindzey (eds.), *Handbook of social psychology* (4th ed., pp. 868–912). New York: McGraw-Hill.

Tetlock, P. E. (2005). *Expert political judgment: How good is it? How can we know?* Princeton, NJ: Princeton University Press.

Tooby, J., & Cosmides, L. (2003). The evolutionary psychology of the emotions and their relationship to internal regulatory variables. In M. Lewis, J. M. Haviland-Jones, & L. F. Barret (eds.), *The Handbook of Emotions* (3rd ed., pp. 114–137). New York: Guildford Press.

Tversky, A., & Kahneman, D. (1973). Availability: A heuristic for judging frequency and probability. *Cognitive psychology, 5,* 207–232.

Tversky, A., & Kahneman, D. (1974). Judgment under uncertainty: Heuristics and biases. *Science, 185,* 1124–1131.

Tversky, A., & Kahneman, D. (1982). *Judgment under uncertainty: Heuristics and biases.* New York: Cambridge University Press.

Tversky, A., & Kahneman, D. (1983). Extensional vs. intuitive reason: The conjunction fallacy in probability judgment. *Psychological Review, 90,* 293–315.

Tversky, A., & Kahneman, D. (1992). Advances in prospect theory: Cumulative representation of uncertainty. *Journal of Risk and Uncertainty, 5,* 297–323.

Von Winterfeldt, D., & Edwards, E. (1986). *Decision analysis and behavioral research.* New York: Cambridge University Press.

Walt, S. M. (1985). Alliance formation and the balance of world power. *International Security, 9,* 3–43.

Winkielman, P., & Berridge, K. C. (2004). Unconscious emotion. *Current Directions in Psychological Science, 13,* 120–123.

Wohlforth, W. (2009). Unipolarity, status competition, and great power war. *World Politics, 61,* 28–57.

CHAPTER 13

....

CRISIS MANAGEMENT

....

STEPHEN BENEDICT DYSON AND PAUL 'T HART

POLITICAL crises—episodes of threat, uncertainty, and urgency—present a devilish problem: A literal meaning of crisis is "turning point," and the practical experience is one of high stress and complex choices. In crises, then, decision-making is both unusually consequential and unusually difficult.

Under these trying circumstances, is human psychology an aid or a hindrance to good decision-making? The long-dominant "errors and biases" perspective suggests that the influence is malign: the ideal of synoptic rationality is said to be muddled by the introduction of cognitive and affective biases, and the stress of crisis magnifies the problem and raises the specter of disastrous misjudgment. Crisis literature has cataloged the errors made by decision-makers, while prescribing procedures designed to ameliorate the ill effects of human psychology.

Much of this research remains valid and useful, and is covered in depth in the chapters on the psychology of threat perception (Stein, chapter 12, this volume) and foreign policy generally (Levy, chapter 10, this volume), as well as many excellent reviews of the psychology of crisis management (e.g. Holsti, 1989; Jervis, Lebow, & Stein, 1985). In this chapter, though, we aim to move the study of crisis forward. We first offer a schema of types of crisis that is broader than the usual focus upon acute international confrontation, and suggest that tasks of reality testing, sense making, narrative framing, and lesson learning confront decision-makers.

Second, we incorporate work on dual-process models that differentiates between automatic-affective and deliberative-cognitive systems (Chaiken & Trope, 1999; Sloman, 2002). This paradigm portrays human psychology as a mixture of automatic reactions and shortcuts on the one hand, and effortful, comprehensive processing on the other. The picture is more nuanced than the traditional errors-and-biases approach and finds, for example, that emotion is helpful and necessary in cueing effortful processing, and that the stress of crisis can lead to quicker and better decisions. Dual-process models provide a framework for understanding the interplay of cognitions, emotions, and stress that are cued by circumstances of threat, uncertainty, and urgency.

The chapter proceeds as follows. We define the tasks of crisis decision-making, generating a schema that can be applied beyond the foreign policy realm. We then trace the development of a political psychology approach to crisis. The tenets of this are a focus upon decision process as well as outcome, and the treatment of rationality as a heuristic rather than descriptive model of decision-making. This leads, in the balance of the chapter, to investigation of the stress-motivation nexus; cognitive complexity under stress; the use of decision heuristics; the mood and affective state of decision-makers during crises; the impact of specific emotions on crisis response; and an examination of small-group psychology. Throughout, we relate the dual process revolution in social psychology to the field of crisis decision-making, and consider a fuller range of hypotheses than that represented by the errors and bias tradition.

1. CRISES

What distinguishes a state of crisis from business as usual in politics and government? Definitional discussions of crisis and closely associated concepts like "emergency," "disaster," and "catastrophe" have been widespread in a range of social science disciplines (Hermann, 1969; 1972; Brecher, 1979; Rosenthal, Charles, & 't Hart, 1989; Pearson & Clair, 1998; Quarantelli, 1998; Boin, McConnell, t Hart, 2008). Despite ongoing debate at the margins, there is agreement in the literature that events or conditions that are experienced as crises share three characteristics.

First, core values or vital systems of a community are seen as under *threat*. Widely shared values such as safety and security, welfare and health, integrity and fairness can be shattered as a result of (looming) violence, physical destruction, government incompetence, institutional corruption, or other agents of destabilization. Threat perception is subjective and contextual: it cannot be predicted by simply counting the numbers of bodies, jobs, or dollars affected (Cohen, 1980). The anthrax scare and the Washington Beltway snipers caused the death of relatively few people in the fall of 2001, but nevertheless evoked widespread fear among the public and severely affected community life in significant parts of the United States for weeks. A flood killing 100 people may be a routine occurrence in Bangladesh, but would be considered a national crisis in most Western nations. The psychological impact of adverse events is a function of the state of mind of the perceivers of these happenings, as determined by a range of factors including their beliefs about order, normality, and control. These vary widely within and between different individuals and groups, partly depending upon existing levels of preparedness and prior experience with crisis situations (Quarantelli, 1998).

Second, crises are associated with a *sense of urgency*. Governments and bureaucracies can deal with tough problems if they have time to work them through. They commission studies, conduct negotiations, and use trial and error to learn what policies work to tame the problem. When problems escalate very quickly and no time is available, the political system is forced into improvisational mode. While operational agencies like police and the military are generally well equipped to make that transition to real-time response modes, this is much harder for all-round policymakers and policy bureaucracies. A sense of urgency may also be self-generated: in cases of conflict and negotiation, every policymaker who seeks to pressure demonstrators, terrorists, or states by setting a deadline or issuing an ultimatum also puts pressure on him- or herself (Rosenthal et al., 1989). When the deadline approaches with no solution in sight, the pressure to act builds. Sometimes, this mechanism is used deliberately, for example, to soften up parties in international trade negotiation conferences or dispute resolution summits.

Finally, crises are characterized by a high degree of *uncertainty*. The uncertainty pertains to both the nature and the potential consequences of the developing threat: What is happening? How did it happen? What is next? How bad will it be? More importantly, uncertainty clouds the search for solutions: What can we do? What happens if we select this option? How will people respond? The collapse of Lehman Brothers in September 2008 generated acute uncertainty on global markets and forced governments around the world to contemplate grim possibilities concerning the viability of their financial systems and economies. With experts disagreeing about what had happened and what could happen, what were policymakers to think? And yet they were forced to take far-reaching decisions committing billions and billions of tax dollars to try to prop up public confidence over the course of a weekend.

Combining these three features, we speak of crises when events occur that communities and/or their political elites interpret as *a serious threat to the basic structures or fundamental values and norms underpinning the status quo, creating highly uncertain circumstances that call for urgent responses*. Many different phenomena can be experienced as a crisis. For a political psychology approach, it is the perception or internalization of the crisis that is important, rather than the objective seriousness of the situation (Billings, Milburn, & Schaalman, 1980). Panic in a community over a comparatively insignificant threat is still a crisis for policymakers when it generates intense pressure for remedial action (Ben-Yehuda & Goode, 2009). A government that erroneously believes its country is about to be attacked will nevertheless base its actions upon that belief, potentially setting in motion a self-fulfilling prophecy (e.g., Holsti, 1972).

The locus of action (i.e., local-national-international; diplomatic-military; technological-social) and the immediate causes (natural or man-made; human-systemic) of crises can also differ markedly. It is useful to classify crises in terms of the nature of the problem. The classic and most intensely studied category is what we might call *situational* crises where the main challenge is perceived to be responding to havoc inflicted by adverse forces, whether they be the deliberate actions of political opponents or lawbreakers, turbulence in money markets, forces of nature, or human and organizational error in critical infrastructures. But increasingly, analysts have distinguished a further category of critical episodes that we might call *institutional* crises. These occur when the performance of public officeholders, organizations, or governments itself is so widely and vehemently called into question that they interpret the situation as an acute threat to their legitimacy, their political survival, or even the stability of the administrative, political, or constitutional order in which they are embedded. These latter type of threats may be just as real, urgent, and stressful in the minds of (some) policymakers as those associated with violent conflict or natural disaster. Richard Nixon's study *Six Crises* (1962), focused upon what were essentially political crises imperiling his career progress, provides vivid illustrations, as do studies of Nixon's physical and mental condition and capacity for judgment during the height of the Watergate scandal (at the same time as his administration faced a major situational crisis following the outbreak of the 1973 Yom Kippur War in the Middle East) (Ambrose, 1991; Black, 2007; Siniver, 2008).

As table 13.1 suggests, crises that are defined as situational require mainly operational-technical management of their implications. Government is seen as part of the solution, though government elites may be faced with extraordinarily difficult decisions about interpreting signals by adversaries, communicating resolve, controlling the escalation of conflict, mass evacuations of populations, rationing of scarce resources, or the use of emergency bylaws and physical force to maintain or restore order. Institutional crises, in contrast, require strategic-political management to address the illegitimacy of existing practices, policies, and organizations. Government is seen as part of the problem, perhaps even its root. Whereas situational crises may entail a struggle for physical and economic survival of entire communities, institutional crises are about the political survival of elites and organizations.

This distinction is most usefully thought of as a continuum along which particular crisis episodes move over time as events unfold and various parties produce differing accounts of them. One type of crisis may evolve into the other, thus changing the nature of the required response. For example, a situational crisis such as the 9/11 terrorist attacks became an institutional one when it forced onto the agenda urgent questions about the US government's capacity to foresee, forestall, and respond to terrorist phenomena. Urban riots, such as those in London and other UK cities during August 2011, may turn the spotlight onto the unresolved tensions, blatant inequalities, and everyday injustices that low-opportunity, socially stigmatized groups suffer. Even natural disasters such as Hurricane Katrina can become reframed as institutional crises when allegations of government negligence in prevention and preparedness, and incompetence, in-fighting, and indifference in emergency response gain credence in the aftermath (Boin et al., 2008; Boin, McConnell, 't Hart, & Preston, 2010).

2. COPING WITH CRISES: CHALLENGES AND RESPONSES

Once perceptions of crisis take hold, communities and their leaders face a number of response challenges that can be summarized under the rubrics of sense making, decision-making, meaning making, and learning (Boin, 't Hart, Stern, & Sundelius, 2005; 't Hart & Tindall, 2009).

Table 13.1 Situational and Institutional Crises

Situational crises: Scenarios	Institutional crises: Scenarios	Situational crises: Dynamics	Institutional crises: Dynamics
		Play out in the physical world:	Play out in the political world:
Acute	*Acute*	signals, shocks, systems	passions, players, positions
Classic natural disasters	Politicization of ineffective crisis/ emergency prevention, preparedness and response practices	Citizens as victims, audiences	Citizens as advocates, arbiters
Industrial accidents		Media report events	Media frame interpretations
Riots, revolts, revolutions		Key arenas:	
Terrorist attacks	High-impact institutional fraud, waste and abuse	- the field	Key arenas:
Pandemics		- executive government	- the public sphere
International brinkmanship	Elite scandals and "coverups"	- command, control, and coordination centers	- the polity as a whole
Creeping	*Creeping*	Key stakes:	- accountability forums (parliament inquiries, courts)
Tipping points in critical resource depletion	Ethnic ecological, social "time bombs"	- physical damage control	Key stakes:
Toxic dumps	"Permanently failing" organizations	- containing external adversaries	- symbolic damage control
Overcrowded, dilapidated prisons ("powder kegs")	Erosion of trust in public institutions Infrastructural decay	- community recovery	- containing "political" adversaries
		- re-equilibration of systems and relationships	- community anger
			- distribution of political, policy and organizational consequences

2.1. Sense Making: Testing Crisis Realities

Crises, especially in the very early stages, produce vague, ambivalent, and often conflicting signals, which policymakers must interpret as indicative of serious rather than routine problems that can be dealt with using standard processes and procedures. Sense making is about diagnosing the nature of the situation in the face of "unness": unwanted, unpleasant, unplanned, and unexpected circumstances. Policymakers must cognitively "test the realities" of the events as they unfold (Burke & Greenstein, 1989). Leaders need to determine in their own minds the likely level of threat, who or what will be affected, the scope for operational and strategic interventions, and how the crisis is likely to develop before they can decide to take action and communicate to the public and other actors. Signals come from many sources: some loud, some soft, some accurate, some rumor and speculation, and some bearing no relation to reality. How can policymakers judge which is which? How can they extract coherent and credible signals from the noise of crisis? How can they prevent a wholesale collapse of sense making? (Weick, 1993).

2.2. Decision-Making: Shaping Crisis Responses

Responding to crises confronts governments and public agencies with pressing choices amid conflicting values and major political risks: about backing down or stepping up, helping or standing by, doing deals or acting on principle, speaking out or keeping silent, denying or accepting responsibility, using force or persuasion, and so on. For example, in disasters, urgent and legitimate demand for collective resources and special benefits almost always exceeds supply. Moreover, in the heat of an emergency it can be very difficult to discern legitimate from opportunistic and even criminal demands, but the pressure on responsible policymakers to show solidarity and generosity can be immense.

It is these kinds of choices on the edge of peace or war, order or chaos, helping or standing by, and negotiated or imposed conflict resolution that political psychologists study to understand when and how leaders and governments can produce well-considered responses to unsettling, even extreme, events. Consequently, political psychologists have focused on the effects of time pressure on judgment, the use of information and expertise in crisis decision-making, the role of intuition and emotion, factors affecting the quality of group deliberation, and leaders' flexibility and rigidity in making and revising critical decisions.

2.3. Meaning Making: Framing Crisis Narratives

In times of crisis, public leaders must not just make sense of events in their own minds as a precondition for purposeful action; they must also make meaning for their constituencies, the nation and sometimes the wider world. Meaning-making efforts are aimed at quelling public uncertainty by producing an authoritative account of what is happening, what caused it to happen, and what action needs to be taken. Meaning making involves several layers of discursive reconstruction and public persuasion. First and foremost there is the need to communicate the *significance* of the events: how bad is the situation, who will be affected, how long will it last? In addition, leaders need to explain the *causes* of the events, as many people will wonder how and why such unpalatable events could occur in the first place.

This puts leaders in a delicate spot. One of their chief roles is to protect public order, health and safety, and the national interest. The very occurrence of crisis imperils this role, particularly in the event of institutional crises ('t Hart, 1993, p. 39). The public, the media, and political opponents want to know what went wrong and who should be held responsible. Causal frames that emphasize factors deemed to be foreseeable and controllable focus blame on identifiable individuals and the policies they embody.

Frames that attribute the cause of events to unforeseeable or uncontrollable forces get policymakers off the accountability hook and deflate the case for sanction or policy change (Bovens & 't Hart, 1996). Crafting a particular interpretation of a crisis can also be of strategic use to policymakers. Once a dominant "crisis narrative" takes hold, it can be an important force for change in policy arenas that are normally stabilized by the forces of path dependence, inheritance, and veto playing (Hay, 2002; Kuipers, 2006).

In this context of public anxiety and political risk and opportunity, leaders must give meaning to the unfolding crisis. Meaning-making efforts are complicated because of the need to persuade publics that are already aroused and opinionated. Policymakers must avoid the danger of their public meaning-making distorting their own, private sense-making processes. Publicly committing to an interpretation of events triggers cognitive biases that bolster that interpretation in private cognition, potentially leading to cognitive closure and the discounting of new information (Janis & Mann, 1977). Moreover, in the age of global and social media, policymakers do not have a monopoly on framing the crisis narrative. Opposition to and distrust in government do not necessarily disappear just because a crisis has arisen. Actors inside and outside government will strive to have their particular interpretations of the crisis accepted in the media and by the public as the authoritative account. Silencing or crowding out such voices is not only unacceptable in a democracy, it has become nearly impossible given the prevalence of social media.

The study of public meaning-making in crises has been dominated by students of political communication, social conflict, and policy dynamics. They have developed a separate body of knowledge on crisis rhetoric and crisis exploitation focusing on the conditions under which persuasive mechanisms such as framing, impression management, image repair, fear appeals, stereotyping, and apology affect public perceptions of a crisis and work politically for or against those who employ them (Masters & 't Hart, 2012). International relations scholars have demonstrated that leaders sometimes initiate or verbally escalate external confrontations in order to promote domestic political cohesion, deflect attention from current controversies and scandals (now often referred to as the "Wag the Dog" effect, following the 1997 Hollywood pastiche of this type of diversionary leader behavior; see also Levy, 1988), or simply create a justification for a war they had already made up their minds to wage (Lebow, 1981).

2.4. Learning: Distilling Crisis Implications

Postcrisis learning is an exercise in retrospective sense-making and accountability involving many unanswerable counterfactual questions, taking place in an often politically charged environment in which actors are primarily motivated by the desire to avoid blame. The more painful the crisis, the stronger the imperative to avoid its repetition ("never again"). Yet determining what the right lessons are and what level of investment is warranted to learn them is a major leadership challenge (Neustadt & May, 1986). It is a political as much as an analytical process. Policymakers have to balance the necessity of managing accountability and blame in charged postcrisis political arenas with their stewardship role of making it safe for their own organizations to engage in the rigorous soul-searching that learning from crisis requires. The dilemma is real: research suggests that hasty symbolic gestures and policy overreaction in the wake of crisis can preempt learning (Rose & Davies, 1994); that the lessons of history can be invoked rhetorically to serve strategic purposes (Levy, 1994; Levy, chapter 10, this volume;; and that truly debating the hard questions in internal learning exercises can pose political and legal liability risks that policymakers are keen to avoid (Boin et al., 2008).

3. The Development of a Political Psychology Approach to Crises

What constitutes a distinctively political-psychological approach to the study of crisis management? Political psychologists have focused upon the process of decision-making as much as the outcome of the crisis, and have utilized rational utility models as baselines rather than descriptively accurate accounts of choice processes. While we believe, as stated above, the way forward for studying crises comes from a broad conception of the domains in which they occur, many of the examples in what follows are from foreign policy, reflecting the dominant focus of the existing literature.

3.1. Decision-Making

The decision-making approach takes individuals in executive positions as constitutive of the state (Snyder, Bruck, & Sapin, 1962). The spotlight is on how these individuals perceive, experience, and respond to the crisis situation (Snyder & Diesing, 1977, pp. 282–418). This focus upon individuals and their subjective approach to policy problems provides a natural entry point for the political psychology study of crises (Falkowski, 1978). Most fundamentally, the study of decision-making from a psychological viewpoint requires a study of process, not just outcome. Indeed, as George Ball famously put it, in many cases "[t]he process was the author of the policy" (quoted in Holsti, 1972, p. 204).

Other approaches, drawing upon models of rationality, regard the process of decision-making as relatively unproblematic and hence irrelevant to what happens. Understand the stimulus, and you can understand the response. Nothing of interest happens between stimulus and response. Graham Allison's *Essence of Decision* (1971) was among the pathbreaking works (along with Snyder et al., 1962) that sensitized scholars to the importance of process. Allison, of course, famously set a model of simple stimulus–response rationality in competition with models of stimulus–*process*–response in explaining decision-making during the Cuban Missile Crisis. Allison did not deploy models drawing upon psychological variables (for which he has been criticized, see Kellerman, 1983), but his contribution was to highlight the necessity of understanding decision-making process in order to account for policy choice and crisis outcome.

3.2. Rationality

After Allison, political psychology studies of crisis have used rational choice theories as a foil—a first cut that probably will not suffice as an explanation but will help to identify what is to be explained. Whatever looks puzzling or odd from a simple stimulus / response rationality model is fodder for investigation using the tools of political psychology. This is true in terms of both crisis outcome and decision processes within crises. Models of utility maximization provide a baseline for understanding policy outcomes. If the outcome was suboptimal, perfect rationality cannot have held. The question becomes whether psychological approaches can explain the outcome more accurately.

Just as importantly, the stipulations of procedural rationality—gathering all pertinent information, systematically considering each piece of information in an unbiased manner, rendering global judgments with strict ranking of policy choices—allow for an understanding of a normatively "perfect" policy process and allow us to recognize deviations from it (Schafer & Chrichlow, 2010; see also Redlawsk & Lau, chapter 5, this volume; Chong, chapter 4, this volume). Was relevant information missed? Was it processed in an idiosyncratic manner? Was a policy chosen because it fulfilled one goal that had become valued above all others for no good reason? These are dynamics that psychology recognizes and can explain.

As a matter of intellectual history, much of the initial impetus for the political psychological study of crisis came from a belief that rationality models were not only substantively incorrect, but that some of their policy implications were profoundly dangerous (Lebow, 1987). Proponents of rational deterrence models such as Thomas Schelling had, so students of the burgeoning political psychology field believed, sold an overly sanguine view of the workings of rationality in crisis to decision-makers such as John Foster Dulles (Holsti, 1980, p. 670; Jervis et al., 1985). An interesting abstract model had begun to be prescribed as a normative guide to actual policy decisions (George & Smoke, 1974, pp. 58–87). The prescriptions of models like Schelling's—such as to make the most aggressive deterrent commitment possible, because the other side would calculate that to challenge that commitment was irrational—were likely, once one understood psychological processes of threat perception and conflict escalation, to be extraordinarily dangerous (Jervis, 1976; Lebow & Stein, 1994).

However, this focus on disabusing the dominant policy narrative of the easy assumptions of rationality during crisis—combined with the state of social psychology at the time that classic works on crises were written (the dominant paradigms being the "cognitive miser," seeking to expend as few cognitive resources as possible, and the "naive scientist," seeking to understand cause and effect but with a shaky grasp of scientific method—see Larson, 1985)—contributed to a narrow and hypercritical agenda among political psychologists. Rationality models saw crisis decision-making as easy and the decision-maker as irrelevant, so early political psychology models countered that crisis decision-making was difficult and the decision-maker was deeply flawed, riddled by errors-and-biases.

There is often a lag between the literatures in psychology proper and political psychology. Many political scientists do not engage with new intellectual currents in psychology, but rely instead on classics in political science that have a psychology focus. The errors and biases approach, a derivative of the cognitive miser and naive scientist paradigms, persists in political science—or at least in foreign policy analysis and studies of crisis decision-making—while it has been substantially modified in the parent discipline of psychology.

It is now time to take account of developments in dual-process accounts of psychology and broaden our hypotheses on the impact of human psychology on crisis decision-making. We should stress how human psychology can be adaptive to the challenges of crisis management, rather than assume a perfectly rational ideal to which the human element contributes only error (Snyder & Lopez, 2002; Mercer, 2005). To take the most obvious example of the importance of so doing, rationality, we now know, is not harmed by emotion but is impossible without it. Emotionless people (those who have suffered damage to the relevant parts of the brain) are unmotivated to make decisions of any kind—sensible or otherwise. They spend weeks pondering trivialities such as the best time of day to get a haircut. People without emotion are inert, not efficient (Damasio, 1994; Brader & Marcus, chapter 6, this volume; Stein, chapter 12, this volume). Not only is it intellectually moribund to castigate decision-makers for psychological violations of rationality, the very concept of human psychology and rationality as in opposition to one another is a neurobiological nonsense.

Social psychology has progressed from seeing rationality as a normative goal and benchmark against which to measure error, to seeing rationality as essentially a function of what makes most sense given the decision task at hand and the resources of the decision-maker (Fiske & Taylor, 2007; Stanovich & West, 2002). Studies of crisis decision-making should make the same move, and we offer a guide to doing so.

4. DUAL-PROCESS MODELS AND CRISIS DECISION-MAKING

The dual-process view of the mind (also variously referred to as "dual mode" or "two systems") identifies automatic, rapid, and effortless features as well as more conscious, deliberative, and effortful features (Evans, 2008; Dijksterhuis & Aarts, 2010). Two systems of reasoning are posited: System 1, which responds rapidly, automatically, and is largely affect-driven, and System 2, which is slower, deliberative, and cognitive (Sloman, 2002; Fiske & Taylor, 2007, pp. 25–50).

Psychologists disagree over whether the two processes operate sequentially or in parallel (Gilbert, 1999). Affect enters the process almost immediately on reception of an environmental stimulus, and cues various concepts and associations before conscious consideration has begun (Zajonc, 1980). Indeed, much of psychological life is preconscious and nondeliberative (Bargh & Chartrand, 1999). If initial system 1 processing reveals a routine stimulus that requires no action or for which a satisfactory response is readily available, then the level of conscious cognitive deliberation may be slight (so-called "mindless" low-effort processing, or System 1 dominance). If, however, the initial rapid appraisal indicates danger, novelty, or some other aspect requiring attention, then more effortful conscious and "mindful" processes are cued (System 2 takes over, enriching, modifying or rejecting the efforts of System 1). Many researchers into these dual processes suggest that the level of cognitive effort expended is determined by a sufficiency principle—individuals will seek to match the cognitive strategy and level of effort to the requirements and importance of the decision task (Chen & Chaiken, 1999, p. 74).

The conscious part of deliberation can be deeply influenced by the rapid and automatic initial response, which is to say that we cannot just study cold cognition as a proximate cause of behavior and claim explanatory completeness. The errors and biases approach was based upon the assumption that conscious cognition was the cause of behavior. But given that System 1 processes are often preconscious, decision-makers may be unaware of the extent to which the effortful and careful deliberations they believe constitute their response are in fact shaped by rapid reactions occurring milliseconds after an environmental stimulus is received (Bargh & Chartrand, 1999; Dijksterhuis & Aarts, 2010).

The importance for the study of crises is that these types of high-stakes situations provide stimuli that will shape the responses of the dual systems. System 1 processing alone—the type of automaticity suited for routine tasks—is unlikely to characterize crisis decision-making. Crises provide the motivational cues and task complexity that should lead us to expect effortful System 2 processing. However, the initial affective associations and automatic encoding of stimuli will continue to play a role in the effortful deliberation. If time pressure and stress become acute, System 2 resources may become depleted, and System 1 may reenter the frame through the use of decision heuristics and emotional reactions as cues to choice. Decision-making in crises, then, should be a fertile area of application for the newer dual process psychological models.

5. STRESS

The crucial link between dual-process models and political crises is stress. Most research on stress begins with the Yerkes-Dodson law on arousal and performance (Yerkes

& Dodson, 1908; Hermann, 1979). The Yerkes-Dodson model posited an "inverted U-curve" of the impact of stress on performance. As stress increases from low to moderate levels, performance improves as attention is given to the task at hand. As stress moves from moderate to high levels, performance declines as the decision maker becomes overwhelmed. The Yerkes-Dodson law can be re-interpreted in light of the dual-process perspective. Low levels of stress provide little motivation to engage in much cognitive activity, and so decision-making is automatic or partially automatic (System 1). A moderate amount of stress provides the motivation for effortful cognition and a thorough consideration of actions (System 2). High stress may overwhelm effortful cognition, and System 1– processes such as emotions and heuristics can re-enter decision-making. At extreme stress levels, the decision-maker becomes overwhelmed and performance collapses (Holsti, 1972, p. 12; Post, 1991, p. 474; Lebow, 1987, pp. 144–147).

Consistent with the general focus of political psychology on mistakes and failures, much work has assumed the extreme case—that crises overwhelm decision-makers—and searched the record for correspondingly poor decision-making performance. Irving Janis, who had a career-long interest in decision-making under stress, provided the most extensive consideration of these processes with his "conflict-theory model" (Janis & Mann, 1977).

Janis was interested in when individuals made decisions according to rational postulates versus when their decision processes were defective, increasing the likelihood of suboptimal outcomes. Individuals faced with potentially stressful stimuli quickly appraise three key variables, Janis argued: are there serious risks associated with changing course and/or doing nothing? Is there a realistic hope of finding a better alternative than those immediately available? Is there sufficient time to carefully search for and evaluate alternatives? The answers to these questions, Janis argued, determined which of five patterns of decision-making will predominate:

1. Do nothing ("unconflicted inertia")
2. Do the obvious thing ("unconflicted change")
3. Avoid the decision ("defensive avoidance")
4. Panic ("hypervigilance")
5. Respond rationally ("vigilance")

For Janis, decision patterns 1 and 2 carried potential danger due to their blasé, nature; pattern 3 solved little and just wasted time, quite commonly resulting in the frantic, disastrous, pattern 4. Here, a hypervigilant decision-maker, out of time and options, "impulsively seizes upon a hastily contrived solution that seems to offer immediate relief" (Janis, 1993, pp. 71–75). Janis's model had the virtue of focusing attention on decision process as an influence on outcome, and on the fact that decision-makers have to solve not just the objective problem (which is the facet stressed by rational and purely cognitive theory), but also to manage their internal state and potential feelings of panic, shame, humiliation, and regret. Janis's theory remains broadly useful and mirrors prominent psychological theories of dealing with crises in personal health and life circumstances such as Coping Theory (Folkman, Lazarus, Dunkel-Schetter, DeLongis, & Gruen, 1986) and Crisis Decision Theory (Sweeny, 2008).

Yet Janis's work was focused upon the rationality versus human psychology-as-disaster dichotomy that has been prevalent in the field. When he brings emotion into the framework, it is as a solely negative factor. We can broaden our view of the impact of stress by incorporating newer psychological literature. One amendment is the finding that the total collapse of a decision-maker's ability to cope is probably quite rare (George, 1986, p. 531). Modifying the inverted U-curve model in light of newer research, it seems that there is a large set of fairly adaptive responses between the optimum high point of the performance curve (under moderate stress), and the collapse of performance at extreme stress levels.

Dual-process models would suggest that as stress increases beyond a moderate level while the person is tackling complex tasks, System 2 resources become depleted. The affective System 1 reenters decision-making as a supplement, providing simpler, faster decision strategies (Kahneman & Frederick, 2002). System 1 acts as a crutch that bolsters the sagging System 2 and prevents decision-makers from collapsing in a paroxysm of panic or paralysis.

For example, there is evidence for increased reliance on heuristics (a decision aid discussed more extensively later in the chapter) while under high levels of stress. Thus, processing is "mindless," automatic, and heuristic-driven at low levels of stress, "mindful" and comprehensive at moderate levels, and returns to a partially heuristic-driven state under high stress. The dual systems bolster one another at high levels of stress, preventing total collapse of performance.

Providing support for this hypothesis, Kassam, Koslov, and Mendes (2009, p. 1395) found that the ability to modify initial diagnoses reached through the application of heuristics was diminished by high levels of stress. Absent stress, decision-makers could expend cognitive effort to make the estimates provided by an initial heuristic more precise, but under stress they had fewer cognitive resources and so relied more fully on the anchor provided by the unadjusted heuristic. As explained below, however, heavy reliance upon an initial heuristic does not necessarily result in a worse decision.

A second new area of research questions the universality of the Yerkes-Dodson view of stress. While much research assumes this "inverted U-curve" to be applicable to all decision-makers, there are important findings that suggest different individuals react to stress in different ways. Post (1991, p. 476) made this point some time ago, suggesting that tolerance for the stress and uncertainty of crises varies considerably by personality type. Post, though, focused entirely upon the negative side of the ledger: the degree to which extreme types—the compulsive, narcissistic, and paranoid personalities—were especially prone to suboptimal behavior during crises. Post's focus on negative personality types and stress has been broadened by Robins & Dorn (1993), who suggest that some political leaders flourish under high stress and actively seek it out. They develop a typology of leaders and stress: *sturdy warriors* cope well with and enjoy stressful crises, *battle-hungry warriors* are compulsively drawn to crises but may not be as skillful at handling stress as they believe (Richard Nixon being the exemplar), while *frail warriors* are overwhelmed by and unable to cope with stressful situations.

Research based upon the "Big Five" personality characteristics found that the strongest predictor of negative stress reactions was neuroticism. Neurotics perceived more situations as stressful, perceived stress more intensely, and coped less well with the stressful situations (Suls, 2001). An individual's capacity for cognitive complexity, treated in depth below, is also of relevance to coping with stress. Kowert (2002, p. 18) found evidence that closed-minded decision-makers suffered performance deterioration at lower levels of stress than open-minded decision-makers. Interestingly, several researchers have noted that John F. Kennedy's level of performance was maintained if not improved as the Cuban Missile Crisis reached the point of maximum danger (Blight, 1992; Lebow & Stein, 1994, pp. 331–338).

Kemeny (2003) and Folkman and Moskowitz (2000) point out that whether stress is helpful or not depends upon the interaction of the degree of stress with the resources of the decision-maker. When a decision-maker's resources are sufficient to cope with the level of stress, they enter a "challenge" state of arousal and motivation that is useful in dealing with the situation. When a decision-maker's resources are overwhelmed by the magnitude of the stress, they enter a "threat" state that can lead to the defensive coping pathologies identified by Janis. The key resources for the decision-maker are cognitive capacity and perceived degree of control over the situation—the higher the perceived control, the more likely it is that stress will provoke a challenge rather than threat state.

These findings offer some explanation for what had for some time been a disjunction between the theorized impact of stress on crisis decision-making and the observed effects. The most focused series of studies on stress and crises—the volumes of the *International Crisis Behavior* series—had shown that stress often improved performance, and that observed decision-making pathologies such as those of Hitler at Stalingrad where probably due to preexisting personality or situational factors rather than stress per se (Brecher, 1980; Richardson, 1988). Given the variability in the impact of stress on decision-making identified within the context of dual-process models, these empirical results are less surprising in retrospect.

6. Cognitive Complexity

With the onset of crisis a rapidly increasing cognitive load begins to press upon the decision-maker. Information-processing tasks accumulate, new information is received at a high rate, and decision deadlines loom (Suedfeld, 1992, p. 437). Premature cognitive closure—the failure to perceive alternative points of view and to seek out the information necessary to evaluate them—has been identified as "the most widespread and fundamental decision-making problem" during crises (Lebow, 1981, p. 293). Catastrophic cognitive closure comes, for example, when the decision-maker sees war as inevitable and stops trying to avoid it. What if war wasn't inevitable, and keeping options open would have led to a solution?

Succumbing to cognitive closure, or being able to keep options open, is a feature of different levels of cognitive complexity, which alongside stress may be the most extensively studied psychological factor influencing crisis decisions.

Lower complexity entails seeing fewer dimensions and nuances in the environment. This has a wide variety of implications: narrowed information search, discounting of information inconsistent with preexisting views, encoding information into fewer and starker categories, holding views with certainty, and reliance on a single schema and action-script when determining responses to stimuli. As complexity increases, the individual perceives a greater variety and subtlety of actors, motivations, issues, and ideas. The person searches for longer, and from a wider variety of sources for relevant information. Their cognitive architecture incorporates a greater number of schema with more connections between them. The decision-maker moves comfortably between different levels of abstraction when thinking about a situation. Categories resemble fuzzy-sets rather than sharply distinct boxes, and action-scripts are composed of overlapping, integrated responses.

Cast in the light of dual-process theories, higher complexity can be seen as associated with effortful, System 2 processing. Lower complexity could be an indicator of System 1 processing: the automatic application of well-learned schematic responses, or the application of simplified heuristics under conditions of task complexity and stress.

M. Hermann's (2003) *conceptual complexity* and Suedfeld's (2010) *integrative complexity* are the major research programs in this area. They are separated by two differences. The first is definitional—is complexity a matter simply of perceiving differentiated aspects of the environment ("there are three opinions on this issue"), or is the degree to which differentiated aspects are reintegrated also relevant ("the three opinions can be reconciled when we consider the underlying problem")? Hermann's measure focuses solely on differentiation while, as the name implies, the Suedfeld construct considers reintegration to be a feature of higher complexity.

The second difference concerns the "state versus trait" debate. Is complexity, as the Hermann construct assumes, a broadly stable trait component of individual personality, varying from situation to situation within a truncated range around a chronic level? Or is complexity, as Suedfeld avers, a highly variable state affected strongly by situational factors such as stress, personal investment in the situation, and cognitive load? Both constructs have have been applied with some success to crisis decision-making (Dyson & Preston, 2006, pp. 267–269; Suedfeld, 2010)..

Viewing complexity as a chronic state—perhaps even a facet of personality—leads to the hypothesis that individuals with differing levels of complexity will handle crises in fundamentally different ways. Dyson used the Iraq decision-making of President George W. Bush (lower complexity) and Secretary of Defense Donald Rumsfeld (higher complexity) as a natural experiment—two leaders with different levels of complexity dealing with the same policy issues—and found the expected variation in both policy choice and decision style (Dyson, 2009a). Where Bush was definitive, Rumsfeld would vacillate. Following the emergence of the Iraq insurgency, Bush cried "Bring 'em on" while Rumsfeld asked aides for the dictionary definitions of "insurgency, guerilla war, and belligerency"—being sure that calibrating the terminology was an important starting point in dealing with the problem (Dyson, forthcoming). A study of a single leader across multiple crises—former British prime minister Margaret Thatcher—found an invariant low level of complexity and the corresponding behaviors (Dyson, 2009b). According to one of her ministers, the expectation of a Thatcher cabinet meeting was not that there would be a nuanced discussion of the views of ministerial colleagues, but rather "tremendous battle lines will be drawn up and everyone who doesn't fall into line will be hit on the head" (Dyson, 2009b, p. 33). This lowered tolerance for conflicting opinions is characteristic of lower complexity leaders.

Suedfeld's *integrative complexity* is a tracking approach that expects to observe significant variability in complexity levels over very short periods of time, as individuals manage the cognitive resources they have at their disposal(Suedfeld, 1992). A wide variety of individuals dealing with both personal and political crises have been studied, and the key findings are these:

1. Complexity drops prior to the onset of war for the initiating side. The side that is attacked exhibits no drop prior to war, but does see a drop after hostilities begin (Suedfeld & Bluck, 1988).
2. Maintaining higher levels of complexity increases the chances of a crisis being resolved through negotiation rather than violence (Suedfeld & Tetlock, 1977).
3. Military leaders able to maintain higher complexity tend to be more successful in battle (Suedfeld, Corteen, & McCormick, 1986).
4. Political leaders able to maintain higher complexity in crises have a greater chance of remaining in office for unusually long time-periods (Wallace & Suedfeld, 1988).
5. As crises intensify, complexity tends to decrease. This is referred to as the "disruptive stress hypothesis," and posits that crises overwhelm an individual's cognitive resources, leading to lowered complexity as a coping mechanism. While some support has been found for this effect (Wallace, Suedfeld, & Thachuk, 1993) there have also been contraindications (Levi & Tetlock, 1980).

7. HEURISTICS

Under crisis conditions, decision-makers need to cope with a great deal of information. Heuristics—shortcuts for identifying the core features of a situation while ignoring peripheral features—are necessary. Tversky and Kahneman's seminal article (1974) identified three major heuristics (availability, representativeness, and anchoring-and-adjustment) that have been the focus of much attention. In fact, many political psychologists continue to utilize Tversky and Kahneman's three examples of heuristics as if they were exhaustive of the concept, whereas there are a multitude of possible heuristics across every human decision situation: the term merely denotes a decision strategy that focuses attention on part of the problem and ignores other aspects. (On heuristics see also Redlawsk & Lau, chapter 5, this volume; Taber & Young, chapter 17, this volume.)

The traditional thrust of the heuristics-in-crises work has been that heuristics purchase speed and conserve cognitive resources, but do so at the price of accuracy (Mercer, 2005, p. 87). The new "fast and frugal" perspective on heuristics overturns this assumption. In certain environments characterized by information scarcity, time pressure, and information redundancy (many pieces of information point toward a similar conclusion), simple heuristic strategies such as "take the best" single cue and make a decision without collecting more information can represent the optimal strategy (Gigerenzer, Czerlinski, & Martignon, 2002).

The key question concerning heuristics, then, is not, how can policymakers avoid being led astray by them, but rather *under what circumstances are heuristics necessary, acceptable, or even superior alternatives to comprehensive information processing?* (Gigerenzer & Gaissmaier, 2011). Gerd Gigerezer argues for resituating the study of heuristics within a paradigm of "ecological rationality": "A heuristic is ecologically rational to the degree that it is adapted to the structure of the environment" (Gigerenzer, Todd, & ABC Research Group, 1999, p. 13). Crucially, heuristics that are ecologically rational are close to equally accurate if not superior to the most stringent "rational choice" decision strategy.

In the crisis in Iraq following the 2006 Samarra mosque bombing and descent into civil war, President Bush employed a simple heuristic as a decision aid: withdrawal is not an option. This heuristic eliminated the majority of options proposed at the time and stimulated the generation of a "surge" plan that eventually reduced the level of violence. While this heuristic violated many principles of a rational choice approach to decision-making, the policy outcome was positive—in fact it achieved a better policy result than would the recommendations of the much-feted Iraq Study Group, which had engaged in a more comprehensive and leisurely review of information and options (Dyson, 2010–2011).

This new approach to heuristics can be helpful in understanding not only the temptation but also the variable success of decision-making through the use of analogy during international crises (Khong, 1992; Neustadt & May, 1986; Levy, chapter 10, this volume). Decision-makers are drawn toward seeking to interpret a current situation in terms of a similar situation from the past and often use the "lessons" of the past to guide their expectations and actions in the present (Houghton, 1998). Much work on analogical reasoning has focused upon the instances where policymakers were led astray during crises, often relying upon the availability heuristic (drawing analogies from those events they most easily recalled rather than those that were most appropriate) and the representativeness heuristic (assuming that an event of the past was representative of a whole class of events, and so the past event could be applied to the current circumstance). In particular, the ubiquitous "Munich analogy," which counsels that instances of aggression must be met firmly now in order to avoid a more costly stand later, has been linked to subrational crisis decision-making and/or manipulative use for policy justification purposes in the Vietnam War (Khong, 1992) and post-9/11 foreign policy (Record, 2008).

That said, decision-makers often use analogies that are appropriate and helpful. The most famous example of this is perhaps President Kennedy's analogizing between the outbreak of the First World War (he had recently read Barbara Tuchman's argument in *The Guns of August* that the war was inadvertent, a result of poor crisis management in July 1914) and the October 1962 Cuban Missile Crisis. Kennedy drew upon the lessons of 1914 and exercised supreme caution in 1962. The analogy sensitized him to ignore parts of the situation that were irrelevant—the differences in the machinery of war, for example—and focus on the core feature of the risk of military procedures leading both sides into conflict. The analogy was, then, "ecologically rational" and arguably superior to a full and leisurely consideration of every facet of the information and every available strategy (Dyson & Preston, 2006).

Returning to the dual-process frame, heuristics should be most prevalent for low stress, System 1 decision-making, and for high-stress decision-making where deliberative System 2 resources have been overwhelmed (that is to say, heuristic-based decision-making occurs at both low and high levels of stress, although for different reasons). In moderate stress circumstances, heuristics may still play a role, but they are likely to provide initial framings that are carefully modified by deliberative "adjustment" processes, tweaking the heuristic frame in accordance with the nuance of the situation (Epley & Gilovich, 2001). Interestingly, although the original Kahneman and Tversky discussion of heuristics focused almost entirely on cognition—representing the dominant approach in social psychology at the time—there have been moves to incorporate affective processes into the heuristic research program. The "affect heuristic," wherein emotions and moods become informative decision cues, is a fertile area of research for crisis scholars (Slovic et al., 2002). With the affect heuristic in operation, feelings become information about what to do (Schwartz, 2002).

8. Emotions and Emotional States during Crises

Josef Stalin, according to political psychologist Raymond Birt, followed the classic paranoid depressive response to receiving devastating information (Birt, 1993). When Hitler invaded the USSR, Stalin retreated psychologically more rapidly than his battered troops retreated physically. He cycled, Birt argues, through feelings of victimization, depression, revenge plotting, and, finally, getting even. Stalin's idiosyncratic behavior led to an extended period of chaos as Soviet forces lacked strategic direction from their supreme commander. British prime minister Anthony Eden, who suffered from depression exacerbated by chronic illness, also exhibited erratic decision-making during the Suez crisis of 1956. Jerrold Post drew strong predictions about Iraq president Saddam Hussein's likely behavior during the crisis leading to the first Gulf War through developing a diagnosis of the Iraqi leader as a malignant narcissist prone to emotional grandiosity (Post, 1991; chapter 15, this volume).

In important episodes of crisis decision-making, then, the emotional state of the decision-maker is a major determinant of how they cope. Earlier treatment of these issues—as illustrated in the three examples above—focused on only part of the universe of possibilities: the impact of chronically negative moods (and even mental illnesses) such as depression and paranoia on crisis performance. The major hypotheses concerned the erratic behavior and decisional paralysis that would afflict a crisis manager beset with these conditions.

Studies of crisis management can broaden their hypotheses on affective states and crisis decision-making from this purely negative focus. We know, for example, that a person's baseline or default mood is not neutral, but slightly positive, and that this "Pollyanna effect" causes negative information to stand out as it differs from the norm (Matlin & Stang, 1978). This is an evolutionarily adaptive reaction as it ensures that negative information—such as the onset of a crisis—is less likely to be missed by the decision-maker and more likely, as something new and discrepant in the environment, to cue effortful deliberative processes. In fact, the desire to restore mood to a positive state is a motivational stimulus to solving the crisis (Fiske, 1980). This is a paradigmatic example of the interaction between System 1 and System 2 processes, and one that is highly relevant to crisis decision-making.

Affective state also bears upon decision-making style (Bodenhausen et al., 2001). Individuals in a good mood exhibit more creative and flexible decision-making. Individuals feeling sad or anxious tend to be more careful, cautious, and detail oriented in their decision-making: "happier moods promote a greater focus on the forest and sadder moods a greater focus on the trees" (Gasper & Clore, 2002, p. 34). In terms of crisis management, of course, it is not clear that we should necessarily prefer creative, flexible decision-making over cautious, detail-oriented decision-making. It is reasonable to hypothesize, given that crises almost by definition indicate something is amiss and are likely to shift a decision-maker's mood state in an initially negative direction, that crisis decision-making as affected by mood will be more cautious and careful than noncrisis decision-making. Crises that end with a particularly virtuoso display of creative, nonconventional thinking, however, would be good candidates for an investigation focused upon the affective mood-state of the decision-makers at the crucial point.

The emotions literature should be of great interest to students of crises. It is however, a challenging area of psychology to apply. Emotions are not directly observable and their effects can be hard to distinguish from those of cold cognitions predicting the same behaviors. Within the parent discipline of psychology, the literature on emotions is disparate and uneven, depriving us of a body of settled theory to draw upon (Fiske & Taylor, 2007, p. 311).

Emotions can be of relevance to crisis decision-making in two ways. First, as discussed above, emotion and cognition are essentially intertwined. Affect prompts effortful cognitive operations. As Izard (2009, p. 18) points out, the most basic emotion is that of being interested in what is occurring. If we find a situation uninteresting, we do not expend cognitive resources upon it. Second, specific emotions can be cued by the special features of a crisis situation. Very basic emotions with evolutionary and biological roots—such as fear and anger—can play an important role in crisis management (Izard, 2009, p. 7). Challenge and threat as motivational states are accompanied by affective responses, according to Smith and Kirby (2001, p. 83). Threat provokes fear, anxiety, and sadness, whereas challenge may produce anger. Folkman and Moskowitz (2000, p. 117) also find that the affective experience of crisis is not necessarily, as we might expect, centered upon the negative emotions of sadness, despair, and frustration. Indeed, they endorse a bipolar view of emotion that suggests that the experience of stress can cue the positive emotions of elation, joy, and well-being. A challenge state—high arousal in a circumstance where individuals believe they can cope with and overcome the situation—is especially likely to produce elation.

The emotional stimulus of *fear* is especially potent, and of great relevance to international politics. The political psychologist Jacques Hymans (2006) has linked the experience of fear by high-level decision-makers to three tendencies. First, fear leads to inflated threat assessments and a heightened sense of danger in the external environment. Second, fear leads to lowered cognitive complexity. Perceptions become more absolute when fear is driving cognitive processing (the intervention of a System 1 process on the operations of System 2). Third, fear produces a desire to take action. Fear is an uncomfortable emotional state, and it motivates the decision-maker to seek to escape the feeling. Taking some action—any action—can offer the fearful decision-maker a potential escape, leading to a preference for quick decisions over lengthy deliberation. (For other perspectives on responses to fear and anger see Brader & Marcus, chapter 6, this volume; Stein, chapter 12, this volume.)

The much-studied principle of "loss aversion," one of the tenets of prospect theory (McDermott, 1998; Levy, chapter 10, this volume), may have roots in the emotion of fear. Prospect theory's relevance to crisis decision-making is the prediction that, when faced with a loss relative to a reference point (i.e., precrisis situation), decision-makers will become risk acceptant in seeking to restore the status quo. Research driven by the study of economic losses has posited "preconscious encoding" in situations that are antecedent to loss aversion. Information relevant to the choice of alternatives is encoded with "somatic markers" of negative emotions that then shape conscious deliberation away from those alternatives (Damasio, 1994; Loewenstein, Rick, & Cohen, 2008, p. 653).

Evidence from fMRI testing found activation of the fear centers of the brain of those making choices in situations framed as losses. As the size of the loss increased, so did the level of activation in the fear center (Loewenstein, Rick, & Cohen, 2008, p. 654). Prospect theory, then, may describe a preconscious, fear-driven decision process, rather than being driven, as we had assumed, by a cognitive "avoid losses" heuristic (Mercer, 2010, p. 17). The affective tags with which a situation is framed by System 1 seem to carry over into the conscious, System 2 processing that has been the focus of prospect theory research.

A natural concomitant of *fear*, Hymans (2006) suggests, is the emotion of *pride*—the "general sense of one's proper dignity and value, and a specific pleasure or satisfaction taken from (actual or expected) achievement or possession." Pride acts as the switching mechanism between the two natural responses to fear: backing down and fleeing ("flight") or standing one's ground and counterattacking ("fight"). When pride is ascendant, in the form of the decision-maker's assessment of his or her nation's strength and proper position in the world, the "fight" response is activated. When pride is lower, and the decision-maker is concerned about or shameful of his or her nation's weakness, "flight" is the response. More specifically, Hyman notes, *pride* leads to several distinct behavioral tendencies: an enhanced sense of "the nation's 'natural' capability, *if it exerts itself*, to affect others behavior," a higher feeling of control and a "sense that we are not mistake—or accident prone," and a *need to act autonomously*, producing "positive utility from the *act* of 'standing alone,' even if the ultimate material objective of that act could be more easily or more fully achieved by cooperation" (Hymans, 2006, p. 34). While fear and pride can occur separately, the mix is most potent when both are activated.

9. GROUPTHINK

While the chapter thus far has focused upon factors affecting individual decision-making, almost all decisions in crises will involve a leader and their associates. During crises, bureaucracies become timid and possess fewer of the relevant attributes (rapidity and flexibility) necessary for effective response. Simultaneously, the top leadership—chief executive and key lieutenants—begin to pay very close attention to what is happening. The combination of the two factors often (but not always; see 't Hart et al., 1993) leads to a concentration of authority and decision-making at the top of government (Bennett & Monten, 2010, pp. 490–493; Krebs, 2009). When it does occur, the concentration of decision-making in the hands of a leader and associated small groups should magnify the importance of their characteristics to state behavior (Verbeek, 2003).

Groupthink—one of the most famous concepts to emerge not only from political psychology but from political science in general—was defined by Irving L. Janis as "a mode of thinking that people engage in when they are deeply involved in a cohesive in-group, when the members' strivings for unanimity override their motivation to realistically appraise alternative courses of action" (Janis, 1982, p. 9). With defective appraisals of courses of action, Janis argued, the probability of choosing a successful policy was lowered.

Janis's original work on groupthink problematized two tenets of folks wisdom: that "two heads are better than one" and that "a problem shared is a problem halved." Janis suggested that groups often made worse decisions than individuals. And he argued that collegiality and comfort within the group, commonly thought to lead to concentration on the task at hand in a supportive atmosphere, could have a dampening effect on the critical faculties of decision-makers. This was an important finding for students of crises, who had been attracted to the intuitive assumption that decision-makers under stress would benefit from sharing the load within a group. Janis found that stress impacts decision processes in groups in many of the same ways it does in individuals: the collective does not provide a ready diffusion mechanism for crisis-induced stress (Kerr & Tindale, 2004, p. 630).

Groupthink rapidly became a classic of crisis decision-making and political psychology ('t Hart, 1919). However, it has become apparent to researchers studying groups under pressure that Janis may have been too negative about the effects of group cohesion, strong leadership, and time pressure. Absent these factors, groups are just as prone to poor performance, and in the presence of these factors they are capable of good performance (George, 1998, pp. 40–41; Kerr & Tindale, 2004, p. 640). Cohesive groups, as with heuristics, can be adaptive responses to the situation—the issue is again one of ecological rationality—does the group process fit the situation at hand?

Groupthink is fundamentally "a theory of poor decision making in relation to maximizing decision quality" (McCauley, 1998, p. 144), yet groups make decisions for many reasons besides decision quality—creating investment in the decision in order to improve implementation; sharing responsibility, out of a normative commitment to democratic processes; and so on. Each of these rationales and patterns of group decision-making may be important during crises. A decision categorized as suboptimal in objective quality may reflect the trade-offs necessitated by the need to generate support among colleagues and the wider public and the need to conserve time and other decision-making resources (George, 1998, p. 45).

Excessive concurrence-seeking, moreover, is just one possible dynamic of a group under pressure (Stern & Sundelius, 1997. Excessive group conflict—paralysis, competition, and manipulation—is also a plausible result of crisis stimuli (see 't Hart, 1994). While Janis constructed a simple dichotomy of groupthink vigilance, then, a more promising approach is to regard both processes as on a continuum encompassing different types of conformity, conflict, and hybrid patterns (Stern & Sundelius, 1997, pp. 132–133).

10. CONCLUSION

We suggest that the new political psychology of crisis management has three core principles. First, crises occur in all realms of political life. Restricting the concept to acute international conflict is conceptually unnecessary and empirically restrictive. Common tasks of sense-making, meaning-making, decision-making, and learning confront those who manage crises in whatever realm of political life they occur.

Second, crises present stimuli that are best understood within the context of newer dual-process models of psychology. The dual-process paradigm makes sense of the stimulus of stress and accounts for its nuanced impact upon decision-making. Cognitive processes, such as the complexity of information processing and the sophistication of heuristic use, are shaped by both the conscious cognitive system and the unconscious affective system. Affective state and the experience during crises of specific emotions can be key determinants of perception and choice.

Third, the errors and biases approach of much existing literature offers a narrow and scolding view of the impact of human psychology on decision-making quality. Heuristics, for example, are often quicker and more accurate than fully comprehensive decision strategies. Affect does not equal disaster, but cues important decision processes necessary at the most basic level to purposive choice and action.

References

Allison, G. (1971). *Essence of decision: explaining the Cuban Missile Crisis*. Boston: Little, Brown.

Ambrose, S. (1991). *Nixon: Ruin and recovery*. New York: Simon and Schuster.

Bargh, J. A., & Chartrand, T. L. (1999). The unbearable automaticity of being. *American Psychologist, 54*(7), 462–479.

Ben-Yehuda, N., & Goode, E. (2009). *Moral panics: The social construction of deviance*. New York: Wiley.

Billings, R. S., Milburn, T. W., & Schaalman, M. L. (1980). A model of crisis perception. *Administrative Science Quarterly 25*(3), 300–316.

Birt, R. J. (1993). Personality and foreign policy: The case of Stalin. *Political Psychology, 14*, 607–625.

Black, C. (2007). *Richard Nixon: A life in full*. New York: Public Affairs Press.

Blight, J. G. (1992). *The shattered crystal ball: Fear and learning in the Cuban Missile Crisis*. New York: Rowman & Littlefield.

Bodenhausen, G. V., Mussweiler, T., Gabriel, S., & Moreno, K. N. (2001). Affective influences on stereotyping and intergroup relations. In J. P. Forgas (Ed.), *Handbook of affect and social cognition* (pp. 319–343). Mahwah, NJ: Erlbaum.

Boin, A., 't Hart, P., Stern, E., & Sundelius, B. (2005). *The politics of crisis management: Public leadership under pressure*. Cambridge: Cambridge University Press.

Boin, A., McConnell, A., & 't Hart, P. (Eds.). (2008). *Governing after crisis: The politics of investigation, accountability and learning*. Cambridge: Cambridge University Press.

Boin, A., McConnell, A., 't Hart, P., & Preston, T. (2010). Leadership style, crisis response and blame management: The case of Hurricane Katrina. *Public Administration, 88*, 706–723.

Bovens, M., & 't Hart, P. (1996). *Understanding policy fiascoes*. New Brunswick, NJ: Transaction.

Brecher, M. (1979). State behavior in international crisis. *Journal of Conflict Resolution, 23*(3), 446–480.

Brecher, M. (1980). *Decisions in Crisis: Israel, 1967 and 1973*. Berkeley: University of California Press.

Burke, J., & Greenstein, F. (1989). *How presidents test reality*. New York: Russell Sage.

Chaiken, S., & Trope, Y. (1999). *Dual-process theories in social psychology*. New York: Guilford Press.

Chen, S., & Chaiken, S. (1999). The heuristic-systematic model in its broader context. In S. Chaiken & Y. Trope (eds.), *Dual-process theories in social psychology* (pp. 73–96). New York: Guilford Press.

Cohen, R. (1980). *Threat perception in international crisis.* Madison: University of Wisconsin Press.

Damasio, A. (1994). *Descartes' error.* New York: Grosset/Putnam.

Dijksterhuis, A., & Aarts, H. (2010). Goals, attention, and (un)consciousness. *Annual Review of Psychology, 61,* 467–490.

Dyson, S.B. (forthcoming). *Leaders in conflict: Bush and Rumsfeld in Iraq.* Manchester: Manchester University Press.

Dyson, S. B. (2010–2011). George W. Bush, the surge, and presidential leadership. *Political Science Quarterly, 125*(4), 557–585.

Dyson, S. B. (2009a). Stuff happens: Donald Rumsfeld and the Iraq war. *Foreign Policy Analysis, 5*(4), 327–348.

Dyson, S. B. (2009b). Cognitive style and foreign policy: Margaret Thatcher's black-and-white thinking. *International Political Science Review, 30*(1), 33–49.

Dyson, S. B., & Preston, T. (2006). Individual characteristics of political leaders and the use of analogy in foreign policy decision making. *Political Psychology, 27,* 249–272.

Epley, N., & Gilovich, T. (2001). Putting adjustment back in the anchoring and adjustment heuristic: Differential processing of self-generated and experimenter-provided anchors. *Psychological Science, 12,* 391–396.

Evans, J. S. B. T. (2008). Dual-processing accounts of reasoning, judgment, and social cognition. *Annual Review of Psychology, 59,* 255–278.

Falkowski, L. S. (1978). *Presidents, secretaries of state, and crises in U.S. foreign relations: A model and predictive analysis.* Boulder, CO: Westview.

Fiske, S. T. (1980). Attention and weight in person perception: The impact of negative and extreme behavior. *Journal of Personality and Social Psychology, 38,* 889–906.

Fiske, S. T., & Taylor, S. E. (2007). *Social Cognition.* New York: McGraw Hill.

Folkman, S., Lazarus, R. S., Dunkel-Schetter, C., DeLongis, A., & Gruen, R. J. (1986). Dynamics of a stressful encounter: Cognitive appraisal, coping, and encounter outcomes. *Journal of Personality and Social Psychology, 50*(5), 992–1003.

Folkman, S., & Moskowitz, J. T. (2000). Positive emotion and coping. *Current Directions in Psychological Science, 9,* 115–118.

Gasper, K., & Clore, G. L. (2002). Attending to the big picture: Mood and global versus local processing of visual information. *Psychological Science, 13*(1), 34–40.

George, A. L., & Smoke, R. (1974). *Deterrence in American foreign policy.* New York: Columbia University Press.

George, A. L. (1986). The impact of crisis-induced stress on decision making. In F. Solomon & R. Q. Marston (eds), *The medical implications of nuclear war* (pp. 529–552). Washington, DC: National Academy Press.

George, A. L. (1998). From groupthink to contextual analysis of policy-making groups. In P. 't Hart, E. K. Stern, & B. Sundelius (eds.), *Beyond groupthink: Political group dynamics and foreign policy-making* (pp. 35–54). Ann Arbor: University of Michigan Press.

Gigerenzer, G., Czerlinski, J., & Martignon, L. (2002). How good are fast and frugal heuristics? In T. Gilovich, D. Griffin, & D. Kahneman (eds.), *Heuristics and biases: The psychology of intuitive judgment* (pp. 559–581). New York: Cambridge University Press.

Gigerenzer, G., & Gaissmaier, W. (2011). Heuristic decision making. *Annual Review of Psychology*, 62, 451–482.

Gigerenzer, G., Todd, P. M., & ABC Research Group. (1999). *Simple heuristics that make us smart*. New York, Oxford University Press.

Gilbert, D. T. (1999). What the mind's not. In S. Chaiken & Y. Trope (eds.), *Dual-process theories in social psychology* (pp. 3–11). New York: Guilford Press.

't Hart, P. (1991). Irving L. Janis' *Victims of groupthink*. *Political Psychology*, 12, 247–278.

't Hart, P. (1993). Symbols, rituals and power. *Journal of Contingencies and Crisis Management*, 1, 57–63.

't Hart, P. (1994). *Groupthink in government: Small groups and policy failure*. Baltimore: Johns Hopkins University Press.

't Hart, P., & Tindall, K. (Eds.). (2009). *Framing the global meltdown*. Canberra: ANU E-Press.

Hay, C. (2002). *Political analysis*. Basingstoke: Palgrave.

Hermann, C. F. (1969). *Crises in foreign policy: A simulation analysis*. Indianapolis, IN: Bobbs-Merrill.

Hermann, C. F. (Ed.). (1972). *International crises: Insights from behavioral research*. New York: Free Press.

Hermann, M. G. (1979). Indicators of stress in policy makers during foreign policy crises. *Political Psychology*, 1, 27–46.

Hermann, M. G. (2003). Assessing leadership style: Trait analysis. In J. M. Post (ed.), *The psychological assessment of political leaders* (pp. 178–214). Ann Arbor: University of Michigan Press.

Holsti, O. R. (1972). *Crisis, escalation, war*. Montreal: McGill-Queen's University Press.

Holsti, O. R. (1980). Historians, social scientists, and crisis management: An alternative view. *Journal of Conflict Resolution*, 24, 665–682.

Holsti, O. R. (1989). Crisis decision making. In P. E. Tetlock, J. L Husbands, R. Jervis, P. C. Stern, & C. Tilly (eds.), *Behavior, society, and nuclear war* (vol. 1, pp. 8–84). New York: Oxford University Press.

Houghton, D. P. (1998). Analogical reasoning and policymaking: Where and when is it used? *Policy Sciences*, 31, 151–176.

Hymans, J. E. C. (2006). *The psychology of nuclear proliferation: Identity, emotions, and foreign policy*. New York: Cambridge University Press.

Izard, C. E. (2009). Emotion theory and research: Highlights, unanswered questions, and emerging issues. *Annual Review of Psychology*, 60, 1–25.

Janis, I. L. (1982). *Groupthink*. (2nd ed.) Boston: Houghton Mifflin.

Janis, I. L. (1993). Decision making under stress. In L. Goldberger & S. Breznitz (eds.), *Handbook of stress: Theoretical and clinical aspects* (pp. 69–87). New York: Free Press.

Janis, I. L., & Mann, L. (1977). *Decision making: A psychological analysis of conflict, choice, and commitment*. New York: Free Press.

Jervis, R. (1976). *Perception and misperception in international politics*. Princeton, NJ: Princeton University Press.

Jervis, R., Lebow, R. N., & Stein, J. G. (1985). *Psychology and deterrence*. Baltimore: Johns Hopkins University Press.

Kahneman, D., & Frederick, S. (2002). Representativeness revisited: Attribute substitution in intuitive judgment. In T. Gilovich, D. Griffin, & D. Kahneman (eds.), *Heuristics and biases: The psychology of intuitive judgment* (pp. 49–81). New York: Cambridge University Press.

Kassam, K. S., Koslov, K., & Mendes, W. B. (2009). Decisions under distress: Stress profiles influence anchoring and adjustment. *Psychological Science, 20*, 1394–1399.

Kellerman, B. (1983). Allison redux: Three more decision making models. *Polity, 15*, 351–367.

Kemeny, M. E. (2003). The psychobiology of stress. *Current Directions in Psychological Science, 12*, 124–129.

Kerr, N. L., & Tindale, R. S. (2004). Group performance and decision making. *Annual Review of Psychology, 55*, 623–655.

Khong, Y. F. (1992). *Analogies at war*. Princeton, NJ: Princeton University Press.

Kowert, P. A. (2002). *Groupthink or deadlock: When do leaders learn from their advisors?* New York: SUNY Press.

Krebs, R. J. (2009). In the shadow of war: The effects of conflict on liberal democracy. *International Organization, 66*, 177–210.

Kuipers, S. (2006). *The crisis imperative: Crisis rhetoric and welfare state reform in Belgium and the Netherlands in the early 1990s*. Amsterdam: Amsterdam University Press.

Larson, D. W. (1985). *Origins of containment: a psychological explanation*. Princeton: Princeton University Press.

Lebow, R. N. (1987). *Nuclear crisis management: A dangerous illusion*. Ithaca, NY: Cornell University Press.

Lebow, R. N. (1981). *Between peace and war: The nature of international crisis*. Baltimore, MD: Johns Hopkins University Press.

Lebow, R. N., & Stein, J. G. (1994). *We all lost the cold war*. Princeton, NJ: Princeton University Press.

Levi, A., & Tetlock, P. E. (1980). A cognitive analysis of Japan's 1941 decision for war. *Journal of Conflict Resolution, 24*, 195–211.

Levy, J. S. (1988). Domestic politics and war. *Journal of Interdisciplinary History, 18*, 653–673.

Levy, J. S. (1994). Learning and foreign policy: Sweeping a conceptual minefield. *International Organization 48*, 279–312.

Loewenstein, G., Rick, S., & Cohen, J. D. (2008). Neuroeconomics. *Annual Review of Psychology, 59*, 647–672.

Masters, A., & 't Hart, P. (2012). Prime ministerial crisis rhetoric and recession politics: Meaning making in economic crisis management. *Public Administration, 90*, 759–780.

Matlin, M. W., & Stang, D. J. (1978). *The pollyanna principle: Selectivity in language, memory, and thought*. Cambridge: Schenkman Publishing Company.

McCauley, C. (1998). Group dynamics in Janis' theory of groupthink: Backward and forward. *Organizational Behavior and Human Decision Processes, 73*, 142–162.

McDermott, R. (1998). *Risk taking in international politics*. Ann Arbor: University of Michigan Press.

Mercer, J. (2010). Emotional beliefs. *International Organization, 64*, 1–31.

Mercer, J. (2005). Rationality and psychology in international politics. *International Organization, 59*, 77–106.

Monten, J., & Bennett, A. (2010). Models of crisis decision making and the 1090–91 gulf war. *Security Studies, 19*, 486–520.

Neustadt, R. E., & May, E. R. (1986). *Thinking in time*. New York: Free Press.

Nixon, R. M. (1962). *Six crises*. New York: Doubleday.

Pearson, C., & Clair, J. (1998). Reframing crisis management. *Academy of Management Review, 23*(1), 59–76.

Post, J. M. (1991). The effect of crisis induced stress on policymakers. In A. L. George (ed.), *Avoiding war: Problems of crisis management* (pp. 471–494). New York: Praeger.

Quarantelli, E. (Ed.). (1998). *What Is a disaster?* New York: Routledge.

Record, J. (2008). Retiring Hitler and appeasement from the national security debate. *Parameters, 38,* 91–101.

Richardson, J. L. (1988). New insights on international crises. *Review of International Studies, 14*(4), 309–316.

Robins, R. S., & Dorn, R. M. (1993). Stress and political leadership. *Politics and the Life Sciences, 12,* 3–17.

Rose, R., & Davies, P. L. (1994). *Inheritance in public policy: Change without choice in Britain.* New Haven, CT: Yale University Press.

Rosenthal, U., Charles, M., & 't Hart, P., (Eds). (1989). *Coping with crises.* Springfield, IL: Charles C. Thomas.

Rosenthal, U., & Kouzmin, A. (1997). Crises and crisis management: Toward comprehensive government decision making. *Journal of Public Administration Research and Theory, 7,* 277–304.

Schafer, M., & Chrichlow, S. (2010). *Groupthink versus high quality decision making.* New York: Columbia University Press.

Schwartz, N. (2002). Feelings as information: Moods influence judgments and processing strategies. In T. Gilovich, D. Griffin, & D. Kahneman (eds.) *Heuristics and biases: The psychology of intuitive judgment* (pp. 534–547). New York: Cambridge University Press.

Siniver, A. (2008). *Nixon, Kissinger, and U. S. foreign policy making: The machinery of crisis.* Cambridge: Cambridge University Press.

Sloman, S. A. (2002). Two systems of reasoning. In T. Gilovich, D. Griffin, & D. Kahneman (eds.) *Heuristics and Biases: The psychology of intuitive judgment* (pp. 379–396). New York: Cambridge University Press.

Slovic, P., Finucane, M. L., Peters, E., & MacGregor, D. G. (2002). The affect heuristic. In T. Gilovich, D. Griffin, & D. Kahneman (eds.) *Heuristics and Biases: The psychology of intuitive judgment* (pp. 397–420). New York: Cambridge University Press.

Smith, C. A., & Kirby, L. D. (2001). Affect and cognitive appraisal processes. In J. P. Forgas (ed.), *Handbook of affect and social cognition* (pp. 75–94). Mahwah, NJ: Lawrence Erlbaum.

Snyder, C. R., & Lopez, S. J. (2002). *Handbook of positive psychology.* New York: Oxford University Press.

Snyder, G. H., & Diesing, P. (1977). *Conflict among nations.* Princeton, NJ: Princeton University Press.

Snyder, R. C., Bruck, H. W., & Sapin, B. (Eds.) (1962). *Decision making as an approach to international politics.* New York: Free Press.

Stanovich, K. E., & West, R. F. (2002). Individual differences in reasoning: Implications for the rationality debate? In T. Gilovich, D. Griffin, & D. Kahneman (eds.) *Heuristics and biases: The psychology of intuitive judgment* (pp. 421–440). New York: Cambridge University Press.

Stern, E., & Sundelius, B. (1997). Understanding small group decisions in foreign policy: Process diagnosis and research procedure. In P. 't Hart, E. Stern, & B. Sundelius (eds.), *Beyond groupthink* (pp. 123–150). Ann Arbor: University of Michigan Press.

Suedfeld, P. (2010). The complexity construct in political psychology: Personological and cognitive approaches. Available at www.pubs.drdc.gc.ca/.../CEBsupport.100218_0834. Toronto_CR_2010_022.pdf.

Suedfeld, P. (1992). Cognitive managers and their critics. *Political Psychology, 13,* 435–453.

Suedfeld, P., & Bluck, S. (1988). Changes in integrative complexity prior to surprise attacks. *Journal of Conflict Resolution, 32,* 626–635.

Suedfeld, P., Corteen, R. S., & McCormick, C. (1986). The role of integrative complexity in military leadership: Robert E. Lee and his opponents. *Journal of Applied Social Psychology, 16*, 498–507.

Suedfeld, P., & Granatstein, J. L. (1995). Leader complexity in personal and professional crises: concurrent and retrospective information processing. *Political Psychology, 16*, 509–522.

Suedfeld, P., & Tetlock, P. (1977). Integrative complexity of communications in international crises. *Journal of Conflict Resolution, 21*, 169–184.

Suls, J. (2001). Affect, stress and personality. In J. P. Forgas (ed.), *Handbook of affect and social cognition* (pp. 392–409). Mahwah, NJ: Lawrence Erlbaum.

Sweeny, K. (2008). Crisis decision theory: Decisions in the face of negative events. *Psychological Bulletin, 134*(1), 61–76.

Tversky, A., & Kahneman, D. (1974). Judgment under uncertainty: Heuristics and biases. *Science, 185*, 1124–1130.

Verbeek, B. (2003). *Decision making in Great Britain during the Suez crisis: Small groups and a persistent leader*. Aldershot: Ashgate.

Wallace, M. D., & Suedfeld, P. (1988). Leadership performance in crisis: The longevity-complexity link. *International Studies Quarterly, 32*, 439–451.

Wallace, M. D, Suedfeld, P., & Thachuk, K. (1993). Political rhetoric of leaders under stress in the Gulf crisis. *Journal of Conflict Resolution, 37*, 94–107.

Weick, K. (1993). The collapse of sensemaking in organizations. *Administrative Science Quarterly, 38*(4), 628–652.

Yerkes, R. M., & Dodson, J. D. (1908). The relation of strength of stimulus to rapidity of habit formation. *Journal of Comparative Neurology and Psychology, 18*, 459–482.

Zajonc, R. B. (1980). Feeling and thinking: Preferences need no inferences. *American Psychologist, 35*, 151–175.

CHAPTER 14

PERSONALITY PROFILES
OF POLITICAL ELITES

DAVID G. WINTER

ONE of the central axioms of political psychology is that political outcomes are shaped and channeled by personalities of leaders and other significant elite groups—that is, by their individually patterned integration of perceptions, memories, emotional reactions, judgments, goal seeking, and choices. History, institutions, structures of allies and opponents, and the characteristics of their own people furnish opportunities and set limits on what leaders can do. However, in the end "the goals, abilities, and foibles of *individuals* are crucial to the intentions, capabilities, and strategies of a state" (Byman & Pollack, 2001, p. 109; emphasis added). As former US secretary of state Henry Kissinger put it in an interview with journalists, "as a professor, I tended to think of history as run by impersonal forces. But when you see it in practice, you see the difference personalities make" (Isaacson, 1992, p. 13).

Whenever an unexpected crisis develops or a new leader emerges, diplomats, military planners, and even heads of government want information about the characteristics and personalities of the key players (Carey, 2011). Even journalists sometimes need assistance from psychology; thus in reviewing two biographies of Mao Zedong, Burns (2000) confessed:

> For myself, I wish now that in covering China, South Africa under apartheid, the Soviet Union and wars in Afghanistan and the former Yugoslavia, among other places—scars, all, on the conscience of the 20th century—I had made fuller allowance for, or understood better, the role of wounded psyches in producing the Maos, Stalins, Vorsters, Najibullahs, Karadzics and Arkans I wrote about along the way. (p. 7)

Policymakers need personality profiles of living foreign leaders, often in urgent contexts where the usual kinds of information may be sparse, such as North Korean leader Kim Jong-un. Thus in 1960, Wedge (1968) prepared a profile on Soviet leader Nikita Khrushchev for incoming US president Kennedy, while Soviet psychologists (Egorova, 1982) prepared profiles of American leaders. To assist President Carter's successful management of the Camp David summit, Post (1979) prepared profiles of Egyptian president Sadat and Israeli prime minister Begin.

Finally, policymakers prefer and often expect unambiguous answers to specific questions about leaders' future actions. These requirements impose special constraints and obstacles on the profiler who would prefer to make "if/then" statements and probabilistic predictions in a complex and multivariate world.

In contrast, academic political psychologists are driven more by intellectual curiosity and questions of historical interest than by the needs of government policy. They are certainly interested in working out the puzzling personality dynamics of leaders from the past, but there are no longer pressing policy reasons for rushing the job. For example, Leonardo da Vinci—perhaps the first person studied by a psychologist at a distance—had been dead almost 400 years when Freud ([1910] 1957) published his landmark analysis.

For all their importance to policymakers and academic researchers, however, leaders' personalities are not accessible to the usual psychological methods of assessment and measurement. The important leaders of history are dead and (adapting a quotation from Glad, 1973) they have taken their personality characteristics—Oedipus complexes, authoritarianism, or power motivation—with them. Living leaders are protected from direct intrusions of psychological inquiry, so that one cannot even imagine giving them standard personality tests, questionnaires, surveys, or even psychological interviews. For these reasons, this chapter focuses on ways of measuring leaders' personalities indirectly, at a distance (see Winter, 2003a, for a review of the history of this academic enterprise). After a brief prologue discussing when and how personality might be expected to affect political outcomes, I survey the major methods political psychologists have employed to study the personalities of individual actors. I use a fourfold framework of the different elements or variables of personality to discuss the many specific variables commonly used in these at-a-distance studies, focusing particularly on successful leadership and conflict escalation.

1. PROLOGUE: WHEN DOES PERSONALITY AFFECT POLITICS?

It seems easy to give examples of the effect of personality on politics: thus Woodrow Wilson lost the peace in 1919 because he negotiated ineptly, confused rhetoric with substance, and refused to compromise. Adolf Hitler set Europe aflame with a foreign policy rooted in personal pathology. The grandiose self-conceptions of Saddam Hussein and Mu'ammar al-Gaddafi brought cruel oppression to their own people and trouble to their neighbors. Perhaps driven by a "Nobel Prize complex" (Post, 2004, p. 269), Egypt's Anwar Sadat was able to do the unthinkable—visiting Jerusalem and making peace with Israel. Bill Clinton's inability to control himself jeopardized his presidential accomplishments. In each case, the intrusion of a leader's personal appetites, needs, aspirations, fears, and obsessions shaped highly consequential public actions—in ways that were sometimes self-defeating or violently aggressive and sometimes brave and heroic. Other cases where personal characteristics of leaders clearly affected international relations outcomes are cited by Byman and Pollack (2001), Kennedy (1982), Hamby (1991), and Friedlander and Cohen (1975).

Yet even as we recognize the importance of individual leaders and their personalities, we should be cautious about neglecting the importance of constraints and opportunities in the roles and situations in which leaders operate. Thus in 1918 Americans wanted to "bring the troops home" and were reluctant to cede national sovereignty to a League of Nations, which made Wilson's weakness a matter of position as much as personality. And whatever the role of Hitler's personal demons in the origins of the Holocaust, without the support of many other persons and institutions (see Kershaw, 1999) he would have remained a failed artist haunting the streets and opera house of Vienna. Events in Iraq since the removal and execution of Saddam Hussein suggest that he was not the sole source of cruelty and oppression in that country. Even Anwar Sadat's heroic peacemaking depended on Menachem Begin being a willing (if suspicious) counterplayer and Jimmy Carter a mediator.

Thus the scholarly terrain of this chapter is defined by two boundaries: on the one hand the naive view of political outcomes as merely the projection of leaders' personalities, and on the other the equally simplistic view that individual personalities have no effect. Charting a course between these extremes, Greenstein ([1969] 1987, chap. 2) and Byman and Pollack (2001) suggest that the personalities of political leaders are likely to be especially important under certain conditions: when power is concentrated; when leaders occupy strategic positions; when institutions are in conflict; when the situation is novel, ambiguous, unstable, or complex (without clear precedents, expectations, or routine role requirements); and when the situation is laden with symbolic and emotional significance. These conditions tend to hold when the leader first organizes the administrative apparatus after assuming power, during crises (especially foreign policy crises involving "enemy" nations), and whenever events pose a threat to deeply held values. For this reason, personality and political behavior studies typically involve topics such as how leaders structure their advising staff and organize the process of making decisions, how they act during escalating crises and war, and how they respond to threats.

In these situations, personality factors affect the arousal and weighting of leaders' goals and preferences, as well as conflicts and fusions among their different goals. They affect how leaders respond to (or resist) cues, symbols, and signs; how they seek out and interpret "stimuli" and then transform them into "information." Finally, personality affects leaders' persistence, endurance, and management of emotions. Seen in this way, "personality" explanations do not replace "rational choice" explanations, but rather supply the coefficients necessary to fill out the abstract terms of rational choice (nature of goals, choice of maximizing strategy, information-seeking style, and time span).

2. What Is Personality?

2.1. A Conception of Personality

It is easy to think of people's personalities as a "thing"—a set of fixed qualities based on a genetic blueprint and developed by life experience. A more complex conception would recognize that people have many "possible selves"; thus "personality" ought to be viewed as an array of capacities or dispositions that may be engaged, primed, or brought forward depending on the demands of the situation and the person's own "executive apparatus." On this view, personality is like a personal computer: there are some relatively fixed "hardware" characteristics, but also many "software" applications, each of which can be "opened" or "closed" by the operator. Some of these applications typically run in a prominent "window" at the center of the screen; others are available in the immediate background "windows," and a few run almost undetected in "deeper" background.

Two political examples will illustrate how this conception of personality can be useful in understanding some otherwise complicated and perplexing actions of political leaders. For example, as mentioned above, US president Woodrow Wilson is usually described as an idealistic, highly moral, and inflexible political leader—repeatedly sabotaging his goals and programs by his stubborn refusal to compromise. On the other hand, Wilson often displayed extraordinary flexibility and leadership skill, as in 1912 when he ran for governor of New Jersey as a "reform" candidate while at the same time securing the support of the state's political bosses. George ([1971] 1987) reconciled these seemingly inconsistent styles as consistent responses ("software programs," in the above terminology) to different situations: flexible when he was *seeking power*, and stubborn when he encountered opposition while *exercising power*. Wilson's personality did not "change" back and forth from flexibility to inflexibility; rather, his adult personality always included both patterns, each primed by different social contexts.

The political career of Italian fascist dictator Benito Mussolini furnishes another example of situations priming different software programs. From 1922 through 1937, he "recorded an impressive string of accomplishments, including creating an empire and improving Italy economically" (N. Winter, 1992, p. 2). After meeting with Hitler in Berlin for several days in September 1937, however, he returned to Italy a changed man—adopting Nazi policies, alienating many supporters, and ultimately ruining Italy economically and militarily. Winter suggested that meeting Hitler primed in Mussolini a pattern of "powerful and grandiose leader" (reflected in sharp increases in power motivation), crowding out his prior pattern of "achieving leader who improves things" (decreases in achievement motivation). Rather than saying that Mussolini changed, our understanding might be enhanced by viewing this sequence as the emergence of an alternative that was always present in Mussolini's enduring personality, primed by a specific set of circumstances—a context skillfully planned and manipulated by Nazi officials (Kershaw, 2000, pp. 44–45).

2.2. Four Elements of Personality

What are these "software applications" of personality? Some theorists have argued that personality consists only of traits (Allport, 1961) or motives (Murray, 1938), but most consider that personality is made up of several fundamentally different kinds of variables (Winter, 1996; see also Barenbaum & Winter, 2008; Winter, John, Stewart, Klohnen, & Duncan, 1998). For convenience, I divide personality into four elements or classes of variables, as illustrated in table 14.1: social contexts, traits, cognitions, and motives. While some writers use the word "trait" to cover different elements—for example, power motivation, cognitive complexity, or authoritarianism—I suggest that analytic precision will be enhanced by using different words for things that are essentially different.

The four elements can be described in terms of two dimensions: (*a*) whether they are public and observable, or else "inner" and therefore inferential; and (*b*) whether they are relatively stable across situations and can therefore be described in terms of "typical" levels, or else are highly dependent on situations and contexts. (The difference is relative: probably all aspects of personality are affected to *some* extent by situations.) The table lists major theorists and typical personality variables associated with each element.

Social contexts include both immediate or short-term situations and also broader and enduring environments such as gender, social-economic class, race and ethnicity, culture, history, religion, family, and significant institutions such as universities, corporations, and the military. These are usually assessed from traditional sources of biographical information. Some readers may find it strange to consider social contexts as an element of personality. Usually, these contexts are conceived as marking the field on which personality plays out, rather than as dispositions within the person. While social contexts do channel the expression of personality by furnishing opportunities and constraints, they also become internalized as aspects of personality itself (see Moen, Elder, & Lüscher, 1995; also Winter & Stewart, 1995). In fact, personality can be viewed as a series or *accumulation of past "embodied contexts"*; once formed, these internalizations are resistant to change (or at least harder to change than to acquire).

Traits are the public, observable element of personality, consistencies of style readily noticed by other people. They reflect the language of "first impressions," the adjectives and adverbs of everyday language that we use to describe other people. Thus traits are usually assessed by means of observers' ratings. (Self-reports are also widely used, but they run the danger of confounding people's beliefs about themselves with the impressions that others have of them.) While the number of separate "traits" is only limited by the number of person-descriptors in the language (Allport and Odbert, 1936, identified 4,504 trait words in English), over the past few decades personality psychologists have settled on a few basic trait clusters or factors—the "Big Five"—that seem to emerge in most cultures, at least those using an Indo-European language: *extraversion* (or

Table 14.1 The Four Elements of Personality

	Private, Inferential	Public, Observable
Trans-situational	**Cognitions**	**Temperament, Traits**
	Typical variables:	*Typical variables:*
	Beliefs	Extraversion
	Attitudes	Agreeableness
	Values	Conscientiousness
	Self concept(s)	Neuroticism
	Operational codes	Openness to experience
	Major theorists:	Energy level
	Gordon Allport	*Major theorists:*
	George Kelly	Gordon Allport
	Carl Rogers	Hans Eysenck
		Carl Jung
Situation-dependent	**Motives**	**Social Context**
	Typical variables:	*Microcontext:*
	Motives	Immediate situations
	Goals	*Macrocontexts:*
	Regulating mechanisms	Gender
	Defense mechanisms	Social-economic class
	Major theorists:	Ethnicity
	Sigmund Freud	RaceCulture
	David McClelland	Generation
	Abraham Maslow	History
	Henry Murray	Family
		Major theorists:
		Erik Erikson
		Walter Mischel
		B. F. Skinner
		Abigail Stewart

surgency), *agreeableness, conscientiousness, emotional stability* (or its opposite, *neuroticism*), and *openness to experience* (but see Ashton, Lee, & Goldberg, 2004, on the possibility of additional factors).

Cognitions include a wide variety of mental representations: beliefs, values, and attitudes; more technical psychological concepts such as categories, schemas, and models; representations of the self and "personal identity," as well as of other people, groups, and social-political systems; and for political leaders especially beliefs about the scope and nature of politics.

Motives involve the anticipation goals, or desired end states. Over time, they organize and guide actions in pursuit of goals (or avoidance of undesired states and negative goals). Motives are latent dispositions: over time, they wax and wane in response to internal states and external opportunities. When and how any given motive is expressed depends on the perceived situation: think of the variety of ways in which we satisfy our hunger motive, depending on available food resources, the time of day, and the physical and social setting. Thus any particular motive does not always drive one consistent pattern of action. Moreover, people's motives are often not apparent to other people (particularly if they have not observed the person over time), or even to themselves. Thus motives are *implicit* and are assessed through indirect means such as content analysis of imaginative texts (see Schultheiss & Bronstein, 2010, for a review of implicit motives).

3. HOW CAN WE MEASURE PERSONALITY WITHOUT DIRECT ACCESS?

Some traditional direct methods for assessing personality apparently can be used only up to a certain level of power or prominence—for example, state legislators in the United States (Altemeyer, 1996)—or under unusual circumstances, such as the Rorschach testing of indicted Nazi war criminals during the Nuremberg trials (Zillmer, Harrower, Ritzler, & Archer, 1995). For almost all significant living or dead political leaders, however, these methods cannot be applied. In consequence, political psychologists have developed a variety of indirect measurement techniques that can be applied at a distance.

3.1. Political Psychobiography

Assessment without access can lead to undifferentiated and unhelpful clichés, speculation (e.g., Frank, 2004, on George W. Bush), or in extreme cases character assassination (e.g., a poll of US psychiatrists about Barry Goldwater's fitness to be president; see Boroson, 1964). Several political psychologists have formulated principles of constructing political psychobiography (see Schultz, 2005; Renshon, 2003; Walter, 2007). Thus Greenstein ([1969] 1987, chap. 3) described three stages of the process: (1) Identify and describe the *phenomenology*; that is, the particular actions or outcomes that are to be explained by the use of psychology. Typically these are surprising and unusual actions, not explicable by the routine requirements of the leader's role or the logic of the situation. (2) Formulate a *dynamic* explanation for these actions or outcomes. What psychological mechanisms can best "explain" the phenomenology? (3) As an optional further step, identify the *genesis* or origin of the dynamic in the leader's childhood experiences (see Elms, 1994; Schultz, 2005; and Winter, 2003a; but also see the critical comments by Walter, 2007 for discussions of the history, methods, and issues of psychobiography as well as extensive references).

Drawing on conceptions of personality (usually psychoanalysis, object relations theory, or the work of Erikson) and clinical experience, many psychobiographers (e.g., Post, 2004) often select whatever concepts seem most promising for the explanation of the person whose actions they are studying. Others draw on everyday language to design more idiographic concepts to explain particular leaders (e.g., Hargrove, 2008). In recent years, however, some psychobiographers have introduced systematic conceptual frameworks. In his studies of American presidents, for example, Greenstein (2009a; 2009b; 2013) identified six dimensions of analysis and comparison: *communication to the public, organizational capacity, political skill, policy vision, cognitive style,* and *emotional intelligence.* Other systematically applied concepts include level of *activity* and *positive/negative* affect (Barber, 1992; see also Henderson, 2001), *extent of desired change* and *breadth of scope* (Blondel, 1987; see also Fukai, 2001), and *personalization* of leadership (Blondel & Thiébault, 2010).

3.2. Theory-Based Rating Scales

Several political psychologists have adapted some of the ordinary techniques of personality measurement to at-a-distance assessment of theoretically important leader personality characteristics. The trait domain of personality, for example, is usually measured by adjective checklists or rating scales filled out either by the person or by someone who knows that person well, as in Simonton's (1986, 1988) studies of US presidents. Rubenzer and Faschingbauer (2004) asked experts who knew a lot about presidents—115 authors of book-length presidential biographies, and authors of reference books on the presidency—to fill out standard measures of the five trait factors (the Revised NEO Personality, Costa & McCrae, 1992; phrases from the California Q-Sort, Block, 1961; 2010; and clusters of ordinary English adjectives, Goldberg, 1990).

Immelman (1993) developed a more elaborate inventory of personality ratings, based on Millon's (1990) theoretical conception of personality as involving *syndromes* or prototypes—eight "normal" patterns (e.g., forceful, confident, sociable, cooperative) and corresponding "pathological" patterns (e.g., sadistic, narcissistic, histrionic, dependent). One or more people familiar with the leader codes the presence or absence of various diagnostic criteria according to a manual developed by Immelman (2004). Millon's theory and the specific descriptors are derived from the psychiatric *Diagnostic and Statistical Manual,* which means that many of its concepts reflect a medical or psychopathology orientation.

Some researchers use the Q-sort technique (Block, 2010; see also Brown, 1986), in which knowledgeable experts are asked to sort a large number of adjectives or statements into a forced-normal distribution of several categories, ranging from "apply-ing" to "not applying" to the leader (Kowert, 1996).

3.3. Content Analysis

While past and present political leaders are not accessible to direct methods of personal-ity measurement, they do *talk*, and the words of their speeches, news conferences, and often their informal remarks are preserved and archived, in great abundance. Content analysis exploits this resource and has become one of the most widely used techniques for measuring personality at a distance. The essential feature of content analysis is cod-ing for the presence of certain categories in written text or transcriptions of verbal text. Many other kinds of documents can be scored: personal letters and diaries, diplomats' reports and summaries, government-to-government communications, parliamentary debates, media commentary, and works of fiction.

Some sets of content analysis categories are drawn from theory (e.g., the operational code coding system; see Walker, 1990), whereas other are developed through experi-mental manipulation of the relevant personality variable (see Winter, 1998b). Some content analysis systems can be used after minimal preparation; others require consid-erable training of scorers and monitoring of interscorer reliability. Many content analy-sis systems are applied manually (e.g., integrative complexity, see Suedfeld, Guttieri, & Tetlock, 2003; motive imagery, see Winter, 2003b). Some use computer-assisted manual scoring (e.g., the Verbs in Context System developed to score operational codes; see Schafer & Walker, 2006; Walker et al., 2003). A few systems have been fully automated (e.g., the DICTION system developed by Hart, 2001; the Linguistic Inquiry and Word Count [LIWC] system developed by Pennebaker, Booth, and Francis, 2007; frame anal-ysis developed by Sanfilippo et al., 2008; and Leadership Trait Analysis developed by Hermann, 2003). Detailed discussions of methods and issues of psychological content analysis can be found in Schafer (2000), Walker (2000), Winter (1992), and Winter and Stewart (1977).

Making personality assessments of political leaders based on content analysis of their spoken or written words raises a major issue: do the results reflect the personalities of the leaders themselves or of their speechwriters? This issue has led some researchers to prefer "spontaneous" rather than "prepared" material; this distinction tends to break down as leaders are extensively prepared for "spontaneous" remarks and press con-ferences. Other researchers (Winter, 2002, pp. 46–47; Suedfeld, 2010, pp. 1677–1678) argue that although speechwriters may draft the words and images, leaders select their speechwriters and review and edit their work. Furthermore, good speechwriters know how to adapt to the goals and style of their clients, to craft words that seem "natural" to both speaker and audience. However, as an alternative interpretation, it is possible to view the speeches (and assessments) as actually reflecting the personalities of the loose collectivity that is often called "the administration" or "the government." For many pur-poses the conceptual status of assessments derived from content analysis may not be important if the resulting scores lead to accurate predictions about the leaders' actions and political outcomes.

4. Social Contexts and Political Elites

In constructing a personality profile of any person—leader, follower, cabinet minister, diplomat, legislator, protest organizer, or voter—it is advisable to begin with a description of that person's social contexts. Since people exist in particular social contexts, the meaning of their behavior and its diagnostic relevance cannot be fully understood without considering these contexts. Actions that to observers might appear to reflect individual personality may to the actor seem compelled by the immediate political, economic, diplomatic, or military microcontexts. More broadly, actions or words that are really characteristic of entire groups—the "macrocontext" of cultures or ethnicities, social-economic classes, genders, religions, or members of particular institutions—may be inappropriately taken as signs only of individual personality characteristics. Thus when studying leaders from outside one's own country, or leaders from a variety of countries, it is even more important to begin with their social contexts.

Fortunately, the social contexts of political leaders can usually be described by drawing on accessible sources such as biographies and histories, supplemented by concepts from anthropology and sociology, gender studies, and other disciplines such as comparative religion.

4.1. Culture

Culture provides shared meanings and a shared sense of what is "normal" or "pathological." Much of the influence of culture can be seen in *language*. Consider the concept of power, fundamental to any political system. The Russian language uses a single word—*vlast*—to mean both "power" and "authority." Perhaps this linguistic fact is related to alleged Russian cultural themes identified by Ihanus (2001, pp. 131–134) of absolute autocracy, the "ecstasy of submission" to charismatic leaders, and leader transition by overthrow. Shestopal (2000a, 2008) has used survey data to study contemporary images of power in Russia. In the Western political tradition and perhaps especially in the United States, "power" means making decisions. In China, however, power has the connotation of being spared the burden of decision-making. It is bound up with themes of patron/client dependency, consensus versus competition, and matters ethical propriety as well as practical instrumentality (Pye & Pye, 1985).

Abstractions such as "honor" and "freedom" have very different meanings and importance in different cultures. In many cultures, an insult to religious or family honors "requires" aggressive public punishment or even killing. One example is the 2005 controversy about cartoons published in a Danish newspaper: Muslims found them offensive and blasphemous; to many westerners they represented freedom of expression. Nisbett and Cohen (1995) documented the existence of an aggressive "culture of honor" in the US South. In Japan, however, "honor" has a different meaning: a dishonored leader may resign or in an extreme case commit suicide.

While the every culture may have its own unique configuration, Hofstede (2001) has proposed several dimensions useful for comparing cultures, thus cultural backgrounds of different leaders: *power distance* (i.e., power inequality), *individualism* (vs. collectivism), *uncertainty avoidance, future time orientation*, and *gendering*. (Hofstede's label is "masculinity," but since he means *differentiation* between women and men in roles, socialization, and occupations, "gendering" seems a more accurate label.)

4.2. History

Every leader is from a particular nation, and every nation has constructed a particular history. Often these accounts—sometimes shrouded in the dim mists of history—are constructed around memories of defeats or other traumatic events, as Volkan (2001) points out. Thus for thousands of years, Jews have commemorated (with the traditional hope of "next year in Jerusalem") their Exodus from oppression in Egypt. Shite Muslim history is focused on the assassination of Ali, son of the Prophet, in 661 B.C.E. The 1389 defeat at Kosovo is the defining episode of Serbian identity. In South Africa, the Great Trek of 1835–1840, in which over 10,000 Boers left Cape Colony to escape British domination, became the foundation of Afrikaans identity.

The Arab historical narrative involved rapid initial success, followed by "crusades" and defeats by the West, compounded by forced conversions and expulsions in Spain after the Reconquest (Carr, 2009), and broken Allied promises of independence after World War I. The historical narrative of Armenians focuses on the genocidal events of 1915–1918. Nazi leaders fanned and then exploited German humiliation growing out of the sudden military defeat in 1918 and the Versailles Treaty. For many Palestinians, the *Nakba* or "catastrophe" associated with expulsions and departures during the 1947–1948 Arab-Israeli conflict is the defining trauma that has dominated their history for more than six decades (see Nets-Zehngut, 2011). What makes this conflict intractable is that these events are also associated with the 1948 creation of Israel, which is—for its Jewish citizens—closely related to the trauma of the 1933–1945 Holocaust.

4.3. Age

Leaders come in a wide range of ages. Since 1900, for example, US presidents ranged from age 45 (Theodore Roosevelt) to 69 (Reagan) when they assumed office; British prime ministers from 43 (David Cameron) to 69 (Henry Campbell-Bannerman). Prime ministers of India showed an even greater age-range: 40 (Rajiv Gandhi) to 81 (Morarji

Desai). Young leaders may be less experienced and mature, whereas older leaders are vulnerable to the physical and psychological effects of aging (Post, 1980; see also Gilbert, 2006).

Perhaps even more important than chronological age, however, is the leader's age in relation to the culture's conception of stages of life. Erikson's (1982) familiar framework of eight life stages, each with its own crisis and source of strength, can be applied to European and North American leaders—for which the middle-adulthood concept of *generativity* (Erikson, Erikson, & Kivnick, 1986; McAdams & de St. Aubin, 1998; de St. Aubin, McAdams, & Kim, 2003) may be especially relevant to the study of political leaders. Other cultures, however, may have different conceptions of the human life cycle (Kakar, 1968).

4.4. Generation

Generation is the intersection of individual age and collective history. Leaders are often marked by their generation—a component of social identity formed around whatever events occurred during their transition to adulthood. Mannheim ([1928] 1952) introduced "generation" as an important concept in social science (see also Kertzer, 1983). Stewart and Healy (1989) have elaborated the concept into a general model for understanding the effects of historical events and social trends occurring at different ages. Using survey research, Shestopal (2000b) has analyzed generational differences in Russia on key variables of political experience and perception, as shown in table 14.2, which locates Russian leaders since the break-up of the Soviet Union in their appropriate generational row.

Russian survey results reported by Evgenieva (2008) suggest an important generational difference about what people think the boundaries of Russia "should" be. Older people would include all of the former Soviet Union; younger people would also add Finland, Poland, Turkey, Afghanistan, Mongolia, and Alaska.

4.5. Hegemony: Social Class, Ethnicity, and Discrimination

Societies are organized in hierarchies or structures of power—economic or social power, hierarchies of relative ethnic prestige, in extreme cases even the power to imprison. In the course of growing up, and then in their adult lives, leaders occupy locations in these hierarchies. The resulting experiences of *hegemony*—whether of being on top or being on the bottom of a power hierarchy—can play a critical role in determining a leader's personality and future actions. For example, growing up in a privileged position at the top of a hierarchy, or even having everyday experiences of wielding power over others, may affect how a leader handles power. Power can increase the power holder's psychological distance from "subordinate" persons and groups—creating the sense that they are not fully human. From there, it is only a short step to moral indifference and exploitation (see Kipnis, 1976; Winter, 2010a).

Table 14.2 Generational Differences in Political Experience and Perception in Russia

Born	Age 20 in	Russian leader of this cohort	Key events of young adulthood	Contemporary political attitude	Typical response to probe: "democracy is…"
Generation of the Revolution and Civil War					
1906–1929	1926–1949	Brezhnev Andropov Chernenko	Stalinist collectivism and repressions World War II victory	Angry that the state no longer takes care of people	"submission to the state."
Children of the War, who grew up to become "Sixties People"					
1929–1939	1949–1959	Gorbachev Yeltsin	Stalin's death Cold War Possibility of nuclear war Spy mania	This cohort tended to disappear from politics after 1990.	"economic equality."
Post–World War II generation					
1939–1949	1959–1969		End of Stalin cult of personality	Anger at post-1990 crime and nationalistic politicians	"following the law, human rights."
Children of Khrushchev's "thaw"					
1949–1964	1969–1984	Putin (older part) Medvedev (younger part)	Brezhnev "Freezing" in political life Afghan war	Very interested in politics Hopeful, anxious	"having a powerful state."
Generation of Brezhnev epoch and stagnation					
1965–1977	1985–1997		Indoctrination, followed by traumatic changes Dissolution of the USSR	Cynicism about politics Russia is a mighty country Authorities are incompetent but accepted	"voting [and other specific political practices]."
Children of Perestroika					
1977–1982	1997–2002		"New Russia" Market economy	Critical of growing economic inequality	"not really legitimate."
Post-Soviet Children					
1982–1995	2002–2015			"Slogans are an eyesore." "Leaders' speeches are like the sound of a rattling tractor."	"personal freedom and independence, not responsibility or participation"

Note: Adapted from Shestopal (2000b).

On the other hand, experiences at the bottom of a hegemonic hierarchy can drive a variety of later responses: from sheer reactance and revenge ("fighting back"), to identification with the aggressor, or transcendence and efforts to reduce or eliminate power hierarchies. Which response leaders display may have enormous consequences for themselves and their country. For example, consider the enormous difference in the responses of Robert Mugabe and Nelson Mandela, both of whom were imprisoned for years by a white government for struggling against racial oppression. Decades after becoming leader of an independent Zimbabwe, Mugabe (2008) continued to blame Zimbabwe's enormous economic and social problems on the original white colonizers, the British— "who planted their children here to oppress us," "are planning to plunder our country," and "are now using local puppets that they fund to fight us." In contrast, Nelson Mandela assumed the office of president of a transformed South Africa with words and deeds of reconciliation (Mandela, 1994): "We speak as fellow citizens to heal the wounds of the past with the intent of constructing a new order based on justice for all."

4.6. Gender

History, age, generation, and social class are all sharply differentiated by another aspect of social context, namely gender. The impact of history, cultural conceptions of the life cycle, and the sense of generational identity are often very different for women and men. Consider how their lives and political roles might have turned out if Eleanor Roosevelt had been born 80 years later (in 1964 instead of 1884), if Margaret Thatcher had been the child of an Afghan family, or if Indira Gandhi had been born into a low-caste poor South Indian family instead of a Kashmiri Brahman family. A broad discussion of the importance of gender in political psychology can be found in Sapiro (2003). Eagly and Carli (2007) discuss issues of gender and leadership, while Steinberg (2001; 2008) has studied particular women heads of government. Traister (2010) provides a gender perspective on the landmark 2008 US presidential campaign of Hillary Rodham Clinton.

4.7. Social Contexts of Particular Leaders

The importance of social contexts as well as the range of their variation can be demonstrated with sketches of three world leaders of major powers in the early years of the 21st century.

Vladimir Putin, president (1999–2008 and 2012–) and prime minister (1999-2000 and 2008-2012) of Russia. Although Putin was born in the former Leningrad (now St. Petersburg) in 1952, seven years after the end of World War II, the "Great Patriotic War" (as it is called in Russia) was for him an important historical context. His family lived through the terrible 900-day siege of Leningrad. Over a million Russians in that city died from starvation, freezing, or combat—including Putin's older brother, who died of diphtheria; his father was severely injured in the fighting. Thus he was in effect an only child. Although his family was not prominent, they did have low-level family connection to the Communist regime: his grandfather had been a cook for Lenin and later Stalin, and his father did sabotage work for the NKVD (now the KGB) behind German lines. After law studies at Leningrad State University, Putin served in the KGB. He was stationed in Dresden in the former East Germany at the time of the fall of the Berlin Wall and the collapse of East Germany.

Mariano Rajoy, prime minister of Spain (2011–). Rajoy's cultural and historical heritage encompasses the Golden Age of 16th-century Spain—a superpower at the center of a vast world economic and religious empire—and its subsequent decline, a vicious civil war in the 1930s, the Franco dictatorship and diplomatic isolation, and finally a return to constitutional democracy in the 1970s. His father was a judge in the Franco era, which suggests high social status, but within a now-discredited dictatorship tradition. Rajoy served in both the bureaucracy and the parliament. He said his military experience, involving cleaning duties, taught him "pride in a job well done," and made him "a real expert" in cleaning (Minder, 2011). Rajoy became prime minister in the immediate context of Spain's severe economic difficulties and the ongoing eurozone debt crisis.

Barack Obama, president of the United States (2009–). For Obama, as the first African American president, *race*—with all that means in terms of history, discrimination, social change, and finally how he is perceived by majority and minority Americans—is a supremely important social context. Yet his social contexts are actually many and varied. He is of mixed race. He lived in Indonesia for four years, then from the age of 10 he lived in Hawaii with his maternal (white) grandparents. He attended colleges in California and New York, worked as a community organizer in Chicago, and then graduated from Harvard Law School. Thus by the age of 30, Obama—with cultural roots in both white America and Africa—had lived in the eastern, midwestern, and Pacific regions of the United States, as well as in Hawaii and Asia. Finally, his adult political skills were honed in the legendary crucible of the Chicago Democratic political "machine" (see Winter, 2011).

4.8. The Importance of Social Contexts

Social contexts were placed first and treated at length because they establish and channel other elements of personality. They can *affect the levels* of certain personality variables. For example, certain religious beliefs and practices, by influencing independence training or permissiveness, can affect the development of achievement or power motives (McClelland, 1985, pp. 255–265, 325–328). Contexts also provide *networks of meanings*, customs, and relationships in which personality and behavior are embedded, which determine whether actions and dispositions are considered "normal" or pathological. For example, many Americans consider extraversion to be healthy and well adjusted, but to many Chinese *introversion* is normal and high levels of extraversion slightly abnormal. Third, certain personality characteristics may be unique or at least widespread (thus "typical") in certain cultures. For example, "amok" (a state of destructive, maddened excitement) in Southeast Asia and "amae" (a sense of entitled dependency) in Japan (see Berry, Poortinga, Segall, & Dasen, 1992, pp. 89–93).

Finally, social contexts *channel the expression* of all personality characteristics. For example, extraversion is associated with drinking coffee and smoking—but extraverted people who are also devout Mormons are unlikely to smoke or drink coffee because these actions are proscribed by their religion. As a "thought experiment," consider some clearly defined and familiar personality variables such as power motivation, optimistic explanatory style, extraversion, and conscientiousness. Each is associated with a recognized and characteristic set of observable behaviors. Yet imagine how differently each would have been expressed on the morning of June 6, 1944, by (1) a 20-year-old white American man storming "Utah Beach" during the World War II invasion of Normandy in France, and (2) a middle-aged Japanese American woman in an internment camp set up in the Utah desert at the beginning of the war by the US government for citizens and residents of Japanese ancestry. Clearly there would be enormous context effects on the expression of these four personality variables, such that predicting actions only from these variables would be difficult if not impossible, though a careful observer would probably be able to "recognize" expressions of the variables in the two different contexts.

Many structural and political variables also channel the expression of political leaders' personalities: the structure of the particular political system, the array of supporting and opposing political forces, the nature and tractability of social, economic, and political issues, and the existence and nature of external enemies and allies.

5. TRAITS AND POLITICAL ELITES

Because traits can be observed in a person's public behavior, they are encoded or represented in the adjectives and adverbs of everyday language. As a result, most traits can be assessed by asking those who know the person. As mentioned above, the current consensus in personality research is that trait terms cluster into five factors—often called the "Big Five" (see Wiggins, 1996). While the five factors are fairly robust across Indo-European languages (McCrae & Costa, 1997), some differences do emerge in studies based on languages such as Mandarin, especially when the researchers begin with indigenous adjectives rather than translations of imported words (see, for example, Cheung, Zhang, & Cheung, 2010). Table 14.3 presents the most common labels for the five trait factors, along with a brief description of politically relevant behaviors of people who score high and low on each factor.

5.1. Measuring Traits at a Distance

To measure traits at a distance, many political psychologists use raters—sometimes experts, sometimes college undergraduates, sometimes simply "raters." Expert

Table 14.3 Politically Relevant Behavior Associated with Five Trait Factors

	Politically relevant behavior of	
Trait factor number and names	High scorer	Low scorer
1. Extraversion-surgency	A leader, dominant, aggressive	Loyal follower
2. Warmth, agreeableness	Congenial	Remote, hostile
3. Conscientiousness	Responsible, gets things done, does the "dirty work"	Irresponsible, cuts losses, sociopathic; may discover creative shortcuts
4. Emotional stability, (low) neuroticism	Stable, "unflappable"	Can't make up mind, depressed, neurotic
5. Openness to experience	Curious, learns from experience	Rigid, close-minded

raters—those with extensive knowledge of the person or persons to be rated—are asked to draw on their knowledge. Less knowledgeable raters are usually supplied with standardized information or biographical sketches on which to base their ratings, as in the work of Simonton (1986; 1988). In the research of Rubenzer and Faschingbauer (2004) cited above, only openness to experience was significantly related to presidential success (as rated by historians in a prior study by Murray and Blessing, 1994), while extraversion showed a positive but nonsignificant trend. Perhaps there are many different styles of successful leadership. Alternatively, variation in other personality characteristics, as well as the situations, problems, and opportunities leaders face, may wash out the effects of broad trait factors.

Leaders' traits can also be assessed by analyzing how other people describe them, using everyday conversational or written language (see Winter, 1996, pp. 481–485, for an example). While it may be cumbersome to assemble a panel of experts to fill out personality questionnaires about leaders, for most leaders there is no shortage of descriptions by people who know and observe them—associates, friends, rivals, clients, enemies, journalists, and of course historians. The first step in such an analysis is to extract adjectives and adverbs that are described as "characteristic" or "typical" of the person. The contribution of each word or phrase to the leader's "score" on any given trait factor can be determined by tables that group adjectives into the five trait factors (see Goldberg, 1990; 1992; also Ashton et al., 2004, for factor loadings of 1,719 English descriptor root words, and Lee & Ashton, 2008, for loadings of 449 English adjectives). Descriptions drawn from ordinary language can also be mapped on the three factors of descriptive meaning (evaluation, potency, and activity) identified by Osgood, Suci, and Tannenbaum (1957) by using the tables in Heise (1965).

The five-factor model of traits is intended as a universal framework applicable to all persons, leaders and ordinary people alike. Some political psychologists have identified and measured more specific traits especially relevant to leadership and political elites. As discussed above, Greenstein and Barber each developed their own list of characteristics relevant to the performance of US presidents. Sigelman (2002) developed a content-analysis measure of Barber's "activity-passivity" dimension. Other political psychologists have adapted conventional psychological traits and concepts to at-a-distance measurement: for example, charismatic style (House, Spangler, & Woycke, 1991), proactivity (Deluga, 1998), and rigidity versus pragmatism (Keller, 2009). Simonton (2006) reported measures of IQ, "intellectual brilliance," and openness to experience of US presidents.

5.2. Traits as Perceived by Other Leaders

Do the five trait factors identified by psychologists have anything to do with the actual language that political leaders actually use to describe other leaders? Swede and Tetlock (1986) studied the memoirs of Henry Kissinger, former US national security adviser and secretary of state under presidents Nixon and Ford. First, they extracted Kissinger's descriptions of several other leaders. Then, rather than simply "mapping" the adjectives that Kissinger used to describe each leader onto the five-factor framework, as discussed in the previous paragraph, they used clustering procedures to identify the implicit dimensions that Kissinger himself used to describe other leaders. The results, presented in table 14.4, show that he did indeed use five clusters or factors. Some seem close to the standard five factors; others involved combinations of two or more factors. Swede and Tetlock then used their analysis to show how Kissinger described individual leaders, differentiated among different leaders, and organized leaders into implicit types. This technique suggests a way of assessing the cognitive dimensions of leaders' person-perceptions.

As a limitation broad trait factors, it is worth noting that when Kissinger described leaders he knew really well, he used exquisitely subtle and differentiated phrases that go well beyond trait factors. For example, he described former French president Charles de Gaulle as having "the natural haughtiness of a snow-capped Alpine peak," and former US president Lyndon Johnson as a "caged eagle" (Swede & Tetlock, 1986, p. 641).

5.3. Problems with Trait Descriptions of Leaders

Rubenzer and Faschingbauer (2004) described US president Abraham Lincoln as scoring high on openness to experience and low on emotional stability. These scores were based on biographers' judgments, which were in turn based on their knowledge of the facts of Lincoln's life. In other words, the trait "scores" are really summary descriptions of Lincoln's consistent public behavior. If we then use these scores to *explain* specific Lincoln behaviors—for example, that some neurotic action, such as calling off his initial engagement with Mary Todd, was "caused" by Lincoln's low emotional stability—we are in danger of circular reasoning.

Table 14.4 Henry Kissinger's Implicit Dimensions of Person–Perception

Cluster name	Description	Examples	Possible five-factor "translation"
Revolutionary greatness	Great, ruthless, self-assured, revolutionary	Mao Zedong Anwar Sadat	High extraversion
Realistic friendship	Friendly, decisive, ambivalent, close	Nelson Rockefeller Georges Pompidou	High agreeableness
Ambitious patriotism	Patriotic, suspicious, ambitious, ungenerous	Richard Nixon Nguyen Van Thieu	High extraversion Low agreeableness Low emotional stability
Professional anguish	Insecure, lonely, tough, proud	Indira Gandhi Kissinger himself	High conscientiousness Low emotional stability
Intellectual sophistication	Humorous, knowledgeable, skilled, subtle	Le Duc Tho Zhou Enlai	High openness to experience

Note: Based on Swede and Tetlock (1986).

Furthermore, does a trait-factor description of Lincoln, for all its "scientific" basis, really tells us anything about him that we didn't already know—that he was curious and read widely, and that he suffered inner torments? And wouldn't such a description apply to a very large number of people in the United States—calculating from his percentile scores and the size of the US population, perhaps over 300,000 in Lincoln's time and 3 million in the second decade of the 21st century? We have surely not achieved any deep understanding of Lincoln's personality by analyzing his trait factors. As McAdams (1992) wrote, the five-factor trait model uses the language of first impressions and provides only the "psychology of the stranger." It is a useful starting point in describing Lincoln to someone who doesn't know him, but there must be more to the personality of Abraham Lincoln or any other leader.

6. Cognitions and Political Elites

The cognitions of personality include specific and general beliefs (what is the case) and values (what ought to be; what is worth struggling and sacrificing to get or keep). Beliefs involve conceptions of human nature, morality, society, and the world order, as well as images of the self, one's associates, the nation, and the international system. Cognitions have both *content* (particular beliefs and values) and *structure* (how the individual cognitive elements are arranged and integrated).

6.1. Operational Code

One of the most widely used cognitive variables in elite personality profiles is the *operational code*. The concept was originally introduced by Leites (1951) as a way of organizing his Cold War–era study of Soviet leaders in terms of a "code" or set of operational rules that could supply coherent explanations of the Soviet behavior. George (1969) reframed the concept in terms of two kinds of beliefs: *philosophical beliefs* about the nature of political life (harmony or conflict), the predictability of the future, optimism versus pessimism, and the relative influence of human control versus chance on outcomes; and *instrumental beliefs* about selecting goals (maximizing or satisfying), tactics in pursuit of these goals (words versus deeds, rewards versus sanctions), and controlling risks. Walker and his colleagues (Schafer & Walker, 2006; Walker et al., 2003) have further refined the concept and developed methods of measuring operational codes through content analysis of texts, culminating in the quantitative computer-assisted Verbs In Context System (VICS), which calculates quantitative measures of operational code components as well as overall patterns (Schafer, 2000).

Using VICS, several researchers have constructed operational codes for leaders such as British prime ministers Margaret Thatcher (Crichlow, 2006) and Tony Blair (Schafer & Walker, 2001), US presidents George W. Bush (Renshon, 2008; Robison, 2006), Theodore Roosevelt, and Woodrow Wilson (Walker & Schafer, 2007), Cuban leader Fidel Castro and North Korean leader Kim Il Sung (Malici & Malici, 2005), leaders of the People's Republic of China (Feng, 2006), and terrorists (Lazarevska, Sholl, & Young, 2006). The usefulness of the operational code concept is not restricted to political leaders: thus Thies (2006) analyzed bankers during the 1997–1999 Asian financial crisis.

Other researchers have studied variation of operational codes within individual political leaders; for example, the difference between John F. Kennedy's "public" and "private" operational codes during the 1962 Cuban Missile Crisis (Marfleet, 2000; see also Renshon, 2009), differences across domains (Walker & Schafer, 2000), and consistency over time (Schafer & Crichlow, 2000; Dille, 2000).

6.2. Cognitive Complexity

The cognitive elements of personality include not only the content of specific beliefs, but also how they are arranged. Do leaders process information in simplistic ways, focusing only on a single perspective or black-and-white alternatives; or do they recognize different points of view and integrate them into broader complex perspectives? The content analysis measure of *integrative complexity* developed by Suedfeld and his colleagues (Suedfeld, 2010; Suedfeld et al., 2003) reflects these two processes of *differentiation* and *integration*. Suedfeld suggests that integrative complexity can reflect stable individual differences among leaders, but also more variable *states* brought on by external factors such as threats, dangers, and time pressure, as well as internal factors such as stress or emotional arousal.

Researchers have studied integrative complexity in several different groups of political leaders: members of the British House of Commons (Tetlock, 1984); Canadian prime ministers (Suedfeld, Conway, & Eichhorn, 2001), US presidents (Thoemmes & Conway, 2007) and Supreme Court justices (Tetlock, Bernzweig, & Gallant, 1985), traditionalist and reformist Soviet politicians during the 1980s (Tetlock & Boettger, 1989), Soviet and American foreign policy elites during the 1970s and early 1980s (Tetlock, 1985), and successful versus unsuccessful revolutionaries (Suedfeld and Rank, 1976). Specific individuals whose levels of integrative complexity have been assessed include Saddam Hussein (Suedfeld, 2003), Soviet president Gorbachev (Wallace, Suedfeld, & Thachuk, 1996), British prime ministers Neville Chamberlain (Walker & Watson, 1994) and Winston Churchill (Tetlock & Tyler, 1996), and US presidents Barack Obama (Suedfeld, Cross, & Brcic, 2011) and Bill Clinton (Suedfeld, 1994; Suedfeld & Tetlock, 2003). Suedfeld, Leighton, and Conway (2006) reported a parallel study of British prime minister Neville Chamberlain and German Führer Adolf Hitler during the fateful negotiations for the Munich agreement of 1938. Perhaps because of his ambivalence about reconciling conflicting imperatives of "standing up" to the Nazi leader and yet avoiding war, Chamberlain's level of complexity was almost twice as high as that of the single-minded and relentless Hitler. The Munich example suggests that high integrative complexity does not always lead to good decisions and political success. (Shakespeare's Hamlet was arguably too complex for his own good!)

6.3. Explanatory Style

How people explain events—particularly bad events and outcomes—reflects their balance of optimism and pessimism and may affect how long they persist after failure. Peterson, Seligman, and their colleagues (see Peterson, 1992) developed a measure of optimistic explanatory style based on explaining bad outcomes as the result of *external* (versus internal), *specific* (versus global), and *temporary* (versus enduring) factors. Among major world leaders, such optimism is associated with crisis escalation and aggression (Satterfield & Seligman, 1994; Satterfield, 1998), perhaps because it renders leaders vulnerable to misperceptions typically associated with starting wars (see White, 1990). More broadly, optimistic people are more comfortable with rejecting the status quo in ordinary politics (Niven, 2000). For US presidential candidates, optimism tends to predict victory (Zullow & Seligman, 1990).

6.4. Specific Cognitive Variables

Authoritarianism. The concept of authoritarianism is one of the most widely studied personality variables. It involves a set of beliefs about power, morality, and the social order, emphasizing obedience to authorities and the norms of conventional morality, as well as aggression toward those who are perceived as "different." Authoritarianism is measured by a self-report questionnaire, usually Altemeyer's (1996) measure of *right-wing authoritarianism*, which has replaced the classic but flawed F-scale originally developed by Adorno, Frenkel-Brunswik, Levinson, & Sanford (1950). The *concept* of authoritarianism is undoubtedly relevant to the study of many political elites and leaders. Judging by their actions, for example, it seems quite likely that among leaders of the former Soviet Union, Mikhail Gorbachev would have scored lower in authoritarianism than his predecessor Leonid Brezhnev, and Nikita Khrushchev (at least after 1953) lower than Joseph Stalin (see Naumov, 2000). However, without a validated at-a-distance measure, we cannot be sure. Molano and Winter (1998) used three content analysis measures developed by Hermann (1980b)—ethnocentrism, low cognitive complexity, and distrust—as a proxy measure for authoritarianism in their study of ethnopolitical war.

Cognitions related to the self. Self-esteem or self-confidence is an important feature of the self-concept. People will sometimes go to extraordinary lengths to preserve a high estimation of themselves along whatever dimensions are important to them and their culture. Threats to that self-esteem may be felt as an insult, requiring retaliation. Thus upon learning about the Soviet missiles in Cuba, John F. Kennedy responded with startled anger: "He can't do that to *me*!" (Neustadt & Allison, 1971, p. 122). Shortly thereafter, he told his advisers that "we're going to take out these missiles." Fortunately for the peace of the world, however, Kennedy's cooler instincts prevailed and war was avoided. In February 2011, as NATO forces launched air attacks on his military forces, Libyan leader Mu'ammar al-Gaddafi (2011) made extravagant public claims: Referring to himself as "a fighter" who would "die a martyr at the end," he claimed that "I am an international leader and millions defend me. I will extend a call to millions from the Sahara to the Sahara and we will march, I and the millions, to cleanse Libya inch by inch." Sometimes the maintenance of self-esteem pushes the leader to suicide. In April 1945, as the Red Army was conquering Berlin, Adolf Hitler (1945) decided to stay in the German capital and kill himself, "in order to escape the disgrace of deposition or capitulation" and because "I do not wish to fall into the hands of an enemy who requires a new spectacle."

In extreme cases, grandiose self-images, along with lack of empathy and rage in the face of frustration of self are signs of narcissistic disorder and "malignant narcissism" (Post, 1993a), concepts drawn from psychoanalytic theory (especially the work of Kohut, 1985). Narcissism is clearly relevant to the understanding of many leaders—perhaps especially as they age (Post, 1993b). For example, Mao Zedong (Sheng, 2001) was a highly successful strategist during his early and middle years, but as his grandiosity increased in his midsixties, he overestimated resources and ignored difficulties. The result was a series of ill thought-out and unrealistic plans, such as the breakneck industrialization of the "Great Leap Forward" of 1958–1960 or the Taiwan Straits crisis of 1958. The inevitable failures increased his paranoia and grandiosity, culminating in the Cultural Revolution of 1966–1976.

More quantitative content analysis measures have been developed for narcissism (Deluga, 1997) and the related "normal" concept of self-confidence (Hermann, 1980b). Schütz (1993; 2001) developed content analysis measures of the related concepts of assertive, aggressive, and defensive styles of self-presentation to analyze German political leaders of the 1990s.

Values. Values are those goals or standards of judgment that people refer to as if self-evidently desirable (White, 1951, p. 13). Because values are consciously endorsed and held, they are usually measured by asking people directly, for example with the widely used Schwartz Value Inventory (1992). However, White developed a content analysis system for scoring 50 values in written or spoken text. Eckhardt (1965) applied this system to political speeches and documents, and Eckhardt and White (1967) used it to compare value profiles of Khrushchev and Kennedy. More recently, Smith (2004) adapted White's coding system in a study comparing matched terrorist and nonterrorist groups and leaders (see also Smith, Suedfeld, Conway, & Winter, 2008).

7. Implicit Motives and Political Elites

Motives involve tendencies to approach desired goals or end-states, or avoid undesired or feared end-states. While the number of different human goals is potentially without limit, many psychologists have followed Murray (1938) in identifying 20 broad classes of goals as able to account for the major trends or strivings in people's lives. Drawing on theory and a variety of studies, Winter (1996, chaps. 4 and 5) argued that Murray's "catalog" of motives can be represented in spatial terms, organized by three *dimensions of motivated behavior*—achievement (forward/backward), affiliation (near/far), and power (up/down).

Since the best way to reach a goal depends on the opportunities and obstacles at the moment, any particular goal is likely to be associated with a wide variety of different actions, depending on the situation. (In contrast, traits involve consistency of action across situations.) Moreover, motives often operate at an *implicit* or even unconscious level: partly because of social desirability and defense mechanisms, but also because people may not attend to or verbalize the long-term trends of their actions. When asked about their motives, people often reply with cognitions or beliefs about what led them to act. For these reasons, implicit motives are usually measured through content analysis of verbal or written texts, using empirically derived scoring systems (see Winter, 1994; 1998b; 2003b; also Smith, 1992).

7.1. Studies of Political Leaders

Using content analysis of speeches, interviews, and other texts, researchers have studied the achievement, affiliation, and power motives of several key groups of US political leaders: presidents (Winter, 2002) and presidential candidates (Winter, 1995), Supreme Court justices (Aliotta, 1988), and state governors (Ferguson & Barth, 2002). Other studies produced motive profiles of southern Africa political leaders in the 1970s (Winter, 1980), candidates in the 1996 Russian presidential election (Valenty & Shiraev, 2001), key figures in the Northern Ireland peace talks that led to the 1998 Good Friday Agreement (Valenty & Carroll, 2002), and matched terrorist and nonterrorist groups

(Smith, 2008; see also Smith et al., 2008). Hermann included an adaptation of the power and affiliation motive measures in her studies of world leaders (Hermann, 1980b), members of the Politburo of the Communist Party of the Soviet Union in the 1970s (Hermann, 1980a), and sub-Saharan Africa leaders (Hermann, 1987).

Several studies have constructed motive profiles of individual leaders in order to understand their past actions or make predictions about future actions. Thus Winter and Carlson (1988) used the motive profile of former US president Richard Nixon to resolve several of the apparent paradoxes of his political career. For example, his changing political beliefs ("almost populist" during college, conservative "Redhunter" as a new member of Congress in 1947, and presidential guest of Communist Chinese leader Mao Zedong in 1972) arguably reflect the tendency of people who, like Nixon, score high in achievement motivation to modify their actions on the basis of feedback. And his bizarre behavior on the night of May 8–9, 1970—an aggressive press conference, followed by 51 telephone calls and finally a 4:30 A.M. visit to protesting college students at the Lincoln Memorial—can be understood as a reflection of his very high affiliation motive finally prevailing over his more moderate level of power motivation. Winter (1998a) related the increase of Bill Clinton's level of power motivation (relative to achievement) to the dramatic turnaround of his political fortunes from the early years of his first term to his landslide re-election in 1996. Hermann produced a profile of former Syrian president Hafiz al-Assad (Hermann, 1988). Suedfeld, Bluck, Ballard, and Baker-Brown (1990) analyzed the motives and integrative complexity of rival party leaders in Canadian general elections from 1945 to 1974. More recently, Winter analyzed motives and made predictions about George W. Bush (2001; 2005) and Barack Obama (2009; 2011; 2012).

Overall, these studies suggest that leaders scoring high in power motivation are inclined toward strong, forceful actions; as a result, they may be charismatic to their followers (House et al., 1991), but aggressive and warlike to opponents (Winter, 1980; 1987; 2004). Affiliation-motivated leaders, in contrast, are more peaceable and cooperative—so long as they are surrounded by like-minded others, and do not feel threatened. Achievement motivation, which is usually associated with entrepreneurial success, does not appear to make for success in politics, particularly if it is higher than power motivation (Winter, 2010b). Achievement-motivated leaders tend to become frustrated by some many inherent features of political life: for example, one leader's conception of "the best" is likely to be disputed or opposed by others, it will likely cost too much, and its implementation usually depends on bureaucrats whom the leader did not select and cannot dismiss.

7.2. Leader-Society Motive Congruence

Several studies have examined the relationship between motives of a leader (measured through content analysis of speeches) and motives of that leader's society (measured through content analysis of popular literature). Winter (1987) found that the closer the president's motive profile to that of US society at the time, the higher that president's margin of victory—thus supporting theories of leadership that emphasize psychological congruence between leaders and followers. Ethington (2001) found a similar relationship in a study of short-term fluctuations of candidate speeches and polling data during the 2000 US presidential campaign. Schmitt and Winter (1998) studied leaders and society in the Soviet Union between 1924 and 1986 and found a different kind of leader-society congruence: the motive profile of Soviet society came to resemble that of the leader during the years *after* the leader's accession.

8. Toward a Multivariate, Integrative Study of Personality

While personality researchers are still looking for the ideal research strategy and statistical algorithms for dealing with the complexity of personality, one general guideline seems important: if personality comprises different independent elements, it follows that the most complete personality assessments and the most accurate predictions from personality to political behavior will use *combinations* of multiple variables, preferably reflecting the four elements of personality described in this chapter.

As an example, Hermann (2003) developed a method for assigning leaders to one of six integrated *orientations* on the basis of their scores on several different motivational, cognitive, and trait-style component variables. Hermann's system has been used in numerous comparative studies: world leaders (Hermann, 1980a), Soviet Politburo members during the mid-1970s (Hermann, 1980b), British and German prime ministers (Kaarbo, 2001; Kaarbo & Hermann, 1998), British leaders' decisions to stay out of Vietnam but participate in the Iraq war (Dyson, 2007), Lyndon Johnson and the Vietnam war (Preston & t'Hart, 1999), and former Iranian president Khatami (Taysi & Preston, 2001).

Another promising development is the appearance of collaborative studies, in which different political psychologists join together—employing their own methods for studying leaders and elites at a distance—to produce an integrative profile. For example, Winter, Hermann, Weintraub, and Walker (1991b; 1991a) applied their own methods of personality measurement to make comparative assessments of US president George H. W. Bush and Soviet president Mikhail Gorbachev. Post (2003) brought together a group of political psychologists who carried out parallel and comparative assessments of Bill Clinton and Saddam Hussein, using their different methods and measures (political personal profiling, verbal behavior assessment, scoring for motive imagery and integrative complexity, operational code analysis, and Hermann's multivariate profiling). As mentioned above, Smith et al. (2008) used their individual content analysis measures to compare terrorist and nonterrorist groups. Expanded versions of these studies were published in 2011 in a special issue of *Dynamics of Asymmetric Conflict* (volume 4, issue 2).

9. THE FUTURE OF AT-A-DISTANCE ASSESSMENT: A LESSON IN HUMILITY

With the growing use of digitally based systems for the analysis of verbal content, we may expect that computerized scoring procedures for many more personality characteristics will be developed in the future, although on account of the incredible subtlety and complexity of human language, such goals may be farther away and more difficult to achieve than "cyber-optimists" imagine.

At the same time, we must recognize that even with the best measures, predictions of political leaders' behavior must always be phrased in contingent or conditional, "if/then" terms (Wright & Mischel, 1987; 1988). For example, Winter et al. (1991b) described George H. W. Bush as a "peacemaker, concerned with development and not prone to seek political ends through violence and war" (p. 237). Yet during the autumn of 1990 Bush threatened military action against Iraq, and in January 1991, this affiliation-motivated president began a devastating (if mercifully short) war. Of course the proximate cause of Bush's aggressive policy was the August 1990 Iraqi invasion of Kuwait, which certainly could not have been predicted from any knowledge of Bush's personality. That conceded, however, many features of Bush's policy and conduct of the war *can* be derived from the personality portrait sketched by Winter et al. (1991b): impulsivity, angry, and defensive reactions to perceived threat, demonizing dissimilar others, and alliance-building with similar others via extensive communication.

The effects of leaders' personalities always depend on the situations in which they find themselves—and by itself personality profiling cannot precisely predict those situations. Nevertheless, in most situations we can trace the effects of personality. Perhaps a certain amount of humility is appropriate to the task of profiling leaders and elite groups, with predictions "conditionally hedged," to take account of unpredictable changes in the situation.

REFERENCES

Adorno, T. W., Frenkel-Brunswik, E., Levinson, D. J., & Sanford, R. N. (1950). *The authoritarian personality*. New York: Harper.

Aliotta, J. M. (1988). Social backgrounds, social motives and participation on the U.S. Supreme Court. *Political Behavior, 10*, 267–284.

Allport, G. W. (1961). *Pattern and growth in personality*. New York: Holt, Rinehart, & Winston.

Allport, G. W., & Odbert, H. S. (1936). Trait-names: A psycho-lexical study. *Psychological Monographs, 47*(1). (Whole number 211).

Altemeyer, B. (1996). *The authoritarian specter*. Cambridge, MA: Harvard University Press.

Ashton, M. C., Lee, K., & Goldberg, L. R. (2004). A hierarchical analysis of 1,710 English personality-descriptive adjectives. *Journal of Personality and Social Psychology, 87*(5), 707–721.

Barber, J. D. (1992). *The presidential character: Predicting performance in the White House* (4th ed.). Englewood Cliffs, NJ: Prentice-Hall.

Barenbaum, N. B., & Winter, D. G. (2008). History of modern personality theory and research. In O. P. John, R. W. Robins, & L. A. Pervin (eds.), *Handbook of personality theory and research* (3rd ed., pp. 3-26). New York: Guilford Press.

Berry, J. W., Poortinga, Y. H., Segall, M. H., & Dasen, P. R. (1992). *Cross-cultural psychology: Research and applications.* New York: Cambridge University Press.

Block, J. (1961). *The Q-sort method in personality assessment and psychiatric research.* Springfield, IL: Charles C Thomas.

Block, J. (2010). *The Q-sort in character appraisal: Encoding subjective impressions of persons quantitatively.* Washington, DC: American Psychological Association.

Blondel, J. (1987). *Political leadership: Towards a general analysis.* London: Sage.

Blondel, J., & Thiébault, J.-L. (Eds.). (2010). *Political leadership, parties and citizens: The personalisation of leadership.* New York: Routledge.

Boroson, W. (1964). What psychiatrists say about Goldwater. *Fact, 1*(5), 24-64.

Brown, S. R. (1986). Q technique and method: Principles and procedures. In W. D. Berry & M. S. Lewis-Beck (eds.), *New tools for social scientists: Advances and applications in research methods* (pp. 57-77). Beverly Hills, CA: Sage.

Burns, J. F. (2000, February 6). Methods of the great leader. *New York Times,* p. 7.

Byman, D., & Pollack, K. (2001). Let us now praise great men: Bringing the statesman back in. *International Security, 25,* 107-146.

Carey, B. (2011, March 29). Teasing out policy insight from a character profile. *New York Times,* pp. D1, 6. Retrieved July 14, 2012, from http://www.nytimes.com/2011/03/29/science/29psych.html?_r=1&scp=2&sq=carey%20character&st=cse.

Carr, M. (2009). *Blood and faith: The purging of Muslim Spain.* New York: New Press.

Cheung, F. M. C., Zhang, J., & Cheung, S. F. (2010). From indigenous to cross-cultural personality: The case of the Chinese Personality Assessment Inventory. In M. H. Bond (ed.), *The Oxford handbook of Chinese psychology* (pp. 295-308). New York: Oxford University Press.

Costa, P. M., & McCrae, R. (1992). *The Revised NEO Personality Inventory professional manual.* Odessa, FL: Psychological Assessment Resources.

Crichlow, S. (2006). The eyes of Kesteven: How the worldviews of Margaret Thatcher and her cabinet influenced British foreign policy. In M. Schafer & S. G. Walker (eds.), *Beliefs and leadership in world politics: Methods and applications of operational code analysis* (pp. 77-100). New York: Palgrave Macmillan.

de St. Aubin, E., McAdams, D. P., & Kim, T.-C. (Eds.). (2003). *The generative society: Caring for future generations.* Washington, DC: American Psychological Association.

Deluga, R. (1997). Relationship among American presidential charismatic leadership, narcissism, and rated performance. *Leadership Quarterly, 8,* 49-65.

Deluga, R. (1998). American presidential proactivity, charismatic leadership, and rated performance. *Leadership Quarterly, 9,* 165-291.

Dille, B. (2000). The prepared and spontaneous remarks of Presidents Reagan and Bush: A validity comparison for at-a-distance measurements. *Political Psychology, 21,* 573-585.

Dyson, S. B. (2007). Alliances, domestic politics, and leader psychology: Why did Britain stay out of Vietnam and go into Iraq? *Political Psychology, 28,* 647-666.

Eagly, A. H., & Carli, L. L. (2007). *Through the labyrinth: The truth about how women become leaders.* Boston: Harvard Business School Press.

Eckhardt, W. (1965). War propaganda, welfare values, and political ideology. *Journal of Conflict Resolution, 9*, 345–358.

Eckhardt, W., & White, R. K. (1967). A test of the mirror-image hypothesis: Kennedy and Khrushchev. *Journal of Conflict Resolution, 11*, 325–332.

Egorova, E. V. (1982). *The influence of the political situation on foreign-policy decision-making in capitalist states: Political-psychological aspects* [Russian language]. Moscow: Nauka.

Elms, A. C. (1994). *Uncovering lives: The uneasy alliance of biography and psychology.* New York: Oxford University Press.

Erikson, E. H. (1982). Psychosexuality and the cycle of generations. In E. H. Erikson, *The life cycle completed* (pp. 25–53). New York: Norton.

Erikson, E. H., Erikson, J. M., & Kivnick, H. Q. (1986). *Vital involvement in old age.* New York: Norton.

Ethington, L. (2001). Election 2000: A time-series analysis of motive profiles and other variables in the U.S. presidential campaign. Honors thesis, Department of Psychology, University of Michigan.

Evgenieva, T. V. (2008). Problems of national identity in contemporary Russia [Russian language]. In E. B. Shestopal (ed.), *Images of the state, nation and leaders* (pp. 167–174). Moscow: Aspect Press.

Feng, H. (2006). Crisis deferred: An operational code analysis of Chinese leaders across the strait. In M. Schafer & S. G. Walker (eds.), *Beliefs and leadership in world politics: Methods and applications of operational code analysis* (pp. 151–170). New York: Palgrave Macmillan.

Ferguson, M. R., & Barth, J. (2002). Governors in the legislative arena: The importance of personality in shaping success. *Political Psychology, 23*, 787–808.

Frank, J. A. (2004). *Bush on the couch: Inside the mind of the president.* New York: HarperCollins.

Freud, S. ([1910] 1957). Leonardo da Vinci and a memory of his childhood. In J. Strachey (ed.), *The standard edition of the complete psychological works of Sigmund Freud* (vol. 11, pp. 63–137). London: Hogarth Press.

Friedlander, S., & Cohen, R. (1975). The personality correlates of belligerence in international conflict. *Comparative Politics, 7*, 155–186.

Fukai, S. N. (2001). Building the war economy and rebuilding postwar Japan: A profile of pragmatic nationalist Nobusuke Kishi. In O. Feldman & L. O. Valenty (eds.), *Profiling political leaders: Cross-cultural studies of personality and political behavior* (pp. 167–184). Westport, CT: Praeger.

Gaddafi, M. al- (2011, February 22). Speech broadcast on Libyan state-run Al-Jamahiriyah TV and transcribed by *BBC Monitoring International Reports*, February 23, 2011. Retrieved, April 16, 2011, from Lexis-Nexus Academic.

George, A. L. (1969). The "operational code": A neglected approach to the study of political leaders and decision-making. *International Studies Quarterly, 13*, 190–222.

George, A. L. ([1971] 1987). Some uses of dynamic psychology in political biography: Case materials on Woodrow Wilson. In T. L. Crosby and G. Cocks (eds.), *Psycho/history: Readings in the method of psychology, psychoanalysis, and history* (pp. 132–156). New Haven, CT: Yale University Press.

Gilbert, R. E. (2006). Psychological illness in presidents: A medical advisory commission and disability determinations. *Political Psychology, 27*, 55–75.

Glad, B. (1973). Contributions of psychobiography. In J. N. Knutson (ed.), *Handbook of political psychology* (pp. 296–321). San Francisco: Jossey-Bass.

Goldberg, L. R. (1990). An alternative "description of personality": The Big-Five factor structure. *Journal of Personality and Social Psychology, 59*, 1216–1229.

Goldberg, L. R. (1992). The development of markers for the Big-Five factor structure. *Psychological Assessment, 4*, 26–42.

Greenstein, F. I. ([1969] 1987). *Personality and politics: Problems of evidence, inference, and conceptualization.* Princeton, NJ: Princeton University Press.

Greenstein, F. I. (2009a). *Inventing the job of president: Leadership style from George Washington to Andrew Jackson.* Princeton, NJ: Princeton University Press.

Greenstein, F. I. (2009b). *The presidential difference: Leadership style from FDR to Barack Obama* (3rd ed.). Princeton, NJ: Princeton University Press.

Greenstein, F. I. (2013). *Presidents and the dissolution of the Union: Leadership style from Polk to Lincoln.* Princeton, NJ: Princeton University Press.

Hamby, A. L. (1991). An American democrat: A reevaluation of the personality of Harry S. Truman. *Political Science Quarterly, 106*, 33–55.

Hargrove, E. C. (2008). *The effective presidency: Lessons on leadership from John F. Kennedy to George W. Bush.* Boulder, CO: Paradigm Publishers.

Hart, R. P. (2001). Redeveloping DICTION: Theoretical considerations. In M. West (ed.), *Theory, method, and practice of computer content analysis* (pp. 43–60). New York: Ablex.

Heise, D. R. (1965). Semantic differential profiles for 1,000 most frequent English words. *Psychological Monographs: General and Applied, 79*(8, Whole No. 601), 1–31.

Henderson, J. (2001). Predicting the performance of leaders in parliamentary systems: New Zealand prime minister David Lange. In O. Feldman & L. O. Valenty (eds.), *Profiling political leaders: Cross-cultural studies of personality and political behavior* (pp. 203–216). Westport, CT: Praeger.

Hermann, M. G. (1980a). Assessing the personalities of Soviet Politburo members. *Personality and Social Psychology Bulletin, 6*, 332–352.

Hermann, M. G. (1980b). Explaining foreign policy behavior using the personal characteristics of political leaders. *International Studies Quarterly, 24*, 7–46.

Hermann, M. G. (1987). Assessing the foreign policy role orientations of sub-Saharan African leaders. In S. G. Walker (ed.), *Role theory and foreign policy analysis* (pp. 161–198). Durham, NC: Duke University Press.

Hermann, M. G. (1988). Syria's Hafez al-Assad. In B. Kellerman & J. Z. Rubin (eds.), *Leadership and negotiation in the Middle East* (pp. 70–95). New York: Praeger.

Hermann, M. G. (2003). Assessing leadership style: Trait analysis. In J. M. Post (ed.), *The psychological assessment of political leaders* (pp. 178–212). Ann Arbor: University of Michigan Press.

Hitler, A. (1945). "Last will" and "My political testament." Retrieved, April 16, 2011, from http://en.wikipedia.org/wiki/Last_will_and_testament_of_Adolf_Hitler.

Hofstede, G. H. (2001). *Culture's consequences: Comparing values, behaviors, institutions, and organizations across nations* (2nd ed.). Thousand Oaks, CA: Sage.

House, R. J., Spangler, W. D., & Woycke, J. (1991). Personality and charisma in the U.S. presidency: A psychological theory of leader effectiveness. *Administrative Science Quarterly, 36*, 364–396.

Ihanus, J. (2001). Profiling Russian leaders from a psychohistorical and a psychobiographical perspective. In O. Feldman & L. O. Valenty (eds.), *Profiling political leaders: Cross-cultural studies of personality and political behavior* (pp. 129–147). Westport, CT: Praeger.

Immelman, A. (1993). The assessment of political personality: A psychodiagnostically relevant conceptualization and methodology. *Political Psychology, 14*, 725–741.

Immelman, A. (2004). *Millon inventory of diagnostic criteria manual* (2nd ed.). Manuscript, Department of Psychology, St. John's University, Collegeville, MN.

Isaacson, W. (1992). *Kissinger: A biography*. New York: Simon and Schuster.

Kaarbo, J. (2001). Linking leadership style to policy: How prime ministers influence the decision-making process. In O. Feldman & L. O. Valenty (eds.), *Profiling political leaders: Cross-cultural studies of personality and political behavior* (pp. 81–96). Westport, CT: Praeger.

Kaarbo, J., & Hermann, M. G. (1998). Leadership styles of prime ministers: How individual differences affect the foreign policymaking process. *Leadership Quarterly, 9,* 243–263.

Kakar, S. (1968). The human life cycle: The traditional Hindu view and the psychology of Erik Erikson. *Philosophy East and West, 18,* 127–136.

Keller, J. W. (2009). Explaining rigidity and pragmatism in political leaders: A general theory and a plausibility test from the Reagan presidency. *Political Psychology, 30,* 465–498.

Kennedy, P. (1982). The Kaiser and German Weltpolitik: Reflexions on Wilhelm II's place in the making of German foreign policy. In J. C. G. Röhl & N. Sombart (eds.), *Kaiser Wilhelm II: New interpretations* (pp. 143–168). New York: Cambridge University Press.

Kershaw, I. (1999). *Hitler, 1889–1936: Hubris*. New York: Norton.

Kershaw, I. (2000). *Hitler, 1936–1945: Nemesis*. New York: Norton.

Kertzer, D. I. (1983). Generation as a sociological problem. *Annual Review of Sociology, 9,* 125–149. Palo Alto, CA: Annual Reviews Press.

Kipnis, D. (1976). *The powerholders*. Chicago: University of Chicago Press.

Kirkpatrick, I. (1964). *Mussolini: A study in power*. New York: Hawthorn Books.

Kohut, H. (1985). *Self psychology and the humanities*. New York: Norton.

Kowert, P. (1996). Where *does* the buck stop? Assessing the impact of presidential personality. *Political Psychology, 17,* 421–452.

Lazarevska, E., Sholl, J. M., & Young, M. D. (2006). Links among beliefs and personality traits: The distinctive language of terrorists. In M. Schafer & S. G. Walker (eds.), *Beliefs and leadership in world politics: Methods and applications of operational code analysis* (pp. 171–186). New York: Palgrave Macmillan.

Lee, K., & Ashton, M. C. (2008). The HEXACO personality factors in the indigenous personality lexicons of English and 11 other languages. *Journal of Personality, 76*(5), 1001–1053.

Leites, N. (1951). *The operational code of the Politburo*. New York: McGraw-Hill.

Malici, A., & Malici, J. (2005). The operational codes of Fidel Castro and Kim Il Sung: The last cold warriors? *Political Psychology, 26,* 387–412.

Mandela, N. (1994, May 9). Address to the people of Cape Town on his inaugural as state president. Retrieved, April 6, 2011, from http://db.nelsonmandela.org/speeches/pub_view.asp?pg=item&ItemID=NMS175&txtstr=inauguration.

Mannheim, K. ([1928] 1952). The problem of generations. In *Essays on the sociology of knowledge,* pp. 276–322. New York: Oxford University Press.

Marfleet, B. G. (2000). The operational code of John F. Kennedy during the Cuban Missile Crisis: A comparison of public and private rhetoric. *Political Psychology, 21,* 545–558.

McAdams, D. P. (1992). The five-factor model in personality: A critical appraisal. *Journal of Personality, 60,* 329–361.

McAdams, D. P., & de St. Aubin, E. (Eds.). (1998). *Generativity and adult development: How and why we care for the next generation*. Washington, DC: American Psychological Association.

McClelland, D. C. (1985). *Human motivation*. Glenview, IL: Scott, Foresman.

McCrae, R. R., &, Costa, P. T., Jr. (1997). Personality trait structure as a human universal. *American Psychologist, 52,* 509–516.

Millon, T. (1990). *Toward a new personology: An evolutionary model*. New York: Wiley.

Minder, R. (2011, December 15). For Spain's next prime minister, rigor is watchword. *New York Times*. Retrieved, July 14, 2012, from http://www.nytimes.com/2011/12/16/world/europe/16iht-spain16.html?pagewanted=all.

Moen, P., Elder, & Lüscher, K. (Eds.). (1995). *Examining lives in context: Perspectives on the ecology of human development*. Washington, DC: American Psychological Association.

Molano, J. R. V., & Winter, D. G. (1998, August). Toward a psychological theory of ethnopolitical war. Paper presented at the International Congress of Applied Psychology, San Francisco.

Mugabe, R. (2008, April 18). Independence Day speech. Text published in BBC Worldwide Monitoring (BBC Monitoring-Africa), April 19, 2008. Retrieved May 12, 2008, from www.lexisnexis.com/us/lnacademic.

Murray, H. A. (1938). *Explorations in personality*. New York: Oxford University Press.

Murray, R. K., & Blessing, T. H. (1994). *Greatness in the White House: Rating the presidents*. University Park: Pennsylvania State University Press.

Naumov, V. (2000). Repression and rehabilitation. In W. Taubman, S. Khrushchev, & A. Gleason (eds.), *Nikita Khrushchev* (pp. 85–112). New Haven, CT: Yale University Press.

Nets-Zehngut, R. (2011). Palestinian autobiographical memory regarding the 1948 Palestinian Exodus. *Political Psychology, 32*, 271–295.

Neustadt, R. E., & Allison, G. T. (1971). Afterword. In R. F. Kennedy, *Thirteen days* (pp. 107–150). New York: Norton.

Nisbett, R., & Cohen, D. (1995). *The culture of honor: The psychology of violence in the South*. Boulder, CO: Westview Press.

Niven, D. (2000). The other side of optimism: High expectations and the rejection of status quo politics. *Political Behavior, 22*, 71–88.

Osgood, C. E., Suci, G. J., & Tannenbaum, P. H. (1957). *The measurement of meaning*. Urbana: University of Illinois Press.

Pennebaker, J. W., Booth, R. J., & Francis, M. E. (2007). *Linguistic inquiry and word count (LIWC2007)*. Austin, TX. Retrieved March 15, 2011, from http://www.liwc.net.

Peterson, C. (1992). Explanatory style. In C. P. Smith (ed.), *Motivation and personality: Handbook of thematic content analysis* (pp. 376–382). New York: Cambridge University Press.

Post, J. M. (1979, Spring). Personality profiles in support of the Camp David summit. *Studies in Intelligence*, 1–5.

Post, J. M. (1980). The seasons of a leader's life: Influences of the life cycle on political behavior. *Political Psychology, 2*(3–4), 35–49.

Post, J. M. (1993a). Current concepts of the narcissistic personality: Implications for political psychology. *Political Psychology, 14*, 99–121.

Post, J. M. (1993b). Dreams of glory and the life cycle: Reflections on the life course of narcissistic leaders. In R. G. Braungart & M. M. Braungart (eds.), *Life course and generational politics* (pp. 49–60). Lanham, MD: University Press of America.

Post, J. M. (Ed.). (2003). *The psychological assessment of political leaders*. Ann Arbor: University of Michigan Press.

Post, J. M. (2004). *Leaders and their followers in a dangerous world*. Ithaca, NY: Cornell University Press.

Preston, T., & t'Hart, P. (1999). Understanding and evaluating bureaucratic politics: The nexus between political leaders and advisory systems. *Political Psychology, 20*, 49–98.

Pye, L. W., & Pye, M. W. (1985). *Asian power and politics: The cultural dimensions of authority*. Cambridge, MA: Harvard University Press.

Renshon, J. (2008). Stability and change in belief systems: The operational code of George W. Bush. *Journal of conflict resolution, 52,* 381–398.

Renshon, J. (2009). When public statements reveal private beliefs: Assessing operational codes at a distance. *Political Psychology, 30,* 649–661.

Renshon, S. A. (2003). Psychoanalytic assessments of character and performance in presidents and candidates: Some observations on theory and method. In J. M. Post (ed.), *The psychological assessment of political leaders* (pp. 105–133). Ann Arbor: University of Michigan Press.

Robison, S. (2006). George W. Bush and the Vulcans: Leader-advisor relations and America's response to the 9/11 attacks. In M. Schafer & S. G. Walker (eds.), *Beliefs and leadership in world politics: Methods and applications of operational code analysis* (pp. 101–126). New York: Palgrave Macmillan.

Rubenzer, S. J., & Faschingbauer, T. R. (2004). *Personality, character, and leadership in the White House: Psychologists assess the presidents.* Washington, DC: Brassey's.

Sanfilippo, A., Franklin, L., Tratz, S., Danielson, G., Mileson, N., Riensche, R., & McGrath, L. (2008). Automating frame analysis. In H. Liu, J. Salerno, & M. Young (eds.), *Social computing, behavioral modeling, and prediction* (pp. 239–248). New York: Springer.

Sapiro, V. (2003). Theorizing gender in political psychology research. In D. O. Sears, L. Huddy, & R. Jervis (eds.), *Oxford handbook of political psychology* (pp. 601–634). New York: Oxford University Press.

Satterfield, J. M. (1998). Cognitive-affective states predict military and political aggression and risk taking: A content analysis of Churchill, Hitler, Roosevelt, and Stalin. *Journal of Conflict Resolution, 42,* 667–690.

Satterfield, J. M., & Seligman, M. E. P. (1994). Military aggression and risk predicted by explanatory style. *Psychological Science, 5,* 77–82.

Schafer, M. (2000). Issues in assessing psychological characteristics at a distance: An introduction to the symposium. *Political Psychology, 21,* 511–527.

Schafer, M., & Crichlow, S. (2000). Bill Clinton's operational code: Assessing source material bias. *Political Psychology, 21,* 559–571.

Schafer, M., & Walker, S. G. (2001). Political leadership and the democratic peace: The operational code of Prime Minister Tony Blair. In O. Feldman & L. O. Valenty (eds.), *Profiling political leaders: Cross-cultural studies of personality and political behavior* (pp. 21–35). Westport, CT: Praeger.

Schafer, M., & Walker, S. G. (Eds.). (2006). *Beliefs and leadership in world politics: Methods and applications of operational code analysis.* New York: Palgrave Macmillan.

Schmitt, D. P., & Winter, D. G. (1998). Measuring the motives of Soviet leadership and Soviet society: Congruence reflected or congruence created? *Leadership Quarterly, 9,* 181–194.

Schultheiss, O. C., & Bronstein, J. C. (2010). *Implicit motives.* New York: Oxford University Press.

Schultz, W. T. (2005). *Handbook of psychobiography.* New York: Oxford University Press.

Schütz, A. (1993). Self-presentational tactics used in a German election campaign. *Political Psychology, 14,* 471–493.

Schütz, A. (2001). Self-presentation of political leaders in Germany: The case of Helmut Kohl. In O. Feldman & L. O. Valenty (eds.), *Profiling political leaders: Cross-cultural studies of personality and political behavior* (pp. 217–232). Westport, CT: Praeger.

Schwartz, S. H. (1992). Universals in the content and structure of values: Theoretical advances and empirical tests in 20 countries. In M. Zanna (ed.), *Advances in experimental social psychology, 25,* 1–65. New York: Academic Press.

Sheng, M. M. (2001). Mao Zedong's narcissistic personality disorder and China's road to disaster. In O. Feldman & L. O. Valenty (eds.), *Profiling political leaders: Cross-cultural studies of personality and political behavior* (pp. 111–127). Westport, CT: Praeger.

Shestopal, E. B. (2000a). *Images of power in the political culture of Russia* [Russian language]. Moscow: Moskovskii ob-nyi nauch Fond.

Shestopal, E. B. (2000b). *A psychological profile of Russian politics of the 1990s: Theoretical and applied problems of political psychology* [Russian language]. Moscow: Rosspen.

Shestopal, E. B. (2008). *Images of Russian power: From Yeltsin to Putin* [Russian language]. Moscow: Rosspen.

Sigelman, L. (2002). Two Reagans? Genre imperatives, ghostwriters, and presidential personality profiling. *Political Psychology, 23,* 839–851.

Simonton, D. K. (1986). Presidential personality: Biographical use of the Gough Adjective Check List. *Journal of Personality and Social Psychology, 51,* 149–160.

Simonton, D. K. (1988). Presidential style: Personality, biography, and performance. *Journal of Personality and Social Psychology, 55,* 928–936.

Simonton, D. K. (2006). Presidential IQ, openness, intellectual brilliance, and leadership: Estimates and correlations for 42 U.S. chief executives. *Political Psychology, 27,* 511–526.

Smith, A. G. (2004). From words to action: Exploring the relationship between a group's value references and its likelihood of engaging in terrorism. *Studies in Conflict and Terrorism, 27,* 409–437.

Smith, A. G. (2008). The implicit motives of terrorist groups: How the needs for affiliation and power translate into death and destruction, *29,* 55–75.

Smith, A. G., Suedfeld, P., Conway, L. G., & Winter, D. G. (2008). The language of violence: Distinguishing terrorist from non-terrorist groups using thematic content analysis. *Dynamics of Asymmetrical Conflict, 1,* 142–163.

Smith, C. P. (Ed.). (1992). *Motivation and personality: Handbook of thematic content analysis.* New York: Cambridge University Press.

Steinberg, B. S. (2001). The making of female presidents and prime ministers: The impact of birth order, sex of siblings, and father-daughter dynamics. *Political Psychology, 22,* 89–110.

Steinberg, B. S. (2008). *Women in power: The personalities and leadership styles of Indira Gandhi, Golda Meir, and Margaret Thatcher.* Montreal: McGill-Queen's University Press.

Stewart, A. J., & Healy, J. M., Jr. (1989). Linking individual development and social change. *American Psychologist, 44,* 30–42.

Suedfeld, P. (1994). President Clinton's policy dilemmas: A cognitive analysis. *Political Psychology, 15,* 337–349.

Suedfeld, P. (2003). Saddam Hussein's integrative complexity under stress. In J. M. Post (ed.), *The psychological assessment of political leaders* (pp. 391–396). Ann Arbor: University of Michigan Press.

Suedfeld, P. (2010). The cognitive processing of politics and politicians: Archival studies of conceptual and integrative complexity. *Journal of Personality, 78,* 1669–1702.

Suedfeld, P., Bluck, S., Ballard, E. J., & Baker-Brown, G. (1990). Canadian federal elections: Motive profiles and integrative complexity in political speeches and popular media. *Canadian Journal of Behavioural Science, 22,* 26–36.

Suedfeld, P., Conway, L. G., & Eichhorn, D. (2001). Studying Canadian leaders at a distance. In O. Feldman & L. O. Valenty (eds.), *Profiling political leaders: Cross-cultural studies of personality and political behavior* (pp. 3–19). Westport, CT: Praeger.

Suedfeld, P., Cross, R. W., & Brcic, J. (2011). Two years of ups and downs: Barack Obama's patterns of integrative complexity. *Political Psychology, 32*, 1007–1033.

Suedfeld, P., Guttieri, K., & Tetlock, P. E. (2003). Assessing integrative complexity at a distance: Archival analyses of thinking and decision making. In J. M. Post (ed.), *The psychological assessment of political leaders* (pp. 246–270). Ann Arbor: University of Michigan Press.

Suedfeld, P., Leighton, D. C., & Conway, L. G., III. (2006). Integrative complexity and decision-making in international confrontations. In M. Fitzduff & C. E. Stout (eds.), *The psychology of resolving global conflicts: Nature vs. nurture* (vol. 1, pp. 211–237). Westport, CT: Praeger.

Suedfeld, P., & Rank, A. D. (1976). Revolutionary leaders: Long-term success as a function of changes in conceptual complexity. *Journal of Personality and Social Psychology, 34*, 169–178.

Suedfeld, P., & Tetlock, P. E. (2003). President Clinton: Cognitive manager in trouble. In J. M. Post (ed.), *The psychological assessment of political leaders* (pp. 328–332). Ann Arbor: University of Michigan Press.

Swede, S. W., & Tetlock, P. E. (1986). Henry Kissinger's implicit theory of personality: A quantitative case study. *Journal of Personality, 54*, 617–746.

Taysi, T., & Preston, T. (2001). The personality and leadership style of President Khatami: Implications for the future of Iranian political reform. In O. Feldman & L. O. Valenty (eds.), *Profiling political leaders: Cross-cultural studies of personality and political behavior* (pp. 57–77). Westport, CT: Praeger.

Tetlock, P. E. (1984). Cognitive style and political belief systems in the British House of Commons. *Journal of Personality and Social Psychology, 46*, 365–375.

Tetlock, P. E. (1985). Integrative complexity of American and Soviet foreign policy rhetoric: A time-series analysis. *Journal of Personality and Social Psychology, 49*, 1565–1585.

Tetlock, P. E., Bernzweig, J., & Gallant, J. L. (1985). Supreme Court decision making: Cognitive style as a predictor of ideological consistency of voting. *Journal of Personality and Social Psychology, 48*, 1227–1239.

Tetlock, P. E., & Boettger, R. (1989). Cognitive and rhetorical styles of traditionalist and reformist Soviet politicians: A content analysis study. *Political Psychology, 10*, 209–232.

Tetlock, P. E., & Tyler, A. (1996). Churchill's cognitive and rhetorical style: The debates over Nazi intentions and self-government for India. *Political Psychology, 17*, 149–170.

Thies, C. G. (2006). Bankers and beliefs: The political psychology of the Asian financial crisis. In M. Schafer & S. G. Walker (eds.), *Beliefs and leadership in world politics: Methods and applications of operational code analysis* (pp. 219–236). New York: Palgrave Macmillan.

Thoemmes, F. J., & Conway, L. G. (2007). Integrative complexity of 41 U.S. presidents. *Political Psychology, 28*, 193–226.

Traister, R. (2010). *Big girls don't cry: The election that changed everything for American women.* New York: Free Press.

Valenty, L. O., & Carroll, M. E. (2002). Motive imagery and integrative complexity: Bill Clinton, George Mitchell, and the Northern Ireland peace talks. In L. Valenty & O. Feldman (eds.), *Political leadership for the new century: Personality and behavior among American leaders* (pp. 65–80). Westport, CT: Praeger.

Valenty, L. O., & Shiraev, E. (2001). The 1996 Russian presidential candidates: A content analysis of motivational configuration and conceptual/integrative complexity. In O. Feldman & L. O. Valenty (eds.), *Profiling political leaders: Cross-cultural studies of personality and political behavior* (pp. 37–56). Westport, CT: Praeger.

Volkan, V. D. (2001). Transgenerational transmissions and chosen traumas: An aspect of large-group identity. *Group Analysis, 34*, 79–97.

Walker, S. G. (1990). The evolution of operational code analysis. *Political Psychology, 11,* 403–418.

Walker, S. G. (2000). Assessing psychological characteristics at a distance: Symposium lessons and future research directions. *Political Psychology, 21,* 597–602.

Walker, S. G., & Schafer, M. (2000). The political universe of Lyndon Johnson and his advisors: Diagnostic and strategic propensities in their operational codes. *Political Psychology, 21,* 529–543.

Walker, S. G., & Schafer, M. (2007). Theodore Roosevelt and Woodrow Wilson as cultural icons of U.S. foreign policy. *Political Psychology, 28,* 747–776.

Walker, S. G., Schafer, M., & Young, M. D. (2003). Profiling the operational codes of political leaders. In J. M. Post (ed.), *The psychological assessment of political leaders* (pp. 215–245). Ann Arbor: University of Michigan Press.

Walker, S. G., & Watson, G. L. (1994). Integrative complexity and British decisions during the Munich and Poland crises. *Journal of Conflict Resolution, 38,* 3–23.

Wallace, M. D., Suedfeld, P., & Thachuk, K. A. (1996). Failed leader or successful peacemaker? Crisis, behavior, and the cognitive processes of Mikhail Sergeyevitch Gorbachev. *Political Psychology, 17,* 453–472

Walter, J. (2007). Book review: *Handbook of psychobiography. Political Psychology, 28,* 257–259.

Wedge, B. (1968, October). Khrushchev at a distance: A study of public personality. *Trans-Action, 5,* 24–28.

White, R. K. (1951). *Value-analysis.* Ann Arbor, MI: Society for the Psychological Study of Social Issues.

White, R. K. (1990). Why aggressors lose. *Political Psychology, 11,* 227–242.

Wiggins, J. S. (Ed.). (1996). *The five-factor model of personality: Theoretical perspectives.* New York: Guilford Press.

Winter, D. G. (1980). An exploratory study of the motives of southern African political leaders measured at a distance. *Political Psychology, 2*(2), 75–85.

Winter, D. G. (1987). Leader appeal, leader performance, and the motive profiles of leaders and followers: A study of American presidents and elections. *Journal of Personality and Social Psychology, 52,* 196–202.

Winter, D. G. (1992). Content analysis of archival data, personal documents, and everyday verbal productions. In C. P. Smith (ed.), *Motivation and personality: Handbook of thematic content analysis* (pp. 110–125). New York: Cambridge University Press.

Winter, D. G. (1994). *Manual for scoring motive imagery in running text* (Version 4.2). Ann Arbor: University of Michigan Department of Psychology.

Winter, D. G. (1995). Presidential psychology and governing styles: A comparative psychological analysis of the 1992 presidential candidates. In S. A. Renshon (ed.), *The Clinton presidency: Campaigning, governing and the psychology of leadership* (pp. 113–134). Boulder, CO: Westview.

Winter, D. G. (1996). *Personality: Analysis and interpretation of lives.* New York: McGraw-Hill.

Winter, D. G. (1998a). A motivational analysis of the Clinton first term and the 1996 presidential campaign. *Leadership Quarterly, 9,* 253–262.

Winter, D. G. (1998b). "Toward a science of personality psychology:" David McClelland's development of empirically derived TAT measures. *History of Psychology, 1,* 130–153.

Winter, D. G. (2001). Measuring Bush's motives. *ISPP News: International Society of Political Psychology, 12*(1), 9.

Winter, D. G. (2002). Motivation and political leadership. In L. Valenty & O. Feldman (eds.), *Political leadership for the new century: Personality and behavior among American leaders* (pp. 25–47). Westport, CT: Praeger.

Winter, D. G. (2003a). Assessing leaders' personalities: A historical survey of academic research studies. In J. Post (ed.), *The psychological assessment of political leaders* (pp. 11–38). Ann Arbor: University of Michigan Press.

Winter, D. G. (2003b). Measuring the motives of political actors at a distance. In J. M. Post (ed.), *The psychological assessment of political leaders* (pp. 153–177). Ann Arbor: University of Michigan Press.

Winter, D. G. (2004). Motivation and the escalation of conflict: Case studies of individual leaders. *Peace and Conflict: Journal of Peace Psychology, 10,* 381–398.

Winter, D. G. (2005). Continuity and change in George Bush's motive profile. *ISPP News: International Society of Political Psychology, 16*(1), 10–11.

Winter, D. G. (2009). Predicting the Obama presidency. *ISPP News: International Society of Political Psychology, 20*(1), 6–8.

Winter, D. G. (2010a). Power in the person: Exploring the psychological underground of power. In A. Guinote & T. Vescio (eds.), *The social psychology of power* (pp. 113–140). New York: Guilford Press.

Winter, D. G. (2010b). Why does achievement motivation predict success in business but failure in politics? The importance of personal control. *Journal of Personality, 78,* 1637–1667.

Winter, D. G. (2011). Philosopher-king or polarizing politician? A personality profile of Barack Obama. *Political Psychology, 32,* 1059–1081.

Winter, D. G. (2012). Tracking Obama's motives. *ISPP News, 23*(1), 8–9.

Winter, D. G., & Carlson, L. (1988). Using motive scores in the psychobiographical study of an individual: The case of Richard Nixon. *Journal of Personality, 56,* 75–103.

Winter, D. G., Hermann, M. G., Weintraub, W., & Walker, S. G. (1991a). The personalities of Bush and Gorbachev at a distance: Follow-up on predictions. *Political Psychology, 12,* 457–464.

Winter, D. G., Hermann, M. G., Weintraub, W., & Walker, S. G. (1991b). The personalities of Bush and Gorbachev at a distance: Procedures, portraits, and policy. *Political Psychology, 12,* 215–245.

Winter, D. G., John, O. P., Stewart, A. J., Klohnen, E., & Duncan, L. E. (1998). Traits and motives: Toward an integration of two traditions in personality research. *Psychological Review, 105,* 230–250.

Winter, D. G., & Stewart, A. J. (1977). Content analysis as a technique for assessing political leaders. In M. G. Hermann (ed.), *A psychological examination of political leaders* (pp. 28–61). New York: Free Press.

Winter, D. G., & Stewart, A. J. (1995). Commentary: Tending the garden of personality. *Journal of Personality, 63,* 711–727.

Winter, N. J. G. (1992, July). The effects of the Hitler relationship on Mussolini's motive profile. Paper presented at the Annual Meeting of the International Society of Political Psychology, San Francisco.

Wright, J. C., & Mischel, W. (1987). A conditional approach to dispositional constructs: The local predictability of social behavior. *Journal of Personality and Social Psychology, 53,* 1159–1177.

Wright, J. C., & Mischel, W. (1988). Conditional hedges and the intuitive psychology of traits. *Journal of Personality and Social Psychology, 55,* 454–469.

Zillmer, E. A., Harrower, M., Ritzler, B. A., & Archer, R. P. (1995). *The quest for the Nazi personality: A psychological investigation of Nazi war criminals.* Hillsdale, NJ: Erlbaum.

Zullow, H. M., & Seligman, M. E. (1990). Pessimistic rumination predicts defeat of presidential candidates, 1900 to 1984. *Psychological Inquiry, 1*(1), 52–61.

CHAPTER 15

···

PSYCHOBIOGRAPHY

"the child is father of the man"

···

JERROLD M. POST

No more suitable subtitle for this chapter on psychobiography could be found than the poetic epigram "The child is father of the man," a line of William Wordsworth's ode "My Heart Leaps Up When I Behold" (Palgrave, 1875). For it poetically connotes that it is the shaping, formative experiences of childhood and youth that produce the adult. In trying to understand the psychogenesis of the leader's character and personality, it is imperative to search for the foundations of that personality in the life course of the leader (Winter, chapter 14, this volume; for a lengthier treatment of political socialization see Sears & Brown, chapter 3, this volume).

This chapter will be concerned with elaborating the theory and practice of the craft of psychobiography. It will describe the evolution of psychobiography, emphasizing the history and utilization of psychological theories that depict the formative influences that shape the emerging political personality and that give rise to its psychodynamic features. In the age of Freud, any biography that did not try to make psychological sense of the subject's life would be considered insufficient. The chapter will begin with a discussion of some of Freud's theoretical contributions, and his pioneering efforts at psychohistory and psychobiography. It will then review a spectrum of psychoanalytic perspectives that derived, but differed in emphasis, from Freud's original contributions to psychoanalytic theory. Runyan's important scholarship on biography contributes significantly to this discussion, with its emphasis on relativism or perspectivism. It then considers the important contributions of Harold Lasswell, who is widely considered the father of political psychology, and who applied psychodynamic theory to understanding what psychological forces impel political leaders, conceptualizing the "power seeker."

This led to Alex and Juliet George's psychobiography of President Woodrow Wilson, considered an exemplar of psychobiography, which was developed to test Lasswell's theory. The chapter then discusses a different interpretation of Wilson's rigidity and failure to compromise, which fatally wounded two of his most cherished political goals.

It contrasts the psychodynamic approach of the Georges with a medical explanation by the neurologist and psychoanalyst Edwin Weinstein, leading to a major academic dispute, which is next discussed. This emphasizes the effects of medical illness, the next topic of discussion, with examples of the Shah of Iran and Israeli prime minister Menachem Begin.

The importance of the contributions of Erik Erikson to the theory and practice of psychobiography can scarcely be overestimated. In the next section of the essay, his contributions are presented, both the psychosocial stages of the life cycle and his important emphasis on development always occurring in a particular political/social/historical context. Through his psychobiography of Martin Luther, he focused especially on the identity crisis of adolescence and youth. Drawing strongly on Erikson, Daniel Levinson's important work on the major transitions of the life cycle is then presented. Erikson's emphasis on the psychosocial context is further developed by the psychohistorian Peter Loewenberg, with the example of the Hitler war youth, followed by a discussion of the psychohistorian Robert Lifton's work.

Gandhi, in addition to Vladimir Lenin and Leon Trotsky, is the subject of an interesting typological study by Victor Wolfenstein of what he calls "ascetic revolutionaries." Tucker's nuanced psychobiography of Lenin's revolutionary successor, Joseph Stalin, is then considered.

The development of psychobiographies in support of government policy is next addressed, with discussions first of *The Mind of Adolf Hitler*, prepared for the Office of Strategic Services by the psychoanalyst Walter Langer during World War II, and then of the Camp David profiles of Menachem Begin and Anwar Sadat prepared for President Jimmy Carter by the CIA's Center for the Analysis of Personality and Political Behavior. Discussed next is a contemporary example of a psychobiographic profile of a "power seeker" who impacted government policy—that of Saddam Hussein. In this discussion, using the theoretical perspective of self psychology, he is seen as a prime example of the malignant narcissistic personality, who, on the basis of a wounded self, compensates with grandiose dreams of glory. Indeed, the trauma of his earliest years was so severe as to color his political behavior throughout his life.

Finally, in addition to the dramatic example of Saddam Hussein as malignant narcissist, attention is given more broadly to the impact of narcissistic personality features on many of the political leaders under study, a central aspect of their psychobiographies. First is a discussion of Vamik Volkan's psychoanalytic study of the founder of the modern state of Turkey, *The Immortal Ataturk*, written with the Middle East historian Norman Itzkowitz. This is written from the object relations psychoanalytic framework of Otto Kernberg. Then discussed are two psychobiographies written from the perspective of Heinz Kohut, a psychobiography of the shah of Iran, *Majestic Failure: The Fall of the Shah*, by Marvin Zonis, and Charles Strozier's psychoanalytically informed psychobiography of Abraham Lincoln, *Lincoln's Quest for Union*. Another pathway to dreams of glory, in contrast to that of Saddam Hussein, is that of parents who seek to have their children be the vehicle of their own success, with the dramatic examples of General Douglas MacArthur and Woodrow Wilson.

The chapter concludes with a contemporary example of the manner in which some of the life course features delineated above contribute usefully to the understanding of political events, in particular the Arab Spring, both aging autocrats and rebellious youth.

1. In the Beginning: The Foundational Influence of Sigmund Freud

No discussion of the development of personality would be complete without beginning with the seminal work of Sigmund Freud. Freud's foundational writings concerning personality development, especially his early works, are focused on the developing child in the family context.

A particularly important work by Freud, which has foundational influence in psychobiography, is his 1914 *On Narcissism*, published in a 1959 collection of his papers. He focuses on the entitled individual who, in effect, acts as if he is governed by the statement, "I want what I want when I want it, and I want it now," the imperious demanding quality referred to by Freud as "His Majesty the Baby" (p. 90). In understanding the developmental pathways of narcissism, he observes: "If we look at the attitude of affectionate parents towards their children, we have to recognize that it is a revival and reproduction of their own narcissism, which they have long since abandoned" (p. 90).

The reaction of parents to the miracle of the birth of the newborn, their adoration of their own child, who is perfect in every way, and has a future without limits in its potential, is palpable. The dreams of parents for their newborn children soar: "The child shall fulfill those wishful dreams of the parents which they never carried out—the boy shall become a great man and a hero in his father's place, and the girl shall marry a prince as a tardy compensation for her mother.... Parental love, which is so moving, and at bottom so childish, is nothing but the parents' narcissism born again" (pp. 90–91).

The excessive and overinflated praise such parents bestow upon their proud creations leads inevitably to an unconscious awareness that "the lady doth protest too much," producing an insatiable appetite for praise lest the underlying inadequacy be revealed. As a consequence, in the narcissistic individual there comes to be an idealized self-concept, or "good self," and an inadequate devalued "bad self."

Healthy parents progressively guide their children through the shoals of reality, helping them to cope with its frustrations, to learn how to delay their quest for immediate gratification. They learn to integrate the "good self" and "bad self" into a realistic self-concept.

It is important to emphasize that we are speaking of a continuum. After all, it is the mother's praise and love, communicated in the context of reality with an appreciation of the child's individuality and limitations, that lead to a healthy self-concept and healthy self-esteem. But some parents are so consumed by their need for their children to be special that they fail to help their children develop a realistic self-concept.

While this theoretical elaboration of the psychology of narcissism is illuminating, when Freud applied his psychoanalytic concepts to history and psychobiography, the results were decidedly mixed. His book *Leonardo da Vinci and a Memory of His Childhood* (1957) is considered by his biographer and colleague Ernest Jones as "the first real psychoanalytic biography" (1981,p. 345). As Jones summarizes, Freud studied the known history of Leonardo's infancy—an illegitimate child who lived alone with his mother for several years "until his father, who had married a wife who bore no children took him away and adopted him" (p. 345). From this, Freud traces the struggles that dominated da Vinci's life between art and science, and also his homosexuality. This work stimulated great interest and is considered now to be the first psychobiography.

Employing what might generously be termed creative imagination, Freud applied his theories to history, emphasizing psychopathology, and dealt with the psychopathology of a collective interacting with the psychopathology of an individual great man. In his book *Moses and Monotheism* (1964), he hypothesizes that Moses appealed to the aggressive instincts of the collective. He concludes that Moses was an Egyptian and credits him with creating the Jews and, as the eminent psychohistorian Robert Lifton (1974) observes, goes on to suggest that Moses " 'chose' the Hebrews as his people and gave them the gift of monotheism...only to be murdered by his 'chosen people,' his symbolic sons" (p. 24), thus endowing the legend of Moses with the elements of the Oedipus complex. Lifton calls attention to the following remarkably cavalier footnote in this book:

> I am very well aware that in dealing so autocratically and arbitrarily with Biblical tradition—bringing it up to confirm my views when it suits me and unhesitatingly rejecting it when it contradicts me—I am exposing myself to serious methodological criticism and weakening the convincing force as of my arguments, But this is the only way in which one can treat material of which one knows definitely that its trustworthiness has been severely impaired by the distorting influences of tendentious purposes. It is to be hoped that I shall find some degree of justification later on, when I come upon the track of these secret motives. Certainly it is any case unattainable and moreover it may be said that every other writer on the subject has adopted the same procedure. (Cited in Lifton, 1974, p. 30)

A venture into psychobiography for which Freud has been deservedly criticized is his 1967 book with William Bullitt, *Thomas Woodrow Wilson, Twenty Eighth President of the United States: A Psychological Study*. Textual analysis makes it clear that, with the exception of the introduction, Freud did not write this, but he nevertheless lent his name to this vicious attack on Wilson by Bullitt, which masks the motivated attack on Wilson with pseudoscientific psychological language. In referring to this work in his 1979 book *Truth in History*, Oscar Handlin, with wry understatement and with reference to the emerging enterprise of psychohistory, said that the Freud and Bullitt psychobiography of Woodrow Wilson had "not commanded confidence" (p. 14, as cited in Runyan, 1988, p. 4). An eminent scholar of biography, Runyan has also noted this withering critique of psychohistory by Stannard (1980):

> From the earliest endeavors to write psychohistory to those of the present, individual writings of would-be psychohistorians have consistently been characterized by a cavalier attitude towards fact, a contorted attitude towards logic, an irresponsible attitude towards theory validation, and a myopic attitude towards cultural difference and anachronism. (p. 147, as cited in Runyan, 1988, p. 4)

Freud's revealing footnote in *Moses and Monotheism*, cited above, is an exemplar of the "cavalier attitude towards fact" and the "irresponsible attitude towards theory validation" of which Stannard complains.

Cocks and Crosby (1987) have edited a book on psychohistory that considers the methods of psychology, psychoanalysis, and history. Beginning with a chastening critique by Hans Eysenck of psychoanalysis as not being a theory because it is not, in his estimation, testable, the book contains important articles by Peter Loewenberg, Robert Tucker, Alexander George, and Charles Strozier, who review the contributions of Erik Erikson. The book is notable for containing major articles bearing on the Woodrow Wilson controversy earlier mentioned, including a trenchant review by Robert Tucker of the field of psychobiography, with reference to the Georges' psychobiography of Wilson.

2. A Spectrum of Psychoanalytic Perspectives

Runyan (1982) has wrestled with the diversity of biographical accounts, illustrating his discussion with the diverse accounts of the life of Jesus, Shakespeare, and Lincoln. He argues for what he terms "epistemological relativism that is capable of coming to terms with a diversity of accounts" (p. 34). This is starkly different from the approach confessed to by Freud, above, where he acknowledges with disarming candor choosing confirming evidence for his theories, and rejecting disconfirming evidence. Runyan goes on to observe that

> Relativism (or perspectivism) is frequently contrasted with objectivity, but this can be a meaningless dichotomy. A more illuminating comparison is between multiple perspectives or a singular perspective, between diversity or a uniformity of viewpoint. Just because analyses and accounts of lives are embedded in and relative to particular personal, social, intellectual and historical conditions, does not mean they cannot be objective or cannot be rigorously examined. Relativism does not mean that one ignores evidence or throws out procedures of rigorous inquiry, but rather that empirical and logical inference are employed within the context of a particular perspective. (p. 35)

In a chapter entitled "Why Did Van Gogh Cut Off His Ear? The Problem of Alternative Explanations in Psychobiography," Runyan identifies no less than 13 alternative psycho-dynamic explanations. He emphasizes the distinction made by Popper (1962) between conjectures and refutation: some of the explanations offered, on rigorous examination, have not a shred of evidence supporting them, whereas for others there is substantial supporting or disconfirming evidence.

Psychoanalytic theory has proliferated since Freud, with a number of schools developing: Karl Jung's emphasis on myth and the collective unconscious; the ego psychology school, with its emphasis on adaptation, associated with Heinz Hartmann, Ernst Kris, and Rudolph Loewenstein; the interpersonal school associated with Harry Stack Sullivan, Eric Fromm, and Karen Horney; the object relations school, associated with Melanie Klein, and contemporaneously with Otto Kernberg; self psychology, associated with Heinz Kohut; and the relational school, associated with Stephen Mitchell. To review these schools comprehensively and contrast them is not the task of this chapter, but rather, considering personality as a jewel, each school can be considered to be a facet of that jewel through which to look at the developing personality, a particular perspective. They all derive from Freudian psychoanalysis but emphasize different elements. It is not so much that they are in conflict as taking differing perspectives.

2.1. The Political Psychology of Psychoanalysis

In a remarkable account of the origins of psychoanalysis, in which he describes the fractious, often contentious history of this discipline, George Makari, in *Revolution in Mind* (2008), describes the political psychology of this field—the rivalries, the power struggles, the requirements for unquestioning loyalty, and so on. Referring to the feud between Freud and Adler, who in his writings addressed the centrality of the power motive, Popper (1962) has observed that

> Every conceivable case could be interpreted in light of Adler's theory or of Freud's. . . . I could not think of any behavior which could not be interpreted in terms of either theory. It was precisely this fact—that they always fitted, that they were always confirmed—which in the eyes of admirers constituted the strongest argument in favor of these theories. It began to dawn on me that this apparent strength was in fact their weakness. (p. 33, as cited in Runyan, 1982, p. 48)

In effect, Popper is asserting that if a psychoanalytic theory cannot be refuted, it is not a scientific theory, but rather more an ideology or religious faith. When Freud, in the foot-note to *Moses and Monotheism* quoted above, and in referring to the lack of supportive evidenced, states, "It is to be hoped that I shall find some degree of justification later on, when I come upon the track of these secret motives," he is in effect stating, "I know my theory is correct. And I hope later on the facts will emerge to confirm it." Not exactly an objective scientific attitude!

The psychohistorian Peter Loewenberg has noted the importance of the shift from libidinal-drive theory, Freud's earliest formulations, to ego psychological and object relations paradigms in applying psychoanalysis to history. He also emphasizes the importance of the countertransference of the psychohistorian/psychobiographer, what he describes as "the researcher's subjective reactions to the material" (Loewenberg, 1988, p. 127). It should be added that a preexisting negative bias toward the subject of study, as was clearly the case with the psychobiography of Woodrow Wilson by Bullitt and Freud, will inevitably interfere with objective dispassionate research.

Robert Tucker reflected in his biographer's memoir on the influence of the interpersonal psychoanalytic perspective of Karen Horney, in her classic *Neurosis and Human Growth* (1950), which he read while working in the American embassy in Moscow upon his authoritative biography of Stalin (Tucker, 1988). He found particularly clarifying Horney's concept that a background characterized

> by adverse emotional circumstances in early life may seek and find a rock of inner security by forming an idealized image of himself or herself. The content of the self-image will depend on the direction the child takes in relations with others—moving against, toward, or away from them. One whose tendency is to move against others may idealize himself as a great warrior, while one whose tendency is to move toward others may imagine himself to be saintlike. (Tucker, p. 63)

It was Harold Lasswell, the political scientist considered the founding father of political psychology, who saw in Freud's theories important implications for the study of political leadership, explored first in his 1930 book *Psychopathology and Politics*. In his 1948 book, *Power and Personality*, Lasswell explores the development of political man, the power seeker, who seeks political power to overcome low estimates of himself.

2.2. The Psychodynamics of the Power Seeker: Harold Lasswell

In his 1948 *Power and Personality*, Lasswell conceptualizes the psychodynamics of the power seeker, hypothesizing that he "pursues power as a means of compensation against deprivation. *Power is expected to overcome low estimates of the self*" (p. 39). This concept was first introduced in his 1930 *Psychopathology and Politics*, where, in considering political movements, Lasswell suggests that "political movements derive their vitality from the displacement of private affects upon public objects" (p. 173). He further refines this concept in *Power and Personality*, where he develops this concept as a general formula that describes the developmental history of the political man, in effect hypothesizing the nature of the psychobiographic roots of the power seeker, that is, the psychogenetics. The first element in this equation is private motives, which he designates as p. The second term, d, refers to displacement of private motives from family objects to public objects. As an example, Lasswell (1960) suggests that "the repressed father-hatred may be turned against kings or capitalists, which are social objects playing a role before and within the community" (p. 75). Finally, the third element, *r*, signifies the rationalization of the displacement as being in terms of public interests. Lasswell here is referring to a key element of the Oedipus complex, an important theoretical contribution of Freud. What Lasswell is suggesting here is that when the leadership of the country is corrupt, it provides a conduit for the youth, who, in struggling to establish his own identity and displace paternal authority, to turn against the national authority. Lasswell then combines these terms into the following general formula that expressed the developmental facts about the fully developed political man:

$$p\} \, d\} \, r = \mathrm{P},$$

where } equals "transformed into" (p. 76). In *Power and Personality*, Lasswell indicates that "our political man"

1. Accumulates power
2. Demands power (and other values) for the self (the primary ego plus incorporated symbols of other egos)
3. Accentuates expectations concerning power
4. Acquires at least a minimal proficiency in the skills of power. (p. 57)

This breathtaking psychodynamic insight can be considered the mother lode of psychobiography.

2.3. The Georges' Psychobiography of Woodrow Wilson: Testing Lasswell's Theory

The exemplary psychobiography of Woodrow Wilson, *Woodrow Wilson and Colonel House* (1956) was written by Alexander and Juliet George to test the hypotheses of Harold Lasswell concerning "the power seeker" and explore the degree to which this helped explain Woodrow Wilson's political crises, especially his failure to win endorsement of more lenient conditions for the Versailles Treaty.

Woodrow Wilson and Colonel House: A Personality Study is widely considered an exemplar of the psychological biography or psychobiography. In his 1968 article "Power as a Compensatory Value for Political Leaders," Alexander George describes the analytic rigor with which he and his wife tested Lasswell's theory, using the case of Woodrow Wilson. In particular, he examines the manner in which high need for power is related to low self-estimates, namely how damaged self-esteem can lead some individuals to develop an unusually strong need for power. He reflects on an observation by Erik Erikson (1964) of common features in five individuals who were reformers or innovators. The memoirs of Martin Luther, Mohandas Gandhi, Søren Kierkegaard, Woodrow Wilson, and Eleanor Roosevelt all reflected low self-estimates, but also manifested a "strong conscience," precocious attention to "ultimate concerns," and a responsibility for a segment of mankind. Erikson also found special characteristics of the child's conflicted relationship with the father, and how it was resolved.

In systematically attempting to operationalize Lasswell's formula for the development of "the power seeker," George (1968) found it necessary to define the key elements of the formula: low self-estimates, power, and compensation. He identified examples of feelings that would convey low self-estimates: (*a*) feelings of unimportance; (*b*) feelings of moral inferiority; (*c*) feelings of weakness; (*d*) feelings of mediocrity; and (*e*) feelings of intellectual inadequacy. He identified six possible behavioral indicators of a striving for power gratification on the part of a compensation-seeking personality (p. 32):

1. *Unwillingness to permit others to share* in his actual or assumed field of power
2. *Unwillingness to take advice* regarding his proper functioning in his actual or assumed field of power
3. *Unwillingness to delegate* to others tasks that are believed to belong to his regularly constituted field of power
4. *Unwillingness to consult* with others who have claim to share power, regarding his functioning in his actual or assumed field of power
5. *Unwillingness to inform* others with respect to his actual or assumed field of power
6. *Desire to devise and impose orderly systems* upon others in the political arena

George then describes how, in conducting the research for *Woodrow Wilson and Colonel House*, he and his wife examined the copious writings of Wilson to confirm or refute the hypothesized feelings and indicators listed above. This resulted in a thoroughly evidenced psychobiography of Woodrow Wilson, which persuasively confirms that Wilson well fit the formula of "the power seeker" hypothesized by Lasswell, and that these personality dynamics helped explain the failure of Wilson to achieve his two most cherished goals: American membership in the League of Nations, and moderate conditions for the Versailles Treaty.

George lays the basis for Wilson's hypothesized damaged self-esteem to the difficult relations with his father, a Presbyterian minister who had very high expectations of his firstborn son, indeed demanded that he measure up to very high intellectual and moral attainments. The Georges suggest that Wilson internalized these demanding standards, becoming a perfectionist. (This is an example of the defense mechanism identified by Anna Freud, identification with the aggressor.) His failure to make even minor compromises in the language establishing the League of Nations in order to win Senate endorsement and the participation of his arch-rival, Henry Cabot Lodge, reflected this perfectionistic bent. The Georges note that when the French ambassador indicated to Wilson that the Allies would be glad to accept American membership in the League even with a set of reservations that would satisfy influential Republicans, Wilson reportedly snapped, "Mr. Ambassador, I shall consent to nothing, The Senate must take its medicine" (1956, p. 289).

2.4. When Illness Strikes the Leader

The study of Wilson introduces another important theme, namely the impact of medical illness on political behavior, referring to the medical psychobiography of Woodrow Wilson by Edwin Weinstein. Concealing a leader's illness and denial of illness can have serious political consequences, as exemplified by the Shah of Iran and Menachem Begin, discussed in section 2.5.

One should not consider the Georges' psychobiography of Woodrow Wilson without referring to its central role in what is considered one of the great academic disputes. Edwin Weinstein, a psychoanalyst and neurologist, and a close friend of Arthur Link, the editor of the Wilson papers at Princeton, debunked the Georges' psychological explanation for Wilson's rigid insistence that every word be accepted as drafted, and his refusal to compromise that doomed his cherished League of Nations to defeat. Rather, Weinstein posits that Wilson suffered from early onset of arteriosclerosis (hardening of the arteries) of the brain, and had suffered a series of strokes dating back to his presidency of Princeton that accounted for his rigidity (1970 1981). These hypothesized "strokes" are referred to as established facts in the Wilson papers, to the great objection of the Georges. Weinstein also disputed the Georges' central argument, asserting that Wilson's relationship with his father was unambivalently positive and admiring.

A debate was scheduled for the 1982 Annual Scientific Meeting of the International Society of Political Psychology in Washington, DC, to be held in the Woodrow Wilson house with a jury to be composed of physicians and political scientists. When Weinstein withdrew at the last minute, the convener of the debate, Jerrold Post, decided instead to hold the debate in the pages of the journal *Political Psychology*. In his own summary, Post observed that the neurologist and the ophthalmologist on his jury concluded that there was no definitive medical evidence that Wilson had suffered from strokes before 1919. He also observed that the question being debated need not be dichotomous—that is, was the behavior in question of psychological or of neurological origin? Wilson probably did have some cerebral arteriosclerosis leading up the disabling stroke he suffered in 1919 while campaigning for ratification of the Versailles Treaty. But that did not negate the psychological explanation posited by the Georges. To the contrary, citing a geriatric psychiatry aphorism, "as a man grows older, he becomes more like himself," he indicated that the aging, ailing Wilson may well have been become all the more rigid and uncompromising, leading to the defeat of his long-cherished goals (Post, 1983).

2.5. Terminal Urgency: The Impact of Age and Terminal Illness on Political Decisions

The dispute over the sources of Wilson's behavior highlights the importance of considering all aspects of the leader, including his medical health, in developing psychobiographies. For leaders, after all, are human beings, subjects to the same vicissitudes of the life cycle that affect us all. But leaders have the burden of needing at all times to be all-wise, all-powerful, and a leader's illness can have major effects on political behavior, especially when the leader is consumed by dreams of glory and illness strikes when his dreams have not yet been achieved.

2.5.1. The Shah of Iran's Terminal Urgency

Consider the impact of the Shah of Iran's serious illness, which first became symptomatic in 1973, 32 years after he succeeded to power, and six years before his regime was overthrown in the violent Islamist revolution of 1979 (Post & Robbins, 1993, pp. 2–7). He had a sallow complexion, was weak, had experienced weight loss, all with abdominal bloating and pain. When his physicians examined him, they were alarmed to find an enlarged liver and spleen and called in French physicians, who found him to be suffering from Waldenstrom's macroglobulinemia, a disease of the bone marrow. He was informed that he had a serious illness, with a life expectancy of perhaps seven years. In his 1961 book, *Mission for My Country*, he had spelled out a development plan for his country that would take perhaps 20 years to implement. But the shah did not have 20 years. And in 1973, the year he first became ill, the shah broke with OPEC, quadrupling oil prices, leading to a large flow of money into Iran, which did not have the infrastructure for which his plan called. A revolution of rising expectations followed, destabilizing Iran's rigid structure and paving the way for Khomeini's Islamic revolution. The shah had superimposed his truncated personal timetable on the nation's political timetable because of his terminal urgency (for lengthier discussion of crisis decision making see Dyson & t'Hart, chapter 13, this volume).

2.5.2. Begin's Weakness and Compensatory Political Strength

Similarly, two of the most controversial policy decisions of Israeli prime minister Menachem Begin were made in reaction to his age and illness. Before he yielded to terminal despair, Begin had fought with single-minded devotion for the Zionist dream of establishing a Jewish homeland in the biblical land of Israel. The hallmark of his political career, for which he, with President Sadat of Egypt, was awarded the Nobel Peace Prize in 1978, was the successful negotiations with President Sadat of the Camp David Accords in 1978 in which "land for peace" was the basis for a peace treaty with Israel's enemy Egypt.

Begin was a man of fragile health, whose leadership was punctuated by health reverses, including three coronaries and a stroke. These were pointed reminders that his time was limited, and the dream he had cherished throughout his lifetime, a Jewish homeland at peace, was not to be achieved in his lifetime. Like Moses, he would not enter that promised land. But if he could not achieve an Israel at peace, then in the time remaining he would fight to ensure a secure Jewish state.

As each illness underlined the brevity of his remaining time, in the wake of serious illness came some of his most dramatic political moves. Two of his most controversial political actions not only occurred in relationship to illness, but in fact the decisions were actually made from his hospital bed!

In June 1980, Begin suffered a minor coronary occlusion. While recuperating in the hospital, he became obsessed with the need to declare unambiguously to the world his commitment to the integrity of the biblical land of Israel. To his doctor's dismay, he received political advisers daily. From his hospital bed he crafted a statement that was read to the press on July 6.

> It is the national consensus and the policy of the Government of Israel that Jerusalem, which has been reunited as a result of a successful legitimate self-defense, will remain forever united, forever indivisible, and forever the capital city of the State of Israel by virtue of right. (Middle East Report, 1980)

This was a highly provocative and unnecessary statement coming as it did during an American presidential campaign. It led to tension with the United States, Israel's strongest supporter, for the incumbent president, Jimmy Carter, whose proudest accomplishment was in bringing Israel and its enemy Egypt together at Camp David, was in a close, heated, and ultimately losing campaign against Ronald Reagan, who was sharply critical of Carter's foreign policy, especially his handling of the Iran hostage crisis. It also strengthened the hands of the Arab states who wished to perpetuate the state of hostility with Israel. They could point to Israel's intransigence to justify their own. When Begin was released from hospital on July 14, upon leaving the hospital he said that he personally endorsed the statement and spoke again of his vision of Jerusalem as capital.

> If the Arab countries recognize the State of Israel and Jerusalem as its capital, 20 Arab flags would fly in Jerusalem, the capital of Israel, which would be recognized by all the Arab countries.

On November 26, 1981, Begin tripped in the bathroom of his home and fell. He suffered a fractured hip, a frequent affliction of the aged. The fracture required surgical repair, and the postoperative hospital stay was painful. But during this hospitalization, too, he became preoccupied with Israel's security. On December 14, the day of his discharge, Begin called Ariel Sharon and asked him to call an emergency meeting of the cabinet that day and, still in his hospital bathrobe, announced the extension of Israeli law to the Golan Heights, the equivalent of annexation (*Jerusalem Post*, 1980). The Golan Heights, which had been captured from Syria in the 1967 war, had long been a source of menace to Israel, with nightly rocket bombardments of the helpless settlements below in northern Galilee. "Never again," vowed Begin, would Israel be exposed to that mortal danger. Once again, physical weakness had precipitated a politically "strong" response, an affirmation of Begin's lifelong creed, "I fight, therefore I am!"

Begin's aim was to establish an eternally secure Israel. Weak physically, he was demonstrating his strength as a leader. But politically, as with the annexation of East Jerusalem, this provocative policy of annexing the Golan Heights damaged Israel's standing in the West and his ability to deal with moderate Arab governments.

3. THE LIFE CYCLE AND THE PSYCHOSOCIAL CONTEXT: ERIK ERIKSON

In a chapter entitled "The Eight Ages of Man" in his 1950 book *Childhood and Society*, Erik Erikson drew our attention to the manner in which each subsequent phase of the life cycle has its own developmental crisis, and the manner in which an individual progresses through the life cycle depends upon how he or she negotiates these crises. Erikson emphasized the influence of the broader sociopolitical context on personality development, with a particular emphasis on the establishment of identity.

Erikson has importantly emphasized how the individual life cycle must be understood in the context of the historical moment (Erikson, 1975). Thus he identified eight stages of psychosocial development, emphasizing the importance of the social context in which psychological development is occurring. In contrast to Freud, he emphasized that psychological growth and development occur during the entire life cycle. Moreover, and quite importantly, the success or failure of managing the crisis of each developmental stage impacts upon subsequent stages.

Drawing on Freud's concepts of the foundations of narcissism and positive self-esteem, Erikson drew attention to the importance of the earliest years. It is the parents, especially the mother, in providing a sense of warmth, affection, and continuity in providing for basic needs, that set the stage for healthy self-esteem and trust. Neglect or abuse during infancy sets the stage for distrust and insecurity. The developing infant introjects outer goodness, its parents' adoration, within him, which becomes the foundation of inner certainty, of positive self-esteem. In contrast, he projects outward the harm within, "endowing significant people with the evil that is actually within us" (p. 221). Thus the central challenge of Erikson's first stage, from birth to 12–18 months, the period of infancy, is that of trust versus mistrust, and failures to transcend this challenge can have consequences for the entire life span.

The psychological challenge of the second stage, from 18 months to three years, is that of will, what Erikson conceptualizes as autonomy versus shame and doubt. The parents foster autonomy, as the growing child is beginning to explore the world around him or her, and is beginning to interact with the world with curiosity. It is also a time of potential danger, as the healthy parents negotiate the perilous path between fostering increasing autonomy and protecting their child.

The central challenge of the third stage, from 6 to 12 years old, that is, childhood, is that of competence: industry versus inferiority. During this stage, children are eager to learn and are able to manage most matters of personal hygiene with little or no parental guidance. These elementary school years are crucial for the development of self-confidence, but children can develop a sense of inferiority if teased or ridiculed during this period.

Identity versus role confusion is the central challenge of adolescence, 12 to 18 years. This is the era when identity, including political identity, is being consolidated. This is a transitional era, between childhood and young adulthood, from being a child with awe-like reverence (or fear) for the admired, powerful parent, to becoming an adult in one's own right. It is frequently a time of adolescent rebelling, which, rather than striving for independence, is often characterized by antidependence. In his psychobiographies *Young Man Luther* (1958) and *Gandhi's Truth* (1969), Erikson emphasizes the political and cultural context in which these two important figures lived and developed. His aphorism "We cannot lift a case history out of history" well sums this up (Erikson, 1958, pp. 15–16). Indeed, it was his study of Martin Luther that led Erikson to focus on the psychology of adolescence and identity formation. Luther's own rebellion against paternal authority, so characteristic of adolescent psychology, became the powerful dynamic that led to the Protestant Reformation. So, in contrast to Freud in *Moses and Monotheism*, who sought to depict his psychological development in terms of inner conflicts, for Erikson it was the junctures of the great man of history with the historical context that told the story of the individual's unique impact on society and in history.

Erikson emphasized the continuity of the life cycle and the challenges that continue throughout. The central challenge of young adulthood, 19 to 40 years old, is that of love: intimacy versus isolation. This conflict often comes to a height at age 30. Successful resolution of the challenge of this life stage rests on successful accomplishment of identity consolidation during the previous stage of adolescence. An individual who is not secure with his emerging identity will have great difficulty in achieving intimate relationships.

The challenge of middle adulthood, ages 40–65, concerns generativity versus stagnation. The predominant question of this era is, "Will I produce something of value?" both contributing to society and to future generations. These are the parenting years, and the years of peak career accomplishments.

And finally, the challenge of the last psychosocial stage, late adulthood, is that of ego integrity versus despair. It is a time of taking stock, of retrospective reflection. "What have I accomplished?" "Have I lived up to the goals I had set for myself, the dreams and aspirations of my youth?" Some are able to reflect with quiet satisfaction on the accomplishments of a lifetime and are able to pass on wisdom to the next generation, while others, seeing the gap between the dreams of one's youth and reality, sink into despair. The prior section demonstrates how serious illness can intensify the psychology of aging, as the individual seeks to accomplish his life goals in the brief time remaining.

3.1. Key Life Transitions: Daniel Levinson

Drawing on Erikson's emphasis on the effects of the entirety of the life cycle, from infancy through old age, on human psychology, in *The Seasons of a Man's Life*, Daniel Levinson (1978) has focused our attention on three key life transitions: the Young Adult Transition, the Midlife Transition, and the Late Adult Transition, depicted in figure 15.1 (Post, 2004, p. 23).

Levinson has delineated four major phases of the life cycle: childhood and adolescence (birth to 22), young adulthood (17–45), middle adulthood (40–65), and late adulthood (60–?). It should be noted that in contrast to Erikson's psychosocial life stages, where

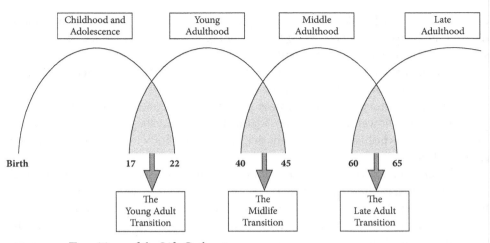

FIGURE 15.1 Transitions of the Life Cycle

the work of one era concludes as that of the next era commences, Levinson considers that the work of the next era commences while the task of the preceding era has not yet been concluded. As illustrated in the schematic, this produces three important life transitions. If childhood and adolescence are from birth to age 22, and Young Adulthood is from age 17 to 45, the period 17 to 22 is one of transition, the Young Adult Transition, called the period of the identity crisis by Erikson. Similarly, if Young Adulthood is from ages 17 to 45, and midlife begins at age 40, the period 40 to 45 is the period of the Midlife Transition, for some the period of "the midlife crisis." And if midlife is from 40 to 65, and late adulthood begins at age 60, the period 60 to 65 is the period of the Late Adult Transition. The issue is less the specificity of the numbers, which will vary from culture to culture, than the psychological issues at play during these transition periods.

During these transition periods, the work of one era is being brought to a close, while the succeeding era is getting underway. They are times of psychological stress when personality organization may be especially fluid, with a consequent potential for significant change and growth (Post, 2004). During the Young Adult Transition, identity is consolidating, including political identity. The Midlife Transition marks the end of youth and is regularly accompanied by a retrospective reflection on the degree to which youthful dreams and ambitions have been achieved, with a frequent intensified need for self-actualization and assertive action. The psychology of the period of old age should be of particular interest to the field of political psychology, for the judgment and emotional stability of aging leaders is often of critical concern at times of political crisis.

3.2. Understanding the Individual in the Political and Historical Context

The foregoing studies emphasize the importance of accurately locating the subject in the historical and political context when conducting psychobiographic research, a central theme of Erik Erikson's treatment of Luther, as indicated above, and even more directly the focus of his later (1975) *Life History and the Historical Moment*. The construction of parallel timelines to identify the political crisis during key developmental epochs of the subject aids in this task. In *Decoding the Past* (1983), the noted psychohistorian Peter Loewenberg plays a seminal role in applying a psychoanalytic perspective to the study of history. He makes an especially valuable contribution by placing the study of leader-follower relations in broader historical contexts, calling attention to the manner in which the historical moment shapes the followers, who in turn influence the choice of leaders.

In the chapter titled "The Psychohistorical Origins of the Nazi Youth Cohort," Loewenberg details the shared life experiences of Nazi youth, who were at the core of Hitler's support. As a consequence of the harsh conditions of the Versailles Treaty at the conclusion of World War I, unemployment was rampant in Germany, with one in three unemployed, as the Great Depression mounted in the early 1930s. Those who were to become the Nazi youth cohort often had had fathers unavailable to provide for their families, due to the disruptions of World War I, in many cases due to the soldiers' deaths. These youths were especially vulnerable to the appeal of Adolf Hitler's externalizing rhetoric and the promise of being the strong leader for their country, a vivid contrast to their weak or absent fathers. Consider the emphasis on strength in Hitler's speeches, the reviling of weakness, the stress on the strength of the German people. This was especially true when speaking of German youth: "...look at our splendid youth...I do not want anything weak or tender in them..." (Bychowski, 1948, pp. 172–173). Hitler would not have been able to cast his charismatic spell over his wounded nation, especially its youth, at a time of peace and prosperity. It was a powerful fit, an exemplar of the Canadian psychoanalyst Irvine Schiffer's concept in *Charisma* that all leaders—especially charismatic leaders—are, at heart, the creation of their followers (1973).

In his 1974 edited collection *Explorations in Psychohistory*, Robert Lifton extols the significance of Erik Erikson's work in calling attention to the critical importance of the historical context in developing psychobiographies. He particularly cites Erikson's 1958 *Young Man Luther* as being of pivotal importance, of being at the intersection of individual and collective histories. He observes the book's "painstaking exploration of the very tenuous psychic boundaries between identity crisis, psychosis, theological innovation, and individual and historical revitalization.... For Luther to emerge from his own identity crisis, he had to bring about a shift in the historical identity of his epoch" (p. 29). In the same collection, Erikson, using his study of Mohandas Gandhi as a vehicle, addresses the nature of psychohistorical evidence and the requirement for the biographer not only to address the historical context of his individual subject, but also to address that of his community (1974). In *Biography and Society* (1981), Daniel Bertaux brings together a number of social scientists who address the social psychology of the community, and the issue of how to employ diaries and biographical accounts to understand the dominant psychological motifs within that community.

4. COMMON PSYCHOBIOGRAPHIC FEATURES OF REVOLUTIONARIES

Gandhi has provided rich material for many studies of psychobiography. E. Victor Wolfenstein (1971) identified a class of leaders, tracing what drove their leadership to conflicts from their pasts. He developed a collective comparative analysis of what he called "revolutionary ascetics." Seeking to answer the question of why a man becomes a revolutionary, he examined from a psychoanalytic perspective the life courses of three notable revolutionary leaders, one of which was Gandhi, the others Lenin and Trotsky. Wolfenstein found interesting features in common. In particular, as was the case with Woodrow Wilson, each had an unusually ambivalent relationship with his father. Noting that such ambivalence is not unusual in adolescents, he observed that for such feelings to be transformed into revolutionary energy, these feelings must be accentuated as adolescence progresses. Moreover, there must be political circumstances that facilitate the transfer from the father to the national father figure that permit, in Lasswell's formulation, the displacement of a personal grievance to a public cause that can be rationalized in the public good. In Lenin's case, for example, he observed that the death of his father and brother, the latter indirectly at the hands of the czar, animated Lenin's revolutionary quest. This was the political precipitant that served as the conduit for Lenin, channeling his adolescent rebellious energy into the revolutionary cause of overthrowing the czar.

While Wolfenstein was attempting to identity a subspecies of revolutionary leader, the ascetic revolutionary, analyzing Lenin, Trotsky, and Gandhi, implying similar psychodynamic features, it is interesting to observe that Erik Erikson wrote a major psychobiography of Gandhi. Erikson, too, observed the ambivalent relationship of Gandhi with his father, and the manner in which his humiliating experiences in South Africa caused by his being a colored person provided the conduit to rebel against authority, setting the stage for his remarkable nonviolent resistance against British colonial domination of India. Erikson, of course, focused especially on the establishment of political identity and the political/historical/cultural context during which his identity was consolidating, but in fact, in shorthand, this is very much what Wolfenstein was addressing.

Another Russian revolutionary, whose life course well demonstrates that the political context can affect how personal developmental struggles can shape the revolutionary personality, especially during the consolidation of personal and political identity in late adolescence, is Joseph Stalin, the subject of a notable psychologically sophisticated political biography by Robert Tucker (1973).

Stalin was 15 in 1894 when he entered the Tiflis Theological Seminary, a repressive and authoritarian institution where rebellion was a tradition (student strikes took place in 1890 and 1893). His initial form of rebellion was to read "outside" books, a forbidden pastime for which he was punished on numerous occasions. He became fascinated with political history, and there read *Das Kapital*, becoming immersed in Russian Marxist literature. By the time he left the seminary in 1899, at the age of 20, he was already a committed revolutionary. He came progressively to admire Vladimir Lenin and came to identify Lenin as an idealized hero (so characteristic of youth—the rebel against authority who seeks a new authority). By 1905, Stalin was in direct contact with Lenin, who, impressed by the ardor of his young admirer, became his mentor and helped foster Stalin's rise in the revolutionary cause.

Attaching oneself to a mentor, as Stalin attached himself to Lenin, is a common pattern for the young adult. The young adult, on the one hand, benefits from the wisdom and experience of the mentor, often, as Stalin did, idealizing him as a heroic idol, while the mentor, on the other hand, may view himself as extending his influence through his protégé and often come to see his young apprentice as a younger version of himself. In Levinson's sample, the average age of the mentor tended to be some 8 to 15 years older than the young adult (1978). In the process of "becoming one's own man, to which epoch (ages 35 to 38) Levinson has assigned the acronym BOOM, the mentee may come to view his idol as having feet of clay and to see the mentor as responsible for blocking fulfillment of his youthful dreams. When he was 43, squarely in the Midlife Transition, Stalin, restive for power in his own right, confronted Lenin, who shortly thereafter suffered a debilitating stroke, and Stalin went on to consolidate power in his own right.

5. Psychobiographic Leader Personality Assessments in Support of Government Policy

As these developments were occurring in the academic world, application of psychobiography to the study of political leaders was also occurring in government. After discussing the seminal work by the psychoanalyst Walter Langer, "The Mind of Adolph Hitler," prepared the Office of Strategic Services during the 1940s, I give consideration to the establishment of the Center for the Analysis of Personality and Political Behavior, illustrating its contributions with the Camp David profiles of Menachem Begin and Anwar Sadat, prepared for President Jimmy Carter.

5.1. The Mind of Adolph Hitler: Walter Langer

No essay on psychobiography would be complete without discussion of what is considered the pioneering effort of at-a-distance leader personality assessment in support of government policy. That is the personality analysis of Adolf Hitler prepared by the psychoanalyst Walter Langer in 1943 at the request of "Wild Bill" Donovan, director of the Office of Strategic Services (OSS), the predecessor of the Central Intelligence Agency. Declassified in 1969, it was published in 1972 as *The Mind of Adolf Hitler*. (A detailed summary of Langer's psychobiographic study can be found in Post, 2003.) It was largely based on a psychobiographic reconstruction of the life of Hitler, drawing psychoanalytic inferences on the manner in which his troubled life shaped his personality, positing the powerful psychodynamic forces that were to play out so destructively on the political stage. How, Langer wondered, could this shiftless ne'er-do-well, who had never been promoted above the rank of lance corporal, "in the course of a relatively few years, talk his way into the highest political office, hoodwink the experienced leaders of the major powers, turn millions of highly civilized people into barbarians, order the extermination of a large segment of the population, build and control the mightiest war machine ever known, and plunge the world into history's most devastating war?" (Langer, 1972, p. 11). He found that Hitler's messianic sense of his own destiny was remarkable. Hitler believed himself to be possessed of special gifts both in his role as statesman and on the field of battle. In his messianic gifts, he associated himself with Jesus Christ, not the loving Christ but a hard Lord and Savior who was a fighter. To contradict him was a crime, for he was never mistaken. This posture of conviction and strength was very appealing to the wounded German people. Hitler was attuned to his audience in a remarkable fashion. His fiery oratory drove the masses to a frenzy. But underneath this messianic facade was emptiness. Hitler's father, Alois, was illegitimate at birth, and Langer suggested that Hitler may have feared that his grandfather may have been one of the Rothschilds, a wealthy Jewish family for which Hitler's grandmother was a maid. Was this the passion that drove him to eliminate the Jews? (This theme, with supporting evidence, was later to be developed in Waite's *The Psychopathic God*, 1977.) Developed two years before the end of the war in Europe, the study predicted with uncanny accuracy how the conflict would end, including both the "scorched earth" policy and Hitler's terminal suicide.

5.2. The Camp David Profiles

The use to which the Langer study was put is not clear. What is clear, though, is the degree to which the psychobiographic political personality studies of Menachem Begin and Anwar Sadat later informed the accomplishment of President Jimmy Carter at Camp David in 1979. In his memoir *Keeping Faith* (1982), Carter recalled studying the profiles on his trip to the Snake River just before the Camp David summit:

> I had to understand these men! I was poring over psychological analyses of two of the protagonists which had been prepared by a team of experts within our intelligence community. This team could write definitive biographies of any important world leader, using information derived from a detailed scrutiny of events, public statements, writings, known medical histories and interviews with personal acquaintances of the leaders under study. I wanted to know all about Begin and Sadat. What had made them national leaders? What was the root of their ambition? What were their most important goals in life? What events during past years had helped to shape their characters? What were their religious beliefs? Family relations? State of their health? Political beliefs and constraints? Relations to other leaders? Likely reactions to intense pressure in a time of crisis? Strengths and weaknesses? Commitments to political

constituencies? Attitudes towards me and the United States? Whom did they *really* trust? What was their attitude towards one another? I was certain they were preparing for our summit conference in a similar manner.

From time to time I paused to consider the negotiating strategy I would follow at Camp David. I made careful notes. These few quiet evenings away from Washington were an ideal time for me to concentrate almost exclusively on a single major challenge—peace in the Middle East. During my coming days at Camp David, my studies at the foot of the Grand Tetons were to pay rich dividends.

Afterward, referring to the Camp David profiles, Carter was to remark that after spending thirteen days with the participants, he would not change a word of the prepared profiles.

That most of Begin's family was killed during the Holocaust was seared into his political psychology, becoming the foundation of the vow "Never again!" that so shaped his policies as leader of Israel (Post, 1979). Thus Begin, putting this in Lasswellian terms, took the personal tragedy that led to the murder of most of his family in the Holocaust and transformed it into a credo for Israel: never again would the Jewish people passively yield to superior force. He came to exemplify the "fighting Jew" as national leader.

This emphasizes the iterative aspect of the craft of psychobiography. Obviously not everyone who lost family in the Holocaust went on to become a national leader. But when a person does rise to leadership, in tracing the origins of his national policies one seeks to find powerful experiences that shaped these attitudes. Begin was a key disciple of the fiery revisionist Zionist Vladimir "Ze'ev" Jabotinsy, who was known for his militant nationalist views. The leadership of the right-wing Likud Party, ultimately resulting in his become prime minister of Israel, provided the opportunity for Begin to make as a matter of national policy the "Never again!" doctrine in which he had long been steeped.

The profile of Sadat, entitled "Sadat's Nobel Prize Complex," traced his special sense of self and belief that he was a man of destiny back to his boyhood, a point emphasized by President Carter in his description of Sadat as a latter-day pharaoh. As a boy, he identified himself with Mohandas Gandhi and, wrapped in a sheet, would fast for several days, his only company a goat on a tether.

Particularly important was the third profile, which contrasted Sadat's "big picture" mentality with Begin's preoccupation with detail, with implications for difficulties in simultaneous negotiations. It was argued that if Begin and Sad totally agreed on substance, the different shapes of their minds would make it difficult for them to negotiate directly with each other. This led to the recommendation that Carter play an intermediary role in order to bridge this gap (Post, 1979).

5.3. Saddam Hussein: Contemporary Exemplar of the Power Seeker

Psychobiographic material suggests that Saddam Hussein was a contemporary exemplar of Lasswell's "power seeker," or *homo politicus*. In that crucial first stage of life, described by Erikson as being of foundational importance to subsequent psychological growth and maturation, Saddam experienced massive trauma that was profoundly damaging to his self-esteem.

It is rare that information concerning the earliest years of development of political leaders is available. When such information becomes available, it can be of immense help in understanding what shaped the leader's political personality. Through the assiduous sleuthing of Amatzia Baram, a noted Israeli scholar of Iraqi history, remarkable information about Saddam's earliest years has been revealed, which was of central importance to the political personality profile of Saddam this author developed after the Iraqi invasion of Kuwait in July 1990, on the basis of which he testified twice before Congress in December 1990 before the conflict began (Post, 1990).

The origins of Saddam's wounded self can be traced back to the womb. During the fourth month of his mother's pregnancy with him, Saddam's father died of cancer. During the eighth month of the pregnancy, her firstborn son died under the surgeon's knife. Saddam's mother first tried to abort herself of the pregnancy with Saddam, and then to commit suicide, but was prevented from doing so by an Iraqi Jewish couple now living in a suburb of Tel Aviv. Revealing the magnitude of the depression she was understandably suffering from, when Saddam was born, his mother turned away and would not accept her son to breast. Her brother Khairallah was enlisted to care for the newborn, and Saddam was raised by Khairallah's extended family until he was two and a half. It was then that his mother remarried. For the first time he was with his mother and new stepfather, who was abusive psychologically and physically to Saddam. It is difficult to imagine a more traumatic early childhood. The first years of life are of crucial importance to developing healthy self-esteem and confidence, a reflection of the adoration of the mother for her newborn. Saddam was deprived of this "mirroring." Most individuals so wounded would be deeply scarred, unable to function effectively as adults.

But for Saddam, life took a different course. When he was eight, he asked his parents to send him to school like his cousin. When they refused, he left his home and went back to his Uncle Khairallah, who filled him with dreams of glory, telling Saddam that he would have an important role in Iraqi history, like his granduncle, and that he would follow in the heroic path of Nebuchadnezzar and Saladin, who had rescued the Kingdom of Jerusalem from the Crusaders. For high school, his uncle brought Saddam to Baghdad, which was throbbing with excitement over the successful coup d'état in Egypt by the Arab nationalist hero Gamal Abdel Nasser and his Free Officers Movement. Nasser became a model for young Saddam, who someday hoped to wear his mantle as Arab nationalist leader.

To put the above into psychoanalytic perspective, using the self psychology framework of Heinz Kohut, Saddam had experienced major traumas during his earlier years, producing a profoundly wounded self, with major damage to his self-esteem. With his leaving the family home and coming again under the influence of his uncle Khairallah, he was filled with compensatory dreams of glory, the basis of a fixated grandiose self. But always under that grandiose self was extreme insecurity. This, in turn, produced Saddam's sensitivity to criticism and the consequent development of a sycophantic circle surrounding him, which told him what he wanted to hear rather than what he needed to hear, a major contribution to his often errant decision-making.

When Saddam did come to power, he dotted the landscape of Iraq with magnificent palaces, with inlaid wood, marble floors, fine carpets, bathrooms with gold faucets. These represented his dreams of glory, his grandiose self, just as the mud hut in which he was born in Tikrit represented the psychological and economic poverty and trauma of his origins, the "wounded self" at his core. And what underlay the palaces? Underground bunkers, bristling with weapons and communications equipment, representing the default position in his psychology, the psychological siege state, ready to be attacked, ready to counterattack (Post & Panis, 2005).

Throughout his totalitarian rule, Saddam believed he should be recognized as one of history's great socialist leaders, to be ranked with Joseph Stalin, Mao Zedong, Ho Chi Minh, Marshal Tito, and Fidel Castro. But he was largely ignored until the summer of 1990, when Iraq invaded Kuwait. The invasion was not a reckless grab for power, but only occurred after he was reassured by US ambassador April Glaspie, acting on instructions, that any dispute between Arab neighbors was not a matter of concern to the United States.

After the invasion, suddenly Saddam's name filled the headlines. When he made an aggressive comment, oil barrel prices spiked and the Dow Jones stock average plummeted. He had the world by the throat. At last he was recognized as a powerful world leader. Adding to his triumph, the Palestinian people came to see him as their new hero, who would return Jerusalem to them, fulfilling his uncle's prophecy of occupying a heroic place in Arab history. It was dreams of glory fulfilled, producing an explosion of narcissistic gratification for Saddam.

And the notion that he would retreat ignominiously to his previous position of obscurity in the face of the impending massive military assault by the US-led coalition was psychologically impossible. In the assessment presented to Congress, it was emphasized that Saddam considered himself a "revolutionary pragmatist" and that he had in the past reversed himself. But there were two conditions thta had to be satisfied for Saddam to reverse himself and withdraw from Kuwait: he must be able to save face, and he must be assured that his power would be preserved. As the deadline approached, George H. W. Bush, at a press conference, pounded on the table as he declared: "There will be no face saving!" The story leaked from a general (who was subsequently forced to retire) concerning contingency plans to eliminate Saddam and effect a regime change. Thus the two conditions necessary to permit Saddam to reverse himself were not met. Saddam expected a massive air campaign and was prepared to survive it. Convinced that the United States still suffered from a "Vietnam complex," when American boots were on the ground, and the flower of American youth were again being sent back in body bags, Saddam concluded that this would be intolerable to the American public. There would be protest demonstrations at the White House and the Pentagon, which would lead to a political-military impasse. Saddam would have "won" by demonstrating that he had the courage to stand up against the most powerful nation on earth, consolidating his place in Arab history as a worthy successor to Nasser.

As it was, on the third day of the air campaign, acting on Saddam's instructions, his minister of information, Latif Jassim, declared victory, to the astonishment of the assembled press. He went on to explain that it was widely expected that Iraq would crumble in two days, but that they had already survived for three days, and each passing day would only magnify the scope of the victory. In commemoration of the victory, the "Mother of all Battles Mosque" was built in the aftermath, with four parapets shaped like Scud missiles, each 43 meters high to commemorate the 43 days of the US military campaign.

In the run-up to the 2003 war, the two reasons proffered by the Bush administration for the war were that Saddam Hussein and Osama bin Laden were in league, and that Saddam was developing a nuclear capability and would endanger the United States by providing a weapon of mass destruction to terrorists. Analysis of profiles of both Saddam Hussein and Osama bin Laden revealed that they were bitter rivals, and the notion that they were conspiring was risible. As for the expressed concern that Saddam would make such a weapon available to terrorists, analysis based on his political personality profile made clear that this was inconceivable. Saddam was a prudent decision-maker, with a fixed address, and would never give up control of a nuclear weapon. He knew that if the provenance of such a weapon were traced back to Iraq, his country would be incinerated.

When Saddam went into hiding after the brief conflict, on the basis of the profile it was possible to predict that he would not suicide or go into exile, but would await what he believed were his still loyal followers rising up to support him. When he was found in a spider hole under a mud hut near Tikrit, where he was born, initially the wounded self came into view, as he meekly bowed his head to be inspected for lice, and docilely opened his mouth to have his teeth inspected. But within a short time, his characteristic grandiose self was in evidence. He identified himself as "president of Iraq" and asked who was negotiating with him. This posture characterized him throughout his trial, as predicted, where he denied the legitimacy of the court and made a mockery of the proceedings (Post & Panis, 2005).

6. NARCISSISM AND THE LIFE COURSE

It is perhaps not too large an exaggeration to say that if the ranks of political leaders were stripped of those with significant narcissistic personality features, the ranks would be perilously impoverished. With the development of psychoanalytic theory, increasing attention has been devoted to the etiology and clinical manifestations and treatment of the narcissistic personality, especially reflected in the work of two leading psychoanalysts, Otto Kernberg, a training analyst at the New York Psychoanalytic Institute, and Heinz Kohut, the founding father of "self psychology" and a training analyst at the Chicago Institute of Psychoanalysis. A number of important psychobiographies have been strongly influenced by their formulations. A principal difference between these two schools is that Kernberg views all narcissism as pathological, whereas Kohut considers that there is a healthy line of narcissistic development. (For a review of the implications of the narcissistic personality for political psychology, including psychobiography, see Post, 1993. This review also enumerates points in common and differentiating features of the Kernbergian (object relations) and Kohutian (self psychology) schools.)

6.1. *The Immortal Ataturk*: Volkan and Itzkowitz

Vamik Volkan's scholarship is notable for the systematic manner in which he elucidates how narcissistic dynamics affect political behavior. His psychobiography of Ataturk, the founding father of the modern state of Turkey, written with the Middle East historian Norman Itzkowitz, is an exemplar of accurately relating individual psychogenetic development to the complex political context of Turkey in transition, alternating chapters by Volkan on the individual, and by Itzkowitz on history, politics, and culture (1984). Volkan, trained in the New York Psychoanalytic Institute, which reflects the theoretical perspectives of Otto Kernberg, has written about the "reparative charismatic," who in effect heals the wounds in his own psychology as he heals the wounds in his society. This stands in contrast to the "destructive charismatic," such as Hitler, who unifies his people against the enemy. He identifies the origins of Ataturk's sense of specialness in the influence of his mother's special nurturing. Volkan powerfully conveys the manner in which Ataturk rescued the Turkish people at a critical time in their national history, with the development of a cult of personality, and Ataturk being accorded godlike status. His exalted status is still reflected in Turkey, where every aspiring politician to this day makes a pilgrimage to Ataturk's grave. Furthermore, the name "Ataturk" literally means "Father Turk." The authors make a persuasive case to indicate that Ataturk, whose father died when he was but seven years old, sustained within him an idealized father who was at the heart of Ataturk's becoming father to his nation. He was an example of the reparative charismatic, which is discussed in Volkan's 1988 seminal book *The Need to Have Enemies and Allies*, and which makes a major contribution to understanding leader-follower relationships and helps elucidate charismatic leader-follower relationships.

A student of the self psychology school of Heinz Kohut, Marvin Zonis (1991) has authored a comprehensive psychobiography of the shah of Iran, which relates his fragile narcissistic grandiosity to the troubled course of his nation. Zonis persuasively documents the father's preference for the shah's twin sister, and the manner in which the father's disapproval shaped the inner doubts of the shah, which underlay his grandiose self-concept. Zonis suggests that this, in turn, influenced his capacity to take risks, reflecting his compensatory sense of omnipotence and invulnerability. The very magnitude of the risks he took led, according to Zonis, to the shah's "magnificent fall." His compensatory grandiosity and dreams of glory for his nation also underlay the terminal urgency when he became seriously ill, as described earlier.

6.2. Lincoln's Quest for Union: Charles Strozier

Charles Strozier, also trained in self psychology, wrote a compelling psychobiography of Abraham Lincoln, in which he applied psychoanalytic concepts to elucidate the complex political personality of Abraham Lincoln (1982). The title, a play on words, reflects Lincoln's difficulty with intimacy and guilt over his tortured relationship with his own family. Thus he posits personal resonance with the threat posed by the secession of the South from the union, contributing to his powerful leadership to maintain the integrity of the nation.

6.3. Children Raised Specially to Be the Vehicle of Their Parents' Success

Dreams of glory can also be instilled by parents who see their own path to fame through their children's success. Indeed, while the materials bearing on Wilson's mother's role in shaping his own dreams of glory were not available at the time the Georges were crafting *Woodrow Wilson and Colonel House*, there is fascinating material in her letters to her son that can be seen as setting the foundation for a narcissistic personality consumed by high ambition (Post, 1983).

Similarly, the communications from General Douglas MacArthur's mother to her son are powerful evidence of the role she played in shaping his dreams of glory. In his memoirs, MacArthur includes a poem from his mother:

> Like mother, like son, is saying so true
> The world will judge largely of mother by you.
> Be this then your task, if task it shall be
> To force this proud world to do homage to me.
> Be sure it will say, when its verdict you've won
> She reaps as she sowed: "this man is her son!"
> (MacArthur, 1964, p. 32)

This is clear evidence in and of itself that Mrs. MacArthur viewed much of her own worth and importance in how her son presented himself to the world. That she took an apartment at West Point during his education there to watch over him certainly suggests an unusual closeness, and, with the poem, speaks to the origins of his dreams of glory.

Dreams of glory, combined with talent and opportunity, can propel some to achieve greatness. But dreams die hard, and for the consummate narcissist, especially at the end of life, exaggerated reactions to frustrated dreams of glory can cause nightmares for us all. That leaders in the late life transition can hold too tightly to the reins of power, leading to major psychopolitical dislocations is well illustrated by what came to be called "the Arab Spring" of 2011.

7. AGING AUTOCRATS

At the time of this writing, international attention has focused on the political decisions and actions of aging Middle Eastern autocrats, with the so-called Arab Spring. First is the 74-year-old Zine al-Abidine Ben Ali, leader of Tunisia for 30 years. Then there is 82-year-old Hosni Mubarak, the autocratic leader of Egypt, who was at its helm for 30 years, from 1979 to 2011. Both left office after facing mammoth political demonstrations. Their overthrows, in turn, led to the uprising in Libya, led for 42 years by Mu'ammer al-Gaddafi, 68 years old, who was killed by the rebels after being forced from power; and to demonstrations in Yemen against the leadership of 65-year-old president Ali Abdullah Saleh, in power since 1994, who under duress agreed to a transfer of power in November 2011. Aging dictators may increasingly come to see themselves as synonymous with their countries and, protected by sycophantic subordinates, may be late in recognizing how much discontent has been brewing in response to their repressive policies. Mubarak showed a very paternalistic attitude to his people, initially characterizing the protestors as thugs. He related to Egypt and its people as if he were their king, their pharoah.

For the intensely narcissistic dictator such as Gaddafi, it was inconceivable that everyone in Libya did not love him; after all, he had created Libya (Post, 2011a). Therefore, anyone protesting must have been provoked to do so by al-Qaeda or the West. He suggested that al-Qaeda had slipped hallucinogenic drugs in the Nescafe of the crazed youthful protestors, and when the drugs wore off, they would lay down their guns. From the beginning and throughout the protests, speaking in his characteristic first-person singular, he repeated, "They love me. All my people are with me. They all love me. They will die to protect me, my people." He went on to say, "I am resistant, I am the creator of tomorrow, I am here, I am here, I am here" (Amanpour, 2011). His use of the first-person singular stands in striking contrast to Churchill's use of the first-person plural, Churchill always spoke of "*our* struggle," "*our* duties," "what *we* must do" (Post, 2011b). Gaddafi indeed earlier stated that Libya was "my country. I created it and I can destroy it" (*The Economist*, 2011).

While Gaddafi had been characterized as "insane," "a madman," "the mad dog of the Middle East" (in President Reagan's words), for the most part he was "crazy like a fox," the consummate survivor and in touch with reality, shrewdly assessing his situation. But there were two circumstances when he could slip below the border of reality, showing faulty judgment and erratic behavior: when he was winning and when he was losing. When he was winning, as represented by his triumphal march toward the rebel headquarters in Benghazi before the UN resolution and the alliance campaign to create a no-fly zone, he seemed swollen with pride, invulnerable, expansive in his predictions of total victory, committing himself to "show no mercy." But in the beginning, when, inspired by the revolutions in Tunisia and Egypt, the rebel forces were surging ahead, he was under massive pressure and he was losing. He went into a stance he had demonstrated throughout his life: the outsider, standing up courageously against superior forces, the heroic Muslim warrior.

This pattern can be traced to his boyhood. Born in a tent in the desert to Bedouin parents, Gaddafi was sent to Tripoli for schooling, where he was teased by the sons of Libyan elites for his coarse manners. This resentment of the establishment contributed to his leadership of the coup that toppled King Idris, to his support of terrorists internationally, and to his enmity toward the United States. It was predictable that he would not suicide or go into a lush exile, but meant it when he said he would go down "to the last drop of his blood."

In the age of the Internet, with the possible exception of North Korea, dictators can no longer control information, and the ability of citizen journalists with their cell phone cameras to post pictures of violent government suppression and galvanize opposition to autocratic dictators is a major quantum shift. And for youth, in the forefront of the uprisings, rebelling against the leadership of corrupt old men fits well the psychology of the young adult transition.

8. CLOSING NOTE

All too often, a leader comes to power with relatively sparse information available concerning his formative years. But to fully understand a leader's personality and political behavior, it is imperative to understand the manner in which the life course shaped the leader, that is, the psychobiographic influences. This chapter began with a discussion of the seminal contributions of Freud and the influence of his psychoanalytic theory on psychobiography. After reviewing the seasons of a leader's life as set out by Erikson and Levinson, drawing on Harold Lasswell's foundational work, the theory of the "power seeker" was reviewed and then the manner in which Alexander and Juliette George tested Lasswell's hypotheses in the case of Woodrow Wilson. The origins of "dreams of glory" were reviewed, using Saddam Hussein as an example of the traumatized "wounded self," but also reviewing the influences of parents who shape their sons and daughters to be special and fulfill their parents' destiny. This gives emphasis to the importance of the shaping of narcissistic personalities and their overrepresentation among major political leaders.

The question might well be asked, "How do we 'know' that Saddam's traumatic early life experiences shaped his political personality in the manner suggested, or that the killing of most of his family in the Holocaust influenced Menachem Begin's 'Never again' vow that he translated into national policy when he became prime minister?" In his 1989 National Endowment of the Humanities Jefferson lecture, entitled "The Fateful Rift: The San Andreas Fault in the Modern Mind," Walker Percy discusses the inherent "unknowability" of mind and decries attempting to apply criteria from the physical sciences to the social sciences, observing there is an unbridgeable gap, a "San Andreas fault," between the two types of science.

Psychobiography in general wrestles with this dilemma. It attempts to address the manner in which formative life experiences shape adult personality, and for political leaders, how the resultant psychodynamic forces within the personality shape and influence political behavior. While we can never "know" with certainty, by rigorously searching for data that confirm or deny the hypotheses deriving from the varying psychogenetic and psychodynamic theories, we can identify patterns and connections and identify understandings of "what makes X tick." Still, we will never "know" with full certainty. Not all theories are created equal, and, as Runyan has suggested, theory should guide a rigorous search for evidence. Some psychodynamic theories have been applied with wild abandon, ignoring evidence entirely in flights of fancy, whereas other psychobiographers, as exemplified by the Georges, seek rigorously to search for evidence to test their hypotheses.

References

Amanpour, C. (2011, February 28). "My People Love Me": Moammar Gadhafi denies demonstrations against him anywhere in Libya. *ABC News*. http://abcnews. go.com/International/christiane-amanpour-interviews-libyas-moammar-gadhafi/ story?id=13019942#.TtfYKI48rG8.

Bertaux, D. (1981). *Biography and society: The life history approach to the social sciences*. Beverly Hills, CA: Sage.

Bychowski, G. (1948). *Dictators and disciples from Caesar to Stalin: A psychoanalytic interpretation of history*. New York: International Universities Press.

Carter, J. (1982). *Keeping faith: Memoirs of a president*. New York: Bantam Books.

Cocks, G., & Crosby, T. (1987). *Psychohistory: Readings in the methods of psychology, psychoanalysis, and history*. New Haven, CT: Yale University Press.

Economist, The. (2011, February 24). Endgame in Tripoli: The bloodiest of the North African rebellions so far leaves hundreds dead. [http://www.economist.com/node/18239888]

Erikson, E. (1950). *Childhood and society*. New York: Norton.

Erikson, E. (1958). *Young man Luther: A study in psychoanalysis and history*. New York: Norton .

Erikson, E. (1964). *Insight and responsibility*. New York: Norton.

Erikson, E. (1969). *Gandhi's truth: On the origins of militant nonviolence*. New York: Norton.

Erikson, E. (1974). On the nature of psychohistorical evidence. In R. J. Lifton & E. Olson (eds.), *Explorations in psychohistory: The Wellfleet Papers* (pp. 42–77). New York: Simon and Schuster.

Erikson, E. (1975). *Life history and the historical moment*. New York: Norton.

Freud, S. (1957). Leonardo da Vinci and a memory of his childhood. In *The standard edition of the complete psychological works of Sigmund Freud*, vol. 11: *Five lectures on psycho-analysis, Leonardo da Vinci and other works* (ed. James Strachey). London: Hogarth Press.

Freud, S. (1959). *On narcissism: An introduction*. Vol. 14 of the *Collected Papers*, American Edition. New York: Basic Books.

Freud, S. (1964). *Moses and monotheism*. In *The standard edition of the complete psychological works of Sigmund Freud*, vol. 23: *Moses and monotheism, An outline of psychoanalysis, Analysis terminable and interminable, and other works* (J. Strachay, ed.). London: Hogarth Press.

Freud, S., & Bullitt, W. C. (1967). *Thomas Woodrow Wilson, twenty-eighth president of the United States*. Boston, MA: Houghton-Mifflin.

George, A. L. (1968). Power as a compensatory value for political leaders. *Journal of Social Issues, 24*, 24–49.

George, A. L., & George, J. L. (1956). *Woodrow Wilson and Colonel House: A personality study.* New York: John Day.

Handlin, O. (1979). *Truth in history.* Cambridge, MA: Belknap Press of Harvard University Press.

Horney, K. (1950). *Neurosis and human growth: The struggle toward self-realization.* New York: Norton.

Jones, E. (1981). *The life and work of Sigmund Freud* (vol. 2). New York: Basic Books.

Langer, W. (1972). *The mind of Adolf Hitler: The secret wartime report.* New York: Basic Books.

Lasswell, H. D. (1930). *Psychopathology and politics.* Chicago: University of Chicago Press.

Lasswell, H. D. (1948). *Power and personality.* New York: Norton.

Lasswell, H. D. (1960). *Psychopathology and politics.* New York: Viking.

Levinson, D. (1978). *The seasons of a man's life.* New York: Knopf.

Lifton, R. J., & Olson, E. (Eds.). (1974). *Explorations in psychohistory: The Wellfleet Papers.* New York: Simon and Schuster.

Loewenberg, P. (1983). *Decoding the past: The psychohistorical approach.* Berkeley: University of California Press.

Loewenberg, P. (1988). Psychoanalytic models of history: Freud and after. In W. M. Runyan (ed.), *Psychology and historical interpretation.* New York: Oxford University Press, p. 126–156.

MacArthur, D. (1964). *Reminiscences.* New York: McGraw-Hill.

Makari, G. (2008). *Revolution in mind: The creation of psychoanalysis.* New York: Harper Collins.

Palgrave, F. T. (Ed.). (1875). *The golden treasury of the best songs and lyrical poems in the English language.* London: Macmillan.

Popper, K. Raimund Sir (1962). *Conjectures and refutations: The growth of scientific knowledge.* New York: Basic Books.

Post, J. (1979, Spring). Personality profiles in support of the Camp David summit. *Studies in Intelligence*, 1–5.

Post, J. (1983). Woodrow Wilson reexamined: The mind-body controversy redux and other disputations. *Political Psychology*, 4(2), 289–306.

Post, J. (1990, December). A political personality profile of Saddam Hussein. Testimony to House Foreign Affairs Committee, Lee Hamilton, Chairman.

Post, J. (1993). Current concepts of the narcissistic personality: Implications for political psychology. *Political Psychology*, 14(1), 99–120.

Post, J. (Ed.). (2003). *The psychological assessment of political leaders.* Ann Arbor: University of Michigan Press.

Post, J. (2004). *Leaders and their followers in a dangerous world: The psychology of political behavior.* Ithaca, NY: Cornell University Press.

Post, J. (2011a, March 15). Qaddafi under siege: A political psychologist assesses Libya's mercurial leader. *Foreign Policy.* http://www.foreignpolicy.com/articles/2011/03/15/qaddafi_under_seige.

Post, J. (2011b, August 26). Moammar Kadafi's inner "I": The Libyan leader's speeches are full of first-person self-aggrandizement. *Los Angeles Times.* http://articles.latimes.com/2011/aug/26/opinion/la-oe-post-kadafi-churchill-libya-20110826.

Post, J., & Panis, L. (2005). Tyranny on trial: The personality and trial conduct of Slobodan Milosevic and Saddam Hussein. *Cornell University International Law Review*, 38(3), 823.

Post, J., & Robins, R. S. (1993). *When illness strikes the leader: The dilemma of the captive king.* New Haven, CT: Yale University Press.

Runyan, W. M. (1982). *Life histories and psychobiography: Explorations in theory and method.* New York: Oxford University Press.

Runyan, W. M. (Ed.). (1988). *Psychology and historical interpretation*. New York: Oxford University Press.

Schiffer, I. (1973). *Charisma: A psychoanalytic look at mass society*. Toronto: University of Toronto Press.

Stannard, D. E. (1980). *Shrinking history: On Freud and the failure of psychohistory*. New York: Oxford University Press.

Strozier, C. B. (1982). *Lincoln's quest for union: Public and private meanings*. New York: Basic Books.

Tucker, R. (1973). *Stalin as revolutionary, 1879–1929*. New York: Norton.

Tucker, R. (1988). A Stalin biographer's memoir. In W. M. Runyan (ed.), *Psychology and historical interpretation* (pp. 63–81). New York: Oxford University Press.

Volkan, V. (1988). *The need to have enemies and allies: From clinical practice to international relationships*. New York: Jason Aranson.

Volkan, V., & Itzkowitz, N. (1984). *The immortal Ataturk: A psychobiography*. Chicago: University of Chicago Press.

Waite, R. (1977). *The psychopathic god: Adolf Hitler*. New York: Basic Books.

Weinstein, E. A. (1970). Woodrow Wilson's neurological illness. *Journal of American History, 57*, 324–351.

Weinstein, E. A. (1981). *Woodrow Wilson: A medical and psychological biography*. Princeton, NJ: Princeton University Press.

Wolfenstein, V. E. (1971). *The revolutionary personality: Lenin, Trotsky, Gandhi*. Princeton, NJ: Princeton University Press.

Zonis, M. (1991). *Majestic failure: The fall of the shah*. Chicago: University of Chicago Press.

CHAPTER 16

CONFLICT ANALYSIS AND RESOLUTION

RONALD J. FISHER, HERBERT C. KELMAN,
AND SUSAN ALLEN NAN

THIS chapter presents a social-psychological approach to the analysis and resolution of international and intercommunal conflicts. At the level of practice, its central focus is on *interactive conflict resolution* (cf. Fisher, 1997), a family of models for intervening in deep-rooted, protracted conflicts between identity groups, which is anchored in psychological principles At the level of analysis, the social-psychological approach gained increasing favor in the 1960s and is now more or less an accepted part of the multidiscipline of international relations and the interdisciplinary field of political psychology (Kelman, 1965; Jervis, 1976; Levy, 2003; Rosati, 2000; Stein, 2001). Given that political psychology involves the application of human psychology to the study of politics, the social-psychological perspective has relevance to many of the areas of political psychology, including the study of images, threat perception, decision-making, foreign policy, political communication, intergroup relations, and political mobilization. The social-psychological approach assumes that (1) subjective elements are central in determining perceptions of reality and responses to that reality; (2) perceptual and cognitive processes need to be understood in the context of group dynamics and intergroup relations; (3) interaction between the parties is fundamental in understanding the course and outcomes of conflict; and (4) a multilevel systems analysis is necessary to understand the phenomenon (Fisher, 1990; Fisher & Kelman, 2011).

The chapter begins with a presentation of a social-psychological perspective on the nature of international conflict and a discussion of the perceptual and normative processes that contribute to its escalation and perpetuation. The analysis has clear implications for the outcomes that accrue and for the practice of interactive conflict resolution. To illustrate the family of approaches subsumed under this rubric, we proceed to a more detailed description of the assumptions and procedures of its primary prototype, the problem-solving workshop, and describe applications of the method to three different ethnopolitical conflicts on which the authors have worked. The chapter concludes with an identification of some of the challenges confronting scholar-practitioners in the field of conflict analysis and resolution with particular reference to interactive conflict resolution.

1. The Nature of International Conflict

A social-psychological perspective can expand on the view of international conflict provided by the realist and neorealist schools of international relations or other, more traditional approaches focusing on structural or strategic factors (Kelman, 2007). Social-psychological approaches enrich the analysis in a variety of ways: by exploring the subjective factors that set constraints on rationality; by opening the black box of the state as unitary actor and analyzing processes within and between the societies that underlie state action; by broadening the range of influence processes (and, indeed, of definitions of power) that play a role in international politics; and by conceiving international conflict as a dynamic process, shaped by changing realities, interests, and relations between the conflicting parties.

Social-psychological analysis suggests four propositions about the nature of international conflict that are particularly relevant to existential conflicts between identity groups—conflicts in which the collective identities of the parties are engaged and in which the continued existence of the group is seen to be at stake. Thus, the propositions apply most directly to ethnopolitical or ideological conflicts, but they also apply to more mundane interstate conflicts insofar as issues of national identity and existence come into play—as they often do.

First, *international conflict is a process driven by collective needs and fears,* rather than entirely a product of rational calculation of objective national interests on the part of political decision-makers. Human needs are often articulated and fulfilled through important collectivities, such as the ethnic group, the national group, and the state. Conflict arises when a group is faced with nonfulfillment or threat to the fulfillment of basic needs: not only such obvious material needs as food, shelter, physical safety, and physical well-being, but also, and very centrally, such psychological needs as identity, security, recognition, autonomy, self-esteem, and a sense of justice (Burton, 1990). Moreover, needs for identity and security and similarly powerful collective needs, and the fears and concerns about survival associated with them, contribute heavily to the escalation and perpetuation of conflict. Even when the conflicting parties have come to the conclusion that it is in their best interest to put an end to the conflict, they resist going to the negotiating table or making the accommodations necessary for the negotiations to move forward, for fear that they will be propelled into concessions that in the end will leave their very existence compromised. The fears that drive existential conflicts lie at the heart of the relationship between the conflicting parties, going beyond the cycle of fears resulting from the dynamics of the security dilemma (Jervis, 1976).

Collective fears and needs combine with objective factors—for example, a state's resources, the ethnic composition of its population, or its access to the sea—in determining how different segments of a society perceive state interests, and what ultimately becomes the national interest as defined by the dominant elites. Similarly, all conflicts represent a combination of rational and irrational factors, and in each type of conflict the mix may vary from case to case. Furthermore, in all international conflicts, the needs and fears of populations are mobilized and often manipulated by the leadership, with varying degrees of demagoguery and cynicism. Even when manipulated, collective needs and fears represent authentic reactions within the population and become the focus of societal action. They may be linked to individual needs and fears. For example, in highly violent ethnic conflicts, the fear of annihilation of one's group is often (and for good reason) tied to a fear of personal annihilation.

The conception of conflict as a process driven by collective needs and fears implies, first and foremost, that conflict resolution—if it is to lead to a stable and just peace and to a new relationship that enhances the welfare of the two societies—must address the fundamental needs and deepest fears of the populations. From a normative point of view, such a solution can be viewed as the operationalization of justice within a problem-solving approach to conflict resolution (Kelman, 1996). Another implication of a human-needs orientation is that the psychological needs on which it focuses—security, identity, recognition—are not inherently zero-sum (Burton, 1990), although they are usually seen as such in deep-rooted conflicts. Thus, it may well be possible to shape an integrative solution that satisfies both sets of needs, which may then make it easier to settle issues like territory or resources through distributive bargaining. Finally, the view of conflict as a process driven by collective needs and fears suggests that conflict resolution must, at some stage, provide for interactions that take place at the level of individuals, such as taking the other's perspective (or realistic empathy) (White, 1984), creative problem solving, insight, and learning.

Second, *international conflict is an intersocietal process*, not merely an intergovernmental or interstate phenomenon. The conflict, particularly in the case of protracted ethnopolitical struggles, becomes an inescapable part of daily life for each society and its component elements. (See also Bar-Tal & Halperin's discussion of intractable conflicts in chapter 28 of this volume.) Thus, analysis of conflict requires attention, not only to its strategic, military, and diplomatic dimensions, but also to its economic, psychological, cultural, and social-structural dimensions. Interactions along these dimensions, both within and between the conflicting societies, shape the political environment in which governments function and define the political constraints under which they operate.

An intersocietal view of conflict alerts us to the role of internal divisions *within* each society, which often play a major part in exacerbating or even creating conflicts *between* the societies. They impose constraints on political leaders pursuing a policy of accommodation, in the form of accusations by opposition elements that they are jeopardizing national existence, and of anxieties and doubts within the general population that are both fostered and exploited by the opposition elements. The internal divisions, however, may also provide potential levers for change in the direction of conflict resolution, by challenging the monolithic image of the enemy that parties in conflict tend to hold and enabling them to deal with each other in a more differentiated way. They point to the presence on the other side of potential partners for negotiation and thus provide the opportunity for forming pro-negotiation coalitions across the conflict lines (Kelman, 1993). To contribute to conflict resolution, any such coalition must of necessity remain an "uneasy coalition," lest its members lose their credibility and political effectiveness within their respective communities.

Another implication of an intersocietal view of conflict is that negotiations and third-party efforts should ideally be directed not merely to a political *settlement* of the conflict, but to its *resolution*. A political agreement may be adequate for terminating relatively specific, containable interstate disputes, but conflicts that engage the collective identities and existential concerns of the adversaries require a process conducive to structural and attitude change, to reconciliation, and to the transformation of the relationship between the two societies. Finally, an intersocietal analysis of conflict suggests a view of diplomacy as a complex mix of official and unofficial efforts with complementary contributions.

Third, *international conflict is a multifaceted process of mutual influence*, not only a contest in the exercise of coercive power. Each party seeks to protect and promote its own interests by shaping the behavior of the other. Conflict occurs when these interests clash: when attainment of one party's interests (and fulfillment of the needs that underlie them) threatens, or is perceived to threaten, the interests (and needs) of the other. In pursuing the conflict, therefore, the parties engage in mutual influence, designed to advance their own positions and to block the adversary. Similarly, in conflict management, the parties exercise influence to induce the adversary to come to the table, to make concessions, to accept an agreement that meets their interests and needs, and to live up to that agreement. Third parties also exercise influence in conflict situations, by backing one or the other party, by mediating between them, or by maneuvering to protect their own interests.

Influence in international conflict typically relies on a mixture of threats and inducements, with the balance often on the side of force and the threat of force. Thus, the US-Soviet relationship in the Cold War was predominantly framed in terms of an elaborate theory of deterrence—a form of influence designed to keep the other side from doing what you do not want it to do (George & Smoke, 1974; Jervis, Lebow, & Stein, 1985; Schelling, 1960). In other conflict relationships, the emphasis may be on compellence—a form of influence designed to make the other side do what you want it to do, or to stop doing something, or to undo what it has already done. Such coercive strategies entail serious costs and risks, and their effects may be severely limited. For example, they are likely to be reciprocated by the other side and thus lead to escalation of the conflict, and they are unlikely to change behavior to which the other is committed. Thus, the effective exercise of influence in international conflict requires a broadening of the repertoire of influence strategies, at least to the extent of combining "carrots and sticks"—of supplementing the negative incentives that typically dominate international conflict relationships with positive incentives (cf. Baldwin, 1971; Kriesberg, 1982), such as economic benefits, international approval, or a general reduction in the level of tension. An example of an approach based on the systematic use of positive incentives is Osgood's (1962) GRIT (Graduated and Reciprocated Initiatives in Tension Reduction) strategy.

Effective use of positive incentives requires more than offering the other whatever rewards, promises, or confidence-building measures seem most readily available. It requires actions that address the fundamental needs and fears of the other party. Thus, the key to an effective influence strategy based on the exchange of positive incentives is *responsiveness* to the other's concerns. The advantage of a strategy of responsiveness is that it allows each party to exert influence on the other through positive steps (not threats) that are within its own capacity to take. The process is greatly facilitated by communication between the parties in order to identify actions that are politically feasible for each party and yet likely to have an impact on the other.

A key element in an influence strategy based on responsiveness is *mutual reassurance*. The negotiation literature suggests that parties are often driven to the table by a mutually hurting stalemate, which makes negotiations more attractive than continuing the conflict (Zartman & Berman, 1982; Touval & Zartman, 1985, p. 16). But parties in existential conflicts are afraid of negotiations, even when the status quo has become increasingly painful and they recognize that a negotiated agreement is in their interest. To advance the negotiating process under such circumstances, it is at least as important to reduce the parties' fears as it is to increase their pain.

Mutual reassurance can take the form of acknowledgments, symbolic gestures, or confidence-building measures. To be maximally effective, such steps need to address the other's central needs and fears as directly as possible. When Egyptian president Sadat spoke to the Israeli Knesset during his dramatic visit to Jerusalem in November 1977, he clearly acknowledged Egypt's past hostility toward Israel and thus validated Israelis' own experiences. In so doing, he greatly enhanced the credibility of the change in course that he was announcing. At the opening of this visit, Sadat's symbolic gesture of engaging in a round of cordial handshakes with the Israeli officials who had come to greet him broke a longstanding taboo. By signaling the beginning of a new relationship, it had an electrifying effect on the Israeli public. In deep-rooted conflicts, acknowledgment of what was heretofore denied—in the form of recognition of the other's humanity, nationhood, rights, grievances, and interpretation of history—is an important source of reassurance that the other may indeed be ready to negotiate an agreement that addressees your fundamental concerns. By signaling acceptance of the other's legitimacy, each party reassures the other that negotiations and concessions no longer constitute mortal threats to its security and national existence. By confirming the other's narrative, each reassures the other that a compromise does not represent an abandonment of its identity.

An influence strategy based on responsiveness to each other's needs and fears and the resulting search for ways of reassuring and benefiting each other has important advantages from a long-term point of view. It does not merely elicit specific desired behaviors from the other party, but can contribute to a creative redefinition of the conflict, joint discovery of mutually satisfactory solutions, and transformation of the relationship between the parties.

Fourth, *international conflict is an interactive process with an escalatory, self-perpetuating dynamic*, not merely a sequence of action and reaction by stable actors In intense conflict relationships, the natural course of interaction between the parties tends to reinforce and deepen the conflict, and is governed by a set of norms and guided by a set of images that create an escalatory, self-perpetuating dynamic. This dynamic can be reversed through skillful diplomacy, imaginative leadership, third-party intervention, and institutionalized mechanisms for managing and resolving conflict.

The needs and fears of parties engaged in intense conflict impose perceptual and cognitive constraints on their processing of new information, with the resulting tendency to underestimate the occurrence and the possibility of change. The ability to take the role of the other is severely impaired. Dehumanization of the enemy makes it even more difficult to acknowledge and access the perspective of the other. Conflicting parties display particularly strong tendencies to find evidence that confirms their negative images of each other and to resist evidence that would seem to disconfirm these images. Thus, interaction not only fails to contribute to a revision of the enemy image, but actually helps to reinforce and perpetuate it. Interaction guided by mirror images of a demonic enemy and a virtuous self (cf. Bronfenbrenner, 1961; White, 1965) creates self-fulfilling prophecies by inducing the parties to engage in the hostile actions they expect from one another.

Self-fulfilling prophecies are also generated by the conflict norms that typically govern the interaction between parties engaged in an intense conflict. Expressions of hostility and distrust toward the enemy are not just spontaneous manifestations of the conflict, but are normatively prescribed behaviors. Political leaders' assumption that the public's evaluation of them depends on their adherence to these norms influences their tactical and strategic decisions, their approach to negotiations, their public pronouncements, and, ultimately, the way they educate their own publics. For the publics, in turn, adherence to these norms is often taken as an indicator of group loyalty. Thus, the discourse in deep-rooted conflicts is marked by mutual delegitimization and dehumanization. Interaction governed by this set of norms—at the micro and macro levels—contributes to escalation and perpetuation of the conflict. Parties that systematically treat each other with hostility and distrust are likely to become increasingly hostile and untrustworthy.

The dynamics of conflict interaction create a high probability that opportunities for conflict resolution will be missed. Conflict resolution efforts, therefore, require promotion of a different kind of interaction, capable of reversing the escalatory and self-perpetuating dynamics of conflict: an interaction conducive to sharing perspectives, differentiating the enemy image, and developing a language of mutual reassurance and a new discourse based on the norms of responsiveness and reciprocity.

2. CONTRIBUTIONS TO CONFLICT ANALYSIS

The social-psychological perspective can be particularly helpful in explaining why and how, once a conflict has started, perceptual and normative processes are set into motion that promote conflict escalation and perpetuation, and create or intensify barriers to conflict resolution. By the same token, social-psychological analysis, in helping to identify and understand these barriers, can also suggest ways of overcoming them.

2.1. Perceptual Processes

Perceptual and cognitive processes—the ways in which we interpret and organize conflict-related information—play a major role in the escalation and perpetuation of conflict and create impediments to redefining and resolving the conflict despite changing realities and interests. Since the 1950s, social psychology in North America has concentrated on the study of social cognition and has typically focused on individual-level processes with little reference to their social context. In contrast, we explore the ways social perception and cognition operate in the social and relational environment. The concept of stereotype provides a good example, in that it goes beyond the individual-level process of categorization to find meaning in the context of group identities and intergroup relations.

The concept of *stereotype* has a considerable history in social psychology (Kinder, chapter 25, this volume), and has typically been defined as a set of simplified beliefs about the attributes of an out-group. Stereotypes build on the social categorization effect of perceived out-group similarity, but also incorporate the out-group derogation side of ethnocentrism, in that the simplistic beliefs typically have negative connotations. Stereotypes abound in the world of intergroup relations at low levels of conflict escalation and can be relatively innocuous misperceptions of group reality. However, at higher levels of escalation, stereotypes can drive more insidious processes, such as self-fulfilling prophecies, and can provide part of the justification for destructive behaviors such as discrimination, dehumanization, and ultimately genocide.

The concept of *image* builds on that of stereotype and has gained greater currency in the study of international relations than the concept of attitude, even though the two can be similarly defined as consisting of cognitive, affective, and behavioral components (Scott, 1965; Herrmann, chapter 11, this volume). One important application of the concept is the proposition that parties in conflict often hold *mirror images* of each other, seeing themselves in a similarly stereotypical positive light and the enemy in a similarly negative light. A classic study of American and Russian images of each other during the Cold War demonstrated that the Americans' distorted view of Russia was surprisingly similar to the Russians' image of America; for example, each saw the other as the aggressor who could not be trusted (Bronfenbrenner, 1961). Similar mirror images have been documented in a variety of intergroup and international conflicts in different parts of the world, and their significance lies in the effects they have on driving increasingly escalatory behavior by the parties. Thus, a number of commentators have stressed the value of images in the study of international relations and foreign policy and have called for a more differentiated view of images as they affect foreign-policy making (e.g., Herrmann & Fischerkeller, 1995).

Once established, typically through in-group socialization, stereotypes and images serve as cognitive structures that drive *selective and distorted perception*. Unfortunately, in the intergroup context, the effects of social categorization and ethnocentrism appear to increase as the distinguishing characteristics of groups—for example, in language, manner of dress, or skin color—are clearer and more marked. Thus, stronger stereotypes between such groups become filters through which information consonant with the stereotype is perceived and assimilated while contrary information is ignored or discounted (Hamilton, 1979; Schneider, 2004). (See also the discussions of motivated reasoning by Stein, chapter 12, this volume; and by Taber & Young, chapter 17, this volume.) The pressures of conflict escalation, with its attendant perception of threat, distrust, and hostility, tend to enhance these distortions.

The positive, in-group side of ethnocentrism also involves perceptual selectivity and distortion, which now operate in the direction of elevating and glorifying the in-group. According to social identity theory (see below), the self-serving biases that operate here are due to the need for enhanced self-esteem that comes from heightened in-group distinctiveness and out-group derogation through invidious comparisons. Simply put, individuals tend to perceive positive behaviors more on the part of in-group members and negative behaviors more on the part of out-group members, and even evaluate the same behaviors differently when they are associated with in-group versus out-group members (Pruitt & Kim, 2004).

Causal attribution plays an increasingly important role as intergroup conflict escalates over time. It refers to the judgments individuals make about the reasons for their own and other people's behavior, and the inferences they draw about the characteristics of the actor. Attributions are significant in human interaction, because they tend to affect responses (both emotional and behavioral) to other people's actions. A key distinction in the attribution of the causes of behavior is between attribution to internal or dispositional characteristics of the person versus external or situational factors. A common cognitive bias in attribution appears to be the tendency to attribute one's own behavior to situational causes, but the behavior of others to dispositional factors (Jones & Nisbett, 1971). Ross (1977) described the latter tendency as the *fundamental attribution error*. At the level of intergroup relations, a more insidious bias enters in—the so-called *ultimate attribution error* (Pettigrew, 1979). Assuming social categorization and a degree of ethnocentrism, a prejudiced individual will tend to attribute undesirable actions by an out-group member to dispositional (i.e., group) characteristics, whereas desirable actions will be attributed to situational circumstances. Concurrently, undesirable behavior by an in-group member will be attributed to situational determinants, while desirable actions will be attributed to dispositional (i.e., in-group) characteristics.

According to Pettigrew, the effect of this cognitive bias will be stronger when there are highly negative stereotypes and intense conflict between the groups. What is happening in this process is that prejudiced individuals are able to confirm their negative expectations and discount information that runs counter to their out-group stereotypes.

As conflict escalates, a series of transformations occur in the orientations and behavior of each party and thereby in their interaction (Pruitt & Kim, 2004). One of these changes relates to the motivation of the parties, which shifts from doing well in achieving their goals, to winning over the other party, and finally to hurting the other party. At a middle level of escalation, a competitive and increasingly hostile interaction induces the parties toward further perceptual and cognitive biases. Essentially, this is where negative expectations become increasingly confirmed, mirror images develop, and cognitive dissonance influences parties toward consistent systems of thinking and behaving.

The *self-fulfilling prophecy* is a type of expectancy effect in which a person's stereotypes regarding an out-group member lead that person to behave in ways that confirm the stereotype. In intergroup conflict, the stereotyped expectancies that one group holds of another group—for example, as untrustworthy—are communicated through behavior, such as cautiousness and skepticism. These behaviors may then be reciprocated by the target group members—for example, through unwillingness to trust and cooperate—thus confirming the initial views of the first group. In this way, stereotypes are not only confirmed, but strengthened for the next round of interactions. The pervasive effects of stereotypes on intergroup relations are among the enduring potential contributions of social psychology to the understanding of intergroup and international conflict (Fiske, 2002).

Many of the perceptual biases and cognitive distortions that afflict parties in conflict can be partly explained through the effects of *cognitive dissonance*, an unpleasant state of tension that is hypothesized to exist whenever any two cognitive elements (e.g., beliefs, perceptions of behavior) are incongruent (Festinger, 1957). Individuals are predisposed to reduce cognitive dissonance through a variety of possible changes, such as modifying one of the elements, adding new elements, or changing their behavior. Related conceptualizations, including Heider's balance theory, also identify the need for cognitive consistency as a prime motivator in supporting biases and distortions (Heider, 1958). The initial application of these concepts to international conflict in a comprehensive manner was undertaken by Robert Jervis, whose analysis and case examples emphasized how policymakers assimilated new information into preexisting beliefs and categories in ways that rendered the information cognitively consistent (Jervis, 1976).

At higher levels of escalation, all of the aforementioned misperceptions and biases find their expression in more extreme forms. Each perceptual and cognitive distortion becomes more pronounced and thus has a larger effect on interaction and escalation. Mirror images, based on an ethnocentric perspective, produce a spiraling effect in which each party's interpretation of the other's difficult or hostile behavior reinforces attributions of aggressive intent and untrustworthiness (Fisher & Kelman, 2011). Mirror images develop beyond the moderately good-bad distinction toward more exaggerated and variegated forms, identified by White as including the *diabolical enemy image, the virile self-image,* and the *moral self-image* (White, 1970).

The diabolical enemy image finds its expression in the *demonization* of the enemy, which White determined to be not only the most common, but also an almost universal misperception, in his 40 years of studying the most serious conflicts of the past 100 years (White, 2004). Demonization is also linked to the process of *dehumanization*, in which members of the enemy group are seen as less than human, thus justifying or rationalizing aggressive behavior toward them. Dehumanization, in turn, is linked to the phenomenon of *deindividuation*, in which group members experience a loss of personal identity and become submerged in the group's cognitive reality (Festinger, Pepitone, & Newcomb, 1952). As a consequence, members of one's own group or other groups are seen less as individual persons than as members of a social category (Pruitt & Kim, 2004). In intergroup conflict, this process appears to reduce constraints within groups on aggressive behavior by reducing individual responsibility, and at the same time reduce the perception of out-group members as individual human beings deserving of morally acceptable treatment. The accumulation of all of these processes allows for more severe aggressive responses toward members of the enemy group, which in turn, escalates the intensity of the conflict. The *mutual victimization* characteristic of highly destructive intergroup conflicts is in part due to the enabling effects of extreme images and the cognitive biases that go with them.

Also at higher levels of escalation, an insidious cognitive process known as *entrapment* becomes a driver in the intractable nature of the conflict. Entrapment is a cognitive process in which the parties become increasingly committed to costly and destructive courses of action that would not be prescribed by rational analysis (Brockner & Rubin, 1985). Thus, each party in an escalated conflict pursues its goals by expending more resources than would seem to be justifiable by objective or external standards (Pruitt & Kim, 2004). In a related vein, Deutsch (1983) has identified the cognitive error of unwitting commitment in his largely cognitive analysis of the escalatory dynamics of what he terms the *malignant social process,* that is, one that is increasingly costly and dangerous and from which the parties see no way of extricating themselves without unacceptable losses. The dynamics behind unwitting commitment are seen to include a more general phenomenon identified as postdecision dissonance reduction: Once an alternative has been chosen, it becomes evaluated more positively in order to increase cognitive consistency (Brehm, 1956). A connection can also be made between entrapment and some of the hypothesized effects of prospect theory, especially loss aversion, which might help explain why parties persist in failing policies much longer than a rational, cost-benefit analysis would prescribe (Levy, 1996; and chapter 10, this volume).

2.2. Group and Normative Processes

Adding to the complexity and intractability of escalated and destructive conflict induced by perceptual processes is another set of insidious dynamics at the group and societal levels. The evolving course of the conflict is governed by a powerful set of norms that encourage attitudes, actions, and decision-making processes that are conducive to the generation, escalation, and perpetuation of conflict between distinct identity groups. Furthermore, these same factors inhibit the perception and occurrence of change in the direction of tension reduction and conflict resolution (Kelman, 2007).

Social identity theory (SIT) provides important linkages between the individual and group levels, and thereby a context for the operation of individual cognitive and emotional processes (Tajfel, 1982; Tajfel & Turner, 1986; Huddy, chapter 23, this volume). SIT is a complement to realistic group conflict theory (RCT), which posits that real differences in interests are necessary for the causation of intergroup conflict (Brown & Capozza, 2000; LeVine & Campbell, 1972). According to RCT, conflicts of interests based on incompatible goals and competition for scarce resources (especially in situations of relative deprivation) result in the perception of threat, which then increases ethnocentrism and drives invidious group comparisons. RCT also posits that threat causes awareness of in-group identity and solidarity, while at the same time causing hostility to the source of the threat.

Theorizing on SIT was stimulated by the finding that mere cognitive categorization tends to produce an exaggeration of both intraclass similarities and interclass differences. The theory was extended by the minimal group experiments, which showed that even the most trivial and arbitrary group assignments created intergroup discrimination favoring the in-group in the absence of a conflict of interests (Tajfel, 1970). A series of propositions was then developed to link social categorization and social identity to individual self-esteem and positive identity through the mechanism of self-serving social comparisons with other groups. The motivating force for intergroup discrimination was thus found in the concept of self-esteem, in that a positive social identity created by group formation and enhanced by positive in-group evaluations and negative out-group comparisons enhances the in-group member's self-concept. SIT thus links individual-level cognitive variables (categorization effects), motivational variables (need for self-esteem), and emotional variables (attachment to the in-group) to the social levels of group functioning and intergroup relations. The central point here is that when individuals or groups interact in the context of their respective memberships in social categories, their functioning can only be understood at the levels of group and intergroup behavior (Tajfel & Turner, 1986). At the same time, research on SIT provides stronger support for in-group positiveness and favoritism than for out-group denigration and discrimination (Brewer, 1979). It appears that competition or conflict between groups (as posited by RCT) is necessary to produce the full effects of ethnocentrism (Brewer, 2007).

The important role of social identity processes in the causation and maintenance of protracted intercommunal and international conflict is now generally accepted in the field (Stein, 2001). Particularly in situations of intractable conflict, threats to identity are seen as playing a pivotal role in the escalation and persistence of the conflict, to the point that the parties unwittingly collude in maintaining the conflict, because it has become part of their identities (Northrup, 1989). Kelman (2001) explores the role of national identity in exacerbating intercommunal or international conflict, with particular reference to the Israeli-Palestinian conflict. Although national identity is part of the social identity of individual members of the group, it can be conceptualized as a collective phenomenon—as a property of the group: "Insofar as a group of people have come to see themselves as constituting a unique, identifiable entity, with a claim to continuity over time, to unity across geographical distance, and to the right to various forms of self-expression, we can say that they have acquired a sense of national identity. National identity is the group's definition of itself as a group—its conception of its enduring characteristics and basic values; its strengths and weaknesses; its hopes and fears; its reputation and conditions of existence; its institutions and traditions; and its past history, current purposes, and future prospects" (Kelman, 1997b, p. 171).

Kelman (2001) asserts that the threat to collective identities posed by existential conflict between peoples is a core issue, in that identity is not only a source of distinctiveness and belongingness, but also constitutes the justification for each group's claim to territory and other resources and is bolstered by each group's national narrative. Thus, the national identity of the out-group becomes a threat to the in-group, leading to a zero-sum struggle over not only territory, but also identity, in that acknowledging the out-group's identity becomes tantamount to jeopardizing or denying one's own. The mutual denial of identity therefore creates serious obstacles to conflict resolution, in that all issues are rendered existential ones—matters of life and death—and as such are nonnegotiable.

At the societal level, public support is an essential resource for political leaders engaged in a conflict, both in ensuring the public's readiness to accept the costs that their policies may entail and in enhancing the credibility of their threats and promises to the other side. The primary means of gaining public support is *the mobilization of group loyalties*. Arousal of nationalist and patriotic sentiments, particularly in a context of national security and survival, is a powerful tool in mobilizing public support. The nation generates such powerful identifications and loyalties because it brings together two central psychological dispositions: the needs for self-protection and self-transcendence (Kelman, 1969; 1997b).

Group loyalties can potentially be mobilized in support of conciliatory policies. Political leaders may promote painful compromises and concessions to the adversary on the grounds that the security, well-being, integrity, and survival of the nation require such actions. Indeed, leaders with impeccable nationalist credentials—such as Charles de Gaulle, Yitzhak Rabin, or F. W. de Klerk—are often most effective in leading their populations toward peaceful resolution of conflicts, once they have decided that this approach best serves the national interest. In general, however, group loyalties are more readily available to mobilize support for aggressive policies than for conciliatory ones.

Processes of group loyalty create barriers to change in a conflict relationship. Group loyalty requires adherence to the group's norms—which, in an intense conflict, call for a militant, unyielding, and suspicious attitude toward the enemy. Hence, particularly in situations of perceived national crisis, the militants exercise disproportionate power and often a veto over official actions and policies. They impose severe constraints on the ability of leaders to explore peaceful options. Dissent from the dominant conflict norms becomes defined as an act of disloyalty and is suppressed.

Another insidious process supporting conflict norms is the *formation of collective moods* (Stein, chapter 12, this volume). With periodic shifts in collective mood, public opinion can act as both a resource and a constraint for political leaders in the foreign policy process. In principle, it can provide support for either aggressive or conciliatory policies, but under the prevailing norms in an intense, protracted conflict, leaders are more likely to expect—and to mobilize—public support for the former than for the latter. Apart from transitory moods, certain pervasive states of consciousness underlie public opinion in a society engulfed in a deep-rooted conflict, reflecting the existential concerns and the central national narratives widely shared within the population. In many cases—such as Serbia, Northern Ireland, and the Middle East—historical traumas serve as the points of reference for current events. These memories are part of the people's consciousness available for manipulation. The effect of such collective moods is to bring to the fore powerful social norms that support escalatory actions and inhibit moves toward compromise and accommodation. When fundamental concerns about identity and survival are tapped, national leaders, with full expectation of public support, are far more ready to risk war than to take risks for peace—again in line with the proposition derived from prospect theory that people are more reluctant to take risks to achieve gains than to avoid losses (Levy, 1992). Any change in the established view of the enemy and of the imperatives of national defense comes to be seen as a threat to the nation's very existence.

Decision-making processes (see the chapters in this volume by Redlawsk & Lau, chapter 5; Levy, chapter 10; and Dyson & 't Hart, chapter 13) in a conflict situation tend to inhibit the search for alternatives and the exploration of new possibilities, particularly when decision-makers are operating in an atmosphere of crisis. These tendencies are by no means inevitable, and there are historical instances—such as the Cuban Missile Crisis—of creative decision-making in dangerous crisis situations (Allison, 1971; Lebow, 1981). Conflict norms do, however, impose serious burdens on the decision-making process.

A major source of reluctance to explore new options is the domestic constraints under which decision-makers labor. In an intense conflict situation, adherence to the conflict norms tends to be seen as the safest course of action. The search for alternatives in response to changing realities is also inhibited by institutionalized rigidities in the decision-making apparatus. Decision-makers and their bureaucracies operate within a framework of assumptions about available choices, effective strategies, and constituency expectations, shaped by the conflict norms, which may make them unaware of the occurrence and possibility of change. Furthermore, they often rely on established procedures and technologies, which are more likely to be geared toward pursuing the conflict—by military and other means—than toward resolving it.

The microprocesses of action and interaction in crisis decision-making further inhibit the exploration of new options. At the level of individual decision-makers, the stress they experience in situations of crisis—when consequential decisions have to be made under severe time pressures—limits the number of alternatives they consider and impels them to settle quickly on the dominant response, which, in intense conflicts, is likely to be aggressive and escalatory (Holsti, 1972; Lebow, 1987).

At the level of decision-making groups, crisis decision-making often leads to "group-think" (Janis, 1972; 1982; Dyson & 't Hart, chapter 13, this volume), a concurrence-seeking tendency designed to maintain the cohesiveness of the group. Janis (1972) defined groupthink as a process by which a cohesive and insulated elite decision-making group develops concurrence seeking to the extent that it overrides a realistic appraisal of alternative courses of action, thus producing suboptimal outcomes. He identified three symptoms of the groupthink syndrome: (1) the overestimation of the group, including an illusion of invulnerability and a belief in the group's inherent morality, (2) closed-mindedness, including stereotypes of out-groups and collective rationalization, and (3) pressures toward uniformity, including self-censorship, an illusion of unanimity, group pressure on dissenters, and the use of self-appointed "mindguards" to enforce conformity with the leader's initial direction. Groupthink results in a poor information search, a selective bias in information processing, an incomplete survey of alternatives, the failure to examine the risks of the preferred choice, a failure to work out contingency plans, and other shortcomings that produce a low probability of success (Janis, 1982). Decision-making under these circumstances is much more likely to produce policies and actions that perpetuate and escalate the conflict in line with group norms than innovative ideas for conflict resolution.

The norms governing *negotiation and bargaining processes* between parties involved in longstanding conflict strongly encourage zero-sum thinking, which equates the enemy's loss with one's own gain. Negotiation—even distributive bargaining in its narrowest form—is possible only when both parties define the situation, at least at some level, as a mixed-motive game, in which they have both competitive and cooperative goals. While pursuing its own interests, each party must actively seek out ways in which the adversary can also win and appear to be winning. But this is precisely the kind of effort that is discouraged by the conflict norms.

At the micro level, negotiators in an intense conflict tend to evaluate their performance by the forcefulness with which they present their own case and by their effectiveness in resisting compromise. To listen to what the other side needs and help the other side achieve its goals would violate the conflict norms and might subject the negotiators to criticism from their own constituencies and particularly from their hard-line domestic opposition. At the macro level, the parties—even when they recognize their common interest in negotiating certain specific issues—tend to pursue an overall outcome that strengthens their own strategic position and weakens the adversary's. Such a strategy reduces the other's incentive for concluding an agreement and ability to mobilize public support for whatever agreement is negotiated. Zero-sum thinking at both levels undermines the negotiating process, causing delays, setbacks, and repeated failures.

Finally, conflict creates certain *structural and psychological commitments*, which then take on a life of their own (see Pruitt & Gahagan, 1974; Pruitt, & Kim, 2004). Most obviously, in a conflict of long standing, various individuals, groups, and organizations—military, political, industrial, scholarly—develop a vested interest in maintaining the conflict as a source of profit, power, status, or raison d'être. Others, though not benefiting from the conflict as such, may have a strong interest in forestalling a compromise solution, because it would not address their particular grievances or fulfill their particular aspirations. Vested interests do not necessarily manifest themselves in deliberate attempts to undermine efforts at conflict resolution. They may take indirect and subtle forms, such as interpreting ambiguous realities and choosing between uncertain policy alternatives in ways that favor continuation of the conflict.

Vested interests and similar structural commitments to the conflict are bolstered by psychological commitments. People involved in a longstanding and deep-rooted conflict tend to develop a worldview that is built around the conflict and would be threatened by an end to the conflict. Resistance to change is likely to be more pronounced, the more elaborate the cognitive structure or ideology in which the view of the conflict is embedded, since changing this view would have wider ramifications. In an intense conflict, the image of the enemy is often a particularly important part of people's worldview, with implications for their national identity, view of their own society, and interpretation of history.

Despite all the reasons why conflict images and conflict norms are resistant to change, they are not immutable. Social-psychological evidence suggests that they can change, and historical evidence shows that they do change (Chong, chapter 4, this volume; Stein, chapter 12, this volume). The challenge for scholars and practitioners of international conflict resolution is to devise the means to overcome these resistances to change. Interactive conflict resolution is specifically designed to address these kinds of resistances, along with the other social-psychological processes that contribute to the escalation and perpetuation of intergroup and international conflict.

3. Interactive Conflict Resolution

The practice of interactive conflict resolution and the rationale behind it are anchored in a social-psychological perspective. John Burton, whose first degree was in psychology, is credited not only with challenging the dominant paradigm of realism in international relations, but also with the creation of an alternative problem-solving approach to international conflict analysis and resolution, which he initially termed *controlled communication* (Burton, 1969). Following Burton's method, high-level representatives of parties in destructive conflict are brought together in unofficial discussions under the guidance of a third-party panel of social scientists, who work to build an open and supportive climate in which the antagonists can analyze their situation, examine their perceptions and evaluations, and create mutually acceptable options for conflict resolution. Herbert Kelman was a panel member in one of Burton's early workshops on the Cyprus conflict, and went on to develop his own method of *interactive problem solving*, which he has applied over many years to the Israeli-Palestinian conflict. A variety of interventions and studies applying these types of methods to intergroup and international conflict are reviewed by Fisher (1972; 1983), who also developed a generic model of *third-party consultation* to represent the essential components of the approach.

Fisher (1997, p. 8) has captured the work of Burton, Kelman, and others under the rubric of *interactive conflict resolution,* which is defined in a focused manner as "small-group, problem-solving discussions between unofficial representatives of identity groups or states engaged in destructive conflict that are facilitated by an impartial third party of social scientist-practitioners." Given the proliferation of interactive methods over the past decade, Fisher (1997) also provides a broader view of interactive conflict resolution as involving facilitated, face-to-face activities in communication, training, education, or consultation that promote collaborative conflict analysis and problem solving among antagonists. In either case, the method is based in social-psychological assumptions about intergroup and international conflict, which see the importance of subjective factors (attitudes, perceptions, emotions) alongside objective elements, and which propose that a different form of meaningful interaction among conflicting parties is necessary to de-escalate the conflict. In addition, the method takes a system perspective, knowing that any changes in individuals that take place in problem-solving workshops or other interactive forums must be transferred successfully to the level of political discourse and policymaking for conflict resolution to occur. Interactive methods are also becoming increasingly important in postconflict peace-building, to help implement settlements and rebuild war-torn relationships, so that re-escalating cycles of violence are prevented.

There are a variety of different forms of interactive conflict resolution in addition to the classic problem-solving workshop model articulated by Burton (1987), Mitchell (1981), Kelman (1986), Azar (1990), Fisher (1983), and others. Vamik Volkan and his colleagues have developed a psychodynamic approach to both understanding and ameliorating ethnopolitical conflict among contesting communal groups. Volkan (1991) contends that deeper psychological processes, such as projection and victimization, need to be addressed along with political and economic issues, and he has developed a workshop methodology for bringing together influential members of conflicting groups to establish workable relationships and develop mutually acceptable options. The approach has been successfully applied to the Arab-Israeli conflict (Julius, 1991) and to conflicts in the post-Soviet Baltic republics between majority populations and Russian minorities (Volkan & Harris, 1993). Although the psychodynamic underpinnings of Volkan's method are different from those of the social-psychological model, the design of the workshops and role of the third-party facilitators are remarkably similar.

Another form of interactive conflict resolution has been developed by Harold Saunders, a former US diplomat and policymaker, who has worked as a member of the third-party team in workshops organized by both Volkan and Kelman. For many years, Saunders was involved in the Dartmouth conference, bringing together Soviet (now Russian) and American influentials to engage in citizen-to-citizen dialogue. He served as the American cochair of the regional conflict task force, which examined superpower interaction in Cold War hot spots as a means of understanding the relationship between the two countries. Based on this experience, Chufrin and Saunders (1993) articulated a public peace process involving five stages of unofficial dialogue between conflicting groups. Following the end of the Cold War, Saunders and Randa Slim worked with American and Russian colleagues to apply the dialogue model with considerable success to the civil war in the former Soviet republic of Tajikistan (Saunders, 1995). Based on this and other experiences, including a dialogue on race relations in the United States, Saunders (1999) has articulated a broadly applicable model of facilitating *sustained dialogue* between members of conflicting groups.

3.1. Problem-Solving Workshops

The focused definition of interactive conflict resolution is essentially coterminous with the method of the problem-solving workshop, which brings together unofficial yet influential representatives of parties engaged in destructive and protracted conflict for informal small-group discussions facilitated by an impartial (or multipartial) third-party team of skilled and knowledgeable scholar-practitioners, often based in academia. The objectives are to develop a shared analysis of the conflict and to create options or directions that might help lead the parties out of their impasse. The nature and characteristics of the problem-solving workshop have been articulated by a number of authors, and the description here will follow most closely the approach associated with *interactive problem solving*, as articulated by Kelman and his colleagues. The following passage is a recent attempt to capture the essence of the problem-solving workshop succinctly (Fisher, 2004):

> Regardless of the label applied, the workshop method evidences a number of essential characteristics (Kelman, 1972; Kelman & Cohen, 1976; 1986). A small group of individuals (usually three to six from each side) are invited by a third party team (usually three to five) to engage in low risk, noncommittal, off-the-record discussions over a period of three to five days in a neutral and secluded setting conducive to a relaxed atmosphere and devoid of intrusions. While the meetings are not secret, they are quiet, that is, held out of the public and media view with clear assurances of confidentiality stressing the non-attribution of comments made in the workshop. The participants are typically influential individuals in their communities who are not in official policy-making roles, but have access to the political leadership. Some variations involve officials, but in a private, unofficial capacity. The role of the third party is to facilitate the discussions in an impartial manner and to suggest conceptual tools that might be useful to the participants in analyzing their conflict. The objective is to create an informal atmosphere in which participants can freely express their views, while respecting those of the other side, and can move from adversarial debate to a joint analysis of the conflict and the creation of problem solutions that might help address it. Following agreement on ground rules, the third party provides a rough agenda for the sessions, starting with an initial exchange of perceptions, to an analysis of the attributions, interests and needs underlying incompatible positions

and escalatory interactions, to the application and development of insights and models of understanding, to the creation of ideas for peacebuilding and resolution, and finally to considering the constraints and resistances to these options. (p. 387)

It is evident that much of the potential power of the problem-solving workshop to influence the course of a conflict lies in its *social-psychological assumptions and principles*. Some of these assumptions relate to the nature of human social conflict in general (Fisher, 1990), others relate more specifically to the nature of the international system and conflicts within it (Kelman, 2007), and yet others underlie the structure, process, and content of workshops (Kelman, 1992; Kelman & Cohen, 1986). The focus here is on how conflict perceptions, interactions, and systems can be influenced through such workshops to help bring about changes that lead to conflict resolution.

It is assumed that all conflicts are a mix of objective and subjective factors, and that both of these sets must be addressed for resolution to occur. Therefore, workshops focus on a range of perceptual, motivational, and interactional factors such as misperceptions, misattributions, self-serving biases, unwitting commitments, mistrust, miscommunication, adversarial interactions, self-fulfilling prophecies, and unmet human needs for security, identity, and distributive justice, all of which play important roles in causing and escalating the conflict. It is also assumed that authentic and constructive face-to-face interaction is necessary to confront and overcome these distorted and invalid cognitive elements and to change the adversarial orientations and patterns of interaction that characterize destructive conflict. As Kelman (1992) writes:

> Workshops are designed to promote a special kind of interaction or discourse that can contribute to the desired political outcome....the setting, ground rules, and procedures of problem-solving workshops encourage (and permit) interaction marked by the following elements: an emphasis on addressing each other (rather than one's constituencies, or third parties, or the record) and on listening to each other; analytical discussion; adherence to a 'no-fault' principle; and a problem-solving mode of interaction. This kind of interaction allows the parties to explore each other's concerns, penetrate each other's perspectives, and take cognizance of each other's constraints. As a result they are able to offer each other the needed reassurances to engage in negotiation and to come up with solutions responsive to both sides' needs and fears. (p. 85)

To promote this kind of interaction, the facilitative and diagnostic role of an impartial and skilled third party is essential. The third party helps to elicit and maintain problem-solving motivation, to support constructive and respectful interaction, to encourage a joint analysis that transcends biased narratives, and to create directions and options for de-escalating and resolving the conflict (Fisher, 1972).

To have an effect on the larger conflict system, the changes in individuals' perceptions and attitudes that occur as a result of participation in a workshop must be transferred to their respective societies. Individual participants can influence public opinion and policymaking in their societies in many ways through the various roles they enact—for example, as advisers to decision-makers, political activists, journalists, or academic analysts.

It must be emphasized that problem-solving workshops and related activities are not negotiating sessions. Negotiations can be carried out only by officials authorized to conclude binding agreements, and workshops—by definition—are completely nonbinding. Their nonbinding character, in fact, represents their special strength and is the source of their unique contribution to the larger process: They provide a context for sharing perspectives, exploring options, and engaging in joint thinking.

Even though workshops must be clearly distinguished from official negotiations, they can be viewed as an integral part of the larger negotiating process, relevant at all stages of that process. At the prenegotiation stage, they can help the parties move toward the negotiating table by contributing to the creation of a political environment conducive to negotiation. At the negotiation stage itself they can perform useful para-negotiation functions: They can contribute to overcoming obstacles to the negotiations, to creating momentum and reviving the sense of possibility, and to identifying options and reframing issues so that they can be negotiated more effectively once they get to the table. Finally, at the postnegotiation stage, workshops can contribute to resolving problems in the implementation of negotiated agreements, as well as to the process of peace-building and reconciliation in the aftermath of an agreement and to the transformation of the relationship between the former enemies.

Workshops have a *dual purpose*. They are designed, first, to produce change—new learning, in the form of new understandings, new insights, and new ideas for resolving the conflict—in the particular individuals who participate in the workshop; and, second, to transfer these changes into the political debate and the decision-making process in the two societies. An important theoretical and practical consequence of the dual purpose of workshops is that the two purposes may create contradictory requirements. The best example of these dialectics is provided by the selection of participants. *Transfer* into the political process would be maximized by officials who are close to the decision-making apparatus and thus in a position to apply immediately what they have learned. *Change*, however, would be maximized by participants who are removed from the decision-making process and therefore less constrained in their interactions and freer to play with ideas and explore hypothetical scenarios. To balance these contradictory requirements, selection has focused on participants who are not officials, but who are politically influential. They are thus relatively free to engage in the process, but, at the same time, any new ideas they develop in the course of a workshop can have an impact on the thinking of decision-makers and the society at large.

As noted above, problem-solving workshops follow a set of ground rules, which are presented to the participants in detail. The central ground rule, *privacy and confidentiality*, is important for the protection of the participants in the face of political, legal, and even physical risks, but it is equally important for protection of the process that workshops seek to promote. This process is captured by the next three ground rules: Participants are asked to *focus on each other*, rather than on their constituencies, third parties, an audience, or the record; to enter into an *analytic (nonpolemical) discussion*, seeking to explore each other's perspective and gain insight into the causes and dynamics of the conflict; and to move to a *problem-solving (nonadversarial) mode of interaction*, sidestepping the usual attempt to allocate blame and, instead, taking the conflict as a shared problem that requires joint effort to find a mutually satisfactory solution.

An additional ground rule, *equality of the two parties* within the workshop setting, assures that each party has the same right to serious consideration of its needs, fears, and concerns. Regardless of asymmetric power or moral standing, each side has the right to be heard in the workshop, and each side's needs and fears must be given equal attention in the search for a mutually satisfactory solution. Finally, the ground rules specify a *facilitative role of the third party*. The third party does not take part in the substantive discussion, give advice, or offer its own proposals, nor does it take sides, evaluate the ideas presented, or arbitrate between different interpretations of historical facts or international law. Its task is to create the conditions that allow ideas for resolving the conflict to emerge out of the interaction between the parties themselves. The third party sets the ground rules and monitors adherence to them; it helps to keep the discussion moving in constructive directions, tries to stimulate movement, and intervenes as relevant with questions, observations, and even challenges, relating both to the content and to the process of the interaction. It also serves as a repository of trust for parties who, by definition, do not trust each other.

In the typical one-time, freestanding workshop, the *workshop agenda* is relatively open and unstructured with respect to the substantive issues under discussion. The way in which these issues are approached, however, and the order of discussion are structured so as to facilitate the kind of discourse that the ground rules are designed to encourage. A similar structure, with some necessary modifications, characterizes the agenda within and across the meetings of a continuing workshop.

Workshops usually begin with an *exchange of reports about recent developments*, which provides a shared base of information and sets a precedent for the two sides to deal with each other as mutual resources, rather than solely as combatants. The agenda then typically turns to a *needs analysis*, in which members on each side discuss their central concerns in the conflict—the fundamental needs that would have to be addressed and the existential fears that would have to be allayed if a solution is to be satisfactory to them. The purpose is for each side to gain an adequate understanding of the other's needs, fears, and concerns, from the perspective of the other. The next phase of the agenda, *joint thinking about possible solutions*, seeks to develop ideas about the overall shape of a solution for the conflict as a whole or, perhaps, a particular issue in the conflict that would address the needs and fears of *both* sides. As participants develop common ground in this process of joint thinking, they turn to discussion of the *political and psychological constraints* within the two societies that would create barriers to carrying out the ideas for solution that they have developed. Finally, depending on how much progress has been made and how much time is left, the parties are asked to engage in another round of joint thinking—this time about ways of *overcoming* the *constraints* that have been presented. (For further details about the workshop agenda, as well as about the ground rules, see Kelman, 2010).

3.2. Israeli-Palestinian Case Illustration

Kelman's and his colleagues' Israeli-Palestinian work has sought to contribute to all three of the stages of the negotiating process over the course of the years. All of the workshops in the 1970s and 1980s took place, of course, in the prenegotiation stage and were designed to explore the possibilities for movement toward the negotiating table. A variety of workshops were carried out during that period—in different contexts and with different types of participants. All of the participants, however, were members (or soon-to-be members) of the political elite. Moreover, all of the workshops during this period were "one-time" events: The particular group of Israelis and Palestinians who took part in a given workshop convened only for this one occasion— usually over an extended weekend. Some of the individuals participated in more than one such workshop, and the one-time workshops held over the years had a cumulative effect within the two societies and helped to inject new ideas into the two political cultures.

In 1990, for the first time in this program, Kelman and Nadim Rouhana organized a continuing workshop: a group of highly influential Israelis and Palestinians—six on each side—who agreed to participate in a series of three meetings over the course of a year, and in the end continued to meet (with some changes in personnel) until August 1993 (Rouhana & Kelman, 1994). As it happened, with the onset of official negotiations in 1991, first in Madrid and then in Washington, this continuing workshop also provided the organizers' first experience with interactive problem solving as a para-negotiation process. The political relevance of this work was enhanced by the appointment, in 1991, of four of the six initial Palestinian participants in the group to key positions in the official negotiating teams, and, in 1992, of several Israeli participants to ambassadorial and cabinet positions in the new Rabin government.

These efforts from the 1970s to the early 1990s, along with other unofficial efforts, helped to lay the groundwork for the Oslo agreement of September 1993 (Kelman, 1995; 1997a). They contributed by developing cadres prepared to carry out productive negotiations; by sharing information and formulating new ideas that provided substantive inputs into the negotiations; and by fostering a political atmosphere that made the parties open to a new relationship.

After the Oslo agreement, Kelman and Rouhana initiated a Joint Working Group on Israeli-Palestinian Relations, which met regularly between 1994 and 1999. For the first time in this program, the group set itself the goal of producing written documents: joint concept papers on the issues in the final-status negotiations, viewed in the context of what would be required to establish a long-term peaceful and mutually enhancing relationship between the two societies. The group thus intended to contribute both to the negotiations themselves and to the postnegotiation process of peace-building and reconciliation. Three papers were published (Joint Working Group, 1998; 1999; Alpher, Shikaki, et al., 1998) and translated into Arabic and Hebrew.

With the failure of the Camp David summit and the onset of the Second Intifada in 2000, Kelman's work entered a new phase, marked by the breakdown of once-promising negotiations. The main thrust of the work since then has been a new joint working group, co-facilitated by Shibley Telhami, focusing on the theme of rebuilding trust within the two communities in the availability of a credible negotiating partner and of a mutually acceptable framework for a two-state solution. The group (with some changes in membership) continues to meet and is now working on a proposal for a new framework to restart negotiations toward a two-state solution.

3.3. Cyprus Case Illustration

The frozen ethnopolitical conflict in Cyprus between the Greek and Turkish communities has long been a focus of both official and unofficial conflict resolution efforts, with more of the latter since 1990 (Broome, 2005; Fisher, 2001; Hadjipavlou and Kanol, 2008). An early problem-solving workshop (PSW) organized by John Burton was followed by a long hiatus, until the now defunct Canadian Institute for International Peace and Security sponsored a series of PSWs in the early 1990s, organized by Ronald Fisher (Fisher, 1997). An initial workshop in 1990 brought together Greek and Turkish Cypriot community leaders living in Canada at the Institute to focus on the creation of ideas for de-escalation and resolution, and to establish the credibility of the third-party initiative. A second workshop, held near London in 1991, brought together influentials from the two communities on the island, including informal advisers to the two leaders as well as academics, journalists, and businesspersons. The participants achieved consensus on the nature of the desired future relationship between the two communities, and a number of peace-building projects resulted from the workshop. Two further workshops followed in 1993, with a focus on the role of education in maintaining the conflict and its potential role in helping to de-escalate and resolve the conflict. Following the two meetings, participants were brought together to form joint teams to address particular issues and develop specific proposals, including cross-line visits by teachers, the development of common teaching materials on the conflict, and the revision of existing history and social studies textbooks. The workshops thus planted some seeds that continue to find expression in later projects on education (see Hadjipavlou and Kanol, 2008).

In the mid-1990s, no PSWs were held, but an American-sponsored training project in conflict resolution led by Louise Diamond and Diana Chigas brought together hundreds of Greek and Turkish Cypriots to learn concepts and skills that they could use to address conflicts within and between their communities, with no intention of influencing the official peace process (Broome, 2005; Chigas, 2007; Hadjipavlou and Kanol, 2008). However, during 1999 to 2003, the training project morphed into a series of five PSWs augmented with the technique of facilitated brainstorming to develop options relevant to the negotiation process. The so-called "Harvard Study Group" was organized by Robert Rotberg, along with Diamond and Chigas, and brought together influential participants, many of whom were graduates of the training program and some of whom were very well connected politically to the current administrations on the island (Chigas, 2007; in press). The sessions produced a comprehensive document for a "United States of Cyprus," and some of these ideas found their way into the "Annan Plan." However, the effects of the intervention were muted as participants better represented the Greek Cypriot leadership at the time as opposed to the governing coalition that came to power in 2003, and the intervention and its outcome were also attacked in the Greek Cypriot media.

Following the referendum defeat of the Annan Plan in the Greek Cypriot community in 2004, the peace-building community on the island was demoralized and in disarray, and few bicommunal projects were initiated. A small symposium organized by Ronald Fisher and Tamra Pearson d'Estree in 2007 at the University of Denver brought together a collection of Cypriot and American peace-builders to discuss the current environment and propose possible strategies for reinvigorating conflict resolution work. This resulted in the organization of two PSWs, the first in 2009, which engaged longtime Cypriot peace-builders from the two communities to assess the current state of the renewed peace process and to develop ideas for how civil society could support the negotiations. One conclusion emerging from the workshop was the importance of the two motherlands in supporting the two leaderships in developing and promoting a mutually beneficial settlement in their communities. This led to a second PSW in 2011, which first brought together some of the same Cypriot peace-builders for two days followed by the inclusion of Greek and Turkish influentials (policy advisers, journalists) for three days. Although many strategies were identified for positively influencing the peace process by both Cypriot civil society and by the Greek and Turkish leaderships, these were seen as contingent upon positive developments in the negotiations themselves, an outcome that continues to be elusive.

3.4. Georgian-South Ossetian Case Illustration

Just after the August 2008 war between Georgians, South Ossetians, and Russians, official negotiations ended with "procedural difficulties" (Higgins, 2008). Experienced Georgian and South Ossetian conflict-resolvers remembered the strong positive impact of a series of workshops in the late 1990s that had contributed to stability, freedom of movement, and trade across the conflict divide (Nan, 2005). They lamented the lack of workshops in the increasingly tense years preceding the renewed fighting.

As no contact across the ceasefire line was possible locally, Susan Allen Nan, Paula Garb, Ekaterina Romanova, and colleagues convened Georgians and South Ossetians at Point of View, George Mason University's conflict resolution retreat center. The goal was to explore what peace-builders on each side could do to rebuild confidence in the aftermath of the war. That workshop launched a three-year series of 13 problem-solving workshops that was dubbed the Point of View process. Rather than aiming at an immediate political agreement, the conflict analysis within the workshops suggested a focus on confidence-building measures as being more realistic for the immediate post-war phase. The experienced local conflict resolvers provided substantive input to the facilitation team, resulting in several variations on the classic problem-solving workshop design.

One variation the participants suggested was a simple press release after each meeting. These few paragraphs provided participants with general descriptions of the workshops that allowed them to acknowledge their participation and the topics discussed, without breaking confidentiality. These press releases then led to a simple project website, where individual participants posted their personal reflections on the process.

At the second and subsequent workshops in Istanbul, officials coming in their personal capacities from both sides and individuals from villages most affected by the war participated alongside a core group of the unofficial peace-builders. The villagers focused discussion on basic human needs, particularly the needs of individuals living very close to the ceasefire line. The officials (some directly involved in the official negotiations) spoke in their personal capacity, but brought clarity on the stumbling blocks preventing cooperation and a political settlement.

The workshop focus on analyzing prospects for particular confidence-building measures allowed the workshops to take on a catalytic function. Workshop discussions allowed planning on particularly promising confidence-building measures. Following the workshops, pairs of participants jointly led confidence-building measures such as cross-conflict women's dialogues, visiting prisoners, encouraging prisoner releases, and a visit across the ceasefire line by two of the Georgian workshop participants.

In addition, the workshops analyzed particular sticking points in the official talks and developed innovative ways to allow unofficial exploration on specialized areas of potential confidence building. Special groups met on occasion to address technical issues such as water and gas flow across the ceasefire line, inviting appropriate engineers to engage in problem solving. Core participants from the ongoing workshop series facilitated these special technical meetings. Another workshop within the larger problem-solving workshop series included four health experts (two from each side) who engaged with the workshop team to identify confidence-building measures within the health sector. In sum, these workshops diverged from the classic problem-solving workshop process by including some officials (in their personal capacities), catalyzing confidence-building measures directly, engaging villagers from close to the ceasefire line, and focusing on a particular sector (such as health or water) as that sector became relevant to confidence building.

4. Challenges Facing the Field

Conflict analysis and resolution from a social-scientific base with a professional practice orientation is a relatively new field of endeavor, which in addition to the fundamental complexity and intractability of the phenomenon that it addresses, must also confront and overcome many difficult issues. This brief section will only be able to identify a number of the most important of these.

4.1. Culture and Gender

Scholars and practitioners of conflict resolution need to take the questions of cultural and gender influences seriously (Avruch, 1998; Taylor & Miller, 1994). It is not appropriate to assume the universality of concepts and methods, given that each society has its "culture of conflict," which incorporates the beliefs, practices, and institutions relevant to managing differences and which affects what is defined as conflict and how it is addressed (Ross, 1993a). A first step is to carry out a cultural analysis of the situation, so that the effects of cultural differences on the etiology and expression of the conflict are clearly understood (Avruch & Black, 1993). Similar points can be made about gender differences as they are expressed in conflict, especially given the patriarchal and hierarchical nature of most societies, which incorporates significant differences in status and power. Unfortunately, the conflict resolution literature is largely silent on gender differences in the enactment of third-party roles, particularly at the international level. This may be due to the near-total absence of women in peace processes at the elite level, probably because of a combination of sexism and structural exclusion (Anderlini, 2007). In an analysis of Israeli-Palestinian problem-solving workshops, d'Estrée and Babbitt (1998) conclude that women tend to engage in deeper self-disclosure, leading to empathy for the enemy and a reciprocal acknowledgment of concerns, coupled with an orientation to build relationships and a capacity to bring to the surface emotional as well as strategic issues. This implies that women may be better equipped to build relationships in the prenegotiation phase and to craft more integrative and hence sustainable agreements. Continuing attention to both gender and cultural issues is thus warranted.

4.2. Professionalization and Training

Many individuals who come to the work of conflict analysis and resolution are professionals from a related field, such as international relations, law, psychology, human relations, diplomacy, or psychiatry, which enables them to analyze social problems and provide some form of service. Only recently have a number of interdisciplinary graduate programs been established to train scholar-practitioners in the many intricacies of conflict and its resolution, and few of these are at the doctoral level. Such training is a daunting task that involves the application of a variety of concepts and models from social science, and the acquisition of a range of strategies and skills from various domains of social practice. Many practitioners thus begin their practice with only a modicum of the analytical tools and social skills they need, and must learn through experience from more seasoned professionals. There is a challenge, therefore, to develop professional training programs, both at the graduate and midcareer levels, that will provide practitioners with the knowledge and capacities they require to engage successfully as negotiators, mediators, third-party consultants, dialogue facilitators, or trainers in conflict resolution. There is also a need to provide opportunities in continuing professional development for scholar-practitioners to broaden their conceptual knowledge and to enhance their strategic and tactical repertoire. Such offerings now exist, but there is little assessment of their quality or depth, or how some collection of them might coalesce toward an adequate level of professional competence. Thus, it would be valuable to initiate activities that would assist in the professionalization of the field at the international level, so that knowledge bases and best practices could be shared toward the improvement of human welfare.

4.3. Evaluation

One of the key challenges confronting the field of interactive conflict resolution is evaluation of the effectiveness of its efforts in achieving the goals it sets out to achieve. As a field that proposes to introduce innovative, academically based forms of intervention in conflict into the larger diplomatic process, interactive conflict resolution has a special obligation to demonstrate its utility and success by way of systematic, empirical evidence consistent with scholarly standards. Writers in the field have increasingly moved to respond to this challenge (e.g., Chataway, 2004; d'Estrée, Fast, Weiss, & Jacobsen, 2001; Kelman, 2008; Ross & Rothman, 1999; Rouhana, 2000; Saunders, 2000). The ultimate goal of interactive conflict resolution is to *contribute* to the achievement of a negotiated agreement that is mutually satisfactory and lasting and that transforms the relationship between the conflicting parties. Since interactive problem solving—which is not in the business of negotiating agreements—cannot *produce* such an outcome, but only *contribute* to it, the most relevant criteria for evaluating it refer to its success in achieving its intermediate goals, rather than its ultimate goal. The intermediate goals constitute changes in the political cultures of the conflicting parties that would make them more receptive to negotiation with each other (Kelman, 2008). Standard models of evaluation—such as the experimental field test—are not applicable to this problem. Furthermore, the use of obtrusive observations and experimental manipulations is often ethically or methodologically unacceptable in research on ongoing interventions. The challenge, therefore, is to develop evaluation models and research methods that are appropriate to the nature and purpose of the enterprise.

4.4. Complementarity of Interventions

One of the challenges to the field is to understand how different third-party roles contribute to negotiation success and sustainable conflict resolution. The early proponents of interactive conflict resolution were clear about its potential as a useful prenegotiation activity (e.g., Burton, 1969; Kelman & Cohen, 1976), in line with a rationale more fully articulated by Fisher (1989). However, it is now evident that it can make contributions at all stages of negotiation (Kelman, 1992; 1998). Given that conflict, especially ethnopolitical conflict between identity groups, is a potent mix of objective and subjective factors, interventions are required to address the subjective factors—the misperceptions, misattributions, hostile images, mistrust, and vengeance—that fuel escalation and intractability. In fact, it is difficult to see how identity-based conflicts can be addressed without methods that focus on the human and psychological side of the equation (Rothman, 1997; Ross, 1993b). The question is how these methods can be related to and sequenced with the more traditional forms of conflict management.

Fisher and Keashly (1991) developed a contingency approach to third-party intervention, proposing that different methods be matched to the stage of conflict escalation for maximum utility. They also propose that methods need to be sequenced in a complementary fashion, so that a lead intervention gives way to others designed to de-escalate and resolve the conflict. There are two points of complementarity between interactive conflict resolution (represented by third-party consultation) and mediation, in both its pure and power forms. (Pure mediation involves the third party facilitating an agreement on substantive issues through reasoning, persuasion, the control of information and the suggestion of alternatives. Power mediation incorporates these elements, but goes beyond to apply leverage in the form of promised rewards or threatened punishments and often involves the third party as a guarantor.) At the first point of complementarity, consultation can serve as a premediation activity that improves understanding and builds trust in the relationship so that pure mediation can deal more effectively with objective issues. Second, consultation can follow power mediation, after it has achieved a ceasefire or initial settlement on substantive issues, in order to rebuild the torn relationship toward a comprehensive agreement and a sustainable peace. While a limited amount of experimental and empirical research supports the contingency approach (Fisher, 2007; Keashly & Fisher, 1996), it remains a skeletal representation of a complex set of relationships that may not play out as diagrammed in the complexity of real-world dynamics. Nonetheless, the contingency model and similar attempts (e.g., Kriesberg, 1996) challenge theorists and practitioners to think more seriously about the coordination and complementarity of interventions that may well be required to adequately address intractable ethnopolitical conflicts.

An intersocietal view of conflict, as we have proposed, calls for a complex mix of official and unofficial processes, complementing each other in the achievement of the overall diplomatic goal. The challenge is to make effective use of the potential contributions of interactive conflict resolution and other unofficial tracks in the official diplomatic process. Ideally, problem-solving workshops and related activities can be used for exploring possibilities, formulating options, and framing issues in ways that can advance negotiations at its various stages. This has indeed happened on occasion, but it needs to be done systematically, while making sure that track two efforts maintain their integrity and independence and do not become—or come to be seen as—merely another component of the track one process. Official negotiations can also benefit from adopting some of the exploratory, analytical, and problem-solving methods of interactive conflict resolution in their own proceedings, insofar as they can be accommodated within the constraints of the official process (Kelman, 1996).

4.5. Institutionalization

At the level of a particular conflict, it might be useful to institutionalize interactive conflict resolution as part of the peace-building process that must accompany and follow the negotiation of a peace agreement. At the global level, the persistence and proliferation of deadly conflicts between identity groups around the world suggest the urgent need for a large, well-endowed, mostly nongovernmental organization devoted to monitoring such conflicts as they evolve and ready to intervene with efforts to help prevent and resolve them (cf. Burton, 1983). The purpose would be to supplement the work of existing governmental, intergovernmental, and nongovernmental organizations devoted to peacemaking, peacekeeping, and postconflict humanitarian aid by bringing together politically influential representatives of the opposing sides in an active or impending conflict for joint exploration, within a problem-solving framework, of steps toward preventing, de-escalating, or resolving the conflict. The institution might include a permanent staff to monitor conflict regions and provide the infrastructure for workshops as the need arises; a cadre of regional and conflict resolution specialists available to organize and lead workshops; and a cadre of local representatives to recommend appropriate actions or evaluate proposals from the staff and to assist by organizing and participating in workshops as needed (Kelman, 2006). If the resources needed for a large-scale effort of this kind can be generated, there is at least the hope that it can begin to tackle the problem of intercommunal violence that has been plaguing the international scene for centuries.

REFERENCES

Allison, G. T. (1971). *Essence of decision: Explaining the Cuban Missile Crisis.* Boston, MA: Little, Brown.

Alpher, J., & Shikaki, K., with the participation of the additional members of the Joint Working Group on Israeli-Palestinian Relations. (1998). The Palestinian refugee problem and the right of return. Weatherhead Center for International Affairs Working Paper No. 98-7. Cambridge, MA: Harvard University. Reprinted in *Middle East Policy, 6*(3), (1999), 167–189.

Anderlini, S. (2007). *Women Building Peace: What They Do, Why It Matters.* Boulder, CO: Lynne Rienner.

Avruch, K. (1998). *Culture and conflict resolution.* Washington, DC: United States Institute of Peace.

Avruch, K., & Black, P. (1993). Conflict resolution in intercultural settings: Problems and prospects. In D. J. D. Sandole & H. van der Merwe (eds.), *Conflict resolution theory and practice: Integration and application* (pp.131–145). Manchester: Manchester University Press.

Azar, E. E. (1990). *The management of protracted social conflict.* Hampshire, UK: Dartmouth Publishing.

Baldwin, D. (1971). The power of positive sanctions. *World Politics, 24,* 19–38.

Brehm, J. W. (1956). Postdecision changes in the desirability of alternatives. *Journal of Abnormal and Social Psychology, 52,* 384–389.

Brewer, M. B. (1979). Ingroup bias in the minimal intergroup situation: A cognitive-motivational analysis. *Psychological Bulletin, 86,* 307–324.

Brewer, M. B. (2007). The importance of being we: Human nature and intergroup relations. *American Psychologist, 62,* 728–738.

Brockner, J., & Rubin, J. Z. (1985). *Entrapment in escalating conflicts: A social psychological analysis.* New York: Springer-Verlag.

Bronfenbrenner, U. (1961). The mirror image in Soviet-American relations: A social psychologist's report. *Journal of Social Issues, 17*(3), 45–56.

Broome, B. (2005). *Building bridges across the Green Line.* Nicosia, Cyprus: United Nations Development Program.

Brown, R., & Capozza, D. (2000). Social identity theory in retrospect and prospect. In D. Capozza & R. Brown (eds.), *Social identity processes: Trends in theory and research* (pp. vii–xv). London: Sage.

Burton, J. W. (1969). *Conflict and communication: The use of controlled communication in international relations.* London: Macmillan.

Burton, J. W. (1983, April). A continuing seminar and an international facilitating service. A proposal by members of the Centre for the Analysis of Conflict (University of Kent, Canterbury, England), presented at the Annual Meeting of the International Studies Association, Mexico City.

Burton, J. W. (1987). *Resolving deep-rooted conflict: A handbook.* Lanham, MD: University Press of America.

Burton, J. W. (Ed.). (1990). *Conflict: Human needs theory.* New York: St. Martin's Press.

Chataway, C. (2004). Assessing the social psychological support for Kelman's interactive problem-solving workshops. In A. Eagly, R. M. Baron, & V. L. Hamilton (eds.), *The social psychology of group identity and social conflict: Theory, application, and practice* (pp. 213–225). Washington, DC: American Psychological Association.

Chigas, D. (2007). Capacities and limits of NGOs as conflict managers. In C. Crocker, F. O. Hampson, & P. Aall (eds.), *Leashing the dogs of war* (pp. 553–581). Washington, DC: United States Institute of Peace.

Chigas, D. (In press). Contributions and constraints of non-official problem solving: The Harvard Study Group on Cyprus. In H. Wolpe & M. Lund (eds.), *Building leadership and state capacity.* Washington, DC: Woodrow Wilson Center Press.

Chufrin, G. I., & Saunders, H. H. (1993). A public peace process. *Negotiation Journal, 9,* 155–177.

d'Estrée, T. P., & Babbitt, E. F. (1998). Women and the art of peacemaking: Data from Israeli-Palestinian interactive problem-solving workshops. *Political Psychology, 19,* 185–209.

d'Estrée, T. P., Fast, L. A., Weiss, J. N., & Jacobsen, M. S. (2001). Changing the debate about "success" in conflict resolution efforts. *Negotiation Journal, 17,* 101–113.

Deutsch, M. (1983). The prevention of World War III: A psychological perspective. *Political Psychology, 4,* 3–32.

Festinger, L. (1957). *A theory of cognitive dissonance.* Stanford, CA: Stanford University Press.

Festinger, L., Pepitone, A., & Newcomb, T. (1952). Some consequences of deindividuation in a group. *Journal of Abnormal and Social Psychology, 47,* 382–389.

Fisher, R. J. (1972). Third party consultation: A method for the study and resolution of conflict. *Journal of Conflict Resolution, 16,* 67–94.

Fisher, R. J. (1983). Third party consultation as a method of intergroup conflict resolution: A review of studies. *Journal of Conflict Resolution, 27,* 301–334.

Fisher, R. J. (1989). Prenegotiation problem-solving discussions: Enhancing the potential for successful negotiation. In J. G. Stein (ed.), *Getting to the table: The process of international prenegotiation* (pp. 206–238). Baltimore, MD: Johns Hopkins University Press.

Fisher, R. J. (1990). *The social psychology of intergroup and international conflict resolution.* New York: Springer-Verlag.

Fisher, R. J. (1997). *Interactive conflict resolution.* Syracuse, NY: Syracuse University Press.

Fisher, R. J. (2001). Cyprus: The failure of mediation and the escalation of an identity based conflict to an adversarial impasse. *Journal of Peace Research, 38,* 307–326.

Fisher, R. J. (2004). The problem-solving workshop as a method of research. *International Negotiation, 9,* 385–395.

Fisher, R. J. (2007). Assessing the contingency model of third party intervention in successful cases of prenegotiation. *Journal of Peace Research, 44,* 311–329.

Fisher, R. J., & Keashly, L. (1991). The potential complementarity of mediation and consultation within a contingency model of third party intervention. *Journal of Peace Research, 28,* 29–42.

Fisher, R. J., & Kelman, H. C. (2011). Perceptions in conflict. In D. Bar-Tal (ed.), *Intergroup conflicts and their resolution: Social psychological perspectives* (pp. 61–81). London: Psychology Press.

Fiske, S. (2002). What we know about bias and intergroup conflict, the problem of the century. *Current Directions in Psychological Science, 11*(4), 123–128.

George, A. L., & Smoke, R. (1974). *Deterrence in American foreign policy: Theory and practice.* New York: Columbia University Press.

Hadjipavlou, M., & Kanol, B. (2008). *Cumulative impact case study: The impacts of peacebuilding work on the Cyprus conflict.* Cambridge, MA: Collaborative for Development Action.

Hamilton, D. L. (1979). A cognitive-attributional analysis of stereotyping. In L. Berkowitz (ed.), *Advances in experimental social psychology* (vol. 12, pp. 53–84). New York: Academic Press.

Heider, F. (1958). *The psychology of interpersonal relations.* New York: Wiley.

Herrmann, R., & Fischerkeller, M. P. (1995). Beyond the enemy image and spiral mode: Cognitive-strategic research after the Cold War. *International Organization, 49*(3), 415–450.

Higgins, A. G. (2008, October 20). Georgia-Russia talks off to shaky start in Geneva. Associated Press.

Holsti, O. R. (1972). *Crisis, escalation, war.* Montreal: McGill-Queen's University Press.

Janis, I. L. (1972). *Victims of groupthink.* Boston, MA: Houghton Mifflin.

Janis, I. L. (1982). *Groupthink* (2nd ed.). Boston, MA: Houghton Mifflin.

Jervis, R. (1976). *Perceptions and misperceptions in international politics.* Princeton, NJ: Princeton University Press.

Jervis, R., Lebow, R. N., & Stein, J. G. (Eds.). (1985). *Psychology and deterrence.* Baltimore, MD: Johns Hopkins University Press.

Joint Working Group on Israeli-Palestinian Relations. (1998). General principles for the final Israreli-Palestinian agreement. PICAR Working Paper. Cambridge, MA: Program on International Conflict Analysis and Resolution, Weatherhead Center for International Affairs, Harvard University. Reprinted in *Middle East Journal, 53*(1) (1999), 120–175.

Joint Working Group on Israeli-Palestinian Relations. (1999). The future Israeli-Palestinian relationship. Weatherhead Center for International Affairs Working Paper No. 99-12. Cambridge, MA: Harvard University. Reprinted in *Middle East Policy, 7*(2) (2000), 90–112.

Jones, E. E., & Nisbett, R. E. (1971). The actor and the observer: Divergent perceptions of the causes of behavior. In E. E. Jones et al. (eds.), *Attribution: Perceiving the causes of behavior* (pp. 79–94). Morristown, NJ: General Learning Press.

Julius, D. A. (1991). The practice of track two diplomacy in the Arab-Israeli conferences. In V. D. Volkan, J. V. Montville, & D. A. Julius (eds.), *The psychodynamics of international relationships,* vol. 2: *Unofficial diplomacy at work* (pp. 193–205). Lexington, MA: Lexington Books.

Keashly, L., & Fisher, R. J. (1996). A contingency perspective on conflict interventions: Theoretical and practical considerations. In J. Bercovitch (ed.), *Resolving international conflicts: The theory and practice of mediation* (pp. 235–261). Boulder, CO: Lynne Rienner.

Kelman, H. C. (Ed.). (1965). *International behavior: A social-psychological analysis.* New York: Holt, Rinehart & Winston.

Kelman, H. C. (1969). Patterns of personal involvement in the national system: A social-psychological analysis of political legitimacy. In J. N. Rosenau (ed.), *International politics and foreign policy: A reader in research and theory* (rev. ed., pp. 276–288). New York: Free Press.

Kelman, H. C. (1972). The problem-solving workshop in conflict resolution. In R. L. Merritt (ed.), *Communication in international politics* (pp. 168–204). Urbana: University of Illinois Press.

Kelman, H. C. (1986). Interactive problem solving: A social-psychological approach to conflict resolution. In W. Klassen (ed.), *Dialogue: Toward interfaith understanding* (pp. 293–314). Tantur, Jerusalem: Ecumenical Institute for Theological Research.

Kelman, H. C. (1992). Informal mediation by the scholar/practitioner. In J. Bercovitch & J. Z. Rubin (eds.), *Mediation in international relations: Multiple approaches to conflict management* (pp. 64–96). New York: St. Martin's Press.

Kelman, H. C. (1993). Coalitions across conflict lines: The interplay of conflicts within and between the Israeli and Palestinian communities. In S. Worchel & J. Simpson (eds.), *Conflict between people and groups* (pp. 236–258). Chicago: Nelson-Hall.

Kelman, H. C. (1995). Contributions of an unofficial conflict resolution effort to the Israeli-Palestinian breakthrough. *Negotiation Journal, 11,* 19–27.

Kelman, H. C. (1996). Negotiation as interactive problem solving. *International Negotiation: A Journal of Theory and Practice, 1*(1), 99–123.

Kelman, H. C. (1997a). Some determinants of the Oslo breakthrough. *International Negotiation, 2,* 183–194.

Kelman, H. C. (1997b). Nationalism, patriotism, and national identity: Social-psychological dimensions. In D. Bar-Tal & E. Staub (eds.), *Patriotism in the lives of individuals and nations* (pp. 165–189). Chicago: Nelson-Hall.

Kelman, H. C. (1998). Social-psychological contributions to peacemaking and peacebuilding in the Middle East. *Applied Psychology: An International Review, 47,* 5–28.

Kelman, H. C. (2001). The role of national identity in conflict resolution: Experiences from Israeli-Palestinian problem-solving workshops. In R. D. Ashmore, L. Jussim, & D. Wilder (eds.), *Social identity, intergroup conflict, and conflict reduction* (pp. 187–212). New York: Oxford University Press.

Kelman, H. C. (2006). The role of an international facilitating service for conflict resolution. *International Negotiation, 11,* 209–223.

Kelman, H. C. (2007). Social-psychological dimensions of international conflict. In I. W. Zartman (ed.), *Peacemaking in international conflict: Methods and techniques* (rev. ed., pp. 61–107). Washington, DC: U.S. Institute of Peace.

Kelman, H. C. (2008). Evaluating the contributions of interactive problem solving to the resolution of ethnonational conflicts. *Peace and Conflict: Journal of Peace Psychology, 14,* 28–60.

Kelman, H. C. (2010). Interactive problem solving: Changing political culture in the pursuit of conflict resolution. *Peace and Conflict: Journal of Peace Psychology, 16,* 389–413.

Kelman, H. C., & Cohen, S. P. (1976). The problem-solving workshop: A social-psychological contribution to the resolution of international conflict. *Journal of Peace Research, 13,* 79–90.

Kelman, H. C., & Cohen, S. P. (1986). Resolution of international conflict: An interactional approach. In S. Worchel & W. G. Austin (eds.), *Psychology of intergroup relations* (2nd ed., pp. 323–342). Chicago: Nelson-Hall.

Kriesberg, L. (1982). Non-coercive inducements in international conflict. In C. M. Stephenson (ed.), *Alternative methods for international security* (pp. 105–120). Washington, DC: University Press of America.

Kriesberg, L. (1996). Varieties of mediating activities and mediators in international relations. In J. Bercovitch (ed.), *Resolving international conflicts: The theory and practice of mediation* (pp. 219–233). Boulder, CO: Lynne Rienner.

Lebow, R. N. (1981). *Between peace and war.* Baltimore, MD: Johns Hopkins University Press.

Lebow, R. N. (1987). *Nuclear crisis management: A dangerous illusion.* Ithaca, NY: Cornell University Press.

LeVine, R. A. & Campbell, D. T. (1972). *Ethnocentrism: Theories of conflict, ethnic attitudes and group behavior.* New York: Wiley.

Levy, J. S. (1992). Prospect theory and international relations: Theoretical applications and analytical problems. *Political Psychology, 13,* 283–310.

Levy, J. S. (1996). Loss aversion, framing, and bargaining: The implications of prospect theory for international relations. *International Political Science Review, 17,* 177–193.

Levy, J. S. (2003). Political psychology and foreign policy. In D. O. Sears, L. Huddy, & R. Jervis (eds.), *Oxford handbook of political psychology* (pp. 253–284). Oxford: Oxford University Press.

Mitchell, C. R. (1981). *Peacemaking and the consultant's role.* Westmead, UK: Gower.

Nan, Susan Allen. (2005). Track one-and-a-half diplomacy: Contributions to Georgian-South Ossetian peacemaking. In R. J. Fisher (ed.), *Paving the way: Contributions of interactive conflict resolution to peacemaking* (pp. 161–173). Lanham, MD: Lexington Books, 2005.

Northrup, T. A. (1989). The dynamic of social identity in personal and social conflict. In L. Kriesberg, T. A. Northrup, & S. J. Thorson (eds.), *Intractable conflicts and their transformation* (pp. 35–82). Syracuse, NY: Syracuse University Press.

Osgood, C. E. (1962). *An alternative to war or surrender.* Urbana: University of Illinois Press.

Pettigrew, T. F. (1979). The ultimate attribution error: Extending Allport's cognitive analysis of prejudice. *Personality and Social Psychology Bulletin, 5,* 461–476.

Pruitt, D. G., & Gahagan, J. P. (1974). Campus crisis: The search for power. In J. T. Tedeschi (ed.), *Perspectives on social power* (pp. 349–392). Chicago: Aldine.

Pruitt, D. G., & Kim, S. H. (2004). *Social conflict: Escalation, stalemate, and settlement* (3rd Ed.). New York: McGraw-Hill.

Rosati, J. A. (2000). The power of human cognition in the study of world politics. *International Studies Review, 2*(3), 45–75.

Ross, L. (1977). The intuitive psychologist and his shortcomings: Distortions in the attribution process. In L. Berkowitz (ed.), *Advances in experimental social psychology* (vol. 10, pp. 173–220). New York: Academic Press.

Ross, M. H. (1993a). *The culture of conflict: Interpretations and interests in comparative perspective.* New Haven, CT: Yale University Press.

Ross, M. H. (1993b). *The management of conflict.* New Haven, CT: Yale University Press.

Ross, M. H., & Rothman, J. (1999). *Theory and practice in ethnic conflict management: Theorizing success and failure.* London: Macmillan.

Rothman, J. (1997). *Resolving identity-based conflict.* San Francisco, CA: Jossey-Bass.

Rouhana, N. N. (2000). Interactive conflict resolution: Issues in theory, methodology, and evaluation. In P. C. Stern & D. Druckman (eds.), *International conflict resolution after the Cold War* (pp. 294–337). Washington, DC: National Academy Press.

Rouhana, N. N., & Kelman, H. C. (1994). Promoting joint thinking in international conflicts: An Israeli-Palestinian continuing workshop. *Journal of Social Issues, 50* (1), 157–178.

Saunders, H. H. (1995). Sustained dialogue on Tajikistan. *Mind and Human Interaction, 6*(3), 123–135.

Saunders, H. H. (1999). *A public peace process*. New York: St. Martin's Press.

Saunders, H. H. (2000). Interactive conflict resolution: A view for policy makers on making and building peace. In P. C. Stern & D. Druckman (eds.), *International conflict resolution after the Cold War* (pp. 251–293). Washington, DC: National Academy Press.

Schelling, T. C. (1960). *The strategy of conflict*. Cambridge, MA: Harvard University Press.

Schneider, D. J. (2004). *The psychology of stereotyping*. New York: Guilford Press.

Scott, W. A. (1965). Psychological and social correlates of international images. In H. C. Kelman (ed.), *International behavior: A social-psychological analysis* (pp. 71–103). New York: Holt, Rinehart & Winston.

Stein, J. G. (2001). Image, identity, and the resolution of violent conflict. In C. A. Crocker, F. O. Hampson, & P. Aall (eds.), *Turbulent peace: The challenges of managing international conflict* (pp. 189–208). Washington, DC: United States Institute of Peace.

Tajfel, H. (1970). Experiments in intergroup discrimination. *Scientific American, 223*, 96–102.

Tajfel, H. (Ed.). (1982). *Social identity and intergroup relations*. Cambridge UK: Cambridge University Press.

Tajfel, H., & Turner, J. C. (1986). The social identity theory of intergroup behavior. In S. Worchel & W. G. Austin (eds.), *Psychology of intergroup relations* (2nd ed., pp. 7–24). Chicago: Nelson-Hall.

Taylor, A., & Miller, J. B. (Eds.). (1994). *Conflict and gender*. Cresskill, NJ: Hampton Press.

Touval, S., & Zartman, I. W. (Eds.). (1985). *International mediation in theory and practice*. Boulder, CO: Westview Press.

Volkan, V. D. (1991). Psychological processes in unofficial diplomacy meetings. In V. D. Volkan, J. V. Montville, & D. A. Julius (eds.), *The psychodynamics of international relationships,* vol. 2: *Unofficial diplomacy at work* (pp. 207–222). Lexington, MA: Lexington Books.

Volkan, V. D., & Harris, M. (1993). Vaccinating the political process: A second psychopolitical analysis of relationships between Russia and the Baltic states. *Mind and Human Interaction, 4*(4), 169–190.

White, R. K. (1965). Images in the context of international conflict: Soviet perceptions of the U.S. and the U.S.S.R. In H. C. Kelman (ed.), *International behavior: A social-psychological analysis* (pp. 238–276). New York: Holt, Rinehart & Winston.

White, R. K. (1970). *Nobody wanted war: Misperception in Vietnam and other wars*. Garden City, NY: Doubleday.

White, R. K. (1984). *Fearful warriors: A psychological profile of U.S.-Soviet relations*. New York: Free Press.

White, R. K. (2004). Misperception and war. *Peace and Conflict: Journal of Peace Psychology, 10*, 399–409.

Zartman, I. W., & Berman, M. R. (1982). *The practical negotiator*. New Haven, CT: Yale University Press.

PART III

MASS POLITICAL BEHAVIOR

CHAPTER 17

POLITICAL INFORMATION PROCESSING

CHARLES S. TABER AND EVERETT YOUNG

In this chapter we review modern public opinion research from an information-processing and political-cognition perspective. We focus microscopically on individual-level psychological processes that give rise to individual political opinions—on *private* opinion—and turn away from a discussion of how those private opinions aggregate in broader democratic politics. Our emphasis will be on the distinctively cognitive psychology of opinion formation, which distinguishes our approach from social-process models of ideological thinking that focus on the person-to-person transmission of political ideology, or from more traditional class-based or self-interest models. Our mission is to review research that suggests answers to the question: Does the manner in which individual citizens process political information systematically affect the content of the political attitudes they end up holding? That is, does *how* people think about politics give rise to *what* they think?

1. SOME BASIC CONCEPTS OF POLITICAL INFORMATION PROCESSING

The political cognition approach to opinion formation is explicitly *not* behaviorist. Rather than treating the individual as a "black box" that responds in systematic and measurable ways to environmental stimuli, *cognitivists attempt some account of the actual mechanisms that intervene between stimulus and response*. To be precise, the information-processing perspective rests on the following basic assumptions (adapted from Eysenck & Keane, 2010):

- Citizens are viewed as individual information processors embedded within an information environment, and their mental processing is interactive between environmental and internally stored information.

- This information is perceived, changed, and stored in symbolic form by the mind, which is viewed as a symbol processor.
- Mental processes take time and effort, which may be measured through timing or interference experiments—or, increasingly, by hemodynamic response in functional brain imaging.
- The symbol processing of the mind rests on an underlying physiological system.

1.1. The Associative Network Model of Memory

Human memory is remarkable for its contrasts: a nearly unlimited storage capacity but relatively inefficient retrieval processes; the ability to vividly recall events from early childhood coupled with an inability to keep in mind the lunch menu at McDonald's; the capacity to process staggering amounts of information automatically (that is, out of awareness) along with an attentional focus for conscious processing so narrow as to almost debilitate complex thought. The dominant structural model of the mind for social and political cognitivists, based on the classic architectural distinction between long-term memory (LTM) and working memory (WM), was developed in cognitive psychology out of the effort to reconcile these contrasts (Anderson, 1983; Atkinson & Shiffrin, 1968; Miller, 1957).

Human long-term memory is organized associatively in networks of meaning. When people are asked to freely recall what they know on some topic—say terrorism—what they say seems often to be remarkably structured, as though each memory triggers additional thoughts in a cognitive chain reaction. Precisely *how* memory is organized remains controversial; that it is organized associatively is not. LTM provides primary storage for information processing, for recording experience and mental activity. Working memory (WM) corresponds to the portion of LTM that receives the focus of attention at any given moment. Quite literally, the processing limitations that led Herbert Simon to his notion of bounded rationality (1978) derive from the inefficiencies of WM. There are three primary bottlenecks in WM:

- A very limited capacity—we are able to hold only seven plus or minus two chunks of information in awareness at the same time (Miller, 1957).
- Attention is serial—in order for new information to enter WM from LTM or from sensory experience, old information must be displaced (Payne, 1982).
- The fixation rate for recording information from WM to LTM is very slow—it takes on the order of 8–10 seconds to organize new information and "write" it to LTM (Simon, 1978).

The primary mechanism for memory retrieval is *spreading activation* in LTM. At any moment, all objects in memory (i.e., nodes) have some arousal level that can go up or down as a result of conscious or unconscious processing. Since the probability that a node will pop into conscious WM is an increasing function of its level of activation, these activation processes are critically important (for a formal discussion, see Kim, Taber, & Lodge, 2010). First, conscious thought increases the activation level of implicated memory objects; reading about Barack Obama activates the corresponding node(s) in LTM. Second, activation spreads automatically through LTM from highly aroused nodes to all directly linked nodes, and from there to second-order nodes, and so on, in what is known as the fan effect. Third, activation decays rapidly and with it accessibility to conscious processing, though some memory objects may be chronically highly accessible.

1.2. Grounded Cognition

A powerful extension to the cognitive architecture of associative network theory has recently been proposed (see Barsalou, 2008). Grounded cognition theories argue that "modal" sensory, motor, emotional, and cognitive centers do *not* pass information to a separate "amodal" symbol processing mechanism. That is, the brain does not have a separate "general processing CPU" that applies universal processing rules to modal input from various senses. Rather, cognition consists of "simulations" of multimodal states—simulations that recruit the modal centers themselves for processing. When the concept "gun" is processed (perhaps in a gun control debate), its activation occurs across the brain's and body's modalities that have interacted with guns in the real world: a mental image of a gun may activate (Kosslyn, Thompson, & Ganis, 2006); the feeling of a gun in one's hand may be simulated in sensorimotor areas; the emotions one has felt at hearing of a gun death may be replayed in appropriate neural pathways. Simulations need not be full recreations of experience, and need not even reach conscious activation levels.

One flavor of grounded cognition theories likely to have implications for political thinking is "situated cognition." Human cognitive architecture evolved to support action in specific situations, particularly social interactions, and social cognition is accomplished by brain systems that exist to "do" social interaction in goal-oriented states. Situated cognition theories suggest that objects of cognition do not have meaning outside the situations in which we encounter them. This suggests that the activation of such mental objects as affective tags and semantically related concepts may be moderated by *which* modalities are actively simulating the concepts. For example, a word such as "punishment" might engage a sensory modality in the context of spanking, and a very different set of modalities—perhaps ones evolved to handle norm enforcement and cooperative living—when crime is salient. Across the two situations, "punishment" might have very different associations in a cognitive network.

Another variation with political implications is grounded linguistics theory, which essentially proposes that people think about politics in metaphors, which are grounded in modal states. Lakoff and Johnson (1999), for example, propose that abstract concepts are grounded in bodily states and situated knowledge: people make metaphorical use of concrete states they've experienced to make sense of abstract ideas such as politics. Increasing evidence shows that metaphors are more than linguistic conventions— which is to say they're more than metaphors. They're real elements of thought, abstract concepts simulated in concrete modalities.

1.3. Opinion Formation

The fundamental task of the citizen in forming opinions is evaluative. In conversation, in the voting booth, on opinion surveys, citizens are asked to report their considered evaluations of candidates, groups, or issues, and there is in this a presumption that citizens *have* opinions to report. Converse (1964) thought, rather provocatively, that most did not hold political attitudes worthy of the name. Do people even have retrievable political attitudes?

We limit our commentary on the "nonattitudes" debate to two key replies to Converse. First, it may be that inadequate measurement was more to blame for response instability than inadequate citizens, a possibility powerfully demonstrated by Achen (1975). But how is one to interpret this measurement error? Is it unsystematic, as implied by Achen, or might there be good information-processing explanations for question wording order, or context effects that could be included in models of opinion expression? This question takes us to a second response to Converse, which suggests that people do not *hold* attitudes for retrieval and report; rather, they *construct* attitudes out of the particular sample of considerations that they recall from LTM at the time they respond to a survey question (Tourangeau, Rips, & Rasinski, 2000; Zaller & Feldman, 1992). Since memory recall in the associative network model is cued by the specific context of the moment, the sample considerations retrieved into WM will be mightily affected by the wording of the question, the nature of the preceding questions, and a host of contextual factors. Far from being empty-headed, say John Zaller and Stanley Feldman (1992), many citizens possess multiple, conflicting considerations relevant to a given topic; their unstable responses to survey questions simply reflect this ambivalence.

The Zaller and Feldman model is memory-based, in the sense that evaluations are formed from the likes and dislikes that citizens can recall at the time a judgment is needed. By contrast, online models of political evaluation (Lodge, McGraw, & Stroh, 1989; Lodge, Steenbergen, & Brau, 1995) claim that "citizens spontaneously extract the evaluative implications of political information as soon as they are exposed to it, integrate these implications into an ongoing summary counter or running tally, and then proceed to forget the nongist descriptive details of the information" (Lavine, 2002, p. 227). The citizen in the voting booth need not reconsider pros and cons, for an evaluation has already been made.

These two models are often presented as competing or even incompatible—with memory-based processes being seen as more applicable to complex, ambivalent attitude objects (issues) and online processes as more applicable to simpler, univalent objects (candidates). But the "debate" is an unproductive one, driven by extreme interpretations nobody really believes. The online model cannot mean that all details are forgotten; such an organism would not have in LTM the ingredients necessary to discern the evaluative implications of new information at the time of exposure. And the memory-based approach cannot mean that people refrain from all evaluation of information at the time of exposure; such an organism would have no ability to resist persuasion or otherwise maintain beliefs through time. A far more plausible account of impression formation builds on hybrid models (Hastie & Pennington, 1989). For example, evaluative tags created through an online process may become activated and enter working memory along with other considerations; a strong evaluative tag might heavily constrain the construction of a judgment (and in the extreme, may determine it), while a weak tag might act as one among many considerations (Lavine, 2002).

2. Sources of Opinion Formation

In his 1998 commentary on the field, Donald Kinder identifies three broad types of information that may be of special concern to citizens as they form opinions about political persons, groups and issues: "(1) the material interests that citizens see at stake, (2) the sympathies and resentments that citizens feel toward social groupings, and (3) commitment to the political principles that become entangled in public issues" (p. 800). Each of these provides some "motivational orientation" for opinion-forming citizens. We suggest an additional class of variable that we believe must be regarded as a powerful input to opinion formation: individual differences in *cognitive process*.

2.1. Material Self-Interest

Political theorists from Marx to Mosca have built their diverse understandings of political systems on the seemingly solid foundation of self-interest. But surprisingly, there are powerful reasons to question the empirical importance of self-interest (Citrin & Green, 1990; Sears & Funk, 1991). So long as self-interest is defined in a reasonably tangible and material way—that is, by ruling out forms of "psychological utility" such as intrapsychic gratification (rendering *any* opinion self-interested to the extent that one "likes" holding it)—then self-interest turns out in study after study to have remarkably little to do with public opinion on a wide range of political issues. Overall, self-interest appears to matter only when material stakes are high and when the personal benefit is obvious and imminent (Sears & Funk, 1991). Nonetheless, self-interest *does* influence attention: Citizens whose interests are implicated in an issue tend to consider that issue important (Boninger, Krosnick, Barent, & Fabrigar, 1995; Sears & Citrin, 1982; see also Chong, chapter 4, this volume).

2.2. Group Orientations

If narrow self-interest is not a central guide to opinion, perhaps basic orientations to social and political groups will prove more potent. After all, we have long understood the importance of social identity to the development of social and political attitudes (Brewer & Brown, 1998; Converse, 1964). Affiliations with, and affinities for, politically relevant social groups can guide political opinion formation, as do negative identifications, feelings toward groups to which we do not belong (Conover & Feldman, 1981).

Social group cleavages, from gender to generation, socioeconomic class to regionalism, have been found to be important determinants of opinion on a wide range of issues (Kinder, 1998). One of the most firmly established findings in this literature, for example, is that black and white Americans differ in their positions on many political issues, often markedly. Race clearly remains a potent orienting force for many Americans (Bobo & Kluegel, 1993; Gerber, Huber, Doherty, Dowling, & Ha, 2010; Kinder & Sanders, 1996; Kinder, chapter 25, this volume). Attitudes on welfare (Gilens, 1999), immigration (Pettigrew & Meertens, 1995), and AIDS policy (Price & Hsu, 1992) all turn on hostility toward the out-group.

One rather obvious potential source of group influence on opinion is political parties. Wherever party identification comes from—family transmission is certainly one well-documented source (Jennings & Niemi, 1981)—it is reasonable to suggest that people adopt the policy positions of their party (Sears & Brown, chapter 3, this volume). Indeed, Goren (2005) found that party identification exerts an across-time influence on political values (with no across-time causation in the opposite direction). And Cohen (2003) manipulated party endorsement to induce liberal and conservative subjects to support policies that appeared to be in direct opposition to their principles (though Cohen's careful interpretation of these results is more nuanced than this implies).

2.3. Political Values

Politics is contentious in part because it brings values into conflict, certainly on a societal scale (Stoker, 1992) but also within individual citizens (Tetlock, 1986). Values are seen by political psychologists as key elements in the *structure* of political knowledge (i.e., memory), providing constraint across issues and response stability across time for at least some citizens (Feldman, 1988), even unsophisticated ones (Goren, 2004). Their strong relationship with issue positions is well documented (Feldman & Steenbergen, 2001; Caprara, Schwartz, Capanna, Vecchione, & Barbaranelli, 2006). For example, "rugged individualism" and "egalitarianism" clearly do help to explain policy attitudes such as those toward government assistance programs (Feldman & Johnston, 2009) and normative beliefs that the poor are to blame for their condition (Sniderman & Brody, 1977). The chapters in this volume by Caprara and Vecchione (chapter 2) and Feldman (chapter 19) discuss values at greater length.

2.4. Individual Differences in Cognitive Process

Political and social values—egalitarianism and humanitarianism (Feldman & Steenbergen, 2001), collectivism, individualism, communitarianism, universalism, and countless other isms (Schwartz, 1990)—do reliably correlate with policy positions. Understanding how "broader" values relate to "narrower" policy positions can certainly support our understanding of how people think about politics. However, we believe political psychologists are being forced, by much of the evidence we present below, to attend to another source of opinion formation: individual differences in the way people think give rise to differences in the content of their political opinions.

We note, however, that many studies supporting a connection between "cognitive style" and opinion formation measure cognitive style using traitlike self-report scales, and these scales can be infected by a problem that, it is also important to point out, plagues studies that "explain" opinions with values: many of the explanatory variables such as "Openness to Experience" or "Ambiguity Intolerance"—ostensibly measures of cognitive style—contain items that themselves sound strikingly ideological. We worry that the routine practice of explaining attitudes with other attitudes may invite a sort of shell game in which more general attitude statements (values endorsements, "trait" measurements that amount to expressions of cultural preferences) act in analyses as the exogenous "causes" of what amount to merely narrower or more concrete expressions of the very same attitudes ("opinions")—a central critique of *The Authoritarian Personality* that we think continues to apply to much opinion-formation research.

We believe the more promising pathway forward in opinion-formation research involves explaining thought *content* with real measures of cognitive *process*: explaining *what* we think by measuring *how* we think. This is not a call to halt all values-oriented, self-reported-trait-oriented, or "content-causes-content"-oriented public opinion research, but it is a call to devote a greater portion of our energy to using individual-difference measurements in cognitive process as our independent variables. This will mean more reaction-time measures, measures of performance on tasks unrelated to politics or culture, and other culture-irrelevant measures, and, most important, fewer explicit self-descriptions.

As we review research findings on the ostensibly psychological causes of opinion formation below, we roughly distinguish research designs by whether they explain content with content or with process. While fewer studies have attempted to traverse the latter, more challenging, pathway, fortunately many "content-causes-content" research results do strongly *imply* a "process-causes-content" hypothesis.

So with caveats noted, we can continue by stating emphatically that the interindividual difference in cognitive style that is most often suggested as a predictor of opinion is cognitive "flexibility" versus "rigidity" or "structure," with flexibility generally thought positively related to more liberal or left-wing political opinions (e.g., Jost, Kruglanski, Glaser, & Sulloway, 2003; Gerber et al., 2010). Although this is not the only hypothesized process-level predictor, it will certainly be a recurrent theme.

3. Explaining Opinions with Other Thought Content

3.1. "Big Five" Traits

The "Big Five" (B-5; Saucier & Goldberg, 1998) and the "five-factor model" (FFM; Costa & McCrae, 1988) are two highly parallel models of personality that have become a standard for describing individual differences in personality. The dimensions, generally, can be described as extraversion (roughly, assertiveness and forwardness); openness to experience (being introspective, philosophizing, thinking abstractly); conscientiousness (working hard, keeping an orderly space); agreeableness (compassion, approachability); and neuroticism (anxiousness, depression). These traits are expressed at an earlier age than most believe political ideology develops and are relatively stable over a lifetime, implying they tap something temporally and causally prior to political opinion formation (McGhee, Ehrler, & Buckhalt, 2007).

By far the most common findings regarding the relationships between B-5 traits and political ideology have to do with openness, a measure of cognitive flexibility. The finding that experiential openness is associated with liberalism versus conservatism is by now firmly established, both for social-moral and economic dimensions of ideology, with correlations sometimes exceeding .3, depending on how traits and ideology are measured. Right-wing affiliations and attitudes also appear positively related to conscientiousness. In at least the economic and other nonmoral dimensions (such as issues related to immigration, militarism, and crime), left-wing affiliations and attitudes appear to be positively related to agreeableness and negatively related to extraversion (Caprara et al., 2006; Gerber et al., 2010; Young, 2009). And Gerber and colleagues (2010) found neuroticism positively related to liberal attitudes and self-placement.

In these and numerous other studies, liberals and conservatives certainly *describe themselves* as having different personality profiles. But what do these findings suggest about possible differences in *how* liberals and conservatives *process* political information? It seems there is a relationship between conservatism and cognitive rigidity or high levels of cognitive structure, as well as a decisiveness (in the extraversion and, perhaps, conscientiousness results), which seems resonant with the rigidity hypothesis. The implication is that quick decisions, seizing on what is most salient, most apparent, or most concretely understood, and a tendency to avoid overthinking, describe an information-processing style characteristic of people on the political right.

3.2. Cognitive-Motivational Variables

A family of self-descriptive "need-for" measures that attempt to capture chronic motivational tendencies populates a number of studies of opinion formation and the analysis of leadership (Winter, chapter 14, this volume). Need for cognition, need for closure (Kruglanski & Webster, 1996), personal need for structure (Neuberg & Newsom, 1993), ambiguity intolerance (Sidanius, 1978) and others have been found to be related to ideology. Unlike the "openness" traits, these "need-for" measures are conceptualized as drives to satisfy intrapsychic needs rather than unmotivated tendencies.

The broad findings in this area are entirely unsurprising: motives to be cognitively rigid or structured predict conservatism. Many of the findings relating motivations to ideology are reviewed in the landmark 2003 meta-analysis of Jost, Kruglanski, Glaser, and Sulloway, who construct a motivational theory of conservative thinking in which needs to reduce fear and uncertainty are satisfied by conservative ideas.

3.3. Variables from the Prejudice Research Tradition

Research on authoritarianism and social dominance orientation documents strong relationships with a variety of cognitive-rigidity measures (Heaven & Bucci, 2001; Cunningham, Raye, & Johnson, 2004; Jugert, Cohrs, & Duckitt, 2009; Caprara & Vecchione, chapter 2, this volume, discuss authoritarianism at greater length). In a recent review, Sibley and Duckitt (2008) find that Right Wing Authoritarianism (RWA) is negatively correlated with openness in 46 out of 47 samples, while SDO is negatively related to openness in 30 out of 30 samples and negatively correlated with agreeableness in 31 out of 31 samples.

Duckitt and colleagues (e.g., Sibley & Duckitt, 2008) base a prejudice-oriented research program on a dual-process motivational model that has clear implications for the relationship between cognitive process and opinion formation. Their results show that SDO and RWA are independent predictors of ethnocentrism and right-wing political association, and these two predictors have distinct psychological bases. RWA is associated with dangerous-world beliefs, which themselves are based in low openness, high conscientiousness, and an orientation toward social conformity. SDO is, by contrast, associated with a competitive-jungle worldview, driven by low agreeableness. The implications for our discussion are that economic conservatism, however imperfectly proxied by SDO, is painted as an eagerly competitive, aggressively decisive orientation, while social ideology is more driven by fear and uncertainty.

3.4. Why Would Cognitive Rigidity Cause Conservatism?

Openness and needs for structure, order, closure, certainty—all seem to covary positively with conservatism. Why? Indeed, why generally would any personality traits predict certain patterns of opinion formation? In some cases, the ideology-traits connection seems straightforward. High agreeableness reflects compassion and empathy—of which welfare is a policy embodiment. Extraversion contains a component of assertiveness, which, in the formulation of Caprara & Zimbardo (2004), is associated with the "energy" of the business world. And in the case of moral ideology, it's not difficult to see resonance between a craving for certainty and the safety of tradition.

Probably the most ambitious attempt to develop theory explaining how this concatenation of psychological variables "goes with" ideology is Jost and colleagues' theory of political conservatism as motivated social cognition (Jost et al., 2003). Adding to the familiar rigidity-conservatism findings with additional results showing that conservatism is related to fear of threat and loss, the authors suggest that the contents of conservative ideologies match the existential and epistemic "needs" tapped by these variables. They argue that two major components of conservatism—resistance to change and inequality endorsement—are essentially uncertainty-reducing and hence intrapsychically pleasing to some people.

Other theoretical possibilities come to mind, including that an inflexible cognitive style characterized by "seizing and freezing" (Kruglanski & Webster, 1996) would *inherently* prefer conservative policies without need of motivational drives. The "weak" form allows that such effects exist but could be culture-bound. Hence, an inflexible psychology that produced decisive, unreconsidered opinions would favor capitalism when it resides in a predominantly capitalist culture, but not necessarily when residing in a more collectivist culture. In the "strong" form, cognitive rigidity is related to at least some aspects of conservatism *universally* and across cultural contexts, a view Rokeach (1960) seems to have articulated when he wrote, "If a person's underlying motivations are served by forming a closed belief system, then it is more likely that his motivations can also be served by embracing an ideology that is blatantly anti-equalitarian" (p. 127).

4. "Explaining What with How": Thought *Process* as Independent Variable

We turn now to a sparser literature: attempts to explain why people hold the opinions they hold using not other attitudes, self-descriptions, or motivations, but rather variables that try to capture more purely the *way* in which people think. Some such measures still retain an element of attitude measurement, but even where they do, their focus is on capturing cognitive style, not self-described beliefs or values.

4.1. Performance Measures of Rigidity and Flexibility

Young (2009) used a factor-analytic approach to develop an issues-based measure of ideology, finding three empirically distinguishable dimensions: economic, social/moral, and a third "toughness" dimension that tapped militarism, foreign-policy toughness, and toughness on criminals and immigrants. He then sought to predict left-right opinion on this ideology measure using cognitive-process variables. Two new independent variables are worth mentioning—*Categorization Strength* (CS) and *Deliberative Complexity* (DC).

CS is a measure of performance on a visual categorization task on which subjects classify nonpolitical objects or concepts, of various prototypicality levels, into one of two boxes, or alternately place an object *between* the boxes to indicate the object's belongingness is indeterminate. The tendency to definitively categorize an object into a box is considered a measure of cognitive rigidity based on theory not dissimilar to that of Rosch (1975). Young found that CS significantly predicted conservatism in all three dimensions and in multiple convenience samples, some consisting of students, others of adults.

DC is a set of items that presents respondents with an outcome in need of explanation ("What makes a great fish dish great?") and asks them to select among ordered response options bounded on one end by a simple, concrete explanation ("A great cut of fish") and on the other by a more verbose, variegated one that spreads the antecedent across multiple causes. No "attitude" or self-description is required, only an expression of which causal antecedent seems most likely. The selection of simpler, more concrete causes is regarded as a measure of rigidity, a tendency to see causation in certain and concrete terms. Young (2009) found that lower complexity predicted all three dimensions of conservatism, and in fact DC mediated the effects of CS on opinion formation.

4.2. Attributional Style

The notion that cognitive flexibility differences arise because conservatives and liberals perceive causality differently has most often been investigated in the attributional-style research paradigm. The nearly universal finding here is that liberals are more likely to understand behaviors—especially negative ones—as the result of complex and situational causal antecedents rather than being internally caused or trait-driven (e.g., Zucker & Weiner, 1993). Cozzarelli, Wilkinson, and Tagler (2001), for example, found that internal (versus external) attributions were related to ideologically relevant cognitions such as negative stereotypes of the poor and the belief in a just world (BJW—that people tend to get what they deserve).

Many parallel results emerge from the criminal-justice literature, where attributing criminal behavior to "situational" rather than "dispositional" causes is consistently associated with preferences for lighter punishments or more rehabilitation (Cochran, Boots, & Heide, 2003). Grasmick and McGill (1994) find that a dispositional attribution style links religious conservatism to punitive attitudes. Tam and colleagues (e.g., Tam, Au, & Leung, 2008) have found in multiple studies that need for cognition predicts situational as opposed to individual attributions, low punitiveness, and support for rehabilitation.

Tetlock and colleagues (2007) manipulated the perception of the society-wide prevalence and severity of crime, and generated an increased tendency to attribute a crime to internal-controllable causes, and to increase punitiveness. The increases in internal attributions and punishment came about through the activation of anger-charged retributive goals and *not* by more reason-based deterrence goals. Outside the criminal justice literature, Bryan, Dweck, Ross, Kay, and Mislavsky (2009) manipulated college students' attributions of their own success getting into a top university to be either more merit-based (internal) or more luck-based (situational). Activating the meritocratic schema resulted in more conservative opinion output across numerous issues, mostly of the fiscal and toughness type.

In sum, attributional style is an area with great potential for advances in studying apolitical correlates of political thinking (but see Skitka, Mullen, Griffin, Hutchinson, & Chamberlain, 2002). It is challenging to devise task-based measures of attributional style that are truly scrubbed of political content. For example, whether a businessman's success is attributed to internal versus external sources can be easily seen as a politically loaded question, especially for the politically sophisticated who "know" that conservatives more than liberals are "supposed" to regard businesspeople as "deserving" of their reward. But the ideology-scrubbing appears well worth the effort.

5. AUTOMATICITY AND EMOTION

A previous edition of this chapter predicted that "in the next decade…we will have to come to grips with what John Bargh (1999) has called 'the cognitive monster': the unconscious and automatic underpinnings of thought." Indeed, there has been an explosion of new research. By automatic, we mean processes or behaviors uncontrolled by conscious deliberation, and although automatic processes often remain out of conscious awareness, cognitive psychologists are increasingly realizing that conscious processes themselves reflect automatic processing (see Lodge & Taber, 2013).

Probably the most famous, and reliable, automatic effects observed have been implicit negative evaluations of minority ethnic groups. Indeed, many implicit attitude measurements were designed to work around social-desirability effects that make the measurement of racism difficult (see Fazio & Olson, 2003, for a review). But even beyond survey research and its desirability effects, evidence has been growing for decades that a great deal of the work of thinking is in fact submerged in automatic processes (Bargh & Chartrand, 1999; Bargh & Ferguson, 2000). We discuss emotion and automaticity under the same rubric because it turns out that some of the most important automatic processes are affective.

How can we study thoughts and feelings that are outside of awareness? Most empirical research draws on associative network theory and measures the *associational strength* between an "implicit" or unconsciously held attitude and some "explicit" behavioral measure. In *postconscious automaticity* paradigms, participants are aware of a stimulus but not of how their responses to it are affected. For example, Bassili (1995) uses people's response times in answering survey questions to measure the accessibility of attitudes. The Implicit Association Test (Greenwald, McGhee, & Schwartz, 1998) is a postconscious-automaticity measure that requires respondents to categorize words or objects quickly into "right" and "left" categories, using keys or buttons, under time pressure. Two categories are assigned to the right button, and two to the left. The logic of the test is that when evaluatively or semantically similar categories are assigned to the same button, the task is easier and requires less deliberation, hence less time. The IAT is probably the most popular tool for eliciting automatic associations and preferences.

Preconscious automaticity paradigms utilize implicit priming—in which the evaluated object is typically presented subliminally, as a prime, and subjects react to a target, presented supraliminally and immediately after the prime. In implicit evaluation experiments, facilitated (faster) responses to unambiguously valenced targets are thought to indicate an association between the subliminal prime and the positivity or negativity of the target. Another behavioral measure observed in response to either post- or preconscious primes is word-fragment completions. Rather than measuring reaction-time facilitation, subjects are given ambiguous word fragments that, completed in one of two obvious ways, form words whose valence or semantic meaning presumably is related to that of the prime. Other measurement techniques exist, and it is important to note that correlations between various different implicit measures are historically disappointingly low, so exactly what is being captured is not always clear (see Fazio & Olson, 2003; Burdein, Lodge, & Taber, 2006).

5.1. Political Effects of Automaticity and Emotion

That unconscious evaluation occurs is well established, as is its faster speed relative to more deliberative or conscious cognitions (Ferguson & Zayas, 2009). Taber and Lodge (2005; 2013) have grounded a research program on the "hot cognition hypothesis," which holds that all cognitive objects are linked to affective tags in LTM via an associative network, and *cannot be activated without simultaneously activating their affective tags.* The implication is simple: "cold" cognitive deliberation on political objects is not possible. Affect influences political information processing automatically and regardless of our determination to be "rational."

There is emerging, if inchoate, evidence that automatic attitudes have their own separable effects on opinion formation, even when they remain consciously unrecognized. It is good to be familiar with a number of recent findings: Pérez (2010) found that implicit attitudes toward Latino immigrants captured on an IAT predicted opinions on immigration policy, controlling for ideology *and* explicit measures of attitudes toward immigrants and outgroups. Arcuri and colleagues (Arcuri, Castelli, Galdi, Zogmaister, & Amadori, 2008) used the IAT to predict the future voting behavior of participants who had explicitly denied any preference. Carraro, Gawronski, and Castelli (2010) demonstrate that implicit and explicit political attitudes don't always function equivalently. They found that negative campaigning has negative effects on *explicit* evaluations of the source (the negative campaigner) only—but that *implicit* evaluations of *both* source and target suffered. There is in fact an emerging literature showing that changes in implicit attitudes are possible while leaving explicit attitudes intact (for a review, see Blair, 2002). Implicit and explicit attitudes do appear to interact, however. Galdi, Arcuri, and Gawronski (2008) found that the implicit political attitudes of undecided people (using the IAT) predicted their explicit policy choice, about enlargement of a US military base, measured one week later, while the *explicit* ideological attitudes of *decided* people predicted *changes* in their *implicit* attitudes one week later.

Amodio and Devine (2006) take a powerful theoretical step toward linking *particular* automatic processes both forward to particular effects, and backward to neurophysiological activation differences. Neuroanatomically, stereotyping and prejudice arise from different brain substrates associated with semantic (stereotyping) versus affective (prejudice) memory systems. Amodio and Devine provide evidence that implicit stereotyping and implicit evaluation are independent processes (both automatic) and produce different behavioral responses. Implicit *evaluation* conditions approach-avoid responses; implicit *stereotyping* conditions "instrumental" behaviors, such as ideological positions. There is evidence that implicit racial attitudes drive interpersonal behavior more than explicit attitudes do (Fazio, Jackson, Dunton, & Williams, 1995; Dovidio, Kawakami, & Gaertner, 2002), and Dasgupta and Rivera (2006) found that automatic attitudes toward gays (by IAT) affected behavior toward a gay confederate in predicted ways, when subjects were distracted from conscious egalitarian beliefs.

Not only can attitudes merely exist at the implicit level, but they can be affected by stimuli that are themselves not consciously attended to (Dijksterhuis, Aarts, & Smith, 2005). Weinberger and Westen (2008) subliminally presented the word RATS to subjects and thereby increased negative evaluations of an unknown candidate. Erisen, Lodge, and Taber (forthcoming) find that being subliminally primed with smiling or frowning faces has effects on the number of positive or negative thoughts people list about policy positions in an "affective contagion" process. Though not an example of preconscious priming, Berger, Meredith, and Wheeler's (2008) finding that voting in a school as opposed to a firehouse or church increased support for school budgets indicates the power of unconscious contextual influences on evaluations (for a related discussion of media priming and framing see Valentino and Nardis, chapter 18, this volume).

Going beyond automatic evaluation, Petersen, Slothuus, Stubager, and Togeby (2011) provide evidence that cues in the environment can unconsciously affect the way people frame and thereby understand an issue. They find that an automatically activated "deservingness heuristic" causes people to conceptualize welfare issues in individualistic terms, with implications for policy support. More generally, social emotions—compassion and anger—can automatically affect opinion independently of abstract values (Petersen, Sznycer, Cosmides, & Tooby, 2012). People across cultures spontaneously judge the motivations of the needy—a sign that this is an evolved mechanism. In the work by Petersen and colleagues, perceptions of effort drive welfare opinions, while anger and compassion mediate such perceptions. More importantly, the *accessibility* of welfare attitudes was driven by anger and compassion, *not* by ideological extremity, pointing to the existence of an evolved, automatic, emotional mechanism for making deservingness judgments about resource distribution.

Perhaps the most often hypothesized effects of emotion in politics have to do with fear and anxiety. The affective intelligence research program addresses the effect of anxiety on individuals' motivation to be vigilant (Marcus & Mackuen, 1993; Marcus, Neuman, & Mackuen, 2000; see also Brader & Marcus, chapter 6, this volume). Here we focus on a somewhat different question: do *fear* and the perception of threat drive people systematically to form certain types of opinions? Broadly, there appear to be two perspectives, both of which accept that threat increases levels of cognitive narrowing and rigidity. One perspective—deriving from Terror Management Theory (Greenberg, Pyszczynski, & Solomon, 1986; Greenberg et al., 1990)—holds that people under threat cling to their preexisting ideologies—liberals to liberal ideas, conservatives to conservative ideas. The other perspective holds that threat systematically produces more conservative thinking via cognitive narrowing and motivational needs (Jost et al., 2003). Both camps can point to supporting findings.

Thorisdottir & Jost (2010) manipulated a subjective sense of terrorism threat with an extremely subtle manipulation, and the high-threat condition was significantly associated with greater cognitive closure, and just as importantly, with postmanipulation conservative self-identification. Cognitive narrowing may, then, explain how threat makes people more receptive to conservative ideas. This experimental result, exciting for its rather direct showing that cognitive *process* might *cause* ideology, follows upon a long line of findings connecting threat with conservative or authoritarian thinking (Doty, Peterson, & Winter, 1991; McCann, 1997). For example, Vigil (2010) found that Republican sympathizers, more than Democratic, interpret ambiguous facial expressions as threatening; Landau et al. (2004) found that mortality salience and September 11 reminders increased support for President George Bush in experimental subjects; Willer (2004) showed that raising the terror alert level increased support not only for President Bush, but for conservative *economic* policies; death primes have been found to increase support for Bush among liberals and conservatives alike (Landau et al., 2004); and Lavine, Lodge, Polichak, and Taber (2002) found high-RWA individuals responded more quickly to threatening words in a lexical-decision task; Greenberg et al. (1990) found high-authoritarians but not low-authoritarians reacted especially negatively to an attitudinally dissimilar other under mortality salience. And finally, Jost and colleagues (2007) measured sensitivity to threat and uncertainty avoidance across three studies, finding that self-identified conservatism was related to the aversion to uncertainty and threat, while ideological extremity was not, undercutting the basic claim of TMT.

TMT suggests that death anxiety has special effects that work through people's existential fears, and that the salience of mortality should cause people to cling to any already-accepted value orientation. Kosloff, Greenberg, Weise, and Soloman (2010) found that mortality salience increased liking for particularly charismatic candidates who matched the observer's ideology—*not* just conservative candidates. In perhaps the most definitive demonstration, Castano et al. (2011) manipulated death salience using questionnaires about either death or a neutral subject. Then, subjects completed ideological measures—RWA, issue positions, broader values-type questions, or tolerance.

Regardless of the measures, mortality salience caused the liberals in the mostly liberal samples to become more liberal. The few conservatives became more conservative.

So the debate rages on. But we see a rather easy way out. Note that the Jost et al. (2007) study was not experimental: mortality salience was not manipulated, and the finding was that (presumably chronic) levels of death fear are associated with conservatism. And the main result of Thorisdottir and colleagues (2010) was that death-anxiety manipulations produce cognitive narrowing, not across-the-board conservative attitudes. The TMT studies are quite different. Castano et al. (2011) manipulated mere death anxiety—not a perception of threat from a politically charged source such as terrorists—and measured political *attitudes* as the dependent variable. Hence, it's entirely possible that death anxiety could lead to cognitive narrowing that, in the brief course of an experimental session, causes people to express greater certainty about attitudes they've previously held. By contrast, years of high levels of perceived threat could produce chronically narrowed thinking and, with that, increasing conservatism in the polity. A test of this hypothesis would represent a significant advance.

Having reviewed a large and somewhat disparate group of studies, how to summarize? Though difficult to measure, implicit attitudes surely exist. They are not the same thing as consciously recognized attitudes; they have a more evaluative, affective character than "explicit" attitudes; they are "faster"; and they certainly do interact with explicit attitudes, though exactly how has not been worked out. And it is ultimately conceivable (we think likely) that all attitudes, including explicit ones, are essentially automatically determined. Increasingly, we can say more about some particular automatic and affective processes and the particular kinds of attitudes, ideologically speaking, they give rise to: there is evidence that anger and resentment are automatic responses to certain social stimuli and systematically produce more recognizably "conservative" thinking. And the same can be said of fear and anxiety, with some caveats drawn from the TMT research program. Finally, despite an explosion of research in the last decade, automatic opinion formation is still a very young field of study, and we expect much more progress in the next decade.

5.2. Other Emotion-Relevant Results: Avoidance Motivations and Happiness

Much of the cited work suggests conservative attitudes are, in part, a defensive response to aversive stimuli or a result of a focus on prevention (Jost et al., 2003; Thorisdottir & Jost, 2010). Other research has suggested that having one's self-regulative motivations dominated by avoidance concerns is a cause of mental rigidity (Friedman & Forster, 2005; Crowe & Higgins, 1997). Anxiety appears to have the same effect (Mikulincer, Kedem, & Paz, 1990). Using a self-regulatory paradigm, Rock and Janoff-Bulman (2010) found that, in fact, avoidance-motivation causes abstractly measured cognitive rigidity. Their dependent variable was the Rosch (1975) categorization task in which people indicate the belongingness to categories of items varying in prototypicality. They manipulated approach-versus-avoidance motivation in apolitical ways, such as having participants indicate which movies people should see versus avoid. Avoidance manipulations caused more decisive category-exclusion in the Rosch task. Most relevantly, though, the effect occurred only for conservatives, suggesting a three-way affinity between conservatism, avoidance motivation, and a categorizing cognitive style.

One curious "emotional" predictor of conservative opinion appears to be subjective reports of happiness. Napier and Jost (2008) begin with an acknowledgment that "endorsement of system-justifying beliefs"—a variable with an economically conservative flavor—"is generally associated with high personal satisfaction, as well as increased positive affect and decreased negative affect" (p. 565). They then find that conservatives are indeed subjectively happier than liberals. Why? A tendency to overthink (need for cognition) does not appear to be the cause; rather, in meditational analyses, American conservatives appear to have been buffered against unhappiness by higher levels of "inequality rationalization."

6. NEUROPOLITICS

Modern political psychologists seeking to understand how opinions are formed should become acquainted with a host of results from the relatively young subfield of neuropolitics. It is now clear that liberals and conservatives differ in terms of uncontrolled *physiological* responses to stimuli, brain function, and even static brain anatomy. Indeed, *whether* liberal and conservative brains "look different" is probably no longer a question worth taking up, and neuroscientific findings are now taking sufficient shape to yield implications for the refinement of theory about what *mental* processes give rise to opinion formation. A helpful oversimplification suggests that at least three common themes in the explanation of ideological opinion formation—the role of fear in generating conservatism; the acceptance of change, innovation, and the unexpected in generating liberalism; and the role of empathy in differentiating liberals and conservatives—have all been "spoken to" by the neuroimaging literature, alongside a panoply of other findings. That is, the neuroimaging literature seems largely to parallel, if not outright confirm, other, typically trait- and survey-based research suggesting liberal thinking, relative to conservative, is related to greater cognitive flexibility, more empathy, and less concern with fear. That, it seems to us, is the emerging, though still far from complete, story.

Our review of findings below, not exhaustive in any way, will recurrently touch on three important brain regions: the amygdala, the anterior cingulate cortex (ACC), and the insular cortex, or insula. For nonneuroscientists, reading brain-imaging studies can be daunting, especially when trying to gain some purchase on what the *psychological* implications are. Countless brain regions are typically described as being more or less active under varying conditions, and it can sometimes seem as though every region does a little bit of everything. For our purposes, we need to boil a few important brain regions down to their most well understood functions. Taking cues from dozens of articles, then, we can say that the amygdala, a subcortical structure, is described as being involved in habituated, conditioned emotional responses in the presence of emotionally salient stimuli (see, e.g., Stanley, Phelps, & Banaji, 2008) and is most consistently implicated in fear-based learning, such as the conditioning of responses to aversive stimuli. The ACC is known to be involved in the monitoring of conflict between expectation and external environment, or perhaps for general error detection, and is also known to be involved in the "affective" component of pain experience. And the insular cortex is most often discussed as involved with representing internal states, and in particular with negative emotional experience, the emotional aspect of pain (along with the ACC), interoceptive awareness, self-awareness, and interpersonal experience including imagining pain in others. Note importantly that both ACC and insula structures seem implicated in empathy, or in "feeling another's pain." With these simplified concepts in mind, we review some of the most interesting findings and encourage readers to think beyond our own formulations, about what the broad psychological implications might be, using this review as a "quick reference."

The amygdala seems certain to be involved in political thinking. It is involved in the expression of implicit attitudes, including those involved with racial bias (Hart et al., 2000; Stanley et al., 2008). For example, Cunningham et al. (2004) found using fMRI that whites' amygdala responses were stronger when presented subliminally with black faces than supraliminally. When presented supraliminally, activity in cognitive control and monitoring regions such as the dorsolateral prefrontal cortex (DLPFC) and the ACC suggested the suppression, perhaps itself automatic, of automatic amygdala response (Knutson, Mah, Manly, & Grafman, 2007; Richeson et al., 2003). Interestingly, however, Kaplan, Freedman, and Iacoboni (2007) did *not* find amygdala activation related to perception of the opposite-party presidential candidate in 2004.

Due to its association with fear, a hypothesized link between the amygdala and ideological conservatism seems almost too obvious. Well, as of this writing emerging evidence appears to establish exactly that. Kanai, Feilden, Firth, and Rees (2011) used anatomical MRI (with no time-varying measurement of function) and found in a young-adult British sample that liberal-conservative self-identification covaries with brain structure in a surprisingly straightforward manner: right amygdala volume predicts conservatism, while gray matter volume in the ACC predicts liberalism. While the authors are careful to say that political attitudes are surely related to brain processes in complex ways, they do not miss the obvious implications, suggesting that the amygdala's role in fear processing and its greater volume in conservatives is congruent with theories such as that of Jost et al. (2003). And they suggest that the ACC's role in uncertainty and conflict monitoring is congruent with liberals' greater tolerance for uncertainty and conflicts.

Outside of the brain itself but on a strongly similar note, Oxley et al. (2008) found that participants with lower eyeblink amplitudes in response to sudden noises and lower skin-conductance changes in response to threatening visual images were more likely to support foreign aid, liberal immigration policies, pacifism, and gun control than individuals who had stronger physiological reactions to these threatening stimuli. Strong reactions were associated with favoring higher defense spending, the death penalty, and patriotism. The authors suggest that physiological responsiveness to threat indicates advocacy of policies that protect the "existing social structure from both external (out-group) and internal (norm-violator) threats" (Oxley et al., 2008, 1667).

Perhaps the first study to document neurological differences explicitly between liber-als and conservatives dates only to 2007. Amodio and colleagues (Amodio, Jost, Master, & Yee, 2007), used an electroencephalogram to monitor brain activity during a Go/No-Go task. The Go/No-Go task involves habituating a dominant response (to the Go stimulus) and observing behaviors when the "alternate" No-Go stimulus is presented. When the No-Go response was called for, conservatives not only committed more errors of commission—suggesting greater habituation—but liberals exhibited more neural activity localized to the ACC, as might be expected for a conflict-monitoring area. The authors interpret the result as consistent with liberals' particular ability to "de-habituate" and conservatives' "structured" and "persistent" style of judgment.

In a study conducted by Schreiber and colleagues (2009), subjects' brains were monitored by fMRI during an abstract risk-taking decision task. When making win-ning risky versus winning safe decisions, Republicans showed greater activation in the bilateral amygdala and ventral ACC, while Democrats showed greater activation in the right anterior insula. The authors interpret this as an indication of external versus inter-nal orientation while attempting risk-oriented tasks. "It appears," they write, that "our Republican participants, when making a risky choice, are predominantly externally ori-ented, reacting to the fear-related processes with a tangible potential external conse-quence. In comparison, risky decisions made by Democratic participants appear to be associated with monitoring how the selection of a risky response might feel internally."

Chiao, Mathur, Harada, and Lipke (2009) found that anterior insula and ACC activa-tion correlate negatively and *very* strongly with SDO in 14 female subjects who were imaged while watching people experiencing pain (physical and emotional). They write that the results complement growing evidence of a role for the insular cortex, and social emotions generally, in fairness judgments. Going further, the authors draw on the prev-alence of dominance hierarchies across species to suggest that the extent to which one can share in another's misfortune—as measured by ACC and insula activation—may interfere with the evolved inclination to accept hierarchy.

Inzlicht, McGregor, Hirsh, and Nash (2009) used EEGs to find, incredibly, that height-ened ACC activity (measured after a Stroop-task error) is associated with being less religious. The ACC is presented, as usual, as the structure involved in being an "alarm system" detecting expectation-outcome mismatches in the environment. The authors do not suggest that the ACC drives a lack of religiosity, though; rather, they suggest that religious conviction curbs ACC activity by buffering people against the affective con-sequences of errors. Curiously and perhaps importantly, the highly religious commit slightly, but significantly, *fewer* errors despite their apparently lower conflict-monitoring activity, suggesting that religious conviction is "not the result of some inflexible persis-tence of habitual response patterns. Rather, . . . it appears to be associated with deliberate and careful responding" (pp. 4–5). The religious, in fact, sacrificed speed for accuracy. In another curious study, the ACC appears to be involved in susceptibility to media framing. Deppe et al. (2007) found that the perceived credibility of a magazine advertisement depended on the magazine brand just to the extent that a subject's ACC was activated (but see also Deppe et al., 2005). ACC activation may point in this instance to the extent to which people (perhaps nonconsciously) attend to peripheral aspects of a communication. One wonders whether liberals, with their less "categorical" minds, are susceptible to a wider range of peripheral cues. A testable hypothesis is certainly suggested.

In a powerful result that suggests liberalism is in some way associated with insular cortex activation, Hsu, Anen, and Quartz (2008) find that, while the putamen encodes efficiency, the insula encodes equity and fairness. In their experiment, subjects allocate meals to African orphans under scarcity conditions. The relative efficiency and equity of allocation choices are manipulated, and activity in the insular cortex is found to be correlated with the inequity manipulations such that high insula activity predicts more equitable allocation choices. The authors' interpretation of results suggests that emotional empathy is driven by insula activation and can push people, through an "affective signal," to make inefficient allocations for the sake of fairness: justice is rooted in fairness, but moral sentimentalism, not reason, drives the conceptualization of fairness. Putamen activation, on the other hand, correlates with the efficiency manipulations. The putamen is part of the striatum, which is a dopaminergic region involved in reward computation. The authors interpret the putamen activation as a utilitarian or efficiency-reward computation in the relative absence of strong emotional signals from the insula. Once again, causality is indeterminate, but the parallels with liberal (empathy-driven) versus conservative (reward-calculation-driven) economic thinking are hard to miss.

Scale measures of empathy, unsurprisingly, are known to correlate with liberal attitudes on social spending (Smith, 2006). Is there a neural signature of empathy? The insula and ACC would seem to be places to look. According to Decety and Jackson (2004), the ACC and insula are parts of the pain-mediating network that are active during empathy. Jackson, Meltzoff, and Decety (2005) found that the anterior insula and ACC displayed heightened activity when assessing strangers' physically painful situations. Activity in the ACC was strongly correlated with *ratings* of others' pain, indicating the ACC is not just a conflict-monitoring station; it is involved with the perception of pain in others as well as self. Recall that the ACC and insula are understood by neuroscientists as contributing to the "affective" but not the sensory component of pain processing (e.g., Morrison, Lloyd, di Pellegrino, & Roberts, 2004). It would appear, then, that lower levels of ACC and insula activation may be associated with the relative failure to even perceive that others are in pain. Singer and colleagues (2004) observed heightened ACC activation and insula activation, in response to the observation of a loved one in pain, in those who scored highest on two empathy scales.

The emotional response of "shared pain" with others is, in fact moderated by evolved top-down processes that recognize when shared pain is not adaptively functional (Shamay-Tsoory, 2011; Xu, Zuo, Wang, & Han, 2009). For example, Decety, Echols, and Correll (2010), during fMRI imaging, showed subjects video clips of people experiencing physical pain and manipulated the targets' level of social stigma

(AIDS patients versus non-AIDS patients) and their level of apparent internal responsibility for their condition (infected by blood transfusion versus intravenous drug use). "Blameless" AIDS transfusion targets received higher empathy ratings, their pain was perceived as greater, and they generated more hemodynamic activity in participants' ACCs and insulae. For AIDS patients who were drug users, hemodynamic activity in the ACC was lower than for healthy targets. The authors' takeaway is that the "perception of pain is not the exclusive domain of automatic bottom-up processing of nociceptive information, but . . . is profoundly modulated by top-down considerations, including how observers conceptualize both the situation [how the person got AIDS] and the person [whether he's to blame] who is expressing pain" (p. 994).

And outside of empathy, one last finding on the insula and ACC: Westen, Blagov, Harenski, Kilts, and Hamann (2006) find evidence for an emotional basis of motivated reasoning using fMRI. Presented with threatening information about a preferred political candidate, subjects engage in motivated reasoning, and most importantly display more activation in emotional centers—the familiar ACC and insular cortex, among others—and *not* in the dorsolateral prefrontal cortex, known to be involved with "cold" cognition and explicit emotion regulation and suppression.

In sum, we believe a familiarity with the emerging understanding of the functioning of different brain regions, and of politically relevant findings such as those above, is a powerful engine for theory generation. As Kahneman and Frederick (2006) write, "Translating the imaging findings into psychological propositions is helpful to the theoretical analysis of decision making" (p. 45). To recap and simplify again: the amygdala is important for fear. The ACC is important for conflict monitoring, which seems to have implications for handling the unexpected with greater facility, and the insular cortex (along with the ACC) seems important for empathy, particularly with imagining others' pain, and with perceptions of justice, which are inseparable from affect. But ultimately, it matters little exactly where this or that function is located. What matters is the implication these findings have for theory about how opinions are generated in the brain and why people arrive at different opinions at all. First, we believe the findings we've reviewed support a broad story that the fear, conflict-handling, and empathy associated with these regions have the rather obvious and expected effects on political thinking. Perhaps most importantly, the observation of the political brain's modularity at work is, by itself, a revolution in the conceptualization of how political information processing works: in theorizing about how cognition produces opinion, if your background model of the mind is not modular, then your model risks being antiquated: neuroscience suggests a conceptualization of the individual citizen as, in a very literal sense, not a single political actor but multiple political actors competing for influence over an organism's political behavior. But the science goes further: rather than leave us to intuit what the different "modules" might be psychologically, neuroscience helps identify them and points to physical substrates that justify the existence of those modules empirically. That's a powerful and irreplaceable look inside the black box.

7. Not Rational Man, but . . .

Given the evidence cited so far, the question of whether political thought could ever amount to a normatively satisfying rational-choice process is probably not even a subject for debate. But the question has not always seemed so quaint, and here we identify two perspectives on political thought that arose largely in response to the influence of rational choice models of individual political behavior: the motivated-reasoning (MR) and political heuristics approaches.

7.1. Motivated Reasoning

There was, in the 1990s and 2000s, a resurgence in motivational models of information processing (Kunda, 1990; Lodge & Taber, 2000; Taber & Lodge, 2006; Taber, Lodge, & Glather, 2001). As in earlier cognitive consistency theories (Festinger, 1957; Heider, 1958), these frameworks assert that the pressure for evaluative consistency in attitudes is a powerful motivational force in information processing. Lodge and Taber built a theory of motivated political reasoning on the hot-cognition idea discussed earlier. Citizens display automatic affect toward candidates, groups, and issues, and it is expected that this affect should color their processing of issue-relevant information. Indeed, an oft-repeated finding in the motivated-reasoning literature is that subjects display a "disconfirmation bias" (Edwards & Smith, 1996; Taber & Lodge, 2006): subjects with strong prior affect on a variety of issues are biased in their processing of counter-attitudinal arguments—they spend more time reading them than reading pro-attitudinal arguments, and that time is spent "arguing against." They also display "confirmation bias" in their attentional focus on *pro*-attitudinal arguments. The result is not only resistance to persuasion, but that subjects *polarize* in the direction of previously held attitudes in response to counter-attitudinal arguments. This effect is strongest among the politically sophisticated and robust to changes in argument format (Taber, Cann, & Kucsova, 2009). The backfire effect and sophistication interaction have also been observed in Danish samples in response to arguments presented as coming from a more right-wing or left-wing party (Slothus & de Vreese, 2010). And it certainly applies to political candidates as well as issues (Redlawsk, 2002; Meffert, Chung, Joiner, Waks, & Garst, 2006). It is clear that the backfire effect is driven by affect, and not by "cold" cognitive balance-seeking (Morris, Squires, Taber, & Lodge, 2003; Redlawsk, 2002; Westen et al., 2006).

Nyhan and Reifler (2010) extended the classic opinion-polarization finding to demonstrate that not only attitudes but factual beliefs can be motivated. Shown a news story about the failure to find weapons of mass destruction in Iraq, conservatives displayed greater certainty that in fact Iraq did possess them, while liberals showed the more "rational" belief updating. The authors then attempted to "catch" liberals in similar motivated belief-updating by presenting a factual story to counteract the false but prevalent belief that President Bush had "banned" stem cell research. The results: liberals did *not* change significantly in the predicted direction (i.e., did not increase their belief that Bush had banned stem cells), but at least conservatives did accept the factual story and updated their beliefs "rationally." (Most curiously, in both experiments, without the "factual correction" it was conservatives who were the more misinformed). Redlawsk, Civettini, and Emmerson (2010) do show that an "affective tipping point" can be reached, such that an ever-increasing onslaught of counter-attitudinal information does not cause attitudes to polarize without bound.

An effect related to motivated reasoning is *selective exposure*—the idea that people engage in belief-protection by exposing themselves primarily to pro-attitudinal arguments. Surprisingly, the large literature on selective exposure that came out of the cognitive dissonance tradition does not provide much support for the hypothesis (Eagly & Chaiken, 1993; Frey, 1986; Sears & Freedman, 1967). Perhaps the clearest evidence of selective exposure in processing political information comes from the Taber-Lodge experimental subjects (Taber & Lodge, 2006), who actively sought out opinion-supporting information on an information board, especially when they were politically sophisticated. In other findings, Lavine, Lodge, and Freitas (2005) found that selective exposure was enhanced particularly for authoritarians under a mortality salience (MS) condition—suggesting a potential relationship between ideology (authoritarianism) and motivated reasoning that is largely unexplored.

7.2. Heuristic Usage

One of the most influential ideas of recent years concerning citizen rationality is that "individuals use heuristics—mental shortcuts that require hardly any information to make fairly reliable political judgments" (Kuklinski & Quirk, 2000, p. 153; see also Redlawsk & Lau, chapter 5, this volume). Party identification (Campbell, Converse, Miller, & Stokes, 1960), candidate traits (Popkin, 1991), trusted elites (Mondak, 1993), interest groups (Lupia, 1994), public mood (Rahn, 2000), and liberals or conservatives (Sniderman, Brody, & Tetlock, 1991) all provide useful cues to citizens in their information processing, so long as such orientations themselves are accessible and involve sufficiently strong attitudes (Huckfeldt, Levine, Morgan, & Sprague, 1999). Such heuristics, it is suggested, may allow "low information rationality" (Popkin, 1991), with the strongest claims being that ill-informed citizens behave just as they would if fully informed and that such a process saves democracy from the ignorance of its citizens. But work on heuristics *in social psychology* emphasizes not only the utility of shortcuts to information processing but also the inferential shortcomings (Druckman, Kuklinski, & Siegelman, 2009; Nisbett & Ross, 1980). Heuristic reasoning may mislead citizens, sometimes quite seriously (Kuklinski & Quirk, 2000; Lau & Redlawsk, 2001). Poorly informed citizens, for example, do not distribute their votes in presidential elections as do their well-informed counterparts (Bartels, 1996; Gilens, 2001). At least two sources of error intervene: the information provided by cue sources may not be accurate, and it may not be perceived accurately. Indeed, a variety of systematic biases stand in the way of the straightforward use of political heuristics.

We know that the most sophisticated are not insulated from motivated reasoning, but are *especially* subject to it. But do they make less frequent use of heuristics, choosing to deliberate effortfully on politics instead? Kam (2005), basing her research on the dual-process Heuristic-Systematic model (Chen & Chaiken, 1999) showed that high levels of political knowledge decreased reliance on party cues and increased reliance on "issue relevant" values in support for a proposed policy, concluding that for the sophisticated, values and not heuristics "cause opinion formation"—although there is no evidence in the paper that, for the very knowledgeable, the use of values is particularly effortful. Yet Miler (2009) shows that political elites—in this case legislative staffers attempting to discern constituent preferences—are susceptible to the "accessibility heuristic." The point Huckfeldt et al. (1999) make is salient here: everyone uses heuristics, but not everyone uses the same ones, and it is unwise to assume heuristic processing approximates rationality, even in the aggregate (Kuklinski & Quirk, 2000).

A fresh view is found in Petersen's (2009) notion of "moral heuristics," an evolutionary-psychological notion wherein adaptive problems such as sharing, collective action, and punishing free-riders "carry deep structural similarities to modern political issues such as welfare, tax payments, criminal sanctions," and so forth, facilitating low-deliberative-effort political judgments (Cosmides & Tooby, 2006; Alford & Hibbing, 2004). It is essentially heuristic usage, says Petersen, when people form opinions on political issues using their sense of moral approval or outrage according to whether stereotypes of entire classes of people (welfare recipients, criminals, immigrants) "fit" the input conditions of the evolved social judgment mechanism.

8. Conclusions: Avoiding the Shell Game, and a Future of Promise

Does openness to experience *cause* liberalism? Or would it be more accurate to say that liberalism and conservatism form a "politics" facet of a broad phenomenon we could call "openness?" Some versions of the scale used to measure openness to experience do, after all, contain the item, "I tend to vote for liberal political candidates."

We ask to illustrate a problem we believe has been common in political psychology. Political opinions are routinely "predicted" using, as independent variables, values, traits, motivations, and belief scales that come dangerously near to constituting measurements of the dependent variable. Ambiguity intolerance scales ask whether people agree that there is a right and a wrong way to do things; the need-for-cognition scale contains such a strong cultural component that anyone suspicious of people who fit the "intellectual" (liberal) cultural type might have a very hard time scoring highly on it, however much they thrived on cognition; Jost and colleagues' economic system justification (ESJ) scale, which has been used to predict conservative attitudes, might, if one were unfamiliar with it, be mistaken for a measurement of economic conservatism itself.

There is nothing wrong with knowing that need for cognition or ESJ is associated with liberalism or conservatism. We do not deny that some ground is gained when we verify that these various latent constructs are interrelated—just as knowledge would be gained if we learned that openness items, ambiguity intolerance items, need-for-cognition items, and certain issue positions all "loaded on a single common factor." Such a study would not be without value.

In general, though, we argue that the more often self-reports are used to predict self-reports; the more often attitudes are used to predict attitudes; the more often self-descriptions are infused with cultural descriptions (I like art; I like philosophical conversations; I like jobs that don't require a lot of thought)—the more we use these kinds of variables, the more strongly we step away from *explaining* opinion formation and toward merely *characterizing* the opinions by their associations with other constructs that bear strong resemblances to the opinions themselves.

Our argument here is simple. *Explanation* is better accomplished with independent variables that are truly scrubbed of political content, and explaining "what with how" should generally be preferred to explaining "what with what." For example, no independent variable is more apolitical than the random assignment to an experimental group, which also has the advantage of offering a strong causal claim. Considering the number of claims in the literature that cognitive style of some kind affects opinion formation, it is shocking how few experiments attempt to *manipulate* cognitive style to produce an ideological outcome (Thorisdottir & Jost, 2010, does come to mind as a rare example).

But even outside of experimentation, political psychologists intent on correlating static psychological with static ideological measures can develop psychological measures that are more careful not to sneak ideology in through the back door, even if this involves abandoning the "safety" of more well-known scales. We'd be most excited if such new psychological measures were, as directly as possible, measures of *how* people think, which will often mean fewer self-reports and more implicit and task-based measures.

But let us not end our chapter by griping, when we actually find our field at an exciting turning point, perhaps already a step ahead of our complaints. We are looking inside the black box already. The explosion of findings in automaticity and brain-imaging research relevant to opinion formation represents a strong step in the direction of explaining what we believe with how we think. In automaticity and emotion research, we can observe effects on opinion-formation outputs depending on whether the specter of "deservingness" is raised, or whether threat or death is in the air. Motivated reasoning research affords us a glimpse inside the box revealing how people can defend beliefs—and along with brain imaging reveals that affective investment in these beliefs is an indispensable catalyst in the process. And with brain imaging, we are beginning to see how differential activation of various brain "modules" correlates with differential opinion formation. While, obviously, observing increased blood flow is not the same thing as observing semantic meaning itself as the *mind* processes it, taken together the neuroscience is beginning to tell a stunningly coherent story of a modular mind, composed of different mechanisms for handling the unexpected, for empathizing, for anger, for fear, for conceptualizing justice. And of course when this chapter is rewritten again, perhaps in another decade, what we understand about how the brain produces attitudes will make today's chapter sound downright naive. More modules will have been identified. The functions of the ones we know of today will be understood at a greater level of nuance. And the connections between them will be far better understood. And although we've not discussed it here, the causal role of genes—and how they affect brain function—in opinion formation will be a major part of the story.

Indeed we think, concomitant with such developments, political psychologists will quite naturally continue to develop more abstract, task-based, and apolitical measures, and to turn to experimentation, to keep pace. The latest research on political heuristics is already, for example, taking a view of the brain as modular and is strongly experimental in its methodology. The next decade of research in political information processing will, then, be strongly multidisciplinary, and, while we do not anticipate (nor even hope for) the demise of traditional personality-trait scales, it will be characterized by a dramatic and more direct revealing of the engines inside the black box.

References

Achen, C. H. (1975). Mass political attitudes and the survey response. *American Political Science Review, 69,* 1218–1231.

Alford, J. R., and Hibbing, J. R. (2004). The origin of politics: An evolutionary theory of political behavior. *Perspectives on Politics, 2,* 707–723.

Amodio, D. M., & Devine, P. G. (2006). Stereotyping and evaluation in implicit race bias: Evidence for independent constructs and unique effects on behavior. *Journal of Personality and Social Psychology, 91,* 652–661.

Amodio, D. M., Jost, J. T., Master, S. L., & Yee, C. M. (2007). Neurocognitive correlates of liberalism and conservatism. *Nature Neuroscience, 10,* 1246–1247.

Anderson, J. R. (1983). *The architecture of cognition.* Cambridge, MA: Harvard University Press.

Arcuri, L., Castelli, L., Galdi, S., Zogmaister, C., & Amadori, A. (2008). Predicting the vote: Implicit attitudes as predictors of the future behavior of decided and undecided voters. *Political Psychology, 29,* 369–387.

Atkinson, R. C., & Shiffrin, R. M. (1968). Human memory: A proposed system and its control processes. In K. W. Spence & J. T. Spence (eds.), *The psychology of learning and motivation* (vol. 2, pp. 89–195). London: Academic Press.

Bargh, J. A. (1999). The cognitive monster: The case against controllability of automatic stereotype effects. In S. Chaiken & Y. Trope (eds.), *Dual-process theories in social psychology* (pp. 361–382). New York: Guilford Press.

Bargh, J. A., & Chartrand, T. L. (1999). The unbearable automaticity of being. *American Psychologist, 54,* 462–479.

Bargh, J. A., & Ferguson, M. L. (2000). Beyond behaviorism: On the automaticity of higher mental processes. *Psychological Bulletin, 126,* 925–945.

Barsalou, L. W. (2008). Grounded cognition. *Annual Review of Psychology, 59*, 617–645.

Bartels, L. M. (1996). Uninformed votes: Information effects in presidential elections. *American Journal of Political Science, 40*, 194–230.

Bassili, J. N. (1995). Response latency and the accessibility of voting intentions: What contributes to accessibility and how it affects vote choice. *Personality and Social Psychology Bulletin, 21, 7*.

Berger, J., Meredith, M., & Wheeler, S. C. (2008). Contextual priming: Where people vote affects how they vote. *Proceedings of the National Academy of Sciences of the United States of America, 105*, 8846–8849.

Blair, I. V. (2002). The malleability of automatic stereotypes and prejudice. *Personality and Social Psychology Review, 6*, 242–261.

Bobo, L., & Kluegel, J. R. (1993). Opposition to race targeting: Self-interest, stratification ideology, or racial attitudes? *American Sociological Review, 58*, 443–464.

Boninger, D. S., Krosnick, J. A., Barent, M. K., & Fabrigar, L. R. (1995). *The causes and consequences of attitude importance. Attitude strength: Antecedents and consequences.* Mahwah, NJ: Erlbaum.

Brewer, M. B., & Brown, R. J. (1998). Intergroup relations. In D. T. Gilbert, S. T. Fiske, & G. Lindzey (eds.), *Handbook of social psychology* (4th ed., pp. 554–594). London: Oxford University Press.

Bryan, C. J., Dweck, C. S., Ross, L., Kay, A. C., & Mislavsky, N. O. (2009). Political mindset: Effects of schema priming on liberal-conservative political positions. *Journal of Experimental Psychology, 45*, 890–895.

Burdein, I., Lodge, M., & Taber, C. (2006). Experiments on the automaticity of political beliefs and attitudes. *Political Psychology, 27, 3*, 359–371.

Campbell, A., Converse, P., Miller, W., & Stokes, D. (1960). *The American voter.* New York: John Wiley and Sons.

Caprara, G. V., Schwartz, S., Capanna, C., Vecchione, M., & Barbaranelli, C. (2006). Personality and politics: Values, traits, and political choice. *Political Psychology, 27*, 1–28.

Caprara, G. V., & Zimbardo, P. G. (2004). Personalizing politics: A congruency model of political preference. *American Psychologist, 59*, 581–594.

Carraro, L., Gawronski, B., & Castelli, L. (2010). The effects of negative versus positive person-based campaigns on implicit and explicit evaluations of political candidates. *British Journal of Social Psychology, 49*, 453–470.

Castano, E., Leidner, B., Bonacossa, A., Nikkah, J., Perrulli, R., Spencer, B., & Humphrey, N. (2011). Ideology, fear of death and death anxiety. *Political Psychology, 32*, 601–621.

Chen, S., & Chaiken, S. (1999). The heuristic-systematic model in its broader context. In S. Chaiken, and Y. Trope (eds.), *Dual-process theories in social psychology* (pp. 73–96). New York: Guilford Press.

Chiao, J. Y., Mathur, V. A., Harada T., & Lipke, T. (2009). Neural basis of preference for human social hierarchy versus egalitarianism. *Values, Empathy, and Fairness across Social Barriers: Annals of the New York Academy of Sciences, 1167*, 174–181.

Citrin, J., & Green, D. (1990). The self-interest motive in American public opinion. *Research in Micropolitics, 3*, 1–27.

Cochran, J. K., Boots, D. P., & Heide, K. (2003). Attribution styles and attitudes toward capital punishment for juveniles, the mentally incompetent, and the mentally retarded. *Justice Quarterly, 20*, 65–93.

Cohen, G. L. (2003). Party over policy: The dominating impact of group influence on political beliefs. *Journal of Personality and Social Psychology, 85*, 808–822.

Conover, P., & Feldman, S. (1981). The origins and meaning of liberal-conservative self-identifications. *American Journal of Political Science, 25,* 617–645.

Converse, P. E. (1964). The nature of belief systems in mass publics. In D. Apter (ed.), *Ideology and discontent.* New York: Free Press.

Cosmides, L., & Tooby, J. (2006). Evolutionary psychology, moral heuristics, and the law. In G. Gigerenzer & Engel, C. (eds.), *Heuristics and the law* (pp. 182–212). Cambridge, MA: MIT Press.

Costa, P. T., Jr., & McCrae, R. R. (1988). From catalog to classification: Murray's needs and the five-factor model. *Journal of Personality and Social Psychology, 55,* 258–265.

Cozzarelli, C., Wilkinson, A. V., & Tagler, M. J. (2001). Attitudes toward the poor and attributions for poverty. *Journal of Social Issues, 57,* 207–227.

Crowe, E., & Higgins, E. T. (1997). Regulatory focus and strategic inclinations: Promotion and prevention in decision-making. *Organizational Behavior and Human Decision Processes, 69,* 117–132.

Cunningham, W. A., Raye, C. L., & Johnson, M. K. (2004). Implicit and explicit evaluation: fMRI correlates of valence, emotional intensity, and control in the processing of attitudes. *Journal of Cognitive Neuroscience, 16,* 1717–1729.

Dasgupta, N., & Rivera, L. M. (2006). From automatic anti-gay prejudice to behavior: The moderating role of conscious beliefs about gender and behavioral control. *Journal of Personality and Social Psychology, 91,* 268–280.

Decety, J., Echols, S., & Correll, J. (2010). The blame game: The effect of responsibility and social stigma on empathy for pain. *Journal of Cognitive Neuroscience, 22,* 985–997.

Decety, J., & Jackson, P. L. (2004). The functional architecture of human empathy. *Behavioral and Cognitive Neuroscience Reviews, 3,* 71–100.

Deppe, M., Schwindt, W., Kramer, J., Kugel, H., Plassmann, H., Kenning, P., & Ringelstein, E. B. (2005). Evidence for a neural correlate of a framing effect: Bias-specific activity in the ventromedial prefrontal cortex during credibility judgments. *Brain Research Bulletin, 67,* 413–421.

Deppe, M., Schwindt, W., Piepera, A., Kugel, H., Plassmann, H., Kenning, P., Deppe, K., & Ringelstein, E. B. (2007). Anterior cingulate reflects susceptibility to framing during attractiveness evaluation. *Neuroreport, 18,* 1119–1123.

Dijksterhuis, A., Aarts, H., & Smith, P. K. (2005). The power of the subliminal: On subliminal persuasion and other potential applications. In R. R. Hassin, J. S. Uleman, & J. Bargh (eds.), *The new unconscious* (pp. 77–106). New York: Oxford University Press.

Doty, R. M., Peterson, B. E., & Winter, D. G. (1991). Threat and authoritarianism in the United States, 1978–1987. *Journal of Personality and Social Psychology, 61,* 629–640.

Dovidio, J. F., Kawakami, K., & Gaertner, S. L. (2002). Implicit and explicit prejudice and interracial interaction. *Journal of Personality and Social Psychology, 82,* 62–68.

Druckman, J. N., Kuklinski, J. H., & Sigelman, L. (2009). The unmet potential of interdisciplinary research: Political psychological approaches to voting and public opinion. *Political Behavior, 31,* 485–510.

Eagly, A. H., & Chaiken, S. (1993). *The psychology of attitudes.* Fort Worth, TX: Harcourt, Brace, Jovanovich.

Edwards, K., & Smith, E. E. (1996). A disconfirmation bias in the evaluations of arguments. *Journal of Personality and Social Psychology, 71,* 5–24.

Erisen, C., Lodge, M., & Taber, C. S. (forthcoming). Affective contagion in effortful political thinking. *Political Psychology.*

Eysenck, M. W., & Keane, M. T. (2010). *Cognitive Psychology* (6th edi.). Hove: Psychology Press.

Fazio, R. H., Jackson, J. R., Dunton, B. C., & Williams, C. J. (1995). Variability in automatic activation as an unobtrusive measure of racial attitudes: A bona fide pipeline? *Journal of Personality and Social Psychology, 69,* 1013–1027.

Fazio, R. H., & Olson, M. A. (2003). Implicit measures in social cognition research: Their meaning and use. *Annual Review of Psychology, 54,* 297–327.

Feldman, S. (1988). Structure and consistency in public opinion: The role of core beliefs and values, *American Journal of Political Science, 32,* 416–440.

Feldman, S., & Johnston, C. (2009). Understanding political ideology: The necessity of a multidimensional conceptualization. Paper presented at the Annual Meeting of the American Political Science Association.

Feldman, S., & Steenbergen, M. (2001). The humanitarian foundation of public support for social welfare. *American Journal of Political Science, 45,* 658–677.

Ferguson, M., & Zayas, V. (2009). Automatic evaluation. *Current Directions in Psychological Science, 18,* 362–366.

Festinger, L. (1957). *A theory of cognitive dissonance.* Palo Alto, CA: Stanford University Press.

Frey, D. (1986). Recent research on selective exposure to information. In *Advances in Experimental Social Psychology* (vol. 19, pp. 41–80). New York: Academic.

Friedman, R. S., & Forster, J. (2005). The influence of approach and avoidance cues on attentional flexibility. *Motivation and Emotion, 29,* 69–81.

Galdi, S., Arcuri, L., & Gawronski, B. (2008). Automatic mental associations predict future choices of undecided decision-makers. *Science, 321,* 1100–1102.

Gerber, A. S., Huber, G. A., Doherty, D., Dowling, C. M., & Ha, S. E. (2010). Personality and political attitudes: Relationships across issue domains and political contexts. *American Political Science Review, 104,* 111–133.

Gilens, M. (1999). *Why Americans hate welfare: Race, media, and the politics of anti-poverty policy.* Chicago: University of Chicago Press.

Gilens, M. (2001). Political ignorance and collective policy preferences. *American Political Science Review, 95,* 379–396.

Goren, P. (2004). Political sophistication and policy reasoning: A reconsideration. *American Journal of Political Science, 48,* 462–478.

Goren, P. (2005). Party identification and core political values. *American Journal of Political Science, 49,* 881–896.

Grasmick, H. G., & McGill, A. L. (1994). Religion, attribution style, and punitiveness toward juvenile offenders. *Criminology, 32,* 23–46.

Greenberg, J., Pyszczynski, T., & Solomon, S. (1986). The causes and consequences of a need for self-esteem: A terror management theory. In R. F. Baumeister (ed.), *Public self and private self* (pp. 189–212). New York: Springer-Verlag.

Greenberg, J., Pyszczynski, T., Solomon, S., Rosenblatt, A., Veeder, M., Kirkland, S., & Lyon, D. (1990). Evidence for terror management theory: II. The effects of mortality salience on reactions to those who threaten or bolster the cultural worldview. *Journal of Personality and Social Psychology, 58,* 308–318.

Greenwald, A. G., McGhee, D. E., & Schwartz, J. L. K. (1998). Measuring individual differences in implicit cognition: The implicit association test. *Journal of Personality and Social Psychology, 74,* 1464–1480.

Hart, A. J., Whalen, P. J., Shin, L. M., McInerney, S. C., Fischer, H., & Rauch, S. L. (2000). Differential response in the human amygdala to racial outgroup vs ingroup face stimuli. *Neuroreport, 11,* 2351–2355.

Hastie, R., & Pennington, N. (1989). Notes on the distinction between memory-based and on-line judgment. In J. Bassili (ed.), *On-line cognition in person perception* (pp. 1–17). Hillsdale, NJ: Lawrence Erlbaum.

Heaven, P. C. L., & Bucci, S. (2001). Right-wing authoritarianism, social dominance orientation and personality: An analysis using the IPIP measure. *European Journal of Personality*, *15*, 49–56.

Heider, F. (1958). *The psychology of interpersonal relations*. New York: Wiley.

Hsu, M., Anen, C., & Quartz, S. R. (2008). The right and the good: Distributive justice and neural encoding of equity and efficiency. *Science, 320*, 1092–1095.

Huckfeldt, R., Levine, J., Morgan, W., & Sprague, J. (1999). Accessibility and the political utility of partisan and ideological orientations. *American Journal of Political Science, 43*, 888–911.

Inzlicht, M., McGregor, I., Hirsh, J. B., & Nash, K. (2009). Neural markers of religious conviction. *Psychological Science, 3*, 1–8.

Jackson, P. L., Meltzoff, A. N., & Decety, J. (2005). How do we perceive the pain of others? A window into the neural processes involved in empathy. *Neuroimage, 24*, 771–779.

Jennings, M. K., & Niemi, R. G. (1981). *Generations and politics: A panel study of young Americans and their parents*. Princeton, NJ: Princeton University Press.

Jost, J. T., Kruglanski, A. W., Glaser, J., & Sulloway, F. J. (2003). Political conservatism as motivated social cognition. *Psychological Bulletin, 129*, 339–375.

Jost, J. T., Napier, J. L., Thorisdottir, H., Gosling, S. D., Palfai, T. P., & Ostafin, B. (2007). Are needs to manage uncertainty and threat associated with political conservatism or ideological extremity? *Personality and Social Psychology Bulletin, 33*, 989–1007.

Jugert, P., Cohrs, C., & Duckitt, J. (2009). Inter- and intrapersonal processes underlying authoritarianism: The role of social conformity and personal need for structure. *European Journal of Personality, 23*, 607–621.

Kahneman, D., & Frederick, S. (2006). Frames and brains: elicitation and control of response tendencies. *Trends in Cognitive Sciences, 11*, 45–46.

Kam, C. (2005). Who toes the party line? Cues, values, and individual differences. *Political Behavior, 27*, 163–182.

Kanai, R., Feilden, T., Firth, C., & Rees, G. (2011). Political orientations are correlated with brain structure in young adults. *Current Biology, 21*, 677–680.

Kaplan, J. T., Freedman, J., & Iacoboni, M. (2007). Us versus them: Political attitudes and party affiliation influence neural response to faces of presidential candidates. *Neuropsychologia, 45*, 55–64.

Kim, S., Taber, C. S., & Lodge, M. (2010). A computational model of citizen as motivated reasoner: Modeling the 2000 presidential election. *Political Behavior, 37*, 1–28.

Kinder, D. R. (1998). Opinion and action in the realm of politics. In D. T. Gilbert, S. T. Fiske, & G. Lindzey (eds.), *Handbook of Social Psychology* (4th ed., vol. 2, pp. 778–867). London: Oxford University Press.

Kinder, D. R., & Sanders, L. M. (1996). *Divided by color: Racial politics and democratic ideals*. Chicago: University of Chicago Press.

Knutson, K. M., Mah, L., Manly, C. F., & Grafman, J. (2007). Neural correlates of automatic beliefs about gender and race. *Human Brain Mapping, 28*, 915–930.

Kosloff, S., Greenberg, J., Weise, D., & Soloman, S. (2010). The effects of mortality salience on political preferences: The roles of charisma and political orientation. *Journal of Experimental Psychology, 46*, 139–145.

Kosslyn, S. M., Thompson, W. L., & Ganis, G. (2006). *The case for mental imagery.* New York: Oxford Press.

Kruglanski, A. W., & Webster, D. M. (1996). Motivated closing of the mind: "Seizing" and "freezing." *Psychological Review, 103,* 263–283.

Kuklinski, J. H., & Quirk, P. J. (2000). Reconsidering the rational public: Cognition, heuristics, and mass opinion. In A. Lupia, M. D. McCubbins, & S. L. Popkin (eds.), *Elements of reason: Cognition, choice, and the bounds of rationality* (pp. 153–182). Cambridge: Cambridge University Press.

Kunda, Z. (1990). The case for motivated reasoning. *Psychological Bulletin, 108,* 480–498.

Lakoff, G., & Johnson, M. (1999). *Philosophy in the flesh: The embodied mind and its challenge to Western thought.* New York: Basic Books.

Landau, M. J., Solomon, S., Greenberg, J., Cohen, F., Pyszczynski, T., Arndt, J., Miller, C. H., Ogilvie, D. M., & Cook, A. (2004). Deliver us from evil: The effects of mortality salience and reminders of 9/11 on support for President George W. Bush. *Personality and Social Psychology Bulletin, 30,* 1136–1150.

Lau, R. R., & Redlawsk, D. P. (2001). Advantages and disadvantages of cognitive heuristics in political decision making. *American Journal of Political Science, 45,* 951–971.

Lavine, H. (2002). On-line vs. memory-based process models of political evaluation. In K. R. Monroe (ed.), *Political psychology* (pp. 225–247). Mahwah, NJ: Lawrence Erlbaum.

Lavine, H., Lodge, M., & Freitas, K. (2005). Threat, authoritarianism, and selective exposure to information. *Political Psychology, 26,* 219–244.

Lavine, H., Lodge, M., Polichak, J., & Taber, C. (2002). Explicating the black box through experimentation: Studies of authoritarianism and threat. *Political Analysis, 10,* 342–360.

Lodge, M., McGraw, K., & Stroh, P. (1989). An impression-driven model of candidate evaluation. *American Political Science Review, 83,* 399–419.

Lodge, M., Steenbergen, M., & Brau, S. (Eds). (1995). The responsive voter: Campaign information and the dynamics of candidate evaluation. *American Political Science Review, 89,* 309–326.

Lodge, M., & Taber, C. S. (2000). Three steps toward a theory of motivated political reasoning. In A. Lupia, M. D. McCubbins, & S. L. Popkin (eds.), *Elements of reason: Cognition, Choice, and the bounds of rationality* (pp. 183–213). Cambridge: Cambridge University Press.

Lodge, M., & Taber, C. S. (2013). *The rationalizing voter.* New York: Cambridge University Press.

Lupia, A. (1994). Shortcuts versus encyclopedias: Information and voting behavior in California insurance reform elections. *American Political Science Review, 88,* 63–76.

Marcus, G. E., & MacKuen, M. B. (1993). Anxiety, enthusiasm and the vote: On the emotional underpinnings of learning and involvement during presidential campaigns. *American Political Science Review, 87,* 672–685.

Marcus, G. E., Neuman, W. R., & Mackuen, M. (2000). *Affective intelligence and political judgment.* Chicago: University of Chicago Press.

McCann, S. J. H. (1997). Threatening times, "strong" presidential popular vote winners, and the victory margin, 1824–1964. *Journal of Personality and Social Psychology, 73,* 160–170.

McGhee, R. M., Ehrler, D. J., & Buckhalt, J. (2007). *Five factor personality inventory—Children (FFPI-C).* Austin, TX: Pro-Ed.

Meffert, M. F., Chung, S., Joiner, A. J., Waks, L., & Garst, J. (2006). The effects of negativity and motivated information processing during a political campaign. *Journal of Communication, 56,* 27–51.

Mikulincer, M., Kedem, P., & Paz, D. (1990). The impact of trait anxiety and situational stress on the categorization of natural objects. *Anxiety Research*, 2, 85–101.

Miler, K. C. (2009). The limitations of heuristics for political elites. *Political Psychology*, 30, 863–894.

Miller, G. A. (1957). The magic number seven, plus or minus two: Some limits on our capacity for processing information. *Psychological Review*, 63, 81–93.

Mondak, J. J. (1993). Source cues and policy approval: The cognitive dynamics of public support for the Reagan agenda. *American Journal of Political Science*, 37, 186–212.

Morris, J., Squires, N., Taber, C. S., & Lodge, M. (2003). The activation of political attitudes: Psychophysiological evidence for the hot cognition hypothesis. *Political Psychology*, 24, 727–745.

Morrison, I., Lloyd, D., di Pellegrino, G., & Roberts, N. (2004). Vicarious responses to pain in anterior cingulate cortex is empathy a multisensory issue? *Cognitive and Affective Behavioural Neuroscience*, 4, 270–278.

Napier, J. L., & Jost, J. T. (2008). Why are conservatives happier than liberals? *Psychological Science*, 19, 565–572.

Neuberg, S. L., & Newsom, J. T. (1993). Personal Need for Structure: Individual differences in the desire for simple structure. *Journal of Personality and Social Psychology*, 65, 113–131.

Nisbett, R. E., & Ross, L. (1980). *Human inference: Strategies and shortcomings of social judgment.* Englewood Cliffs, NJ: Prentice-Hall.

Nyhan, B., & Reifler, J. (2010). When corrections fail: The persistence of political misperceptions. *Political Behavior*, 32, 303–330.

Oxley, D. R., Smith, K. B., Alford, J. R., Hibbing, M. V., Miller, J. M., Scalora, M., Hatemi, P. K., & Hibbing, J. R. (2008). Political attitudes vary with physiological traits, *Science*, 321, 5896.

Payne, J. W. (1982). Contingent decision behavior. *Psychology Bulletin*, 92, 382–402.

Pérez, E. O. (2010). Explicit evidence on the import of implicit attitudes: The IAT and immigration policy judgments. *Political Behavior*, 32, 517–545.

Petersen, M. B. (2009). Public opinion and evolved heuristics: The role of category-based inference. *Journal of Cognition and Culture*, 9, 367–389.

Petersen, M. B., Slothuus, R., Stubager, R., & Togeby, L. (2011). Deservingness versus values in public opinion on welfare: The automaticity of the deservingness heuristic. *European Journal of Political Research*, 50, 24–52.

Petersen, M. B., Sznycer, D., Cosmides, L., & Tooby, J. (2012). Who deserves help? Evolutionary psychology, social emotions, and public opinion on welfare. *Political Psychology*, 33, 395–418.

Pettigrew, T., & Meertens, R. W. (1995). Subtle and blatant prejudice in Western Europe. *European Journal of Social Psychology*, 25, 57–75.

Popkin, S. L. (1991). *The reasoning voter: Communication and persuasion in presidential campaigns.* Chicago: University of Chicago Press.

Price, V., & Hsu, M. (1992). Public opinion about AIDS policies: The role of misinformation and attitudes toward homosexuals. *Public Opinion Quarterly*, 56, 29–52.

Rahn, W. M. (2000). Affect as information: The role of public mood in political reasoning. In A. Lupia, M. D. McCubbins, & S. L. Popkin (eds.), *Elements of reason: Cognition, Choice, and the bounds of rationality* (pp. 130–152). Cambridge: Cambridge University Press.

Redlawsk, D. P. (2002). Hot cognition or cool consideration? Testing the effects of motivated reasoning on political decision making. *Journal of Politics*, 64, 1021–1044.

Redlawsk, D. P., Civettini, A. J., & Emmerson, K. M. (2010). The affective tipping point: Do motivated reasoners ever "get it"? *Political Psychology, 31*, 563–593.

Richeson, J., Baird, A., Gordon, H., Heatherton, T., Wyland, C., Trawalter, S., & Shelton, J. (2003). An fMRI investigation of the impact of interracial contact on executive function. *Nature Neuroscience, 6*, 1323–1328.

Rock, M. S., & Janoff-Bulman, R. (2010). Where do we draw our lines? Politics, rigidity, and the role of self-regulation. *Social Psychological and Personality Science, 1*, 26–33.

Rokeach, M. (1960). *The open and closed mind.* New York: Basic Books.

Rosch, E. (1975). Cognitive representation of semantic categories. *Journal of Experimental Psychology: General, 104*, 192–233.

Saucier, G., & Goldberg, L. R. (1998). What is beyond the Big Five? *Journal of Personality, 66*, 495–524.

Schreiber, D. M., Simmons, A. N., Dawes, C. T., Flagan, T., Fowler, J. H., & Paulus, M. P. (2009). Red brain, blue brain: Evaluative processes differ in Democrats and Republicans. Paper presented to the Annual Meeting of the American Political Science Association, Toronto. Available at SSRN: http://ssrn.com/abstract=1451867.

Schwartz, S. H. (1990). Individualism-collectivism: Critique and proposed refinements. *Journal of Cross-Cultural Psychology, 21*, 139–157.

Sears, D. O., & Citrin, J. (1982). *Tax revolt: Something for nothing in California.* Cambridge, MA: Harvard University Press.

Sears, D. O., & Freedman, J. L. (1967). Selective exposure to information: A critical review. *Public Opinion Quarterly, 31*, 194–213.

Sears, D. O., & Funk, C. L. (1991). The role of self-interest in social and political attitudes. *Advances in Experimental Social Psychology, 24*, 1–91.

Shamay-Tsoory, S. G. (2011). The neural bases for empathy. *Neuroscientist, 17*, 18–24.

Sibley, C. G., and Duckitt, J. (2008). Personality and prejudice: A meta-analysis and theoretical review. *Personality and Social Psychology Review, 12*, 248–279.

Sidanius, J. (1978). Intolerance of ambiguity and socio-politico ideology: A multidimensional analysis. *European Journal of Social Psychology, 8*, 215–235.

Simon, H. A. (1978). Rationality as process and as product of thought. *American Economic Review, 68*, 1–16.

Singer, T., Seymour, B., O'Doherty, J., Kaube, H., Dolan, R. J., & Frith, C. D. (2004). Empathy for pain involves the affective but not sensory components of pain. *Science, 303*, 1157–1161.

Skitka, L. J., Mullen, E., Griffin, T., Hutchinson, S., & Chamberlain, B. (2002). Dispositions, scripts, or motivated correction? Understanding ideological differences in explanations for social problems. *Journal of Personality and Social Psychology, 83*, 470–487.

Slothuus, R., & de Vreese, C. H. (2010). Political parties, motivated reasoning, and issue framing effects. *Journal of Politics, 72*, 630–645.

Smith, T. W. (2006). *Altruism and empathy in America: Trends and correlates.* Chicago: National Opinion Research Center, University of Chicago.

Sniderman, P. M., & Brody, R. A. (1977). Coping: The ethic of self-reliance. *American Journal of Political Science, 21*, 501–522.

Sniderman, P. M., Brody, R. A., & Tetlock, P. E. (1991). *Reasoning and choice: Explorations in political psychology.* New York: Cambridge University Press.

Stanley, D., Phelps, E. A., & Banaji, M. R. (2008). The neural basis of implicit attitudes. *Current Directions in Psychological Science, 17*, 164–170.

Stoker, L. (1992). Interests and ethics in politics. *American Political Science Review, 86*, 369–380.

Taber, C. S., Cann, D., & Kucsova, S. (2009). The motivated processing of political arguments. *Political Behavior*, *31*, 137–155.

Taber, C. S., & Lodge, M. (2003). First steps toward a dual-process accessibility model of political beliefs, attitudes, and behavior. Paper presented at the Shambaugh Conference on Emotion and Politics, University of Iowa.

Taber, C. S., & Lodge, M. (2006). Motivated skepticism in the evaluation of political beliefs. *American Journal of Political Science*, *50*, 755–769.

Taber, C., Lodge, M., & Glather, J. (2001). The Motivated construction of political judgments. In J. Kuklinski (ed.), *Citizens and politics: Perspectives from political psychology* (pp. 198–226). New York: Cambridge University Press.

Tam, K., Au, A., & Leung, A. K. (2008). Attributionally more complex people show less punitiveness and racism. *Journal of Research in Personality*, *42*, 1074–1081.

Tetlock, P. E. (1986). A value pluralism model of ideological reasoning. *Journal of Personality and Social Psychology*, *50*, 819–827.

Tetlock, P. E., Visser, P. S., Singh, R., Polifroni, M., Scott, A., Elson, B., Mazzocco, P., & Rescober, P. (2007). People as intuitive prosecutors: The impact of social-control goals on attributions of responsibility. *Journal of Experimental Social Psychology*, *43*, 195–209.

Thorisdottir, H., & Jost, J. T. (2010). Motivated closed-mindedness mediates the effect of threat on political conservatism. *Political Psychology*, *31*, 1–38

Tourangeau, R., Rips, L. J., & Rasinski, K. (2000). *The psychology of the survey response*. Cambridge: Cambridge University Press.

Vigil, J. M. (2010). Political leanings vary with facial expression processing and psychosocial functioning: Group process. *Intergroup Relations*, *13*, 547–558.

Weinberger, J., & Westen, D. (2008). RATS, we should have used Clinton: Subliminal priming in political campaigns. *Political Psychology*, *29*, 631–651.

Westen, D., Blagov, P. S., Harenski, K., Kilts, C., & Hamann, S. (2006). Neural bases of motivated reasoning: An fMRI study of emotional constraints on partisan political judgment in the 2004 U.S. presidential election. *Journal of Cognitive Neuroscience*, *18*, 1947–1958.

Willer, R. (2004). The effects of government-issued terror warnings on presidential approval ratings. *Current Research in Social Psychology*, *10*, 1–12.

Xu, X., Zuo, X., Wang, X., & Han, S. (2009). Do you feel my pain? Racial group membership modulates empathic neural responses. *Journal of Neuroscience*, *29*, 8525–8529.

Young, E. (2009). Why we're liberal, why we're conservative: A cognitive theory on the origins of ideological thinking. PhD dissertation, Stony Brook University.

Zaller, J. R., & Feldman, S. (1992). A simple theory of the survey response. *American Journal of Political Science*, *36*, 579–616.

Zucker, G. S., & Weiner, B. (1993). Conservatism and perceptions of poverty: An attributional analysis. *Journal of Applied Social Psychology*, *23*, 925–943.

CHAPTER 18

....

POLITICAL COMMUNICATION

*form and consequence of the
information environment*

....

NICHOLAS A. VALENTINO AND
YIORYOS NARDIS

1. INTRODUCTION

....

SCHOLARS in the early to mid 20th century were quite concerned about the potential for mass media to have profound persuasive impact on citizens. The genocides of Europe and Asia, political purges in the Soviet Union, and bloody revolutions around the world cried out for explanation so that we might reduce the incidence of these horrifyingly destructive events in the future. A natural place to look was the power of mass media. It seemed obvious that mass media were critical for helping organize the world outside the direct experience of the average citizen (Lippmann, 1922). The ability of charismatic leaders to project their voice and image via radio, film, and television was assumed necessary, if not sufficient, for their success in mobilizing support for their genocidal plans. Audiences, it was thought, were captive to the media, so that simple repetition of the message would eventually yield large-scale changes in attitudes and behavior. This simple persuasion process—whereby a sophisticated messenger would simply inject new information into the brains of vulnerable citizens and induce behavioral change—became known as the "hypodermic needle" model of media effects. Scholars focused primarily on the skill of the messenger and the characteristics of the message, paying little attention to the possibility that the audience was actually quite well equipped to resist.

Fears of massive media effects, particularly of the kind Nazi propaganda minister Joseph Goebbels was so confident he commanded, abated as the first generation of scientific studies on the topic revealed quite weak results. For example, merely repeating a message did not seem to boost the likelihood of its acceptance by the mass public (Hyman & Sheatsley, 1947). Several other surprises emerged from experimental work on behalf of the US War Department during World War II. Films devoted to boosting a soldier's motivation to fight had nearly no such effect, and one-sided messages were often *not* more effective than two-sided messages (Hovland et al., 1949).

These findings suggested audiences were much less pliable, attentive, and captive than previously assumed. Elites who would try to change mass preferences about important political matters of the day had a tough row to hoe (Klapper, 1960). Citizens, it seemed, didn't pay much attention to politics, and when they did receive new information it was primarily from friends and relatives they considered authorities on the subject (Katz & Lazarsfeld, 1955). This "Two-Step Flow" notion of media influence—where political media content is filtered through "opinion leaders" in a social network and then relayed to less interested members of the group—helped to explain why mass opinion change seemed so rare. Opinion leaders tend to be similar in many ways to those in their discussion networks, leaving few opportunities for wholesale shift in opinion as a result of exposure (see Huckfeldt, Mondak, Hayes, Pietryka, & Reilly, chapter 21, this volume, for a review of the subsequent work on the impact of social networks). In the end, it seemed political campaigns seemed to do a much more effective job of reinforcing existing predispositions and, perhaps, mobilizing voters (Lazarsfeld, Berelson, & Gaudet, 1948; Berelson, Lazarsfeld, & McPhee, 1954).

Politicians, candidates, news journalists and pundits continue to behave as if the media can have massive effects, even though empirical demonstrations of such massive effects are rare. The public also persists in the belief that the masses are susceptible to a variety of media influences, and, perhaps ironically, this fact alone may be enough to influence elite behavior (Davison, 1983). Of course, much has changed in recent times with regard to the structure and content of political messages in the media environment. The amount of money spent by political candidates in the United States and around the world has increased sharply over the last several decades: In 2008 spending exceeded 1.5 billion dollars in the US presidential election according to the Federal Election Commission. Much of this money is spent on campaign communication, including advertising via television and radio, but also on Internet websites, mailings, and consulting fees for free media strategy. Citizens are bombarded with information during the campaigns, and the campaign has become a nearly permanent endeavor (Blumenthal, 1982).

A 2010 Pew Research Center survey found that Americans are spending less time consuming traditional news, but are making up for it via online political content. Radio and newspaper exposure to public affairs has declined precipitously over the past two decades in the United States, whereas since the mid-1990s, after a period of decline, television viewership has remained quite stable. Meanwhile, online political information is proliferating as people get more and more of their news online every year. In fact, digital consumption of news may completely account for decreases in traditional news consumption since the mid-1990s. Changing exposure patterns, technological affordances, and candidate strategies in the shift to an online, 24-hour information environment might alter the impact of political communication either positively or negatively.

Advances in our understanding of the impact of political communication have been built on the hunch that several causal steps must take place between message sending and behavioral change. Lasswell and his colleagues were among the first to recognize this, as is evidenced by his well-worn definition of political communication as "who says what to whom with what effect" (Lasswell, 1948). McGuire (1985) specified in more detail these steps in his model of persuasion/communication. For a message (say, "Obama handled the debt crisis debate in 2011 poorly") to persuade, it must be received, the receiver must pay attention to it, comprehend it, encode it in memory, and yield to it. When subsequently faced with a behavioral decision –say, her vote choice in 2012—the receiver must recall the information and decide to act on it. Only after each of these steps has taken place could behavior—turnout and vote choice in 2012—be affected.

While the conception of media persuasion as a linear and stepwise process is plausible, we now know that all these steps are not necessary (Petty, Brinol, & Priester, 2009). Sometimes people change their minds without paying very much attention, or without seeming to learn any new information as a result of exposure. Sometimes people change their behavior but continue to hold attitudes contradicting those choices. The factors that explain variation in the process of political communication effects fall into four categories: Source cues, features of media technology, message content, and human information processing. We turn to these now.

2. Moderators of Media Effects: Source, Medium, Message, and Information Processing

Carl Hovland and his colleagues speculated early on about specific forces that might moderate the effectiveness of communication (Hovland, Janis, & Kelley, 1953). With regard to source cues, specific attributes of communicators such as their credibility or likeability (Chaiken, 1980) moderate the influence of media messages on attitudes. In addition, media technology—the specific features a medium uses to convey information—vary widely, and this is especially important as we think about the impact of new media (Chaiken & Eagly 1976). These technological factors might, for example, alter the amount and ideological diversity of new information citizens encounter. With regard to content, the organization of the argument—for example, the explicit versus implicit cues in the message—might also moderate its impact. Information quality—news bias, for example—might also moderate the impact of the media.

Finally, systematic biases in human information processing seem to strongly moderate the impact of the media on attention, learning, attitude and action. Other chapters in this publication will provide much more detail about this important step in the persuasion process (see especially Taber & Young, chapter 17; Redlawsk & Lau, chapter 5), but we will briefly review them here since they enter into most contemporary discussions of the impact of political communication.

One of the most important insights guiding media effects research is that human information-processing capacity is quite limited (Simon, 1979). We simply cannot hold all pieces of information relevant to a decision in working memory, weigh their value accurately, and consciously calculate the "correct" answer. Instead, humans seem to do the best they can with what they have cognitively available at the moment—to satisfice. This fact has led to theories about subtle media influences such as priming, agenda setting, and framing.

A second insight is that attitude objects held in long-term memory, including political objects, carry an affective "charge" such that people *always* call to mind how much they like an object (Fazio, Sanbonmatsu, Powell, & Karkes, 1986; Lodge & Stroh, 1993). Third, we now know that much of what happens in reaction to new information occurs automatically, before the receiver is even consciously aware she is evaluating (Bargh & Pietromonaco, 1982; Bargh & Ferguson, 2000). The recognition that much of human cognition occurs outside of awareness has begun to influence a wide variety of theories about the impact of political communication, including those involving the role of emotions on attention, learning, attitude change, and action (Marcus, Neuman, & MacKuen, 2000).

Finally, one of the more important insights regarding human information processing for theories involving the impact of political communication is that under different circumstances, and across different individuals, the motivation to process new information varies. The concern with motivation as a moderator of mass media effects draws its inspiration from *dual process* theories of persuasion (Petty & Cacciopo, 1986; Eagly & Chaiken, 1993; Cialdini & Goldstein, 2004; Petty et al., 2009). The assumption underlying these models is that humans are motivated to hold accurate beliefs and reasonable attitudes, but often are unable or unwilling to expend the cognitive resources necessary to carefully consider whether new information should make them change their minds. When motivation is low, a peripheral process dominates in which simple heuristics such as the quantity of information will be the most influential elements of a given message, and persuasion will be weaker and short lived. When processing motivation is high, however, the quality of the arguments will matter and counterarguing will take place. If persuasion results, then it will likely be more lasting.

More recently, however, we have begun to recognize that humans are motivated not only to be accurate but also to defend their existing views even if they are incorrect (Kunda, 1990). Understanding the relative influence of *directional* versus *accuracy* motivations—and the circumstances and individual characteristics that determine which is strongest—will have large consequences for understanding the impact of political communication. In fact, the combination of these insights about human information processing undergirds theories of motivated reasoning that are beginning to bear fruit in political science (Taber & Lodge, 2006; Lodge & Taber, 2013). For example, motivated reasoning theory predicts that citizens with the strongest prior beliefs and highest levels of political sophistication are most likely to counterargue information that contradicts their points of view and to uncritically accept confirmatory evidence. This psychological process has obvious implications for the impact of political communication on democratic accountability, as we will discuss.

In summary, we will discus four major domains of media influence: *attention, learning, attitude change,* and *action*. The media can alter political outcomes by influencing the public's attention to major issues of the day, leading citizens to learn new information, changing attitudes about objects in the political world, and mobilizing or demobilizing political action. The careful reader will wonder why the category *persuasion* is not one of our major foci. The reason is that we think of persuasion as the combination of attitude change and action. Persuasive communication is, in other words, a message that changes attitudes in ways significant and lasting enough to alter later behavior (McGuire, 1985). Throughout our discussion of these effects, we will pay special attention to the important external moderators of media influence: Source cues, features of the medium, and message factors. We argue that these moderating effects are best understood from a psychological perspective: Contemporary accounts of information processing shed considerable light on how a credible source, specific argument, or vivid image can alter a message's persuasiveness.

3. POLITICAL COMMUNICATION AND ATTENTION

If media influence mass attitudes and behavior, they first must penetrate the clutter of people's daily lives and capture their attention (Neuman, 1991; 2000). This was a big enough obstacle when the media environment for the average citizen consisted of a few television and radio stations, a newspaper or two, and perhaps a national newsmagazine. The expansion and fragmentation of the media environment makes the study of information seeking and attention even more central. The recognition that exposure and attention are not constants led scholars to wonder about their antecedents beginning in the 1970s. Advances in *selective exposure*, focusing on biases in the ways people are exposed to attitudinally consonant versus dissonant information, and media *agenda setting*, focusing on the impact of the news environment on attention to some issues and not others, resulted. These theories, in turn, led to speculation about how the media might alter political cognition via *priming*—elevating the salience of some considerations over others in memory during the evaluation of leaders and policies. Finally, psychological theories of risk and decision-making influenced the development of *framing* research, which explores the consequences of elite choices about how social problems are described in the media. We will review these processes in turn.

3.1. Selective Exposure

One of Klapper's (1960) explanations for the puzzling null results in media effects research was the power of *selective exposure*: People seemed rarely exposed to messages that challenged their existing viewpoints. One way this might happen is if people are motivated to avoid attitudinally discrepant information, a prediction made by Cognitive Dissonance Theory (Festinger, 1957). This theory posited that holding contradictory attitudes, or behaving in ways that contradicted one's attitudes, caused psychological discomfort that we are all motivated to reduce. This provided an explanation for why so few people changed their mind in response to persuasive media messages: The motivation to hold logically consistent attitudes and beliefs would lead to the avoidance of counter-attitudinal messages in the first place. Media messages could have little effect on attitudes and behavior if people were rarely exposed to views that differed from their own. This logic became the basis for much research on selective exposure (Frey, 1986).

However, empirical research found very little support for the notion that people consciously attempted to avoid attitudinally discrepant information (Sears & Freedman, 1967). In fact, it seemed quite common for people to actually *prefer* such information, especially when it was deemed useful for future decision-making or for defending one's own point of view. These findings were consistent with the general notion that people are motivated to hold accurate beliefs and defensible attitudes. Instead, information selectivity—when it occurred—seemed to be driven by a much more passive process, what Sears & Freedman (1967) labeled "de facto selectivity," in which people would simply find themselves in politically homogeneous discussion networks (Huckfeldt & Sprague, 1995) that naturally reinforce their standing views. Bankers and factory line workers not only have different points of view, they are also unlikely to run into each other at the bar after work. Observational tests mostly confirmed the experimental work, finding quite small amounts of bias in information seeking (Chaffee & Miyo, 1983; Milburn, 1979).

One of the contextual forces undermining selective exposure was the structure of the news industry of the 20th century. This is a factor determined by the medium itself, which biased the supply of information in a particular way. Each night, beginning at around suppertime, the big three networks and their local affiliates would supply news programing that conformed to a set of rules mandating the airing of politically contrapuntal viewpoints (Neuman, 1991; Mutz & Martin, 2001). Even if people were motivated to seek out attitudinally consistent viewpoints, it was quite difficult to avoid at least incidental exposure to the other side. The rules of newsmaking and dissemination, however, have changed dramatically over the last 20 years. The big three American news networks have been joined by myriad cable news channels, newspaper readership has experienced a long and not so slow decline, and political voices both elite and mass have exploded on the World Wide Web. The same flexibility and interactivity that make the Internet rich with normatively beneficial political potential (Hill & Hughes, 1998) may also trigger concerns about information bubbles where people become impervious to differing points of view (Negroponte, 1995; Sunstein, 2002). Whereas it was once impossible to completely avoid attitudinally discrepant information unless you tuned out news entirely (a phenomenon we will discus below), it is now at least possible to surround oneself in a comfortable bubble of consonant points of view, gently soothing away any facts that undermine one's beliefs. Such a process might reduce the power of media messages to persuade people to change their attitudes or behavior (Bennett & Iyengar, 2008).

Indeed, correlational evidence of selectivity in contemporary news consumption continues to emerge (Stroud, 2008). However, people still seem to be encountering quite a bit of counter-attitudinal information online (Garrett, 2009). One reason for this may have to do with the accuracy motivation discussed above: When counter-attitudinal information will be *useful* for some future decision or interaction, people will seek it out even when it challenges their beliefs, and the Internet makes that effort less costly (Valentino, Banks, Hutchings, & Davis, 2009). Further, the correlation between seeking attitudinally consonant and attitudinally discrepant information is positive, not negative (Garrett, Carnahan, & Lynch, 2013), as would be the case if directional motivations completely override the motivation to hold accurate views. While people prefer information that corresponds to their beliefs, they do not avoid discrepant information at all costs. Such findings provide only small comfort to those who worry that such normative benefits are outweighed by the costs of the new media system on the quality and quantity of public discourse and deliberation.

3.2. Agenda Setting

Given the practically infinite universe of issues available for consideration by government, understanding the causes of the public's issue priorities is of obvious importance. Might exogenously determined changes in the media environment influence the public's attention to specific issues, groups, problems, and policy solutions? The answer seems to be a confident yes. Cohen (1963) was perhaps only modestly exaggerating when he claimed that "while the press may not be successful much of the time in telling people what to think, it is stunningly successful in telling its readers what to think about" (p. 13). McCombs and Shaw (1972) found nearly perfect correspondence between the rank ordering of issue priorities of the public and that of attention given to said issues in the news. Of course, such correlations were open to multiple causal interpretations, including the possibility that journalists were merely focusing on issues the public already viewed as important or that both news and the public attention to issues were triggered by real-world events. Subsequent time-series demonstrations of the effect, whereby studies tracked changes in the media agenda and found subsequent changes in public opinion, were more convincing (Funkhouser, 1973; Behr & Iyengar, 1985). Finally, controlled lab experiments that manipulated the amount of news attention given to a particular issue powerfully altered respondents' subsequent importance ratings (Iyengar & Kinder, 1987). The agenda-setting effect is one of the most powerful media influences in the political arena both in the United States and abroad.

3.3. Media Priming

Confidence in media agenda setting led to speculation about related effects on political decision-making. Iyengar and Kinder (1987) proposed that news attention might alter the salience of issues during the formation of candidate preferences. At first blush, media priming is straightforward: by paying attention to some issues, events, candidate traits, and not others, the media alters the categories on the public's political scorecard. This process, changing the ingredients of evaluations of presidents, policies, and other attitude objects, is one of the most important ways in which the information environment during and between electoral campaigns affects public opinion.

Media priming has been demonstrated via changes in the association between an attitude dimension and global candidate evaluations or policy opinions after exposure to a message relevant to the attitude. News about defense spending, for example, boosts the association between a candidate's performance on defense and his overall approval rating (Iyengar & Kinder, 1987). The assumed psychological mechanism driving the media-priming effect draws on the same limited-information processing abilities of the human brain discussed above (Simon, 1979). Because citizens cannot hold all possible evaluative criteria in memory at the same time, they base their choices disproportionately on candidate performance on currently salient issues. Ample evidence indicates the recent or frequent activation of ideas in memory automatically facilitates their use in subsequent judgment tasks (Higgins, Bargh, & Lombardi, 1985; Higgins, Rholes, & Jones, 1977; Srull & Wyer, 1979; Bargh & Pietromonaco, 1982). This notion is consistent with a view of memory as organized in an associative network of "schemas," or related opinion nodes (Anderson, 1983). When one node is given attention, say via media attention, it activates other relevant nodes in memory. This process has been dubbed "spreading activation" (Collins & Loftus, 1975). Given the complexity of the political world, therefore, citizens typically base their judgments only on those considerations that are most salient or accessible—those that are at the "top of the head" (Iyengar & Kinder, 1987; Zaller, 1992).

Over the past two decades, research on this topic has intensified, and many dozens of studies have demonstrated priming effects via a wide variety of media content including campaign advertising (Ansolabehere & Iyengar, 1995), general news coverage (Iyengar, 1991; Iyengar & Kinder, 1987; Valentino, 1999; Miller & Krosnick, 2000), and campaign news (Krosnick & Brannon, 1993; Jacobs & Shapiro, 1994). These studies also demonstrate that a variety of politically relevant attitudinal dimensions can be "primed," including issue preferences (Iyengar & Kinder, 1987), economic interests (Iyengar & Simon, 1993), racial attitudes (Mendelberg, 2001; Valentino, 1999; Valentino, Hutchings, & White, 2002), broad-based racial and gender schemas (Winter,

2008), foreign policy attitudes (Peffley & Hurwitz, 1993), and ideology and moral values (Stoker, 1993). Petrocik (1996) argues that campaigns are, at their heart, priming competitions in which the parties seek to raise the salience of their traditionally "owned" issues or performance issues on which they enjoy recent success.

One concern about the nature of media-priming effects is based on the fact that many studies measure the "primed" dimension *after* exposure to the media message that presumably does the priming. As a result of this design feature, one cannot be sure whether the media message activated an existing attitude or altered it directly, thereby bringing it into line with some policy opinion or candidate evaluation (Huber & Lapinski, 2006). Iyengar and Kinder (1987) labeled this alternative to priming "projection": the association between some issue-specific performance dimension and global candidate evaluations increases because the voter changes his evaluation of the candidate's issue-specific performance in order to rationalize his candidate preference. Lenz (2009) shows this is often just what happens: many (but not all) so-called priming effects are in fact examples of citizens learning new information about where parties or candidates stand on issues, and *adjusting their own issue stands to match*. For example, heavy news attention to Social Security in 2000 led people to learn that Bush favored investing Social Security funds in the stock market. In turn, these individuals became more favorable toward this alternative. This effect, while not priming, is still important: How can democratic citizens hold elected officials accountable to their interests if they change those interests to be in line with the candidate they prefer? In any case, work on media priming needs to become much more careful about the causal pathways that lead to increases in the correlation between specific issue concerns and evaluations of political candidates.

Even if media priming is not simply projection or learning, questions have still been raised about whether the psychological process underlying the effect is automatic and unconscious or more reflective and controlled. The original definition assumed an automatic process based on the accessibility of thoughts in short-term memory (Iyengar & Kinder, 1987). Unfortunately, direct measures of changes in the accessibility of primed schemas are almost always absent. Valentino et al. (2002), however, confirmed the priming of racial attitudes via subtle cues in political advertising via a response latency task that measured how quickly respondents could identify schema-relevant words. Miller and Krosnick (2000), however, argue that a more conscious process underlies the effect: Media attention changes how important people consider an issue to be, and these importance ratings alter judgment criteria. Future work must follow up on these early leads in order to find out more about the contours of media-priming effects in politics, and to better understand the psychological process that underlies the effect.

3.4. Media Framing

The conceptual definition of media framing has suffered from a lack of precision, and several theorists have noticed that this ambiguity undermines the construct's value as an analytical tool (Entman, 1993; Druckman, 2001b; 2004; Sniderman & Theriault, 2004).

Gamson and Modigliani (1987) provide a useful if broad definition: media frames present "a central organizing idea or story line that provides meaning to an unfolding strip of events, weaving a connection among them" (p. 143). Frames are particularly important given that politics is multifaceted and public policy at times abstract. Multiple considerations about an issue exist, and a frame emphasizes one (or more) of them. They suggest how political issues should be thought about, allowing citizens to understand them by creating a sensible narrative that conforms to established habits of mind (Berinsky & Kinder, 2006). Frames include the language and expressions politicians use to develop their positions. These ideas are a good start, but they do not nail down exactly how one would identify a frame, or understand its effects compared to some alternative.[1] Significant theoretical development over the last decade has thus been quite helpful.

Druckman (2001b) identifies an important distinction between *equivalency* and *emphasis* frames. Equivalency frames are messages that present information in logically equivalent ways but nonetheless lead to changes in preferences over policy alternatives. The effects of such frames are most easily recognized in Tversky and Kahneman's (1981) groundbreaking discoveries regarding the asymmetric effects of describing a policy in terms of *losses versus gains*. When a policy choice is described in terms of gains (200 out of 600 people suffering from a disease will be saved versus a two-thirds chance that no one will be saved), people overwhelmingly prefer the sure (first) alternative. When the same policy choice is described in terms of losses (400 out of 600 people will die versus a one-third chance no one will die), people prefer the risky (second) alternative. This psychological bias for taking risks to avoid losses but avoiding risk to secure gains can trigger large opinion shifts. Since it was framed as necessary to prevent future losses, an expensive and risky policy such as the invasion of Iraq in 2003 might have received more support than if it would have were framed as a way to secure gains already achieved.

Equivalency framing effects demonstrate an important way in which political communication can lead citizens to violate one of the basic tenets of rational decision-making—the invariance of logically equivalent alternatives. If people do not have stable preferences over competing policies, as Downs's (1957) economic theory of democracy demands, constructing a government that effectively translates majority preferences into policies is impossible (Bartels, 2003).

The other common usage of media framing refers to the effects of changing the set considerations relevant to a given issue—what Druckman (2001b) dubs *emphasis* frames. When the debate over illegal immigration hinges on cultural threats posed by newcomers, we might expect different mass opinions than when the focus is on the benefits of low-wage labor for consumer prices. In the most straightforward case, framing effects mean that opinion on immigration that is driven by a negative consideration (cultural threats) is replaced with one on which many are favorable (lower prices). Politics, it seems, is often framed by elites in terms of the large social groups in conflict over rights and resources (Nelson & Kinder, 1996), and this is consistent with the finding that most citizens organize politics according to their ideas about group interests rather than more abstract ideological values (Converse, 1964). Media framing has been shown to move opinions about government spending (Jacoby, 2000), social welfare (Gilens, 1999), affirmative action (Kinder & Sanders, 1996), foreign affairs (Berinsky & Kinder, 2006), crime (Iyengar, 1991), and many other issues.

So how, psychologically speaking, does framing work? It works in a way quite similar to media priming, many theorists believe. By explaining events one way or another, the media affects the public's understanding of the issue by automatically altering the mix of considerations that are accessible in the mind (Iyengar, 1991; Gamson & Modigliani, 1987). When public affairs news highlights elites who describe the problem of terrorism as caused by a small number of violent foreigners motivated by hatred, it can strongly shape the policy responses an individual would support in dealing with the threat. On the other hand, if the news identifies the economic and structural factors in the United States and in other countries that lead people to consider violent acts, different policy solutions might become viable. Media framing, therefore, helps to define the set of appropriate policy solutions in much the same way that media priming helps to determine which issues are salient when candidates are evaluated.

Iyengar (1991) investigated the possibility that alternate news frames for an identical act of terrorism might bring about changes in attributions of responsibility for the problem simply by making individual (*episodic*) versus societal (*thematic*) causes salient. Episodic news frames take the form of a case study or event-oriented report and portray social issues in terms of concrete instances (e.g., an actual terrorist). Thematic frames place public issues in more broad and abstract circumstances (e.g., terrorism as a whole). When subjects read stories about terrorism as a broad sociopolitical phenomenon, respondents were more likely to ascribe wider social explanations for its causes, and thus favored systemic solutions. For those exposed to news stories that focused on individual cases of terrorism and the terrorists themselves, respondents were more likely to blame individuals and support harsh punishments. As a result, journalistic workways that favor episodic coverage may inadvertently lead citizens to shift blame away from the political institutions and elected officials for social problems.

Price and Tewksbury (1997) offer a different psychological account of framing effect. While media priming effects are driven by changes in the automatic accessibility of specific information, framing effects may represent changes in the *applicability* of that information to explanations of social problems in the news. This is a much more conscious and deliberative process, and would suggest framing is a very different psychological process than priming. This view is consistent with the emphasis framing effects discovered by Nelson, Clawson, and Oxley (1997). They explore how the framing of a Klu Klux Klan group impacted support for the group's right to hold a rally. Participants were exposed to local news broadcasts that framed the rally either in terms of the group's free speech rights or as a risk to public safety. The perceived importance of free speech versus public safety, not the cognitive accessibility of these values, mediated the effect of the frame. Those randomly assigned to read a frame emphasizing the free speech consequences of banning the group considered free speech more important, and were more likely to permit the rally. Those who read about the rally's threat to public order rated that criterion more important and were less willing to accept the rally.

There remain few studies exploring whether priming and framing effects are driven by distinct psychological processes. We think this is an area that would benefit from additional examination. Our suspicion, however, coincides with the motivated reasoning theory presented by Lodge & Taber (2013): A substantial proportion of reactions to new information occurs automatically, outside awareness. Before we are even aware of how new information is present in our environment, our mind is at work applying cognitive biases that influence its perception, encoding, and application. The provocative conjecture provided by motivated reasoning theory is that what we think of as political deliberation is mostly the post hoc rationalization of preconscious evaluations.

Recent work explores the individual and contextual conditions that moderate the power of frames. First, source credibility boosts the impact of frames (Druckman, 2001a). Prior beliefs, motivation, and expertise also seem important. When confronted with a weak frame, highly motivated citizens may even move in the opposite direction, consistent with the *contrast* effects identified previously (Sherif & Hovland, 1965; Eagly & Chaiken, 1993; Shah, Watts, Domke, & Fan, 2002). Druckman and Nelson (2003) find that regardless of political knowledge, a person who already possesses strong political beliefs less is affected by new information from media frames, possibly because the individual is motivated to defend long-held views. Druckman (2004) offers the fullest theoretical account to date, experimentally demonstrating the moderating impact of deliberation, expertise, and elite competition on the impact of media frames. In general, as these variables increase, the effects of elite frames decline. While these findings of resistance to frames may be encouraging, they are also in line with the information-processing biases discussed above: As motivated reasoners, citizens may sometimes reject new information even when it is accurate and helpful.

4. Political Communication and Learning

Americans seem to carry around less concrete factual information about public affairs than similarly situated citizens of other Western democracies. Dimock and Popkin (1997), for example, find that college-educated Americans are less likely to even know the names of important political figures than non-college-educated citizens of European countries. Delli Carpini and Keeter (1996) searched hundreds of survey items and concluded that some Americans know a lot about many topics, many do not know very much at all, but most seem to grasp at least a few basic truths about issues of importance to them. This vindicates earlier intuitions by Key (1961) and Dahl (1989) that democratic citizens do seem to be able to manage, perhaps just barely, to learn what they need to know in order to hold elected officials accountable. One solution to the problem of low general levels of knowledge is that the voting "errors" of the uninformed might, on any given issue, cancel each other out, leaving more informed citizens to guide the polity in a more or less rational (i.e., majoritarian) way (Page & Shapiro, 1992). The $24,000 question, then, is not *how much* but *what* exactly do we really need to know to keep our democracy functioning (Druckman, 2005a)?

4.1. Democratic Importance of Political Knowledge

To put the point most severely, given most citizens' quite limited time, capacity, and motivation to engage in politics (Simon, 1979), one might wonder how a healthy, fully functioning democracy could exist at all. How much hard political knowledge is actually required to hold elected officials accountable? On the one hand, citizens seem to need very little specific policy information in order to choose elected officials who will best represent their interests in government (Lupia, 1994; Lupia & McCubbins, 1998). Using a field experiment, Arceneaux and Kolodny (2009) verify Lupia's (1994) observational finding: Group endorsements act as powerful heuristics for the least informed. Information shortcuts, in other words, lead the least politically informed citizens to approximate the voting fidelity of their more sophisticated compatriots. Note also that the impression-driven model of candidate evaluation, discussed above, suggests a different sort of shortcut—the summary of all the affective tags relevant to a given object— is all that is needed to make satisfactory decisions.

On the other hand there seems to be little doubt that holding substantive information about issues changes policy opinions in line with the normative expectations of democratic theory. Holding socioeconomic and political characteristics of the voter constant, increasing substantive knowledge changes policy and candidate preferences quite dramatically (Bartels, 1996; Althaus, 1998; Gilens, 2001). An even more dramatic intervention into people's lives, bringing them together in person to deliberate with other citizens about important issues of the day, seems to produce substantial increases in knowledge and shifts in issue preferences that are at least arguably enhanced in quality (Farrar et al., 2010).

4.2. News Media and Knowledge Acquisition

Regardless of exactly how much factual knowledge is necessary to hold democratically elected officials accountable, we need to know whether the media help or hinder the citizenry's ability to become informed. Survey research has long found positive correlations between self-reported exposure to news via a variety of media, especially newspapers, and political knowledge (Chaffee, Ward, & Tipton, 1970). Clarke and Fredin's (1978) analysis of 67 news markets suggests that a decrease in newspaper readership, coupled with an increase in television news viewership, lessens people's comprehension of political candidates. A longitudinal study of adults and adolescents found that for both age groups, newspaper exposure was correlated with knowledge of various general news topics more strongly than television exposure (Chaffee & Schleuder, 1986). Television news is a rather weak but positive predictor of long-term information gain, while newspaper reading is typically stronger (McLeod & McDonald, 1985; Robinson & Levy, 1996). A recent study using panel data (Eveland, Hayes, Shah, & Kwak, 2005) found evidence consistent with the causal impact of news consumption on political knowledge. Taken all together, self-reported exposure to substantive public affairs news content, especially via newspapers but even via television and the Internet, is significantly correlated with political knowledge (Zhao & Chaffee, 1995; Robinson & Levy, 1996; Druckman, 2005b; Eveland et al., 2005).

Unfortunately, these correlations are not clear evidence of the causal impact of media on political knowledge. First, much of what people know at the end of the campaign they knew at the beginning, such that only very distinctive campaign messages are likely to produce significant effects (Bartels, 1993). Second, correlations between self-reported exposure to news and political knowledge could be the result of the reverse causal process: prior knowledge might cause people to consume news in the first place (Price & Zaller, 1993). Alternatively, knowledge and news consumption might both be caused by some third variable (such as interest in politics). In a series of telephone survey experiments, Prior (2009) revealed that inflated self-reports are caused by estimations based on imperfect recall and the use of flawed inference rules. By comparing responses with Nielsen ratings, he finds that on average, self-reported exposure may be triple the true value, and in young people as much as eight times as high. Prior suggests that survey questions should assist respondents in estimation, by providing information on audience size and encouraging them to consider the viewing practices of others.

While new media might complicate our efforts at measuring exposure, technology can also help. Sophisticated analyses of program content can lead to more accurate predictions about the impact of exposure on knowledge. Linking survey data to media market records of political advertising has been particularly useful for estimating exposure to television advertisements (Goldstein & Freedman, 2002). Shaw (1999), for example, used information on television ad purchases acquired from campaigns themselves. Campaign advertising can also be measured using Gross Rating Points (GRPs), which measure the percentage of households viewing a show on which an advertisement appeared (Huber & Arceneaux, 2007). A study by Ridout, Shah, Goldstein, and Franz (2004) also measured campaign advertising exposure in six different ways and found that a multimethod approach—a measure combining ads broadcast in a market plus self-reported television viewing habits—fared better than self-reports, total ads in a market, program measures, and a daypart (i.e., time of day) measure.

Of course it is important to remember that the accountability function of news media in a democracy—which Lasswell (1948) spoke of—can only be achieved if the news represent the world in a more or less unbiased way. Concern about this message factor—the ability and incentives of journalists to present to citizens an unbiased social and political reality—was raised by Lippmann (1922), but remains understudied according to some scholars (Althaus et al., 2011). Content analyses have pointed out, however, that powerful biases exist in the production of news, including a strong overrepresentation of criticism, and underrepresentation of praise, of a sitting president by his own party (Groeling & Baum, 2009) and the overrepresentation of African Americans in news stories about poverty (Gilens, 1999) and crime (Dixon & Linz, 2000). These biases make learning "facts" directly from the media less tenable, and they also lead to powerful framing and priming effects, as we will see below.

Further, given that people are sometimes motivated to defend their existing beliefs in the face of contradictory information (Kunda, 1990), even objective facts can be rejected by those with powerful directional motivations, for example, the strongest partisans (Bartels 2002). Groenendyk (2012) found that when strong partisans receive information that contradicts their beliefs about their party, they do not simply shift their identity toward the other party. Instead, they defend their identity by denigrating the out-party, leaving them in the same position in terms of their relative preference for the parties as before the information came in. This directional motivation also seems stronger among the strongest partisans. This can lead to some ironic consequences from the perspective of democratic theory. Those who care most about politics, and who are motivated to expose themselves to new information, might also be most resistant to substantive information that could potentially help them "get it right" when it comes to the endorsement of policies and candidates that represent their interests (but see Arceneaux, 2008, for an interesting counterargument).

4.3. Knowledge and Advertising

Observers have long been skeptical of political advertising as a conduit of useful information in a democracy (McGinnis, 1969). It is often assumed, but rarely observed systematically, that advertising is devoid of information that would help citizens learn what they need to know in order to make reasonable choices about their representation in government. Some early voices noted the possibility that ads might provide relevant information in an easily digestible and memorable form to the average citizen (Patterson & McClure, 1976). In fact, several studies have shown the journalistic and popular concern about the vacuous nature of political advertising to be unfounded. Content analyses suggest most advertisements focus on substantive issues (Joslyn, 1980; West, 2013). Experimental and observational studies come to similar positive conclusions about the informative power of political advertising (Zhao & Chaffee, 1995; Ansolabehere & Iyengar, 1995; Wattenberg & Brians, 1999; Valentino, Hutchings, & Williams, 2004).

4.4. Online News and Political Knowledge

Are recent advances in media technology—increasing numbers of cable news outlets, social media websites, cellular telephony, Internet political blogs—likely to enhance or depress citizen knowledge? We might begin thinking about the answer simply by describing some of the changes wrought in the structure, amount, and quality of information in the new media environment. On the one hand, cable news and the Internet drastically increase the round-the-clock availability of political information and outlets for discussion at most citizens' fingertips (Neuman, 2000; Graber, 1984; Davis, 1999). Enhancing quantity and access make acquiring information much easier, especially for those with time and money (Prior & Lupia, 2008). This perhaps complicates theories about what knowledge citizens need to carry around in their heads in order to hold elected officials accountable.

The emergence of popular "infotainment" hybrids such as the *Daily Show* and *The Colbert Report* has also led to a flood of new research. One argument suggests that the rise of "soft news" multiplies exposure opportunities for many citizens, because it attracts folks who are not interested in politics (Baum, 2003). War-related human-interest stories on shows like *Inside Edition* and *Entertainment Tonight* seemed to boost public attentiveness to US foreign policy, particularly among the less educated and less interested in public affairs to begin with. So again, we have individual differences in motivation moderating the impact of mass media. These new forms of media content may also produce agenda-setting and priming effects. Crime dramas increase crime-related concerns and prime criminal justice attitudes during evaluations of presidential performance (Holbrook & Hill, 2005).

Empirically speaking, the first elections of the Internet age saw tentative use of the medium for information dissemination but did not take full advantage of the medium's interactive functionality (Bimber & Davis, 2003). Official websites maintained by members of the US House of Representatives in 1996 and 2001 were even less interactive than those of their campaigns, and simply provided more detailed information about issue positions and committee work (Jarvis & Wilkerson, 2005). Deuze (2003), however, found that online news sites have begun to take advantage of the innovations of the World Wide Web such as interactivity, user feedback, and hypertextuality characterized by links to supporting documentation. By 2004, politicians began to use the full functionality of the new technology. Howard Dean's 2004 Democratic primary campaign facilitated communication among supporters and also provided a user-friendly interface for donations and campaign volunteering (Trippi, 2004), an approach Barack Obama's 2008 presidential campaign capitalized upon and expanded. It is now difficult to imagine even local campaign staffs without web-management personnel.

The structural features of the online information environment have led to some perhaps optimistic speculation about enhancing citizen knowledge. If information online is organized and hyperlinked in ways that are similar to the semantic network structure of human memory, won't citizens be more likely to remember political information encountered there? Alas, the answer seems to be no: Eveland and Dunwoody's (2001) rigorous experimental tests suggest people learn more facts from the old-fashioned print news. Tewksbury and Althaus (2000) make precise comparisons between users of the *New York Times* online versus print and corroborate the superiority of the latter. They speculate that the online version of the news provides fewer cues about the relative importance of various stories on a given day because more headlines can fit on the "front page" of a news website. In addition, online news outlets are designed to enhance the reader's control, permitting a variety of motivations to impact the exposure process. In other words, the flexibility and interactivity of new media technologies might lead fundamental biases of human information processing to have a greater impact.

Prior (2007) provides another example of how changing media technology can interact with mass-level variation in psychological dimensions such as interest and attention. He examines the impact of changing media institutions on knowledge of public affairs and electoral participation, and draws a conclusion much less optimistic than Baum (2003), discussed above. When three major broadcast networks dominated US television, a heterogeneous audience was exposed to homogeneous content: the national nightly news. This system reduced the disparities in knowledge and turnout between the most and least educated citizens. The proliferation of cable entertainment television (and more recently, Internet blogs and news outlets) boosted choice. This allowed politically motivated citizens to seek out *more* news than they had previously, while others were be able to avoid news altogether. Media choice, then, can boost knowledge gaps between the least and most interested citizens.

5. POLITICAL COMMUNICATION AND ATTITUDE CHANGE

The preceding discussions about media impacts on attention and learning are important in their own right, but many would insist that to influence politics, media messages must alter attitudes and political behavior. Recall, however, that evidence for the direct effects of media on such outcomes is scarce. The debate about when and how media messages influence political attitudes has revolved around more direct, memory-based models (Zaller, 1992) versus less deliberative, online decision-making (Lodge, McGraw, & Stroh, 1989; Lodge, Steenbergen, & Brau, 1995). Taber and Young's chapter (chapter 17) in this volume provides a useful review of concepts fundamental to this discussion, especially involving the architecture of human memory.

Zaller (1992) offers the Receive Accept Sample (RAS) model of public opinion formation that is based on a few simple axioms, drawing on earlier insights from Converse (1962) and McGuire (1968). First, people arrive at their views on issues at any given moment by sampling across all the relevant considerations they hold in their memory. This *sampling* axiom is identical to the priming process discussed above, and insists that considerations most recently or frequently accessed be brought to bear more readily on current decisions. Second, people will be more likely to *receive* a new message if they are interested in politics in the first place. This second assumption explicitly incorporates ideas about motivation into the attitude change process—those at the high end of attentiveness will be much more likely to receive new information that contradicts their views. But according to the third *(acceptance)* axiom, these citizens will also be better armed at rebutting such messages because they maintain a more impressive arsenal of defensive arguments. Those who are lowest in political motivation are most vulnerable to attitude change but are least likely to be exposed to new information in the first place because they are not interested. The model thus predicts that those in the *middle* of the distribution of motivation will often display the largest shifts in attitude as a result of exposure to new information, because they are more likely than the least motivated to be exposed, but not as likely as the most motivated to counterargue. Empirically, the model seems to be able to explain a variety of puzzles, including the changing distribution of opposition over time to the Vietnam War and the incumbency advantage in Congress.

Another possibility is that a different media effects process occurs for less politically informed and sophisticated citizens. Lodge and his colleagues (Lodge et al., 1989; Lodge, Steenbergen, & Brau, 1995) offer an "impression driven" model of opinion formation that differs from Zaller's in several important ways. First, they note that most citizens, most of the time, do not have even a concrete set of considerations that can be sampled from memory and then brought to bear on political decisions of the day. Upon reflection, people might be able to come up with concrete reasons for choosing one candidate or another, or one policy over another, but these are only post hoc rationalizations for the outcome of a nearly information-free mental process. The "impression driven" model of decision-making leans heavily on online psychological decision-making models offered by Hastie and Park (1986). The online model is a heuristic process whereby the individual maintains a running tally of affective tags associated with events from the past. These tags cumulate, with some negative and some positive, adding up to a general impression associated with a given candidate or policy. In the voting booth, the individual does not need to recall all relevant information but is still able to do better than using only the most frequently or recently activated considerations from memory, as Zaller's model supposed. Recalling the running tally is all that is necessary.

The media environment is filled with heuristics that might influence the opinions of those who are paying only peripheral attention to the political world. For example, even the dissemination of information about public opinion itself can sway individual views (Mutz, 1998). The rise of scientific polling based on random samples in the second half of the 20th century led to a dramatic rise in news media reliance on polling to measure opinions about a wide range of important issues both in the United States and around the world (Herbst, 1993). Media were drawn to this information because it fit their demand for "objective" political facts (Patterson, 1993). When credible and accurate information about public opinion became available to the masses, however, some theorists predicted that this information might trigger an unhealthy spiral of opinion "bandwagons." Once an opinion majority was established, those in the minority would keep quiet out of a fear of social isolation and those in the middle would feel social pressure to be on the winning side (Noelle-Neumann, 1974). This would lead to even more pressure for the minority to shut up and thus be shut out of policy compromises. During primaries, this motivation to be on the popular side could manifest in what is commonly known as "electoral momentum" (Bartels, 1988), whereby a marginal advantage in early polling leads to increased coverage, fundraising and primary victories, thus prematurely short-circuiting a careful and deliberate candidate vetting process.

Once again, the story seems to be more complicated. Under some circumstances, people hold fast to their minority view—a phenomenon referred to as an "underdog" or "boomerang" effect (Mutz, 1998). Vivid examples of this in contemporary American politics are abundant, from the resilient minority views of the Tea Party to support for candidates like Michelle Bachmann who have little chance of success. Mutz (1998) employs insights from the *cognitive response model* to predict that, as with the dual-process models discussed at the outset, the effect of information about the public's views differs with political involvement. This model posits a strong role for motivation as a moderator of reactions to information about public opinion. Politically involved, knowledgeable citizens will tend to view public opinion as a weak reason to change their minds and will react to such news by rehearsing justifications for their previous view. Those least interested in politics, having fewer counterarguments ready, tend to be influenced in the direction of the majority. This set of findings is representative of much of the work reviewed so far: The intrinsic motivation to engage with politics significantly moderates the impact of media messages.

How do changes in media content fit into these models of opinion formation? One interesting development is the rise of explicitly comedic programming that involves politics. In the United States, political humor can take the form of late-night comedic talk shows such as *The Late Show with David Letterman* and satirical news shows such as *The Daily Show with Jon Stewart* and *The Colbert Report*. The former have arguably stepped away from a pure comedic role and now tend to be more political than late-night comedy, which tends to focus narrowly on presidential candidates (Niven, Lichter, & Amundson, 2003). In a 2005 sample of *The Daily Show* content, more than half addressed political topics (Brewer & Marquardt, 2007). These new media forms may lend themselves to persuasion via the peripheral, low-motivation route described by the Elaboration Likelihood Model (ELM, Petty & Cacciopo, 1986). Some tantalizing empirical evidence has begun to emerge suggesting this may in fact be the case (Nabi, MoyerGuse, & Byrne, 2007; Baumgartner, 2007; Young, 2008; Polk, Young, & Holbert, 2009). Even completely nonpolitical content can have political effects: exposure to certain dramas and sitcoms may reinforce the relationship between sexism and opinions about women's rights (Holbert, Shah, & Kwak, 2003).

6. COMMUNICATION AND POLITICAL ACTION

Last we will review work on the relationship between mass communication and participation in the political sphere. Theoretical explanations of participation traditionally do not explore the impact of mass media exposure (Wolfinger & Rosenstone,

1980), or they do not find much evidence of a relationship when they look for one (Verba, Scholzman, & Brady, 1995; Rosenstone & Hansen, 1993). On the other hand, elite communication—citizen contacting by party representatives (Eldersveld, 1956; Rosenstone & Hansen, 1993) or direct personal canvassing (Gerber & Green, 2000)— boosts turnout quite substantially. These models focus on long-term material resources and skills that help people overcome obstacles to participation. They also include stable motivational factors such as civic duty, civic engagement, trust, and efficacy toward the political system that help explain why rational citizens turn out even when the chance that action will be decisive is vanishingly small (Riker & Ordeshook, 1968). One possible route of influence entertained by a substantial number of communication scholars focuses on the presumed causal linkage between media use and these motivational factors.

A strong positive relationship exists between public affairs consumption and civic engagement, while overall television viewing is often negatively correlated with such outcomes (Putnam, 2000; Shah, 1998). With regard to Internet use, social and recreational uses are negatively related to social trust and civic engagement (Shah, Kwak, & Holbert, 2001). A more recent study of youth by Romer, Jamieson, and Pasek (2009) found that television consumption is inversely related to trust and civic engagement, suggesting perhaps that civic engagement enhances trust by reducing time spent with television.

A great deal of attention has focused on whether campaign advertising mobilizes or demobilizes political participation. Pundits, commentators, and candidates themselves had long bemoaned negativity in politics, and polls suggest the American people do not like it either. The concern was that campaign negativity was on the rise (West, 2013) and it might sour mass attitudes toward the political system itself, undermining the motivation to pay attention, learn about politics, and get involved before and on Election Day (Jamieson, 1992). Changing workways of campaign journalism, stimulated by changing primary rules that favored individual candidate image over party platforms (Patterson, 1993) led to dramatic increases in the portrayal of political actors as strategic, cynical, and selfish, and these portrayals were then blamed for increases in cynicism about and distrust of public officials (Cappella & Jamieson, 1997).

An impressive set of controlled experiments run by Ansolabehere, Iyengar, and their colleagues tested the demobilization hypothesis and found negative advertising to be powerfully demobilizing, especially among nonpartisans (Ansolabehere, Iyengar, Simon, & Valentino, 1994; Ansolabehere & Iyengar, 1995). The presumed causal mechanism was that negative ads undermined internal efficacy or perceived government responsiveness to average citizens. The key advantage to these studies was their internal validity: The manipulations used the same narration and images, changing only a few words so that the advertisement criticized the opponent rather than promoted the sponsor. The results bolstered the conventional wisdom about the potential dangers of excessive negativity in politics, and prompted a large wave of follow-on studies.

Subsequent tests of the demobilization hypothesis, however, came to a very different conclusion: Negativity often seemed to *enhance* engagement and participation rather than depress it, perhaps because it was more memorable (Wattenberg & Brians, 1999; Finkel & Geer, 1988; Freedman & Goldstein, 1999; Goldstein & Freedman, 2002). In addition, negative advertisements seem to have more concrete policy information—presumably the type of information that citizens need to differentiate between elected officials and thus hold them accountable (Garramone, Atkin, Pinkleton, & Cole, 1990; Geer, 2006).

Finally, negative information can powerfully boost the short-term motivation to participate by generating negative emotions (Valentino, Brader, Groenendyk, Gregorowicz, & Hutchings, 2011). Some early work suggested both anxiety and anger could be powerfully mobilizing, perhaps because threats quite automatically break citizens out of their normal cognitive routines and trigger increased vigilance to new information (Marcus et al., 2000; Brader, 2006; Valentino et al. 2008). Later work, drawing on the expectations of cognitive appraisal theories of emotion, predicted anger and anxiety might have very different consequences for participation (Valentino et al., 2011). Anxiety, it was found, mobilized low-cost, expressive acts like talking with others about politics. Higher-risk, costly participatory acts like donating money and attending rallies seemed to require the combination of anger and resources. Brader and Marcus (chapter 6, this volume) review research on a wide range of political implications of emotion.

Meta-analyses of accumulated findings in 1999 and 2007 both concluded that, on average, negative advertisements have very little if any net effect on participation, either up or down (Lau, Sigelman, Heldman, & Babbitt, 1999; Lau, Sigelman, & Rovner, 2007). These general findings would seem to put the nail in the coffin of a several-decade-old debate over the effects of campaign negativity on political action. Not so fast, argues Krupnikov (2011). Her theory suggests both sets of findings may be entirely correct: The impact of negativity during campaigns may depend on when it appears. Before people make up their minds, negativity might have exactly the kinds of effects those who tout its benefits predict: It will boost the intention to participate by providing critical information that can help people discriminate between candidates. After their minds are made up, however, negativity tends to demobilize by discouraging people about the potential benefits of their preferred candidate. In other words, once a choice is made, the media environment tends to influence the motivation to act on that choice, not on revising the decision. Once the previous studies were disaggregated by when during the campaign they took place, the null result disappeared and a clearer relationship between negativity and participation came into focus.

Recent scholarship has also explored the potential impact of new media technology on civic engagement, volunteering, and collective action. Valenzuela, Park, and Kee (2009) find a positive—albeit small—correlation between the use of social networking sites like Facebook and trust, civic engagement, and political participation. Nondemocratic governments attempt to maintain power via strict control over communication media, including online social networking. Indeed, public protest against authoritarian regimes may be powerfully catalyzed by the simple knowledge of the popularity of antiregime viewpoints (Kuran, 1991; Lohmann, 1994). Popular uprisings across the Maghreb and into the Middle East in 2011 led many pundits to speculate about the power of the social media. That the social media were *conveying* important information between protestors is beyond dispute; it is only the causal impact of this information on the success or failure of movements that is still unclear. What is clear is that the government of Egypt decided to launch a coordinated effort to staunch the flow of point-to-point communication via cell phones and social networking Internet sites on January 27, 2011. The blackout was temporary, but revealed the regime's concern about unfettered communication networks. It would seem plausible that knowledge of others' willingness to participate in risky public demonstrations may help individuals overcome their reluctance to attend. Klandermans and van Stekelenburg (chapter 24, this volume) review research on collection action in greater detail. They suggest that media information may provide a source of identification, grievances, and self-efficacy, all of which in turn drive collection action. The role of social media on large-scale movements is therefore likely to be indirect, but not insignificant.

7. CONCLUSIONS

One of the goals of any review of political communication should be a thorough understanding of the effects that *matter*. The focus on psychological theories of cognition and attitude change, while interesting, may not seem critical to most macrotheories of politics. They do not seem to help us explain why, for example, some democracies thrive while others do not, why a protest movement succeeds or fails, or why a government chooses to commit genocide against its own citizens. This charge is a tough one, and political psychology has some way to go before it can bridge these gaps in scope of the dependent phenomena (policy attitudes versus policy outcomes), units of analyses (individual decision-makers versus nations), and theoretical breadth (single electoral outcomes versus the long-term survival of regimes).

What democratic citizens need to pay attention to, know, feel, and do in order to hold their elected officials accountable is of fundamental theoretical and normative importance. The evidence we have reviewed suggests media have a role to play. Macroscopic but well-defined changes in patterns of news coverage of social welfare are clearly linked to support for basic programs that affect the lived conditions of millions of our fellow citizens (Gilens, 1999). Changes in media institutions over the past 30 years seem to exacerbate gaps in knowledge and participation based on socioeconomic status and engagement (Prior, 2007). The focus on emotion as a potential mechanism that carries the effect of political communication on political action has led us to better insights about why some Americans—those who feel threatened but not anxious—might trade freedom for security in response to terrorist threats while others—those who just feel anxious—would not (Huddy, Feldman, Tabler, Lahav, 2005). We now know more about how and why negativity in campaigns may mobilize citizens and improve their decisions at some moments, but demobilize and discourage them at others (Krupnikov, 2011). These breakthroughs should be of interest to many political scientists outside the subfield of political psychology. They are focused on the causal mechanisms that drive individual behaviors that, when aggregated, weave the fabric of politics writ large.

Viewed from above, the vast and yet rapidly burgeoning literature on the effects of political communication is tied together with an important thread. The motivation to hold accurate beliefs and *also* to defend existing attitudes plays a consistent and very large role in who is exposed to communication in the first place, who learns from it, who changes his or her mind, and who participates as a result. One question that jumps to mind, then, is "Where does individual variation in these motivations come from?" Why are some people so interested in public affairs and others not at all? In the last decade we have begun to understand the causal antecedents of short-term fluctuations in interest and political engagement. This may well be the largest and most reliable contribution to date of the research in our field deploying psychological theories of emotion (Marcus et al., 2000; Brader, 2006; Huddy, Feldman, & Cassese, 2007). Perhaps most of the variation in this critical moderating variable, however, springs from much deeper and more stable roots in childhood (Prior, 2010) or even genetics (Alford, Funk, & Hibbing, 2005). Funk (chapter 8, this volume) reviews the literature on the role of genetic predispositions as predictors of political attitudes and behaviors. Personality has also come back into vogue as an area of inquiry in political psychology. Gerber et al. (2011) find strong correlations between some of the Big Five personality dimensions of extraversion and emotional stability and political participation. The speculation here is that stable personality traits may explain variation in long-term motivations to learn more about politics, participate, and defend ones' partisan views against new and potentially challenging information. A more thorough understanding of the variation in trait-level political interest and other individual-level motivational factors, therefore, is critical.

While we continue to move toward results of general relevance to other subfields, we should also take pride in our commitment to achieving a truly scientific discipline. Political psychology utilizes rigorous observational and experimental methods, provides consistent innovation in the conceptualization and measurement of important concepts, and takes replication seriously. This is the only way to make progress answering important questions, solving empirical puzzles, and testing causal claims. These advances, we hope, would please Simon, Lippmann, Lasswell, Lazarsfeld, Hovland, Klapper, and the other pioneers of our field.

ACKNOWLEDGMENT

The authors would like to thank Donald Kinder and Leonie Huddy for their excellent advice on this chapter.

Notes

1. Other chapters in this publication (Chong, chapter 4; Kinder, chapter 25) provide additional detailed discussions of framing.

References

Alford, J. R., Funk, C. L., & Hibbing, J. R. Are political orientations genetically transmitted? *American Political Science Review, 99*, 1–15.

Althaus, S. L. (1998). Information effects in collective preferences. *American Political Science Review, 92*, 545–558.

Althaus, S. L., Swigger, N., Chernykh, S., Hendry, D. J., Wals, S. C., & Tiwald, C. (2011). Assumed transmission in political science: A call for bringing description back in. *Journal of Politics, 73*, 1065–1080.

Anderson, J. R. (1983). *The architecture of cognition.* Cambridge, MA: Harvard University Press.

Ansolabehere, S. D., & Iyengar, S. (1995). *Going negative: How political advertising shrinks and polarizes the electorate.* New York: Free Press.

Ansolabehere, S. D., Iyengar, S., Simon, A., & Valentino, N. (1994). Does attack advertising demobilize the electorate? *American Political Science Review, 88*, 829–838.

Arceneaux, K. (2008). Can partisan cues diminish accountability? *Political Behavior, 30*, 139–160.

Arceneaux, K., & Kolodny, R. (2009). Educating the least informed: Group endorsements in a grassroots campaign. *American Journal of Political Science, 53*, 755–770.

Bargh, J. A., & Ferguson, M. L. (2000). Beyond behaviorism: On the automaticity of higher mental processes. *Psychological Bulletin, 126*, 925–945.

Bargh, J. A., & Pietromonaco, P. (1982). Automatic information processing and social perception: The influence of trait information presented outside of conscious awareness on impression formation. *Journal of Personality and Social Psychology, 55*, 1173–1182.

Bartels, L. M. (1988). *Presidential primaries and the dynamics of public choice.* Princeton, NJ: Princeton University Press.

Bartels, L. M. (1993). Messages received: The political impact of media exposure. *American Political Science Review, 87*, 267–285.

Bartels, L. M. (1996). Uninformed votes: Information effects in presidential elections. *American Journal of Political Science, 40*, 194–230.

Bartels, L. M. (2002). Beyond the running tally: Partisan bias in political perceptions. *Political Behavior, 24*(2), 117–150.

Bartels, L. M. (2003). Democracy with attitudes. In M. MacKuen & G. Rabinowitz (eds.), *Essays in honor of Philip Converse* (pp. 48–82). Ann Arbor: University of Michigan Press.

Baum, M. A. (2003). *Soft news goes to war: Public opinion and American foreign policy in the new media age.* Princeton, NJ. Princeton University Press.

Baumgartner, J. C. (2007). Humor on the next frontier: Online political humor and its effects on youth. *Social Science Computer Review, 29*, 319–338.

Behr, R. L., & Iyengar, S. (1985). Television news, real-world cues, and changes in the public agenda. *Public Opinion Quarterly, 49*, 38–57.

Bennett, W. L., & Iyengar, S. (2008). A new era of minimal effects? The changing foundations of political communication. *Journal of Communication, 58*, 707–731.

Berelson, B., Lazarsfeld, P., & McPhee, W. N. (1954). *Voting: A study of opinion formation in a presidential election*. Chicago: University of Chicago Press.

Berinsky, A. J., & Kinder, D. R. (2006). Making sense of issues through frames: Understanding the Kosovo crisis. *Journal of Politics, 68*, 640–656.

Bimber, B. A., & Davis, R. (2003). *Campaigning online: The Internet in U.S. elections.* Oxford: Oxford University Press.

Blumenthal, S. (1982). *The permanent campaign.* New York: Simon & Schuster.

Brader, T. (2006) *Campaigning for hearts and minds.* Chicago: University of Chicago Press.

Brewer, P. R., & Marquardt, E. (2007). Mock news and democracy: Analyzing *The Daily Show. Atlantic Journal of Communication, 15*, 249–267.

Cappella, J. N., & Jamieson, K. H. (1997). *Spiral of cynicism: The press and the public good.* New York: Oxford University Press.

Chaffee, S. H., & Miyo, Y. (1983). Selective exposure and the reinforcement hypothesis. *Communication Research, 10*, 3–36.

Chaffee, S. H., & Schleuder, J. (1986). Measurement and effects of attention to media news. *Human Communication Research, 13*, 76–107.

Chaffee, S. H., Ward, L. S., & Tipton, L. P. (1970). Mass communication and political socialization. *Journalism Quarterly, 57*, 647–659.

Chaiken, S. (1980). Heuristic versus systematic information processing and the use of source versus message cues in persuasion. *Journal of Personality and Social Psychology, 39*, 752–766.

Chaiken, S., & Eagly, A. H. (1976). Communication modality as a determinant of message persuasiveness and message comprehensibility. *Journal of Personality and Social Psychology, 34*, 605–614.

Cialdini, R. B., & Goldstein, N. (2004). Social influence: Compliance & conformity. *Annual Review of Psychology, 55*, 591–621.

Clarke, P., & Fredin, E. (1978). Newspapers, television and political reasoning. *Public Opinion Quarterly, 42*, 143–160.

Cohen, B. (1963). *The press and foreign policy.* Princeton, NJ: Princeton University Press.

Collins, A., & Loftus, E. (1975). A spreading-activation theory of semantic memory. *Psychological Review, 82*, 407–428.

Converse, P. E. (1962). Information flow and the stability of partisan attitudes. *Public Opinion Quarterly, 26*, 578–599.

Converse, P. E. (1964). The nature of belief systems in mass publics. In D. E. Apter (ed.), *Ideology and discontent* (pp. 206–261). New York: Free Press.

Dahl, R. A. (1989). *Democracy and its critics.* New Haven, CT: Yale University Press.

Davis, R. (1999). *The web of politics.* Oxford: Oxford University Press.

Davison, W. P. (1983). The third person effect in communication. *Public Opinion Quarterly, 47*, 1–15.

Delli Carpini, M. X., & Keeter, S. (1996). *What Americans know about politics and why it matters.* New Haven, CT: Yale University Press.

Deuze, M. (2003). The Web and its journalisms: Considering the consequences of different types of newsmedia online. *New Media & Society, 5*, 203–230.

Dimock, M., & Popkin, S. (1997). Political knowledge in comparative perspective. In S. Iyengar & R. Reeves (eds.), *Do the media govern?* (pp. 217–224). Thousand Oaks, CA: Sage.

Dixon, T. L., & Linz, D. (2000). Overrepresentation and underrepresentation of African Americans and Latinos as lawbreakers on television news. *Journal of Communication, 50*(2), 131–154.

Downs, A. (1957). *An economic theory of democracy*. New York: Harper and Row.

Druckman, J. N. (2001a). On the limits of framing effects. *Journal of Politics, 63*, 1041–1066.

Druckman, J. N. (2001b). The implications of framing effects for citizen competence. *Political Behavior, 23*, 225–256.

Druckman, J. N. (2004). Political preference formation: Competition, deliberation, and the (ir) relevance of framing effects. *American Political Science Review, 98*, 671 686.

Druckman, J. N., & Nelson, K. R. (2003). Framing and deliberation: How citizens' conversations limit elite influence. *American Journal of Political Science, 47*, 729–745.

Druckman, J. N. (2005a). Does political information matter? *Political Communication, 22*, 515–519.

Druckman, J. N. (2005b). Media matter: How newspapers and television news cover campaigns and influence voters. *Political Communication, 22*, 463–481.

Eagly, A. H., & Chaiken, S. (1993). *The psychology of attitudes*. Fort Worth, TX: Harcourt, Brace, Jovanovich.

Eldersveld, S. J. (1956). Experimental propaganda techniques and voting behavior. *American Political Science Review, 50*, 154–165.

Entman, R. M. (1993). Framing: Toward clarification of a fractured paradigm. *Journal of Communication, 43*, 51–58.

Eveland, W. P., Jr., & Dunwoody, S. (2001). User control and structural isomorphism or disorientation and cognitive load? Learning from the Web versus print. *Communication Research, 28*, 48–78.

Eveland, W. P., Jr., Hayes, A. F., Shah, D. V., & Kwak, N. (2005). Understanding the relationship between communication and political knowledge: A model comparison approach using panel data. *Political Communication, 22*, 423–446.

Farrar, C., Fishkin, J. S., Green, D. P., List, C., Luskin, R. C., & Paluck, E. L. (2010). Disaggregating deliberation's effects: An experiment within a deliberative poll. *British Journal of Political Science, 40*, 333–347.

Fazio, R. H., Sanbonmatsu, D. M., Powell, M. C., & Kardes, F. R. (1986). On the automatic activation of attitudes. *Journal of Personality and Social Psychology, 50*, 229–238.

Festinger, L. (1957). *A theory of cognitive dissonance*. Evanston, IL: Row, Peterson.

Finkel, S. E., & Geer, J. G. (1998). A spot check: Casting doubt on the demobilizing effect of attack advertising. *American Journal of Political Science, 42*, 573–595.

Freedman, P., & Goldstein, K. (1999). Measuring media exposure and the effects of negative campaign ads. *American Journal of Political Science, 43*, 1189–1208.

Frey, D. (1986). Recent research on selective exposure to information. In L. Berkowitz (ed.), *Advances in experimental social psychology* (pp. 41–80). San Diego, CA: Academic Press.

Funkhouser, G. R. (1973). The issues of the sixties: An exploratory study in the dynamics of public opinion. *Public Opinion Quarterly, 37*, 62–75.

Gamson, W. A., & Modigliani, A. (1987). The changing culture of affirmative action. In R. A. Braumgart (ed.), *Research in political sociology* (pp. 137–177). Greenwich, CT: JAI.

Garramone, G. M., Atkin, C. K., Pinkleton, B. E., & Cole, R. T. (1990). Effects of negative political advertising on the political process. *Journal of Broadcasting and Electronic Media, 34*, 299–311.

Garrett, R. K. (2009). Echo chambers online? Politically motivated selective exposure among Internet news users. *Journal of Computer-Mediated Communication, 14*(2), 265–285.

Garrett, R. K., Carnahan, D., & Lynch, E. K. (2013). A turn toward avoidance? Selective exposure to online political information, 2004-2008. *Political Behavior, 35*, 113–134.

Geer, J. G. (2006). *In defense of negativity: Attack ads in presidential campaigns.* Chicago: University of Chicago Press.

Gerber, A. S., & Green, D. P. (2000). The effects of personal canvassing, telephone calls, and direct mail on voter turnout: A field experiment. *American Political Science Review, 94,* 653–663.

Gerber, A. S., Huber, G. A., Doherty, D., Dowling, C. M., Raso, C., & Ha, S. E. (2011). Personality traits and participation in political processes. *Journal of Politics, 73,* 692–706.

Gilens, M. (1999). *Why Americans hate welfare.* Chicago: University of Chicago Press.

Gilens, M. (2001). Political ignorance and collective policy preferences. *American Political Science Review, 95,* 379–396.

Goldstein, K., & Freedman, P. (2002). Campaign advertising and voter turnout: New evidence for a stimulation effect. *Journal of Politics, 64,* 721–740.

Graber, D. (1984). *Processing the news: How people tame the information tide.* New York: Longman.

Groeling, T., and Baum, M. A. (2009). Journalists' incentives and media coverage of elite foreign policy evaluations. *Conflict Management and Peace Science, 26,* 437–470.

Groenendyk, E. W. (2012). Justifying party identification: A case of identifying with the lesser of two evils. *Political Behavior, 34,* 453–475.

Hastie, R., & Park, B. (1986). The relationship between memory and judgment depends on whether the task is memory-based or on-line. *Psychology Review, 93,* 258–268.

Herbst, S. (1993). *Numbered voices: How opinion polling has shaped American politics.* Chicago: University of Chicago Press.

Higgins, E. T., Bargh, J. A., & Lombardi, W. (1985). The nature of priming effects on categorization: Learning, memory, and cognition. *Journal of Experimental Psychology, 11,* 59–69.

Higgins, E. T., Tory, E., Rholes, W. S., & Jones, C. R. (1977). Category accessibility and impression formation. *Journal of Experimental and Social Psychology, 13*(2), 141–154.

Hill, K. A., & Hughes, J. E. (1998). *Cyberpolitics: Citizen activism in the age of the Internet.* Lanham, MD: Rowman & Littlefield.

Holbert, R. L., Shah, D. V., & Kwak, N. (2003). Political implications of prime-time drama and sitcom use: Genres of representation and opinions concerning women's rights. *Journal of Communication, 53,* 45–60.

Holbrook, R. A., & Hill, T. (2005). Agenda-setting and priming in prime time television: Crime dramas as political cues. *Political Communication, 22,* 277–295.

Hovland, C. I., Janis, I. L., & Kelley, H. H. (1953). *Communication and persuasion.* New Haven, CT: Yale University Press.

Hovland, C. I., Lumsdaine, A. A., & Sheffield, F. D. (1949). *Experiments on mass communication.* Princeton, NJ: Princeton University Press.

Huber, G. A., & Arceneaux, K. (2007). Identifying the persuasive effects of presidential advertising. *American Journal of Political Science, 51,* 957–977.

Huber, G. A., and Lapinski, J. S. (2006). The "race card" revisited: Assessing racial priming in policy contests. *American Journal of Political Science, 50*(2), 421–440.

Huckfeldt, R., & Sprague, J. (1995). *Citizens, politics, and social communication: Information and influence in an election campaign.* Cambridge: Cambridge University Press.

Huddy, L., Feldman, S., & Cassese, E. (2007). On the distinct political effects of anxiety and anger. In W. R. Neuman, G. E. Marcus, & A. N. Crigler (eds.), *The affect effect: Dynamics of emotion in political thinking and behavior* (pp. 202–230). Chicago: University of Chicago Press.

Huddy, L., Feldman, S., Tabler, C., & Lahav, G. (2005). Threat, anxiety, and support of antiterrorism politics. *American Journal of Political Science, 49*, 593–608.

Hyman, H. H., & Sheatsley P. B. (1947). Some reasons why information campaigns fail. *Public Opinion Quarterly, 11*, 413–423.

Iyengar, S. (1991). *Is anyone responsible? How television frames political issues.* Chicago: University of Chicago Press.

Iyengar, S., & Kinder, D. (1987). *News that matters: Television and American opinion.* Chicago: University of Chicago Press.

Iyengar, S., & Simon, A. F. (1993). News coverage of the Gulf crisis and public opinion: a survey of effects, *Communication Research*, 365–383.

Jacobs, L. R., & Shapiro, R. Y. (1994). Issues, candidate image, and priming: The use of private polls in Kennedy's 1960 presidential campaign. *American Political Science Review, 88*, 527–540.

Jacoby, W. G. (2000). Issue framing and public opinion on government spending. *American Journal of Political Science, 44* (4), 750–767.

Jamieson, K. H. (1992). *Dirty politics: Deception, distraction, and democracy.* New York: Oxford University Press.

Jarvis, S. E., & Wilkerson, K. (2005). Congress on the Internet: Messages on the homepages of the U.S. House of Representatives, 1996 and 2001. *Journal of Computer-Mediated Communication, 10*, 00.

Joslyn, R. A. (1980). The content of political spot ads. *Journalism Quarterly, 57*, 92–98.

Katz, E., & Lazarsfeld, P. F. (1955). *Personal influence: The part played by people in the flow of mass communication.* New York: Free Press.

Key, V. O., Jr. (1961). *Public opinion and American democracy.* New York: Knopf.

Kinder, D. R., & Sanders, L. M. (1996). *Divided by color: Racial politics and democratic ideals.* Chicago: University of Chicago Press.

Klapper, J. T. (1960). *The effects of mass communications.* Glencoe, IL: Free Press.

Krosnick, J. A., & Brannon, L. A. (1993). The impact of the Gulf War on the ingredients of presidential evaluations: Multidimensional effects of political involvement. *American Political Science Review, 87*, 963–975.

Krupnikov, Y. (2011). When does negativity demobilize? Tracing the conditional effect of negativity on voter turnout. *American Journal of Political Science, 55*, 797–813.

Kunda, Z. (1990). The case for motivated reasoning. *Psychological Bulletin, 108*(3), 480–498.

Kuran, T. (1991). Now out of never: The element of surprise in the East European revolution of 1989. *World Politics, 44*, 7–48.

Lasswell, H. (1948). The structure and function of communication in society. In L. Bryson (ed.), *The communication of ideas* (pp. 37–51). New York: Harper.

Lau, R. R., Sigelman, L., Heldman, C., & Babbitt, P. (1999). The effects of negative political advertisements: A meta-analytic assessment. *American Political Science Review, 93*, 851–876.

Lau, R. R, Sigelman, L., & Rovner, I. B. (2007). The effects of negative political campaigns: A meta-analytic reassessment. *Journal of Politics, 69*, 1176–1209.

Lazarsfeld, P., Berelson, B., & Gaudet, H. (1948). *The people's choice* (2nd ed.). New York: Columbia University Press.

Lenz, G. S. (2009). Learning and opinion change, not priming: Reconsidering the evidence for the priming hypothesis. *American Journal of Political Science, 53*(4): 821–837.

Lippmann, W. (1922). *Public opinion.* New York: Macmillan.

Lodge, M., McGraw, K. M., & Stroh, P. (1989). An impression-driven model of candidate evaluation. *American Political Science Review, 83*, 399–419.

Lodge, M., Steenbergen, M., & Brau, S. (1995). The responsive voter: Campaign information and the dynamics of candidate evaluation. *American Political Science Review, 89,* 309–326.

Lodge, M., & Stroh, P. (1993). Inside the mental voting booth. In S. Iyengar & W. McGuire (eds.), *Explorations in political psychology* (pp. 225–263). Durham, NC: Duke University Press.

Lodge, M., & Taber C. S. (2013). *The rationalizing voter.* Cambridge: Cambridge University Press.

Lohmann, S. (1994). The dynamics of informational cascades: The Monday demonstrations in Leipzig, East Germany, 1989–1991. *World Politics, 47,* 42–101.

Lupia, A. (1994). Shortcuts versus encyclopedias: Information and voting behavior in California insurance reform elections. *American Political Science Review, 88,* 63–76.

Lupia, A., & McCubbins, M. D. (1998). *The democratic dilemma: Can citizens learn what they need to know?* New York: Cambridge University Press.

Marcus, G. E., Neuman, W. R., & MacKuen, M. (2000). *Affective intelligence and political judgment.* Chicago: University of Chicago Press.

McCombs, M. E, & Shaw, D. L. (1972). The agenda-setting function of the media. *Public Opinion Quarterly, 36,* 176–187.

McGinnis, J. (1969). *The selling of the president.* New York: Simon & Shuster.

McGuire, W. J. (1968). Personality and susceptibility to social influence. In E. F. Borgatta & W. W. Lambert (eds.), *Handbook of personality theory and research* (pp. 1130–1187). Chicago: Rand McNally.

McGuire, W. J. (1985). Attitudes and attitude change. In G. Lindzey and E. Aronson (eds.), *Handbook of social psychology* (3rd ed., vol. 2, pp. 233–246). New York: Random House.

McLeod, J. M., & McDonald, D. G. (1985). Beyond simple exposure: Media orientations and their impact on political processes. *Communication Research, 12,* 3–33.

Mendelberg, T. (2001). *The race card.* Princeton, NJ: Princeton University Press.

Milburn, M. A. (1979). A longitudinal test of the selective exposure hypothesis. *Public Opinion Quarterly, 43,* 507–517.

Miller, J. M., & Krosnick, J. A. (2000). News media impact on the ingredients of presidential evaluations: Politically knowledgeable citizens are guided by a trusted source. *American Journal of Political Science, 44*(2), 301–315.

Mutz, D. C. (1998). *Impersonal influence: How perceptions of mass collectives affect political attitudes.* Cambridge: Cambridge University Press.

Mutz, D. C., & Martin, P. S. (2001). Facilitating communication across lines of political difference: The role of mass media. *American Political Science Review, 95* (1), 97–114.

Nabi, R. L., MoyerGuse, E., & Byrne, S. (2007). All joking aside: A serious investigation into the persuasive effect of funny social issue messages. *Communication Monographs, 74,* 29–54.

Negroponte, N. (1995). *Being digital.* New York: Knopf.

Nelson, T. H., Clawson, R. A., & Oxley, Z. M. (1997). Media framing of a civil liberties conflict and its effect on tolerance. *American Political Science Review, 91,* 567–583.

Nelson, T. E., & Kinder, D. R. (1996). Issue frames and group-centrism in American public opinion. *Journal of Politics, 58,* 1055–1078.

Neuman, W. R. (1991). *The future of the mass audience.* New York: Cambridge University Press.

Neuman, W. R. (2000). The impact of the new media: Fragmentation, stratification and political evolution. In W. L. Bennett & R. M. Entman (eds.), *Mediated politics: Communication in the future of democracy* (pp. 299–320). New York: Cambridge University Press.

Niven, D., Lichter, S., & Amundson, D. (2003). The political content of late-night comedy. *Harvard International Journal of Press/Politics, 8,* 118–133.

Noelle-Neumann, E. (1974). The spiral of silence: A theory of public opinion. *Journal of Communication, 24*, 43–51.

Page, B. I., & Shapiro, R. Y. (1992). *The rational public*. Chicago: University of Chicago Press.

Patterson, T. E., and McClure, R. D. (1976). *The unseeing eye: The myth of television power in national elections*. New York: G. P. Putnam.

Patterson, T. E. (1993). *Out of order*. New York: Knopf.

Peffley, M., and Hurwitz, J. (1993). International events and foreign policy beliefs: Public response to changing Soviet-US relations. *American Journal of Political Science 36*, 431–461.

Petrocik, J. R. (1996). Issue ownership in presidential elections, with a 1980 case study. *American Journal of Political Science, 40*, 825–850.

Petty, R. E., Brinol, P., & Priester, J. R. (2009). Mass media attitude change: Implications of the Elaboration Likelihood Model of persuasion. In J. Bryant & M. B. Oliver (eds.), *Media effects: Advances in theory and research* (pp.125–164). New York: Routledge.

Petty, R. E., & Cacioppo, J. T. (1986). *Communication and persuasion: Central and peripheral routes to attitude change*. New York: Springer-Verlag.

Pew Research Center for the People & the Press. 2010. Americans spending more time following the news. Ideological news sources: Who watches and why. http://people-press. org/report/652/.

Polk, J., Young, D. G., & Holbert, R. L. (2009). Humor complexity and political influence: An elaboration likelihood approach to the effects of humor type in *The Daily Show with Jon Stewart*. *Atlantic Journal of Communication, 17*, 202–219.

Price, V., & Tewksbury, D. (1997). News values and public opinion: A theoretical account of media priming and framing. In G. A. Barnett & F. J. Boster (eds.), *Progress in the communication sciences* (vol. 13, pp. 173–212). New York: Ablex.

Price, V., & Zaller, J. (1993). Who gets the news? Alternative measures of news reception and their implications for research. *Public Opinion Quarterly, 57*, 133–164.

Prior, M. (2007). *Post-broadcast democracy: How media choice increases inequality in political involvement and polarizes elections*. New York: Cambridge University Press.

Prior, M. (2009). Improving media effects research through better measurement of news exposure. *Journal of Politics, 71* (3), 893–908.

Prior, M. (2010). You've either got it or you don't? The stability of political interest over the life cycle. *Journal of Politics, 72* (3), 747–766.

Prior, M., & Lupia, A. (2008). Money, time, and political knowledge: Distinguishing quick recall and political learning skills. *American Journal of Political Science, 52* (1), 168–182.

Putnam, R. D. (2000). *Bowling alone: The collapse and revival of American community*. New York: Simon & Schuster.

Ridout, T. R, Shah, D. V., Goldstein K. M., & Franz, M. (2004). Evaluating measures of campaign advertising exposure on political knowledge. *Political Behavior, 26* (3), 201–225.

Riker, W. H., & Ordeshook, P. (1968). A theory of the calculus of voting. *American Political Science Review, 62*, 25–42.

Robinson, J. P., & Levy, M. R. (1996). News media use and the informed public: A 1990s update. *Journal of Communication, 46*, 129–135.

Romer, D., Jamieson, K. H., & Pasek, J. (2009). Building social capital in young people: The role of mass media and life outlook. *Political Communication, 26*, 1, 65–83.

Rosenstone, S. J., & Hansen, J. M. (1993). *Mobilization, participation and democracy in America*. New York: Macmillan.

Sears, D. O., & Freedman, J. L. (1967). Selective exposure to information: A critical review. *Public Opinion Quarterly, 31*, 195–213.

Shah, D. V. (1998). Civic engagement, interpersonal trust, and television use: An individual-level assessment of social capital. *Political Psychology, 19*(3), 469–496.

Shaw, D. V. (1999). The effect of TV ads and candidate appearances on statewide presidential votes, 1988–1996. *American Political Science Review, 93*, 345–361.

Shah, D. V., Kwak, N., & Holbert, R. L. 2001. "Connecting" and "disconnecting" with civic life: Patterns of Internet use and the production of social capital. *Political Communication, 18* 141–162.

Shah, D. V., Watts, M. D., Domke, D., & Fan, D. P. (2002). News framing and cueing of issue regimes: Explaining Clinton's public approval in spite of scandal. *Public Opinion Quarterly, 66*, 339–370.

Sherif, M., & Hovland, C. I. (1965). *Social judgment: Assimilation and contrast effects in communication and attitude change.* New Haven, CT: Yale University Press.

Simon, H. A. (1979). *Models of thought.* New Haven, CT: Yale University Press.

Sniderman, P. M., & Theriault, S. M. (2004). The dynamics of political argument and the logic of issue framing. In W. E. Saris, & P. M. Sniderman (eds.), *Studies in public opinion* (pp. 133–165). Princeton, NJ: Princeton University Press.

Srull, T. K., & Wyer, R. S. (1979). The role of category accessibility in the interpretation of information about persons: Some determinants and implications. *Journal of Personality and Social Psychology, 37*, 1660–1672.

Stoker, L. (1993). Judging presidential character: The demise of Gary Hart. *Political Behavior, 15*, 193–223.

Stroud, N. J. (2008). Media use and political predispositions: Revisiting the concept of selective exposure. *Political Behavior, 30*, 341–366.

Sunstein, C. R. (2002). *Republic.com.* Princeton, NJ: Princeton University Press.

Taber, C. S., & Lodge, M. (2006). Motivated skepticism in the evaluation of political beliefs. *American Journal of Political Science, 50*, 755–769.

Tewksbury, D., & Althaus, S. (2000). Differences in knowledge acquisition among readers of the paper and online versions of a national newspaper. *Journalism & Mass Communication Quarterly, 77*, 457–479.

Trippi, J. (2004). *The revolution will not be televised: Democracy, the Internet, and the overthrow of everything.* New York: Regan Books.

Tversky, A., & Kahneman, D. (1981). The framing of decisions and the psychology of choice. *Science, 211*, 453–458.

Valentino, N. A. (1999). Crime news and the priming of racial attitudes during evaluations of the president. *Public Opinion Quarterly, 63*, 293–320.

Valentino, N. A., Banks, A. J., Hutchings, V. L., & Davis, A. K. (2009). Selective exposure in the Internet age: The interaction between anxiety and information utility. *Political Psychology, 30*, 591–613.

Valentino, N. A., Brader, T., Groenendyk, E., Gregorowicz, K., & Hutchings, V. L. (2011). Election night's alright for fighting: The role of emotions in political participation. *Journal of Politics, 73*, 156–170.

Valentino, N. A., Hutchings, V. L., Banks, A. J., & Davis, A. K. (2008). Is a worried citizen a good citizen? Emotions, political information seeking, and learning via the Internet. *Political Psychology, 29*, 247–273.

Valentino, N. A., Hutchings, V. L., & White, I. (2002). Cues that matter: How political ads prime racial attitudes during campaigns. *American Political Science Review, 96*, 75–90.

Valentino, N. A., Hutchings, V. L., and Williams, D. (2004). The impact of political advertising on knowledge, Internet information seeking, and candidate preference. *Journal of Communication, 54*, 337–354.

Valenzuela, S., Park, N., & Kee, K. F. (2009). Is there social capital in a social network site? Facebook use and college students' life satisfaction, trust, and participation. *Journal of Computer-Mediated Communication, 14*, 875–901.

Verba, S., Schlozman, K. L., & Brady, H. E. (1995). *Voice and equality: Civic voluntarism in American politics.* Cambridge, MA: Harvard University Press.

Wattenberg, M. P., & Brians, C. L. (1999). Negative campaign advertising: Demobilizer or mobilizer? *American Political Science Review, 93*, 891–899.

West, D. (2013). *Television advertising and social media in election campaigns, 1952–2012.* 6th ed. Washington, DC: CQ Press.

Winter, N. J. G. (2008). *Dangerous frames: How ideas about race and gender shape public opinion.* Chicago: University of Chicago Press.

Wolfinger, R. E., & Rosenstone, S. J. (1980). *Who votes?* New Haven, CT: Yale University Press.

Young, D. G. (2008). The privileged role of the late-night joke: Exploring humor's role in disrupting argument scrutiny, *Media Psychology, 11*, 119–142.

Zaller, J. (1992). *The nature and origin of mass opinion.* Cambridge: Cambridge University Press.

Zhao, X., & Chaffee, S. H. (1995). Campaign advertisements versus television news as sources of political issue information. *Public Opinion Quarterly, 59*, 41–64.

CHAPTER 19

POLITICAL IDEOLOGY

STANLEY FELDMAN

1. INTRODUCTION: DILEMMAS OF POLITICAL IDEOLOGY

As Walter Lippmann ([1922] 1997) long ago noted, politics is a complex and confusing arena of modern life: Most people relate to it only indirectly, and it occupies a relatively minor place in their day-to-day lives. Yet democracy requires that voters choose between candidates and parties that offer alternatives on a multitude of issues. How can people make sensible political choices given this "great buzzing, blooming confusion" (p 81)? Ideology is one way to navigate a complex political world.[1] Choosing a candidate or party whose ideology is closest to your own reduces a complex, multiple-dimensional problem to a simpler matter of comparing positions on a single or small number of ideological dimensions.

However, as attractive as this may be, the concept of ideology can be difficult to reconcile with empirical research on political knowledge and belief system organization. First, ideology is a construct that is used at multiple levels. Political ideologies exist as formal systems of political thought. Texts on Marxism, liberalism, conservatism, and fascism develop elaborate interpretations of social, economic, and political arrangements and offer prescriptions for political actions (see, for example, Heywood, 2007). In somewhat less structured ways, ideologies operate at the societal level to organize political debate by allowing political parties to offer more or less coherent policy platforms (Gabel & Huber, 2000; Lijphart, 1990). And, in the primary focus of this chapter, ideology is also used to describe the ways in which people organize their political attitudes and beliefs. It is easy to introduce confusion into discussions of ideology by blurring the lines between these levels of analysis. Some connections between these levels should exist, but we must not make the mistake of assuming that there are straightforward relationships between these varied uses of ideology.

Second, discussions of ideology at the individual level have to contend with scholars who argue that most people are "innocent of ideology" (Kinder, 2006; Luskin, 1987). Low levels of political knowledge are a thorn in the side of those who wish to describe the ideological orientations of members of the public (Delli Carpini & Keeter, 1997). John Zaller (1992) has made a compelling argument that responding to political debates in an ideologically consistent manner requires high levels of political information, or sophistication (but see Goren, 2004).

More critical to any discussion of the psychology of political ideology is Converse's (1964; 1970) argument that many people don't even have real attitudes on specific issues—a phenomenon he labeled "non-attitudes." Using panel data, Converse demonstrated that the low test-retest correlations found for most political issues are consistent with a simple model in which some people have perfectly stable attitudes while others (typically a majority on most issues) respond in a manner that is essentially random. How could the search for ideological structure among political attitudes proceed if many of those attitudes don't even exist? Of all of the critical findings in the public opinion literature, this one presents the most significant hurdle for the study of political ideology. Pushed to one extreme, this research could mean that only a thin slice of the public in any country will exhibit the sort of attitudinal coherence that merits the label ideology—the conclusion reached by Converse almost 50 years ago.[2]

A number of researchers have criticized the non-attitudes thesis. Some have attributed the lack of stability in reported issue preferences to measurement error in survey questions (Achen, 1975; Erikson, 1979; Feldman, 1989). These studies appear to turn Converse's conclusion on its head—once this measurement error is accounted for issue preferences appear to be almost perfectly stable for virtually everyone (strictly speaking, for everyone who offers any response). However, even if measurement error is admitted as a significant cause of response instability, Feldman (1989) has shown that political knowledge is inversely correlated with response error—more knowledgeable citizens have more stable political attitudes (see also Zaller, 1992).

Using a more sophisticated statistical model, Hill and Kriesi (2001) show that response instability comes in shades of grey, not just the two classes of attitudes and non-attitudes that Converse suggested. That grey area is consistent with a model of question answering proposed by Zaller and Feldman (1992; see also Zaller, 1992). They suggest that many people respond to questions about policy preferences by searching their memories for "considerations" that are relevant to that policy. Responses are therefore constructed and over-time variability may result from things like probabilistic memory search and accessibility (see Taber and Young, chapter 17, this volume). Many people may not have the fixed issue preferences that Converse looked for, though lack of stability in this model is not an indication of random responses.

Another version of the measurement argument has been advanced by Ansolabehere, Rodden, and Snyder (2008). They argue that if responses to individual issue questions are affected by random error, then one solution is to combine the individual items into scales that are more reliable. Indeed, they find that scales created to represent broad issue domains (economic, social issues) are much more stable and have more explanatory power than individual issue questions. However, the Ansolobehere et al. analysis cannot really answer a key question: Is the random noise seen in responses to individual issue questions a function of poorly written survey questions or to a lack of crystalized opinions among the respondents?

The Ansolobehere et al. study points to another consistent finding from studies of public opinion: To the extent that latent dimensions of policy preferences exist, they are only weakly related to each other and only weakly consistent with an overall liberal-conservative (left-right) dimension (see Peffley & Hurwitz, 1985). And while Goren (2004) shows that even people relatively low in political knowledge (sophistication) can link domain-specific values such as limited government and traditional morality to political choices, this is not the case for liberal-conservative self-identification in the United States. The ability to connect a general ideological dimension to vote choice is strongly moderated by political sophistication.[3] Thus, while ordinary people may be able to make use of fairly narrow and concrete policy attitudes, broad, abstract ideological reasoning may be limited to the most politically sophisticated.

A detailed discussion of the political science literature on civic competence and sophistication would take up more space than is available here. There are many good reviews of this topic that should be on the reading list of anyone interested in political ideology (see Kinder, 2006). Some students of public opinion remain as pessimistic about the likelihood of observing political ideology at the individual level as Converse and Lippmann were. Others suggest that the search for the sources of structure in political belief systems is far from hopeless. While I will review a great deal of important research on the structure and determinants of political ideology in the rest of this chapter, it is important not to lose sight of the implications of low levels of political knowledge, instability in measures of issues preferences, and multiple dimensions of issue preferences, when evaluating research on individual-level political ideology. At a minimum, these findings encourage us to consider models of ideology that do not require a great deal of sophistication from most people and to be aware of the limits of ideology among nonelites. As I will show, however, people may not need to be ideologues in order to have ideological proclivities. And the continuing relevance of ideology in Western democracies (Bobbio, 1996) makes it important to look more carefully at the determinants of political ideology.

2. The Structure of Political Ideology

One of the central questions in the study of political ideology is the structure of belief systems. Our ability to understand the determinants of ideology depends on a good conceptualization of the construct. There are several issues that have complicated discussions of this topic. The multiple levels at which ideology is used become particularly problematic here. In modern discussions of ideology it has been common to discuss specific ideologies as if they could be located along a single dimension: Left to right or liberal to conservative (Bobbio, 1996; Laponce, 1981). In traditional terms, left-wing ideologies (e.g., socialism) are based on the values of equality, social justice, and widespread involvement in the political system. Right-wing ideologies (e.g., nationalism, fascism) emphasize social control and unequal influence over political and economic systems (Heywood, 2007). Although it is unclear if this is a completely adequate model for political systems (i.e., Singapore's authoritarian political system and free market economy) or formal ideological structures (libertarianism), the critical question for political psychology is whether this unidimensional conceptualization is a good basis for understanding how people organize their political beliefs.

One-dimensional models provide a straightforward connection between people and political elites. Parties and politicians only need to broadcast a single cue—a location on this dimension—in order to communicate their positions on a full range of issues (Downs, 1957). A large fraction of the ideology literature in political psychology assumes that this is a good model of mass belief systems. Many research studies rely on a single measure of ideology—often a single question on liberal-conservative or left-right self-placement—as the key dependent variable.[4] This assumes, implicitly or explicitly, that psychological models can provide a good explanation of variations in ideology by focusing on this single dimension. Two very different lines of reasoning lead to this conclusion.

Converse's (1964) classic paper on mass belief systems began with the premise that any constraint between elements in a belief system stems from similar constraints within elite discourse. People will connect beliefs A and B if they regularly hear elites packaging those beliefs together. Since Converse argued that American political elites held ideologies that ranged on a single dimension from liberal to conservative, by his logic belief systems among citizens must reflect the same single dimensional structure. It is important to note that unidimensionality is not an inherent characteristic of ideologies in this perspective. Belief system constraint for Converse is always top-down (social) in origin, so belief system organization in the public will be a function of ideological structure among elites. If the latter is multidimensional, so will be the former. Converse's conclusion about liberal-conservative organization in belief systems depends on these two key assumptions—the social learning of constraint and the structure of elite discourse. And since constraint depends on social learning (attention and sophistication), it should only be found among the politically attentive members of the public.

Coming from a very different perspective, Jost, Glaser, Kruglanski, and Sulloway (2003) offer a theoretically sophisticated and influential unidimensional theory of political ideology.[5] Starting from the assumption that all beliefs are psychologically motivated, they argue that both economic and social aspects of conservatism serve the same basic needs for order, certainty, and security. What fundamentally differentiates conservatives from liberals in their model is that the former have substantially stronger needs to create order and minimize insecurity. Social (or moral) conservatism flows directly from this psychological mechanism since defending traditional social and moral values provides a buffer against change and uncertainty in the world. They go on to argue that acceptance of social and economic inequality also reduces uncertainty and threat "insofar as preserving the [inegalitarian] status quo allows one to maintain what is familiar and known while rejecting the risky, uncertain prospect of social change" (Jost et al., 2007, p. 990). Thus, while economic and social conservatism may be distinct conceptually, they tend to be related in practice due, in part, to their common origins in these psychological antecedents. By this account, we should expect to find that those on the political left endorse both egalitarian economic views and modern, tolerant views on matters of personal conduct and morality, whereas those on the right should hold the opposite positions.

Despite the popularity of a unidimensional model, there are many reasons to doubt that citizens' political ideology can be adequately reduced to a single dimension. A large number of studies, spanning well over 50 years, have examined the dimensionality of political beliefs and issue preferences among people in many different countries. In virtually no case is a single factor (left-right) model an adequate fit to the data. The most common finding is a two-dimensional space in which economic preferences (greater equality / compassion vs. market outcomes / self-interest) form one dimension and social preferences (modern vs. traditional values or social freedom vs. order) form the second (Ashton et al., 2005; Feldman & Johnston forthcoming; Kerlinger, 1967; Treier & Hillygus, 2009; Heath, Evans, & Martin, 1994; Evans, Heath, & Lalljee, 1996). This two-dimensional structure is reproduced in very similar ways in North America and western Europe (and, in one study, in Hong Kong and Ghana as well; see Ashton et al., 2005).

As Jost, Federico, and Napier (2009) note, some studies that examine these two dimensions also find a correlation between them: Egalitarian economic views tend to be associated with valuing freedom in social interactions. The relationship between economic and social ideology can be fairly modest, however. In US national data, for example, the correlation between latent factors (thus taking account of measurement error) corresponding to each dimension is approximately .3 across several studies (Feldman & Johnston, forthcoming; Treier & Hillygus, 2009). Even in some highly sophisticated samples—very informed respondents in the United States (Feldman & Johnston, forthcoming) and politicians in Canada (Choma, Ashton, & Hafer, 2010)—a two-factor model is a much better fit to data than a single-factor model. And some studies using non–North American data (Cochrane, 2010; Achterberg & Houtman, 2009) find no significant correlation at all between the two dimensions. The results from non–North American samples suggest that caution is required even when generalizing from the modest correlations found in North American samples. Using data from the European Social Survey and the World Values Survey, Cochrane (2010) finds only one exception to the nonsignificant correlation between economic and social ideology—the United States.

Jost et al. (2003) go on to argue that the correlation between economic and social issues observed in the United States indicates that there is a natural (psychological) connection between the two dimensions. The relationship between economic and social ideology is consistent with their model, in which conservative economic and social beliefs arise as a way to resist social change and minimize insecurity. Those who are psychologically insecure should gravitate strongly to the conservative pole of both dimensions, thus producing a significant correlation between them.

It is, however, important to consider other ways of understanding the connection between these two ideology dimensions. First, several studies have shown that the correlation between the economic and the social dimensions of ideology—often measured as Right-Wing Authoritarianism (RWA) and social dominance orientation (SDO) (see Caprara & Vecchione, chapter 2, this volume)—varies substantially across contexts and people (Mirisola, Sibley, Boca, & Duckitt, 2007; Roccato & Ricolfi, 2005). The correlation can range from vanishingly small to substantial. At least some of the variation across countries appears to be a function of ideological polarization: The greater ideological polarization, the higher the correlation between the two dimensions (Roccato & Ricolfi, 2005). This is consistent with the existence of social or elite-based constraint (Converse, 1964; Zaller, 1992), which leads to a stronger association between the two ideological dimensions when ideological elites strongly compete with each other and generate politically divergent discourses. In more highly ideological Western societies—where parties are likely to be tightly arrayed along a left-right dimension and ideological differences between parties are more clear—citizens will be exposed to elite debate and rhetoric that closely combines social and economic ideology. This could also explain why the correlation between the two dimensions increases with political sophistication in the United States: More sophisticated citizens are likely to have greater exposure to ideological rhetoric that currently links the two dimensions (see Johnston, 2011).[6]

2.1. Determinants of Social and Economic Ideology

If the correlation between economic and social ideology reflects the same underlying psychological dynamics, then the two dimensions should share key predictors. For the most part, researchers do not find that the same variables predict economic and social ideological dimensions when their determinants are examined simultaneously. To the contrary, economic and social views seem to be predicted by different factors, which strongly suggests that they are grounded in very different social, psychological, and motivational forces.

For example, using US national survey data, Feldman and Johnston (forthcoming) show that authoritarianism, need for cognitive closure, and need for cognition are significant predictors of social preferences; none of these variables have a significant effect on economic preferences in their analyses. Van Hiel and Mervielde (2004) similarly found that openness to experience, one of the Big Five personality dimensions, correlated strongly with different measures of social conservatism but very weakly with economic conservatism. A similar pattern emerged in the one study reported in Carney, Jost, and Gosling (2008) that distinguished between economic and social dimensions of ideology. Crowson (2009) found substantial effects of dogmatism, need for cognition, belief in certain knowledge, and fear of death on a measure of cultural conservatism. None of these variables were significant predictors of economic conservatism.

In a multinational investigation of the structure and determinants of political ideology, Ashton et al. (2005) found that economic and social dimensions of ideology (which they labeled compassion vs. competition and moral regulation vs. individual freedom) had very different relationships with social values as measured by the Schwartz (1992) values inventory (see section 3.1). Ashton et al. showed that the economic dimension was strongly related to values that contrast self-enhancement with self-transcendence, while the social dimension was related to values of openness to change versus conservation. No significant cross-correlations emerged. A measure of social dominance orientation was strongly correlated with the economic ideology dimension but not at all with social ideology. Right-wing authoritarianism was significantly correlated with both.

For some of their samples Ashton et al. constructed measures of compassion and social freedom. The former correlated with economic preferences and the latter with social preferences. No significant correlations were observed between compassion and social preferences or between social freedom and economic preferences. The compassion and social freedom scales were also uncorrelated in several cross-national samples. This strongly suggests that the two ideology dimensions have very distinct characteristics.

The differential relationships between core dimensions of the Schwartz value typology and economic and social ideology mirror results found for RWA and SDO. In an early study that compared these two measures, Altemeyer (1998) found that they had very different correlations with the value dimensions and several other predictors. In a pattern similar to the Ashton et al. results, RWA was most strongly related to the Schwartz dimension of conservation versus openness to change, while SDO correlated with the dimension of concern with self-enhancement versus self-transcendence. Importantly, these two value dimensions are virtually orthogonal.

The dual-process model of prejudice and ideology developed by Duckitt (2001) underscores the motivational differences between economic and social aspects of ideology. As with many of the other studies noted in this section, the dependent variables in Duckitt's model are RWA and SDO, which Duckitt conceptualizes as social attitudes or ideological dimensions, not personality measures. In Duckitt's model, RWA and SDO have distinct origins in personality and social worldviews. Underlying RWA is a personality that emphasizes social conformity and a corresponding view of the world as a dangerous place. This bears some similarity to the Jost et al. model of conservatism as a motivated response to psychological insecurity. Duckitt traces the origins of SDO to a tough-minded personality type that produces a view of the world as a competitive jungle.

Studying the determinants of ideology with a unidimensional model also assumes that the structure and predictors of ideology are consistent across this dimension. A few studies suggest that this assumption may not be generally accurate. Conover and Feldman (1981) argue attitudes toward liberals and conservatives in the United States are not bipolar. The correlation between these attitudes is negative but only modestly so (but see

Green, 1988). Their analysis also suggests that those who identify as liberal and conservative have different ways of understanding ideology. Asymmetry between those on the left and right in the organization of political beliefs is well illustrated in comparative survey data by Cochrane (2010). Among those on the political left (especially those who are politically engaged), egalitarian views on the economy cohere with left-wing opinions on social ideology and immigration. Not so for those on the right; their views on economic equality are almost entirely unrelated to their opinions on social issues and immigration. As Cochran (2010, p. 109) concludes: "Free-market supporters oppose left-wing economic outlooks; social conservatives oppose left-wing moral values; and those who are hostile toward outgroups oppose left-wing positions on immigration. But there is no inherent predisposition that brings these opinions together for those on the right."[7]

2.2. Heterogeneity in Political Beliefs Structures

If core ideological dimensions are not highly correlated, is a single measure of liberal-conservative or left-right self-identification meaningful? Using cross-national data, Cochran (2010) shows that economic and social preferences, as well as attitudes toward immigrants, independently predict left-right self-placement even though these attitudes are largely uncorrelated.[8] Left-right thus reflects disparate underlying beliefs. Feldman and Johnston (forthcoming) attempt to reconcile these findings by showing that the meaning of liberal-conservative self-identification is heterogeneous in the United States. Their analysis shows that Americans have at least three different ways of understanding the liberal-conservative dimension. For some the dimension closely approximates a broad ideology dimension—both economic and social issues preferences are linked to variation along this dimension. Another group of people connect liberal/conservative differences only to preferences on social (moral) issues, while a contrasting group only connect the dimension to economic issues. This suggests that a single ideology dimension can be a meaningful predictor of political attitudes and behavior even when it is understood very differently by people in a society.

More generally, focusing on the forces that produce a positive relationship between economic and social conservatism can also obscure the fact that the low to moderate correlations between these dimensions leaves many people with political beliefs that are not well described by the standard pair of ideological labels. Some of this "inconsistency" may be due to the relatively low levels of political sophistication that political scientists have extensively documented (Converse, 1964; Luskin, 1987). It is also possible that "nonstandard" belief systems may result from the varying combinations of social and psychological factors that some people experience.

Consider a study of ideological structure in the Netherlands by Achterberg and Houtman (2009). Using measures of authoritarianism and egalitarianism, they not only found that a two-factor model fit their data much better than a single-factor model, the correlation between the two dimensions was not statistically significant (−.02). Exploring further, they found that this correlation varied substantially across educational levels. As with the sample as a whole, no correlation between egalitarianism and authoritarianism was found for those in the middle education levels. A significant negative relationship was found for those high in education. By itself, this is consistent with studies that suggest that ideological consistency will be found only among the most politically sophisticated citizens. But they also found a significant *positive* relationship between egalitarianism and authoritarianism among those low in education; high authoritarianism among this group was connected to greater egalitarianism. In a follow-up analysis, Achterberg and Houtman found that some of this ideological "inconsistency" was a result of a combination of economic and cultural insecurity.[9] This bears a strong resemblance to the phenomenon of "working-class authoritarianism" that Lipset (1959) described.

What is often ignored when looking at correlations that are far from perfect is that low to moderate correlations can hide a great deal of underlying heterogeneity. A correlation of zero between two variables could be found if half of the population had a strong positive relationship between the variables while the other half had an equally strong negative relationship. This is what was observed in the Dutch study—an overall correlation of zero between authoritarianism and egalitarianism obscured subgroups with positive, negative, and zero relationships between those dimensions.

There is some intriguing evidence from the United States suggesting that substantial heterogeneity in belief system structure may be common. Ellis and Stimson (2007) have explored heterogeneity in self-identification as a conservative. They first note that many people who choose the conservative label have policy preferences that are better described as liberal (see also Ellis & Stimson, 2009). A large majority of self-identified conservatives do not have consistently conservative beliefs. Ellis and Stimson go on to identify three groups of self-identified conservatives—"constrained conservatives," who do have consistently conservative policy views, "moral conservatives," who are conservative only on traditional morality issues, and "conflicted conservatives," who have largely liberal views on both economic and moral issues.

Similar heterogeneity in conservative self-identification is also seen in Feldman and Johnston's (forthcoming) analysis: Conservative self-identifiers in the United States are made up of those with consistently conservative policy views, those with conservative economic but liberal social views (libertarians), and another group with conservative social views and moderate views on economic issues. Zumbrunnen and Gangl (2008) explored another aspect of structural complexity of American conservatism by tracing its roots in cultural conservatism and market conservatism—dimensions that are only weakly related in their data. At a minimum, this suggests that researchers should be cautious in using self-identification as a simple indicator of people's underlying belief systems.

2.3. Toward a Broader Typology of Political Ideology

Two different studies of policy preferences in the United States show the degree to which ideological perspectives other than simple left-right or liberal-conservative can be lost if ideology is assumed to be unidimensional. Feldman and Johnston (forthcoming) used latent class analysis, a method for identifying classes, or groups, of people who share similar patterns of issue preferences to explore the structure of political ideology in the United States. Their results indicated that six latent classes were required to account for the grouping of respondents in their national survey data. Two of these classes were consistent liberals and conservatives—people who had liberal (conservative) views on both economic and social policies. Two other groups reversed this pattern, combining liberal (conservative) economic attitudes with conservative (liberal) social positions. Two other groups had economic preferences that were consistently moderate with one expressing liberal social policy preferences and the other conservative social policy preferences.

Using a very different methodology, Baldassarri and Goldberg (2010) used a network methodology to identify groups of people who organize their political attitudes in similar ways. Three groups of people were identified in this way: "Ideologues," whose views on a range of issues were organized in the standard liberal-conservative manner; "Alternatives," who combined economic and social ideology in the opposite pattern; and "Agnostics," who demonstrated little evidence of ideological structure. Importantly, the Alternatives were not simply people who lacked sufficient sophistication to organize their beliefs in a simple liberal-conservative fashion. Rather, they exhibited a conflict between their economic status and their religious beliefs. For example, lower-income religious people are pushed in a more liberal direction on economic issues but in a more conservative direction on social policies. This study also makes it clear that social positions in society, not just psychological predispositions, can have substantial effects on the structure of political ideology.

Another way to think about the complexity of political ideology is to go back to the core two-dimensional structures of economic and social ideology. If these dimensions are not highly correlated, then people should be distributed across the two-dimensional space. Dividing this space into four quadrants yields people consistently on the left and right in the "ideologically consistent" regions of the space. It also defines two other "off-diagonal" ideological regions (see Swedlow, 2008 for an extended discussion of typologies of this sort). One is typically identified as libertarianism (Boaz, 1998; Murray, 1997). In terms of the two-dimensional space, libertarians are economically conservative and socially liberal. More fundamentally, they are people who value freedom and individualism above all else.

A critical question is whether libertarians are simply some mixture of liberalism and conservatism or if they are a distinct ideological group. An analysis of U.S. survey data by Swedlow and Wyckoff (2009) demonstrated that libertarians do have a distinctive affinity for the value of freedom, with a mean score on this value substantially higher than both liberals and conservatives (who did not significantly differ in their endorsement of this value). A paper by Iyer, Koleva, Graham, Ditto, and Haidt (2012) makes a major contribution to our psychological understanding of libertarianism. Using a large Internet sample of Americans who selected libertarianism as the best description of their ideology, Iyer et al. also found that libertarians value liberty more than liberals and conservatives *"at the expense of other moral concerns"* (p. 28, italics in original). In addition to confirming the distinctive value priorities of libertarians, Iyer et al. also show that they have a number of distinctive psychological attributes: They are less emotional than liberals and conservatives; they enjoy reasoning (they are high on need for cognition); they were the only ideological group that scored higher on a scale of systematizing than on a scale of empathy (Baron-Cohen, Richler, Bisarya, Gurunathan, & Wheelwright, 2003); and they scored low on measures tapping close connections with, and identity with others.

This study strongly suggests that libertarians are not just some mixture of liberal and conservative positions, as they are often described. They appear to have a very distinctive set of psychological attributes and personality traits, and their political preferences are a direct reflection of those characteristics. This raises an interesting question for comparative research. People with the psychological attributes described in the Iyer et al. paper can easily express libertarian ideological views in the United States, which has a long cultural tradition of libertarianism. What would a person like this do in a society such as a western European nation with a strong and unchallenged social welfare state that did not offer a contemporary political home for libertarians?

The fourth cell of this typology has received little attention in the empirical literature. Generally described as "populism," this ideological framework combines liberal economic preferences with conservative views on social issues (sometimes associated with ethnocentrism as well). As described by Swedlow (2008, p. 169), "Populism seeks to enlist an interventionist, nationalistic state on behalf of traditional, culturally conservative, small town, rural folks to level the concentrations of power and wealth found in big government and big business." An alternative interpretation of this attitudinal configuration is "communitarianism": A political view that promotes both social order (moral values) and greater equality to maintain social cohesion (Etzioni, 1996).

It is unfortunate that so little empirical research has focused on the psychological appeal of populism. While a comprehensive discussion of populism and its history is well beyond the scope of this chapter, many populist movements have had significant effects on politics in the United States, Europe, and Latin America (see Taggart, 2004 for a very good introduction to this topic). Swedlow and Wyckoff (2009) find that people fitting this description combine above average support for the values of equality and caring with unusually low levels of concern for freedom. One of the groups that emerged in the Feldman and Johnston (forthcoming) latent structure analysis combined economic liberalism and social conservatism. People in this group valued equality but had very high scores on a measure of authoritarianism. It is also possible, based on the Achterberg and Houtman (2009) Dutch study and the Baldassarri and Goldberg (2010) US analysis, that people with these political views are socially conflicted between their low socioeconomic status and religious/morally conservative beliefs. The psychological roots of populism remain an interesting, unexplored question.

3. Origins of Political Ideology

Significant progress in understanding the psychological determinants of ideology has been made in recent years. Researchers have explored a number of possible origins of ideology ranging from values to brain structure to genetics. While I will review some of this psychologically oriented research here, it is critical to recognize that the political environment also plays a very large role in the formation of political attitudes and beliefs. For example, studies of "framing effects" in political science show that the ways in which political issues are structured and presented in political debate and the media can have substantial effects on people's responses to those issues (see chapters in this volume by Chong, chapter 4; and Valentino and Nardis, chapter 18).

There is also a wealth of evidence that partisan cues and media coverage can move public opinion. Zaller (1992) presents a number of clear examples of this. In one extended case study he shows that public opinion toward the Vietnam War in the United States changed dramatically as Democratic elites and the media became more critical of US military involvement from 1966 to 1970. Many liberals who supported the war prior to 1966 (when the war was directed by liberal, Democratic presidents) become opposed, but only after the partisan and media environment changed.

In addition, Stimson (1991) and Erikson, MacKuen, and Stimson (2002) have shown that political ideology can change significantly in response to the broader political and social environment. Stimson created a time series of political ideology (or, in his terminology, public mood) using US public opinion data from 1952 to the present. His data show large swings in ideology—preferences for activist government—over time. And these movements in ideology are systematically related to factors such as government policies and the state of the economy.

It is also important to remember one of the striking results of Converse's (1964) study of mass belief systems: There is a great deal of instability in the policy preferences expressed by people in political surveys. Even if there are doubts about the extreme version of the nonattitudes thesis, there is no question that responses to specific survey questions exhibit substantial amounts of instability. For all of these reasons, it is critical to remember that psychological factors can only produce general proclivities, not fixed ideological positions. While such proclivities are important, they leave plenty of room for environmental and elite effects on political attitudes and beliefs.

3.1. Values: Social and Political

Values appear at the core of a number of models of political ideology. Values, it is often argued, are the ultimate underpinnings of attitudes.[10] Values have characteristics that appear to lend themselves to the analysis of political attitudes and ideology (see also Caprara and Vecchione, chapter 2, this volume). They are assumed to be relatively few in number. Thus they could provide a basis for reducing the complexity of political judgments and for creating consistency among attitudes. On the other hand, all discussions of values suggest that they are more numerous than the single left-right ideological dimension that is typically used to understand political conflict. Political attitudes that are structured by values therefore may not exhibit any simple unidimensional structure. In addition, many theorists argue that values exist, not in isolation, but as systems. The structure of values could therefore provide an underlying basis for political ideology. Finally, values are also assumed to be relatively stable, a property necessary for them to act as ongoing standards of evaluation. Value priorities may change slowly over time, as may be necessary for people to adapt to a nonconstant environment. They should be inertial enough, however, to lend stability to evaluations and behavior.

According to Schwartz (1992, p. 4) "values (1) are concepts or beliefs, (2) pertain to desirable end states or behaviors, (3) transcend specific situations, (4) guide selection or evaluation of behavior and events, and (5) are ordered by relative importance. Values, understood this way, differ from attitudes primarily in their generality or abstractness (feature 3) and in their hierarchical ordering by importance (feature 5)." Since values refer to a preferable mode of conduct or desirable end-state, it is likely that an individual will positively evaluate most, if not all values. It is therefore common to speak of value priorities: the relative endorsement of values with respect to each other. People may think that, taken individually, ambition, success, responsibility, and social justice are all desirable values. Yet one person may attach a higher priority to ambition and success, while another person may see responsibility and social justice as more important.

Empirical research on the relationship between values and political attitudes has generally taken two tracks, largely divided by academic discipline. Political science research has typically examined the effects of individual values like egalitarianism and individualism (but see Jacoby, 2006). In contrast, social psychologists have focused more on the role of value systems. As research based on measures of individual values is both empirically and conceptual more straightforward, I will begin by discussing work on value systems.

Although empirical research on values has a relatively long history in the social sciences, contemporary research in social psychology derives largely from the work of Rokeach (1973) and Schwartz (1992). Schwartz, working from the foundation created by Rokeach, has constructed a model of human values that motivates much of the current work on values. Schwartz began by developing a theory that specifies the types of values that should be found in all human societies (see Schwartz & Bilsky, 1987; 1990). He reasons that underlying specific values are a smaller number of goals or motivations: "needs of individuals as biological organisms, requisites of coordinated social interaction, and survival and welfare needs of groups" (Schwartz, 1992, p. 4).

Schwartz's model specifies 10 fundamental value types, often measured by a substantially larger number of individual values (Schwartz, 1994, p. 22):

1. Power: social status and prestige, control or dominance over people and resources
2. Achievement: personal success through demonstrating competence according to social standards

3. Hedonism: pleasure and sensuous gratification for oneself
4. Stimulation: excitement, novelty, and challenge in life
5. Self-direction: independent thought and action—choosing, creating, exploring
6. Universalism: understanding, appreciation, tolerance, and protection for the welfare of all people and for nature
7. Benevolence: preservation and enhancement of the welfare of people with whom one is in frequent personal contact
8. Tradition: respect, commitment, and acceptance of the customs and ideas that traditional culture or religion provide
9. Conformity: restraint of actions, inclinations, and impulses likely to upset or harm others and violate social expectations or norms
10. Security: safety, harmony, and stability of society, of relationships, and of self

Schwartz's conceptualization of values is especially interesting because it also suggests how value systems are organized. For example, benevolence and universalism should be compatible since they both reflect (different aspects of) prosocial orientations. On the other hand, universalism and power should stand in opposition to each other since power involves personal dominance and control of resources while universalism is concerned with protecting the welfare of all people. These relationships suggest that the individual value items can be arrayed in two-dimensional space with the 10 values types emerging as areas in that space with compatible values next to each other and opposing values opposite. Schwartz (1992) provides empirical evidence from samples collected in many countries to support this model.[11]

A two-dimensional space can also be defined by two axes crossing at the center of the space. Schwartz proposes two such dimensions that suggest an even simpler understanding of overall value structure and a key link to political ideology. One dimension, running from self-direction and stimulation at one end through security, conformity, and tradition, is labeled openness to change versus conservation. The second, self-transcendence versus self-enhancement, is located at an approximately 90-degree angle to the first and has the universalism and benevolence value types at one end and achievement and power at the other.

Numerous studies have found evidence of relationships between values and political attitudes. Research has demonstrated consistent effects of values on policy preferences (Feldman, 1988; Goren, 2001; 2004; Pollock, Lilie, & Vittes, 1993; Zaller, 1992; Peffley & Hurwitz, 1985), attitudes toward social groups (Kinder & Sanders, 1996; Biernat, Vescio, Theno, & Crandall, 1996; Sagiv & Schwartz, 1995), and politicians and parties (Miller & Shanks, 1996; Knutsen, 1995). Many of these studies have used measures of specific political or social values rather than drawing on a full model of value structure consistent with the treatment of values within political science research.

The ways in which values help to structure political ideology are well illustrated in an analysis of the European Social Survey data from 20 countries by Piurko, Schwartz, and Davidov (2011). They examined the value correlates of left-right orientation (self-designation by the respondents). They divided those countries into three groups: Liberal countries, those with a political history of liberal democracy and social welfare; Traditional countries, where religion and nationalism remain intertwined with politics; and Post Communist countries. In the Liberal countries, left-right was best predicted by the contrast between power, security, conformity, and tradition versus universalism and benevolence. There appears to be an asymmetry in Liberal nations between right and left. The values underlying right-wing views largely reflect a desire to maintain the status quo and reduce insecurity (security, conformity, and tradition). Left-wing views, on the other hand, seem to derive from egalitarianism and concern for other people. A somewhat different configuration emerged in the Traditional countries, with security, conformity, and tradition opposing universalism, self-direction, and stimulation. Ideology in these countries seems more closely bound to the conflict over the maintenance of older (religious) moral values, with left-wing values reflecting a rejection of those moral codes (self-direction and stimulation). No strong associations between values and ideology emerged in the Post Communist countries, suggesting that the left-right dimension had not yet taken on a clear meaning in these countries (as of 2002–2003).

Several studies have examined the effects of the full set of Schwartz values on political ideology or ideology as reflected in vote choice. Evidence from Israel and Italy demonstrates substantively large effects of values on preferences for political parties. Importantly, the values that best predict vote choices appear to depend on the way in which political debate is organized. For example, Barnea and Schwartz (1998) showed that in Israel (in 1990) ideological competition between the political parties was structured largely in terms of security versus civil liberties and the role of religion. Framed this way, party choice was best predicted by a function that contrasted tradition and conformity with self-direction, hedonism, stimulation, and achievement. In contrast, Caprara, Schwartz, Capanna, Vecchione, and Barbaranelli (2006), analyzing data from Italy, showed that when political conflict is structured more along a traditional left-right dimension of limited government and economic markets versus the welfare state and social justice, conflict is best predicted by the contrast between universalism and benevolence versus conformity, security, power, and achievement.

The two axes that Schwartz uses to describe the dimensional space among the values—openness to change versus conservation and self-transcendence versus self-enhancement—provide another way to link values and ideology. Schwartz (1994) argues that these two dimensions correspond to two dimensions of ideology. The first, which he labels classical liberalism, "refers to whether government should devote more to guarding and cultivating individual freedoms and civil rights or to protecting the societal status quo by controlling deviance from within or enemies from without" (Schwartz, 1994, p. 39). This ideological dimension should be most closely related to the openness to change versus conservation value dimension. The second ideological dimension, economic egalitarianism, "refers to whether government should devote itself more to promoting equality by redistributing resources or to protecting citizens' ability to retain the wealth they generate in order to foster economic growth and efficiency" (Schwartz, 1994, p. 40). The self-transcendence versus self-enhancement value dimension should be most closely linked to economic egalitarianism. This two-dimensional values model thus corresponds closely (as noted earlier) to the two dimensions often found in factor analyses of issue preferences: social and economic ideology.

There is evidence that these two value dimensions are correlated with RWA and SDO as predicted by Schwartz's model. Several researchers (Rohan & Zanna, 1996; Altemeyer, 1998; Duriez & Van Hiel, 2002) have found that RWA is strongly related to the openness to change versus conservation dimension. Its strongest positive correlations are with the conformity and tradition value types, and it is most negatively correlated with the self-direction and stimulation values. Altemeyer and Duriez and Van Hiel also report evidence showing that social dominance orientation is related to the self-enhancement versus self-transcendence dimension. As I noted earlier, if RWA and SDO are reasonable proxies for social and economic ideology respectively, these relationships strongly suggest that these ideological dimensions have very different motivational bases in human values.

3.2. Values: Moral

There is another important approach to understanding human values that has been recently linked to political ideology: moral values. While the social values identified by Rokeach and Schwartz are not devoid of morality—benevolence and tradition values are not very far removed from moral prescriptions, for example—there is a long social science tradition of identifying the bases of moral judgments. In psychology this work can be traced back to Piaget ([1932] 1997) and, especially, to Kohlberg (1969). More important for understanding political ideology is the work of Haidt and his colleagues. Haidt (see Haidt & Joseph, 2004; 2007) begins by arguing that the underlying framework for moral reasoning is innate or hardwired in humans. This doesn't mean that people are born with specific moral values. Rather, people start out with a basic structure for developing and understanding a small number of moral values: "We propose that human beings come equipped with an *intuitive ethic*, an innate preparedness to feel flashes of approval or disapproval toward certain patterns of events involving other human beings" (Haidt & Joseph, 2007, p. 56, italics in original). A key feature of Haidt's framework is that moral judgments are, most of the time, based on fast intuitive responses. While people may provide justifications for their responses, these are generally rationalizations of their quick affective judgments.

The brain may be wired for morality; society, however, provides much of the content. Arguing from an evolutionary perspective, Haidt suggests that humans and human culture coevolved moral rules to deal with fundamental social or adaptive challenges. From his reading of the moral philosophy literature, as well as anthropological studies, Haidt argues that there are five basic domains of human moral judgment (Haidt, Graham, & Joseph, 2009, p. 111):

1. Harm/care: basic concerns for the suffering of others, including virtues of caring and compassion

2. Fairness/reciprocity: concerns about unfair treatment, inequality, and more abstract notions of justice
3. Ingroup/loyalty: concerns related to obligations of group membership, such loyalty, self-sacrifice and vigilance against betrayal
4. Authority/respect: concerns related to social order and the obligations of hierarchical relationships, such as obedience, respect, and proper role fulfillment
5. Purity/sanctity: concerns about physical and spiritual contagion, including virtues of chastity, wholesomeness, and control of desires

One of the most interesting features of this mapping of moral domains is its implications for our understanding of the cross-cultural bases of morality. The first two of these domains, harm/care and fairness/reciprocity, have been the dominant concerns of liberal political theory and much of the work in moral psychology. Haidt and his colleagues argue that a singular focus on these two domains—and only on the protection of individuals—misses key aspects of moral judgment in non-Western cultures and in nonliberal (conservative) Western ideological groups.

Haidt's key contribution to understanding political ideology stems from the relationship between these five moral foundations and political attitudes. In several studies he and his colleagues (Graham, Haidt, & Nosek, 2009; Haidt, Graham, & Joseph, 2009) show that liberals (in the United States) base their moral judgments primarily on the harm/care and fairness/reciprocity domains. Conservatives, on the other hand, draw more uniformly on all five moral domains, balancing concerns about ingroup loyalty, authority, and purity with the more individualistic values of harm and fairness.

Understanding ideology through this lens of moral concerns provides a more balanced way of understanding the differences between liberals and conservatives. Not surprisingly, conservatives often object to descriptions of them that highlight traits like authoritarianism and intolerance of ambiguity. Conservatives, in this model, are people whose moral values include a concern for the well-being of the collective, as well as the individual. As with all correlational studies, however, the sticking point is causality. As Graham et al. (2009, p. 1042) themselves note, "Do people first identify with the political left or right and then take on the necessary moral concerns, or do the moral concerns come first, or is there a reciprocal influence or even an unidentified third variable at the root of both?"

Lakoff (1996) has offered a different and somewhat idiosyncratic approach to understanding the moral basis of liberalism and conservatism in the United States. Lakoff's field is cognitive linguistics, and he has applied that methodology to describe the moral metaphors that liberals and conservatives use to reason about politics. By analyzing the rhetoric of liberals and conservatives, Lakoff argues that these two ideologies can be understood as conflicting visions of the ideal family structure. Lakoff views the family in metaphorical terms as the way in which people understand the nation, in particular, the relationship between the government and citizens.

Liberals, according to Lakoff, believe in a "nurturant family" model. From this perspective, the role of parents is to provide a warm, caring, and supportive environment so that children can develop their potential and find happiness in life. Nurturing parents help protect helpless children from threats and dangers. Empathy and social responsibility are important qualities, and parents have an obligation to help foster them. Children's obedience comes from love and the respect that loving parents engender through their care and warmth.

The conservative worldview is based on the "strict parent" model. The challenge of raising children from this perspective is dealing with a dangerous world in which evil is a lurking presence. Children must therefore be raised to be strong, self-reliant, and to know the difference between right and wrong. Only through tough love can parents mold the character traits necessary for their children to succeed in life.[12]

Even though these moral worldviews are described directly in terms of the family, Lakoff believes that people understand government and politics through this lens. Thus, in the liberal worldview governments should care about the well-being of their citizens, protect them from a range of external dangers, and foster a caring and empathetic society. For conservatives, governments should maintain and enforce clear normative standards and encourage the development of citizens who have self-discipline and take personal responsibility for their lives.

As a cognitive linguist, Lakoff comes to his interpretations by attending closely to the rhetoric and language of political debate. For him, that is sufficient evidence of the validity of his model. Some additional evidence can be found in two very different studies that were designed to test this framework.

Using US national survey data, Barker and Tinnick (2006) attempted to test Lakoff's framework using people's responses to three questions about childrearing values. Specifically, respondents were asked: "Although there are a number of qualities that people feel children should have, every person thinks that some are more important than others. I am going to read you pairs of desirable qualities. Please tell me which one you think is more important for children to have: independence or respect for elders? Curiosity or good manners? Being considerate or well behaved?" (Barker & Tinnick, 2006, p. 253). Barker and Tinnick assumed that those who chose respect for elders, good manners, and well behaved fit Lakoff's description of the strict father model, while those choosing independence, curiosity, and considerate resemble the nurturant parent model. In a series of multivariate models Barker and Tinnick found many significant effects of the child values on political attitudes and political ideology, even with extensive statistical controls. These relationships were consistent with the predictions of Lakoff's model.

It is interesting to note that the questions used by Barker and Tinnick to measure Lakoff's two family structures have been used by others to measure authoritarianism (Feldman & Stenner, 1997; Feldman, 2003a; Stenner, 2005; Hetherington & Weiler, 2009). Seen in this light, there is a close resemblance between Lakoff's description of the contrasting family structures (and the moral values that they represent) and conceptualizations of authoritarianism. This raises important questions about the ultimate roots of ideology in factors like personality and values, to which I will return.

McAdams et al. (2008) coded written statements provided by a sample of midlife adults who were active members of Christian congregations and who were also active in politics. Each subject wrote open-ended accounts of 12 important "scenes" in their lives. This was defined as "a particular episode or event in one's life that was circumscribed in time and space and that entailed an important or memorable sequence of behaviors, thoughts, and feelings" (McAdams et al. 2008, p. 981). These open-ended statements were then coded for four themes that were considered central to Lakoff's description of liberal and conservative worldviews: nurturant caregiving, empathy-openness, rules-reinforcements, and self-discipline. Three of these themes were significantly related to ideology in their data. The interesting exception was the nurturant caregiving theme, which was noted frequently by liberals and conservatives. McAdams et al. concluded that what most distinguished liberals and conservatives was not the nature and quality of the caregiving but the outcomes: Conservatives value being self-disciplined and rule abiding, while liberals value empathy and openness.

McAdams et al. also coded the same open-ended statements for references that related to the five moral domains in Haidt's model. They found significant correlations between ideology and references to the moral domains. Liberals were more likely to refer to harm-care and fairness-reciprocity when describing important events in their lives, while conservatives were more likely to mention in-group loyalty, purity-sanctity, and, especially, authority-respect. The McAdams et al. study suggests that when liberals and conservatives in the United States are asked to describe important events in their lives, they use concepts consistent with Haidt's and Lakoff's theoretical frameworks. Whether this is because political ideology arises directly out of these moral frameworks or because liberals and conservatives have adopted differing languages to communicate their preferences is less clear.

3.3. Personality and Political Ideology

It is difficult to do justice to the large literature on personality and political ideology in a single chapter. The history of research on this relationship virtually parallels the history of the field of political psychology. *The Authoritarian Personality* (Adorno et al., 1950) was perhaps the first systematic attempt to understand the bases of ideology in terms of personality. Although their focus was on the dynamics of prejudice, Adorno, Frenkel-Brunswik, Levinson, and Sanford (1950) observed relationships between personality (conceptualized in terms of Freudian psychodynamics) and what they labeled a "pseudo-conservative" ideology. A few years later, Eysenck (1954) published an extensive analysis of the structure of political ideology. Joining in a growing critique of the Adorno et al. work, he argued that ideology is two dimensional: A left-right dimension and a tender-minded versus tough-minded dimension. He also speculated about the deeper origins of these dimensions in personality.[13] Other significant contributions were made by McClosky (1958), Tomkins (1964), and Wilson (1973).[14] Approaching the study of ideology from a different theoretical perspective, Jost et al. (2003) presented a large body of findings that draw on and parallel much of this research on personality and ideology.

Despite the very different theoretical approaches represented in this large body of research on personality and ideology a few major threads run through the literature. As well summarized by Carney et al. (2008, p. 816), conservatives are typically described as rigid, fearful, conventional, organized, and self-controlled. Liberals are characterized as open to experience, imaginative, sensation seeking, and impulsive.[15]

For most of its long history, studies of the relationship between personality and ideology failed to produce a truly cumulative body of evidence due to the diverse theoretical frameworks that motivated individual studies. In part that was a function of the state of theory and research on personality. That situation is beginning to change. Contemporary research on the personality-ideology connection has begun to use the framework of the Big Five personality model (McCrae and Costa, 1999). A trait model of personality, it identifies five continuous dimensions that parsimoniously describe differences in human temperament and behavior: extraversion, neuroticism (or its flip side, emotional stability), conscientiousness, agreeableness, and openness to experience. (For a very good introduction to the Big Five model and examples of its application in political psychology see Mondak, 2010; and Caprara and Vecchione, chapter 2, this volume). Cross-national research appears to validate the universality of this five-factor model of personality (see McCrae & Allik, 2002).

While trait models have been common in the personality literature for decades, the Big Five model is the first one that seems to have generated something approaching a consensus among students of personality. It is important to recognize that identification of these five traits was based on empirical evidence. There was no grand theory that predicted the number or identity of the dimensions in this theory. The inductive origins of this model will be an important issue to consider as research into the origins of ideology reaches into deeper levels of neuropsychology and biology.

While the "standard" measure of the Big Five traits (the NEO Personality Inventory) is quite long, the availability of shorter measures has made it possible to investigate empirical connections between these five trait dimensions and ideology by including the personality measures on political questionnaires. Research on this relationship has now been conducted in numerous nations including the United States, Germany, Italy, Spain, Greece, and Poland (Caprara et al., 2006; Gerber, Huber, Doherty, Dowling, & Ha, 2010; Schoen & Schumann, 2007; Vecchione et al., 2011). There are two relatively consistent empirical findings that emerge from these studies. First, openness to experience is the dimension most related to political ideology, with people higher on this dimension more likely to be on the political left. The second consistent predictor is conscientiousness, with higher scores associated with more conservative political attitudes. While the effect of conscientiousness is relatively consistent across studies, the magnitude of its effect is generally smaller than openness. When the dependent variable is some measure of, or proxy for, left-right (liberal-conservative) ideology, other of the Big Five dimensions have been predictive in some studies but not consistently across studies. Vecchione et al. (2011) examined the effects of the Big Five traits on party choice in five European nations and found some differences in the effects of personality traits both across nations and in paired comparisons among choices in multiparty systems. For example, openness to experience has significant effects on vote for center-right versus center-left parties in Italy, Spain, Germany, and Poland, but not in Greece. In Germany, conscientiousness is significantly related to choices involving the center-right parties and those of the left (the center-left and greens), but it does not distinguish in the choice between the center-left and greens. These different relationships could be, as they suggest, a function of party and policy differences in these countries. However, these findings need to be replicated (using better samples) before we can be confident about the detailed effects that they find. Caprara and Vecchione (chapter 2, this volume) have a longer discussion of many of these studies.

One concern about many of these studies is that the effect of personality traits is assessed against a single dimensional model of ideology (but see Gerber et al., 2010). This is problematic for two reasons. As I argued earlier in this chapter, there is a great deal of evidence suggesting that political ideology is at least two dimensional. Research that focuses on a single ideological dimension may be obscuring some important relationships. Second, if the salience of subdimensions of ideology varies across nations, some of the inconsistency in these studies could be a function of variation in the meaning of ideology.

Some evidence on the differential effects of the Big Five dimensions on economic versus social ideology comes from a meta-analysis reported by Sibley and Duckitt (2008). The results they report are somewhat indirect for our purposes as they review studies of the relationship between the Big Five and measures of Right-Wing Authoritarianism (RWA) and social dominance orientation (SDO). As I noted earlier, RWA overlaps significantly with social conservatism, while SDO is much more strongly related to economic conservatism. Summarizing the results of 71 studies, Sibley and Duckitt found two distinct patterns of relationships. RWA was most strongly predicted by openness to experience. Conscientiousness was a consistent, but much weaker predictor. The strongest personality effect on SDO came from agreeableness—higher scores on this trait are associated with lower levels of SDO. Openness to experience was a much weaker predictor of this dimension. Conclusions about the effects of personality on ideology thus depend significantly on how ideology is conceptualized and measured. And null findings with respect to agreeableness may be partly a function of not distinguishing economic from social ideology. As with studies of the effects of the Big Five on a left-right dimension, Sibley and Duckitt found some variations across cultures, though the differences were relatively small.[16]

It is also important to determine whether the conceptualization of personality traits captured by the Big Five is the best way to understand the personality basis of political ideology. This model was derived to provide a parsimonious representation of trait variation. While these five dimensions do appear in many data sets and across cultures, five factors is not the only empirical fit to trait data. It is well known that each of the

Big Five dimensions can be subdivided into more fine-grained "facets" that distinguish aspects of each dimension. It is possible that examining personality at a finer level of detail could add to our understanding of ideology. One recent study shows how valuable this could be. Hirsh, DeYoung, Xu, and Peterson (2010) examined the effects of two correlated but distinct components of agreeableness: Empathy (compassion) and politeness. They found countervailing effects of these two subdimensions: Empathy was positively associated with liberalism, while politeness was negatively correlated. The typical null finding for effects of agreeableness on ideology may be due to these opposing effects of its major components. Students of ideology need to think carefully before assuming that the Big Five traits are a sufficient basis for understanding the personality basis of political ideology.

Correlations between personality measures and ideology are almost always interpreted as evidence of a causal effect of personality on ideology. If personality takes form early in life and is then relatively stable (or even has biological/genetic origins), it is certainly plausible that personality is causally prior to political ideology. One potential problem with this argument is that personality is almost always measured via questionnaire items—the very same type of questions used to measure ideology. It is possible both that personality is truly exogenous to ideology *and* that the measures used to assess personality are significantly reactive to political ideology.

Two studies suggest that the personality-ideology relationship may not be spurious. In an interesting set of studies, Carney et al. (2008) employed indirect measures of openness to experience and conscientiousness. In one study they coded nonverbal interactions between the subjects and researchers for evidence related to these two traits. In a second study they examined subjects' bedrooms or offices for indicators of openness and conscientiousness. Although the effect sizes were not large, there was evidence that ideology (measured with a single liberal to conservative item) is significantly related to personality, especially to openness to experience. There need to be more studies that examine personality effects on political attitudes using nonquestionnaire measures that are more confidently exogenous.

A very different research design was used in a study by Block and Block (2006). The analysis draws on a 20-year longitudinal study that followed a group of people from nursery school (approximately 3 years old) until they were young adults (23 years old). Teachers employed by the researchers rated the children on a wide range of personality and social/cognitive attributes. Twenty years later, the subjects completed a long battery of political attitude measures ranging from questions on public policy issues to political tolerance to political activism. From these measures a single liberal-conservative ideology scale was constructed. Correlations between the childhood personality measures and young adult political ideology revealed a number of significant relationships, with some differences between males and females. Most generally, those children who became conservative adults "were viewed as uncomfortable with uncertainty, as susceptible to a sense of guilty, and a rigidifying when experiencing duress" (Block & Block, 2006, p. 745). Liberals, on the other hand, "were viewed as resourceful, autonomous, expressive, and self-reliant" (Block & Block, 2006, p. 746).

While this research design clearly avoids the potential problem of having personality measures affected by political ideology, some issues with this study need to be considered. The single measure of political ideology in this paper includes a wide range of content that many researchers would consider conceptually distinct. Are conservatives necessarily political inactive and intolerant? It would have been very helpful to see the correlations of childhood temperament with each of the individual measures. The nature of the sample is also somewhat problematic. The children who began the study were living in Berkeley and Oakland, California, and were born about 1966. This part of Northern California is one of the most liberal (left-wing) areas in the United States. Growing up to be conservative would have been somewhat unusual, and the consequences of this for the relationship of childhood personality to ideology must be taken into account.

3.4. Biology, Genetics, and Ideology

Most research on the psychological origins of ideology has roots that extend back to the earliest data of empirical social science. One recent research area, however, breaks new ground: studies of the neurological, biological, and genetic bases of ideology. Many of these studies have only appeared in the last several years. With a couple of notable exceptions, replication of their findings has been rare, and so some caution is necessary in assessing the contribution of this work to our understanding of political ideology.[17]

Perhaps the most compelling evidence that there is some biological origin to ideology comes from studies of twins (see Funk, chapter 8, this volume, and Medland & Hatemi, 2009 for detailed discussion of twin study methodology). The standard twin design compares the relationship (correlation) for some phenotype—an observable characteristic—between monozygotic (MZ) and dizygotic (DZ) twins.[18] The heritability of a particular trait or behavior can be estimated from such data since we know that MZ twins share 100% of their genetic makeup, while DZ twins share, on average, 50%. Given some assumptions (see Medland & Hatemi, 2009), it can be easily shown that $2 \times (r_{MZ} - r_{DZ})$ is an estimate of the proportion of variance in a trait or behavior that can be attributed to genetic factors. In a similar way, it is possible to estimate the proportion of variance due to shared and unshared environmental influences. In most recent twin studies structural equation models are used to obtain more precise estimates of the sources of variance in phenotypes and confidence intervals for those parameters.

A number of studies conducted in the United States, Australia, Germany, and Canada have used twin data to examine the heritability of political ideology (see Funk, chapter 8, this volume, for a discussion of these studies). The results of these studies are surprisingly similar. Heritability of ideology is estimated in the range of 40% to 60%. Shared environmental effects—effects of the environment that impinge on both twins equally—are typically near zero. Many of these studies rely on unidimensional measures of ideology, often using the Wilson-Patterson ideology scale (Wilson & Patterson, 1968). A few studies have looked at subdimensions of ideology and found similar levels of heritability for those. A twin study using a sample from Canada is one of the few to examine more specific dimensions of political attitudes (Bell, Schermer, & Vernon, 2009). The authors found that heritability estimates varied substantially across the dimensions. Heritability was estimated to be quite high for "religiosity/social conservatism" (.73), and high for economic equality and attitudes toward ethnic and racial minorities (.58 and .52). Their best-fitting model for two other attitude dimensions—environmentalism and "activist state on social issues"—suggested no heritability at all. Unfortunately, there have been no other studies that measure political attitudes at this level, so it is impossible to know if results like this would generalize. In general, the small number of twin studies that go beyond a single liberal-conservative dimension suggest that major subdimensions of ideology have substantial levels of heritability, though there is a little evidence that this may not extend to all domains of political attitudes.[19]

Some caution is needed when interpreting estimates of the heritability of any observable characteristic. First, estimates of heritability can only be interpreted in terms of variance across people. Thus, an estimate that a trait is 50% heritable means that 50% of the variability of that trait across people can be attributed to differences in their genetic makeup. It does not mean that 50% of any individual's value on that trait is due to his or her genotype. Second, estimates from twin studies are population specific; they indicate the amount of heritability of a characteristic in a specific population at a specific point in time. For example, many studies show that height is highly heritable—approximately 80% of the variance in any population is genetically determined (Silventoinen et al., 2003). At the same time, there are substantial variations in height across populations and over time within populations. A great deal of this cross-cultural variation can be explained by factors like health and nutrition (Silventoinen, 2003). Thus, a high level of heritability within a population does not rule out substantial environmental effects on that characteristic. This is a critical issue for studies of the heritability of ideology, which have been based, to date, on samples of twins within a specific nation at a specific point in time. But ideology varies significantly across national contexts. We cannot fully understand the genetic and environmental origins of ideology without considering the sources of cross-national differences as well as intranational variation.

Twin studies may provide evidence that a person's genetic makeup contributes to his or her ideology, but they do not give any indication of how political orientations result from one's genetic makeup. In effect, twin studies are a giant black box showing potential biological effects on ideology without suggesting any mechanism producing those effects. There have been a few studies that attempt to link particular genes—allelic variants in specific genes—with political attitudes and behavior (Dawes & Fowler, 2009; Fowler & Dawes, 2008; Settle, Dawes, Christakis, & Fowler, 2010). However, the effect sizes in all of these studies have been quite small, and none of the findings have been replicated. Given all of the complexities involved in the determination of social behavior, it is highly unlikely that specific genes will have more than a trivial effect on specific political attitudes and behaviors (Charney & English, 2012).

One genome-wide association study (GWAS)[20] (Hatemi et al., 2011) reported some significant or near significant associations between a few genetic markers and a measure of liberal-conservative ideology. The interpretation of these relationships remains quite speculative, however, and there doesn't appear to be any replication of these findings. On the other hand, attempts to find genetic markers for core personality traits have been largely unsuccessful. For example de Moor et al. (2010) conducted a meta-analysis of GWAS studies of personality as measured by the Big Five model. Some weak associations were found for openness to experience and conscientiousness, but these findings were not completely replicable. No significant results emerged for the other three personality traits. It appears that we are a long way from understanding the genetic mechanisms underlying the heritability estimates of social traits like personality and ideology.

Some research has begun to look at biological and neurological mechanisms that may influence the development of ideology. Kanai, Feilden, Firth, and Rees (2011) used magnetic resonance imaging (MRI) to examine the relationship between variations in gray matter volume in the brain with liberal-conservative ideology in a sample of college students in London. They found two significant associations with self-described conservatism: Increased gray matter volume in the anterior cingulate cortex (ACC) and in the right (but not left) amygdala. These findings do not appear to have been replicated, and their interpretation is somewhat speculative. For example, it is tempting to interpret variation in the size of the amygdala with sensitivity to threat or anxiety. However, studies have shown that the amygdala is involved in the processing of emotional stimuli in general, not just threatening ones (see Balleine & Killcross, 2006). And the causal relationship between brain volume and social attitudes is not entirely clear. As Kanai et al. recognize, longitudinal data is required to determine whether ideology is a function of these differences in gray matter volume of if they are instead a function of social learning and/or experiences that contribute to the development of ideology.

Instead of measuring gray matter sizes, Zamboni et al. (2009) used fMRI to observe patterns of brain activation when subjects were asked to respond to political stimuli. They also used multidimensional scaling to obtain a more nuanced representation of political attitudes and beliefs. Based on the MDS solution, they identified three dimensions of political attitudes: "individualism," "conservatism," and "radicalism." The first looks similar to measures of economic ideology, while the second resembles social or moral ideology. The third dimension, radicalism, is somewhat harder to relate to other studies of political ideology. Using another group of subjects, they observed differences in fMRI activation in response to political stimuli that were associated with each of the three dimensions in the first set of subjects. Their data seemed to show that different patterns of brain activation were associated with each of the three dimensions. As with the Kanai et al. study, replication of this study is needed to generate confidence in the findings, and the interpretation of the patterns of brain activation is speculative.

Two recent studies have suggested significant differences in the way that liberals and conservatives respond to nonpolitical stimuli. Amodio, Jost, Master, and Yee (2007) used a Go/No-Go task to investigate differences between liberals and conservatives in conflict monitoring, "a general mechanism for detecting when one's habitual response

tched with responses required by the current situation" (Amodio
his design, subjects are repeatedly presented with a Go stimulus so
become habitual. On a small number of trials a No-Go stimulus is
lead to a nonresponse. Amodio et al. measured areas of brain acti-
encephalograhics (EEG). There were two notable relationships with
scribed liberal-conservative ideology in this study. First, liberals (compared to
conservatives) were more accurate in the No-Go trials (i.e., they appropriately did not
respond). Second, the EEG results showed stronger responses in the dorsal ACC in the
No-Go trials among liberals.

Oxley et al. (2008) examined physiological measures of responses to threat and their
relationship to political ideology. Using a sample of residents of Lincoln, Nebraska,
Oxley et al. measured skin conductance and startle-blink responses to nonpolitical
threatening stimuli (a very large spider, an individual with a bloody face, and an open
wound covered with maggots). Ideology was measured by responses to a series of statements on social/moral issues including military spending, patriotism, and the death
penalty that Oxley et al. collectively labeled "protecting the social unit." Significant
relationships with both measures were observed indicating that those most concerned
with protecting the social unit exhibited stronger physiological responses to threatening
stimuli than those least concerned.

One interesting area of research in which there are a sufficient number of studies
to generate some confidence in their findings focuses on disgust sensitivity. In studies
using questionnaire measures of disgust sensitivity (Inbar, Pizarro, & Bloom, 2009) and
physiological measures (Smith et al., 2011), conservatives were found to have higher
levels of disgust sensitivity than liberals. Importantly, these differences were largely confined to specific social/moral issues: Abortion and gay marriage (see also Inbar, Pizarro,
Knobe, & Bloom, 2009). No significant effects were found for a wide range of other
issues. A recent study (Inbar, Pizarro, & Bloom, 2012) demonstrated that exposing people to a noxious odor increased dislike of homosexuals. The manipulation had no effect
on attitudes toward other social groups nor on a range of political issues.

4. CONCLUDING THOUGHTS

It should be clear from this review that a substantial amount of research has been done in
recent years on the psychological origins of ideology. Our understanding of the nature
and roots of political attitudes has certainly grown as a result of this work. Still, it is hard
to come away from an assessment of this literature without wondering if the whole is
really the sum of the parts. In concluding I would like to raise two questions about the
current state of research on political ideology.

First, how do we conceptualize and measure ideology? As I have discussed, there is
abundant evidence of (at least) two distinct ideological dimensions. More importantly,
social and economic ideology are grounded in different social values and personality

traits (and degree of disgust sensitivity) and thus have very different psychological origins. A long line of research beginning with *The Authoritarian Personality* links social conservatism to a lack of openness to experience, intolerance of ambiguity, and the need to manage threat and insecurity. At the same time, what is not sufficiently appreciated is that these types of predictors explain only a modest amount of the variance in social conservatism. Thus, something else must account for at least as much variance in this dimension of ideology as does psychological insecurity. We still know very little about what those other factors may be.

The psychological origins of economic ideology are much less well understood. The personality trait of agreeableness, or empathy, appears to have appreciable effects on this dimension, as does the Schwartz value dimension of self-transcendence versus self-enhancement, but little else can be gleaned from the literature at this point. One reason that economic ideology is so poorly understood may be the structure of the modern social welfare state. Liberal economic policy can serve two functions. On the one hand it can redistribute income and regulate market forces. As Jost et al. (2003) argue, this can be seen as threatening to the status quo of a free market and economic individualism (particularly in the United States). The modern welfare state also *provides security* in the form of retirement benefits, medical care, and unemployment benefits. As Johnston (2011) shows, the relationship between measures of psychological insecurity and economic conservatism in the United States is dependent on how people understand these alternative functions. Psychological insecurity predicts greater economic conservatism only when elite rhetoric associates it with threats to the status quo. Absent those elite cues, psychological insecurity is associated with economic *liberalism*.

A closer look at the structure of political ideology also suggests that a more fine-grained understanding the construct could be enlightening. The recent paper by Iyer et al. (2012) strongly suggests that at least one additional ideology perspective, libertarianism, may be characterized by psychological dynamics that clearly distinguish it from more conventionally understood left-wing and right-wing ideologies. A closer look at populism, or communitarianism, might similarly be worthwhile.

Second, a large number of theoretical approaches have now been employed to understand the origins of ideology: Values, morality, personality, cognitive functioning, biological processes, and genetics. Each seems to offer some insight into the dynamics of ideology. The problem is that we know far too little about how these theoretical perspectives relate to each other. It is simply impossible that all of the various constructs and measures that have been used in this literature are unrelated to each other, but very few studies examine multiple determinants of ideology simultaneously. In other cases, disparate findings are seen as part of a single psychological process even when evidence supporting those conclusions is absent.

As I discussed, both social values (Schwartz) and moral values (Haidt) have been shown to correlate significantly with ideology. But aspects of these two systems look similar. There are also significant correlations between personality measures and both social and moral values. As Caprara et al. (2006) and Lewis and Bates (2011) have shown, most of the effects of (Big Five) personality traits on ideology are mediated by values—in the first case by social values and in the second by moral values. Both sets of values *independently* mediate the same effects of personality on ideology. Could these results really be independent? Haidt, Graham, and Joseph (2009) report that a measure of one of the moral foundations, purity, is correlated ($r = .34$) with disgust sensitivity and ($r = .65$) with RWA. If measurement error is taken into account, are purity and RWA distinguishable?

Other connections are drawn with little or no empirical support. Are the effects of conflict monitoring (Amodio et al., 2007) and physiological reactions to threatening stimuli (Oxley et al., 2008) on ideology understandable from a single theoretical perspective? It is entirely possible that these are different psychological processes. And is variability in either conflict monitoring or physiological reactions to threat correlated with openness to experience or need for cognitive closure or the size of the amygdala or disgust sensitivity? It is also tempting to suggest that the genetic variance in ideology that has been observed in twin data is accounted for by core personality characteristics that also appear to have a very large heritable component. A study by Kandler, Bleidorn, and Riemann (2012) supports this conclusion, while another study by Verhulst, Eaves, and Hatemi (2011) suggests that personality does not have a direct effect on political ideology, with both being a function of a common underlying genetic cause. Seemingly obvious relationships require careful empirical verification.

It is too much to ask every researcher to develop a fully integrative mode of the determinants of political ideology. However, real progress in understanding ideology will ultimately depend on research that attempts to link these diverse perspectives in order to identify the causal origins of political ideology.

Notes

1. I will forgo a long discussion on the definition of ideology since, as Gerring (1997) ably demonstrates, a multitude of definitions have been offered that at times contradict each other. Searching for a common core among these definitions, Gerring arrives at the following: "Ideology, at the very least, refers to a set of idea-elements that are bound together, that belong to one another in a non-random fashion" (Gerring, 1997, p. 980).

2. For evidence that low levels of political sophistication are not just a US phenomenon see Converse and Pierce (1986) for comparable data from France.

3. Even in-depth interview studies show that people rarely use any simple, overarching standard for evaluating politics (Lane, 1962; Hochschild, 1981).

4. The Wilson-Patterson ideology scale (Wilson & Patterson, 1968) is another popular unidimensional measure of ideology in this literature.

5. To be clear, Jost et al. do not argue that a one-dimensional model will account for all of the variance in political beliefs. Rather, they suggest that an important core of belief systems can be described in this way. Moreover, this underlying dimension is, in their model, the crucial component of political ideology both psychologically and politically.

6. There is another explanation for the higher correlation among the more sophisticated and in more ideological societies that has not received any attention. Something like

social desirability pressure may be at work. People for whom politics is important may understand what *should go* with what. When they are confronted with explicit questions on surveys, consistency pressures may lead to answers that suggest greater left-right consistency. This is even likely with measures like SDO and RWA. The "correct left- and right-wing answers" for most questions in these measures are fairly clear for those paying a reasonable amount of attention to politics. It would be interesting to see if the correlation between implicit measures of these two dimensions varies in the same way as the explicit measures.

7. Lachat (2011) proposes an alternative asymmetric model in which variations in left-wing positions in western Europe are a function of economic beliefs, while variation in right-wing positions are a function of cultural beliefs.

8. Attitudes toward immigrants and social preferences are modestly correlated; both are uncorrelated with economic preferences.

9. McClosky and Zaller (1984) found a similar belief structure in the United States that they labeled an "anti-regime" pattern. They attributed this to low political sophistication, though the Achterberg and Houtman (2009) study suggests that social factors associated with low sophistication could also be responsible.

10. See Feldman (2003b) for a more extensive discussion of the relationship between values and political attitudes.

11. To get more information about the full two-dimensional structure of the Schwartz value model (including empirically derived representations of the two dimensional space) see Schwartz (1992) and Feldman (2003b).

12. Lakoff's model bears a clear resemblance to Tompkin's (1964) distinction between normative and humanistic scripts, with conservatives emphasizing norms and rules and liberals stressing empathy and warmth.

13. Eysenck's interpretation of the factor analysis results was soon called into question (Rokeach and Hanley, 1956), with others arguing that a 45-degree rotation of those axes produced dimensions that look like economic and social ideology. His claims of left-wing authoritarianism (tough-minded leftists) have also not fared well in subsequent research (see Stone, 1980).

14. See Carney, Jost, and Gosling (2008) for a very good discussion of research on personality and political ideology.

15. Interestingly, the literature reviewed by Carney et al. provides a much richer description of the personality traits of conservatives than it does of liberals.

16. One recent study that examined the effects of Big Five measures on economic and social ideology was reported by Gerber et al., 2010). Contrary to many other studies, Gerber et al. found that openness to experience was strongly related to both social and economic ideology, as was conscientiousness. It isn't obvious why their results diverged from other studies. They used a very short (10-item) measure of the Big Five dimensions, and it's unclear what impact this may have had. And they used a sample of registered voters that (in the United States) is more sophisticated than a representative adult sample would be.

17. Replication is particularly important in this sort of research since it is often exploratory and frequently (but not always) large numbers of tests are conducted simultaneously (large numbers of genotypes or very small brain regions in an fMRI study). This raises concerns about type I errors.

18. MZ and DZ twins are often referred to as identical and fraternal twins in popular discourse.

19. Two key assumptions are generally needed to estimate heritability from twin data: Equal environments and no assortative mating. Funk (chapter 8, this volume) has a very good discussion of both of these assumptions.

20. A genome-wide association study examines a large number of genetic variants (genotypes) simultaneously. The goal is to identify specific genotypes that are related to particular phenotypes.

REFERENCES

Achen, C. H. (1975). Mass political attitudes and the survey response. *American Political Science Review, 69*(4), 1218–1231.

Achterberg, P., & Houtman, D. (2009). Ideologically illogical? Why do the lower-educated Dutch display so little value coherence? *Social Forces, 87*(3), 1649–1670.

Adorno, T. W., Frenkel-Brunswik, E., Levinson, D. J., & Sanford, R. N. (1950). *The authoritarian personality*. Oxford: Harpers.

Altemeyer, R. (1998). The other "authoritarian personality." *Advances in Experimental Social Psychology, 30,* 47–92.

Amodio, D. M., Jost, J. T., Master, S. L., & Yee, C. M. (2007). Neurocognitive correlates of liberalism and conservatism. *Nature Neuroscience, 10*(10), 1246–1247.

Ansolabehere, S., Rodden, J., & Snyder, J. M. (2008). The strength of issues: Using multiple measures to gauge preference stability, ideological constraint, and issue voting. *American Political Science Review, 102*(2), 215–232.

Ashton, M. C., Danso, H. H., Maio, G. R., Esses, V. M., Bond, M. H., & Keung, D. K. Y. (2005). Two dimensions of political attitudes and their individual difference correlates: A cross-cultural perspective. *Culture and social behavior: The Ontario symposium* (vol. 10, pp. 1–29). Hillsdale, NJ: Lawrence Erlbaum.

Baldassarri, D., & Goldberg, A. (2010). Political belief networks: Socio-cognitive heterogeneity in American public opinion. Retrieved from http://papers.ssrn.com/sol3/papers.cfm?abstract_id=1642641.

Balleine, B. W., & Killcross, S. (2006). Parallel incentive processing: An integrated view of amygdala function. *Trends in neurosciences, 29*(5), 272–279.

Barker, D. C., & Tinnick, J. D. (2006). Competing visions of parental roles and ideological constraint. *American Political Science Review, 100*(2), 249–263.

Barnea, M. F., & Schwartz, S. H. (1998). Values and voting. *Political Psychology, 19*(1), 17–40.

Baron-Cohen, S., Richler, J., Bisarya, D., Gurunathan, N., Wheelwright, S., Baron-Cohen, S., Richler, J., et al. (2003). The systemizing quotient: An investigation of adults with Asperger syndrome or high-functioning autism, and normal sex differences. *Philosophical Transactions of the Royal Society of London. Series B: Biological Sciences, 358,* 361–374.

Bell, E., Schermer, J. A., & Vernon, P. A. (2009). The origins of political attitudes and behaviours: An analysis using twins. *Canadian Journal of Political Science, 42*(4), 855–879.

Biernat, M., Vescio, T. K., Theno, S. A., & Crandall, C. S. (1996). Values and prejudice: Toward understanding the impact of American values on outgroup attitudes. In C. Seligman, J. M. Olson, & M. P. Zanna (eds.), *The psychology of values: The Ontario symposium,* The Ontario symposium on personality and social psychology (vol. 8, pp. 153–189). Hillsdale, NJ: Lawrence Erlbaum.

Block, J., & Block, J. H. (2006). Nursery school personality and political orientation two decades later. *Journal of Research in Personality, 40*(5), 734–749.

Boaz, D. (1998). *Libertarianism: A primer*. New York: Free Press.

Bobbio, N. (1996). *Left and right: The significance of a political distinction*. Chicago: University of Chicago Press.

Caprara, G. V., Schwartz, S., Capanna, C., Vecchione, M., & Barbaranelli, C. (2006). Personality and politics: Values, traits, and political choice. *Political Psychology, 27*(1), 1–28.

Carney, D. R., Jost, J. T., Gosling, S. D., & Potter, J. (2008). The secret lives of liberals and conservatives: Personality profiles, interaction styles, and the things they leave behind. *Political Psychology, 29*(6), 807–840.

Carpini, M. X. D., & Keeter, S. (1997). *What Americans know about politics and why it matters*. New Haven, CT: Yale University Press.

Charney, E., & English, W. (2012). Candidate genes and political behavior. *American Political Science Review, 1*(1), 1–34.

Choma, B. L., Ashton, M. C., & Hafer, C. L. (2010). Conceptualizing political orientation in Canadian political candidates: A tale of two (correlated) dimensions. *Canadian Journal of Behavioural Science, 42*(1), 24–33.

Cochrane, C. (2010). Left/right asymmetries in a multidimensional universe: Citizens, activists, and parties. PhD dissertation, University of Toronto. Retrieved from https://tspace.library.utoronto.ca/handle/1807/24414.

Conover, P. J., & Feldman, S. (1981). The origins and meaning of liberal/conservative self-identifications. *American Journal of Political Science, 25,*(4), 617–645.

Converse, P. (1964). "The Nature of Belief Systems in Mass Publics." In D. Apter (ed.), *Ideology and discontent* (pp. 206–261). New York: Free Press.

Converse, P. (1970). Attitudes and non-attitudes: Continuation of a dialogue. In E. Tufte (ed.), *The quantitative analysis of social problems* (pp. 168–189). Reading, MA: Addision-Wesley.

Converse, P. E., & Pierce, R. (1986). *Political representation in France*. Cambridge, MA: Belknap Press of Harvard University Press.

Crowson, H. M. (2009). Are all conservatives alike? A study of the psychological correlates of cultural and economic conservatism. *Journal of Psychology, 143*(5), 449–463.

Dawes, C. T., & Fowler, J. H. (2009). Partisanship, voting, and the dopamine D2 receptor gene. *Journal of Politics, 71*(3), 1157–1171.

de Moor, M. H. M., Costa, P. T., Terracciano, A., Krueger, R. F., De Geus, E. J. C., Toshiko, T., Penninx, B., et al. (2010). Meta-analysis of genome-wide association studies for personality. *Molecular psychiatry, 17*, 337–349.

Downs, A. (1957). *An economic theory of democracy*. New York: Harper and Row.

Duckitt, J. (2001). A dual-process cognitive-motivational theory of ideology and prejudice. *Advances in experimental social psychology, 33*, 41–113.

Duriez, B., & Van Hiel, A. (2002). The march of modern fascism: A comparison of social dominance orientation and authoritarianism. *Personality and Individual Differences, 32*(7), 1199–1213.

Ellis, C., & Stimson, J. A. (2007). On symbolic conservatism in America. Paper presented at the Annual Meetings of the American Political Science Association. Chicago, IL.

Ellis, C., & Stimson, J. A. (2009). Symbolic ideology in the American electorate. *Electoral Studies, 28*(3), 388–402.

Erikson, R. S. (1979). The SRC panel data and mass political attitudes. *British Journal of Political Science, 9*(01), 89–114.

Erikson, R. S., MacKuen, M., & Stimson, J. A. (2002). *The macro polity*. New York: Cambridge University Press.

Etzioni, A. (1996). *The new golden rule: Community and morality in a democratic society.* New York: Basic Books.

Evans, G., Heath, A., & Lalljee, M. (1996). Measuring left-right and libertarian-authoritarian values in the British electorate. *British Journal of Sociology, 47*(1), 93–112.

Eysenck, H. J. (1954). *The psychology of politics.* London: Routledge and Kegan Paul.

Feldman, S. (1988). Structure and consistency in public opinion: The role of core beliefs and values. *American Journal of Political Science, 32*(2), 416–440.

Feldman, S. (1989). Measuring issue preferences: The problem of response instability. *Political Analysis, 1*(1), 25–60.

Feldman, S. (2003a). Enforcing social conformity: A theory of authoritarianism. *Political psychology, 24*(1), 41–74.

Feldman, S. (2003b). Values, ideology, and the structure of political attitudes. In D. O. Sears, L. Huddy, & R. Jervis (eds.), *Oxford handbook of political psychology* (pp. 477–508). New York: Oxford University Press.

Feldman, S. & Johnston, C. (Forthcoming). Understanding the determinants of political ideology: Implications of structural complexity. *Political Psychology.*

Feldman, S., & Stenner, K. (1997). Perceived threat and authoritarianism. *Political Psychology, 18*(4), 741–770.

Fowler, J. H., & Dawes, C. T. (2008). Two genes predict voter turnout. *Journal of Politics, 70*(3), 579–594.

Gabel, M. J., & Huber, J. D. (2000). Putting parties in their place: Inferring party left-right ideological positions from party manifestos data. *American Journal of Political Science, 44*(1), 94–103.

Gerber, A. S., Huber, G. A., Doherty, D., Dowling, C. M., & Ha, S. E. (2010). Personality and political attitudes: Relationships across issue domains and political contexts. *American Political Science Review, 104*(01), 111–131.

Gerring, J. (1997). Ideology: A definitional analysis. *Political Research Quarterly, 50*(4), 957–994.

Goren, P. (2004). Political sophistication and policy reasoning: A reconsideration. *American Journal of Political Science, 48*(3), 462–478.

Graham, J., Haidt, J., & Nosek, B. A. (2009). Liberals and conservatives rely on different sets of moral foundations. *Journal of personality and social psychology, 96*(5), 1029–1046.

Green, D. P. (1988). On the dimensionality of public sentiment toward partisan and ideological groups. *American Journal of Political Science, 32*(3), 758–780.

Haidt, J., Graham, J., & Joseph, C. (2009). Above and Below Left–Right: Ideological Narratives and Moral Foundations. *Psychological Inquiry, 20*(2-3), 110–119.

Haidt, J., & Joseph, C. (2004). Intuitive ethics: How innately prepared intuitions generate culturally variable virtues. *Daedalus, 133*(4), 55–66.

Haidt, J., & Joseph, C. (2007). The moral mind: How five sets of innate intuitions guide the development of many culture-specific virtues, and perhaps even modules. In P. Carruthers, S. Laurence, & S. Stich (eds.), *The innate mind, Vol. 3,* 367–392, Oxford University Press.

Hatemi, P. K., Gillespie, N. A., Eaves, L. J., Maher, B. S., Webb, B. T., Heath, A. C., Medland, S. E., et al. (2011). A genome-wide analysis of liberal and conservative political attitudes. *Journal of Politics, 73*(1), 271–285.

Heath, A., Evans, G., & Martin, J. (1994). The measurement of core beliefs and values: The development of balanced socialist/laissez faire and libertarian/authoritarian scales. *British Journal of Political Science, 24*(1), 115–132.

Hetherington, M. J., & Weiler, J. D. (2009). *Authoritarianism and polarization in American politics.* New York: Cambridge University Press.

Heywood, A. (2007). *Political ideologies: An introduction* (4th ed.). New York: Palgrave Macmillan.

Hiel, A. V., & Mervielde, I. (2004). Openness to experience and boundaries in the mind: Relationships with cultural and economic conservative beliefs. *Journal of Personality, 72*(4), 659–686.

Hill, J. L., & Kriesi, H. (2001). An extension and test of Converse's "black-and-white" model of response stability. *American Political Science Review, 95*(2), 397–414.

Hirsh, J. B., DeYoung, C. G., Xu, X., & Peterson, J. B. (2010). Compassionate liberals and polite conservatives: Associations of agreeableness with political ideology and moral values. *Personality and Social Psychology Bulletin, 36*(5), 655–664.

Hochschild, J. (1981). *What's fair? Americans' attitudes toward distributive justice.* Cambridge, MA: Harvard University Press.

Inbar, Y., Pizarro, D. A., & Bloom, P. (2009). Conservatives are more easily disgusted than liberals. *Cognition and Emotion, 23*(4), 714–725.

Inbar, Y., Pizarro, D. A., & Bloom, P. (2012). Disgusting smells cause decreased liking of gay men. *Emotion, 12*(1), 23–27.

Inbar, Y., Pizarro, D. A., Knobe, J., & Bloom, P. (2009). Disgust sensitivity predicts intuitive disapproval of gays. *Emotion, 9*(3), 435–439.

Iyer, R., Koleva, S., Graham, J., Ditto, P., & Haidt, J. (2012). Understanding libertarian morality: The psychological dispositions of self-identified libertarians. *PLoS ONE, 7*(8), e42366.

Jacoby, W. G. (2006). Value choices and American public opinion. *American Journal of Political Science, 50*(3), 706–723.

Johnston, C. (2011). *The motivated formation of economic preferences.* PhD dissertation, Stony Brook University.

Jost, J. T., Federico, C. M., & Napier, J. L. (2009). Political ideology: Its structure, functions, and elective affinities. *Annual Review of Psychology, 60*, 307–337.

Jost, J. T., Glaser, J., Kruglanski, A. W., & Sulloway, F. J. (2003). Political conservatism as motivated social cognition. *Psychological Bulletin, 129*(3), 339–375.

Jost, J. T., Napier, J. L., Thorisdottir, H., Gosling, S. D., Palfai, T. P., & Ostafin, B. (2007). Are Needs to Manage Uncertainty and Threat Associated With Political Conservatism or Ideological Extremity? *Personality and Social Psychology Bulletin, 33*(7), 989–1007

Kanai, R., Feilden, T., Firth, C., & Rees, G. (2011). Political orientations are correlated with brain structure in young adults. *Current Biology, 21*(8), 677–680.

Kandler, C., Bleidorn, W., & Riemann, R. (2012). Left or right? Sources of political orientation: The roles of genetic factors, cultural transmission, assortative mating, and personality. *Journal of Personality and Social Psychology, 102*(3), 633–645. doi:10.1037/a0025560

Kerlinger, F. N. (1967). Social attitudes and their criterial referents: A structural theory. *Psychological Review, 74*(2), 110–122.

Kinder, D. R. (2006). Belief systems today. *Critical Review, 18*(1–3), 197–216.

Kinder, D. R., & Sanders, L. M. (1996). *Divided by color: Racial politics and democratic ideals.* Chicago: University of Chicago Press.

Knutsen, O. (1995). The impact of Old Politics and New Politics value orientations on party choice—a comparative study. *Journal of Public Policy, 15*, 1–63.

Kohlberg, L. (1969). *Stage and sequence: The cognitive-developmental approach to socialization.* Chicago: Rand McNally.

Lachat, R. (2011). The issue basis of citizens' ideological self-placement. Retrieved from http://www.romain-lachat.ch/papers/left_right.pdf.

Lakoff, G. (1996). *Moral politics: What conservatives know that liberals don't.* Chicago: University of Chicago Press.

Lane, R. E. (1962). *Political ideology.* New York: Free Press.

Laponce, J. A. (1981). *Left and right: The topography of political perceptions.* Toronto: University of Toronto Press.

Lewis, G. J., & Bates, T. C. (2011). From left to right: How the personality system allows basic traits to influence politics via characteristic moral adaptations. *British Journal of Psychology,* *102*(3), 546–558.

Lijphart, A. (1990). *Dimensions of ideology in European party systems.* New York: Oxford University Press.

Lippmann, W. ([1922] 1997). *Public opinion.* New Brunswick, NJ: Transaction.

Lipset, S. M. (1959). Democracy and working-class authoritarianism. *American Sociological Review,* *24*(4), 482–501.

Luskin, R. C. (1987). Measuring political sophistication. *American Journal of Political Science,* *31*(4), 856–899.

McAdams, D. P., Albaugh, M., Farber, E., Daniels, J., Logan, R. L., & Olson, B. (2008). Family metaphors and moral intuitions: How conservatives and liberals narrate their lives. *Journal of Personality and Social Psychology,* *95*(4), 978–990.

McClosky, H. (1958). Conservatism and personality. *American Political Science Review,* *52*(1), 27–45.

McClosky, H., & Zaller, J. (1984). *The American ethos: Public attitudes toward capitalism and democracy.* Cambridge, MA: Harvard University Press.

McCrae, R. R., & Costa, P. T., Jr. (1999). A five-factor theory of personality. *Handbook of personality: Theory and research* (2nd ed., pp. 139–153). New York: Guilford Press.

McCrae, R. R. & Allik, J. (2002). *The five-factor model of personality across cultures.* New York: Kluwer Academic.

Medland, S. E., & Hatemi, P. K. (2009). Political science, biometric theory, and twin studies: A methodological introduction. *Political Analysis,* *17*(2), 191–214.

Miller, W. E., & Shanks, J. M. (1996). *The new American voter.* Cambridge, MA: Harvard University Press.

Mirisola, A., Sibley, C. G., Boca, S., & Duckitt, J. (2007). On the ideological consistency between right-wing authoritarianism and social dominance orientation. *Personality and Individual Differences,* *43*(7), 1851–1862.

Mondak, J. J. (2010). *Personality and the foundations of political behavior.* New York: Cambridge University Press.

Murray, C. (1997). *What it means to be a libertarian: A personal interpretation.* New York: Broadway Books.

Oxley, D. R., Smith, K. B., Alford, J. R., Hibbing, M. V., Miller, J. L., Scalora, M., Hatemi, P. K., et al. (2008). Political attitudes vary with physiological traits. *Science,* *321*(5896), 1667–1670.

Peffley, M. A., & Hurwitz, J. (1985). A hierarchical model of attitude constraint. *American Journal of Political Science,* *29*(4), 871–890.

Piaget, J. (1997). *The moral judgment of the child.* New York: Free Press.

Piurko, Y., Schwartz, S. H., & Davidov, E. (2011). Basic personal values and the meaning of left-right political orientations in 20 countries. *Political Psychology* *32*(4), 537–561.

Pollock, P. H., Lilie, S. A., & Vittes, M. E. (1993). Hard issues, core values and vertical constraint: The case of nuclear power. *British Journal of Political Science,* *23*(1), 29–50.

Roccato, M., & Ricolfi, L. (2005). On the Correlation between Right-Wing Authoritarianism and social dominance orientation. *Basic and Applied Social Psychology,* *27*(3), 187–200.

Rohan, M. J., & Zanna, M. P. (1996). Value transmission in families. *The psychology of values: The Ontario symposium* (Vol. 8, pp. 253–276). Hillsdale, NJ: Lawrence Erlbaum.

Rokeach, M. (1973). *The nature of human values*. New York: Free Press.

Rokeach, M., & Hanley, C. (1956). Eysenck's tendermindedness dimension: A critique. *Psychological Bulletin, 53*(2), 169–176.

Sagiv, L., & Schwartz, S. H. (1995). Value priorities and readiness for out-group social contact. *Journal of Personality and Social Psychology, 69*(3), 437–448.

Schoen, H., & Schumann, S. (2007). Personality traits, partisan attitudes, and voting behavior. Evidence from Germany. *Political psychology, 28*(4), 471–498.

Schwartz, S. H. (1992). Universals in the content and structure of values: Theoretical advances and empirical tests in 20 countries. *Advances in Experimental Social Psychology, 25*(1), 1–65.

Schwartz, S. H. (1994). Are there universal aspects in the structure and contents of human values? *Journal of Social Issues, 50*(4), 19–45.

Schwartz, S. H., & Bilsky, W. (1987). Toward a universal psychological structure of human values. *Journal of Personality and Social Psychology, 53*(3), 550–562.

Schwartz, S. H., & Bilsky, W. (1990). Toward a theory of the universal content and structure of values: Extensions and cross-cultural replications. *Journal of Personality and Social Psychology, 58*(5), 878–891.

Settle, J. E., Dawes, C. T., Christakis, N. A., & Fowler, J. H. (2010). Friendships moderate an association between a dopamine gene variant and political ideology. *Journal of Politics, 72*(4), 1189–1198.

Sibley, C. G., & Duckitt, J. (2008). Personality and prejudice: A meta-analysis and theoretical review. *Personality and Social Psychology Review, 12*(3), 248–279.

Silventoinen, K. (2003). Determinants of variation in adult body height. *Journal of Biosocial Science, 35*(2), 263–285.

Silventoinen, K., Sammalisto, S., Perola, M., Boomsma, D. I., Cornes, B. K., Davis, C., Dunkel, L., et al. (2003). Heritability of adult body height: A comparative study of twin cohorts in eight countries. *Twin Research, 6*(5), 399–408.

Smith, K. B., Oxley, D. R., Hibbing, M. V., Alford, J. R., & Hibbing, J. R. (2011). Disgust Sensitivity and the Neurophysiology of Left-Right Political Orientations. *PLoS One, 6*(10), e25552.

Stenner, K. (2005). *The Authoritarian Dynamic*. Cambridge University Press.

Stimson, J. A. (1991). *Public opinion in America: Moods, cycles, and swings*. Boulder, CO: Westview Press.

Stone, W. F. (1980). The myth of left-wing authoritarianism. *Political Psychology, 2*(3–4), 3–19.

Swedlow, B. (2008). Beyond liberal and conservative: Two-dimensional conceptions of ideology and the structure of political attitudes and values. *Journal of Political Ideologies, 13*(2), 157–180.

Swedlow, B., & Wyckoff, M. L. (2009). Value preferences and ideological structuring of attitudes in American public opinion. *American Politics Research, 37*(6), 1048–1087.

Taggart, P. (2004). Populism and representative politics in contemporary Europe. *Journal of Political Ideologies, 9*(3), 269–288.

Tomkins, S. (1964). Left and right: A basic dimension in personality and ideology. In R. W. White (ed.), *The study of lives*. New York: Atherton.

Treier, S., & Hillygus, D. S. (2009). The nature of political ideology in the contemporary electorate. *Public Opinion Quarterly, 73*(4), 679–703.

Vecchione, M., Schoen, H., Castro, J. L. G., Cieciuch, J., Pavlopoulos, V., & Caprara, G. V. (2011). Personality correlates of party preference: The Big Five in five big European countries. *Personality and Individual Differences 51*(6), 737–742.

Wilson, G. D. (1973). *The psychology of conservatism*. New York: Academic Press.

Wilson, G. D., & Patterson, J. R. (1968). A new measure of conservatism. *British Journal of Social and Clinical Psychology*, *7*(4), 264–269.

Zaller, J. (1992). *The nature and origins of mass opinion*. New York: Cambridge University Press.

Zaller, J., & Feldman, S. (1992). A simple theory of the survey response: Answering questions versus revealing preferences. *American Journal of Political Science*, *36*(3), 579–616.

Zamboni, G., Gozzi, M., Krueger, F., Duhamel, J. R., Sirigu, A., & Grafman, J. (2009). Individualism, conservatism, and radicalism as criteria for processing political beliefs: A parametric fMRI study. *Social Neuroscience*, *4*(5), 367–383.

Zumbrunnen, J., & Gangl, A. (2008). Conflict, fusion, or coexistence? The complexity of contemporary American conservatism. *Political Behavior*, *30*(2), 199–221.

CHAPTER 20

SOCIAL JUSTICE

TOM R. TYLER AND
JOJANNEKE VAN DER TOORN

THIS chapter reviews the political psychology literature on social justice. Justice in the political arena involves reactions to the decisions and policies of political authorities and institutions that are based upon whether they act in ways that are right and proper, that is, achieve fair ends, enact just procedures, and appropriately punish wrongdoing. Central to all such judgments, evaluations, and reactions is the role of ethical or value-based judgments about what is right, proper, and/or just and fair.

Our focus is upon subjective approaches to justice and explores the influence of whether people evaluate decisions and policies as consistent with or discrepant from their judgments about what is right or wrong. This psychological approach can be contrasted to a philosophical approach in which scholars define objective criteria for evaluating the justice or injustice of authorities and institutions and their policies and practices. Such criteria are often based upon a philosophical normative analysis of factors that shape fairness.

Perhaps the best way to define justice is to contrast it to its major competing theory: perceived self-interest. Self-interested actors are viewed as behaving in ways that maximize their perceived gains or minimize their losses. Such gains and losses are often defined in material terms (e.g., money) but can also refer to such intangible entities as love, honor, and status. Actors are thought of as making decisions about how to behave by considering the anticipated impact of actions upon their own personal psychological "bottom line." People do those things that they think will bring them rewards and avoid those behaviors that are likely to lead to costs (for greater detail on self-interest see Chong, chapter 4, this volume).

Self-interest and justice theories may lead to divergent predictions in the political arena, for example predictions about how authorities effectively gain followership. One way authorities may motivate others to follow them and to accept their decisions is by exerting their power to threaten punishment or promise reward. Another way is by creating a sense among followers that their rule is appropriate and right. These judgments that an authority or institution in its decisions or policies is acting in ways that are consistent with what people believe is just or fair are of value if and when followers are motivated by more than anticipated punishments and rewards. Justice can at times conflict with self-interest and the prediction of which will win out in a given situation is not as straightforward as is often assumed. Do people prefer a just leader, or someone who delivers greater resources and opportunities to them? Are people troubled if they see evidence that others are being treated unfairly? These questions raise issues about the range and depth of people's commitments to justice in their political lives. The literature we review in this chapter demonstrates that justice judgments are strongly felt and can sometimes motivate people to act in ways and make choices that go against their self-interest. Citizens might, for example, reject a policy that favors them or their own groups because they think it is unfair.

Justice has a long history as it relates to politics and governance. It was around 380 B.C. that Plato discussed the nature of justice and of the ideal community in his classic work *The Republic*. And issues of justice and injustice have been recognized as central to the study of political order and stability as well as being among the most important antecedents of rebellions and revolutions ever since (Gurr, 1970; Moore, 1978). As we have noted, people do not simply respond to the exertion of power when dealing with others but are also concerned about what they think is fair. This centrality of justice to political issues is a core theme throughout history and well justifies the normatively based statement of Rawls that "justice is the first virtue of social institutions" and, therefore, that "laws and institutions no matter how efficient and well-arranged must be reformed or abolished if they are unjust" (Rawls, 1971). It also underscores Henry Lewis Mencken's assertion that "If you want peace work for justice" and explains the widespread concern about justice in the literatures on governance and political philosophy (Barry, 2005; Brighouse, 2004; Clayton & Williams, 2004; Fleischacker, 2004; Miller, 1999; Sandel, 2009; Sen, 2009; White, 2007).

Our goal for this chapter is not to review the long history of justice as a political and philosophical idea (and ideal) but instead to focus on the recent empirical literature on the connections of social justice to governance. To this end, we will address a series of questions central to the study of the psychology of justice in political contexts. The first question is whether justice matters. Are people's thoughts, feelings, and actions actually impacted by their evaluations of fairness or unfairness? It is only if justice makes a distinct impact upon people beyond judgments about their personal or group self-interest that it assumes importance, and several bodies of theory dispute the importance of justice (e.g., self-interest-based rational choice theories; see Green & Shapiro, 1994). Second, we address the question of what is considered just, that is, the rules that people apply to define justice in different types of settings. Research suggests that there is no universal rule indicating what is right or wrong in all settings and that context can have a distinct influence on justice judgments. Third, we consider the different levels at which justice may be framed: the level of the individual, the group, and society as a whole. The level at which people think of justice or injustice is important because it determines both the degree to which they see injustice and how they respond to it. Of course, even objectively unfair events may not necessarily be interpreted as unfair because people may be motivated to accept or justify their unwelcome realities. The fourth question we address is, therefore, when people would engage in efforts to restore actual justice and when they would be motivated to restore a psychological sense of justice through justification. A fifth question concerns the scope of justice, that is, the range of cases to which considerations of justice are applied. People may use a justice frame to structure and interpret events involving human beings but think nothing of eating a cow, squashing a bug, or cutting down a tree. Also, within the category of human beings, people may limit justice to those who share their community, nationality, ethnicity, or religion.

Finally, we discuss the relationship between justice and other social and political values. While distinct in some ways, justice and fairness share features with morality and ethicality, all being values of varying types. We conclude by commenting on the importance of the psychology of justice to the broader issues addressed within political psychology, arguing that justice is a core organizing principle within groups, organizations, and societies and hence central to discussions of a broad variety of topics within the study of governance.

1. DOES JUSTICE MATTER?

Researchers have explored whether justice matters by considering to what extent three distinct types of justice influence people's thoughts, feelings, and actions. Distributive justice concerns the fairness of the allocations of resources and opportunities across people, groups, and societies. For example, when a group of people divide a cake or a bag of cookies based on some principle of deservingness, they are concerned with distributive justice. Procedural justice focuses on the fairness of the procedures, rules, institutions, and authorities through which allocations are made. For example, a trial can be conducted by the adversarial or the inquisitorial method, which are different procedures that may or may not be viewed as a fair way to decide guilt or innocence. Retributive justice concerns what is considered fair punishment of those who break rules. If people steal from others, we may feel that they should apologize, should compensate the victims, and/or should spend time in jail. Each involves a question of appropriate justice in response to wrongdoing and may depend not only on the type of offense but also on who the offender is and what the circumstances are.

Within each of these three areas of justice, researchers have demonstrated that justice generally shapes people's attitudes, feelings, and behaviors in ways that are distinct from simply acting based on material self-interest (Sauermann & Kaiser, 2010; Tyler, Boeckmann, Smith, & Huo, 1997). People are not primarily interested in maximizing their personal or group-based self-interest in collective settings but also have a powerful desire to receive and to provide others with justice.

1.1. Distributive Justice

Distributive justice is concerned with the fairness of allocations. Principles of distributive justice define the rules that govern fair outcome distributions among people within the context of groups, organizations, communities, and societies. The three most typically articulated distributive justice principles are equity, equality, and need (Deutsch, 1975). Each provides a way to move from people's inputs to their outcomes. Equality provides equal resources or opportunities to all regardless of their inputs. Equity distributes resources or opportunities by merit, productivity, or effort. Need distributes resources or opportunities by giving the most to those with the fewest prior resources or the least capability to obtain them for themselves. While these principles of distributive justice are often applied to the allocation of material outcomes, they can in fact refer to the distribution of anything that people find to be of worth (whether it be money, status, honor, etc.).

Two assumptions underlie distributive justice research. The first is that people evaluate and react to their outcomes not simply in terms of how much they receive but also by comparing their outcomes to a standard, which could potentially be their own outcomes at other points in time and/or the outcomes of others. The second assumption is that the standards people use reflect a principle of justice, that is, people's reactions are shaped by their views about what people deserve or are entitled to. The first principle is central to relative deprivation models that link discontent to temporal and social comparisons. The second principle reflects distributive justice because people are making their comparison using a standard of justice when they consider what they deserve or are entitled to receive.

The psychological literature on distributive justice demonstrates that people care about whether or not their outcomes are fair and become upset when they receive too little or too much compared to a standard of what is appropriate or deserved. These standards can be derived from many sources. For example, assessments of deservedness may be based upon people's status; how hard they have worked; or how much they are in need, either relative to others or to themselves at other points in time. Irrespective of where such standards come from, people may feel that what they receive departs from their sense of entitlement or deservingness.

Two types of people are potentially politically interesting: those who have too little and those who have too much. It is not surprising that underbenefited people may feel angry, since this reaction is predicted by both justice theories and theories of self-interest, and a large political psychology literature links disadvantage to discontent and engagement in unconventional political behaviors ranging from voting for the opposition to demonstrations and riots (e.g., Crosby, 1976). It is equally interesting that when the disadvantaged choose not to act, they may still be influenced by their feelings of unfair disadvantage and show signs of stress and depression, which may lead to drinking, drug use, and suicide (see Tyler et al., 1997, chap. 7).

In addition, one of the most striking and potentially important aspects of distributive justice theories is the prediction that overbenefited people will also be dissatisfied with their situation. This runs contrary to self-interest theories, which would expect these people to be highly satisfied. If a sense of justice can motivate the well-off to redistribute resources to the disadvantaged, many of whom lack the political power they would need to mandate such a redistribution by themselves, then it can be an important source of social change and progress. In other words, concerns about justice help those who are unlikely to be able to prevail based upon their power.

A number of empirical studies support the above-mentioned predictions by showing that people become upset either if they have too little or if they have too much. In the context of work, research shows that employees who believe they are over- or underpaid are less satisfied than those who believe they are being fairly paid (Adams, 1965; Walster, Walster, & Berscheid, 1978). Studies also suggest that workers adjust their level of effort and productivity (Greenberg, 1988) and even steal (Greenberg, 1990) to restore equity. Finally, people leave situations characterized by distributive unfairness and move to situations where they feel fairly compensated, even if that means they will be earning less (Schmitt & Marwell, 1972). In the context of relationships, studies show that those characterized by distributive justice are more satisfying and long-lasting than relationships characterized by injustice (Van Yperen & Buunk, 1994). For example, when both parties in a relationship indicate that what they receive is "fair" in relation to what they give, the relationship is more likely to last.

The two literatures noted above illustrate the two approaches commonly taken to distributive justice studies. In experimental studies of justice participants tend to be explicitly told that they are either receiving more or that they are receiving less than they deserve. For example, they will be told that their payment is appropriate, "too much," or "too little" compared to the effort they put into a task or compared to specific others. By manipulating the perceived fairness of the distribution, the experimenter can be sure that any differences in some outcome variable (e.g., satisfaction or willingness to engage in another task) are due to the difference between the conditions. In natural situations, studies tend to be based upon questionnaires. The power of justice judgments in these real-world settings is tapped by asking people to rate their inferences on scales (e.g., scales running from "not at all fair" to "very fair"). Their answers are subsequently correlated with some outcome variable to examine their relationship.

Theories of distributive justice also apply to people's reactions to governance. In particular, evaluations of public policy are rooted in judgments about the application of fair distribution principles (Michelbach, Scott, Matland, & Bornstein, 2003). For example, opposition to affirmative action can be understood through an equity framework in which rewards are evaluated through judgments of individual-level effort and ability rather than group memberships (Reyna, Tucker, Korfmacher, & Henry, 2005; Taylor & Moghaddam, 1994). This perspective suggests that the person who is better educated, brighter, or harder working should be hired or promoted. Similarly, judgments of equity, equality, and need have been shown to shape public policy support in general (Pratto, Tatar, & Conway-Lanz, 1999), support for the poor (Appelbaum, 2001), and support for the elderly (Huddy, Jones, & Chard, 2001). In each case people express the highest levels of support for policies that they think support the distribution of resources to those who deserve them. In the case of the elderly, for example, people support aid to the elderly when they feel that elderly people deserve to receive those resources because of their actions (they worked earlier in their lives) or their status (they are in need) or for other reasons. Hence, it is important to know which distributive justice principles people apply when considering a particular policy toward a specific group since a group might be deserving based upon one principle but not deserving based upon another principle. We will further discuss this issue below.

1.2. Procedural Justice

Procedural justice refers to the fairness of the procedures through which decisions about allocation, conflict resolution, and leadership or policy formation are made. Whenever people are involved in interactions with others (e.g., situations that involve authorities, rules, and institutions), they care about the procedures being used to make decisions. One example is markets. Although we often talk about "free markets," the perceived desirability of these markets is influenced by whether people believe them to operate according to fair procedures (Sondak & Tyler, 2007). Another example is negotiation, where people are found to focus upon the degree to which they feel that their partner is following "fair procedures" when negotiating (Hollander-Blumoff & Tyler, 2008).

While procedural justice may be broadly important, most studies of procedural justice are concerned with formal leaders and authorities, and large literatures exist on procedural justice involving law, management, and governnance. While it is possible to imagine that societies could function without hierarchies, authorities, and institutions, the reality is that people typically organize themselves into political groups that have authority structures. As a consequence, it is important to identify fair procedures for creating authorities and institutions and, once created, for those authorities and institutions to fairly exercise their authority to make policies, to allocate resources, and to resolve conflicts.

Procedural justice is particularly important in this regard because recent research suggests that it is a key aspect of people's relation to authorities and institutions. Procedural justice shapes the legitimacy of authorities and institutions and, through it, the willingness of people to defer to the decisions of authorities and to the rules created by institutions (Grimes, 2006; Hibbing & Theiss-Morse, 1995; 2001; 2002). This procedural justice effect on legitimacy and deference is found to be widespread and robust and occurs in legal, political, educational, and managerial settings (Tyler, 2006a; 2006b; 2011). Similarly, political authorities and institutions lose legitimacy when they do not adhere to procedural fairness norms (Baird & Gangl, 2006; Clawson, Kegler, & Waltenberg, 2001; Farnsworth, 2003; Gangl, 2003; Hibbing & Theiss-Morse, 2002; Murphy, 2004).

Recent research on political institutions and authorities in new democracies supports the argument that procedural issues underlie the perceived legitimacy of political authorities and institutions. A study of eastern European countries by Kluegel and Mason (2004) suggests that both procedural and distributive justice judgments about the economic system shape political support, and studies conducted in other developing societies show that evidence of procedural injustice, in the form of corruption (i.e., unfair decision-making procedures), undermines political support (Seligson, 2002).

The procedural base of legitimacy has widespread implications for the legitimation of authority figures since it suggests why people do or do not view their leaders as legitimate (Tyler, 2006a; 2006b). It is often believed that leaders are legitimate if they solve problems or deliver "the goods." However, the research outlined suggests that people also focus on how their leaders govern, and view those who exercise their authority in fair ways as legitimate.

One key issue is the procedure by which an authority is established. In democracies elections play a central role in establishing the legitimate authority of an executive or legislative leader. What is crucial to a democratic state is that the losers in an election defer to the will of the majority and accept the right of the winner to rule in the name of the entire group. It is this ability to gain "losers' consent" that is the central consequence of procedural fairness (Anderson, Blais, Bowler, Donovan, & Listhaug, 2005; Anderson & LoTempio, 2002).

The potentially facilitative role of elections in conferring legitimacy upon authorities has been long recognized within political science (Gonzalez & Tyler, 2008), but it is not automatic and depends upon many factors, including the procedural fairness of the election process (Craig, Martinez, Gainous, & Kane, 2006; Moehler, 2009). It is for this reason that many scholars were concerned about the potential for illegitimacy following the Bush versus Gore election, which was, in effect, decided by the Supreme Court (Sunstein & Epstein, 2001).

In addition, procedures are important when policies are being implemented (Lind & Tyler, 1988; Thibaut & Walker, 1975). In political processes the widespread effort to create deliberative political procedures for implementing public policies is motivated, in part, by the demonstration that public participation in such procedures both facilitates policy acceptance and enhances political legitimacy (Delli, Carpini, Cook, & Jacobs, 2004). The efforts of the legal system to create more informal legal procedures such as mediation reflect the similar recognition that the public experiences these procedures as fairer and that their use enhances the legitimacy of legal authorities (Landsman, 2003; Shestowsky, 2004). Similarly, in work settings, the use of open and participatory styles of leadership has been linked to the desire to build legitimacy and gain cooperation from employees (DeCremer & van Knippenberg, 2002; Keyes, Hysom, & Lupo, 2000).

Political scientists have long recognized the link between institutional legitimacy and procedure. For example, Murphy and Tanenhaus (1969) draw upon the writing of Easton (1965) and focus on the key role of the perceived fairness of the rules by which courts operate in creating legitimacy ("the rules of the game"). They argue that courts gain legitimacy when they are believed to be generally "impartial, just and competent" in their decision-making procedures (p. 359), even when people disagree with the substance of their decisions. Indeed, people distinguish support for particular decisions or justices (specific system support) from support for the fairness of the manner in which the court carries out its decision-making responsibilities (diffuse system support; Murphy & Tanenhaus, 1969).

A number of studies support the suggestion that decision-making that is based upon legal guidelines tends to be viewed as a fair procedure for exercising legal authority

(Baird & Gangl, 2006; Hibbing & Theiss-Morse, 1995). For example, Gibson, Caldeira, and Spence (2005) argued that the United States Supreme Court could legitimate policy decisions; Tyler and Mitchell (1994) found that the Court could legitimate deference to decisions about abortion; and Ramirez (2008) linked perceived procedural fairness to general support for the Court. Internationally, Gibson and Caldeira (2003) found that the South African Supreme Court had only a limited ability to legitimate decisions through the use of fair procedures. Similar procedural justice arguments have been made concerning other forms of political authority (Dahl, 1971; 1989), and more recent studies support this connection in terms of political action. As an example, Gibson (1996; 1997) demonstrated that support for the institutions and processes of democratic governance led to opposition to an undemocratic coup in the USSR.

Experimental studies of established political authority also support the basic procedural justice argument that fair procedures facilitate decision acceptance. In such studies procedural justice is the independent (i.e., manipulated) variable, and higher levels of decision acceptance are a consequence of using a fairer procedure to make the decision. Tyler and Degoey (1995) showed that people were more willing to accept water use rules from political authorities who made decisions about the distribution of water in fair ways. Studies of land-use policy demonstrated that people who evaluated political decisions as made using fair procedures had higher levels of trust and were more willing to accept decisions (Grimes, 2006) and that the procedural justice of land-use hearings in South Africa legitimated eviction decisions (Gibson, 2008). Terwel, Harinck, Ellemers, and Daamen (2010) examined the willingness of interest groups to accept environmental rules and found that people who had a voice during the decision-making process were more trusting of authorities and more willing to accept their decisions. In addition, Hibbing and Alford (2004) found that people reacted negatively to unfair allocations and were especially upset when the procedures that the allocator used to decide on a particular distribution suggested that it was their intention to treat them unfairly (i.e., by evidence of procedural injustice).

A quite different viewpoint to which we will return is to view legitimacy as a consequence of the motivation to justify the status quo and, hence, of existing power differences (Van der Toorn, Tyler, & Jost, 2011). From this perspective people do not only judge the fairness of procedures; they are also motivated to view existing authorities and institutions as desirable, fair, and legitimate. As a consequence, people may distort their perceptions when their experiences raise questions about justice. We will address this view of justice in more detail later in this chapter.

1.3. Retributive Justice

The section on procedural justice already discussed people's natural inclination to create structures of governance that include authorities and institutions. Those authorities and institutions create informal rules and more formal laws and take on the responsibility to enforce them. Breaking these laws results in receiving punishment. The desire to punish can be especially strong among other members of the collectivities to which the wrongdoer belongs because part of being a member of a group, community, or society is a presumed commitment to the norms and values of the group. Rule breaking raises questions about whether the rule breaker is in fact committed to those norms. It also raises doubts about whether those norms and values are strong enough to constrain the behavior of the members of a collectivity and through that constraint maintain social order. For these reasons punishment is a way to restore a sense of both material and identity balance between the wrongdoer and the victims, as well as to maintain the more general sense that there is a moral balance within the larger collectivity. In the absence of punishment people lose respect for the law and for political and legal institutions (Hogan & Emler, 1981; Miller & Vidmar, 1981; Vidmar & Miller, 1980; Vidmar, 2000).

The state claims a monopoly on the right to use force to uphold social rules, and consequently people hold political and legal authorities accountable for whether they do in fact appropriately identify and punish criminals. One of the universal features of political authorities is that they have to be able to enforce the core rules defining their political group to be viewed as legitimate, credible, and effective in their roles (Hogan & Emler, 1981; Miller & Vidmar, 1981; Vidmar & Miller, 1980; Vidmar, 2000). It is the ability of the state to enact justice that prevents people from engaging in acts of retaliation and revenge. In such cases the people involved must restrain themselves from acting upon their emotional feelings desiring revenge and follow rules. Their willingness to do so is conditioned upon the belief that the state will, in fact, see that justice is done.

One area in which the question of retribution has recently been studied by political psychologists is the area of transitional justice (Staub, 2006). When a government changes and especially when an authoritarian regime becomes more democratic the question arises of whether and how to punish those authority figures who committed crimes in the former regime. This issue has been important in a wide variety of settings, including the former Communist bloc countries, the Balkans, Cambodia, and South Africa (Whitt & Wilson, 2007). For example, Gibson (2007) studied the effort to deal with transitional issues through "truth commissions" in South Africa. Based upon a survey of South Africans, he argues that the truth-seeking process did contribute to reconciliation. Gibson argues that the primary element of a successful truth-seeking commission is the legitimacy gained by using fair procedures, in particular by being seen as even-handed (Gibson, 2007). Others suggest that procedures work when those procedures involve apologies (Blatz, Schumann & Ross, 2009) and accord with local views of procedural fairness (Duch & Palmer, 2004). Others suggest that reframing the issue from retribution toward principles of redistribution (i.e., distributive justice) by focusing upon equalizing resources also facilitates reconciliation (David & Choi, 2009).

1.4. Justice and Social Coordination

Three types of justice have been considered: distributive, procedural, and retributive justice. In each case there is evidence that people care about justice. People are more willing to accept social decisions they view as just, independent of whether they benefit personally. And they will accept losses to defend justice principles, supporting the argument that people value justice in political settings.

Justice is particularly important when people are functioning within a group, an organization, a community, or a society. If people are going to reap the benefits of living in social arrangements led by authorities and institutions, they must have rules and procedures for determining how to distribute benefits among the people with whom they interact (who gets what and why), as well as procedures for dealing with those who violate rules. The effectiveness of such rules is largely determined by whether they are widely shared within the group, organization, community, or society. Evidence suggests that such consensus on social rules, which although not universal is widespread, facilitates efficient and effective interactions. People are able to conduct their lives in a series of interactions with others and can within those interactions both act fairly and expect fairness from others, with all parties agreeing about how fairness will be defined. Shared rules also allow people to evaluate whether their commitment to a collectivity is reasonable or whether they should reevaluate their connection.

To be most effective, conceptions of fair rules, procedures, and principles of justice need to be shared. As an example, to the extent that there are ideological differences and liberals think that equality is more important in shaping fair distributions than do conservatives, it is hard to use distributive justice to make allocations that will be acceptable to everyone involved. Procedural justice judgments are particularly important in this regard, since ideology influences evaluations of distributive and retributive justice, but has at best a minimal influence upon evaluations of procedural justice. Liberals and conservatives generally agree about the procedural justice principles that define a fair procedure for deciding what welfare policy should be. Those principles are provide voice; be neutral; treat people with respect; and consider people's needs and concerns. Hence, a focus on procedural justice is less likely to lead to political polarization, a situation in which one group of people feels that justice has been done, while another does not.

2. What Is Just?

Within each of these three justice literatures a second important issue is identifying the principles that people use to decide whether something is fair. As said, the three most typically articulated distributive justice principles are equity, equality, and need (Deutsch, 1975). Within procedural justice people generally define the fairness of procedures by referring to four procedural principles: the procedure provides voice; decisions are made neutrally; the authorities are acting in a sincere, benevolent, and trustworthy manner; and people and their rights are treated with respect during the decision-making process. Finally, retributive justice typically involves decisions about the intention of the actor(s) and through that assessment the social implications of the rule-breaking incident (Okimoto, Wenzel, & Feather, 2011; Wenzel, Okimoto, Feather, & Platow, 2008).

2.1. Distributive Justice

Studies suggest that people generally associate equity with the distribution of rewards in work settings; equality with political settings; and need with family or friendship settings (for a lengthier discussion of egalitarianism see Feldman, chapter 19, this volume). Deutsch (1975; 1982; 1985) theorizes that the principle that people use is based upon the goal they want to achieve. He suggests that equity is viewed as leading to productivity; equality to social harmony; and need to social welfare. While all of these principles can apply to any arena of life, the Barrett-Howard and Tyler findings suggest that people view social harmony as a particularly important aspect of political systems, productivity of economic systems, and social welfare of social systems (Barrett-Howard & Tyler, 1986).

Why should equality promote social harmony? Of the different principles of distributive justice equality has the virtue of simplicity and straightforwardness. Political principles such as "one person, one vote" are clear and easy to implement. In contrast, equity and need both require individual-level evaluations, one of effort or ability and the other of need, and are therefore more open to disputes about how they should be applied. Studies suggest, for example, that equity is not as effective an allocation mechanism when people exaggerate the value of their contributions to groups. Conversely, studies of social welfare find that people disagree about who is in need and whether they should be helped. Such differences are especially problematic in political settings because they are linked to ideology, with liberals more concerned with need and conservatives with effort (Skitka & Tetlock, 1992).

2.2. Procedural Justice

Equality is a simple rule of distributive justice because it is easy to implement. However, to apply evaluations of merit or need someone has to decide how much merit people have or how much need they are in. It is hard to trust the actual people to whom resources would be allocated because they may be motivated to exaggerate their effort or their need so as to benefit themselves. Hence, to make decisions involving merit or need it is beneficial to have a neutral person make evaluations of deservedness. What is needed is an authority or institution that has procedures for weighing claims and evidence, as well as determining which decision rules are appropriate and which can provide judgments that are neutral and hence more acceptable to all parties. For this reason, as has been noted, in complex social situations people typically shift their focus away from distributive rules to procedural ones. For example, Thibaut and Walker (1975) found that people focused upon their opportunities to present their evidence to a neutral decision-maker, assuming that that authority would then be able to make a decision that would reflect relevant rules of distributive justice (in this case they studied equity). In other words, they expected that procedural justice would lead to distributive justice.

Studies typically identify four key components of procedural justice that people consider when evaluating an allocation or dispute resolution procedure (Blader & Tyler, 2003; Tyler & Lind, 1992). Two are linked to decision-making. They are voice and neutrality. Two are linked to interpersonal treatment. They are trust and courtesy (or, treatment with respect). Studies generally suggest that courtesy and treatment with respect dominate reactions to personal experiences with authorities (Tyler & Huo, 2002). This factor is closely intertwined with trust in the motives of authorities.

When authorities give honest explanations and when they treat people and their concerns respectfully, they are viewed as both trustworthy and fair. And, of course, allowing people voice so that their concerns can be considered and showing evidence of good intentions through neutral and fact-based decision-making involving the consistent application of rules also promotes inferences of trustworthiness and perceptions of fairness.

2.3. Retributive Justice

While people feel that some form of response to rule breaking is required, there are widespread differences in the severity and form of response that is viewed as appropriate. One core distinction is made between retribution—punishing the offender—and restoration—repairing the damage via compensation, restitution, or apology. In retributive justice the state unilaterally imposes a punishment upon an offender. Restoration, in contrast, is a consensual effort by the parties, including the offender, to reaffirm the values violated by the offender and to find a way to restore those values. Traditional treatments of reactions to wrongdoing focus on punishment of the offender (Darley, 2002; Feather, 1999; Vidmar, 2000). The suggestion is that wrongdoing disturbs the moral balance in society and punishment restores it (Carlsmith, Darley, & Robinson, 2002; Darley, Carlsmith, & Robinson, 2000). The victim has been degraded and diminished and his or her status needs to be restored (Murphy & Hampton, 1988). Studies show this by demonstrating that the degree to which people want to punish an offender is not linked to the extent of the material harm done or the degree of future danger. Instead, it is a reflection of the degree to which people think that the crime damaged social norms and/or diminished the status and undermined the identity of the victim (Darley & Pittman, 2003).

An alternative conception of retributive justice is that it should be less linked to the state and that more responsibility and decision-making authority should be given to the victims, offenders, and communities affected by the rule breaking. Such approaches emphasize identifying and clarifying local social norms and renewing a social consensus about the harm done and the appropriate ways to correct that harm, as occurs in restorative justice conferences (Wenzel et al., 2008). Restorative justice conferences proceed from the perspective of "good person, bad action." In them efforts are made to encourage offenders to recognize their commitment to adhering to social rules. People from the community, the offender's family, and the victim work together to reengage the offender in the community while also identifying actions he or she can take to atone for the wrongdoing (restitution, apology, etc.). This approach has the advantage of being more satisfactory to victims, who often feel excluded from the procedures used by the state to manage reactions to crimes. It is also more likely to lower subsequent recidivism on the part of the offender, who feels fairly treated and consequently is more likely to view social rules as legitimate and to obey them in the future.

However, the effective use of restorative procedures that aim to reconcile the offender and the offended requires a willingness among the various parties to engage in a sincere effort to develop a shared understanding of the social implications of the offense and how to respond to it. If, for example, the "wrongdoer" denies having broken the rules or fails to express any regret, to acknowledge any harm, to apologize, or to offer some form of compensation, then restorative approaches cannot be effective in situations in which the victim's identity has been harmed by the offense (Okimoto et al., 2011). An example is a situation in which the "wrongdoer" refuses to acknowledge that he or she committed the behavior or refuses to express regret for the harm inflicted. In extreme cases harm doers even belittle or ridicule the victim in an effort to justify their behavior, arguing that those harmed "deserved" what happened because they were careless or weak, as when people dehumanize victims (Kelman & Hamilton, 1989). Many historical examples can be cited, such as the racism and negative stereotyping targeted toward African Americans through much of American history.

Certainly victims find it hard to forgive a wrongdoer who is not repentant because this leaves them with diminished status and a damaged social identity. Thus, in situations in which responses to rule breaking are difficult to frame in restorative terms, the state, as the entity with a legitimate right to use coercion and force, remains the backup option for responding to rule breaking.

2.4. Consensus about Justice

In the case of each type of justice—distributive, procedural, or retributive—no single principle defines the meaning of that form of justice. What is just depends upon the nature of the social situation and upon the individual characteristics of the perceiver. For example, in America equality is seen as distributively just in political settings, but not in economic situations. On the other hand, studies suggest that within a given society there is typically broad consensus among different types of people about what type of rules define justice in a given type of setting (Tyler, 1985, 2012). This consensus can be overstated because there are differences of opinion among liberals and conservatives (Mitchell, Tetlock, Newman, & Lerner, 2003), but it is this general consensus that is important to the ability of justice to facilitate social interactions and diminish conflicts. For justice to be of value in the exercise of authority the type of principle involved is less central than whether people agree about which principles apply. Similarly, people are found to view different procedures to be appropriate for resolving different types of conflict, but within any given situation different types of people generally agree about what is a fair procedure. And, finally, within a given society people generally agree as to how to handle a particular type of wrongdoing (Tyler, 1985).

The fact that people within societies agree is striking given that differences between societies are large in terms of whether and how they punish wrongdoing. Studies show that there is considerable cross-national variation as to which justice principle is appropriate in a given setting (e.g., Van der Toorn, Berkics, & Jost, 2010). This seems consistent with the suggestion that it is agreement among interacting parties that is central to the effectiveness of justice as a facilitator of social life. It also highlights the difficulties that can arise when people from different collectivities try to interact with one another. Because people within a particular group, community, or society are likely to view their justice principles as self-evidently correct, the potential for conflict in intergroup situations is high.

Given that people typically want to achieve multiple goals in any situation, while each justice principle is primarily associated with one goal, groups often find ways to make decisions in ways that combine justice rules. For example, many work organizations divide up annual compensation increases into two parts, giving everyone some set raise (equality) and then allocating some money to those who work harder or produce more (equity). This addresses the goals of social harmony and productivity at the same time.

Okun (1975) talked about such trade-offs in the political arena. He suggested that there is a trade-off between equality and equity, with equity promoting productivity and equality promoting social harmony. This political argument is widely used to justify inequalities in income and wealth by contending that inequality results from the desirable use of the productivity-promoting allocation principle of equity. However, it has been disputed based upon empirical research in work settings, which suggests that equality can lead to equally high levels of productivity (Deutsch, 1985). Similarly, systems of hierarchy and command and control are often justified in productivity terms. Research does not support this argument in all settings. Instead, studies suggest that procedures that are fairer in the sense of allowing greater input and participation in decision-making often lead to greater productivity (Tyler & Blader, 2000). This is the case because these fairer procedures encourage people to more strongly identify with the collectivities involved and to become more motivated to act on behalf of those collectivities by working for their success.

One very salient example of the consequences of retributive justice principles is the use of unusually punitive punishment policies in the United States relative to other societies. This approach has widespread public support in terms of American conceptions of appropriate or just punishment, but it also has important societal consequences. For example, it requires a large societal allocation of resources to build and staff prisons, as well as a large police presence in disadvantaged communities to manage the high rates of recidivism among ex-inmates. Other societies in comparison are more likely to view informal justice, including apology, restitution, and rehabilitation, to be fair ways to deal with wrongdoing. Of course, there are likely types or levels of wrongdoing that no society can or will forgive. For example, leaders who engage in violence toward people under their authority may find that their victims are unwilling to forgo vengeance and punishment no matter how much regret they express over their actions.

3. Individual, Group-Based, and Societal Justice

One level of justice is the individual or personal level, but justice can also be conceptualized at the group level or at the societal or system level (Tyler, 2012). Individual justice refers to what a particular person receives, as in "My raise was less than I deserved." Group-based justice claims are framed in terms of group membership, for example, "African Americans are unfairly treated" or "Gays deserve more rights." Finally, societal judgments speak to the overall distribution of resources or opportunities in society. We might say, for example, that it is "unfair" that 1 percent of our society's population controls such a large share of our total wealth.

As the issue of affirmative action illustrates, a policy can be both fair and unfair at the same time depending upon the level at which it is examined. Affirmative action is often suggested to be fair at a group level in that it attempts to achieve a fair distribution of opportunities between groups (e.g., it redresses past disadvantage of qualified women in employment situations), but is equally often argued to be unfair to individuals because members of disadvantaged groups are (as individuals) given preferential treatment (e.g., it may disadvantage the qualified male vying for the same job as a qualified female applicant; see Crosby & Konrad, 2002 for a review of the public debate). Similarly, income redistribution may make society fairer in macro terms, but can again be seen as an unfair measure to particular individuals or groups, for example, the wealthy individuals who pay higher tax rates than others because they got rich through hard work. These issues have led to hotly contested political debates that revolve around the different conceptions of justice. Our goal is not to take a position on these debates but rather to illustrate how opinions may differ based upon the level at which justice is framed. However, although this means that different sides to a debate can legitimately claim to be motivated by a desire to see justice done, social implications may differ depending on the type of framing.

Whereas affirmative action procedures are often based on considerations of group membership in addition to considerations of merit, it is commonly viewed as based on group membership alone (Crosby & Konrad, 2002). This has pernicious consequences. Heilman, Block, and Lucas (1992), for example, showed that students rated women described as an affirmative action hire as less competent than men or than women without such designation. Kinder (chapter 25, this volume) discusses how support for racial affirmative action policies varies with how the policy is framed.

Laboratory studies have demonstrated that people react more negatively to selection procedures when group membership is considered in addition to consideration of merit (e.g., Heilman, Battle, Keller, & Lee, 1998). Similarly, people who believed they were selected on the basis of group membership rather than merit evaluated their own general and task-specific performance as lower (Heilman et al., 1998), but when the beneficiaries of affirmative action were told that their qualifications were high, they did not show the same negative effects as when they believed their abilities were not a factor in selection (Heilman, Rivero, & Brett, 1991).

3.1. Distributive Justice

Relative deprivation, a term originally coined by Merton (1938; see also Merton & Kitt, 1950), refers at the individual level to the perceived discrepancy between a person's value expectations and his or her value capabilities, in other words, between what one has and what one feels one should have (Folger, 1986; Runciman, 1966). Relative deprivation theory assumes that feelings of relative deprivation result from a comparison of one's situation with a certain standard, which may be one's past situation, someone else's situation, or a desired situation following from considerations of justice principles (Folger, 1986). If a comparison results in the conclusion that one is not receiving what one deserves, a person is relatively deprived.

A critical distinction is made in this literature between relative deprivation at the personal (i.e., I get less than I should) and the group level (i.e., my group gets less than it should; Kelly & Breinlinger, 1996; Runciman, 1966). This framing issue is important because it shapes whether people respond to injustice as individuals or as groups. In particular, the group-level framing of injustice may lead to collective action (Major, 1994; Martin, 1986), which has been defined as acts by which people act as representatives of the group and when the action is directed at improving the conditions of the group as a whole (Wright, Taylor, & Moghaddam, 1990; Klandermans & van Stekelenburg, chapter 24, this volume). In his seminal work *Why Men Rebel* Gurr (1970) contends that feelings of economic relative deprivation are at the roots of political violence, as people collectively voice their discontent with the discrepancy between their group's expected and actual material conditions.

In addition to felt grievances associated with perceived deprivation (e.g., Gurr, 1970; Klandermans, 1997), various other factors have been identified as influencing the likelihood of collective (i.e., group) action: felt grievances associated with perceived deprivation (e.g., Klandermans, 1997), a sense of collective efficacy (e.g., van Stekelenburg & Klandermans, 2007; van Zomeren, Spears, Fischer, & Leach, 2004), embeddedness in civil society networks (Klandermans, Van der Toorn, & van Stekelenburg, 2008), and identification with the group (e.g., Tajfel & Turner, 1979).

Research on the latter demonstrates that the more people identify with a group, the more likely it is that they will participate in action on behalf of the group (Abrams, 1992;

Simon & Klandermans, 2001; Sabucedo, Rodrigues, & de Weerd, 2002; see also O'Brien & Major, 2005). This suggests that people participate in collective action not only for instrumental reasons but also to fulfill identity needs.

More recent research has looked at the role of emotions in collective action and suggests that when injustice elicits feelings of anger and contempt, the likelihood of protest increases, whereas fear reduces its likelihood (van Stekelenburg & Klandermans, 2007; Tausch et al., 2011; van Zomeren et al., 2004). Each emotion motivates people to engage in particular actions, with anger and contempt being linked to promotion-focused actions and fear being linked to prevention-focused actions.

3.2. Procedural Justice

Most discussions of collective action have focused upon the outcomes that people receive (e.g., money, jobs, opportunities) rather than the procedures by which these outcomes are determined. Relative deprivation has typically been conceptualized as involving outcomes, but, in examining the influence of various forms of relative deprivation upon social discontent, Tyler and Lind (2002) found that group-based procedural deprivations were particularly upsetting and in at least some cases more influential than group-based outcome comparisons. For example, a procedural deprivation may be some people (whites) receiving better treatment (considerate; respectful) from the police and the courts than other people (minorities), whereas an outcome-based argument would be that some people get more lenient sentences than other people. Hence, relative deprivation can also concern procedures. Such procedural deprivation could potentially occur at the individual level (e.g., a boss who favors a pretty employee in a promotion situation), the group level (e.g., systematic disenfranchisement based on group membership), and the societal or system level (e.g., government corruption or federal violations on the First Amendment). People may be upset about deprivations of their rights to voice and fair decision-making, just as they would be upset about unfair outcomes.

Given the relative importance people place on procedures over outcomes, it has been suggested that grievances stemming from perceived procedural injustice might be a more powerful predictor of collective action than those stemming from distributive injustice (Tyler & Smith, 1998). Indeed, Blader (2007) found that procedural justice judgments predicted people's support for union certification and the votes they cast in a union certification election, even after accounting for the influence of their economic concerns (see Klandermans et al., 2008 for a similar finding with regard to procedural injustice experienced at the individual level).

Whereas collective action is an attempt to redress injustice and restructure society through actions aimed at social change, it does not necessarily mean it is directed at overhauling the system as a whole. Protests can signify efforts to overhaul a form of governmental regime (such as occurred during the large-scale protests in the Middle East, known as the Arab Spring) or signify acts of political participation within democratic systems (see Klandermans et al., 2008).

In evaluating collective action, a distinction is often made between normative (or conventional, nondisruptive activities such as signing petitions, sending letters, and making donations) and nonnormative (or unconventional, more disruptive activities such as occupying buildings and setting cars on fire) forms of protest. Tausch et al. (2011) showed that the antecedents of these forms of action are different. Whereas anger and high collective efficacy predict normative protest, contempt and a belief in the low efficacy of conventional actions are predictors of nonnormative protest.

When group-based injustice is framed (by a victim or abuser) at the individual level, the likelihood of collective protest is low, as people may revert to individual strategies (Dubé & Guimond, 1986). That is, they may try to distance themselves from their disadvantaged group and engage in actions designed to raise their own status and improve their personal identity (Tajfel, 1974; 1978; Tajfel & Turner, 1979). For example, Wright et al. (1990) found that people often respond to membership in a disadvantaged group by making individual efforts to move out of that group. When, however, group boundaries are perceived to be impermeable and people cannot leave their group, the likelihood of a collective response to change the status or predicament of their group increases. And, of course, many acts of injustice are just personal, as when a boss shows favoritism to a relative or when a foster parent abuses a child. The question is how the victim frames the injustice: as something that is individual or that is linked to groups and group membership.

Even when injustice is framed at the group level, it doesn't necessarily follow that people will take action to advance the well-being of their group. Felt grievances, collective efficacy, and group identification have been shown to increase the likelihood of protest, and although resistance would seem to be the most obvious or appropriate response to perceived injustice (Gurr, 1970; Hirschman, 1970; Klandermans, 1997; Reicher, 2004), its occurrence is relatively rare (Huddy, chapter 23, this volume). Instead, people, including members of disadvantaged groups, frequently acquiesce in the social order and, in so doing, violate their own objectively defined social interests (e.g., Jost & Van der Toorn, 2012).

4. JUSTIFICATION IN THE FACE OF INJUSTICE

Justice research finds that people balance between two types of motivation. One motivation is to do what is just. This leads to a desire to give back resources among the advantaged and to a motivation to demand justice among the disadvantaged (distributive justice), as well as to a general willingness to incur losses or exert effort when needed to enforce justice rules (procedural justice). The other motivation is to justify advantages and disadvantages by making psychological adjustments to make them appear appropriate and reasonable.

4.1. Distributive Justice as a basis for justification

People may respond to perceptions of injustice by either taking action to restore justice or by restoring justice psychologically through the reevaluation of different aspects of the situation, for example by changing estimates of inputs and outputs or which justice principles apply.

A variety of social psychological researchers have studied the phenomenon of the motivated justification of injustice (e.g., Jost & Banaji, 1994; Pratto, Sidanius, Stallworth, & Malle, 1994). For example, system justification theory suggests that both advantaged and disadvantaged group members have a motivation to justify existing social arrangements (Jost & Van der Toorn, 2012). While for advantaged groups this motivation is in accord with needs to feel good about their group and the self (Tajfel & Turner, 1986), for disadvantaged groups endorsing the fairness and legitimacy of the system implies acceptance of their subordinated status (i.e., accepting "injustice"). Indeed, disadvantaged group members (e.g., women, African Americans, gay people) have been shown to exhibit implicit preferences for higher status out-groups (e.g., men, European Americans, straight people; Jost, Pelham, & Carvallo, 2002), endorse negative stereotypes of their own group (e.g., Eagly, Makhijani, & Klonsky, 1992), and come up with complementary attributions to rationalize their disadvantage (e.g., "I'm poor but happy"; Kay & Jost, 2003). There is evidence that justification of unequal economic arrangements is associated with self-deception (Jost, Blount, Pfeffer, & Hunyady, 2003), suggesting that justification is a motivated, though not necessarily conscious, process (see Jost et al., 2010 for further evidence for this assertion).

Studies show that people feel better after they psychologically adjust their views about injustice. Wakslak, Jost, Tyler, and Chen (2007), for example, showed that believing the world is a fair place dampens moral outrage in the face of injustice and eliminates the need to redistribute resources to produce actual justice. Other reasons that the advantaged may justify their advantage are to deal with the feelings of guilt and the emotional unease that comes from having too much. Indeed, Wakslak et al. (2007) found that the endorsement of system justification is negatively associated with existential guilt and general emotional distress. Justifying beliefs may take the form of the advantaged exaggerating the role of effort and ability in the attainment of their privileges. For example, children that have been admitted to elite schools as "legacies" are found to emphasize stories of effort and hard work that cloak their advantage in an image of merit. These stories convince both the advantaged and others that privileges are earned, and therefore not unjust (Chen & Tyler, 2001).

The situation for the disadvantaged is more complex. Obvious reasons for justification among the disadvantaged are the practical difficulties and social costs that are associated with the pursuit of actual justice restoration. Yet research suggests that the disadvantaged may be motivated to justify the system for psychological reasons too. While seemingly antithetical to their personal and group interest, researchers have argued that system justification also serves a palliative function for the disadvantaged and thus has (at least short-term) positive consequences for their well-being

(Jost & Hunyady, 2002). Hierarchy legitimizing myths are endorsed to satisfy basic epistemic, existential, and relational needs to reduce the experience of uncertainty, manage threat, and maintain a sense of shared reality with others. System justification motivation is increased when the system is perceived to be threatened, when the system is seen as inevitable, and when people are dependent on the system (Jost & Van der Toorn, 2012; Kay & Zanna, 2009). For example, perceived dependence increases justification of the social and economic system, even in the case of blatant inequality (Van der Toorn, Feinberg, et al., 2013). Similarly, feeling that one is dependent on an authority for desired resources increases legitimation of that authority, regardless of whether it acts in procedurally and distributively fair ways (Van der Toorn, Tyler, & Jost, 2011).

4.2. Procedural Justice as a basis for justification

People are found to view procedures as fair that in objective terms are not fair. Extensive research now supports the argument that such views may be motivated by the palliative benefits of justification (Jost et al., 2010). In other words, people feel less upset and threatened after they have adjusted their beliefs to view existing social and political arrangements as fair. In conducting studies on this issue one key concern is distinguishing when people are appraising fairness realistically and without bias and when they are rationalizing the status quo.

Studies of public views on markets are an example of justifying ideologies that concern allocation and decision-making procedures (e.g., Jost, Blount, et al., 2003). Societal allocations are legitimated through the fairness of the procedures that produce them; in other words fair procedures can act as justifications for outcomes (Jost, Blount, et al., 2003). That is, people defer to individual and group-based inequities because they believe that the use of markets to make economic allocations is a fair, and therefore legitimate, procedure for determining who receives what in society. People are found to focus first on the fairness of market procedures and to use these procedural judgments to determine whether they support government controls over markets or government corrections for market outcomes via procedures such as affirmative action (Tyler, 2004). Such influences are found to be distinct from the impact of ideology. If people view market procedures as fair, they give little weight to evidence of potential distributive unfairness in the form of individual or group-based outcome differences. When either disadvantage or advantage is viewed as legitimate, people are more willing to accept it (Tyler, 2006b).

As a further example, the differences in the economic and social status of white and ethnic minority group members raise questions about the legitimacy of the economic and social system. In other words, legitimation is not just about particular authorities or decisions. It occurs more broadly when people are evaluating overall societies and their institutions. One important example is the economic system—the primary system for the allocation of social benefits and burdens. Within the American economic system the primary allocation system for economic outcomes is the market (Dye, 1990), although markets are conditioned by many social safety nets including Social Security and Medicare.

People are found to accept a variety of types of legitimating beliefs about markets. They uncritically accept meritocratic explanations for economic inequality (Jost, Pelham, Sheldon, & Sullivan, 2003), and they focus blame for failure on individuals, not the system (Kluegel & Smith, 1986). As a consequence, they believe that people deserve the outcomes they receive from markets and resist governmental interventions in the economic sphere through policies such as affirmative action (Tyler, 2004). Such procedural legitimation of the economic system has increasingly pernicious consequences as income inequality has increased in recent years in the United States (Norton & Ariely, 2011). Americans believe that the allocation of economic outcomes within our society occurs through a system that provides people with equal opportunities to compete for wealth and status by working hard and achieving success (Weiss, 1969). The view that economic achievement is the end product of a fair and open contest in which energy and talent shape outcomes leads workers (Lane, 1967) and the members of minority groups (Hochschild, 1996) alike to accept both their personal economic disadvantage and that of their social and ethnic groups.

When do people protest in response to injustice and when do they justify? Research has been conducted to determine when group members will be most likely to acquiesce in the face of injustice or to act against authority to change the social hierarchy. Walster et al. (1978) showed that the key situational factor that shapes the likelihood that people would engage in actual as opposed to psychological restoration of distributive justice is ambiguity. When the appropriate outcome distribution is not clearly and publicly articulated (e.g., by a politician), people are more likely to justify the unequal distribution as opposed to redistributing resources. Of course, views on what constitutes an appropriate distribution may differ based on people's position in society as well as their ideology (see also Klandermans & van Stekelenburg, chapter 24, this volume).

Martorana, Galinsky, and Rao (2005) identified certain boundary conditions that predict whether low-power individuals will condemn rather than justify the system. For condemnation to occur, it is necessary that people experience anger and pride, that they feel a sense of power, and that they perceive the existing hierarchy as unstable and illegitimate with few opportunities for social mobility (see Brader & Marcus, chapter 6, this volume, for a more complete account of political emotions). In investigating the antecedents of protest, Jost et al. (2012) showed that system justification and group identification have parallel but opposite effects on protest tendencies. While group identification increases the likelihood of protest by increasing anger, system justification reduces the likelihood that people will engage in collective action by decreasing anger. Wakslak et al. (2007) further showed that system justification dampens moral outrage and as such decreases people's interest in policies aimed at redressing injustice.

More research is needed to identify the factors that influence when people do or do not act on injustice, and this is one area where political psychologists can make important contributions. A large body of research has focused on the ways in which social change is inhibited by the belief that the status quo is legitimate. The positive consequences of system justification occur at the individual level in that they may help people cope with unwelcome realities. Namely, system justification may in the short term alleviate the anxiety, uncertainty, and fear elicited by threats to the societal status quo (e.g., Jost & Hunyady, 2002; Jost, Wakslak, & Tyler, 2008). At the societal level, on the other hand, it certainly inhibits support for change. And for individuals, the long-term implications of pursuing the system justification goal can be negative, especially for members of disadvantaged groups (e.g., Jost & Thompson, 2000; O'Brien & Major, 2005; Rankin, Jost, & Wakslak, 2009). Understanding the factors that influence whether people will strive for justice versus justification is thus important for the effectiveness of social interventions.

5. IS THERE A SCOPE OF JUSTICE?

One view of justice is that concerns about justice reflect a fundamental human motivation that is found in all social settings. An example of such a motivation is the belief that we live in a world in which people get what they deserve and deserve what they get ("just world theory"; Lerner, 1980). Other models of justice argue for a scope of justice outside of which people do not consider justice issues. Such a scope, for example, may be reflected in people's interactions with animals or plants. It may also be reflected in their dealings with strangers or outsiders. In both cases people with a limited scope of justice would not feel compelled to treat the animals, plants, or outsiders with respect and dignity.

One model of the scope of justice argues that people extend justice to those with whom they have productive exchange relationships (Deutsch, 1985). Another suggests that people's justice concerns extend to the boundaries of groups with whom they share a common identity and shared values (Tyler & Lind, 1990). Both of these models, however, suggest that people do not automatically view justice as relevant to all social situations. There are situations that exist outside of the scope of justice.

An example of the potential political importance of the scope of justice is the inclusion or exclusion of groups from the rights and protections of group membership. Nagata (1993) examines how JapaneseAmericans living in the United States during World War II suddenly found themselves viewed as outside the community of Americans and no longer entitled to the rights of citizens. Huo (2002) examined this issue experimentally and showed in two studies that university students think that excluding disliked groups from society can occur at three levels: resource denial; denial of rights; and denial of treatment with dignity. Of these harms denial of treatment with dignity was regarded as the most serious denial, while denial of resources was the least serious.

6. Justice and Values

Justice is one of a broader set of normative orientations that includes morality and values. In contrast to the idea of justice, social psychology has a longer history of concern with issues of morality and moral values. This concern was rooted in the work of Freud, for whom the development of functionally autonomous moral motivations is an important aspect of the overall childhood socialization process. His work focuses particular attention on the internalization of values during childhood. Through this internalization process children become internally motivated to act in ways that are consistent with their sense of right and wrong. The core point made by Freud and others is that such values, once acquired, shape people's behavior in social settings, leading them to act in ways that differ from their material self-interest based upon the motivation to adhere to principles of right and wrong.

Irrespective of how it is acquired, morality is commonly defined as a desirable end state that motivates actions (Hitlin & Piliavin, 2004; Schwartz, 1992). In particular, morality is a value-based system that is linked to responsibility and obligation to engage in conduct that conforms to principles of right and wrong. The core argument is that people develop such values and act in ways consistent with them, even when such values conflict with what other people want them to do or are not in their self-interest. A number of studies by psychologists now support the basic premise that people's morality shapes their actions in social settings (Eisenberg, 2000; Tangney & Dearing, 2002; Turiel, 2002).

Moral values are general principles of right and wrong that people use to decide what actions to take. Much of the research on morality has been about moral reasoning and has focused upon situations in which moral values are in conflict with each other. A classic example is the work of Kohlberg (1969) on conflicts between following rules versus principles of right and wrong. In his studies people consider following the law if that results in harm to someone versus breaking the law if that helps someone. Kohlberg is interested in how people reason when trying to solve this moral dilemma. More recently, Sandel (2009) has popularized reasoning about situations of moral conflict, for example, the trolley problem in which a person must decide whether to kill one person to save the lives of many others. Sandel finds that people are more willing to passively stand by and let one person die to save multiple others than to actively kill a person to save the same number of people.

Distributive and retributive justice principles can be seen as a subset of moral principles because they represent ideas of what is right and wrong in social settings. Procedural justice may also reflect such ideas, as in the suggestion that the right to liberty and self-governance is a universal and potentially "natural" right. Psychologists have sometimes speculated that people have an innate sense of justice (Lerner, 1980). Thibaut and Walker (1975), for example, speculated that all people view being given voice as an element of just treatment and suggest that it will be associated with justice in all societies. While this argument is difficult to test empirically, their research does show that in European societies in which the legal system does not give people personal voice in legal proceedings, people evaluate the higher voice associated with American procedures as reflecting a more just procedure. Since people in these societies are presumably socialized toward the belief that their own legal procedures are fairer, Thibaut and Walker suggest that their finding is consistent with the argument that there is some core sense of innate justice that manifests itself in spite of contrary socialization pressures. That core sense of justice is that people are entitled to voice.

Both sociologists and political scientists have also been interested in people's values, defined as the goals that they seek to achieve. One widely studied example is Inglehart's effort to study materialist versus postmaterialist values (Inglehart, 1977; 2008); another is the study of values by Baker (2005). These studies of values focus upon people's most desirable end states for a society. The Inglehart studies ask whether people would prefer: "maintaining order," "fighting rising prices," "protecting freedom of speech," or "giving people more say in important political decisions." While not framed in terms of justice, the postmaterial end states could also be seen as reflecting key elements of procedural justice, including voice and respect for people's rights. Hence, people who value free speech and voice are showing a postmaterialist desire for justice over a materialist desire for order and security.

In an influential American Psychological Association presidential address, Donald Campbell provocatively argued that the development of moral and social values could be viewed as an example of social evolution (Campbell, 1975). He suggested that these values, and the institutions that maintain them, serve the useful function of helping people to control "human nature"—that is, the biological tendency to act in one's immediate self-interest. Campbell suggested that behavior arising from self-interest was not adaptive in many situations and that people who live in social groups that have developed effective mechanisms for minimizing such behavioral tendencies will be more likely to flourish. Those groups have taught their members to identify with their group and to hold group values and norms. Increasingly, such socially superior groups dominated over others, leading to our present highly socialized world. This culture-based view of values is consistent with recent arguments that values are not universal (Fiske, 1992; Schwartz, 1992) and evolve as cultures change (Baker, 2005; Inglehart & Welzel, 2005).

This argument draws morality and justice together by suggesting that both are socially created and transmitted mechanisms for managing problems of coordination in groups, organizations, and societies. Principles of justice and the development of supportive values both facilitate people's efforts to control their motivation to pursue short-term self-interest, a motivation that may well have a biological basis but that nonetheless is an approach to interactions with others that can create societal difficulties. Put simply, social motivations function to overcome biological tendencies. Of course, there are also institutional mechanisms, such as the free market, that constrain people's desire to pursue self-interest. This chapter, however, emphasizes the virtue of values as a regulatory mechanism.

While one line of research has emphasized the commonality of morality and justice, another has focused upon the distinction between morality and empathy. In a series of studies Batson has demonstrated that people can experience conflicts between following abstract principles of morality and their empathetic liking for particular individuals. For example, while people may want to allocate scarce resources using general principles of morality, they may also want to ignore those rules and give resources to people that they find particularly likable and sympathetic (Batson, 1999; 2002; 2003; 2005).

Individuals can also have a general inclination toward cooperation or competition. Morality can be viewed as linked to these orientations. Van Lange, Otten, De Bruin, and Joireman (1997) argue that these orientations reflect values and distinguish between prosocial, individualistic, and competitive value orientations. All are motivated to maximize their own outcomes, but prosocials also want to maximize outcomes for others and minimize the difference between their own and others' outcomes, whereas competitors want to maximize their advantage over others. Individualists, on the other hand, have little or no regard for others' outcomes. Because social value orientations are predictive of helping behavior and judgments of cooperation and competition (McClintock & Allison, 1989; Van Vugt, Meertens, & Van Lange, 1995), they are of interest to the study of governance.

7. CONCLUSION

The findings of justice research are important for political psychology in several ways. First, they contribute to the demonstration that people's thoughts, feelings, and behaviors are determined by their internally held views concerning what is just or fair. These views play an important role in making social life possible because they provide a basis for cooperation among people in groups, organizations, and societies. And, as the literature on social justice makes clear, they provide an important confirmation that the social ties between people are central to their actions in social settings. People in social settings do not act simply as self-interested actors, pursuing individual or group gains and losses. Rather their feelings, thoughts, and behaviors are shaped by their judgments concerning what is appropriate, reasonable, and fair.

The demonstration that people are justice-based actors provides a clear demonstration of the centrality of social motivations to people's actions in groups, communities, organizations, and societies (Tyler, 2011). Justice and morality are both found to be important social judgments that influence how people act when dealing with others. And since both reflect a sense of what is appropriate within a given setting, their influences show that people are concerned with questions of right and wrong. Their actions do not simply reflect material gain/loss judgments.

Beyond the overall finding that justice matters, demonstrating the particular importance of procedural justice is a distinct contribution of this literature, that is, the finding that people care about the fairness of government procedures, for example, whether there are elections and whether government decisions are made in fair ways (e.g. open hearings; transparent procedures). It is not self-evident a priori that people's engagement in political groups would be the result of procedural justice judgments. People could potentially consider a wide variety of aspects of their relationship to their group when they are evaluating the degree to which they want to engage themselves in a group, organization, community, or society. One thing that we might expect people to consider is reward level—that is, people might consider their salaries, the number of resources they are given to manage, and/or the size of their office, their car, or their home as key inputs in their judgments about how much to engage themselves in a collectivity. Or, at least, they might consider outcome fairness, that is, whether they get the resources and opportunities they feel they deserve, as suggested by Thibaut and Walker (1975).

Because an outcome focus is an intuitively obvious basis for making decisions (e.g., cost-benefit analysis of gains and losses), the finding that procedural justice is so central to people's thinking is striking. It is especially striking because, of the procedural elements considered, questions of interpersonal treatment consistently emerge as important. In other words, people's focus is upon those aspects of their experience that communicate messages about identity and status, rather than upon those more directly related to issues of decision-making. This supports the argument that it is status issues that most importantly define people's relationship to groups, organizations, communities, and societies (Tyler & Blader, 2000; 2003).

Overall, the literature on political justice contributes to a social vision of the person on several levels: first, because people care about justice, a socially constructed idea, and view it as a core element of social groups; second, because people think of justice in very relational terms (i.e., in terms of their connections to others); and, third, because studies of how justice influences people's behavior suggest that the key connection between people and groups, communities, organizations, and societies is rooted in their concerns about self and identity. In all of these ways, people show themselves to be fundamentally social animals.

Following World War II the field of social psychology was infused with excitement and energy by the sense that many of the aspects of the recent world conflict could be understood in terms of social psychological issues linked to authority relations and intergroup relations. This led to the social psychological study of leadership styles; authoritarianism/prejudice, propaganda/attitude change, childrearing, mass communication, and intergroup dynamics. Of particular relevance to the field of justice was the work of Kurt Lewin and his efforts to understand and explain authority structures and styles of leadership (Lewin, 1951).

The socially relevant element of social psychology, with its emphasis upon the psychology of group functioning and authority dynamics in groups, led to the field of social justice. In turn, the literature on justice has strongly supported the image of the person as a social being who reacts to social experiences in terms of his or her values concerning what is just and morally right, values that are socially created and collectively held. As the field of social psychology has moved in an increasingly intrapersonal direction

in the intervening years through successi
bution, social cognition, and recently soci
within the field of social justice is a reminc
social psychology that examine groups, or
their importance in arenas such as governal

654 MASS POLITICAL BEHAVI

Chen, E., & Tyler, T. R. (20(
the advantaged. In J. /
241–261). Philadelp
Clawson, R. A., K(
of the U.S. S
Clayton, M
Craig, S
co

REFERENCES

Abrams, D. (1992). Processes of social identificat
  of the self-concept (pp. 57–100). London: Aca(

Adams, J. S. (1965). Injustice in social exchang
  (vol. 2, pp. 267–299). New York: Academic Pr

Anderson, C. J., Blais, A., Bowler, S., Donovan, T.,
  and democratic legitimacy. Oxford: Oxford Ui

Anderson, C. J., & LoTempio, A. J. (2002). Winning, losing and political trust in America.
  British Journal of Political Science, 32, 335–351.

Appelbaum, L. D. (2001). The influence of perceived deservingness on policy decisions
  regarding aid to the poor. Political Psychology, 22, 419–442.

Baird, V. A., & Gangl, A. (2006). Shattering the myth of legality: The impact of the media's
  framing of Supreme Court procedures on perceptions of fairness. Political Psychology, 27,
  597–614.

Baker, W. (2005). America's crisis of values. Princeton, NJ: Princeton University Press.

Barrett-Howard, E., & Tyler, T. R. (1986). Procedural justice as a criterion in allocation decisions.
  Journal of Personality and Social Psychology, 50, 296–304.

Barry, B. (2005). Why social justice matters. Cambridge: Polity Press.

Batson, C. D. (1999). Two threats to the common good: Self-interested egoism and empathy-
  induced altruism. Personality and Social Psychology Bulletin, 25, 3–16.

Batson, C. D. (2002). Justice motivation and moral motivation. In M. Ross and D. T. Miller
  (eds.), The justice motive in everyday life (pp. 41–63). New York: Cambridge University Press.

Batson, C. D. (2003). As you would have them do unto you: Does imagining yourself in
  the other's place stimulate moral action? Personality and Social Psychology Bulletin, 29,
  1190–1201.

Batson, C. D. (2005). Similarity and nurturance: Two possible sources of empathy for strangers.
  Basic and Applied Psychology, 27, 15–25.

Blader, S. L. (2007). What Leads organizational members to collectivize? Injustice and
  identification as precursors of union certification. Organization Science, 18, 108–126.

Blader, S. L., & Tyler, T. R. (2003). A four component model of procedural justice. Personality
  and Social Psychology Bulletin, 29, 747–758.

Blatz, C. W., Schumann, K., & Ross, M. (2009). Government apologies for historical injustices.
  Political Psychology, 30, 219–241.

Brighouse, H. (2004). Justice. Cambridge: Polity Press.

Campbell, D. T. (1975). On the conflicts between biological and social evolution and between
  psychology and moral tradition. American Psychologist, 30, 1103–1126.

Carlsmith, K. M., Darley, J. M., & Robinson, P. H. (2002). Why do we punish? Deterrence and
  just deserts as motives for punishment. Journal of Personality and Social Psychology, 83,
  284–299.

1). Cloaking power: Legitimizing myths and the psychology of
. Bargh and A. Y. Lee-Chai (eds.), *The use and abuse of power* (pp.
nia: Psychology Press.

gler, E. R., & Waltenberg, E. N. (2001). The legitimacy-conferring authority
preme Court. *American Politics Research, 29*, 566–591.

& Williams, A. (2004). *Social justice*. Malden, MA: Blackwell.

C., Martinez, M. D., Gainous, J., & Kane, J. G. (2006). Winners, losers, and election
ntext: Voter responses to the 2000 presidential election. *Political Research Quarterly, 59*,
579–592.

Crosby, F. J. (1976). A model of egoistical relative deprivation. *Psychological Review, 83*, 85–113.

Crosby, F. J., & Konrad, A. (2002). Affirmative action in employment. *Diversity Factor, 10*, 5–9.

Dahl, R. A. (1971). *Polyarchy*. New Haven, CT: Yale University Press.

Dahl, R. A. (1989). *Democracy and its critics*. New Haven, CT: Yale University Press.

Darley, J. M. (2002). Just punishments: Research on retributional justice. In M. Ross & D. T. Miller (eds), *The justice motive in everyday life* (vol. 17, pp. 314–333). New York: Cambridge University Press.

Darley, J. M., Carlsmith, K. M., & Robinson, P. H. (2000). Incapacitation and just deserts as motives for punishment. *Law and Human Behavior, 24*, 659–683.

Darley, J. M., & Pittman, T. S. (2003). The psychology of compensation and retributive justice. *Personality and Social Psychology Review, 7*, 324–336.

David, R., & Choi, S. Y. P. (2009). Getting even or getting equal? Retributive desires and transitive justice. *Political Psychology, 30*, 161–192.

DeCremer, D., & van Knippenberg, D. (2002). How do leaders promote cooperation?: The effects of charisma and procedural fairness. *Journal of Applied Psychology, 87*, 858–866.

Delli Carpini, M. X. D., Cook, F. L., & Jacobs, L. R. (2004). Public deliberation, discursive participation, and citizen engagement. *Annual Review of Political Science, 7*, 315–344.

Deutsch, M. (1975). Equity, equality, and need: What determines which value will be used as the basis for distributive justice? *Journal of Social Issues, 31*, 137–149.

Deutsch, M. (1985). *Distributive justice*. New Haven, CT: Yale University Press.

Dubé, L., & Guimond, S. (1986). Relative deprivation and social protest: The personal-group issue. In J. M. Olson, C. P. Herman, & M. P. Zanna (eds.), *Relative deprivation and social comparison: The Ontario symposium* (vol. 4, pp. 57–77). Hillsdale: Erlbaum.

Duch, R. M., & Palmer, H. D. (2004). It's not whether you win or lose, but how you play the game: Self-interest, social justice, and mass attitudes toward market transition. *American Political Science Review, 98*, 437–452.

Dye, T. (1990). *The political legitimacy of markets and governments*. Greenwich, CT: JAI Press.

Eagly, A. H., Makhijani, M. G., & Klonsky, B. G. (1992). Gender and the evaluation of leaders: A meta-analysis. *Psychological Bulletin, 111*, 11–22

Easton, D. (1965). *A systems analysis of political life*. Chicago: University of Chicago Press.

Eisenberg, N. (2000). Emotion, regulation, and moral development. *Annual Review of Psychology, 51*, 665–697.

Farnsworth, S. J. (2003). Congress and citizen discontent: Public evaluations of the membership and one's own representative. *American Politics Research, 21*, 66–80.

Feather, N. T. (1999). *Values, achievement, and justice: Studies in the psychology of deservingness*. New York: Kluwer Academic / Plenum Press.

Fiske, A. (1992). The four elementary forms of sociality. *Psychological Review, 99*, 689–723.

Fleischacker, S. (2004). *A short history or distributive justice*. Cambridge, MA: Harvard University Press.

Folger, R. (1986). A referent cognition theory of relative deprivation. In J. M. Olson, C. P. Herman, and M. Zanna (eds.), *Relative deprivation and social comparison: The Ontario symposium* (vol. 4, pp. 33–56). Hillsdale: Lawrence Erlbaum.

Gangl, A. (2003). Procedural justice theory and evaluations of the lawmaking process. *Political Behavior, 25*, 119–149.

Gibson, J. L. (1996). A mile wide but an inch deep? The structure of democratic commitments to the former USSR. *American Journal of Political Science, 40*, 396–420.

Gibson, J. L. (1997). Mass opposition to the Soviet putsch of August 1991: Collective action, rational choice, and democratic values in the former Soviet Union. *American Political Science Review, 91*, 671–684.

Gibson, J. L. (2007, March 30–31). On legitimacy theory and the effectiveness of truth commissions. Paper presented at Vanderbilt Law School.

Gibson, J. L. (2008). Group identities and theories of justice: An experimental investigation into the justice and injustice of land squatting in South Africa. *Journal of Politics, 70*, 700–716.

Gibson, J. L., & Caldeira, G. A. (2003). Defenders of democracy? Legitimacy, popular acceptance, and the South African Constitutional Court. *Journal of Politics, 65*, 1–30.

Gibson, J. L., Caldeira, G. A., & Spence, L. K. (2005). Why do people accept public policies they oppose? *Political Research Quarterly, 58*, 187–201.

Gonzalez, C., & Tyler, T. R. (2008). The psychology of enfranchisement: Engaging and fostering inclusion of members through voting and decision-making procedures. *Journal of Social Issues, 64*, 447–466.

Green, D., & Shapiro, I. (1994). *Pathologies of rational choice theory*. New Haven, CT: Yale University Press.

Greenberg, J. (1988). Equity and workplace status: A field experiment. *Journal of Applied Psychology, 73*, 606–613.

Greenberg, J. (1990). Employee theft as a reaction to underpayment inequity: The hidden cost of pay cuts. *Journal of Applied Psychology, 75*, 561–568.

Grimes, M. (2006). Organized consent: The role of procedural fairness in political trust and compliance. *European Journal of Political Research, 45*, 285–315.

Gurr, T. (1970). *Why men rebel*. Princeton, NJ: Princeton University Press.

Heilman, M. E., Battle, W. S., Keller, C. E., & Lee, R. A. (1998). Type of affirmative action policy: A determinant of reactions to sex-based preferential selection? *Journal of Applied Psychology, 83*, 190–205.

Heilman, M. E., Block, C. J., & Lucas, J. A. (1992). Presumed incompetent? Stigmatization and affirmative action efforts. *Journal of Applied Psychology, 77*, 536–544.

Heilman, M. E., Rivero, J. C., & Brett, J. F. (1991). Skirting the competence issue: Effects of sex-based preferential selection on task choices of women and men. *Journal of Applied Psychology, 76*, 99–105.

Hibbing, J. R., & Alford, J. R. (2004). Accepting authoritative decisions: Human as wary cooperators. *American Journal of Political Science, 48*, 62–76.

Hibbing, J. R., & Theiss-Morse, E. (1995). *Congress as public enemy: Public attitudes toward American political institutions*. Cambridge: Cambridge University Press.

Hibbing, J. R., & Theiss-Morse, E. (2001). *What is it about government that Americans dislike?* Cambridge: Cambridge University Press.

Hibbing, J. R., & Theiss-Morse, E. (2002). *Stealth democracy: Americans' beliefs about how government should work*. Cambridge: Cambridge University Press.

Hirschman, A. O. (1970). *Exit, voice, and loyalty: Responses to decline in firms, organizations, and states*. Cambridge, MA: Harvard University Press.

Hitlin, S., & Piliavin, J. (2004). Values: Reviving a dormant concept. *Annual Review of Sociology*, 30, 359–394.

Hochschild, J. L. (1996). *Facing up to the American dream: Race, class and the soul of the nation*. Princeton, NJ: Princeton University Press.

Hogan, R., & Emler, N. P. (1981). Retributive justice. In M. J. Lerner & S. C. Lerner (eds.), *The justice motive in social behavior*. New York: Academic Press.

Hollander-Blumoff, R., & Tyler, T. R. (2008). Do nice guys finish last? Procedural justice and negotiation outcomes. *Law and Social Inquiry*, 33, 473–500.

Huddy, L., Jones, J. M., & Chard, R. E. (2001). Compassionate politics: Support for old-age programs among the elderly. *Political Psychology*, 22, 443–471.

Huo, Y. J. (2002). Justice and the regulation of social relations: When and why do group members deny claims to social goods? *British Journal of Social Psychology*, 41, 535–562.

Inglehart, R. (1977). *The silent revolution*. Princeton, NJ: Princeton University Press.

Inglehart, R. (2008). Changing values among Western publics from 1970 to 2006. *Western European Politics*, 31, 130–146.

Inglehart, R., & Welzel, C. (2005). *Modernization, cultural change, and democracy*. Cambridge: Cambridge University Press.

Jost, J. T., & Banaji, M. R. (1994). The role of stereotyping in system-justification and the production of false consciousness. *British Journal of Social Psychology*, 33, 1–27.

Jost, J. T., Blount, S., Pfeffer, J., & Hunyady, G. (2003). Fair market ideology: Its cognitive-motivational underpinnings. *Research in Organizational Behavior*, 25, 53–91.

Jost, J. T., Chaikalis-Petritsis, V., Abrams, D., Sidanius, J., Van der Toorn, J., & Bratt, C. (2012). Why men (and women) do and do not rebel: System justification and willingness to participate in disruptive and nondisruptive protest. *Personality and Social Psychology Bulletin*, 38, 197–208.

Jost, J. T., & Hunyady, O. (2002). The psychology of system justification and the palliative function of ideology. *European Review of Social Psychology*, 13, 111–153.

Jost, J. T., Liviatan, I., Van der Toorn, J., Ledgerwood, A., Mandisodza, A., & Nosek, B. (2010). System justification: How do we know it's motivated? In D. R. Bobocel, A. C. Kay, M. P. Zanna, & J. M. Olson (eds.), *The psychology of justice and legitimacy: The Ontario symposium* (vol. 11, pp. 173–203). Hillsdale, NJ: Erlbaum.

Jost, J. T., Pelham, B. W., & Carvallo, M. R. (2002). Non-conscious forms of system justification: Implicit and behavioral preferences for higher status groups. *Journal of Experimental Social Psychology*, 38, 586–602.

Jost, J. T., Pelham, B. W., Sheldon, O., & Sullivan, B. N. (2003). Social inequality and the reduction of ideological dissonance on behalf of the system. *European Journal of Social Psychology*, 33, 13–36.

Jost, J. T., & Thompson, E. P. (2000). Group-based dominance and opposition to equality as independent predictors of self-esteem, ethnocentrism, and social policy attitudes among African Americans and European Americans. *Journal of Experimental Social Psychology*, 36, 209–232.

Jost, J. T., & Van der Toorn, J. (2012). System justification theory. In P. A. M. van Lange, A. W. Kruglanski, & E. T. Higgins (eds.), *Handbook of theories of social psychology* (pp. 313–343). London: Sage.

Jost, J. T., Wakslak, C., & Tyler, T. R. (2008). System justification theory and the alleviation of emotional distress: Palliative effects of ideology in an arbitrary social hierarchy and in society. In K. Hegtvedt & J. Clay-Warner (eds.), *Advances in group processes* (pp. 181–211). Bingley, UK: Emerald Group Publishing Limited.

Kay, A. C., & Jost, J. T. (2003). Complementary justice: Effects of "poor but happy" and "poor but honest" stereotype exemplars on system justification and implicit activation of the justice motive. *Journal of Personality and Social Psychology*, 85, 823–837.

Kay, A. C., & Zanna, M. (2009). A contextual analysis of the system justification motive and its societal consequences. In J. T. Jost, A. C. Kay, & H. Thorisdottir (eds.), *Social and psychological bases of ideology and system justification* (pp. 158–181). New York: Oxford University Press.

Kelly, C., & Breinlinger, S. (1996). *The social psychology of collective action*. Basingstoke: Taylor and Francis.

Kelman, H. C., & Hamilton, V. L. (1989). *Crimes of obedience*. New Haven, CT: Yale University Press.

Keyes, C. L., Hysom, S. J., & Lupo, K. L. (2000). The positive organization: Leadership legitimacy, employee well-being and the bottom line. *Psychology of Management Journal*, 4, 143–153.

Klandermans, B. (1997). *The social psychology of protest*. Oxford: Blackwell.

Klandermans, B., Van der Toorn, J., & Van Stekelenburg, J. (2008). Embeddedness and identity: How immigrants turn grievances into action. *American Sociological Review*, 73, 992–1012.

Kluegel, J. R., & Mason, D. S. (2004). Fairness matters: Social justice and political legitimacy in post-communist Europe. *Europe-Asia Studies*, 56, 813–834.

Kluegel, J. R., & Smith, E. R. (1986). *Beliefs about inequality: Americans' view of what is and what ought to be*. Hawthorne, NJ: Gruyter.

Kohlberg, L. (1969). Stage and sequence: The cognitive-developmental approach to socialization. In D. A. Goslin (ed.), *Handbook of socialization theory and research* (pp. 347–480). Chicago: Rand McNally.

Landsman, S. (2003). Lay participation in legal processes and the development of democracy. *Law and Policy*, 25, 173–178.

Lane, R. (1967). *Political ideology*. New York: Simon and Schuster.

Lerner, M. (1980). *The belief in a just world*. New York: Plenum Press.

Lewin, K. (1951). *Field theory in social science*. Westport, CT: Greenwood Press.

Lind, E. A., & Tyler, T. R. (1988). *The social psychology of procedural justice*. New York: Plenum Press.

Major, B. (1994). From social inequality to personal entitlement: The role of social comparisons, legitimacy appraisals, and group membership. *Advances in experimental social psychology*, 26, 293–355. New York: Academic Press.

Martin, J. (1986). The tolerance of injustice. In J. M. Olson, C. P. Herman, and M. P. Zanna, *Relative deprivation and social comparison: The Ontario symposium* (vol. 4, pp. 217–242). Hillsdale, NJ: Lawrence Erlbaum.

Martorana, P. V., Galinsky, A. D., & Rao, H. (2005). From system justification to system condemnation: Antecedents of attempts to change status hierarchies. In M. A. Neale, E. A. Mannix, & M. Thomas-Hunt (eds.), *Research on managing groups and teams: Status* (vol. 7, pp. 283–313). Greenwich, CT: JAI Press.

McClintock, C. G., & Allison, S. (1989). Social value orientation and helping behavior. *Journal of Applied Social Psychology*, 19, 353–362.

Merton, R. K. (1938). Social structure and anomie. *American Sociological Review*, 3, 672–682.

Merton, R. K., & Kitt, A. S. (1950). Contributions to the theory of reference group behavior. In R. K. Merton & P. F. Lazersfeld (eds.). *Continuities in social research: Studies in the scope and method of "The American Soldier"* (pp. 40–105). Glencoe, IL: Free Press.

Michelbach, P. A., Scott, J. T., Matland, R. E., & Bornstein, B. H. (2003). Doing Rawls justice: An experimental study of income distribution norms. *American Journal of Political Science*, 47, 523–539.

Miller, D. (1999). *Principles of social justice.* Cambridge, MA: Harvard University Press.

Miller, D. T., & Vidmar, N. (1981). The social psychology of punishment reactions. In M. J. Lerner & S. C. Lerner (eds.), *The justice motive in social behavior* (pp.145–172). New York: Academic Press.

Mitchell, G., Tetlock, P. E., Newman, D. G., & Lerner, J. S. (2003). Experiments behind the veil: Structural influences on judgments of social justice. *Political Psychology, 24,* 519–547.

Moehler, D. C. (2009). Critical citizens and submissive subjects: Election losers and winners in Africa. *British Journal of Political Science, 39,* 345–366.

Moore, B. (1978). *Injustice: The social bases of obedience and revolt.* White Plains, NY: M. E. Sharpe.

Murphy, K. (2004). The role of trust in nurturing compliance: A study of accused tax avoiders. *Law and Human Behavior, 28,* 187–209.

Murphy J. G., & Hampton, J. (1988). *Forgiveness and mercy.* Cambridge: Cambridge University Press.

Murphy, W. F., & Tanenhaus, J. (1969). Public opinion and the United States Supreme Court: A preliminary mapping of some prerequisites for court legitimation of regime changes. In J. B. Grossman & J. Tanenhaus (eds.), *Frontiers of Judicial Research* (pp. 273–303). New York: John Wiley.

Nagata, D. (1993). *Legacy of injustice.* New York: Plenum Press.

Norton, M., & Ariely, D. (2011). Consensus on building a better America—one wealth quartile at a time. *Perspectives on Psychological Science, 6,* 9–12.

O'Brien, L. T., & Major, B. (2005). System-justifying beliefs and psychological well-being: The roles of group status and identity. *Personality and Social Psychology Bulletin, 31,* 1718–1729.

Okimoto, T. G., Wenzel, M., & Feather, N. T. (2011). Conceptualizing retributive and restorative justice. Manuscript, School of Management, Yale University.

Okun, A. M. (1975). *Equality and efficiency: The big tradeoff.* Washington, DC: Brookings Institution.

Pratto, F., Sidanius, J., Stallworth, L. M., & Malle, B. F. (1994). Social dominance orientation: A personality variable predicting social and political attitudes. *Journal of Personality and Social Psychology, 67,* 741–763.

Pratto, F., Tatar, D. G., & Conway-Lanz, S. (1999). Who gets what and why: Determinants of social allocations. *Political Psychology, 20,* 127–150.

Ramirez, M. D. (2008). Procedural perceptions and support for the US Supreme Court. *Political Psychology, 29,* 675–698.

Rankin, L. E., Jost, J. T., & Wakslak, C. J. (2009). System justification and the meaning of life: Are the existential benefits of ideology distributed unequally across racial groups? *Social Justice Research, 22,* 312–333.

Rawls, J. (1971). *A theory of justice.* Cambridge, MA: Harvard University Press.

Reicher, S. (2004). The context of social identity: Domination, resistance, and change. *Political Psychology, 20,* 921–945.

Reyna, C., Tucker, A., Korfmacher, W., & Henry, P. J. (2005). Searching for common ground between supporters and opponents of affirmative action. *Political Psychology, 26,* 667–682.

Runciman, W. G. (1966). *Relative deprivation and social justice.* London: Routledge and Kegan Paul.

Sabucedo, J. M., & Rodriguez, M. (2002). Politicization of collective identity: Farmer's identity and farmer's protest in the Netherlands and Spain. *Political Psychology, 23,* 235–252.

Sandel, M. J. (2009). *Justice: What's the right thing to do?* New York: Farrar, Straus and Giroux.

Sauermann, J., & Kaiser, A. (2010). Taking others into account: Self-interest and fairness in majority decision making. *American Journal of Political Science, 54,* 667–685.

Schmitt, D. R., & Marwell, G. (1972). Withdrawal and reward allocation as responses to inequity. *Journal of Experimental Social Psychology, 8,* 207–221.

Schwartz, S. H. (1992). Universals in the content and structure of values. *Advances in experimental social psychology* (vol. 25, pp. 1–65). New York: Academic Press.

Seligson, M. A. (2002). The impact of corruption on regime legitimacy. *Journal of Politics, 64,* 408–433.

Sen, A. (2009). *The idea of justice.* Cambridge, MA: Harvard University Press.

Shestowsky, D. (2004). Procedural preferences in alternative dispute resolution. *Psychology, Public Policy, and Law, 10,* 211–249.

Simon, B., & Klandermans, B. (2001). Politicized collective identity: A social psychological analysis. *American Psychologist, 56,* 319–331.

Skitka, L., & Tetlock, P. E. (1992). Allocation of scarce resources. *Journal of Experimental Social Psychology, 28,* 491–522.

Sondak, H., & Tyler, T. R. (2007). How does procedural justice shape the desirability of markets. *Journal of Economic Psychology, 28,* 79–92.

Staub, E. (2006). Reconciliation after genocide, mass killing, or intractable conflict. *Political Psychology, 27,* 867–894.

Taylor, D. M., & Moghaddam, F. M. (1994). *Theories of intergroup relations.* New York: Praeger.

Sunstein, C. R., & Epstein, R. A. (2001). *The vote: Bush, Gore & the Supreme Court.* Chicago: University of Chicago Press.

Tajfel, H. (1974). Social identity and intergroup behavior. *Social Science Information, 13,* 65–93.

Tajfel, H. (1978). *Differentiation between social groups: Studies in the social psychology of intergroup relations.* London: Academic Press.

Tajfel, H., & Turner, J. (1979). An integrative theory of intergroup conflict. In W. G. Austin and S. Worchel (eds.), *The social psychology of intergroup relations* (pp. 33–47). Monterey, CA: Brooks-Cole.

Tajfel, H., & Turner, J. C. (1986). The social identity theory of inter-group behavior. In S. Worchel & L. W. Austin (eds.), *Psychology of intergroup relations* (pp. 7–24). Chicago: Nelson-Hall.

Tangney, J. P., & Dearing, R. L. (2002). *Shame and guilt.* New York: Guilford Press.

Tausch, N., Becker, J., Spears, R., Christ, O., Saab, R., Singh, P., & Siddiqui, R. N. (2011). Explaining radical group behavior: Developing emotion and efficacy routes to normative and non-normative collective action. *Journal of Personality and Social Psychology, 101,* 129–148.

Taylor, D. M., & Moghaddam, F. M. (1994). *Theories of intergroup relations: International social psychological perspectives* (2nd. ed.). New York: Praeger.

Terwel, B. W., Harinck, F., Ellemers, N., & Daamen, D. L. D. (2010). Voice in political decision-making. *Journal of Experimental Social Psychology, 16,* 173–186.

Thibaut, J., & Walker, L. (1975). *Procedural justice.* Hillsdale: Erlbaum.

Turiel, E. (2002). *The culture of morality.* Cambridge: Cambridge University Press.

Tyler, T. R. (1985). Justice in the political arena. In R. Folger (ed.), *The sense of injustice* (pp. 189–226). New York: Plenum.

Tyler, T. R. (2004). Affirmative action in an institutional context. *Social Justice Research, 17,* 5–24.

Tyler, T. R. (2006a). *Why people obey the law.* Princeton, NJ: Princeton University Press.

Tyler, T. R. (2006b). Psychological perspectives on legitimacy and legitimation. *Annual Review of Psychology, 57,* 375–400.

Tyler, T. R. (2011). *Why people cooperate.* Princeton, NJ: Princeton University Press.

Tyler, T. R. (2012). Justice and effective cooperation. *Social Justice Research, 25,* 355–375.

Tyler, T. R., & Blader, S. L. (2000). *Cooperation in groups: Procedural justice, social identity and behavioral engagement.* Philadelphia: Psychology Press.

Tyler, T. R., & Blader, S. L. (2003). The group engagement model: procedural justice, social identity, and cooperative behavior. *Personality and Social Psychology Review, 7,* 349–361.

Tyler, T. R., Boeckmann, R., Smith, H. J., & Huo, Y. J. (1997). *Social justice in a diverse society.* Boulder, CO: Westview.

Tyler, T. R., & Degoey, P. (1995). Collective restraint in social dilemmas. *Journal of Personality and Social Psychology, 69,* 482–497.

Tyler, T. R., & Huo, Y. J. (2002). *Trust in the law: Encouraging public cooperation with the police and courts.* New York: Russell Sage.

Tyler, T. R., & Lind, E. A. (1990). Intrinsic versus community-based justice models: When does group membership matter? *Journal of Social Issues, 46,* 83–94.

Tyler, T. R., & Lind, E. A. (1992). A relational model of authority in groups. In M. Zanna (ed.), *Advances in experimental social psychology* (vol. 25, pp. 115–191). New York: Academic Press.

Tyler, T. R., and Lind, E. A. (2002). Procedural justice and relative deprivation. In I. Walker and H. J. Smith (eds.), *Relative deprivation: Specification, development, and integration* (pp. 44–68). Boulder, CO: Westview.

Tyler, T. R., & Mitchell, G. (1994). Legitimacy and the empowerment of discretionary authority. *Duke Law Journal, 43,* 703–814.

Tyler, T. R., & Smith, H. (1998). Social justice and social movements. In D. Gilbert, S. T. Fiske, and G. Lindzey (eds.), *Handbook of social psychology* (4th ed., pp. 595–626). New York: McGraw-Hill.

Van der Toorn, J., Berkics, M., & Jost, J. T. (2010). System justification, satisfaction, and perceptions of fairness and typicality at work: A cross-system comparison involving the U.S. and Hungary. *Social Justice Research, 23,* 189–210.

Van der Toorn, J., Feinberg, M., Jost, J. T., Kay, A. C., Tyler, T. R., Willer, R., & Wilmuth, C. (in press). A sense of powerlessness fosters system justification: On the legitimation of authority, hierarchy, and government. *Political Psychology.*

Van der Toorn, J., Tyler, T. R., & Jost, J. T. (2011). More than fair: Outcome dependence, system justification, and the perceived legitimacy of authority figures. *Journal of Experimental Social Psychology, 47,* 127–138.

Van Lange, P. A. M., Otten, W., De Bruin, E. M. N., & Joireman, J. A. (1997). Development of prosocial, individualistic, and competitive orientations: Theory and preliminary evidence. *Journal of Personality and Social Psychology, 73,* 733–746.

Van Stekelenburg, J., & Klandermans, B. (2007). Individuals in movements: A social psychology of contention. In B. Klandermans and C. Roggeband (eds.), *Social movements across disciplines* (pp. 157–204). New York: Springer.

Van Vugt, M., Meertens, R., & Van Lange, P. A. M. (1995). Car versus public transportation? The role of social value orientations in a real life social dilemma. *Journal of Applied Social Psychology. 25,* 258–278.

Van Yperen, N. W., & Buunk, B. P. (1994). Social comparison and social exchange in marital relationships. In M. J. Lerner & G. Mikula (eds.), *Entitlement and the affectionate bond* (pp. 89–116). New York: Plenum Press.

Van Zomeren, M., Spears, R., Fischer, A. H., & Leach, C. W. (2004). Put your money where your mouth is! Explaining collective action tendencies through group-based anger and group efficacy. *Journal of Personality and Social Psychology, 87,* 649–664.

Vidmar, N. (2000). Retribution and revenge. In J. Sanders & V. L. Hamilton (eds.). *Handbook of justice research in law* (pp. 31–63). New York: Kluwer.

Vidmar, N., & Miller, D. T. (1980). The social psychology of punishment. *Law and Society Review, 14*, 565–602.

Wakslak, C. J., Jost, J. T., Tyler, T. R., & Chen, E. S. (2007). Moral outrage mediates the dampening effect of system justification on support for redistributive social policies. *Psychological Science, 18*, 267–274.

Walster, E., Walster, G. W., & Berscheid, E. (1978). *Equity: Theory and research*. Boston: Allyn and Bacon.

Weiss, R. (1969). *The American myth of success: From Horatio Alger to Norman Vincent Peale*. New York: Basic Press.

Wenzel, M., Okimoto, T. G., Feather, N. T., & Platow, M. J. (2008). Retributive and restorative justice. *Law and Human Behavior, 32*(5), 375–389.

White, S. (2007). *Equality*. Cambridge: Polity Press.

Whitt, S., & Wilson, R. K. (2007). The dictator game, fairness and ethnicity in postwar Bosnia. *American Journal of Political Science, 51*, 655–668.

Wright, S. C., Taylor, D. M., & Moghaddam, F. M. (1990). Responding to membership in a disadvantaged group: From acceptance of collective protest. *Journal of Personality and Social Psychology, 58*, 994–1003.

CHAPTER 21

....

NETWORKS, INTERDEPENDENCE, AND SOCIAL INFLUENCE IN POLITICS

....

ROBERT HUCKFELDT, JEFFERY J. MONDAK,
MATTHEW HAYES, MATTHEW T. PIETRYKA,
AND JACK REILLY

ONE could craft an example of citizenship in which a person engages the political world while having few, if any, politically relevant encounters with other people. Our hypothetical citizen might follow politics solely by reading a local newspaper, watching political programs on television, and checking out political reports and commentary on the Internet. Together, these news sources may provide a solid base of information, one that enables the person to hold well-grounded opinions on various issues of the day. As to electoral politics, upon selecting favored candidates, the person might visit those candidates' websites, and even send in financial contributions to their campaigns. On Election Day, our isolated citizen would fill out the ballot while standing in the privacy of the voting booth, having had only the most cursory of interactions with election workers before receiving a ballot. The person we have described may well be a functional, competent citizen. However, what he or she never does is discuss politics with others. No complaints are voiced to friends about the state of the economy, the sluggishness of the bureaucracy, or the corruption of a scandal-plagued legislator. No jokes are shared with coworkers about a politician's embarrassing blunder at an international forum or a candidate's gaffe during a recent debate. Our hypothetical citizen experiences politics alone.

The citizen we have described here is not entirely far-fetched. Some people surely do strive to keep their political views entirely to themselves, and to avoid all conversations, and indeed all social interactions, that touch on politics. However, extreme political recluses such as the individual in our example are rather uncommon. Most citizens are of a different sort. Some might prefer not to discuss politics, yet be unable to escape the proselytizing of highly politicized relatives, neighbors, or coworkers. Others acknowledge and perhaps even welcome multiple social processes and encounters that carry political significance. Examples of the social aspects of politics abound. People attend town hall meetings. They go to rallies to hear candidates' speeches. They join associations, volunteer for campaigns, and go door-to-door to work on behalf of petition drives. Or, more mundanely, they have casual conversations with friends, relatives, and other acquaintances, conversations that sometimes include the exchange of information about politics and sometimes are marked by disagreement over the merits of a new policy proposal or the attributes of a public official or political candidate.

Research on social influence in politics considers the possibility that these various types of social interaction are politically consequential. By *social influence in politics*, we mean interpersonal encounters that affect at least one of the participants' subsequent patterns of political behavior, such as by prompting the formation of a new attitude, inducing change in an existing attitude, or motivating the person to take action, such as by voting in an election. For most people, citizenship includes a social component; the hypothetical political recluse we have described is an exception, not the norm. If most people experience at least occasional social interactions that involve politics, then scholars have the potential to improve our understanding of mass political behavior by exploring the nature and significance of those exchanges. In this chapter, we review research in this area. We do so with an eye toward demonstrating the value of scholarly attention to social influence in politics. In short, our contention is that full answers to pivotal questions about how and how well people execute the tasks of citizenship require acknowledgment of the social component of politics (see also Searing, Solt, Conover, & Crewe, 2007).

The examples of politically relevant social interaction cited above are sufficient to support a few basic premises regarding the social components of political behavior. First, social interactions relevant for politics come in many forms, from the casual chat that touches on politics, to a spur-of-the-moment choice to attend a campaign rally, to membership and participation in a public interest group. The possible social aspects of politics are broader still if we include matters such as seeing political yard signs and bumper stickers while driving through one's neighborhood, or reading about the opinions of others, such as in a news report regarding a recent public opinion poll, or by scanning letters to the editor in the local paper. Second, people vary in their levels of social exposure to political information. Our friends and acquaintances may talk about politics nearly every time we see them, or only from time to time. Our neighborhood may be a hotbed of campaign activity, or a place where campaign signs and political bumper stickers are quite scarce. Third, people have some control—but not full control—over social exposure to political information. We can choose our friends, but we may not always be able to steer conversations with them toward or away from politics. We can choose which neighborhood to live in, but not our actual neighbors, and not whether those neighbors knock on our door to ask us to sign petitions or to donate money to social or political causes.

Although research in political psychology about mass politics considers many phenomena, one of the chief concerns of research in this area is information. Scholars seek to understand what information about politics citizens encounter, how that information is processed, and how—and how well—information is used to update political attitudes and to guide political decisions and behaviors. Because some political information is transmitted socially, it follows that part of the effort by political psychologists to study citizen politics will explore relevant aspects of social communication. In political science, this research most often is labeled as being about social influence (for a discussion of political communications, including the news media, see Valentino and Nardis, chapter 18, this volume). Although social influence in politics may come in many forms, this chapter focuses primarily on the political significance of people's everyday encounters with their more or less regular associates—the relatives, friends, coworkers, neighbors, fellow parishioners, and casual acquaintances who make up their *social networks*. In pursuing this topic, we are ignoring large literatures regarding other forms of social influence—for example, literatures on reference groups and social identities (see Huddy, chapter 23, this volume). We justify this omission on two counts. First, a single review could not feasibly do justice to all the literatures relevant to social influence in politics. Second, we believe that network studies constitute an increasingly important area for scholarship on social influence.

Assume for the moment that a person has informed researchers that her social network includes four people, and that she speaks with each of them about politics on at least an occasional basis. If the analyst's ultimate goal in studying social networks is to further our understanding of the role of information in mass politics, it should be apparent that several aspects of our subject's social network will be of interest to us. At the very least we might want to know (1) whether, compared with other people's social networks, this one is large or small; (2) just how often politics comes up in conversation; (3) whether our subject and the members of her social network generally hold similar or dissimilar views about politics; (4) the nature and existence of relationships among the members of our subject's network; and (5) whether these networks of relationships have political consequences for our subject, such as increasing her basic knowledge about politics, influencing her thoughts about an issue or a candidate, or motivating her to vote in an election or volunteer on behalf of some cause. Digging even deeper, we might ask *why* it is that this person has a large or small network, discusses politics with a given level of frequency, does or does not encounter dissimilar points of view, and is or is not influenced by these political conversations.

This is a large number of questions. Fortunately, they can be reduced to two basic categories. The first concerns the *effects of social networks*. That is, does what goes on in people's social networks matter for subsequent patterns in political behavior? If the answer is no, research on social influence in politics can stop at this point. There would be little or no reason for political psychologists to explore the intricacies of social networks if those networks do not matter for politics. If the answer is yes, then we must consider subsidiary questions pertaining to *network content and composition*. In other words, what are the important features of social networks? Possibilities include the size of the network, the frequency with which a person and her conversation partners discuss politics, how politically well informed the network's members are, and whether our subject and the others in her network generally tend to agree or disagree when they talk about politics. Second, some research considers those forces that exert *effects on social networks*. Why do social networks differ in their content, composition, and, ultimately, their effects on political behavior? One factor is individual preference. Some people are social and outgoing, whereas others interact mostly with a few close friends. Some people welcome new ideas and viewpoints, whereas others have made up their minds and are resistant to alternate perspectives. Life circumstances provide a second set of factors. For example, a waiter at the Capitol Diner likely will be drawn into or overhear more conversations about politics while at work than will a tollbooth attendant. And finally, social and political events also may influence social networks. Conversations about politics arise for a reason. Often, that reason is something in the news, such as a dire new report about the state of the economy, the onset of a military invasion, or the occurrence of a major political speech. What goes on *in* social networks is likely shaped by what goes on *outside* of those networks, and whatever influence networks exert may be a product of their capacity to help people to learn about and make sense of the broader political world.

The remainder of this chapter is organized into several sections. The first provides a brief history of early research on social influence in politics. The second discusses the methodological approaches and data sources used in research on social networks. The remaining sections then tackle the core substantive topics we have introduced. Most of these relate to the possible effects of social networks. We walk through the types of effects networks might produce, and what research has found regarding the conditions under which these effects are most likely to be observed. Following review of research on the effects of social networks, the chapter then steps back to consider factors that possibly shape or moderate either patterns in social communication or the effects of such discussions.

1. HISTORICAL PERSPECTIVES ON SOCIAL INFLUENCE IN POLITICS

Scientific research on politics became increasingly common in the 1940s and 1950s, and several of the discipline's most important and influential research traditions trace back to that era. For scholars interested in social communication about politics, the efforts of Columbia University's Paul Lazarsfeld and his colleagues established a vital foundation. The Columbia researchers used panel surveys to explore the interrelationship between news media and interpersonal discussion as influences on electoral decision-making and other forms of social judgment. Their efforts constitute the most important precursors to the subsequent research on social networks discussed later in this chapter.

Their works also outlined an influential perspective on the nature of media effects in American politics and society.

Rather than gathering data using national surveys, the Columbia researchers focused on single locations. Moreover, to facilitate study of the flow of information and possible changes in people's attitudes and behaviors, panel surveys—surveys in which the same individuals are interviewed at multiple points in time—were conducted. The surveys sought to measure the effects of both news media and social communication.

Three central works were published by Lazarsfeld and his colleagues. The first, *The People's Choice: How the Voter Makes Up His Mind in a Presidential Campaign* (Lazarsfeld, Berelson, & Gaudet, 1948), reported on research conducted in Erie County, Ohio, during the 1940 presidential campaign. In this study, news media were observed to exert relatively little impact on voters, especially when compared with the impact of social communication. Lazarsfeld and his colleagues further examined the impact of information on electoral behavior in 1948, reporting their results in *Voting: A Study of Opinion Formation in a Presidential Campaign* (Berelson, Lazarsfeld, & McPhee, 1954). In this project, data were gathered in Elmira, New York. Last, in *Personal Influence: The Part Played by People in the Flow of Mass Communication* (Katz and Lazarsfeld, 1955), the researchers considered not only information about politics, but also social information such as people's views of new movie releases. Of particular interest in this study was the possibility that information in the news was disseminated through the mass public as a result of interpersonal communication initiated by a relatively small number of opinion leaders via what was referred to as a two-step flow of communication.

Soon after the onset of the Columbia research program, scholars at the University of Michigan launched the American National Election Studies (ANES; e.g., Campbell, Converse, Miller, & Stokes, 1960). Although a tremendously valuable resource for the study of elections and voting, one legacy of the Michigan approach was a relative lack of attention to social communication. Consideration of possible social influence was pushed to the back burner largely as an artifact of methodological approach. ANES data are drawn from national surveys, making it difficult to study the effects of any given individual's social context and interpersonal network. If we have data from 1,500 survey respondents and we wish to study the interconnections among them, doing so logically will be dramatically more challenging if our 1,500 respondents are drawn randomly from across an entire nation than if they are drawn from a single city or county. Compared with the Columbia scholars' focus on individual localities, the ANES approach enjoys an overwhelming advantage in terms of breadth of scope. However, that advantage is gained partly at the expense of depth of insight regarding the intricate networks and contexts possibly operating on the individual. In any case, as a consequence of the growing prominence of the ANES data following publication of *The American Voter* in 1960, it was some time before scholars began reconsidering the questions regarding social influence highlighted by Lazarsfeld and his colleagues. Today, research on social influence in politics enjoys unprecedented breadth and vibrancy. Much of this work makes use of survey-based methodological approaches that build on those pioneered by the Columbia researchers, but other methods also are important in contemporary research on networks and politics.

2. MEASURES AND METHODS

Scientific inquiry on political discussion networks takes several forms. As was the case in the 1940s and 1950s in the research conducted by Lazarsfeld and his colleagues, the most commonly used approach involves gathering data via surveys. As an alternate to surveys, other research makes use of qualitative, or observational, methods. Laboratory experiments also have been conducted to study particular aspects of discussion networks. In this section, we first will review some of the key approaches and issues in survey-based research on discussion networks. Following this, the unique properties of observational and laboratory designs will be considered, and examples of both will be introduced.

There are two basic variants in survey questions about political discussion. One type of question asks about overall patterns in political discussion, without making reference to particular individuals. For example, respondents may be asked how many days in the past week they have discussed politics, or how often they have attempted to convince a friend or acquaintance which way to vote in an upcoming election. These questions can be useful because responses can be contrasted with similar measures pertaining to other behaviors. For instance, in addition to asking about the frequency of political discussion, a survey may include items using the same format to measure how many days in the past week the respondent has read a newspaper or watched the news on television. Similarly, the question about efforts at persuading others how to vote may be asked along with questions about the frequency of donating money to candidates, attending campaign rallies, and other forms of participation. Collectively, data from these items permit political discussion to be assessed within broader information and participatory contexts.

The second survey-based approach to gathering data about political discussion is to ask respondents to identify particular individuals with whom they discuss politics or other important matters. Using this method, the first step is for the survey interviewer to obtain a list of names from the respondent. Depending on the survey, the respondent may be asked to provide up to three, four or five names. Collectively, the discussion partners identified by a given respondent operationally constitute that person's *network*. Respondents vary in how many discussion partners, or discussants, they identify. Therefore, a simple count provides a measure of *network size*. Network size may offer an indication of how politically engaged the respondent is, and it also may matter for social influence. For instance, the impact of a particular discussion partner on the respondent intuitively might be expected to lessen as network size increases—as the individual discussion partner becomes one voice among many.

Given the right prompt, many people probably could name more than three or four individuals with whom they have conversations about politics or important matters. For these people, the three or four discussants identified on a survey represent a larger network. It follows that it may be important which discussants the respondent thinks to list. Outside of the realm of political discussion, it is well established that survey respondents often offer very different answers depending on how questions are phrased and framed. This implies that the prompt used on surveys to induce respondents to think about their discussion partners also might be consequential. The prompt, or introduction, read by the survey interviewer in an effort to elicit the names of respondents' discussants is referred to as a *name generator*. One type of name generator asks respondents to list individuals with whom they discuss "important matters." The "important matters" name generator gained popularity among sociologists, and it is the approach that has been used when the General Social Survey has included questions about discussion networks (e.g., Burt, 1984; Marsden, 1987; McPherson, Smith-Lovin, & Brashears, 2006).

When asked about "important matters," the respondent could have a great diversity of considerations in mind. In an effort to focus attention on conversations—and conversation partners—specific to the domain of politics, an alternate to the "important matters" name generator makes reference to government, elections, or political affairs. Huckfeldt and Sprague (1995) used this approach in their 1984 South Bend Study, asking respondents after the November 1984 US elections, "Can you give me the first names of the three people you talked with most about the events of the past election year?" Since that 1984 study, variants of the "political affairs" name generator have been employed on several other surveys.

The difference in name generators gives rise to questions regarding whether the two approaches yield consistent depictions of respondents' social networks. Much of the leverage on this question emerged through examination of data from the 1996 Indianapolis–St. Louis survey (Huckfeldt, Levine, Morgan, & Sprague 1998; Huckfeldt and Mendez, 2008; Klofstad et al., 2009). On that survey, respondents were randomly assigned to be read one of two name generators, one focused on "important matters" or one involving "government, elections and politics." Upon comparing networks identified using these differing approaches, Klofstad, McClurg, and Rolfe (2009) found relatively minor differences and arrived at the justifiable conclusion that political networks are not constructed to create a politically safe haven of like-minded associates. That is, since political communication networks resemble "important matters" networks in most respects, it would appear that a great deal of political conversation occurs with the people who are readily at hand—the same people with whom the respondents discuss most matters of interest.

At the same time, there is a substantial body of evidence to suggest that political communication networks do not perfectly overlap with the networks measured using an "important matters" name generator. Most importantly, some people who play significant roles in political communication networks are likely to be excluded by an "important matters" name generator. First, it would appear that the important matters networks run the risk of underrepresenting workplace associates (Mutz & Mondak, 2006). This is important because these associates are encountered through a shared environment (the workplace) that is nonvoluntary and instrumentally oriented, and hence they hold out the promise of being the "weak ties" who expose individuals to a wider variety of information and viewpoints (Granovetter, 1973; Huckfeldt, Beck, Dalton, & Levine, 1995). Second, other analyses of the Indianapolis–St. Louis survey demonstrate subtle but important effects due to the name generator. In spite of the fact that the identified networks are likely to overlap, the mean frequency of political communication is higher in politically defined networks, and respondents report a somewhat higher mean frequency of political disagreement (Huckfeldt & Mendez, 2008). Once again, the important matters name generator would appear to exclude some potentially important discussants. Finally, Huckfeldt, Levine, et al. (1998) show differences in the cognitive processes underlying the two alternative means of identifying network associates, with important implications for network identification.

The analyses of Klofstad et al. (2009) and Huckfeldt and Mendez (2008) reach the important conclusion that, because "important matters" and "politics" name generators produce similar depictions of networks, most people discuss politics with many of the same individuals with whom they have other sorts of conversations. Rather than forming topic-specific networks, most people appear to converse with *many* of the same discussants regardless of whether the topic is a generic "important matter," something pertaining to "government, elections and politics," or perhaps even more mundane issues such as a new movie or restaurant. At the same time, it would be a mistake to conclude that there are *no* important differences between important matters networks or political networks or other specialty topic networks (see Katz & Lazarsfeld, 1955; Schneider, Teske, Roch, & Marschall, 1997). Hence, and most crucially, the important matters network name generator runs the risk of excluding political discussants who play particularly important roles in the political communication process.

Once a name generator has been used to identify a survey respondent's discussion partners, several follow-up questions are asked about those discussants. The specific questions differ across surveys. However, it is common for these batteries of network items to ask about matters such as how it is that the respondent and the discussant know one another, how frequently they talk, how often politics comes up as a topic of conversation, the discussant's levels of interest in and knowledge about politics, how often the respondent and discussant agree or disagree with one another, and what the respondent perceives the discussant's political views to be—what party the discussant supports, which candidate the discussant voted for in a recent election, and so on. Data from these various follow-up items enable researchers to explore which types of relationships and which attributes of discussants are most strongly associated with particular effects.

A limitation of asking respondents about their discussion networks is that the resulting data tell only one side of the story. The analyst sees a given discussion dyad—the relationship between two conversation partners—from the point of view of the survey respondent, but not from the point of view of the identified discussant. It could be, for instance, that the respondent has misidentified the discussant's party affiliation, or that the respondent and discussant disagree about how often they disagree. Some network studies have addressed this concern by surveying respondents about their discussion partners and then contacting some of those discussants and also surveying them (e.g., Huckfeldt & Sprague, 1995). The second sample, the one composed of the discussants named by the original respondents, is referred to as a *snowball sample*. This is because this second group of respondents is not identified via conventional random sampling techniques; instead, these respondents are identified as a byproduct of the initial survey. By merging data from the initial respondents with those obtained from their discussion partners, numerous important questions can be considered. Chief among these is the accuracy of social perception: if the respondent perceived that the discussant voted for the winning candidate in the most recent national election, how likely is it that this perception is accurate? Reciprocity also can be examined. For instance, the respondent named the discussant as one of his or her top three (or four or five) discussion partners, but did the discussant, in turn, name the respondent, or did the discussant identify different individuals?

These questions are central in research on the effects of social communication, and we will return to them below. Survey-based research has been the dominant approach in the study of political discussion networks, and most of the works described in later sections of this chapter examine survey data. First, though, a brief mention of two additional approaches in the study of social networks, observational studies and laboratory experiments, is warranted.

Using survey data, researchers can identify properties of individuals' networks and can devise statistical tests designed to attempt to measure whether social communication matters for subsequent patterns in political behavior. However, one area in which survey applications do not fare well is in providing insight regarding the actual content of people's political conversations. How does politics come up as a topic of conversation? What subjects are discussed? Do these exchanges bring some sort of give and take, do they spark disagreement, or do they lead to feelings of awkwardness and discomfort among participants? With survey data alone, these are difficult questions to answer. As an alternative, researchers sometimes attempt to observe the occurrence of actual conversations about politics. Field research of this type can offer a useful complement to other methodological approaches.

In the past decade, Walsh (2004; 2007) has observed political conversations as part of two major projects. In the first, the investigation focused primarily on a diner at which a large group of men, mostly senior citizens, met each morning. Part of the challenge in this research was for Walsh to meet, be accepted by, and ultimately join the discussion group in question. Once this hurdle had been crossed, actual conversation, including conversation about politics, could be observed. Among other noteworthy findings, Walsh saw that discussion moved fluidly from one topic to another, with political matters coming and going mostly as unplanned elements of the conversation. This observation supports the conclusion that political discussion often is simply a subset of discussion in general rather than being a deliberate focal point for conversations with select discussion partners. Walsh also found that news coverage often provided a starting point for political discussion, but that participants frequently supplied their own frames to help make sense of what was in the news rather than relying exclusively on how news media had depicted a story. Consistent with this, Walsh observed that identity was an important component of political discussion. Most members of the group had known one another for decades, and many saw one another nearly every day. Consequently, the conversation partners shared a strong sense of group identity. In Walsh's view, a participant's identity with the group led the person to understand political issues via a shared perspective with other group members.

Walsh's second observational study (2007) considered political exchanges in a more formalized setting, community-sponsored forums on race. Although these forums differ in structure from casual conversations about politics, suggestive insights still emerged regarding the nature of political discussion. For instance, Walsh noted that personal anecdotal experiences were highly influential on forum participants' views. That is, if a participant conveyed the story of a relevant personal experience, that anecdote would strongly influence the opinions and interpretations of other members of the discussion forum. This observation brings insight regarding both the occurrence of social influence and a key aspect of social communication—the reporting of a relevant personal experience—that gives rise to such influence.

Laboratory experiments provide a second alternative to survey research as a means to study social networks. As with laboratory research on other topics, a chief benefit of laboratory methods for network studies is that experiments permit careful attention to matters of process. In particular, the analyst's capacity to derive causal inferences is expanded. With survey data on discussion networks, analyses are inherently correlational. The research can demonstrate, for instance, that a person's exposure to conservative viewpoints via political discussion corresponds with an increased likelihood that the person will vote for a conservative candidate, but the evidence will not be definitive that the network exerted a causal influence. Greater certainty about cause and effect can emerge using experimental designs.

Several types of experiments have been employed in research on social networks. We will offer a few illustrative examples. Parker, Parker, and McCann (2008) embedded experimental treatments in a panel survey of undergraduates to determine if social communication produced lasting effects on individuals' judgments regarding public hazards. Students were recruited to discuss with their friends hazards such as mercury levels in canned tuna, and the friends were later surveyed as a means to gauge the impact of social communication on the message recipients' policy views. Ahn, Huckfeldt, and Ryan (2010) conducted small-group experiments using a computerized platform as a means to study the relative value people assign to the effects of expertise and shared values on social cue-taking. Participants were charged with the task of obtaining information about candidates from one another in an interactive setting. Mondak (1995a; 1995b) introduced a quasi experiment, or natural experiment, by capitalizing on the fact that a strike had shut down the city of Pittsburgh's newspapers during the 1992 US elections. Data from Pittsburgh were contrasted with data from Cleveland, a demographically similar city in which newspapers remained available. Absent newspapers in

Pittsburgh, political discussion of local elections decreased, but the influence of socially communicated political views on the vote choice increased.

The studies mentioned here provide a sense of the diversity of topics and experimental methods researchers have introduced in the study of social networks. In each of these studies, aspects of the information context were varied, whether by the researcher or by unique circumstances. As a result, the researchers were on relatively firm ground when seeking to identify causal effects on participants' attitudes and behaviors.

Surveys, observational approaches, and experiments all are means to an end. Regardless of method, the goal in this stream of research involves improving our understanding of social networks and their possible effects on political behavior. We should also note that research on social influence in politics is not limited to these approaches. For instance, some studies have used mathematical models and computer simulations to examine phenomena such as the social diffusion of information (Albert & Barabasi, 2002; Axelrod, 1997). Others have mapped out patterns of linkages among individuals in varied contexts, such as among members of the US House of Representatives (Cho and Fowler, 2010; Fowler, 2006) and users of Facebook (Gaines & Mondak, 2009). Regardless of how social networks are studied, the forms that network effects might take require careful consideration. We turn next to an overview of the two basic manners in which political discussion might alter a person's patterns of political engagement, by providing a person with new information and by influencing the person's judgments and behaviors. Following this overview, we delve deeper into the conditions under which social communication should be expected to be the most consequential.

3. Possible Effects of Social Communication about Politics: Information and Influence

When a person engages a conversation partner in political discussion, what outcome might we expect? One possibility, of course, is that the discussion will produce no discernible impact. People chat with one another all of the time about a plethora of subjects, and it seems unlikely that each such exchange would bring notable lasting effects for the participants. In the political domain, it is entirely possible—indeed, perhaps likely—that when two people talk about a candidate, policy, or public official, their casual endeavor to pass the time will fail to alter either person's future attitudes and behaviors. Keeping this potential for an absence of effects in mind, we must consider what sorts of tangible results political discussion might produce, and in what circumstances. When studying social networks, effects will not be observed in the absence of communication, but the sheer existence of communication does not ensure that effects will be seen (McClurg, 2003). In other words, communication is a necessary, but not a sufficient, condition for exchanges within networks to give rise to discernible effects on political attitudes and behavior.

As with exposure to any form of communication, exposure to social communication can produce two broad classes of effects: the first focused on influence and the second focused on information. As will become clear, information and influence often are closely interrelated. The first type of effect associated with social networks is influence. With respect to political discussion, influence occurs when a conversation leads one of the participants to form an opinion, to change an opinion, or to engage in some behavior. One example of this type of influence might be an update in a person's evaluation of the president. Another example is if the discussion leads one of the individuals to finalize his or her vote choice in an upcoming election. Or, with respect to political participation, the conversation might convince a person to vote (or not to vote) in that election. The empirical record abounds with important works that have generated evidence pointing toward these forms of social influence (e.g., Pattie & Johnston, 2001). In addition to the actual identification of social influence, other research in this area focuses largely on exploration of the conditions that foster influence. Scholars examine what it is about a person, the person's discussion partner, and their dyadic relationship that makes influence more or less likely to occur.

Among the several issues to be examined below, two require preview. First, demonstration that influence has occurred, particularly within the parameters of survey-based research on social networks, is not an easy task. In many instances, self-selection stands as a plausible alternate to influence. For instance, suppose that a person identifies with the Blue Party, but has three political discussion partners who identify with the Yellow Party, and the person in question also ends up voting for the Yellow Party in the next national election. The person's decision to vote Yellow may be the product of social influence. After hearing for weeks or months from friends and acquaintances about the merits of the Yellow Party, the person may, at last, have been influenced to vote against the Blue ticket. However, an alternate possibility is that, prior to any conversations, the person already was leaning toward the Yellow Party in this year's election. Indeed, this emerging preference may be why the person was willing to take on supporters of the Yellow Party as political discussion partners. Thus, it may be that no actual social influence took place. As we will see, differentiating influence from self-selection can be a vexing task.

Second, how a person's initial views relate to those of a discussion partner affect the possibilities for influence to occur. If two people agree on everything, if they are always on the some page as one another, then influence will not be observed. Minds cannot change when the speakers are always in perfect harmony. Instead, it is only where initial points of view differ—where the conversation is marked by at least some level of implicit or explicit disagreement—that influence can take place. Although the presence of disagreement is a logical precondition for influence, it is one that brings its own complications. Intuitively, we should expect that many individuals will prefer to avoid disagreement. If this is the case, then opportunities for social influence are closed off from the start. Further, even if people are exposed to different points of view, they may be resistant to those perspectives. Rather than yielding to their conversation partners' points of view, people may instead dig in their heels and cling to their own opinions. The particular significance of disagreement will receive expanded attention below.

In addition to influence, social communication may produce political effects by fostering the dissemination of information. Political discussion results in an information effect when a participant learns something new or otherwise acquires expanded political competence. Facts are transmitted. Expertise is gained. The individual comes away from the conversation at least somewhat more capable of understanding one or more aspects of the political world, and perhaps somewhat more capable of forming evaluative judgments about political phenomena. The occurrence of such information effects presupposes (1) that one of the discussion partners entered into the conversation knowing something that the other person did not, (2) that the individual attempted to share this information, and (3) that the information was received by the second individual. Thus, similar to much of the research on the effects of news media, research on the capacity of social communication to foster an increase in participants' information levels examines the circumstances under which these three conditions are or are not met. In other words, this research investigates the possible social transmission of political expertise.

4. INFLUENCE VERSUS SELF-SELECTION

The occurrence of a conversation about politics between any two individuals can be viewed as the culmination of a complex process, a process that brought the two people together, and that did so in a manner in which one or both ultimately felt comfortable raising politics as a topic of discussion. Some of the forces that brought the two conversation partners together were within their direct control, others were ones for which the individuals perhaps had an indirect say, and still others may have operated independently from the discussants' personal choices and preferences. Acknowledging the presence of these various interrelated forces is essential if scholars are to succeed in distinguishing between possible social influence and self-selection. Failure to take the issue of self-selection seriously leads to the temptation to overstate the prevalence and magnitude of social influence.

If life unfolded like a laboratory experiment, social influence would be easy to demonstrate. Encounters with political discussion partners would be completely exogenous to personal preferences, political or otherwise, much as exposure to an experimental manipulation occurs entirely outside of the control, and even awareness, of the study's participants. In this context, we merely would need to observe whether an encounter with a discussion partner led the individual to form a new attitude or change an old one. If such an effect were to be observed, we would conclude that social influence occurred.

Juxtaposed against the laboratory experiment, consider the case of two coworkers chatting about politics during a coffee break. The fact that these individuals work together at all may be the consequence of macro processes of sorting and mixing, processes that, as Schelling (1978) noted, can create homogeneity absent individual intention and communication (see also Achen & Shively, 1995). After all, something led the two coworkers to be employed at the same company at the same time. Perhaps, for example, they are young engineers working in a midsized electronics development company. Market forces outside of their control created incentives that encouraged them to acquire training in engineering and then to seek employment in this particular company. Once cast together as coworkers, the two may have found one another as discussion partners because they were rationally motivated to search for trustworthy informants who shared their interests and preferences (Downs, 1957), or because they carefully constructed amenable friendship circles within an otherwise diverse workplace context (Finifter, 1974). Last, when their conversation turns to politics, one or both of the coworkers may engage in self-censoring to avoid the unpleasantness of political disagreement with an associate (MacKuen, 1990) or even because aspects of the broader political context creative disincentives for political discourse (Conover, Searing, & Crewe, 2002; Mondak & Gearing, 1998).

In this example, the coworkers certainly did not choose careers in engineering so as to alter their future exposure to political discussion, yet their choices had this effect, nonetheless. Upon finding themselves together at work, each of the two enjoyed at least some capacity to seek out or to avoid conversation with the other, and, once conservation ensued, to seek out or to avoid politics as a topic of discussion. By the time one of the workers complained to the other about the president's poor handling of a recent issue, it is far from certain that room for social influence remained. Instead, it may be the case that the second worker selected into this conversation due to his or her own concern with the president's performance, and a corresponding desire to hear a coworker support this critical perspective. The endogeneity of this real-world example contrasts starkly with the exogeneity of the laboratory experiment. The critical lesson is that identification of a causal relationship—in this case, the occurrence of social influence—is an extraordinarily challenging task.

Apart from caution in the interpretation of statistical results, what can be done to address self-selection and the corresponding problem of endogeneity? A first step, albeit not a definitive one, is to ensure that statistical models fully account for a person's own circumstances, values, and political predispositions before seeking to determine whether the person's attitudes were influenced by those of a discussion partner. In the example of the two coworkers, the dependent variable might be the first coworker's assessment of the president's handling of the economy. In a statistical model, individual-level predictors might include the person's education level, job status, personal economic situation, partisan affiliation, and support or opposition to the president in the last election. The last variable to add to the model is a measure of the coworker's views, whether it be this person's partisanship or opinion about the president's handling of the economy. If this variable yields a significant effect on the dependent variable over and above any influences of the individual-level controls, we would have reasonable grounds for confidence that social influence has occurred—that is, the second coworker's views truly have influenced the first's. Unfortunately, this analytical structure brings no means for self-selection to be ruled out conclusively, because it remains possible that selection, and thus endogeneity, took place via some other factor that has been omitted from the model. In short, this design may enable the researcher to rule out the obvious threats to the inference that social influence has transpired, but it does not enable the researcher to rule out all such threats.

A related concern with this approach is that any correlation between the preferences of the respondent and the discussant would be assumed to represent the impact of the latter on the former even though reciprocal or reverse influence is possible. That is, perhaps the respondent influenced the discussant rather than vice versa, or each influenced the other. Scholars have addressed this concern by representing the discussant's political views with an instrumental variable, one that is presumably immune to reciprocal effects (e.g., Huckfeldt & Sprague, 1991; 1995). For example, the discussant's partisan affiliation can be represented with data about the discussant's parents' partisan preferences. Those parental partisan affiliations cannot have been affected by a conversation between the survey respondent and the respondent's discussion partner, yet those affiliations will predict, at least coarsely, the discussant's current views. Thus, an instrument reliant on parental partisanship will capture some of the partisan flavor of the subsequent political conversation without falling victim to the tangle of possible reciprocal influence.

A second step toward assessing the problems of self-selection and endogeneity is to demonstrate that the composition of political discussion networks is at least partly beyond the control of any individual participant. Several forms of evidence support this conclusion. For one, to a substantial extent, the composition of interpersonal political discussion networks is a function of the composition of the larger environment. For instance, people who reside among conservatives are more likely to converse with conservatives, quite apart from their own political predispositions (Huckfeldt & Sprague, 1988). The implication is that people generally do not exert ardent control over their discussion networks, but instead merely take political discussion as it comes. Consistent with this view, a second point is that political discussion often is unplanned. When talking, people jump from topic to topic, as different statements cue new thoughts and recollections (Walsh, 2004). The stochastic nature of conversation itself inherently constrains an individual's capacity for selective avoidance of politics or any other topic. Last, researchers have capitalized on the two types of name generators addressed above, the "important matters" and "politics" generators, to show that political discussion networks are no more homogeneous or free from disagreement than more generalized networks (Huckfeldt & Mendez, 2008; Klofstad, McClurg, & Rolfe, 2009). Thus, if social influence occurs outside of the realm of political discussion, then it quite likely also occurs when conversations turn toward political matters.

A third approach to demonstrating social influence despite the possible effects of self-selection entails differentiating among the contexts in which communication networks are formed. For instance, research on political discussion within the workplace, an important source of communication networks, establishes that conversation often occurs among coworkers and other casual acquaintances who are cast together for economic rather than social reasons (Mondak & Mutz, 2001; Mutz & Mondak, 2006). When asked about patterns of political discussion at work, many respondents indicate that it was their discussion partners, not themselves, who typically brought up politics as a topic of conversation, and that, given a choice, many respondents would have preferred not to discuss politics. In these instances, political discussion is the product of involuntary association, not purposive self-selection. Partly as a result of these patterns of interaction, individuals are more likely to be exposed to heterogeneous preferences at work than in many other contexts. When apparent social influence is identified within workplace-based discussion networks, the unique properties of these networks bring analytical leverage useful for distinguishing actual influence from self-selection.

More recently, a new wave of experiments (Visser & Mirabile, 2004), field experiments (Levitan & Visser, 2009), and longitudinal research (Lazer, Brian, Carol, Katz, & Neblo, 2010) has addressed the endogeneity problem head-on, with focus on the formation of political communication networks among new students enrolled as freshmen at the University of Chicago and as first-year graduate students at Harvard University's Kennedy School of Government. In these studies, the researchers either could construct social networks in the laboratory or could monitor students' patterns of behavior as they arrived on campus and experienced the formation of new networks. Although there is evidence of sorting and homophily in these studies, the sorting is not based on politics or political preferences, even for the Lazer et al. (2010) study of graduate students in public affairs. Further, although politics was not central to the formation of students' networks, all three studies document important patterns of social influence among the students. The point is not that people fail to pursue personal preferences in selecting associates. Rather, this work suggests that maintaining political agreement is a relatively unimportant criterion for network formation. As a consequence, individuals end up being located in politically diverse networks, networks that carry a large potential for political influence.

A related literature addresses the endogeneity of social interaction effects within the context of partisan canvassing and contacting strategies that take place as part of voter mobilization efforts. In an innovative series of field experiments, Gerber and Green (1999; 2000) study mobilization efforts initiated by canvassers who are typically unknown to the people who are contacted. These studies demonstrate significant and consistent effects on the likelihood that, upon being contacted by a canvasser, a person will turn out and vote. Moreover, Nickerson (2008) identifies second-order consequences that arise due to these contacts. Specifically, not only does the contact affect the likelihood of turnout by the person who is contacted, but also the likelihood that others in the household will vote as well. Social influence can be inferred in this case. In Nickerson's field experiment, canvassers knocked on doors and either encouraged a resident to vote or delivered a message regarding the value of recycling. If a woman was assigned to the voter turnout treatment and an effect was later observed on the likelihood that her husband voted, communication between the wife and the husband about the party canvasser's message—that is, social influence—almost certainly drives the effect.

None of the studies discussed here claims that self-selection and the associated issue of endogeneity are unproblematic for research on social influence. Indeed, establishing causal relationships in research on social influence remains both a serious concern and a vibrant topic of scholarly exchange (e.g., Cohen-Cole & Fletcher, 2008; Fowler, Heaney, Nickerson, Padgett, & Sinclair, 2011). People choose neighborhoods in which to reside, churches to attend, and career paths to follow. People choose friends and acquaintances. People choose to enter into conversations with others, and they choose to steer those conversations toward or away from politics. The accumulated research does not deny self-selection, but it does establish that self-selection is insufficient to preclude social influence, including in the political domain. First, politics is not the only criterion that is invoked when people select their associates, and it does not appear to be a particularly important one. Second, discussion networks are, by and large, representative of the communities (e.g., neighborhoods, workplaces) from which they are drawn. Third, although many people might prefer to avoid hearing wrongheaded opinions from their colleagues and acquaintances, avoidance is not always a practical or even a viable option.

5. THE IMPORTANCE OF DISAGREEMENT

When two people discuss politics, the potential for social influence hinges in part on the mix of their initial positions and on their receptivity to alternate points of view. If two discussion partners absolutely always agree with one another, their conversations never will result in opinion change. Information may be exchanged, as would be the case if one of the individuals learned something new and shared it with the other. But one discussion partner's opinions would never move toward the other's if they always began in the same place. Thus, at least some level of disagreement must exist if social influence is to be observed. However, it is logically the case that too much disagreement is also problematic. If two discussion partners absolutely always disagree with one another, then, once again, their conversations will never result in opinion change. At least in terms of an impact on opinion, social influence presupposes that discussion partners disagree at least some of the time, but also that at least one of the individuals is occasionally receptive to the other's perspectives.

Recognizing the important role disagreement plays in establishing the potential for social influence, scholars have devoted particular attention to studying the bases and consequences of disagreement in political discussion. More specifically, research has examined how much disagreement actually exists in social networks, the factors that lead disagreement to be sustained rather than snuffed out, the possible positive effects of exposure to diverse perspectives through social communication, and the potential for disagreement to result in unexpected adverse consequences. Each of these lines of inquiry warrants consideration.

Previously, we noted that in survey-based research on social networks, a respondent's interpersonal discussion network is operationally defined as being composed of the individuals the respondent names when asked to list conversation partners. Some respondents name zero discussion partners, others name one or two, and still others provide the maximum number of names requested (typically either three, four, or five). Disagreement between the respondent and his or her discussants can be represented in numerous manners. One criterion might be the vote choice in the most recent national election. A respondent and discussant would be coded as being in agreement if they voted for the same candidate. Similarly, partisan affiliation could be used as the basis for determining whether a respondent and discussion partner are in agreement. In the United States, for example, disagreement would be recorded if a Republican respondent has a Democratic discussion partner. Yet another means to measure levels of disagreement is to ask the respondents to gauge it. For example, a survey might ask, "When you talk with (name) about politics, how often do you disagree: always, sometimes, rarely or never?" Last, a researcher might measure disagreement by using data from each of these approaches to form a summative index.

Disagreement can be represented at the level of the discussion dyad or at the level of a survey respondent's full discussion network. In the latter case, the key distinction in the literature is whether the person's network is wholly homogeneous or whether at least some disagreement is present. For instance, suppose that the Republican respondent from the example above names four discussion partners, including three fellow Republicans and one Democrat. In this case, we would characterize the respondent's network as including a diversity of partisan viewpoints because the network is not fully homogeneous.

Viewed at the dyadic level, most political discussion dyads, or pairs of discussion partners, are characterized by agreement, not disagreement. As our analysis of self-selection highlighted, there are two key reasons for this. First, macro-level sorting processes work to bring similar people together and to keep dissimilar people apart. We resemble our neighbors in terms of socioeconomic status, our coworkers in terms of education level and professional interests, and our fellow parishioners in terms of faith. Each of these dimensions correlates at least modestly with political predispositions. A liberal surrounded only by other liberals faces only two choices in terms of political discussion: talk with a fellow liberal, or do not talk at all. Second, although, as we have seen, it has its limits, some self-selection takes place. Disagreement is, well, disagreeable. Consequently, many people prefer to avoid it and are willing to expend at least some effort to do so.

Although the odds of encountering disagreement in any given discussion dyad are relatively low, diversity within three- or four-person interpersonal networks is considerably more common. Indeed, in an analysis of data from the 2000 US presidential election between George Bush and Al Gore, Huckfeldt, Johnson, and Sprague (2004) note that the modal condition in interpersonal discussion networks was exposure to disagreement. In other words, all Bush voters did not converse exclusively with fellow Bush voters, and all Gore voters did not converse exclusively with other Gore voters. It is not uncommon, for instance, to observe a Gore voter with a four-person discussion network composed of three fellow Gore voters and one Bush supporter. Precise interpretation of the data depends partly on how nonvoters, undecided voters, and supporters of other candidates (e.g., third-party candidates Pat Buchanan and Ralph Nader) are categorized. On this point, Mutz (2006) indicates that fewer networks would be labeled as including diverse points of view if the definition were limited to include only (a) Bush voters with at least one discussant who voted for Gore, and (b) Gore voters with at least one discussant who voted for Bush. Regardless of how one classifies respondents and discussants who are other than Bush or Gore voters, two clear points remain. First, political conversations, whether at the dyadic or network level, are more likely to be characterized by similarity in viewpoints than by dissimilarity. But second, for a large portion of citizens, at least some exposure to cross-cutting perspectives takes place.

The continued presence of some diversity of viewpoints in many individuals' discussion networks can, itself, be assessed from two perspectives. One question we already have considered is why levels of diversity are not greater than they are. The combination of structural forces and self-selection helps foster homogeneity in interpersonal discussion networks. But this question also can be turned on its head: why is it that disagreement is observed at all? In light of the factors that act to discourage the occurrence of conversations between individuals with differing political views, why is it that political disagreement survives rather than being pushed to the point of extinction?

The puzzle posed by the persistence of disagreement arguably is more challenging than the question of why levels of disagreement are not even greater than they are. First, as we have emphasized, key factors work to discourage the airing of diverse political points of view. But second, given the potential for social influence, the *persistence* of disagreement may seem curious. Suppose, for example, that a person who considers herself to be a Blue Party supporter finds herself, despite the factors that discourage exposure to disagreement, having a series of conversations about politics with an affiliate of the Yellow Party. If social influence occurs, what would we observe over time? Logically, disagreement between our subject and her discussion partner should not persist for long. One option, of course, is that the each will throw up her hands in despair over the other's obstinacy, and they will stop having these disagreeable conversations, or even break off their relationship. Alternately, social influence could take place. In this scenario, the strength of our Blue Party supporter's positions could eventually wear down her Yellow Party acquaintance, and eventually convert the latter to the Blue side (or at least to becoming an independent). And the opposite process obviously is possible as well, with the Yellow Party gaining a new supporter when our erstwhile Blue Party subject is persuaded to switch sides.

The potential for social influence to extinguish political disagreement seems all the more plausible when we step back and consider such influence from the perspective of broader psychological research. Relevant and important work has been conducted on an interrelated array of topics, including conformity effects (Asch, 1955), cognitive dissonance (Festinger, 1957), attitudinal consistency (Heider, 1958), the rational use of socially supplied information to reduce information costs (Downs, 1957), and, more recently, motivated reasoning (Lodge & Taber, 2000; Taber & Lodge, 2006; see also Taber & Young, chapter 17, this volume). All of these research traditions and their associated empirical works point to the conclusion that people generally seek to resolve—not maintain—dissonance. Collectively, these research traditions would seem to suggest that if individuals do not avoid disagreeable messages, they ought to be convinced by them. That is, if social communication is influential, and if avoidance fails, one would expect that communication to be persuasive. Over time, either our Blue Party supporter or her Yellow Party acquaintance should exhibit changing preferences. But, as we have seen, research on political discussion networks establishes that some diversity of views is present in a substantial portion of them. If social communication is persuasive, how can we account for the persistence of political diversity within interpersonal networks (Abelson, 1964; 1979)?

Disagreement can be found in some individuals' networks, but not in others. *Network density* has emerged as a key determinant of whether disagreement persists. Network density refers to the relationships among all of the members of a network. A high level of density exists if all of the members are tightly connected to one another. Suppose, for example, that Alice and Emma were each asked to name three political discussion partners. Alice names Bonnie, Carol, and Denise. The four all attended high school together, and they have been close friends ever since. Alice's network would have the maximum value on a measure of density, because all four of the individuals in the network know one another well. In contrast, Emma names as discussion partners her sister Faye, her college roommate Grace, and her coworker Hanna. Faye, Grace, and Hanna either do not know one another at all, or they have met in passing solely due to their mutual acquaintance with Emma. In this case, network density would be categorized as low.

Network density matters because disagreement is more likely to occur between individuals who do not share a common circle of friends. Put differently, a person is more likely to be exposed to disagreement if her network has a low level of density. In the case of the present examples, it is far more likely that we would observe political disagreement in Emma's discussion network than in Alice's. With Alice, we would expect disagreement, if it was ever present at all, to have been resolved long ago. If Alice were the only Blue Party supporter among her circle of friends, she either would have dropped Bonnie, Carol, and Denise in favor of a more congenial set of associates, or she would have been persuaded to switch to the Yellow Party. With Emma, it may be that Emma herself and Faye and Grace all support the Blue Party, but disagreement persists within Emma's network because Hanna sides with the Yellow Party. And, for her part, Hanna's only Blue Party discussion partner may be Emma. That is, Hanna is the source of political diversity in Emma's network, and Emma is the source of diversity in Hanna's. Apart from one another, their respective networks are homogeneous.

These examples suggest that disagreement can be sustained by the nonoverlapping structure of an individual's network, a key lesson emphasized in Huckfeldt, Johnson, and Sprague (2004). For Alice, there is not a nonoverlapping component to the network because Alice and her three discussants all are tightly linked to one another. As a result, disagreement has no grounds on which to flourish. In contrast, Emma's discussion partners do not all know one another, and conversations with Hanna expose Emma to different points of view. Emma is willing to engage in these discussions, and perhaps even welcomes them, partly because the rest of her network—that is, Faye and Grace—is congenial to her perspectives, and thus Emma is not being bombarded with exclusively contrary viewpoints. Critically, the very same aspect of Emma's network that facilitates her exposure to disagreement also acts to constrain opportunities for social influence. That is, consonant discussion with Faye and Grace acts both to increase Emma's willingness to hear a different point of view from Hanna and to make it difficult for Hanna to influence Emma's political opinions. After all, influence could occur only if Hanna's discourse was so compelling as to counter the inertia of Emma's existing views and their reinforcement via discussion with Faye and Grace. In more technical terms, what this implies is that complex networks of association foster agreement, but also sustain disagreement. Therefore, dyadic influence cannot be understood apart from attention to other aspects of the discussion partner's networks and contexts. Ultimately, the residual components of a network (Faye and Grace, in our example) mean that social influence can be self-limiting, but also that disagreement can be sustained.

Our point is that situating dyads within broader networks and contexts is vital to understanding both the persistence of disagreement and the potential for social influence. Individuals are embedded in networks and contexts of social and political communication. In our examples, each hypothetical person we have mentioned is embedded within a network, and each also is embedded in multiple contexts—the neighborhood, church, workplace, and so on. If individuals are embedded in networks and contexts, then so, too, are dyads. Whether communication within a dyad is politically influential depends on the wider distribution of opinions and beliefs (Huckfeldt, Beck, Dalton, Levine, & Morgan, 1998; McClurg, 2006a; 2006b; Jang, 2009). More specifically, the influence of any message depends on messages previously received from others in the network (Huckfeldt, Johnson, & Sprague, 2002; McClurg, 2004; Nickerson, 2008). When it comes to political opinions and beliefs, individuals rarely adopt views that receive minority support within their communication networks (Huckfeldt, Johnson and Sprague, 2004). Thus, as in our example involving Emma and her three discussion partners, circumstances external to Emma and Hanna's dyadic relationship—namely, the fact that Emma is in agreement with her other two discussion partners—facilitate the persistence of disagreement (Emma retains Hanna as a discussion partner), but also limit the potential for social influence.

Thus far, we have examined the importance of disagreement as a precondition for the occurrence of social influence, and we have addressed the puzzle about why disagreement persists in some networks rather than being extinguished. The final matters regarding disagreement to be considered involve its effects. Social influence is, of course, one possible effect of exposure to diverse political viewpoints. That is, upon hearing the case for an opposing perspective, a person could change her mind and adopt her discussion partner's position (thereby eliminating their disagreement). Apart from such a stark attitudinal transformation, several other possible effects of exposure to disagreement have been the targets of empirical study. Some of these are generally considered to be positive in the sense of improving the quality of citizenship, but other consequences of disagreement may be less desirable.

In terms of citizenship, the chief advantage of cross-cutting political conversations—exchanges in which multiple perspectives are voiced, and participants thus are exposed to diverse points of view—may be their capacity to promote civility and understanding. Three related effects have been considered in empirical research. First, engaging in a conversation marked by political disagreement may help the discussion partners to understand the rationales underlying opposing viewpoints. Thus, rather than dismissing the other side as misguided, uninformed, or even unpatriotic, the person who is exposed to disagreement through social communication may learn that there are legitimate, reasoned bases for holding opposing views. Consistent with this hypothesis, Mutz (2002a; 2006) demonstrates that survey respondents' levels of awareness of the rationales underlying opposing political views increase as a function of exposure to disagreement in political discussion, and that political conversations in the workplace are especially well suited to fostering such awareness (Mutz & Mondak, 2006).

A second, and similar, possible effect of exposure to political disagreement is an increase in tolerance. Political tolerance exists when a person is willing to extend the full rights of citizenship to all others, including to members of controversial or disliked groups (Sullivan, Piereson, & Marcus, 1982; Mondak & Sanders, 2003). Participation in cross-cutting political conversations has been hypothesized to heighten the extent to which individuals value the free exchange of ideas, including unpopular ones, thereby increasing levels of tolerance. Evidence consistent with this hypothesis has been reported in several studies (e.g., Mutz, 2002a; 2006; Mutz & Mondak, 2006; Pattie & Johnston, 2008).

The third seemingly positive effect of political disagreement examined in recent research is a decrease in polarizing emotions. The logic is that exposure to cross-cutting views will temper a person's emotional enthusiasm for the in-party candidate, and also reduce negative emotions toward the out-party candidate (for a lengthier discussion of political emotions see Brader & Marcus, chapter 6, this volume). As a result, the gap in emotions toward the two candidates will shrink, leaving emotional responses that are less polarized. Parsons (2010) reports evidence that disagreement produces such a decrease in polarizing emotions. However, that effect, in turn, corresponds with a decline in political interest and a reduced likelihood of subsequent political participation. This suggests that exposure to disagreement may be something of a mixed blessing. Although at first glance, especially in an era marked by heated political rhetoric, a decrease in the intensity of emotions about politics may seem to be a positive result, muting those emotions may have the effect of lessening some people's commitment to civic engagement.

The broader implication is that political disagreement, regardless of whatever other benefits it may engender, conceivably has the effect of demobilizing prospective voters. Mutz (2002b; 2006) called attention to this possibility. Examining data from the United States, Mutz found that exposure to disagreement corresponds with a reduced propensity for political participation. One explanation for this is that exposure to mixed political signals may foster ambivalence. However, Mutz identified no support for this account. Instead, an individual-level disposition, conflict avoidance, was found to be central to the demobilizing influence of political disagreement. Specifically, a decrease in participation levels was most apt to occur among individuals who scored high in conflict avoidance and who were exposed to disagreement through social communication.

Mutz's (2002b; 2006) findings sparked several follow-up investigations designed to assess whether the demobilizing impact of political disagreement is present in all conditions and contexts. Subsequent studies have suggested that demobilization occurs only among individuals who are part of the political minority within the broader context (McClurg, 2006a), and that the occurrence of demobilization hinges in part on how disagreement is defined (Nir, 2011) and on the actual substantive content of cross-cutting political conversations (Lee, 2012). Further, outside of the United States, exposure to disagreement has been shown to correspond with increases, not decreases, in participation levels in Belgium (Quintelier, Stolle, & Harell, 2012) and Britain (Pattie & Johnston, 2009).

Huckfeldt, Mendez, and Osborn (2004) address the issue of political engagement within the context of network size, based on an analysis of candidate evaluation in the 2000 presidential election. First, their analyses show that people located within larger political networks are more likely to be politically interested and engaged, but they are also more likely to encounter political disagreement. As a consequence, attitude *polarization* regarding candidates is reduced—people are more likely to see both the strengths and the weaknesses of candidates. At the same time, attitude *intensity* is increased—people are able to provide more reasons for their attitudes toward the candidates (see Thompson, Zanna, & Griffin, 1995). The implications for political mobilization are partially offsetting, since the lack of polarization retards political engagement, while higher levels of intensity encourage it. Perhaps more importantly, these effects suggest a qualitative change in the basis for political involvement, moving away from the more partisan to the more thoughtful and balanced.

Collectively, these studies suggest that the possible negative influence of social exposure to disagreement on political participation is neither ironclad nor unconditional. As research in this area proceeds, the growing empirical record will help to determine whether the net effect of disagreement on civic engagement is positive or negative. Likewise, further refinement should be expected in our understanding of how disagreement interacts with individual-level dispositions and features of the social context.

In the past two sections, our review of research on self-selection and disagreement has concerned the broader issue of social influence. The guiding questions have been whether, and under what circumstances, political discussion holds the potential to influence participants' attitudes and patterns of behavior. But social influence is only one of two general effects associated with interpersonal discussion networks. The other is the possible social communication of political expertise. Irrespective of any direct influence on attitudes and behaviors, political discussion may increase a person's available stock of information, or it may improve the quality of the person's political judgments. In short, talking about politics may help people to better perform the duties of citizenship. Numerous studies have examined this possibility.

6. POLITICAL DISCUSSION AND THE TRANSMISSION OF EXPERTISE

Some individuals thrive on politics and political information. For them, attending to politics involves more than the fulfillment of civic duty. Following politics may constitute something of a hobby, or even a passion. These individuals voraciously read newspapers and magazines, they watch programs about politics on television, and they regularly consult various politically oriented websites. And, in the process, they accumulate large amounts of information about politics.

Whenever people develop expertise in an area, many will seek to share that expertise with others. This is true, for example, of our friends and acquaintances with gourmet tastes in food and wine, those who are highly attuned to the world of independent film, and those who are diehard fans of professional soccer. Likewise, it holds in the political realm. Many individuals are political experts who realize psychic and social rewards from engaging in political discussion (Ahn, Huckfeldt, & Ryan, 2010). We might even say that these individuals experience negative information costs (Fiorina, 1990). For people such as these, political arguments, observations, and facts come readily to mind. Moreover, they willingly share this information. Whether documented by their own self-reports or the reports of their associates, individuals with high levels of expertise also demonstrate relatively high levels of political discussion (Huckfeldt, 2001).

Political experts lie at the heart of democratic politics, and they may play a central role in fostering political discussion (see also Chong, chapter 4, this volume). This status has been acknowledged in research dating back to the Columbia studies (Lazarsfeld et al., 1948; Berelson et al., 1954). These efforts differentiated between citizens who were opinion leaders and those who were opinion followers, although later work (Katz, 1957) suggested that the distinction was not so clear-cut in that even would-be opinion leaders can be susceptible to external influence.

Differences in levels of political expertise can matter in two important ways for social communication about politics. First, variation across individuals in political expertise may shape patterns in the *occurrence* of political discussion—that is, which types of individuals do the most talking, which types of people are sought out as discussion partners, and so on. Second, expertise also may be consequential for the *effects* of political discussion. What a person's discussion partner brings to the table in terms of political expertise logically places an upper bound on what the person can gain from chatting with that discussant. It the discussion partner knows nothing about politics, then the person who talks with that discussion partner will learn nothing. Discourse with an expert discussant does not guarantee that a person's own level of political expertise will be elevated, but the social transmission of political information is precluded from the outset if neither conversation partner possesses any political expertise.

Individuals with high levels of political expertise generally also prefer to engage in relatively high levels of political discussion, but do people with lower levels of political information welcome these experts as discussion partners? Downs (1957, p. 229) suggested that they should. More specifically, Downs argued that political discussion minimizes the information costs of political engagement. Hence, reasonable, efficiency-minded citizens should search for well-informed associates who share their political orientations and draw cues from them via social communication (see also Mondak & Huckfeldt, 1992). Calvert (1985) also focused on the utility of socially communicated information, arguing that information is more useful if it is acquired from someone with a clear bias independent of the recipient's own perspective. Of course, the recipient's bias adds a serious potential wrinkle. The value of communication with experts may be lost if recipients overestimate the expertise of those with whom they agree and underestimate it among those with whom they disagree (Lord, Ross, & Lepper, 1979; Lodge and Taber, 2000).

The empirical record provides grounds for cautious optimism regarding the social communication of political expertise. First, people engage in political discussion more frequently with discussion partners they judge to be politically expert, and this impact of expertise on discussion frequency is independent from the effects of agreement and disagreement (Huckfeldt, 2001). In short, people talk the most with the people whom they think know the most. Second, people's judgments regarding the expertise of their discussion partners are rooted in reality. On a snowball survey of individuals' discussion partners, the discussants were asked a series of factual political knowledge questions. How well the discussants fared in answering these questions was correlated with how favorably the original respondents rated these discussants in terms of political expertise (Huckfeldt, 2001). In other words, people accurately perceive whether their political discussion partners are well informed or poorly informed. But third, there is no evidence to suggest that people weight expert discussants' views more heavily than nonexperts' views (Huckfeldt & Sprague, 1995). This means that people may not listen to experts with more respect. Nonetheless, they do converse with them with greater frequency.

What this suggests as a bottom line is that the dynamics of social communication produce the right result, but arguably for the wrong reason. Expert voices trump nonexperts in political discussion networks, but they do so because experts speak, and are listened to, with greater frequency, not because their views are held in higher esteem. In the aggregate, social communication exerts a positive impact on the level of citizen competence. The key reason that it does so is that those individuals with the greatest political expertise do the most talking.

The research on discussion and expertise reviewed thus far supports the inference that social communication bolsters aggregate levels of citizen competence. Still, a more direct test of this possibility would be useful. Toward this end, several recent studies have examined network effects on expertise by invoking the perspective of "voting correctly." Lau and Redlawsk's (1997; 2006; Lau, Andersen, & Redlawsk, 2008; Redlawsk & Lau, chapter 5, this volume) original investigation of correct voting did not explicitly involve social networks. Instead, the driving question in that research was how well citizens voted with access to less than full information. To gauge this, Lau and Redlawsk contrast the vote choices of experimental subjects in a mock election with their selections upon receiving all available information, and they contrast the votes of survey respondents with ideal votes as defined by the respondents' political predispositions and policy preferences. Results from both methods support the conclusion that voters vote correctly a solid majority of the time—about 70% of the time, on average—but also that many apparently incorrect votes are cast.

Richey (2008), Ryan (2011), and Sokhey and McClurg (2012) all explore the possible effects of social communication on correct voting. Richey (2008) examines survey data. His key predictor is a measure of political knowledge in a person's discussion network, as perceived by the respondent. Richey finds that the likelihood of correct voting increases as individuals converse with more knowledgeable discussion partners. Ryan (2011) uses a laboratory experiment to study the impact of social communication on correct voting. Participants who are uninformed and politically independent fare better in terms of correct voting due to the positive impact of political discussion, but similar gains are not realized among participants who are partisans. Last, Sokhey and McClurg (2012) examine survey data in an effort to uncover the mechanism linking social communication and correct voting. Like Richey (2008), they find that political discussion exerts a positive effect on the quality of electoral decision making. However, rather than signaling the occurrence of learning, this effect is found to represent a simple heuristic process in which voters draw guidance from their discussion partners. Collectively, these recent studies demonstrate that social communication fosters citizen competence, but also that the effects are modest and limited in scope.

Thus far, the bulk of this chapter has examined research regarding the effects of social networks. Attention has been devoted primarily to the possibility of social influence, including the accompanying matters of self-selection and political disagreement. Extending beyond the question of influence, the present section has considered a second possible effect of political discussion, the potential for social communication to transmit political expertise. What we have not yet considered, except in passing, are the factors that operate to shape patterns in social communication. Political discussion may be influential, but what influences political discussion? We address this question in the chapter's final substantive section.

7. Determinants of Variance in Patterns of Political Discussion

Neither political discussion networks nor the conversations within them emerge independent of external forces. It follows that the failure to acknowledge these forces could lead analysts to overstate the independent impact of social communication for political behavior, and, correspondingly, to understate the significance of antecedent factors. In this section, two very different types of external forces will be considered. The first, which we have noted previously, is the impact of situational, or environmental, constraints on the formation, composition, and content of interpersonal discussion networks. At question is the extent to which factors outside of the individual's immediate control operate to shape the information the person encounters via social communication. Second, we will address the possibility that people's core psychological dispositions, or personality traits, influence their likelihood of engaging in and being receptive to political discussion. In this scenario, factors internal to the individual but external to the other members of the network may shape the potential for social influence. In the extreme, environmental and psychological influences on discussion networks may be thought of as competing. If networks were purely a product of the environments in which they are embedded, no room would exist for psychological dispositions to alter patterns of social communication. Conversely, if people's personality traits were the sole determinants of with whom, how often, and with what effects political discussion transpires, any influence of extraneous environmental factors would be precluded. In actuality, neither environmental nor psychological factors are all-powerful. Thus, a full understanding of the bases of variation in patterns of political discussion requires attention to both.

Earlier, while addressing the limits of self-selection, it was noted that networks must be seen within the contexts that house them (Huckfeldt & Sprague, 1987; 1995). In extreme cases, aspects of the surrounding environment can establish upper and lower bounds on numerous facets of networks, from size to content to density. If everyone in a person's context is a conservative, all of the person's discussion partners necessarily will be conservative. If no one in the context is willing to talk about politics, the person will be prevented from engaging in political discussion. If the available discussion partners all lack political expertise, conversations with them will not improve the quality of the individual's political decision-making. For most people, the contextual supply of potential discussion partners likely is not nearly so one-sided as in our examples. Nonetheless, it remains the case that where a person lives, works, and worships can affect how diverse and how well-informed the person's political discussants are and how many she has.

The reality that the surrounding context impinges on interpersonal discussion networks brings implications for efforts to foster political discourse. If it were decided, for instance, that steps should be taken by community leaders or workplaces to increase the frequency with which citizens discuss politics, or to increase the level of cross-cutting political exchanges (or if people took it upon themselves to seek out more political discussion), the impact of context in structuring opportunities for interpersonal interaction would have to be acknowledged. Much as in Schelling's (1978) artful discussion of phenomena such as the inescapable mathematics of musical chairs, best wishes cannot overcome structural reality. If liberals in a given context outnumber conservatives by three to one, then we cannot pair up every liberal with a conservative discussion partner unless each conservative is called on for triple duty. If each person in a context has one discussion partner, and if half have discussants with more political expertise than the person himself, then members of the second half will be destined to find the conversations relatively uninformative.

Apart from structuring opportunities for networks to form and take shape, the external context also may matter for the topical content of political discussion. News media are thought to be especially important in this regard. With their two-step model, Lazarsfeld and his colleagues (Lazarsfeld et al., 1948; Katz & Lazarsfeld, 1955) provided early guidance regarding the possible interrelationship between news media and social communication. In the two-step framework, news reports are seen as fueling political discussion because opinion leaders take what they learn from the news and disseminate it via conversations with their associates. Lazarsfeld and his colleagues addressed the two-step model primarily in terms of the value of social communication in expanding the reach of stories that originated in news reports. However, the dynamic they outline also can be considered from the perspective of media's influence on political discussion: if the two-step model is accurate, then news media play an important role in shaping the content of—that is, of setting the agenda for—social communication (Valentino & Nardis, chapter 18, this volume). Logically, this rings true. It seems unlikely that many political topics, especially those on the national and international scenes, become the subjects of interpersonal discussion without first having been the subjects of news reports.

Subsequent works have built on the Lazarsfeld et al. perspective while incorporating insights from the media effects literature. Contemporary research that examines both news media and social communication suggests that the relationship between the two is complex. One study, which treated a newspaper strike as the centerpiece of a natural experiment, found that the occurrence of political discussion declined due to the dearth of raw material from news sources, but also that the influence of discussion rose because of the vacuum left by the shortage of news coverage of local elections (Mondak, 1995a; 1995b). Hence, news media and social communication were complements at one level, but competitors at another. A second study contrasted news media frames with those employed by acquaintances conversing about those same issues (Walsh, 2004). The frames used as part of social communication were a subset of those provided in news reports, suggesting that news frames and selectivity on the part of discussion partners combine to influence the eventual content of political discussion. Druckman and Nelson (2003) tackled a related question experimentally and found that elite framing of a topic is consequential in the absence of subsequent discussion, but that elite frames become irrelevant once a topic has been bandied about by a politically mixed group of discussants.

The upshot of all of this is that the flow of political information involves complex interactions among elite cues, news reports, and social communication. Although this complexity has long been noted, most theoretical and empirical frameworks continue to focus on individual elements of the information environment rather than endeavoring to integrate the study of elite messages, news media, and political discussion. Situating these three elements relative to one another is no easy task, yet doing so is essential if we are ever to have a holistic, comprehensive model of political communication.

Macro-level forces shape key aspects of social networks, but so, too, do micro-level psychological dispositions, or personality traits. Work in this area holds that core personality traits influence people's basic patterns of behavior. In the realm of social communication, psychological dispositions may matter for phenomena such as how talkative the person is, how receptive to exposure to disagreement, and how susceptible to social influence. We will expand on these possible effects below. First, though, it is important to note that any such influence of personality traits presupposes selectivity on the part of the individual. For instance, the introvert may prefer to avoid political discussion, but that preference only will be consequential for actual patterns of social communication to the extent that macro-level factors do not fully determine network structure and content. The more that political discussion is constrained by context, the less room remains for personal preferences—and thus personality traits—to play a role. Extant research reveals that both macro-level and micro-level factors influence social networks. Hence, our point is not that social communication is either environmentally or psychologically determined, but rather that variables at each level operate within parameters established by other very different types of variables.

Research on personality and politics has experienced a resurgence in recent years due to the emergence of the five-factor, or Big Five, framework (for reviews, see Caprara and Vecchione, chapter 2, this volume; Mondak & Hibbing, 2012). Proponents of the five-factor approach contend that the bulk of variation in personality trait structure can be represented with attention to five broad trait dimensions: openness to experience, conscientiousness, extraversion, agreeableness, and emotional stability. Applications of the five-factor framework in research on political behavior explore the possibility that personality differences influence numerous components of citizenship. Recently, several works have considered specific links between personality and multiple aspects of political discussion. This research advances two interrelated themes. First, people's basic psychological characteristics affect the attributes and consequences of their social networks. Second, it follows that personality traits may bring heterogeneity to social communication. This implies that when other research identifies effects of social networks, those are average effects across all individuals in a sample, and they may mask considerable personality-based individual-level variation.

Among studies examining personality effects on social communication, Kalish and Robins (2006) found relationships between extraversion and both network density and network size. Subsequently, several studies have considered personality as it relates specifically to patterns of political discussion. Positive effects of openness to experience and/or extraversion have been found on the frequency of political discussion (Gerber, Huber, Doherty, & Dowling, 2012; Hibbing, Ritchie, & Anderson, 2011; Mondak, 2010; Mondak & Halperin, 2008) and network size (Mondak, 2010; Mondak, Hibbing, Canache, Seligson, & Anderson, 2010).

Beyond aspects of network structure and composition, personality effects also have been observed with respect to the key issues of social influence and exposure to disagreement. Hibbing et al. (2011) report that social influence on political judgments peaks among individuals who score high in openness to experience. This is a sensible finding in that people low in openness to experience—people who are characteristically closed-minded—should be resistant to efforts to change their views. As to disagreement, a question in the literature has been whether larger networks generally promote higher levels of exposure to diverse points of view (Huckfeldt, Johnson, & Sprague, 2004; Mutz, 2006). Research invoking the five-factor framework has found that the extent to which network size yields greater exposure to disagreement hinges partly on personality. Specifically, larger networks bring more exposure to cross-cutting views for individuals with high levels of extraversion and low levels of agreeableness (Mondak, 2010; Mondak et al., 2010). Extraverts value social interaction for its own sake and are relatively indiscriminate in terms of the selection of discussion partners, whereas introverts strongly emphasize maintenance of congenial social relations and thus steer clear of disagreement. Likewise, people high in agreeableness fundamentally dislike dissonant social relations and seek to avoid them; conversely, people who are psychologically prone to be disagreeable do not value consonance in social interactions—indeed, they often may be the source of disagreement in political discussion networks.

The recent resurgence in attention to personality and politics corresponds with, and is linked to, the flurry of work being conducted on biology and politics (see Funk, chapter 8, this volume, for a review). Students of biology and politics rightly acknowledge that most or all of the effects of biology on political behavior are indirect. It is implausible, for example, that there would be a gene for whether a person will discuss the candidates in an upcoming election or will have a one-person rather than three-person political discussion network. This means that biological variables must operate on politics indirectly, via some linkage mechanism. Students of both biology and politics (e.g., Alford, Funk, & Hibbing, 2005; Fowler, Baker, & Dawes, 2008; Smith, Oxley, Hibbing, Alford, & Hibbing, 2011) and personality and politics (e.g., Mondak, 2010; Mondak et al., 2010) have called attention to the possibility that biology matters for politics partly because biological influences contribute to the shape of people's core personality traits, which, in turn, affect political behavior (for direct tests of this thesis, see Dawes et al., 2011; Hibbing, 2011). In other words, personality traits may be key mechanisms connecting biology to political behavior.

We mention the possible linkages among biology, personality, and politics for two reasons. First, some studies have identified biological bases for differences in social communication. Using a twin study approach, Fowler, Dawes, and Christakis (2009) demonstrated that several facets of social interaction are heritable, which means that some portion of their variation is rooted in biology. More recently, Fowler, Settle, and Christakis (2011) identified correlations in genotypes among individuals in friendship networks. This research even has contemplated the effects of particular genes. For instance, Settle, Dawes, Christakis, and Fowler (2010) found that an individual's number of adolescent friendships predicts subsequent self-identification as an ideological liberal, but only among persons possessing the 7R variant of the dopamine receptor D4 gene.

A second reason to contemplate linkages among biology, personality, and social influence is that doing so may help us to gain leverage on the problem of endogeneity in social influence. For example, we might wish to assess the possible impact of Jane's political views on Joe's, while acknowledging the possible reciprocal effect of Joe on Jane. One approach might be to construct an instrument for Jane's ideology, one informed only by biology and/or personality. With a biology-based instrument for Jane's ideology, for example, we would be able to rule out the possibility of reciprocal influence; that is, Jane's interaction with Joe would not have altered Jane's genetic profile. Consequently, if any correspondence we identify between the instrument for Jane's political dispositions and Joe's actual political views stems from social influence, it would have to be the result of Jane's impact on Joe.

As these examples highlight, emerging research on personality, biology, and politics brings the potential for scholars to produce new insights on many of the enduring questions central to the social communication literature. By doing so, this research promises to add precision to our understanding of the complex interplay between the macro-level and micro-level factors that shape political discussion and its effects. As such research proceeds, it will be important for scholars to keep in mind the key lessons learned about social networks over the past several decades, and to identify the central questions for which further clarification is needed. We briefly revisit these matters in this chapter's final section.

8. Conclusion and Prognosis

At the outset of this chapter, we introduced a person who is a rarity in modern polities, a political recluse. In contrast with that hypothetical figure, most people have at least occasional social encounters that expose them to other people's opinions and understandings of the political world. This chapter has examined research regarding the significance of those social encounters. Our primary focus has been people's day-to-day conversations, and the potential of those conversations to produce social influence and to transmit political expertise.

Research on the role of social influence on political behavior has continued to gain refinement and precision. In this chapter, we have sought to review these developments as a means both to survey what has been accomplished thus far and to suggest areas in which additional inquiry is needed. A primary argument of this effort is that progress in studying social influence in politics depends on continued innovation in observation and measurement. First, studies of social influence depend on the ability to observe individuals in relationship to other individuals. This requires moving beyond investigations of isolated individuals either in surveys or in laboratories. Studying social influence depends on the capacity to consider the messenger, the message, and the message's recipient. Moreover, while social influence occurs through these dyadic encounters, the dyads are not self-contained. Instead, each dyad is part of each participant's broader social network and is located within a particular social context. This means that continued progress in research concerning social influence in politics depends on the ability to observe the opportunities and constraints for communication and influence that these networks and contexts create.

Second, we are rapidly gaining new knowledge regarding the microfoundations of perception, cognition, and hence influence. In particular, progress regarding the biological and personality foundations of communication and influence lead us to reconsider the nature of social influence. Not only do studies of social influence in politics build on an observational commitment to the careful consideration of interdependence among participants in the communication process, but this work also requires a careful consideration of the exogenous contribution of inherently individual-level characteristics and predispositions. In short, it is neither nature nor nurture but rather the interplay between the two that is responsible for social communication and influence in politics.

Finally, the interaction between messenger, message, and recipient is necessarily based on stochastic processes of communication and influence that cannot be understood apart from their underlying dynamic logics. At one level this means continued efforts must address problems related to self-selection. At another level, it means developing a more complete understanding of the dynamic structures that are responsible for creating various forms of interdependence among actors.

Enormous progress has been made on all these fronts since the pathbreaking work of Lazarsfeld and his colleagues at Columbia University (Lazarsfeld et al., 1948; Berelson et al., 1954), but a great deal remains to be accomplished. Progress is driven both by theory and observation. Theoretical imagination is required to formulate new questions and methods of observation. These questions and methods, in turn, not only provide answers to existing questions but also the theoretical vision to ask new ones.

REFERENCES

Abelson, R. P. (1964). Mathematical models of the distribution of attributes under controversy. In Norman Fredriksen and Harold Gulliksen (eds.), *Contributions to mathematical psychology* (pp. 142–160). New York: Holt, Rinehart, and Winston.

Abelson, R. P. (1979). Social clusters and opinion clusters. In P. W. Holland & S. Leinhardt (eds.), *Perspectives on social network research* (pp. 239–256). New York: Academic Press.

Achen, C. H., & Shively, W. P. (1995). *Cross level inference.* Chicago: University of Chicago Press.

Ahn, T. K., Huckfeldt, R., & Ryan, J. B. (2010). Communication, influence, and informational asymmetries among voters. *Political Psychology 31*(5), 763–787.

Albert, R., & Barabasi, A. L. (2002). Statistical mechanics of complex networks. *Reviews of Modern Physics, 74*(1), 41–96.

Alford, J. R., Funk, C. L., & Hibbing, J. R. (2005). Are political orientations genetically transmitted? *American Political Science Review, 99*(2), 153–167.

American National Election Studies. *The ANES guide to public opinion and electoral behavior.* Ann Arbor: University of Michigan, Center for Political Studies [producer and distributor]. Retrieved from www.electionstudies.org.

Asch, S. E. (1955). Opinions and social pressure. *Scientific American, 193,* 31–35.

Axelrod, R. (1997). The dissemination of culture: A model with local convergence and global polarization. *Journal of Conflict Resolution, 41*(2), 203–226.

Berelson, B., Lazarsfeld, P. F., & McPhee, W. N. (1954). *Voting: A study of opinion formation in a presidential campaign*. Chicago: University of Chicago Press.

Burt, R. S. (1984). Network items and the general social survey. *Social Networks*, 6(4), 293–339.

Calvert, R. L. (1985). The value of biased information: A rational choice model of political advice. *Journal of Politics*, 47, 530–555.

Campbell, A., Converse, P. E., Miller, W. E., & Stokes, D. F. (1960). *The American voter*. Chicago: University of Chicago Press.

Cho, W. K. T., & Fowler, J. H. (2010). Legislative success in a small world: Social network analysis and the dynamics of congressional legislation. *Journal of Politics*, 72(1), 124–135.

Cohen-Cole, E., & Fletcher, J. M. (2008). Detecting implausible social network effects in acne, height, and headaches: Longitudinal analysis. *British Medical Journal*, 337, a2533.

Conover, P. J., Searing, D. D., & Crewe, I. M. (2002). The deliberative potential of political discussion. *British Journal of Political Science*, 32(1), 21–62.

Dawes, C., Cesarini, D., Fowler, J. H., Johannesson, M., Magnusson, P. K. E., & Oskarsson, S. (2011). Do psychological traits mediate the relationship between genes and political participation? Manuscript.

Downs, A. (1957). *An economic theory of democracy*. New York: Harper and Row.

Druckman, J. N., & Nelson, K. R. (2003). Framing and deliberation: How citizens' conversations limit elite influence. *American Journal of Political Science*, 47, 728–744.

Festinger, L. (1957). *A theory of cognitive dissonance*. Palo Alto, CA: Stanford University Press.

Finifter, A. (1974). The friendship group as a protective environment for political deviants. *American Political Science Review*, 68, 607–625.

Fiorina, M. (1990.) Information and rationality in elections. In J. Ferejohn & J. Kuklinski (eds.), *Information and democratic processes* (pp. 329–342). Urbana: University of Illinois Press.

Fowler, J. H. (2006). Legislative cosponsorship networks in the US House and Senate. *Social Networks*, 28(4), 454–465.

Fowler, J. H., Baker, L. A., & Dawes, C. T. (2008). Genetic variation in political participation. *American Political Science Review*, 102(02), 233–248. doi:10.1017/S0003055408080209

Fowler, J. H., Dawes, C. T., & Christakis, N. A. (2009). Model of genetic variation in human social networks. *Proceedings of the National Academy of Sciences*, 106(6), 1720–1724.

Fowler, J. H., Heaney, M. T., Nickerson, D. W., Padgett, J. F., & Sinclair, B. (2011). Causality in political networks. *American Politics Research*, 39(2), 437–480.

Fowler, J. H., Settle, J. E., & Christakis, N. A. (2011). Correlated genotypes in friendship networks. *Proceedings of the National Academy of Sciences*, 108(5), 1993–1997.

Gaines, B. J., & Mondak, J. J. (2009). Typing together? Clustering of ideological types in online social networks. *Journal of Information Technology and Politics*, 6(3–4), 216–231.

Gerber, A. S., Huber, G. A., Doherty, D., & Dowling, C. M. (2012). Personality traits, disagreement, and the avoidance of political discussion: Putting political discussion networks in context. *American Journal of Political Science*, 56(4), 849–874.

Gerber, A. S., & Green, D. P. (2000). The effects of canvassing, telephone calls, and direct mail on voter turnout: A field experiment. *American Political Science Review*, 94(3), 653–663.

Gerber, A., & Green, D. P. (1999). Does canvassing increase voter turnout? *Proceedings of the National Academy of Sciences of the United States of American*, 19, 10939–10942.

Granovetter, M. S. (1973). The strength of weak ties. *American Journal of Sociology*, 78, 1360–1380.

Heider, F. (1958). *The psychology of interpersonal relations*. New York: Wiley.

Hibbing, M. V. (2011). Unifying behavioral inquiry: Integrating personality traits and situational effects in the study of political behavior. PhD dissertation, University of Illinois.

Hibbing, M. V., Ritchie, M., & Anderson, M. R. (2011). Personality and political discussion. *Political Behavior, 33*(4), 601–624.

Huckfeldt, R. (2001). The social communication of political expertise. *American Journal of Political Science, 45*, 425–438.

Huckfeldt, R., Beck, P. A., Dalton, R. J., & Levine, J. (1995). Political environments, cohesive social groups, and the communication of public opinion. *American Journal of Political Science, 39*, 1025–1054.

Huckfeldt, R., Beck, P. A., Dalton, R. J., Levine, J., & Morgan, W. (1998). Ambiguity, distorted messages, and nested environmental effects on political communication. *Journal of Politics, 60*, 996–1030.

Huckfeldt, R., Johnson, P. E., & Sprague, J. (2002). Political environments, political dynamics, and the survival of disagreement. *Journal of Politics, 64*(1), 1–21.

Huckfeldt, R., Johnson, P. E., & Sprague, J. (2004). *Political disagreement: The survival of diverse opinions within communication networks.* New York: Cambridge University Press.

Huckfeldt, R., Levine, J., Morgan, W., & Sprague, J. (1998). Election campaigns, social communication, and the accessibility of discussant preference. *Political Behavior, 20*, 263–294.

Huckfeldt, R., & Mendez, J. M. (2008). Moths, flames, and political engagement: Managing disagreement within communication networks. *Journal of Politics, 70*, 83–96.

Huckfeldt, R., Mendez, J. M., & Osborn, T. (2004). Disagreement, ambivalence, and engagement: The political consequences of heterogeneous networks. *Political Psychology, 25*(1), 65–95.

Huckfeldt, R., & Sprague, J. (1987). Networks in context: The social flow of political information. *American Political Science Review, 81*(4), 1197–1216.

Huckfeldt, R., & Sprague, J. (1988). Choice, social structure, and political information: The informational coercion of minorities. *American Journal of Political Science, 32*(2), 467–482.

Huckfeldt, R., & Sprague, J. (1991). Discussant effects on vote choice: Intimacy, structure, and interdependence. *Journal of Politics, 53*(1), 122–158.

Huckfeldt, R., & Sprague, J. (1995). *Citizens, politics, and social communication: Information and influence in an election campaign.* New York: Cambridge University Press.

Jang, S. J. (2009). Are diverse political networks always bad for participatory democracy? *American Politics Research, 37*(5), 879–898.

Kalish, Y., & Robins, G. (2006). Psychological predispositions and network structure: The relationship between individual predispositions, structural holes and network closure. *Social Networks, 28*(1), 56–84.

Katz, E. (1957). The two step flow of communication: An up-to-date report on an hypothesis. *Public Opinion Quarterly, 21*, 67–81.

Katz, E., & Lazarsfeld, P. F. (1955). *Personal influence: The part played by people in the flow of mass communications.* New York: Free Press.

Klofstad, C. A., McClurg, S. D., & Rolfe, M. (2009). Measurement of political discussion networks: A comparison of two "name generator" procedures. *Public Opinion Quarterly, 73*, 462–483.

Lau, R. R., Andersen, D. J., & Redlawsk, D. P. (2008). An exploration of correct voting in recent U.S. presidential elections. *American Journal of Political Science, 52*(2), 395–411.

Lau, R. R., & Redlawsk, D. P. (1997). Voting correctly. *American Political Science Review, 91*, 585–598.

Lau, R. R., & Redlawsk, D. P. (2006). *How voters decide: Information processing during election campaigns.* New York: Cambridge University Press.

Lazarsfeld, P. F., Berelson, B., & Gaudet, H. (1948). *The people's choice: How a voter makes up his mind in a presidential campaign.* New York: Columbia University Press.

Lazer, D., Brian, R., Carol, C., Katz, N., & Neblo, M. (2010). The coevolution of networks and political attitudes. *Political Communication, 27,* 248–274.

Lee, F. L. F. (2012). Does discussion with disagreement discourage all types of political participation? Survey evidence from Hong Kong. *Communication Research, 39*(4), 543–562.

Levitan, L. C., & Visser, P. S. (2009). Social network composition and attitude strength: Exploring the dynamics within newly formed social networks. *Journal of Experimental Social Psychology, 45*(5), 1057–1067.

Lodge, M., & Taber, C. (2000). Three steps toward a theory of motivated political reasoning. In A. Lupia, M. D. McCubbins, & S. L. Popkin (eds.), *Elements of reason: Cognition, choice, and the bounds of rationality* (pp. 183–213). New York: Cambridge University Press.

Lord, C. G., Ross, L., & Lepper, M. R. (1979). Biased assimilation and attitude polarization: The effects of prior theories on subsequently considered evidence. *Journal of Personality and Social Psychology, 37,* 2098–2109.

MacKuen, M. B. (1990). Speaking of politics: Individual conversational choice, public opinion and the prospects for deliberative democracy. In J. A. Ferejohn & J. H. Kuklinski (eds.), *Information and democratic processes* (pp, 59–99). Urbana: University of Illinois Press.

Marsden, P. V. (1987). Core discussion networks of Americans. *American Sociological Review, 52*(1), 122–131.

McClurg, S. D. (2003). Social networks and political participation: The role of social interaction in explaining political participation. *Political Research Quarterly, 56*(4), 449–464.

McClurg, S. D. (2004). Indirect mobilization: The social consequences of party contacts in an election campaign. *American Politics Research, 32*(4), 406–443.

McClurg, S. D. (2006a). The electoral relevance of political talk: Examining the effect of disagreement and expertise in social networks on political participation. *American Journal of Political Science, 50*(3), 737–754.

McClurg, S. D. (2006b). Political disagreement in context: The conditional effect of neighborhood context, discussion, and disagreement on electoral participation. *Political Behavior, 28*(4), 349–366.

McPherson, M., Smith-Lovin, L., & Brashears, M. E. (2006). Social isolation in America: Changes in core discussion networks over two decades. *American Sociological Review, 71*(3), 353–375.

Mondak, J. J. (1995a). Media exposure and political discussion in U.S. elections. *Journal of Politics, 57*(1), 62–85.

Mondak, J. J. (1995b). *Nothing to read: Newspapers and elections in a social experiment.* Ann Arbor: University of Michigan Press.

Mondak, J. J. (2010). *Personality and the foundations of political behavior.* New York: Cambridge University Press.

Mondak, J. J., & Gearing, A. F. (1998). Civic engagement in a post-communist state. *Political Psychology, 19,* 615–637.

Mondak, J. J., & Halperin, K. D. (2008). A framework for the study of personality and political behavior. *British Journal of Political Science, 38,* 335–362.

Mondak, J. J., & Hibbing, M. V. (2012). Personality and public opinion. In A. J. Berinsky (ed.), *New directions in public opinion* (pp. 217–238). New York: Routledge.

Mondak, J. J., Hibbing, M. V., Canache, D., Seligson, M. A., & Anderson, M. R. (2010). Personality and civic engagement: An integrative framework for the study of trait effects on political behavior. *American Political Science Review, 104,* 85–110.

Mondak, J. J., & Huckfeldt, R. (1992). Mixed signals: Source cues and social cues as information sources. Paper presented at the Annual Meeting of the American Political Science Association, Chicago.

Mondak, J. J., & Mutz, D. C. (2001). Involuntary association: How the workplace contributes to American civic life. Paper presented at the Annual Meeting of the Midwest Political Science Association, Chicago.

Mondak, J. J., & Sanders, M. S. (2003). Tolerance and intolerance, 1976–1998. *American Journal of Political Science, 47*(3), 492–502.

Mutz, D. C. (2002a). Cross-cutting social networks: Testing democratic theory in practice. *American Political Science Review, 96*, 111–126.

Mutz, D. C. (2002b). The consequences of cross-cutting networks for political participation. *American Journal of Political Science, 46*, 838–855.

Mutz, D. C. (2006). *Hearing the other side: Deliberative versus participatory Democracy.* New York: Cambridge University Press.

Mutz, D. C., & Mondak, J. J. (2006). The workplace as a context for cross-cutting political discourse. *Journal of Politics, 68*(1), 140–155.

Nickerson, D. (2008). Is voting contagious? Evidence from two field experiments. *American Political Science Review, 102*, 49–57.

Nir, L. (2011). Disagreement and opposition in social networks: Does disagreement discourage turnout? *Political Studies, 59*(3), 674–692.

Parker, S. L., Parker, G. R., & McCann, J. A. (2008). Opinion talking within friendship networks. *American Journal of Political Science, 52*(2), 412–:420.

Parsons, B. M. (2010). Social networks and the affective impact of political disagreement. *Political Behavior, 32*(2), 181–204.

Pattie, C., & Johnston, R. J. (2001). Talk as a political context: Conversation and electoral change in British elections, 1992–1997. *Electoral Studies, 20*(1), 17–40.

Pattie, C. J., & Johnston, R. J. (2008). It's good to talk: Talk, disagreement and tolerance. *British Journal of Political Science, 38*(4), 677–98.

Pattie, C. J., & Johnston, R. J. (2009). Conversation, disagreement and political participation. *Political Behavior, 31*(2), 261–285.

Quintelier, E., Stolle, D., & Harell, A. (2012). Politics in peer groups: Exploring the causal relationship between network diversity and political participation. *Political Research Quarterly, 65*(4), 868–881.

Richey, S. (2008). The social basis of voting correctly. *Political Communication, 25*(4), 366–376.

Ryan, J. B. (2011). Social networks as a shortcut to correct voting. *American Journal of Political Science, 55*(4), 753–766.

Schelling, T. C. (1978). *Micromotives and macrobehavior.* New York: Norton.

Schneider, M., Teske, P., Roch, C., & Marschall, C. (1997). Networks to nowhere: Segregation and stratification in networks of information about schools. *American Journal of Political Science, 41*, 1201–1223.

Searing, D. D., Solt, F., Conover, P. J., & Crewe, I. (2007). Public discussion in the deliberative system: Does it make better citizens? *British Journal of Political Science, 37*(4), 587–618.

Settle, J. E., Dawes, C. T., Christakis, N. A., & Fowler, J. H. (2010). Friendships moderate an association between a dopamine gene variant and political ideology. *Journal of Politics, 72*(4), 1189–1198.

Smith, K. B., Oxley, D. R., Hibbing, M. V., Alford, J. R., & Hibbing, J. R. (2011). Linking genetics and political attitudes: Reconceptualizing political ideology. *Political Psychology, 32*(3), 369–397.

Sokhey, A. E., & McClurg, S. D. (2012). Social networks and correct voting. *Journal of Politics,* *74*(3), 751–764.

Sullivan, J. L., Piereson, J., & Marcus, G. E. (1982). *Political tolerance and American democracy.* Chicago: University of Chicago Press.

Taber, C., & Lodge, M. (2006). Motivated skepticism in the evaluation of political beliefs. *American Journal of Political Science, 50,* 755–769.

Thompson, M. M., Zanna, M. P., & Griffin, D. W. (1995). Let's not be indifferent about (attitudinal) ambivalence. In R. E. Petty & J. A. Krosnick (eds.), *Attitude strength: Antecedents and consequences* (pp. 361–386). Mahwah, NJ: Erlbaum.

Visser, P. S., & Mirabile, R. R. (2004). Attitudes in the social context: The impact of social network composition on individual-level attitude strength. *Journal of Personality and Social Psychology, 87*(6), 779–795.

Walsh, K. C. (2004). *Talking about politics: Informal groups and social identity in American life.* Chicago: University of Chicago Press.

Walsh, K. C. (2007). *Talking about race: Community politics and the politics of difference.* Chicago: University of Chicago Press.

CHAPTER 22

POLITICAL DELIBERATION

C. DANIEL MYERS AND TALI MENDELBERG

1. INTRODUCTION

Deliberation is an increasingly common form of political participation (Jacobs, Cook, & Delli Carpini, 2009) and already plays a role, direct or indirect, in society and politics. Government bodies use deliberative forums to consult citizens in various policy decisions (Gastil, 2000; Karpowitz, 2006; Rosenberg, 2007). For example, citizen deliberations in Chicago provide input on school and police issues, a process that has deepened citizen engagement with both institutions (Fung, 2004). Juries make decisions that affect industry, commerce, rights, and a variety of life outcomes for people and organizations (Gastil, Deess, Weiser, & Simmons, 2010). Some deliberating groups issue official recommendations that can become the basis of constitutional change (e.g., the British Columbia constitutional assembly) (Warren & Pearse, 2008). Deliberation is increasingly featured in developing or postconflict societies as a way to repair breaches of trust and establish democratic procedures or institutions (Humphreys, Masters, & Sandbu, 2006), while many localities in the United States organize deliberating groups to encourage dialogue across racial lines (Walsh, 2007). Finally, deliberation is used to measure considered public opinion in environmental, health, and urban planning policy (De Vries et al. 2011; Forrester, 1999; Owens, 2000).

However, deliberation is more than just another form of political participation. Deliberation is a longstanding element of, and has played an increasingly important role in, democratic theory (Thompson, 2008). From Aristotle's vision of the polity (Wilson, 2011), to grass-roots visions of American democracy in the writings of Tocqueville, deliberation has been identified as significant to democratic societies. However, the last several decades have seen a "deliberative turn" in democratic theory (Dryzek, 2000) that has increased the emphasis on deliberation, in contrast to other features of democratic government such as free and fair elections. Much of the empirical research on deliberation in political science takes this recent scholarship as its inspiration and point of departure. We will discuss this literature in greater depth below.

The explosion in interest in deliberation has created multiple definitions of "deliberation." This presents problems for research, causing scholars to talk past each other and making it difficult for new results to build on past research. But the diverse definitions also have advantages, by including a broader set of discursive phenomena and allowing researchers to study more variables, enriching our overall understanding. In this chapter we *define deliberation as small-group discussion intended to make a decision or to change the content or basis of public opinion that is either prompted by or speaks to a governmental unit or political actor.* The political actor need not be the government; it can be any person or organization with power or authority in society. For example, Mansbridge studied deliberative decision-making within a nongovernmental organization (Mansbridge, 1980). The decision need not be binding, and need not be directly on a policy matter. For example, in Deliberative Polls deliberators reach an agreement only on what questions to pose to policy experts or candidates running for elected office. In some deliberations citizens merely provide input to officials who eventually make a collective decision. All these count as deliberation by our definition.

Our definition still encompasses a wide variety of phenomena, but does narrow our focus in a few important ways. Most notably, it excludes deliberation that takes place in everyday talk between citizens (Conover, Searing, & Crewe, 2002, Mutz, 2006; Huddy, chapter 23, this volume; Green & Staerklé, chapter 26, this volume), "deliberation within," or internal reflection (Goodin & Niemeyer, 2003), and the question of what kinds of citizens tend to attend deliberative forums (Karpowitz, 2006; Jacobs et al., 2009, chap. 3; Neblo, Esterling, Kennedy, Lazer, & Sokhey, 2010). We limit our discussion primarily to the literature within political psychology and, when appropriate, political communication. We do not attempt a comprehensive review of the large literature in social psychology on small-group process (see Mendelberg, 2002 for a review), but refer to these sources when helpful.

The chapter proceeds as follows. We briefly review the normative literature on deliberation and then discuss the contribution of political psychology to the study of deliberation. We structure our discussion in three sections: outcomes, processes, and context. We will discuss these in reverse order—outcomes, then processes, then context—because understanding research on the processes of deliberation generally requires understanding the outcomes that these processes might influence; similarly, research on the context of deliberation is generally interested in how these contextual variables affect the process of deliberation, the outcomes it produces, or both. We conclude with thoughts on the future of this burgeoning field.

1.1. Normative Theory and the Requirements of Deliberation

In this section we review some of the central requirements of normative theories of deliberation. We focus on those aspects of deliberative theory that are most relevant for empirical investigators. Given that the focus on deliberation in the normative literature on democratic theory is a relatively recent phenomenon, it is not surprising that a variety of normative theories exist and central aspects of what constitutes deliberative democracy are still up for debate. Nevertheless, most contemporary theories agree on most of the following points.

At its core, deliberation is the free, equal, and open-minded dialogue about a matter of public concern among anyone affected by the issue (Cohen, 1989; Gutmann & Thompson, 1996; 2004; Benhabib, 1996; Habermas, 1975; 1996; Neblo, 2005). The content of this exchange can take many forms, such as evidence, reasons, or questions, and more controversially, personal testimony, storytelling, or expressions of emotion (Sanders, 1997; Young, 1996), but they should all consist of communication that the interlocutor can understand. Deliberative democrats hold that deliberation is necessary to justify a decision and render it legitimate. Proponents of a policy should offer the people who would be affected by that policy reasons in support of that policy that they might be able to accept (Gutmann & Thompson, 2004). Further, all affected by a policy should have a chance to address these arguments and provide their own arguments or perspectives. The information exchanged should be considered with an open mind by everyone involved, and hence be uncontaminated by force or its close cousins, deception and manipulation (Habermas, 1975). Most deliberative democrats agree that conversation must at some point end with a vote (Cohen, 1989, p. 348), though some argue that the goal of deliberation can be more amorphous, such as greater understanding, enlightenment, or consensus (Gutmann & Thompson, 1996).

Democracy demands equal power and access to influence among its participants. Power in deliberative democracy lies in the ability to convince others through the discursive process, and the kind of equality required by deliberative democracy should reflect what Knight and Johnson term "equal opportunity to access political influence" (1997, p. 280). At minimum, this means equal access to the floor. In the words of Lynn Sanders, "If it's demonstrable that some kinds of people routinely speak more than others in deliberative settings . . . then participation isn't equal, and one democratic standard has fallen" (1997, p. 365; see also Thompson, 2008, p. 501). In addition, deliberators should have an equal ability to voice their perspectives effectively and to be heard with full consideration. This is a particular concern for socially disadvantages groups like women and minorities. If inequalities in resources such as education or wealth mean that some are more effective speakers, then equality has not been achieved even if all speakers have *de jure* equal access to the deliberative forum (Mansbridge, 1980). Equal resources to participate may still not be enough; factors such as prejudice may mean that perspectives associated with lower status and power in society may be less likely to get floor time, to be fully articulated, and to receive an open-minded hearing (Karpowitz, Mendelberg & Shaker, 2012; Thompson, 2008, p. 501).

In addition to equal chance to voice one's distinctive views and to be heard, deliberation demands an absence of coercion. Deliberators should be free to speak as they choose and to adopt whatever position that the debate leads them toward. To use Habermas's felicitous phrase, the "forceless force of the better argument" should carry the day (Habermas, 1975, p. 108). However, this freedom from coercion does not extend to allowing listeners to ignore the speech of those they disagree with. Participants in deliberation should maintain an open mind to perspectives other than their own, an understanding and respect for differences. Finally, most deliberative theorists agree that this open-mindedness should be accompanied by a concern for the good of others, either from a deliberator's empathy for the other; from the deliberator's ability to conceive of her interests in an enlarged form that encompasses the collective; or from a principled commitment to fairness and justice (Cohen, 1989; Benhabib, 1996; Gutmann & Thompson, 1996). Such open-mindedness should include an element of self-reflectiveness. While deliberation should respect the deeply held views of deliberators (Gutmann & Thompson, 1996), these deliberators should be willing to reflect on their positions and change them if the course of deliberation leads them to do so (Dryzek, 2000). Deliberation may not change any minds, but it should still lead deliberators to better understand their own positions and which reasons are legitimate or illegitimate as a basis for them (Gutmann & Thompson, 1996).

1.2. Political Psychology and Deliberative Democracy

Political psychology, and empirical political science more broadly, can make two contributions in this area. The first is to help define what good deliberation is in practical terms. Any definition of good deliberation must start with standards identified by normative theory. However, political psychology can give empirical meaning to these standards and identify ways in which these standards might be successfully implemented, or violated, in the real world (Mutz, 2008). Political psychology can also help identify the conditions under which these standards are more or less likely to be met, such as the formal rules of deliberation or the degree of racial heterogeneity in a group. For example, Karpowitz et al. (2012) find that a group's gender composition and its decision rule can ameliorate or exacerbate the bias against women's participation and influence. Specifically, women are much less disadvantaged in groups that decide with majority rule and contain a large majority of women, as well as in groups that decide unanimously and contain a small proportion of women.

As Mutz (2008) argues, deliberation may be located on a point along a continuum from very close to very far from the ideal. The requirements of deliberation should also be operationalized sufficiently concretely that they can be measured, so that, using these measures, the quality of any particular deliberation can be judged. Consider the discussion of equality in the example above. Equality is a standard that might be measured in a number of ways, each with particular strengths and weaknesses. Karpowitz et al. (2012) operationalize the equality standard by a one-to-one ratio of the talk time taken by women relative to men. On the other hand, Myers (2012a) judges equality by asking whether an item of information has the same influence in discussion regardless of who introduces it into deliberation. Either of these measures may be appropriate, depending on the research question at hand; as we discussion below, developing a set of deliberative quality measures and understanding the situations where each is appropriate is an important task.

1.3. Studying the Political Psychology of Deliberation: Context, Process, and Outcomes

To examine the current state of work on the political psychology of deliberation we will break research into three areas or clusters of variables: The *context* in which deliberation takes place, the *process* by which deliberation proceeds, and the *outcomes* that deliberation produces.[1] The border between these categories is far from absolute; nevertheless, we believe that this division provides a useful framework.

Outcomes are the products of deliberation. Some of these outcomes are familiar to students of political psychology, like knowledge gain or changed attitudes. Other outcomes of interest are particular to deliberation. For example, deliberation is supposed to increase deliberators' familiarity with opposing views and the rationales underlying them as well as provide more legitimate, reasonable bases for deliberators' own views. Ideally, this familiarity creates greater tolerance for those who hold opposing views, in turn resulting in more expansive self-conceptions that include others and their needs (Walsh, 2007). A final set of outcome variables concerns perceptions of the deliberative process itself, such as its fairness or legitimacy.

Process variables describe what happens once a group has started deliberating. The importance of some process variables is anchored in the normative literature and is not necessarily connected to good outcomes that these processes may produce. For example, deliberative theorists argue that good deliberation requires deliberators to justify their positions to each other; thus deliberative processes that include more justifications are preferable, *ceteris paribus*, to deliberations that do not. Other process research is motivated by empirical literatures, particularly the literatures on racial and gender inequality and other literatures about psychological processes that may harm group deliberation. Finally, some process research, primarily qualitative in nature, aims at developing a better understanding of the inner workings of small-group conversation.

The context of deliberation includes those factors that exist before deliberation begins and influence its process or outcomes. Most research on contextual factors examines the effects of the institutional structure of a deliberative group such as the decision rule that a group uses, whether the deliberation takes place face-to-face or over the Internet. Others focus on the place deliberation occupies in the broader political system (e.g., Karpowitz, 2006). In many ways these variables are the most important for practical empirical research, as they are frequently the only variables that institutional designers can directly control.

2. OUTCOMES OF DELIBERATION

While deliberation presents interesting questions for normative theory, more empirically minded scholars study deliberation because they think it can enhance democracy and the quality of governance. In short, we start with the question "What can deliberation do?" This question is particularly important given the great amount of time and, frequently, money that must be expended to hold deliberative forums. If deliberation has little effect on subsequent behaviors and attitudes, or if it is actively harmful to civic culture, as hypothesized by Hibbing and Theiss-Morse (2002, chaps. 7 and 8), then it may not be worth these valuable resources. The variables that we group under the heading of "outcomes" attempt to address these concerns. In addition to establishing the value of deliberation, these variables can serve as dependent variables for analyses involving the process and context variables. In this section we focus on three outcome variables at the core of most research on deliberation: opinion change, knowledge gain, and post-deliberation behavior (e.g., subsequent political participation). We then discuss several other outcomes that may be important products of public deliberation.

2.1. Opinion Change

Perhaps the most basic outcome produced by deliberation is the effect it has on participants' opinions. As Cohen (1989) says, "ideal deliberation aims to arrive at a rationally motivated *consensus*," something that is obviously impossible if deliberation is incapable of changing deliberators' minds. And in fact, a variety of studies show that deliberation can cause opinion change. This research includes reports from a large number of Deliberative Polls showing that deliberation is capable of changing attitudes (e.g., Luskin, Fishkin, & Jowell, 2002; Andersen & Hansen, 2007; Fishkin, 2009), as well as evidence from other deliberative forums (e.g., Barabas, 2004; Gastil, Black, & Moscovitz, 2008; Esterling, Fung, & Lee, 2012). Opinion change is not universal. Gilens (2011) argues that the magnitude of opinion change in Deliberative Polls is not large, especially given the intensity of the experience. Wojcieszak and Price (2010) found minimal effects of deliberation on attitudes about gay rights, and Farrar et al. (2010) found little attitude change on a highly salient local political issue, suggesting that attitude change will not happen in all deliberations.

More research on this question would be welcome, but research should more precisely link the quality of the deliberative process to the magnitude of attitude change, or focus on change in attitudes that can objectively be defined as undesirable by some established normative criteria. Simply demonstrating opinion change tells us little about the meaning of that opinion change, or of the quality of deliberation that produced it. Many processes that are not deliberative, such as manipulation by powerful actors, can cause opinion change and yet run against the salient interests of deliberators or their communities (Eliasoph, 1998); preference change may be produced predominantly by prejudice, xenophobia, or aggression toward out-groups (Mansbridge, 1980; Mendelberg & Oleske, 2000); or preferences may be shaped by discussion that focuses disproportionately on knowledge known by members of the majority group (Myers, 2012b). Further, a lack of opinion change should not be taken as a sign that deliberation has failed. Deliberators might engage in reasoned discussion, learn a great deal about the issue at hand, and end discovering that their original policy preferences were correct, albeit for reasons that they were not aware of. While a lack of opinion change should trigger some scrutiny given that it may be caused by any of several normatively suspect processes, it is the scrutiny of the process that matters. Normative theorists are understandably reluctant to set criteria for desirable outcomes from deliberation since it is not easy to link the standards for good outcomes, which tend to rest on less objective criteria and are often contested, with the standards for good processes, which are far less so (Gutmann & Thompson, 2004).

Several studies address this concern by examining the kind of opinion change caused by deliberative processes and comparing it to some standard for high-quality public opinion. This research takes a valuable step beyond simply measuring opinion change, though the importance of any finding depends a great deal on the standard that the study's authors use. For example, Gastil and Dillard (1999) examined changes in attitudes on seven issues among participants in National Issues Forums and found that participation increased attitude certainty and modestly increased schematic integration and differentiation—the degree to which participants consistently held liberal or conservative beliefs (see also Gastil, Deess, Weiser, & Meade, 2008). However, Sturgis et al. (2005) examined changes in attitude constraint across five Deliberative Polls conducted in the United Kingdom and found inconsistent evidence of increased constraint. Thus, if attitude coherence is our standard for "high-quality" opinion, following Converse's classic argument (1964), there is some evidence for a modest positive effect of deliberation. However, some critics might argue that attitude constraint is not necessarily a sign of "high-quality" public opinion if it is driven by ideological rigidity. Again, the key is to examine whether attitude change is rooted in each of the desirable processes of deliberation, which include open-mindedness.

Alternately, Farrar et al. (2010) examined the effect of deliberation on how "single-peaked" citizens' preferences are. When policies can be described along a single dimension, preferences are single-peaked when a person always prefers policies that are closer on this dimension to a single, most-preferred, policy over those that are further from the most-preferred outcome. Single-peaked preferences are important in many social choice accounts of democracy because they avoid cycling, when a collective voting by majority rule prefers x to y, y to z, and z to x (Arrow, 1953). In social choice accounts, cycling and related phenomena render the idea of a single public preference incoherent. Farrar et al. (2010) found that participation in a Deliberative Poll led deliberators to have more single-peaked preferences on individual issues. Again, those who do not think that single-peakedness is an important quality for democratic public opinion will not be impressed.

A final standard for opinion quality is "argument repertoire" (Cappella, Price, & Nir, 2002). In these studies, researchers solicit a person's opinion and then ask them to list reasons for holding that opinion as well as reasons why someone might hold the opposite opinion. A large number of reasons is taken as an indicator that the person has a well-thought-out opinion, though it might also be thought of as a measure of political knowledge. People with a high AR on an issue are more likely to engage in deliberation on that issue, and, further, deliberation increases the AR of one's own and of the opposition position. Once again, the validity of this measure depends on whether one thinks that being able to recall the reasons for an opinion is a valid measure of the quality of that opinion; proponents of online models of political information processing may be skeptical (Chapter 17).

Finally, some studies look at deliberative situations where there is arguably an objectively correct or more just outcome. For example, Simon and Sulkin (2002) use a multiple-player "divide the dollar" game to test the effect of discussion on equitable outcomes. The more equal the division of the group's resource, the more the outcome is deemed fair by the researchers. They found that deliberation produces more fair outcomes by this standard. Several experimental studies of rational choice models of deliberation use decisions where there is an objectively best choice for the group to make (Guarnaschelli, McKelvey, & Palfrey, 2000; Goeree & Yariv, 2011; Myers, 2012a). However, most of these studies use highly stylized forms of communication where players send signals (e.g., "red" or "blue") over computers but do not actually talk face to face (for an exception see Myers, 2012a). Finally, Karpowitz, Mendelberg, and Shaker (2012) have subjects deliberate and decide between different rules for redistributing income that they will earn in a subsequent, unknown experimental task (see also Karpowitz et al., 2012, Mendelberg, Karpowitz, & Goedert, 2013). In this deliberation task, which loosely mirrors Rawls's original position (1971), groups' decisions can be judged as more or less just based on how generously they decide to redistribute income to the poor, though such judgment obviously requires a commitment to a particular substantive conception of justice (such as Rawls's; see also Guttmann & Thompson, 1996).

Setting aside questions of opinion quality, Gastil, Bacci, and Dollinger (2010) look at the ideological direction of opinion change caused by Deliberative Polls. Critiques of deliberation have argued that deliberation is little more than a way for highly educated, liberal professors to harangue the masses into adopting their views (Posner, 2004). Gastil, Bacci, and Dollinger (2010) examined opinion change on 65 items from several Deliberative Polls and found no tendency for deliberators to change their attitudes in a more liberal direction. However, deliberators did tend to adopt attitudes that were more egalitarian, cosmopolitan, and collective-focused after participating in deliberation. Whether these tendencies represent an ideological bias in deliberation is open to debate. They do conform to some theorists' normative standard for good deliberative outcomes, which include transforming deliberators' self-concepts to be more inclusive of others (Gutmann & Thompson, 1996; Rosenberg, 2007).

Another important question is determining whose attitudes change during deliberation. Gastil, Black, and Moscovitz (2008) find greater attitude change on the parts of liberals and moderates than conservatives. Fishkin (2009) shows that attitudes change the most among those with the highest level of knowledge at the end of Deliberative Polls, though there is no relationship between attitude change and change in knowledge between the start of the poll and the end of the poll. Fishkin and coauthors argue that measures of knowledge at the end of deliberation are more accurate measures of learning than the difference between pre- and post-deliberation measures of knowledge (Luskin et al., 2002, pp. 480–483; also Luskin, Helfer, & Sood, 2011), and thus that their findings tell us that attitude change is greatest among those who gain the most knowledge. However, if gaining knowledge is the best measure of learning, then we should conclude that opinion change is not produced by learning. As with much research on deliberation, the quality of the measures scholars use to assess successful deliberation is a key issue; not only do scholars need to calibrate variables to normative standards of good deliberation, but they also must develop instruments with adequate psychometric measurement properties.

2.2. Knowledge Gain

While the value of opinion change as a measure of quality deliberation is debatable, most would agree that good deliberation should increase relevant knowledge. Most studies of deliberation that measure knowledge gain find an increase, including studies in the Deliberative Polling tradition (e.g., Andersen & Hansen, 2007) and outside of it (e.g., Barabas, 2004). Participants retain knowledge gains for a least a little while after the deliberative experience (Jacobs et al., 2009, chap. 6). Interestingly, a fair amount of learning appears to happen before discussion begins (Farrar et al., 2010) and continues after the deliberative exercise as deliberators pay increased attention to politics (Esterling, Neblo, & Lazer, forthcoming). Thus studies that measure only the knowledge gained during the deliberative exercise may miss much of its positive effect. On the other hand, much of the benefit of deliberation might not be caused by deliberation per se, but rather by anticipating or taking part in a novel and intensive form of political participation.

While an increase in average knowledge is good, the value of this knowledge gain may depend on who is learning from deliberation. Esterling et al. (forthcoming) found that knowledge gain is widely distributed and is not dependent on prior political knowledge. Similarly, Jacobs et al. (2009) found no significant interactions between any demographic characteristics and knowledge gain.

2.3. Post-deliberation Behavior

The effect of deliberation on participants goes beyond their attitudes about and knowledge of the issue under discussion. Since Mill and Tocqueville, theorists have argued that participation in the democratic process improves the civic character of the participant (see Mansbridge, 1999 for a review). John Gastil and a team of collaborators test this theory by examining the effect of participation in jury deliberation on later political involvement. They found that service on criminal juries can increase jurors' subsequent rates of voting. Jurors in civil trials saw no boost to turnout. The authors argue that this is because of the public nature of the issues decided by criminal juries, where the state is prosecuting a violation of the law, as compared to civil juries who adjudicate disputes between private parties. They helpfully show that the effect holds only for jurors whose trial actually reaches the point of jury deliberation, and not for alternate jurors or those whose trial ended in a mistrial (Gastil, Deess, et al., 2008; Gastil, Deess, et al., 2010). Gastil, Deess et al. (2010) go on to demonstrate that jurors who felt engaged and satisfied as jurors subsequently paid more attention to civic affairs and became more active in their communities beyond the voting booth. They further found that jury service could boost jurors' efficacy and faith in the political system, though these effects depended on the characteristics of the juror and his or her subjective experience.

The effect of deliberation on subsequent political participation seems to extend beyond juries. Jacobs et al. (2009, chap. 5) use US national survey data to show that participating in face-to-face deliberation, defined as attending a meeting that was organized to discuss a public issue, increases subsequent political participation, controlling for demographic characteristics and social capital factors like belonging to community organizations. Wantchekon (2011) randomly assigned candidates in Benin to campaign using either town hall meetings or traditional clientelist methods (distributing money to voters) and found that the former produced greater turnout. Finally, Lazer, Sokhey, Neblo, and Esterling (2010) found that participation in a deliberative event increased the number of subsequent discussions held outside the event.

While Gastil and coauthors suggest that satisfaction with a deliberative experience can drive participation, Karpowitz's study (2006) of deliberations about town planning in the United States found that it was those who were *dissatisfied* with the decisions made by a deliberative forum who participated in subsequent town council meetings held to discuss the results of those forums. Thus the effects of deliberation on subsequent action depend on the larger context for the deliberation. The political context for deliberation may determine whether the deliberation is primarily a civic exercise (meant to promote learning or dialogue, or attracting citizens out of a sense of civic duty) or whether it feeds into a process of conflicting interests in a larger adversary system (Karpowitz and Mansbridge, 2005). If the former, then it is satisfaction that drives action; if the latter, then it is dissatisfaction that does so, though the ability of dissatisfaction to drive participation may depend on the availability of alternative venues where the deliberative decision can be contested.

The effect of deliberation on subsequent participation may be heterogeneous across individuals. In a study of deliberation about the rights of sexual minorities in Poland, Wojcieszak (2011b) found that deliberation had a small, negative effect on intentions to participate—except for participants who held extreme opinions. These participants reported higher intentions to participate, but only when they reported encountering a lot of disagreement. Wojcieszak, Baek, and Delli Carpini (2010) report a similar finding based on survey data. In this data, subsequent participation among moderates was mediated by their affective responses to deliberation, while subsequent participation among weak ideologues was mediated by cognitive reactions to deliberation, and subsequent participation by strong ideologies was not mediated by any reaction to deliberation. These findings offer evidence that analyses that ignore differences among deliberators may miss important effects of deliberation, and that both negative and positive experiences and reactions can mediate these effects.

2.4. Other Outcomes

Three other outcome variables are of particular interest: tolerance for opposing views, feelings of political efficacy, and satisfaction with the deliberative procedure and the policy it produces. Many theorists believe that deliberation will increase tolerance for opposing views by increasing awareness of the reasons underlying these views as well as establishing common ground across differences (Gutmann & Thompson, 1996; Sanders, 1997). Indeed, Walsh (2007) found that interracial dialogue groups foster greater understanding of other racial groups. Participants in a discussion across racial lines "compel each other to face the reality of different realities" (p. 8) by balancing the search for common ground with the attempt to listen to, acknowledge, and respect difference. By intertwining unity and difference, deliberations can render difference less threatening. However, Andersen and Hansen (2007) found participating in a Deliberative Poll had little effect on tolerance, though anticipation of a deliberative experience might actually reduce tolerance. The difference between these findings may lie in Walsh's (2007) groups' specific focus on learning and understanding others' views.

Evidence about whether deliberation increases general social tolerance is mixed. Weber (2001) found that deliberation about the degree of freedom that should be granted to a politically extreme group increased tolerance for that group. However, Wojcieszak and Price (2010) found that deliberation about same-sex marriage does not increase support for the rights of sexual minorities. Thus the tolerance that is promoted by deliberation may be limited to tolerance of the expression of opposing or extreme views.

Finally, we might expect that deliberation increases citizens' belief in their ability to participate in politics (internal efficacy) and their belief that government will respond to their demands (external efficacy). Results on deliberation's effect on political efficacy are mixed, suggesting that deliberation increases external efficacy but does not affect internal efficacy. Walsh's early (2003) work on intergroup dialogue programs found this pattern, though she notes that participants began with high efficacy (Walsh, 2003). Morrell (2005) found that deliberation does not increase general internal political efficacy, but that it does increase deliberator's sense of efficacy to participate in future deliberations—that is, deliberating makes citizens think they are more capable of deliberating. Nabatchi (2010) examines changes in efficacy among participants in an America*Speaks* town hall meeting and found increased external efficacy, but no change in internal efficacy; these results persisted after 24 months. Andersen and Hansen (2007) found a similar pattern of changes in political efficacy in a Deliberative Poll about whether Denmark should adopt the euro. However, Pierce, Neeley, and Budziak (2008) discovered that college students participating in a deliberation about university issues with administrators and faculty members felt more comfortable expressing their views (similar to internal efficacy), but not more confident that those in authority cared about their views (similar to external efficacy). The evidence, then, is mixed.

Several studies treat measure how satisfied deliberators are with the deliberative process and its products as important outcome variables (Gastil et al., 2010; Simon & Sulkin, 2002; Stromer-Galley & Muhlberger, 2009; Esterling et al., 2012). It is tempting to use these as measures of the quality of the process. For example, after deliberation Esterling et al. (2012) asked deliberators for their level of agreement with such statements as "People at this meeting listened to one another respectfully and courteously" and used these to measure the quality of the deliberative.[2] Better is the approach of Stromer-Galley and Muhlberger (2009) who used these responses as outcomes of rather than indicators of the process, and directly measured the process (specifically, the number of statements where deliberators agreed or disagreed with each other). Satisfaction with the deliberative process (as well as the policies it produces) again raises the two questions we have encountered throughout this section: does the measure fit a normative standard of good deliberation, and are the measures adequate for the underlying standard? It is not clear that normative theories require satisfaction with the outcome under any circumstance; or that they require satisfaction with the process of deliberation after the fact, and especially when that satisfaction is divorced from more objectives measures of process quality.

2.5. Conclusion

In sum, there is good and bad news. The bad news: opinions can change with deliberation, but the evidence is inconsistent, the magnitude is small, and the change does not satisfy any normative standard of deliberation (for example, it is not always produced by knowledge gain). Deliberation produces more constrained attitudes—sometimes. It can produce outcomes judged just or accurate by an objective standard, though more troubling is evidence that it can also produce opinions more in line with the organizers' political agenda, and all this depends greatly on process and context variables (to which we turn below). Alienation as much as satisfaction can produce the increases in later political participation and engagement. There is no effect on internal efficacy. On the plus side: Deliberation can help make preferences single-peaked, though more work on this result is needed; and it increases the argument repertoire for and against one's side. It increases knowledge, though perhaps not solely from deliberation but also from the hoopla surrounding it. It can elevate citizens' external efficacy and, especially, their political engagement well after it is over. Finally, deliberators generally like deliberating—no small matter for the generally apathetic and apolitical citizen. Deliberation is best at giving people more specific knowledge about the issues and positions at hand, and when the experience is meaningful, either negatively or positively, it can elevate political participation and engagement. So we can learn something useful from studies of outcomes.

However, there is a danger in using outcomes as measures of processes and contexts. Many of these outcomes can be produced by a number of non-deliberative processes. The normative value of the *outcome* may depend on the *process* that produced it.

A great deal of research remains to be done on the outcomes of deliberation. Findings on some important outcome variables, such as tolerance for the views of others, are still inconclusive. Other outcome variables could gain from greater detail in their specification. For example, we might be interested in learning if the informal political discussion spurred by participating in a deliberative experience is itself deliberative, and if subsequent knowledge-seeking is open-minded (Conover et al., 2002). Finally, deliberative theory suggests some outcome variables that have yet to be widely tested. For example, deliberation is supposed to produce opinions and decisions that are more "public-spirited" (Gutmann & Thompson& 1996, p. 51). We need more empirical work to operationalize and measure the relevant variables.

3. Processes

Establishing the normative value of deliberation requires looking at processes, not just outcomes. For example, a lecture by a well-informed individual may greatly increase knowledge. However, such a one-sided communication would hardly count as deliberation. This point is worth reinforcing; while some process variables are important because they lead to good outcomes, some have value in and of themselves. For example, deliberation that allows all participants to speak might produce less learning than deliberation where only the most knowledgeable members of the community speak. Despite the fact that learning is an important outcome variable, we may nevertheless favor the equal deliberation because equality is a process variable with value in its own right, and because the participatory aspect of deliberative theory means that speaking matters along with listening. In other words, process variables can be dependent variables as well as independent variables in the study of deliberation. Like Thompson (2008), we believe that some of the requirements of deliberation have value independent of any outcome they may produce; here, the goal of empirical research should be to determine whether deliberation can have these traits at all, and whether some structural factors (e.g., the presence of moderators) are more likely to produce these traits than others.

We organize this section around three kinds of process research. First, we describe measurements of deliberative processes that are motivated directly by the normative literature. This kind of research takes the procedural requirements described by theorists (e.g., the requirement to respect other deliberators) and seeks to judge whether a particular deliberation or deliberative institution meets these requirements. We then discuss process research that is motivated by literatures in political psychology such as the literatures on race and gender. This research identifies processes that take place in deliberation and then suggests why these processes might be good or bad for deliberation. Finally, we end with a discussion of the qualitative research on the kinds of speech used in deliberation. While this topic is not generally discussed under the rubric of political psychology, we believe that examining what is said in deliberation can offer valuable lessons to students of the psychology of small-group deliberation.

3.1. Process Measurement Motivated by Normative Theory

A prime example of research motivated directly by normative theory is the Discourse Quality Index (DQI) (Steenbergen, Bächtiger, Spörndli, & Steiner, 2003, Steiner, Bächtiger, Spörndli, & Steenbergen, 2004). The DQI is intended as a measure of how well discourse in parliamentary debates approximates the ideal discourse described in Habermas's discourse ethics. It codes each speech during a legislative debate along seven dimensions, listed in table 22.1, and grouped into broad areas for the purposes of comparison. The DQI is primarily a measure of parliamentary speeches, which differ in many important ways from the kind of small-group deliberation that we describe here. Nevertheless, it can be used in a variety of settings.

Stromer-Galley (2007) introduces a similar coding scheme for coding conversation among average citizens. While the DQI draws primarily on Habermas for its coding categories, Stromer-Galley (2007) draws on a number of definitions of deliberation, including Habermas but also communications scholars and sociologists. Stromer-Galley's method (2007) also uses a much smaller unit of analysis, analyzing each thought expressed by a speaker instead of entire parliamentary speeches. The coding categories reflect these differences. While Stromer-Galley (2007) includes measures of whether speech takes the form of reasoned opinions and whether it is supported by sources (as well as what those sources are), she codes specifically for a number of areas glossed over by the DQI such as equality in speech, whether speech is on topic, and whether speech engages with the prior speech of others.

We advocate measuring the process directly rather than relying on deliberators' reports post-deliberation. As we noted, several studies measure the quality of the deliberative process by asking participants about their perceptions of the deliberative process after discussion is over (e.g., Gastil, Black, & Moscovitz, 2008; Stromer-Galley & Muhlberger, 2009). In one study where post-deliberation self-reports of deliberative quality are compared to the observations of third-party coders, these two quantities have different relationships with outcome measures (Gastil, Black, & Moscovitz, 2008, p. 37). Self-ratings are generally problematic indicators of an objective reality, and from a psychometric perspective they are suspect until proven otherwise. For example, participants may report, or even actually come to believe, that the discussion was high quality because the organizers or fellow members expect it to be so or because of the need to

Table 22.1 Elements of the Deliberative Coding Schemes

General area	DQI coding dimension	Definition	Stromer-Galley coding dimension	Definition
Equality	Participation	Can the speaker communicate freely in debate?	Equality	Do deliberators take advantage of formal equality in opportunities to speak?
Reasoning	Level of justification	How sophisticated is the justification offered by the speaker?	Reasoned opinion expression	Is speech a reasoned expression of a relevant opinion?
	Content of justification	Does the justification appeal to the common good?	Sourcing	Do deliberators refer to a source to support their opinions?
			Topic	Does the speech deal with the topic at hand?
Respect	Respect for groups	Does the speaker show respect for groups affected by the policy?	Engagement	Do deliberators demonstrate that they are listening to and responding to the speech of others?
	Respect for demands	Does the speaker show respect for the demands of those who disagree with his/her view?		
	Respect for counterarguments	Does the speaker address and acknowledge the value of counterarguments?		
Consensus	Constructive politics	Does the speaker suggest alternative proposals that could be the basis for consensus?	None	

Source: Adapted from Steiner et al., 2004, chap. 3; Stromer-Galley, 2007.

reduce the dissonance that they would experience if they invested in the effortful activity of deliberation and then repudiated the worth of that activity. The variety of different measurements used also makes comparison across studies difficult.

3.2. Process Research Motivated by Psychological Theory

One element of group information processing commonly noted in the psychological literature is polarization. This is the well-known finding that the post-deliberation group average position on an issue tends to be a more extreme version of the pre-deliberation average. Polarization is the product of two distinct processes. The first, *social comparison*, describes the tendency of deliberators to adopt whatever position appears to be the norm within the group. (See also the discussion in Huddy, chapter 23, this volume.) For example, in a group where the average position on an issue tilts liberal, all deliberators will feel pressure to adopt a position at least as liberal as the perceived norm; as those below the average move toward the group's mean, they push the new group mean higher, and those at the old mean may shift higher as well (for a review see Mendelberg, 2002, pp. 158–161; see also the discussion of "groupthink" by Dyson & 't Hart, chapter 13, this volume). The second process, *persuasive arguments*, suggests that in a group with a starting majority, the pool of arguments that can be introduced in conversation consists mainly of arguments that support the majority view. For example, in a group of liberals, the pool of available arguments will be mostly liberal, and sharing these arguments will tend to push deliberators in an even more liberal direction. This explanation emphasizes a more rational process of persuasion through the balance of arguments for one side, in contrast to the first explanation, which emphasizes the desire for social acceptance. However, these explanations may interact; members of groups with a liberal median may feel uncomfortable expressing conservative arguments, further biasing the argument pool.

Schkade, Sunstein, and Hastie (2007) demonstrated polarization in an explicitly political environment by putting deliberators in ideologically homogeneous groups, but do not examine which if either of these processes produced the polarization that they observed. However, Price, Nir, and Cappella (2006) found evidence of both processes in online deliberation about candidates' tax policy plans.

Some work from social psychology suggests that the relative weight of these two forces may depend on whether the issue under discussion is a matter of facts or values. Vinokur and Burnstein (1978) look at discussions of several public issues for evidence of both processes. They find evidence supporting persuasive arguments theory on most issues except for capital punishment, the most value-laden issue under discussion. Similarly, Kaplan and Miller's examination (1987) of mock jury verdicts finds that argumentation can account for the value of compensation damages, but social comparison for the value of punitive damages.

While the role of norms versus informational influence in driving polarization is unsettled, proponents of Deliberative Polling claim that polarization is not present in

Deliberative Polls (Luskin, Fishkin, & Hahn, 2007; Fishkin, 2009). Sunstein (2002) offers a number of hypotheses related to the structure of Deliberative Polls that might account for why groups in Deliberative Polls do not polarize. Specifically, he argues that the lack of a collective decision on the issue, the availability of balanced briefing materials, the diversity of opinions within deliberative polling groups, and the presence of a neutral moderator might account for the observed lack of polarization. These Hypotheses regarding the effect of structural variables on polarization remain untested (see section 4).

A concept related to polarization is attitude convergence (or homogenization), which measures the degree to which the attitudes of a group move toward the prediscussion group mean, regardless of whether the group is ideologically homogeneous. While attitude polarization is generally seen as a normatively negative outcome (Sunstein, 2002), attitude convergence may not be a universal negative, particularly if it is the product of meaningful compromise and learning. Again, it helps to separate the outcome from the process.

Evidence for convergence is, at any rate, mixed. In addition to finding group polarization, Schkade et al. (2007) report that the variance of attitudes within groups drops as a result of deliberation. However, Farrar, Green, Green, Nickerson, and Shewfelt (2009) found that attitude convergence happens inconsistently in Deliberative Polls and is generally of a small magnitude. Again, this finding may depend in part on the unique structure of the Deliberative Poll. Others find similarly mixed evidence for attitude convergence and suggest some conditions under which it might or might not happen. Gastil, Black, and Moscovitz (2008) found a relationship between the quality of deliberation, as measured by the post-deliberation perceptions of deliberators, and the amount that group members' attitudes converged. It is unclear if deliberators were more satisfied with deliberation that ended with more agreement or if better deliberation produced more satisfaction and more agreement. Additionally, there was no relationship between deliberative quality and attitude convergence when deliberative quality was measured by third-party observers. Barabas (2004) found that deliberators change their minds only when there is verbal consensus within the group at the end of group deliberation. Lacking a consensus, deliberators tend to retain their original opinion. This finding echoes the classic finding from Asch that pressure on a dissenter to conform was greatly reduced when at least one member agreed with the dissenter. Finally, Wojcieszak (2011a) found that deliberators discussing the rights of sexual minorities in politically heterogeneous groups tended to move further apart instead of converging; this was particularly true among deliberators who began with relatively extreme views. Taken together, this evidence suggests that deliberation often, but not always, causes convergence.

Polarization has received a great deal of attention, but it is far from the only finding from the group processes literature that might affect political deliberation (see Mendelberg, 2002 for a review). Another is the Common Knowledge Effect (also known as the Hidden Profile finding), which predicts that groups will focus discussion on information that all members know before discussion begins, ignoring novel information that is known by only one or a few deliberators. While this is a well-established finding in psychology (Lu 2012), and one that has sparked concern among deliberative theorists (Sunstein 2006), Myers (2012b) finds no evidence that the Common Knowledge Effect affects political deliberation. He suggests that this is because, unlike other forms of group discussion, political deliberation it usually includes deliberators with conflicting interests, which motivates greater information search. Thus while the group processes literature can be a valuable source of hypotheses about political deliberation, deliberative democratic institutions are unique in ways that mean that these results must be replicated in the political arena.

Research on deliberation is not restricted to examinations of group processes such as polarization or convergence. Other research examines how deliberation affects individual information processing. For example, Druckman (2004) and Druckman and Nelson (2003) exposed experimental subjects to newspaper articles that frame an issue in one of two ways. Framing effects are problematic because they imply that public opinion shifts for arbitrary reasons and can be manipulated easily. Group discussion greatly reduced framing effects, but the composition of the discussion group mattered. (For more on framing see Chong, chapter 4, this volume.) Mixed groups, where half had been exposed to one frame and half to another, saw framing effects disappear; in same-frame groups framing effects were only diminished if members of the group had high motivation and ability to think about the issue. Hopefully, future research will examine the effect of discussion on other processes known to affect political information processing (e.g., emotional arousal, see Morrell 2010).

3.3. Heterogeneity of Identities and the Process of Deliberation

Understanding the effect of group diversity is important for determining whether deliberation can meet the normative standard of equality in deliberation, and in particular whether it can offer an equal voice to marginalized groups in society. (See also the discussion by Kurzban & Sidanius, chapter 7, this volume.) One of the most persistent critiques of deliberative democracy claims that deliberation privileges members of socially dominant groups because they have a greater ability to present their views in the language of rational discourse (Young, 1996; Sanders, 1997). In some cases this is the result of better access to education, skilled occupations, and other resources that make people rhetorically capable and self-confident and thus more likely to dominate deliberation. However, even in the absence of material privilege, minorities and other dominated groups may be at a disadvantage because they lack access to the cultural background of the dominant group and the set of assumed knowledge and perspectives that this background entails. Sanders (1997), drawing on research on juries, argues that "jurors who are privileged in terms of race, economic background, or gender tend to have perspectives quite different from those who are not, belying the expectation that deliberation might inspire, or help recall, a sense of community. The distance between jurors' perspectives may be sufficient so that less privileged jurors feel that their views are discounted" (p. 369). If this is true, then deliberation may accomplish little more than validate the perspectives of the dominant group. Protected "enclave" deliberation may be an alternative in these cases (Karpowitz, Raphael, & Hammond, 2009; see Harris-Perry, 2004 for an example of similar informal discussion).

Some research, primarily qualitative in nature, validates these concerns. As part of her exploration of democracy at the radically egalitarian workplace Helpline, Mansbridge (1980) stresses that even in environments where white deliberators are committed to racial equality, deliberation often rests on unarticulated class- and race-specific assumptions that are alien to members of minority groups, making it harder for them to fully participate (pp. 195–198). One African American member of Helpline reported, "I needed help understanding Helpline. I didn't know what people were talking about half the time.... It was an enormous culture shock" (p. 196). Even egalitarian members of the majority group may be blind to the disadvantages that minority group members face; Mansbridge herself admits that she did not realize until late in her research that race was a salient dividing line at Helpline (p. 195). Further, Mansbridge notes that such "color-blind" environments can make explicit discussions of race difficult, as white group members perceive suggestions that race is important as personal attacks, or marginalize the person bringing up race as someone outside the mainstream of the group (p. 197).

Mendelberg and Oleske (2000) offer similar findings about racial discussion in a comparative study of two town meetings. The meetings discussed a proposal to combine two school districts, one of which was racially mixed and one almost entirely white. At the meeting in the white school district race was rarely brought up directly, and racial motivations were explicitly disavowed. However, the authors argue that several of the common arguments against integration contained racial undertones. At the racially mixed meeting, racial minorities attempted to point out the racial implications of arguments against integration; these attempts were seen by white attendees as unfair attacks, and deliberation shut down as the two sides refused to listen to each other. On the other hand, Walsh (2007) paints a brighter picture in her study of interracial dialogue groups, finding that deliberation can be used to build understanding across racial groups. Still, even in these settings racial minorities speak less and are asked to justify their remarks more frequently (p. 188), echoing Mansbridge's finding that even egalitarian settings can be difficult for minority deliberators because egalitarianism hides unshared cultural assumptions.

A final finding suggests that while racial minorities may be at a disadvantage relative to members of a racial majority, their presence may nevertheless improve the quality of deliberation in a group. Sommers (2006) finds that racially diverse juries "deliberated longer, discussed more trial evidence, and made fewer factually inaccurate statements in discussing evidence than did all-White juries" (p. 182; for a review of related studies see Sommers, 2007). The effects of racial diversity began before deliberation even started: whites on racially diverse juries were less likely to vote for guilt in a pre-deliberation poll than whites on all-white juries. Thus even if racial minorities have less direct influence in discussion, their very presence may give them indirect influence over deliberative outcomes. The results point both to the processes deliberative theorists would be glad to see—better information-processing—and to those they might treat with suspicion, such as socially motivated conformity.

Combined, these studies suggest that deliberation about racial issues is difficult, though not impossible in the right context. However, minorities are likely to be at a disadvantage, as deliberation is likely to depend on cultural assumptions that are not shared across racial groups. Minorities tend to be the deliberators who bring these assumptions to light, a difficult task.

Research on gender and deliberation reaches similar conclusions about the subtle but important effects of unequal social identities. In the two sites she studied, Mansbridge finds that being female "limited one's power and participation in ways that are subtle and difficult to measure" (Mansbridge, 1980 pp. 105–107, 191–193). In Mansbridge's study, women appeared to be less confident in their ability to communicate effectively, and more likely to be intimidated by others' speech. This conclusion is seconded by a comprehensive study of Vermont town meetings (Bryan, 2004).

In a series of studies, Karpowitz, Mendelberg, and several coauthors build on these insights. They show a considerable effect of the gender composition of a group and of its decision rule on levels of gender inequality in deliberating groups. In situations characterizing most real-world deliberative settings, women are a numerical minority and decisions are reached by majority rule. In experimental simulation of these conditions, women speak far less during deliberation than men, are less likely to be judged as influential by other deliberators and in their own assessment, are less likely to mention issues typically of distinctive concern to women (children, families, the poor), and are less likely to articulate preferences for group decisions that favor generous redistribution. However, in groups assigned to have a majority of women and decide by majority rule, these inequalities disappear; women in these groups have equal participation, equal influence, a higher number of references to women's issues, and the group chooses a more generous redistribution policy. In addition, unanimous rule protects the numerical minority of women and mutes the inequalities with men in their group (Mendelberg, Karpowitz, & Goedert 2013; Karpowitz et al., 2012). The findings are robust to various controls, such as the ideology of the participants. These findings reinforce earlier findings from social psychology that men wield more influence on juries by, for example, being more likely to volunteer to serve as foreperson (Strodtbeck & Lipinski, 1985). They are replicated in a study of local school boards (Karpowitz & Mendelberg, 2012). These studies further support concerns raised by feminist critics of deliberation that deliberation has the potential to marginalize the views and concerns of socially dominated groups (Young, 1996; Sanders, 1997), but locate settings and institutional procedures that can mitigate the problem.

Other forms of unequal status may also affect deliberation. Pierce et al. (2008) examined deliberation about campus issues between students, faculty and administrators, and found that deliberation, rather than being hindered by the status differences between these groups, can help overcome these status differences. However, they only examined deliberators' perceptions of the fairness of discussion, not whether the lower-status members of groups, in this case students, actually influenced deliberation. Ban and Rao (2009) examined deliberation in Indian villages and found that when groups include village officials, those officials tend to dominate discussion. However, such officials were more likely to mention the preferences of others and more likely to make substantive contributions to deliberation. In general, unequal status may have a variety of sources beyond race and gender, and the normative and empirical role of deliberators with role expertise or authority on the topic under discussion requires further study (Estlund, 2000, Myers, 2011). Studies outside advanced industrial countries find severe problems of inequality and disadvantages for people who are illiterate, landless, or members of lower castes (Besley, Pande, & Rao, 2005).

However, Fishkin (2009) argues that inequalities of influence based on social status do not appear in Deliberative Polls. He presents data showing that the post-deliberation attitudes of a group are not particularly correlated with the pre-deliberation attitudes of white, male, and highly educated deliberators. Based on this, he claims that deliberation does not disadvantage socially marginalized groups. These conflicting results may be the result of different measures of deliberator influence. Karpowitz et al. (2012) and Mendelberg et al. (2013) measure influence using the gender gap in volume of speech, in the topics discussed, in ratings of influence, and in influence over outcomes, while Fishkin (2009) uses the relationship between pre- and post-deliberation attitudes. If the issue under discussion is characterized by broad agreement to begin with, the pre-post correlation will not reveal unequal influence. A range of indicators of unequal voice and influence may be needed. Finally, inequalities in deliberation may not be constant and inevitable but rather created by the conditions of discussion. For example, the group composition and norms of the group may determine whether inequalities exist and how severe they are (Karpowitz et al., 2012). Enclave spaces play an important empowering role (Harris-Perry, 2004; Karpowitz et al., 2009). The issue under discussion may widen or close the gender gap (Hannagan & Larimer, 2010). Female officeholders or the presence of authoritative officials who actively bring marginalized perspectives into discussion may help (Ban & Rao, 2009; Karpowitz & Mendelberg, 2014).

3.4. Heterogeneity of Interests and Attitudes

A range of research examines the effect of heterogeneous interests and attitudes in deliberation. At stake is the normative criterion of rationality; if people only hear their own view, discussion fails to expose people to disagreement and they lose the opportunity to learn new information and arguments and to improve the quality of their reasoning (Mutz, 2006). The representation of diverse interests is also necessary for the transformational aspiration of deliberation, which seeks to enlarge people's capacity to think of the common good (Mansbridge, 1980).

Esterling et al. (2012) found that groups with either high or low levels of preference heterogeneity produce lower-quality deliberation, as compared to groups with moderate levels of disagreement, though quality here is measured with self-reports. In addition, this study found that moderately heterogeneous groups display more preference convergence. As we noted, Wojcieszak and Price (2010) found that online deliberation in ideologically mixed groups about the rights of sexual minorities produced the opposite—a movement away from the group mean among conservatives but not among liberals. These findings are not necessarily in conflict; disagreement on issues like gay marriage may be particularly intractable, at least for conservatives, and Wojcieszak and Price (2010) do not report variation in the level of disagreement within groups. The effects of heterogeneity remain an open research topic.

A key question is whether minority preferences can find an adequate voice. That they do so is a fundamental requirement of all normative models of deliberation, and a large literature in psychology tackles this question (see Mendelberg, 2002 for a review). Myers (2012a) tests several conditions that could promote equal voice and representation for interest minorities in group decisions, using lab and field settings. He experimentally varies whether the identical piece of relevant information is given to a member who is in the majority in terms of interest in the decision being made or is in the minority. He finds that groups are more likely to ignore the information when it is given to the minority. A group needs diverse preferences to produce learning and eliminate priming effects, but when interests conflict, the learning process is directed by the majority to the disadvantage of the minority.

3.5. Kinds of Speech in Deliberation

Studies that examine the nature of language and the contents of speech are valuable for political psychology because they open a window on the process and mechanisms that drive the cause and effect we observe. Studies in this vein seek to classify aspects of speech in order to analyze concepts of interest to political psychology and deliberation. These studies tend to be qualitative; quantitative content analysis is a little-explored frontier of research on language (but see Myers, 2011; Mendelberg et al., 2013).

One focus of these studies is storytelling. Black (2009) argues that storytelling is the primary way that deliberators share information and manage disagreement, and that the use of these stories is closely connected to the identities available to the storyteller (See also Ryfe, 2006). Storytelling was also a key feature of deliberation's ability to prompt exchanges across lines of social difference in the interracial dialogue groups that Walsh studied (2007). Stories allow speakers to introduce controversial issues and train listeners' attention on differences between the speaker's experience and their own, but in a way that may create empathy. However, debate also plays an important role; by using debate, participants identify and delimit differences while still showing respect for others. Black develops a typology of stories; this typology and Walsh's distinction between dialogue and debate can prove useful lenses for understanding speech in deliberation. Future research may focus on how effective these different forms of dialogue are.

Polletta (2008) took a different approach by examining the "mode" or model of conversation that deliberators employ. On the surface deliberation appears to follow the mode of sociable conversation: pleasant, but not leading to attitude change and avoiding conflict between different opinions. However, she found that deliberators make use of other conversation modes: "educational," "negotiation," and "advocacy" that differ from social conversation by allowing for disagreement. Rather than avoid conflict, as is usually done in sociable conversation (Eliasoph, 1998), deliberators were able to express disagreement respectfully and reach compromise using these alternative conversational modes.[3] Importantly, compromise was favored over avoidance because conversation in the advocacy mode led the groups to believe that they had a mandate to come to conclusions, even though the groups were not formally charged with reaching a consensus.

Another approach is to assess the level of discourse at which deliberators engage each other. Rosenberg (2007) classifies conversation into three types discourse. Each level has its own understanding of what discourse is intended to achieve and what rules govern social interaction. In the simplest level of *conventional discourse* deliberators try to find a solution to a well-defined problem while "maintaining conventional social roles." In *cooperative discourse* deliberators share perspectives on the problem in order to redefine the problem as well as the kinds of considerations that might be relevant to solving the problem. At the highest and most transformative level, *collaborative discourse*, deliberators reflect on "the process whereby rules of argumentation are formulated, basic assumptions regarding nature, society, and individuals are defined, and the social conditions of discourse are understood and institutionalized." That is, at the highest level, participants question the notion that they already share fundamental understandings of the issues and of the process of discussion, and explicitly examine their assumptions and perspectives. Rosenberg presents empirical results from group discussions of school reform that suggest that deliberators are rarely willing or able to engage in discourse beyond the conventional level (Rosenberg, 2007).

These studies are valuable because they offer categories of analysis for understanding speech, and suggest ways in which speech might reflect, implement, or alter individuals' motivations, reasoning, social identities, and other concepts of interest to political psychologists. Future studies could fruitfully seek a more explicit connection between outputs such as group polarization and processes such as storytelling, or outputs such as self-understanding and self-awareness and processes such as collaborative discourse.

3.6. Conclusion

As we elaborate in the next section, the conditions of deliberation shape the process, and few processes can be regarded as a sure and fixed characteristic of deliberation. For example, deliberation may produce attitude polarization and convergence in some cases, but it is premature to declare a "law" of group polarization (Sunstein, 2002).

Still, tentative conclusions can be drawn in some areas, while in others the need for more research is clear. Deliberators do articulate relevant arguments and information, and these do shape their views at the end of the day. Deliberation can help correct some of the pathologies of individual information processing, for example, by eliminating framing effects, although it can lead to other information-based or socially based pathologies, such as group polarization or convergence. Whatever its normative value, storytelling appears to play a major role in how people deliberate about political issues. However, while deliberation is supposed to result in more inclusive decision-making, and racially heterogeneous groups may provide information-processing benefits just as full inclusion of women can alter the agenda and decisions of the group, the process of deliberation is rarely free of the inequalities of social status, race, and gender. These problems can be addressed, but specific conditions must be in place to do so. As Esterling et al. (2012) show, other forms of heterogeneity, such as preference heterogeneity, can have complicated effects on the quality and outcomes of deliberation. Process research can also identify biases that are not anticipated by normative scholars, such as Myers's finding (2012a) that the influence of an argument depends on whether the argument is introduced by someone who shares the majority's interests, not just on the informational value of the argument.

A number of factors that make research on deliberative processes particularly difficult are worth noting. Process variables can be difficult to operationalize, particularly when they are drawn from normative theory. Notice, for example, the different ways that the DQI and Stromer-Galley (2007) operationalize key normative concepts, and the fact that even their extensive and detailed typologies ignore storytelling, an element that Black (2009) and Polletta (2008) find to be crucial (see also Ryfe, 2006). Other key concepts, such as a speaker's direct engagement of other speakers, are rarely operationalized (see Kathlene, 1994 and Karpowitz & Mendelberg, 2014 for an attempt that relies on interruptions). Self-report measures of process are highly problematic, and both psychological and normative theories require attention to the actual words that are spoken in deliberation, but coding conversation is difficult and time-consuming.

4. CONTEXT OF DELIBERATION

Small-group deliberation does not happen in a vacuum and rarely happens spontaneously (Ryfe, 2002). It is generally organized by some existing group[4] and is shaped by the broader political context in which it takes place. For example, the alternatives to deliberation in the broader political context shape the deliberation; Karpowitz (2006) suggests that the availability of adversarial political means for influencing the policy process can cause people who feel that they are disadvantaged in deliberation to disengage from it. Deliberation is also shaped by the decisions made by organizers about how to structure group discussion: procedural and decision rules and practices, settings, moderators, and so on. Organizers of a deliberation may have their own policy agenda (Cramer-Walsh, 2007), and there is a danger that they may use control over agendas, briefing materials or procedural rules to shape debate. Jacobs et al. (2009, chaps. 4 and 6) find much diversity in the topics and institutional structures of deliberation. We refer to these variables as the context of deliberation.[5]

4.1. The Medium of Deliberation: Face to Face versus Online

While deliberation is naturally conceived of as occurring face-to-face, holding deliberative forums online can reduce costs and make them more accessible to citizens (Price & Cappella, 2007). While proponents of online deliberation acknowledge that such deliberation is different in a number of ways, including "reduced social cues, [the] relative anonymity of participants, and a reliance on text-based exchanges lacking non-verbal, facial and vocal cues," they argue that such differences are not fatal flaws. Indeed, they might prove advantageous by "facilitat[ing] open exchanges of controversial political ideas" (Price, 2009, p. 37). At the very least, these differences in the deliberative experience may create significant differences in the psychological processes involved in deliberation.

Several major research projects have examined the effects of online deliberation on opinion formation (Luskin, Fishkin, & Iyengar, 2004, Price & Cappella, 2007).[6] Like face-to-face deliberation, online deliberation appears to increase political sophistication, foster opinion change, and drive higher levels of social trust and political participation (Price & Cappella, 2007; 2009). These results suggest that online deliberation affects a range of outcome variables similar to those affected by face-to-face deliberation.

Only a few experimental studies explicitly compare online deliberation to offline deliberation, making it hard to tell whether the differences between the formats result in meaningful differences in the size of these effects. What research exists suggests that the context-poor condition of online deliberation means that effects of online deliberation are similar to offline, but smaller in magnitude. (Luskin et al., 2004; Min, 2007; Grönlund, 2009). Min (2007) found that online deliberation produced slightly less of an increase in efficacy than offline deliberation on the same topic, and unlike face-to-face deliberation produced no statistically significant increase in intentions to engage in political participation. Further, what evidence exists suggests that the lack of social context does not make online deliberation more conducive to the exchange of controversial ideas. Min (2007) found that participants in face-to-face deliberation were more likely to feel that deliberation had been characterized by a high level of respect than participants in online deliberation. Luskin et al. (2004) claim that the attitudes of groups engaged in online deliberation are somewhat more likely to polarize and converge within groups, paradoxically suggesting that the forces of social conformity discussed in the processes section are harder to resist in the online environment.

Baek, Wojcieszak, and Delli Carpini (2012) and Wojcieszak, Baek, and Delli Carpini (2009) used survey data of people who report participating in face-to-face or online deliberation to compare the two formats. They found that participants in online deliberation are more likely to be white and male, and not notably more diverse in other respects than face-to-face deliberators. Interestingly, participants in online deliberation perceive their fellow deliberators as more diverse than participants in face-to-face deliberation. Online deliberation does attract more moderates, perhaps because of its lower cost to participants. Participation in the two formats appears to be motivated differently; face-to-face deliberators report more community focused motivations, while online deliberators more individualistic motivations. Online deliberators were less likely to report that their discussion produced consensus, prodded participants to take further action, or taught factual knowledge than offline deliberators, and online deliberators reported experiencing more negative emotions during discussion.

4.2. Moderators

Designers of deliberative institutions believe that moderators can improve deliberation by keeping groups on task, managing conflict, and ensuring that everyone has a chance to speak (Mansbridge, Hartz-Karp, Amengual, & Gastil, 2006). Others argue that moderators have a negative effect by using their privileged position to exert influence over the outcome of deliberation (e.g., Humphreys et al., 2006). These concerns stem from research in the psychology on jury forepersons. While dormant recently, this literature suggests that forepersons tend to be of higher SES than the average juror and exert disproportionate influence, relative to other jurors, over jury decisions and the content of deliberation (Hastie, Penrod, & Pennington, 1983, Strodtbeck & Lipinski, 1985; see Devine, Clayton, Dunford, Seying, & Pryce, 2001 for a review). This evidence suggests to critics of deliberation that the presence of moderators will bias discussion toward those already privileged by the political system (Sanders, 1997).

Surprisingly little research has examined the possible positive and negative effects of moderation. Pierce et al. (2008) found that moderators increase low-status deliberators' perceptions that all participants had an opportunity to participate and make these deliberators feel more comfortable. A study of online discussions assigned some groups to trained, active facilitators and other groups to basic, bare-bones facilitation. It found that active facilitation limits the gap between men's and women's participation in the forum, though it did not include a "no facilitation" control condition (Trénel, 2009). On the negative side, Humphreys et al. (2006) used the random assignment of discussion leaders to groups in a national forum in São Tomé and Principe to show that the policy preferences of these leaders exert a great deal of influence over the decisions groups reached (though see Imai & Yamamoto, 2010 for a methodological critique of this finding). Spada and Vreeland (2011) found that moderators who made semiscripted, nonneutral interventions during the deliberation were successful at shifting group opinion toward the side favored by the minority, but less successful at reinforcing the view supported by a majority in the group. Thus the possible benefits of facilitators in increasing

social equality and airing a variety of views may be offset by the possible disproportionate and perhaps unnoticed influence that they have on the direction of discussion
and the group's ultimate decision. Still, no published study looking at possible negative
influences of moderators compares moderated groups to unmoderated groups, and
the theory of how moderators might have either positive or negative effects remains
underdeveloped.

4.3. Decision Rules

When group deliberation ends with a decision, the decision rule used may have a significant impact on the form discussion takes. Much of the evidence in this regard comes
from the study of juries, which usually decide by unanimous rule but occasionally use
majority rule. Such studies have found that unanimous rule can lead groups to spend
more time talking (Davis, Hulbert, Au, Chen, & Zarnoth, 1997), to focus more on normative arguments (Kaplan & Miller, 1987), to believe more often that the deliberation
was fair and comprehensive (Kameda, 1991; Kaplan & Miller, 1987), to accept the group
decision more frequently (Kameda, 1991), and more frequent shifting of individual
jurors' views (Hastie et al., 1983). Group consensus generated through talk can also lead
to increased cooperative behavior (Bouas & Komorita, 1996). In sum, unanimous rule
appears to create the expectation that the group will behave as one, while majority rule
implies that individuals are expected to focus more on individual interests (Mansbridge,
1980). If consensus aids otherwise quiescent participants with distinct views, it will contribute to the exchange of diverse perspectives.

However, the literature also offers contradictory findings. Consensus pressures can
silence participants and are not always conducive to airing deep conflicts (Mansbridge,
1980; Karpowitz & Mansbridge, 2005). Falk and Falk (1981) found that majority decision rule may counteract inequities of influence more effectively than unanimous
rule. Miller, Jackson, Mueller, and Schersching (1987) conclude that the unanimity
requirement sometimes increases rejection of minority views. When simulated juries
are instructed to choose unanimously or with near unanimity, they frequently adopt
an implicit norm that squashes the minority view (Davis, Kameda, Parks, Stasson, &
Zimmerman,1989; Davis, Stasson, Ono, & Zimmerman, 1988). Finally, a substantial
game-theoretic literature claims that unanimous rule encourages jurors to strategically hide information that points toward innocence, as conviction requires unanimous
assent (Guarnaschelli et al., 2000, Austen-Smith & Feddersen, 2006; Goeree & Yariv,
2011). Unanimous rule may thus exacerbate rather than remedy the quiescence of
minority members. Finally, little is known about the effects of not having a group decision at all such as in Deliberative Polls. Removing the need to reach a decision may ameliorate some of the pressures that lead to group polarization or silence minority views
(Luskin et al., 2007), but a sense that a decision is not required may remove the need to
compromise (see Black, 2009).

4.4. Conclusion

Small group deliberation is shaped by a large number of contextual factors. While these factors have received less attention than some process or outcome variables, existing research sheds light on some of their effects. Online deliberation is cheaper and easier, but the less intensive format results in fewer gains from deliberation. The familiarity of deliberators with the issue under discussion as well as the place of that issue and of the deliberation effort in the broader political context can affect the outcomes deliberation produces. Decision rules appear to have large effects on the process and outcome of deliberation. Finally, the effect of moderators on the process of deliberation is complex and deserves further research attention.

As this review should make clear, a wide range of contextual factors remain un- or under-investigated. While we know something about online forums and about moderators, much remains to be learned; the explosion of opportunities for discourse online, in particular, is underexplored. Two still more neglected variables are group size and meeting length and repetition. For example, Jacobs et al. (2009, chap. 4) report substantial variance in the size of deliberative forums. Research on juries suggests that size matters (Devine et al., 2001); future research on deliberation should explore how and when. In addition, deliberations vary from a few minutes to days, and from one-time to a long series of iterations (e.g., Warren & Pearse, 2008). Longer deliberations may allow for more interpersonal connections between deliberators that change the process of discussion, and some studies argue that the nature of personal connections is crucial (Mansbridge, 1980). While certainly not exhaustive, this list suggests that like other areas of deliberation research, contextual research on deliberation remains an open field.

5. Conclusion

Empirical research on political deliberation is in its infancy. Despite this, the existing literature contains a wealth of studies that have begun to identify and illuminate the important questions in the field. In addition to reviewing this literature, we hope that we have provided a useful structure for thinking about deliberation in terms of three categories of variables: outcomes, process, and context. Research on outcomes has shown what outcomes deliberation *can* produce. As the literature develops, we hope that more research will examine *how* these outcomes are produced by the process and context of deliberation. Focusing on the *how* of deliberation has practical as well as normative benefits. As a practical matter, understanding how contexts and processes produce different outcomes will help policymakers with the complicated institutional design questions that come with planning deliberative forums. On the normative side, the same outcome may be more or less normatively preferable depending on the process that produces it. Indeed, simply knowing the outcome of deliberation may tell us little about the normative value of the process that produced it.

Research on deliberation is shaped by its connection to contemporary democratic theory, a connection that sets it apart from much of the other research discussed in this handbook (Mutz, 2008; Thompson, 2008). The best research in the studies we have reviewed makes use of this connection by taking seriously the demands of normative theory and turning these demands into usable empirical measures. Echoing Mutz (2008), we agree that empirical political science cannot "test" deliberative democracy because deliberative democracy is an ideal. Instead, empirical research on deliberation can take the yardstick of that ideal and use it to create better, more legitimate deliberative institutions that come closer to the deliberative ideal, as well identifying those situations where deliberation is so difficult or detrimental that it is not worthwhile. Like any political process, deliberation can never reach the ideal. Nevertheless, finding ways to bring political institutions closer to the deliberative ideal is a useful and laudable project for political psychology.

As deliberation becomes a more important part of political process, the research discussed in this chapter will only grow in importance. Jacobs et al. (2009) show that deliberation, broadly defined, is a fairly common form of political participation—more common than frequently studied forms of participation such as volunteering or giving money to a campaign. While some fear that deliberation might be harmful to democracy (Hibbing & Theiss-Morse, 2002), or that deliberation is at odds with participatory democracy (Mutz, 2006), other research suggests that deliberation is uniquely well suited to increasing the participation of citizens who feel alienated from normal politics (Neblo et al., 2010). Further, research is beginning to point to structures and processes that can be used to actualize deliberation's potential (Karpowitz & Mendelberg, 2012; Wantchekon, 2011). Deliberative methods are now used in policy fields as diverse as criminal justice, environmental policy, international development, and bioethics. Empirical guidance from political psychology can help ensure that these efforts achieve the goals of normative theory.

Notes

1. We are building on other overviews here: Neblo (2007), Mutz (2008) Ryfe (2005), and De Vries et.al. (2011).
2. See also Gastil et. al. 2008a, Andersen and Hansen, 2007.
3. For related experimental evidence see Stromer-Galley and Muhlberger (2009).
4. For more on groups that organize deliberative forums, see Jacobs et al. (2009, ch. 7) and Ryfe (2002).
5. One topic requiring more research is the effect of the issue. Existing research has shown that attitude change is greater on unfamiliar than on familiar issues (Farrar et al. 2010). Also, the issue can shape inequality; local boards dealing with topics that society constructs as more feminine tend to have much higher proportions of women (Hannagan and Larimer, 2010). More research is needed on issue type and its effects.
6. There is, of course considerable variation in the format of online deliberation. For example, Luskin et. al. (2004) conduct an online deliberation where deliberators speak into a

microphone, allowing for voice communication, while most online deliberation uses text communication (Min, 2007). The effects of these specific variations are an interesting topic for future research.

References

Andersen, V. N., & Hansen, K. M. (2007). How deliberation makes better citizens: The Danish Deliberative Poll on the euro. *European Journal of Political Research, 46*, 531–556.

Arrow, K. (1953). *Social choice and individual values.* New York: Wiley.

Austen-Smith, D., & Feddersen, T. J. (2006). Deliberation, preference uncertainty, and voting rules. *American Journal of Political Science, 100*, 209–217.

Baek, Y. M., Wojcieszak, M., & Delli Carpini, M. X. (2012). Online versus face-to-face deliberation: Who? Why? What? With what effects? *New Media & Society, 14*, 363–383.

Ban, R., & Rao, V. (2009). Is deliberation equitable? Evidence from transcripts of village meetings in South India. World Bank Policy Research Working Paper No. 4928.

Barabas, J. (2004). How deliberation affects policy opinions. *American Political Science Review, 98*, 687–701.

Benhabib, S. (Ed.). (1996). *Democracy and difference: Contesting the boundaries of the political.* Princeton, NJ: Princeton University Press.

Besley, T., Pande, R., & Rao, V. (2005). Participatory democracy in action: Survey evidence from South India. *Journal of the European Economic Association, 3*, 648–657.

Black, L. W. (2009). Listening to the city: Difference, identity, and storytelling in online deliberative groups. *Journal of Public Deliberation, 5*, Article 4.

Bouas, K. S., & Komorita, S. S. (1996). Group discussion and cooperation in social dilemmas. *Personality and Social Psychology Bulletin, 22*, 1144–1150.

Bryan, F. M. (2004). *Real democracy: The New England town meeting and how it works.* Chicago: University of Chicago Press.

Cappella, J. N., Price, V., & Nir, L. (2002). Argument repertoire as a reliable and valid measure of opinion quality: Electronic dialogue during campaign 2000. *Political Communication, 19*(1), 73–93.

Conover, P. J., Searing, D. D., & Crewe, I. M. (2002). The deliberative potential of political discussion. *British Journal of Political Science, 32*, 21–62.

Converse, P. E. (1964). The nature of belief systems in mass publics. In D. E. Apter (ed.), *Ideology and its discontents* (pp. 206–261). New York: Free Press of Glencoe.

Cohen, J. (1989). Deliberation and democratic legitimacy. In A. Hamlin & P. Pettit (eds.), *The good polity: Normative analysis of the state* (pp. 17–34). Cambridge: Basil Blackwell.

Davis, J. H., Hulbert, L., Au, W. T., Chen, X., & Zarnoth, P. (1997). Effects of group size and procedural influence on consensus judgments of quantity: The examples of damage award and mock civil juries. *Journal of Personality and Social Psychology, 73*, 703–718.

Davis, J. H., Kameda, T., Parks, C., Stasson, M., & Zimmerman, S. (1989). Some social mechanics of group decision making: The distribution of opinion, polling sequence, and implications for consensus. *Journal of Personality and Social Psychology, 57*, 1000–1012.

Davis, J. H., Stasson, M., Ono, K., & Zimmerman, S. (1988). Effects of straw polls on group decision making: Sequential voting pattern, timing, and local majorities. *Journal of Personality and Social Psychology, 55*, 918–926.

Devine, J., Clayton, L. D., Dunford, B. B., Seying, R., & Pryce, J. (2001). Jury decision making: 45 years of empirical research on deliberating groups. *Psychology, Public Policy, and Law, 7,* 622–727.

De Vries R., Stanczyk A., Ryan K., & Kim, S. Y. (2011). A framework for assessing the quality of democratic deliberation: Enhancing deliberation as a tool for bioethics. *Journal of Empirical Research on Human Research Ethics, 6*(3), 3–17.

Druckman, J. N. (2004). Political preference formation: Competition, deliberation, and the (ir) relevance of framing effects. *American Political Science Review, 98,* 671–686.

Druckman, J. N., & Nelson, K. R. (2003). Framing and deliberation: How citizens' conversations limit elite influence. *American Journal of Political Science, 47,* 729–745.

Dryzek, J. K. (2000). *Deliberative democracy and beyond: Liberals, critics, contestation.* Oxford: Oxford University Press.

Eliasoph, N. (1998). *Avoiding politics: How Americans produce apathy in everyday life.* Cambridge: Cambridge University Press.

Esterling, K. M., Fung, A., & Lee, T. (2012). How much disagreement is good for democratic deliberation? The California Speaks health care experiment. Presented at the University of Michigan Health Policy Research Seminar Series, Ann Arbor.

Esterling, K. M., Neblo, M. A., & Lazer, D. M. J. (2011). Means, motive, & opportunity in becoming informed about politics: A deliberative field experiment with members of Congress and their constituents. *Public Opinion Quarterly, 75,* 483–503.

Estlund, D. (2000). Political quality. *Social Philosophy and Policy, 17,* 127–160.

Falk, G., & Falk, S. (1981). The impact of decision rules on the distribution of power in problem solving teams with unequal power. *Group and Organization Studies, 6,* 211–223.

Farrar, C., Fishkin, J. S., Green, D. P., List, C., Luskin, R. C., & Paluck, E. L. (2010). Disaggregating deliberation's effects: An experiment with a Deliberative Poll. *British Journal of Political Science, 40,* 333–347. doi:10.1017/S0007123409990433

Farrar, C., Green, D. P., Green, J. E., Nickerson, D. W., & Shewfelt, S. (2009). Does discussion group composition affect policy preferences? Results from three randomized experiments. *Political Psychology, 30,* 615–647.

Fishkin, J. S. (2009). *When the people speak: Deliberative democracy and public consultation.* Oxford: Oxford University Press.

Forester, J. (1999). *The deliberative practitioner: Encouraging participatory planning processes.* Cambridge, MA: MIT Press.

Fung, A. (2004). *Empowered participation: Reinventing urban democracy.* Princeton, NJ: Princeton University Press.

Gastil, J. (2000). *By popular demand: Revitalizing representative democracy through deliberative elections.* Berkeley: University of California Press.

Gastil, J., Bacci, C., & Dollinger, M. (2010). Is deliberation neutral? Patterns of attitude change during "the Deliberative Polls." *Journal of Public Deliberation, 6*(2), Article 3.

Gastil, J., Black, L., & Moscovitz, K. (2008). Ideology, attitude change, and deliberation in small face-to-face groups. *Political Communication, 25,* 23–46.

Gastil, J., Deess, E. P., Weiser, P., & Meade, J. (2008). Jury service and electoral participation: A test of the participation hypothesis. *Journal of Politics, 70,* 1–16. doi:10.1017/S0022381608080353

Gastil, J., Deess, E. P., Weiser, P. J., Simmons, C. (2010). *The jury and democracy: How jury deliberation promotes civic engagement and political participation.* New York: Oxford University Press.

Gastil, J., & Dillard, J. P. (1999). Increasing political sophistication through public deliberation. *Political Communication, 16*, 3–23. doi:10.1080/105846099198749

Gilens, M. (2011). Two-thirds full? Citizen competence and democratic governance. In A. J. Berinsky (ed.), *New Directions in Public Opinion* (pp. 52–76). New York: Taylor and Francis.

Goeree, J. K., & Yariv, L. (2011). An experimental study of collective deliberation. *Econometrica, 79*, 893–921.

Goodin, R. E., & Niemeyer, S. J. (2003). When does deliberation begin? Internal reflection versus public discussion in deliberative democracy. *Political Studies, 51*, 627–649.

Grönlund, K., Strandberg, K., & Himmelroos, S. (2009). The challenge of deliberative democracy online—a comparison of face-to-face and virtual experiments in citizen deliberation. *Information Polity, 14*, 187–201. doi:10.3233/IP-2009-0182

Guarnaschelli, S., McKelvey, R. D., & Palfrey, T. R. (2000). An experimental study of jury decision rules. *American Political Science Review, 94*, 407–423.

Gutmann, A., & Thompson, D. (1996). *Democracy and disagreement.* Cambridge, MA: Harvard University Press.

Gutmann, A., & Thompson, D. (2004). *Why deliberative democracy?* Princeton, NJ: Princeton University Press.

Habermas, J. (1975). *Legitimation crisis* (T. McCarthy, trans.). (Boston, MA: Beacon.

Habermas, J. (1996). *Between facts and norms: Contributions to a discourse theory of law and democracy* W. Rehg, trans.). Cambridge, MA: MIT Press.

Hannagan, R. J., & Larimer, C. W. (2010). Does gender composition affect group decision outcomes? Evidence from a laboratory experiment. *Political Behavior, 32*, 51–67.

Harris-Perry, M. V. (2004). *Barbershops, Bibles, and BET: Everyday talk and black political thought.* Princeton, NJ: Princeton University Press.

Hastie, R., Penrod, S. D., & Pennington, N. (1983). *Inside the jury.* Cambridge, MA: Harvard University Press.

Hibbing, J. R., & Theiss-Morse, E. (2002). *Stealth democracy: Americans' beliefs about how government should work.* Cambridge: Cambridge University Press.

Humphreys, M., Masters, W. A., & Sandbu, M. E. (2006). The role of leaders in democratic deliberations: Results from a field experiment in São Tomé and Príncipe. *World Politics, 58*, 583–622.

Imai, K., & Yamamoto, T. (2010). Causal inference with differential measurement error: Nonparametric identification and sensitivity analysis. *American Journal of Political Science, 54*, 543–560.

Jacobs, L. R., Cook, F. L., & Delli Carpini, M. X. (2009). *Talking together: Public deliberation and political participation in America.* Chicago: University of Chicago Press.

Kameda, T. (1991). Procedural influence in small-group decision making: Deliberation style and assigned decision rule. *Journal of Personality and Social Psychology, 61*, 245–256.

Kaplan, M. F., & Miller, C. E. (1987). Group decision making and normative vs. informational influence: Effects of type of issue and assigned decision rule. *Journal of Personality and Social Psychology, 53*, 306–313.

Karpowitz, C. F. (2006). Having a say: Public hearings, deliberation, and democracy in America. PhD dissertation, Princeton University.

Karpowitz, C. F., & Mansbridge, J. (2005). Disagreement and consensus: The importance of dynamic updating in public deliberation. In J. Gastil & P. Levine (eds.), *The deliberative democracy handbook: Strategies for effective civic engagement in the 21st century* (pp. 237–253). San Francisco, CA: Jossey-Bass.

Karpowitz, C. F., & Mendelberg, T. (2014). *The silent sex: Gender, deliberation and institutions.* Princeton, NJ: Princeton University Press.

Karpowitz, C. F., Mendelberg, T., & Shaker, L. (2012). Gender inequality in deliberation. *American Political Science Review, 106,* 533–547.

Karpowitz, C. F., Raphael, C., & Hammond, A. S., IV. (2009). Deliberative democracy and inequality: Two cheers for enclave deliberation among the disempowered. *Politics & Society, 37,* 576–615.

Kathlene, L. (1994). Power and influence in state legislative policymaking: The interaction of gender and position in committee hearing debates. *American Political Science Review, 88,* 560–576.

Knight, J., & Johnson, J. (1997). What sort of equality does deliberative democracy require? In J. Bohman & W. Rehg (eds.), *Deliberative democracy: Essays on reason and politics* (pp. 279–320). Cambridge, MA: MIT Press.

Lazer, D. M., Sokhey, A. E., Neblo, M. A., & Esterling, K. M. (2010). Expanding the conversation: Ripple effects from a deliberative field experiment. Working paper, Ohio State University.

Lu, L., Yuan, Y. C., & McLeod, P. L. (2012). Twenty-five years of hidden profiles in group decision making: A meta-analysis. *Personality and Social Psychology Review, 16,* 54–75.

Luskin, R. C., Fishkin, J. S., & Hahn, K. S. (2007). Consensus and polarization in small group deliberations. Prepared for presentation at the annual meeting of the American Political Science Association, Chicago, IL.

Luskin, R. C., Fishkin, J. S., & Iyengar, S. (2004). Considered opinions on U.S. foreign policy: Face-to-face versus online Deliberative Polling. Working paper, Center for Deliberative Democracy, Stanford University.

Luskin, R. C., Fishkin, J. S., & Jowell, R. (2002). Considered opinions: Deliberative polling in Britain. *British Journal of Political Science, 32,* 455–487. doi:10.1017/S0007123402000194

Luskin, R. C., Helfer, A., & Sood, G. (2011). Measuring learning in informative processes. Working paper, University of Texas, Austin.

Mansbridge, J. J. (1980). *Beyond adversary democracy.* New York: Basic Books.

Mansbridge, J. J. (1999). On the idea that political participation makes better citizens. In S. L. Elkin & K. E. Soltan (eds.), *Citizen competence and democratic institutions* (pp. 291–326). University Park: Pennsylvania State University Press.

Mansbridge, J. J., Hartz-Karp, J., Amengual, M., & Gastil, J. (2006). Norms of deliberation: An inductive study. *Journal of Public Deliberation, 2,* Article 7.

Mendelberg, T. (2002). The deliberative citizen: Theory and evidence. In M. X. Delli Carpini, L. Huddy, & R. Shapiro (eds.), *Research in micropolitics: Political decisionmaking, deliberation and participation,* (6th ed., pp. 151–193). Greenwich, CT: JAI Press.

Mendelberg, T., & Oleske, J. (2000). Race and public deliberation. *Political Communication, 17,* 169–191.

Mendelberg, T., Karpowitz, N., & Goedert, N. (2013). Does descriptive representation facilitate women's distinctive voice? How gender composition and decision rules affect deliberation. Paper presented at the John F. Kennedy School of Government, March 14.

Miller, C. E., Jackson, P., Mueller, J., & Schersching, C. (1987). Some social psychological effects of group decision rules. *Journal of Personality and Social Psychology, 52*(2), 325–332.

Min, S.-J. (2007). Online vs. face-to-face deliberation: Effects on civic engagement. *Journal of Computer-Mediated Communication, 12,* 1369–1387. doi:10.1111/j.1083-6101.2007.00377.x

Morrell, M. E. (2005). Deliberation, democratic decision-making and internal political efficacy. *Political Behavior, 27,* 49–69.

Morrell, M. E. (2010). *Empathy and Democracy*. University Park, PA: The Pennsylvania State University Press.

Mutz, D. C. (2006). *Hearing the other side: Deliberative versus participatory democracy*. Cambridge: Cambridge University Press.

Mutz, D. C. (2008). Is deliverable democracy a falsifiable theory? *Annual Review of Political Science, 11*, 521–538. doi:10.1146/annurev.polisci.11.081306.070308

Myers, C. D. (2011). Information use in small group deliberation. PhD dissertation, Princeton University.

Myers, C. D. (2012a). Interests, information, and minority influence in political deliberation. Paper presented at the Annual Meeting of the Midwest Political Science Association, April, Chicago, IL.

Myers, C. D. (2012b). Political Deliberation, Interest Conflict and the Common Knowledge Effect. Paper presented at the Annual Meeting of the International Society for Political Psychology, July, Chicago, IL.

Nabatchi, T. (2010). Deliberative democracy and citizenship: In search of the efficacy effect. *Journal of Public Deliberation, 6*, Article 8.

Neblo, M. A. (2005). Thinking through democracy: Between the theory and practice of deliberative politics. *Acta Politica, 40*, 169–181.

Neblo, M. A., Esterling, K. M., Kennedy, R. P., Lazer, D. M. J., & Sokhey, A. E. (2010). Who wants to deliberate—and why? *American Political Science Review, 104* (3). doi:10.1017/S0003055410000298

Owens, S. (2000). "Engaging the public": Information and deliberation in environmental policy. *Environment and Planning A, 32*, 1141–1148.

Pierce, J. L., Neeley, G., & Budziak, J. (2008). Can deliberative democracy work in hierarchical organizations? *Journal of Public Deliberation, 4*, Article 14.

Polletta, F. (2008). Just talk: Public deliberation after 9/11. *Journal of Public Deliberation, 4*(1), Article 2.

Posner, R. (2004). Smooth sailing. *Legal Affairs*, January–February, Article 3.

Price, V. (2009). Citizens deliberating online: Theory and some evidence. In T. Davies & S. Gangadharan (eds.), *Online deliberation: Design, research, and practice* (pp. 37–58). Stanford, CA: CSLI Publications.

Price, V., & Cappella, J. N. (2007). Healthcare dialogue: Project highlights. The Proceedings of the Eighth Annual International Digital Government Research Conference.

Price, V., Nir, L., & Cappella, J. N. (2006). Normative and informational influence in online political discussions. *Communication Theory, 16*(1), 47–74.

Rawls, J. (1971). *A theory of justice*. Cambridge, MA: Belknap Press of Harvard University Press.

Rosenberg, S. W. (2007). Types of discourse and the democracy of deliberation. In S. Rosenberg (ed.), *Deliberation, participation and democracy: Can the people govern?* Basingstoke, UK: Palgrave Macmillan, pp. 130-158.

Ryfe, D. M. (2002). The practice of deliberative democracy: A study of 16 deliberative organizations. *Political Communication, 19*, 359–377.

Ryfe, D. M. (2005). Does deliberative democracy work? *Annual Review of Political Science, 8*, 49–71. doi:0.1146/annurev.polisci.8.032904.154633

Ryfe, D. M. (2006). Narrative and Deliberation in Small Group forums. *Journal of Applied Communication Research, 34*, 72–93.

Sanders, L. M. (1997). Against deliberation. *Political Theory, 25*, 347–376.

Schkade, D., Sunstein, C. R., & Hastie, R. (2007). What happened on deliberation day? *California Law Review, 95*, 915–940.

Simon, A. F., & Sulkin, T. (2002). Discussion's impact on political allocations: An experimental approach. *Political Analysis, 10*, 403–412. doi:10.1093/pan/10.4.403

Sommers, S. R. (2006). On racial diversity and group decision-making: Identifying multiple effects of racial composition on jury deliberations. *Journal of Personality and Social Psychology, 90*, 597–612.

Sommers, S. R. (2007). Race and the decision making of juries. *Legal and Criminological Psychology, 12*, 171–187.

Spada, P., & Vreeland, J. R. (2011). Participatory decision making: A field experiment on manipulating the votes. Working paper, Yale University.

Steenbergen, M. R., Bächtiger, A., Spörndli, M., & Steiner, J. (2003). Measuring political deliberation: A discourse quality index. *Comparative European Politics, 1*(1), 21–48.

Steiner, J., Bächtiger, A., Spörndli, M., & Steenbergen, M. R. (2004). *Deliberative politics in action: Analysing parliamentary discourse.* New York: Cambridge University Press.

Strodtbeck, F. L., & Lipinski, R. M. (1985). Becoming first among equals: Moral considerations in jury foreman selection. *Journal of Personality and Social Psychology, 49*, 927–936.

Stromer-Galley, J. (2007). Measuring deliberation's content: A coding scheme. *Journal of Public Deliberation, 3*(1), Article 12.

Stromer-Galley, J., & Muhlberger, P. (2009). Agreement and disagreement in group deliberation: Effects on deliberation satisfaction, future engagement, and decision legitimacy. *Political Communication, 26*, 173–192.

Sturgis, P., Roberts, C., & Allum, N. (2005). A different take on the Deliberative Poll information, deliberation and attitude constraint. *Public Opinion Quarterly, 69*, 30–65.

Sunstein, C. R. (2002). The law of group polarization. *Journal of Political Philosophy, 10*, 175–195.

Sunstein, C. R. (2006). *Infotopia.* Oxford: Oxford University Press.

Thompson, D. F. (2008). Deliberative democratic theory and empirical political science. *Annual Review of Political Science, 11*, 497–520. doi:10.1146/annurev.polisci.11.081306.070555

Trénel, M. (2009). Facilitation and inclusive deliberation. In T. Davies & S. P. Gangadharan (eds.), *Online deliberation: Design, research, and practice* (pp. 253–257). Stanford, CA: CSLI Publications.

Vinokur, A., & Burnstein, E. (1978). Depolarization of attitudes in groups. *Journal of Personality and Social Psychology, 36*, 872–885.

Walsh, K. C. (2003). The democratic potential of civic dialogue on race. Paper prepared for presentation at the Annual Meeting of the Midwest Political Science Association, April, Chicago, IL.

Walsh, K. C. (2007). *Talking about race: Community dialogues and the politics of difference.* Chicago: University of Chicago Press.

Wantchekon, L. (2011). Deliberative electoral strategies and transition from clientelism: Experimental evidence from Benin. Working paper, Princeton University.

Warren, M., & Pearse, H. (2008). *Designing deliberative democracy: The British Columbia citizens' assembly.* Cambridge: Cambridge University Press.

Weber, L. M. (2001). The effect of democratic deliberation on political tolerance. PhD dissertation, University of Colorado, Boulder.

Wilson, J. L. (2011). Deliberation, democracy, and the rule of reason in Aristotle's Politics. *American Political Science Review, 105*, 259–275. doi:10.1017/S0003055411000086

Wojcieszak, M. (2011a). Deliberation and attitude polarization. *Journal of Communication, 61*(4), 596–617.

Wojcieszak, M. (2011b). Pulling toward or pulling away: Deliberation, disagreement, and opinion extremity in political participation. *Social Science Quarterly, 92*(1), 207–225.

Wojcieszak, M., Baek, Y. M., & Delli Carpini, M. X. (2009). What is really going on? *Information Communication & Society, 12*(7), 1080–1102.

Wojcieszak, M., Baek, Y. M., & Delli Carpini, M. X. (2010). Deliberative and participatory democracy? Ideological strength and the processes leading from deliberation to political engagement. *International Journal of Public Opinion Research, 22*(2), 154–180.

Wojcieszak, M., & Price, V. (2010). Bridging the divide or intensifying the conflict? How disagreement affects strong predilections about sexual minorities. *Political Psychology, 31*, 315–339. doi: 10.1111/j.1467-9221.2009.00753.x

Young, M. I. (1996). Communication and the other: Beyond deliberative democracy. In S. Benhabib (ed.), *Democracy and difference: Contesting the boundaries of the political* (pp. 120–136). Princeton, NJ: Princeton University Press.

PART IV

INTERGROUP
RELATIONS

CHAPTER 23

FROM GROUP IDENTITY TO POLITICAL COHESION AND COMMITMENT

LEONIE HUDDY

GROUP identities are central to politics, an inescapable conclusion drawn from decades of political behavior research (Huddy, 2003). Partisan identities such as Republican and Democrat in the United States, Conservative and Labour in the UK, Social Democrat and Christian Democrat in Germany, or Labor and Likud in Israel play a very central role in shaping the dynamics of public opinion and electoral choice (Dalton & Wattenberg, 2000; Lewis-Beck, Jacoby, Norpoth, & Weisberg, 2008). Social identities based on race, ethnicity, religion, gender, and other characteristics can generate political cohesion through a shared outlook and conformity to norms of political activity (Miller, Gurin, Gurin, & Malanchuk, 1981). Within a democratic polity, national identities boost support for civic norms, drive democratic engagement, and increase support for a muscular response to national threat (Huddy & Khatib, 2007; Theiss-Morse, 2009). Other specific issue and ideological identities such as pro-environment, feminist, conservative, or right-to-life also generate strong political cohesion and drive commitment to political action (Simon & Klandermans, 2001). An understanding of the psychology of group identification is central to the study of political behavior.

The political relevance of explicitly political identities such as partisanship and left-right ideology is self-evident. The political cohesion of certain racial, ethnic, and religious groups within specific polities such as African Americans in the United States or religious Jews in Israel is also chronically apparent (Shamir & Arian, 1999; Tate, 1994). But most social groups do not cohere politically, or do not do so to any great degree. Sociodemographic groups based on social class, age, gender, or marital status exhibit only very modest levels of political cohesion in the United States and other Western democracies (Dalton, 1996; Huddy, Cassese, & Lizotte, 2008; Lewis-Beck et al., 2008; Wattenberg, 2008). On occasion, a subset of group members develops a cohesive political ideology and outlook. Feminists are an example of a politicized subgroup of women, and gay and lesbian activists form a politicized subgroup of all gays and lesbians (Simon & Klandermans, 2001). Such politicized group identities can merge with explicitly partisan identities to enhance a group's political impact. The conditions under which group identities become politicized, the psychology underlying this process, and the consequences of political identities for political cohesion and engagement are the subject of the current chapter.

The focus throughout this review is on the *political* effects of group membership, although I pay greater attention to political attitudes and electoral behavior than collective action, which is discussed by Klandermans and van Stekelenburg (chapter 24, this volume). I also stress the consequences of group membership for in-group solidarity but spend little time discussing its implications for out-group antipathy, a topic covered by Kinder (chapter 25, this volume). In reviewing a very large literature in both psychology and political science I cannot hope to comprehensively cover psychological research or major theoretical approaches to social identity and intergroup relations, which are well reviewed elsewhere (Ashmore, Deaux, & McLaughlin-Volpe, 2004; Brown, 2000; Ellemers & Haslam, 2012; Hornsey, 2008; Simon, 2004).

1. Group Membership, Group Identification, and Social Identity

Several key definitions are required to better understand the conditions under which group membership leads to a politicized identity. *Group membership* is based on objective inclusion in a group and does not necessitate an internalized sense of membership, although objective group membership is not always clear-cut. Social class in the United States is a classic case of an ambiguous group membership in which the criteria for class membership are not well defined, resulting in Americans of the same income and occupational group varying as to whether they consider themselves working or middle class. Race and ethnic categories are similarly complex and constantly undergoing change in the US census, revealing their subjective underpinnings (Martin, DeMaio, & Campanelli, 1990). Racial and ethnic categories are further complicated for individuals with mixed ancestry. In addition, membership is inherently vague for many if not most political groups. It is difficult, for example, to define membership in a political party when individuals are not required to formally join a political organization.

The ambiguous nature of various social and political groups and the failure of some objective group members to internalize membership heightens the importance of *group identification*, a more restrictive, subjective, and internalized sense of group belonging. I define group identification as an internalized state confined to a subset of objective group members. Objective membership can be difficult to ascertain, but in the end, I regard group membership as a precursor to identification, even if membership is fuzzy or ill-defined.

A *social identity* is a common form of group identification that involves the incorporation of group membership into the self-concept. According to Tajfel, a social identity involves an individual's "knowledge of his membership in a social group (or groups) together with the value and emotional significance attached to the membership" (Tajfel, 1981, p. 255). This also fits Campbell, Converse, Miller, and Stokes's (1960) definition of partisan identification in *The American Voter* as not only a set of beliefs but also feelings that culminate in a sense of "psychological attachment" to a political group—in this instance, Democrats and Republicans. An emphasis on a subjective sense of belonging or identification as a precursor to political cohesion helps to explain why not all groups cohere politically.

Finally, a *political identity* is a social identity with political relevance. Many social identities, such as Asian in the United States, Chinese in Indonesia, or Turk in the Netherlands, lack a distinct political outlook (Freedman, 2000; Junn & Masuoka, 2008; Phalet, Baysu, & Verkuyten, 2010). A political identity can emerge in formerly apolitical groups, however, when group members develop a similar set of political beliefs and adhere to group norms in support of a specific political party, candidate, policy issue, or course of political action (Campbell et al., 1960). Some identities such as being an American Republican or a German Christian Democrat are inherently political. Other political identities emerge from social identities that have gained political content. The concept of political identity lays the groundwork for the development of group-based political cohesion.

2. Major Theoretical Approaches

I consider five broad classes of theory each of which highlights a somewhat different set of active ingredients in the development of group-based political cohesion (for a more exhaustive list, see Brewer & Brown, 1998).[1] My goal is not to evaluate how well each approach accounts for the emergence of group solidarity, but rather to derive a set of underlying factors that account for cohesion. I define *political cohesion* as the existence of shared political attitudes, beliefs, and behavior among group members that can be directly attributed to group membership. A subjective group identity lies at the core of political cohesion and helps to distinguish group-based cohesion from a common political outlook derived from the simple aggregation of individual members' political beliefs.

2.1. Cognitive Approach: Categorization and Group Salience

A cognitive approach underscores the importance of categorization to the development of group cohesion. Self-categorization theory (SCT) attributes group cohesion to cognitive factors such as the situational salience of a group identity that arouses a collective sense of self. The shift from personal to collective identity is accompanied by increased adherence to group norms and heightened self-stereotyping, factors that are logical precursors to political cohesion (Hogg, Hardie, & Reynolds, 1995; Terry & Hogg, 1996; Turner, Hogg, Oakes, Reicher, & Wetherell, 1987). Salience is typically defined as a combination of the readiness to adopt an identity and the relevance of an identity to a given situation, although SCT researchers have paid greater attention to situational factors such as salience than a preexisting readiness to identify with a group (Simon, 2004). Self-categorization is best captured by measures that tap an internalized sense of group belonging, although SCT researchers have typically assumed rather than measured group identity under conditions of group salience (see the exchange on this point between Huddy, 2002 and Oakes, 2002).

Self-categorization theorists have an especially labile view of social identities and their meaning. They draw extensively on categorization research to argue that perceived similarity to a prototypic group member (e.g., Barack Obama for Democrats) plays a key role in the formation and development of a social identity and the emergence of group conformity (Hogg & Hains, 1996; McGarty, Turner, Hogg, David, & Wetherell, 1992; Turner et al., 1987). According to SCT researchers social identities are driven almost completely by one's immediate perceptual context. From their perspective, identities vary, in part, because social categories such as age or gender vary in salience across situations. Indeed, one of the key tenets of self-categorization theory is that individuals constantly shift back and forth between an individual and a social identity (Turner et al., 1987). Thus, within a cognitive approach group cohesion and conformity rest heavily on the salience of group membership.

2.2. Realistic Interest Approaches

Realistic interest approaches include realistic group conflict, relative deprivation, social dominance theory, and Blumer's sense of group position (Blumer, 1958; Bobo & Hutchings, 1996; Sidanius & Pratto, 2001; see Brown, 2010 for an overview). They suggest collectively that group membership is politically consequential to the extent that tangible group gains and losses drive group members' political decisions. Realistic interest theories include the protection of self-interests and group interests that might indicate short-term or long-term interests that are objective or subjective, direct or indirect (Bobo, 1983). Thus the unemployed might cohere politically around their mutual reliance on monthly unemployment benefits; the elderly could unite over threats to cut Social Security benefits or other national old-age pensions; and immigrants could unify in opposition to programs that deny them national rights and benefits.

In most studies of Americans' policy preferences, self-interest has had very circumscribed and limited effects on a range of policies, including support for unemployment policies, taxation, busing, women's issues, bilingual education, and immigration (Hainmuller & Hiscox, 2010; Sears & Funk, 1991). The political effects of self-interest are most pronounced when government decisions or actions have large, clear, and certain effects on an individual's interests (Sears & Funk, 1991). At times, self-interest can motivate political action (Begley & Alker, 1982; Green & Cowden, 1992). But the political effects of self-interest need to be disentangled from those of group interest, which is often more powerful politically (Bobo, 1983). For example, perceived economic and political interdependence with other blacks is often used to measure common fate among African Americans (Bobo & Johnson, 2000; Tate, 1994).

Some theorists argue that additional beliefs are needed to create political cohesion even when group members share a sense of common fate (Simon & Klandermans, 2001). Subjective deprivation is critical to *relative deprivation theory*—the perception that one's group's finances, access to power, or other tangible interests are deteriorating or worse than those of other groups (Gay, 2006). Relative deprivation theorists refer to this as a sense of fraternal deprivation and contrast it with egoistic deprivation, which arises when an individual feels personally deprived when compared to an individual or group (Brown, 2010).

2.3. Symbolic Approaches: Social Identity Theory

Social identity theory emphasizes the importance of symbolic concerns such as a group's social standing as central to the development of group cohesion. There are two distinct branches of social identity theory (SIT): the version developed by Tajfel (1981) and Tajfel and Turner (1979) known as social identity theory, and self-categorization theory referred to earlier as a cognitive elaboration of SIT (Turner et al., 1987). Both theories acknowledge the origins of social identity in cognitive and motivational factors, although SCT places greater emphasis on cognitive factors (Hogg, 1996, p. 67). Tajfel concluded that cognitive factors could not solely explain the emergence of intergroup discrimination and believed that motivational factors linked to the protection of group status were central to intergroup behavior. The earliest versions of social identity theory developed by Tajfel (1981) and Tajfel and Turner (1979) placed key emphasis on the need among group members "to differentiate their own groups positively from others to achieve a positive social identity" (Turner et al., 1987, p. 42).

The need for positive group distinctiveness has important political consequences. For instance, it means that group identity and in-group bias emerge readily among members of high-status groups because membership positively distinguishes group members from outsiders (Bettencourt, Dorr, Charlton, & Hume, 2001). In contrast, the development of group identity is less certain among members of low-status groups who need to additionally develop an identity around alternative, positively valued group attributes (social creativity) or fight to change the group's negative image (social change) before membership can enhance their status (Tajfel & Turner, 1979).[2] The motives that contribute to the development of in-group cohesion have been expanded beyond positive distinctiveness to include basic needs such as inclusiveness, distinctiveness, and a need for certainty (Hogg, 2007; Leonardelli, Pickett, & Brewer, 2010).

These motives are discussed in greater detail in reference to individual differences in identity development.

2.4. Social Constructivism and the Meaning of Group Membership

The reach of social constructivism extends well beyond the dynamics of identity, but I include it here for its insight into the development of political cohesion (Duveen, 2001; Erikson, 1993). Social constructivism—the notion that concepts attain meaning through social processes—is implicit within social identity and self-categorization theory, which stress the ease with which social groups and social identities can be created among members of arbitrarily designated groups. As a number of critics have noted, however, social identity theorists have explored the socially fluid nature of identities but have not closely examined or analyzed their meaning (Duveen, 2001; Huddy, 2001; Reicher, 2004). From a social constructivist perspective, it is difficult to understand the consequences of group identification without understanding its subjective meaning to group members (Billig, 1995). This may be especially true for politically relevant identities that are often the target of political manipulation—efforts by politicians and group entrepreneurs to create, define, and redefine identities to serve their political ends (Erikson, 1993; Reicher, 2004).

From a social constructivist perspective, the emphasis on arbitrary groups formed in the laboratory in research on social identity and self-categorization theory may seriously hamper an understanding of both identity acquisition and its consequences (Huddy, 2001). For example, members of diverse subgroups may attach a different meaning to the same identity, such as national identity, depending on their race or ethnicity or the region of the country in which they live (Reicher & Hopkins, 2001; Schildkraut, 2011). Group membership can also take on diverse connotations when its meaning is contested, perhaps for political reasons. To complicate matters further, the internal meaning of a group can be quite different from its external meaning as group members actively reject external derogatory views of the group, for example (Reicher, 2004). Group members may even choose to internalize a group identity because they hold a different conception of what group membership means than objective members who fail to adopt the identity.

2.5. An Evolutionary Perspective

Evolutionary psychologists highlight the functional underpinnings of group identity. They stress the necessity of group coordination for human existence, including basic activities such as childrearing, food gathering, tool development, food production, and group defense (see Sidanius & Kurzban, chapter 7, this volume). From this perspective, an internalized attachment to a small group evolved as a functional necessity for survival. Brewer (2007) argues that the key motive for group cohesion is not to maintain social status or positive distinctiveness, as claimed by SIT researchers, but rather the need to cooperate with other group members for survival purposes (Brewer, 2007; Brewer & Caporael, 2006). She argues that social identity lies at the center of this evolutionary process and believes it plays a critical role in helping group members to keep track of those with whom they need to cooperate and trust.

An evolutionary approach is consistent with evidence that social identities form rapidly on a very minimal basis, and that group members react more strongly to the emotions of in-group than out-group members (Chaio, Bowman, & Gill, 2008; van Bavel, Packer, & Cunningham, 2008). The approach also fits with a nascent body of research hinting at a genetic and biological basis to identity and group cooperation (Dawes & Fowler, 2009; De Dreu, Greer, Van Kleef, Shalvi, & Handgraaf, 2011; Lewis & Bates, 2010).

Several key insights emerge from an evolutionary approach to group cohesion. First and most important, group identities do not necessarily foster out-group antipathy since their primary function is to promote internal cooperation (Halevy, Bornstein, & Sagiv, 2008). A link between identity and out-group hostility arises, however, when the group is threatened, since group defense is a key facet of cooperation for which identities developed (Brewer &Caporael, 2006). Thus the link between in-group identity and out-group hostility revolves around the existence of perceived group threat (Brewer, 2007).

Second, an emphasis on cooperation provides a correction to research that has focused inordinately on the consequences of identities for political conflict. Political psychologists are only now beginning to address a number of intriguing questions concerning the link between identity and political cooperation: To what extent do group identifiers favor government programs that assist fellow group members (Theiss-Morse, 2009)? Follow politics, vote, and engage in other forms of collective political activity (Huddy & Khatib, 2007)? Or value the lives of fellow group members to a greater degree than those of outsiders (Pratto & Glasford, 2008)?

Third, an evolutionary approach underscores the importance to group cohesion of group norms that foster cooperation and promote the punishment of transgressors. This insight fits with a growing body of research that emphasizes group norms as a key to understanding political cohesion.

2.6. Contrasting the Five Approaches

These five theoretical approaches highlight differing sources of commonality among members, place differing emphasis on the importance of conflicting interests with an out-group, emphasize different types of groups as candidates for political mobilization, and stress different types of issues around which members are likely to mobilize. The cognitive approach predicts cohesion among the members of a politically salient group; realistic interest theory confines cohesion to groups whose members share a common fate; social identity theory points to heightened unity among members of groups whose status is threatened; a social constructivist perspective predicts cohesion among members who share a common understanding of the political implications of group membership; and an evolutionary approach stresses the importance of identity for the development of cooperation and the emergence of intergroup conflict under conditions of threat.

3. From Social Identity to Political Cohesion

Membership in a social group does not necessarily prescribe a specific political outlook, nor does it dictate political action on a group's behalf. Several factors are central to the development of political cohesion: the existence of strong identities, convergent identities, the political meaning of group membership, the existence of symbolic and realistic threats and grievances, and group consciousness.

3.1. Strong, Subjective Group Identity

Political cohesion rests on the development of strong, subjective identities. But even weak subjective identities have a more powerful influence on political membership than objective group membership. The earliest voting studies provided evidence of greater support for the Democratic Party among Jews, union leaders, and blacks who felt close to their respective membership groups (Berelson, Lazarsfeld, & McPhee, 1954; Campbell et al., 1960). Within contemporary American politics, African Americans have remained politically cohesive, and this is driven in large part by subjective identity. Blacks who identify strongly with their race are more likely than others to support the Democratic Party and take a progroup, liberal position on a variety of racial and social welfare issues (Tate, 1994). The political power of racial and ethnic identity extends to other groups as well. Sidanius, Levin, van Laar, and Sears (2008) found that UCLA students who were strongly identified with their ethnic group (white, African American, Latino, Asian) were more inclined to vote for a group member and were more willing to demonstrate and sign a petition on behalf of a group-related cause.

Strong identities are equally important in explaining the political effects of identities based on partisanship and ideology. Strong partisans are more likely than weak partisans to exhibit partisan bias in their evaluations of a president and assessment of factual economic and social conditions (Bartels, 2002). Malka and Lelkes (2010) provide experimental evidence that such effects are linked to identity, not beliefs, demonstrating that strong ideologues (liberal or conservative) were more persuaded then weak ideologues to support an American farm subsidy policy if advocated by those who were described as being in their ideological camp regardless of the liberal or conservative thrust of arguments advanced in support of the program (see also Cohen, 2003).[3] When leaders of the major political parties differ in their support of a specific policy, strong, well-informed partisans are the most likely to be exposed to these disagreements and fall in step with party leaders (Green, Palmquist, & Schickler, 2002; Zaller, 1992).

Several studies demonstrate that group salience further enhances the political effects of a strong identity. White Americans are more supportive of spending on minority education when their national identity is salient but are less supportive of the·same program when their racial identity is salient (Transue, 2007). The 9/11 terrorist attacks may have had a similar effect on white Americans. In one study, experimental exposure to information about the events of 9/11 heightened American identity and increased support for multiculturalism policies (Davies, Steele, & Markus, 2008). Partisan and ideological identities are chronically salient within American politics, but others wax and wane in political influence depending on their salience within current political debate. Kam and Ramos (2008) found that national identity shapes presidential approval in periods of national threat, but partisan identity is more powerful in "normal" political times.

Political action is also more common among strong group identifiers. Strong partisans are more likely than weak partisans to have given money or volunteered their time to work for a political candidate or political party, voted, or engaged in other political activities (Fowler & Kam, 2008; Mason, Huddy, & Aarøe, 2012), and strongly identified Americans are more likely to vote (Huddy & Khatib, 2007). There is ample evidence that strong identities also fuel collective action and related forms of group-based political activity (Simon et al., 1998; Klandermans & van Stekelenburg, chapter 24, this volume). Van Zomeren, Postmes, and Spears (2008) offer compelling evidence of the connection between identity and action in a meta-analysis of over 60 studies. In general, the link between identity strength and political action is larger for explicitly political identities such as feminist, conservative, and pro-environment.

Other nonpolitical aspects of group cohesion are also more common among strongly identified group members, helping to explain the maintenance of strong identities over time. For example, strong identifiers feel more positive about members of their group (Simon, Kulla, & Zobel, 1995). At work, a strong company or organizational identity leads to greater job satisfaction, loyalty, and compliance (Tyler & Blader, 2000). In several western European countries, a greater sense of national pride increases tax compliance, an indicator of national cooperation (Torgler & Schneider, 2007). Strongly identified Americans place a higher value on the loss of American than Iraqi lives, leading to their greater opposition to government policies in Iraq that involved the loss of US military troops (Pratto & Glasford, 2008). A strong social identity even provides protective psychological effects under conditions of intense intergroup conflict, as observed in Northern Ireland (Muldoon, Schmid & Downes, 2009).

Finally, a strong identity generates defensiveness in the face of group criticism. For example, priming societal (as opposed to individual) explanations for a lack of African American success resulted in greater defensiveness among white students strongly identified with their race but led to greater support for blacks among weakly identified whites (Andreychick et al., 2009). Strong identifiers tend to draw group boundaries more tightly and are more careful about whom they include within the in-group. They are more exclusive, take longer to decide that a racially ambiguous face belongs to their group than reject an ambiguous face as belonging to the out-group, and define their national group more exclusively in terms of race and ethnicity (Castano, Yzerbyt, Bourguignon, & Seron, 2002; Theiss-Morse, 2009).

In essence, group behavior is heavily dependent on gradations in identity strength, which needs to be well measured to detect its political effects. The measurement of group identification and social identity has taken different paths over time and across social science disciplines (for a more extensive discussion see Huddy, 2003). In political science, partisanship, which is the most common political identity, is usually measured with a single question. In the United States and elsewhere, respondents are generally asked whether, and the degree to which, they think of themselves as belonging to one or another political party to yield roughly three or four levels of partisan identification strength.

In contrast, social psychologists typically rely on different multiple-item identity scales, including the assessment of subscales that are combined to form an overall measure of identity (Ashmore et al., 2004; Cameron, 2004; Ellemers, Kortekaas, & van Ouwerkerk, 1999; Jackson & Smith, 1999; Luhtanen & Crocker, 1992). Four identity subscales have been used by political psychologists with some frequency. They include the subjective importance of an identity, a subjective sense of belonging, feeling one's status is interdependent with that of other group members, and positive feelings for members of the in-group. These various elements are found in scales developed to measure national (Huddy & Khatib, 2007; Schildkraut, 2011; Sniderman, Hagendoorn, & Prior, 2004; Theiss-Morse, 2009), partisan (Greene, 1999; Mason et al., 2012), and ethnic (Sidanius et al., 2008) identity. The scales exhibit good internal reliability that is reasonably robust to the inclusion of questions with slightly different wording.

3.2. Convergent Identities

Political cohesion may be especially likely when multiple identities, one of which contains strong political content, converge. Roccas and Brewer (2002) develop the concept of identity complexity to capture identity overlap, measuring it as the degree to which groups share similar members or attributes. Political identities have exhibited this type of fusion in the United States in recent years as political partisans become sorted more fully along the lines of political ideology (Levendusky, 2009). Mason (2012) examined this process and found that convergent partisan and ideological identities lead to greater political activism and more cohesive political attitudes. Roccas and Brewer (2002) found that a less complex (and more convergent) set of identities decreases tolerance of various out-groups in the United States and Israel. And factors such as threat promote identity convergence. For example, in Northern Ireland threat reduced social identity complexity, leading to increased overlap between an identity as Catholic and Irish, and Protestant and British (Schmid, Tausch, Hewstone, Hughes, & Cairns, 2008).

The overlap between national and ethnic or racial identities among members of minority groups has particular importance for political engagement and citizenship. Simon and colleagues report that a dual identity as a Russian-German or Turkish-German, indicated by statements such as "Sometimes I feel more as a German and sometimes more as a Turk," enhances political activity and support of group-related political issues among immigrants in Germany (Simon & Grabow, 2010; Simon & Ruhs, 2008). These dual identities exhibit attributes of Brewer and Roccas's complex identities in which no one of the two identities dominates, and together foster electoral engagement on behalf of the minority group.

3.3. Group Meaning

Not all strong, subjective group identities translate readily into group-based solidarity, however, and other factors are needed to understand the development of political cohesion. The second factor considered here is the meaning of group membership, especially its political content (Deaux, 1993). Groups attain political content through norms and beliefs that connect group membership to specific political attitudes and actions. As noted, some groups, based, for example, on partisanship and ideology, are inherently political and automatically generate political cohesion among strong identifiers. Other groups attain political meaning through norms that prescribe specific beliefs or actions for members. Groups can also acquire political meaning through the influence of group leaders who advocate certain beliefs and policy positions or take specific political action.

3.3.1. Group Norms and National Identity

National identity provides a fascinating example of an identity that differs in meaning even among citizens of the same nation, helping to explain variation among citizens in their support for aggressive national security policies, civic engagement, immigration, and other policies. National identity researchers frequently tap support for group norms by asking about the desired attitudes and behaviors of "true" or "good" citizens. Citrin and colleagues explore the subjective meaning of being American and uncover widespread consensus that it depends on support for the fundamental American values of equality and individualism consistent with the view of the United States as a civic nation defined by normative beliefs and ideals. Nonetheless, they also discover contested aspects of American identity that are endorsed by a subset of Americans such as the need to believe in God or speak up for one's country in order to be considered a "true American" (Citrin, Reingold, & Green, 1990; Citrin, Wong, & Duff, 2001; Citrin & Wright, 2009). Researchers working in this area contrast such ethnocultural conceptions of national identity with civic conceptions that rest on shared values such as individualism or freedom.

Other researchers pursue a slightly different approach to the study of national identity and its meaning, identifying three subjective facets of national attachments. Measures of *patriotism* or symbolic patriotism assess positive feelings of pride toward the nation and support for national symbols such as the flag and anthem. Political symbols such as the flag can be politically polarizing, resulting in greater symbolic patriotism among conservatives than liberals in the United States (Huddy & Khatib, 2007). A second form of national attachment involves a sense of national superiority and is referred to variously as *nationalism*, chauvinism, blind patriotism, or uncritical patriotism; it also tends to be more strongly endorsed by American conservatives than liberals (De Figueiredo & Elkins, 2003; Herrmann, Isernia, & Segatti, 2009; Kosterman & Feshbach, 1989; Parker, 2010; Schatz, Staub, & Lavine, 1999). Finally, Schatz et al. (1999) developed a measure of *constructive patriotism* that assesses the degree to which someone believes Americans should speak up and criticize the nation when deemed necessary. All three types of national attachments are linked to a strong national identity but have different content (Theiss-Morse, 2009; Herrmann et al., 2009).

Not surprisingly, many of the political effects of national identity depend on its subjective meaning. Individuals who endorse an ethnocultural view of American identity are more likely to oppose policies designed to benefit new immigrants, view negatively the impact of immigration, support English-only vote ballots, endorse ethnic profiling of Arab Americans, and generally support restrictions on civil liberties for noncitizens (Citrin et al., 1990; Citrin et al., 2001; Schildkraut, 2011; Wong, 2010). Those who rank highly the civic aspects of American identity are more supportive of increased immigration and less supportive of policies that favor English-speaking immigrants (Citrin & Wright, 2009). They are also more inclined than others to think that volunteering, donating money to charity, and serving in the military are obligations they owe to other Americans (Schildkraut, 2011).

In an international context, the meaning of national identity affects the formation of larger regional identities that transcend national boundaries. Breakwell (1996) documents differences among Europeans in the extent to which they see European identity as compatible with their existing national identity. In Eurobarometer data from 1992, as few as 13% of Italians but as many as 32% of Irish and 38% of those in the UK felt they would lose their national identity if all European countries came together in a European union. Clearly, a greater number of individuals living in the British Isles than other European nations see European identity as incompatible with their existing national identity. Hooghe and Marks (2004) report that Europeans who choose their nation but not Europe when asked whether they think of themselves in terms of their nation, nation and Europe, Europe and nation, or just Europe are far less likely to support European integration. The overlap between European and national identity thus influences support for policies designed to create a single community, affecting levels of national cohesion on the issue.

The direction of causality between meaning and political attitudes can be questioned, however: does the meaning of group membership drive policy attitudes, or vice versa? Evidence that the political effects of meaning are conditioned by identity strength in cross-sectional data circumvents this empirical impasse to some degree. Sindic and Reicher (2009) demonstrate that group meaning has its most marked political effects among the strongest group identifiers. In their research, strongly identified Scots who viewed Scotland as dominated by the English, felt their identity was undermined by a union with Britain, and saw the two identities as incompatible were far more likely than others to support Scottish nationalism and political independence from Britain. But in the absence of a strong Scottish national identity, these beliefs had far less political impact.

In summary, group norms are central to the development of political cohesion. Research on the meaning of national identity, especially its association with norms of civic participation, helps to explain levels of political engagement and action. But even highly normative aspects of national identity are not entirely consensual. For example, blind patriots hold a strong national identity but are less likely than others to vote (Huddy & Khatib, 2007). The political implications of group membership are less clear in the absence of widely shared norms that dictate political attitudes and behavior. In general, political cohesion emerges in groups with large numbers of strongly identified members who adhere to common norms of political belief and action.

3.3.2. Prototypes and Leadership

The characteristics, beliefs, and actions of prototypic group members provide a second source of group meaning. In self-categorization theory, groups are viewed as fuzzy sets with unclear boundaries and a "graded" or probabilistic structure (Turner et al., 1987). From this vantage point, typical members define the group, and group identity is driven by feeling similar to the typical or prototypic group member. When group identity is salient, group members conform to the behaviors and beliefs of prototypic group members. The political beliefs, ideology, or actions of prototypic group members can also influence the emergence of political cohesion.

Group prototypes influence political cohesion in at least two ways. First, they help to establish group boundaries and place limits on political assistance to and cooperation with outsiders. In the context of national identity, an ethnocultural conception of national identity results in a group prototype constituted of majority group members exclusive of immigrants and ethnic minorities. Some Americans define American identity in this way by confining it to individuals who are Christian, speak English, or are born in the United States (Citrin & Wright, 2009). Theiss-Morse (2009) demonstrates that placing such boundaries on the group prototype limits support for government policies that benefit members of ethnic and racial minority groups such as spending on welfare, education, urban areas, or improving the condition of blacks. In this way, the group prototype defines who constitutes "we" and places boundaries on in-group cooperation.

Second, when it comes to political groups such as nations or political parties, the group prototype is often a national or political leader whose beliefs, actions or exhortations to action directly influence group members. John F. Kennedy's admonition to Americans to "ask not what your country can do for you—ask what you can do for your country" is a direct appeal to American civic engagement and a clear example of prototypic influence at work. In one sense, a prototype associated with specific beliefs is not very different from a norm that prescribes what group members ideally believe, although prototypes are more descriptive and less prescriptive than norms (cf. Hogg & Reid, 2006). Once again, the influence of group prototypes is greatest among strong group identifiers, who are most likely to conform to the group prototype, a process that has been well documented for partisan and ideological groups (Malka & Lelkes, 2010; Cohen, 2003).

In general, group leaders are expected to play a powerful role in forging political cohesion. According to Hogg and Reid (2006), group leaders are individuals who communicate their prototypicality to their followers through the use of pronouns such as "we," and in reference to common goals and concerns, language that is very common in political speeches. Such leaders can be regarded as identity entrepreneurs who manage norms and prototypes through their verbal and nonverbal communication. When George W. Bush identified Osama bin laden and al-Qaeda as the enemy after 9/11, he went out of his way to make clear that Muslims and Muslim Americans were not the target of US military action. His position was generally adopted by Americans and serves as a marked contrast to the vilification and internment of Japanese Americans after the attack on Pearl Harbor (Schildkraut, 2002). Of course, a group leader considered atypical by some members is far less likely to wield this kind of influence.

Leaders can influence a group in other ways as well. Reicher and Hopkins (2001) highlight the politics of national identity in the context of Scottish independence. In the 1992 Scottish elections, the Scottish National Party, which favored independent statehood, emphasized that Scottish identity was incompatible with English identity. In contrast, the conservatives, who supported continued ties with Britain, emphasized Britishness and the commonalities between the Scots and English while downplaying Scottish distinctiveness. Leaders can also directly mobilize members by manufacturing and shaping group grievances as observed within social movements (Klandermans & van Stekelenburg, chapter 24, this volume). Group members' awareness of grievances is strengthened by the way in which politicians and group leaders respond to and interpret ongoing political events.

3.4. Shared Interests, Grievances, and Threat

Subjective identity is insufficient to motivate group-based political action, according to realistic interest theory. In addition, group members need to share common interests or at least perceive that they do. From this perspective, affluent whites band together against affirmative action to protect what they see as threatened privileges, and women cohere around issues linked to gender discrimination (Lowery, Unzueta, Knowles, & Goff, 2006). In the first instance, common group interests are at risk and need to be defended, while in the second group members feel aggrieved and wish to improve their position. The existence or perception of common fate and threats to shared interests is the fourth factor considered here as a basis for political cohesion.

Researchers typically equate common fate with the existence of shared material interests. I extend this discussion to include both shared *material* interests, such as income and employment, and *symbolic* concerns, such as the esteem and respect that group members receive from nongroup members. A sense of common fate concerning material outcomes is derived from realistic interest theory and includes a sense that group members share similar economic and material outcomes. A sense of symbolic common fate touches on concerns about group status and esteem, linked to social identity theory and related approaches. The distinction between the two types of interests matters because they hint at the emergence of political cohesion in different types of groups— high-status groups whose status is threatened are more likely to cohere according to social identity theory, whereas realistic interest approaches suggest political cohesion among members who share a similar economic fate. Stephan and Stephan (2000) incorporate both symbolic and material threats in their influential approach to the study of threat.

3.4.1. *Material Interests*

Material shared interests have been assessed in two ways. First, researchers have examined the political consequences of a sense of perceived common fate and deteriorating group finances. Drawing on data from the 1984 American National Election Studies (ANES), Kinder, Adams, and Gronke (1989) examined the impact of perceived common economic interests on vote choice. Americans who felt a sense of economic interdependence with other group members such as the elderly, farmers, or the middle class and who saw their group situation as deteriorating were more likely to rate the national economy negatively and vote on that basis. In Kinder et al.'s research, a sense of common fate worked in conjunction with a sense of economic grievance to promote political cohesion. Lowery et al. (2006) experimentally manipulated the effects of various employment-related affirmative action programs and found lowered program support among whites with a strong white identity when the program was framed in terms of white job loss (as opposed to black gains). In this instance, a strong identity combined with worsened group outcomes increased opposition to affirmative action programs.

More commonly, however, shared economic interests have been examined in a second form—as a function of fraternal deprivation, the sense that one's group is doing worse than another. This research provides consistent evidence that fraternal deprivation drives political cohesion. Whites who felt they were doing worse than blacks were more inclined to support George Wallace's candidacy in 1968 (Vanneman & Pettigrew, 1972) and become involved in the Boston antibusing movement (Begley & Alker, 1982). Other studies reveal similar findings (Guimond & Dubé-Simard, 1983; Tripathi & Srivastava, 1981).[4] It would be tempting to conclude from these studies that a sense of fraternal deprivation drives political cohesion. But in some research the impact of fraternal deprivation is confined to individuals who strongly identify with their group, revealing an interaction between identity and perceived deprivation (Struch & Schwartz, 1989; Brown, Maras, Masser, Vivian, & Hewstone, 2001).

Group identity also colors reactions to intergroup events, enhancing the perception of fraternal deprivation. Gibson (2008) finds, for example, that black South Africans who identify strongly with their ethnic group are far less likely to believe that justice has been adequately performed when asked to react to an experimental vignette in which a black squatter is evicted from land on which she is squatting. Typically, procedural justice (which is manipulated in the study) increases the perceived fairness of the eviction, but this is less true for the majority of black South Africans who identify with either their racial or ethnic group (e.g., Zulu, Xhosa) as opposed to South Africa as a nation. The clear implication of these findings is that principles of justice are applied more broadly by those who identify with the nation. Without a sense of national identity, black South Africans question the fairness of government actions and harbor a standing sense of grievance.

Overall, shared material interests and related grievances play a role in producing political cohesion, either directly or in combination with group identification. But some caution is needed in interpreting these results. Typically, fraternal deprivation is assessed subjectively. But there is reason to believe that subjective material grievances are intensified among strong group identifiers, raising questions about the origins of perceived common fate. In-group identification heightens a sense of in-group grievance in both experimental and correlational studies (Dambrun, Taylor, McDonald, Crush, & Méot, 2006; Gurin & Townsend, 1986, Kawakami & Dion, 1993; Smith, Spears, & Oyen, 1994). Riek, Mania, Gaertner, McDonald, and Lamoreaux (2010) even find that making salient a shared American identity reduces perceived partisan threat among Democrats and Republicans. Findings such as these have prompted Simon and Klandermans (2001, p. 325) to conclude that the "relationship between collective identity and awareness of shared grievances is therefore bi-directional."

3.4.2. *Symbolic Interests*

In contrast to material interests focused on tangible economic and related concerns, social identity theory shifts the focus to the defense of group status as a source of political cohesion. There is ample evidence that symbolic concerns can increase political cohesion. Group power, status, and culture all constitute symbolic interests, and their possible loss can produce opposition to a threatening out-group and support for government policies designed to minimize the threat. Sniderman et al. (2004) exposed Dutch participants to various scenarios concerning new immigrants and found less opposition to unskilled immigrants who might pose an economic threat than to immigrants who did not fit into Dutch culture and thus posed a symbolic threat. Moreover, a strong Dutch identity increased the perception that immigrants posed a cultural threat to the Netherlands, in a process akin to the intensification of realistic grievances among strong group identifiers. Symbolic grievances may be especially prone to identity-based intensification since they are highly subjective and more difficult to document than economic grievances. In addition, priming Dutch national identity increased opposition to the entry of new immigrants, especially among Dutch participants who initially saw little cultural threat from immigrants. Other studies report similar findings in which cultural threat interacts with national identity to increase out-group discrimination (Falomir-Pichastor, Gabarrot, & Mugny, 2009).

Biological indicators underscore the power of status threat. In an innovative study, Scheepers and Ellemers (2005) demonstrate that group members react physically to both low status and a threat to high status. They measured blood pressure among participants assigned to a group with low or high status who were then told that their status could change in a second round of the study. As expected, those assigned to a low-status group experienced an increase in blood pressure after learning of their low status, whereas blood pressure declined among those in the high-status group. When subjects were told that their group status could change, blood pressure increased among the high-status group and declined among the low. A possible decline in high status was just as stressful in this study as being assigned a low status. Scheepers (2009) followed up on this work, confirming the stressful effects of unstable high-group status.

Strong group identification amplifies the cohesive effect of symbolic threat. Voci, (2006) gave false feedback to northern and southern Italians on how they were viewed by the other group. One half learned that they were viewed positively and the other half negatively. When told that they were disliked by Italians in the other region, strongly identified northern or southern Italians rated their in-group more positively than in the positive feedback condition. Similar findings are observed in Northern Ireland. Northern Irish who are strongly identified with their religion are far more likely than weak identifiers to translate perceived threats to their values or political power into negative out-group attitudes (Tausch, Hewstone, Kenworthy, Cairns, & Christ, 2007). Haslam and Reicher (2006) found suggestive evidence that a strong group identity reduces stress as measured by cortisol levels in response to a threat to group status.

The effects of threat on group cohesion may depend on whether or not group members have an opportunity to affirm the positive attributes of the group and thus defuse a threat to their status. In research by Glasford, Dovidio, and Pratto (2009), strongly identified Americans felt less psychological discomfort when told that the United States had bombed civilians if they also had an opportunity to affirm the group's status by ranking positive American values such as freedom. Without such an opportunity, discomfiting information about US action increased out-group negativity among strong identifiers. In the same study, strongly identified Americans who valued universal healthcare and learned that the United States failed to provide it chose to express their views on Muslims and thus express out-group animosity rather than express their support for a positive change to US policy.

3.5. Group Consciousness

Group consciousness models link cohesion to identity and grievances, the two factors discussed so far, along with a third element: blaming the system for grievances and group disparities. The model thus underscores the additional importance of political beliefs to the emergence of political cohesion and action. Miller et al. (1981) defined group consciousness as subjective group closeness (identification), feelings of power deprivation (grievances), polar affect (akin to in-group bias), and blaming the system for group-based disparities. In their analysis of the 1972 and 1976 ANES data, political participation was enhanced among subjectively identified group members (based on age, class, race, and gender) who felt fraternally deprived and viewed this as the result of unfair systemic factors such as discrimination. A growing number of scholars see beliefs about group power and consciousness as central to political action among members of racial and ethnic minority groups (Dawson, 1994; Junn and Masuoka, 2008).

Tajfel and Turner (1979) share a group consciousness perspective by arguing that grievances are necessary but not sufficient to motivate group-based action. According to Tajfel and Turner, group members need to identify with their group, perceive intergroup status differences, and view status differences as illegitimate before action is likely. This model has not been tested as a precursor to the development of political cohesion, but Ellemers, Wilke, and Van Knippenberg (1993) found related evidence in an experimental setting. Beliefs can also influence how one reacts to status threat. Townsend, Major, Gangi, and Mendes (2011) subjected women to a sexist rejection in which they learned that they had been rejected as a coworker in an experimental study because they would be "probably too emotional and won't be a strong partner." Women in the study reacted with greater stress, as assessed by higher levels of cortisol, if they chronically perceived sexism, whereas women who saw little sexism in the world were not threatened by the incident. In this instance, status threats combined with an existing ideology affected reactions to an intergroup encounter.

In sum, there is extensive evidence that symbolic and material concerns can drive political cohesion, a process that is most evident among strong group identifiers. Few studies directly contrast the role of material and symbolic concerns, although research hints at the greater power of symbolic than material threats (Sniderman et al., 2004). The wealth of evidence from minimal intergroup studies underscores that economic competition is not a necessary condition for the development of group cohesion (Brewer, 1979; Brewer & Brown, 1998). The dual influence of group-linked interests and group identity on the development of political cohesion is consistent with popular models of collective action that center on grievances and identity as two of its three central ingredients (van Zomeren et al., 2008). It remains unclear whether political cohesion additionally requires a sense that group deprivation derives from unfair systemic inequity and discrimination.

4. EMOTION AS A CATALYST FOR GROUP-BASED ACTION

Emotions play an important role in conveying and amplifying the political effects of strong group identities by reinforcing group cohesion and strengthening or weakening the willingness to act in defense of the group. Positive emotions consistently increase group commitment, whereas negative emotions have divergent effects: anger motivates an active response to group threat, whereas anxiety leads to the avoidance of action and may dampen group commitment. Intergroup emotions theory (IET; Mackie, Devos, & Smith, 2000), a combination of emotional appraisal theory (see Marcus & Brader, chapter 6, this volume) and social identity theory, lends insight into the conditions most likely to generate anger and anxiety. From the perspective of IET, threat is most likely to produce anger among strongly identified group members who view their group as likely to prevail over a threatening out-group. In contrast, members of a weaker group should feel anxiety in response to a threat from a stronger out-group. Moreover, anger leads to action to deal with a threatening group whereas anxiety fosters avoidance and disengagement (Berkowitz & Harmon-Jones, 2004; Carver, 2004; Lambert et al., 2010).

When applied to a threatening international situation, for example, intergroup emotions theory predicts that citizens who view their country as strong militarily are most likely to feel outraged and angry at an attack by a weaker opponent. Citizens of weaker countries are more inclined to feel anxious in the same situation. In essence, members of stronger groups can afford to feel angry at an opponent because they are more certain that retaliatory action against their weaker opponent will succeed. As a corollary to this prediction, IET also states that individuals who identify most strongly with their nation are most likely to overestimate their country's might and thus get far angrier than weak identifiers when the nation is threatened (Mackie et al., 2000). This expectation stems from social identity theory's notion that strong group identifiers are motivated to view their group positively and thus see it as stronger than a threatening opponent.

4.1. Identity Strength and Emotional Reactivity

There is growing support for the various predictions of intergroup emotions theory. First, there is evidence that strong group identifiers react more angrily to group threat (Musgrove & McGarty, 2008; Rydell et al., 2008; van Zomeren, Spears, & Leach, 2008). Strong American patriots reacted with greater anger toward terrorists in the lead-up to the Iraq war (Feldman, Huddy, & Cassese, 2012), and in response to an insulting message about the United States and Americans written by a foreigner (Rydell et al., 2008). Strong Democrats and Republicans react with greater anger to a threatened electoral loss (Mason et al., 2012). Experimentally heightened identity salience also increases anger among group members in response to threat or victimization (Yzerbyt, Dumont, Wigboldus, & Grodijn, 2003). For example, Fischer, Haslam, and Smith (2010) made salient British subjects' national or gender identity and then exposed them to photos of the July 7, 2005, London bombings. Subjects whose British identity was made salient were more likely to report feeling aggression and expressed greater support for the war on terror than those for whom gender identity was made salient.

Anger and identity may also be mutually reinforcing. In a series of studies, Thomas & McGarty (2009; Thomas, McGarty, & Mavor, 2009) assigned subjects to small groups and asked them to craft an information campaign to arouse interest in the lack of clean drinking water in the developing world. Some groups were told that such information campaigns were successful if they convinced people that programs work, creating a norm of efficacy. Others learned that the campaign would be more successful if it aroused a sense of outrage on the issue. Generating a norm of outrage among group members was far more effective than the norm of efficacy in arousing anger, a commitment to action, and in boosting group identity. In this research, anger strengthened group identity, a finding that has obvious implications for the formation and cohesion of political groups.

Strongly identified group members also feel other emotions more intensely than weak identifiers in response to threat and reassurance. Strong partisans in the United States feel increased schadenfreude, a complex positive emotion, when they read about bad things happening or reflecting poorly on a political candidate of the other party, even when an event, such as increased US military deaths in Iraq, is clearly negative (Combs, Powell, Schurtz, & Smith, 2009). Strong partisans feel more positive than weak partisans when exposed to a reassuring message about future electoral victory (Mason et al., 2012).

4.2. Group Strength and Anger

Research findings support a second prediction from IET—that anger will be more pronounced among members of a group seen as strong in the face of threat. Mackie et al. (2000) sorted subjects into those for and against gay rights and then manipulated the group position by exposing members to a series of news headlines in support (strong) or opposed (weak) to the group position. In the "strong" group condition, group members felt angrier at out-group members than those in the "weak" condition and were more action-oriented, wanting to engage in an argument with an out-group member. Musgrove and McGarty (2008) examined reactions to the war on terror in Australia and found that confidence in the government's ability to respond to terrorism was associated with anger at international terrorists.

Group strength does not just lie with military might or an electoral victory, it also includes a sense of moral strength. Mendes, Major, McCoy, and Blascovich (2008) found, for example, that an interracial rejection by someone of the other race was viewed as a challenge that increased anger and physical activation (cardiovascular efficiency) among both white and black subjects. In contrast, subjects rejected by a member of their own race reacted to this as a threat that decreased cardiac efficiency and did not increase anger. Other group-related moral transgressions can also be equated with group strength and lead to increased anger and a commitment to action. The experience of collective guilt and responsibility for moral injustice has the opposite effect, weakening the group position and leading to conciliation and support for reparations (Doosje, Branscombe, Spears, & Manstead, 1998).

4.3. Anger and Action

Finally, there is considerable research support for IET's prediction that group-based anger increases a commitment to action whereas anxiety decreases it (Leach, Iyer, & Pederson, 2007; Mackie et al., 2000; Musgrove & McGarty, 2008; Thomas & McGarty, 2009). Consider reactions to terrorism. American anger toward Saddam Hussein and terrorists prior to the Iraq war was linked to the view that a war in Iraq was not risky and increased overall support for the war (Huddy, Feldman, & Cassese, 2007). In contrast, terrorism-related anxiety lead Americans to view war in Afghanistan and Iraq as risky and decreased war support overall (Huddy, Feldman, Taber, & Lahav, 2005; Huddy et al., 2007; Sadler, Lineberger, Correll, & Park, 2005; Skitka, Bauman, Aramovich, & Morgan, 2006). Self-reported fear and anxiety after the 2004 Madrid terrorist bombings also increased avoidant behaviors such as staying at home, avoiding air travel, and avoiding contact with Muslims among Spanish respondents (Conejero & Etxebarria, 2007).

Similar findings have been observed in research that experimentally arouses anger or anxiety (Fischhoff, Gonzalez, Small, & Lerner, 2005; Lerner, Gonzalez, Small, & Fischhoff, 2003). For example, Lambert et al. (2010) undertook a series of carefully crafted experiments to demonstrate the existence and differing political consequences of anger and anxiety in reaction to 9/11. They randomly assigned subjects to watch a video about 9/11 and found that it generated both anger and anxiety. The two emotions had differing political effects: anger increased support for war, whereas anxiety undercut it. They also demonstrated that experimentally aroused anger unrelated to 9/11 increased support for prowar political candidates, whereas experimentally heightened feelings of anxiety (again unrelated to terrorism) undercut support for such candidates.

Overall, there is much that is intuitively appealing in an intergroup emotions explanation of political reactions to group threat and reassurance. It is easy to understand, for example, why Americans felt angry after the 9/11 terrorist attacks: levels of patriotism among Americans are generally high and increased after 9/11, and Americans are likely to see the United States as far more powerful militarily than Iraq or al-Qaeda. In general, intergroup emotions theory predicts that citizens of strong military entities such as Israel or the United States should feel more angry than anxious when threatened, inclining them to respond with disproportionate force in response to threat. Of course, the logic and reality of guerilla warfare underscores the point that members of weaker entities will also engage in action if they believe they can defeat a strong military entity.

5. DEVELOPMENT OF GROUP IDENTITY

One of the crucial ingredients in the development of political cohesion is the existence of a strong, internalized subjective group identity. This finding raises an additional challenge for political psychologists: How do we explain an individual's decision to identify as a group member? Research on this question has moved well beyond Campbell et al.'s (1960) notion that subjective identification is simply a function of the percentage of one's life spent as a group member. Influenced in part by social identity theory, there is growing evidence on several factors that promote the development of strong social identities.

5.1. Salient Identity

Self-categorization theory underscores the situational nature of identity as individuals constantly shift back and forth between an individual and a social identity (Turner et al., 1987). Thus, if a national figure contrasts the valor of one ethnic group of citizens against the sloth of another, ethnic identities rise to the fore. But if, in contrast, the politician rails against the evils of an opposing nation, national identity is transcendent. Social identity researchers consider group salience an essential ingredient in the development of identity and group political cohesion. According to Oakes (in Turner et al., 1987) salience is heightened by any factor that increases the "separateness" and "clarity" of a category, and one of the factors most likely to increase a category's clarity is minority status, when group members are outnumbered by members of an out-group (see also Brewer & Brown, 1998).

Category salience plays a clear role in shaping identity. Eifert, Edward, and Posner (2010) provide an interesting example of group salience at work within a political context. Drawing on data in the Afrobarometer, they record an increase in the intensity of ethnic identity and a decline in occupational and class identities closer to elections, especially competitive elections. They attribute the increase in ethnic identity to the increased salience of ethnicity in African elections, during which politicians emphasize ethnic loyalties and distribute goods along ethnic lines. In essence, the authors argue that African politicians exploit ethnic identities to gain electoral support and thus increase the salience of ethnic identities around election time. The importance of group salience is further confirmed in a meta-analysis in which group salience promoted the development of in-group bias across a large number of studies (Mullen, Brown, & Smith, 1992).

Political behavior research also points, however, to the limits on category salience in the development of social identity. Members of diverse ethnic and racial groups in the United States, who form salient minorities, identify primarily as American and only secondarily as members of their ethnic or racial group, despite the greater salience of minority group status in the United States (Citrin et al., 2001; Sears, Citrin, Cheleden, van Laar, 1999). Hispanic students who attended a high school with relatively few other Hispanics, and whose ethnic group membership was thus highly salient, were less likely to identify as Hispanic than Hispanic students attending schools in heavily Hispanic areas (Eschbach & Gomez, 1998). In a similar vein, blacks living in more segregated areas expressed higher levels of racial identification than those in integrated areas, where race is more chronically salient (Postmes

& Branscombe, 2002). This evidence raises important questions about the extent to which the salience of one's ethnic or racial group—the key ingredient in identity development for many social identity researchers—explains the emergence of ethnic and racial identities.

5.2. Meaning and Valence of Identity

If salience has a limited impact on the development of social identity, other factors are needed to account for their emergence. The meaning of group membership is a crucial additional ingredient in identity development, especially in large groups with competing conceptions of membership (Huddy, 2001). As already noted, national identity is typically fraught with disputes over who qualifies as a "good" citizen, and national identities are often weaker among members of minority groups who do not fit the national prototype. Identity meaning also revolves around the normative *values* with which an identity is associated. Schwartz, Struch, and Bilsky (1990) illustrate one way in which to assess the values underlying group membership. They asked German and Israeli students to rank 19 terminal and 18 instrumental values on the basis of their own preference order and that of their national group. Not surprisingly, one's own views and that of one's group are related, although the link is stronger for Israeli than for German students. This suggests that an important source of national identity—shared values—is stronger among Israeli than among German students and hints at an important source of weakened national identity among Germans.

Valence plays a further role in affecting identity development; a negatively regarded group will have *greater* difficulty eliciting strong group members, all else being equal. There is evidence that ethnic identity is more strongly developed among members of objectively identified, higher-status groups and among individuals who perceive their group as holding higher societal status (Ethier & Deaux, 1994). For example, national identity is more strongly developed among Cubans in the United States than among other Latinos because they believe their social status far exceeds that of Mexican Americans or Puerto Ricans (Huddy & Virtanen, 1995). Junn and Masuoka (2008) were able to strengthen Asian identity by experimentally increasing group status through photos of powerful Asian political figures. And good news about Europe increased, and bad news decreased, a sense of European identity (Bruter, 2009).

5.3. Acquired versus Ascribed Identities

Identity strength is also related to identity choice. Acquired identities, adopted by choice, are likely to be stronger than ascribed identities. Turner, Hogg, Turner, and Smith (1984) report a study in which subjects were either ascribed or could choose to belong to one of two teams competing in a problem-solving exercise. Members of winning teams indicated higher self-esteem and cohesion when they had been ascribed to the team. But members who voluntarily chose their team were more likely to report high self-esteem and group cohesion when they lost, suggesting a stronger sense of group commitment when identity is acquired than when ascribed. Perreault and Bourhis (1999) extended this research to include the effects of identity acquisition on the development of out-group discrimination. They found that group identification increased in strength with the sense that lab group membership was voluntary.

5.4. Permeable Group Boundaries

One of the most important implications of identity choice is that it allows members of low-status groups to abandon group identity because of permeable group boundaries. Tajfel and Turner (1979) refer to this strategy as social mobility, and several researchers provide evidence of its existence among members of low-status groups (Jackson, Sullivan, Harnish, & Hodge, 1996; Wright, Taylor, & Moghaddam, 1990). Wright (1997) found that boundary permeability does not have to be very extensive for group members to contemplate individual rather than collective solutions to problems of low in-group status. Permeability is not just a feature of highly fluid groups but can also characterize membership in relatively fixed groups based on ethnic and regional boundaries. For example, East Germans who thought it was easy to be considered West German were more likely to think of themselves as simply German and had weaker East German identities than those who thought it was difficult to pass as West German (Mummendey, Kessler, Klink, & Mielke, 1999).

Finally, there is some intriguing evidence that upward mobility may weaken race identification. Race is far from permeable in the United States. Nonetheless, a sense of black identity appears to weaken among blacks who move to better neighborhoods or who grow up in less segregated neighborhoods, in part, because they feel rejected by other blacks and worry that they have effectively abandoned their racial grouping (Gay, 2004; Postmes & Branscombe, 2002). In contrast when group boundaries are impermeable, there is evidence that members of low-status groups bolster their identity and enhance their group's standing through the strategies of social creativity and social change (Tajfel & Turner, 1979; Jackson et al., 1996).

Overall, questions of group permeability raise concomitant questions about the influence of *external labeling* on identity acquisition. If group membership is obvious to others, it will be more difficult for a group member to avoid external identification. It may be relatively easy for an East German to pass as someone from the West but much more difficult for an African American to escape the label black. Less permeable group boundaries and a higher incidence of external labeling should increase the likelihood that a group member will internalize group identity. Relevant external cues include skin color, gender, group-specific physical features, language, and cultural practices. Conversely, attributes that can be hidden or disguised enhance the role of choice in identity acquisition.

5.5. Group Size

Group identification is typically more pronounced among members of minority than majority groups, and Brewer developed optimal distinctiveness theory to account for this asymmetry (Leonardelli et al., 2010). Brewer views group life as characterized by two competing needs—the need to belong to a group, and the need to differentiate oneself from others. From this perspective, members of large, majority groups evince weaker in-group identities than do members of smaller, minority groups because a majority identity confers insufficient distinctiveness. Group identities develop to the extent that a group satisfies both needs by providing a sense of inclusiveness within the group and distinctiveness between an in-group and out-group. Optimal distinctiveness theory hints at the difficulty in forging political cohesion among members of large majority groups, among whom identity provides too little differentiation, and among members of very small groups, who feel overly distinct and insufficiently collective.

One problem with the approach, however, is that there are many numerically large political entities that elicit strong group identities. Political parties, for example, comprise an amorphous group of unknown size yet elicit powerful emotions, identities, and a commitment to action. The same holds for nations. Are small nations more likely to hold strong national identities than larger nations? There is no supportive evidence for this. The tendency for minority groups such as African Americans or Latinos to evince political cohesion in the United States may have more to do with their common interests and grievances than optimal group size.

5.6. Individual Differences

Social identity researchers have largely ignored individual variation in the general proclivity to identify with social groups but others have been digging profitably into this question. Several basic personality traits are associated with the tendency to affiliate with political groups (for a discussion of personality traits see Caprara & Vecchione, chapter 2, this volume). Gerber, Huber, Doherty, and Dowling (2011) analyzed the origins of partisan identity strength in the Big Five personality traits using data from a 2010 national US survey. They found that extraverts and those who score highly on agreeableness exhibited the strongest partisan identities, attesting to the social and emotional motivational basis of partisan identification. Those low in openness to experience are also stronger partisans, suggesting that strong partisanship may provide cognitive certainty and coherence.

The role of cognitive uncertainty in the development of group identification is further developed in a program of research by Hogg (2007). While he regards uncertainty as more situational than personality-based, his findings complement those emerging in research on personality and politics by highlighting the strong link between identity and uncertainty reduction. In his view, group members "need to feel certain that their perceptions, attitudes, and behaviors are correct," which pushes them to identify with a group (Grieve & Hogg, 1999, p. 927). In a politically relevant example, Hohman, Hogg, and Bligh (2010) manipulated certain or uncertain feelings by assigning research participants to read and mark sections in a speech on the environment by President George W. Bush. Some participants were randomly assigned to mark passages that made them feel certain about their place in the world and others were assigned to mark sections that made them feel uncertain. Both Democrats and Republicans reported stronger partisanship in the uncertain than in the certain condition.

5.7. Threat

I have focused so far on in-group cohesion and, for the most part, put aside discussion of intergroup hostilities. But the notion of threat—which typically involves an external threat from a known out-group—is relevant here because it can strengthen in-group unity, in addition to inflaming out-group hostilities (a topic discussed in greater detail by Kinder, chapter 25, this volume). An external threat enhances in-group solidarity and tightens in-group boundaries in direct proportion to the degree of threat (Coser, 1956; Levine & Campbell, 1972).[5] The rise in American patriotism after the 9/11 terror attacks provides a compelling example of this process at work (Gallup, 2005). This truism has its parallel in an important and continuing line of research in international relations—the diversionary theory of war—in which a leader focuses a nation's attention on an external enemy to shore up domestic support (Levy, 1989).

Threat may have its strongest effects on those who already hold a strong group identity, as seen in research by Ethier and Deaux (1994). They found that Hispanics with an initially strong Hispanic identity attending Ivy League schools increased the strength of their Hispanic identification over time. In contrast, students with a weak initial identity perceived greater anti-Hispanic threat in the school environment, and their Hispanic identity weakened over time. Verkuyten and Nekuee (1999) observed a similar process among Iranian immigrants to the Netherlands. Iranians who identified strongly with their nationality group and who perceived the Dutch as discriminatory toward their group were more likely to self-stereotype themselves as typically Iranian. The impact of perceived anti-Iranian discrimination on self-stereotyping was less pronounced among those who identified less strongly as Iranian.

Finally, existential threats to the self can also intensify group attachment and identity. Research within the paradigm of terror management theory demonstrates heightened in-group cohesion when one's mortality is made salient. Greenberg et al. (1990) found that Christians who were asked to form an impression of a Jewish and Christian individual evaluated the Christian more positively and the Jew more negatively when their mortality had been made salient. In other studies, mortality salience heightens in-group identification (Castano, Yzerbyt, Paladino, & Sacchi, 2002).

6. CONCLUSION

One thing is resoundingly clear from this review. Group membership may be a necessary condition for the development of political cohesion, but it is certainly not sufficient. This analysis has focused on several factors that are pivotal to the development of a cohesive political outlook and a strong group identity. But there is more to be done. As a starting point, political psychologists could profitably shift frameworks to view and study partisanship and political ideology as social identities. The approach is gaining traction but remains understudied even though the benefits of this perspective are considerable. When examined as a social identity, partisanship may be weakened by a threatened electoral loss, especially among partisans whose identity is not especially strong. An identity approach also underscores the role of emotions in motivating political action and reveals the emotionality of strong partisans. Strong partisans and ideologues are typically the most passionate about their political group and seem far from the rational decision-makers envisioned by democratic theorists.

Other interesting questions concerning political identity also remain unanswered. To what extent are leaders able to influence the views of their followers? Are there certain kinds of people who develop a sense of group identification more readily and hang on to this identity more firmly than others, and do genetic and biological factors underlie this process? To what extent do political systems influence the emergence and character of political identities? Are strong political identities more common in systems with many smaller political parties characterized by tightly convergent social and political identities? Is this identity convergence occurring in the United States, despite the existence of two large omnibus parties, as the country fractures politically along the lines of urban versus others, secular versus religious, North versus South, and the wealthy versus the rest? Are such forces counteracted by an increasingly globalized world of extensive immigration, vast international social networks, emergent cosmopolitanism, and growing preoccupation with global problems such as the environment? Answers to these questions will be central to an understanding of public opinion, political action, and democracy in the coming decades.

ACKNOWLEDGEMENT

Thanks to Vicky D'Anjou-Pomerlau for prompt and thorough research assistance.

NOTES

1. This is a selective account of the major theoretical approaches to in-group cohesion. Other approaches not covered here include a psychodynamic approach (see Post, chapter 15, this volume) and social comparison theory (Brewer and Brown, 1998).

2. For a more detailed overview of social identity theory see Brown (2010) and Brewer and Brown (1998).

3. There are also limits to the power of partisan reasoning. Nicholson (2012) did not find partisan cue-taking on familiar issues and Bullock (2011) found that policy information is just as powerful as party in shaping opinion on modifications to Medicaid.

4. Other beliefs, such as blaming inequality on an external enemy or the perceived efficacy of protest, may be additionally needed to translate realistic grievances into political action (Klandermans & van Stekelenburg, chapter 24, this volume).

5. Threat can also splinter a group if threat is directed at a subset or the group lacks any initial solidarity (Coser, 1956).

References

Andreychick, M. R., & Gill, M. J. (2009). Ingroup identity moderates the impact of social explanations on intergroup attitudes: External explanations are not inherently prosocial. *Personality and Social Psychology Bulletin, 35*(12), 1632–1645.

Ashmore, R. D., Deaux, K., & McLaughlin-Volpe, T. (2004). An organizing framework for collective identity: Articulation and significance of multidimensionality. *Psychological Bulletin, 130*(1), 80–114.

Bartels, L. M. (2002). Beyond the running tally: Partisan bias in political perception. *Political Behavior, 24*(2), 117–150.

Begley, T. M., & Alker, H. (1982). Anti-busing protest: Attitudes and actions. *Social Psychology Quarterly, 45*, 187–197.

Berelson, B. R., Lazarsfeld, P. F., & McPhee, W. N. (1954). *Voting: A study of opinion formation in a presidential campaign.* Chicago: University of Chicago Press.

Berkowitz, L., & Harmon-Jones, E. (2004). Towards an understanding of the determinants of anger. *Emotion, 4*, 107–130.

Bettencourt, B. A., Dorr, N., Charlton, K., and Hume, D. L. (2001). Status differences and ingroup bias: A meta-analytic examination of status stability, status legitimacy, and group permeability. *Psychological Bulletin, 127*(4) 520–542.

Billig, M. (1995). Rhetorical psychology, ideological thinking, and imagining nationhood. In H. Johnston & B. Klandermans (eds.), *Social movements and culture* (pp. 64–81). Minneapolis: University of Minnesota Press.

Blumer, H. (1958). Race and prejudice as a sense of group position. *Pacific Sociological Review, 1*, 3–7.

Bobo, L. D. (1983). Whites' opposition to busing: Symbolic racism or realistic group conflict? *Journal of Personality and Social Psychology, 45*, 1196–1210.

Bobo, L. D., & Hutchings, V. L. (1996). Perceptions of racial group competition: Extending Blumer's theory of group position to a multiracial context. *American Sociological Review, 61*, 951–972.

Bobo, L. D., & Johnson, D. (2000). Racial attitudes in a prismatic metropolis: Mapping identity, stereotypes, competition, and views on affirmative action. In L. D. Bob, O. L. Melvin, J. H. Johnson Jr., & A. Valenzeual Jr. (eds.), *Prismatic metropolis: Inequality in Los Angeles* (pp. 81–163). New York: Russell Sage Foundation.

Breakwell, G. M. (1996). Identity Processes and Social Change. In Breakwell, G. M., & Lyons, E. (eds.), *Changing European identities: Social psychological analyses of social change* (pp. 13–30). Oxford: Butterworth-Heinemann.

Brewer, M. B. (1979). In-group bias in the minimal inter-group situation: A cognitive motivational analysis. *Psychological Bulletin, 86*, 307–324.

Brewer, M. B. (2007). The importance of being we: Human nature and intergroup relations. *American Psychologist, 62*(8): 728–738.

Brewer, M. B., & Brown, R. (1998). Intergroup relations. In D. Gilbert, S. Fiske, & G. Lindzey (eds.) *Handbook of Social Psychology* (4th ed., vol. 2, pp. 554–594). New York: McGraw-Hill.

Brewer, M. B., and Caporael, L. R. (2006). An evolutionary perspective on social identity: Revisiting groups. In M. Schaller, J. A. Simpson, & D. T. Kenrick (eds.), *Evolution and social psychology* (pp. 143–162). New York: Psychology Press.

Brown, R. (2000). Social identity theory: Past achievements, current problems and future challenges. *European Journal of Social Psychology, 30*, 745–778.

Brown, R. (2010). *Prejudice: Its social psychology.* Oxford: John Wiley & Sons.

Brown, R., Maras, P., Masser, B., Vivian, J., & Hewstone, M. (2001). Life on the ocean wave: Testing some intergroup hypotheses in a naturalistic setting. *Group Processes and Intergroup Relations, 4*, 81–97.

Bruter, M. (2009). Time bomb? The dynamic effect of news and symbols on the political identity of European citizens. *Comparative Political Studies, 42*(12), 1498–1536.

Bullock, J. G. (2011). Elite influence on public opinion in an informed electorate. *American Political Science Review, 105*(3), 496–515.

Cameron, J. E. (2004). A three-factor model of social identity. *Self and Identity, 3*, 239–262.

Campbell, A., Converse, P., Miller, W. E., & Stokes, D. E. (1960). *The American voter.* New York: John Wiley & Sons.

Carver, C. S. (2004). Negative affects deriving from the behavioral approach system. *Emotion, 4*, 3–22.

Castano, E., Yzerbyt, V. Y., Bourguignon, D., & Seron, E. (2002). Who may enter? The impact of in-group identification on in-group/out-group categorization. *Journal of Experimental Social Psychology, 38*, 315–322.

Castano, E., Yzerbyt, V. Y., Paladino, M. P., & Sacchi, S. (2002). I belong, therefore, I exist: Ingroup identification, ingroup entitativity, and ingroup bias. *Personality and Social Psychology Bulletin, 28*, 135–143.

Chaio, J. Y., Bowman, N. E., & Gill, H. (2008). The political gender gap: Gender bias in facial inferences that predict voting behavior. *PLoSONE, 3*(10), e3666.

Citrin, J., Reingold, B., & Green, D. P. (1990). American identity and the politics of ethnic change. *Journal of Politics, 52*, 1124–1154.

Citrin, J., Wong, C., & Duff, B. (2001). The meaning of American national identity: Patterns of ethnic conflict and consensus. In R. D. Ashmore & L. Jussim (eds), *Social identity, intergroup conflict, and conflict reduction* (pp. 71–100). London: Oxford University Press.

Citrin, J., & Wright, M. (2009). Defining the circle of we: American identity and immigration policy. *Forum, 7*(3), Article 6. http://www.bepress.com/forum/vol7/iss3/art6/.

Cohen, G. L. (2003). Party over policy: The dominating impact of group influence on political beliefs. *Journal of Personality and Social Psychology, 85*, 808–822.

Combs, D. J. Y., Powell, A. J., Schurtz, D. R., & Smith, R. H. (2009). Politics, schadenfreude, and ingroup identification: The sometimes happy thing about a poor economy and jobs. *Journal of Experimental Social Psychology, 45*, 635–646.

Conejero, S., & Etxebarria, I. (2007). The impact of the Madrid bombing on personal emotions, emotional atmosphere and emotional climate. *Journal of Social Issues, 63*, 273–287.

Coser, L. (1956). *The functions of social conflict.* New York: Free Press.

Dalton, R. J. (1996). Political cleavages, issues, and electoral change. In L. LeDuc, R. G. Niemi, & P. Norris (eds.) *Comparing democracies: Elections and voting in global perspective* (pp. 319–342).

Dalton, R. J., & Wattenberg, M. P. (2000). *Parties without partisans: Political change in advanced industrial democracies.* Oxford: Oxford University Press.

Dambrun, M., Taylor, D. M., McDonald, D. M., Crush, J., & Méot, A. (2006). The relative deprivation-gratification continuum and the attitudes of South Africans toward immigrants: A test of the V-curve hypothesis. *Interpersonal Relations and Group Processes, 91*(6), 1032–1044.

Davies, P. G., Steele, C. M., & Markus, H. R. (2008). A nation challenged: The impact of foreign threat on America's tolerance for diversity. *Interpersonal Relations and Group Processes, 95*(2), 308–318.

Dawes, C. T., & Fowler J. T. (2009). Partisanship, voting, and the dopamine D2 Receptor gene. *Journal of Politics, 71*(3), 1157–1171.

Dawson, M. C. (1994). *Behind the mule: Race and class in African-American politics.* Princeton, NJ: Princeton University Press.

Deaux, K. (1993). Reconstructing social identity. *Personality & Social Psychology Bulletin, 19*, 4–12.

De Dreu, C. K. W., Greer, L. L., Van Kleef, G. A., Shalvi, S., & Handgraaf, M. J. J. (2011). Oxytocin promotes human ethnocentrism. *Proceedings of the National Academy of Sciences, 108* (4), 1262–1266.

De Figueiredo, R. J. P., & Elkins, Z. (2003). Are patriots bigots? An inquiry into the vices of in-group pride. *American Journal of Political Science, 47*(1), 171–188.

Doosje, B., Branscombe, N. R., Spears, R., & Manstead, A. S. R. (1998). Guilt by association: When one's group has a negative history. *Journal of Personality and Social Psychology, 75*(4), 872–886.

Duveen, G. (2001). Representations, identities, resistance. In K. Deaux & G. Philogene (eds.) *Representations of the Social* (pp. 257–270). Malden, MA: Blackwell.

Eifert, B., Edward, M., & Posner, D. N. (2010). Political competition and ethnic identification in Africa. *American Journal of Political Science, 54*(2), 494–510.

Ellemers, N., & Haslam, A. S. (2012). Social identity theory. In P. A. M. van Lange, A. W. Kruglanski, & E. T. Higgins (eds.), *Handbook of theories of social psychology* (vol. 2, pp. 379–398). Thousand Oaks, CA: Sage.

Ellemers, N., Kortekaas, P., & van Ouwerkerk, J. P. (1999). Self-categorisation, commitment to the group and group self-esteem as related but distinct aspects of identity. *European Journal of Social Psychology, 29*, 371–389.

Ellemers, N., Wilke, H., &. Van Knippenberg, A. (1993). Effects of the legitimacy of low group or individual status as individual and collective status-enhancing strategies. *Journal of Personality and Social Psychology, 64*, 766–778.

Erikson, T. H. (1993). *Ethnicity and nationalism: Anthropological perspectives.* Boulder, CO: Pluto Press.

Eschbach, K., & Gomez, C. (1998). Choosing Hispanic identity: Ethnic identity switching among respondents to high school and beyond. *Social Science Quarterly, 79*, 74–90.

Ethier, K. A., & Deaux, K. (1994). Negotiating social identity when contexts change: Maintaining identification and responding to threat. *Journal of Personality & Social Psychology, 67*, 243–251.

Falomir-Pichaster, J. M., Gabarrot, F., & Mugny, G. (2009). Group motives in threatening contexts: When loyalty conflict paradoxically reduces the influence of an anti-discrimination ingroup norm. *European Journal of Social Psychology, 39*, 196–206.

Feldman, S., Huddy, L., & Cassese, E. (2012). Emotions, threat, and political reasoning. In Ron Sun (ed.), *Grounding social sciences in cognition* (pp. 127–156). Cambridge, MA: MIT Press.

Fischer, P., Haslam, A. S., & Smith, L. (2010). If you wrong us, shall we not revenge? Social identity salience moderates support for retaliation in response to collective threat. *Group Dynamics: Theory, Research, and Practice, 14*, 143–150.

Fischhoff, B., Gonzalez, R. M., Small, D. A., & Lerner, J. S. (2005). Evolving judgments of terror risks: Foresight, hindsight and emotion. *Journal of Experimental Psychology: Applied, 11*, 124–139.

Fowler, J. H., and Kam, C. D. (2008). "Beyond the self: Social identity, altruism, and political participation. *Journal of Politics, 69*(3), 813–827.

Freedman, A. L. (2000). *Chinese overseas in Malaysia, Indonesia, and the United States.* New York: Routledge.

Gallup. (2005). Post-9/11 patriotism remains steadfast. http://www.gallup.com/poll/17401/post911-patriotism-remains-steadfast.aspx.

Gay, C. (2004). Putting race in context: Identifying the environmental determinants of black racial attitudes. *American Political Science Review, 98*(4), 547–562.

Gay, C. (2006). Seeing difference: The effect of economic disparity on black attitudes toward Latinos. *American Journal of Political Science, 50*, 982–997.

Gerber, A. S., Huber, G. A., Doherty, D., & Dowling, C. M.. (2011). Personality and the Strength and Direction of Partisan Identification. *Political Behavior, 34*(4), 653–688.

Gibson, J. L. (2008). Group identities and theories of justice: An experimental investigation into the justice and injustice of land squatting in South Africa. *Journal of Politics, 70*(3), 700–716.

Glasford, D. E., Dovidio, J. F., & Pratto, F. (2009). I continue to feel so good about us: Ingroup identification and the use of social identity-enhancing strategies to reduce intragroup dissonance. *Personality and Social Psychology Bulletin, 35*(4), 415–427.

Green, D. P., & Cowden, J. A. (1992). Who protests: Self-interest and white opposition to busing. *Journal of Politics, 54*, 471–496.

Green, D. P., Palmquist, B., & Schickler, E. (2002). *Partisan hearts and minds: Political parties and the social identities of voters.* New Haven, CT: Yale University Press.

Greenberg, J., Pyszczynski, T., Solomon, S., Rosenblatt, A., Veeded, M., & Kirkland, S. (1990). Evidence for terror management theory II: The effects of mortality salience on reactions to those who threaten or bolster the cultural world view. *Journal of Personality and Social Psychology, 58*, 308–318.

Greene, S. (1999). Understanding party identification: A social identity approach. *Political Psychology, 20*, 393–403.

Grieve, P. G., & Hogg, M. A. (1999). Subjective uncertainty and intergroup discrimination in the minimal intergroup situation. *Personality and Social Psychology Bulletin, 25*, 926–940.

Guimond, S., & Dubé-Simard, L. (1983). Relative deprivation theory and the Quebec nationalist movement: The cognition-emotion distinction and the personal-group deprivation issue. *Journal of Personality and Social Psychology, 44*, 526–535.

Gurin, P., & Townsend, A. (1986). Properties of gender identity and their implications for consciousness. *British Journal of Social Psychology, 25*, 139–148.

Hainmueller, J., & Hiscox, M. J. (2010). Attitudes toward highly skilled and low-skilled immigration: Evidence from a survey experiment. *American Political Science Review, 104*, 61–84.

Halevy, N., Bornstein, G., & Sagiv, L. (2008). "In-group Love" and Out-group Hate" as motives for individual participation in intergroup conflict. *Psychological Science, 19*(4), 405–411.

Haslam, A. S., & Reicher, S. (2006). Stressing the group: social identity and the unfolding dynamics of responses to stress. *Journal of Applied Psychology*, *91*(5), 1037–1052.

Herrmann, R. K., Isernia, P., & Segatti, P. (2009). Attachment to the nation and international relations: dimensions of identity and their relationship to war and peace. *Political Psychology*, *30*(5), 721–754.

Hogg, M. A. (1996). Intragroup processes, group structure, and social identity. In Robinson, W. P (Ed.), *Social Groups and Identities: Developing the Legacy of Henri Tajfel*, Oxford: Butterworth-Heinemann, (pp. 65–93).

Hogg, M. A. (2007). Uncertainty-identity theory. *Advances in Experimental Social Psychology*, *39*, 69–126.

Hogg, M. A., & Hains, S. C. (1996). Friendship and group identification: A new look at the role of cohesiveness in groupthink. *European Journal of Social Psychology*, *28*, 323–41.

Hogg, M. A., Hardie, E. A., & Reynolds, K. J. (1995). Prototypical similarity, self-categorization, and depersonalized attraction: A perspective on group cohesiveness. *European Journal of Social Psychology*, *25*, 159–177.

Hogg, M. A, & Reid, S. A. (2006). Social Identity, self-categorization, and the communication of group norms. *Communication Theory*, *16*, 7–30.

Hohman, Z. P., Hogg, M. A., & Bligh, M. C. (2010). Identity and intergroup leadership: Asymmetrical political and national identification in response to uncertainty. *Self and Identity*, *9*, 113–128.

Hooghe L., & Marks, G. (2004). Does identity or economic rationality drive public opinion on European integration? *Political Science and Politics*, *37*(3), 415–420.

Hornsey, M. J. (2008). Social Identity theory and self-categorization theory: A historical review. *Social and Personality Psychology Compass*, *2*(1), 204–222.

Huddy, L. (2001). From social to political identity: A critical examination of social identity theory. *Political Psychology*, *22*, 127–156.

Huddy, L. (2002). Context and Meaning in Social Identity Theory: A Response to Oakes. *Political Psychology*, *23*, 825–838.

Huddy, L. (2003). "Group Identity and Political Cohesion." In Sears, D. O., Huddy, L., & Jervis, R. (Eds.) *Oxford Handbook of Political Psychology*. New York: Oxford University Press (pp. 511–558).

Huddy, L., Cassese, E., & Lizotte, M.-K. (2008). Gender, public opinion, and political reasoning. In Wolbrecht, C., Beckwith, K., & Baldez, L. (Eds.), *Political Women and American Democracy*. Cambridge University Press, (pp. 31–49).

Huddy, L., Feldman, S., & Cassese, E. (2007). On the distinct political effects of anxiety and anger. In Neuman, W. R., Marcus, G. E., Crigler, A., & MacKuen, M. (eds.). *The Affect Effect: Dynamics of Emotion in Political Thinking and Behavior*. Chicago: University of Chicago Press, (pp. 202–230).

Huddy, L., Feldman, S., Taber, C., & Lahav, G. (2005). Threat, anxiety, and support of anti-terrorism policies. *American Journal of Political Science*, *49*(3), 610–625.

Huddy, L., & Khatib, N. (2007). American patriotism, national identity, and political involvement. *American Journal of Political Science*, *51*(1), 63–77.

Huddy, L., & Virtanen, S. (1995). Subgroup differentiation and subgroup bias among Latinos as a function of familiarity and positive distinctiveness. *Journal of Personality and Social Psychology*, *68*(1), 97.

Jackson, J. W., & Smith, E. R. (1999). Conceptualizing social identity: A new framework and evidence for the impact of different dimensions. *Personality and Social Psychology Bulletin*, *25*, 120–135.

Jackson, L. A., Sullivan, L. A., Harnish, R., & Hodge, C. N. (1996). Achieving positive social identity: Social mobility, social creativity, and permeability of group boundaries. *Journal of Personality and Social Psychology, 70,* 241–254.

Junn, J., & Masuoka, N. (2008). Asian American identity: shared racial status and political context, *Perspectives on Politics, 6,* 729–740.

Kam, C. D., & Ramos, J. M. (2008). Joining and leaving the rally understanding the surge and decline in presidential approval following 9/11. *Public Opinion Quarterly, 72*(4), 619–650. doi:10.1093/poq/nfn055

Kawakami, K., & Dion, K. (1993). The impact of salient self-identities on relative deprivation and action intentions. *European Journal of Social Psychology, 23,* 525–540.

Kinder, D. R., Adams, G. S., & Gronke, P. W. (1989). Economics and politics in the 1984 American presidential election. *American Journal of Political Science, 33,* 491–515.

Kosterman, R., & Feshbach, S. (1989). Toward a measure of patriotic and nationalistic attitudes. *Political Psychology, 10*(2), 257–274.

Lambert, A. J., Scherer, L. D., Schott, J. P., Olson, K. R., Andrews, R. K., O'Brien, T. C., & Zisser, A. R. (2010). Rally effects, threat, and attitude change: An integrative approach to understanding the role of emotion. *Journal of Personality and Social Psychology, 98*(6), 886–903.

Leach, C. W., Iyer, A., & Pederson, A. (2007). Angry opposition to government redress: When the structurally advantaged perceive themselves as relatively deprived. *British Journal of Social Psychology, 46,* 191–204.

Leonardelli, G. J., Pickett, C. L., & Brewer, M. B. (2010). Optimal distinctiveness theory: A framework for social identity, social cognition, and intergroup relations. In Zanna, M. P., & Olson, J. M. (Eds.) *Advances in Experimental Social Psychology* (Vol. 43, pp. 63–114).

Lerner, J. S., Gonzalez, R. M., Small, D. A., & Fischhoff, B. (2003). Effects of fear and anger on perceived risks of terrorism: A national field experiment. *Psychological Science, 14,* 144–150.

Levendusky, M. (2009). *The partisan sort: How liberals became Democrats and conservatives became Republicans.* Chicago: University of Chicago Press.

LeVine, R. A., & Campbell, D. T. (1972). *Ethnocentrism: theories of conflict, ethnic attitudes and behavior.* New York: John Wiley.

Levy, J. S. (1989) "The diversionary theory of war: a critique." In Manus I. Midlarsky, ed., *Handbook of war studies.* Boston: Unwin Hyman. pp. 259–88.

Lewis, G. J., & Bates, T. C. (2010). Genetic evidence for multiple biological mechanisms underlying in-group favoritism. *Psychological Science, 21*(11), 1623–1628.

Lewis-Beck, M. S., Jacoby, W. G., Norpoth, H., & Weisberg, H. E. (2008). *The American voter revisited.* Ann Arbor: University of Michigan Press.

Lowery, B. S., Unzueta, M. M., Knowles, E. D., & Goff, P. A. (2006). Concern for the in-group and opposition to affirmative action. *Journal of Personality and Social Psychology, 90*(6), 961–974.

Luhtanen, R., & Crocker, J. (1992). A collective self-esteem scale: Self-evaluation of one's social identity. *Personality & Social Psychology Bulletin, 18,* 302–318.

Mackie, D. M., Devos, T., & Smith, E. R. (2000). Intergroup emotions: Explaining offensive action tendencies in an intergroup context. *Journal of Personality and Social Psychology, 79*(4), 602–616.

Malka, A., & Lelkes, Y. (2010). More than ideology: conservative-liberal identity and receptivity to political cues. *Social Justice Research, 23*(2–3), 156–188.

Martin, E., DeMaio, T. J., & Campanelli, P. C. (1990). Context effects for census measures of race and Hispanic origin. *Public Opinion Quarterly, 54*, 551–566.

Mason, L. (2012). "The rise of uncivil agreement: issue versus behavioral polarization in the American electorate," *American Behavioral Scientist, 57*, 140–159.

Mason, L., Huddy, L., & Aaroe, L. (2012). *Measuring partisanship as a social identity, predicting political activism*. Stony Brook, NY: Unpublished manuscript.

McGarty, C., Turner, J. C., Hogg, M. A., David, B., & Wetherell, M. S. (1992). Group polarization as conformity to the prototypical group member. *British Journal of Social Psychology, 31*, 1–20.

Mendes, W. B., Major, B., McCoy, S., & Blascovich, J. (2008). How attributional ambiguity shapes physiological and emotional responses to rejection and acceptance. *Journal of Personality and Social Psychology, 94*(2), 278–291.

Miller, A. H., Gurin, P., Gurin, G., & Malanchuk, O. (1981). Group consciousness and political participation. *American Journal of Political Science, 25*, 494–511.

Muldoon, O. T., Schmid, K., & Downes, C. (2009). Political violence and psychological well-being: The role of social identity. *Applied Psychology: An International Review, 58*(1), 129–145.

Mullen, B., Brown, R., & Smith, C. (1992). Ingroup bias as a function of salience, relevance, and status: An integration. *European Journal of Social Psychology, 22*, 103–122.

Mummendey, A., Kessler, T., Klink, A., & Mielke, R. (1999). Strategies to cope with negative social identity: Predictions by social identity theory and relative deprivation theory. *Journal of Personality & Social Psychology, 76*(2), 229–245.

Musgrove, L., & McGarty, C. (2008). Opinion-based group memberships as a predictor of collective emotional responses and support for pro- and anti-war action. *Social Psychology, 39*(1), 37–47.

Nicholson, S. P. (2012). Polarizing cues. *American Journal of Political Science 56*(1), 52–66.

Oakes, P. (2002). Psychological groups and political psychology: A response to Huddy's "Critical examination of social identity theory." *Political Psychology, 23*(4), 809–824.

Parker, C. S. (2010). Symbolic versus blind patriotism: Distinction without difference? *Political Research Quarterly, 63*, 97–114.

Perreault, S., & Bourhis, R. Y. (1999). Ethnocentrism, social identification, and discrimination. *Personality and Social Psychology Bulletin, 25*(1), 92–103.

Phalet, K., Baysu, G., & Verkuyten, M. (2010). Political mobilization of Dutch Muslims: Religious identity salience, goal framing, and normative constraints. *Journal of Social Issues, 66*(4), 759–779.

Postmes, T., & Branscombe, N. R. (2002). Influence of long-term racial environmental composition on subjective well-being in African Americans. *Journal of Personality and Social Psychology, 83*(3), 735–751.

Pratto, F., & Glasford, D. E. (2008). Ethnocentrism and the value of human life. *Journal of Personality and Social Psychology, 95*(6), 1411–1428.

Reicher, S. (2004). The context of social identity: Domination, resistance, and change. *Social Psychology, 25*(6), 921–945.

Reicher, S., & Hopkins, N. (2001). *Self and nation: categorization, contestation and mobilization*. London: Sage.

Riek, B. M., Mania, E. W., Gaertner, S. L., McDonald, S. A., & Lamoreaux, M. J. (2010). Does a common ingroup identity reduce intergroup threat? *Group Processes & Intergroup Relations, 13*(4), 403–423.

Roccas, S., & Brewer, M. B. (2002). Social identity complexity. *Personality and Social Psychology Review, 6*(2), 88–106.

Rydell, R. J., Mackie, D. J., Maitner, A. T., Claypool, H. M., Ryan, M. J., & Smith, E. R. (2008). Arousal, processing, and risk-taking: Consequences of intergroup anger. *Personality and Social Psychology Bulletin, 34*(8), 1141–1152.

Sadler, M. S., Lineberger, M., Correll, J., & Park, B. (2005). Emotions, attributions, and policy endorsement in response to the September 11th terrorist attacks. *Basic and Applied Social Psychology, 27,* 249–258.

Schatz, R. T., Staub, E., & Lavine, H. (1999). On the varieties of national attachment: Blind versus constructive patriotism. *Political Psychology, 20,* 151–174.

Scheepers, D. (2009). Turning social identity threat into challenge: Status stability and cardiovascular reactivity during inter-group competition. *Journal of Experimental Social Psychology, 45*(1), 228–233.

Scheepers, D., & Ellemers, N. (2005). When the pressure is up: The assessment of social identity threat in low and high status groups. *Journal of Experimental Social Psychology, 41,* 192–200.

Schildkraut, D. J. (2002). The more things change... American identity and mass and elite responses to 9/11. *Political Psychology, 23*(3), 511–535.

Schildkraut, D. J. (2011). *Americanism in the twenty-first century. Public opinion in the age of immigration.* New York: Cambridge University Press.

Schmid, K., Tausch, N., Hewstone, M., Hughes, J., & Cairns, E. (2008). The effects of living in segregated vs. mixed areas in Northern Ireland: A simultaneous analysis of contact and threat effects in the context of micro-level neighborhoods. *International Journal of Conflict and Violence, 2,* 56–71.

Schwartz, S. H., Struch, N., & Bilsky, W. (1990). Values and intergroup social motives: A study of Israeli and German students. *Social Psychology Quarterly, 53,* 185–198.

Sears, D. O., Citrin, J., Cheleden, S. V., & van Laar, C. (1999). Cultural diversity and multicultural politics: Is ethnic balkanization psychologically inevitable? In Prentice, D. & Miller, D. (Eds.), *Cultural divides: The social psychology of cultural contact* (pp. 35–79). New York: Russell Sage Foundation.

Sears, D. O., & Funk, C. (1991). The role of self-interest in social and political attitudes. *Advances in Experimental Psychology, 24,* 1–91.

Shamir, M., & Arian, A. (1999). Collective identity and electoral competition in Israel. *American Political Science Review, 93,* 265–277.

Sidanius, J., Levin, S., van Laar, C., & Sears, D. O. (2008). *The diversity challenge. Social identity and intergroup relations on the college campus.* New York: Russell Sage.

Sidanius, J., & Pratto, F. (2001). *Social dominance: An intergroup theory of social hierarchy and oppression.* New York: Cambridge University Press.

Simon, B. (2004). *Identity in modern society: A social psychological perspective.* Malden, MA: Blackwell.

Simon, B., & Grabow, O. (2010). The politicization of migrants: Further evidence that politicized collective identity is a dual identity. *Political Psychology, 31*(5), 717–738.

Simon, B., & Klandermans, B. (2001). Politicized collective identity: A social psychological analysis. *American Psychologist, 56,* 319–331.

Simon, B., Kulla, C., & Zobel, M. (1995). On being more than just a part of the whole: Regional identity and social distinctiveness. *European Journal of Social Psychology, 25,* 325–340.

Simon, B., Loewy, M., Sturmer, S., Weber, U., Freytag, P., Habig, C., et al. (1998). Collective identification and social movement participation. *Journal of Personality and Social Psychology, 74,* 646–658.

Simon, B., & Ruhs, D. (2008). Identity and politicization among Turkish immigrants in Germany: The role of dual identification. *Journal of Personality and Social Psychology, 95*(6), 1354–1366.

Sindic, D., & Reicher, S. D. (2009). "Our way of life is worth defending": Testing a model of attitudes towards superordinate group membership through a study of Scots' attitudes towards Britain. *European Journal of Social Psychology, 39,* 114–129.

Skitka, L. J., Bauman, C. W., Aramovich, N. P., & Morgan, G. S. (2006). Confrontational and preventative policy responses to terrorism: Anger wants a fight and "fear" wants them to go away. *Basic and Applied Social Psychology, 28,* 375–384.

Smith, H. J., Spears, R., & Oyen, M. (1994). People like us: The influence of personal deprivation and group membership salience on justice evaluations. *Journal of Experimental Social Psychology, 30,* 277–299.

Sniderman, P., Hagendoorn, L., & Prior, M. (2004). Predispositional factors and situational triggers: Exclusionary reactions to immigrant minorities. *American Political Science Review, 98*(1), 35–49.

Stephan, W. G., & Stephan, C. W. (2000). An integrated threat theory of intergroup behavior. In S. Worchel & W. G. Austin (eds.), *Psychology of intergroup relations* (pp. 7–24). Chicago: Nelson-Hall.

Struch, N., & Schwartz, S. H. (1989). Intergroup aggression: Its predictors and distinctness from in-group bias. *Journal of Personality and Social Psychology, 56,* 364–373.

Tajfel, H. (1981). *Human groups and social categories.* Cambridge: Cambridge University Press.

Tajfel, H., & Turner, J. C. (1979). An integrative theory of intergroup conflict. In W. G. Austin and S. Worchel (eds.), *The social psychology of intergroup relations* (pp. 33–47). Monterey, CA: Brooks/Cole.

Tate, K. (1994). *From protest to politics: The new black voters in American elections* (enlarged ed.). Cambridge, MA: Harvard University Press.

Tausch, N., Hewstone, M., Kenworthy, J., Cairns, E., & Christ, O. (2007). Cross-community contact, perceived status differences, and intergroup attitudes in Northern Ireland: The mediating roles of individual-level versus group-level threats and the moderating role of social identification. *Political Psychology, 28*(1), 53–68.

Terry, D. J., & Hogg, M. A. (1996). Group norms and the attitude-behavior relationship: A role for group identification. *Personality and Social Psychology Bulletin, 22,* 776–793.

Theiss-Morse, E. (2009). *Who counts as an American: The boundaries of national identity.* Cambridge: Cambridge University Press.

Thomas, E. F., & McGarty, C. (2009). The role of efficacy and moral outrage norms in creating the potential for international development activism through group-based interaction. *British Journal of Social Psychology, 48,* 115–134.

Thomas, E. F., McGarty, C., & Mavor, K. I. (2009). Aligning identities, emotions and beliefs to create commitment to sustainable social and political action. *Personality and Social Psychology Review, 13*(3), 194–218.

Torgler, B., & Schneider, F. (2007). What shapes attitudes toward paying taxes? Evidence from multicultural European countries. *Social Science Quarterly, 88*(2), 443–470.

Townsend, S. S., Major, B., Gangi, C. E., & Mendes, W. B. (2011). From "in the air" to "under the skin": Cortisol responses to social identity threat. *Personality and Social Psychology Bulletin, 37*(2), 151–164.

Transue, J. E. (2007). Identity salience, identity acceptance, and racial policy attitudes: American national identity as a uniting force. *American Journal of Political Science, 51,* 78–91.

Tripathi, R. C., & Srivastava, R. (1981). Relative deprivation and intergroup attitudes. *European Journal of Social Psychology, 11,* 313–318.

Turner, J. C., Hogg, M. A., Oakes, P. J., Reicher, S. D., & Wetherell, M. S. (1987). *Rediscovering the social group: A self-categorization theory.* Oxford: Basil Blackwell.

Turner, J. C., Hogg, M. A., Turner, P. J., & Smith, P. M. (1984). Failure and defeat as determinants of group cohesiveness. *British Journal of Social Psychology, 23,* 97–111.

Tyler, T. R., & Blader, S. L. (2000). *Cooperation in groups. Procedural justice, social identity, and behavioral engagement.* Philadelphia, PA: Psychology Press.

van Bavel, J. J., Packer, D. J., & Cunningham, W. A. (2008). The neural substrates of ingroup bias. *Psychological Science, 19*(11), 1131–1139.

Vanneman, R. D., & Pettigrew, T. F. (1972). Race and relative deprivation in the urban United States. *Race, 13,* 461–486.

van Zomeren, M., Postmes, T., and Spears, R. (2008). Toward an integrative social identity model of collective action: Quantitative research synthesis of three socio-psychological perspectives. *Psychological Bulletin, 134*(4), 504–535.

van Zomeren, M., Spears, R., & Leach, C. W. (2008). Exploring psychological mechanisms of collective action: Does relevance of group identity influence how people cope with collective disadvantage? *British Journal of Social Psychology, 47,* 353–372.

Verkuyten, M., & Nekuee, S. (1999). Ingroup bias: The effect self-stereotyping, identification, and group threat. *European Journal of Social Psychology, 29,* 411–418.

Voci, A. (2006). The link between identification and in-group favouritism: Effects of threat to social identity and trust-related emotions. *British Journal of Social Psychology, 45,* 265–284.

Wattenberg, M. P. (2008). *Is voting for young people? With a postscript on citizen engagement.* New York: Pearson Longman.

Wong, C. J. (2010). *Boundaries of obligation in American politics: Geographic, national, and racial communities.* New York: Cambridge University Press.

Wright, S. C. (1997). Ambiguity, social influence, and collective action: Generating collective protest in response to tokenism. *Personality and Social Psychology Bulletin, 23,* 1277–1290.

Wright, S. C., Taylor, D. T., & Moghaddam, F. M. (1990). Responding to membership in a disadvantaged group: From acceptance to collective protest. *Journal of Personality and Social Psychology, 58,* 994–1003.

Yzerbyt, V., Dumont, M., Wigboldus, D., & Grodijn, E. (2003). I feel for us: The impact of categorization and identification on emotions and action tendencies. *British Journal of Social Psychology, 42,* 533–549.

Zaller, J. R. (1992). *Nature and nature of mass ideology.* Cambridge: Cambridge University Press.

CHAPTER 24

SOCIAL MOVEMENTS AND THE DYNAMICS OF COLLECTIVE ACTION

BERT KLANDERMANS AND JACQUELIEN VAN STEKELENBURG

PROTESTS in the "new" democracies in central Europe about "stolen elections," street demonstrations in the "old" democracies against austerity measures, ongoing protests in the Arab world for more democracy, and occupied city squares throughout the world to denounce inequality and to demand better governance: Almost daily our news media report on how people try to influence politics in contentious manners. This is not to say that political protest is something people regularly do. In fact, participants in political protest are most of the time a minority. Even mass mobilization rarely encompasses more than a few percent of the population. This raises a question that has always occupied students of social movements and collective action, especially social and political psychologists: *Why do some individuals participate in collective action while others don't?* The answer to that question is less obvious than many assume.

In 1965 Mancur Olson published his *Logic of Collective Action*. The core of the book was the argument that rational actors will *not* take part in collective action unless selective incentives persuade them to do so. Olson's reasoning was soon applied to social movement participation, as it helped to explain why so often people do not participate in social movements despite the interest they have in the achievement of the movement's goals. Movement scholars argued that movement goals are collective goods. Therefore, if the goal is achieved, people will enjoy the benefits irrespective of whether they have participated in the effort. In view of a goal for which achievement is uncertain, but for which benefits—if materialized—can be reaped anyway, rational actors will take a free ride, so the Olsonian reasoning goes.

The problem with Olson's logic of collective action is that indeed it provides an explanation for why people do not participate in collective action (although one of us demonstrated that nonparticipation often has reasons other than free riding—Klandermans,

1988), but fares poorly in explaining why people do participate. While we are writing, the world witnesses the uproar in the Arab world, worldwide protests against austerity measures, and the Occupy movement demonstrating if anything that people *do* protest. A recurring criticism is that Olson's model assumes that individuals make their decisions in isolation, as if there are no social media, no other people with whom they interact, with whom they feel solidary, and by whom they are kept to their promises. Yet Olson's dilemma of collective action can serve well to explain why participation in collective action cannot be taken for granted even if it seems to be in someone's interest. This is the paradox that lies at the roots of the argument we will unfold in the pages to come. We propose a political psychology of collective action participation. In doing so, we will introduce dynamics of collective action of engagement, sustainable participation, and disengagement. But we will begin with a definition of social movements and collective action, the phenomena we are interested in.

1. Defining Social Movements and Collective Action

"Social movements are collective challenges by people with common purposes and solidarity in sustained interaction with elites and authorities" (Klandermans, 1997, p. 2; Tarrow, 1998, p. 4). This definition includes three key elements that deserve elaboration. First, social movements are *collective challenges*. They concern disruptive collective direct action against elites, authorities, other groups, or cultural codes. There is an obvious reason why this is the case. Social movements typically though not always encompass people who lack access to politics. Had they had access, there would have been no need for a social movement. Disruptive collective action forces authorities to pay attention to the claims brought forward. Second, it concerns people with a *common purpose and solidarity*. Social movement participants rally behind common claims; they want authorities to do something, to change a state of affair or to undo changes. Such common claims are rooted in feelings of collective identity and solidarity. Third, isolated incidents of collective action are not social movements. Only *sustained collective action* turns contention into a social movement.

Although movement participants are a minority, several authors have observed that movement types of action has become more frequent over the last 30 years (Jenkins, 1995; Mayer, 2013; but see McCarthy, Rafail, & Gromis, 2013 for diverging figures on the United States; Meyer & Tarrow, 1998; Neidhart & Rucht, 1993; van Stekelenburg & Boekkooi, 2013; 2010). Others have argued that social movements have become a regular phenomenon in democratic societies (Goldstone, 2003; Johnston, 2011). Some of these authors have labeled this trend "movimentization of politics" (Neidhardt & Rucht, 1993), while others coined the term "movement society" (Meyer & Tarrow, 1998; Johnston, 2011). This is also observed at the individual level by Dalton, Van Sickle, and

Weldon (2009). With data from the 1999–2002 wave of the World Values Survey (WVS), they demonstrate that political protest is seemingly a ubiquitous aspect of politics in contemporary advanced industrial societies, and that its use may be spreading to less developed nations as well.

Engaging in social movements most of the time implies taking part in some form of collective action. In the words of Wright, Taylor, and Moghaddam (1990) an individual takes part in collective action "any time that [she or he] is acting as a representative of the group and the action is directed at improving the conditions of the entire group." Wright (2001) proposes a simple taxonomy of possible forms of political action. In response to some political issue, people can chose to stay inactive; if they get into action, they can engage in individual or collective action; and collective action can be noncontentious or contentious. Participation can further be distinguished in terms of duration (ad hoc versus sustained) and effort (weak versus strong) (figure 24.1).

Some activities require little effort, others a lot, and some are limited in time, while others are unlimited. Activities in the low-effort/limited duration square typically require large numbers to make any impression on policymakers. It does not make much sense to have a petition with only 10 signatures; you need thousands if not hundreds of thousands. People know this, and thus for them to be motivated it is important to know that some threshold level will be reached. Therefore, an important element of the persuasion strategy must be how to convince people that enough other people will participate. Activities in the high-effort/unlimited duration square, on the other hand, must solve the free-rider dilemma. For high-effort/long duration activities it usually suffices to have only a few participants who are willing to make an effort. As a consequence, many people can afford to take a free ride. Willingness to participate in this type of activity thus implies readiness to give 90% or more of the supporters that free ride. The social psychological dynamics vary, as the story of thresholds and free riders illustrate. Attempts to explain (non)participation must thus take into account the kind of activity we are talking about.

DURATION

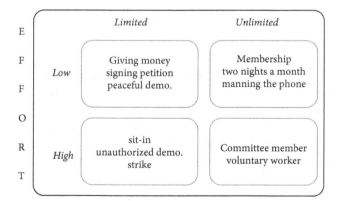

FIGURE 24.1 The process of participation (Klandermans, 1997)

In this chapter we focus on individuals—what are their fears, hopes, and concerns? What are the choices they make and the motives they have? These questions bring us to the level of analysis of the individual and therefore to the realm of political and social psychology. Obviously, other disciplines like sociology and political science have social movements and collective action as their study object too; in this chapter we will focus on the political psychological approach and will point to literature from sociology and political science where applicable. People live in a perceived world. They respond to the world as they perceive and interpret it. Indeed, this is what a political psychology of social movements and collective action is about—trying to understand why people who are seemingly in the same sociopolitical configuration respond so different. As political psychology explores the causes of the thoughts, feelings, and actions of people—and primarily how these are influenced by sociopolitical context—it has a lot to offer to the study of protest participation. Indeed, context matters. Therefore, questions we want to ask as well include the following: How are citizens embedded in their social environment, and how does that influence their political orientation and behavior? What kind of politics do citizens encounter? In this chapter we concentrate on movement politics, but we must not forget that movement and party politics are counterparts and that contextual factors influence whether citizens choose to employ one or the other.

2. WHY SOCIAL MOVEMENTS EMERGE

In this chapter we concentrate on why individuals participate in movement activities. The question of why social movements come into being and why they have become common practice is not our focal question. There is a rich literature available on that matter (for instance, Buechler, 2000; della Porta & Diani, 2006; Klandermans, 2001; McAdam, McCarthy, & Zald, 1996; McAdam, Tarrow, & Tilly, 2001; Meyer & Tarrow, 1998; Snow, Soule, & Kriesi, 2004; Tarrow, 2011). For our purpose it suffices to summarize the global answers that have been forwarded, in brief: because people are aggrieved, because people have the resources to mobilize and seize the political opportunity to protest, and because their collective identities politicize. These answers parallel the history of theoretical approaches to collective action. Research began in the 1950s and 1960s with classical theories such as symbolic interactionism, structural functionalism, and relative deprivation theory. Buechler (2000) classified these theories as classical collective behavior theories, a category that he characterizes as theories that understand social movements as a reaction to social stress, strain, or breakdown. The direct causes of collective behavior are seen as rooted in individuals who are experiencing various forms of discontent or anxiety. Basically, discontent is viewed as the origin of protest. In social movement literature these theories have also been labeled "breakdown theories," which alludes to the fact that researchers conceived of social movements as indicators of the existence of major cleavages in a society and of societal tension or even breakdown as a consequence. The works of Blumer (1951), Turner and Killian (1987), Smelser (1962),

Davies (1962), and Gurr (1970) are classic examples of this research tradition. The first two are associated with symbolic interactionism, describing social movements as phenomena emerging in the interaction between dissatisfied people. Smelser is associated with structural functionalism, an approach that defines social movements as a process to restore equilibrium in a society. Davies and Gurr brought relative deprivation to the field, explaining the emergence of social movements from high levels of relative deprivation in a society. But it was obvious that many aggrieved people never engage in protest. Indeed in the early 1970s protagonists of resource mobilization theory began to argue that grievances are ubiquitous and that the real question is not so much what makes people aggrieved but what makes aggrieved people participate in social movements (McCarthy & Zald, 1976; Oberschall, 1973).

Resource mobilization theorists saw social movements as normal, rational, institutionally rooted political challenges by aggrieved people. Differential availability of resources explains in their eyes why some aggrieved people become involved in social movements while others don't. It was argued that people need resources to stage collective political action, and a key resource for such action is organizations and networks that exist among the affected population (so-called indigenous organizations, Morris, 1984). Applying an economic metaphor, McCarthy and Zald (1976) made the distinction between social movements (beliefs that represent a preference for change in a society), social movement organizations (organizations that identify with a social movement), social movement industries (social movement organizations that belong to the same social movement), and social movement sectors (all social movement industries in a society). Within the resource mobilization framework, participation in collective action was analyzed in terms of the costs and benefits associated with it. Rational choice models of behavior (Klandermans, 1984; Oberschall, 1973; Opp, 1988) and Olson's theory of collective action (1965) were employed as models to explain individuals' participation and nonparticipation in collective action. When the potential benefits outweigh the anticipated costs, people opt to participate. Paradoxically, the same deprivation that might motivate people to stage collective action might deprive them of the resources needed for such action. Indeed, it was proposed that external resources could tip the balance. Soon a variant of resource mobilization theory developed within political science—the political process approach—which proposed that political opportunities available to aggrieved groups with the resources to take action make the difference (McAdam, 1982). Political opportunities are "those consistent—but not necessarily formal or permanent—dimensions of the political environment that provide incentives for people to undertake collective action by affecting their expectations of success and failure" (Tarrow, 1998, p. 85). Among the many aspects of the political environment that have been referred to as factors influencing success expectations are the strength of the state, the level of repression, the party system, the degree of access to policy, and the dividedness of elites.

In the late 1980s and early 1990s, partly as the result of exchanges between American and European social movement scholars (Klandermans, Kriesi, & Tarrow, 1988), an interest began to develop in the cognitive and affective origins of social movements. In response to the structuralist approach of the then dominant paradigms—resource mobilization and political process theories—social movement scholars from various angles began to highlight the processes of interaction, the symbolic definition and negotiation among participants, opponents, and bystanders of collective action. Grievances, resources, and opportunities are all needed for social movements to develop, but these scholars hold that they are also the result of the presence of social movements. They are in the eyes of the beholder and thus socially constructed. Moreover, researchers working from this perspective argued that aggrieved people might have the resources and opportunities to protest, but they still need to construct a politicized collective identity to engage in collective political action. Over the last decade and a half this new approach to collective action has been elaborated in studies of framing, collective identity, and emotions in the context of social movements. Together they have been labeled social constructionist approaches to protest. Snow, Rochford, Worden, and Benford (1986) were among the first to elaborate on the role of cognitive processes in their treatment of frame alignment—that is, attempts by movement organizers to persuade people to adopt the movement's reading of the situation. At the same time, Melucci (1989) began to point to the importance of collective identity (Cohen, 1985). In social psychology, scholars began to elaborate social identity theory and intergroup emotions theory (see Huddy, chapter 23, this volume). Soon cognition and identity began to proliferate in social movement literature (see Morris & McClurg Mueller, 1992 for an overview of scholarly work at that time). The most recent social constructionist attempt to move away from structural approaches such as resource mobilization and political process concerns the role of emotions in collective action (Goodwin, Jasper, & Polleta, 2001; van Stekelenburg & Klandermans, 2007). By way of conclusion it suffices to assert that social constructionism has carved out its own niche as a legitimate approach to the analysis of social movements (Buechler, 2000, p. 54).

In sum, breakdown theories, resource mobilization and political process theories, and social constructionist theories all tried to account for the emergence of social movements in our societies. All agree that somehow grievances are at the roots of social movements and contention, but they diverge in their explanations of what makes aggrieved people protest. While breakdown theories offer little in terms of mobilization processes beyond high levels of discontent, resource mobilization and political process theory point to resources and political opportunities as factors in the environment that impact on the formation and fate of social movements. Social constructionists, on the other hand, focus more on processes of interaction and sense-making among the aggrieved as internal factors stimulating the emergence of social movements. The remainder of this chapter will be devoted to the mechanisms of engagement and disengagement in collective action as they are currently conceived in social and political psychology.

3. THE DYNAMICS OF COLLECTIVE ACTION

Dynamics of collective action can be decomposed into dynamics of demand, supply, and mobilization (Klandermans, 2004). Dynamics of demand are about people and their motives, dynamics of supply about organizations and their appeals, and dynamics of mobilization about the convergence of demand and supply. Although the three are interdependent, each concerns different aspects of the dynamics of collective action, refers to different mechanisms, and relates to different literatures.

The *demand side* of collective action concerns characteristics of a social movement's mobilization potential. What is its demographic and political composition? Which collective identities does it comprise? What are the shared grievances and emotions? What is the composition of its organizational field; and to what extent are individuals socially and virtually embedded? The *supply side* of collective action concerns the characteristics of the movement. Is it strong; is it effective? Is it likely to achieve its goals at affordable costs? Does it have charismatic leaders? Is it an organization people can identify with? What does its action repertoire look like? Does it stage activities that are appealing to people? Which ideology does the movement stand for, and what constituents of identification does it offer? Demand and supply do not automatically come together. In a market economy, marketing is employed to make sure that the public is aware of a supply that might meet its demand. *Mobilization* is—so to speak—the marketing mechanism of the movement domain. The study of mobilization concerns such matters as the effectiveness of (persuasive) communication, the influence of social networks, and the role of new media such as the Internet, (smart)phones, and social media.

Studies of participation tend to concentrate on mobilization and to neglect the development of demand and supply factors. Yet there is no reason to take either for granted. To be sure, grievances abound in a society, but that does not mean that there is no reason to explain how grievances develop and how they are transformed into a demand for protest. Nor does the presence of social movement organizations in a society mean that there is no need to understand their formation and to investigate how they stage opportunities to protest and how these opportunities are seized by aggrieved people.

Between the paradigms a division of labor seems to exist in terms of the study of demand and supply. Whereas resource mobilization and political process theorists typically study supply factors, social constructionists study demand factors, and all three study mobilization. As we are concentrating on the study of collective action in social and political psychology, we will put an emphasis on demand and mobilization, but we cannot do without a brief discussion of the dynamics of supply.

3.1. Dynamics of Demand

Little is known about how exactly demand is formed. A few decades ago Klandermans introduced the distinction between *consensus mobilization* and *consensus formation* (1984; 1988). While consensus mobilization concerns "the deliberate attempts to spread the view of a social actor among parts of the population," consensus formation concerns "the unplanned convergence of meaning in social networks and subcultures" (Klandermans, 1988, p. 175). Gamson (1992) in his *Talking Politics* shows that people use any kind of information source if they talk with their friends about politics. Employing time-series analysis Vliegenthart (2007) demonstrated for the issues of immigration and integration that in a complex interplay between real-life events, media attention, debates in the parliament, and debates between politicians, public opinion is formed and converted into anti-immigrant party support in the Netherlands. In research she has yet to report on, van Stekelenburg investigates how, in a newly built neighborhood, demand for protest develops as a function of the development of formal, informal, and virtual networks. These days the Internet and social media play a crucial role in this regard (Earl & Kimport, 2011; van Stekelenburg, Petrovic, Pouw, Limburg, & Nederlof, 2012).

Indeed, the formation of demand is a process that takes place in social interaction. Individuals are embedded in formal, informal, and virtual networks, which in turn are embedded in multiorganizational fields. Taylor (2013) proposes the concept of *discursive communities* to signify these settings in which consensus formation takes place. Understanding the formation of demand in a society requires insight in these processes of consensus mobilization and formation. We will return to the subject in our section on mobilization.

3.1.1. Grievances

Grievances concern "outrage about the way authorities are treating a social problem" (Klandermans, 1997, p. 38). In *The Social Psychology of Protest*, while expanding on this definition, Klandermans made the distinction between illegitimate inequality, suddenly imposed grievances, and violated principles. The notions of suddenly imposed grievances and violated principles, in fact, originate in the sociological social movement literature. Walsh & Warland (1983) coined the first and Kriesi (1993) the second. Suddenly imposed grievances—such as the establishment of a waste incinerator or a highway trajectory—are powerful mobilizers, as are violated principles. Illegitimate inequality is dealt with in the literatures on relative deprivation and social justice. Relative deprivation theory holds that feelings of relative deprivation result from a comparison of one's situation with a certain standard—one's past, someone else's situation, or an ideological standard such as equity or justice (Folger, 1986). If a comparison results in the conclusion that one is not receiving what one deserves, a person experiences relative deprivation. The literature further distinguishes between relative deprivation based on personal comparisons (i.e., individual deprivation) and relative deprivation based on group comparisons (i.e., group deprivation; Kelly & Breinlinger, 1996). Research demonstrates that group relative deprivation is particularly important for engagement in collective action (Major, 1994), but work by Foster and Matheson (1999) suggests that so-called "double deprivation," that is, a combination of group and individual deprivation, is even more effective. On the basis of a meta-analysis, van Zomeren, Postmes, and Spears (2008) conclude that the cognitive component of relative deprivation (i.e., the observation that one receives less than the standard of comparison) has less influence on action participation than does the affective component (i.e., such feelings as dissatisfaction, indignation, and discontent about outcomes).

Social psychologists have applied social justice theory to the study of social movements (Tyler & Smith, 1998). The social justice literature distinguishes between two classes of justice judgments: distributive and procedural justice. Distributive justice is related to relative deprivation in that it refers to the fairness of outcome distributions. Procedural justice, on the other hand, refers to the fairness of decision-making procedures and the relational aspects of the social process, that is, whether authorities treat people with respect and can be trusted to act in a beneficial and unbiased manner (Tyler & Lind, 1992). Research has found that people care more about how they are treated than about outcomes. Based on these findings, Tyler and Smith (1998) propose that procedural justice might be a more powerful predictor of social movement participation than distributive justice; that is what we found indeed both in our research in South Africa (Klandermans, Roefs, & Olivier, 2001) and among migrants in the Netherlands and New York (Klandermans, Van der Toorn, & van Stekelenburg, 2008).

Political trust and political cynicism further influence the formation of grievances. Folger (1986) argues that perceived inequalities will not turn into discontent if people trust responsible actors (mostly authorities) to deal with the problem. Indeed, we found in our research in South Africa that relative deprivation is substantially reduced when people display trust in government (Klandermans et al., 2001). On the other hand, if people are cynical about politics, feelings of injustice are more likely to turn into contestation, as our migrants study demonstrated (Klandermans, Van der Toorn, & van Stekelenburg, 2008).

Table 24.1 summarizes what grievances are strong motivators: suddenly imposed grievances, group and double deprivation rather than individual deprivation, procedural justice rather than distributive justice, the emotional component of grievances rather than the cognitive component, violated principles and threatened interests, and political cynicism rather than trust.

3.1.2. Efficacy

It would be hard to deny that people who are part of a movement's mobilization potential are aggrieved, but as we know meanwhile grievances do not provide a sufficient reason to participate in collective action. Therefore, the key question of any grievance theory to address is: why do some aggrieved people protest, while others do not? The

Table 24.1 Strongly Motivating Grievances

Suddenly imposed grievances

Group and double deprivation

Procedural justice

The emotional component of grievances

Violated principles and threatened interests

Political cynicism

first to raise that question were the resource mobilization theorists (e.g., Oberschall, 1973; McCarthy and Zald, 1976) and a social psychological expansion thereof (Klandermans, 1984). More recently, in a large comparative study based on WVS surveys, Dalton et al. (2009) found that grievances are weak predictors of protest. Rather than aggrieved people, it is those who possess political skills and resources who generally protest more, independent of their level of grievances. The underlying political psychological concept is efficacy. People are more likely to participate in movement activities when they believe this will help to redress their grievances at affordable costs (Klandermans, 1984). The more effective an individual believes collective action participation to be, the more likely the person is to participate. Van Zomeren, Spears, Fischer, and Leach (2004) propose efficacy as the core of what they call problem-focused coping—one of the two pathways to collective action they define, the other being emotion-focused coping, with group-based anger at its core (see below). In a cross-national study Corcoran, Pettinicchio, and Young (2012) demonstrated the significant role of efficacy for protest participation across 48 countries. Qualifying the assertions of political process approaches, these authors report important contextual influences. Feelings of efficacy make people more likely to participate in collective action, especially if they are faced with closed political opportunities. But for those who feel efficacious, opportunities or lack of repression don't make any difference. Efficacious people participate in collective action no matter what the opportunities are. Indeed, opportunities or absence of repression only make fatalistic people take part in collective action. The authors report that social embeddedness is of crucial importance for the generation and role of feelings of efficacy in that respect. We will come back to that later.

3.1.3. *Identity*

Next to efficacy, identity, specifically collective identity, became an important concept in the social movement literature in the past 25 years. Melucci was among the first to emphasize the significance of collective identity (1981). In the years to follow the concept began to gain prominence in the social movement literature (see Stryker, Owens, & White, 2000). Meanwhile, social psychologists began to explore the role of group identification in movement participation (Kelly & Breinlinger, 1996; Simon et al., 1998; de Weerd & Klandermans, 1999; Simon & Klandermans, 2001; Stürmer & Simon, 2004) and concluded that the more one identifies with a group involved in a protest activity, the more likely one is to take part in that activity.

A complicating matter in this respect is the fact that people simultaneously hold multiple identities, while movements tend to emphasize a single identity and refer to a single place in society. As a consequence, people may experience being steered in different directions by conflicting identities (cf. Kurtz, 2002). Individuals might find themselves under cross-pressure when two groups they identify with are on opposite sides of a controversy (e.g., union members faced with the decision to strike against their own company). Indeed, workers who go on strike or movement activists who challenge their government are often accused of being disloyal to the company or the country. This problem is especially relevant in the case of protest participation by immigrants, these days specifically Muslim immigrants, which can easily be (mis)interpreted as disloyalty to their new country of residence. González and Brown (2003) coined the term "dual identity" to point to the concurrent workings of supra- and subordinated identities. They argue that identification with a subordinate entity (e.g., ethnic identity) does not necessarily exclude identification with a supraordinate entity (e.g., national identity). In fact, they claim that dual identity is a healthy configuration, as it implies sufficient identification with one's subgroup to experience basic security *and* sufficient identification with the overarching group to preclude divisiveness.

There is evidence that indeed people who hold a dual identity are more satisfied with their situation than people who do not (González & Brown, 2003; Simon, 2010). Furthermore, studies of Spanish and Dutch farmers, South African citizens, and immigrants in the Netherlands and New York suggest that individuals who report holding a dual identity are more satisfied with their social and political situation than those who do not hold a dual identity (Klandermans et al., 2001; Klandermans, Sabucedo, & Rodriguez, 2004; Klandermans et al., 2008). However, if they are dissatisfied, individuals who hold a dual identity are more likely to participate in collective action.

Simon and his students (Simon & Grabow, 2010; Simon & Ruhs, 2008) have argued that a politicized collective identity is by definition a dual identity. In 2001 Simon and Klandermans published their influential paper on the politicization of collective identity (PCI). In order to become the vehicle of collective action, collective identity must politicize, they argued. Shared grievances, common enemies, and a search for third-party support are the building blocks of PCI the authors refer to. Some sense of identification with the superordinate political entity seems to be a basic requirement of social and political mobilization in that it ensures that this entity is acknowledged as *one's own* social or political habitat or arena. More specifically, to the extent that one identifies with the superordinate entity, one should feel entitled to make political claims, because identity confers rights. Similarly, one should feel motivated to get actively involved in the political game, because it becomes one's own game, and one should feel encouraged to approach third parties as potential allies, because they can be viewed as in-group members at the superordinate level (Simon and Ruhs, 2008). Politicization divides people's social environment into allies and opponents and results in polarization. Polarization concerns the process of distancing of the opposing camps. The more polarized the relationship becomes, the less deviation from own opinions and actions is accepted and the more opinions and acts of the opponents are rejected. Eventually, this may result in radicalization. Simon suggests that in a polarized situation, to the extent that PCI is a dual identity including identification with the superordinate polity, PCI has a pacifying effect on politicization and associated collective action in that it prioritizes normative claims and actions (i.e., claims and actions that stay within the limits of normative acceptance in the larger polity). In contrast, collective identities lacking this pacifying effect, such as separatist identities based on more exclusive cultural, ethnic, or religious allegiances, should be more prone to nonnormative escalation and radicalization.

3.1.4. *Emotions*

Recent work in sociology and social and political psychology has brought emotions to the study of social movements (Goodwin et al., 2001; Jasper, 1998; van Stekelenburg, 2006; van Zomeren et al., 2004). For those of us who have been part of protest events or watched reports on protest events in the news media, this is hardly surprising. Indeed, it is hard to conceive of protest detached from emotions. Emotions can be avoidance or approach oriented. Fear, which makes people refrain from taking action, is an example of an avoidance-oriented emotion. Anger is an approach oriented emotion and is known to be an antecedent of protest participation (van Zomeren et al., 2004). There appears to be a relation between emotions and efficacy. When people do not feel efficacious, they are more likely to experience fear; feeling efficacious, on the other hand, is associated with experiencing anger (Mackie, Devos, & Smith, 2000). Findings from our study among migrants confirm this: feelings of efficacy reinforced anger and reduced fear, while in their turn anger fostered collective action participation, while fear undermined it (Klandermans et al., 2008). Van Zomeren et al. (2004) show that anger is an important motivator of protest participation of *disadvantaged* groups. Leach, Iyer, & Pedersen (2006) examined readiness for political action among *advantaged* Australians to oppose government plans to redress disadvantaged Aborigines. They found that symbolic racism and relative deprivation evoked group-based anger, which in turn promoted willingness for political action. But advantaged group members can also perceive the in-group advantage as unfair and feel guilt and anger about it. Anger related to in-group advantage, and to a lesser degree guilt, appears to be a potent predictor for protest (Leach et al., 2006). Anger, guilt, and fear are not the only emotions relevant in the context of movement participation; indeed other emotions such as hope and despair are proposed as well (D. Gould, 2009; Stürmer & Simon, 2009; Taylor, 2013). Anger moves people to adopt a more challenging relationship with authorities than subordinate emotions such as shame and despair (Taylor, 2009) or fear (Klandermans et al., 2008).

In explaining different tactics, efficacy appears to be relevant, too. Anger is mainly observed in normative actions were efficacious people protest. However, in nonnormative violent actions contempt appears to be the more relevant emotion (Fischer & Roseman, 2007; Tausch, Becker, Spears, & Christ, 2008). This suggests two emotional routes to protest (cf. van Stekelenburg & Klandermans, 2010): an anger route based on efficacy leading to normative action, and a contempt route when legitimate channels are closed (Wright et al., 1990) and the situation is seen as hopeless, invoking a "nothing to lose" strategy leading to nonnormative protest (Kamans, Otten, & Gordijn, 2010).

3.1.5. *An Integrating Framework*

Strikingly, a comprehensive framework integrating identities, grievances, and emotions into a single model was lacking for a long time. Recently, however, Simon et al. (1998), van Zomeren et al. (2008), van Stekelenburg and Klandermans (2007), and van Stekelenburg, Klandermans, and van Dijk (2009) have each attempted to build

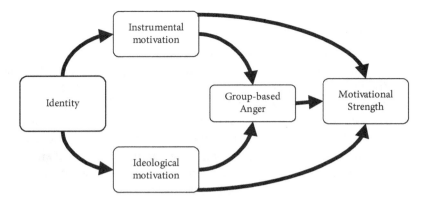

FIGURE 24.2 Motivational dynamics of collective action participation

such models. The three models these authors have offered have in common that they distinguish various pathways to collective action. While Simon et al. distinguish an instrumental and identity pathway, and van Zomeren et al. distinguish between an emotion- and a problem-focused pathway, van Stekelenburg and Klandermans distinguish instrumentality, identity, ideology, and anger as determinants of participation in collective action. Central to all three models are processes of identification; in order to develop the shared grievances and shared emotions that characterize demand, a shared identity is needed. Similarly, all three models include an instrumentality component with efficacy as a key aspect. In a comparison of the three models van Zomeren et al. concluded that injustice, identity, and efficacy each contributed to the explanation of collective action participation (2008).

Figure 24.2 depicts our summary of the various models. As dependent variable we took the strength of the motivation to participate in collective action. Motivational strength results from group-based anger, and instrumental and/or ideological motivation. Instrumental and ideological motivation each result from grievances and feelings of efficacy shared with a group that the individual participants identify with. Grievances may originate from interests and/or principles that are felt to be threatened. The more people feel that interests of the group and/or principles that the group values are threatened, the angrier they are and the more they are prepared to take part in collective action to protect their interests and/or to express their indignation. Whether a specific level of motivation turns into actual participation depends also on the supply of opportunities to act.

3.2. Dynamics of Supply

Social movement organizations are more or less successful in satisfying demands for collective political participation, and we may assume that movements that are successfully supplying what potential participants demand gain more support than movements that fail to do so. Movements and movement organizations can be compared in terms of their effectiveness in this regard. This is not to say that it is easy to assess effectiveness (Giugni, 1998; 2004; Giugni, McAdam, & Tilly, 1999). Measures of effect differ (e.g., impact on and access to polity, impact on public opinion, attention of mass media) and people's assessment of effectiveness differs as well. A movement organization's effectiveness can also be assessed on its ability to provide selective incentives (McCarthy & Zald, 1976; Oliver, 1980). Nonetheless, movement organizations try to convey the image of an effective political force. They can do so by pointing to the impact they have had in the past, or to the powerful allies they have. Of course, they may lack all this, but then, they might be able to show other signs of strength. A movement may command a large constituency, as witnessed by turnout on demonstrations, or by membership figures, or large donations. It may comprise strong organizations with strong charismatic leaders who have gained respect, and so on.

The political system and the organizational field movement organizations are embedded in may also show considerable variation that influences the supply side of movement participation. Repressive political environments may increase the costs of participation considerably: people may lose friends, they may risk their jobs or otherwise jeopardize their sources of income, they may be jailed, and they may even lose their lives (Davenport, Johnston, & Mueller, 2005; Tilly, 1978).

An important element of the supply side of participation is the provision of information about the behavior of others. Social networks—real and virtual—are of strategic importance in this respect, because it is through these networks that people are informed about the behavior or intentions of others (Chew, 1999; Earl & Kimport, 2011; Kim & Bearman, 1997; Oegema & Klandermans, 1994; Passy, 2001). In his paper on the Chinese student movement of 1989, Zhao (1998) gives a striking illustration of this mechanism. He describes how the ecological circumstance that most students in Beijing live in the same part of town made the success of the movement in terms of mobilization visible in the streets in front of the dormitories. In the virtual world, social media such as Facebook do the same (van Stekelenburg & Klandermans, 2012)

Movements offer the opportunity to act on behalf of one's group. This is most attractive if people identify strongly with their group (de Weerd & Klandermans, 1999; Kelly & Breinlinger, 1996; Klandermans, 2002; Simon et al., 1998; Stürmer & Simon, 2004). Interestingly, all these studies show that identification with the more exclusive group of movement participants is far more influential than identification with the more inclusive category. Indeed, in addition to the opportunity to act on behalf of the group, collective political action participation offers further constituents of identification: the leader of the movement; the movement's cause; the people in the movement, the movement organization, or the group one is participating in. Not all these sources of identification are always equally appealing. Movement leaders can be more or less charismatic, or the people in the movement can be more or less attractive. Moreover, movements and movement organizations may be, and in fact often are, controversial. As a consequence, movement participants are frequently stigmatized (Klandermans & Mayer, 2006; Linden & Klandermans, 2006). Within the movement's network, this is, of course, completely different. There the militant does have the status society is denying him or her. Indeed, it is not uncommon for militants to refer to the movement organization as a second family, a substitute for the social and associative life society is no longer offering them (Orfali, 1990; Tristan, 1987). Movement organizations not only supply sources of identification, they also offer all kinds of opportunities to enjoy and celebrate the collective identity: marches, rituals, songs, meetings, signs, symbols, and common codes (see Stryker et al., 2000 for an overview).

Social movements play a significant role in the diffusion of ideas and values (Eyerman & Jamison, 1991). Rochon (1998) makes the distinction between "critical communities," where new ideas and values are developed, and "social movements," which are interested in winning social and political acceptance for those ideas and values. "In the hands of movement leaders, the ideas of critical communities become ideological frames" (Rochon, 1998, p. 31). Through processes such as consensus mobilization (Klandermans, 1988), framing (Snow et al., 1986), or dialogue (Steinberg, 1999) movements seek to disseminate their definition of the situation to the public at large. Such definitions of the situation have been labeled "collective action frames" (Gamson, 1992; Klandermans, 1997). Collective action frames can be defined in terms of injustice—that is, some definition of what's wrong in the world; identity—that is, some definition of who is affected and who is responsible; and agency—that is, some beliefs about the possibilities of changing society. We may assume that people who join a movement come to share some part of the movement's ideas and values.

Social movements do not invent ideas from scratch; they build on an ideological heritage as they relate their claims to broader themes and values in society. In so doing they relate to societal debates that have a history of its own, and that history is usually much longer than that of the movement itself. Gamson (1992), for example, refers to the "themes" and "counterthemes" that in his view exist in every society. One such paired theme and countertheme he mentions is "self-reliance" versus "mutuality," that is, the belief that individuals must take care of themselves versus the belief that society is responsible for its less fortunate members. In a study of the protests about disability payments in the Netherlands we demonstrated how in the Netherlands these two beliefs became the icons that galvanized the debates (Klandermans & Goslinga, 1996). While "self-reliance" became the theme of those favoring restrictions on disability payments, "mutuality" was the theme of those who defended the existing system. Another example is what Tarrow (1998) calls "rights frames": human rights, civil rights, women's rights, animal rights, and so on, in other words, collective action frames that relate a movement's aims to some fundamental rights frame. For decades Marxism has been such an ideological heritage movements identified with, positively by embracing it or negatively by distancing themselves from it. In a similar vein, fascism and Naziism form the ideological heritage right-wing extremism must come to terms with either by identifying with it or by keeping it at a distance.

The supply side of collective action is not static or a constant. In fact, it has to be constructed again in every mobilization campaign. McAdam et al. (1996) have defined this phenomenon as *mobilizing structures*, which are "those collective vehicles, informal as well as formal, through which people mobilize and engage in collective action" (McAdam et al., 1996, p. 3). Mobilizing structures are the connecting tissue between organizers and participants. At any time, all kinds of groups, organizations, and networks that exist in a society can become part of a mobilizing structure. However, none can be assumed to automatically become part of it. Networks need to be adapted, appropriated, assembled, and activated by organizers in order to function as mobilizing structures (Boekkooi, Klandermans, & van Stekelenburg, 2011). Many studies have shown that networks are important in explaining differential recruitment and mobilization (e.g., Klandermans & Oegema, 1987; Snow, Zurcher, & Ekland-Olson, 1980; Walgrave & Klandermans, 2010). Assembling a mobilizing structure is an important step in the process of micromobilization. Which organizations join the mobilizing coalition is an important predictor of who will participate in the protest (e.g., Heaney and Rojas, 2011). Most studies assessing organizational affiliations show that organizations predominantly mobilize their own members. Similarly, networks tend to reach those who are embedded in their structures. Thus, organizers who assemble different mobilizing structures, be they coalitions of formal organizations or networks of informal networks or both, reach different subsets of a movement's mobilization potential (Boekkooi et al., 2011).

Roggeband and Duyvendak (2013) raise the question of whether traditional networks and organizations such as parties, unions, or churches have lost their mobilizing force and are being replaced by light communities and highly fluid mobilizing structures. They suggest that more and more people avoid "heavy" long-term engagements and leave more formal institutions for looser engagements in informal, sometimes temporary, or issue-specific networks. As they also see a change from "identity politics" to "issue politics," these authors speculate that the emergence of "light" communities will be accompanied by a process of individualization resulting in a shift from collective to individual action. It does not come as a surprise that the Internet and virtual networks are central in their reasoning. Although the authors admit that much of their argument is speculative, developments like these raise important questions for social movement researchers.

In processes of framing social movements, organizations work hard to turn grievances into claims, to point out targets to be addressed, to create moral outrage and anger, and to stage events where all this can be vented. They weave together a moral, cognitive, and ideological package and communicate that appraisal of the situation to the movement's mobilization potential. In doing so, social movement organizations play a significant role in the process of construction and reconstruction of collective beliefs and in the transformation of individual discontent into collective action. Grievances can be framed in terms of violated *interests* and/or violated *principles*. We demonstrated that campaigns that emphasize the violation of interests more likely resonate with instrumental motives, while campaigns that emphasize the violation of principles more likely resonate with ideological motives (van Stekelenburg, Klandermans, & van Dijk,, 2009). With the concept of resonance we have entered the terrain of mobilization.

3.3. Mobilization

Mobilization is the process that gets the action going; demand and supply would remain potentials if processes of mobilization did not bring the two together. Social networks are indispensable in the processes of mobilization. Individual grievances and feelings are transformed into group-based grievances and feelings within social networks. As early as 1965, Almond and Verba observed a positive correlation between active engagement in voluntary associations and political efficacy. Hence, a movement's mobilization potential can be described in terms of the *social capital* accumulated in it. Lin (1999, p. 35) defined social capital as "resources embedded in a social structure which are accessed and/or mobilized in purposive actions." Paxton (2002) argued that associational life cumulates social capital, which "provides space for the creation and dissemination of discourse critical of the present government, and it provides a way for active opposition to the regime to grow" (p. 257).

3.3.1. Social Embeddedness

The concept of social capital has important implications for advancing our understanding of the role of social embeddedness in protest participation. Exploring the impact of social capital takes into account the social context in which the decision to participate or not is taken. As a set of relationships, social capital has many different attributes, which are categorized into three components: a structural, a relational, and a cognitive component (Nahapiet & Ghoshal, 1998). The *structural* component of social capital refers to the presence or absence of network ties between actors, and it essentially defines *who* people can reach. Structural social capital encourages cooperative behavior, thereby facilitating mobilization and participation. The *relational* component of social capital concerns the kinds of personal relationships people have developed through a history of interaction (Granovetter, 1973). It focuses on the particular relationships people have, such as respect, trust, and friendship. The structural position may be necessary, but it does not appear sufficient to help individuals overcome the collective action dilemma. Relational capital implies *what* people are actually able to receive in terms of informational, physical, and emotional support. When trust is built between people, they are more willing to engage in cooperative activity through which further trust can be generated (on trust: Lind & Tyler, 1988; on respect: Simon & Stürmer, 2003). The third—*cognitive*—component is defined as those resources providing shared representations, interpretations, and systems of meaning. It constitutes a powerful form of social capital in the context of protest (and politics in general, as Huckfeldt, Mondak, Hayes, Pietryka, & Reilly, chapter 21, this volume, argue). The cognitive dimension is in protest literature referred to as raised consciousness—a set of political beliefs and action orientations arising out of an awareness of similarity (Gurin, Miller, & Gurin, 1980, p. 30). Consciousness-raising takes place within social networks. It is within these networks that individual processes such as grievance formation, strengthening of efficacy, identification, and group-based emotions all synthesize into a motivational constellation preparing people for action and building mobilization potential. Both resource mobilization theory and political process theory emphasize the structural component, the role of social networks, especially as mobilizing structures (Diani & McAdam, 2003; Kitts, 2000; McAdam et al., 1996). Social constructivistic approaches put more emphasis on the relational and cognitive component.

Part of the infrastructure of a movement's mobilization potential is the communication networks that connect individuals. Walgrave and Klandermans (2010) demonstrate how open and closed communication channels and weak and strong ties weave a web of connections that influence how easy or difficult it is to reach a movement's mobilization potential. Polletta, Chen, Gardner, and Motes suggest that the Internet plays an important role in grievance formation (2013). This corroborates van Stekelenburg and Klandermans' observation that technologies such as mobile phones, the Internet, Facebook, and so on, played a crucial role in the mobilization of high school students in the Netherlands in a protest campaign against educational policy (2012).

Social embeddedness—be it in formal, informal, or virtual networks—plays a pivotal role in the context of protest, but why? The effect of interaction in networks on the propensity to participate in politics is contingent on the amount of political discussion that occurs in social networks and the information that people are able to gather about politics as a result (McClurg, 2003). Klandermans et al. (2008) provide evidence for such mechanisms: immigrants who felt efficacious were more likely to participate in protest provided that they were embedded in social networks, especially ethnic networks, which offer an opportunity to discuss and learn about politics. In other words, this is where people talk politics and thus where the factuality of the sociopolitical world is constructed and people are mobilized for protest. Being integrated in a network increases the chances that one will be targeted with a mobilizing message and that people are kept to their promises to participate. For example, people with friends or acquaintances who are already active within social movements are more likely to take part in movement actions than others (R. Gould, 1993; Klandermans, 1997). Social networks function as communication channels, discursive processes take place to form consensus that makes up the symbolic resources in collective sense-making (Gamson, 1992), and people are informed of upcoming events and social capital as trust and loyalty accumulates in networks to provide individuals with the resources needed to invest in protest.

3.3.2. The Process of Mobilization

Mobilization is a complicated process that can be broken down into several conceptually distinct steps. Klandermans (1988) proposed to break the process of mobilization down into consensus and action mobilization. *Consensus mobilization* refers to dissemination of the views of the movement organization, while *action mobilization* refers to the transformation of those who adopted the view of the movement and turned into active participants. The more successful consensus mobilization is, the larger the pool of sympathizers a mobilizing movement organization can draw from. In their frame

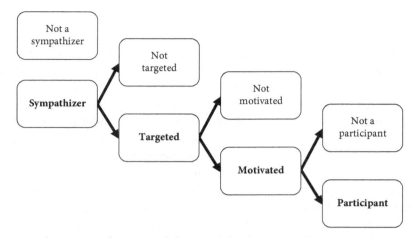

FIGURE 24.3 The process of action mobilization (Klandermans & Oegema, 1987).

alignment approach to mobilization Snow and Benford and their colleagues elaborated consensus mobilization much further (see Benford, 1997 for a critical review; and Snow, 2004 for an overview). Klandermans and Oegema (1987) broke the process of action mobilization down further into four separate steps: people (1) need to *sympathize* with the cause, (2) need to *know* about the upcoming event, (3) must *want* to participate, and (4) must be *able* to participate (see figure 24.3).

Each step brings the supply and demand of protest closer together until an individual eventually takes the final step to participate in an instance of political protest. The first step accounts for the results of consensus mobilization. It divides the general public into those who sympathize with the cause and those who do not. A large pool of sympathizers is of strategic importance, because for a variety of reasons many a sympathizer never turns into a participant. The second step is equally obvious as crucial; it divides the sympathizers into those who have been the target of mobilization attempts and those who have not. The third step concerns the social psychological core of the process. It divides the sympathizers who have been targeted into those who are motivated to participate in the specific activity and those who are not. Finally, the fourth step differentiates the people who are motivated into those who end up participating and those who do not.

In their research on the mobilization campaign for a peace demonstration Klandermans and Oegema (1987) found that three-quarters of the population of a community south of Amsterdam felt sympathy for the movement's cause. Of these sympathizers, three-quarters were somehow targeted by mobilization attempts. Of those targeted, one-sixth were motivated to participate in the demonstration. And finally, of those motivated, one-third ended up participating. The net result of these different steps is some (usually small) proportion of the general public that participates in protest. With each step smaller or larger numbers drop out, but the better the fit between demand and supply, the smaller the number of dropouts.

3.3.3. Mobilization with Minimal Organization

Sometimes the demand for protest can be so overwhelming that very little is needed to bring large numbers onto the streets. In the context of the massive indignation regarding the kidnapping and serial killing of children by Dutroux and judicial errors in Belgium in dealing with it, television and newspapers sufficed as mobilizing actors (Walgrave & Manssens, 2000). Yet the mobilizing power of the media should not be overestimated (Kingdon, 1984). They only have the power to mobilize in case of so-called consensual issues (Verhulst, 2011), that is, issues that root in suddenly imposed grievances that evoke a communal sense of repulsion and indignation. Examples are the death of a child caused by drunken driving (McCarthy & Wolfson, 1996) or sense-less violence (Lodewijkx, Kersten, & van Zomeren, 2008). The salience and the consensual character of the issues compensate for the lack of organizational brokerage, making mobilization via the mass media possible. Similarly, Walgrave & Klandermans (2010) report findings from a demonstration against the Iraq war revealing that appeals via mass media were more effective in countries with high levels of opposition against the war.

Mobilization with minimal organization has become more effective with the appearance of virtual networks and social media. In November 2007, we conducted a study on protests staged in the absence of any form of organization (van Stekelenburg & Boekkooi, 2013; van Stekelenburg & Klandermans, 2012). That week in November 20,000 Dutch secondary school pupils took to the streets protesting the deteriorating quality of their education. The movement took the shape of protests by several groups geographically scattered and diffused over a period of time that were impromptu and short-lived. They were initiated by the stereotypical guy next door, Kevin, whose call for action was "virally" spread via face-to-face personal and virtual networks (e.g. MSN, social network sites). Via mobile phones, videos of unrest were uploaded on YouTube, and the YouTube films facilitated frame-alignment. In nearly real-life time, *would-be* protesters came to share grievances and emotions with *actual* protesters. Questions related to expected participation of others were instantly answered by the uploaded films and instant messages. Social media, smartphones, and YouTube facilitated organizing without organizations.

The secondary school protests are examples of so-called connective action (cf. Bennett and Segerberg, 2012; van Stekelenburg & Klandermans, 2012). Mobilization for connective action moves from one person to another—individually, as part of a larger email list, a listserv, or a social network such as Facebook or MySpace. In a process that continues to reproduce itself, the message is copied and redistributed. An original sender cannot know where or when the message stops traveling, stops being copied and redistributed, stops being translated. Messages with higher degrees of resonance will be dispersed in greater densities. The Arabian revolutions from Tunisia to Syria and earlier the Green Protests in Iran are all examples of the power of connective action. The working of these new forms of mobilization is far from clear. What at first sight seems mobilization without organization, may in hindsight appears to be more organized than presumed. For the time being, there are more questions than answers.

4. Dynamics of Sustained Participation

Most research on protest concerns a comparison of participants and nonparticipants in a specific instance of participation at a specific point in time—be it a demonstration, a boycott, a sit-in, a rally, or a petition. In terms of our participation typology, this concerns short-term, most of the time low-risk or little effort participation, and sometimes high risk or effort. We argue that such short-term activities have different motivational dynamics than sustained participation, be it low or high risk or effort. Our research among long-term extreme right activists corroborates that assumption (Klandermans & Mayer, 2006). Life-history interviews with long-term extreme right activist in Belgium, France, Italy, Germany, and the Netherlands reveal that such activism has significant impact on someone's life and sometimes comes with serious measures of stigmatization. Therefore, long-term activists tend to be true believers; otherwise someone would not be prepared to take such consequences (Van Laer, 2011). Nonetheless, even true believers do not always take the repercussions of their activism easily.

A movement has only a limited number of core activists. For example, 5%–10% of the membership of the Dutch labor unions is core activists. Empirical evidence suggests that most core activists are perfectly aware of the fact that they are giving 90% or more of the movement's supporters a free ride, but do not care. On the contrary, this is what seems to motivate them to take the job (Oliver, 1984). They care so much for the movement's cause that they are prepared to make that effort knowing that most others won't. Indeed, for 29% of the core activists within Dutch unions, this was the single most important motivation for their sustained participation.

Becoming a long-term activist is to a large extent a matter of biographical availability. After all, sustained participation requires discretionary time for an extended period. The concept of biographical availability was proposed by McAdam in his study of participation in the Mississippi Freedom Summer (McAdam, 1988). What McAdam had in mind was freedom from other societal commitments. "If college students are uniquely free of life-course impediments to activism, the Freedom Summer applicants were freer still. And the actual volunteers were the freest of all" (Goldstone & McAdam, 2001). Indeed, participants in the Mississippi Freedom Summer Campaign were students who were biographically available. But in terms of a life history, there is more than available time, there is also *mental* availability, that is, susceptibility to the ideas a movement is propagating.

Activism frequently persists despite pessimism regarding the action's ostensible goals (Louis, 2009). Why do people continue participating in movements even if it does not effectuate their goals? Drury and Reicher (2009) suggest that participation generates a "positive social-psychological transformation." They argue that participation strengthens identification and induces collective empowerment. The emergence of an inclusive self-categorization as "oppositional" leads to feelings of unity and expectations of support. This *empowers* people to offend authorities. Such action, they continue, defines the participant's oppositional identity vis-à-vis the dominant out-group. Protest participation strengthens empowerment and politicization, paving the path to sustained participation. Sustained participation need not necessarily take the form of the same activity all the time. People often go from one activity to another, sometimes from one movement to another, and in so doing build activist careers (Andrews, 1991).

Paths to sustained participation vary. Linden and Klandermans (2007) distinguish four trajectories: revolutionaries, wanderers, converts, and compliants. The first two trajectories are instances of biographical continuity (Roth, 2003), that is, life histories whereby participation appears as the logical result of political socialization from someone's youth onwards. Revolutionaries are convinced right-wingers early on, while wanderers are life-long political homeless, wandering from one political shelter to the other. The latter two are examples of conversion (Blee, 2002), trajectories that imply a break with the past—in the case of converts because some critical events made their minds turn; in the case of compliants because a significant other persuaded them to become involved.

Critical events are supposed to play a crucial role in both continuity and conversion. In the context of biographical continuity the event means the last push or pull in a direction in which the person is already going, whereas in the context of conversion the event means an experience that marks a change of mind. Obviously, such conversion does not come out of the blue. It is rooted in a growing dissatisfaction with life as it is. The critical event is the last push toward change. Teske (1997) describes the example of a journalist who ends up in front of the gate of a nuclear weapons plant and whose experience with the authorities' suppressive response to that demonstration turns him into an activist. The story of this journalist made clear that on the one hand it was no accident that he ended up at that gate, but on the other hand, had the demonstration not taken that dramatic turn, it would not have had this impact on his life.

Sustained participation is surprisingly absent in the social movement literature—surprisingly, because long-term participants keep the movement going. Knowing the motives, conditions, and mechanisms that facilitate or hinder people to become and continue to be activists is essential for social movements to secure continuity. Therefore, understanding the mechanisms that make people become activists and persist in their activism, and which make protest veterans terminate their active involvement, is of crucial importance not only theoretically, but also for understanding the growth and decline of social movement involvement.

5. Dynamics of Disengagement

The dynamics of sustained participation in social movements have a clear counterpart, namely, the dynamics of disengagement. Indeed, the sustainability of a fit between demand and supply is by no means obvious. Why do people defect from the movement

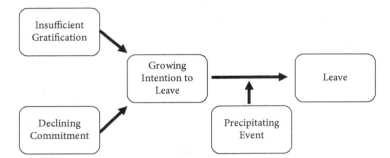

FIGURE 24.4 The dynamics of disengagement

they have worked so hard for? Surprisingly little attention has been given to that question. Compared to the abundant literature on why people join movements, literature on why they exit is almost nonexistent (but see Fillieule, in press; Fillieule & Broqua, 2005). The guiding principle of our discussion of disengagement is the simple model shown in figure 24.4.

Insufficient gratification in combination with declining commitment produces a growing intention to leave. Eventually, some critical event tips the balance and makes the person quit. Obviously, the event itself only triggers the final step. Against that background, its impact may be overestimated. After all, it was the decline in gratification and commitment that causes defection; the critical event only precipitated matters.

5.1. Insufficient Gratification

The integrated motivational framework presented at the end of the demand section distinguishes three fundamental motives for participation: identification, instrumental, and ideological motivation. Social movements may supply the opportunity to fulfill these demands, and the better they do, the more movement participation turns into a satisfying experience. However, movements may also fall short on each of these motives. The most likely reason for movements to fall short is inadequate instrumentality. Although it is difficult to assess the effectiveness of social movements, it is obvious that many a movement goal is never reached. Opp (1988) has argued that indeed people are very well aware of the fact that movement goals are not always easy to achieve, but that they reason that nothing happens in any event if nobody takes any action. Yet sooner or later some success must be achieved for instrumental motivation to continue to fuel participation. In addition to not being achieved, movement goals may lose their urgency and drop lower on the societal agenda. Finally, the individual costs or risks of participation may be too high compared to the attraction of the movement's goals. Repression adds to the costs and might make participation too costly for people (Tilly, 1978).

Movements offer the opportunity to act on behalf of one's group. This is the most attractive if people identify strongly with their group. But the composition of a movement may change, and as a consequence people may feel less akin to the others in the movement (Whittier, 1997). Schisms are another reason why movements fail to satisfy identity motives. Sani and Reicher (1998) and Catellani et al. (2006) demonstrate that schisms result from fights over the core identity of a movement and that people who leave no longer feel that they can identify with the movement. Finally, people occupy a variety of positions in society, and consequently identify with a variety of collectives. A change in context may make one collective identity more and the others less salient, and therefore identification with a movement may wither. For example, in their study of farmers' protests in the Netherlands and Spain, Klandermans, Sabucedo, Rodriguez, and de Weerd (2002) observed that in Spain during a campaign for local and provincial elections the identification with other farmers declined.

Social movements provide the opportunity to express one's views. This is not to say that they are always equally successful in that regard. Obviously, there is not always full synchrony between a movement's ideology and a person's beliefs. Indeed, many a movement organization ends in fights between ideological factions, with schisms and defection as a consequence (Gamson, 1975).

5.2. Declining Commitment

Movement commitment does not last by itself. It must be maintained via interaction with the movement, and any measure that makes that interaction less gratifying helps to undermine commitment. Downton and Wehr (1997) discuss mechanisms of social bonding that movements apply to maintain commitment. Leadership, ideology, organization, rituals, and social relations, which make up a friendship network, each contribute to sustaining commitment, and the most effective context is, of course, a combination of all five. Although not all of them are equally well researched, each of these five mechanisms is known from the literature on movement participation as a factor that fosters people's attachment to movements. For example, it is known from research on union participation that involving members in decision-making processes increases commitment to a union. Taylor and Whittier (1995) demonstrated how rituals in lesbian movement groups strengthened the membership's bond to the movement. Unions and other movement organizations have developed many kinds of services for their members to make membership more attractive. Selective incentives may seldom be sufficient reasons to participate in a movement, but they do increase commitment.

5.3. The Role of Precipitating Events

When gratification falls short and commitment declines, an intention to leave develops. Yet this intention does not necessarily turn into leaving. Many participants maintain a marginal level of participation for extended periods until some critical event makes them quit. For example, Goslinga (2002) calculated that a stable 25% of the membership of Dutch labor unions considered leaving. Such critical events can have many different appearances, and sometimes even appear trivial. When some decades ago Dutch labor unions changed to a different system of dues collection and members had to sign an agreement to participate in the new system, quite a few members chose not to sign. A change of address may be seized as an opportunity to leave the movement, simply by not renewing contacts in the new place of residence. More substantial reasons might be a conflict with others in the organization, disappointing experiences in the movement, a failed protest, and so on.

5.4. Disengagement versus Radicalization

When a movement declines, many activists quit. But becoming inactive is not the only response to movement decline. Indeed, radicalization appears as an alternative response to movement decline (della Porta, 1995). Although violence tends to be present from the very beginning of a protest cycle, the more dramatic forms of violence occur when the mass phase of the protest cycle is over (della Porta, 1995). Violence as mobilization declines is attributed to people's dissatisfaction with protest outcomes and their attempts to compensate for the "reduction in numbers" (della Porta, 1995), At the same time the repression apparatus becomes more effective toward the end of a cycle. Against that background, sustained participation can take the form of radicalization, making radical, sustained participation and disengagement different sides of the same coin.

6. Conclusion

A decade has passed since the first edition of the *Handbook of Political Psychology* was published. In those years protest participation has gained the interest of social and political psychologists. This resulted in a whole host of studies, of which we have tried to take stock in this chapter. Has this burgeoning scholarship moved the field ahead? Let us return to the unanswered questions Klandermans closed with in 2003. These were questions concerning the formation of demand and supply and how they affect mobilization; questions about the relative weight of instrumentality, identity, and ideology and how these motivations interact; and questions about the role of identity in the context of movement participation, the formation of collective identity, and the politicization of collective identity. Equally understudied were the roles of ideology and emotions, and despite all the work done on networks, their exact roles remained unclear. Little was known about leadership in social movements, and, finally, many unanswered questions regarded sustained participation, commitment, disengagement, and the life course.

Indeed, we have made progress with regard to the dynamics of demand, especially the role of identity, emotions, and motivation. Compared to a decade ago, the social and political psychology of protest has become richer, more sophisticated, and more rooted in state-of-the-art social and political psychology. Yet students of social movements have for too long neglected social and political psychology. At the same time, social and political psychologists have for too long neglected to study such phenomena as social movements and collective action. As a consequence, social movement scholars are not aware of new developments in social and political psychology, while social and political psychologists are unaware of the many unanswered questions that they could help to find an answer to. We hope this chapter has been useful in exemplifying what political psychology has to offer to the study of social movements and where we stand.

So, where are we heading the next 10 years? One unanswered question a decade ago that remains largely unanswered concerns sustained participation, disengagement, and the life course. Basically, many of the same questions are still waiting for answers. Fillieule & Broqua (2005) edited a volume on disengagement (unfortunately for English-language scholars, in French, which makes the work less accessible to the non-French community). More generally, the theme of sustained participation raises another underexplored issue, namely the *personal consequences* of movement participation. But in recent studies Drury et al. (Drury, Cocking, Beale, Hanson, & Rapley, 2005; Drury and Reicher, 1999; 2000; 2009); Louis (2009), and van Zomeren and colleagues (2012) have begun to investigate the individual consequences of participation in collective action.

This brings us to probably the most important challenge of the political psychology of protest, namely to move from static decontextualized explanations of protest to more dynamic, contextualized models of protest. In 2007 we made a plea for more dynamic models (van Stekelenburg and Klandermans, 2007). We argued that a more dynamic approach would provide the opportunity to study mechanisms through concepts like identification, participation motives, efficacy, emotions, and feelings of injustice as consequence and antecedent of collective action. This approach is not easy, as Ellemers, Spears, and Doosje observe: "From an investigational point of view, it is difficult to deal with a variable that, at the same time, can be a dependent and an independent variable, can develop over time or change across contexts" (1999, p. 3). Yet studying protest participation in a more dynamic way would do more justice to the theoretical and empirical richness of the concepts and may be crucial to gain better insights in the processes at hand (cf. McAdam et al., 2001). An example of such a dynamic model, in addition to those we discussed in the previous pages, is van Zomeren et al.'s dual pathway model of protest (van Zomeren, 2013; van Zomeren, Leach, & Spears, 2012). These authors introduce a dynamic model that integrates many common explanations of collective action (i.e., group identity, unfairness, anger, social support, and efficacy). The model conceptualizes collective action as the outcome of two distinct processes: emotion-focused and problem-focused coping. The former revolves around the experience of group-based anger, while the latter revolves around beliefs in the group's efficacy. The model makes explicit the dynamic nature of collective action by explaining how undertaking collective action leads to the reappraisal of collective disadvantage, thus inspiring future collective action. Tausch and colleagues are among the first to report empirical findings on how emotions affect the dynamic nature of collective action participation. They show that protest participants experience more out-group-directed anger and contempt, and self-directed positive affect. Out-group anger and contempt, rather than self-directed positive affect, inspire future collective action (Becker, Tausch, & Wagner, 2011). In yet another study—a two-wave longitudinal field study—they examined how emotional responses to success and failure of collective action inspire future collective action (Tausch & Becker, 2013). They found that both pride (in relation to success) and anger (in response to failure) motivated future collective action. While anger stemming from failure predicted future protest directly, pride resulting from success enhanced feelings of efficacy that inspired future actions. These few examples are an excellent start for the years to come; taking the dynamic nature of collective action seriously will shed light on the many unanswered questions related to sustained participation and disengagement—and indeed on another question: Protest, and then what? (Louis, 2009).

In addition to antecedents and consequences of protest, our plea for dynamic models also alludes to the thorny issue of causality. Indeed, the majority of the findings and relations we reported are based on correlational data. Correlational data can be interpreted in causal terms based on the theories we have, but cannot demonstrate causality. Take, for instance, the relation between efficacy, embeddedness, and protest. Based on social capital theories, we interpreted our correlational data in causal terms: that is, the more embedded people are, the more efficacious they feel and the more they protest. However, are more efficacious people more inclined to become members of organizations, or do people become more efficacious in their networks? We simply do not know. Social psychologists attempt to overcome the problem of causality by employing experimental methods. These experiments have a high internal validity and have the potential to make strong causal statements. However, laboratory experiments are often detached from natural settings, resulting in low ecological validity. Indeed, are students in the lab who report strong intentions to protest really willing to take onto the streets? We cannot be sure about it. First of all, this is because the correlation between intentions and actual participation is moderate at best (Oegema and Klandermans, 1994), but perhaps more important, we simply do not know whether artificially created grievances, identification, and efficacy are comparable to real-life indignation stemming from imperiled interests or violated principles. In a longitudinal field study in a natural setting we are seeking to address this issue of causality (van Stekelenburg et al., 2012). Longitudinal data were collected in a newly built Dutch neighborhood. Within approximately a month of their arrival inhabitants received a questionnaire with four follow-up surveys, which encompasss predictors of protest, several protest intentions, and actual participation and network questions. Thus, we monitor the development of demand and supply of protest as it starts from scratch. This means moving beyond correlation studies *and* studies of isolated individuals in surveys or laboratories (see also Huckfeldt et al., chapter 21, this volume). In that way, we hope to be able to shed more light on causality issues in protest participation.

The second challenge we envision is to develop protest models that incorporate contextual variation. Little political psychological research has focused on the subjective experience of meso- and macro-level factors. Nonetheless, at the meso or macro level, variables can be identified that affect peoples' subjective interpretations of their situation in terms of identities, opportunities, or constraints and injustice. Koopmans and Statham (2000) and Roggeband (2002, 2004), for example, acknowledge that the dynamics of participation are created and limited by characteristics of the national contexts in which people are embedded. Collective action participation is context dependent (van Stekelenburg et al., 2009), but political psychology theories are not always good at taking that into account and in conceptualizing how contextual factors impact on social psychological mechanisms. In a large-scale study of participation in street demonstrations in different countries and on different issues, we sought to assess the combined impact of national and mobilizing context on who participates in street demonstrations (Klandermans et al., 2010). In that way, we hoped to be able to demonstrate the context-dependency of action participation.

One such matter of contextualization concerns the conceptualization of political protest, that is, social movement participation (movement politics) vis-à-vis that other form of political behavior, namely participation in the electoral arena (party politics). Movement politics centers around active participation in protest events, such as mass demonstrations, occupations of public sites, boycotts, blockades, and riots. The modal form of participation in the electoral arena consists of a vote for a candidate (person or party) who seeks a public office. In a recent paper, reflecting on the state of the art of the study of contentious politics, McAdam & Tarrow (2013) observe that scholars of social movements have largely neglect to pay attention to elections, while on the other hand election researchers have failed to include social movements in their designs. Two assumptions regarding party and movement politics are encountered in the literature (Hutter, 2010). (1) The two reinforce each other—people who engage in party politics are more likely to engage in movement politics as well and vice versa. In statistical terms one would expect a positive correlation. (2) The two alternate—that is, people who participate in the one activity are less likely to participate in the other (a negative correlation). Recently, Hutter (2010) proposed and found empirical support for a third option, namely, that (3) the two follow a logic of their own (hence, no correlation). We take as our point of departure that any kind of arrangement between movement and party politics is conceivable. Movements and parties may compete, complement each other, or collaborate (Goldstone, 2003; Johnston, 2011). If movements institutionalize, citizens may opt for party politics, a decision then reflected in electoral successes and declining protest activity. Conversely, if party politics fail, citizens may resort to movement politics, a change reflected in declining votes and rising protest activity. We know that all these options exist and are actually practiced by citizens who want to influence politics (cf. Teorell, Torcal, & Montero, 2007), but we know very little about the conditions and mechanisms that make citizens want to influence politics and to take the one option or the other.

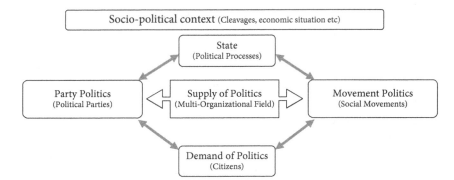

FIGURE 24.5 Routes to political influence

We propose that the relative importance of movement and party politics is context dependent (see also McAdam & Tarrow, 2013). Figure 24.5 maps the political landscape citizens are faced with if they want to influence the state. Sociopolitical context can be described in terms of political opportunities and cleavages that divide citizens along lines of interests and principles. The social cleavages that are prevalent in a society shape its multiorganizational field. Political parties and movement organizations are embedded in such organizational fields. Within the multiorganizational field, movements and parties assemble mobilizing structures that offer opportunities to participate in politics—party politics, movement politics, or both (supply of politics). Citizens who want to promote or protect their interest or principles (demand of politics) may take one or more of these opportunities to act. Capitalizing on their abilities to mobilize, the political parties and movement organizations are more or less able to put pressure on the state.

Evidence underscores the context dependency of the relative importance of movement and party politics. McAdam and Tarrow (2013) illustrate this with examples from US history of how electoral politics have influenced protest politics and vice versa. In the United States, so these authors argue, protest politics increasingly interferes in electoral politics. They refer to the Tea Party movement as an example. In Europe they observe the opposite pattern. Movements institutionalize into parties, while parties professionalize. As a consequence, there is a growing gap between politicians and citizens, which in its turn results in the growth of populist parties. Hutter (2010) similarly observed the growth of populist parties, but interprets this development as a consequence of processes of globalization. Hutter's observation is made in the context of a study regarding the question of how electoral politics relates to protest politics. Building on a study in six European countries, he observes three patterns of relations between the two forms of politics: congruence—more contestation in the electoral arena goes with more contestation in the protest arena; counterweight—more contestation in the electoral arena comes with less contestation in the other; different logic—the direction of the relationship differs depending on the political orientation of the actors involved.

Burstein (1999) suggests that as long as public opinion is unified and clear, politicians do not need social movement organizations to define their politics. This implies that movement politics gains significance if public opinion on an issue is polarized or diffuse. In other words, according to this reasoning the social movement sector has grown so much because Western societies have become less hegemonic. A different sort of reasoning takes the movement sector's relative effectiveness as its point of departure (Giugni et al., 1999; Jenkins, 1995). If party politics fails, movement politics takes over, and, indeed, compared to working one's way through political institutions, contentious collective actions can be remarkably effective provided that the right ingredients are in place, as so convincingly demonstrated by the "Colored Revolutions" and the events in the Arab world.[1] Indeed, some 20 years ago one of us estimated on the basis of an overview of various literature reviews that approximately one-third of the instances of collective political action had some degree of success (Klandermans, 1989). We are not aware of similar estimates for political parties, but we may assume that experiencing success encourages similar actions in the future, while seeing others succeed is an incentive to try oneself (Eisinger, 1973; see Tunisia and Egypt for recent examples). And yet another process of reasoning reveals that protest is the continuation of party politics because, as Dalton and colleagues show, protesters are those citizens who already *have* access to party politics (Dalton et al., 2009).

In other words, evidence underscores that citizens attempt several routes to political influence, but so far, it is inconclusive and unclear who takes what route and how that choice is influenced by contextual variation. As political psychology explores the causes of the thoughts, feelings, and actions of people—and primarily how these are influenced by sociopolitical context—we believe it has a lot to offer to future work that will attempt to incorporate contextual variation in protest models.

Notes

1. Although the failed revolutions in Azerbaijan and Syria also reveal what happens when the right ingredients are not in place.

References

Andrews, M. (1991). *Lifetimes of commitment: Ageing, politics, psychology*. New York: Cambridge University Press.

Becker, J., Tausch, N., & Wagner, U. (2011). Emotional consequences of collective action participation: Differentiating self-directed and outgroup-directed emotions. *Personality and Social Psychology Bulletin, 37*, 1587–1598.

Benford, R. (1997). An insider's critique of the social movement framing perspective. *Sociological Inquiry, 67*(4), 409–430.

Bennett, W. L., & Segerberg, A. (2012). The Logic of Connective Action. *Information, Communication & Society, 15*(5), 739–768.

Burstein, P. (1999). Social movements and public policy. In M. Giugni, D. McAdam, & C. Tilly (eds.), *How social movements matter* (pp. 3–21). Minneapolis: University of Minnesota Press.

Blee, K. M. (2002). *Inside organized racism: Women in the hate movement.* Berkeley: University of California Press.

Blumer, H. (1951). Social movements. In A. M. Lee (ed.), *New outline of the principles of sociology* (pp. 199–220). New York: Barnes & Noble.

Boekkooi, M. E., Klandermans, B., & van Stekelenburg, J. (2011). Quarrelling and protesting: How organizers shape a demonstration. *Mobilization, 16*(2), 498–508.

Buechler, S. M. (2000). *Social movements in advanced capitalism.* Oxford: Oxford University Press.

Catellani, P., Milesi, P., & Crescentini A. M. (2006). One root, different branches: Identity, injustice and schism. In B. Klandermans & N. Mayer (eds.), *Extreme right activists in Europe: Through the magnifying glass* (pp. 204–223). New York: Routledge.

Chew, M. S.-Y. (1999). Structure and strategy in collective action. *American Journal of Sociology, 105*, 128–156.

Cohen, J. (1985). Strategy or identity? New theoretical paradigms and contemporary social movements. *Social Research, 52*, 663–716.

Corcoran, K., Pettinicchio, D., & Young, J. (2012). The context of control: A cross-national investigation of the link between structure, efficacy, and collective action. *British Journal of Social Psychology. 50*(4), 575–605.

Dalton, R., Van Sickle, A., & Weldon, S. (2009). The individual-institutional nexus of protest behaviour. *British Journal of Political Science, 40*(1), 51–73.

Davenport, C., Johnston, H., & Mueller, C. (Eds.). (2005). *Repression and mobilization.* Minneapolis: University of Minnesota Press.

Davies, J. (1962). Toward a theory of revolution. *American Sociological Review, 27*, 5–19.

della Porta, D. (1995). *Social movements, political violence and the state.* Cambridge: Cambridge University Press.

della Porta, D., & Diani, M. (2006). *Social movements. An introduction.* Oxford: Blackwell.

de Weerd, M., & Klandermans, B. (1999). Group identification and political protest: Farmers' protest in the Netherlands. *European Journal of Social Psychology, 29*, 1073–1095.

Diani, M., & McAdam, D. (Eds.). (2003). *Social movement analysis: The network perspective.* New York: Oxford University Press.

Downton, J., Jr., & Wehr, P. (1997). *The persistent activist: How peace commitment develops and survives.* Boulder, CO: Westview.

Drury, J., Cocking, C., Beale, J., Hanson, C., & Rapley, F. (2005). The phenomenology of empowerment in collective action. *British Journal of Social Psychology, 44*, 309–328.

Drury, J., & Reicher, S. (1999). The intergroup dynamics of collective empowerment: Substantiating the social identity model of crowd behavior. *Group Processes Intergroup Relations, 2*(4), 381–402.

Drury, J., & Reicher, S. (2000). Collective action and psychological change: The emergence of new social identities. *British Journal of Social Psychology, 39*(4), 579–604.

Drury, J., & Reicher, S. (2009). Collective psychological empowerment as a model of social change: Researching crowds and power. *Journal of Social Issues, 65*(4), 707–725.

Earl, J., & Kimport, K. (2011). *Digitally enabled social change: Activism in the Internet age.* Cambridge, MA: MIT Press.

Eisinger, P. K. (1973). The conditions of protest behavior in American cities. *American Political Science Review, 67*, 11–28.

Ellemers, N., Spears, R., & Doosje, B. (1999). Introduction. In N. Ellemers, R. Spears, & B. Doosje (eds.), *Social identity: Context, commitment, content* (pp. 1–5). Oxford: Basil Blackwell.

Eyerman, R., & Jamison, A. (1991). *Social movements: A cognitive perspective.* Oxford: Polity Press.

Fillieule, O. (in press). Disengagement processes from radical organizations. What is so different when it comes to exclusive groups? In B. Klandermans & C. van Stralen (eds.), *Movements in times of transition*. Philadelphia: Temple University Press.

Fillieule, O., & Broqua, C. (2005). La défection dans deux associations de lutte contre le sida: Act Up et AIDES. In O. Fillieule (ed.), *Le désengagement militant* (pp. 189–228). Paris: Belin.

Fischer, A., & Roseman, I. (2007). Beat them or ban them: The characteristics and social functions of anger and contempt. *Journal of Personality and Social Psychology 93*, 103–115.

Folger, R. (1986). Rethinking equity theory: A referent cognitions model. In H. W. Bierhoff, R. L. Cohen, & J. Greenberg (eds.), *Justice in social relations* (pp. 145–162). New York: Plenum.

Foster, M. D., & Matheson, K. (1999). Perceiving and responding to the personal/group discrimination discrepancy. *Personality and Social Psychology Bulletin, 25*(10), 1319–1329.

Gamson, W. A. (1975). *Strategy of social protest*. Homewood, IL: Dorsey Press.

Gamson, W. A. (1992). *Talking politics*. New York: Cambridge University Press.

Giugni, M. (1998). Was it worth the effort? The outcomes and consequences of social movements. *Annual Review of Sociology, 85*, 1017–1042.

Giugni, M. (2004). Personal and biographical consequences. In D. A. Snow, S. A. Soule, & H. Kriesi (eds.), *The Blackwell companion to social movements* (pp. 389–507). Oxford: Blackwell.

Giugni, M., McAdam, D., & Tilly, C. (Eds.). (1999). *How social movements matter*. Minneapolis: University of Minnesota Press.

Goldstone, J. A. (Ed.). (2003). *States, parties, and social movements: Protest and the dynamics of institutional change*. Cambridge: Cambridge University Press.

Goldstone, J. A., & McAdam, D. (2001). Placing contention in demographic and life-course context. In R. Aminzade, J. A. Goldstone, D. McAdam, E. Perry, J. William Sewell, S. Tarrow, & C. Tilly (eds.), *Silence and voice in the study of contentious politics* (pp. 195–221). New York: Cambridge University Press.

González, R., & Brown, R. (2003). Generalization of positive attitudes as a function of subgroup and superordinate group identifications in intergroup contact. *European Journal of Social Psychology, 33*, 195–214.

Goodwin, J., Jasper, J. M., & Polleta, F. (2001). *Passionate politics: Emotions and social movements*. Chicago: University of Chicago Press.

Goslinga, S. (2002). Binding aan de vakbond [Union commitment]. PhD dissertation, Vrije Universiteit, Amsterdam.

Gould, D. (2009). *Moving politics: Emotion and ACT UP's fight against AIDS*. Chicago: University of Chicago Press.

Gould, R. (1993). Collective action and network structure. *American Sociological Review, 58*, 182–196.

Granovetter, M. (1973). The strength of weak ties. *American Journal of Sociology, 78*(6), 1360–1380.

Gurin, P., Miller, A. H., & Gurin, G. (1980). Stratum identification and consciousness. *Social Psychology Quarterly, 43*(1), 30–47.

Gurr, T. (1970). *Why men rebel*. Princeton, NJ: Princeton University Press.

Heaney, M. T., & Rojas, F. (2011). The Partisan dynamics of contention: Demobilization of the antiwar movement in the U.S., 2007–2009. *Mobilization, 16*, 44–64.

Hutter, S. (2010). Protest politics and the right populist turn: A comparative study of six West European countries, 1975–2005. PhD dissertation, University of Munich.

Jasper, J. (1998). The emotions of protest: Affective and reactive emotions in and around social movements. *Sociological Forum, 13*(3), 397–424.

Jenkins, J. C. (1995). Social movements, political representation, and the state: An agenda and comparative framework. In J. C. Jenkins & B. Klandermans (eds.), *The politics of social protest: Comparative perspectives on states and social movements* (pp. 14–35). Minneapolis: University of Minnesota Press.

Johnston, H. (2011). *States and social movements*. Cambridge: Polity Press.

Kamans, E., Otten, S., & Gordijn, E. H. (2011). Threat and power in intergroup conflict: How threat determines emotional and behavioral reactions in powerless groups. *Group Processes & Intergroup Relations, 14*(3), 293–310.

Kelly, C., & Breinlinger, S. (1996). *The social psychology of collective action: Identity, injustice and gender*. London: Taylor & Francis.

Kim, H., & Bearman, P. S. (1997). The structure and dynamics of movement participation. *American Sociological Review, 62*(1), 70–93.

Kingdon, J. W. (1984). *Agendas, alternatives and public policies*. New York: Harper Collins.

Kitts, J. A. (2000). Mobilizing in black boxes: Social networks and participation in social movement organizations. *Mobilization, 5*(2), 241–257.

Klandermans, B. (1984). Mobilization and participation: Social-psychological expansions of resource mobilization theory. *American Sociological Review, 49*(5), 583–600.

Klandermans, B. (1988). The formation and mobilization of consensus. In B. Klandermans, H. Kriesi, & S. Tarrow (eds.), *From structure to action: Comparing social movement research across cultures* (vol. 1, pp. 173–196). Greenwich, CT: JAI Press.

Klandermans, B. (1989). Does happiness soothe political protest? In R. Veenhoven (ed.), *How harmful is happiness?* (pp. 61–78). Rotterdam: University Press.

Klandermans, B. (1997). *The social psychology of protest*. Oxford: Blackwell.

Klandermans, B. (2001). Why movements come into being and why people join them. In J. Blau (ed.), *Blackwell's compendium of sociology* (pp. 268–281). Oxford: Blackwell.

Klandermans, B. (2002). How group identification helps to overcome the dilemma of collective action. *American Behavioral Scientist, 45*(5), 887–900.

Klandermans, B. (2004). The demand and supply of participation: Social-psychological correlates of participation in social movements. In D. A. Snow, S. A. Soule, & H. Kriesi (eds.), *The Blackwell companion to social movements* (pp. 360–379). Oxford: Blackwell.

Klandermans, B., & Goslinga, S. (1996). Media discourse, movement publicity, and the generation of collective action frames: Theoretical and empirical exercises in meaning construction in comparative perspectives on social movements. In D. McAdam, J. D. McCarthy, & M. N. Zald (eds.), *Political opportunities, mobilizing structures, and cultural framings* (pp. 312–337). New York: Cambridge University Press.

Klandermans, B., Kriesi, H., & Tarrow, S. (Eds.). (1988). *From structure to action: Comparing social movement research across cultures* (vol. 1). Greenwich, CT: JAI Press.

Klandermans, B., & Mayer, N. (Eds.). (2006). *Extreme right activists in Europe: Through the magnifying glass*. New York: Routledge.

Klandermans, B., & Oegema, D. (1987). Potentials, networks, motivations, and barriers: Steps toward participation in social movements. *American Sociological Review, 52*, 519–531.

Klandermans, B., Roefs, M. M. I., & Olivier, J. (2001). Grievance formation in a country in transition: South Africa 1994–1998. *Social Psychology Quarterly, 64*, 41–54.

Klandermans, B., Sabucedo, J. M., & Rodriguez, M. (2004). Inclusiveness of identification among farmers in the Netherlands and Galicia (Spain). *European Journal of Social Psychology, 34*(3), 279–295.

Klandermans, B., Sabucedo, J. M., Rodriguez, M., & de Weerd, M. D. (2002). Identity processes in collective action participation: Farmers' identity and farmers' protest in the Netherlands and Spain. *Political Psychology, 23*(2), 235–251.

Klandermans, B., van der Toorn, J., & van Stekelenburg, J. (2008). Embeddedness and identity: How immigrants turn grievances into action. *American Sociological Review, 73*, 992–1012.

Klandermans, B., van Stekelenburg, J., van Troost, D., van Leeuwen, A., Walgrave, S., Verhulst, J., et al. (2010). *Manual for data collection on protest demonstrations. Caught in the act of protest: Contextualizing Contestation (CCC-project):* VU University/Antwerpen University.

Koopmans, R. & Statham P. (eds.) (2000). *Challenging immigration and ethnic relations politics: comparative european perspectives.* Oxford: Oxford University Press.

Kriesi, H. (1993). *Political mobilization and social change.* Aldershot: Avebury.

Kurtz, S. (2002). *All kinds of justice: Labor and identity politics.* Minneapolis: University of Minnesota Press.

Leach, C. W., Iyer, A., & Pedersen, A. (2006). Anger and guilt about in-group advantage explain the willingness for political action. *Personality and Social Psychology Bulletin, 32*, 1232–1245.

Lind, E. A., & Tyler, T. R. (1988). *The social psychology of procedural justice.* New York: Plenum Press.

Linden, A., & Klandermans, B. (2006). Stigmatization and repression of extreme-right activism in the Netherlands. *Mobilization: An International Journal, 11*(2), 213–228.

Linden, A., & Klandermans, B. (2007). Revolutionaries, wanderers, converts, and compliants: Life histories of extreme right activists. *Journal of Contemporary Ethnography, 36*, 184–201.

Lodewijkx, H. F. M., Kersten, G. L. E., & van Zomeren, M. (2008). Dual pathways to engage in "silent marches" against violence: Moral outrage, moral cleansing and modes of identification. *Journal of Community and Applied Social Psychology, 18*, 153–167.

Louis, W. (2009). Collective action—and then what? *Journal of Social Issues, 65*(4), 727–748.

Mackie, D. M., Devos, T., & Smith, E. R. (2000). Intergroup emotions: Explaining offensive action tendencies in an intergroup context. *Journal of Personality and Social Psychology, 79*(4), 602–616.

Major, B. (1994). From social inequality to personal entitlement: The role of social comparisons, legitimacy appraisals, and group memberships. *Advances in Experimental Social Psychology, 26*, 293–355.

Mayer, N. (2013). The "contentious French" revisited. In J. van Stekelenburg, C. M. Roggeband, & B. Klandermans (eds.), *The future of social movement research. Dynamics, mechanisms, processes.* Minnesota: University of Minnesota Press.

McAdam, D. (1982). *Political process and the development of black insurgency, 1930–1970.* Chicago: University of Chicago Press.

McAdam, D. (1988). *Freedom summer.* New York: Oxford University Press.

McAdam, D., McCarthy, J. D., & Zald, M. N. (1996). *Comparative perspectives on social movements.* New York: Cambridge University Press.

McAdam, D., & Tarrow, S. (2013). Social movements and elections: Toward a broader understanding of the political context of contention. In J. van Stekelenburg, C. M. Roggeband, & B. Klandermans (eds.), *The future of social movement research. Dynamics, mechanisms, processes.* Minnesota: University of Minnesota Press.

McAdam, D., Tarrow, S., & Tilly, C. (2001). *Dynamics of contention.* New York: Cambridge University Press.

McCarthy, J. D., Rafail, P., & Gromis, A. (2013). Recent trends in public protest in the U.S.A.: The social movement society thesis revisited. In J. van Stekelenburg, C. M. Roggeband, & B. Klandermans (eds.), *The future of social movement research. Dynamics, mechanisms, processes*. Minnesota: University of Minnesota Press.

McCarthy, J. D., & Wolfson, M. (1996). Resource mobilization by local social movement organizations: Agency, strategy, and organization in the movement against drinking and driving. *American Sociological Review, 61*(6), 1070–1088.

McCarthy, J. D., & Zald, M. N. (1976). Resource mobilization and social movements: A partial theory. *American Journal of Sociology, 82*, 1212–1241.

McClurg, S. D. (2003). Social networks and political participation: The role of social interaction in explaining political participation. *Political Research Quarterly, 56*, 448–464.

Melucci, A. (1981). Ten hypotheses for the analysis of social movements. In D. Pinto (ed.), *Contemporary Italian sociology* (pp. 173–194). New York: Cambridge University Press.

Melucci, A. (1989). Nomads of the present: Social movements and individual needs in contemporary society. London: Hutchinson Radius.

Meyer, D. S., & Tarrow, S. (1998). *The social movement society: Contentious politics for a new century*. Lanham, MD: Rowman & Littlefield.

Morris, A. D. (1984). *The origins of the civil rights movement*. New York: Free Press.

Morris, A. D., & McClurg Mueller, C. (Eds.). (1992). *Frontiers in social movement theory*. Binghampton, NY: Vail-Ballou Press.

Nahapiet, J., & Ghoshal, S. (1998). Social capital, intellectual capital, and the organizational advantage. *Academy of Management Review, 23*(2), 242–266.

Neidhardt, F., & Rucht, D. (1993). Auf dem Weg in die "Bewegungsgesellschaft"? Über die Stabilisierbarkeit sozialer Bewegungen. *Soziale Welt, 44*(3), 305–326.

Oberschall, A. (1973). *Conflict and social movements*. Englewood Cliffs, NJ: Prentice-Hall.

Oegema, D., & Klandermans, B. (1994). Why social movement sympathizers don't participate: Erosion and nonconversion of support. *American Sociological Review, 59*(5), 703–722.

Oliver, P. (1980). Rewards and punishments as selective incentives for collective action: Theoretical investigations. *American Journal of Sociology, 85*(6), 1356–1375.

Oliver, P. (1984). Rewards and punishments as selective incentives: An apex game. *Journal of Conflict Resolution, 28*(1), 123–148.

Olson, M. (1965). *The logic of collective action: Public goods and the theory of groups*. Cambridge, MA: Harvard University Press.

Opp, K. D. (1988). Grievances and social movement participation. *American Sociological Review, 53*(6), 853–864.

Orfali, B. (1990). *L'adhésion au Front national, de la minorité active au mouvement social*. Paris: Kimé.

Passy, F. (2001). Socialization, connection, and the structure/agency gap: A specification of the impact of networks on participation in social movements. *Mobilization: An International Journal, 6*(2), 173–192.

Paxton, P. (2002). Social capital and democracy: An interdependent relationship. *American Sociological Review, 67*, 254–277.

Polletta, F., Chen, P. C. B., Gardner, B. G., & Motes, A. (2013). Is the Internet creating new reasons to protest? In J. van Stekelenburg, C. M. Roggeband, & B. Klandermans (eds.), *The future of social movement research. Dynamics, mechanisms, processes*. Minnesota: University of Minnesota Press.

Rochon, T. R. (1998). *Culture moves: Ideas, activism, and changing values*. Princeton, NJ: Princeton University Press.

Roggeband, C. M. (2002). *Over de grenzen van de politiek. Een vergelijkend onderzoek naar de opkomst en ontwikkeling van de vrouwenbeweging tegen seksueel geweld in Nederland en Spanje.* Assen: Van Gorcum.

Roggeband, C. M. (2004). Instantly I thought we should do the same thing. International inspiration and exchange in feminist action against sexual violence. *European Journal of Women's Studies, 11,* 159–175.

Roggeband, C. M., & Duyvendak, J. W. (2013). The changing supply side of mobilization: Questions for discussion. In J. van Stekelenburg, C. M. Roggeband, & B. Klandermans (eds.), *The future of social movement research. Dynamics, mechanisms, processes.* Minnesota: University of Minnesota Press.

Roth, S. (2003). *Building movement bridges. The coalition of labor union women.* Westport, CT: Praeger.

Sani, F., & Reicher, S. (1998). When consensus fails: An analysis of the schism within the Italian Communist Party (1991). *European Journal of Social Psychology, 28,* 623–645.

Simon, B. (2010). Collective identity and political participation. In A. Azzi, X. Chryssochoou, B. Klandermans, & B. Simon (eds.), *Identity and participation in culturally diverse societies: A multidisciplinary perspective* (pp. 89–91). Oxford: Blackwell Wiley.

Simon, B., & Grabow, O. (2010). The politicization of migrants: Further evidence that politicized collective identity is a dual identity. *Political Psychology, 31,* 717–738.

Simon, B., & Klandermans, B. (2001). Towards a social psychological analysis of politicized collective identity: Conceptualization, antecedents, and consequences. *American Psychologist, 56*(4), 319–331.

Simon, B., Loewy, M., Stürmer, S., Weber, U., Freytag, P., Habig, C., et al. (1998). Collective identification and social movement participation. *Journal of Personality and Social Psychology, 74*(3), 646–658.

Simon, B., & Ruhs, D. (2008). Identity and politicization among Turkish migrants in Germany: The role of dual identification. *Journal of Personality and Social Psychology, 95*(6), 1354–1366.

Simon, B., & Stürmer, S. (2003). Respect for group members: Intragroup determinants of collective identification and group-serving behavior. *Personality and Social Psycholol gy Bulletin, 29*(2), 183–193.

Smelser, N. J. (1962). *Theory of collective behavior.* New York: Free Press.

Snow, D. (2004). Framing processes, ideology and discursive fields. In D. A. Snow, S. A. Soule, & H. Kriesi (eds.), *The Blackwell companion to social movements* (pp. 380–412). Oxford: Blackwell.

Snow, D., Rochford, E. B., Worden, S. K., & Benford, R. (1986). Frame alignment processes, micromobilization, and movement participation. *American Sociological Review, 51,* 464–481.

Snow, D., Soule, S. A., & Kriesi, H. (Eds.). (2004). *The Blackwell companion to social movements.* Oxford: Blackwell.

Snow, D., Zurcher, L. A., & Ekland-Olson, S. (1980). Social networks and social movements: A microstructural approach to differential recruitment. *American Sociological Review, 45*(5), 787–801.

Steinberg, M. W. (1999). The talk and back talk of collective action: A dialogic analysis of repertoires of discourse among nineteenth-century English cotton spinners. *American Journal of Sociology, 105,* 736–780.

Stryker, S., Owens, T. J., & White, R. W. (Eds.). (2000). *Self, identity, and social movements* (vol. 13). Minneapolis: University of Minnesota Press.

Stürmer, S., & Simon, B. (2004). Collective action: Towards a dual-pathway model. *European Review of Social Psychology, 15,* 59–99.

Stürmer, S., & Simon, B. (2009). Pathways to collective protest: Calculation, identification, or emotion? A critical analysis of the role of group-based anger in social movement participation. *Journal of Social Issues, 65*(4), 681–705.

Tarrow, S. (1998). *Power in movement: Social movements, collective action, and politics.* New York: Cambridge University Press.

Tarrow, S. (2011). *Power in movement: Social movements, collective action, and politics* (3rd ed.). New York: Cambridge University Press.

Tausch, N., & Becker, J. (2013). Emotional reactions to success and failure of collective action as predictors of future action intentions: A longitudinal investigation in the context of student protests in Germany. *British Journal of Social Psychology.* in press.

Tausch, N., Becker, J., Spears, R., & Christ, O. (2008). Emotion and efficacy pathways to normative and non-normative collective action: A study in the context of student protests in Germany. Paper presented at the Intra- and Intergroup Processes' Pre-conference to the 15th General Meeting of the EAESP, Opatija, Croatia.

Taylor, V. (2009). The changing demand side of contention: From structure to meaning. Paper presented at the Conference on Advancements in Social Movement Theories, Amsterdam, September 30–October 2.

Taylor, V. (2013). Social movement participation in the global society: Identity, networks and emotions. In J. van Stekelenburg, C. M. Roggeband, & B. Klandermans (eds.), *The .future of social movement research. Dynamics, mechanisms, processes.* Minnesota: University of Minnesota Press.

Taylor, V., & Whittier, N. E. (1995). Analytical approaches to social movement culture: The culture of the women's movement in social movements and culture. In H. Johnston & B. Klandermans (eds.), *Social movements and culture* (pp. 163–187). Minneapolis: University of Minnesota Press.

Teorell, J., Torcal, M., & Montero, J. R. (2007). Political participation: Mapping the terrain. In J. W. van Deth, J. R. Montero, & A. Westholm (eds.), *Citizenship and involvement in European democracies: A comparative analysis* (pp. 384–414). New York: Routledge.

Teske, N. (1997). *Political activists in America: The identity construction model of political participation.* New York: Cambridge University Press.

Tilly, C. (1978). *From mobilization to revolution.* Reading, MA: Addison-Wesley.

Tristan, A. (1987). *Au front.* Paris: Gallimard.

Turner, R. H., & Killian, L. M. (1987). *Collective behavior* (3rd ed.). Englewood Cliffs, NJ: Prentice-Hall.

Tyler, T. R., & Lind, E. A. (1992). A relational model of authority in groups. *Advances in Experimental Social Psychology, 25,* 115–191.

Tyler, T. R., & Smith, H. J. (1998). Social justice and social movements. In D. Gilbert, S. T. Fiske, & G. Lindzey (eds.), *Handbook of social psychology* (pp. 595–629). New York: McGraw-Hill.

Van Laer, J. (2011). *Why people protest.* PhD Dissertation, University of Antwerp.

van Stekelenburg, J. (2006). Promoting or preventing social change: Instrumentality, identity, ideology and groups-based anger as motives of protest participation. PhD dissertation, VU University, Amsterdam.

van Stekelenburg, J., & Boekkooi, M., E. (2013). Mobilizing for change in a changing society. In J. Van Stekelenburg, C. M. Roggeband, & B. Klandermans (eds.), *The future of social movement research. Dynamics, mechanisms, processes.* Minnesota: University of Minnesota Press.

van Stekelenburg, J., & Klandermans, B. (2007). Individuals in movements: A social psychology of contention. In B. Klandermans & C. M. Roggeband (eds.), *The handbook of social movements across disciplines* (pp. 157–204). New York: Springer.

van Stekelenburg, J., & Klandermans, B. (2010). The social psychology of protest *Sociopedia.isa*. Retrieved from http://www.sagepub.net/isa/admin/viewPDF.aspx?&art=Protest.pdf.

van Stekelenburg, J., & Klandermans, B. (2012). Uploading unrest: Comparing mobilization and participation in traditional and rhizomatical mobilized protest. Forthcoming.

van Stekelenburg, J., Klandermans, B., & van Dijk, W. W. (2009). Context matters: Explaining why and how mobilizing context influences motivational dynamics. *Journal of Social Issues*, 65(4), 815–838.

van Stekelenburg, J., Klandermans, B., & van Dijk, W. W. (2011). Combining motivations and emotion: The motivational dynamics of collective action participation. *Revista de Psicología Social*, 26(1), 91–104.

van Stekelenburg, J., Petrovic, I., Pouw, W., Limburg, N., & Nederlof, N. (2012). Societies from scratch: How collective action emerges in evolving neighbourhoods. Paper presented at the International Society of Political Psychology, Annual Meeting, July 6–9.

van Zomeren, M. (2013). Opening the black box of "dynamics" in theory and research on the demand side of protest. In J. van Stekelenburg, C. M. Roggeband, & B. Klandermans (eds.), *The future of social movement research. Dynamics, mechanisms, processes*. Minnesota: University of Minnesota Press.

van Zomeren, M., Leach, C. W., & Spears, R. (2012). Protesters as "passionate economists": A dynamic dual pathway model of approach coping with collective disadvantage. *Personality and Social Psychology Review*, 16, 180–198.

van Zomeren, M., Postmes, T., & Spears, R. (2008). Toward an integrative social identity model of collective action: A quantitative research synthesis of three socio-psychological perspectives. *Psychological Bulletin*, 134, 504–535.

van Zomeren, M., Spears, R., Fischer, A. H., & Leach, C. W. (2004). Put your money where your mouth is! Explaining collective action tendencies through group-based anger and group efficacy. *Journal of Personality and Social Psychology*, 87(5), 649–664.

Verhulst, J. (2011). *Mobilizing issues and the unity and diversity of protest events*. PhD Dissertation, University of Antwerp.

Vliegenthart, R. (2007). *Framing immigration and integration: Facts, parliament, media and anti-immigrant party support in the Netherlands*. PhD Dissertation. VU University Amsterdam.

Walgrave, S., & Klandermans, B. (2010). Open and closed mobilization patterns: The role of channels and ties. In S. Walgrave & D. Rucht (eds.), *The world says no to war: Demonstrations against the war in Iraq* (pp.169–193). Minneapolis: University of Minnesota Press.

Walgrave, S., & Manssens, J. (2000). The making of the white march: The mass media as a mobilizing alternative to movement organisations. *Mobilization*, 5(2), 217–239.

Walsh, E. J., & Warland, R. H. (1983). Social movement involvement in the wake of a nuclear accident: Activists and freeriders in the Three Mile Island area. *American Sociological Review*, 48(6), 764–780.

Whittier, N. E. (1997). Political generations, micro-cohorts, and the transformation of social movements. *American Sociological Review*, 62, 760–778.

Wright, S. C. (2001). Strategic collective action: Social psychology and social change. In R. Brown & S. Gaertner (eds.), *Intergroup processes: Blackwell handbook of social psychology* (vol. 4, pp. 409–430). Oxford: Blackwell.

Wright, S. C., Taylor, D. M., & Moghaddam, F. M. (1990). Responding to membership in a disadvantaged group: From acceptance to collective protest. *Journal of Personality and Social Psychology*, 58, 994–1003.

Zhao, D. (1998). Ecologies of social movements: Student mobilization during the 1989 predemocracy movement in Beijing. *American Journal of Sociology*, 103, 1493–1529.

CHAPTER 25

....

PREJUDICE AND POLITICS

....

DONALD R. KINDER

In the early decades of the 20th century, legislative assemblies and constitutional conventions throughout the American South passed into law a series of devices designed to remove African Americans from political life. Onto the scene came the poll tax, literacy and property tests, the understanding and good character clauses, and, not least, the white primary. Blacks held meetings, initiated legal actions, organized campaigns, circulated petitions, and where permitted, voted against the new suffrage restrictions. Their efforts were unavailing. African Americans disappeared from politics (Key, 1949; Kousser, 1974; Valelly, 2004).

All these formal obstacles are gone now, done in by Supreme Court decisions, the Voting Rights Act, the threat of federal intervention, and scores of local struggles.[1] Black participation in political life towers over what it was just a generation or two ago. And largely as a consequence of *that*, many African Americans now hold positions of political authority: as mayors of important cities, members of Congress, and on school boards, city councils, and state assemblies in every corner of the nation. In 2008, American voters chose Barack Hussein Obama, dark-skinned, the son of a Kenyan immigrant, as their president.

From separate and unequal to Obama's historic victory, the country has come a long way. By almost any measure, the quality of life experienced by black Americans has notably improved over this period. And yet imposing racial differences remain and on things that really matter: education, health, employment, income, wealth, and more. Mindful of this history, and informed by current realities, my purpose here is to assess the part prejudice plays in American politics today.

It is not a small task. Some years ago David Sears and I wrote that empirical examination of the relationship between prejudice and politics was suffering from "benign neglect" (Kinder & Sears, 1981). No longer. The field is overflowing with findings, interpretations, and claims. For the most part this is a good thing—an excellent thing—but it means a comprehensive review is beyond my reach. Instead, I will do my best to highlight recent developments, clarify key concepts, and condense the multiplicity of results into orderly patterns.[2]

Any serious discussion of race prejudice presupposes that we know both what race is and what prejudice is—and neither is entirely straightforward. Accordingly, the chapter begins by spelling out the meaning of these two central concepts: first "race" and then "prejudice." With these elementary matters disposed of, I move on to review what we know about the origins of race prejudice, distinguishing between the social conditions that give rise to prejudice in general and the factors that predispose some individuals to embrace prejudice and others to reject it. In the next section of the chapter, I argue that race prejudice comes in more than a single variety and that the varieties of prejudice can be classified in terms of three basic distinctions: prejudice may emphasize biological differences or cultural differences; prejudice may be primarily cognitive in nature or primarily affective in nature; and prejudice may exist in the mind in conscious form or it may exist in the mind in unconscious form. The next section, and the heart of the chapter, summarizes evidence on the political consequences of prejudice (keeping track, insofar as it is possible to do so, of the different varieties of prejudice just introduced). Here we will see to what extent, and under what conditions, prejudice has consequences for what Americans do in politics—for the political party they join, the candidates they back, and the policies they favor. The next and penultimate section carries us outside the United States to western Europe, there to explore the part played by prejudice in the politics of immigration. The chapter concludes with a quick recapitulation of what we have learned so far and some advice on how we might profitably move forward.

1. THE IDEA OF RACE

According to *The Oxford English Dictionary*, race refers to "One of the great divisions of mankind, having certain physical properties in common." This seems straightforward enough. But then comes the warning, in small print, that "race" is often used imprecisely "even among anthropologists." This turns out to be an understatement of some magnitude.

Perhaps it would be best to abandon the term altogether. That is a common recommendation today from both biology and anthropology (e.g., Lewontin, 1995). Such advice is ironic, in that these two disciplines did their best for a very long time to place race at the center stage of science. Throughout the 19th century, biologists and naturalists used the term "race" to refer to fundamentally different kinds, and their empirical research was devoted to establishing a racial hierarchy, with the "Caucasian" at the top and the "African" (or "Ethiopian") at the bottom. Well into the 20th century, race retained respectability and widespread use as a scientific category. Differences between races—inherent and immutable—continued to be regarded as established matters of fact, and "the inferiority of certain races was no more to be contested than the law of gravity to be regarded as immoral" (Barkan, 1992, p. 3).

Modern biology and anthropology now say that this was a terrible mistake. Migration and conquest are central and recurrent features of human history. Genetic diversity in human groups is overwhelmingly a matter of individual variation within local populations; only a tiny fraction can be assigned to differences between geographically separated groupings (e.g., Lewontin, 1974; 1995).

That race has largely disappeared from science is interesting and important, but it doesn't settle anything here. Our interest is in race as understood by everyday people. That racial categories are largely social inventions with little basis in biological reality does not mean that they are therefore inconsequential. Throughout American history people have been classified as black based on "a single drop of blood": that is, any known or visible sign of African ancestry is sufficient to classify a person as a member of the black "race." This is, one might say, merely convention. But it is a durable and consequential convention: inscribed in law, entrenched in social experience, imprinted on economic life, and influential, still today, as we will see, in the organization of politics.[3]

2. The Nature of Prejudice

The idea of race and the idea of prejudice are closely intertwined.[4] Prejudice takes race for granted; that is, prejudice presumes that human populations can be partitioned into distinct kinds on the basis of their concrete, physical differences. Indeed, racial categories make no sense without prejudice. In the absence of prejudice, physical features that distinguish one group from one another would hold no significance. It is not the presence of objective physical differences that creates races, but the social interpretations that are imposed upon such differences (van den Berghe, 1967; see also Sidanius & Kurzban, chapter 7, this volume).

To the prejudiced person, objective physical differences like the color of skin or the texture of hair are more than mere curiosities. Physical manifestations of difference are outward signs of underlying and deep differences in capacity, temperament, and character. Such differences are systematic; prejudice entails hierarchy. To the person in possession of prejudice, members of another race are not merely different, but inferior.

Prejudice encompasses both beliefs about another group's inferiority *and* feelings of animosity directed at the group. Emotion—negative emotion—is a central ingredient of prejudice. Such emotion can assume a variety of kinds and intensities: from hatred and disgust at one end of the spectrum, through anger and resentment in the midrange, and then on to condescension, discomfort, or utter indifference, at the other (Pettigrew, 1982). The essential point here is that prejudice is not just a way of thinking about others. Prejudice is a belief system infused with emotion.

Finally, prejudice is both categorical and dimensional. It is categorical in that it takes for granted the presence of racial groups as natural kinds. Prejudice is directed toward a group as a whole or toward specific individuals because they are members of that group. At the same time, prejudice is dimensional. People vary in the degree to which they approach the social world from a prejudiced point of view. It would be a mistake to conceive of prejudice as a type, and to assume that people either are prejudiced or they are not. People are more or less prejudiced. Prejudice is a quantity, not a kind.[5]

3. THE ORIGINS OF PREJUDICE

In seeking the origins of prejudice, it is useful to distinguish between two complementary levels of explanation. The first attempts to identify the social conditions that give rise to prejudice in a society. The second attempts to explain why some individuals accept prejudice while others reject it.

3.1. Social Conditions That Give Rise to Prejudice

3.1.1. Prejudice as a Consequence of Persistent Inequality

In the United States, as in other advanced industrial societies, individuals vary enormously in wealth, power, and status. Such inequality is generated in part by individual differences in talent and enterprise; in part by luck and misfortune; and, of interest here, in part by recurrent social processes, whereby different social groups are subject to systematically different treatment (Tilly, 1998).

Race provides an excellent case in point. Persistent inequality between blacks and whites is a central theme of American history, beginning with the degradations of slavery and continuing on after emancipation through the Jim Crow regime of racial oppression. Today, one-third of black children in the United States live in poverty, more than three times the rate of white children. Black children are more than twice as likely to die in their first year than are white children, and those who survive their first year face poorer health, more illness—asthma, diabetes, heart disease, and cancer—and, on average, a shorter life. Black adults are twice as likely to be unemployed as whites, and when they are employed, they earn less. On average, black households command less than *one-tenth* the financial assets of the average white household.[6]

The persistence of racial inequality is important for many reasons. It is important here because persistent inequality is the rich soil from which prejudice grows. Glaring differences between groups in wealth, power, and status are understood among the advantaged to reflect corresponding differences in talent and virtue. Inequality does not require but it certainly encourages the creation of stereotypes (Campbell, 1967) and what Anderson (2010, p. 19) calls "stigmatizing stories"—stories that explain and justify inequality.

3.1.2. Prejudice as a Consequence of Group Conflict

A second and complementary proposition regarding the origins of prejudice derives from realistic group conflict theory (Blumer, 1958; Bobo, 1999; Sherif, Harvey, White, Hood, & Sherif, 1961; see also Huddy, chapter 23, this volume). From this perspective, animosity between groups is rooted in conflict. Groups have incompatible goals and they compete for scarce resources. Conflict is most intense where competition is keenest, where contending groups have the most at stake. Under realistic group conflict theory, racial groups are "vehicles for the pursuit of interest in modern pluralist societies...participants in ongoing competition for control of economic, political, and social structures" (Giles & Evans, 1986, pp. 470, 471).

As such, realistic group conflict theory can account for perhaps the most robust empirical finding in the entire American race relations literature: namely, the finding of a strong association between the threat that blacks pose to whites (or *seem* to pose), on the one hand, and the hostility of whites' political response, on the other. In *Southern Politics in State and Nation*, V. O. Key (1949) showed in masterful detail that politics in the American South through the middle of the 20th century was most reactionary where black people lived in concentrated numbers. Key's observations have been corroborated by scores of subsequent investigations. When and where blacks appear to threaten the interests and privileges of whites, prejudice flourishes (e.g., Bobo & Hutchings, 1996; Bobo & Tuan, 2006; Glaser, 1994; Giles and Hertz, 1994).[7]

3.2. Factors That Affect Acceptance of Prejudice

In *The Authoritarian Personality* (1950), Adorno, Frenkel-Brunswik, Levinson, and Sanford organized their massive project around an explicitly psychological question: why do some individuals but not others find antidemocratic ideas appealing? Taking for granted that such ideas would be available in any society, they set their aim on identifying those who were drawn to antidemocratic ideas, those who were repelled by such ideas, and on explaining the difference. That's what we are up to here but with race prejudice specifically in mind.

3.2.1. *Genetic Predispositions*

In his influential essay in the first edition of *The Handbook of Social Psychology*, Gordon Allport (1935) offered three conjectures about the origins of attitudes. Attitudes may be built up through the gradual accretion of experience; they may reflect a single dramatic emotional experience; or they may be adopted ready-made from parents, teachers, and friends. Allport took for granted that attitudes are learned, and so, in overwhelming numbers, have those who have written about attitudes since.[8]

Prejudice is an attitude, and so it may seem ridiculous to propose that differences in prejudice can be traced, even in part, to differences in genetic predispositions. But this is what is suggested by recent results from research in human behavioral genetics.

The primary goal of quantitative behavioral genetics is to partition the observed variation in human traits into genetic and environmental sources. In one respect, the genotype and the environment are equally important, in that each is indispensable to human development. Any observed behavior—any phenotype—is the result of a continuous interaction between genes and environment (for greater detail on behavioral genetics see Funk, chapter 8, this volume). This still leaves an important question: to what extent do the differences observed among people—say differences among them in prejudice—reflect differences in their genotypes and to what extent do they reflect differences in their environments?

The most straightforward empirical method for partitioning phenotypic variation into genetic and environmental sources capitalizes on the difference between monozygotic (MZ) twins (who share an identical genetic inheritance, genetic relatedness of approximately 1.0) and dizygotic (DZ) twins (who develop from two separate eggs, fertilized by two separate sperm, genetic relatedness of approximately .5). Insofar as "identical" twins are more similar than "fraternal" twins on a particular trait, to that degree the trait can be said to be due to genetic differences (other things equal).[9]

Behavioral genetics research began with a focus on illness and achieved some striking successes. Scores of debilitating diseases have been traced to genetic sources, including cystic fibrosis, hemophilia, color blindness, and schizophrenia. More recently, research in the field has expanded its focus, taking up the heritability of personality traits and social attitudes. The seminal paper in this line of research was published in 1986 in the *Proceedings of the National Academy of Sciences*. N. G. Martin and his colleagues compared a large Australian sample of MZ and DZ twins on a measure of general conservatism. Their analysis suggested not just a genetic component to conservatism, but a *large* genetic component: more than half of the observed variation in conservatism was attributed to genetic difference. Other studies, employing different designs, samples, and statistical techniques, arrive at essentially the same conclusion (e.g., Alford, Funk, & Hibbing, 2005; Bouchard, Lykken, McGue, Segal, & Tellegen, 1990; Eaves et al., 1999; Olson, Vernon, & Jang, 2001).

Conservatism is not the same thing as prejudice, of course. To assess conservatism, most studies in this tradition have relied on the Wilson-Patterson Conservatism Scale (Wilson, 1973). The 50 items that comprise the complete scale are intended to tap conservatism in a broad sense, but a handful of questions deal explicitly with race—with white superiority, apartheid, "coloured" immigration, and mixed marriages. Results suggest that as in the case of conservatism generally, roughly half of the observed variation in these items can be ascribed to genetic factors.

It is much too early to draw settled conclusions. But we do know enough now to recognize that the genetic hypothesis needs to be taken seriously. The mystery of individual differences in prejudice—of who is drawn to prejudice and who is not—may lie partly in our genes.

3.2.2. *The Return of Authoritarianism*

Theodor Adorno and his colleagues who together produced *The Authoritarian Personality* (1950) famously concluded that prejudice—anti-Semitism, racism, hostility toward refugees, suspicion of "foreign" ideas, and more—is "an expression of deep-lying trends in personality" (1950, p. 1). When *The Authoritarian Personality* was published, it was greeted with widespread acclaim, and then, in the space of a few years, buried under an avalanche of criticisms. Is prejudice in fact rooted in authoritarianism? Nearly a thousand pages long, strikingly ambitious in purpose and intermittently brilliant in analysis, *The Authoritarian Personality* cannot tell us.[10]

If it has been left to others to make the case, they have now made it. Karen Stenner and Stanley Feldman (Feldman, 2003; Stenner, 2005) offer fresh theoretical perspectives on authoritarianism. In the new view, authoritarianism emerges out of a universal human dilemma. Living alongside others inevitably generates tension between personal autonomy and social cohesion. How to strike a proper balance between group authority and uniformity, on the one side, and individual autonomy and diversity, on the other? Authoritarians choose the former over the latter: they are inclined to glorify, encourage, and reward uniformity, while disparaging, suppressing, and punishing difference. Using modern experimental and statistical methods, Feldman and Stenner demonstrate that authoritarians are inclined towards narrow-mindedness—they tend to support such initiatives as suppressing constitutionally protected speech or keeping "undesirables" out of the neighborhood. These results suggest that race prejudice may arise in part from authoritarianism.[11]

3.2.3. Education

Formal education is widely thought to supply the moral values and cognitive skills that enable people to overcome prejudice. This argument is made forcefully in the literature on political tolerance, where democratic regimes and citizens are said to be tested by their willingness to tolerate the expression of offensive points of view. Tolerance "implies a willingness to 'put up with' those things that one rejects" (Marcus, Sullivan, Theiss-Morse, & Wood, 1995, p. 28).

If political tolerance is an acquired taste, then the evidence is overwhelming that many Americans have failed to acquire it. In Samuel Stouffer's famous study carried out in the 1950s as the McCarthy hearings on domestic subversion were underway, for example, relatively few Americans were prepared to grant constitutional rights of speech and assembly to communists, atheists, or other unsavory types. Stouffer's results shattered the assumption that Americans would apply democratic procedures and rights to all. Subsequent research has massively reinforced the point (e.g., McClosky & Brill, 1983; Sullivan, Piereson, & Marcus, 1982).

Of course, some Americans *are* prepared to defend ideas and activities they find distasteful. A very reliable source of discriminating between those who are and those who are not is education. From Stouffer's results on communists to contemporary disputes over gay marriage, more education means more tolerance. This is true in general, and it is true in the specific case of race prejudice (e.g., Sears, 1969; Schuman, Steeh, Bobo, & Krysan, 1997; Sniderman & Piazza, 1993). Education, it would seem, imparts knowledge, values, and a subtlety of thinking that together act as a counterweight to the "natural" inclination towards intolerance. Americans are more or less prejudiced because of differences in education.

This is the standard story, and it very well may be correct. Education and prejudice are correlated, that's for sure. But individuals who pursue more education differ systematically from those who do not. This means that the various characteristics that are responsible for greater education (e.g., superior cognitive skills, engagement in school and community life, self-confidence, politically engaged parents, privileged back-grounds) might be responsible for the observed correlation between education and prejudice. Disentangling causality from selection in this case is far from straightforward (e.g., Kam & Palmer, 2008). Whether education plays an important role in reducing prejudice remains an open question.

4. Varieties of Prejudice

Prejudice comes in more than a single variety. In this section of the chapter I will argue that it is useful to classify types of American prejudice according to three sets of binary distinctions: biological versus cultural; cognitive versus affective; and conscious versus unconscious.

4.1. Biological versus Cultural

The first distinction contrasts biological as against cultural forms of prejudice. The biological variety emerged in clearest and most complete form as a defense of American slavery. In response to northern abolitionists, southern slaveholders, intel-lectuals, and statesmen argued that slavery was a just and virtuous institution and that the Negro was "destined by providence" for slavery. They insisted that Negroes and whites constituted separate and fundamentally distinct races. Differences in intel-lectual capacity and moral character were inborn and permanent. Sexual liaisons between black men and white women were an abomination. A racially integrated society was inconceivable.

The Civil War brought an end to slavery, but other forms of racial oppression survived and still more were invented. After Reconstruction, African Americans were excluded from politics, ostracized from social life, and confined to the meanest work. For all of this, biological racism provided justification and, insofar as it was needed, moral conso-lation (Fredrickson, 1971; 2002; Myrdal, 1944; Litwack, 1998).

The biological form of race prejudice persisted well into the 20th century—endorsed not just by ordinary citizens, but by scientists, intellectuals, church leaders, and states-men alike. This is no longer so. Elite expressions of biological racism are today much harder to find in books, journals, sermons, and speeches (Degler, 1991; Myrdal, 1944), and perhaps for this reason, biological racism is much harder to find in the American public. The best evidence on this point comes from a series of careful studies under-taken by Charles Glock and his colleagues in the early 1970s, set in the San Francisco Bay Area and recounted in *The Anatomy of Racial Attitudes* (Apostle, Glock, Piazza, & Suelzle et al., 1983). In this research, Americans were questioned about the differences they saw between blacks and whites and then about how they explained the differences they saw. Relatively few whites attributed racial inequalities to inborn differences: to differences in intellectual capacity, differences "in the genes," in the "makeup" of blacks and whites, or to differences "in the blood." Roughly 6% of Bay Area whites were in possession of a pure version of a biological account for racial differences, and another 16% or so incorporated such thinking partially. From other studies we know that support for the core tenets of biological racism has diminished notably in recent decades. The notion of genetic difference, of permanent disadvantage, is much less prominent now than it once was (Schuman et al., 1997).

Even if biological racism were to disappear completely, it would not mean the end of racism. Among others, George Fredrickson (2002) contends that a distinctive form of racism has recently arisen in the United States, one that emphasizes *cultural* as against *biological* differences. The crucial point here is that prejudice does not require "an ideology centered on the concept of biological inequality." Discrimination, neglect, and exclusion can be justified just as well by what are understood to be "deep-seated cultural differences."

In the analysis of race and politics in the United States, the new cultural racism travels under various names, most notably "symbolic racism" (Sears, 1988), "modern racism" (McConahay, 1986), "racial resentment" (Kinder & Sanders, 1996), "subtle prejudice" (Pettigrew & Meertens, 1995), "aversive racism" (Gaertner & Dovidio, 1986), and "laissez faire racism" (Bobo & Smith, 1998).

The emergence of a cultural form of prejudice is a reflection, in part, of dramatic transformations in American society: the passing of slavery and end of the plantation economy; the great migration of African Americans out of the rural South into national urban centers; and perhaps especially, the success of the modern civil rights movement in securing basic rights of citizenship and dismantling the legal foundations underpinning discrimination (Bobo & Smith, 1998; Kinder & Sanders, 1996). Many white Americans wondered why, after all that government had done for African Americans—landmark legislation, executive orders, Supreme Court decisions, dramatic expansion of social programs the likes not seen since FDR and the New Deal—did they continue to lag so far behind? Discrimination no longer stood in the way. Opportunities abounded—indeed, government and other major institutions were showering blacks with programs and advantages. Instead of complaining about their problems and demanding special treatment, blacks should buckle down, work hard, and take advantage of the abundant opportunities now provided them. Majorities of white Americans believed that discrimination had been eradicated and that if blacks would only try harder they could be just as well off as whites (Sears & Henry, 2005).

Biological and cultural forms of prejudice are alike in several important respects. Both emerged out of a national crisis: in the case of biological racism, the debate over slavery that eventually sundered the country; in the case of cultural racism, the collision between the civil rights movement and the oppressions of Jim Crow that galvanized the nation's attention in the middle of the 20th century. Cultural racism offers an account of racial differences in wealth, status, and power that is flattering to whites and denigrating to blacks, just as biological racism does.

Both biological and cultural racism provide alibis for neglect, but they do so in different ways. Biological racism understands differences between blacks and whites to be biologically determined and therefore (in folk understanding) permanent, arising from differences in genetic endowments. Racial differences are deep and unalterable, rooted "in blood." So said science, and so said the leading intellectuals and statesmen of the day. On the account offered by cultural racism, however, blacks do poorly not because of their biological endowments but because of their creation of a culture that promotes unhealthy values and bad habits. Racial inferiority is cultural not biological, seen in the customs and folkways of black life: idleness, violence, drug abuse, teenage mothers—the whole "tangle of pathology" that many whites see as characteristic of life in black neighborhoods.

If differences between blacks and whites are less stark and immutable under cultural racism than under biological racism—if racial categories are perhaps less essentialized—racial differences remain morally charged. Cultural racism is preoccupied with matters of poor choices and bad habits. From the perspective of cultural racism, black Americans fail to display the virtues and practices that white Americans claim as central to the moral ordering of their own lives and to the life of their society.

At the same time, cultural racism, one might say, is a softer variety of prejudice than the biological racism it has largely replaced. The modern form of prejudice is less degrading and vicious. The distance between blacks and whites is not so vast: not the qualitative differences that separate one biological species from another, but rather the graded and overlapping differences between varieties of humankind. Cultural racism is typically accompanied by feelings of resentment and condescension, not the hatred and disgust of biological racism. Compared to days gone by, political appeals to prejudice today are more subtle and indirect (Kinder & Sanders, 1996; Mendelberg, 2001).

4.2. Cognition versus Emotion

"Stereotype" is the name psychology gives to the beliefs we possess about social groups: "poets, professors, professional wrestlers, and film stars," among others (Brown, 1986, p. 188). Stereotypes capture—or rather they seem to capture—the characteristics that define a group: that Jews are shrewd, say, or that Italians are impulsive. Over the past 30 years, as part of a more general "cognitive turn," social psychology has invested heavily in the study of stereotypes and stereotyping.[12]

From one point of view, stereotyping is a completely ordinary manifestation of the ubiquitous process of categorization. To negotiate and make sense of the world, stereotypes and stereotyping are indispensable. "Life is so short, and the demands upon us for practical adjustments so great, that we cannot let our ignorance detain us in our daily transactions. We have to decide whether objects are good or bad by classes" (Allport, 1954, p. 9).

But if stereotypes are grounded in ordinary cognitive processes, and if they reduce the social world to manageable size, they are very much a mixed blessing. For one thing, stereotypes exaggerate differences and sharpen boundaries: in-groups and out-groups appear more different from each other than they actually are (e.g., Campbell, 1967; Taylor, Fiske, Etcoff, & Ruderman, 1978; Krueger, Rothbart, & Sriram, 1989). For another, stereotypes portray members of out-groups as though they were all the same: individual variation is flattened; anomalous cases are set aside (e.g., Kunda & Oleson, 1995; 1997; Kinder & McConnaughy, 2006; Park & Rothbart, 1982). And for a third, although stereotypes are occasionally flattering, much more often they are not: stereotypes generally traffic in defects and deficiencies (Bobo & Massagli, 2001; Kinder & Kam, 2009).

Stereotypes have been measured in a variety of ways: through rating scales, checklists, free response, and more (Biernat & Crandall, 1999). Especially useful for the study of prejudice and politics is the inventory developed by the National Opinion Research Center at the University of Chicago for the General Social Survey. On the NORC inventory, white Americans display subtle but consistent racial stereotyping. Stereotyping is subtle, in that whites do not regard racial groups as categorical opposites; they do not say that all blacks are stupid and that all whites are smart. At the same time, stereotyping is consistent, in that most whites believe that blacks are not as bright as whites; that blacks apply themselves with less determination and resolve; and that blacks can't be trusted as much. Moreover, these specific beliefs are connected to one another: whites who regard blacks as not that bright also tend to think of them as relatively lazy and as comparatively untrustworthy. Stereotypes, that is to say, are not just a jumble of beliefs; they reflect a consistent outlook, a general claim of racial superiority (e.g., Bobo & Massagli, 2001).

Stereotypes represent prejudice in its cognitive aspect. But prejudice is not only cognition. As I stipulated earlier, emotion—negative emotion—is a central ingredient of prejudice. This point is given special force by Robert Zajonc's (1980) provocative claim that cognition and affect constitute separate and partially independent systems, and that between the two, affect is often the more important. According to Zajonc, affect is both more basic—infants cry and smile long before they acquire language—and inescapable—affective reactions occur rapidly and automatically, whether we wish them to or not. Consistent with Zajonc's broad claim, Kahneman (2003) argues that basic assessments of whether objects are good or bad are carried out quickly and efficiently by specialized neural circuitry. Kahneman regards these rapid and automatic affective reactions as especially potent, shaping subsequent judgment and behavior through a process of "affective swamping" (for more on automaticity see Taber & Young, chapter 17, this volume).

In light of these arguments, it is disappointing to discover how little effort has been invested in the direct measurement of emotional aspects of prejudice. As things now stand, if not the best certainly the most widely used measure of the affective component of prejudice is the thermometer rating scale. The thermometer scale was invented for use on the National Election Study as a general purpose measure of feelings toward social and political groups. The scale arrays feelings from very cold and highly unfavorable (0 degrees), on one end, to very warm and highly favorable (100 degrees), on the other. Among the objects regularly rated in this way are Catholics, the working class, women—and blacks. Using the NES thermometer scale, white Americans rate black Americans much less warmly than the rate their own racial group, and variation in such ratings are consistently associated with whites' views on policy in the racial domain (e.g., Kinder & Drake, 2009; Kinder & Winter, 2001; White, 2007; Winter, 2008).

4.3. Implicit versus Explicit

In a society permeated by public opinion polls, we take for granted that attitudes can be measured. We might disagree over the best method for doing so but not over the possibility of the enterprise itself. It was not always so. In 1928, to a discipline dominated by behavioralism, L. L. Thurstone famously suggested that "Attitudes Can Be Measured." At the time, this was something of a revolutionary proclamation. Thurstone readily conceded that mental constructs like attitudes were exceedingly complex and that the task of measurement was daunting. Nevertheless, he proceeded to spell out a method for doing so. Thurstone's pioneering venture was soon followed by Likert, Guttman, Combs, Osgood, Campbell, and others. These "measurement men," as Banaji and Heiphetz (2010) call them, "achieved the previously unthinkable; for the first time ever, they took the ephemeral mental quality of *favoring* and *disfavoring* and rendered it the subject of scientific study" (p. 349).

These various efforts at measuring attitudes share one thing: they all rely on direct procedures. In one way or another, under standard measurement protocol, people are asked to reflect on some object, retrieve their attitude, and report it.

Deliberately echoing Thurstone, Banaji (2001) has more recently issued an equally bold declaration: "Implicit Attitudes Can Be Measured." By "implicit attitudes" Banaji means to refer to attitudes that are introspectively inaccessible (see also Taber & Young, chapter 17, this volume). In contrast to their explicit counterparts, implicit attitudes elude the conscious mind. Judgments and behaviors informed by implicit attitudes "are under the control of automatically activated evaluations, without the performer's awareness of that causation" (Greenwald, McGhee, & Schwartz, 1998, p. 1464; Greenwald & Banaji, 1995).

Within social psychology, interest in implicit attitudes is skyrocketing. Following publication of a set of seminal papers demonstrating that implicit attitudes could indeed be measured (e.g., Devine, 1989; Dovidio, Kawakami, Johnson, Johnson, & Howard, 1997; Fazio, Jackson, Dunton, & Williams, 1995; Greenwald & Banaji, 1995; Greenwald et al., 1998), hundreds of studies have been carried out and published. The signs of academic celebrity abound: conferences, edited collections, review chapters, even entire handbooks. The sheer volume of research is staggering. Evidently, implicit attitude is an idea whose time has come.[13]

Implicit attitudes require new and subtle methods of measurement, methods that bypass the conscious mind. On their face, such methods offer a way to get at those attitudes—like race prejudice—that people might not care to express to others or even acknowledge to themselves. Conveniently for our purposes, race prejudice is among implicit attitude researchers' favorite objects of study.

Of the several methods of measuring implicit attitudes now available, the Implicit Association Test (IAT) is used most widely. As do most other procedures for measuring implicit attitudes, the IAT requires exact measurement of speed of mental response. The IAT presumes that mental tasks are performed more rapidly when they run on well-practiced associations. In the basic IAT setup, participants move through a series of tasks administered by computer. The first might be to classify names as white ("Stewart") or as black ("Darius"). A name appears on the computer screen, and the task is to classify the name as prototypically white, by tapping a computer key on the left, or as prototypically black, by tapping a computer key on the right, and to do so as fast as possible. Over many trials, latency of response—the time elapsed between presentation of the name and the tap of the computer key—is measured in milliseconds. In the next phase, participants might be presented with words and asked to classify each as pleasant or as unpleasant. This task is easy. The presented words belong obviously to one category (e.g., "gift") or to the other ("disaster"). Once again, over many trials, latency of response is measured and recorded. The third task superimposes the second task on the first. On alternate trials, either a white or black name *or* a pleasant or unpleasant word appears. Participants are asked to classify each as either white or pleasant (left key) or as black or unpleasant (right key). In the fourth and final stage, the associations are reversed. Now the task is to classify each presentation as either white or unpleasant or as black or pleasant.

The key assumption underlying the IAT is this: if the white versus black distinction is positively associated with the pleasant versus unpleasant distinction, then the third task should be easier than the fourth: that is, classifications should be made faster. And so they are. Averaged over many trials and many participants, the typical difference is about is 200 milliseconds. On average, white Americans respond roughly 0.2 seconds faster to black-unpleasant and white-pleasant pairings than to the reverse.[14]

This result is extremely robust. Racial bias, measured by the IAT, shows up in scores of studies. It shows up among white Americans—but also among Hispanics, Asians, and Native Americans, and in equal measure. Only African Americans score as "color-blind" on the IAT (Nosek et al., 2007).[15]

This result leaves open the question of whether racial bias assessed by the IAT can operate as a measure of attitude. Does the IAT uncover reliable individual differences in racial prejudice? The answer is yes (Nosek et al., 2007). In fact, the IAT can uncover two different forms of implicit prejudice: implicit prejudice expressed as affective bias, where the objects of classification are pleasant and unpleasant words ("smile" and "death"); and implicit prejudice expressed as cognitive bias, where the objects of classification are positive and negative stereotypes ("ambitious" and "lazy"). In short, like explicit prejudice, implicit prejudice appears to feature both affective and cognitive components. Furthermore, like standard measures of explicit prejudice, standard measures of implicit prejudice perform well in construct validity tests: that is, the measures prove useful in the prediction of a wide range of judgments and behaviors (e.g., Greenwald, Poehlman, Uhlmann, & Banaji, 2009; Fazio & Olson, 2003).

4.4. Distinct but Correlated Varieties of Prejudice

Drawing conceptual distinctions among kinds of prejudice is one thing. Assessing whether conceptual differences carry empirical consequences is another. In the end, the value of measurement should be assessed on instrumental grounds (Kaplan, 1964). How *useful* is it to distinguish between kinds of prejudice?

An important first step to take in answering this question is to examine correlations between the main varieties of prejudice. Within the domain of explicit kinds, a very general result emerges: different explicit measures represent distinct but correlated varieties of prejudice (e.g., Henry & Sears, 2002; Kinder & Drake, 2009; Tarman & Sears, 2005). That they are correlated supports the conclusion that biological racism, cultural racism, racial stereotyping, and racial affect all belong to the same family. That they are empirically distinct makes it possible that they will have separable consequences for politics.

What about the relationship between these various manifestations of explicit prejudice, on the one hand, and implicit prejudice, on the other? Alas, there is no general result to report. In the psychological literature, the association between implicit and explicit measures of prejudice is sometimes zero; it is sometimes sizable; most often, it is modest (e.g., Cunningham, Preacher, & Banaji, 2001; Dovidio et al., 1997; Fazio & Olson, 2003; Greenwald et al., 2009; Payne, Burkley, & Stokes, 2008).

Many of these estimates come from studies run on college students participating for course credit. Others arise from huge but unrepresentative opt-in samples. In many cases, the estimates are based on studies that included top-of-the-line measures of implicit prejudice but off-hand measures of explicit prejudice. When these problems are corrected, the association between implicit and explicit prejudice turns out to be slight. With excellent samples, best measures, and with or without statistical adjustments for unreliability, implicit and explicit prejudice are largely distinct (e.g., Kinder & Ryan, 2013).

Moreover,, the correlation between implicit and explicit measures of prejudice is lower than it is for less socially delicate attitudes (Greenwald et al., 2009). This result is consistent with the idea that explicit measures of prejudice are contaminated by social desirability and implicit measures are not—or at least, are contaminated less. Implicit components of attitudes appear to be distinguishable from explicit components of attitude at neural levels as well (Phelps et al., 2000; Cunningham et al., 2004). And as we are about to see, implicit and explicit measures of prejudice predict different kinds of political outcomes.

4.5. Is Prejudice Declining?

The answer to this important question depends on exactly what we mean by prejudice. If prejudice is taken to mean biological racism or racial stereotyping, then the answer is yes. Both these forms of prejudice have diminished—though it would be a mistake to conclude that they have disappeared altogether (Katz and Braly, 1933; Gilbert, 1951;

Karlins, Coffman, & Walters, 1969; Kinder & Sanders, 1996).[16] But if by prejudice we mean racial animosity based in cultural differences—the "new racism" of Europe and the United States (Fredrickson, 2002)—then there is no evidence that prejudice is declining. The same can be said for the affective component of prejudice: on average, white Americans express just as much coolness toward African Americans today as they did a half-century ago (Kinder & Drake, 2009; Schuman et al., 1997).

5. Consequences

My purpose here is to ascertain to what extent and under what conditions prejudice spills into politics. I review evidence on the part played by prejudice in shaping the political lives of Americans in three domains: for the political party they identify with, the candidates they choose to support, and the government policies they favor.

5.1. Prejudice and Partisanship

As political parties are central to the functioning of American politics (e.g., Aldrich, 2011), party identification is central to the workings of the American political mind. Most Americans think of themselves as Democrats or as Republicans. The connection between citizen and party is psychological, requiring neither legal recognition nor evidence of formal membership, and it is consequential: "To the average person, the affairs of government are remote and complex, and yet the average citizen is asked periodically to formulate opinions about these affairs.... In this dilemma, having the party symbol stamped on certain candidates, certain issue positions, certain interpretations of reality is of great psychological convenience" (Stokes, 1966, pp. 126–127; also see Campbell, Converse, Miller, & Stokes, 1960; Bartels, 2000; 2002; Converse, 1966; Gerber, Huber, & Washington, 2010; and Green, Palmquist, & Schickler, 2002).

Party identification is abiding. It is a "durable attachment, not readily disturbed by passing events and personalities" (Campbell et al., 1960, p. 151), and not "to be confused with any short-term surge of approval at some triumph of a party or its leadership" (Converse & Pierce, 1985, p. 145; for a discussion of partisanship as a social identity see Huddy, chapter 23, this volume). Under normal conditions, the American political system is characterized by partisan stability.

Conditions are not always normal. Prior to 1964, most African Americans identified with the Democratic Party. After 1964, nearly all did, north and south. In the meantime, as blacks were moving wholesale into the Democratic Party, whites were moving out. More precisely, *southern* whites were moving out. In the 1950s, southern whites were overwhelmingly Democratic in their party identification. By the turn of the new century, southern whites were as likely to identify with the Republican Party—the party of Lincoln and abolition—as they were to think of themselves as Democrats. This is a staggering change, as unusual as it is important, and the political ramifications are still reverberating through the political system (Black & Black, 1987; 2002). What role, if any, did prejudice play in this transformation?

The precipitating event for partisan change in the South would appear to be the sudden shift in the position of the parties on matters of race, made dramatically visible in the 1964 presidential election (Carmines & Stimson, 1989).[17] Kinder and Sanders (1996) interpret the 1964 election as an exemplary case of what V. O. Key Jr. meant by a "realignment," one induced by changes in the parties over the question of race. In Key's treatment, realignments require party shifts on issues of great concern to voters. For whites in the South and for African Americans everywhere, no issue was as important as race. Many southern whites saw the coming of the civil rights movement as a challenge to an entire way of life, just as many African Americans saw the protests, sit-ins, and marches as a way to finally redeem the American promise of equality for all.

Whites in the South and blacks nationwide were vitally concerned about civil rights before the 1964 campaign, but race was central to neither party's agenda. This changed dramatically and suddenly in 1964, when Senator Goldwater came charging out of the conservative wing of his party to win the Republican presidential nomination. The 1964 presidential campaign played out against a backdrop of racial crisis: sit-ins, freedom rides, marches, and other forms of public protest were spreading, racial violence erupted in New York and other major American cities, and Congress passed the most important civil rights legislation since Reconstruction. In the campaign proper, Goldwater argued against the encroachments of the federal government in general and against the civil rights legislation sponsored by the Johnson administration in particular. As he made his case, Goldwater moved the Republican Party sharply to the right on matters of race, just as President Johnson hauled the Democratic Party sharply to the left. President Johnson said one thing, Senator Goldwater said another, and voters reacted accordingly. According to the 1964 National Election Study, Johnson received 99.6% of the vote among blacks. While Johnson was elected in a landslide of epic proportions, inside the Deep South, Goldwater did remarkably well—87% of the vote in Mississippi, nearly 70% in Alabama, 59% in South Carolina, 57% in Louisiana, and 54% in Georgia—all states that had eluded the Republican Party since Reconstruction.

The parties changed and the voters reacted—but to what, exactly? Carmines and Stimson (1989) argue that Senator Goldwater injected a new idea into American politics in 1964: "racial conservatism," the application of conservative principles to issues of employment discrimination, school desegregation, and voting rights that were suddenly occupying the center of national political debate. In their view, Goldwater was articulating a *principled* opposition to federal intervention on race, one rooted in a philosophical view about government in general. According to Black and Black (1987), white southerners were drawn to the Republican Party primarily by the promise of lower taxes, limited government, reduced regulation, and restored patriotism—not by opposition to civil rights initiatives. Kinder and Sanders (1996) argue otherwise; they say that southern whites moved so decisively to Goldwater and then on to the Republican Party for reasons of race. Prejudice, not conservatism, principled or otherwise, drove white southerners out of the Democratic Party.

Whatever it was that voters were acting on, the changes set in motion by the 1964 election have persisted; indeed, they have grown larger (Burns, Jardina, Kinder, & Reynolds, 2011). The South, solidly Democratic since the Civil War, is now preponderantly Republican. According to Carmines and Stimson (1989), the principal mechanism driving the persistence of partisan differences over race is population replacement. Older generations of white Southerners have remained strongly Democratic in their political leanings over the past 40 years, but they are fading away, replaced by younger generations without historic ties to the Democratic Party (Green et al., 2002).

This account is fine as far as it goes, but for our purposes it does not go far enough. In particular, it is silent on whether the new partisans in the South have been choosing the Republican Party motivated, at least in part, by prejudice. On this point, the literature is sharply divided. Carmines and Stimson (1989) say no; that it is principled conservatism, not prejudice, that is the real driving force. Black and Black (2002) argue that it is conservatism as articulated by Ronald Reagan—limited government, strong defense, family values—that have propelled young southern whites to the Republicans. Taking notice of the economic transformation that has come to the South over the past half-century, Shafer and Johnston (2006) contend that partisan change is a story of class overtaking race as the basis for politics. And Valentino and Sears (2005), mindful of the history of racism in the American South, make a strong case that the rapid and remarkable rise of the Republican Party below the Mason-Dixon line must be attributed, in important part, to prejudice.

5.2. Prejudice and the Vote

If prejudice is part of partisanship, then prejudice is also part of voting, for partisanship is the single most important factor in determining the vote. My interest here is in ascertaining the impact of prejudice on vote over and above the effect due to partisanship—prejudice as a short-term electoral force. At the outset, I presume that prejudice will be more or less potent in this role depending on the prominence and clarity of cues signaling that the candidates differ substantially in the racial groups they favor and oppose. The magnitude of the difference, the clarity of the difference, and the prominence of the difference: together, these three constitute the preconditions for the electoral effect of prejudice.

Cues signaling a candidate's alignment with or opposition to racial groups can take various forms. Candidates can propose particular policies that visibly favor one group at the expense of another: think of Senator Goldwater's attack on the 1964 Civil Rights Act. They can emphasize or neglect problems that are of special concern to a particular group: think of President Clinton's pledge to "end welfare as we know it." They can keep certain company, spending time in the public eye with iconic representatives of one group or another: think of Richard Nixon's foray into the Deep South in

1968 accompanied by Senator Strom Thurmond of South Carolina, a hero of southern resistance. Perhaps the most effective signaling device of all is actual membership in a subordinate and therefore marked racial group—think of Jesse Jackson's run for the Democratic nomination in 1988.

Is a candidate's racial identity as black or African American sufficient to activate prejudice? So it seems. This conclusion is supported by three distinct kinds of evidence. First are experiments run on broad community samples that manipulate the racial identity of fictitious candidates while holding other candidate characteristics constant. These experiments demonstrate that white voters generally prefer candidates of their own race (though the experimental effects are sometimes quite subtle); prejudice is irrelevant to white voters' reactions to white candidates; and prejudice is central to white voters' reactions to black candidates (Moskowitz & Stroh, 1994; Reeves, 1997; Sigelman, Sigelman, Walkosz, & Nitz, 1995; Terkildsen, 1993).

A second source of evidence is the statistical analysis of election returns in contests where a white candidate is opposed by a black candidate. Time and again, in races for Congress, the statehouse, or the mayor's office, the same result is observed: African Americans vote almost unanimously for the black candidate while white Americans vote overwhelmingly for the white candidate. Some of this racial divide is due to persistent differences between blacks and whites in party identification, of course, but racial polarization appears to go beyond partisanship. With partisanship taken into account, black candidates run stronger among African American voters—by 4 or 5 percentage points—and weaker among white voters—by roughly 10 percentage points—than they would in the absence of racial considerations (e.g., Bullock & Dunn, 1999; Grofman, Handley, & Lublin, 2001; Lublin, 1997; Sass & Pittman, 2000; Sass & Mehay, 1995; for an exception to this pattern, see Highton, 2004).

Case studies provide a third batch of evidence. Included here are investigations of Edward Brooke's successful run for the Senate in Massachusetts in 1966 (Becker & Heaton, 1967); Tom Bradley's first two races for the mayor's office in Los Angeles in 1969 and 1973 (Kinder & Sears, 1981) and then his unsuccessful try for the California governorship in 1982 (Citrin, Green, & Sears, 1990); Harold Washington's narrow election as mayor of Chicago in 1983 (Kleppner, 1985); and Jesse Jackson's runs for the Democratic Party's presidential nomination in 1984 and again in 1988 (Sears, Citrin, & Kosterman, 1987; Kinder & Dale-Riddle, 2011). Taken together, these studies suggest that racial identity activates prejudice.

Not surprisingly, Barack Obama's historic victory in the 2008 American presidential election has drawn special attention. Various studies, relying on different data, measures, and methods, all find that prejudice predicted white opposition to Obama powerfully. Obama gained votes among African Americans; lost votes among white Americans; and overall lost more than he gained. By several calculations, Obama paid a race penalty of roughly five percentage points. If race as a short-term force could somehow have been erased in 2008, Obama would have won in a landslide. Put another way, had the fundamentals been less favorable to the Democrats in the fall of 2008—an apparently failing war in Iraq and an impending economic catastrophe, both presided over by a Republican administration—Obama would not have been elected at all (Kinder & Dale-Riddle, 2012; Pasek et al., 2009; Payne et al., 2010; Piston, 2010; Tesler & Sears, 2010).

One way to understand this apparently general result—prejudice predicting vote when black candidates run for office—is through stereotyping. From this point of view, the key question voters ask themselves is this: Is the candidate one of *us*, or one of *them*? When a candidate is classified as a member of a marked group, then the stereotypic characteristics associated with the group are transferred onto the candidate. Because the stereotypic characteristics that white Americans associate with black Americans are on the whole negative, black candidates typically pay a penalty for their race.[18]

An alternative mechanism for understanding the connection between prejudice and vote when black candidates run for office points to the activation of cultural racism. From this perspective, the key question voters ask themselves is: Is the candidate *for us*, or *for them*? Under this account, racial identity is just one of many possible cues signaling alignment or opposition to racial groups. This implies that black public figures could be rewarded by racially conservative whites and punished by racially liberal whites insofar as they are seen to stand against the interests of their "people." Consistent with this, white Americans who score high on cultural racism tend to admire Supreme Court Justice Clarence Thomas, famous for his conservative positions, and Condoleezza Rice, former national security adviser and secretary of state under President G. W. Bush (Kinder & Dale-Riddle, 2012).

Another implication of this perspective is that prejudice can be activated by *white* candidates. An obvious case in point is Governor George C. Wallace of Alabama, who first came to national attention for his forceful defense of segregation. In his independent run for the presidency in 1968, Wallace railed against the federal government's intrusion upon the rights of ordinary citizens to send their children to the schools they wished and against the outlaws and thugs who felt free to burn and loot American cities. Wallace campaigned without finances or organization and yet collected almost 10 million votes—13.5% of the national total—and amassed 46 electoral votes, all from states of the Deep South (Black & Black, 1992).

A more subtle case of activation is provided by the 1988 presidential campaign and the well-coordinated Republican initiative to portray the Democratic presidential nominee, Governor Dukakis, as soft on crime. Ostensibly about crime, the campaign was at least as much about race, featuring the horrific story of Willie Horton. A black man convicted of murder and sentenced to life imprisonment, Horton was granted a weekend leave by the Massachusetts prison furlough program while Dukakis was governor. Horton fled the state and terrorized a white couple in Maryland, beating the man and raping the woman before being captured and returned to prison. Horton became a fixture in Bush's speeches, in Republican campaign fliers, and in a set of memorable television advertisements. As the campaign wore on, prejudice became more and more important to the vote, moving racially conservative Democrats and independents into the Republican column (Kinder & Sanders, 1996; Mendelberg, 2001).

5.3. Prejudice and Opinions on Policy

A crucial test of democracy is the responsiveness of public officials to the opinions of their constituents on matters of government policy. But policy is a difficult subject, and we know that Americans, for the most part, are engaged in other pursuits: family, work, friends, and, not least, their own entertainment. In the United States (as in most other places), "politics is a sideshow in the great circus of life" (Dahl, 1961, p. 305; Delli Carpini & Keeter, 1996). How do Americans manage to form opinions on policy?

5.3.1. *Group-centrism*

In his famous essay on belief systems in mass publics, Philip Converse (1964) concluded that the American mass public—*any* mass public, really—is largely innocent of ideology (for an extended discussion of the political psychology of ideology see Feldman, chapter 19, this volume). Given that ideological reasoning was out of reach, Converse suggested that citizens might deduce their opinions on policy from what they felt toward the social groups that the policy seemed to benefit or harm. To illustrate what he had in mind, Converse fabricated a series of hypothetical policies so as to emphasize a highly visible and familiar social group—in his example, using the vernacular of the time, "Negroes"—whose fortunes appear to be advanced or impaired by each of the policies: for example, "The government should see to it that Negroes get fair treatment in jobs and housing" or "Even though it may hurt the position of the Negro in the South, state governments should be able to decide who can vote and who cannot." Converse argued that what looms large in these various policy proposals is the social group itself, not abstract arguments over states' rights or the proper role of the federal government. Because such abstractions "take on meaning only with a good deal of political information and understanding"—precisely what the typical citizen lacks—"the attitude items given would tend to boil down for many respondents to the same single question: 'Are you sympathetic to Negroes as a group, are you indifferent to them, or do you dislike them?'" (Converse, 1964, p. 235).[19]

   Converse's argument was all conjecture; he presented no real evidence to speak of. Now we know he was right. Scores of studies have demonstrated that public opinion on matters of policy is in fact "group-centric": that is, shaped in powerful ways by the attitudes citizens harbor toward the social groups they see as the principal beneficiaries or victims of the policy. This is so for social groups in general, and it is so for racial groups in particular. On such matters as equal opportunity in employment, fair housing, school desegregation, contract set-asides, affirmative action in college admissions, and racial quotas in hiring and promotion, racially prejudiced whites line up on one side of the issue, and racially tolerant whites line up on the other. Of course, prejudice is not the only factor at work, but in all these cases, prejudice is an important factor (e.g., Alvarez & Brehm, 2002; Kinder & Sanders, 1996; Kuklinski et al., 1997; Sears, Hensler, & Speer, 1979; Sniderman, Brody, & Kuklinski, 1984).[20]

5.3.2. Prejudice's Reach

The effect of prejudice on opinion is most pronounced on policies where the racial consequences are explicit and clear, like school desegregation or affirmative action. But prejudice also has strong effects on opinion on issues where race is present only by implication.
Welfare reform, crime and punishment, and immigration: in all three instances, prejudice figures importantly in public opinion (e.g., Brader, Valentino, & Suhay, 2008; Gilens,
1999; Gilliam & Iyengar, 2000; Hurwitz & Peffley, 1997; Kinder & Kam, 2009; Kinder &
Sanders, 1996; Peffley & Hurwitz, 2007; Peffley, Hurwitz, & Sniderman 1997; Tesler,
2012; Valentino, 1999; Winter, 2006). Why?

Winter (2008) offers a general framework that seems helpful in clarifying when
and where prejudice comes into play. Drawing on the literature in cognitive psychology on reasoning by analogy, Winter argues that for predispositions like racial prejudice to influence citizens' views on matters of policy they must be activated. Activation
takes place when the predisposition is psychologically accessible. Predispositions can
be chronically accessible as a result of "upbringing, socialization, and life experience."
They can be episodically accessible as a consequence of prominent current events (e.g.,
Kinder & Drake, 2009). Activation also requires a good fit, a close correspondence,
between the issue and the predisposition. Prejudice, in Winter's telling, consists of three
fundamental and connected elements: a distinction between in-group (white) and out-
group (black); a recognition of pervasive and significant inequalities between in-group
and out-group; and an explanation for how such inequalities arise. When an issue—any
issue—is understood in a way that corresponds to the way that prejudice is structured,
then prejudice will be activated—then, as Winter says, people "will apply their thoughts
and feelings about race relations to the issue" (p. 7).

Issues in the domain of welfare, crime, and immigration are often presented in terms
that match the underlying structure of prejudice. In popular understanding, welfare
invokes a distinction between those who work hard and those who loaf; crime invokes
a distinction between law-abiding and predator; immigration invokes a distinction
between real Americans and foreign intruders. In these ways, welfare, crime, and immigration may be understood in racial terms.

5.3.3. Prejudice, Opinion, and Framing

Citizens are constantly being bombarded by external sources encouraging them to think
about issues in particular ways. Presidents, members of Congress, corporate publicists,
activists, policy analysts, reporters and editors, all are perpetually engaged in a competition about how issues are to be understood—or as the contemporary vocabulary would
have it, in how issues are *framed*. Frames encompass both the rhetorical tools fashioned
by political elites to advance their ideas and the often-unarticulated rules of selection,
emphasis, and presentation governing the work of journalism (Chong & Druckman,
2007; Gamson & Modigliani, 1987; Valentino & Nardis, chapter 18, this volume).

An emphasis upon frames presumes that politics is, at least in part, a competition of
ideas. Every issue is contested; advocates of one persuasion or another attempt to define

the issue their way. Public opinion depends not only on the circumstances and sentiments of individual citizens—their interests, partisanship, political principles, and their feelings toward social groups including prejudice—but also on the ongoing debate among parties and elites. The issues taken up by government are always complex; they are always subject to alternative interpretations. What exactly *is* affirmative action? Is it reverse discrimination? Is it compensation for the injustices of the past? Is it a general remedy, or is it to be applied only under specific and special circumstances? Which of these interpretations prevails in popular discourse may substantially affect how citizens understand affirmative action, and, in the end, what their opinions on affirmative action turn out to be.

For example, support for government requiring large companies to give a certain number of jobs to blacks increases when the question is framed to include the information that such companies have been found to discriminate against blacks in the recent past (Stoker, 2001). This experimental manipulation was designed to mirror the contingent thinking evident in recent Supreme Court decisions on affirmative action. In recent cases, the Court has ruled that affirmative action is to be applied, and preferential treatment policies are appropriate, only as a narrowly tailored remedy for discriminatory practice. In effect, the Court has decided, as Stoker puts it, "Because *this* institution has been discriminating against blacks, it is *this* institution whose procedures must change, and those subject to this discrimination that deserve restitution." Stoker's result suggests that affirmative action programs that follow the Court's rulings are more likely to earn public approval.

More generally, opinion on policy in the domain of race is contingent on how policy is framed. Support for government providing assistance to African Americans increases when justified on grounds of a general principle—equal opportunity—than when justified in racially specific terms—to overcome the legacy of slavery and discrimination (Sniderman, Carmines, Layman, Carter, 1996). Opposition to affirmative action in university admissions diminishes when presented as making sure that all qualified black applicants are considered as against affirmative action described as giving qualified blacks preference in admissions decisions (Stoker, 1998). Approval of antipoverty policies increases when the policies are described as targeted on the poor and the disadvantaged regardless of race (Bobo & Kluegel, 1993; Kinder & Sanders, 1996). Backing for fair housing collapses when Americans are reminded of the argument against fair housing based in property rights (Sniderman, Crosby, & Howell, 2000). All these results are consistent with the claim that frames matter and with the more general proposition that politics is about the choices "citizens make in the face of arguments crafted to win their support" (Sniderman et al., 2000, p. 262).

Over the last 50 years or so, the framing of race in elite discourse has undergone a transformation. In his successful campaign for governor in 1959, Ross Barnett told Mississippi voters:

> I don't believe God meant for the races to be integrated. God placed the black man in Africa and separated the white man from him with a body of water ... Integration has ruined every community in which it has been practiced. I would rather lose my life than to see Mississippi schools integrated. (Black, 1971)

Barnett's remarks were quite representative for his time—but his time was passing. The passionate defense of segregation and the deliberate appeal to racism that characterized Barnett's campaign was about to disappear. As a rule, we don't hear this kind of talk any longer—not from public officials, or from candidates, or from those in public life more generally. When it comes to race, political rhetoric has been sanitized.

Does this mean that appeals to prejudice have disappeared? Not necessarily. Perhaps truculent defense of segregation has given way to more euphemistic language. Perhaps appeals to prejudice continue but take an indirect and surreptitious form (Black, 1976; Kinder & Sanders, 1996).

Mendelberg (1997; 2001) goes so far as to claim that to be effective, appeals to prejudice *must* take this form. Under current conditions, straightforward appeals to prejudice are recognized as such and backfire; only subtle appeals that activate prejudice outside awareness will have the intended effect. Consistent with this strong claim, Mendelberg finds that prejudice has a big effect on opposition to welfare programs when an advertisement attributed to a fictitious gubernatorial candidate is accompanied by visual depictions of African Americans as the principal beneficiaries of welfare; the same advertisement is less effective in triggering prejudice when it not only portrays African Americans but also names African Americans as welfare's primacy beneficiaries. Mendelberg argues that the latter frame is less effective because it is more obvious. By explicitly drawing attention to race, the message provides citizens with the opportunity to self-consciously override their prejudices and decide the matter on other grounds.

Whether the effect of prejudice on opinion increases only when prejudice is activated surreptitiously remains in dispute (Huber & Lapinsky, 2006; 2008; Mendelberg, 2008a; 2008b). What is beyond dispute is the more general claim that prejudice can be successfully activated by appeals that are (or seem) remarkably subtle. Take, for example, White's (2007) finding that prejudice affects opinion on war with Iraq when the argument is made that war should be opposed because it drains resources away from domestic programs (also see Valentino, Hutchings, & White, 2002). A second example: prejudice comes into play on the question of whether the government should invest either in building prisons or reducing poverty when the prison option is framed as locking up violent *inner city* criminals but not when the business of prisons is described as locking up violent criminals (Hurwitz & Peffley, 2005). Here, the insertion of a single phrase—"inner city"— makes all the difference. A final example: Winter (2008) demonstrates that when issues that on their face have nothing at all to do with race are framed in such a way as to match the underlying structure of prejudice—issues like grandparent's visitation rights—then prejudice is activated. These results add to the case that the power of prejudice depends on framing, and that in the realm of race, framing may be an increasingly subtle art.

5.3.4. *Types of Prejudice*

Earlier in the chapter I argued that prejudice may take various forms: biological versus cultural; cognitive versus affective; conscious versus unconscious. Here I want to suggest that keeping these distinctions in mind can enrich our understanding of how prejudice spills into politics.

First of all, in politics in the United States today, the cultural form of prejudice is more important than the biological. It was not always so, but it is so today. And it is so in two senses: cultural prejudice is both more popular and more potent (e.g., Henry & Sears, 2002).

There appears to be one exception to this empirical regularity, however. Biological racism is more important than cultural racism on policies involving interracial mixing: ensuring that black and white children attend school together, ruling out discrimination in the housing market, and especially on permitting blacks and whites to marry (Kinder, 2013). This finding fits with Myrdal's (1944) argument that the cornerstone of biological racism is an obsession with racial purity. If blacks and whites constitute fundamentally different kinds, and if blacks are mired in a state of permanent inferiority, then racial intermingling in schools or in neighborhoods or worse yet, in the creation of offspring, is at least misguided and perhaps even unnatural.

A second empirical regularity, less well established, is that judgment and action are predicted better by affective components of prejudice than by cognitive components (Esses, Haddock, & Zanna, 1993; Fiske, 1998; Stangor, Sullivan, & Ford, 1991). This result (if it really is a result) is consistent with Zajonc's (1980) general claim regarding the primacy of affect and with Allport's (1954) conjecture in his classic and encyclopedic analysis of prejudice. Allport believed that the essence of prejudice was to be found in feelings of hostility. Stereotypes were not unimportant, in Allport's view—they justify and rationalize hostility—but it was hostility that was hard to change and that provided the primary motivation for opinion and action.[21]

What can be said about the distinction between conscious and unconscious prejudice? Not as much as I would like. Almost all of the evidence reviewed so far on the consequences of prejudice relies on explicit measures. We know much less about the political consequences of implicit prejudice. The psychological literature is almost entirely silent on the extent to which implicit prejudice influences political judgment, and indirect measures of prejudice are just beginning to attract the attention of political scientists. Some of this new evidence suggests that implicit prejudice makes a difference in political assessments (Knowles, Lowery, & Schaumberg, 2010), though most of the evidence runs the other way (Ditoni, Lau, & Sears 2013; Dovidio et al., 1997; Fazio et al., 1995; Kalmoe & Piston, 2012; Kinder & Ryan 2013; Pasek et al., 2009; Payne et al., 2010).

I do not mean to imply that unconscious—or implicit—prejudice is innocuous. To the contrary. The psychology literature is brimming with demonstrations that implicit prejudice predicts judgment and action of real social consequence (e.g., Dovidio et al., 1997; Dovidio, Kawakami, & Gaertner, 2002; Fazio et al., 1995; Greenwald et al., 2009; and for an especially troubling example, Green et al., 2007). Implicit measures of prejudice seem especially useful in predicting "spontaneous" judgments and behaviors, those that occur without planning and deliberation. Quillian (2006) suggests that implicit prejudice may be responsible for everyday acts of discrimination. Since the 1964 Civil Rights Act, discrimination by race has been illegal, and surely it is neither as flagrant nor as pervasive today as it once was. But it is far from gone. Scores of careful studies convincingly establish that African Americans still face discrimination at work; are still steered away from white neighborhoods when looking for housing; and still endure racist epithets on the streets, harassment by police officers in public spaces, rudeness, excessive surveillance, and higher prices while they shop, coolness from their teachers and bosses, and racist jokes from their coworkers.[22]

6. PREJUDICE AND POLITICS ELSEWHERE

My focus so far has been on the interplay between race prejudice and politics in the contemporary United States. But of course the United States is not the only nation beset by racial discord. In this section I summarize what we have learned recently about race and politics in contemporary Europe.

For some time now, guest workers, labor migrants, ex-colonials, refugees, and asylum seekers have been pouring into Amsterdam, Brussels, Frankfurt, London, and other major European cities. By 2005, about 10% of residents of western European countries were born abroad. Many of the new immigrants were dark. Their arrival sparked a reaction: a clamoring for restrictions, widespread discrimination, occasional violence, and the rise of right-wing political parties (Kitschelt, 1995; Pettigrew, 1998; Sides & Citrin, 2007).

What lies behind this hostility? Prejudice does, at least in part. Pettigrew and Meertens (1995) show that "subtle prejudice"—which encompasses an exaggeration of cultural differences, a defense of traditional values, especially individualism, and a denial or absence of positive emotions—powerfully predicts opposition to immigration. The same relationship holds for the French reaction to North African and Asian immigrants; the Dutch reaction to Surinamers; the British reaction to West Indians; and the German reaction to Turks. In each instance, prejudice drives opposition. In a similar vein, Sides and Citrin (2007) find that resistance to immigration comes disproportionately from those who embrace an ethnic definition of nationhood, who believe that the nation is stronger when everyone shares the same customs and traditions. Again, this relationship is robust across western Europe, from Austria to Switzerland.

Studies of the foundations of public opinion typically distinguish between identity-based explanations and accounts that highlight economic interests. The principal competitor to prejudice as an explanation for understanding opposition to immigration invokes the economic threat that immigrants pose to native workers. According to this argument, realistic fear over the economic effects of labor-market competition among low-skilled, blue-collar workers is the primary engine of anti-immigrant attitudes. From this perspective, the debate over immigration "is to a large extent about economics, and a critical battle line is the one that separates high-skilled and low-skilled workers" (Hainmueller & Hiscox, 2007, p. 400).

Upon closer examination, this economic argument fails to take us very far in accounting for opposition to immigration. For one thing, economic theory is actually quite equivocal over the effects of immigration on the wages and employment opportunities for native workers. For another, empirical studies find only small wage and employment effects in European labor markets due to immigration. And finally, when measured directly, economic threat appears to have at best small effects on opposition to immigration (Hainmueller & Hiscox, 2007; Sides & Citrin, 2007; Sniderman, Hagendoorn, & Prior, 2004).

There appears to be one patch of blue sky for the economic account: the strong and robust negative relationship between education and disapproval of immigration, interpreted in some quarters as evidence for the role of economic threat (e.g., Scheve & Slaughter, 2001). According to the standard labor-market competition argument, native workers should oppose immigration of workers with skills similar to their own but be indifferent to prospective immigrants with different skills. But Hainmueller and Hiscox (2007; 2010) find that native workers with higher levels of education (and skill sets) are more likely to favor immigration regardless of immigrant education (or skill). Across Europe, higher education means support for immigration of all kinds. Hainmueller and Hiscox conclude "the connection between education or skill levels of individuals and views about immigration appears to have very little, if anything, to do with fears about labor-market competition" (p. 399). Instead, Hainmueller and Hiscox say, the powerful effect attributable to education has to do with cosmopolitanism: better-educated Europeans are more likely to embrace the idea of cultural diversity and less likely to subscribe to prejudiced beliefs—with the consequence that they are substantially more open to immigration.

It seems worth underscoring that this pattern of empirical results on opposition to immigration in western Europe—prejudice dominating interest, education demarcating those who support open immigration from those who do not—is exactly what we see in the prejudice and politics literature in the United States (e.g., Sears et al., 1979; Kinder & Sanders, 1996; Kinder & Sears, 1981).

However methodologically sophisticated or theoretically imaginative research on prejudice and politics in the United States might be, it is necessarily limited by its preoccupation with a single society. Research on opposition to immigration in Europe escapes this particular limitation. By examining the response of publics in many countries simultaneously (or better yet, the response of publics in many countries over time), this research can uncover casual factors that are responsible for *differences* in response to immigration from one country to the next.

One consistent result emerging from research of this kind restores the importance of economic conditions to immigration politics. Quillian (1995) finds that opposition to immigration is accentuated in those European countries characterized by high immigration *and* declining economies. The same result shows up in comparative studies that seek to explain the sharp rise in extreme right parties in western Europe—the National Front in France, the National Alliance in Italy, the Austrian Freedom Party, and the like. Since the 1970s, all across Europe, such parties have grown stronger—but stronger in some places more than in others. Far-right parties prosper when immigration is increasing and unemployment is rising (Golder, 2003; Dancygier, 2010).

Notice the disconnection between the micro and macro results on immigration. Macro research implicates economic conditions as vital in specifying *where and when* opposition to immigration occurs; micro research implicates prejudice and downplays economic motives as vital in specifying *who* opposes immigration. This is an arresting puzzle. Perhaps economic deterioration provides extreme right parties and other "prejudice entrepreneurs" both a platform and an argument. The argument attributes the Nation's decline to the unwelcome and uninvited presence of Others. A platform means that many will hear the message. And of those who hear the message, it is the relatively prejudiced who will respond.

A second macro result points to electoral rules and institutions. Electoral systems vary in their permissiveness. Some set high thresholds for party entry and influence; others are much more permissive. As we've just seen, opposition to immigration rises with increases in the number of foreign-born, especially under conditions of economic decline. But this does not necessarily mean greater electoral success for anti-immigrant political parties. This happens only insofar as the governing electoral system is relatively permissive. National conditions can create a demand for a party like Le Pen's National Front, but electoral institutions determine whether such a demand is translated into actual votes and real political influence (e.g., Golder, 2003; Jackman & Volpert, 1996; Ordeshook & Shvetsova, 1994).

7. CONCLUSIONS

Summarizing a chapter built on summary seems an unprofitable enterprise, and I will not attempt it here. Instead, I will close the chapter with a trio of brief recommendations. I do so in full recognition that scholarship on prejudice and politics appears to be doing just fine without my advice.

First of all, some of the most exciting and informative recent work in the field takes a self-consciously comparative point of view. By this I have in mind the comparison of distinct but related forms of prejudice—prejudice rooted in race, gender, religion, ethnicity, and so on (e.g., Jackman, 1994, Winter, 2008). More of this sort of thing would be good. Second, the substantial investment in the measurement of prejudice, and especially in recent years in the measurement of implicit or unconscious prejudice, should continue. (I'm certain it will.) The measurement of attitudes in general and prejudice in particular is tricky business. The theoretical impurity and factorial complexity of social science measures is a nasty and persistent fact of life, one we should worry over more than we do. Third, as an intellectual puzzle, prejudice and politics sits at the intersection of a number of disciplines. Progress requires interdisciplinary inquiry—to my way of thinking, it calls for social psychology in the grand tradition. A chapter like mine can assemble pieces from different parts of the social sciences. It would have been more fun, and the field would be further ahead, if there were more disciplinary intermingling on the ground.

Conceived of as a political problem, prejudice seems unlikely to disappear anytime soon. Racial inequality is persistent. Segregation is tenacious. Racial differences are embedded in the American party system. The precise political impact of prejudice in the future will likely depend on conditions that are at present difficult to foresee: especially the prominence of racial conflict in social and political life, and the degree to which parties, candidates, and interest groups see it in their interest to frame issues in such a way as to mobilize prejudice for political purposes. But surely the problem is not going away, and the problem is important. What ordinary Americans think and do about race remains a cardinal test of American democracy, a pointed way to gauge the extent to which the United States lives up to its democratic aspirations (Myrdal, 1944).

NOTES

1. Mostly gone, I should have written. Criminal offenders typically forfeit voting rights following felony convictions. Because black Americans are much more likely to be arrested, convicted, and incarcerated than whites are, blacks are also much more likely to have their voting rights revoked on this ground. Many of the state statutes were passed in the late 1860s and 1870s, at a time when the question of voting rights for black Americans was central to the national political debate. Restrictive laws were most common in states with large nonwhite prison populations (Behrens, Uggen, & Manza, 2003).

2. My chapter should be read as complementary to a set of excellent essays: most notably, Brewer and Brown (1998), Duckitt (2003), and Huddy and Feldman (2009).

3. On the invention of the idea of race, see van den Berghe (1967). Hirschfeld (1996) goes furthest in spelling out the folk theory of race—what Americans believe to be true about race. In Hirschfeld's telling, the folk theory begins with the axiom that human populations can be partitioned into distinct types on the basis of their concrete, physical differences. Race itself is transmitted and fixed at birth; it is inherited and immutable. Differences between races are natural, deriving from some underlying essence. This essence gets expressed not only in physical appearance but in qualities of temperament, intellect, and character. Hirschfeld argues that race is not just an accident of how contemporary Americans happen to classify their social world. Rather, Americans, like people everywhere, are predisposed to partition their social worlds into human kinds. All of us, Hirschfeld claims, are endowed with a susceptibility to think in terms of race. From this point of view, race may be a bad idea, but it is a well-worked out and deeply rooted one.

4. The definition I offer here draws on a variety of sources across a range of academic disciplines, especially Allport (1954), van den Berghe (1967), and Fredrickson (2002).

5. I use the terms "prejudice" and "racism" interchangeably. Racism is sometimes distinguished from prejudice on the grounds that racism includes commitment to a political program (e.g., Adorno et al., 1950; Bobo & Smith, 1998; Fredrickson, 2002; and W. Wilson, 1973). My use of the term does not imply this added meaning.

6. The literature on racial differences in economic status is enormous. See, among many others, Blank (2001), Farley (2008), and Farley and Allen (1987). On race and health, see Williams (2001) and Xu, Kochanek, Murphy, and Tejada-Vera (2010).

7. Realistic group conflict theory is not without its problems. One is a preoccupation with conflict over exclusively material resources. In a series of remarkable experiments,

Tajfel (1981) has shown that even "minimal groups" are quite prepared to discriminate against each other (Brewer 2007). A second is the dubious assumption that conflict is always realistic (Kinder & Sanders 1996). Third is the anomalous fact that when conflict subsides, prejudice has proven to be "remarkably hard to eradicate" (Brewer & Brown, 1998, p. 566).

8. On this point, "even theorists who agree on little else are in complete accord" (McGuire, 1969, p. 161). McGuire suggests that "any proposition that everyone agrees with can't be all true; it has probably just been underscrutinized" (1969, p. 161) and goes on to offer prejudice as a promising case of genetic influence.

9. An excellent review of this literature is provided by Caspi, Roberts, and Shiner (2005).

10. On criticism of *The Authoritarian Personality*, see Roger Brown's essay (1965) prepared as a chapter for the first edition of his splendid textbook, *Social Psychology*.

11. Stenner thinks of authoritarianism in terms of personality. In Stenner's analysis, authoritarianism is a universal predisposition: deep-seated, perhaps innate, and difficult to alter. Feldman (2003) thinks of authoritarianism as a choice between competing values. He points out that systematic studies of social values across many countries repeatedly turn up a dimension that runs from social conformity on the one side to self-direction on the other. A related but distinct claim is that prejudice arises from what Sidanius and his colleagues call "social dominance orientation." By social dominance, Sidanius means a basic and universal desire to regard one's own group as superior to others. And by social dominance orientation, he means the extent to which particular individuals "desire social dominance and superiority for themselves and their primordial groups" (Sidanius 1993, p. 209). Social dominance orientation, according to Sidanius, is the fundamental source of oppressive ideologies the world around, including race prejudice in the United States (Sidanius & Pratto, 1999; Sidanius, Pratto, & Bobo, 1996).

12. For a review of the huge literature on stereotypes and stereotyping, see Fiske (1998).

13. A good place to start is Gawronski and Payne (2010).

14. For more on procedures, see Greenwald, McGhee, and Schwartz (1998); Greenwald et al. (2009); and Wittenbrink (2007). The IAT generally turns up larger effects than other procedures and so may offer a more reliable way to detect individual differences: that is, to assess implicit attitudes.

15. Racial bias measured in milliseconds is robust, but not uniform. Implicit prejudice varies as function of a number of contextual factors. For example, implicit prejudice diminishes when study participants are primed with positive African American cases—say, Denzel Washington—and when they are primed with negative white cases—say, Timothy McVeigh (Dasgupta & Greenwald, 2001); when anonymous black exemplars are portrayed as middle class rather than poor (Wittenbrink, Judd, & Park, 2001); or when the experiment is conducted by an affable black person (Lowery, Hardin, & Sinclair, 2001). These results suggest that the extent to which implicit prejudice is activated depends on the goodness-of-fit between particular instances and the underlying attitude (Gawronski & Bodenhausen, 2006).

16. For a skeptical reading of the evidence on stereotype change, see Devine and Elliot (1995) and Sigall and Page (1971).

17. Outside the South, the movement toward racial liberalism among Democratic Party elites started much earlier, beginning in the mid-1940s and continuing on gradually and more or less continuously through the racial crisis of the 1960s (Chen, 2009; Feinstein & Schickler, 2008; Schickler, Pearson, and Feinstein, 2010).

18. This account not only fits the results just reviewed, but also helps us to understand the curious case of Colin Powell (Kinder & McConnaughy, 2006).

19. In this exercise, Converse was using race to make a general point about the potential of sentiments toward social groups to organize political beliefs. He mentioned religion, social class, and nationality as well as race. But Converse also noted the "advantage" of race, in that the markers for group membership in the case of race are highly visible—"in the skin."

20. For policy on race, as for policy in other domains, public opinion is a reflection of not one thing but several: most notably, partisanship, commitment to the ideals of limited government, and egalitarianism.Conspicuous by its omission from this list is self-interest. When it comes to explaining American public opinion, self-interest turns out to be surprisingly unimportant—in general, and in the specific domain of race (e.g., Citrin & Green, 1990; Green, 1992; Kinder & Sears, 1981; Sears, Lau, Tyler, & Allen, 1980). Insofar as interest takes a place in accounts of public opinion, it is group interest—the extent to which a particular policy has implications not for me, but for my group (e.g., Bobo & Hutchings, 1996; Kinder & Sanders, 1996).

21. Allport has a point, but we shouldn't pretend that prejudice is neatly decomposable into its affective and cognitive components, and in particular, we shouldn't imagine that stereotypes are purely cognitive (Mackie & Hamilton, 1993).

22. In my review of research on the consequences of prejudice, I have accentuated points of agreement. All is not sweetness and light in this literature, however. Indeed, sharp and persistent disagreements mark the field—perhaps especially over the nature of the new prejudice in America, and over the relative importance of prejudice and principles in shaping public opinion. As I am a protagonist in these debates, it seemed inappropriate to use the essay to advance my views on these matters. In compensation, here I offer a highly abbreviated (and chronological) guide to the literature.On the meaning of prejudice, old and new: Kinder and Sears (1981); Kinder (1986); Sniderman and Tetlock (1986); Sears (1988); Kinder and Sanders (1996); and Fredrickson (2002).On the measurement of prejudice (and principles): Feldman (1988); Kinder and Sanders (1996); Sniderman et al. (1996); Kinder and Mendelberg (2000); Schuman (2000); Sears, Henry, and Kosterman (2000); Sniderman, Crosby, and Howell (2000); Stoker (2001); Henry and Sears (2002); Tarman and Sears (2005); and Huddy and Feldman (2009).On the relative importance of prejudice and principles: Sniderman and Piazza (1993); Kinder and Sanders (1996); Sidanius et al. (1996); Sniderman et al. (1996); Sniderman and Carmines (1997); Sniderman, Carmines, Howell, and Morgan (1997); Stoker (1998); Sears et al. (2000); Federico and Sidanius (2002); Feldman and Huddy (2005); and Tarman and Sears (2005).

REFERENCES

Adorno, T. W., Frenkel-Brunswik, E., Levinson, D. J., & Sanford, R. N. (1950). *The authoritarian personality*. New York: Harper and Row.

Aldrich, J. H. (2011). *Why parties? The origin and transformation of political parties in America. A second look*. Chicago: University of Chicago Press.

Alford, J., Funk, C., & Hibbing, J. R. (2005). Are political orientations genetically transmitted? *American Political Science Review, 99*(2), 164–167.

Allport, G. W. (1935). Attitudes. In C. A. Murchison (ed.), *A handbook of social psychology* (vol. 2, pp. 798–844). New York: Russell and Russell.

Allport, G. W. (1954). *The nature of prejudice*. Reading, MA: Addison-Wesley.

Alvarez, R. M., & Brehm, J. (2002). *Hard choices, easy answers*. Princeton, NJ: Princeton University Press.

Anderson, E. (2010). *The imperative of integration*. Princeton, NJ: Princeton University Press.

Apostle, R. A., Glock, C., Piazza, T, & Suelzle. M. (1983). *The anatomy of racial attitudes*. Berkeley, CA: University of California Press.

Banaji, M. R. (2001). Implicit attitudes can be measured. In H. L. Roediger, I. N. Naire, & A. M. Suprenant (eds.), *The nature of remembering: Essays in honor of Robert G. Crowder* (pp. 117–149).Washington, DC: APA.

Banaji, M. R., & Heiphetz, L. (2010). Attitudes. In S. T. Fiske, D. Gilbert, & G. Lindzey (eds.), *Handbook of social psychology* (5th ed., vol. 1, pp. 353–393). New York: John Wiley.

Barkan, E. (1992). *The retreat of scientific racism: Changing concepts of race in Britain and the United States between the world wars*. New York: Cambridge University Press.

Bartels, L. M. (2000). Partisanship and voting behavior, 1952–1996. *American Journal of Political Science, 44*, 35–50.

Bartels, L. M. (2002). Beyond the running tally: Partisan bias in political perceptions. *Political Behavior, 24*, 117–150.

Becker, J. F., & Heaton, E. E. (1967). The election of Senator Edward W. Brooke. *Public Opinion Quarterly, 31*(3), 346–358.

Behrens, A., Uggen, C., & Manza, J. (2003). Ballot manipulation and the "menace of Negro domination": Racial threat and felon disenfranchisement in the United States, 1850–2002. *American Journal of Sociology, 109*, 559–605.

Biernat, M., & Crandall, C. S. (1999). Racial attitudes. In J. P. Robinson, P. R. Shaver, & L. S. Wrightman (eds.), *Measures of political attitudes* (pp. 297–412). San Diego, CA: Academic Press.

Black, E. (1971). Southern governors and political change: Campaign stances on racial segregation and economic development. *Journal of Politics, 33*, 719–726.

Black, E., & Black, M. (1987). *Politics and society in the South*. Cambridge, MA: Harvard University Press.

Black, E., & Black, M. (2002). *The rise of southern Republicans*. Cambridge, MA: Harvard University Press.

Blank, R. M. (2001). An overview of trends in social and economic well-being, by race. In N. J. Smelser, W. J. Wilson, & F. Mitchell (eds.), *America becoming: Racial trends and their consequences* (pp. 21–39, vol. 1). Washington, DC: National Academy Press.

Blumer, H. (1958). Race prejudice as a sense of group position. *Pacific Sociological Review, 1*, 3–7.

Bobo, L. (1999). Prejudice as group position: Microfoundations of a sociological approach to racism and race relations. *Journal of Social Issues, 55*, 455–472.

Bobo, L., & Hutchings, V. L. (1996). Perceptions of racial group competition: Extending Blumer's theory of group position to a multiracial social context. *American Sociological Review, 61*, 951–972.

Bobo, L., & Kluegel, J. R. (1993). Opposition to race targeting: Self-interest, stratification ideology, or racial attitudes? *American Sociological Review, 58*, 443–464.

Bobo, L., & Massagli, M. P. (2001). Stereotyping and urban inequality. In A. O'Connor, C. Tilly, & L. Bobo (eds.), *Urban inequality: Evidence from four cities* (pp. 89–162). New York: Russell Sage Foundation.

Bobo, L., & Smith, R. A. (1998). From Jim Crow racism to laissez-faire racism: The transformation of racial attitudes. In W. F. Katkin, N. Landsman, & A. Tyree (eds.), *Beyond pluralism: The conception of groups and group identities in America* (pp. 182–220). Urbana: University of Illinois Press.

Bobo, L. D., & Tuan, M. (2006). *Prejudice and politics: Group position, public opinion, and the Wisconsin treaty rights dispute.* Cambridge, MA: Harvard University Press.

Bouchard, T. J., Lykken, D. T., McGue, M., Segal, N. L., & Tellegen, A. (1990). Sources of human psychological differences: The Minnesota study of twins reared apart. *Science, 250* (October), 223–228.

Brader, T., Valentino, N. A., & Suhay, E. (2008). What triggers public opposition to immigration? Anxiety, group cues, and immigration threat. *American Journal of Political Science, 52*(4), 959–978.

Brewer, M. B. (2007). The importance of being *we*: Human nature and intergroup relations. *American Psychologist, 62,* 728–738.

Brewer, M. B., & Brown, R. J. (1998). Intergroup relations. In D. Gilbert, S. T. Fiske, & L. Gardner (eds.), *Handbook of social psychology* (4th ed., pp. 554–594). Boston, MA: McGraw Hill.

Brown, R. (1965). *Social psychology.* New York: Free Press.

Brown, R. (1986). *Social psychology* (2nd ed.). New York: Free Press.

Bullock, C. S., III, & Dunn, R. E. (1999). The demise of racial districting and the future of black representation. *Emory Law Review, 48,* 1209–1253.

Burns, N., Jardina, A., Kinder, D. R., & Reynolds, M. (2011). Explaining gender gaps and racial divides in American partisanship. Paper delivered at the Annual Meeting of the American Political Science Association, Seattle, Washington, September 1.

Campbell, A., Converse, P. E., Miller, W. E., & Stokes, D. E. (1960). *The American voter.* New York: John Wiley.

Campbell, D. T. (1967). Stereotypes and the perception of group differences. *American Psychologist, 22,* 812–829.

Carmines, E. G., & Stimson, J. A. (1989). *Issue evolution: Race and the transformation of American politics.* Princeton, NJ: Princeton University Press.

Caspi, A., Roberts, B. W., & Shiner, R. L. (2005). Personality development. *Annual Review of Psychology, 56,* 453–484.

Chen, A. (2009). *The fifth freedom: Jobs, politics, and civil rights in the United States, 1941–1972.* Princeton, NJ: Princeton University Press.

Chong, D., & Druckman, J. N. (2007). Framing theory. *Annual Review of Political Science, 10,* 103–126.

Citrin, J., & Green, D. P. (1990). The self-interest motive in American public opinion. *Research in Micropolitics, 3,* 1–27.

Citrin, J., Green, D. P., & Sears, D. O. (1990). White reactions to black candidates. When does race matter? *Public Opinion Quarterly, 54,* 74–96.

Converse, P. E. (1964). The nature of belief systems in mass publics. In D. E. Apter (ed.), *Ideology and discontent* pp. 206–261). New York: Free Press.

Converse, P. E. (1966). The concept of a normal vote. In A. Campbell, P. E. Converse, W. E. Miller, & D. E. Stokes (eds.), *Elections and the political order* (pp. 9–39). New York: Wiley.

Converse, P. E., & Pierce, R. (1985). Measuring partisanship. *Political Methodology, 11,* 143–166.

Cunningham, W. A., Johnson, M. K., Raye, C. L., Gatenby, J. C., Gore, J. C., & Banaji, M. R. (2004). Separable neural components of processing of black and white faces. *Psychological Science, 15*(12), 806–813.

Cunningham, W. A., Preacher, K. J., & Banaji, M. R. (2001). Implicit attitude measures: Consistency, stability, and convergent validity. *Psychological Science, 12,* 163–170.

Dahl, R. A. (1961). *Who governs? Democracy and power in an American city*. New Haven, CT: Yale University Press.

Dancygier, R. M. (2010). *Immigration and conflict in Europe*. New York: Cambridge University Press.

Dasgupta, N., & Greenwald, A. G. (2001). On the malleability of automatic attitudes: Combating automatic prejudice with images of admired and disliked individuals. *Journal of Personality and Social Psychology, 81*, 800–814.

Degler, C. N. (1991). *In search of human nature*. New York: Oxford University Press.

Delli Carpini, M. X., & Keeter, S. (1996). *What Americans know about politics and why it matters*. New Haven, CT: Yale University Press.

Devine, P. G. (1989). Stereotypes and prejudice: Their automatic and controlled components. *Journal of Personality and Social Psychology, 56*, 5–18.

Devine, P. G., & Elliot, A. J. (1995). Are racial stereotypes *really* fading? The Princeton trilogy revisited. *Personality and Social Psychology Bulletin, 21*(11), 62–88.

Ditoni, T. M., Lau, R. R., & Sears, D. O. (2013). AMPing racial attitudes: Comparing the power of explicit and implicit prejudice in 2008. *Political Psychology*.

Dovidio, J. F., Kawakami, K., & Gaertner, S. L. (2002). Implicit and explicit prejudice and interracial interaction. *Journal of Personality and Social Psychology, 82*(1), 510–540.

Dovidio, J. F., Kawakami, K., Johnson, C., Johnson, B., & Howard, A. (1997). On the nature of prejudice: Automatic and controlled processes. *Journal of Experimental Social Psychology, 33*, 510–540.

Duckitt, J. (2003). Prejudice and intergroup hostility. In D. O. Sears, L. Huddy, & R. Jervis (eds.), *Oxford handbook of political psychology* (pp. 559–600). New York: Oxford University Press.

Eaves, L. J., Heath, A., Martin, N., Maes, H., Neale, M., Kendler, K., Kirk, K., & Corey, L. (1999). Comparing the biological and cultural inheritance of personality and social attitudes in the Virginia 30000 study of twins and their relatives. *Twin Research, 2*, 62–80.

Esses, V. M., Haddock, G., & Zanna, M. P. (1993). Values, stereotypes, and emotions as determinants of intergroup attitudes. In D. M. Mackie & D. L. Hamilton (eds.), *Affect, cognition, and stereotyping: Interactive processes in group perception* (pp. 137–166). San Diego, CA: Academic Press.

Farley, R. (2008). The Kerner Commission plus four decades: What has changed? What has not? Unpublished paper, Center for Population Research, Institute for Social Research, University of Michigan.

Farley, R., & Allen, W. R. (1987). *The color line and the quality of life in America*. New York: Russell Sage Foundation.

Fazio, R. H., Jackson, J. R., Dunton, B. C., & Williams, C. J. (1995). Variability in automatic activation as an unobtrusive measure of racial attitudes: A bona fide pipeline? *Journal of Personality and Social Psychology, 69*, 1013–1027.

Fazio, R. H., & Olson, M. A. (2003). Implicit measures in social cognition research: Their meaning and use. *Annual Review of Psychology, 54*, 297–327.

Federico, C. M., & Sidanius, J. (2002). Racism, ideology, and affirmative action revisited. *Journal of Personality and Social Psychology, 82*, 488–501.

Feldman, S. (1988). Structure and consistency in public opinion: The role of core beliefs and values. *American Journal of Political Science, 32*, 416–440.

Feldman, S. (2003). Enforcing social conformity: A theory of authoritarianism. *Political Psychology, 24*(1), 41–74.

Feldman, S., & Huddy, L. (2005). Racial resentment and white opposition to race-conscious programs: Principles or prejudice? *American Journal of Political Science, 49*, 168–183.

Feinstein, B. D., & Schickler, E. (2008). Platforms and partners: The civil rights realignment reconsidered. *Studies in American Political Development, 22*, 1–31.

Fiske, S. (1998). Stereotypes, prejudice, and discrimination. In D. T. Gilbert, S. T. Fiske, & G. Lindzey (eds.), *Handbook of social psychology* (4th ed., vol. 2, pp. 357–414). Boston, MA: McGraw Hill.

Fredrickson, G. M. (1971). *The black image in the white mind: The debate on Afro-American character and destiny, 1817–1914.* New York: Harper and Row.

Fredrickson, G. M. (2002). *Racism: A short history.* Princeton, NJ: Princeton University Press.

Gaertner, S. L., & Dovidio, J. F. (1986). The aversive form of racism. In S. L. Gaertner & J. F. Dovidio (eds.), *Prejudice, discrimination, and racism* (pp. 61–89). Orlando, FL: Academic Press.

Gamson, W. A., & Modigliani, A. (1987). The changing culture of affirmative action. In R. D. Braungart (ed.), *Research in political sociology* (vol. 3, pp. 137–177). Greenwich, CT: JAI Press.

Gawronski, B., & Bodenhausen, G. V. (2006). Associative and propositional processes in evaluation: An integrative review of implicit and explicit attitude change. *Psychological Bulletin, 132*, 692–731.

Gawronski, B., & Payne, B. K. (Eds.). (2010). *Handbook of implicit social cognition: Measurement, theory, and applications.* New York: Guilford Press.

Gerber, A. S., Huber, G. A., & Washington, E. (2010). Party affiliation, partisanship, and political beliefs: A field experiment. *American Political Science Review, 104*(4), 720–744.

Gilbert, G. M. (1951). Stereotype persistence and change among college students. *Journal of Personality and Social Psychology, 46*, 245–254.

Gilens, M. (1999). *Why Americans hate welfare.* Chicago: University of Chicago Press.

Giles, M. W., & Evans, A. (1986). The power approach to intergroup hostility. *Journal of Conflict Resolution, 30*(3), 469–486.

Giles, M. W., & Hertz, K. (1994). Racial threat and partisan identification. *American Political Science Review, 88*(2), 317–326.

Gilliam, F. D., Jr., & Iyengar, S. (2000). Prime suspects: The influence of local television news on the viewing public. *American Journal of Political Science, 44*(3), 560–573.

Glaser, J. M. (1994). Back to the black belt: Racial environment and white racial attitudes in the South. *Journal of Politics, 56*(1), 21–41.

Golder, M. (2003). Explaining variation in the success of extreme right parties in western Europe. *Comparative Political Studies, 36*(4), 432–466.

Green, A. R., Carney, D. R., Pallin, D., Ngo, L. H., Raymond, K. L., Iezzoni, L. I., & Banaji, M. R. (2007). The presence of implicit bias in physicians and its prediction of thrombolysis decisions for black and white patients. *Journal of General Internal Medicine, 22*, 1231–1238.

Green, D. P. (1992). The price elasticity of mass preferences. *American Political Science Review, 86*, 128–148.

Green, D. P., Palmquist, B., & Schickler, E. (2002). *Partisan hearts and minds.* New Haven, CT: Yale University Press.

Greenwald, A. G., & Banaji, M. R. (1995). Implicit social cognition: Attitudes, self-esteem, and stereotypes. *Psychological Review, 102*, 4–27.

Greenwald, A. G., McGhee, D. E., & Schwartz, J. L. K. (1998). Measuring individual differences in implicit cognition: The Implicit Association Test. *Journal of Personality and Social Psychology, 74*, 1464–1480.

Greenwald, A. G., Poehlman, T. A., Uhlmann, E. L., & Banaji, M. R. (2009). Understanding and using the Implicit Association Test: III. Meta-analysis of predictive ability. *Journal of Personality and Social Psychology, 97*(1), 17–41.

Grofman, B., Handley, L., & Lublin, D. (2001). Drawing effective minority districts: A conceptual framework and some empirical evidence. *North Carolina Law Review, 79*, 1383–1430.

Hainmueller, J., & Hiscox, M. J. (2007). Educated preferences: Explaining attitudes toward immigration in Europe. *International Organization*, *61*, 399–442.

Hainmueller, J., & Hiscox, M. J. (2010). Attitudes toward highly skilled and low-skilled immigration: Evidence from a survey experiment. *American Political Science Review*, *104*(1), 61–84.

Henry, P. J., & Sears, D. O. (2002). The symbolic racism 2000 scale. *Political Psychology*, *23*, 253–283.

Highton, B. (2004). White voters and African American candidates for Congress. *Political Behavior*, *26*(1), 1–25.

Hirschfeld, L. A. (1996). *Race in the making*. Cambridge, MA: MIT Press.

Huber, G. A., & Lapinski, J. (2006). The "race card" revisited: Assessing racial priming in policy contests. *American Journal of Political Science*, *48*, 375–401.

Huber, G. A., & Lapinski, J. (2008). Testing the implicit-explicit model of racialized political communication. *Perspectives on Politics*, *6*, 125–134.

Huddy, L., & Feldman, S. (2009). On assessing the political effects of racial prejudice. *Annual Review of Political Science*, *12*, 423–447.

Hurwitz, J., & Peffley, M. (1997). Public perceptions of race and crime: The role of racial stereotypes. *American Journal of Political Science*, *41*, 375–401.

Hurwitz, J., & Peffley, M. (2005). Playing the race card in the post–Willie Horton era. *Public Opinion Quarterly*, *69*, 99–112.

Jackman, M. R. (1994). *The velvet glove: Paternalism and conflict in gender, class, and race relations*. Berkeley: University of California Press.

Jackman, R., & Volpert, K. (1996). Conditions favoring parties of the extreme right in western Europe. *British Journal of Political Science*, *26*, 501–521.

Kahneman, D. (2003). A perspective on judgment and choice: Mapping bounded rationality. *American Psychologist*, *58*, 697–720.

Kalmoe, N. P., & Piston, S. (2013). Is implicit prejudice against blacks politically consequential? Evidence from the AMP. *Public Opinion Quarterly*.

Kam, C. D., & Palmer, C. L. (2008). Reconsidering the effects of education on participation. *Journal of Politics*, *70*(3), 612–631.

Kaplan, A. (1964). *The conduct of inquiry*. Ann Arbor: University of Michigan Press.

Karlins, M., Coffman, T. L., & Walters, G. (1969). On the fading of social stereotypes: Studies in three generations of college students. *Journal of Personality and Social Psychology*, *13*, 1–16.

Katz, D., & Braly, K. W. (1933). Racial stereotypes of 100 college students. *Journal of Abnormal and Social Psychology*, *28*, 280–290.

Key, V. O., Jr. (1949). *Southern politics in state and nation*. New York: Knopf.

Kinder, D. R. (1986). The continuing American dilemma: White resistance to racial change forty years after Myrdal. *Journal of Social Issues*, *42*, 151–172.

Kinder, D. R. (2013). Myrdal's prediction: Principles versus prejudice in American political life. Unpublished manuscript, Department of Political Science, University of Michigan.

Kinder, D. R., & Dale-Riddle, A. (2012). *The end of race? Obama, 2008, and racial politics in America*. New Haven, CT: Yale University Press.

Kinder, D. R., & Drake, K. W. (2009). Myrdal's prediction. *Political Psychology*, *30*, 539–568.

Kinder, D. R., & Kam, C. D. (2009). *Us against them: Ethnocentric foundations of American opinion*. Chicago: University of Chicago Press.

Kinder, D. R., & McConnaughy, C. M. (2006). Military triumph, racial transcendence, and Colin Powell. *Public Opinion Quarterly*, *70*, 139–165.

Kinder, D. R., & Mendelberg, T. (2000). Individualism reconsidered: Principles and prejudice in contemporary American opinion. In D. O. Sears, J. Sidanius, & L. Bobo (eds.), *Racialized politics* (pp. 44–74). Chicago: University of Chicago Press.

Kinder, D. R., & Ryan, T. (2013). Prejudice and politics re-examined: The political significance of implicit racial bias. Unpublished manuscript, Department of Political Science, University of Michigan, Ann Arbor.

Kinder, D. R., & Sanders, L. M. (1996). *Divided by color*. Chicago: University of Chicago Press.

Kinder, D. R., & Sears, D. O. (1981). Prejudice and politics: Symbolic racism versus racial threats to the good life. *Journal of Personality and Social Psychology, 40*, 414–431.

Kinder, D. R., & Winter, N. (2001). Exploring the racial divide. *American Journal of Political Science, 45*, 439–456.

Kitschelt, H. (1995). *The radical right in western Europe: A comparative analysis*. Ann Arbor: University of Michigan Press.

Kleppner, P. (1985). *Chicago divided: The making of a black mayor*. DeKalb: Northern Illinois Press.

Knowles, E. D., Lowery, B. S., & Schaumberg, R. L. (2010). Racial prejudice predicts opposition to Obama and his health care reform plan. *Journal of Experimental Social Psychology, 46*(2), 420–423.

Kousser, J. M. (1974). *The shaping of southern politics*. New Haven, CT: Yale University Press.

Krueger, J., Rothbart, M., & Sriram, N. (1989). Category learning and change: Differences in sensitivity to information that enhances or reduces intercategory distinctions. *Journal of Personality and Social Psychology, 56*, 866–875.

Kuklinski, J. H., Sniderman, P. M., Knight, K., Piazza, T., Tetlock, P. E., Lawrence, G. R., & Mellers, B. (1997). Racial prejudice and attitudes toward affirmative action. *American Journal of Political Science, 41*(2), 402–419.

Kunda, Z., & Oleson, K. C. (1995). Maintaining stereotypes in the face of disconfirmation: Constructing grounds for subtyping deviants. *Journal of Personality and Social Psychology, 68*, 565–579.

Kunda, Z., & Oleson, K. C. (1997). When exceptions prove the rule: How extremity of deviance determines deviants' impact on stereotypes. *Journal of Personality and Social Psychology, 72*, 965–979.

Lewontin, R. C. (1974). *The genetic basis of evolutionary change*. New York: Columbia University Press.

Lewontin, R. C. (1995). *Human diversity*. New York: Scientific American Library.

Litwack, L. F. (1998). *Trouble in mind: Black southerners in the age of Jim Crow*. New York: Knopf.

Lowery, B. S., Hardin, C. D., & Sinclair, S. (2001). Social influence effects on automatic racial prejudice. *Journal of Personality and Social Psychology, 81*, 842–855.

Lublin, D. (1997). *The paradox of representation: Racial gerrymandering and minority interests in Congress*. Princeton, NJ: Princeton University Press.

Mackie, D. M., & Hamilton, D. L. (Eds.). (1993). *Affect, cognition, and stereotyping: Interactive processes in group perception*. San Diego, CA: Academic Press.

Marcus, G. E., Sullivan J. L., Theiss-Morse, E., & Wood, S. (1995). *With malice toward some: How people make civil liberties judgments*. Cambridge: Cambridge University Press.

McClosky, H., & Brill, A. (1983). *Dimensions of tolerance: What Americans think about civil liberties*. New York: Russell Sage.

McConahay, J. B. (1986). Modern racism, ambivalence, and the modern racism scale. In J. F. Dovidio and S. L. Gaertner (Eds.), *Prejudice, discrimination, and racism* (pp. 91–126). New York: Academic Press.

McGuire, W. J. (1969). The nature of attitudes and attitude change. In G. Lindzey & E. Aronson (eds.), *The handbook of social psychology* (pp. 136–314). Reading, MA: Addison-Wesley.

Mendelberg, T. (1997). Executing Hortons: Racial crime in the 1988 presidential campaign. *Public Opinion Quarterly, 61,* 134–157.

Mendelberg, T. (2001). *The race card.* Princeton, NJ: Princeton University Press.

Mendelberg, T. (2008a). Racial priming revived. *Perspectives on Politics, 6,* 109–124.

Mendelberg, T. (2008b). Racial priming: Issues in research design and interpretation. *Perspectives on Politics, 6,* 135–140.

Moskowitz, D., & Stroh, P. (1994). Psychological sources of electoral racism. *Political Psychology, 15*(2), 307–329.

Myrdal, G. (1944). *An American dilemma: The Negro problem and modern democracy.* New York: Harper and Row.

Nosek, B. A., Symthe, F. L., Hansen, J. J., Devos, T., Linder, N. M., Ranganath, K. A., Smith, C. T., Olson, K. R., Chugh, D., Greenwald, A. G., & Banaji, M. R. (2007). Pervasiveness and correlates of implicit attitudes and stereotypes. *European Review of Social Psychology, 18,* 36–88.

Olson, J., Vernon, P., & Jang, K. (2001). The heritability of attitudes: A study of twins. *Journal of Personality and Social Psychology, 80*(6), 845–860.

Ordeshook, P., & Shvetsova, O. (1994). Ethnic heterogeneity, district magnitude, and the number of parties. *American Journal of Political Science, 38*(1), 100–123.

Park, B., & Rothbart, M. (1982). Perception of out-group homogeneity and levels of social categorization: Memory for the subordinate attributes of in-group and out-group members. *Journal of Personality and Social Psychology, 42,* 1051–1068.

Pasek, J., Tahk, A., Lelkes, Y., Krosnick, J. A., Payne, B. K., Akhtar, O., & Tompson, T. (2009). Determinants of turnout and candidate choice in the 2008 U.S. presidential election. *Public Opinion Quarterly, 73,* 943–994.

Payne, B. K., Burkley, M., & Stokes, M. B. (2008). Why do implicit and explicit attitude tests diverge? The role of structural fit. *Journal of Personality and Social Psychology, 94,* 16–31.

Payne, B. K., Krosnick, J. A., Pasek, J., Lelkes, Y., Akhtar, O., & Tompson, T. (2010). Implicit and explicit prejudice in the 2008 American presidential election. *Journal of Experimental Social Psychology, 46,* 367–374.

Peffley, M., & Hurwitz, J. (2007). Persuasion and resistance: Race and the death penalty in America. *American Journal of Political Science, 51*(4), 996–1012.

Peffley, M., Hurwitz, J., & Sniderman, P. M. (1997). Racial stereotypes and whites' political views of blacks in the context of welfare and crime. *American Journal of Political Science, 41,* 30–60.

Pettigrew, T. F. (1998). Reactions toward the new minorities of western Europe. *Annual Review of Sociology, 24,* 77–103.

Pettigrew, T. F., & Meertens, R. W. (1995). Subtle and blatant prejudice in western Europe. *European Journal of Social Psychology, 25,* 57–75.

Phelps, E. A., O'Conner, K. J., Cunningham, W. A., Funayama, E. S., Gatenby, J. C., Clore, J. C., & Banaji, M. R. (2000). Performance on indirect measures of race evaluation predicts amygdala activation. *Journal of Cognitive Neuroscience, 12,* 1–10.

Piston, S. (2010). How explicit racial prejudice hurt Obama in the 2008 election. *Political Behavior, 32,* 431–452.

Quillian, L. (1995). Prejudice as a response to perceived group threat: Population composition and anti-immigrant and racial prejudice in Europe. *American Sociological Review*, *60*, 586–611.

Quillian, L. (2006). New approaches to understanding racial prejudice and discrimination. *Annual Review of Sociology*, *32*, 299–328.

Quillian, L. (2008). Does unconscious racism exist? *Social Psychology Quarterly*, *71*(1), 6–11.

Reeves, K. (1997). *Voting hopes or fears? White voters, black candidates & racial politics in America*. New York: Oxford University Press.

Sass, T. R., & Mehay, S. L. (1995). The Voting Rights Act, district elections, and the success of black candidates in municipal elections. *Journal of Law and Economics*, *38*, 367–391.

Sass, T. R., & Pittman, B. J. (2000). The changing impact of electoral structure on black representation in the South, 1970–1996. *Public Choice*, *104*, 369–388.

Scheve, K., & Slaughter, M. (2001). Labor market competition and individual preferences over immigration policy. *Review of Economics and Statistics*, *83*(1), 133–145.

Schickler, E., Pearson, K., & Feinstein, B. D. (2010). Congressional parties and civil rights politics from 1933 to 1972. *Journal of Politics*, *72*, 672–689.

Schuman, H. (2000). The perils of correlation, the lure of labels, and the beauty of negative results. In D. O. Sears, J. Sidanius, & L. Bobo (eds.), *Racialized politics* (pp. 302–323). Chicago: University of Chicago Press.

Schuman, H., Steeh, C., Bobo, L., & Krysan, M. (1997). *Racial attitudes in America: Trends and interpretations*. Cambridge, MA: Harvard University Press.

Sears, D. O. (1969). Political behavior. In G. Lindzey & E. Aronson (eds.), *Handbook of social psychology* (pp. 315–458, 2nd ed., vol. 5). Reading, MA: Addison-Wesley.

Sears, D. O. (1988). Symbolic racism. In P. Katz & D. A. Taylor (eds.), *Eliminating racism: Profiles in controversy* (pp. 53–84). New York: Plenum.

Sears, D. O., Citrin, J., & Kosterman, R. (1987). Jesse Jackson and the southern white electorate in 1984. In R. P. Steed, L. W. Moreland, & T. A. Baker (eds.), *Blacks and southern politics* (pp. 209-225).New York: Praeger.

Sears, D. O., & Henry, P. J. (2005). Over thirty years later: A contemporary look at symbolic racism. *Advances in Experimental Social Psychology*, *37*, 98–150.

Sears, D. O., Henry, P. J., & Kosterman, R. (2000). Egalitarian values and contemporary racial politics. In D. O. Sears, J. Sidanius, & L. Bobo (eds.), *Racialized politics* (pp. 75–117). Chicago: University of Chicago Press.

Sears, D. O., Hensler, C. P., & Speer, L. K. (1979). Whites' opposition to busing: Self-interest or symbolic politics? *American Political Science Review*, *73*, 369–384.

Sears, D. O., Lau, R. R., Tyler, T., & Allen, A. M., Jr. (1980). Self-interest versus symbolic politics in policy attitudes and presidential voting. *American Political Science Review*, *74*, 670–684.

Tarman, C., & Sears, D. O. (2005). The conceptualization and measurement of symbolic racism. *Journal of Politics*, *67*, 731–761.

Shafer, B. E., & Johnston, R. (2006). *The end of southern exceptionalism. Class, race, and partisan change in the postwar South*. Cambridge, MA: Harvard University Press.

Sherif, M., Harvey, O. J., White, B. J., Hood, W. R., & Sherif, C. W. (1961). *Intergroup conflict and cooperation: The Robbers Cave experiment*. Norman, OK: University Book Exchange.

Sidanius, J. (1993). The psychology of group conflict and the dynamics of oppression: A social dominance perspective. In S. Iyengar & W. J. McGuire (eds.), *Explorations in political psychology* (pp. 183–224). Durham, NC: Duke University Press.

Sidanius, J., & Pratto, F. (1999). *Social dominance: An intergroup theory of social hierarchy and oppression*. New York: Cambridge University Press.

Sidanius, J., Pratto, F., & Bobo, L. (1996). Racism, conservatism, affirmative action, and intellectual sophistication: A matter of principled conservatism or group dominance? *Journal of Personality and Social Psychology, 70*, 476–490.

Sides, J., & Citrin, J. (2007). European opinion about immigration: The role of identities, interests, and information. *British Journal of Political Science, 37*, 477–504.

Sigall, H., & Page, R. (1971). Current stereotypes: A little fading, a little faking. *Journal of Personality and Social Psychology, 18*, 247–255.

Sigelman, C. K., Sigelman, L., Walkosz, B. J., & Nitz, M. (1995). Black candidates, white voters: Understanding racial bias in political perceptions. *American Journal of Political Science, 39*(1), 243–265.

Sniderman, P. M., Brody, R. A., & Kuklinski, J. H. (1984). Policy reasoning and political values: The problem of racial equality. *American Journal of Political Science, 28*, 75–94.

Sniderman, P. M., & Carmines, E. G. (1997). *Reaching beyond race*. Cambridge, MA: Harvard University Press.

Sniderman, P. M., Carmines, E. G., Howell, W., & Morgan, W. (1997). A test of alternative interpretations of the contemporary politics of race: A critical examination of *Divided by color*. Paper presented at the Annual Meeting of the Midwest Political Science Association, Chicago, IL.

Sniderman, P. M., Carmines, E. G., Layman, G. C., & Carter, M. (1996). Beyond race: Social justice as a race neutral ideal. *American Journal of Political Science, 40*, 33–55.

Sniderman, P. M., Crosby, G. C., & Howell, W. G. (2000). The politics of race. In D. O. Sears, J. Sidanius, & L. Bobo (eds.), *Racialized politics: The debate about racism in America* (pp. 236–279). Chicago: University of Chicago Press.

Sniderman, P. M., Hagendoorn, L., & Prior, M. (2004). Predisposing factors and situational triggers: Exclusionary reactions to immigrant minorities. *American Political Science Review, 98*(1), 35–49.

Sniderman, P. M., & Piazza, T. (1993). *The scar of race*. Cambridge, MA: Harvard University Press.

Sniderman, P. M., & Tetlock, P. E. (1986). Symbolic racism: Problems of motive attribution in political analysis. *Journal of Social Issues, 42*, 129–150.

Stangor, C., Sullivan, L. A., & Ford, T. E. (1991). Affective and cognitive determinants of prejudice. *Social Cognition, 9*, 359–380.

Stenner, K. (2005). *The authoritarian dynamic*. Cambridge: Cambridge University Press.

Stoker, L. (1998). Understanding whites' resistance to affirmative action: The role of principled commitments and racial prejudice. In J. Hurwitz & M. Peffley (eds.), *Perception & prejudice: Race and politics in the United States* (pp. 135-170). New Haven, CT: Yale University Press.

Stoker, L. (2001). Political value judgments. In J. H. Kuklinski (ed.), *Citizens and politics: Perspectives from political psychology* (pp. 433–468). New York: Cambridge University Press.

Stokes, D. E. (1966). Party loyalty and the likelihood of deviating elections. In A. Campbell, P. E. Converse, W. E. Miller, & D. E. Stokes (eds.), *Elections and the political order* (pp.125–135). New York: John Wiley.

Sullivan, J. L., Piereson, J. E., & Marcus, G. E. (1982). *Political tolerance and American democracy*. Chicago: University of Chicago Press.

Tajfel, H. (1981). *Human groups and social categories*. Cambridge: Cambridge University Press.

Tarman, C., & Sears, D. O. (2005). The conceptualization and measurement of symbolic racism. *Journal of Politics, 67*, 731–761.

Taylor, S. E., Fiske, S. T., Etcoff, N. L., & Ruderman, A. J. (1978). Categorical bases of person memory and stereotyping. *Journal of Personality and Social Psychology, 36*, 778–793.

Terkildsen, N. (1993). When white voters evaluate black candidates: The processing implications of candidate skin color, prejudice, and self-monitoring. *American Journal of Political Science, 37*, 1032–1053.

Tesler, M. (2012). The spillover of racialization into health care: How President Obama polarizes public opinion by racial attitudes and race. *American Journal of Political Science, 56*(3), 690–704.

Tesler, M., & Sears, D. O. (2010). *Obama's race. The 2008 election and the dream of a post-racial America*. Chicago: University of Chicago Press.

Tilly, C. (1998). *Durable inequality*. Berkeley: University of California Press.

Valelly, R. M. (2004). *The two Reconstructions: The struggle for black enfranchisement*. Chicago: University of Chicago Press.

Valentino, N. A. (1999). Crime news and the priming of racial attitudes during evaluations of the president. *Public Opinion Quarterly, 63*, 293–320.

Valentino, N. A., Hutchings, V. L., & White, I. (2002). Cues that matter: How political ads prime racial attitudes during campaigns. *American Political Science Review, 96*, 75–90.

Valentino, N. A., & Sears, D. O. (2005). Old times there are not forgotten: Race and partisan realignment in the contemporary South. *American Journal of Political Science, 49*, 672–688.

Van den Berghe, P. (1967). *Race and racism: A comparative perspective*. New York: John Wiley.

White, I. K. (2007). When race matters and when it doesn't: Racial group differences in response to racial cues. *American Political Science Review, 101*, 339–354.

Williams, D. R. (2001). Racial variation in adult health status: Patterns, paradoxes, and prospects. In N. J. Smelser, W. J. Wilson, & F. Mitchell (eds.), *America becoming: Racial trends and their consequences* (vol. 2, pp. 371–410). Washington, DC: National Academy Press.

Wilson, G. D. (Ed). (1973). *The psychology of conservatism*. London: Academic Press.

Wilson, W. J. (1973). *Power, racism, and privilege: Race relations in theoretical and sociological perspectives*. New York: Free Press.

Winter, N. J. G. (2006). Beyond welfare: Framing and the racialization of white opinion on Social Security. *American Journal of Political Science, 50*, 400–420.

Winter, N. J. G. (2008). *Dangerous frames: How ideas about race and gender shape public opinion*. Chicago: University of Chicago Press.

Wittenbrink, B. (2007). *Implicit measures of attitudes*. New York: Guilford Press.

Wittenbrink, B., Judd, C. M., & Park, B. (2001). Spontaneous prejudice in context: Variability in automatically activated attitudes. *Journal of Personality and Social Psychology, 81*, 815–827.

Xu, J., Kochanek, K. D., Murphy, S. L., & Tejad-Vera, B. (2010). Deaths: Final data for 2007. *National Vital Statistics Reports, 58*, no. 19.

Zajonc, R. B. (1980). Feeling and thinking: Preferences need no inferences. *American Psychologist, 35*, 151–175.

CHAPTER 26

MIGRATION AND MULTICULTURALISM

EVA G. T. GREEN AND CHRISTIAN STAERKLÉ

"MULTICULTURALISM has utterly failed," German chancellor Angela Merkel declared in October 2010; "immigrants need to do more to integrate in German society." A few months later, in February 2011, British prime minister David Cameron also condemned his country's long-standing policy of multiculturalism as a failure, claiming that many young British Muslims were drawn to violent ideology because they found no strong collective identity in Britain. These two quotes from leading European politicians exemplify how migration and multiculturalism have become key issues in contemporary societies. Virtually all countries in the world need to deal with the steady flow of people crossing international borders that have made societies in our globalized world more and more diverse. Despite its contested nature as a normative model for organizing diversity in receiving societies, multiculturalism has become an inescapable reality to which countries need to adapt.

This chapter is concerned with two major questions concerning migration and multiculturalism. First, it looks at the social and psychological processes at work in the migrant experience. Second, it deals with how members of receiving societies react to the increased and diversified immigrant presence in their societies.[1] Our review draws mainly upon research and theory in political and social psychology. Reflecting the diversity of classic and recent empirical work on migration and multiculturalism, we present research covering a wide range of methodological approaches, including survey, experimental, and qualitative studies. The chapter emphasizes how historical and political contexts affect the nature of intergroup relations between migrant groups and receiving societies. It furthermore highlights the role of widely shared social representations in processes of migration and multiculturalism, expressed in ideological belief systems, political discourse, and everyday cultural repertoires. We argue that a political psychology perspective to migration and multiculturalism will gain from taking a interdisciplinary approach in which different levels of analysis—including individual, group, and societal factors—are combined and articulated (Castles & Miller, 2009; Chryssochoou, 2004; Deaux, 2006; Verkuyten, 2005a).

The chapter is organized in four sections. The first section outlines some historical benchmarks of modern migration and briefly presents two key notions of a psychological approach to migration—assimilation and multiculturalism—in their historical context. In a second section, we summarize empirical research that focuses on the psychological dynamics involved in the migrant experience, in particular the interactionist and complex nature of migrant identities, acculturation and adaptation in receiving societies, and intergroup approaches to acculturation and multiculturalism. The third section analyzes the role of threat regarding immigrants and immigration in the reactions, attitudes, and beliefs of majority populations in receiving societies. The fourth section presents recent multilevel research on the effects of contextual factors on attitudes towards immigration held by national majority groups.

This chapter specifically analyzes diversity and multiculturalism as the outcome of international migration. Moreover, although migration is a global phenomenon, we focus our discussion mainly on those migration flows that end up in Western countries since it is mostly in these contexts that empirical research has studied the psychological processes involved in the migrant experience and the public reactions to immigration.

1. Assimilation and Multiculturalism in Context

Early works on immigration and incorporation of immigrants (e.g., Park & Burgess, 1921; Thomas & Znaniecki, 1918) reflected questions arising from voluntary and permanent forms of migration, especially to the United States. Incorporation of immigrants in the host society was seen as a one-way street toward the hegemonic white Anglo-Saxon Protestant "WASP" norm in which immigrants gradually lose their ties with their country of origin while picking up the values of the receiving society (Kivisto, 2002). In this model of migrant *assimilation*, the identity of origin was to be replaced with the host identity, and ethnic distinctions as well as the cultural and social practices that express it were bound to disappear (see Alba & Nee, 2003, for a contemporary analysis of assimilation). Assimilation therefore relies on the principle of *similarity* between migrant groups and the receiving society: Such intergroup similarity is deemed to foster successful integration into mainstream society and to promote harmonious intergroup relations within receiving societies. Largely taken for granted in the early times of immigration, it was the sole conceivable form of migrant incorporation. The "melting pot" of American society was for a long time the key metaphor to figuratively describe assimilation, referring to the dissolving of various ethnic and national identities into a new cultural identity.

European diversity, in contrast, is historically due to migration from former colonial countries and the presence of different cultural and linguistic groups on national territories, for example Wallonian and Flemish populations in Belgium, or Finnish- and Swedish-speaking and native Sami populations in Finland. In "multination" states where cultural diversity arises from the incorporation of territorially concentrated cultures into a larger state, the political debate has been more concerned with political rights of resident cultures than with their assimilation into receiving societies (Kymlicka, 1995). In these contexts, minority cultures typically claim self-government rights that demand some form of political autonomy (e.g., the province of Quebec in Canada) or special representation rights in order for the groups' views and interests to be effectively represented in the political process, for example by reserving a certain number of seats in the legislature for members of minority groups.

After World War II, the nature of international migration gradually changed. Migration volume increased drastically due to armed conflicts and large-scale natural disasters, growing global inequalities pushing people to search for a better life, and new international agreements liberalizing person movements (Castles & Miller, 2009). The United States was confronted with new waves of mass immigration from Latin America (especially Mexico), Asia, and the Caribbean after the Immigration Act of 1965. This migration was characterized by unprecedented numbers of undocumented "illegal" immigrants, by religious identities different from those of American mainstream society, by a tendency to maintain closer ties with their countries of origin, and often by a reluctance or incapacity to learn the English language. Thus, in the 21st century, migrants originate from increasingly diverse economic, social, and cultural backgrounds, giving rise to differentiated forms of migration in receiving countries, including voluntary and involuntary migration, temporary and permanent labor migration, as well as refugee, asylum seeker, and family reunion migration. Migration has also become increasingly politicized, in particular with respect to domestic politics, which are ever more marked by public debates about immigration, by the tendency of political parties in the Western world to define their identity through tough stances toward migration and multiculturalism, and by hostile and xenophobic attitudes of large segments of national majority populations in receiving societies (Kivisto, 2002). The classical understanding of assimilation as a general settlement policy has therefore become ever more questioned. In this context of "new immigration," immigrants can no longer be seen as definitely leaving their country of origin or permanently taking residence in the receiving society, the receiving society cultures have become too heterogeneous to provide a single cultural model toward which immigrants should strive, and in light of the difficult experiences of increasing numbers of immigrants, the notion of inevitable assimilationist progress has become untenable (Deaux, 2006).

The response to the limitations of an assimilationist view of migrant incorporation was the gradual development of "difference"-based conceptions of citizenship, based on the formal recognition of migrant and other minority identities and legal accommodation of their difference (Isin & Wood, 1999; Taylor, 1992). One of the major models of this differentialist turn (Brubaker, 2001) was *multiculturalism*, a term that covers multiple realities and presents a number of ambiguities (Glazer, 1997). In a descriptive sense, multiculturalism refers to the diverse ethnic makeup of contemporary societies, be they the product of existing ethnocultural groups within countries or the outcome of international migration. In this sense, virtually all countries in the world are multicultural. In a normative and prescriptive sense, in turn, multiculturalism is a desirable way of organizing diversity within a country. Offering a positive view of cultural identity maintenance, it considers that cultural diversity *as such* has positive effects on a society, by contributing fresh perspectives, promoting openness towards others, and preventing discrimination (Kymlicka, 1995).

Multiculturalism is implemented with legal and political dispositions that accommodate claims for the recognition of group-specific identities, for example rights for political representation, legal protection of cultural practices, or language and educational rights (see Licata, Sanchez-Mazas, & Green, 2011, for a social psychological recognition approach of immigration and prejudice in Europe). Such group-differentiated policies formally recognize the legitimacy of differences between ethnic and cultural groups residing in a country and aim at promoting equal treatment and equal rights of these groups (Kymlicka, 1995). The passionate debates about the legitimacy of civil, social, or political rights of specific migrant groups, for example affirmative action policies or group-specific clothing regulations (e.g., concerning headscarves and veils of Muslim women, Joppke, 2009) reveal that the question of group rights is one of the most pressing issues in contemporary societies struggling with multicultural demands (Ingram, 2000; Koopmans, Statham, Giugni, & Passy, 2005).

Much like assimilation, the normative model of multiculturalism has also come increasingly under pressure (see Bloemraad, Korteweg, & Yurdakul, 2008, for an overview). Multiculturalism is accused of undermining national cohesion, of exacerbating intergroup divisions rather than overcoming them, of essentializing and reifying group boundaries, and ultimately of compartmentalizing ethnic groups into segregated urban ghettos (Barry, 2001). As a result, multiculturalism would fuel negative attitudes toward migrant groups rather than alleviate them. Such disillusionment with multiculturalism is also observable on the political level, as illustrated by our opening quotes from Angela Merkel and David Cameron. There is today increasing evidence of a backlash against multiculturalism, at the level of public opinion, political discourse, immigration policy, and political theory (Castles & Miller, 2009). Brubaker (2001), for example, observes the rise of new forms of assimilation policies that no longer expect immigrants to be completely absorbed in the receiving society. These policies place a stronger emphasis on the progressive process rather than on the desired end-state of becoming similar to the receiving society, for example in the form of proposed or encouraged language courses for immigrants or in the easing of strict naturalization rules. As a result, many countries that formerly had a strong policy emphasis on multiculturalism, such as the Netherlands, Sweden, and Australia have shifted to policies that require more "adaptation" and "integration" from immigrants, often under pressure of rising right-wing populist parties (Joppke, 2007).

The emergence of transnational and diaspora communities is another key feature of contemporary migration (Faist, 2009; Kivisto, 2002; Portes & Rumbaut, 2006). Owing to new modes of online communication and decreasing travel costs, migrants more easily maintain relationships with their societies of origin across national borders. Transnational social spaces are expressed in political engagement of migrants in their country of origin, as financial support for homeland networks, or as regular traveling between the receiving society and the country of origin. Transnationalism thereby de-emphasizes the importance of physical location of migrants in the receiving society and extends multiculturalism and ethnic loyalties across the national borders of the receiving society.

So what is left when the two major paradigms of migrant incorporation—assimilation, based on the principle of intergroup similarity, and multiculturalism, based on the principle of intergroup difference—are both questioned in contemporary societies? A first answer to this question is provided by the meanings migrants themselves give to their experiences in a receiving society and the strategies they enact to construe their migrant identities.

2. THE MIGRANT EXPERIENCE

2.1. Contemporary Migrant Identities

The concept of *ethnic identity* captures the dynamics that are involved in the negotiation of cultural and ethnic boundaries in receiving societies (see Verkuyten, 2005a). Ethnic identities involve beliefs in commonality, shared kinship, or ancestry; they are historically defined and involve a sense of temporality and continuity that sets them apart from other social identities (see Sani, 2008; for a general description of social identities see Huddy, chapter 23, this volume). Yet, in contemporary research, ethnic groups are not bounded cultural entities to which people naturally belong, but are rather *social constructions* that emerge from continuous social interactions *between* the migrant and the majority group and *within* migrant groups themselves (Barth, 1969). Migrant identities are therefore the product of both "other-definition" and "self-definition." "Other-definition means ascription of undesirable characteristics and assignment of inferior social positions by dominant groups. Self-definition refers to the consciousness of group members of belonging together on the basis of shared cultural and social characteristics. The relative strength of these processes varies. Some minorities are mainly constructed through processes of exclusion (which may be referred to as racism) by the majority. Others are mainly constituted on the basis of cultural and historical consciousness (or ethnic identity) among their members" (Castles & Miller, 2009, p. 33). As a consequence of this interactionist view, ethnic group boundaries may be legitimized and maintained (as in multicultural discourses) or on the contrary challenged and eventually dissolved (as in assimilationist discourses). The disappearance of formerly important distinctions, for example between Irish immigrants and American mainstream society (Ignatiev, 1995), illustrates how boundaries of ethnic groups may be transformed and their meaning reassessed.

The negotiation of migrant identities within ethnic groups concerns, for example, normative pressures to conform to in-group obligations (such as the maintenance of cultural traditions) and out-group expectations (such as labor market integration). These negotiations may take place between first- and second-generation immigrants, between parents and children, or between high- and low-status group members (Wimmer, 2004). As a result, any characteristics, beliefs, or practices associated with ethnic groups may change over time, for example when longstanding traditions are replaced with modern customs. This emphasis on within-group variation and the active self-construal of ethnic groups is an antidote to widespread views of migrant groups as homogenous entities and helpless victims of majority discrimination (see Brubaker, Feischmidt, Fox, & Grancea, 2006).

Ethnic identification, that is, the subjective importance of membership in an ethnic group, has been shown to be particularly strong for migrant groups in receiving societies in which the legitimacy of their norms and values—and even their mere presence on national soil—is questioned. In a study on religious identification by Muslim (Sunni) migrants in the Netherlands, Verkuyten (2007) found that over half of the participants had the highest possible score on scales of religious identification. For these "total" identifiers, identification with the receiving Dutch society was lower than for those Muslims with lower levels of religious identification. These findings suggest that Muslim migrants are prone to stress their ethnic identity in a context of increasing tensions with the receiving society. The degree and nature of in-group identification with migrant groups thus depends on the specific intergroup configurations in receiving societies. Migrants differentially construe their in-group identities as a function of the intergroup relations with national majorities (Hopkins & Kahani-Hopkins, 2006). Hence, ethnic identifications by migrant groups are flexible and change as a function of the intergroup context in receiving societies.

In contrast to classical intergroup research in social psychology, which treats social categories as unproblematic and defines them with unambiguous boundaries, migrant identities are often "messy" and group boundaries "blurry" (Alba, 2005), especially those of second-generation immigrants (see Lamont & Molnar, 2002). The variety of migration contexts, in terms of countries of origin and receiving societies, of migration history, of duration of residence and political grievances, gives rise to a wide range of possible migrant identity configurations and forms of interdependence between migrant groups and receiving societies. Contemporary migrant identities combine cultural origins in different ways and thus give rise to new and complex identities, described as multiple, mixed, hybrid, or hyphenated identities (Ashmore, Deaux, & McLaughlin-Volpe, 2004; Chen, Benet-Martinez, & Bond, 2008; Phinney, 1990; Verkuyten; 2005a; see also Huddy, chapter 23, this volume).

The issue of category labeling captures the often difficult task of using appropriate names for migrant categories whose status in the receiving society is changing. Category names are malleable and strategic constructs. Category labels make a statement about the norms, values, and cultural history of the group, and they convey a sense of position of the group in the larger society (Reicher & Hopkins, 2001). Examples include the continuous debate about the use of "Latino," "Hispanic," or hyphenated category labels (e.g., "Mexican-American") to describe immigrant groups of Spanish and Portuguese descent in the United States (Deaux, 2006; Portes & Rumbaut, 2006) or the shift in usage from "Negroes" to "blacks" to "African Americans" (Philogène, 1999).

One of the striking features of migrant identities is the often huge gap between the way migrant groups are categorized by national majorities and by migrant groups themselves. National majority discourse appeals to inclusive and generalizing categories with often negative connotations such as "foreigners" or "immigrants" (Kosic & Phalet, 2006), while migrants themselves use more fine-grained and less inclusive categories, distinguishing, for example, between different religious orientations, national and regional origins, or first-, second-, and third-generation immigrants. In a study based on a discursive approach to social identity theory, Hopkins and Kahani-Hopkins (2004) illustrate how widespread majority representations of a homogeneous and unified Muslim category are challenged by Muslim activists in Britain: some activists put forward a political understanding of Muslim identity and restrict the boundaries of Muslim identity to those members who conform to central Muslim practices such as the hajj (the Mecca pilgrimage) or the daily prayers. Others, in contrast, promote a more inclusive and spiritual view of Muslim identity and feel affiliated with "people [throughout the world] who are struggling to have their voices heard" (p. 53).

In another study, Hopkins and Kahani-Hopkins (2006) contrasted two views by Muslim representatives on intergroup contact and Islamophobia. One view sought to rectify widespread negative attitudes toward Muslims through raising awareness of variation within the Muslim group and challenging prevalent views about the fundamentally antagonistic nature of relations between Muslims and Westerners. The other view was more polemic and suggested that Islamophobia was a struggle between falsity and truth and between unbelief and belief, thereby urging Muslim community members to unite and enter into negotiations with the non-Muslim other with a single voice. Similar variation was observed in a survey study among more secular and less identified Turkish Alevi Muslims and more religious and highly identified Sunni Muslims in the Netherlands (Verkuyten & Yildiz, 2009). The point here is that migrant identities are actively construed and contested both from within the migrant groups themselves and from the outside, through majority discourses on Muslim and other migrant groups.

Discursive research contextualizes migrant experiences within particular social settings and analyzes migrant identities as flexible and dynamic resources, showing how they change as a function of both social situations and the historical and political context of receiving societies. The analysis of situated discursive practices thus enables a detailed analysis of the subjective understanding of the migrant experience, such as an unfavorable social status of migrant groups or the suffering of discrimination (Deaux, 2006; Verkuyten, 2005c). Studies have, for example, analyzed how migrants reconcile multiple identities or how demeaning representations associated with ethnic minority neighborhoods (Howarth, 2002), pervasive discrimination (Hopkins & Kahani-Hopkins, 2006) and historical collective memories (Ali & Sonn, 2010) shape the construction of migrant identities.

Another key aspect of migrant identities concerns their relationship with the political involvement of migrants. Research has investigated the role of politicized migrant identities as determinants of collective action associated with migrant group membership, including social movements in favor of migrants' position in society and civil society participation in associations defending the rights of migrant groups (see Azzi, Chryssochoou, Klandermans, & Simon, 2011). In a longitudinal survey study on Turkish migrants in Germany, for example, Simon and Ruhs (2008) showed that dual identification with the Turkish migrant group and the superordinate German national group uniquely predicted political involvement in the form of support for political claims in favor of Turks living in Germany, while no relation was found between dual identification and radical or violent politicization. These findings suggest that while identification with the aggrieved in-group is necessary to foster involvement on behalf of the ingroup (Spears, Jetten, & Doosje, 2001), identification with the superordinate group is also required to foster normative collective action, since it reflects the acknowledgment that political action needs to be taken within the limits of general acceptance of the larger polity (see Klandermans & van Stekelenburg, chapter 24, this volume, for dynamics of political mobilization by migrant groups).

2.2. Acculturation and Adaptation of Migrants

Acculturation research focuses on the determinants and consequences of different strategies migrants employ to adapt to new cultural milieus. It has its roots in cross-cultural psychology and studies the individual- and group-level changes resulting from intercultural contact (see Sam & Berry, 2006). The classical definition states that acculturation refers to "those phenomena which result when groups of individuals having different cultures come into continuous first-hand contact, with subsequent changes in the original culture patterns of either or both groups" (Redfield, Linton, & Herskovits, 1936, p. 149).

The most influential model of acculturation has been proposed by Berry (1990). His model emphasizes the bidimensional nature of acculturation processes where the maintenance of relationships with one's country of origin and the development of new ties with the receiving society are independent of each other and may therefore combine in different ways. Four basic types of acculturation strategies result from crossing these two dimensions: *integration* reflects a desire to simultaneously maintain ties with the country of origin and establish strong contacts with members of the receiving society, whereas *separation* denotes the wish to maintain one's migrant identity while minimizing contacts with the receiving society. *Assimilation* refers to the abandonment of one's original cultural identity and the pursuit of contacts with the receiving society, whereas *marginalization* describes the rejection of both the original culture and the receiving society.

More recently, Berry's model has been extended into the *interactive acculturation model* (IAM, Bourhis, Moïse, Perreault, & Senécal, 1997; Bourhis, Montaruli, El-Geledi, Harvey, & Barrette, 2010). This model adds to the acculturation *orientations* adopted by migrant groups the acculturation *expectations* held by members of receiving society toward specific groups of immigrants. Members of the receiving society may, for example, expect immigrants to fully abandon their original culture and follow an assimilation strategy. The IAM thus recognizes that not only the immigrants, but also the receiving society may undergo transformations as a result of the arrival of immigrants (as already implied in the original definition of acculturation), thereby emphasizing the intergroup nature of acculturative processes. The IAM further adds *individualism* as an alternative strategy to marginalization, denoting an orientation that stresses personal characteristics rather than group membership in both migrant and receiving society acculturation orientations. The IAM also highlights the fact that integration policies adopted at the national, regional, and municipal levels of government can both reflect and influence the acculturation orientations adopted by receiving society and migrant communities.

A large body of research has investigated the individual and social factors that determine the preferences for any one of these acculturation strategies. Studies find that integration (e.g., Berry, 1990; van Oudenhoven, Prins, & Buunk, 1998) and separation (e.g., for Turks in Germany, Piontkowski, Florack, Hoelker, & Obdrzálek, 2000) are the preferred modes of acculturation for minorities. Majorities, in turn, expect migrants to endorse either integration or assimilation strategies (Ryder, Alden, & Paulhus, 2000; Zagefka & Brown, 2002; Roccas, Horenczyk, & Schwartz, 2000; Nesdale & Mak, 2000), though exceptions to these patterns are not uncommon. A number of factors have been shown to account for the endorsement of acculturation expectations by majorities, including strength of ethnic and national identification, ethnocentrism, social dominance orientation, political orientation, feelings of threat from the presence of migrant groups, individual networks of ethnic contacts, or perceptions of immigrant discrimination (e.g., Bourhis, Barrette, El-Geledi, & Schmidt, 2009; Montreuil, Bourhis, & Vanbeselaere, 2004). Furthermore, acculturation expectations adopted by majorities depend on the type of migrant groups: Integration is likely to be the preferred strategy for "valued" minorities (in terms of favorable stereotypes associated with them), while assimilation, segregation, and marginalization are more likely to be endorsed for negatively evaluated minorities (Montreuil & Bourhis, 2001).

Nevertheless, the fourfold typology of general acculturation orientations has been criticized for potentially obscuring the wide array of possible forms of interdependence between migrant groups and the receiving society. Migrants' choice of acculturation orientation has been shown to depend on how the relationship between the migrant group and the receiving society is operationalized; whether migrants were asked about willingness for contact with the majority group, adoption of majority cultural values, or identification with the majority group, differently affected their endorsement of acculturation strategies (Snauwaert, Soenens, Vanbeselaere, & Boen, 2003). These varying operationalizations thus reflect different degrees of closeness and different levels of involvement with the receiving society, thereby highlighting the difficulty of defining unambiguous criteria of intergroup similarity, an issue already recognized by Gordon (1964) who differentiated multiple (e.g., cultural, linguistic, behavioral, attitudinal, and identity) dimensions of assimilation. Not surprisingly, then, the rather general measures of endorsement of different acculturation strategies are also controversial (e.g., Arends-Tóth & Van de Vijver, 2006).

Studies have also examined the factors that determine whether acculturation is successful or not, that is, whether migrants are able to appropriately negotiate the demands of the receiving society and adapt to a new cultural context. Successful long-term adaptation is multidimensional and evidenced with migrants' sociocultural and political integration, labor market integration, psychological well-being, and physical health. Cultural learning approaches highlight the need to learn culture-specific skills in order to successfully adapt to a new cultural milieu, in particular communication competence such as proficiency of the language of the receiving society (Jasinskaja-Lahti, 2008) and effective social interaction skills (Masgoret & Ward, 2006). *Acculturative stress* may result from unsuccessfully negotiated cultural contact and manifest itself as depressive symptoms, feelings of anxiety, and psychosomatic disorders (Berry, 2006). Research has generally shown that integration is the most and marginalization the least adaptive strategy to deal with acculturative stress, the integration strategy leading to the most positive outcomes in terms of coping, psychological health, and well-being (Berry & Sabatier, 2010). Yet processes of adaptation develop over time, with acculturative stress increasing soon after the arrival of the migrant in the receiving society, followed by a decrease over time (Berry, 2006).

A key factor that determines the chances of successful adaptation is the experience and perception of *discrimination* by migrants. There is ample empirical evidence showing that perceiving oneself as a target or victim of majority discrimination is a major acculturative stressor, increasing depressive symptoms, distress, and anxiety (Cassidy, O'Connor, Howe, & Warden, 2004; Finch, Kolody, & Vega, 2000; Liebkind & Jasinskaja-Lahti, 2000) and decreasing life satisfaction, well-being, and self-esteem (Vedder, Sam, & Liebkind, 2007). However, in line with the common finding that threats to the in-group encourage group identification, perceived discrimination has also been shown to increase in-group identification (Jetten, Branscombe, Schmitt, & Spears, 2001). As a result, the deleterious effects of perceived discrimination may to some extent be buffered through identification with minority groups (see Schmitt & Branscombe, 2002). Furthermore, extensive social support increases migrant well-being and adjustment (Davis, Morris, & Kraus, 1998; Safdar, Struthers, & van Oudenhoven, 2009), in particular social networks that include members of the receiving society (Jasinskaja-Lahti, Liebkind, Jaakkola, & Reuter, 2006). In addition, illustrating the importance of transnational social spaces as determinants of successful adaptation, ethnic networks *abroad* have been shown to increase migrant well-being (Jasinskaja-Lahti et al., 2006).

The socioeconomic position of the migrant is recognized as a key determinant of adaptation as well. "Segmented assimilation," for example, refers to outcomes where migrants are assimilated into different segments of society as a function of social class (Portes & Rumbaut, 2006). The analysis of second- and higher-generation immigrants shows specific generational paths of incorporation in receiving societies (Levitt & Waters, 2002). For low-status migrants this process may lead to "downward assimilation," whereby young migrants join the most disadvantaged minorities at the bottom of society (Portes & Rumbaut, 2006), an outcome squarely at odds with early assimilationist views of upward mobility and integration in mainstream society. Migrants in low social positions have also been shown to experience greater acculturative stress and to be prone to unsuccessful adjustment (Jasinskaja et al., 2006; Polek, van Oudenhoven, & Ten Berge, 2008).

Critical voices have argued that the distinctly psychological perspective of acculturation research may lead to underestimates of the importance of political connotations of acculturation strategies. In a discursive analysis of acculturation strategies, Bowskill, Lyons, and Coyle (2007) question the seemingly self-evident superiority of the integration strategy. They argue that in the British media integration is often confounded with assimilation and presented as the optimal response to diversity. In media accounts of immigration, separation in turn was positioned as transgressive, thereby delegitimizing possible avenues of collective contestation that require strong identification with migrant groups. Similarly, it is problematic to establish whether or not migrants identify with both groups in an absolute sense, as implied by the definition of the integration orientation. For Verkuyten (2006, p. 158), it is rather the degree to which they do so that is important. A related challenge for future acculturation research consists in addressing the psychological implications of the contemporary backlash against multiculturalism.

2.3. Intergroup Approaches to Acculturation and Multiculturalism

In the wake of the intergroup perspective developed by the interactive acculturation model (Bourhis et al., 1997), recent research has examined the effects of match and mismatch between acculturation orientations held by migrant groups and receiving societies (van Oudenhoven, Ward, & Masgoret, 2006; Roccas et al., 2000; Zagefka & Brown, 2002). Minority and majority attitudes toward acculturation can either be concordant and give rise to consensual relations between majorities and minorities (especially when both groups agree on integration or assimilation as preferred modes of acculturation), or discordant, evidenced by a mismatch between minority preferences and majority expectations, leading to problematic or even conflictual relationships (Bourhis et al., 1997). The relational outcomes of a mismatch of intergroup definitions of acculturation orientations include, for migrants, heightened acculturative stress, and, for members of the receiving society, stereotyping and discriminatory behaviors, for example in educational or healthcare institutions, at the workplace, in housing decisions, or in encounters with the police.

Such mismatch is evidenced in the Netherlands, where Moroccan and Turkish immigrants have been shown to prefer integration, while Dutch nationals believed that separation, their least liked orientation, was mainly chosen by these migrant groups (van Oudenhoven et al., 1998). In Germany, research has similarly shown that whereas migrant groups preferred strategies implying contact with the receiving society, majorities thought they endorsed strategies implying culture maintenance (Zagefka & Brown, 2002). More important, this study revealed that greater perceived mismatch between migrant and majority acculturation orientations at the individual level deteriorated the perceived quality of intergroup relations (in terms of in-group favoritism and perceived discrimination) for both minorities and majorities. Other research has demonstrated that the expectations of the German majority with respect to migrants' modes of acculturation predicted their own attitudes and behavior toward migrants: majority respondents who valued culture maintenance by migrants expressed lower prejudice and less discrimination toward them, with cross-lagged longitudinal analyses showing that the direction of causality between acculturation expectations and discriminatory conduct could go both ways (Geschke, Mummendey, Kessler, & Funke, 2010; see also Zick, Wagner, Van Dick, & Petzel, 2001).

The intergroup nature of migrant incorporation in receiving societies is also evidenced at the level of public attitudes toward multiculturalism and the policies destined to implement its principles (see Verkuyten, 2006). A common finding is that support for multicultural policies is higher among migrant groups than among national majorities (van Oudenhoven et al., 1998; Verkuyten, 2005b). These results imply that in an asymmetrical intergroup context, minorities tend to favor collective forms of social justice that protect their rights against a numerically superior majority. This pattern of greater support by minorities for collective (rather than individual) forms of justice has been experimentally demonstrated in early work on minority rights in South Africa by Azzi (1992), suggesting that minority support for multiculturalism is not a mere product of intergroup competition, but rather the outcome of procedural justice concerns in minority-majority settings. In another study on support for minority rights with Turkish and Kurdish participants in the Netherlands, Verkuyten and Yildiz (2006) experimentally induced either a Dutch or a Turkish context for minority rights. They did not find any difference between the two migrant groups in their support for minority rights in the Dutch context where both groups were minorities. In the Turkish context, however, Kurdish participants showed greater support for minority rights than Turkish participants, who represent the majority group in this context.

Support for multiculturalism has also been examined as a function of perceived essentialism of migrant groups. Verkuyten and Brug (2004) showed that greater perceived essentialism of migrant groups reduced the support for multiculturalism among majority groups, while the opposite was true for minority groups: The more they perceived migrant groups as authentic and permanently different from majority groups, the more they supported multiculturalism. The perception of essentialized migrant groups is thus threatening for majority groups, while it backs claims for recognition and social change among minority groups. A similar pattern of results was evidenced in a study on in-group identification, showing that the more migrants identified with their group, the more they supported multiculturalism, while higher in-group identification by majority members led to opposition to multiculturalism (Verkuyten & Brug, 2004; Verkuyten, 2005b). These findings suggest that in-group identification by minority groups is associated with identity affirmation and the support of group-differentiated policies. In-group identification with majority groups, in turn, highlights the threatening aspects of multiculturalism. This pattern of findings has become known as the "multiculturalism" hypothesis (Verkuyten, 2005b) and has also received experimental support in studies where multicultural versus colorblind ideologies have been manipulated (Wolsko, Park, & Judd, 2006; for a general review of cognitive effects of multiculturalism, see Crisp & Turner, 2011).

3. Majority Attitudes toward Immigration: Threat Perspectives

References to threat are omnipresent in anti-immigrant rhetoric disseminated in the public sphere: Immigrants are depicted as "flooding" the country, "taking" away the jobs of citizens, abusing the welfare system, and undermining national values (e.g., Every & Augoustinos, 2007). In many European countries, for example, following the joining of former eastern European countries in the European Union, the "Polish plumber" has gained some notoriety as an objectification of an immigrant taking away jobs from national plumbers. Such allegations imply that the arrival and presence of immigrants yields various negative consequences for citizens of receiving countries. The virulent French debate about wearing headscarves is an example of supposed threat to national values disseminated in public discourse. Moreover, globally covered events early in the 21st century involving Islamist perpetrators, including terrorist attacks in New York, Madrid, and London, the murder of Dutch film maker Theo Van Gogh in Amsterdam, and the violent reactions to the Prophet Muhammad cartoons in Denmark, have fueled threat perceptions regarding Muslim immigrants in particular. The alleged threats are subsequently used as arguments to oppose rights of immigrants and restrict their entry into receiving societies. In this section, we present research that examines the role of threat in explaining the psychological processes underlying attitudes toward immigrants by members of receiving societies.

The notion of threat is present in a plethora of social psychological theories that are concerned with understanding the underpinnings of anti-immigration attitudes (see Riek, Mania, & Gaertner, 2006). "Threat" is an umbrella term with multiple meanings. Broadly defined, threat appraisals refer to the anticipation of negative consequences related to the arrival and presence of immigrants in a receiving society. Threat research generally differentiates two main routes through which threat relates to anti-immigration attitudes: material or realistic threats on the one hand, and value or symbolic threats on the other (e.g., Huddy, chapter 23, this volume; Riek et al., 2006; Sears & Funk, 1991; Stephan & Renfro, 2003). Material threats anticipate negative consequences with respect to the distribution of valued and usually scarce tangible resources in the receiving society, including economic assets, political power, and physical well-being of national in-group members. Value-based threats, in turn, foresee perceived nontangible negative consequences of immigrant presence and are derived from the assimilationist idea that all members of the national in-group should share the same values and conform to common norms. Threat has also been assessed with intergroup anxiety, involving feelings of uneasiness and awkwardness related to intergroup interactions (Stephan & Stephan, 1985). The psychological nature of threat thus varies, since threat may refer to the perceived likelihood of negative immigration consequences or to an emotional anticipation involving fear and anxiety (Esses, Jackson, & Armstrong, 1998).

Negative outcomes of immigrant presence can furthermore be anticipated on the individual or the collective level, reflecting motivations of individual or collective self-interest (e.g., Burns & Gimpel, 2000; Citrin, Green, Muste, & Wong, 1997; Jackson, Brown, Brown, & Marks, 2001; Stephan & Renfro, 2003). Individual threat perceptions describe situations where members of the receiving society are concerned that their individual interests are menaced by immigration. Collective threat perceptions refer to conditions where the in-group as a whole—be it national, ethnic, or regional—is seen as threatened by immigration.

A potentially confusing issue is that the use and theoretical status of threat as an explanatory variable in immigration attitude research varies widely. Threat has been conceived as a component of prejudice and as an antecedent, mediator, or moderator of the psychological processes underlying anti-immigration stances. Moreover, given the widespread presence of threat rhetoric in the public sphere, perceived threat may also be seen as the expression of endorsement or rejection of threat-based political arguments. Yet, despite their differences in the underlying assumptions and the forms of threats they investigate, the various theories converge in viewing threat as closely related to anti-immigration attitudes.

Threat rhetoric often targets generic immigrants as sources of potential danger to society. However, the way perceived threat affects intergroup attitudes also depends on the specific immigrant group under consideration. "Culturally distant" and stigmatized immigrant groups whose members may wear visible signs of cultural or religious affiliation, or differ in physical appearance, are the most likely targets of value-based threat rhetoric. This is the case, for example, for low-skilled Hispanic laborers in the United States or Muslim immigrants in Europe. Accordingly, immigrants deemed to be "culturally similar" and often originating from wealthier countries are less likely targets of value-based threat rhetoric. These "similar" immigrants may, however, evoke material threat, in particular related to the job market.

In this section we first overview different lines of research investigating material threat and then move on to models of value-based threats. Last, we examine how national identification and intergroup contact affect threat perceptions.

3.1. Material Threats and Immigration Attitudes

Different theoretical models focus on locating the causes of anti-immigrant attitudes in the competitive intergroup *structure* between the national in-group and immigrant out-groups. Based on *realistic conflict theory* (Sherif, 1967), these models assume that competition over scarce resources between social groups leads to intergroup conflict and, consequently, to negative attitudes toward immigrant out-groups. As a result, individuals who perceive themselves to be in competition with an immigrant out-group are most likely to experience material threat and develop negative attitudes toward members of the group. *Group position theory* (Blumer, 1958; Bobo, 1999) and *social dominance theory* (Sidanius & Pratto, 1999; Sidanius & Kurzban, chapter 7, this volume) take a similar approach, underscoring that societies are structured as group-based hierarchies that oppose dominant (national majority) to subordinate (immigrant minority) groups (see also Esses, Jackson, Dovidio, & Hodson, 2005). Dominant national in-groups propagate "legitimizing myths" that portray the majority-immigrant relationship as competitive in order to justify their higher status, resources, and power.

Perceived economic threat has been shown to relate to discriminatory attitudes towards immigrants in Europe (McLaren, 2003; Pereira, Vala, & Costa-Lopes, 2010) and North America (e.g., Citrin et al., 1997; Esses et al., 1998). The differential impact of threat rhetoric as a function of the targeted immigrant group is illustrated in an experimental study by Brader, Valentino, and Suhay (2008) showing that when news reports on Latino immigrants emphasized the costs of immigration (i.e., material threat) instead of its benefits, white US citizens supported reduction of immigration, preferred English-only laws, and requested information from anti-immigration groups. This was far less the case when European immigrants were featured in the reports. In another study, fictitious editorials depicting a highly skilled immigrant group (rather than a vaguely described immigrant group) arriving in a context where jobs are scarce evoked perceptions of competition and resulted in generalized negative attitudes toward immigrants in Canada (Esses et al., 1998).

Perceived material threat does not necessarily affect attitudes directly but may involve mediation and moderation processes. In an Australian study, the relationship between perceived material threat and exclusionary attitudes toward asylum seekers was mediated by procedural and distributive justice perceptions (Louis, Duck, Terry, Schuller, & Lalonde, 2007; for lengthier discussion on the principles of social justice see Tyler & van der Toorn, chapter 20, this volume). The results of a Canadian study, in turn, showed that competitive zero-sum beliefs ("the more for immigrants, the less for us") mediated the relationship between social dominance orientation (SDO) and attitudes toward immigrants (Esses et al., 1998). Individuals high on SDO were more likely to report that gains by immigrants would result in losses for the receiving society, a view that in turn was positively related to anti-immigration stances. In an attempt to understand why immigrants remained a target of prejudice in Switzerland despite prevailing antidiscrimination norms, Falomir-Pichastor, Muñoz-Rojas, Invernizzi, & Mugny (2004) showed that economic threat moderated the impact of antidiscrimination norms on discrimination.

Experimentally induced antidiscrimination norms reduced discrimination of immigrants only when threat was low (i.e., when fictitious research findings demonstrated that a high proportion of immigrants did *not* increase unemployment).

Low-status positions of majority members, assessed with low education and income levels, have been associated with perceived material threat. As immigrants often occupy low-status positions, low- rather than high-status majority members are more likely to be confronted with immigrants. They are therefore also more likely to view themselves in competition for similar resources such as affordable housing and jobs. Indeed, the relationship between low social position and negative immigration and cultural diversity attitudes has often been demonstrated (e.g., Hainmueller & Hiscox, 2007; Scheepers, Gijsberts, & Coenders, 2002; for an overview Ceobanu & Escandell, 2010). Similarly, low-status ethnic minorities such as blacks and Hispanics in the United States are more likely to view themselves in competition with immigrants and thus to be more opposed to immigration (e.g., Burns & Gimpel, 2000). However, competition is not the sole explanation for the links between status, threat perceptions, and anti-immigrant prejudice. Alternative explanations of status differences in the expression of anti-immigration prejudice highlight high-status groups' greater awareness of antidiscrimination norms and more subtle expressions of prejudice (e.g., Jackman & Muha, 1984; Hainmueller & Hiscox, 2007). The symbolic politics approach (e.g., Sears & Funk, 1991) provides yet another explanation by suggesting that the effects of social status are due to differential political socialization of groups, that is, differential socialization experiences rather than status per se is suggested to underlie negative immigration attitudes.

With respect to collective self-interest, Citrin, Sears, Muste, and Wong (2001) have shown that although personal economic circumstances played little role in support for reducing immigration, pessimism about the national economy and beliefs about the negative consequences of immigration on jobs and taxes predicted anti-immigration attitudes (see also Burns & Gimpel, 2000; Stephan & Renfro, 2003). Somewhat paradoxically, while people who see their national in-group as relatively *disadvantaged* in comparison with immigrant out-groups have been shown to display stronger anti-immigrant attitudes (e.g., Pettigrew et al., 2008), this was also the case for those who see their in-group as relatively *advantaged* in relation to immigrant out-groups (Guimond & Dambrun, 2002). In this latter case, immigrant prejudice is interpreted as a strategy to maintain the privileges of the high-status in-group.

3.2. Threatening the Values of the National In-group

In current day Western societies, the worldviews of Muslim immigrants are frequently considered to pose a threat to national values. The November 2009 referendum in Switzerland where 57.5% of the voting population supported a minaret construction ban illustrates the political consequences of such perceptions of value threat. Perceived value threat originates in presumed differences in belief systems, worldviews, and morality between immigrant out-groups and national majorities (e.g., Sears & Funk,

1991). Purportedly incompatible values of immigrant communities are portrayed as a menace to a homogeneous and unified conception of the national in-group based on endorsement of common values (Biernat & Vescio, 2005; Esses, Dovidio, Semenya, & Jackson, 2005). Different lines of value threat research converge in the argument that values and norms of the national majority are used as the sole frame of reference for judging immigrant out-groups (see Joffe & Staerklé, 2007).

Importantly, negative immigration attitudes are triggered by *perceptions* or *beliefs* in profound value differences rather than by any objective difference. Huntington (2004), for example, argued that the continuing immigration from Latin America threatens the linguistic and Anglo-Protestant cultural identity of the United States. Based on both census and survey data, this view was challenged by Citrin, Lerman, Murakami, and Pearson (2007) by showing that by the third generation, most Hispanic immigrants identify as Americans and are monolingual in English, and that therefore alleged value differences no longer exist.

The origins of immigration attitude research on value threat can be found in theories initially developed to understand the continuing racism against blacks in the United States. This research has demonstrated that old-fashioned bigotry has been replaced with a more hidden type of prejudice that is socially more acceptable because it is anchored in the purported lack of conformity with key national values (see Sears & Henry, 2005; Gaertner & Dovidio, 2004; McConahay, 1986; for a more detailed discussion of racial prejudice see Kinder, chapter 25, this volume). In symbolic racism theory, for example, blacks are perceived to violate, more than whites, traditional American values such as self-reliance, the work ethic, and respect for authority (Sears & Henry, 2005). In an influential paper, Pettigrew and Meertens (1995) conceptualized similar ideas in the European context, leading them to distinguish between blatant and subtle forms of prejudice against immigrants. Perceived value violation by immigrants is a central component of subtle prejudice against immigrants, in addition to exaggeration of cultural differences and the denial of positive emotions towards immigrants.

Both symbolic racism and subtle prejudice have been shown to underlie support for various restrictive policies such as expulsion of value-violating immigrants in Europe (Pettigrew & Meertens, 1995) and whites' opposition to immigration and multilingualism in the United States (Sears, Citrin, Cheleden, & van Laar, 1999; see also Huddy & Sears, 1995). Drawing on this seminal work, value-based threats have regularly been shown to be associated with anti-immigrant prejudice (McLaren, 2003; Sides & Citrin, 2007). For example, a study conducted in the Netherlands showed that perceived symbolic, but not material, threat predicted prejudice against Muslim immigrants (Velasco González, Verkuyten, Weesie, & Poppe, 2008). Another study showed that perceived collective cultural threats were the most important types of threat underlying prejudice toward Turks, Moroccans, Surinamese, and refugees in the Netherlands (Sniderman, Hagendoorn, & Prior, 2004).

Although value and material threat are sometimes conceived as rival explanations of anti-immigrant attitudes, some research suggests on the contrary that they are complementary, providing different, but not mutually exclusive, motivational explanations of immigration attitudes (e.g., Huddy & Sears, 1995; Riek et al., 2006; Sniderman et al., 2004). A case can be made that perceptions of material and value-based threat relate to the fundamental processes of dealing with intergroup similarity and difference, respectively. Material threat implies that *similarity* with immigrants is threatening since "they" are motivated to acquire the same resources "we" want. Value threat, in turn, implies that *difference* with immigrants is threatening, since "they" are too different to be integrated in our society. This hypothesis is supported by a study that revealed more negative attitudes toward Mexican immigrants in the United States when participants focused either on intergroup *difference* on positive interpersonal traits such as "generous" and "friendly" (supporting value threat predictions) or on intergroup *similarity* on work-related traits such as "competent" and "hardworking" (supporting material threat predictions) (Zárate, Garcia, Garza, & Hitlan, 2004).

Notwithstanding pressing calls for assimilation and the elimination of intergroup differences, the blurring of boundaries between the national in-group and immigrant out-groups may also lead to perceived threat and thus fuel anti-immigrant attitudes (for distinctiveness threat, e.g., Jetten, Spears, & Postmes, 2004; for threat to the hierarchical status quo, Sidanius & Pratto, 1999). Ideological orientations have been shown to account for some of these different effects of threat by shaping the experience of threat that subsequently drives anti-immigration stances (Cohrs & Stelzl, 2010; Duckitt, 2006; Guimond, Dambrun, Michinov, & Duarte, 2003; see Feldman, chapter 19, this volume). Recent research in the United States and Switzerland demonstrated that when immigrants were portrayed as adapting to the values of the receiving society (i.e., becoming similar to the national majority), antiegalitarian (high SDO) nationals motivated to enforce status boundaries were more willing than low SDO nationals to persecute immigrants than when they did not make such integrative efforts (Thomsen, Green, & Sidanius, 2008). In contrast, right-wing authoritarian (RWA) nationals concerned by conformity with in-group norms were more willing than nationals low on RWA to persecute immigrants when they did *not* make integrative efforts.

3.3. National Identification and Threat

Because immigrants are perceived and constructed as threatening historically developed *national* values, national identification plays an important role in anti-immigrant attitudes. Research has shown that ethnic majorities within countries are more likely to see themselves as legitimate representatives of the nation and are therefore more likely to identify with the nation (Devos & Banaji, 2005; Staerklé, Sidanius, Green, & Molina, 2010). This in-group identification makes members sensitive to things that may harm the group; therefore, individuals who identify strongly with their country are likely to be more concerned by the national interest than less-identified individuals. Accordingly, national identification has been shown to be an antecedent of more intense feelings of threat (e.g., Riek et al., 2006). Threat triggers a motivation to defend the identity of the nation that may lead more strongly identified individuals to hold more negative attitudes towards immigrants (e.g., Blank & Schmidt, 2003; Esses, Dovidio, et al., 2005; Mummendey, Klink, & Brown, 2001). Examining the attitudes of Dutch adolescents, Velasco González et al. (2008) showed that national identification increased anti-Muslim prejudice, but this relationship was fully mediated by perceived symbolic threat. National identification may also influence the way individuals react to threat, by strengthening the link between perceived threats and hostile attitudes toward immigrants (Stephan & Renfro, 2003). The relationship between perceived realistic threat and prejudice toward Russian immigrants in Israel has, for example, been shown to be stronger for high national identifiers (Bizman & Yinon, 2001).

However, not only the degree of national attachment determines whether anti-immigration attitudes are increased, but also its form and content. While an uncritical and idealizing attachment to the nation based on a sense of national superiority is positively related to anti-immigration attitudes, the relationship may be negative when attachment implies pride in the nation and excludes intergroup comparisons (Blank & Schmidt, 2003; Green, Sarrasin, Fasel, & Staerklé, 2011; Mummendey et al., 2001). Thus it is not identification per se that drives anti-immigration stances, but rather the meaning that individuals and groups attribute to identity (Reicher & Hopkins, 2001). Research has, for example, shown that national identification is related to prejudice toward asylum seekers in England only to the extent that people endorse an ethnic conception of the nation, that is, based on ancestry and blood ties (Pehrson, Brown, & Zagefka, 2009; see also Meeus, Duriez, Vanbeselaere, & Boen, 2010). In a study highlighting the importance of representations of national history, the experimentally emphasized Christian roots of Dutch nationhood led low national identifiers to oppose rights of Muslim immigrants to the same extent as did high identifiers (Smeekes, Verkuyten, & Poppe, 2011). Yet, under specific circumstances, national identification has also been shown to improve attitudes toward immigrants. Esses, Dovidio, et al. (2005) demonstrated that immigration attitudes, especially of individuals endorsing high levels of SDO, became less negative when a common national identity and common roots of the national majority and immigrants were experimentally made salient.

3.4. Perceived Threat and Intergroup Contact

Finally, reduction of threat plays an important role in explaining how intergroup contact decreases prejudice (see Hewstone & Al Ramiah, chapter 27, this volume). The classic intergroup contact hypothesis states that positive interaction (i.e., contact) between members of different groups (e.g., through intergroup friendships, Pettigrew, 1997 or transnational social relations, Mau, Mewes, & Zimmermann, 2008) improves intergroup relations, especially when such interaction occurs under favorable conditions (e.g., equal status between groups, common goals, institutional support, Allport, 1954). There is now a considerable body of research on mediating processes showing that contact improves attitudes toward immigrants via reduced intergroup anxiety, which represents a form of perceived threat (Pettigrew & Tropp, 2008; in addition to threat reduction, their meta-analysis identified empathy and knowledge of the immigrant out-group as mediators; see Binder et al., 2009, for longitudinal evidence of threat reduction as a mediator). A study in Italy showed that intergroup anxiety decreased with increasing contact, which then reduced prejudice toward African immigrants (Voci & Hewstone, 2003). In another study, cross-group friendships between white high school pupils and South Asian pupils in England predicted more positive attitudes toward South Asians by the English pupils (Turner, Hewstone, & Voci, 2007). This relationship was mediated by lower intergroup anxiety and increased self-disclosure (i.e., voluntary presentation of information of a personal nature) among English pupils. The same pattern was also found for extended contact (i.e., knowing in-group members who have immigrant friends). Yet another English study showed that the negative effect of direct and extended contact with Muslims on anti-Muslim attitudes was mediated by lower intergroup anxiety (Hutchinson & Rosenthal, 2011).

Although the contact research tradition has advanced our understanding of the mechanisms underlying the reduction of anti-immigrant prejudice, Dixon, Durrheim, and Tredoux (2005) call for research that goes beyond examining the reduction of individual prejudice as the sole possible outcome of contact. While ideal forms of contact (i.e., positive, frequent, among equals, and institutionally sanctioned) indeed reduce threat perceptions, the more common mundane and superficial contacts, or negative contacts, may consolidate or even enhance threat perceptions and intergroup anxiety. Moreover, intergroup contact has been shown to lead to potentially unfavorable outcomes for immigrants at the collective level, since personal contacts across group boundaries may deflect attention from structural inequality between disadvantaged and privileged ethnic groups. As a result, harmonious intergroup contact may paradoxically decrease support for political measures addressing these inequalities (Saguy, Tausch, Dovidio, & Pratto, 2009; Wright & Lubensky, 2009). Contact research should therefore go beyond the analysis of the impact of contact at the individual level and include analyses that demonstrate how contact patterns relate to political outcomes such as institutional discrimination and immigration policies and more broadly to social change.

3.5. Pitfalls in Threat Research

To conclude, some words of caution regarding common pitfalls in threat research are in order. First, the use of threat measures to predict immigration policy attitudes has been criticized as tautological. If there is content overlap in measures of threat and prejudice, then threat may simply be a variant of prejudice (e.g., Sniderman et al., 2004).

Second, sociodemographic factors such as income and education level are rather distal indicators of material threat and do therefore not warrant firm conclusions as to the psychological processes underlying the relationship between material threat and prejudice (Sears & Funk, 1991).

Third, the variety of methods used to study the role of threat in anti-immigration attitudes makes it difficult to establish an equivocal causal order between threat and prejudice. In survey research, threat perceptions are usually assessed by explicitly asking respondents the extent to which they feel immigrants threaten values or job opportunities of the national majority. Threat measures are then used to predict prejudiced policy stances. Such cross-sectional survey research cannot exclude reverse causality. Experimental research, in turn, addresses these critiques by manipulating threat perceptions in various ways (see also Schlueter, Schmidt, & Wagner, 2008, for longitudinal evidence). Many studies use fictitious newspaper articles, editorials, research findings, or policy framings to manipulate threat perceptions, thereby simulating dissemination of threat-based arguments in the media and the public sphere (e.g., Esses et al., 1998; Falomir-Pichastor et al., 2004; Pratto & Lemieux, 2001). However, controlled experiments remain artificial situations—frequently using student populations—and thus cannot conclusively show the conditions under which threat shapes immigration policy stances among the general population in the real world. Similarly, experiments studying the impact of contact on intergroup attitudes are limited due to difficulties in simulating long-term cumulative contact, across different situations, and with different out-group members (for a discussion of methodological issues in intergroup contact research, see Christ & Wagner, 2012).

Thus, any one method alone does not permit unequivocal causal interpretation of the threat-prejudice nexus. Confidence in causal conclusions can only be increased by careful consideration of findings of theory-driven research using several methods on the one hand, and by specifying how specific immigration contexts affect threat-based psychological processes on the other.

4. CONTEXTUAL ANALYSES OF IMMIGRATION ATTITUDES

How do macro-level factors shape individual immigration attitudes, and to what extent do these processes vary over time and across territorial or institutional contexts? In this fourth section of the chapter, we overview how political psychology can benefit from examining the impact of contextual (e.g., national, regional) factors on attitudes related to immigration and multiculturalism. The development of high-quality international social surveys, such as the European Social Survey (ESS) and the International Social Survey Programme (ISSP) has fostered cross-national and cross-regional research that takes into account the impact of contextual factors on individual-level processes and outcomes. The basic rationale for such investigations is that individuals' attitudes toward immigration and multiculturalism are shaped by the social and political contexts in which they develop, over and above the individual-level determinants of political attitudes. In recent years, the necessary multilevel research designs have become common, as they can now be readily implemented with a number of software packages. Multilevel approaches allow the simultaneous examination of different levels of analysis by combining individual-level predictors with national- or regional-level factors in a single explanatory model (e.g., Hox, 2010). Thus, psychological explanations of public opinion toward immigration and immigrants can be complemented with political, historical, and institutional explanations.

The conceptualization of regional and national contexts has up to now mainly relied on competition and threat theories as well as on intergroup contact theory (Ceobanu & Escandell, 2010). The two most studied context-level characteristics relate to national economic conditions (e.g., GDP, unemployment rate) and immigration and diversity patterns (e.g., proportion of immigrants, change in immigrant proportion, ethnic fractionalization). A more recent research trend has examined the impact of the ideological context in which immigration attitudes emerge. In the following, we overview and discuss these different strands of research.

4.1. Extending Threat and Contact Approaches to a Contextual Level

Drawing on both realistic conflict theory and social identity theory, Scheepers et al. (2002) were among the first to theorize threat as a context-level factor in a multilevel perspective, formalized in *ethnic competition theory* (see also Quillian, 1995). On the individual level, ethnic competition theory defines competition in terms of the social conditions (e.g., professional category, income) of members of the receiving society. Low-status conditions elicit perceptions of a competitive relationship with immigrants that in turn give rise to anti-immigration stances. Competition on the contextual level, in turn, is assessed with macro-social, economic conditions of a country or a region, assumed to affect the competitiveness between members of the receiving society and immigrants. In a disadvantaged economic context, indexed by high unemployment rates, for example, competition for scarce resources such as jobs is likely to be greater than in an advantaged economic context. In line with this reasoning, Quillian (1995) showed across 12 European countries that poor economic conditions in a country increased immigrant prejudice over and above individual-level predictors (see also Green, 2009; Kunovich, 2004).

With respect to country-level immigration patterns, the threat approach suggests that a high or increasing proportion of immigrants can elicit both perceived material and value threat. A high number of immigrants may be seen as deteriorating the economic opportunities of receiving country members by increasing competition (material threat), but it may also be seen as challenging the national culture, its values, and lifestyle (value threat). In a study comparing 15 European countries, Scheepers et al. (2002) showed that individuals living in similar conditions as immigrants were more likely to endorse threat perceptions, and that a high proportion of non-EU citizens within a country was directly related to ethnic exclusionism, assessed with opposition to the granting of civil and social rights to immigrants. Comparing measures of immigrant presence, another study showed that while the percentage of *low-status* immigrants in

European countries did not affect individual threat perceptions, a higher percentage of *non-Western* immigrants was associated with higher country average levels of perceived threat related to immigration (Schneider, 2008). Contextual characteristics can also have interactive effects, as already demonstrated by Quillian (1995), who showed that while the proportion of immigrants from non-European countries increased racial prejudice, this relationship was more likely to occur in countries with poor economic conditions.

In addition to territorial contexts, the threat approach has been applied for examining the impact of temporal contexts. *Changes* in immigration and economic conditions as well as the way they are covered in the media affect perceived competition. Pooling Dutch surveys over 1979–2002, Coenders, Lubbers, Scheepers, and Verkuyten (2008, study 1) showed that in times of high levels of immigration and increased unemployment, ethnic discrimination was more widespread (see also Semyonov, Raijman, & Gorodzeisky, 2006). Moreover, birth cohorts having experienced high immigration and unemployment in their formative preadult years also expressed greater ethnic discrimination (for a broad discussion of political socialization see Sears & Brown, chapter 3, this volume). Similar patterns were found across European countries in an examination of a narrower time frame from 2002 to 2007 (Meuleman, Davidov, & Billiet, 2009). This study showed that countries with weaker inflows of immigrants had more tolerant immigration attitudes than those with high levels of immigration, and that attitudes toward immigration became more tolerant particularly in countries where unemployment rates did not increase.

Yet although predictions based on a threat approach have received much empirical support, research has also produced mixed findings (e.g., Hjerm, 2007; Sides & Citrin, 2007; Strabac & Listhaug, 2008). In a comparison of 20 European countries, Sides and Citrin (2007) found, for example, no effects of the economic situation and of the proportion of immigrant populations on hostile attitudes toward immigration. Strabac and Listhaug (2008), in turn, found no effect of the proportion of Muslim populations on anti-Muslim attitudes across European countries. However, the European Value Survey data used in their study were collected prior to the terrorist attacks during the last decade that fueled negative attitudes toward Muslims, which may explain the absence of the effects. Moreover, comparing attitudes toward foreigners in different regions of Germany, Semyonov, Raijman, Yom Tov, and Schmidt (2004) found that the *actual* proportion of the immigrant population in a region did not have effects on such attitudes, whereas a high *perceived* size of the foreign population in the region was associated with perceived threat and discriminatory attitudes toward foreigners.

The processes underlying the impact of the proportion of immigrants in a country on its public opinion remain debated. Predictions derived in recent extensions of intergroup contact theory are indeed at odds with those derived from a threat theory perspective: Contact theorists have established that living in culturally diverse societal contexts, that is, with a high proportion of immigrants, provides more contact opportunities, notably through intergroup friendships, which decreases rather than increases perceived threat and antagonistic attitudes toward immigration and cultural diversity

(Wagner, Christ, Pettigrew, Stellmacher, & Wolf, 2006; see also J. C. Dixon, 2006, for whites' attitudes toward ethnic minorities in the United States). Support for these contentions has been found especially in studies comparing within-country regions. The proportion of immigrants within German districts, for example, was negatively related to immigrant prejudice, and this relationship was mediated by contact at the workplace and in neighborhoods (Wagner et al., 2006). These findings suggest that opportunities for contact explain a part of the relationship between ethnic composition of a community and the level of immigrant prejudice of its members.

Although the contact and threat effects concerning the proportion of immigrants may contradict each other, their opposing effects can nevertheless occur simultaneously. Schlueter and Wagner (2008) demonstrated that the regional proportion of immigrant populations in Europe increased both intergroup contact and perceived threat. Pettigrew, Wagner, and Christ (2010) showed that the effect of contact is based on direct *experience* with immigrants and thus affected by the actual size of immigrant populations within German regions, whereas perceived threat is triggered by the *perception* of immigrant presence. Other studies have shown that the interplay between threat perceptions and intergroup contact affects and is affected by context-level factors. For example, examining 17 European countries, McLaren (2003) revealed that while the percentage of foreigners in a country increases perceived threat, having immigrant friends buffers this effect. Thus, individuals with immigrant friends living in highly diverse contexts will feel less threatened by diversity than those without such friendships. Similarly, the percentage of foreign-born in US regions had less impact on whites' immigration attitudes when their interpersonal networks included nonwhite members (Berg, 2009). Moreover, although positive intergroup contact is negatively related to anti-immigrant stances, this beneficial effect of contact may be more pronounced in diverse contexts where intercultural encounters are commonplace. In line with this idea, the proportion of immigrants in European countries has been shown to moderate the relationship between intergroup contact and anti-immigrant prejudice (Semyonov & Glikman, 2009). Positive contact reduced negative attitudes toward immigrants to a greater degree in countries with a large number of non-Europeans, compared to countries with a smaller number of non-Europeans. Extended, indirect contact (knowing in-group members who have immigrant friends), however, has been shown to be more effective in reducing prejudice for individuals living in segregated neighborhoods with only few direct contact experiences with immigrants, compared to individuals from mixed neighborhoods where more opportunities for direct contact exist (Christ et al., 2010).

The territorial size of the context-level unit of analysis may explain some of the seeming contradictions between the predictions derived from threat and contact approaches. The positive effects of intergroup contact have been suggested to occur at a proximal and local (e.g., municipality, neighborhood, and district) level, where it is plausible that immigrants and members of the receiving society interact in their daily activities (see Wagner et al. 2006; Schmid, Tausch, Hewstone, Hughes, & Cairns, 2008). A large presence of immigrants at a distal, national level, however, may be more likely to enhance threat perceptions due to an increased political concern with immigration, reflected in widespread anti-immigrant discourse using threat discourse in the media. In line with this argument, a US study examining attitudes of Asian Americans, blacks, Latinos, and whites found that interethnic diversity reduced perceived threat and prejudice at the neighborhood level, but increased it at the city ("metropolitan") level (Oliver & Wong, 2003). Similarly, a study across European countries showed that living in mixed—as opposed to homogeneous or highly ethnic—neighborhoods reduced threat perceptions and social distance toward immigrants, whereas the immigrant ratio in the country increased threat perceptions (Semyonov & Glikman, 2009).

4.2. Ideological Climate and Immigration Attitudes

Individuals are embedded in everyday environments that provide normative and ideological reference knowledge guiding their thinking about societal phenomena such as immigration. This normative context can be seen as an "ideological climate" that is institutionalized in national laws and policies and reproduced in a political everyday culture made up by beliefs and values widely shared by members of a community. Ethnic and civic conceptions of national citizenship, for example, are elements of such an ideological climate that exists both at the policy level and at the level of shared values and beliefs in national populations. Across 15 European countries, Weldon (2006) showed that individuals in countries with ethnic citizenship regimes—requiring shared ethnicity and ancestry for citizenship—were less willing to grant political rights to ethnic minorities than individuals in countries with civic citizenship regimes (i.e., assimilationist and pluralistic regimes). Individuals in assimilationist regimes, in turn, were less tolerant than individuals in pluralistic regimes. Furthermore, national identification was related to intolerance only in ethnic citizenship regimes. In another study, Pehrson, Vignoles, and Brown (2009) demonstrated that in countries where the collective representation of nationhood was civic, anti-immigrant prejudice was reduced. Moreover, the relationship between national identification and anti-immigrant prejudice was weaker in these countries, suggesting that national identification defined by shared civic citizenship is related to a lesser degree to a desire to exclude immigrants. This is yet another demonstration that identity content determines whether or not identification relates to anti-immigration stances.

The relative strength of political parties also reflects the ideological climate of countries. A strong presence of right-wing parties, for example, has been shown to increase antiforeigner sentiment across European countries, over and above individuals' political orientation (Semyonov et al., 2006; see also Lahav, 2004). The picture is more complex, however, as specific ideological emphases in political party discourse moderate their impact on individuals' attitudes (Wilkes, Guppy, & Farris, 2007). The presence of extremist parties promoting blatant racism (based on *biological* intergroup differences) did not affect public opinion as a whole, since such views have become socially unacceptable. Instead, the national prevalence of right-wing parties with a culturalist racist agenda (based on essential *cultural* differences) was shown to relate to anti-immigrant attitudes.

Finally, ideological climate has been measured by aggregating individual-level voting results. A study using Swiss national referenda at the level of municipalities provided an indicator of ideological climate based on actual voting behavior on a wide range of social issues (Sarrasin et al., 2012). This study evidenced stronger opposition to antiracism laws in municipalities with conservative ideological climates, after accounting for individual-level ideological stances. Furthermore, in conservative municipalities with a low proportion of immigrants, fewer intergroup contacts were reported: When the proportion of immigrants was high, conservative climate did not affect intergroup contacts. Overall research on ideological climates suggests that whether the climate is defined by institutional factors or by shared representations, it constitutes a framework of normative rules and expectations that individual citizens refer to when taking a stand on immigration.

4.3. Open Issues in Contextual Analyses

Although contextual-level analyses in political psychology have contributed to our understanding of how national, regional, and temporal contexts affect individual opinions regarding immigration, several open questions remain. First, most European studies focus on the proportion of immigrants or non-Europeans in general (for exceptions, e.g., Green, Fasel, & Sarrasin, 2010; Hjerm, 2009; Schneider, 2008; Strabac & Listhaug, 2008), despite the fact that immigrant groups who are targets of prejudice vary widely across countries. The arrival or presence of some immigrant groups (e.g., with Muslim origins) may elicit symbolic threat perceptions related to family or religious values, whereas other immigrant groups (e.g., German professionals coming to Switzerland) may trigger material threat perceptions due to competition in the job market. Thus further research should compare the multilevel impact of the presence of specific immigrant groups. Moreover, there is a growing need to understand how individuals who react with threat perceptions to higher ratios of immigrants differ from those who experience immigrant presence as an opportunity to build intergroup friendships. For example, examining in more detail the meaning individuals give to intergroup interactions is one step in this direction (Dixon et al., 2005).

Second, unraveling the processes that account for the relationship between context and individual attitude remains both a methodological and a theoretical challenge. To this end, new hypotheses are called for in order to better understand this relationship, using novel conceptualizations of contexts as well as mediation and moderation patterns combining different levels of analysis.

Third, most multilevel research on immigration stances only considers the national majority perspective (see, however, Fleischmann, Verkuyten, & Poppe, 2011; Staerklé et al., 2010), presumably because ethnic minorities are under- or misrepresented in national surveys (e.g., Feskens, Hox, Lensvelt-Mulders, & Schmeets, 2006). Examining the minority perspective as well as the interplay between majority and minority perspectives is nevertheless essential for bringing the field forward. Finally, new approaches are needed to circumvent problems in multilevel research related to the small number of context-level units such as countries (Hox, 2010).

5. CONCLUSION

This chapter proposed an overview of research on migration and multiculturalism from the perspective of political psychology. We started our discussion with a historical framing of the two major modes of migrant incorporation, assimilation and multiculturalism. The second section presented research studying the perspective of migrant groups, showing the interactionist nature and the complexity of contemporary migrant identities as well as the pros and cons of various acculturation strategies employed by migrants. We also highlighted the intergroup nature of attitudes toward multiculturalism and of acculturation strategies between national majorities and ethnic migrant minorities. The third section focused on research investigating reactions by national majorities to immigration, in particular the role of various forms of perceived threat associated with migrant groups. The final section featured recent multilevel research on majority attitudes toward migration across national and regional contexts.

An important goal of the chapter was to relate the principles of assimilation and multiculturalism to the dialectic processes of intergroup similarity and differentiation, respectively. The overviewed research clearly indicates that migrant experiences, and reactions to immigration by receiving societies, express the complex and dynamic interplay of similarity and difference, at the level of motivations, perceptions, and normative expectations. For migrant groups, qualified and selective *similarity* with the receiving society's majority is an asset for a successful migrant experience, for example, through language acquisition and awareness of dominant social norms. At the same time, intergroup *difference* and concomitant identification with their ethnic group is likely to help many migrants to construct positive social identities rooted in the everyday experiences and practices associated with their ethnic group. Importantly, research has also emphasized that such differentiation processes do not only operate *between* migrant groups and receiving majorities, but also *within* migrant categories, in particular between early and recent migrants, between first-, second-, and third-generation migrants, between migrant organizations defending contrasting visions of incorporation, and between different ethnic groups.

Yet the demands and practical implications derived from the principle of intergroup similarity may be contradictory: majorities may expect migrants to "adapt" and respect "their values," but when they do so, they may become threatening competitors for jobs and other material resources of the majority group. Intergroup difference can be equally paradoxical: migrants who are portrayed as (too) different from the majority culture allegedly threaten social cohesion and national values. At the same time, majorities may prefer that migrant groups, especially those they dislike, remain apart from them in order to safeguard an imaginary homogeneity of their in-group. Intergroup difference is furthermore enhanced through majority practices that make integration more difficult, such as unequal treatment by authorities, lack of institutional support for integration, widespread discrimination, and segregated housing. Research therefore needs to carefully spell out the specific meaning and practical implications of intergroup similarity and difference that is implied by political rhetoric and hidden in general attitudes toward immigrants. Research should also more clearly differentiate attitude formation toward contrasting types of immigrants, for example, by comparing attitudes toward high- and low-status immigrants or toward immigrants from culturally similar and distant countries. Currently, to maximize cross-national comparability, large international surveys mainly refer to generic immigrants in their item wording. However, additionally assessing attitudes toward immigrants of specific national origin—which may vary from country to country—would allow us to paint a more accurate picture of the psychological processes involved in immigration attitude construction.

During the last two decades, migration and multiculturalism have become one of the most heavily debated issues in contemporary receiving societies, both at the level of political discourse and in everyday conversations. As illustrated in studies on migrant identity construction and ideological climates reviewed in this chapter, this societal communication is likely to affect the way citizens think about immigrants. Politicians, migrant group leaders, members of the civil society, and other "identity entrepreneurs" (Reicher & Hopkins, 2001) participate in the societal immigration debate by strategically communicating specific understandings of assimilation and multiculturalism. In this view, for example, "threat perceptions" are the outcome of social influence processes that deliberately portray certain migrant groups as "different" or "dangerous." These discourses participate in the construction and diffusion of positive and negative meanings of migration, thereby creating socially acceptable, and often simplified, ways of thinking and talking about immigrants and immigration. Both migrant groups and national majorities then rely on such social representations to deal with the realities and difficulties of multicultural societies (see Elcheroth, Doise, & Reicher, 2011; Staerklé, Clémence, & Spini, 2011). In future research, political psychology could gain from placing a stronger emphasis on this ongoing communicative process underlying migrant identities and majority ascriptions of migrant characteristics.

Finally, the variety of methodological and theoretical approaches through which political psychology has studied phenomena of migration and multiculturalism is an important asset for making our research relevant to policymakers and practitioners (see Wills, 2010). Discursive, experimental, and survey research have different stories to tell about migration and immigration. Yet despite their often conflicting theoretical assumptions, we assume they share the normative goal of making our multicultural societies more inclusive and a better place to live for all citizens. Researchers in political psychology should therefore highlight the implications of their studies on migration and immigration policies. As we hope to have shown in this chapter, political psychology has a great deal to offer to promote the chances for successful migrant experiences as well as positive, enriching, and constructive relationships between migrant groups and national majorities.

NOTES

1. Throughout the chapter we use the term "receiving society" instead of "host society" in order to avoid connotations of migrants being passively "hosted" by national majorities. The term "migrant" is used when migration is analyzed from the perspective of those who move into new contexts, while the term "immigrant" is employed to describe the perspective of the receiving society into which migrants immigrate.

REFERENCES

Alba, R. (2005). Bright vs. blurred boundaries: Second-generation assimilation and exclusion in France, Germany, and the United States. *Ethnic and Racial Studies, 28*, 20–49.

Alba, R., & Nee, V. (2003). *Remaking the American mainstream. Assimilation and contemporary immigration.* Cambridge, MA: Harvard University Press.

Ali, L., & Sonn, C. C. (2010). Constructing identity as a second generation Cypriot Turkish in Australia: The Multi hyphenated Other. *Culture and Psychology, 16*, 416–436.

Allport, G. W. (1954). *The nature of prejudice.* Reading, MA: Addison-Wesley.

Arends-Tóth, J. V., & Vijver, F. J. R. v. d. (2006). Assessment of psychological acculturation: Choices in designing an instrument. The Cambridge handbook of acculturation psychology (pp. 142–160). Cambridge: Cambridge University Press.

Ashmore, R. D., Deaux, K., & McLaughlin-Volpe, T. (2004). An organizing framework for collective identity: Articulation and significance of multidimensionality. *Psychological Bulletin, 130*, 80–114.

Azzi, A. (1992). Procedural justice and the allocation of power in intergroup relations. *Personality and Social Psychology Bulletin, 18*, 736–747.

Azzi, A. E., Chryssochoou, X., Klandermans, B., & Simon, B. (Eds.). (2011). *Identity and participation in culturally diverse societies: A multidisciplinary perspective.* Chichester: Wiley.

Barry, B. (2001). *Culture and equality.* Cambridge: Polity Press.

Barth, F. (Ed.). (1969). *Ethnic groups and boundaries: The social organization of cultural difference.* London: Allen & Unwin.

Berg, J. A. (2009). Core networks and whites' attitudes toward immigrants and immigration policy. *Public Opinion Quarterly, 73*, 7–31.

Berry, J. W. (1990). Psychology of acculturation. In J. J. Berman (ed.), *Nebraska Symposium on Motivation, 1989,* vol. 37: *Cross-Cultural perspectives* (pp. 201–234). Lincoln: University of Nebraska Press.

Berry, J. W. (2006). Stress perspectives on acculturation. In D. L. Sam & J. W. Berry (eds.), *The Cambridge handbook of acculturation psychology* (pp. 43–57). Cambridge: Cambridge University Press.

Berry, J. W., & Sabatier, C. (2010). Acculturation, discrimination, and adaptation among second generation immigrant youth in Montreal and Paris. *International Journal of Intercultural Relations, 34*, 191–207.

Biernat, M., & Vescio, T. K. (2005). Values and prejudice: Historical Conceptualizations and current issues. In C. S. Crandall & M. Schaller (eds.), *The social psychology of prejudice: Historical and modern perspectives* (pp. 187–211). Lawrence, KS: Lewinian Press.

Binder, J., Zagefka, H., Brown, R., Funke, F., Kessler, T., Mummendey, A., et al. (2009). Does contact reduce prejudice or does prejudice reduce contact? A longitudinal test of the contact hypothesis among majority and minority groups in three European countries. *Journal of Personality and Social Psychology, 96,* 843–856.

Bizman, A., & Yinon, Y. (2001). Intergroup and interpersonal threats as determinants of prejudice: The moderating role of in-group identification. *Basic and Applied Social Psychology, 23,* 191–196.

Blank, T., & Schmidt, P. (2003). National identity in a united Germany: Nationalism or patriotism? An empirical test with representative data. *Political Psychology, 24,* 289–312.

Bloemraad, I., Korteweg, A., & Yurdakul, G. (2008). Citizenship and immigration: Multiculturalism, assimilation, and challenges to the nation-state. *Annual Review of Sociology, 34,* 153–179.

Blumer, H. (1958). Race prejudice as a sense of group position. *Pacific Sociological Review, 1,* 3–7.

Bobo, L. D. (1999). Prejudice as group position: Microfoundations of a sociological approach to racism and race relations. *Journal of Social Issues, 55,* 445–472.

Bourhis, R. Y., Barrette, G., El-Geledi, S., & Schmidt, R. (2009). Acculturation orientations and social relations between immigrant and host community members in California. *Journal of Cross-Cultural Psychology, 40,* 443–467.

Bourhis, R. Y., Moïse, L. C., Perreault, S., & Senécal, S. (1997). Towards and interactive acculturation model: A social psychological approach. *International Journal of Psychology, 32,* 369–383.

Bourhis, R. Y., Montaruli, E., El-Geledi, S., Harvey, S.-P., & Barrette, G. (2010). Acculturation in multiple host community settings. *Journal of Social Issues, 66,* 780–802.

Bowskill, M., Lyons, E., & Coyle, A. (2007). The rhetoric of acculturation: When integration means assimilation. *British Journal of Social Psychology, 46,* 793–813.

Brader, T., Valentino, N. A., & Suhay, E. (2008). What triggers public opposition to immigration? Anxiety, group cues, and immigration threat. *American Journal of Political Science, 52,* 959–978.

Brubaker, R. (2001). The return of assimilation? Changing perspectives on immigration and its sequels in France, Germany and the United States. *Ethnic and Racial Studies, 24,* 531–548.

Brubaker, R., Feischmidt, M., Fox, J., & Grancea, L. (2006). *Nationalist politics and everyday ethnicity in a Transylvanian town.* Princeton, NJ: Princeton University Press.

Burns, P., & Gimpel, J. G. (2000). Economic insecurity, prejudicial stereotypes, and public opinion on immigration policy. *Political Science Quarterly, 115,* 201–225.

Cassidy, C., O'Connor, R. C., Howe, C., & Warden, D. (2004). Perceived discrimination and psychological distress: The role of personal and ethnic self-esteem. *Journal of Counseling Psychology, 51,* 329–339.

Castles, S., & Miller, M. J. (2009). *The age of migration: International population movements in the modern world* (4th ed.). Hampshire, UK: Palgrave Macmillan.

Ceobanu, A. M., & Escandell, X. (2010). Comparative analyses of public attitudes toward immigrants and immigration using multinational survey data: A review of theories and research. *Annual Review of Sociology, 36,* 309–328.

Chen, S. X., Benet-Martinez, V., & Bond, M. H. (2008). Bicultural identity, bilingualism, and psychological adjustment in multicultural societies: Immigration-based and globalization-based acculturation. *Journal of Personality, 76,* 803–838.

Christ, O., Hewstone, M., Tausch, N., Wagner, U., Voci, A., Hughes, J., et al. (2010). Direct contact as a moderator of extended contact effects: Cross-sectional and longitudinal impact on outgroup attitudes, behavioral intentions, and attitude certainty. *Personality and Social Psychology Bulletin, 36,* 1662–1674.

Christ, O., & Wagner, U. (2012). Methodological issues in the study of intergroup contact: Towards a new wave of research. In G. Hodson & M. Hewstone (eds.), *Advances in Intergroup Contact*. New York: Psychology Press.

Chryssochoou, X. (2004). *Cultural diversity: Its social psychology.* Oxford: Blackwell.

Citrin, J., Green, D. P., Muste, C., & Wong, C. (1997). Public opinion toward immigration reform: The role of economic motivations. *Journal of Politics, 59,* 858–881.

Citrin, J., Lerman, A., Murakami, M., & Pearson, K. (2007). Testing Huntington: Is Hispanic immigration a threat to American identity? *Perspectives on Politics, 5,* 31–48.

Citrin, J., Sears, D. O., Muste, C., & Wong, C. (2001). Multiculturalism in American public opinion. *British Journal of Political Science, 31,* 247–275.

Coenders, M., Lubbers, M., Scheepers, P., & Verkuyten, M. (2008). More than two decades of changing ethnic attitudes in the Netherlands. *Journal of Social Issues, 64,* 269–285.

Cohrs, J. C., & Stelzl, M. (2010). How ideological attitudes predict host society members' attitudes toward immigrants: Exploring cross-national differences. *Journal of Social Issues, 66,* 673–694.

Crisp, R. J., & Turner, R. N. (2011). Cognitive adaptation to the experience of social and cultural diversity. *Psychological Bulletin, 137,* 242–266.

Davis, M. H., Morris, M. M., & Kraus, L. A. (1998). Relationship-specific and global perceptions of social support: Associations with well-being and attachment. *Journal of Personality and Social Psychology, 74,* 468–481.

Deaux, K. (2006). *To be an immigrant.* New York: Russell Sage Foundation.

Devos, T., & Banaji, M. (2005). American = white? *Journal of Personality and Social Psychology, 88,* 447–466.

Dixon, J. C. (2006). The ties that bind and those that don't: Toward reconciling group threat and contact theories of prejudice. *Social Forces, 84,* 2179–2204.

Dixon, J. C., Durrheim, K., & Tredoux, C. (2005). Beyond the optimal contact strategy: A reality check for the contact hypothesis. *American Psychologist, 60,* 697–711.

Dovidio, J. F., & Gaertner, S. L. (2004). Aversive racism. In M. P. Zanna (ed.), *Advances in Experimental Social Psychology* (vol. 36, pp. 1–52). San Diego, CA: Academic Press.

Duckitt, J. (2006). Differential effects of right wing authoritarianism and social dominance orientation on outgroup attitudes and their mediation by threat from and competitiveness to outgroups. *Personality and Social Psychology Bulletin, 32,* 684–696.

Elcheroth, G., Doise, W., & Reicher, S. (2011). On the knowledge of politics and the politics of knowledge: How a social representations approach helps us rethink the subject of political psychology. *Political Psychology, 32,* 729–758.

Esses, V. M., Dovidio, J. F., Semenya, A. H., & Jackson, L. M. (2005). Attitudes towards immigrants and immigration: The role of national and international identity. In D. Abrams, M. A. Hogg, & J. M. Marques (eds.), *The social psychology of inclusion and exclusion* (pp. 317–337). New York: Psychology Press.

Esses, V. M., Jackson, L. M., & Armstrong, T. L. (1998). Intergroup competition and attitudes toward immigrants and immigration: An instrumental model of group conflict. *Journal of Social Issues, 54,* 699–724.

Esses, V. M., Jackson, L. M., Dovidio, J. F., & Hodson, G. (2005). Instrumental relations among groups: Group competition, conflict and prejudice. In J. F. Dovidio, P. Glick, & L. A. Rudman (eds.), *On the nature of prejudice: Fifty years after Allport* (pp. 227–243). O International population movements in the modern xford: Blackwell.

Every, D., & Augoustinos, M. (2007). Constructions of racism in the Australian parliamentary debates on asylum seekers. *Discourse & Society, 18*, 411–436.

Faist, T. (2009). Diversity—a new mode of incorporation? *Ethnic and Racial Studies, 32*(1), 171–190.

Falomir-Pichastor, J. M., Muñoz-Rojas, D., Invernizzi, F., & Mugny, G. (2004). Perceived in-group threat as a factor moderating the influence of in-group norms on discrimination against foreigners. *European Journal of Social Psychology, 34*, 135–153.

Feskens, R., Hox, J., Lensvelt-Mulders, G., & Schmeets, H. (2006). Collecting data among ethnic minorities in an international perspective. *Field Methods, 18*, 284–304.

Finch, B. K., Kolody, B., & Vega, W. A. (2000). Perceived discrimination and depression among Mexican origin adults in California. *Journal of Health and Social Behavior, 41*, 295–313.

Fleischmann, F., Verkuyten, M., & Poppe, E. (2011). Ethnic and republic identification in the Russian Federation and Ukraine: A social dominance perspective. *Journal of Ethnic and Migration Studies, 37*, 23–41.

Geschke, D., Mummendey, A., Kessler, T., & Funke, F. (2010). Majority members' acculturation goals as predictors and effects of attitudes and behaviours towards migrants. *British Journal of Social Psychology, 49*, 489–506.

Glazer, N. (1997). *We are all multiculturalists now*. Cambridge, MA: Harvard University Press.

Gordon, M. (1964). *Assimilation in American life: The role of race, religion and national origins*. New York: Oxford University Press.

Green, E. G. T. (2009). Who can enter? A multilevel analysis on public support for immigration criteria across 20 European countries. *Group Processes & Intergroup Relations, 12*, 41–60.

Green, E. G. T., Fasel, N., & Sarrasin, O. (2010). The more the merrier? The effects of type of diversity on immigration attitudes in Switzerland. *International Journal of Conflict and Violence, 4*, 177–190.

Green, E. G. T., Sarrasin, O., Fasel, N., & Staerklé, C. (2011). Nationalism and patriotism as predictors of immigration attitudes in Switzerland: A municipality-level analysis. *Swiss Political Science Review, 17*, 369–393.

Guimond, S., & Dambrun, M. (2002). When prosperity breeds intergroup hostility: The effects of relative deprivation and relative gratification on prejudice. *Personality and Social Psychology Bulletin, 28*, 900–912.

Guimond, S., Dambrun, M., Michinov, N., & Duarte, S. (2003). Does social dominance generate prejudice? Integrating individual and contextual determinants of intergroup cognitions. *Journal of Personality and Social Psychology, 84*, 697–721.

Hainmueller, J., & Hiscox, M. J. (2007). Educated preferences: Explaining attitudes toward immigration in Europe. *International Organization, 61*, 399–442.

Hjerm, M. (2007). Do numbers really count? Group threat theory revisited. *Journal of Ethnic and Migration Studies, 33*, 1253–1275.

Hjerm, M. (2009). Anti-immigrant attitudes and cross-municipal variation in the proportion of immigrants. *Acta Sociologica, 52*, 47–62.

Hopkins, N., & Kahani-Hopkins, V. (2004). Identity construction and British Muslims' political activity: Beyond rational actor theory. *British Journal of Social Psychology, 43*, 339–356.

Hopkins, N., & Kahani-Hopkins, V. (2006). Minority group members' theories of intergroup contact: a case study of British Muslims' conceptualizations of "Islamophobia" and social change. *British Journal of Social Psychology, 45*, 245–264.

Howarth, C. (2002). "So, you're from Brixton?" The struggle for recognition and esteem in a multicultural community. *Ethnicities*, *2*, 237–260.

Hox, J. (2010). *Multilevel analysis: Techniques and applications*. New York: Routledge.

Huddy, L., & Sears, D. O. (1995). Opposition to bilingual education: Prejudice or the defense of realistic interests? *Social Psychology Quarterly*, *58*, 133–143.

Huntington, S. (2004). The Hispanic challenge. *Foreign Policy*, *141*, 30–45.

Hutchinson, P., & Rosenthal, H. E. S. (2011). Prejudice against Muslims: Anxiety as a mediator between intergroup contact and attitudes, perceived group variability and behavioural intentions. *Ethnic and Racial Studies*, *34*, 40–61.

Ignatiev, N. (1995). *How the Irish became white*. New York: Routledge.

Ingram, D. (2000). *Group rights: Reconciling equality and difference*. Lawrence: University Press of Kansas.

Isin, F. I., & Wood, P. K. (1999). *Citizenship and identity*. London: Sage.

Jackman, M. R., & Muha, M. J. (1984). Education and intergroup attitudes: Moral enlightenment, superficial democratic commitment, or ideological refinement? *American Sociological Review*, *49*, 751–769.

Jackson, J. S., Brown, K. T., Brown, T. N., & Marks, B. (2001). Contemporary immigration policy orientations among dominant-group members in western Europe. *Journal of Social Issues*, *57*, 431–456.

Jasinskaja-Lahti, L. (2008). Long-term immigrant adaptation: Eight-year follow-up study among immigrants form Russia and Estonia living in Finland. *International Journal of Psychology*, *43*, 6–18.

Jasinskaja-Lahti, I., Liebkind, K., Jaakkola, M., & Reuter, A. (2006). Perceived discrimination, social support networks, and psychological well-being among three immigrant groups. *Journal of Cross-Cultural Psychology*, *37*(3), 293–311.

Jetten, J., Branscombe, N. R., Schmitt, M. T., & Spears, R. (2001). Rebels with a cause: group identification as a response to perceived discrimination from the mainstream. *Personality and Social Psychology Bulletin*, *27*, 1204–1213.

Jetten, J., Spears, R., & Postmes, T. (2004). Intergroup distinctiveness and differentiation: A meta-analytic integration. *Journal of Personality and Social Psychology*, *86*, 862–879.

Joffe, H., & Staerklé, C. (2007). The centrality of the self-control ethos in Western aspersions regarding outgroups: A social representational analysis of common stereotype content. *Culture and Psychology*, *13*, 395–418.

Joppke, C. (2007). Transformation of immigrant integration: Civic integration and anti-discrimination in the Netherlands, France, and Germany. *World Politics*, *59*, 243–273.

Joppke, C. (2009). *Veil: Mirror of identity*. Cambridge: Polity Press.

Kivisto, P. (2002). *Multiculturalism in a global society*. Oxford: Blackwell.

Koopmans, R., Statham, P., Giugni, M., & Passy, F. (2005). *Contested citizenship. Immigration and cultural diversity in Europe*. Minneapolis: University of Minnesota Press.

Kosic, A., & Phalet, K. (2006). Ethnic categorization of immigrants: The role of prejudice, perceived acculturation strategies and group size. *International Journal of Intercultural Relations*, *30*, 769–782.

Kunovich, R. M. (2004). Social structural position and prejudice: An exploration of cross-national differences in regression slopes. *Social Science Research*, *33*, 20–44.

Kymlicka, W. (1995). *Multicultural citizenship*. Oxford: Oxford University Press.

Lahav, G. (2004). *Immigration and politics in the new Europe*. Cambridge: Cambridge University Press.

Lamont, M., & Molnar, V. (2002). The study of boundaries in the social sciences. *Annual Review of Sociology, 28*, 167–95.

Levitt, P., & Waters, M. (Eds.). (2002). *The changing face of home: The transnational lives of the second generation.* New York: Russell Sage Foundation.

Licata, L., Sanchez-Mazas, M., & Green, E. G. T. (2011). Identity, immigration, and prejudice in Europe: A recognition approach. In S. J. Schwartz, K. Luyckx, & V. L. Vignoles (eds.), *Handbook of identity theory and research* (pp. 895–916). New York: Springer.

Liebkind, K., & Jasinskaja-Lahti, I. (2000). The influence of experiences of discrimination on psychological stress among immigrants: A comparison of seven immigrant groups. *Journal of Community and Applied Social Psychology, 10*, 1–16.

Louis, W. R., Duck, J. M., Terry, D. J., Schuller, R. A., & Lalonde, R. N. (2007). Why do citizens want to keep refugees out? Threats, fairness and hostile norms in the treatment of asylum seekers. *European Journal of Social Psychology, 37*(1), 53–73.

Masgoret, A.-M., & Ward, C. (2006). Culture learning approach to acculturation. In D. L. Sam & J. W. Berry (eds.), *The Cambridge handbook of acculturation psychology* (pp. 58–77). Cambridge: Cambridge University Press.

Mau, S., Mewes, J., & Zimmermann, A. (2008). Cosmopolitan attitudes through transnational social practices? *Global Networks, 8*, 1–24.

McConahay, J. B. (1986). Modern racism, ambivalence, and the modern racism scale. In J. F. Dovidio & S. L. Gaertner (eds.), *Prejudice, discrimination, and racism* (pp. 91–125). San Diego, CA: Academic Press.

McLaren, L. M. (2003). Anti-immigrant prejudice in Europe: Contact, threat perception, and preferences for the exclusion of migrants. *Social Forces, 81*, 909–936.

Meeus, J., Duriez, B., Vanbeselaere, N., & Boen, F. (2010). The role of national identity representation in the relation between in-group identification and out-group derogation: Ethnic versus civic representation. *British Journal of Social Psychology, 49*, 305–320.

Meuleman, B., Davidov, E., & Billiet, J. (2009). Changing attitudes toward immigration in Europe, 2002–2007: A dynamic group conflict theory approach. *Social Science Research, 38*, 352–365.

Montreuil, A., & Bourhis, R. Y. (2001). Host majority acculturation orientations towards "valued" and "devalued" immigrants. *Journal of Cross-Cultural Psychology, 32*, 718–739.

Montreuil, A., Bourhis, R. Y., & Vanbeselaere, N. (2004). Perceived threat and host community acculturation orientations toward immigrants: Comparing Flemings in Belgium and Francophones in Quebec. *Canadian Ethnic Studies, 36*, 113–135.

Mummendey, A., Klink, A., & Brown, R. (2001). Nationalism and patriotism: National identification and out-group rejection. *British Journal of Social Psychology, 40*, 159–171.

Nesdale, D., & Mak, A. S. (2000). Immigrant acculturation attitudes and host country identification. *Journal of Community & Applied Social Psychology, 10*(6), 483–495.

Oliver, J. E., & Wong, J. (2003). Intergroup prejudice in multiethnic settings. *American Journal of Political Science, 47*, 567–582.

Park, R. E., & Burgess, E. W. (1921). *Introduction to the science of sociology.* Chicago: University of Chicago Press.

Pehrson, S., Brown, R., & Zagefka, H. (2009). When does national identification lead to anti-immigrant prejudice? Cross-sectional and longitudinal evidence for the role of essentialist ingroup definitions. *British Journal of Social Psychology, 48*, 61–76.

Pehrson, S., Vignoles, V. L., & Brown, R. (2009). National identification and anti-immigrant prejudice: Individual and contextual effects of national definitions. *Social Psychology Quarterly, 72*, 21–48.

Pereira, C., Vala, J., & Costa-Lopes, R. (2010). From prejudice to discrimination: The legitimizing role of perceived threat in discrimination against immigrants. *European Journal of Social Psychology, 40*, 1231–1250.

Pettigrew, T. F. (1997). Generalized intergroup contact effects on prejudice. *Personality and Social Psychology Bulletin, 23*, 173–185.

Pettigrew, T. F., Christ, O., Wagner, U., Meertens, R. W., Van Dick, R., & Zick, A. (2008). Relative deprivation and intergroup prejudice. *Journal of Social Issues, 64*(2), 385–401.

Pettigrew, T. F., & Meertens, R. W. (1995). Subtle and blatant prejudice in western Europe. *European Journal of Social Psychology, 25*, 57–75.

Pettigrew, T. F., & Tropp, L. R. (2008). How does intergroup contact reduce prejudice? Meta-analytic tests of three mediators. *European Journal of Social Psychology, 38*, 922–934.

Pettigrew, T. F., Wagner, U., & Christ, O. (2010). Population ratios and prejudice: Modelling both contact and threat effects. *Journal of Ethnic and Migration Studies, 36*, 635–650.

Philogène, G. (1999). *From black to African-American: A new social representation.* Westport, CT: Greenwood-Praeger.

Phinney, J. S. (1990). Ethnic identity in adolescents and adults: Review of research. *Psychological Bulletin, 108*, 499–514.

Piontkowski, U., Florack, A., Hoelker, P., & Obdrzálek, P. (2000). Predicting acculturation attitudes of dominant and non-dominant groups. *International Journal of Intercultural Relations, 24*(1), 1–26.

Polek, E., van Oudenhoven, J. P., & ten Berge, J. M. F. (2008). Attachment styles and demographic factors as predictors of sociocultural and psychological adjustment of eastern European immigrants in the Netherlands. *International Journal of Psychology, 43*, 919–928.

Portes, A., & Rumbaut, R. G. (2006). *Immigrant America: A portrait* (3rd ed.). Berkeley: University of California Press.

Pratto, F., & Lemieux, A. F. (2001). The psychological ambiguity of immigration and its implications for promoting immigration policy. *Journal of Social Issues, 57*, 413–430.

Quillian, L. (1995). Prejudice as a response to perceived group threat: Population composition and anti-immigrant and racial prejudice in Europe. *American Sociological Review, 60*, 586–611.

Redfield, R., Linton, R., & Herskovits, M. (1936). Memorandum on the study of acculturation. *American Anthropologist, 38*, 149–152.

Reicher, S., & Hopkins, N. (2001). *Self and nation.* London: Sage.

Riek, B. M., Mania, E. W., & Gaertner, S. L. (2006). Intergroup threat and outgroup attitudes: A meta-analytic review. *Personality and Social Psychology Review, 10*, 336–353.

Roccas, S., Horenczyk, G., & Schwartz, S. H. (2000). Acculturation discrepancies and well-being: The moderating role of conformity. *European Journal of Social Psychology, 30*, 323–334.

Ryder, A. G., Alden, L. E., & Paulhus, D. L. (2000). Is acculturation unidimensional or bidimensional? A head-to-head comparison in the prediction of personality, self-identity, and adjustment. *Journal of Personality and Social Psychology, 79*, 49–65.

Safdar, S., Struthers, W., & van Oudenhoven, J. P. (2009). Acculturation of Iranians in the United States, the United Kingdom, and the Netherlands. *Journal of Cross-Cultural Psychology, 40*, 468–491.

Saguy, T., Tausch, N., Dovidio, J. F., & Pratto, F. (2009). The irony of harmony. *Psychological Science, 20*(1), 114–121.

Sam, D. L. & Berry, J. W. (Eds.). (2006). *Cambridge handbook of acculturation psychology*. Cambridge: Cambridge University Press.

Sani, F. (Ed.). (2008). *Self continuity: Individual and collective perspectives*. New York: Psychology Press.

Sarrasin, O., Green, E. G. T., Fasel, N., Christ, O., Staerklé, C., & Clémence A. (2012). Opposition to anti-racism laws across Swiss municipalities: A multilevel analysis. *Political Psychology, 33*, 659–681.

Scheepers, P., Gijsberts, M., & Coenders, M. (2002). Ethnic exclusion in European countries. Public opposition to civil rights for legal migrants as a response to perceived ethnic threat. *European Sociological Review, 18*, 17–34.

Schlueter, E., Schmidt, P., & Wagner, U. (2008). Disentangling the causal relations of perceived group threat and outgroup derogation: Cross-national evidence from German and Russian panel surveys. *European Sociological Review, 24*, 567–581.

Schlueter, E., & Wagner, U. (2008). Regional differences matter: Examining the dual influence of the regional size of the immigrant population on derogation of immigrants in Europe. *International Journal of Comparative Sociology, 49*, 153–173.

Schmid, K., Tausch, N., Hewstone, M., Hughes, J., & Cairns, E. (2008). The effects of living in segregated vs. mixed areas in Northern Ireland: A simultaneous analysis of contact and threat effects in the context of micro-level neighbourhoods. *International Journal of Conflict and Violence, 2*, 56–71.

Schmitt, M. T., & Branscombe, N. R. (2002). The meaning and consequences of perceived discrimination in disadvantaged and privileged social groups. In W. Stroebe & M. Hewstone (eds.), *European Review of Social Psychology* (vol. 12, pp. 167–199). Chichester, UK: Wiley.

Schneider, S. L. (2008). Anti-immigrant attitudes in Europe: Outgroup size and perceived ethnic threat. *European Sociological Review, 24*, 53–67.

Sears, D. O., Citrin, J., Cheleden, S., & Van Laar, C. (1999). Cultural diversity and multicultural politics: Is ethnic balkanization psychologically inevitable? In D. Prentice and D. T. Miller (eds.), *Cultural divides: Understanding and overcoming group conflict* (pp. 35–79). New York: Russell Sage.

Sears, D. O., & Funk, C. (1991). The role of self-interest in social and political attitudes. *Advances in Experimental Psychology, 24*, 1–91.

Sears, D. O, & Henry, P. J. (2005). Over thirty years later: A contemporary look at symbolic racism and its critics. In M. P. Zanna (ed.), *Advances in experimental social psychology* (pp. 95–150). New York: Academic Press.

Semyonov, M., & Glikman, A. (2009). Ethnic residential segregation, social contacts, and anti-minority attitudes in European societies. *European Sociological Review, 25*, 693–708.

Semyonov, M., Raijman, R., & Gorodzeisky, A. (2006). The rise of anti-foreigner sentiment in European societies, 1988–2000. *American Sociological Review, 71*, 426–449.

Semyonov, M., Raijman, R., Yom Tov, A., & Schmidt, P. (2004). Population size, perceived threat, and exclusion: A multiple-indicators analysis of attitudes toward foreigners in Germany. *Social Science Research, 33*, 681–701.

Sherif, M. (1967). *Group conflict and cooperation: Their social psychology*. London: Routledge & Kegan Paul.

Sidanius, J., & Pratto, F. (1999). *Social dominance: An intergroup theory of social hierarchy and oppression*. New York: Cambridge University.

Sides, J., & Citrin, J. (2007). European opinion about immigration: The role of identities, interests and information. *British Journal of Political Science, 37*, 477–504.

Simon, B., & Ruhs, D. (2008). Identity and politicization among Turkish migrants in Germany: The role of dual identification. *Journal of Personality and Social Psychology, 95,* 1354–1366.

Smeekes, A., Verkuyten, M., & Poppe, E. (2011). Mobilizing opposition towards Muslim immigrants: National identification and the representation of national history. *British Journal of Social Psychology, 50,* 265–280.

Snauwaert, B., Soenens, B., Vanbeselaere, N., & Boen, F. (2003). When integration does not necessarily imply integration. *Journal of Cross-Cultural Psychology, 34,* 231–239.

Sniderman, P. M., Hagendoorn, L., & Prior, M. (2004). Predisposing factors and situational triggers: Exclusionary reactions to immigrant minorities. *American Political Science Review, 98,* 35–49.

Spears, R., Jetten, J., & Doosje, B. (2001). The (il)legitimacy of ingroup bias: From social reality to social resistance. In J. Jost & B. Major (eds.), *The psychology of legitimacy: Emerging perspectives on ideology, justice and intergroup relations* (pp. 332–362). Cambridge: Cambridge University Press.

Staerklé, C., Clémence, A., & Spini, D. (2011). Social representations: A normative and dynamic intergroup approach. *Political Psychology, 32,* 759–768.

Staerklé, C., Sidanius, J., Green, E. G. T., & Molina, L. (2010). Ethnic minority-majority asymmetry in national attitudes around the world: A multilevel analysis. *Political Psychology, 31,* 491–519.

Stephan, W. G., & Renfro, C. L. (2003). The role of threat in intergroup relations. In D. M. Mackie & E. R. Smith (Eds.), *From prejudice to intergroup emotions: Differentiated reactions to social groups* (pp. 191–207). New York: Psychology Press.

Stephan, W. G., & Stephan, C. W. (1985). Intergroup anxiety. *Journal of Social Issues, 41,* 157–175.

Strabac, Z., & Listhaug, O. (2008). Anti-Muslim prejudice in Europe: A multilevel analysis of survey data from 30 countries. *Social Science Research, 37,* 268–286.

Taylor, C. (1992). *Multiculturalism and the politics of recognition.* Princeton, NJ: Princeton University Press.

Thomas, W. I., & Znaniecki, F. (1918). *The Polish peasant in Europe and in America.* Chicago: University of Chicago Press.

Thomsen, L., Green, E. G. T., & Sidanius, J. (2008). We will hunt them down: How social dominance orientation and right-wing authoritarianism fuel ethnic persecution of immigrants in fundamentally different ways. *Journal of Experimental Social Psychology 44* (6), 1455–1464.

Turner, R. N., Hewstone, M., & Voci, A. (2007). Reducing explicit and implicit prejudice via direct and extended contact: The mediating role of self-disclosure and intergroup anxiety. *Journal of Personality and Social Psychology, 93,* 369–388.

van Oudenhoven, J. P., Prins, K. S., & Buunk, B. P. (1998). Attitudes of majority and minority members towards adaptation of immigrants. *European Journal of Social Psychology, 28,* 995–1013.

van Oudenhoven, J. P., Ward, C., & Masgoret, A.-M. (2006). Patterns of relations between immigrants and host societies. *International Journal of Intercultural Relations, 30,* 637–651.

Vedder, P., Sam, D. L., & Liebkind, K. (2007). The acculturation and adaptation of Turkish adolescents in north-western Europe. *Applied Developmental Science, 11,* 126–136.

Velasco González, K., Verkuyten, M., Weesie, J., & Poppe, E. (2008). Prejudice towards Muslims in the Netherlands: Testing integrated threat theory. *British Journal of Social Psychology, 47,* 667–685.

Verkuyten, M. (2005a). *The social psychology of ethnic identity.* European Monographs in Social Psychology. Hove, UK: Psychology Press.

Verkuyten, M. (2005b). Ethnic group identification and group evaluation among minority and majority groups: Testing the multiculturalism hypothesis. *Journal of Personality and Social Psychology, 88*, 121–138.

Verkuyten, M. (2005c). Immigration discourses and their impact on multiculturalism: A discursive and experimental study. *British Journal of Social Psychology, 44*, 223–240.

Verkuyten, M. (2006). Multicultural recognition and ethnic minority rights: A social identity perspective. *European Review of Social Psychology, 17*, 148–184.

Verkuyten, M. (2007). Religious group identification and inter-religious relations: A study among Turkish-Dutch Muslims. *Group Processes & Intergroup Relations, 10*, 341–357.

Verkuyten, M., & Brug, P. (2004). Multiculturalism and group status: The role of ethnic identification, group essentialism and Protestant ethic. *European Journal of Social Psychology, 34*, 647–661.

Verkuyten, M., & Yildiz, A. A. (2006). The endorsement of minority rights: The role of group position, national context, and ideological beliefs. *Political Psychology, 27*, 527–548.

Verkuyten, M., & Yildiz, A. A. (2009). Muslim immigrants and religious group feelings: self-identification and attitudes among Sunni and Alevi Turkish-Dutch. *Ethnic and Racial Studies, 32*, 1121–1142.

Voci, A., & Hewstone, M. (2003). Intergroup contact and prejudice toward immigrants in Italy: The mediational role of anxiety and the moderational role of group salience. *Group Processes & Intergroup Relations, 6*, 37–54.

Wagner, U., Christ, O., Pettigrew, T. F., Stellmacher, J., & Wolf, C. (2006). Prejudice and minority proportion: Contact instead of threat effects. *Social Psychology Quarterly, 69*, 380–390.

Weldon, S. A. (2006). The institutional context of tolerance for ethnic minorities: A comparative, multilevel analysis of western Europe. *American Journal of Political Science, 50*, 331–349.

Wilkes, R., Guppy, N., & Farris, L. (2007). Right-wing parties and anti-foreigner sentiment in Europe: Comment on Semyonov, Raijman and Gorodzeisky. *American Sociological Review, 72*, 831–840.

Wills, M. (2010). Psychological research and immigration policy. *Journal of Social Issues, 66*, 825–836.

Wimmer, A. (2004). Does ethnicity matter? Social categories and personal networks in three Swiss immigrant neighborhoods. *Ethnic and Racial Studies, 27*, 1–36.

Wolsko, C., Park, B., & Judd, C. (2006). Considering the Tower of Babel: Correlates of assimilation and multiculturalism among ethnic minority and majority groups in the United States. *Social Justice Research, 19*, 277–306.

Wright, S. C., & Lubensky, M. E. (2009). The struggle for social equality: Collective action versus prejudice reduction. In S. Demoulin, J.-P. Leyens, & J. F. Dovidio (eds.), *Intergroup misunderstandings: Impact of divergent social realities* (pp. 291–310). New York: Psychology Press.

Zagefka, H., & Brown, R. (2002). The relationship between acculturation strategies, relative fit and intergroup relations: Immigrant-majority relations in Germany. *European Journal of Social Psychology, 32*, 171–188.

Zárate, M. A., Garcia, B., Garza, A. A., & Hitlan, R. T. (2004). Cultural threat and perceived realistic group conflict as dual predictors of prejudice. *Journal of Experimental Social Psychology, 40*, 99–105.

Zick, A., Wagner, U., Van Dick, R., & Petzel, T. (2001). Acculturation and prejudice in Germany: Majority and minority perspectives. *Journal of Social Issues, 57*, 541–557.

CHAPTER 27

···

DISCRIMINATION

conditions, consequences, and "cures"

···

ANANTHI AL RAMIAH AND MILES HEWSTONE

THE stranglehold of discrimination on minority advancement, and its implications for harmonious intergroup relations, are vital areas of study and vigorous political debate. We review the large body of research on this topic in the broad field of social psychology, focusing where possible on political psychology. We start by defining discrimination and elucidating the extent to which discrimination is determined by prejudice. We argue that social psychology has been dominated by studies that assess prejudice, and strongly urge the necessity of directly studying discrimination. We then outline various conditions under which discrimination is likely to manifest, detail the forms it takes across a range of social and political contexts, and discuss its many consequences. This is followed by a discussion of a variety of strategies that have been shown to be effective at reducing prejudice and stereotyping, and at combatting discrimination directly. We conclude by suggesting that political psychologists have a considerable wealth of knowledge to tap when trying to understand the factors underlying discrimination, its consequences, and its possible "cures."

1. UNDERSTANDING DISCRIMINATION

···

While prejudice, stereotyping, and discrimination are closely linked and often coexist in the individual expressing social bias, social psychologists treat each as a distinct construct with unique properties. Prejudice has been characterized as an individual-level attitude toward, or evaluation of, a group, stereotypes as beliefs about the characteristics and traits of a group, and discrimination as behavior that favors one's group and intentionally or inadvertently harms another group. All three forms of social bias share in common that they sharpen group identities and intergroup differentiation and can lead to preservation of the status quo, particularly when shown by dominant group members.

1.1. Prejudice: The Root of Discrimination?

It has been said that stereotypes and prejudice lie at the root of discrimination. As is the case with all intrapsychic phenomena, none of these social biases can be assessed on the basis of objectively defined criteria. However, there is a range of overt and subtle ways to capture the impulses and evaluations that precede discrimination. In this section, we will discuss what each type of measure actually measures, and its relationship with discriminatory behaviors.

Explicit measures of prejudice are self-report measures in which participants state their attitudes about, or action tendencies toward, a particular target. These measures presume that participants are conscious of their evaluations and behavioral tendencies and are often constructed in a way that aims to reduce the amount of socially desirable responding. Implicit measures of prejudice capture the evaluations and beliefs that are automatically, often unconsciously, activated by the presence or thought of the target group (Dovidio, Kawakami, & Beach, 2001).

The Implicit Association Test (IAT) is the best-known and most widely used measure of implicit attitudes (Greenwald, McGhee, & Schwartz, 1998), which shows that we make connections more quickly between pairs of ideas that are presented to us when these ideas are already related in our minds (e.g., "white-good," "black-bad"), than when they are novel (e.g., "white-bad," "black-good") (for a more detailed explanation of tests of implicit attitudes, see Kinder, chapter 25, this volume; Taber & Young, chapter 17, this volume). The time taken to respond does not depend on any essential or accurate feature of the groups in question, but reflects well-learned cultural associations that automatically come to mind (see Blair, Judd, & Chapleau, 2004) and is one of the features of the IAT that its critics take issue with (Arkes & Tetlock, 2004). Such associations may also be born out of participants' knowledge of the objective association between race, poverty, and crime, or more simply, reactance that may be born out of participants' fear of appearing racist (Mitchell & Tetlock, 2006). Thus, holding certain implicit associations may not indicate that these associations are, in fact, *endorsed* by the individual.

Notwithstanding these reasonable concerns, research has identified the magnitude of the relationship between both explicit and implicit measures of prejudice, and discriminatory behaviors. Meta-analyses of the relationship between explicit prejudice and discrimination have reported a modest correlation between explicit prejudice and discrimination ($r = .32$, Dovidio, Brigham, Johnson, & Gaertner, 1996; $r = .36$, Greenwald, Poehlman, Uhlmann, & Banaji, 2009; $r = .38$, Kraus, 1995). Notwithstanding the moderate effect sizes, the fact that they are derived from studies conducted in a range of situations and intergroup contexts suggests the reliability of the relationships and the value of explicit measures. Meta-analyses of the relationship between implicit prejudice and discrimination have reported a weak to modest relationship ($r = .27$: Greenwald et al., 2009), though in the context of studies that dealt with black-white relations in the United States, Greenwald et al. (2009) found that the relationship between implicit measures and discrimination ($r = .24$) was stronger than that between explicit measures and discrimination ($r = .12$). What do these differences between explicit and implicit measures tell us about what they are measuring?

Greenwald et al. (2009) found that there is incremental validity of implicit and self-report measures, such that each uniquely predicts different aspects of behavior, and certain topics garner significant correlation between the two measures. In particular, when the topic is high in social sensitivity, meta-analytic findings report a weaker correlation between IAT and self-report measures than when the topic is low in sensitivity (Greenwald et al., 2009). It has been argued that the low correlation for high-sensitivity topics may be due to the introspective limits experienced by participants when encountering these issues (Hofmann, Gawronski, Gschwendner, Le, & Schmitt, 2005; Nisbett & Wilson, 1977). In other words, people's implicit attitudes, which are learned through decades of associations between traits/beliefs and the attitude object, may drive their behavior and may diverge from their explicit attitudes (Ranganath, Smith, & Nosek, 2008), which may be shaped, at least in part, by social norms that drive them to hold egalitarian attitudes (Dovidio & Gaertner, 2004).

In terms of implicit attitudes, the nonverbal behavior that may result from them can influence how others perceive us (Dovidio, Kawakami, & Gaertner, 2002) and can lead to a negative response from out-group members (Chen & Bargh, 1997), even if our behavior is inadvertent and at odds with our explicit attitudes toward the out-group, as demonstrated below in the studies by Word, Zanna, and Cooper (1974) and Dovidio et al. (2002). It is therefore vital that we find ways to reduce implicit bias, regardless of whether implicit measures reflect a true attitude or an environmental association (see Dasgupta, 2009, for a review). However, we must not neglect explicit attitudes, because as we will see below, they can also have very serious consequences in a range of social and political scenarios. While some research has demonstrated that implicit attitudes predict nonverbal behaviors and explicit measures predict verbal behaviors (see Dovidio, Kawakami, Johnson, Johnson, & Howard, 1997; Fazio, Jackson, Dunton, & Williams, 1995), recent research has shown that several behaviors depend simultaneously on automatic and controlled processes (Friese, Hofmann, & Schmitt, 2008).

2. Why Studying Prejudice Is Not Enough: An Argument for the Necessity of Studying Discrimination

Allport (1935) wrote that the *attitude* has come to be regarded as social psychology's "most distinctive and indispensable concept" (p. 798). However, what the foregoing discussion demonstrated is that, in general, both explicit and implicit measures of prejudice have, at best, a moderate relationship with discrimination. Thus, discrimination appears to be associated with a range of other factors such as normative and sociostructural features of the environment, and one's motivation and opportunity to control one's prejudice (see the MODE model below; Fazio, 1990)—factors that we will discuss in subsequent sections. Due to the many factors that inform behavior and the difficulty in measuring attitudes accurately (Ajzen & Fishbein, 1977), attitudes will always be imperfect predictors of discrimination. This highlights the necessity of studying prejudicial *behaviors* directly (Al Ramiah, Hewstone, Dovidio, & Penner, 2010).

As Baumeister, Vohs, and Funder (2007) and Simpson (2009) have noted, though the American Psychological Association declared the last decade to be the "Decade of Behavior," there was, and is still, a strong bias in the literature for studies that examine attitudes and stereotypes rather than behaviors. Further, the vast majority of social-psychological studies have investigated weaker forms of bias, as expressed by participants with relatively mild prejudice. Why is this?

Clearly there are cases in which it is unethical or impossible to measure a person's intergroup-related behavior. Studies with behavioral measures also take longer to set up and run and can be quite costly. Internal review boards tend to have fewer objections to studies that ask people questions compared to those in which they are observed in their natural or laboratory settings (Baumeister et al., 2007).

While these are valid concerns, we cannot overlook the danger in relying heavily on attitudinal measures, and this is demonstrated sharply in a set of studies by West and Brown (1975). In a real-life behavioral study, the researchers staged an emergency situation in which the female confederate had been bitten by an animal and asked for a small amount of money from a passing male participant in order to seek medical treatment at the nearby clinic. The severity of the emergency was manipulated, as was the attractiveness of the female confederate in need of help. In a simulation study of self-reported inclination to engage in certain behaviors, participants were given one of the same scenarios to *read* and saw a picture of the confederate who was seeking help. There were two major differences in the findings from the simulation and the real-life study. First, when asked about how much money they would give to help the person in distress, the simulation participants said they would give vastly more than the real-life participants actually gave. Second, the attractiveness of the confederate was an important predictor of how much was given in the real-life setting, with more attractive confederates receiving more money in the severe emergency situation. However, participants in the simulation study responded as if their behavior would not be influenced by the attractiveness of the confederate. These findings demonstrate, unsurprisingly, that people behave differently in the laboratory than they do in real life. Similar divergences have been found in other areas of the social and behavioral sciences (e.g., Holt & Laury, 2002; Nisbett & Wilson, 1977).

3. CONDITIONS FOR, AND CONSEQUENCES OF, DISCRIMINATION

The consequences of discrimination are pervasive, cumulative, and long-lasting. It has been argued that many people occupy segregated areas because of discrimination by members of the majority group, who prefer not to share neighborhoods with minority members and newcomers (Cater & Jones, 1978). Massey and Denton's (1993) seminal study, *American Apartheid*, pointed to the role of segregation in poverty, and more recent work has linked segregation, stress, and poor health (e.g., Massey, 2004). Further, discrimination across situations and time can give rise to cumulative disadvantage. Avoidance may appear harmless in any given situation, but, when aggregated across situations, such rejection can lead to entrenched social hierarchies and reduced social mobility. This is particularly problematic in situations where social networking matters (Heath & McMahon, 1997), such as employment, education, and healthcare. A history of discrimination can also be very damaging to mental health, and those who have been personally discriminated against and live in areas where people have a history of being discriminated against show greater depressive symptoms than those without a history of discrimination, even when controlling for relevant explanatory variables (Simons et al., 2002).

In this section, we will present findings on the extent to which discrimination is shaped by the influence of norms and aversive racism, by the impact of sociostructural relations and stereotyping, and by an individual's resources, disposition, and motivation. These studies will span a range of domains such as academic performance, prosocial behavior, the labor market, the judicial system, public policy, healthcare, and institutional practices. We will conclude this section with a discussion of the effects of discrimination in the domain of political behavior.

3.1. The Influence of Norms and Aversive Racism on Discrimination

It has been argued that many white Americans are afflicted by psychological conflict with regard to their racial attitudes in the post-civil rights era (Dovidio & Gaertner, 2004). Changing social norms prohibit prejudice and discrimination toward minority and other stigmatized groups (Crandall, Eshleman, & O'Brien, 2002), and over time these norms have, to varying degrees, been internalized. Based on explicit and implicit measures of prejudice, it has been demonstrated that a majority of Americans report very low levels of explicit prejudice, while they simultaneously score high on measures of implicit prejudice (Crosby, Bromley, & Saxe, 1980; Greenwald et al., 2009). This complex set of attitudes is said to give rise to aversive racism (Dovidio & Gaertner, 2004), a situation in which people regard prejudice as unjust and offensive, but remain unable to fully suppress their own biases.

According to Aversive Racism Theory, aversive racists tend not to discriminate in situations in which there are a clear set of norms as to what is just and unjust; discrimination would be obvious to others and to oneself, and aversive racists do not want to appear discriminatory and often do not actually want to be discriminatory (see Kinder, chapter 25, this volume, for a related discussion on symbolic racism). In such situations, aversive racists will be highly motivated to "do the right thing" and to avoid being deemed as racist in any way (Dovidio, Gaertner, Shnabel, Saguy, & Johnson, 2010). However, research has shown that aversive racists will systematically discriminate when appropriate behaviors are not clearly prescribed or when they can justify their behavior on the basis of some factor other than race (see Dovidio & Gaertner, 2004). Thus, aversive racism is associated with the same serious and deleterious consequences as the more old-fashioned types of racism.

Dovidio, Kawakami, and Gaertner (2002) conducted a multistage study with white university students, in which participants provided explicit and implicit measures of their attitudes toward blacks and engaged in a videotaped interaction task with white and black confederates separately. In the final stage of the study, the videotaped interactions were rated by independent judges on the friendliness of participants' nonverbal behaviors. The authors found that the explicit measure predicted participants' verbal friendliness and their self-perceived friendliness with the black partner, while the implicit measure predicted participants' nonverbal friendliness and the extent to which both confederate partners and observers felt that the participants were friendlier to white than black partners. The inconsistency of one's implicit and explicit attitudes explains why majority and minority group members may experience interethnic interactions in such divergent ways; majority group members refer to their explicit attitudes when thinking about interactions with out-group members, while minority group members seem to rely more on the majority group member's implicit attitude, as reflected in their nonverbal behaviors, to determine the friendliness of the interaction. Such perceptions on the part of minority group members, partially at least, drive their perceived discrimination (Richeson & Shelton, 2005).

Moving into the arena of prosocial behavior, discrimination against blacks in helping behaviors is more likely when participants could rationalize decisions not to help with reasons that had nothing to do with ethnicity. For example, using university students, Gaertner and Dovidio (1977) showed that, in an emergency situation, white participants were less likely to help black than white victims when the participant had the opportunity to diffuse responsibility over several other people who could potentially be called upon to help; however, black and white victims were helped equally when the participant was the only bystander. In a meta-analysis on helping behaviors, Saucier, Miller, and Doucet (2005) found that when helping was lengthier, riskier, more difficult, more effortful, and when potential helpers were further away from targets, whites gave less help to blacks than to fellow whites.

In terms of employment decisions, aversive racism can have very serious consequences. In Dovidio and Gaertner's (2000) study of how white university student participants made selection decisions in a hiring task, they found that white participants did not discriminate against black (compared to white) candidates when the candidate's qualifications were either strong or weak, but did discriminate when the decision was more ambiguous (i.e., when qualifications were middling). Echoing findings from the helping studies, in the ambiguous qualifications condition, participants were able to find alternative explanations (other than prejudice) for their unwillingness to hire black applicants. Investigating the same paradigm in Canada, Son Hing, Chung-Yan, Hamilton, and Zanna (2008) found that white Canadian participants faced with the task of hiring either an Asian or a white job applicant, both of whom had moderate qualifications, systematically selected the white applicant. The authors also found that implicit bias against Asians (as measured by the IAT) negatively predicted inclination to hire Asian applicants, while explicit bias did not. Augmenting the effect of ambiguous standards, and echoing research on race-based shifting standards (Biernat, Collins, Katzarska-Miller & Thompson, 2009), Hodson, Dovidio, and Gaertner (2002) showed that majority group members systematically altered the importance that they placed on various criteria in order to justify their less favorable views toward minority job applicants, in a way that reduced the importance of the criteria on which minority applicants exceled. These studies show that implicit prejudice has the potential to shape employment-related discrimination in systematic and far-reaching ways. Beyond experimental studies, in a critical review of field methods for studying discrimination, Devah Pager says: "we come to the conclusion that race has large effects on employment opportunities, with a black job seeker anywhere between 50 and 500 percent less likely to be considered by employers as an equally qualified white job applicant" (2007, p. 114). We will examine further implications of these findings in the section below on discrimination and political behavior.

While discrimination in healthcare may seem far removed from the study of political psychology, given the centrality of healthcare to political debate, we briefly discuss some studies that show how discrimination can occur in this arena. Echoing research on discrimination in ambiguous situations, LaVeist, Nuru-Jeter, and Jones (2003) have shown that when physicians had high discretion in their decision-making (such as when making a referral for a procedure), black patients were significantly less likely than white patients to be referred for a cardiac diagnostic test. However, among the black and white patients who *were* referred, there were no differences in the treatment they received. Penner, Albrecht, Coleman, and Norton (2007) argue that this is because treatment (unlike referral) represents an unambiguous situation and so there is less room for the influence of bias. In an experimental version of the LaVeist et al. study, Schulman, Berlin, Harless et al. (1999) found that white physicians were less likely to refer black than white confederate-patients for further testing to investigate their complaints of chest pain.

Penner et al. (2010) studied the effects of physician bias in interactions between black patients and nonblack physicians in a primary care facility in the United States. The patient participants completed a questionnaire on their health, while the physician participants completed measures of their explicit and implicit bias. The interactions between physician and patient were recorded, as were their immediate and longer-term reactions to the interaction. The patients had a less positive view of interactions and talked less with physicians who were low in explicit prejudice and high in implicit prejudice than they did with physicians who had any other combination of implicit and explicit prejudice. The low-explicit-prejudice, high-implicit-prejudice physicians represent the classic aversive racists, and black patients may have responded to these types of physicians most negatively because of the dissonance between the physician's view of themselves (possibly reflected in their friendly verbal behavior) and their actual (likely nonverbal) behaviors that betrayed their implicit prejudice.

3.2. The Impact of Sociostructural Relations and Stereotyping on Discrimination

The Stereotype Content Model (Fiske, Cuddy, Glick, & Xu, 2002) holds that stereotype content ranges along the two fundamental dimensions of warmth and competence (Bakan, 1966; Parsons & Bales, 1955; Wojciszke, 2005) and that each dimension is associated with particular sociostructural and emotional correlates. Social actors are cognizant of the impact of power relations on outcomes; they form—often ambivalent—stereotypes on the basis of the perceived status and competitiveness of groups, such that people tend to dislike those from high-status, and/or competitive, groups (Cuddy, Fiske, & Glick, 2007; Fiske et al., 2002).

The BIAS (Behaviors from Intergroup Affect and Stereotypes) Map extends the Stereotype Content Model's cognitive-affective framework to encompass behaviors (Cuddy et al., 2007). The warmth dimension of stereotypes predicts positive and negative active behavioral tendencies, while the secondary dimension of competence predicts more passive tendencies. Negative active and passive behaviors can be construed by targets as constituting discrimination and can have significant impact on the quality of their lives. Examples of negative passive behaviors are ignoring another's presence, not making eye contact with the person, and denying members of certain groups specific opportunities, while examples of negative active behaviors include supporting institutional racism and voting for anti-immigration political parties. Resonating with findings from aversive racism presented above, these examples show that discriminatory behaviors can range from the subtle to the overt and, further, that the particular views that we have about each out-group can determine the manifestation of discrimination.

Power plays a particularly important role in determining the extent to which people engage in stereotyping, and it has been suggested that people from high-power groups have a greater tendency to stereotype than do those from low-power groups. This tendency is particularly pernicious in domains in which success is stereotypically associated with the high-power group (Cleveland, Vescio, & Barnes-Farrell, 2004). In the labor market, for instance, Glick, Zion, and Nelson (1988) examined gender discrimination in hiring by asking professionals to evaluate bogus résumés of men and women for jobs that were either masculine (sales manager) or feminine (receptionist/secretary) in nature, thereby making gender stereotypes salient. Female applicants were consistently preferred for the job of receptionist or secretary, and male applicants were preferred for the job of sales manager, even when the applicants were not thought to differ in the degree to which they possessed masculine or feminine personality traits. The authors argued that employers may consider certain occupations to be gendered and thus hire on that basis rather than on the basis of individuating nongendered information about the applicant. Thus gender plays a disproportionate role in explaining hiring preferences for traditionally gendered occupations.

Social bias does not always manifest starkly in more/less likelihood of being hired but can have other more subtle manifestations in the labor market. Hebl, Foster, Mannix, and Dovidio (2002) had confederate "applicants" (blind to their condition) wear hats labeled with either "gay and proud" (stigmatizing condition) or "Texan and proud" (neutral condition) and apply for retail jobs. The results revealed that gay and lesbian applicants did *not* experience formal discrimination (i.e., no differences in being told there were jobs available, being able to fill out applications, or in receiving job callbacks) relative to applicants in the neutral condition, but they did experience more subtle and informal discrimination (the average interaction length was shorter with stigmatized applicants, and the interactions were also rated by observers as having less warmth, increased interaction distance, and more rudeness) than did assumed heterosexual applicants. While these results are consistent with expectations based on the BIAS Map, they also resonate with Aversive Racism Theory, because of the nonverbal level at which negative attitudes toward the openly gay confederates were shown, which seems to imply a negative implicit attitude. These results also echo the findings from the classic Word, Zanna, and Cooper (1974, Study 1) research in which white university students interviewed white or black confederate applicants. Black applicants received less immediacy (i.e., less eye contact, more interpersonal distance, less direct shoulder orientation, and more backward leaning; see Mehrabian, 1969), and were given shorter interview times than white applicants.

Moving from the labor market to the legal system, there is disturbing evidence that shows that the process of categorizing people into ethnic groups may call to mind certain stereotypes and evaluations that result in split-second decisions with possibly fatal consequences, such as are routinely taken by armed police officers. Correll, Park, Judd, and Wittenbrink (2002) conducted several studies to understand whether implicit associations of ethnicity with certain group stereotypes might inform a police officer's decision to shoot a suspect. In a simple videogame, black or white targets holding guns or other nonthreatening objects (such as mobile phones), appeared in real-world backgrounds, and the participants (who were white university students and adults from the wider population) were told to "shoot" armed targets and to "not shoot" unarmed targets. The authors found that white participants had a tendency to make more false alarms (i.e., shoot the unarmed target) when the target was black rather than white, and to make more misses (i.e., to not shoot the armed target) when the target was white rather than black. Mirroring this finding, white participants made the correct decision to shoot an armed target more quickly if the target was black than if he was white, while they decided to "not shoot" an unarmed target more quickly if he was white rather than black. Thus, both the response latency and error results show that people use ethnicity to disambiguate potentially threatening stimuli.

In one of the studies, the authors also tapped participants' personal levels of explicit prejudice, their endorsement of negative stereotypes of blacks, and their awareness of the culturally endorsed stereotype of blacks. They did not find personal levels of prejudice or personal endorsement of negative stereotypes to be significantly associated with shooter bias. However, the authors found that people who reported greater awareness of the cultural stereotype were more likely to exhibit shooter bias, even once their personal endorsement of the stereotype was controlled for. This finding suggests that it is knowledge of the cultural stereotype that is at work rather than one's own explicit prejudice. Such cultural associations can be powerful predictors of behavior in situations where we are required to react very quickly, and with little time for controlled or deliberative processes to operate. This research once again demonstrates that "best intentions," while very important in a range of domains, may sometimes be too difficult to access at times of emergency.

Moving away from split-second decisions to those that afford (and demand) greater deliberation, researchers have studied discrimination in criminal sentencing, an especially important issue given the overrepresentation of ethnic minority group members in crime statistics and in the jail system. Blair et al.(2004) studied judge biases in criminal sentencing using data from the Department of Corrections in Florida, which has a web page for every incarcerated inmate (including their criminal record, sentence, and a court "mug shot"), and had raters assess the extent to which inmates possessed Afrocentric features. Afrocentric features refer to features deemed to be typical of African Americans: darker skin, fuller lips, and broader noses (Pizzi, Blair, & Judd, 2005); it is well documented that possession of Afrocentric features is likely to lead to greater categorization as black, which in turn is likely to lead to stereotypic inferences about that individual (Blair, Judd, Sadler, & Jenkins, 2002; Eberhardt, Davies, Purdie-Vaughns, & Johnson, 2006). Controlling for criminal history and crime type, Blair et al. (2004) found that inmates with more Afrocentric features tended to have received a judicial sentence that was on average eight months longer than those with less Afrocentric features.

Up until now, we have considered how stereotypes shape the behaviors of individuals from groups that have the power to discriminate. We will now assess some of the consequences for the targets of stereotypes and discrimination. In their classic research Word et al. (1974, Study 2) randomly assigned white applicants to be interviewed by a confederate who would treat the applicant as if they were either "white" or "black" (based on the subtle discrimination identified in Study 1 and discussed earlier). The authors demonstrated that when white participants were treated like blacks, they responded with nervousness, rated the interviewers as being less adequate and friendly, and performed poorly in the interview, compared to participants who were not shown such subtle discriminatory behavior. This study powerfully illustrates that negative stereotypes about an out-group can give rise to negative passive/subtle behaviors, which in turn can have anxiety-invoking and performance-reducing consequences for the recipients of such subtle behaviors. If people feel that they have been discriminated against (either personally or fraternally), they tend to have a range of negative work-related reactions, such as greater job stress among black women (Mays, Coleman, & Jackson, 1996), mistrust and unresponsiveness to critical feedback among blacks (Cohen, Steele, & Ross, 1999), and lower feelings of power among women (Gutek, Cohen, & Tsui, 1996).

Closely related to this finding is the wealth of research on stereotype threat, which is a debilitating concern that one will be evaluated on the basis of one's negative group stereotype (Steele & Aronson, 1995). This threat has been shown to be related to underperformance in a range of settings such as education (Steele & Aronson, 1995), employment

(Darley & Gross, 1983), and sports (Stone, 2002), and across a range of target groups involving the negative stereotypes associated with ethnicity (Steele & Aronson, 1995), gender (Spencer, Steele, & Quinn, 1999), socioeconomic status (Croizet & Claire, 1998), and mental illness (Quinn, Kahng, & Crocker, 2004). As a consequence of negative stereotyping and subtle discriminatory behaviors, underperformance can lead to the perpetuation of unequal and unfair outcomes. Further, members of lower-status groups may need to become better qualified than powerful group members (Biernat & Kobrynowicz, 1997), in order to compensate for being stereotyped as poorly qualified and incompetent. Thus members of lower-status groups are penalized for their group membership, a phenomenon sometimes referred to in American common parlance as the "black tax." And when members of such groups do succeed, but are then part of a minority group that represents less than 15% of the total group, they fall prey to "tokenism" (Kanter, 1977), where their group membership is highly and consistently salient. Tokens often report feeling vulnerable, have lower performance and appraisals, and are afforded fewer opportunities to advance (Dovidio & Hebl, 2005; Niemann & Dovidio, 1998). Thus it seems that the deck is stacked against members of lower-status groups who risk failing because of self-fulfilling prophecies and stereotype threat, may be liable to a "black tax" that makes them feel as if they need to work harder to compensate for their group's status, and then vulnerable to the negative distinctiveness and pressures that may result from tokenism.

3.3. The Effect of Resources, Dispositions, and Motivation on Discrimination

Given the modest correlation between implicit and explicit attitudes and discriminatory behaviors, in this section we will consider various factors that moderate the relationship between attitudes and behavior in an effort to elucidate when we might be able to reliably expect that a person's group-related attitudes will determine their discriminatory behaviors. Fazio (1990) developed the MODE (Motivation and Opportunities as Determinants of Behavior) model to explain that the extent to which individuals based their decisions and behaviors on deliberative processing, depending on their motivation and opportunity to do so. Recent research has confirmed the importance of these factors and suggests other moderators of the relationship between attitudes and behavior.

In their extensive review of the literature, Friese et al. (2008) found that the ability of implicit measures to predict behavior varied greatly across studies, and that both the opportunity, and, to a lesser degree, the motivation to control one's behaviors are key moderators. Any factors that inhibit opportunity or motivation to control should lead to greater reliance on automatic, as opposed to deliberative, processing, and increase the correspondence between implicit attitude and behavior. For example, implicit measures predict nonverbal behaviors better for individuals with low behavioral control and low awareness of egalitarian beliefs, as compared to individuals who have higher control or who are more conscious of egalitarianism (Dasgupta & Rivera, 2006). Greenwald et al.

(2009) found that explicit attitudes were predictive of deliberative behaviors (such as consumer and political choices) for which we would expect high degrees of controllability. They also found that implicit attitudes were predictive of those behaviors over which the participant could not be expected to have much control, possibly due to long-established associations (e.g., intergroup attitudes).

It has also been shown that dispositional and situational factors unrelated to opportunity and motivation to control can moderate this relationship. For example, from a situational perspective, one's mood impacts the depth of information processing (Bless, 2001), independently of variations in opportunity and motivation, while from a dispositional perspective, one's preference for intuition (over deliberation) guides the way in which people process information, which then determines the extent to which their implicit attitudes predict behavior (Hofmann & Baumert, 2007, as cited in Friese et al., 2008). Friese et al. (2008) suggest that these moderators share in common the degree to which the central executive is impaired. This determines how information is processed and cognitive resources are distributed (Baddeley, 1990), with impairment giving implicit measures increased predictive validity.

3.4. Discrimination and Political Behavior

How do the findings discussed in the preceding sections extend into the realm of political behavior? Kinder (chapter 25, this volume) demonstrates that race plays a pivotal role in voting decisions; when presented with candidates who are equivalent on all characteristics except race, white participant-voters prefer candidates of their own race, and this is more so for participants who are higher in prejudice (e.g., Sigelman, Sigelman, Walkosz, & Nitz, 1995). Echoing Dovidio and Gaertner's (2000) findings with regard to attributional ambiguity in the hiring task discussed above, Moskowitz and Stroh (1994) found that white participants who were prejudiced toward black candidates attributed negative characteristics and unfavorable policy positions to these candidates, thereby justifying their choice not to vote for them.

In the world of real voter choice, there was much talk of a "postracial" America when President Obama won approximately 53% of the vote in 2008. However, an analysis of voting choice by voter race indicates that approximately 95% of blacks, 67% of Hispanics, and 43% of whites voted for Obama, exemplifying in the real world the laboratory finding that whites tend to vote for white candidates and blacks for black candidates (Lublin, 1997). Payne et al. (2010) measured voters' explicit and implicit prejudice several months before the 2008 US presidential elections, and then asked participants whom they voted for after the election. Controlling for party identification, and a range of other variables, they found that people higher in explicit prejudice were more likely to vote for John McCain, the white Republican candidate, and less likely to vote for Barack Obama. Controlling for explicit prejudice, high implicit prejudice also predicted less likelihood of voting for Obama, but did not predict voting for McCain. Rather, voters high in implicit prejudice were more likely to abstain, or vote for an independent candidate.

Racial groups are very broad categories, and, as we know, there is much diversity contained within each. As Blair et al. (2004) showed, prisoners with more Afrocentric features tended to have received harsher judicial sentences than those with less Afrocentric features. What is the impact of such intracategory differentiation on voter decision-making? Terkildsen (1993) examined the effects of black candidates' skin color on white voter choice in her experiment using white adults from Kentucky. She found that controlling for self-monitoring tendencies, dark-skinned black candidates were less likely to garner votes than otherwise identical light-skinned black candidates. Those with high levels of prejudice were particularly negative in their evaluations of dark-skinned black candidates. Thus dark-skinned political candidates face a double jeopardy of having their race and the pigment of their skin count against them, while light-skinned candidates (of whom President Obama is an example) enjoy something of a "pigment-dividend." If these politicians are also ideologically unlike their average black contemporaries (for example, the light-skinned Colin Powell and Condoleeza Rice were Republicans and did not have an overtly problack agenda), they enjoy further dividends, because of the likelihood that they are "subtyped" as unique members of their group, thus protecting them from being enveloped in the negative black stereotype (Kinder, chapter 25, this volume). In the UK, Baroness Sayeeda Warsi, a Muslim woman, who is currently co-chair of the Conservative Party, provides a similar example. Her right-wing political attitudes make her a "safe" choice for party members, who also benefit from being able to hold her up as evidence of their egalitarian attitudes, her personal qualities notwithstanding.

However, as discussed above, such anomalous candidates risk being tokens, rather than necessarily being the forerunners of a significant change in public opinion. For example, being a female candidate with conservative political views can prove to be a more arduous struggle than being a female candidate with liberal views. Given that women are, on the whole, regarded as more liberal than men (Newport, 2009), female Republican candidates may struggle to be endorsed by members of their party (Lawless & Pearson, 2008). This finding is corroborated by statistics that show virtually no increase in the number of female Republican candidates who ran for a seat in the US House of Representatives between 1992 and 2008, compared to a 37% increase in the number of female Democratic candidates in the same period (Center for American Women and Politics, 2008).

Stereotypes play a key role in explaining voters' views of political candidates. Jibing perfectly with the Stereotype Content Model (and based on the agency-communion paradigm; see Powell & Butterfield, 1979), researchers have found that people regard traits related to warmth and communality to be feminine traits, while those related to competence and agency to be male traits (Huddy & Cassese, 2011), and it is the latter that are linked to strong and effective leadership (Eagly & Carli, 2007). Meta-analytic findings by Koenig, Eagly, Mitchell, and Ristikari (2011) support the idea that stereotypes of leaders are culturally masculine—across a range of studies, men are judged to exemplify leaders more than women are; leadership stereotypes are agency- rather than communion-based, and are more masculine than feminine in nature. Hearteningly, the authors found that males rather than females are more likely to subscribe to this masculine view, and that, over time, the masculine construal of leadership has diminished. Further, the effects of gender on actual vote choice are contingent and vary with which issues are most salient in a given context. Experimental evidence has shown that elections that are based on issues that have a strong empathetic tenor (such as education, healthcare and poverty), are believed to favor female politicians, who are, however, at a disadvantage when faced with "tougher" issues such as those to do with the military, defense, and crime (Sanbonmatsu, 2003). However, while some elections may favor female candidates, elections for highest office are believed to accord them a significant disadvantage. Funk (1999) has shown that voters tend to rate typically feminine and communal traits such as warmth and compassion as less essential for presidential personality than masculine and competence traits. Interestingly, voters also tend to rate "masculine" issues such as defense as more pivotal than "feminine" issues such as social welfare policy in the run-up to an election (Dolan, 2009).

3.5. Summary

Many societies around the world espouse egalitarianism, and the evidence seems to suggest that the citizens of these societies are strongly influenced by these norms. Yet they seem to struggle with deeply held, implicit, negative attitudes toward various outgroups. The result is an aversive racism in which people try to be egalitarian in their dealing with others and yet are unable to suppress their implicit biases, which usually surface when people can discriminate against out-group members while attributing their behavior to nonracial reasons. Implicit attitudes are closely connected to the stereotypes that people have about out-groups, because people often learn the content of stereotypes very early in their lives and are constantly exposed to these negative associations over time. While explicit negative stereotypes have been shown to have very negative consequences, implicit stereotypes, which people may not even realize that they hold, can have often subtle, sometimes dire, consequences in everyday life, especially when people have little opportunity for deliberation.

As we will see in the next section, people have a strong motivation to behave in a fair manner, because there are strong sanctions against doing anything else. However, social situations are not always clear-cut, and there is often a great deal of ambiguity and scope for discretion. In such situations, it seems that discrimination is multiply-, possibly even over-, determined. However, if people are given the opportunity to engage in deliberative thinking and can be sufficiently motivated to attend to individuating information, then discrimination need not be an inevitable outcome of ambiguous social situations. In the next section we will discuss various means by which discrimination can be combated.

4. "Curing" and Combating Discrimination

Though there is only a modest relationship between attitudes and behavior, we believe that any effort that aims at creating a fairer world in which people have equal opportunities must be two-pronged and combat both prejudice and discrimination. In this section we discuss some strategies that have been proposed to reduce prejudice and stereotyping, and those that work directly to combat discrimination. Our reasoning is that prejudice has a forward-flowing effect on discrimination, and thus reducing prejudice should result in fewer incidences of discrimination. Simultaneously, combating discrimination should result in people re-evaluating their attitudes over time in order to bring them into line with current norms and laws.

4.1. Reducing Prejudice and Stereotyping

4.1.1. Self-Regulation

Research by Monteith and her colleagues demonstrates that we have the capacity for the de-automatization of our biases (Monteith et al., 2010). They propose a detailed model of the processes through which discriminatory tendencies can be inhibited, and, over time, reversed. The Self-Regulation of Prejudice Model (Monteith, 1993; Monteith & Mark, 2005) presents a series of processes that people—who are intrinsically or extrinsically motivated to be unprejudiced—go through when their automatic stereotypes are activated and brought to consciousness. They posit that the activation of stereotypes leads individuals to engage in a response that may be at odds with internal and/or external standards of behavior, echoing the predictions of Aversive Racism Theory. The awareness of this discrepant response is associated with behavioral inhibition, in which people momentarily interrupt their response. Higgins (1987) has argued that this gives them pause to feel guilty or disappointed (if they are internally motivated to be unprejudiced), or to feel discomfort or threat (if they are externally motivated to be unprejudiced). This is followed by a brief period of retrospective reflection in which individuals will expend resources toward committing to memory various features of the situation and environment, which go on to act as cues for control of discrepant responding in the future. Monteith et al. (2010) explain that, theoretically, this entire process should occur in milliseconds. Research has demonstrated the empirical validity of this model (Monteith, 1993; Monteith, Ashburn-Nardo, Voils, & Czopp, 2002) and it has been validated by social neuroscientific assessments of various brain areas implicated in the processes (Amodio, Devine, & Harmon-Jones, 2007). However, this model will prove ineffective at controlling the experience and expression of bias for those who are uninterested in the equality between groups, and who may be high in social dominance orientation, which is a measure of an individual's preference for hierarchy within a social system (Sidanius, Pratto, Martin, & Stallworth, 1991; see also Sidanius & Kurzban, chapter 7, this volume). For such individuals, discriminatory tendencies may need to be inhibited through external regulation, that is, through powerful sanction by superiors and through discrimination lawsuits (Henry, 2010), as we will see shortly.

4.1.2. *Intergroup Contact*

Intergroup contact has long been put forward as an effective way in which to combat prejudice. Significant support was provided for the prejudice-reducing effects of intergroup contact from a meta-analysis of over 500 studies conducted by Pettigrew and Tropp (2006). The authors found that there was a significant negative relationship between face-to-face intergroup contact and prejudice ($r = -.22$, $p <.0001$), with an effect size comparable to those for the relationship between condom use and sexually transmitted HIV (Weller, 1993) and between passive smoking and the incidence of lung cancer at work (Wells, 1998).

Allport (1954) has argued that effective contact needs to be based on more than a "warm body" (Sampson, 1986, p. 182) approach to desegregated intergroup relations. The contact situation should, if possible, allow participants to interact with equal status; encourage cooperation and promote common goals; and be normative, that is, it should have institutional support (Allport, 1954). This means that political elites and leadership have a strong role to play in demonstrating that intergroup diversity is a valuable aspect of a country/organization and that intergroup contact should be cultivated. In addition, successful contact situations should allow for the development of friendships through meaningful and repeated contact (Amir, 1969; Pettigrew, 1998; Williams, 1947). Pettigrew and Tropp (2006) found that for majority group samples, contact situations that met Allport's conditions resulted in a larger prejudice-reduction effect size than contact situations that did not. It is instructive to think of these conditions as facilitating rather than essential (Pettigrew, 1998), since as Pettigrew and Tropp (2006) demonstrate, positive (but diminished) contact effects exist even in the absence of the fulfillment of all these conditions.

We must, however, be mindful that different factors shape intergroup relations and perceptions for majority and minority group members (Devine, Evett, & Vasquez-Suson, 1996; Devine & Vasquez, 1998). Pettigrew and Tropp conducted a meta-analysis of contact effects by majority versus minority group status (Tropp & Pettigrew, 2005), and found that the contact effect was weaker for members of minority than majority groups, and that the facilitating conditions were not significantly predictive of the contact-prejudice relationship for minority group samples.

In their Mutual Differentiation Model, Hewstone and Brown (1986) and Brown and Hewstone (2005) argue for the maintenance of intergroup salience during contact encounters that otherwise embody the various facilitating conditions discussed above. Group salience is maintained by structuring contact to occur between individuals who are sufficiently typical or representative of their groups. There has been much research to support the roles of group salience and perceived typicality in promoting the effects of contact to generalize beyond the immediate interpersonal contact situation to the out-group as a whole (see Brown & Hewstone, 2005, for a review).

Hewstone and Brown (1986) hold that when maintaining group salience, intergroup comparisons are inevitable. In order to reduce prejudice, the contact situation should allow for the recognition of mutual superiorities and inferiorities in various domains, so that group members can, through socially creative comparisons, maintain positive in-group distinctiveness. Their findings are not, however, without caveats. Brown and Hewstone (2005) caution that in contexts where groups have a history of intergroup tension and animosity, group salience and perceived typicality of out-group members may lead to more prejudice against out-group members. In such fraught contexts, contact may initially best be kept personalized, as suggested by the decategorization model of intergroup contact (Brewer & Miller, 1984; 1988), but we would argue for a move toward group salience as relations between groups became less fraught, in order for the positive effects of contact to generalize to produce group-level prejudice reduction.

Intergroup contact is more powerful if it is able to generalize beyond the immediate contact situation to encompass other groups outside that situation (Brown & Hewstone, 2005; Pettigrew, 2009; 1998; Pettigrew & Tropp, 2006). Several studies have found evidence of what Pettigrew (2009) calls the "Secondary Transfer Effect." Tausch et al. (2010) report data showing that this effect can be explained through attitude generalization, which is the process by which attitudes that one has about one out-group (e.g., an ethnoreligious out-group) generalize to other out-groups (e.g., racial minorities; homosexuals). And moving beyond prejudice, intergroup contact has been shown to have positive effects on a range of other important outcomes such as forgiveness and trust (Hewstone & Cairns, 2001), and attitude strength (Vonofakou, Hewstone, & Voci, 2007).

Several mechanisms have been shown to mediate the contact effect, that is, to explain *how* intergroup contact reduces prejudice. Intergroup anxiety (Stephan & Stephan, 1985), empathy and perspective-taking (Batson, Lishner, Cook, & Sawyer, 2005), knowledge (Robbins, Cooper, & Bender, 1992), realistic and symbolic threat (Stephan & Stephan, 2000), self-disclosure (Turner, Hewstone, & Voci, 2007), and cognitive representations (Dovidio, Gaertner, & Loux, 2000) have all been shown to be consistent mediators of the contact effect. Of all of these, intergroup anxiety has emerged as the most powerful mediator (Pettigrew & Tropp, 2008).

While there has been a treasure trove of work examining the effects of intergroup contact and its processes, relatively little work has assessed the effectiveness of intergroup contact in real-world interventions. We evaluated a nationwide government intervention to reduce prejudice and promote national unity in Malaysia (Al Ramiah & Hewstone, 2012) and found that the intergroup contact-based intervention maintained out-group attitudes (but did not improve them), and the changes associated with the intervention yielded only small effect sizes; on the whole, intervention participants did not show significantly greater improvement than control participants. We highlighted some conditions that may have led to the negligible changes, such as the unbalanced ethnic ratio of majority to minority participants. We believe, like Paluck and Green

(2009), that it is vitally important to study the effectiveness of such interventions in the field, to further understand real-world conditions that may constrain their effectiveness.

Further, Wright and Lubensky (2008) caution that interventions that create situations of pleasant intergroup contact between members of high- and lower-status groups can have the negative effect of reducing subgroup identification for low-status group members, and this, in turn, can make them less likely to support their group in taking collective action aimed at changing the social status quo (Wright, 2001). However, our evaluation of a structured contact intervention in Malaysia showed that Indian participants, who were members of the smallest, and lowest-status, minority group, did not experience a reduction in ethnic identification, and this was despite maintaining high levels of superordinate (national) identification (Al Ramiah & Hewstone, 2012). This finding seems to provide support, particularly for minority group members, for a dual-identity model of intergroup relations, in which people are highly identified simultaneously with their subordinate (ethnic) and superordinate (national) groups (Dovidio, Gaertner, & Kafati, 2000). For further discussion of the role of identity strength (particularly in political cohesion), see Huddy (chapter 23, this volume).

There is often a misunderstanding between "diversity" in terms of people from different groups living in and merely cohabiting the same society, and direct intergroup *contact*, which involves actual, face-to-face contact between members of different groups. Mere cohabitation is an imperfect predictor of contact (see Alexander & Tredoux, 2010; Dixon & Durrheim, 2003), and physical proximity can often be associated with coexistence rather than meaningful contact of the kind that Allport (1954) prescribed (e.g., see Hamilton & Bishop, 1976). Neighborhood studies that aim to assess the effect of diversity on generalized trust and other intergroup perceptions must take into account the amount of actual intergroup contact that neighbors have with one another. Stolle, Soroka, and Johnston (2008) found that people who lived in diverse areas and regularly talked with their neighbors reported higher levels of trust than those living in diverse areas but who spoke only a little or not at all with their neighbors. This finding demonstrates that the absence of contact in the face of diversity may have negative implications for intergroup relations and people's sense of generalized trust.

However, the issue of selection effects in the choice of neighborhood remains a problem for neighborhood studies, particularly with cross-sectional data. How can we be certain that diversity, and the intergroup contact that it can promote, predicts trust, rather than it being the case that people with high levels of trust move into more diverse neighborhoods? To some extent, the selection effects of intergroup contact have been addressed in longitudinal studies that show that there is a reciprocal relationship between intergroup contact and attitudes such that contact predicts attitudes, even when accounting for the effect that attitudes have on contact (e.g., Levin, van Laar, & Sidanius, 2003). Neighborhood studies are somewhat more problematic because the longitudinal horizon necessary in order to determine whether diversity (and contact) predict attitudes or whether people with better attitudes move into more diverse neighborhoods would be considerably longer than the average longitudinal study in the field.

Finally, in the absence of opportunities for direct intergroup contact (or when it is not desirable), indirect forms of contact may also be able to reduce prejudice (Hewstone, 2009). Indirect contact can take several forms, such as extended contact, imagined contact (Turner, Crisp, & Lambert, 2007), contact via the Internet (Amichai-Hamburger & McKenna, 2006), and contact via the media—also known as parasocial contact (Schiappa, Gregg, & Hewes, 2005). Paluck (2009) provides a very compelling evidence from a field experiment in which parasocial contact was used to improve intergroup relations in Rwanda. Of these various indirect forms of contact, extended contact has received the most research attention to date (Dovidio, Eller, & Hewstone, 2011). Extended contact refers to the knowledge that an individual has of an in-group member's direct contact with out-group members. Wright et al. (1997) have shown that when controlling for direct contact, those people who have extended contact report less out-group prejudice than those who do not.

While extended contact has great value in promoting intergroup harmony, particularly in situations where there are few opportunities for contact, or when intergroup relations are fraught, an even more minimalist type of contact also offers promising possibilities. In fact, as argued by proponents of imagined contact theory, actual contact experiences may not be necessary to improve intergroup relations (Turner et al., 2007). These authors showed that simply imagining a conversation with an out-group member resulted in participants having significantly lower levels of prejudice than those who had not imagined such contact, and further, participants viewed the out-group as more variable in the imagined contact condition.

As more research is conducted on indirect forms of contact, meta-analytic work is needed to determine the effectiveness of these various kinds of contact. What is clear at present is that intergroup contact is a powerful and flexible means for reducing prejudice across a wide range of settings.

4.1.3. *Multiple, Cross-Cutting, and Superordinate Identities*

The multiple categorization approach to identification holds that individuals can attend to and make use of multiple categories simultaneously. The logical consequence of this is that individuals are afforded the cognitive capacity to perceive others in a more differentiated manner, and self-definition in terms of such multiple social categories tends to be associated with more positive evaluation of out-groups (Brewer, Ho, Lee, & Miller, 1987; Crisp & Hewstone, 2007). In general, the crossing of two categories to create mixed category groups (an instance of dual identity) has the potential to reduce intergroup prejudice and discrimination (Crisp, Walsh, & Hewstone, 2006).

The common in-group identity model (Gaertner & Dovidio, 2000) proposes the redefinition of group boundaries so that previous out-group members are subsumed into a new superordinate group (Gaertner, Dovidio, Anastasio, Bachman, & Rust, 1993). Gaertner, Mann, Dovidio, Murrell, and Pomare (1990) manipulated categorization by seating participants in either one large group or two smaller groups, where they took part in various cooperative within-group tasks. In the one-group situation (the recategorized group representation), participants reported more positive out-group attitudes than in the two-group (categorization representation) situation. Further, results from research in Northern Ireland (Schmid et al., in press) and Malaysia (Al Ramiah, 2009) show that respondents who self-categorized in terms of the superordinate identity (e.g., Northern Irish or Malaysian) tended to display lower levels of in-group bias than did respondents choosing subordinate categories (e.g., Catholic or Protestant; Malay, Chinese, or Indian).

These results notwithstanding, a common in-group identity may only be short-lived, or unrealistic in the face of powerful ethnic and racial categorizations, and this is especially likely for groups who have a history of intergroup conflict (Hewstone, 1996). Sen (2006), recollecting his experience of Hindu-Muslim riots in his native India, referred to the "speed with which the broad human beings of January were suddenly transformed into the ruthless Hindus and fierce Muslims of July" (p. 2). Further, recategorization may also not be equally effective for majority and minority group members; Mummendey and Wenzel (1999) have argued that when a superordinate category is invoked, the majority group's values and attributes may be treated as the default values and attributes of the superordinate, common identity. Such "in-group projection" can clearly represent a symbolic threat (Stephan & Stephan, 2000) to minority group members and may sow the seeds for intergroup discord (Brown, 2000).

Relatedly, research has found that majority and minority members differ in their acculturation preferences (Plaut, 2002; van Oudenhoven, Prins, & Buunk, 1998) and this leads them to prefer different group representations (Dovidio, Gaertner, & Kafati, 2000; Plaut, Thomas, & Goren, 2009). As stated by Dovidio et al. (2008), majority group members tend toward assimilationist acculturation preferences for minority group members, and a common in-group identity. Minority members, on the other hand, tend toward integrationist acculturation (see also Green & Staerklé, chapter 26, this volume). Based on research with white and minority college students, Dovidio, Gaertner, and Kafati (2000) found that positive intergroup contact led to positive out-group attitudes for both majority and minority group members but was mediated by different group representations dependent on group status. Specifically, for white participants, the effect was mediated by a one-group representation of the groups, while for ethnic minority participants it was mediated by a dual-identity representation. These results suggest the vital importance of paying attention to societal features of the intergroup context, such as the status hierarchy and power relations between groups, when considering the effects of social identification. They also highlight that an intervention or approach that is effective in improving intergroup relations for one group may actually cause them to deteriorate for another group.

Just as there is internal diversity within categories, people also contain diversity within themselves. Social identity complexity refers to the perceived interrelationships among individuals' multiple in-groups, and the degree to which people consider their various in-groups to be similar to one another, and/or to overlap (Roccas & Brewer, 2002). A number of studies have found that social identity complexity was significantly associated with a range of social attitudes and tolerance measures, including greater support for multiculturalism and affirmative action, and attitudes toward specific outgroups

(Brewer & Pierce, 2005; Roccas & Brewer, 2002; Schmid, Hewstone, Tausch, & Cairns, 2009; see also Tyler and van der Toorn, chapter 20, this volume).

4.1.4. *Training to Alter Social-Cognitive Associations*

Kawakami, Dovidio, and Van Kamp (2005) investigated the effects of social cognitive associative training on a job candidate selection. They found that participants who had been trained by making counterstereotypic gender associations were less likely to display gender bias. Other research using the IAT has shown that exposure to counterstereotypic exemplars of a social group decreased bias in both the short term and over longer periods of time (Dasgupta & Rivera, 2008), as did asking participants to visualize a counterstereotypical exemplar (Blair, Ma, & Lenton, 2001). Given that stereotype activation, as we have seen, plays an important role in how political candidates are perceived, this body of research offers promise for reorientating the way people perceive political candidates and make voting choices.

Relatedly, we briefly discuss research on associative training that comes from experience with the attitude object. Correll et al. (2007) were interested in studying whether police officers did better on the shooter-identification task than laypeople (Correll et al., 2002). They conducted a study in which they gave actual police officers the same response latency task as the one described above (in section 3.2). They found that police officers demonstrated bias in the latencies of their correct responses, that is, automatic associations come to mind for them as they do for laypeople. However, the police officers made many more correct decisions than members of the lay population, and their decisions did not appear to be systematically influenced by target ethnicity. This demonstrates the effect of training; the automatic associations were still there, but their impact on final performance could be controlled such that one's bias and cultural associations did not determine behavior.

4.2. Combating Discrimination Directly

While individual-level discrimination is highly prevalent and pernicious, it would be a mistake to conclude that it is only individuals who are prejudiced, or that discrimination *requires* individuals to be prejudiced. Discrimination may occur because of institutional bias, which is enacted by prejudiced and/or unprejudiced social actors and takes the form of "laws, customs, and practices which systematically reflect and produce group-based inequities in any society" (Henry, 2010, p. 427). For example, insurance companies decide house insurance premiums based on a range of objective features such as the value of an applicant's house and the neighborhood in which it is located (Henry, 2010). But this results in some groups, particularly ethnic minorities, systematically paying higher premiums (Squires, 2003) because of historical factors and other institutional biases that they face, which, in part at least, explains minority groups' socioeconomic situation. Thus, such objectively based policies are associated with the entrenchment of inequalities.

In examining the dimensions and consequences of institutional bias, Henry (2010) speaks about the resistance of certain forms of institutional bias (particularly those that involve written or unwritten laws and procedures) to antidiscrimination efforts that are rooted in individual-level theories. Such institutional bias may best be addressed through reparation policies such as affirmative action and equal opportunity legislation.

4.2.1. *Affirmative Action*

Affirmative action has been put forward as a powerful means to address the disparate outcomes that people historically face as a function of their group membership. This policy has been adopted in varying forms in different countries (Sowell, 1989). Political parties across the world have a history of using quotas to increase the representation of women. In the UK for instance, the Labour Party introduced All-Women Shortlists (AWS) at its 1993 Annual Conference in an effort to deal with the very low levels of representation of women in power (Peake, 1997). Though there was considerable opposition to this policy (Wynn Davies, 1995), the Labour Party continues to use AWS, and both the Conservative Party and the Liberal Democrat Party have reversed their opposition to gender quotas and will institute them in the next election (Stratton & Sparrow, 2009). At present, the Sex Discrimination (Election Candidates) Act 2002, which allows parties to use positive discrimination in the selection of candidates, will be in place until 2015, due to the "sunset clause" (Oliver, 2005). Apart from the increased representation of women in politics, the AWS has resulted in greater attention to issues such as women's health, domestic violence, and childcare (Cutts, Childs, & Fieldhouse, 2008). Further, previously underrepresented individuals are able to flourish rather than fall prey to tokenism, as discussed above. Party reservations are also commonplace in countries such as Denmark, Norway, and Sweden.

While much has been written about the effectiveness of affirmative action in reducing unequal outcomes (see Harper & Reskin, 2005, for an extensive review), it remains a contentious and problematic way in which to address the effects of discrimination (D'Souza, 1989). Beneficiaries may gain from greater access to education, employment, and promotions, and this may be extremely valuable to society through the reduction of the size of a disenfranchised minority group, and through gains in productivity and creativity from having a diverse student body (Gurin, 1999) and workforce (Christian, Porter, & Moffitt, 2006; Leung, Maddux, Galinsky, & Chiu, 2008). However, it remains indisputable that such policies raise serious concerns for nonbeneficiaries (Crosby, Iyer, Clayton, & Downing, 2003) who see these policies as discriminatory against them, and this can have negative implications for intergroup relations. This can also lead to increased negative views of affirmative action beneficiaries as incompetent and unworthy (Heilman & Haynes, 2005), and it can lower the performance and self-efficacy of beneficiaries (Heilman & Alcott, 2001). Thus, a program that seeks to combat historical and current discrimination can, ironically, have the result of deepening prejudices and intergroup hostilities. Further, it has been argued that while affirmative action programs are successful in increasing representation in various spheres, minorities continue to face social biases and hostile environments once they are within organizations (Cleveland et al., 2004).

4.2.2. *Equal Opportunity Legislation*

A fundamental way in which to change the discriminatory behaviors of individuals is to inhibit them through societal or legal sanctions. In the United States, the federal government established the Commission on Civil Rights and the Equal Employment Opportunity Commission to monitor discriminatory practices (Henry, 2010), to set standards for what constituted discrimination and procedures for how organizations should try to minimize its occurrence. Such commissions are also powerful monitors and enforcers of social trends in the UK, Australia, and beyond, and have led to the adoption of equal opportunity hiring and promotion practices in organizations around the world. There is, however, the issue that certain minority groups, particularly those that undergo the worst forms of discrimination and persecution (for example, homosexuals or Gypsy communities in some countries) are not recognized by the law as legitimate groups, or where they are, do not have equal protection on all matters. Further, when discrimination takes the form of institutional bias that does not seek to target particular groups, yet unfairly disadvantages particular groups, it is difficult to make the charge of discrimination (Henry, 2010).

4.3. Summary

The foregoing section discussed a range of strategies that could be added to a policy-maker's or institution's toolkit to combat prejudice and discrimination. These strategies work at attacking the bases of discrimination, that is, by reducing the negative stereotypes and prejudice that people hold, and by combating discrimination directly through various legal means. We believe that many of these creative strategies hold great promise and should be employed in concert. In other words, efforts should be made to pass comprehensive legislation that prohibits discrimination and provides equal opportunities for members of all groups, while simultaneously working to reduce the extent to which people reply upon negative associations and attitudes when making decisions. However, we caution, as Paluck and Green (2009) did, that still relatively little is known about whether, why, and under what conditions a particular strategy may work. Without this knowledge it is difficult to make robust recommendations to power-holders on how exactly they should go about combating and curing social bias in the contexts within which they operate.

5. CONCLUSION

Prejudice and discrimination, rather than evaporating in the heat of social change, remain strong and reliable features of intergroup life, across a range of social, economic, and political contexts. What is clear beyond any shadow of a doubt is that discrimination has numerous deleterious consequences for minority groups and stigmatized individuals, and that the disadvantage experienced by any one group in any one generation can have a multiplier effect on intergenerational disadvantage across domains, situations, and group memberships.

We have reported several studies that look at the effects of prejudice and discrimination in political life and have found that both implicit and explicit attitudes and stereotypes play a key role in the decisions made by political actors. While there has been little research on the ways in which discriminatory behaviors may be inhibited in the political sphere, the fact that we understand the factors underlying some of these behaviors in politics, and their resonance with findings from other areas of social psychology, offers great promise in thinking about how discriminatory behaviors in the political sphere can be inhibited, and how people can be encouraged to overcome their biases. Intergroup relations from the perspective of political psychology and broader social psychology share a great deal of common ground: they rely upon the same sociocognitive processes in explaining various phenomena, and are often interested in very similar groups. Political psychologists who deal with issues of gender and race in the political sphere can draw heavily upon research on these social groups outside the political sphere, such as we have reported in this chapter.

References

Ajzen, I., & Fishbein, M. (1977). Attitude-behavior relations: A theoretical analysis and review of empirical research. *Psychological Bulletin, 84*, 888–918.

Al Ramiah, A. (2009). Intergroup relations in Malaysia: Identity, contact and threat. D.Phil. thesis, University of Oxford.

Al Ramiah, A., & Hewstone, M. (2012). "Rallying around the flag": Can an intergroup contact intervention promote national unity? *British Journal of Social Psychology, 51*, 239–256.

Al Ramiah, A., Hewstone, M., Dovidio, J. F., & Penner, L. A. (2010). The social psychology of discrimination: Theory, measurement and consequences. In L. Bond, F. McGinnity, & H. Russell (eds.), *Making equality count: Irish and international approaches to measuring discrimination* (pp. 84–112). Dublin: Liffey Press.

Alexander, L., & Tredoux, C. (2010). The spaces between us: A spatial analysis of informal segregation at a South African university. *Journal of Social Issues, 66*, 367–386.

Allport, G. W. (1935). Attitudes. In C. Murchison (ed.), *Handbook of social psychology* (p. 798). Worcester, MA: Clark University Press.

Allport, G. W. (1954). *The nature of prejudice*. Reading, MA: Addison-Wesley.

Amichai-Hamburger, Y., & McKenna, K. Y. A. (2006). The contact hypothesis reconsidered: Interacting via the Internet. *Journal of Computer-Mediated Communication, 11*, 825–843.

Amir, Y. (1969). Contact hypothesis in ethnic relations. *Psychological Bulletin, 71*, 319–342.

Amodio, D. M., Devine, P. G., & Harmon-Jones, E. (2007). A dynamic model of guilt: Implications for motivation and self-regulation in the context of prejudice. *Psychological Science, 18*, 524–530.

Arkes, H., & Tetlock, P. E. (2004). Attributions of implicit prejudice, or "Would Jesse Jackson 'fail' the Implicit Association Test?" *Psychological Inquiry, 15*, 257–278.

Baddeley, A. D. (1990). *Human memory: Theory and practice.* London: Erlbaum.

Bakan, D. (1966). *The duality of human existence: An essay on psychology and religion.* Oxford: Rand McNally.

Batson, C. D., Lishner, D. A., Cook, J., & Sawyer, S. (2005). Similarity and nurturance: Two possible sources of empathy for strangers. *Basic and Applied Social Psychology, 27,* 15–25.

Baumeister, R. F., Vohs, K. D., & Funder, D. C. (2007). Psychology as the science of self-reports and finger movements: Whatever happened to actual behavior? *Perspectives on Psychological Science, 2,* 396–403.

Biernat, M., Collins, E., Katzarska-Miller, I., & Thompson, E. (2009). Race-based shifting standards and racial discrimination. *Personality and Social Psychology Bulletin, 35,* 16–28.

Biernat, M., & Kobrynowicz, D. (1997). Gender- and race-based standards of competence: Lower minimum standards but higher ability standards for devalued groups. *Journal of Personality and Social Psychology, 72,* 544–557.

Blair, I. V., Judd, C. M., & Chapleau, K. M. (2004). The influence of Afrocentric facial features in criminal sentencing. *Psychological Science, 15,* 674–679.

Blair, I. V., Judd, C. M., Sadler, M. S., & Jenkins, C. (2002). The role of Afrocentric features in person perception: Judging by features and categories. *Journal of Personality and Social Psychology, 83,* 5–25.

Blair, I. V., Ma, J. E., & Lenton, A. P. (2001). Imagining stereotypes away: The moderation of implicit stereotypes through mental imagery. *Journal of Personality and Social Psychology, 81,* 828–841.

Bless, H. (2001). The relation between mood and the use of general knowledge structures. In L. L. Martin & G. L. Clore (eds.), *Mood and social cognition: Contrasting theories* (pp. 9–29). Mahwah, NJ: Erlbaum.

Brewer, M., Ho, H., Lee, J., & Miller, N. (1987). Social identity and social distance among Hong Kong school children. *Personality and Social Psychology Bulletin, 13,* 156–165.

Brewer, M., & Miller, N. (1984). Beyond the contact hypothesis: Theoretical perspectives on desegregation. In N. Miller & M. B. Brewer (eds.), *Groups in contact: The psychology of desegregation* (pp. 281–302). New York: Academic Press.

Brewer, M., & Miller, N. (1988). Contact and cooperation: When do they work? In P. A. Katz & D. A. Taylor (eds.), *Eliminating racism: Profiles in controversy* (pp. 315–326). New York: Plenum.

Brewer, M., & Pierce, K. P. (2005). Social identity complexity and outgroup tolerance. *Personality and Social Psychology Bulletin, 31,* 428–437.

Brown, R. (2000). Social identity theory: Past achievements, current problems and future challenges. *European Journal of Social Psychology, 30,* 745–778.

Brown, R., & Hewstone, M. (2005). An integrative theory of intergroup contact. *Advances in Experimental Social Psychology, 37,* 255–343.

Cater, J., & Jones, T. (1978). Asians in Bradford. *New Society,* 81–82.

Center for American Women and Politics. (2008). *Fact sheet: Women in state legislatures.* New Brunswick, NJ: Eagleton Institute of Politics, Rutgers University.

Chen, M., & Bargh, J. (1997). Nonconscious behavioral confirmation processes: The self-fulfilling consequences of automatic stereotype activation. *Journal of Experimental Social Psychology, 33,* 541–560.

Christian, J. N., Porter, L. W., & Moffitt, G. (2006). Workplace diversity and group relations: An overview. *Group Processes and Intergroup Relations, 9,* 459–466.

Cleveland, J. N., Vescio, T., & Barnes-Farrell, J. (2004). Gender discrimination in organizations. In R. Dipboye & A. Colella (eds.), *Discrimination at work: The psychological and organizational bases* (pp. 149–176). Hilldale, NJ: Erlbaum.

Cohen, G. L., Steele, C. M., & Ross, L. D. (1999). The mentor's dilemma: Providing critical feedback across the racial divide. *Personality and Social Psychology Bulletin, 25*, 1302–1318.

Correll, J., Park, B., Judd, C. M., & Wittenbrink, B. (2002). The police officer's dilemma: Using ethnicity to disambiguate potentially threatening individuals. *Journal of Personality and Social Psychology, 83*, 1314–1329.

Correll, J., Park, B., Judd, C. M., & Wittenbrink, B. (2007). The influence of stereotypes on decisions to shoot. *European Journal of Social Psychology, 37*, 1102–1117.

Crandall, C. S., Eshleman, A., & O'Brien, L. (2002). Social norms and the expression and suppression of prejudice: The struggle for internalization. *Journal of Personality and Social Psychology, 82*, 359–378.

Crisp, R. J., & Hewstone, M. (2007). Multiple social categorization. In M. Zanna (ed.), *Advances in experimental social psychology* (vol. 39, pp. 163–254). San Diego, CA: Academic Press.

Crisp, R. J., Walsh, J., & Hewstone, M. (2006). Crossed categorization in common ingroup contexts. *Personality and Social Psychology Bulletin, 32*, 1204–1218.

Croizet, J. C., & Claire, T. (1998). Extending the concept of stereotype threat to social class: The intellectual underperformance of students from low socioeconomic backgrounds. *Personality and Social Psychology Bulletin, 24*, 588–594.

Crosby, F. J., Bromley, S., & Saxe, L. (1980). Recent unobtrusive studies of black and white discrimination and prejudice: A literature review. *Psychological Bulletin, 87*, 546–563.

Crosby, F. J., Iyer, A., Clayton, S. D., & Downing, R. A. (2003). Affirmative action: Psychological data and the policy debates. *American Psychologist, 58*, 93–115.

Cuddy, A. J. C., Fiske, S. T., & Glick, P. (2007). The BIAS map: Behaviors from intergroup affect and stereotypes. *Journal of Personality and Social Psychology, 92*, 631–648.

Cutts, D., Childs, S., & Fieldhouse, E. A. (2008). This is what happens when you don't listen? All women shortlists at the 2005 general election. *Party Politics, 14*, 575–595.

Darley, J. M., & Gross, P. H. (1983). A hypothesis-confirming bias in labelling effects. *Journal of Personality and Social Psychology, 44*, 20–33.

Dasgupta, N. (2009). Mechanisms underlying the malleability of implicit prejudice and stereotypes: The role of automaticity and cognitive control. In T. Nelson (ed.), *Handbook of prejudice, stereotyping, and discrimination* (pp. 267–284). New York: Psychology Press.

Dasgupta, N., & Rivera, L. M. (2006). From automatic anti-gay prejudice to behavior: The moderating role of conscious beliefs about gender and behavioral control. *Journal of Personality and Social Psychology, 91*, 268–280.

Dasgupta, N., & Rivera, L. M. (2008). When social context matters: The influence of long-term contact and short-term exposure to admired outgroup members on implicit attitudes and behavioral intentions. *Social Cognition, 26*, 54–66.

Devine, P. G., Evett, S. R., & Vasquez-Suson, K. A. (1996). Exploring the interpersonal dynamics of intergroup contact. In R. M. Sorrentino & E. T. Higgins (eds.), *Handbook of motivation and cognition: The interpersonal context* (pp. 423–464). New York: Guilford Press.

Devine, P. G., & Vasquez, K. A. (1998). The rocky road to positive intergroup relations. In J. Ebberhardt & S. T. Fiske (eds.), *Racism: The problem and the response* (pp. 234–262). Thousand Oaks, CA: Sage.

Dixon, J. A., & Durrheim, K. (2003). Contact and the ecology of racial division: Some varieties of informal segregation. *British Journal of Social Psychology, 42*, 1–24.

Dolan, K. (2009). The impact of gender stereotyped evaluations on support for women candidates. Paper presented at the 67th Annual Conference of the Midwest Political Science Association.

Dovidio, J. F., Brigham, J. C., Johnson, B. T., & Gaertner, S. L. (1996). Stereotyping, prejudice, and discrimination: Another look. In N. Macrae, C. Stangor, & M. Hewstone (eds.), *Stereotypes and stereotyping* (pp. 276–319). New York: Guilford.

Dovidio, J. F., Eller, A., & Hewstone, M. (2011). Editorial: Improving intergroup relations through direct, extended and other forms of indirect contact. *Group Processes and Intergroup Relations, 14*, 147–160.

Dovidio, J. F., & Gaertner, S. L. (2000). Aversive racism and selection decisions: 1989 and 1999. *Psychological Science, 11*, 319–323.

Dovidio, J. F., & Gaertner, S. L. (2004). Aversive racism. In M. P. Zanna (ed.), *Advances in experimental social psychology* (pp. 1–51). San Diego, CA: Academic Press.

Dovidio, J. F., Gaertner, S. L., & Kafati, G. (2000). Group identity and intergroup relations: The common in-group identity model. In S. R. Thye, E. J. Lawler, M. W. Macy, & H. A. Walker (eds.), *Advances in group processes* (pp. 1–34). Stamford, CT: JAI Press.

Dovidio, J. F., Gaertner, S. L., & Loux, S. (2000). Subjective experiences and intergroup relations: The role of positive affect. In H. Bless & J. Forgas (eds.), *The message within: The role of subjective experience in social cognition and behavior* (pp. 340–371). Philadelphia, PA: Psychology Press.

Dovidio, J. F., Gaertner, S. L., & Saguy, T. (2008). Another view of "we": Majority and minority group perspectives on a common ingroup identity. *European Review of Social Psychology, 18*, 296–330.

Dovidio, J. F., Gaertner, S. L., Shnabel, N., Saguy, T., & Johnson, J. D. (2010). Recategorization and prosocial behavior: Common identity and a dual identity. In S. Sturmer & M. Snyder (eds.), *The psychology of prosocial behavior* (pp. 191–208). Malden, MA: Wiley-Blackwell.

Dovidio, J. F., & Hebl, M. R. (2005). Discrimination at the level of the individual: Cognitive and affective factors. In R. L. Dipboye & A. Colella (eds.), *Discrimination at work* (pp. 11–35). Mahwah, NJ: Erlbaum.

Dovidio, J. F., Kawakami, K., & Beach, K. (2001). Implicit and explicit attitudes: Examination of the relationship between measures of intergroup bias. In R. Brown & S. L. Gaertner (eds.), *Blackwell handbook of social psychology: Intergroup processes* (pp. 175–197). Oxford: Blackwell.

Dovidio, J. F., Kawakami, K., & Gaertner, S. L. (2002). Implicit and explicit prejudice and interracial interaction. *Journal of Personality and Social Psychology, 82*, 62–68.

Dovidio, J. F., Kawakami, K., Johnson, C., Johnson, B. T., & Howard, A. (1997). The nature of prejudice: Automatic and controlled processes. *Journal of Experimental Social Psychology, 33*, 510–540.

D'Souza, V. S. (1989). *Development planning and structural inequalities: The response of the underprivileged.* New Delhi: Sage.

Eagly, A. H., & Carli, L. L. (2007). *Through the labyrinth: The truth about how women become leaders.* Boston, MA: Harvard Business School Press.

Eberhardt, J. L., Davies, P. G., Purdie-Vaughns, V. J., & Johnson, S. L. (2006). Looking deathworthy: Perceived stereotypicality of black defendants predicts capital-sentencing outcomes. *Psychological Science, 17*, 383–386.

Fazio, R. H. (1990). Multiple processes by which attitudes guide behavior: The MODE model as an integrative framework. In M. P. Zanna (ed.), *Advances in experimental social psychology* (pp. 75–109). San Diego, CA: Academic Press.

Fazio, R. H., Jackson, J. R., Dunton, B. C., & Williams, C. J. (1995). Variability in automatic activation as an unobtrusive measure of racial attitudes: A bona fide pipeline? *Journal of Personality and Social Psychology, 69*, 1013–1027.

Fiske, S. T., Cuddy, A. J. C., Glick, P., & Xu, J. (2002). A model of (often mixed) stereotype content: Competence and warmth respectively follow from perceived status and competition. *Journal of Personality and Social Psychology, 82*, 878–902.

Friese, M., Hofmann, W., & Schmitt, M. (2008). When and why do implicit measures predict behavior: Empirical evidence for the moderating role of opportunity, motivation, and process reliance. *European Review of Social Psychology, 19*, 285–338.

Funk, C. L. (1999). Bringing the candidate into models of candidate evaluation. *Journal of Politics, 61*, 700–720.

Gaertner, S. L., & Dovidio, J. F. (1977). The subtlety of white racism, arousal, and helping behavior. *Journal of Personality and Social Psychology, 35*, 691–707.

Gaertner, S. L., & Dovidio, J. F. (2000). *Reducing intergroup bias: The common ingroup identity model.* Philadelphia, PA: Psychology Press.

Gaertner, S. L., Dovidio, J. F., Anastasio, P. A., Bachman, B. A., & Rust, M. C. (1993). The common ingroup identity model: Recategorization and the reduction of intergroup bias. In W. Stroebe & M. Hewstone (eds.), *European Review of Social Psychology, 4*, 1–26.

Gaertner, S. L., Mann, J. A., Dovidio, J. F., Murrell, A. J., & Pomare, M. (1990). How does cooperation reduce intergroup bias? *Journal of Personality and Social Psychology, 59*, 692–704.

Glick, P., Zion, C., & Nelson, C. (1988). What mediates sex discrimination in hiring decisions? *Journal of Personality and Social Psychology, 55*, 178–186.

Greenwald, A. G., McGhee, D. E., & Schwartz, J. L. K. (1998). Measuring individual differences in implicit cognition: The Implicit Association Test. *Journal of Personality and Social Psychology, 74*, 1464–1480.

Greenwald, A. G., Poehlman, T. A., Uhlmann, E., & Banaji, M. R. (2009). Understanding and using the Implicit Association Test: III. Meta-analysis of predictive validity. *Journal of Personality and Social Psychology, 97*, 17–41.

Gurin, P. (1999). The compelling need for diversity in higher education: Expert testimony in Gratz, et al. v. Bollinger, et al. *Michigan Journal of Race and Law, 5*, 363–425.

Gutek, B. A., Cohen, A. G., & Tsui, A. (1996). Reactions to perceived sex discrimination. *Human Relations, 49*, 791–813.

Hamilton, D. L., & Bishop, G. D. (1976). Attitudinal and behavioral effects of initial integration of white suburban neighbourhoods. *Journal of Social Issues, 32*, 47–67.

Harper, S., & Reskin, B. (2005). Affirmative action at school and on the job. *American Review of Sociology, 31*, 357–379.

Heath, A. F., & McMahon, D. (1997). Education and occupational attainment: The impact of ethnic origins. In V. Karn (ed.), *Education, employment and housing among ethnic minorities in Britain* (pp. 91–113). London: HMSO.

Hebl, M. R., Foster, J. B., Mannix, L. M., & Dovidio, J. F. (2002). Formal and interpersonal discrimination: A field study of bias toward homosexual applicants. *Personality and Social Psychology Bulletin, 28*, 815–825.

Heilman, M. E., & Alcott, V. B. (2001). What I think you think of me: Women's reactions to being viewed as beneficiaries of preferential selection. *Journal of Applied Psychology, 86*, 574–582.

Heilman, M. E., & Haynes, M. C. (2005). No credit where credit is due: Attributional rationalization of women's success in male-female teams. *Journal of Applied Psychology, 90*, 905–916.

Henry, P. J. (2010). Institutional bias. In J. F. Dovidio, M. Hewstone, P. Glick, & V. M. Esses (eds.), *The Sage handbook of prejudice, stereotyping and discrimination* (pp. 426–440). London: Sage.

Hewstone, M. (1996). Contact and categorization: Social psychological interventions to change intergroup relations. In C. N. Macrae, C. Stangor, & M. Hewstone (eds.), *Stereotypes and stereotyping* (pp. 323–357). New York: Guilford.

Hewstone, M. (2009). Living apart, living together? The role of intergroup contact in social integration. *Proceedings of the British Academy, 162,* 243–300.

Hewstone, M., & Brown, R. (1986). Contact is not enough: An intergroup perspective on the "contact hypothesis." In M. Hewstone & R. Brown (eds.), *Contact and conflict in intergroup encounters* (pp. 1–44). Oxford: Blackwell.

Hewstone, M., & Cairns, E. (2001). Social psychology and intergroup conflict. In D. Chirot & M. E. P. Seligman (eds.), *Ethnopolitical warfare: Causes, consequences, and possible solutions* (pp. 319–342). Washington, DC: American Psychological Association.

Higgins, E. T. (1987). Self-discrepancy: A theory relating self and affect. *Psychological Review, 94,* 319–340.

Hodson, G., Dovidio, J. F., & Gaertner, S. L. (2002). Processes in racial discrimination: Differential weighting of conflicting information. *Personality and Social Psychology Bulletin, 28,* 460–471.

Hofmann, W., & Baumert, A. (2010). Immediate affect as a basis for moral judgment: An adaptation of the affect misattribution procedure. *Cognition and Emotion, 24,* 522–535.

Hofmann, W., Gawronski, B., Gschwendner, T., Le, H., & Schmitt, M. (2005). A meta-analysis on the correlation between the Implicit Association Test and explicit self-report measures. *Personality and Social Psychology Bulletin, 31,* 1369–1385.

Holt, C. A., & Laury, S. (2002). Risk aversion and incentive effects. *American Economic Review, 92,* 1644–1655.

Huddy, L. & Cassese, E. (2011). On the complex and varied political effects of gender. In R. Y. Shapiro & L. R. Jacobs (eds.), *Oxford handbook of American public opinion and the media* (pp. 471–487). New York: Oxford University Press.

Kanter, R. M. (1977). *Men and women of the corporation.* New York: Basic Books.

Kawakami, K., Dovidio, J. F., & Van Kamp, S. (2005). Kicking the habit: Effects of nonstereotypic association training and correction processes on hiring decisions. *Journal of Experimental Social Psychology, 41,* 68–75.

Koenig, A. M., Eagly, A. H., Mitchell, A. A., & Ristikari, T. (2011). Are leader stereotypes masculine? A meta-analysis of three research paradigms. *Psychological Bulletin, 137,* 616–642.

Kraus, S. J. (1995). Attitudes and prediction of behaviour: A meta-analysis of the empirical literature. *Personality and Social Psychology Bulletin, 21,* 58–75.

LaVeist, T. A., Nuru-Jeter, A., & Jones, K. E. (2003). The association of doctor-patient race concordance with health services utilization. *Journal of Public Health Policy, 24,* 312–323.

Lawless, J. L., & Pearson, K. (2008). The primary reason for women's under-representation: Re-evaluating the conventional wisdom. *Journal of Politics, 70,* 67–82.

Leung, A. K., Maddux, W. W., Galinsky, A. D., & Chiu, C. (2008). Multicultural experience enhances creativity: The when and how. *American Psychologist, 63,* 169–181.

Levin, S., Van Laar, C., & Sidanius, J. (2003). The effects of ingroup and outgroup friendships on ethnic attitudes in college: A longitudinal study. *Group Processes & Intergroup Relations, 6,* 76–92.

Lublin, D. (1997). *The paradox of representation.* Princeton, NJ: Princeton University Press.

Massey, D. S. (2004). Segregation and stratification: A biosocial perspective. *DuBois Review: Social Science Research on Race, 11*, 1–19.

Massey, D. S., & Denton, N. A. (1993). *American apartheid.* Cambridge, MA: Harvard University Press.

Mays, V. M., Coleman, L. M., & Jackson, J. S. (1996). Perceived race-based discrimination, employment status, and job stress in a national sample of black women: Implications for health outcomes. *Journal of Occupational Health Psychology, 1*, 319–329.

Mehrabian, A. (1969). Significance of posture and position in the communication of attitude and status relationships. *Psychological Bulletin, 71*, 359–372.

Mitchell, G., & Tetlock, P. E. (2006). Antidiscrimination law and the perils of mindreading. *Ohio State Law Journal, 67*, 1023–1121.

Monteith, M. J. (1993). Self-regulation of prejudiced responses: Implication for progress in prejudice-reduction efforts. *Journal of Personality and Social Psychology, 65*, 469–485.

Monteith, M. J., Ashburn-Nardo, L., Voils, C. I., & Czopp, A. M. (2002). Putting the brakes on prejudice: On the development and operation of cues for control. *Journal of Personality and Social Psychology, 83*, 1029–1050.

Monteith, M. J., & Mark, A. Y. (2005). Changing one's prejudiced ways: Awareness, affect, and self-regulation. In M. Hewstone & W. Stroebe (eds.), *European Review of Social Psychology* (pp. 113–154). Hove, UK: Psychology Press / Taylor & Francis.

Monteith, M. J., Mark, A. Y., & Ashburn-Nardo, L. (2010). The self-regulation of prejudice: Toward understanding its lived character. *Group Processes and Intergroup Relations, 65*, 183–200.

Moskowitz, D., & Stroh, P. (1994). Psychological sources of electoral racism. *Political Psychology, 15*, 307–329.

Mummendey, A., & Wenzel, M. (1999). Social discrimination and tolerance in intergroup relations: Reactions to intergroup difference. *Personality & Social Psychology Review, 3*, 158–174.

Newport, F. (2009). Women more likely to be Democrats, regardless of age. *Gallup.* Retrieved from http://www.gallup.com/poll/120839/Women-Likely-Democrats-Regardless-Age.aspx.

Niemann, Y. F., & Dovidio, J. F. (1998). Relationship of solo status, academic rank, and perceived distinctiveness to job satisfaction of racial/ethnic minorities. *Journal of Applied Psychology, 83*, 55–71.

Nisbett, R. E., & Wilson, T. D. (1977). Telling more than we can know: Verbal reports on mental processes. *Psychological Review, 84*, 231–259.

Oliver, J. E. (2005). *Fat politics: The real story behind America's obesity epidemic.* New York: Oxford University Press.

Pager, D. (2007). The use of field experiments for the study of employment discrimination: Contributions, critiques, and directions for the future. *Annals of the American Academy of Political and Social Science, 609*, 104–133.

Paluck, E. L. (2009). Reducing intergroup prejudice and conflict using the media: A field experiment in Rwanda. *Journal of Personality and Social Psychology, 96*, 574–587.

Paluck, E. L., & Green, D. P. (2009). Prejudice reduction: What works? A review and assessment of research and practice. *Annual Review of Psychology, 60*, 339–367.

Parsons, T., & Bales, R. F. (Eds.) (1955). *Family, socialization, and interaction process.* New York: Free Press.

Payne, B. K., Krosnick, J. A., Pasek, J., Lelkes, Y., Akhtar, O., & Tompson, T. (2010). Implicit and explicit prejudice in the 2008 American presidential election. *Journal of Experimental Social Psychology, 46*, 367–374.

Peake, L. (1997). Women in the campaign and in the commons. In J. Tonge & A. Geddes (eds.), *Labour's landslide: The British general election 1997 (pp. 165–178)*. Manchester: Manchester University Press.

Penner, L. A., Albrecht, T. L., Coleman, D. K., & Norton, W. (2007). Interpersonal perspectives on black-white health disparities: Social policy implications. *Social Issues and Policy Review, 1*, 63–98.

Penner, L. A., Dovidio, J. F., West, T. V., Gaertner, S. L., Albrecht, T. L., Dailey, R. K., & Markova, T. (2010). Aversive racism and medical interactions with black patients: A field study. *Journal of Experimental Social Psychology, 46*, 436–440.

Pettigrew, T. F. (1998). Intergroup contact theory. *Annual Review of Psychology, 49*, 65–85.

Pettigrew, T. F. (2009). Contact's secondary transfer effect: Do intergroup contact effects spread to noncontacted outgroups? *Social Psychology, 40*, 55–65.

Pettigrew, T. F., & Tropp, L. R. (2006). A meta-analytic test of intergroup contact theory. *Journal of Personality and Social Psychology, 90*, 751–783.

Pettigrew, T. F., & Tropp, L. R. (2008). How does intergroup contact reduce prejudice? Meta-analytic tests of three mediators. *European Journal of Social Psychology, 38*, 922–934.

Pizzi, W., Blair, I. V., & Judd, C. M. (2005). Discrimination in sentencing based on Afro-centric features. *Michigan Journal of Race and Law, 10*, 1–27.

Plaut, V. C. (2002). Cultural models of diversity: The psychology of difference and inclusion. In R. Shweder, M. Minow, & H. R. Markus (eds.), *Engaging cultural differences: The multicultural challenge in a liberal democracy* (pp. 365–395). New York: Russell Sage.

Plaut, V. C., Thomas, K. M., & Goren, M. J. (2009). Is multiculturalism or colorblindness better for minorities? *Psychological Science, 20*, 444–446.

Powell, G. N., & Butterfield, D. A. (1979). The "good manager": Masculine or androgynous? *Academy of Management Journal, 22*, 395–403.

Quinn, D. M., Kahng, S. K., & Crocker, J. (2004). Discreditable: Stigma effects of revealing a mental illness history on test performance. *Personality and Social Psychology Bulletin, 30*, 803–815.

Ranganath, K. A., Smith, C. T., & Nosek, B. A. (2008). Distinguishing automatic and controlled components of attitudes from direct and indirect measurement. *Journal of Experimental Social Psychology, 44*, 386–396.

Richeson, J. A., & Shelton, J. N. (2005). Thin slices of racial bias. *Journal of Nonverbal Behavior, 29*, 75–86.

Robbins, I., Cooper, A., & Bender, M. P. (1992). The relationship between knowledge, attitudes and degree of contact with AIDS and HIV. *Journal of Advanced Nursing, 17*, 198–203.

Roccas, S., & Brewer, M. (2002). Social identity complexity. *Personality and Social Psychology Review, 6*, 88–106.

Sampson, R. J. (1986). Effects of socioeconomic context on official reaction to juvenile delinquency. *American Sociological Review, 51*, 876.

Sanbonmatsu, K. (2003). Political knowledge and gender stereotypes. *American Politics Research, 31*, 575–594.

Saucier, D. M., Miller, C. T., & Doucet, N. (2005). Differences in helping whites and blacks: A meta-analysis. *Personality & Social Psychology Review, 9*, 2–16.

Schiappa, E., Gregg, P. B., & Hewes, D. E. (2005). The parasocial contact hypothesis. *Communication Monographs, 72*, 92–115.

Schmid, K., Hewstone, M., Tausch, N., & Cairns, E. (2009). Antecedents and consequences of social identity complexity: Intergroup contact, distinctiveness threat and outgroup attitudes. *Personality and Social Psychology Bulletin, 35*, 1085–1098.

Schulman, K. A., Berlin, J. A., Harless, W., & Al, E. (1999). The effect of race and sex on physician's recommendations for cardiac catheterization. *New England Journal of Medicine*, *340*, 618–626.

Sen, A. K. (2006). What do we want from a theory of justice? *Journal of Philosophy*, *103*, 215–238.

Sidanius, J., Pratto, F., Martin, M., & Stallworth, L. M. (1991). Consensual racism and career track: Some implications of social dominance theory. *Political Psychology*, *12*, 691–720.

Sigelman, C. K., Sigelman, L., Walkosz, B. J., & Nitz, M. (1995). Black candidates, white voters: Understanding racial bias in political perceptions. *American Journal of Political Science*, *39*, 243–265.

Simons, R. L., Murry, V., McLoyd, V., Lin, K., Cutrona, C., & Conger, R. D. (2002). Discrimination, crime, ethnic identity, and parenting as correlates of depressive symptoms among African American children: A multilevel analysis. *Development and Psychopathology*, *14*, 371–393.

Simpson, J. A. (2009). Editorial. *Journal of Personality and Social Psychology*, *96*, 60.

Son Hing, L. S., Chung-Yan, G., Hamilton, L., & Zanna, M. P. (2008). A two-dimensional model that employs explicit and implicit attitudes to characterize prejudice. *Journal of Personality and Social Psychology*, *94*, 971–987.

Sowell, T. (1989). *Preferential policies: An international perspective*. New York: Morrow.

Spencer, S. J., Steele, C. M., & Quinn, D. M. (1999). Stereotype threat and women's math performance. *Journal of Experimental Social Psychology*, *35*, 4–28.

Squires, G. (2003). Racial profiling, insurance style: Insurance redlining and the uneven development of metropolitan areas. *Journal of Urban Affairs*, *25*, 391–410.

Steele, C. M., & Aronson, J. (1995). Stereotype threat and the intellectual test performance of African Americans. *Journal of Personality and Social Psychology*, *69*, 797–811.

Stephan, W. G., & Stephan, C. W. (1985). Intergroup anxiety. *Journal of Social Issues*, *41*, 157–175.

Stephan, W. G., & Stephan, C. W. (2000). An integrated threat theory of prejudice. In S. Oskamp (ed.), *Reducing prejudice and discrimination* (pp. 23–45). Mahwah, NJ: Erlbaum.

Stolle, D., Soroka, S., & Johnston, R. (2008). When does diversity erode trust? Neighbourhood diversity, interpersonal trust, and the mediating effect of social interactions. *Political Studies*, *56*, 57–75.

Stone, P. (2002). Multiagent competitions and research: Lessons from RoboCup and TAC. RoboCup 2002 International Symposium.

Stratton, A., & Sparrow, A. (2009, October 20). David Cameron to reverse opposition to all-women shortlists. *The Guardian*. London.

Tausch, N., Hewstone, M., Kenworthy, J. B., Psaltis, C., Schmid, K., Popan, J. R., Cairns, E., et al. (2010). "Secondary transfer" effects of intergroup contact: Alternative accounts and underlying processes. *Journal of Personality and Social Psychology*, *99*, 282–302.

Terkildsen, N. (1993). When white voters evaluate black candidates: The processing implications of candidate skin color, prejudice, and self-monitoring. *Journal of Political Science*, *37*, 1032–1053.

Tropp, L. R., & Pettigrew, T. F. (2005). Allport's intergroup contact hypothesis: Its history and influence. In P. Dovidio, P. Glick, & L. Rudman (eds.), *On the nature of prejudice: Fifty years after Allport* (pp. 262–277). Malden, MA: Blackwell.

Turner, R. N., Crisp, R. J., & Lambert, E. (2007). Imagining intergroup contact can improve intergroup attitudes. *Group Processes and Intergroup Relations*, *10*, 427–441.

Turner, R. N., Hewstone, M., & Voci, A. (2007). Reducing explicit and implicit prejudice via direct and extended contact: The mediating role of self-disclosure and intergroup anxiety. *Journal of Personality and Social Psychology*, *93*, 369–388.

Van Oudenhoven, J. P., Prins, K. S., & Buunk, B. P. (1998). Attitudes of minority and majority members towards adaptation of immigrants. *European Journal of Social Psychology*, 28, 995–1013.

Vonofakou, C., Hewstone, M., & Voci, A. (2007). Contact with out-group friends as a predictor of meta-attitudinal strength and accessibility of attitudes towards gay men. *Journal of Personality and Social Psychology*, 92, 804–820.

Weller, S. C. (1993). A meta-analysis of condom effectiveness in reducing sexually transmitted HIV. *Social Science & Medicine*, 36, 1635–1644.

Wells, A. J. (1998). Re: Breast cancer, cigarette smoking, and passive smoking. *American Journal of Epidemiology*, 147, 991–992.

West, S. G., & Brown, T. J. (1975). Physical attractiveness, the severity of the emergency and helping: A field experiment and interpersonal simulation. *Journal of Experimental Social Psychology*, 11, 531–538.

Williams, R. M. (1947). The reduction of intergroup tensions: A survey of research on problems of ethnic, racial, and religious group relations. *Social Science Research Council Bulletin*, 57, 153.

Wojciszke, B. (2005). Morality and competence in person and self perception. *European Review of Social Psychology*, 16, 155–188.

Word, C. O., Zanna, M. P., & Cooper, J. (1974). The nonverbal mediation of self-fulfilling prophecies in interracial interaction. *Journal of Experimental Social Psychology*, 10, 109–120.

Wright, S. (2001). Strategic collective action: Social psychology and social change. In R. Brown & S. L. Gaertner (eds.), *Intergroup processes* (pp. 223–256). Oxford: Blackwell.

Wright, S., Aron, A., McLaughlin-Volpe, T., & Ropp, S. A. (1997). The extended contact effect: Knowledge of cross-group friendships and prejudice. *Journal of Personality and Social Psychology*, 73, 73–90.

Wright, S., & Lubensky, M. (2008). The struggle for social equality: Collective action vs. prejudice reduction. In S. Demoulin, J. P. Leyens, & J. F. Dovidio (eds.), *Intergroup misunderstandings: Impact of divergent social realities* (pp. 291–310). New York: Psychology Press.

Wynn Davies, P. (1995, August 21). All-women lists face new legal challenge. *The Independent*. London.

....

CHAPTER 28

THE PSYCHOLOGY OF INTRACTABLE CONFLICTS
eruption, escalation, and peacemaking

....

DANIEL BAR-TAL AND ERAN HALPERIN

1. INTRODUCTION

....

THE study of intractable conflicts and their resolution is an examination of a unique context and real-life societal issue. It mandates special efforts to elucidate its dynamics, as intractable conflicts have immense effects on the well-being of the societies involved in them, and often also on the international community in its entirety. The ongoing conflicts in the Middle East, Kashmir, Sri Lanka, Chechnya, and Rwanda constitute prototypical examples of these types of conflict. Of 309 conflicts taking place in the period between 1945 and 1995, Bercovitch (2005) identified 75 serious interstate conflicts that were violent, lasted at least 15 years, and were resistant to any peaceful settlement. But if we extend the scope of the definition, we find that of the 352 violent conflicts that have erupted since World War II, only 144 have concluded in peace agreements (Harbom, Hogbladh, & Wallensteen, 2006). If we assume that it is very difficult in our times to unequivocally win an interethnic or international conflict, it follows that because many of the violent conflicts have been resisting their peaceful resolution, they are protracted.

Conflicts erupt when two or more groups perceive their goals or interests to be in direct contradiction to one another and decide to act on this basis. This very general situation is an inseparable part of human life, and there are thus many different causes for the eruption of conflicts (see Thackrah, 2009). In more specific cases of intractable conflict, the party's goals may include, for example, the rectification of unequal divisions of wealth, power, and/or resources; cessation of occupation, oppression, discrimination, and exploitation practices; satisfaction of national needs and aspirations; achievement

of freedoms; attainment of territorial claims; or achievement of expression or dominance of competing dogma and/or ideology.

From a normative and even moral perspective, conflicts are not necessarily negative
because progress in various domains is often only achieved through them. Even in cases
of intractable conflict, some have been judged by the international community as involving one party with just claims that were, or continue to be, ignored by the opponent (see
Walzer, 2006). Nevertheless, we argue that intractable conflicts, because of their violent
nature, cause the involved society members considerable misery and suffering, and the
challenge for the civilization is therefore to find ways to manage and resolve them in a
constructive way.

Intractable conflicts, by their essence, *are very particular type of severe conflicts that
last for a long period of time, as the parties involved in them can neither win nor are willing to compromise in order to reach their peaceful settlement.* Through the years, different
terms have been proposed to label this type of conflict, among them *protracted conflicts*
(e.g., Azar, 1990), *enduring rivalries* (e.g., Goertz & Diehl, 1993), *malignant conflicts*
(Deutsch, 1985), or *deep-rooted conflicts* (e.g., Burton, 1987).

All the above-mentioned terms imply that this type of conflict is vicious and difficult to resolve. Thus, the term "intractable" has become widely used because it denotes
these conflicts' resistance to peaceful resolution (Coleman, 2000, 2003; Crocker,
Hampson, & Aall, 2005; Kriesberg, 1993; Vallacher, Coleman, Nowak, & Bui-
Wrzosinska, 2010). Throughout the years, the seven following features that underlie the essence of intractable conflicts have been proposed (Kriesberg, 1993, Bar-Tal,
2007a, 2013):

1. *They are total,* being perceived as concerning essential and fundamental goals,
   needs, and/or values that are regarded as indispensable for the group's existence
   and/or survival. (See also the discussion of existential conflicts by Fisher,
   Kelman, & Nan, chapter 16, this volume.)
2. Intractable conflicts involve *physical violence* in which group members,
   combatants and civilians are killed and wounded in either wars, small-scale
   military engagements, or terrorist attacks.
3. Intractable conflicts are *of zero-sum nature,* namely, parties engaged in intractable
   conflict do not see any possibility of compromise and perceive any loss suffered
   by the other side as their own gain, and conversely, any gains of the other side as
   their own loss.
4. They are perceived as *irresolvable,* namely, society members do not perceive a
   possibility of resolving the conflict peacefully.
5. They occupy a *central place* in the lives of the individual group members and the
   group as a whole.
6. Parties engaged in an intractable conflict make *vast material* (i.e., military,
   technological, and economic) *and psychological investments* in order to cope
   successfully with the situation.
7. *They are protracted* in that they persist for a long time, at least a generation.

Different disciplines, like sociology, economy, and political science, contribute to the understanding of the dynamics and foundations of these conflicts. We focus on the socio-political-psychological perspective, which can shed light on some aspects of their major processes. While we acknowledge that these conflicts are over real issues that must be addressed in resolving them, the fact that in their essence they are accompanied by sociopsychological dynamics influences their nature and requires thorough consideration of these factors (see Bar-Tal, 2011, 2013; Fitzduff & Stout, 2006; Kelman, 2007; Tropp, 2012).

Therefore, the socio-political-psychological perspective on intractable conflicts focuses on the study of the beliefs, attitudes, emotions, and behaviors of the individuals and groups involved in the eruption of a conflict, its maintenance, its resolution, and the subsequent reconciliation. These beliefs, attitudes, and emotions play crucial role as a prism through which the involved society members view the realty of conflict and on the basis of this view carry their behaviors. An important assumption in this perspective is that although intractable conflicts differ greatly in their specific context and contents, the general sociopsychological dynamics are similar and can thus be analyzed (see Bar-Tal, 2011, 2013; De Dreu, 2010; Fitzduff & Stout, 2006; Tropp, 2012).

The chapter, focusing on the macro-level analysis, aims mainly to describe the unique nature of intractable conflicts and delineate their major societal emotional-cognitive-behavioral processes, as well as the evolved sociopsychological repertoire that fuels them and the processes that are involved in resolving them peacefully. This goal is achieved by analyzing the course of intractable conflict and its peaceful resolution via its three main phases: eruption of intractable conflict, its escalation and management, and its de-escalation and movement toward peacemaking. Additionally, the chapter strives to make this analysis within a conceptual framework that focuses on the interrelationship between the context and the collective psychological state of society members. This conceptual framework will be now presented.

2. CONCEPTUAL FRAMEWORK AND KEY CONCEPTS

Our analysis of intractable conflict is based on the fundamental and seminal contribution of Kurt Lewin (1951), who proposed that human behavior is a function of an environment in which a person(s) operates with its physical and social factors and his or her tendencies, including ideas, thoughts, intentions, and fantasies. In Lewin's (1951) view, any behavioral analysis must begin with the description of the situation as a whole, because the person's conception of the situation (or environment) determines to a large extent his or her behavioral possibilities and eventually chosen routes of action.

Of special importance for our conception is Lewin's application of the theory to the group situation. He suggested that the behavior of a group, as that of an individual, is affected greatly by the collective perception of the environment and the group's characteristics (Lewin, 1947). On the basis of this classical theoretical framework, which was supported by later conceptions (e.g, Ross & Nisbett, 1991), we suggest that understanding collective behaviors in intractable conflict requires an analysis of the *psychological conditions of the conflict's context* (i.e., an environment, a field) and the *collective psychological state* of the involved societies, which includes the *lasting psychological repertoire* of the collective as well as *immediate psychological response tendencies*. Therefore, our analysis of each phase of the intractable conflict and its resolution will use these two mega-elements, as well as their continuous interaction as building blocks of the conceptual framework.

2.1. The Collective Context and Its Psychological Conditions

Theories in social sciences have generally accepted the basic assumption that the study of a *social context* is essential for understanding the functioning of societies (e.g., Giddens, 1984; Parsons, 1951). Recently, Ashmore, Deaux, and McLaughlin-Volpe (2004) have defined social context as the "general and continuing multilayered and interwoven set of material realities, social structures, and shared belief system that surround any situation" (p. 103). Hence, we begin our presentation with the description of the collective context of intractable conflict. In our view, the collective context's significance lies in the fact that it dictates the society members' needs and goals and the challenges that they have to meet in order to satisfy them. It also provides opportunities and limitations, stimulations and inhibitions, as well as the spaces and boundaries for human behavior.

The collective context of intractable conflict should be seen as a lasting context for decades, as durability is one of the important characteristics of intractable conflict. Thus, the nature of the *lasting context of conflict* has relevance to the well-being of society members—it involves them, occupies a central position in public discourse and the public agenda, supplies information and experiences that compel society members to construct an adaptable worldview, is determinative factor in selection of lines of behaviors, continuously shapes the lives of the involved societies, and imprints every aspect of individual and collective life.

As the lasing context of intractable conflict is durable–at least 25 years—there are short-term contexts of a transitional nature that are embedded into it and turn it into a dynamic phenomenon that develops in a nonlinear fashion. We define this short-term context as *transitional* because it consists of observable and well-defined societal conditions that come about as a result of major events and major information that influence the behavior and functioning of the individuals and collectives who perceive and cognize them (Bar-Tal & Sharvit, 2008).

In any discussion about context, either lasting or transitional, we focus on the *psychological conditions of the conflict's context* that are inherent part of the context. They emerge together with other conditions (physical, political, etc.) and become part of the environment. They provide the signals, stimuli, prompts, and cues that need to be perceived and cognized by individuals and collectives in order for the context to have an impact on them. Some examples of the psychological conditions that are usually formed in the context of intractable conflict are those of threat, danger, stress, and uncertainty (de Rivera & Paez, 2007). These psychological conditions, in turn, trigger perceptions, thoughts, ideas, affects, and emotions that altogether form the *collective psychological state* and lead to various types of behavior.

In this chapter we note additional two contextual features that have an effect on the course of the conflict: societal characteristics typifying societies in conflict and the major entrepreneurs that lead society members and mobilize them for the conflict. Both features function for society members as part of the context. For our conceptual framework the existing levels of openness and freedom of expression are among the most important societal characteristics of the context. They relate to the availability of alternative knowledge and information, which may shed a different light on the conflict. In addition, the entrepreneurs considerably influence the construction of the society members' collective psychological state (Reicher, Hopkins, Levine, & Rath, 2005). They are the agents who diagnose the situation as being conflictive, provide a particular illumination of the situation to society members, and then mobilize them to social action by setting the goals, the rationale behind them, and the means of achieving them, especially by using and forming collective identity through identification (Haslam, Reicher, & Platow, 2010). Subsequently, some of them—or new agents—have to mobilize society members for peacemaking when such an option enters the realm of possibility (Hamburg, George, & Ballentine, 1999).

Finally, any discussion of the context of intractable conflicts has to take into account their diverse natures. In the present chapter, we focus on a particular distinctive dimension of symmetry versus asymmetry (Kriesberg, 2009; Rouhana, 2004). A conflict's location on this dimension is usually evaluated on the basis of the sides' military and economic capabilities. However, the conflict's asymmetry can also be a psychological matter, with both groups perceiving themselves as being weaker party to the conflict because of various reasons (see, for example, Schaller & Abeysinghe, 2006 in the case of Sri Lanka conflict). Finally, this dimension also applies to the international community judgment of the moral justness of the conflict's goals. In some intractable conflicts, the international community may regard the goals of one party as just, while viewing the other party's goals as unjust.

2.2. Collective Psychological State

A collective psychological state consists of the beliefs, attitudes, values, emotions, motivations, intentions, and behavioral practices related to conflict held by the involved society members. It includes an enduring repertoire, as well as immediate psychological reactions that are evoked in specific situations. These two psychological elements feed each other and continuously interact to create the collective psychological state characterizing societies in conflict. While the immediate, transient psychological reactions are somewhat similar to the ones that can be found in other types of intergroup conflicts, the lasting psychological repertoire mostly characterizes intractable conflicts. (See Stein's discussion of collective mood, chapter 12, this volume.)

An important part of the lasting psychological repertoire are societal beliefs, defined as enduring beliefs shared by society members (Bar-Tal, 2000). These beliefs develop as a result of the unique collective experiences and can refer to societal images, norms, values, concerns, and so on. During the intractable conflict many of them are supporting its continuation. In addition, the well-developed system of societal beliefs in intractable conflicts and the strong intragroup connections spur the evolvement of a collective identity that reflects the lasting conditions of intractable conflict. This collective identity indicates the common awareness that members share the recognition that they are members of the same group (David & Bar-Tal, 2009; Huddy, 2001; Klandermans & de Weerd, 2000).

In addition, those who live in societies involved in intractable conflicts also experience long-term emotional sentiments. While emotions are multicomponential responses to specific events, sentiments are enduring configurations of emotions or a temporally stable emotional disposition toward a person, group, or symbol (Arnold, 1960; Frijda, 1986; Halperin, Sharvit, & Gross, 2011). Since most society members do not experience many of the conflict-related events directly, these sentiments should be seen as group-based emotional sentiments, often targeted at another group (Smith, Seger, & Mackie, 2007). That is, they develop and are experienced by society members within the lasting context of intractable conflict because of their identification with the society (de Rivera, 1992; Mackie, Devos, & Smith, 2000; Wohl, Branscombe, & Klar, 2006; Yzerbyt, Dumont, Wigboldus, & Gordin, 2003). The enduring emotional sentiment is frequently associated with its corresponding short-term, group-based emotional reactions (Halperin & Gross, 2011).

Taking the above into account, we would like to note that we do not claim that the resulting psychological state is consensually shared. Nevertheless, we suggest that in many societies in times of intractable conflict (especially during its escalation period) a relatively consensual repertoire evolves regarding the general goals and other conflict-related themes, even when there is no wide consensus on the means.

3. Socio-Political-Psychological Analysis of Conflict Phases

After presenting the general framework, we turn now to the description of the phases of intractable conflict and peacemaking. In the description of these phases, we will focus mainly on those processes that are unique to intractable conflict.

3.1. Eruption of Intractable Conflicts

The fundamental question in this part is how intractable conflicts erupt and what distinguishes their eruption process from the eruption process of other conflicts? Conflict eruption, as the starting phase of any intractable conflict, includes a process in which the parties' conflicting goals rise above the surface and spark the potential for violent intergroup confrontation. Intractable conflicts erupt over goals that are perceived to be of existential importance and often are related to core beliefs associated with group identity. They are based on severe grievances and contentions that are accompanied by strong emotional feelings (Bar-Tal, 2013; Kriesberg, 2007; Coutant, Worchel, & Hanza, 2011). The existential goals appear from the beginning at least on one side, but with time, in cases of intractable conflicts, the features of the intractability appear on both sides. Thus, we will now examine the context and the psychological states of the parties to conflict.

3.1.1. Conflict Eruption: Context and Its Psychological Conditions

Azar (1990) suggested that the basic conditions for eruption of protracted conflicts are deprivation of basic needs related to collective identity (see also Brewer, 2011; Kelman, 2001; Korostelina, 2006; Reicher, 2004; Staub, 2011). These conditions can be classified into several categories (Thackrah, 2009). First, they often develop in a multiethnic community where the resources are unequally divided on the basis of group membership (e.g., the conflicts in Rwanda or South Africa). Second, they pertain to territorial disputes because groups, especially national groups, relate their identity to a specific country they consider their homeland (e.g., the Israeli-Palestinian and Kurdish conflicts). Third, they relate to the political-economic-cultural system in which the societies function (e.g., the conflicts in Nicaragua and Spain). The fourth category is often related to demands of free expression of culture, heritage, tradition, religion, and/or language that are perceived as expressing the essence of group identity (e.g., the conflict in Sri Lanka). Finally, groups may feel that the particular context in which they live threatens their core group identity (e,g,. Protestants in Northern Ireland and Maronites in Lebanon). Importantly, in many cases, the different categories of conditions overlap or appear simultaneously.

The eruption process is driven by intra- as well as intergroup processes that stimulate and motivate the destructive transformation of the disagreements into overt and active conflict. The intragroup processes are led by powerful entrepreneurs, who promote the broad mobilization of society members. The entrepreneurs are those who define the scope of the deprivations, pose the goals of the conflict, construct the epistemic basis and embed it into the social identity, persuade society members to support the conflict's causes, and vigorously recruit active participation in it (Reicher et al., 2005). The challenge of mobilizing society members to actively participate in the intractable conflict is of crucial importance. Many of the ideas related to the psychological processes that underlie collective action (see Klandermans & van Stekelenburg, chapter 24, this volume; Snow, Soule, & Kriesi, 2004; van Zomeren, Postmes, & Spears, 2008) can be applied to mobilization for conflict.

In the discussion of the context we focus on perceived threat as one of the key determinants of conflict eruption. Perceived threat is defined as perceived probability that harm will occur, and it reflects the perceived balance between the magnitude of the outside threat, on the one hand, and one's coping capabilities with such threat, on the other hand (Stephan & Stephan, 2000; Stein, chapter 12, this volume). Threats can be perceived either on the collective or on the personal level. In intractable conflicts in which perceived threat often leads to the fear of the group's possible extinction, society members might experience collective angst (Wohl & Branscombe, 2009; Worchel & Coutant, 2008). Such extreme extinction threat, or collective angst, can stem either from realistic or from symbolic sources (Stephan, Renfro, & Davis, 2008).

Perception of threat increases with the occurrence of violent actions by the rival group (Huddy, Feldman, Taber, & Lahav, 2005; Maoz & McCauley, 2008). Such actions signal the potential of harm and the other group's evil intention. They consequently lead to increased identification, emotional involvement, and enhanced levels of mobilization. Of special importance are brutal acts committed by the other group, which are viewed as unjustified and immoral. These brutal acts serve as traumatic turning-point experiences for group members, as they evoke group outrage, feelings of victimization, and empathy for injured compatriots. In turn, they then increase group members' identification and their willingness to act for the group's cause.

For example, it is assumed that the events in Northern Ireland on Bloody Sunday in 1972 and in South Africa in Sharpeville in 1960 served as major events that increased the readiness of the respective communities of Catholics and blacks to begin actively participating in the conflict. In the former case, British troops fired at a peaceful march of the Northern Ireland Civil Rights Association, killing 14 Catholics (seven of them teenagers) and injuring 13 others. In the latter case, South African police opened fire on a crowd of black protesters, killing 69 of them (including 10 children) and injuring over 180.

Finally, in asymmetrical conflicts the eruption phase develops differently, as institutionalized means for mobilization constitute a determinative factor for its success. When one dominant party has a state anchor, as is the case in asymmetrical conflicts, it has access to state institutions, organizations, resources, and trained personnel. Thus, the powerful party uses institutionalized methods of mobilization, such as the mandatory recruitment of participants, with established procedures, organizations, and training, the use of mass media, and allocation of resources (e.g., the Singhalese, Israeli Jews, government forces in Guatemala, the whites in South Africa, and the French in Algeria).

The party that is not supported by state institutions must employ informal mobilization methods, often relying on volunteers who require training, depending on social networks and trying to raise resources (e.g. Tamils, Palestinians, rebels in Guatemala, the blacks in South Africa, or the Algerians). Moreover, the latter party mobilization methods are often illegal and face active obstruction and prevention by the rival (see, for example, mobilization practices of insurgents in El Salvador, Wood, 2003).

What follows is that the mobilization process of such a party in intractable conflict is especially based on the successful persuasion of society members in the justice of the society's goals and in the ability to carry out the confrontation as well as spontaneous actions that are driven by collective anger. These informal actions are encouraged by the success of militant actions that grant the masses feelings of efficacy and create hope that a violent conflict could fundamentally transform the intergroup power balance (Bandura, 2000).

3.1.2. Conflict Eruption: Collective Psychological States

The context of emerging conflict provides fertile ground for the development of the collective psychological state required for an intractable conflict to erupt. The essential part of this development is the emergence of a strong and salient collective identity that is directed at the evolved goals and the recognition of the need to correct the group's position (Brewer, 2011; Roccas & Elster, 2012; Tajfel, 1982; Huddy, chapter 23, this volume). Other content-based, motivational and structural psychological processes that can potentially promote conflict eruption rely on the existence of this type of strong collective identity (Bar-Tal, 2013).

Indeed, there are empirical indications that social identity becomes a basis for mobilization (Brewer, 2011; Reicher, 2004). The strength of group identification has been found to be related to the level of emotional response to collective threats (Smith et al., 2007)—and to the willingness to engage in political action (Klandermans & de Weerd, 2000; van Zomeren & Iyer, 2009). In addition, in times of intractable conflict, mobilization is facilitated with the strengthening of three generic characteristics of collective identity (see David & Bar-Tal, 2009): *a sense of a common fate* that pertains to the sense of unity and the feelings of mutual dependence (Doosje, Ellemers, & Spears, 1999); *concern for the welfare of the collective and sacrifice for its sake*, which refers to feelings of interest in the experiences of the collective and motivation to act on its behalf, including sacrifice of one's own life (Kashti, 1997; Reykowski, 1997); *coordinated activity by the collective's members*, which refers to the ability of the different groups and sectors that compose the collective to collaborate with one another to achieve societal goals posed in the conflict (van Zomeren & Iyer, 2009). In this vein, the concept of politicized collective identity proposed by Simon and Klandermans (2001) is of special relevance to the present analysis. The concept denotes a mindset based on high identification with the group that leads to involvement and engagement in the group's struggle for its goals (Hunt & Benford, 2004).

Nonetheless, strong collective identity leads to the eruption of conflict only if it is accompanied by the relevant societal beliefs. First and most important is the belief that the in-group is deprived of collective goods (tangible and/or intangible), or that there is some potential for such deprivation. Such a sense of relative deprivation may evolve as a result of comparison between one's own present subjective state of affairs and the state of another group and/or the in-group's own past state, as well as comparison between the present state and an imaginary aspired-to state that the group believes it deserves (Runciman, 1966; Walker & Smith, 2002). An alternative, or complementary belief, may be that another group is harming or poses a continuous potentially existential threat of harm to the in-group.

Second, deprivation or harm potentially lead to conflict eruption if either (*a*) the responsibility or blame for their occurrence can be ascribed explicitly to the actions of a certain out-group and these actions are perceived to be unjust and violating basic norms and values; or (*b*) the out-group possesses the commodity needed to put an end to the experienced deprivation. In both cases, the desired goal of changing this situation must be viewed as justified. These two beliefs, however, may not be enough. A third societal belief often needed for the eruption of intractable conflicts is the conviction that the in-group is strong enough to at least face the out-group successfully in a future confrontation that could be violent (Hirschberger & Pyszczynski, 2010). This perception of strength and controllability (i.e., collective efficacy) provides the confidence necessary to undertake aggressive action and take the inherent risk (Bandura, 2000). Moreover, in most cases, public support for use of violence is highly dependent on the belief that the out-group's hostile actions stem from an evil, stable, and irreversible disposition central to the outg-roup members' character (Halperin, 2008).

Our basic assumption is that the above-mentioned ensemble of societal beliefs leads to the development of the epistemic basis for the goals. The epistemic basis consists of an elaborate belief system (also called a narrative) that explains, rationalizes, legitimizes, and justifies the goals set and later also the means used to achieve these goals. The epistemic basis is necessary because in order to be mobilized for the conflict, group members need to know why the goals are important to them individually and to the group as a whole, and whether the goals are realistic and just. The epistemic basis also addresses the international community in order to receive its support.

In addition, the psychological state in that stage contains the long-term sentiments of despair, frustration, hatred, and fear (Halperin, Sharvit, & Gross, 2011). On the basis of the long-term sentiments and societal beliefs, short-termed emotional and cognitive reactions emerge and transform the long-term beliefs and sentiments into concrete support or even participation in aggressive collective action. These psychological "triggers" of intractable conflict usually appear as a response to what is perceived as out-group provocations or unjustified irritating, aggressive behavior. Emotions, especially negative ones, are the most powerful influential force because they are easily evoked and translated into concrete action tendencies (Lindner, 2006).

The emotion that has been most frequently studied with respect to this stage of the conflict is anger. *Anger* is evoked by events in which the individual perceives the actions of others as unjust, as unfair, or as deviating from acceptable societal norms (Averill, 1982). In addition, it involves appraisals of relative strength and high coping potential (Mackie et al., 2000). The integration of these two characteristics often creates a tendency to confront (Berkowitz, 1993; Mackie et al., 2000), strike, kill, or attack the anger-evoking target.

In line with its characteristics, previous studies conducted in the context of real-world conflicts have consistently found a clear and direct association between anger and the attribution of blame to the out-group (Halperin, 2008; Small, Lerner, & Fischhoff,

2006). Other studies have found that individuals who feel angry appraise future military attacks as less risky (Lerner & Keltner, 2001) and anticipate more positive consequences for such attacks (Huddy, Feldman, & Cassese, 2007; Huddy, chapter 23, this volume). Accordingly, studies conducted in the United States following the 9/11 attacks found that angry individuals were highly supportive of an American military response in Iraq and elsewhere (e.g., Huddy et al., 2007; Lerner, Gonzalez, Small, & Fischhoff, 2003; Skitka, Bauman, Aramovich, & Morgan, 2006). Finally, the central role of group-based anger in motivating conflict eruption and aggression yielded further support in a recent study conducted in Serbia and Republika Srpska (Spanovic, Lickel, Denson, & Petrovic, 2010).

Humiliation is another important emotion that appears in the early phase of conflict eruption. It is defined as "enforced lowering of any person or group by a process of subjugation that damages their dignity" (Lindner, 2006, p. xiv). It creates rifts between groups and breaks relationships (Lindner, 2001). This feeling arises in many of the conflict situations in which societies experience deprivation as a result of discrimination, oppression, and/or exploitation.

On the cognitive level, almost every process of conflict eruption is driven and accompanied by mutual intergroup misperceptions (Fisher & Kelman, 2011; Jervis, 1976; White, 1970). The title of the seminal work of Ralph White, *Nobody Wanted War: Misperception in Vietnam and Other Wars*, accurately captures the role of misperceptions in conflict eruption processes. To demonstrate this process, Keltner and Robinson (1993) have presented evidence for a "false polarization": partisans perceive more disagreement between their own opinions and those of their rivals than exists in reality. This can lead to heightened mistrust, which can potentially result in destructive misinterpretations of the rival's intentions and aspirations (Chambers, Baron, & Inman, 2006).

Another example of misperception in the initial phase of conflict eruption is the tendency to attribute the negative behavior of the rival group to personal characteristics, while disregarding situational factors (see, for example, Pettigrew, 1979, who labeled this tendency the "ultimate attribution error"; also Fisher, Kelman, & Nan, chapter 16, this volume). This tendency is even more profound because the attribution to personal characteristics is often made to innate dispositions (Dweck, 1999). This attribution implies that the rival group is evil and will not change and therefore a confrontation is needed in order to achieve justified demands (Hunter, Stringer, & Watson, 1991; Holt, & Silverstein, 1989).

Hypothetically, situations of deprivation and their appearance on the public agenda could lead the powerful group to recognize the situation as unjust, leading it to attempt to change the situation by correcting the injustice, or dividing the goods in an equal manner, granting autonomy, and possibly compensating the victims for their suffering. In reality, however, this situation almost never happens. When serious demands are posed, a stronger group almost never voluntarily relinquishes its highly valued goods in terms of power, status, privileges, wealth, resources, or territories. Moreover, in almost all the cases when one side characterizes the conflict as being intractable, the other side follows this definition also. In most cases, moral and just reasons do not lead most groups to give up what they think is theirs, or what they think they deserve. Thus, satisfaction of the deprivation usually takes place within the framework of a conflict, after a long, often violent struggle, which may eventually lead to the victory of one side or to the conflict's peaceful settlement.

3.2. Escalation and Conflict Management

The fundamental question of this section is why conflicts escalate and how they are managed in their climax, within the unique framework of intractable conflicts.

3.2.1. *Conflict Escalation: Context and Its Psychological Conditions*

Escalation indicates that the grievances, objections, and contentions raised are not met with understanding and compliance, but rather with dismay, rejection, and even stronger counteractions. Consequently, the party that raised the grievances or objections resorts to harsher steps, in order to make the conflict more salient and more costly to the rival. In other words, the parties gradually adopt increasingly drastic means to promote their goals (Pruitt & Kim, 2004). These steps are met with severe reactions, and both sides thus raise the level of confrontation, entering into cycles of reactions and counter-reactions (Horowitz, 1985; Kriesberg, 2007).

To explain the escalation process we focus on the psychological conditions of the context and specifically on the continuous, vicious cycle of the interactions between these conditions and the collective psychological state. The developed repertoire, as part of the psychological state, leads to actions that escalate the conflict; in turn the escalation reinforces the repertoire that perpetuates the conflict, due to the dominance of the culture of conflict and its bearing on collective identity. In fact, in this stage the parties become entrapped in the conflict because they invest greatly in it and need to justify this investment with the attempt to recoup incurred losses and more forcefully achieve their respective goals (Brockner & Rubin, 1985; Ross, 2010)

The mobilization at this phase is usually successful because the conflict's goals at that stage are often perceived as protected or sacred (Atran & Axelrod, 2008; Landman, 2010), and thus as fundamental for defining the identities, worldviews, and ideologies of society members. Therefore, the goals become resistant to any trade-offs or compromise. Hence, society members become morally invested in the goals of the conflict and morally convinced in the justness of these goals (Tetlock, 2003; Skitka, 2010). The conflict then becomes clearly perceived as being zero sum and unsolvable.

Moreover, this phase is characterized in most of the cases of intractable conflicts as a phase of societal closure. The entrepreneurs of the conflict, on the one hand, propagate information that supports continuation of the conflict and, on the other hand, try to limit the society's access to alternative information that, in their view, could weaken the society's position in the conflict. Thus, the context is often characterized by use of such societal mechanisms as mass media control, censorship of information, delegitimization of alternative information and its sources, and self-censorship (see Bar-Tal, Oren, & Nets-Zehngut, 2012; Burns-Bisogno, 1997; Wolfsfeld, 2004).

The conflict also greatly preoccupies society members and is continuously present on their agenda, as they invest much materially and psychologically in successfully coping with the enemy. Finally, escalation is observed in the context of the intensification of hostile acts, including verbal rhetoric and especially behavioral actions such as killings and injuries of both active participants in the violence and civilians. Paradoxically, the increasing violence and sacrifices usually strengthen the involved parties' commitment to the conflict's continuation, mainly because adhering to this commitment helps society members avoid the cognitive dissonance embedded in behavioral change (Brubaker & Laitin, 1998; Elcheroth & Spini, 2011; Horowitz, 2001; Staub & Bar-Tal, 2003). In line with that rationale, prospect theory suggests that the failure to renormalize reference points after losses leads society members to see these losses as sunk costs, to the overvaluation of those costs, and to risk-acceptant behavior to recover sunk costs and return to the reference point (Levy, 1996; chapter 10, this volume). Thus, the context of the conflict changes significantly and creates very severe experiences for the involved society members. These stressful experiences are part of the psychological conditions of the context that characterize intractable conflicts.

The above-described psychological context poses three basic challenges to the societies involved in intractable conflict (Bar-Tal, 2007a, 2013). First, society members need to somehow satisfy those human needs that remain deprived during intractable conflicts, such as the psychological needs of knowing, feeling certainty, mastery, safety, positive identity, and so on (e.g., Burton, 1990; Maslow, 1954; Reykowski, 1982; Staub, 2003; Tajfel, 1982). Second, they must learn to cope with stress, fears, and other negative psychological experiences that accompany intractable conflict situations (e.g., Hobfoll, Canetti-Nisim, & Johnson, 2006; Shalev, Yehuda, & McFarlane, 2000; Worchel, 1999). Third, the societies must develop psychological conditions that are conducive to successfully withstanding the rival group—that is, to attempt to win the conflict or, at the least, avoid losing it.

Also in this phase, the symmetry versus asymmetry distinction influences the dynamic of the conflict's escalation. The stronger party with a state behind it often has the resources and the military personnel to withstand the escalation and also has at its disposal channels of communication and societal institutions to disseminate the epistemic basis for continuing the conflict. On the other hand, the weaker party must find resources for carrying the escalation, mobilizing volunteers to actively participate in the conflict and to disseminate its messages (Fisher, Kelman, & Nan, chapter 16, this volume). Often in this phase, the weaker party takes violent action, including terror attacks, against civilian targets to harm the stronger party, which often lead, in turn, to retribution and preventative measures (often called terror state's measures) that also widely harm the weaker party's civilian population. Psychologically and morally, this process continuously erodes the epistemic basis for the conflict, on the side of the stronger group, which in turn has to develop further psychological mechanism to mobilize its people to the goals of the conflict (see, for example, Ramanathapillai, 2006).

3.2.2. Conflict Escalation: Collective Psychological States

In discussing the collective psychological state of society members in the escalation phase, we begin with the teleological beliefs, attitudes, feelings, emotions, and motivations that develop as a result of the new experiences of the escalating conflict. They develop in order to allow the societies to meet the described psychological challenges. This proposition on the evolvement of the functional repertoire is based on extensive work in psychology showing that in times of stress, threat, and deprivation, individuals need to form a meaningful worldview that provides a coherent and organized picture (see work by Antonovsky, 1987; Frankl, 1963; Greenberg, Pyszczynski, & Solomon, 1997; Janoff-Bulman, 1992).

It is further proposed that as the intractable conflict persists, the collective psychological state filters into institutions and the communications channels and gradually crystallizes into a sociopsychological infrastructure. This infrastructure has three pillars that constitute the cognitive-emotional basis for the long-term psychological state: collective memory of conflict, ethos of conflict, and collective emotional sentiments that serve as foundations of the developed culture of conflict (Bar-Tal, 2007a; 2013).

3.2.2.1. Collective memory is defined as representations of the past, remembered by society members as the history of the group and providing the epistemic foundation for the group's existence and its continuity (Kansteiner, 2002). Collective memory constructs the narratives, the symbols, the models, and the myths related to the past that mold the culture of the group. Societal beliefs of collective memory, as a narrative, in the case of intractable conflict, evolve to present the history of the conflict to society members (Cairns & Roe, 2003; Halbwachs, 1992; Pennebaker, Paez, & Rimé, 1997; Tint, 2010; Wertsch, 2002).

This narrative develops over time, and the societal beliefs describe the eruption of the conflict and its course, providing a coherent and meaningful picture of what has happened from the society's perspective (Devine-Wright, 2003; Paez & Liu, 2011). The major function of collective memory is to provide the epistemic basis for present societal needs and goals (Liu & Hilton, 2005). Therefore, it is selective, biased and distortive in nature, and it clouds judgment and evaluation of the present (Bar-Tal et al., 2012; Baumeister & Hastings, 1997).

Collective memories of intractable conflict are organized around narratives of transitional contexts or particular major events, with the focus placed on specific individuals who have played major roles in the conflict. These may be short-term events such as battles, or even parts of battles, or prolonged events such as wars or occupations. Indeed, the narrative of collective memory touches on at least four important themes. First, it justifies the eruption of the conflict and the course of its development. Second, it presents a positive image of one's group. Third, it delegitimizes the opponent. Fourth, it presents one's group as being a victim of the opponent.

To develop this narrative, the conflict's collective memory is fed by memories of events that preceded the conflict and/or of events unrelated to the conflict that took place in conjunction with the conflict. These memories are often adapted, reconstructed, and reinvented to serve the needs and goals stemming from the challenges posed by the conflict (e.g., Hammack, 2011; Zerubavel, 1995). Volkan (1997) has proposed that societies especially remember major events that he calls *chosen traumas* and *chosen glories*. These past events, especially chosen traumas, greatly contribute to the definition of group identity and are therefore maintained in the culture and transmitted to new generations, while also occupying a central place in the collective memory of a society involved in intractable conflict (e.g., MacDonald, 2002; Zertal, 2005)

The collective memories of societies involved in intractable conflict provide a black-and-white picture and enable a parsimonious, fast, unequivocal, and simple understanding of the history of the conflict. In fact, the competition over the collective memory constitutes an additional confrontational field where, during the escalation phase of the conflict, each society tries to impart its own collective memory to in-group members and then to persuade the international community of its truthfulness (Bar-Tal et al., 2012; Noor, Brown, & Prentice, 2008).

3.2.2.2. The ethos (of conflict) is defined as "the configuration of central societal beliefs that provide dominant characterization to the society and gives it a particular orientation" (Bar-Tal, 2000, p. xiv). It provides the shared mental basis for societal membership, binds the members of society together, gives meaning to societal life, imparts legitimacy to social order, and enables an understanding of society's present and past concerns as well as its future aspirations.

We suggest that under prolonged conditions of intractable conflict, societies develop a particular ethos of conflict that provides them with a particular dominant orientation and gives meaning to societal life (Bar-Tal, 2000; 2007a; 2012). In the earlier work it was proposed that the ethos of conflict is composed of the following eight interrelated themes of societal beliefs (Bar-Tal, 2000; 2007a; Rouhana & Bar-Tal, 1998) that were found to be dominant in various societies engaged in intractable conflict (Bar-Tal, 2007b; Hadjipavlou, 2007; MacDonald, 2002; Oren, 2009; Papadakis, Perstianis, & Welz, 2006; Slocum-Bradley, 2008).

Societal beliefs about the justness of one's own goals, which first of all outline the goals in conflict, indicate their crucial importance, and provide their justification and rationales. In addition, the societal beliefs negate and delegitimize the goals of the rival group. These societal beliefs play a crucial motivating role because they present the goals as being existential, thus requiring society members to adhere to them and to mobilize.

Societal beliefs about security refer to the appraisal of threats and dangers as well as difficulties in coping with them within the intractable conflict (Bar-Tal & Jacobson, 1998). Their most important function is to satisfy the needs of maintaining safety, which involves the basic human needs for a sense of protection, surety, and survival (Maslow, 1954), but they also play an important role in the mobilization of society members for coping with the perceived threats and dangers.

Societal beliefs of positive collective self-image concern the ethnocentric tendency to attribute positive characteristics, values, norms, and patterns of behavior to one's own society (Baumeister & Hastings, 1997). They frequently relate, on the one hand, to courage, heroism, or endurance and, on the other hand, to humaneness, morality, fairness, trustworthiness, and progress. These beliefs allow a clear differentiation between the in-group and the rival and supply moral strength and a sense of superiority (Sande, Goethals, Ferrari, & Worth, 1989).

Societal beliefs of one's own victimization concern self-presentation as the ultimate victim, with focus on the unjust harm, evil deeds, and atrocities perpetrated by the adversary (Bar-Tal, Chernyak-Hai, Schori, & Gundar, 2009; Vollhardt, 2012). They provide the moral incentive to seek justice and oppose the opponent, as well as to mobilize moral, political, and material support from the international community.

Societal beliefs of delegitimizing the opponent concern beliefs that indicate that the rival group is outside the boundaries of the commonly accepted groups, and should thus be excluded from the international community as a legitimate member worthy of basic civil and human rights and deserving of inhumane treatment (Bar-Tal & Hammack, 2012; Haslam, 2006; Tileaga, 2007). These beliefs serve a special function in justifying the group's own aggressive acts against the rival.

Societal beliefs of patriotism generate attachment to both country and society by propagating loyalty, love, care, and sacrifice (Huddy & Khatib, 2007; Huddy). Patriotic beliefs increase social cohesion and dedication and serve an important function in mobilizing society members to actively participate in the conflict and endure hardships and difficulties, even to the point of sacrificing their lives for the group (Somerville, 1981). When they turn into blind dogma, they close the way to peacemaking (Schatz, Staub, & Lavine, 1999).

Societal beliefs of unity emphasize the importance of staying united in the face of the external threat (Moscovici & Doise, 1994). These beliefs strengthen society from within, develop a consensus and a sense of belonging, increase solidarity, and allow society to direct its forces and energy to dealing with the enemy.

Finally, *societal beliefs of peace* propagate peace as the group's ultimate desire and present society members as peace-loving. Such beliefs play the role of inspiring hope and optimism. They strengthen the positive self-image and a positive self-presentation to the outside world.

An ethos of conflict is a relatively stable worldview, which creates a conceptual framework that allows human beings to organize and comprehend the prolonged context of conflict. Therefore, it can be seen as a type of ideology (Bar-Tal, Sharvit, Halperin, & Zafran, 2012; Cohrs, 2012; Jost, Federico, & Napier, 2009; Van Dijk, 1998). As an ideology, an ethos of conflict represents a coherent and systematic knowledge base that serves as a guide for the coordinated behavior of society members and directs the decisions made by society's leaders, the development of the societal system, and its functioning. It relates to conservative worldviews that intend to preserve the context and societal system as it is (Jost, Glaser, Kruglanski, & Sulloway, 2003).

3.2.2.3. Collective emotional sentiments develop because of the nature of long-term intractable conflicts, which create fertile ground for the continuation and aggregation of emotions beyond the immediate time frame (Bar-Tal, 2013; de Rivera & Paez, 2007; Petersen, 2002; Scheff, 1994). Hence, during the escalation stage societies involved in intractable conflicts develop a set of collective emotional sentiments that is dominated primarily by hatred, despair and fear (see: Halperin, Sharvit, & Gross, 2011).

The most destructive emotional sentiment that influences beliefs, attitudes, and behaviors at the stage of conflict eruption is *hatred*. *Hatred* is a secondary, extreme negative emotion (Halperin, 2008; Sternberg & Sternberg, 2008) that is directed at a particular individual or group and denounces it fundamentally and all-inclusively (Sternberg, 2003). In most cases, hatred involves appraisal of the behavior of an out-group as stemming from a deep-rooted, permanent evil character (Halperin, Sharvit, & Gross, 2011). As a result, hatred is associated with very low expectations for positive change and with high levels of despair, which altogether feed the conflict's continuation and escalation. Indeed the evaluation of short-term conflict-related events through the lens of hatred automatically increases support for initiating violent actions and for intensifying the conflict (Halperin, 2011; Halperin, Canetti-Nisim, & Hirsch-Hoefler, 2009; Staub, 2005). When hatred is accompanied by group-based anger, which dominates the eruption stage, its consequences are even more destructive (Halperin, Russel, Dweck, & Gross, 2011).

While hatred provides the emotional basis for viewing the opponent in the conflict, fear may prevent attempts to break the vicious cycle of violence. Due to recurring experiences of threat and danger resulting from the conflict, society members may become oversensitized to cues that signal danger and exist in a state of constant readiness to defend themselves (Jarymowicz & Bar-Tal, 2006). This oversensitization to fear cues freezes society members in their prior dispositions regarding the conflict and the out-group and prevents them from taking risks or thinking creatively about resolving the conflict. People prefer to suffer with the known than take a risk that comes with possible relief.

Eventually, the sociopsychological infrastructure with its three pillars becomes the foundation of the evolved *culture of conflict*. A culture of conflict develops when societies saliently integrate into their culture tangible and intangible symbols, created to communicate a particular meaning about the prolonged and continuous experiences of living in the context of conflict (Geertz, 1973; Ross, 1997). These symbols of conflict become hegemonic elements and provide a dominant interpretation of the present reality and past and future goals, and an outline acceptable practice. When a culture of conflict becomes dominant, intractable conflicts come to be way of life (Bar-Tal, Abutbul, & Raviv, in press). It serves as the major motivating, justifying, and rationalizing force in the group, playing a highly functional role in addressing the challenges posed by the context (Bar-Tal, 2013).

Additionally, the societal beliefs of culture of conflict provide contents that imbue the collective identity with meaning (Cash, 1996; Cairns, Lewis, Mumcu, & Waddell, 1998; Gillis, 1994; Oren & Bar-Tal, in press). On the individual level, the conflict may change the individuals' definitions of identity and levels of identification, by increasing the importance of both identity and the will to belong to a collective. On the collective level, it may influence the generic characteristics of the shared sense of common fate and continuity, perception of uniqueness, coordination of activity, extent of sharing beliefs, concern for the welfare of the collective, and readiness for mobilization on behalf of the collective (see David & Bar-Tal, 2009; Eriksen, 2001; Reicher, 2004).

Considering that this process occurs simultaneously for both parties to the conflict (each a mirror image of the other), it is obvious how the vicious cycle of violence in intractable conflicts operates (Sandole, 1999). Any negative actions taken by each side toward its rival then serve as information validating the existing collective psychological state and in turn magnify the motivation and readiness to engage in conflict. Both societies practice moral disengagement, moral entitlement, and self-focusing, blocking any empathy and responsibility for the suffering of the rival or responsibility for the group's own actions (Bandura, 1999; Castano, 2008; Čehajić & Brown, 2008; Opotow, in press; Schori, Klar, & Roccas, 2011; Wohl & Branscombe, 2008). Human beings do all the possible psychological acrobatic exercises to continue the conflict and kill rival society members in violent encounters.

Once intractable conflicts become solidified and institutionalized with the culture of conflict, they endure for a very long period of time, fluctuating in their intensity, as powerful barriers prevent their peaceful resolution. We suggest that the same psychological repertoire that helps society members cope with the challenges posed by the conflict, prevents them from identifying and taking advantage of opportunities for peace. Thus, together with more transient cognitive (Ross & Ward, 1995) and emotional (Halperin, 2011) barriers, the enduring sociopsychological repertoire (i.e., ethos of conflict and collective memory) serves as a barrier to conflict resolution. From a broader perspective, sociopsychological barriers *pertain to* an integrated operation of cognitive, emotional, and motivational processes, combined with a preexisting repertoire of rigid conflict-supporting beliefs, worldviews, and emotions that result in selective, biased, and distorted information processing (see details presented in Bar-Tal & Halperin, 2011; also Brader & Marcus, chapter 6, this volume; and Stein, chapter 12, this volume).

This processing obstructs and inhibits the penetration of any new, alternative information that could potentially facilitate progress toward peace. It leads to a selective collection of information, which means that group members tend to search and absorb information that is in line with their repertoire, while ignoring contradictory information, which is viewed as invalid. Furthermore, even when ambiguous or contradictory information is absorbed, it is encoded and cognitively processed in accordance with the held repertoire through bias, addition, and distortion (for example, De Dreu & Carnevale, 2003; Pfeifer & Ogloff, 1991; Shamir & Shikaki, 2002; Sommers & Ellsworth, 2000). This processing takes place because the societal beliefs supporting the continuation of the conflict are rigid due to structural, emotional, contextual, and motivational factors (Bar-Tal & Halperin, 2011; Kruglanski, 2004).

3.3. De-escalation of Intractable Conflicts and Peacemaking

The above barriers indicate that overcoming the core disagreements is a very difficult challenge. Nevertheless, almost every society engaged in intractable conflict contains societal forces (even if they are a small minority) that propagate and press for embarking on a different road—the road of peacemaking. Once these forces grow and become influential, it is possible to say that the process of peace-building has gained momentum. In some societies, this process even ends with a peaceful settlement following negotiations that may extend over many years (see Fisher, Kelman, & Nan, chapter 16, this volume).

There are various terms to describe this process (see Galtung, 1996; Rouhana, 2004). Peace-building processes can be defined as continuous exerted efforts by society members, society's institutions, agents, channels of communications, and the international community to achieve full, lasting peaceful relations with the past rival within the framework of a culture of peace. Peace-building thus includes all the measures taken to facilitate the achievement of this goal, culminating in reconciliation (see also de Rivera, 2009; Lederach, 1997). This is a very long process, commencing when at least a segment of society begins developing activities to promote peace (Lederach, 2005). Peacemaking, as a phase in the peace-building process, focuses only on actions taken to reaching an official settlement of the conflict, in the form of a formal agreement between the rival sides to end the confrontation (see Zartman, 2007). Within the process of peacemaking, conflict resolution refers to the negotiation process that takes place between decision-makers to reach its formal settlement. Hence, the key question in the de-escalation phase is how the process of de-escalation evolves and what factors facilitate it.

3.3.1. Conflict De-escalation: Context and Its Psychological Conditions

In the phase of conflict de-escalation the characteristics of the context change as the intractability becomes less extreme in nature, moving toward the tractable end of the continuum. Embarking on the road of peace-building begins when at least a segment of society members begins to think that the conflict should be resolved peacefully and begins to act to realize this idea. Once such an idea emerges and is propagated by at least some society members, the long process of moving the society toward resolving the conflict peacefully begins.

A substantive change in people's beliefs, as will be described in the following section, may be facilitated in many of the cases by changes in the context, signaling to society members a need to reevaluate the repertoire that has fueled the continuation of the conflict. Such significant change in the context can be driven, among other things, by the accumulation of negative conflict experiences; major events like the eruption of a new harsh conflict with a third, unrelated party; an unexpected conciliatory, trust-building action by the rival; internal non-conflict-related events (for example, economic collapse or internal turmoil); intervention of a third party; geopolitical changes (for example, a fall of a supporting superpower); or the rise of new leaders, who are less committed to the ideology of conflict.

Nonetheless, even such substantial contextual changes do not usually lead to an immediate, dramatic change in public opinion. In many cases, the process of peacemaking begins with a minority who starts to realize that it is necessary to end the conflict by negotiating its resolution with the rival. Those in the minority must possess not only conviction in the justness of the new way but also the courage to present alternative ideas to society members, because they are often viewed by the great majority of society members as, at best, naive and detached from reality, but more often as traitorous. Nevertheless, the emergence of this minority is important not only for the in-group, but also for the rival group, where a similar process may consequently be ignited or reinforced.

As this group develops within society, new entrepreneurs may appear and mobilize society members to support the peace process. In most cases, peacemaking involves, on the one hand, bottom-up processes in which groups, grass-roots organizations, and civil society members support the ideas of peace-building and act to disseminate them among leaders as well, and, on the other hand, top-down processes in which leaders join the efforts, begin persuading society members of the necessity of a peaceful settlement of the conflict, and initiate its implementation (Gawerc, 2006). Peacemaking processes, in order to succeed, must also receive the support of the elites and societal institutions, support that must eventually be shared by at least a substantial portion of society (e.g., Bar-Siman-Tov, 2004; Knox & Quirk, 2000). Of special importance is the role played by the mass media and other societal channels of communication and institutions, which can first promote the formation of a peace orientation and subsequently transmit and disseminate a new system of beliefs among the society members (Wolfsfeld, 2004).

Arriving at a peaceful settlement at the end of the peacemaking process constitutes a turning point in the relations between the rival parties. Still, at least some societies involved in intractable conflict eventually reach this stage through a political process in which both parties eliminate the perceived incompatibility between their goals and interests and establish a new reality of perceived compatibility (Deutsch, 1973; Fisher, 1990; Kriesberg, 2007; also Fisher, Kelman, & Nan, chapter 16, this volume). The formal manifestation of this process is an agreement negotiated by representatives of the two opposing groups, which outlines the settlement's details. The agreement indicates a formal end to the conflict and specifies the terms of its resolution, based on uncertain and ambiguous future benefits. In most cases, the agreement demands the parties put aside certain dreams and aspirations in order to accommodate the possible and practical present. In any event, reaching a peaceful, just, and satisfactory solution to an intractable conflict, supported by both rival parties, is probably one of the most impressive and significant achievements to be attained by human beings.

Nevertheless, a conflict's peaceful resolution does not have a singular meaning, as peace may take on many different forms once it is achieved. It can range from a cold peace that indicates an end to violent acts and minimal diplomatic relations, to a warm peace that is geared toward major transformation—the establishment of entirely novel peaceful relations (see Galtung, 1969).

The period of peacemaking and, even more so, the first stage following the conflict's peaceful settlement is often quite difficult. In this stage, society members move from a well-known and familiar context into an uncertain, ambiguous, and risky context (Bar-Tal, 2013). This context has many of the characteristics of conflict, while at the same time possessing characteristics of the emerging context of peace. On the one hand signs of peacemaking appear, reflected in meetings between the rivals, coordination of some activities, moderation of violence, and so on. On the other hand, violence acts continue, conflict rhetoric continues to be employed, and, most importantly, the culture of conflict remains hegemonic. Adding to the confusion characterizing this period is the fact that the rival parties, avoiding substantial risks, continue to reflect on the possibility that they may be forced to return to the road of violent confrontation. Therefore this period can be seen as a period of duality, where signs of conflict and signs of peace coexist.

Moreover, in most cases, peacemaking is not accepted willingly by all the segments of society. There are often spoilers who exert every effort to foil the process using various tactics of incitement and even violence. Thus, societies making peace are often polarized, with an intrasocietal schism separating those who support peacemaking from those who refuse to compromise toward a peaceful solution. Finally, in many cases of peacemaking and even after the realization of a peaceful settlement, reappearing violence may evoke beliefs and emotions conducive to conflict.

3.3.2. Conflict De-escalation: Collective Psychological State

Changes in the context, as well as the self-enlightenment of some society members, lead to the appearance of new beliefs that must then be adopted and disseminated among society members. This is a necessary condition for the peaceful settlement of a conflict and later for reconciliation. These new beliefs that signal an emergence of an alternative collective psychological state should include many new ideas, such as an idea about the need to resolve the conflict peacefully, about changing the goals that fueled the conflict and posing new goals that can lead to peace, about legitimization, humanization, and trusting the rival, about sharing victimhood, about the history of the conflict, and so on (Bar-Tal, 2013).

This challenging process of cognitive change requires unfreezing, as suggested by classical conception offered by Lewin (1947). Hence, a precondition for the acceptance and internalization of alternative content about the conflict or peace-building depends on the ability to destabilize the rigid structure of the collective psychological state related to the conflict that dominates the involved societies. These new alternative ideas must be spread, legitimized, and eventually institutionalized in society. Legitimization is a stage in which ideas, actions, or agents propagating peacemaking become morally acceptable in view of the norms and values of the group (Kelman, 2001). This important phase moves the minority group to a position in which ideas concerning peacemaking become accepted as part of the legitimate public discourse. Institutionalization indicates penetration of the alternative beliefs supporting peacemaking into societal institutions and channels of communication, such as the formal political system, educational system, cultural products, and mass media. In fact, in this phase, an alternative narrative about the necessity of peacemaking is well established. It contains beliefs that contradict the established collective memory and ethos of conflict and serve as the foundations for an ethos of peace, which sheds new light on the reality.

Alongside the contextual changes that were described above, embarking on the road of peace depends mostly on the psychological states within both societies involved in the severe and harsh conflict. A number of scholars have tried to elucidate the conditions of ripeness that may facilitate peacemaking processes and conflict settlement realization. For example, Zartman (2000, pp. 228–229) proposed that "If the (two) parties to a conflict (a) perceive themselves to be in a hurting stalemate and (b) perceive the possibility of a negotiated solution (a way out), the conflict is ripe for resolution (i.e., for negotiations toward resolution to begin)."

Pruitt (2007) offered a psychological perspective on ripeness theory, by analyzing the case of Northern Ireland. In his view, ripeness reflects each party's readiness to enter and stay engaged in negotiations. Antecedents of readiness include motivation to escape the situation together with optimism about the prospects of reaching a mutually beneficial outcome. We have recently proposed (Bar-Tal & Halperin, 2009) and demonstrated empirically (Gayer, Tal, Halperin, & Bar-Tal, 2009) that societies may begin negotiations for the conflict's peaceful settlement when their members realize that the losses resulting from the continuation of the conflict significantly exceed the losses that a society may incur as a consequence of the compromises and outcomes of peaceful settlement (see also Levy, chapter 10, this volume).

In ending our analysis we would like to make few points that shed light on the macro processes beyond peaceful settlement of intractable conflicts. Eventually, some of the intractable conflicts may de-escalate and move toward their peaceful resolution when society members are demobilized from supporting the goals of the conflict and mobilized for its peaceful resolution (Gidron, Katz, & Hasenfeld, 2002). But it is not enough just to want peace—without determination and persistence by active agents of peace, peace cannot be achieved (Fitzduff, 2006). Almost all human beings cherish the value of peace and wish to live under its wings. But achievement of peace is not that simple—peacemaking requires parting from far-fetched, ideal dreams, resorting to concrete steps of pragmatism, and transforming the psychological repertoire that for many years served as a compass for continuing the conflict. Even goals rooted in justice and moral values must eventually be compromised due to pragmatic considerations that are often required for successful peaceful settlement.

Nevertheless it has become evident that even reaching a formal peace settlement may fall far short of establishing genuine peaceful relations between the former adversaries (e.g., Knox & Quirk, 2000; Lederach, 1997). Formal conflict resolution sometimes obliges only the leaders who negotiated the agreement, the narrow strata around them, or only a small part of the society at large. In these cases, the majority of society members may not accept the negotiated compromises, or even if they do, they may still hold the worldview that has fueled the conflict. As the result, formal resolutions of conflicts may be unstable and may collapse, as was the case in Chechnya following the first war, or they may result in a cold peace, as is the case in Israeli-Egyptian relations. In these and similar cases, hopes of turning the conflictive relations of the past into peaceful societal relations have not materialized because the peace-building process with reconciliation never actually began, was stalled, or has progressed very slowly.

Throughout the last decades social scientists as well as practitioners have come to realize that in order to crystallize peaceful relations between the former rivals and move them into a phase of lasting and stable peace, extensive changes are required in the sociopsychological repertoire of group members on both sides. We regard stable and lasting peace as *consisting of mutual recognition and acceptance, after a reconciliation process, of an invested supreme goal of maintaining peaceful relations that are characterized by full normalization with cooperation in all possible domains of collective life that provide secure and trustful coexistence.* This view provides a compass to the desired nature of peaceful relations that are embedded in a culture of peace.

In this framework, in almost every peace-building process reconciliation between past rival parties is a necessary condition for establishing stable and lasting peace. It pertains to sociopsychological restructuring of relations between past rivals that allows healing from the past wounds of the conflict. This can be achieved through mutual recognition and acceptance, through open and free deliberation about past conflict, and by taking responsibility and correcting past injustices and wrongdoing. Thus, building lasting and stable peace requires, on the one hand, structural changes that restructure the nature of relations between the parties and, on the other hand, fundamental sociopsychological changes that penetrate deep into the societal fabric (Bar-Tal, 2009, 2013; Kelman, 1999; Long, & Brecke, 2003; Nadler, Malloy, & Fisher, 2008; Rouhana, 2011). The former refers to such processes as termination of oppression, discrimination, and occupation; addressing past human rights and justice violations, as well as performance of atrocities; distribution of power, wealth, and resources; demilitarization and disarmament with absolute cessation of violence; and construction of a democratic culture with structural justice. The latter refers to adoption and internalization by society members of values, beliefs, attitudes, emotions, norms, and practices that cherish peace, justice, respect of human rights, cooperation, trust, sensitivity and consideration of the other party's needs, interests, and goals, equality of relations, acceptance and respect of cultural differences—all as foundations of a culture of peace. These processes are interwoven, gradual, nonlinear, reciprocal, planned, voluntary, and very long. Their successful completion can guarantee solidification of peaceful relations between the former rivals, as the processes lay stable foundations, rooted in the new structures and the psyche of the people grounded in a culture of peace.

4. Conclusion

An intractable conflict by its nature is prolonged, vicious, and violent and resists termination because neither of the involved parties can win determinatively or is willing to negotiate a peaceful settlement that will satisfy the needs and goals of a majority of the society. These conflicts do not end, even when one party achieves a temporary military victory, if it does not address properly the grievances and contentions of the rival party that underlay the eruption and continuation of the conflict. Many of these conflicts are a result of unjust practices that were normatively accepted in previous years, and even though the moral codes of intergroup behaviors have changed, it is almost impossible to correct those past injustices. No group yields voluntarily power, dominance, wealth, resources, territories—even when they were obtained in an immoral way in the past. Thus more conflicts are managed by power than by morality and justice, and often powerful third parties have a vested interest in their continuation.

Despite tremendous progress in framing new moral codes of intergroup behaviors, the civilized world has not found ways to bring the rival parties in intractable conflict to a successful, peaceful termination that opens the way for the eventual establishment of the lasting and stable peace. We believe that this is one of the most challenging missions for enlightened civilization: to increase the power of justice and morality and decrease the power of force on the road to establishing international mechanisms that will bring an end to the bloodshed of intractable conflicts. In this mission social scientists can play a major role not only by providing enlightenment about the forces that fuel continuation of the intractable conflicts, but also by elucidating the processes, factors, mechanisms, methods, and ways that can facilitate processes of peace-building.

ACKNOWLEDGMENT

We acknowledge the support of the Maurice and Marilyn Cohen Center for Modern Jewish Studies at Brandeis University, where the first author was a Visiting Scholar during the completion of the chapter.

REFERENCES

Antonovsky, A. (1987). *Unraveling the mystery of health: How people manage stress and stay well.* San Francisco, CA: Jossey-Bass.

Arnold, M. B. (1960). *Emotion and personality* (vols. 1 and 2). New York: Columbia University Press.

Ashmore, R. D., Deaux, K., & McLaughlin-Volpe, T. (2004). An organizing framework for collective identity: Articulation and significance multidimensionality. *Psychological Bulletin, 130,* 80–114.

Atran, S., & Axelrod, R. (2008). Reframing sacred values. *Negotiation Journal, 24,* 221–246.

Averill, J. R. (1982). *Anger and aggression: An essay on emotion.* New York: Springer-Verlag.

Azar, E. E. (1990). *The management of protracted social conflict.* Hampshire, UK: Dartmouth Publishing.

Bandura, A. (1999). Moral disengagement in the perpetration of inhumanities. *Personality and Social Psychology Review, 3*(3), 193–209.

Bandura, A. (2000). Exercise of human agency through collective efficacy. *Current Directions in Psychological Science, 9*(3), 75–78.

Bar-Siman-Tov, Y. (Ed.). (2004). *From conflict resolution to reconciliation.* New York: Oxford University Press.

Bar-Tal, D. (2000). *Shared beliefs in a society: Social psychological analysis.* Thousand Oaks, CA: Sage.

Bar-Tal, D. (2007a). Sociopsychological foundations of intractable conflicts. *American Behavioral Scientist, 50*, 1430–1453.

Bar-Tal, D. (2007b). *Living with the conflict: Socio-psychological analysis of the Israeli-Jewish society* (in Hebrew). Jerusalem: Carmel.

Bar-Tal, D. (2009). Reconciliation as a foundation of culture of peace. In J. de Rivera (Ed.), *Handbook on building cultures for peace* (pp. 363–377). New York: Springer.

Bar-Tal, D. (Ed.). (2011). *Intergroup conflicts and their resolution: Social psychological perspective.* New York: Psychology Press.

Bar-Tal, D. (2013). *Intractable conflicts: Socio-psychological foundations and dynamics.* Cambridge: Cambridge University Press.

Bar-Tal, D., Abutbul, G., & Raviv, A. (in press). Routinization of the intractable conflict. In T. Capelos, H. Dekker, C. Kinvall, & P. Nesbitt-Larkin (Eds.), *The Palgrave handbook of global political psychology.* Houndmills: Palgrave Macmillan.

Bar-Tal, D., Chernyak-Hai, L., Schori, N., & Gundar, A. (2009). A sense of self-perceived collective victimhood in intractable conflicts. *International Red Cross Review, 91*, 229–277.

Bar-Tal, D., & Halperin, E. (2009). Overcoming psychological barriers to peace process: The influence of beliefs about losses. In M. Mikulincer & P. R. Shaver (eds.), *Prosocial motives, emotions and behaviors: The better angels of our nature* (pp. 431–448). Washington, DC: American Psychological Association Press.

Bar-Tal, D., & Halperin, E. (2011). Socio-psychological barriers to conflict resolution. In D. Bar-Tal (ed.), *Intergroup conflicts and their resolution: A social psychological perspective* (pp. 217–240). New York: Psychology Press.

Bar-Tal, D., & Hammack, P. L. (2012). Conflict, delegitimization and violence In L. R. Tropp (ed.), *Oxford handbook of intergroup conflict* (pp. 29–52). New York: Oxford University Press.

Bar-Tal, D., & Jacobson, D. (1998). Psychological perspective on security. *Applied Psychology: An International Review, 47*, 59–71.

Bar-Tal, D., Oren, N., & Nets-Zehngut, R. (2012). Socio-psychological analysis of conflict-supporting narratives. Manuscript submitted for publication.

Bar-Tal, D., & Sharvit, K. (2008). The influence of the threatening transitional context on Israeli Jews' reactions to Al Aqsa Intifada. In V. M. Esses & R. A. Vernon (eds.), *Explaining the breakdown of ethnic relations: Why neighbors kill* (pp. 147–170). Oxford: Blackwell.

Bar-Tal, D., Sharvit, K., Halperin, E. & Zafran, A. (2012). Ethos of conflict: The concept and its measurement. *Peace & Conflict: Journal of Peace Psychology, 18*, 40–61.

Baumeister, R. F., & Hastings, S. (1997). Distortions of collective memory: How groups flatter and deceive themselves. In J. W. Pennebaker, D. Paez, & B. Rimé (eds.), *Collective memory of political events: Social psychological perspectives* (pp. 277–293). Mahwah, NJ: Lawrence Erlbaum.

Bercovitch, J. (2005). Mediation in the most resistant cases. In C. A. Crocker, F. O. Hampson, & P. R. Aall (eds.), *Grasping the nettle: Analyzing cases of intractable conflict* (pp. 99–121). Washington, DC: United States Institute of Peace Press.

Berkowitz, L. (1993). *Aggression: Its causes, consequences and control.* Philadelphia, PA: Temple University Press.

Brewer, M. B. (2011). Identity and conflict. In D. Bar-Tal (ed.), *Intergroup conflicts and their resolution: Social psychological perspectives* (pp. 125–143). New York: Psychology Press.

Brockner, J., & Rubin, J. Z. (1985). *Entrapment in escalating conflicts: A social psychological analysis.* New York: Springer.

Brubaker, R., & Laitin, D. D. (1998). Ethnic and nationalist violence. *Annual Review of Sociology*, *24*, 423–452.

Burns-Bisogno, L. (1997). *Censoring Irish nationalism: The British, Irish and American suppression of Republican images in film and television, 1909–1995.* Jefferson, NC: McFarland.

Burton, J. W. (1987). *Resolving deep-rooted conflict: A handbook.* Lanham, MD: University Press of America.

Burton, J. W. (Ed.). (1990). *Conflict: Human needs theory.* New York: St. Martin's Press.

Cairns, E., Lewis, C. A., Mumcu, O., & Waddell, N. (1998). Memories of recent ethnic conflict and their relationship to social identity. *Peace and Conflict: Journal of Peace Psychology*, *4*, 13–22.

Cairns, E., & Roe, M. (Eds.). (2003). *The role of memory in ethnic conflict.* New York: Palgrave Macmillan.

Cash, J. D. (1996). *Identity, ideology and conflict.* Cambridge: Cambridge University Press.

Castano, E. (2008). On the perils of glorifying the in-group: Intergroup violence, in-group glorification, and moral disengagement. *Social and Personality Psychology Compass*, *2*(1), 154–170.

Čehajić, S., & Brown, R. (2008). Not in my name: A social psychological study of antecedents and consequences of acknowledgment of ingroup atrocities. *Genocide Studies and Prevention*, *3*, 195–211.

Chambers, J. R., Baron, R. S., & Inman, M. L. (2006). Misperception in intergroup conflict: Disagreeing about what we disagree about. *Psychological Science*, *17*, 38–45.

Cohrs, J. C. (2012). Ideologies and violent conflict. In L. R. Tropp (ed.), *Oxford handbook of intergroup conflict* (pp. 53–71). New York: Oxford University Press.

Coleman, P. T. (2000). Intractable conflict. In D. Deutsch & P. T. Coleman (eds.), *The handbook of conflict resolution: Theory and practice* (pp. 428–450). San Francisco, CA: Jossey-Bass.

Coleman, P. T. (2003). Characteristics of protracted, intractable conflict: Towards the development of a metaframework—I. *Peace and Conflict: Journal of Peace Psychology*, *9*(1), 1–37.

Coutant, D. K., Worchel, S., & Hanza, M. (2011). Pigs, slingshots, and other foundations of intergroup conflict. In D. Bar-Tal (ed.), *Intergroup conflicts and their resolution: A social psychological perspective* (pp. 39–59). New York: Psychology Press.

Crocker, C. A., Hampson, F. O., & Aall, P. R. (2005). Introduction: Mapping the nettle field. In C. A. Crocker, F. O. Hampson, & P. R. Aall (eds.), *Grasping the nettle: Analyzing cases of intractable conflict* (pp. 3–30). Washington, DC: United States Institute of Peace Press.

David, O., & Bar-Tal, D. (2009). A socio-psychological conception of collective identity: The case of national identity. *Personality and Social Psychology Review*, *13*, 354–379.

De Dreu, C. K. W. (2010). Social conflict: The emergence and consequence of struggle and negotiation. In S. T. Fiske, D. T. Gilbert, & G. Lindzey (eds.), *Handbook of social psychology* (5th ed., vol. 2, pp. 983–1023). Hoboken, NJ: John Wiley & Sons.

De Dreu, C. K. W., & Carnevale, P. J. (2003). Motivational bases of information processing and strategy in conflict and negotiation. *Advances in Experimental Social Psychology*, *35*, 235–291.

de Rivera, J. (1992). Emotional climate: Social structure and emotional dynamics. In K. T. Strongman (ed.), *International review of studies on emotion* (vol. 2, pp. 199–218). New York: John Wiley.

de Rivera, J. (Ed.). (2009). *Handbook on building cultures for peace.* New York: Springer.

de Rivera, J., & Paez, D. (Eds.). (2007). Emotional climate, human security, and culture of peace. *Journal of Social Issues, 63*(2), 233–460.

Deutsch, M. (1973). *The resolution of conflict*. New Haven, CT: Yale University Press.

Deutsch, M. (1985). *The distributive justice: The social psychological perspective*. New Haven, CT: Yale University Press.

Devine-Wright, P. (2003). A theoretical overview of memory and conflict. In E. Cairns & M. D. Roe (eds.), *The role of memory in ethnic conflict* (pp. 9–33). Houndmills, UK: Palgrave Macmillan.

Doosje, B., Ellemers, N., & Spears, R. (1999). Commitment and intergroup behaviour. In N. Ellemers, R. Spears, & B. Doosje (eds.), *Social identity: Context, commitment, content* (pp. 84–106). Boston: Blackwell.

Dweck, C. S. (1999). *Self-Theories: Their role in motivation, personality and development*. Philadelphia: Taylor and Francis / Psychology Press.

Elcheroth, G., & Spini, D. (2011). Political violence, intergroup conflict, and ethnic categories. In D. Bar-Tal (ed.), *Intergroup conflicts and their resolution: A social psychological perspective* (pp. 175–194). New York: Psychology Press.

Eriksen, T. H. (2001). Ethic identity, national identity, and intergroup conflict. In R. D. Ashomre, L. Jussim, & D. Wilder (eds.), *Social identity, intergroup conflict, and conflict resolution* (pp. 42–68). Oxford: Oxford University Press.

Fisher, R. J. (1990). *The social psychology of intergroup and international conflict resolution*. New York: Springer-Verlag.

Fisher, R. J., & Kelman, H. C. (2011). Perceptions in conflicts In D. Bar-Tal (ed.), *Intergroup conflicts and their resolution: A social psychological perspective* (pp. 61–81). New York: Psychology Press.

Fitzduff, M. (2006). Ending wars: Developments, theories, and practices. In M. Fitzduff & C. E. Stout (eds.), *The psychology of resolving global conflicts: From war to peace* (vol. 1, pp. ix–xl). Westport CT: Praeger Security International.

Fitzduff, M., & Stout, C. E. (Eds.). (2006). *The psychology of resolving global conflicts: From war to peace* (vols. 1–3). Westport, CT: Praeger Security International.

Frankl, V. E. (1963). *Man's search for meaning*. New York: Washington Square Press.

Frijda, N. H. (1986). *The emotions*. Cambridge; Cambridge University Press.

Galtung, J. (1969). Violence, peace, and peace research. *Journal of Peace Research, 6,* 167–191.

Galtung, J. (1996). *Peace by peaceful means: Peace and conflict, development and civilization*. London: Sage.

Gawerc, M. I. (2006). Peace-building: Theoretical and concrete perspectives. *Peace & Change, 31,* 435–478.

Gayer, C., Tal, S., Halperin, E., & Bar-Tal, D. (2009). Overcoming psychological barriers to peaceful conflict resolution: The role of arguments about losses. *Journal of Conflict Resolution, 53,* 951–975.

Geertz, C. (1973). *The interpretation of cultures*: New York: Basic Books.

Giddens, A. (1984). *The constitution of society*. Cambridge: Polity Press.

Gidron, B., Katz, S. N., & Hasenfeld, Y. (Eds). (2002). *Mobilizing for peace: Conflict resolution in Northern Ireland, Israel/Palestine, and South Africa*. Oxford: Oxford University Press.

Gillis J. R. (Ed.). (1994). *Commemorations: The politics of national identity*. Princeton, NJ: Princeton University Press.

Goertz, G., & Diehl, P. F. (1993). Enduring rivalries: Theoretical constructs and empirical patterns. *International Studies Quarterly, 37,* 147–171.

Greenberg, J., Pyszczynski, T, & Solomon, S. (1997). Terror management theory of self-esteem and social behavior: Empirical assessments and conceptual refinements. In M. P. Zanna (ed.), *Advances in experimental social psychology* (vol. 29, pp. 61–139). New York: Academic Press.

Hadjipavlou, M. (2007). The Cyprus conflict: Root causes and implications for peacebuilding. *Journal of Peace Research, 44*, 349–365.

Halbwachs, M. (1992). *On collective memory.* Chicago: University of Chicago Press.

Halperin, E. (2008). Group-based hatred in intractable conflict in Israel. *Journal of Conflict Resolution, 52*, 713–736.

Halperin, E. (2011). Emotional barriers to peace: Negative emotions and public opinion about the peace process in the Middle East. *Peace and Conflict: Journal of Peace Psychology, 17*, 22–45.

Halperin, E., Canetti-Nisim, D., & Hirsch-Hoefler, S. (2009). Emotional antecedents of political intolerance: The central role of group-based hatred. *Political Psychology, 30*, 93–123.

Halperin, E., & Gross, J. (2011). Intergroup anger in intractable conflict: Long-term sentiments predict anger responses during the Gaza war. *Group Processes and Intergroup Relations, 14*(4), 477–488.

Halperin, E., Russel, A. G., Dweck, C. S., & Gross, J. J. (2011). Anger, hatred, and the quest for peace: Anger can be constructive in the absence of hatred. *Journal of Conflict Resolution, 55*(2), 274–291.

Halperin, E., Sharvit, K., & Gross, J. J. (2011). Emotions and emotion regulation in conflicts. In D. Bar-Tal (ed.), *Intergroup conflicts and their resolution: A social psychological perspective* (pp. 83–103). New York: Psychology Press.

Hamburg, D. A., George, A., & Ballentine, K. (1999). Preventing deadly conflict: The critical role of leadership. *Archives of General Psychiatry, 56*, 971–976.

Hammack, P. L. (2011). *Narrative and the politics of identity: The cultural psychology of Israeli and Palestinian youth.* New York: Oxford University Press.

Harbom, L., Hogbladh, S., & Wallensteen, P. (2006). Armed conflict and peace agreement. *Journal of Peace Research, 43*, 617–631.

Haslam, N. (2006). Dehumanization: An integrative review. *Personality and Social Psychology Review, 10*, 252–264.

Haslam, S. A., Reicher, S. D., & Platow, M. J. (2010). *The new psychology of leadership: Identity, influence and power.* New York: Psychology Press.

Hirschberger, G., & Pyszczynski, T. (2010). An existential perspective on ethnopolitical violence. In P. R. Shaver & M. Mikulincer (eds.), *Understanding and reducing aggression, violence, and their consequences.* (pp. 297–314). Washington, DC: American Psychological Association.

Hobfoll, S. E., Canetti-Nisim, D., & Johnson, R. J. (2006). Exposure to terrorism, stress-related mental health symptoms, and defensive coping among Jews and Arabs in Israel. *Journal of Consulting and Clinical Psychology, 74*, 207–218.

Holt, R. R., & Silverstein, B. (1989). On the psychology of enemy images: Introduction and overview. *Journal of Social Issues, 45*(2), 1–11.

Horowitz, D. L. (1985). *Ethnic groups in conflict.* Berkeley: University of California Press.

Horowitz, D. L. (2001). *The deadly ethnic riot.* Los Angeles, CA: University of California Press.

Huddy, L. (2001). From social to political identity: Implication for political psychology. *Political Psychology, 22*, 127–156.

Huddy, L., Feldman, S., & Cassese, E. (2007). On the distinct political effects of anxiety and anger. In A. Crigler, M. MacKuen, G. Marcus, & W. R. Neuman (eds.), *The dynamics of emotion in political thinking and behavior* (pp. 202–230). Chicago: University of Chicago Press.

Huddy, L., Feldman, S., Taber, C., & Lahav, G. (2005). Threat, anxiety, and support of antiterrorism policies. *American Journal of Political Science, 49*, 593–608.

Huddy, L., & Khatib, N. (2007). American patriotism, national identity and political involvement. *American Journal of Political Science, 51*, 63–77.

Hunt, S. A., & Benford, R. D. (2004). Collective identity, solidarity and commitment. In D. A. Snow, A. Soule, & H. Kriesi (eds.), *The Blackwell companion to social movements* (pp. 171–196). Malden, MA: Blackwell.

Hunter, J. A., Stringer, M., & Watson, R. P. (1991). Intergroup violence and intergroup attributions. *British Journal of Social Psychology, 30*, 261–266.

Janoff-Bulman, R. (1992). *Shattered assumptions: Towards a new psychology of trauma.* New York: Free Press.

Jarymowicz, M., & Bar-Tal, D. (2006). The dominance of fear over hope in the life of individuals and collectives. *European Journal of Social Psychology, 36*, 367–392.

Jervis, R. (1976). *Perception and misperception in international politics.* Princeton, NJ: Princeton University Press.

Jost, J. T., Federico, C. M., & Napier, J. L. (2009). Political ideology: Its structure, functions and elective affinities. *Annual Review of Psychology, 60*, 307–337.

Jost, J. T., Glaser, J., Kruglanski, A. W., & Sulloway, F. J. (2003). Political conservatism as motivated social cognition. *Psychological Bulletin, 129*, 339–375.

Kansteiner, W. (2002). Finding meaning in memory: A methodological critique of collective memory studies. *History and Theory, 41*, 179–197.

Kashti, Y. (1997). Patriotism as identity and action. In D. Bar-Tal & E. Staub (eds.), *Patriotism in the lives of individuals and nations* (pp. 213–228). Chicago: Nelson-Hall.

Kelman, H. C. (1999). Transforming the relationship between former enemies: A social-psychological analysis. In R. L. Rothstein (ed.), *After the peace: Resistance and reconciliation* (pp. 193–205). Boulder: Lynne Rienner.

Kelman, H. C. (2001). The role of national identity in conflict resolution. In R. D. Ashmore, L. Jussim, & D. Wilder (eds.), *Social identity, intergroup conflict, and conflict reduction* (pp. 187–212). New York: Oxford University Press.

Kelman, H. C. (2007). Social-psychological dimensions of international conflict. In I. W. Zartman (ed.), *Peacemaking in international conflict: Methods and techniques* (revised ed., pp. 61–107). Washington, DC: United States Institute of Peace.

Keltner, D., & Robinson, R. J. (1993). Imagined ideological differences in conflict escalation and resolution. *International Journal of Conflict Management, 4*(3), 249–262.

Klandermans, B., & de Weerd, M. (2000). Group identification and political protest. In S. Stryker, T. J. Owens, & R. W. White (eds.), *Self, identity, and social movements: Social movements, protest, and contentions* (vol. 13, pp. 68–90). Minneapolis: University of Minnesota Press.

Knox, C., & Quirk, P. (2000). *Peace building in Northern Ireland, Israel and South Africa: Transition, transformation and reconciliation.* London: Macmillan.

Korostelina, K. (2006). National identity formation and conflict intentions of ethnic minorities. In M. Fitzduff & C. E. Stout (eds.), *The psychology of resolving global conflicts: From war to peace* (vol. 2, pp. 147–170). Westport. CT: Praeger Security International.

Kriesberg, L. (1993). Intractable conflict. *Peace Review, 5*, 417–421.

Kriesberg, L. (2007). *Constructive conflicts: From escalation to resolution* (3rd ed.). Lanham, MD: Rowman & Littlefield.

Kriesberg, L. (2009). Changing conflict asymmetries constructively. *Dynamics of Asymmetric Conflict, 2*(1), 4–22.

Kruglanski, A. W. (2004). *The psychology of closed mindedness.* New York: Psychology Press.

Landman, S. (2010). Barriers to peace: Protected values in the Israeli-Palestinian conflict. In Y. Bar-Siman-Tov, *Barriers to peace: The Israeli-Palestinian conflict* (pp. 135–177). Jerusalem: Jerusalem Institute for Israel Studies.

Lederach, J. P. (1997). *Building peace: Sustainable reconciliation in divided societies.* Washington, DC: United States Institute of Peace Press.

Lederach, J. P. (2005). *The moral imagination: The art and soul of building peace.* New York: Oxford University Press.

Lerner, J. S., Gonzalez, R. M., Small, D. A., & Fischhoff, B. (2003). Effects of fear and anger on perceived risk of terrorism: A national field experiment. *Psychological Science, 14*, 144–150.

Lerner, J. S., & Keltner, D. (2001). Fear, anger and risk. *Journal of Personality and Social Psychology, 81*, 1146–1159.

Levy, J. S. (1996). Loss aversion, framing, and bargaining: The implications of prospect theory for international conflict. *International Political Science Review 17*, 179–195.

Lewin, K. (1947). Frontiers of group dynamics: I. *Human Relations, 1*, 5–41.

Lewin, K. (1951). *Field theory in social science.* New York: Harper & Row.

Lindner, E. (2006). *Making enemies: Humiliation and international conflict.* Westport: CT: Praeger.

Lindner, E. G. (2001). Humiliation and the human condition: Mapping a minefield, *Human Rights Review, 2* (2), 46–63.

Lindner, E. G. (2006). Emotion and conflict: Why it is important to understand how emotions affect conflict and how conflict affects emotions. In M. Deutch, P. T. Coleman, & E. C. Marcus (eds.), *The handbook of conflict resolution* (2nd ed., pp. 268–293). San Francisco, CA: Jossey-Bass.

Liu, J. H., & Hilton, D. J. (2005). How the past weighs on the present: Social representations of history and their impact on identity politics. *British Journal of Social Psychology, 44*, 537–556.

Long, W. J., & Brecke, P. (2003). *War and reconciliation: Reason and emotion in conflict resolution.* Cambridge, MA: MIT Press.

MacDonald, D. B. (2002). *Balkan holocausts? Serbian and Croatian victim-centred propaganda and the war in Yugoslavia.* Manchester: Manchester University Press.

Mackie, D. M., Devos, T., & Smith, E. R. (2000). Intergroup emotions: Explaining offensive actions in an intergroup context. *Journal of Personality and Social Psychology, 79*, 602–616.

Maoz, I., & McCauley, C. (2008). Threat, dehumanization, and support for retaliatory aggressive polices in asymmetric conflict. *Journal of Conflict Resolution, 52*, 93–116.

Maslow, A. H. (1954). *Motivation and personality* (2nd ed.). New York: Harper & Row.

Moscovici, S., & Doise, W. (1994). *Conflict & consensus: A general theory of collective decisions.* London: Sage.

Nadler, A., Malloy, T. E., & Fisher, J. D. (Eds.). (2008). *The social psychology of intergroup reconciliation.* New York: Oxford University Press.

Noor, M., Brown, R. J., & Prentice, G. (2008). Precursors and mediators of intergroup reconciliation in Northern Ireland: A new model. *British Journal of Social Psychology, 47*, 481–495.

Opotow, S. (In press). Moral exclusion and moral inclusion: Intergroup conflict, justice, and peace. In L. R. Tropp (ed.), *Oxford handbook of intergroup conflict.* New York: Oxford University Press.

Oren, N. (2009). The Israeli ethos of conflict 1967–2005. Working Paper No. 27. Fairfax, VA: Institute for Conflict Analysis and Resolution, George Mason University. http://icar.gmu.edu/publication/6403.

Oren, N., & Bar-Tal, D. (In press). Collective identity and intractable conflict. In G. M. Breakwell & R. Jaspal (eds.), *Identity process theory: Identity, social action and social change.* Cambridge: Cambridge University Press.

Paez, D., & Liu, J. H. (2011). Collective memory of conflicts. In D. Bar-Tal (ed.), *Intergroup conflicts and their resolution: A social psychological perspective* (pp. 105–124). New York: Psychology Press.

Papadakis, Y., Perstianis, N., & Welz, G. (Eds.). (2006). *Divided Cyprus: Modernity, history, and an island in conflict.* Bloomington: Indiana University Press.

Parsons, T. (1951). *The social system.* Glencoe, IL: Free Press.

Pennebaker, J. W., Paez, D., & Rimé, B. (Eds.). (1997). *Collective memory of political events: Social psychological perspectives.* Mahwah, NJ: Lawrence Erlbaum.

Petersen, R. G. (2002). *Understanding ethnic violence: Fear, hatred, and resentment in twentieth-century eastern Europe.* Cambridge: Cambridge University Press.

Pettigrew, T. F. (1979). The ultimate attribution error: Extending Allport's cognitive analysis of prejudice. *Personality and Social Psychology Bulletin, 5,* 461–467.

Pfeifer, J. E., & Ogloff, J. R. P. (1991). Ambiguity and guilt determinations: A modern racism perspective. *Journal of Applied Social Psychology, 21,* 1713–1725.

Pruitt, D. G. (2007). Readiness theory and the Northern Ireland peace process. *American Behavioral Scientist, 50,* 1520–1541.

Pruitt, D. G., & Kim, S. H. (2004). *Social conflict: Escalation, stalemate, and settlement* (3rd ed.). New York: McGraw-Hill.

Ramanathapillai, R. (2006). The politicizing of trauma: A case study of Sri Lanka. *Peace and Conflict: Journal of Peace Psychology, 12,* 1–18.

Reicher, S. (2004). The context of social identity: Domination, resistance, and change. *Political Psychology, 25,* 921–945.

Reicher, S., Hopkins, N., Levine, M., & Rath, R. (2005). Entrepreneurs of hate and entrepreneurs of solidarity: Social identity as a basis for mass communication. *International Review of the Red Cross, 87*(860), 621–637.

Reykowski, J. (1982). Social motivation. *Annual Review of Psychology, 33,* 123–154.

Reykowski, J. (1997). Patriotism and the collective system of meaning. In D. Bar-Tal & E. Staub (eds.), *Patriotism in the lives of individuals and nations* (pp. 108–128). Chicago: Nelson-Hall.

Roccas, S., & Elster, A. (2012). Group identities. In L. R. Tropp (ed.), *Oxford handbook of intergroup conflict* (pp. 107–122). New York: Oxford University Press.

Ross, L. (2010). Perspectives on disagreement and dispute resolution: Lessons from the lab and the real world. In E. Shafir (ed.), *The behavioral foundations of public policy* (pp. 108–125). Princeton, NJ: Princeton University Press/Russell Sage Foundation.

Ross, L., & Nisbett, R. E. (1991). *The person and the situation: Perspectives of social psychology.* New York: McGraw-Hill.

Ross, L., & Ward, A. (1995). Psychological barriers to dispute resolution. *Advances in Experimental Psychology, 27,* 255–304.

Ross, M. H. (1997). The relevance of culture for the study of political psychology and ethnic conflict. *Political Psychology, 18,* 299–326.

Rouhana, N. N. (2004). Identity and power in the reconciliation of national conflict. In A. Eagly, R. Baron, & V. Hamilton (eds.), *The social psychology of group identity and social conflict: Theory, application, and practice* (pp. 173–187). Washington, DC: American Psychological Association.

Rouhana, N. N. (2011). Key issues in reconciliation: Challenging traditional assumptions on conflict resolution and power dynamics. In D. Bar-Tal (ed.), *Intergroup conflicts and their resolution: A social psychological perspective* (pp. 291–314). New York: Psychology Press.

Rouhana, N. N., & Bar-Tal, D. (1998). Psychological dynamics of intractable conflicts: The Israeli-Palestinian case. *American Psychologist, 53,* 761–770.

Runciman, W. G. (1966). *Relative deprivation and social justice: A study of attitudes to social inequality in twentieth century.* London: Routledge & Kegan Paul.

Sande, G. N., Goethals, G. R., Ferrari, L., & Worth, L. T. (1989). Value-guided attributions: Maintaining the moral self-image and the diabolical enemy-image. *Journal of Social Issues, 45*(2), 91–118.

Sandole, D. (1999). *Capturing the complexity of conflict: Dealing with violent ethnic conflicts of the post–Cold War era.* London: Pinter/Continuum.

Schaller, M., & Abeysinghe, A. M. N. D. (2006). Geographical frame of reference and dangerous intergroup attitudes: A double-minority study in Sri Lanka. *Political Psychology, 27,* 615–631.

Schatz, R. T., Staub, E., & Lavine, H. (1999). On the varieties of national attachment: Blind versus constructive patriotism. *Political Psychology, 20,* 151–174.

Scheff, T. J. (1994). *Bloody revenge.* Boulder, COL.: Westview.

Schori-Eyal, N., Klar, Y., & Roccas, S. (2011). The shadows of the past: Effects of historical group trauma on current intergroup conflicts. Manuscript submitted for publication.

Shalev, A. Y., Yehuda, R., & McFarlane, A. C. (Eds.). (2000). *International handbook of human response to trauma.* Dordrecht, Netherlands: Kluwer Academic Publishers.

Shamir, J., & Shikaki, K. (2002). Self serving perceptions of terrorism among Israelis and Palestinians. *Political Psychology, 23,* 537–557.

Simon, B., & Klandermans, B. (2001). Politicized collective identity: A social psychological analysis. *American Psychologist, 56,* 319–331.

Skitka, L. J. (2010). The psychology of moral conviction. *Social and Personality Psychology Compass, 4,* 267–281.

Skitka, L. J., Bauman, C. W., Aramovich, N. P., & Morgan, G. C. (2006). Confrontational and preventative policy responses to terrorism: Anger wants a fight and fear wants "them" to go away. *Basic and Applied Social Psychology, 28,* 375–384.

Skitka, L. J., Mullen, E., Griffin, T., Hutchinson, S., & Chamberlin, B. (2002). Dispositions, ideological scripts, or motivated correction? Understanding ideological differences in attributions for social problems. *Journal of Personality and Social Psychology, 83,* 470–487.

Slocum-Bradley, N. R. (2008). Discursive production of conflict in Rwanda. In F. M. Moghaddam, R. Harré, & N. Lee (eds.). *Global conflict resolution through positioning analysis* (pp. 207–226). New York: Springer.

Small, D. A., Lerner, J. S., & Fischhoff, B. (2006). Emotion priming and attributions for terrorism: Americans' reactions in a national field experiment. *Political Psychology, 27,* 289–298.

Smith, E. R., Seger, C. R., & Mackie, D. M. (2007). Can emotions be truly group level? Evidence regarding four conceptual criteria. *Journal of Personality and Social Psychology, 93,* 431–446.

Snow, D. A., Soule, A., & Kriesi, H. (Eds.). (2004). *The Blackwell companion to social movements.* Malden, MA: Blackwell.

Somerville, J. (1981). Patriotism and war. *Ethics, 91,* 568–578.

Sommers, S. R., & Ellsworth, P. C. (2000). Race in the courtroom: Perceptions of guilt and dispositional attributions. *Personality and Social Psychology Bulletin, 26,* 1367–1379.

Spanovic, M., Lickel, B., Denson, T. F., & Petrovic, N. (2010). Fear and anger as predictors of motivation for intergroup aggression: Evidence from Serbia and Republika Srpska. *Group Processes and Intergroup Relations, 13*(6), 725–739.

Staub, E. (2003). *The psychology of good and evil: The roots of benefiting and harming other.* New York: Cambridge University Press.

Staub, E. (2005). The origins and evolution of hate, with notes on prevention. In R. J. Sternberg (ed.), *The psychology of hate* (pp. 51–66). Washington, DC: American Psychological Association.

Staub, E. (2011). *Overcoming evil: Genocide, violent conflict, and terrorism.* Oxford: Oxford University Press.

Staub, E., & Bar-Tal, D. (2003). Genocide, mass killing and intractable conflict: Roots, evolution, prevention and reconciliation. In D. O. Sears, L. Huddy, & R. Jervis (eds.), *Oxford handbook of political psychology* (pp. 710–751). New York: Oxford University Press.

Stephan, W. G., Renfro, C. L., & Davis, M. D. (2008). The role of threat in intergroup relations. In U. Wagner, L. R. Tropp, G. Finchilescu, & C. Tredoux (eds.), *Improving intergroup relations* (pp. 55–72). Oxford: Blackwell.

Stephan, W. G., & Stephan, C. W. (2000). An integrated threat theory of prejudice. In S. Oskamp (ed.), *Reducing prejudice and discrimination* (pp. 23–45). Mahwah, NJ: Lawrence Erlbaum.

Sternberg, R. J. (2003). A duplex theory of hate: Development and application to terrorism, massacres and genocide. *Review of General Psychology, 7,* 299–328.

Sternberg, R. J., & Sternberg, K. (2008). *The nature of hatred.* Cambridge: Cambridge University Press.

Tajfel, H. (1982). *Social identity and intergroup relations.* Cambridge: Cambridge University Press.

Tetlock, P. E. (2003). Thinking the unthinkable: Sacred values and taboo cognitions. *Trends in Cognitive Science, 7,* 320–324.

Thackrah, J. R. (2009). *The Routledge companion to military conflict since 1945.* New York: Routledge.

Tileaga, C. (2007). Ideologies of moral exclusion: A critical discursive reframing of depersonalization, delegitimization and dehumanization. *British Journal of Social Psychology, 46,* 717–737.

Tint, B. (2010). History, memory, and intractable conflict. *Conflict Resolution Quarterly, 27*(3), 239–256.

Tropp, L. R. (Ed.). (2012). *Oxford handbook of intergroup conflict.* New York: Oxford University Press.

Vallacher, R. R., Coleman, P. T., Nowak, A., & Bui-Wrzosinska, L. (2010). Rethinking intractable conflict: The perspective of dynamical systems. *American Psychologist, 65,* 262–278.

Van Dijk, T. A. (1998). *Ideology: A multidisciplinary study.* London: Sage.

van Zomeren, M., & Iyer, A. (2009). Toward integrative understanding of the social and psychological dynamics of collective action. *Journal of Social Issues, 65,* 645–660.

van Zomeren, M., Postmes, T., & Spears, R. (2008). Toward an integrative social identity model of collective action: A quantitative research synthesis of three socio-psychological perspectives. *Psychological Bulletin, 134,* 504–535.

Volkan, V. D. (1997). *Blood lines: From ethnic pride to ethnic terrorism.* New York: Farrar, Straus and Giroux.

Vollhardt J. R. (2012). Collective victimization. In L. R. Tropp (ed.), *Oxford handbook of intergroup conflict* (pp. 136–157). New York: Oxford University Press.

Walker, I., & Smith, H. J. (Eds.). (2002). *Relative deprivation: Specification, development and integration.* Cambridge: Cambridge University Press.

Walzer, M. (2006). *Just and unjust wars: A moral argument with historical illustrations.* (4th ed.). New York: Basic Books.

Wertsch, J. (2002). *Voices of collective remembering.* Cambridge: Cambridge University Press.

White, R. K. (1970). *Nobody wanted war: Misperception in Vietnam and other wars.* Garden City, NY: Anchor Books.

Wohl, M. J. A., & Branscombe, N. R. (2008). Collective guilt for current ingroup transgressions. *Journal of Personality and Social Psychology, 94*(6), 988–1006.

Wohl, M. J. A., & Branscombe, N. R. (2009). Group threat, collective angst, and ingroup forgiveness for the war in Iraq. *Political Psychology, 30*, 193–217.

Wohl, M. J. A., Branscombe, N. R., & Klar, Y. (2006). Collective guilt: An emotional response to perceived ingroup misdeeds. *European Review of Social Psychology, 17*, 1–36.

Wolfsfeld, G. (2004). *Media and the path to peace.* Cambridge: Cambridge University Press.

Wood, E. J. (2003). *Insurgent collective action and civil war in El Salvador.* Cambridge: Cambridge University Press.

Worchel, S. (1999). *Written in blood: Ethnic identity and the struggle for human harmony.* New York: Worth.

Worchel, S., & Coutant, D. (2008). Between conflict and reconciliation: Toward a model of peaceful co-existence (pp. 423–446). In A Nadler, J. Fisher, & T. Malloy (eds.), *The social psychology of intergroup reconciliation.* New York: Oxford University Press.

Yzerbyt, V., Dumont, M., Wigboldus, D., & Gordin, E. (2003). I feel for us: The impact of categorization and identification on emotions and action tendencies. *British Journal of Social Psychology, 42*, 533–549.

Zartman, I. W. (2000). Ripeness: The hurting stalemate and beyond. In P. C. Stern & D. Druckman (eds.), *International conflict resolution after the Cold War* (pp. 225–250). Washington, DC: National Academy Press.

Zartman, I. W. (Ed.). (2007). *Peacemaking in international conflict: Methods and techniques* (revised ed.). Washington, DC: United States Institute of Peace.

Zertal, I. (2005). *Israel's Holocaust and the politics of nationhood.* Cambridge: Cambridge University Press.

Zerubavel, Y. (1995). *Recovered roots: Collective memory and the making of Israeli national tradition.* Chicago: University of Chicago Press.

INDEX

Abell, J., 281

Abelson, Robert, 344

abortion, attitudes toward, 12, 72, 115–116, 184, 634

Achen, C., 73, 110, 114–115, 528

Achterberg, P., 598–599

Adams, G.S., 751

Adjective Check List, 29

Adler, Alfred, 464

adolescence: cognitive development in, 67–68; Erikson on, 471–472; identity and, 471–472; socialization and, 59–60, 62–70, 75–76, 81–82; traits measured in, 36

Adorno, Theodor, 14, 28, 444, 609, 816–817

adulthood: cognitive biases during, 10; socialization and, 61–62, 81; stability of political beliefs during, 71–72, 81, 85

advertising. *See* political advertising

affect: behavioral decision theory (BDT) and, 148; cognition and, 13–14, 173, 414, 822; definitions of, 167; demonstrations of, 171; dual process mode of thinking and, 405; implicit attitudes and, 13; political behavior and, 13; racial prejudice and, 13

affirmative action, 631, 641–642, 750–751, 833, 855, 911–912

Afghanistan, 348, 352

African Americans. *See also* discrimination; prejudice: party identification and, 744, 826–827; perceptions of discrimination and, 69–70; political attitudes among, 70; political participation and, 812; racial identity and, 68–70; stereotypes regarding, 12; voting and, 829

age: conservatism and, 79–80; impact on attitudes and, 75–76, 78–80; party identification and, 84–85; personality and, 433–434; political attitudes and, 75–76,

78–80; political behavior and, 32; racism and, 80

Agranat Commission (Israel), 311

Ahn, T.K., 153, 671

Al Ramiah, Anathi, 11, 13

Alexander, M.M., 343

Alford, J., 241, 247, 249–250, 634

Algeria, 78

Allison, Graham, 305–306, 326n48, 348, 402–403

Allport, Gordon, 428, 816, 821, 835, 892, 905, 907

Almond, Gabriel, 306, 790

Altemeyer, R.A., 37, 597, 606

Althaus, S., 107

Altmeyer, B., 248

altruism, 208–210

Alwin, D., 72, 75

American Apartheid (Massey and Denton), 893–894

American National Election Studies (ANES), 71, 75, 120, 150, 666, 693, 751, 754, 822–823, 827

American Political Science Association, 2

American Voter Revisited, The (Lewis-Beck et al.), 62

American Voter, The (Campbell et al.), 61, 71, 83, 149, 666, 739

Amodio, D.M., 244, 538, 543

Anatomy of Racial Attitudes (Glock), 819–820

Andersen, V.N., 709–710

Anderson, D.J., 115

Anderson, E., 815

Angola, 347

Annan Plan (Cyprus), 511

Ansolabehere, S., 578, 592–593

anti-Semitism, 14, 817